March 25–27, 2019
Richardson, TX, USA

I0028981

Association for Computing Machinery

Advancing Computing as a Science & Profession

CODASPY'19

Proceedings of the Ninth ACM Conference on
Data and Application Security and Privacy

Sponsored by:
ACM SIGSAC

Supported by:
The University of Texas at Dallas

Association for Computing Machinery

Advancing Computing as a Science & Profession

The Association for Computing Machinery
2 Penn Plaza, Suite 701
New York, New York 10121-0701

ISBN: 978-1-4503-6099-9 (Digital)

ISBN: 978-1-4503-7058-5 (Print)

Additional copies may be ordered prepaid from:

ACM Order Department
PO Box 30777
New York, NY 10087-0777, USA

Phone: 1-800-342-6626 (USA and Canada)
+1-212-626-0500 (Global)
Fax: +1-212-944-1318
E-mail: acmhelp@acm.org
Hours of Operation: 8:30 am – 4:30 pm ET

Foreword

It is our great pleasure to welcome you to the ninth edition of the *ACM Conference on Data and Application Security and Privacy (CODASPY 2019)*, which follows the successful eight editions held in February/March 2011-2018. This conference series has been founded to foster novel and exciting research in this arena and to help generate new directions for further research and development. The initial concept was established by the two co-founders, Elisa Bertino and Ravi Sandhu, and sharpened by subsequent discussions with a number of fellow data security and privacy researchers. Their enthusiastic encouragement persuaded the co-founders to move ahead with the always daunting task of creating a high-quality conference.

Data and applications that manipulate data are crucial assets in today's information age. With the increasing drive towards availability of data and services anytime and anywhere, security and privacy risks have increased. Vast amounts of privacy-sensitive data are being collected today by organizations for a variety of reasons. Unauthorized disclosure, modification, usage or denial of access to these data and corresponding services may result in high human and financial costs. Important applications such as homeland security, social networking and social computing provide value by aggregating input from numerous individual users, and the mobile devices they carry. The emerging area of Internet of Things also poses serious privacy and security challenges. To achieve efficiency and effectiveness in traditional domains such as healthcare, there is a drive to make these records electronic and highly available. The need for organizations to share information effectively is underscored by rapid innovations in the business world that require close collaboration across traditional boundaries. Security and privacy in these and other arenas can be meaningfully achieved only in context of the application domain. Data and applications security and privacy has rapidly expanded as a research field with many important challenges to be addressed.

In response to the call for papers of CODASPY 2019, 119 papers were submitted from Africa, Asia, Europe, South America and North America. The program committee selected 28 full-length research papers (23.5% acceptance rate). These papers cover a variety of topics, including security issues in web, cloud, IoT, and mobile devices, privacy, access control, authentication, malware, code analysis, and hardware and system security. The program includes a poster paper session presenting exciting work in progress. The program is complemented by two keynote speeches by Anupam Joshi and Engin Kirda. This year's edition also features three workshops: the ACM International Workshop on Security and Privacy Analytics, the ACM International Workshop on Security in Software Defined Networks & Network Function Virtualization, and the ACM Workshop on Automotive Cybersecurity, and a panel on the research challenges at the intersection on AI, Big Data and CyberSecurity.

The organization of a conference like CODASPY requires the collaboration of many individuals. First of all, we would like to thank the authors for submitting to the conference and the keynote speakers for graciously accepting our invitation. We express our gratitude to the program committee members and external reviewers for their efforts in reviewing the papers, engaging in active online discussion during the selection process and providing valuable feedback to authors. We also would like to thank Yuan Cheng (web and publicity chair), Ravi Sandhu (workshop chair), Rhonda Walls (local arrangement chair), Hongxin Hu (poster chair) and the committee of the poster track, and Murtuza Jadliwala (proceedings chair). Finally, we would like to thank our sponsors, ACM SIGSAC and University of Texas at Dallas, for supporting this conference.

We hope that you will find this program interesting and that the conference will provide you with a valuable opportunity to interact with other researchers and practitioners from institutions around the world. Enjoy!

Murat Kantarcioglu, *University of Texas at Dallas, USA*
Ram Krishnan, *University of Texas at San Antonio, USA*
CODASPY'19 Program Co-Chairs

Bhavani Thuraisingham, *University of Texas at Dallas, USA*
Gail-Joon Ahn, *Arizona State University, USA*
CODASPY'19 General Co-Chairs

NOTES

Table of Contents

Session 4: Poster Session

Session 5: Access Control and Information Flow

Session 6: Hardware Assisted Data Security

Session 7: Web Security and Privacy

Session 8: System Security and Authentication

CODASPY 2019 Conference Organization

General Co-Chairs: Gail-Joon Ahn, *Arizona State University, USA*
Bhavani Thuraisingham, *University of Texas at Dallas, USA*

Program Co-Chairs: Murat Kantarcioglu, *University of Texas at Dallas, USA*
Ram Krishnan, *University of Texas at San Antonio, USA*

Poster Chair: Hongxin Hu, *Clemson University, USA*

Workshop Chair: Ravi Sandhu, *University of Texas at San Antonio, USA*

Panel Chair: Latifur Khan, *University of Texas at Dallas, USA*

Publicity and Web Chair: Yuan Cheng, *California State University, Sacramento, USA*

Local Arrangement Chair: Rhonda Walls, *University of Texas at Dallas , USA*

Proceedings Chair: Murtuza Jadliwala, *University of Texas at San Antonio, USA*

Research Award Chair: Bhavani Thuraisingham, *University of Texas at Dallas, USA*

Steering Committee: Elisa Bertino (co-chair), *Purdue University*
Ravi Sandhu (co-chair), *University of Texas at San Antonio, USA*
Gail-Joon Ahn, *Arizona State University, USA*
Alexander Pretschner, *Technische Universität München*

CODASPY 2019 Sponsors & Supporter

Sponsor:

Supporter:

TruZ-View: Developing TrustZone User Interface for Mobile OS Using Delegation Integration Model

Kailiang Ying, Priyank Thavai, and Wenliang Du
Syracuse University, Syracuse, New York, USA
{kying,pthavai,wedu}@syr.edu

ABSTRACT

When OS and hypervisor are compromised, mobile devices currently provide a hardware protected mode called Trusted Execution Environment (TEE) to guarantee the confidentiality and integrity of the User Interface (UI). The present TEE UI solutions adopt a *self-contained design model*, which provides a fully functional UI stack in the TEE, but they fail to manage one critical design principle of TEE: a small Trusted Computing Base (TCB), which should be more easily verified in comparison to a rich OS. The TCB size of the self-contained model is large as a result of the size of an individual UI stack. To reduce the TCB size of the TEE UI solution, we proposed a novel TEE UI design model called *delegation model*. To be specific, our design reuses the majority of the rich OS UI stack. Unlike the existing UI solutions protecting 3-dimensional UI processing in the TEE, our design protects the UI solely as a 2-dimensional surface and thus reduces the TCB size. Our system, called *TruZ-View*, allows application developers to use the rich OS UI development environment to develop TEE UI with consistent UI looks across the TEE and the rich OS. We successfully implemented our design on HiKey board. Moreover, we developed several TEE UI use cases to protect the confidentiality and integrity of UI. We performed a thorough security analysis to prove the security of the delegation UI model. Our real-world application evaluation shows that developers can leverage our TEE UI with few changes to the existing app's UI logic.

CCS CONCEPTS

• **Security and privacy** → **Mobile platform security**;

KEYWORDS

TrustZone, Android, UI safety

ACM Reference Format:
Kailiang Ying, Priyank Thavai, and Wenliang Du. 2019. TruZ-View: Developing TrustZone User Interface for Mobile OS Using Delegation Integration Model. In *Ninth ACM Conference on Data and Application Security and Privacy (CODASPY '19), March 25–27, 2019, Richardson, TX, USA.* ACM, New York, NY, USA, 12 pages. https://doi.org/10.1145/3292006.3300035

1 INTRODUCTION

Nowadays, users perform various essential activities, including banking, shopping, and financing, through the smartphone User Interface (UI). Because of the heavy reliance on this single interface, the security of the mobile software stack controlling UI has become increasingly critical. Unfortunately, CVE results of mobile OSes are not positive [6]. Take Android OS as an example – the number of vulnerabilities has skyrocketed over the last eight years. The mobile OSes cannot prevent untrusted code embedded in applications from running, which then leads to a broad attack surface. Untrusted code can exploit many vulnerabilities and can eventually manage to compromise the OS. Once the mobile OS is compromised, the last UI defense will be gone, and UI will then be controlled by malware. What's worse, malware can spoof actions on behalf of users without their consent.

Trusted Execution Environment (TEE), a technology that can secure the UI when the OS is compromised, has been developed to address this prominent security issue. As the most commonly deployed TEE on mobile devices, ARM TrustZone protects the UI in an isolated environment, *secure world*, inaccessible by the compromised mobile OS and normal apps, while in the *normal world*, untrusted normal apps run freely. We consider that there are mainly two directions to design TrustZone UI, as shown in Figure 1. The current design direction of the TrustZone UI solutions [4, 20, 30] is established to support a fully functional UI stack in the secure world mainly because these UI solutions support the *Trusted Application* (TA) to build isolated UI in the secure world. Such a UI design direction requires an isolated code stack (i.e., UI stack and TA) in the secure world and we call it the *self-contained UI model*, as shown on the left side of the Figure 1. Research works [3, 18, 28, 32] built various UI protection mechanisms (i.e., TAs) on top of the current TrustZone UI solutions [4, 30]. Although the self-contained UI model does provide UI security measures, we consider that the current TrustZone UI model fails to manage one critical design principle of TEE: a small Trusted Computing Base (TCB), which should be more easily verified in comparison to a rich OS. The TCB size of the self-contained model is large because it requires an individually functional UI stack in the secure world.

We intend to reduce the TCB size of the TrustZone UI. Our primary observation is that the functionalities of the secure-world UI stack can be further divided into UI development, UI services, and UI interaction, as shown in Figure 2. The main objective of the TrustZone UI solution is to secure the UI interaction, which involves displaying sensitive data on the screen and taking sensitive input from users. In order to protect the UI interaction, the self-contained UI model decides to also include both the UI development and the UI services in the secure world. When developing UI, developers construct the UI layer by layer. For example, developers can first

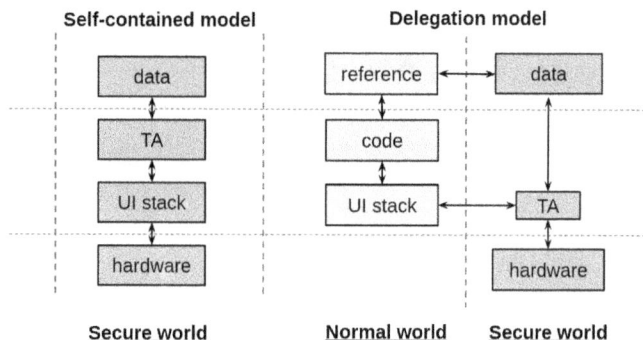

Figure 1: TrustZone UI Design Models

define the background layout (layer 1) and then put buttons (layer 2) on top of the layout (layer 1). The main tasks of the UI services are propagating touch events and compositing the screen content based on the multilayered UI structure defined by developers. Because of the complexity of this multilayered UI processing, the TCB size of the UI development and UI services is large. However, when users interact with the secure-world UI, they solely interact with a 2-dimensional surface on the screen. On a 2-dimensional surface, the protection of displaying the sensitive data is equivalent to the protection of a region on the image and the protection of the users' sensitive input is equivalent to the protection of users' touch coordinates on the screen. We can significantly reduce the TCB size if the secure world solely protects the UI as a 2-dimensional surface and leaves the 3-dimensional UI processing in the rich OS.

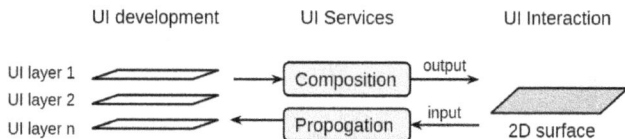

Figure 2: TrustZone UI Stack

Based on our observation, we propose the *delegation UI model* for TrustZone, as shown on the right side of the Figure 1. The main idea of our model is to delegate the UI development and the UI services to the rich OS. The normal world conducts the 3-dimensional UI processing, which does not contain any sensitive data. The output of the normal-world UI stack becomes an image on the screen. To display the sensitive data stored in TrustZone, the secure world takes a screenshot and overlaps the protected data on top of the screenshot before displaying them to users. To protect the users' sensitive input, our design keeps users' touch coordinates on the screenshot in the secure world. The protected data will never be leaked to the normal world. With this new design model, our approach significantly reduces the size of the secure-world UI stack from 3-dimensional UI processing to 2-dimensional UI processing.

This paper makes the following contributions: (1) provides the first study to propose a novel TrustZone UI design model called *delegation model* and to systematically study the properties and design principles of this new model; (2) the implementation of the TrustZone UI solution, called *TruZ-View*, applying the delegation

model to protect UI interaction when the mobile OS is compromised; (3) the performance of a thorough security analysis to prove the security of TruZ-View; (4) the evaluation of our system by using real-world applications.

2 PROBLEM

In this section, we discuss our threat model, research problems, and design challenges when applying the delegation UI model. We systematically compare the design trade-off between the self-contained model and the delegation model.

2.1 Threat Model

The user of the device is trusted. The normal world filled with apps and Android OS is untrusted because it may attempt to take screenshots that contain users' confidential information or to keylog users' confidential input (e.g., password and credit card number), and may spoof an unauthorized action on users' behalf without their confirmation. The secure world that includes the Trusted Applications (TA) and TEE OS is trusted and preserves users' confidentiality and integrity when the normal world is compromised. We assume that the server remains trusted after it is authorized by the user. The authorized server aims to protect the users' confidential data and verify the integrity of the users' request.

2.2 Problem Statement

The research problem of protecting UI can be further broken down into protecting UI display and protecting UI input. In this paper, we apply the delegation UI model and mainly answer (1) how to securely display the protected data, which is downloaded from the server; and (2) how to securely take users' sensitive input in TrustZone.

2.3 UI Design Models Design Trade-off

To better understand characteristics of different design models, we systematically compare the design trade-off between the self-contained UI model and the delegation UI model in three aspects, namely security, system design, and application impact. The comparison result is summarized in Table 1. Relying on the comparison result, we further derive design principles when we apply the delegation UI model.

Security. The TCB size and the isolation boundary are two essential attributes to measure the security of TrustZone solution. The self-contained model requires a separate UI stack to support TAs to write the UI logic, which requires a large TCB in the secure world. By contrast, the delegation model pushes the majority of the UI stack in the normal world and requires a small TCB in the secure world. As a trade-off for the TCB, the self-contained model could maintain a clean isolation boundary between two worlds because the software stacks are completely isolated in two worlds, while the isolation boundary for the delegation model is not clear yet. Therefore, the UI design that applies the delegation model has to answer this challenging question.

System design. The code reusability and the modularity are two critical measurements for the TEE system design. First of all, the code reusability implies that the software stack developed for

Table 1: UI Design Models Comparison Summary

Model	Security		System Design		Application Impact		
	TCB	Isolation	Reusability	Modularity	Transparency	Consistency	Rich Usability
Self-contained	large	clean	low	clean	low	low	high
Delegation	small	unclear	high	unclear	high	high	none

one world can be reused for another world. The software developed based on the self-contained model always suffers a low code reusability because different OSes have different interfaces and development standards. In contrast to the self-contained model, the delegation model reuses the majority of the normal-world software stack including OS level and application level. Therefore, the delegation model can obtain a high code reusability. Secondly, modularity suggests that the system update of one world should not affect the other world. The self-contained model can update systems independently because software stacks of both worlds are entirely separated. As a trade-off for the code reusability, the delegation model cannot merely modularize two worlds into two modules. The UI design that applies the delegation model has to provide an insight to preserve the modularity between two worlds.

Application impact. We use transparency, consistency, and rich usability to assess the TrustZone design impact on applications. Firstly, transparency is how many efforts application developers need to make to integrate the TrustZone UI solution with their applications. The self-contained model requires application developers to work with vendors to develop UI in the secure world, and such an approach requires much effort of application developers to leverage the TrustZone UI. Moreover, putting application-specific logic in the TEE is not secure because it is the reason that broadens the normal-world attack surface. The delegation model has high transparency to applications because our model reuses the normal-world application UI logic to develop the secure-world UI and does not put any application-specific logic in the TEE. Secondly, the consistency means whether users have the same UI experience across worlds. Users usually endure an inconsistent user experience when interacting with the self-contained UI model because the screen images are produced by separate UI stacks. The delegation model can provide consistent UI experiences across worlds because a single UI stack produces screen data for both worlds. Thirdly, the rich usability refers to whether the secure-world UI supports the rich UI functionalities such as animation and UI extensible services such as autocomplete and spell checker. As a trade-off for the TCB, we decide not to support any rich UI functionality like animation inside the secure world while the self-contained model could support rich UI depending on how large its TCB is.

Delegation UI model design principles. To reach a conclusion on the comparison, we summarize design principles of the delegation UI model. When we apply the model to design the TrustZone UI, these principles will help us preserve the aforementioned properties of the delegation model: (1) maintain a small TCB in the secure world and reuse the rich OS for non-sensitive operation as much as possible; (2) find a clean cut for the isolation boundary; (3) require a minimum effort from the TrustZone integration for

applications and the system update; (4) maintain a consistent UI experience across the worlds.

2.4 UI Design Challenges

In this section, we discuss UI design challenges by applying the delegation model. The secure world loses many capabilities during this TCB reduction process because our design model pushes the majority of the UI stack out of the secure world. However, some of the lost capabilities are important for the secure world to protect UI and become challenges for our UI design.

First of all, the secure world loses the capability to develop UI independently. We delegate UI development to the untrusted normal world. The data processed by the normal world is considered as untrusted. How can the secure world leverage the **untrusted** normal-world UI stack to develop UI for the secure world?

Secondly, the secure world loses the UI layer information because the delegation model solely protects the 2-dimensional image in the secure world while all the UI layer information is processed in the normal world. However, some of the UI layer information is important to define how to protect the UI display and the UI input. We need to find way to recover the **lost UI layer information** in the secure world.

3 IDEA

In this section, we discuss our key ideas to leverage the untrusted UI stack and to recover the lost UI layer information.

3.1 Splitting the UI Rendering Process

Our main idea of producing the secure-world UI is to split the normal-world UI rendering process at the last step. We categorize all existing TrustZone UI solutions as splitting the UI rendering process at different layers. The Figure 3 is an abstraction diagram of splitting design options. The first option [4, 20, 30] is to split the UI rendering at the application layer and to put all three layers into the secure world. The second option [32] is to split the UI rendering process at the framework level. Such a splitting option leaves the application logic in the normal world and puts the remaining two layers in the secure world. The challenge of the 2nd option is to maintain the binding between the application code in the normal world and the UI in the secure world. Although these two existing splitting options provide UI security measures, such splitting approaches require a separate UI stack to support the secure-world UI.

We suggest splitting the UI rendering process at the last step. The normal world produces the screen data without having the TrustZone-protected data. Our design takes the normal-world screenshot as the secure-world UI. The secure world protects the sensitive data display by overlapping the protected data on top of the screenshot and protects the users' input by keeping the touch coordinates

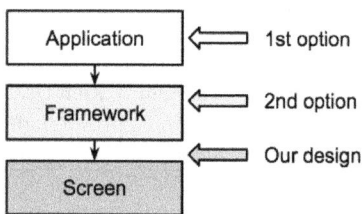

Figure 3: UI Rendering Split Options

inside the secure world. Our splitting option allows us to protect the UI interaction on a 2-dimensional surface.

3.2 Why securing a 2D UI is sufficient?

Here we explain why securing the display of sensitive data on a 2-dimensional surface is sufficient. First of all, users see the UI as a 2-dimensional image. Second, the sensitive data displayed on the UI is also stored in a 2-dimensional format in the secure world. We can directly perform image operation on the 2-dimensional surface to overlap the sensitive data on top of the image, thus protecting a 2-dimensional surface is sufficient to protect the sensitive data display.

Next, we describe why securing the users' sensitive input on a 2-dimensional surface is adequate. First of all, the initial form of the touch event is touch coordinates, which are a pair of float numbers. Second, all security-related inputs (i.e., confidential input, integrity-preserved input) are consumed at the UI's top layer, which users can see. There is no need to propagate such touch events to lower UI layers. For instance, when users type a password (i.e., confidential input) through a keyboard, they intend to click on the keyboard layer that they can see, not on the underlying invisible layers. The touch event is always consumed in an area of the 2-dimensional surface where users can see. Thus protecting the UI's top visible layer, a 2-dimensional surface that is enough to protect the UI input.

In this section, we convey our high-level isolation boundary. We further performed a detailed security analysis in Section 6 to prove the security of the 2-dimensional UI protection.

3.3 Recover UI Layer Information

The UI layer information is missing in the 2-dimensional surface because our design decides to split the UI rendering at the last step. However, some of the layer information is important to preserve the consistent UI experience across worlds. For example, the secure world needs to know how to protect the users' input (e.g., keyboard layout) and know where to display the protected data in the screenshot.

Our main idea of the recovery of the UI layer information is to let the `Android view system` send views' coordinates to TrustZone, as shown in Figure 4. We observe that the UI layer information is initially defined by the UI view that is the basic building block to construct the UI in the normal world. Our design allows developers to label certain views as the TrustZone-protected when they develop the UI. We follow the same UI development workflow and create a TrustZone tag in the view system. Our modified view system sends coordinates of TrustZone-enabled views to the secure world. Based on these coordinates, our design can recover the UI

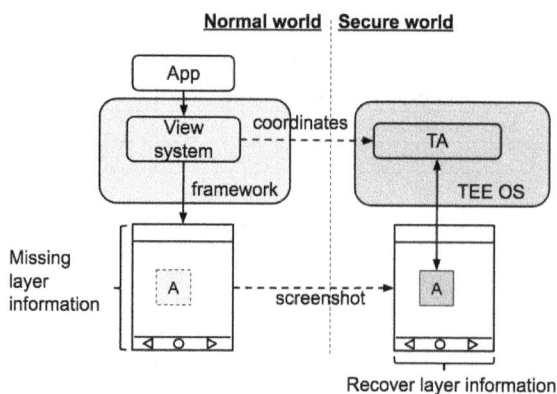

Figure 4: Recover UI Layer Information

layer information on a 2-dimensional surface. We have conducted a thorough security analysis in Section 6 to prove that the normal world cannot misuse the wrong view coordinates.

Our design provides easy-to-use TrustZone UI building blocks for developers. Developers can simply add these UI building blocks into an existing application's UI. We further categorize these UI building blocks into (1) confidential display, (2) confidential input, (3) integrity-preserved interaction. In Section 4, we will describe our UI building blocks design in detail.

4 UI DESIGN

In this section, we discuss our UI building blocks based on three categories: (1) confidential display, (2) confidential input, (3) integrity-preserved UI interaction. We refer to such views as *truz-views*.

4.1 Confidential Display

Application developers can protect users' confidential information displayed on the screen by adding a truz-view.

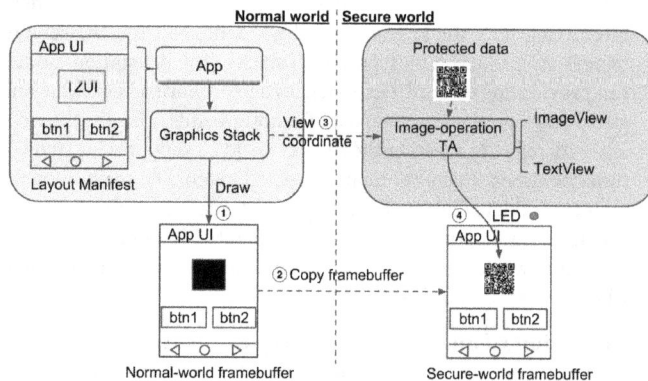

Figure 5: Confidential Display Design

Our confidential display design enables the normal-world graphics stack to recognize the truz-view and to work with TrustZone to display the protected data stored in the secure world. The normal-world graphics stack composites the app's UI into an image but leaves the area of truz-view blank, as shown in Figure 5 ❶.

Users first see the normal-world UI, as shown in Figure 6 WeChat example. To view the TEE-protected data, users click on the truz-view's area. Our design handles this particular click and takes a screenshot of the current UI. The screenshot is then sent to the secure world, as shown in Figure 5 ❷. Our design further transfers the coordinate and size of truz-view to the secure world, as shown in Figure 5 ❸, to guarantee that the protected data is filled in the secure region of the app's UI. The secure world then obtains the exclusive control of the screen hardware and fills in the protected data on the screenshot and displays the complete UI to the user, as shown in Figure 5 ❹. Throughout this process, users see the familiar app's UI with the protected data filled in. We use WeChat barcode payment UI to illustrate our UI in the secure world (Figure 6 WeChat secure world). Users scan the barcode in the secure world and can click the back button to switch the control of the screen to the normal world. When in the normal world, the protected data disappears and the truz-view's area is shown blank on the screen (Figure 6 WeChat normal world). In Section 6.1, we explain why the users' confidential information will not be leaked during the confidential display process.

We totally developed two types of confidential display UI building blocks, namely ImageView and TextView. Developers can simply embed the confidential display UI into the app using the code in Listing 1. They only require the secure world to perform image operation to render the protected data. The confidential information can be downloaded from servers to the secure world. Our design returns a reference to the protected data to the normal world. Developers then use the reference to display the TEE-protected data in the secure world. We will discuss our implementation for data downloading and reference management in Section 5.

Listing 1: Application change for confidential display

```
<View android:tzSecure="true"
android:src="reference to protected data" />
```

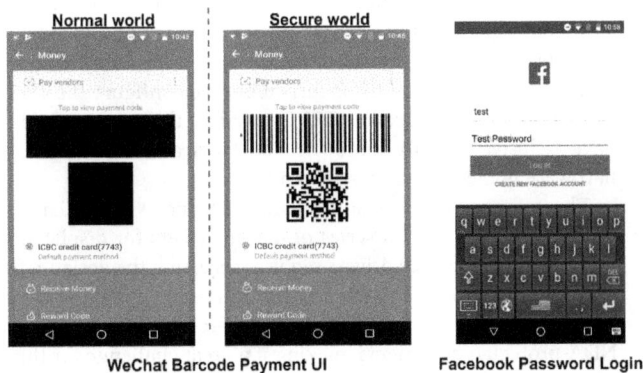

Figure 6: Confidential Display and Input Use Cases

4.2 Confidential Input

Application developers can protect users' confidential input by embedding a truz-view in the app's UI. Apps commonly accept users' confidential input, such as password and account number, through a keyboard, or let users sign on the smartphone to approve a purchase request. Our design mainly focuses on two common confidential input UI: typing password through a keyboard and signing through a signature pad. We use the keyboard to explain our main idea and the concept of securing users' signature is similar.

The keyboard is a standalone application. Android allows apps to use either a system keyboard or a customized keyboard to process users' input. Our design enables both types to protect users' keystroke inside the secure world. To give feedback on users' inputs, the app, which uses the TrustZone-enabled keyboard, needs to display secure-world keystrokes on a text field (i.e., EditText). Application developers can then embed a TrustZone-enabled EditText to be bound with the secure-world keyboard.

The normal world composites the app's UI including the TrustZone-enabled keyboard and EditText into an image. When the normal world displays the UI, our design takes a screenshot and then sends the image to the secure world. Then the secure world takes over the control of the screen and lights on a LED to notify users that they can securely enter their confidential input on the screen.

Users see the same app's UI in the secure world, as shown in Figure 6 Facebook example. To allow the secure world to handle users' click on the keyboard, our design sends the coordinates of truz-views and the layout of the KeyboardView to the secure world. Note that Android requires each Keyboard app to have an XML layout file and our design reuses this file to gain the layout of the keyboard in the secure world. When the user types in the keyboard, the secure world knows how to fill in the corresponding character on the EditText. Once users finish typing, they can click the back button to switch the control of screen to the normal world. Our design stores the user's input in the secure world and returns a reference to the input to the normal world.

The developers can simply embed the confidential input UI into the app using the code in Listing 2. We assume that the input is processed only by the server, not by the client. We will explain our implementation of secret transmission in Section 5. In Section 6.2, we explain why the users' confidential information will not be leaked during the confidential input process.

Listing 2: Application change for confidential input

```
<View android:tzSecure="true" />
```

4.3 Integrity-preserved UI Interaction

App developers desire to obtain the user's consent without it being modified by the compromised OS. Our integrity-preserved UI design focuses on a number of UIs such as Dialog, Confirmation Activity, PIN Pad, Pattern Locker, and Password Locker. The common characteristic of these UIs is that they all require a group of view elements to display the confirmation message to the user and to request the users' agreement to move forward. We use Dialog to illustrate our main idea, and the way to secure other integrity-preserved UIs is similar.

Take Chase monetary transaction Dialog as an example – developers want to allow users to confirm the transaction information displayed in the secure world, as shown in Figure 7. To display the confirmation message, app developers can embed a TrustZone-enabled TextBox. To obtain the user's decision, app developers can embed two TrustZone-enabled buttons, one for a positive decision

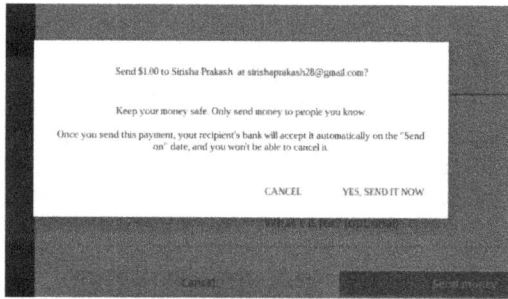

Figure 7: Chase Payment Confirmation Dialog

and the other for a negative decision. Our design recognizes these specialized views and asks the normal-world graphics stack to composite the app's UI including the truz-view's region, as shown in Figure 8 ❶. When the normal world displays the UI, our design takes a screenshot and sends it to the secure world. To fill in the integrity-preserved content on the right region of the app's UI, our design transfers the views' coordinates, the confirmation message, and properties of buttons (i.e., positive or negative) to the secure world, as shown in Figure 8 ❷. The secure world first erases the normal-world text on the TrustZone-enabled views and then fills in the text on these views, as shown in Figure 8 ❸. Two options guarantee the integrity of the text: (1) the TrustZone provides the text content and (2) the server attests the text. For example, the secure world fills in 'Yes' on the positive button and 'Cancel' on the negative button and the confirmation message on the TextView region. Our design prevents the normal world from fooling users. Preserving the integrity of the normal-world UI is nontrivial and we have performed a thorough security analysis in Section 6.3.

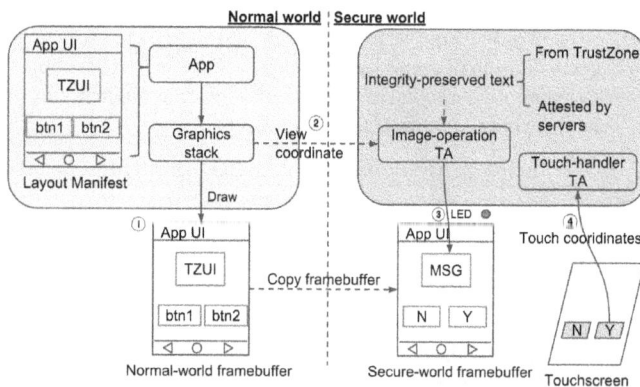

Figure 8: Integrity-preserved UI Interaction Design

Users see the familiar app's UI with the integrity-preserved data filled in. When the user confirms the message, our design generates an attestation of the message inside TrustZone, as shown in Figure 8 ❹. We will explain how the TrustZone and the server exchange the attestation key in Section 5. Once the user clicks on the button, our design injects the user's click along with the attestation back to the normal world. The normal-world OS continues to propagate the touch event to the corresponding Dialog button.

Developers can simply embed the integrity-preserved UI into the app using the code in Listing 3. In Section 6.2, we explain why the

users' confidential information will not be leaked in our injecting click design decision.

Listing 3: Application change for integrity-preserved UI

```
<View android:tzSecure="true"
      android:tzProperty="Positive" />
```

4.4 Hardware Design

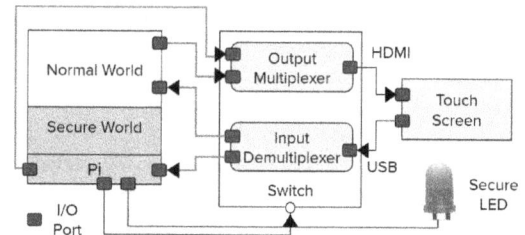

Figure 9: Hardware Design

Our hardware platform runs Android 9.0 in the normal world and OPTEE [22] in the secure world. We built our prototype using the HiKey board as our base platform [1]. We used a TFT LCD panel as the screen. The screen uses the HDMI interface for the display and the USB interface for controlling the touch.

As shown in Figure 9, to allow the secure world to drive the screen, we introduce an additional board (i.e., Raspberry Pi) controlled by the secure world. The secure world communicates with the Raspberry Pi through the serial communication (i.e., UART) and the secure world has the exclusive control of the UART. We achieve the screen isolation at the circuit level. We connect the screen I/O to the multiplexer/demultiplexer. The multiplexer takes the HDMI signal from both worlds and outputs the signal from one of the worlds to the screen. The demultiplexer takes the touch input from the screen and gives it to one of the worlds. The secure world controls the switch of the multiplexer/demultiplexer. Each world has separate I/O ports that are connected to multiplexer/demultiplexer. Users are informed that the screen is controlled by the secure world when an LED is turned on. We configure the Trust-Zone Protection Controller (TZPC) to allow the secure world to have exclusive control of the switch, LED indicator, and UART. Our hardware implementation is shown in Figure 10.

The main reason to use a separate Raspberry Pi is that the OPTEE does not have a series of device drivers for display and input. Developing such drivers requires accessing the design reference documents of the hardware platform (e.g., HiKey). However, the silicon vendors commonly conceal their implementations and NDA-protected documents, making it a great challenge for third-party developers to write drivers. We also consider that writing drivers is unnecessary for our project as our design mainly targets those vendors who have driver stacks for their own hardware. If the vendors adopt our design, they can eliminate the Raspberry Pi in our design by directly deploying the driver stacks in the secure world. Our design only uses Raspberry Pi as a bridge between the secure-world OS and the screen hardware. We do not use any other Linux OS functionalities in Raspberry Pi. We consider that our hardware design provides a reference for the research communities that desire to conduct a hardware-related research but are discouraged by device-driver accessibility in the secure world.

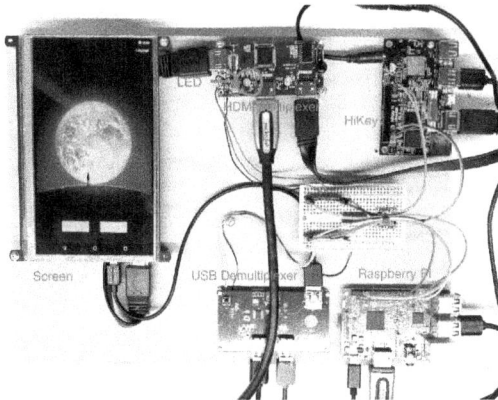

Figure 10: Hardware Implementation

5 DATA PROTECTION AND MANAGEMENT

In this section, we discuss how we protect the data during online data transmission and during the offline data usage. During the online data transmission, our system allows developers to use standard network protocols (e.g., HTTP, SSL) to transfer the confidential data between the server and TrustZone. During the offline data usage, we allow normal-world applications to display the data stored in TrustZone without it leaked into the normal world.

High-level solution. The high-level idea of data protection is shown in Figure 11. Having strong incentives to protect users' sensitive data stored in the cloud, the server establishes a TLS encrypted channel with TrustZone and sends the protected data through HTTPS. The normal world cannot eavesdrop on the network traffic without obtaining the TLS encryption key protected by TrustZone. The secure world decrypts the HTTPS packet and protects the confidential data. Our solution returns a reference to the protected data to the normal world and keeps the data in the secure world. This design ensures that the normal world cannot read and modify the data stored in TrustZone.

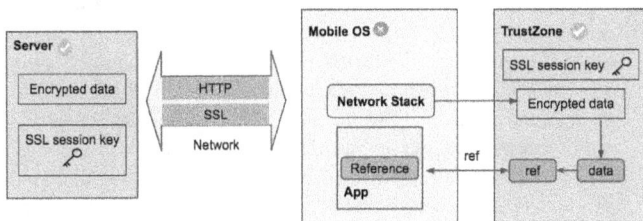

Figure 11: Data Protection High-level Solution

Split SSL. The pioneering researcher has invented a solution called *Split SSL* [32] to protect the online data transmission by using TrustZone. We build on top of the Split SSL to transfer confidential data between the server and TrustZone. The Split SSL secures the server-TEE communication through the TLS protocol and conducts all crypto operations (e.g., encryption, PKI) inside TrustZone. One

advantage is that the Split SSL is entirely transparent to the server so that the server can use standard network protocols for data transmission. The other advantage of the solution is that it allows the TrustZone-protected data and the normal-world data to be mixed in a single HTTPS packet. Their solution is to use an HTTP header to create a boundary between two types of data. They have conducted a thorough security analysis to prove that no information was leaked during the Split SSL connection. The Split SSL allows TrustZone and the server to establish a mutual trust during the login process and exchange the attestation key with TrustZone through the Split SSL. By checking the attestation of the HTTP requests after the login, the server can test whether the request comes from TrustZone.

Engineering Challenges. The Split SSL [32] mainly focuses on uploading a secret to the server. To apply the same solution to the download of the protected data from the server, we need to overcome two additional engineering challenges. Firstly, the HTTP response may be fragmented into multiple TLS records and TEE does not know what to return without having the complete data. The fragmentation is caused due to the limitation of the TLS record length. The protected data will be sealed into multiple TLS records if the data size exceeds the TLS record limitation. Secondly, the secure-world reference may break the normal-world application logic because the logic written by developers should be operated on the actual data, not on the reference to the protected data. The delegation model requires developers to spend the minimum effort integrating TrustZone protection. Thus our design needs to find a way to let the application logic operate on our reference without breaking it.

HTTPS Packet Fragment. The Figure 12 is the overview of our TrustZone-protected HTTPS download. Our system can handle the HTTPS packet fragmentation and return a partial reference to the normal world. One single HTTP packet that is put into the TLS layer could be potentially sealed into multiple TLS records because the TLS record has a maximum of 16KB length, as shown in Figure 12 ❷. Once the secure world knows the size of protected data from the HTTP header, and if the size exceeds the TLS record size limit, the secure world will start to track the offset of currently received data. The protected data will be firstly saved in chunks with the length of the TLS record. Our solution returns a partial reference for each TLS record. The partial reference is combined with the reference to the protected data and the sequence order of the protected data. We embed the reference in a shadow copy of the TLS record, which has the same length as the TLS record, and return the shadow copy to the normal world, as shown in Figure 12 ❹.

Our solution manages all partial references and their corresponding data in a reference management table. Table 2 is a simplified example of our reference management table. We bind the protected data with the server name. If the data is fragmented, we have metadata to describe the sequence and the position of the fragmented data. Once the secure world gets all pieces, our solution concatenates all parts into one buffer and saves it in the secure world.

Reference Design. Applications typically store the data in two places: memory and file. When applications save the data in the memory, our design embeds the reference in a shadow copy that has

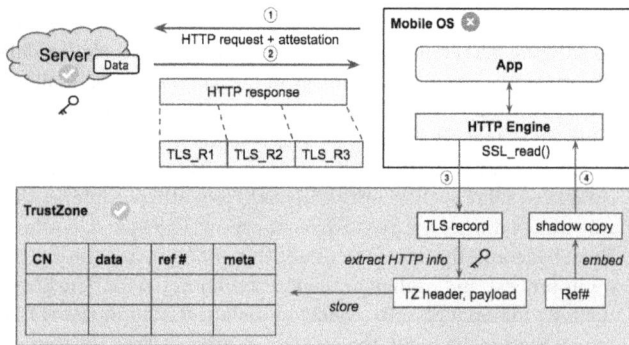

Figure 12: TrustZone-enabled HTTPS Downloading
Table 2: Reference Management Table

CN	data	ref	metadata
a.com	ptr1	12345678(1)	Seq=1,offset=0:16KB
a.com	ptr2	12345678(2)	Seq=2,offset=16:32KB
a.com	ptr3	12345678(3)	Seq=3,offset=32:42KB

the same length as the protected data and returns the shadow copy to the normal world. The shadow copy also preserves the file header in the shadow copy to ensure that the returned reference does not break the normal-world application logic. When applications save the data in the file, the data will be saved in the secure-world file system. The application can ask the secure world to save the content and get a secure-world file path back. Application developers can display the confidential data using both types of reference.

6 SECURITY ANALYSIS

In this section, we present the security analysis of our TrustZone UI design. Our design can guarantee the confidentiality of UI display and UI input, and the integrity of UI interaction when OS and hypervisor are compromised. We also analyze the security of the secure downloading feature that we built on top of the Split SSL [32]. Our analysis assumes that the TrustZone hardware platform is trusted and the secure boot process has initialized the integrity-verified secure-world OS. Hardware attacks, side-channel attacks, shoulder surfing, and DOS attacks are considered out of scope.

6.1 Confidential Display Security Analysis

The objectives of adversary include stealing the TEE-protected data stored in the secure world, accessing the data loaded in the secure-world memory and that displayed on the screen, inferring the data based on the normal-world view information, and accessing the secrets without authorization of the real user.

The normal world cannot steal the protected data stored in the TEE because the protected data is stored in the TEE trusted storage, which is a standard TEE storage solution. When the TA inserts the protected data into the secure-world framebuffer, the TA loads the data into a piece of secure-world memory. Because of the TEE memory isolation, the normal world cannot access the secrets in the secure-world framebuffer.

The normal world cannot access the protected data displayed on the screen. As mentioned in the hardware setup in Section 4.4, the secure world has an exclusive control over the secure-world I/O ports. The normal world thus cannot access the displayed content when the secure world controls the display. We clean up the screen cache before the CPU switches to the normal world to prevent the normal world from reading the cache residue.

The normal world cannot infer the confidential data based on the view information because the content of the view is protected in the secure world. The untrusted normal world can only DOS the confidential display with wrong view coordinates or the wrong framebuffer content.

The unauthorized user who obtains the smartphone cannot see the secrets protected by the secure-world Pattern Locker. For example, some secrets, such as ID card, are visible to users only after the authorization. Our design will not unlock the Pattern Locker if users do not know the pattern and will prevent them from continuing to brute force patterns after 10 failed attempts.

6.2 Confidential Input Security Analysis

The objectives of the adversary include stealing users' inputs, tricking users to type the secret in the normal world, and inferring users' clicks from the secure-world return values.

The normal world cannot get the user's input from the touchscreen. As discussed in Section 6.1, the normal world cannot access the touchscreen when the secure world controls the screen hardware. Therefore, the normal world cannot get the user's touch coordinates generated by the touchscreen.

The normal world cannot fool users into typing secrets. Although the normal world can fake the same UI look and trick the users to type secrets, we use an LED light to indicate to users whether they are typing in the secure world. The secure world obtains the exclusive control over this LED, so the normal world cannot control the indicator. The existing work [32] has done the survey to study whether users can correctly recognize the LED as the world indicator. The study result concludes that users are capable of differentiating worlds based on the LED light.

The normal world cannot infer the touch coordinates from the TA return values because both confidential-display and confidential-input TAs only return the back button event to the normal world. In the case of the Confirmation Activity, only the confirmation button event is returned to the normal world. The normal world cannot use the confirmation button to construct a confidential keyboard and let the secure world return the user's confidential input because only the secure world can render the texts (e.g., Yes, Cancel) for confirmation buttons. The normal world cannot fool users if it cannot render contents on buttons.

The untrusted normal world can only DOS the confidential input with wrong view coordinates or the wrong framebuffer content.

6.3 Integrity-preserved UI Security Analysis

The objectives of the adversary include fooling users into confirming the wrong action, and forging the attestation.

We prevent the normal world from drawing the untrusted confirmation content on the UI. Because the normal world has the full control of the UI drawing, the normal world can draw the UI in a way that makes the user's intended message visible to users and makes the actual attested message inconspicuous to users. To prevent such an attack, the secure world blurs all non-sensitive regions that are not labelled as TrustZone-enabled in the screenshot. Furthermore, before rendering the integrity-preserved text on the truz-view, the TA cleans the secure view region to prevent the normal world from displaying untrusted contents in the secure view region. The TA fills in the text that is either from TrustZone or is verified by the server.

The normal world cannot fool users into making a wrong decision by providing the wrong view coordinates. The normal world can send the wrong coordinates of truz-views to the secure world. For example, the normal world can swap coordinates of positive and negative buttons and send them to the secure world. However, the secure world renders texts including confirmation message and button text. For example, the TA ensures that the negative button only renders the negative text (e.g., Cancel) on the button.

We provide users with solutions to check the identity of the TEE-protected data before the secure world displays the data. The normal world can fool the secure world into displaying the wrong data because the normal world controls the reference to the data. For example, the attacker can ask the bank server to load the attacker's receiving payment barcode into the secure world. When the user receives money by providing the barcode, the normal world can provide the secure world with the reference to the attacker's receiving payment barcode. In that case, users have to check the identity of the data before the secure world shows the data. We allow the authorized server to provide metadata along with the protected data when the secure world downloads data from the server. If the data needs additional metadata to describe the identity of the data (e.g., barcode), the server can use our Pattern Locker to display the barcode's metadata in the secure world before it shows the barcode. The TA allows users to confirm the metadata (e.g., account name) in the secure-world LockPatternView before displaying the content. In our design, we assume that the metadata from the authorized server is trusted and the user can verify the integrity of the data using our TrustZone-enabled LockPatternView.

The normal world cannot forge the secure-world attestation. The server and TrustZone exchange the attestation key through the Split SSL. The normal world cannot forge the attestation without the key. Furthermore, we append a nonce when computing the attestation to avoid replayability.

6.4 Data Download Security Analysis

Attackers' goal includes stealing the protected data and loading malicious data into the TEE.

To prevent the server from leaking the confidential data, when developers send the download request to the server, our solution inserts an attestation that the normal world cannot forge in the HTTP header field. The server always verifies the attestation before sending the protected data.

To avoid attackers from arbitrarily downloading data into the TEE, the secure world has a whitelist that stores servers that users sign in through the secure-world UI. The secure world refuses to save data that comes from an untrusted domain.

The integrity of the HTTPS response cannot be changed by the normal world because the HTTPS packet is first decrypted inside the secure world.

During the data transmission, the untrusted normal world cannot eavesdrop on the encrypted channel because we conduct the SSL key exchange between the server and TrustZone. Without knowing the SSL encryption key, the normal world cannot decrypt the HTTPS response.

After the protected data is stored in the secure world, our design prevents the data from being uploaded to an untrusted domain. Our design binds each piece of data with a whitelist of trusted domains, which can be set by the user or the trusted server.

7 EVALUATION

In Section 4, we have demonstrated applications of our design (i.e., ImageView, KeyboardView, etc.). In this section, we further evaluate TruZ-View from three aspects: TCB reduction, ease of adoption, and performance. For TCB reduction, we compare our TCB size with a standard UI stack and network stack. We quantified the effort that developers take to adapt our solution using the real-world apps and measured the performance overhead that we introduced to both the normal world and secure world. We conducted the evaluation on HiKey 620 board [1], which runs both Android 9.0 in the normal world and OPTEE OS [22] in the secure world.

7.1 TCB Reduction

Our solution eliminates large swaths of code, compared with the existing TrustZone UI works [4, 20, 30], which installed an individual UI framework in the TEE. The comparison result is summarized in the table 3. Take a standard UI stack as an example - Xlib [10] is used for the UI display and the UI input. Xlib has more than 100k LOC. The widget toolkit called tk [8] that runs on top of Xlib contains half a million LOC.

We installed a modified font rendering library [7] that contains 1453 LOC in the secure world. Our TA code is only approximately 2000 LOC. Notably, we require screen drivers in the secure world for display and input. All existing works [4, 20, 30] also installed drivers in the TEE to keep a robust TCB. Our solution only requires a SSL crypto library in the secure world for secure server communication.

Table 3: TCB Reduction

Component	Existing TCB size	Our TCB size
UI stack	100k LOC	1453 LOC
UI widget	500k LOC	2000 LOC

7.2 Ease of Adoption

Methodology. We evaluated the ease of adoption of our design by measuring how much effort developers need to take to add TrustZone support to protect apps' existing UI and to conduct a system update. We quantify the effort as Line of code (LOC) added to use our solution, time spent on making the change, and success rate. We conducted the application evaluation using both open- and closed-source apps. We downloaded the code of open-source apps from F-Droid [2] and the closed-source apps from Google Play. We manually identify the UI risks (e.g., screenshot attack, keylog attack, etc) from the collected apps. Then we applied truz-views to eliminate the UI risks. For open-source apps, we count the LOC changes and modification time in order to integrate our solution into apps. For closed-source apps, we count the success rate of our integration. We initially implemented our solution on Android 7.0 and recorded the time to incorporated our solution on Android 9.0.

We need to solve one engineering challenge in order to evaluate our system on closed-source apps. Our design is mainly designed for open-source applications where we can label the view as TrustZone-enabled. To overcome the limitation that we cannot label views as TrustZone-enabled for closed-source apps, we customized the view system just for the purpose of evaluation. Our main idea is that each view object has a unique resource ID during runtime. We provide a configure file for Android view system. We can label the closed-source app's view by adding the resource ID of view into the configuration file. Our evaluation methodology on closed-source apps does not need to repackage the binary files and thus avoids all types of app crash caused by repackaging.

For use cases, we let apps display various types of sensitive data in the secure world by using our ImageView and TextView. Apps can further use our LockPatternView to display the data identity or authenticate users. We allow apps to secure the users' input in the secure world using our KeyboardView and SignatureView, and to confirm an important action inside the secure world using our Confirmation Dialog and Confirmation Activity.

Result. We totally modified 14 open-source apps, and results are shown in Table 4. It takes fewer than 5 minutes to modify all apps. Most apps take 2 LOC. One of the 2 LOC labels the view as TrustZone-enabled and the other LOC provides the reference to the TEE-protected data. The Confirmation Activity depends on how many views are needed to display in the secure world. The dialog has a fixed pattern, which is two buttons (i.e., positive and negative button) and a TextView for the confirmation message. Both Dialog and Confirmation Activity need 1 LOC to extract the attestation result from the MotionEvent.

Table 4: Evaluation Results for Open-Source Apps

App name	Test Case	LOC	Time (min)
Bitcoin wallet	ImageView	2	2
Bitcoin wallet	LockPatternView	2	2
Loyalty card	ImageView	2	3
Loyalty card	LockPatternView	2	3
andOPT	TextView	2	2
NoteCrypt	TextView	2	2
Signal	KeyboardView	1	1
Telegram	KeyboardView	1	1
Android-Signaturepad	SignatureView	2	2
Signatureview	SignatureView	2	2
UPM	Dialog	2	3
NoteCrypt	Dialog	2	3
Peanut Encryption	Confirmation	6	5
Note Buddy	Confirmation	6	5
Keypass DX	LockPatternView	2	2
Sealnote	LockPatternView	2	2

We collected 42 apps, including Chase, WeChat, Facebook, Linkedin, Instagram, Twitter, Alipay, etc. We used 10 apps for each use cases. Our result is shown in Table 5. All experiments were successful.

We migrated our design from Android 7.0 to 9.0. It took 6 hours to migrate our design to the new view system. Our system update is quick because our design of the view system follows its existing workflow.

7.3 Performance

In this section, we present results of performance evaluation for each major component in our system.

View system overhead. Our design modifies the view system in the Android graphics stack. We measure the performance overhead introduced to the Android graphics stack by running the benchmark tool called Basemark OS, which runs a series of test cases and provides a score report. We conducted the benchmark ten times, with a reboot to remove the impact caused by other factors, and then calculated the average score. As shown in Table 6, the major impact is caused by our modification in Android view system and by the memory access of framebuffer.

Input event latency. We calculated the touch input overhead by measuring the additional logic added to the onTouchEvent() in the view system. Because the logic added to each view is almost the same, we used the ImageView to measure the touch input overhead. The touch response overhead is less than 1 ms.

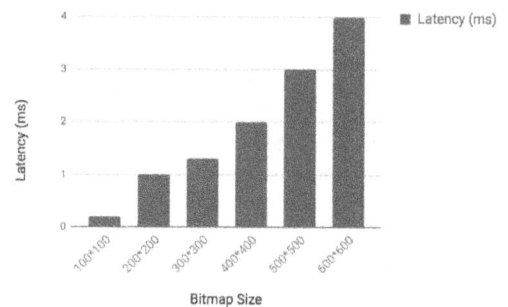

Figure 13: Image Rendering Overhead

Secure-world rendering overhead. Our image-operation TA renders content on the secure-world framebuffer. We measured the performance of the bitmap operations for both image and text in OPTEE OS [22]. We measured the time needed to construct the final framebuffer for various image sizes, word lengths, and font sizes. Figure 13 shows the image rendering overhead with common image sizes from 100*100 to 600*600. The overhead is less than 4 ms. Figure 14 shows the text rendering overhead with different lengths from 100 to 300 and different font sizes from 10 to 30. The overhead is less than 5 ms for the largest combination. Our rendering performance evaluation shows that our bitmap rendering approach is feasible to the real TrustZone platform with a low-performance cost.

Framebuffer sharing overhead. We measured the overhead of copying the normal-world framebuffer to the secure world. Because we introduce a separate Raspberry Pi to control screen, the actual

Table 5: Evaluation Result for Closed-Source Apps

Test Case	EditText	ImageView	TextView	SignaturePadView	Dialog/Confirmation	LockPatternView
Success/Total	10/10	10/10	10/10	10/10	10/10	10/10

Table 6: Framebuffer Transfer Performance Overhead

Benchmark	Origin	Modified	Overhead
System	1506	1499	0.4%
Graphics	306	302	1.4%

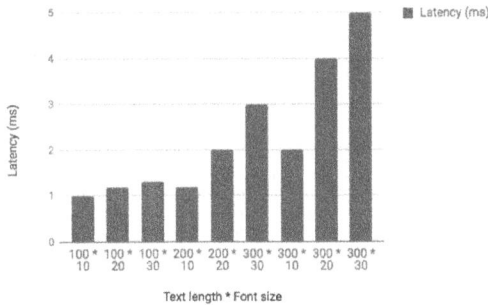

Figure 14: Text Rendering Overhead

Table 7: Framebuffer Transfer Performance Overhead

Data Size	TCP (second) for Emulation	SHM (second) for Real System
2MB	2.28	0.013
4MB	4.45	0.025
8MB	8.76	0.046

framebuffer memory sharing is over TCP (from the normal world to the Raspberry Pi). We also measured the OPTEE shared memory to transfer various sizes of framebuffer (2 MB - 8 MB). Table 7 shows both our framebuffer transferring overhead and the projected overhead. We argue that when vendors adopt our solution, the extra cost introduced by the Raspberry Pi can be reduced easily and replaced with the projected overhead because all vendors have drivers to their screen hardware, but rare research groups can obtain the access to drivers to a particular model of SOC.

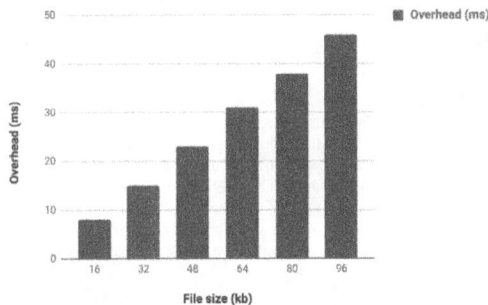

Figure 15: Data Download Performance Overhead

Download data overhead. We measured the overhead of our secure downloading feature. The overhead (average of 20 trails) is calculated based on the downloading time of various file size (16KB - 96KB). To eliminate the overhead caused by the Split SSL solution,

we only calculated the overhead introduced by the SSL_read() and excluded the time for the TLS handshake. To eliminate the fact of the network bandwidth, we used the following way to calculate the overhead:

overhead = TZ download time - normal download time

Figure 15 summarizes our performance result. The main overhead is caused by the world switch of each TLS record decryption.

8 DISCUSSION

Limitation. Our current approach cannot support dynamic UI features, such as animation, scroll up/down, a timer, and touch event propagation, in the secure world. Our design is mainly used for static UI, which requires the TrustZone assistance. However, most of the security-related tasks do not involve these dynamic UI features (e.g., animation, timer, etc). If users need to use the dynamic UI features, users can interact with the same app's UI (without the protected data on the UI) in the normal world. We consider that the security benefits of our design are worth the cost of these UI dynamic features in the secure world.

9 RELATED WORK

In this section, we compare our work with other TrustZone UI solutions. Our UI solution can benefit all research works that build on top the TrustZone UI solution. We also list present Android UI security-related research.

TrustZone UI solutions. TrustZone UI solutions provide applications a development platform to build secure-world UI. Our work fits into this category. Several TrustZone UI solutions [4, 20, 30] follow a self-contained model. These solutions require a large TCB in the secure world. Another category of the solution [11] leverages the normal-world hypervisor protection. Our work is different from ShrodinText [11] in two aspects: (1) our threat model is stronger. ShrodinText requires a trusted hypervisor in the normal world to secure screen. We do not trust any normal-world components including hypervisor since hypervisor can be compromised by the untrusted OS [9, 25]; (2) our solution has a comprehensive UI coverage. Our design offers a generic UI solution to protect both UI input and UI display while ShrodinText mainly focuses on a single use case of UI display (i.e., display text). It is difficult to generalize ShrodinText design to protect both UI input and output like what we do.

TrustZone UI applications. Several research works identified the security UI risks and develop various solutions on top of the TrustZone UI. Li et al. [17, 18] built on top of T6 [4] and improve the integrity of mobile UI. Samsung KNOX [27] built on top of Trustonic [30] and protected the confidentiality and integrity of the UI interaction. TruZ-UI [32] provided generic secure-world UI and bound with the normal-world application code. TrustOTP [28] leveraged TrustZone UI to protect the one-time password display.

TrustPay [35] proposed a mobile payment framework on the Trust-Zone platform to protect the display of the user's payment information. IM-Visor [29] and Li et al. [19] protected the users' inputs by capturing the users' sensitive keystrokes inside the secure world. Dmitrienko et al. [14] proposed a security architecture for the protection of electronic health records and authentication credentials used to access e-health services. AEP-M [31] adapted TrustZone to protect users' money and critical data during the e-payment process. Our research benefits all these works that built on top of the TrustZone UI solution and provides an easy-to-use UI solution for them.

Android UI Security. Researchers have discovered various vulnerabilities [12, 13, 15, 16, 24, 34] in Android UI system and proposed several solutions [5, 12, 23, 26, 33] to mitigate the problems. Different from TEE researches, Android UI researches assume that the Android OS is robust and the malware wants to gain unauthorized access to the UI. Researchers discovered several UI task hijacking techniques [13, 15, 24, 34] to render phishing UI. Antonio et al. [12] and WindowGuard [23] proposed solutions to mitigate the UI task hijacking. Yanick et al. [15] and Luo et al. [21] discovered touch jacking in the Android UI. Android has been aware of the screenshot attack and has allowed developers to set a secure window to prevent the app's UI from being taken screenshots [5]. However, the Android secure window cannot protect the UI in the event of a compromised OS.

10 SUMMARY

In this paper, we proposed a TrustZone UI design model called *delegation model* and systematically studied the design properties of the delegation model. Based on our new model, we developed truz-views that includes confidential display, confidential input, and integrity-preserved interaction. We implemented our design on the HiKey board and evaluated our system using real-world apps. The evaluation results show that our solutions can be adopted easily by existing apps with a low-performance overhead.

11 ACKNOWLEDGMENTS

We would like to thank our anonymous reviewers for their insightful comments. This project was supported in part by the NSF grant 1718086. We also thank Xiaoyun Shen-Krizic for her detailed editing suggestion.

REFERENCES

[1] 2017. Android Developers: Selecting Devices. https://source.android.com/source/devices.html. (2017).
[2] 2017. F-Droid repository. https://f-droid.org/en/packages/. (2017).
[3] 2017. Samsung Pay. http://www.samsung.com/us/samsung-pay/. (2017).
[4] 2017. TrustKernel T6 Secure OS. https://www.trustkernel.com/en/products/tee/t6.html. (2017).
[5] 2018. Android WindowManager FLAG SECURE. https://developer.android.com/reference/android/view/WindowManager.LayoutParams. (2018).
[6] 2018. Google Android: Vulnerability Statistics. http://www.cvedetails.com/product/19997/Google-Android.html?vendor_id=1224. (2018).
[7] 2018. MCUFont. https://github.com/mcufont/mcufont. (2018).
[8] 2018. Tk graphical user interface toolkit. https://www.tcl.tk/. (2018).
[9] 2018. XEN security vulnerability. https://www.cvedetails.com/vulnerability-list/vendor_id-6276/XEN.html. (2018).
[10] 2018. Xlib X Language X Interface. https://www.x.org/archive/X11R7.5/doc/libX11/libX11.html. (2018).
[11] Ardalan Amiri Sani. 2017. SchrodinText: Strong Protection of Sensitive Textual Content of Mobile Applications. In *Proceedings of the 15th Annual International Conference on Mobile Systems, Applications, and Services (MobiSys '17)*. ACM, New York, NY, USA, 197–210. https://doi.org/10.1145/3081333.3081346
[12] Antonio Bianchi, Jacopo Corbetta, Luca Invernizzi, Yanick Fratantonio, Christopher Kruegel, and Giovanni Vigna. 2015. What the App is That? Deception and Countermeasures in the Android User Interface. (2015).
[13] Qi Alfred Chen, Zhiyun Qian, and Z. Morley Mao. 2014. Peeking into Your App without Actually Seeing It: UI State Inference and Novel Android Attacks. In *23rd USENIX Security Symposium (USENIX Security 14)*.
[14] Alexandra Dmitrienko, Zecir Hadzic, Hans Löhr, Ahmad-Reza Sadeghi, and Marcel Winandy. 2013. Securing the Access to Electronic Health Records on Mobile Phones. In *Biomedical Engineering Systems and Technologies*.
[15] Yanick Fratantonio, Chenxiong Qian, Simon Chung, and Wenke Lee. 2017. Cloak and Dagger: From Two Permissions to Complete Control of the UI Feedback Loop. In *Proceedings of the IEEE Symposium on Security and Privacy (Oakland)*.
[16] Tongxin Li, Xueqiang Wang, Mingming Zha, Kai Chen, XiaoFeng Wang, Luyi Xing, Xiaolong Bai, Nan Zhang, and Xinhui Han. 2017. Unleashing the Walking Dead: Understanding Cross-App Remote Infections on Mobile WebViews. In *Proceedings of the 2017 ACM SIGSAC Conference on Computer and Communications Security (CCS '17)*.
[17] W. Li, H. Li, H. Chen, and Y. Xia. 2015. AdAttester: Secure Online Mobile Advertisement Attestation Using TrustZone. In *Proceedings of the 13th Annual International Conference on Mobile Systems, Applications, and Services*. NY, USA.
[18] Wenhao Li, Shiyu Luo, Zhichuang Sun, Yubin Xia, Long Lu, Haibo Chen, Binyu Zang, and Haibing Guan. [n. d.]. VButton: Practical Attestation of User-driven Operations in Mobile Apps. In *Proceedings of the 16th Annual International Conference on Mobile Systems, Applications, and Services (MobiSys '18)*.
[19] W. Li, M. Ma, J. Han, Y. Xia, B. Zang, C. Chu, and T. Li. 2014. Building trusted path on untrusted device drivers for mobile devices. In *Proceedings of 5th Asia-Pacific Workshop on Systems*. Beijing, China.
[20] D. Liu and L. Cox. 2014. VeriUI: Attested Login for Mobile Devices. In *Proceedings of the 15th Workshop on Mobile Computing Systems and Applications*. CA, USA.
[21] T. Luo, X. Jin, A. Ananthanarayanan, and W. Du. 2012. Touchjacking Attacks on Web in Android, iOS, and Windows Phone. In *Proceedings of the 5th International Symposium on Foundations & Practice of Security*.
[22] OP-TEE. 2015. OPTEE OS. (2015). https://github.com/OP-TEE/optee_os
[23] Chuangang Ren, Peng Liu, and Sencun Zhu. 2017. WindowGuard: Systematic Protection of GUI Security in Android. In *NDSS*.
[24] Chuangang Ren, Yulong Zhang, Hui Xue, Tao Wei, and Peng Liu. 2015. Towards Discovering and Understanding Task Hijacking in Android. In *24th USENIX Security Symposium (USENIX Security 15)*.
[25] B. Robert, V. Julian, and N. Jan. 2016. The Threat of Virtualization: Hypervisor-Based Rootkits on the ARM Architecture. In *Information and Communications Security*.
[26] Franziska Roesner and Tadayoshi Kohno. 2013. Securing Embedded User Interfaces: Android and Beyond. In *Presented as part of the 22nd USENIX Security Symposium (USENIX Security 13)*. USENIX.
[27] Samsung. 2013. KNOX White Paper. (2013).
[28] H. Sun, K. Sun, Y. Wang, and J. Jing. 2015. TrustOTP: Transforming Smartphones into Secure One-Time Password Tokens. In *Proceedings of the 22nd ACM Conference on Computer and Communications Security*. Denver, Colorado, USA.
[29] Chen Tian, Yazhe Wang, Peng Liu, Qihui Zhou, Chengyi Zhang, and Zhen Xu. 2017. IM-Visor: A Pre-IME Guard to Prevent IME Apps from Stealing Sensitive Keystrokes Using TrustZone. *2017 47th Annual IEEE/IFIP International Conference on Dependable Systems and Networks (DSN)* (2017).
[30] Trustonic. 2012. Trustonic TEE Trusted User Interface. (2012).
[31] Bo Yang, Kang Yang, Zhenfeng Zhang, Yu Qin, and Dengguo Feng. 2016. AEP-M: Practical Anonymous E-Payment for Mobile Devices Using ARM TrustZone and Divisible E-Cash. In *Information Security*.
[32] Kailiang Ying, Amit Ahlawat, Bilal Alsharifi, Yuexin Jiang, Priyank Thavai, and Wenliang Du. 2018. TruZ-Droid: Integrating TrustZone with Mobile Operating System. In *Proceedings of the 16th ACM International Conference on Mobile Systems, Applications, and Services* (June 10-15) (MobiSys '18). Munich, Germany.
[33] Xiao Zhang, Yousra Aafer, Kailiang Ying, and Wenliang Du. 2016. Hey, You, Get Off of My Image: Detecting Data Residue in Android Images. In *Computer Security – ESORICS 2016*.
[34] Xiao Zhang, Kailiang Ying, Yousra Aafer, Zhenshen Qiu, and Wenliang Du. 2016. Life after App Uninstallation: Are the Data Still Alive? Data Residue Attacks on Android. In *NDSS*.
[35] Xianyi Zheng, Lulu Yang, Jiangang Ma, Gang Shi, and Dan Meng. 2016. TrustPAY: Trusted mobile payment on security enhanced ARM TrustZone platforms.. In *ISCC*.

Understanding the Responsiveness of Mobile App Developers to Software Library Updates

Tatsuhiko Yasumatsu
Waseda University
Tokyo, Japan
ty@nsl.cs.waseda.ac.jp

Takuya Watanabe
NTT Secure Platform Labs
& Waseda University
Tokyo, Japan
watanabe.takuya@lab.ntt.co.jp

Fumihiro Kanei
NTT Secure Platform Labs
Tokyo, Japan
kanei.fumihiro@lab.ntt.co.jp

Eitaro Shioji
NTT Secure Platform Labs
Tokyo, Japan
shioji.eitaro@lab.ntt.co.jp

Mitsuaki Akiyama
NTT Secure Platform Labs
Tokyo, Japan
akiyama@ieee.com

Tatsuya Mori
Waseda University
& RIKEN AIP
Tokyo, Japan
mori@nsl.cs.waseda.ac.jp

ABSTRACT

This paper reports a longitudinal measurement study aiming to understand how mobile app developers are *responsive* to updates of software libraries over time. To quantify their responsiveness to library updates, we collected 21,046 Android apps, which equated 142,611 unique application package kit (APK) files, each corresponding to a different version of an app. The release dates of these APK files spanned across 9 years. The key findings we derived from our analysis are as follows. (1) We observed an undesirable level of responsiveness of app developers; 50% of library update adoptions by app developers were performed for more than 3 months after the release date of the library, and 50% of outdated libraries used in apps were retained for over 10 months. (2) Deploying a security fix campaign in the app distribution market effectively reduced the number of apps with unfixed vulnerabilities; however, CVE-numbered vulnerabilities (without a campaign) were prone to remain unfixed. (3) The responsiveness of app developers varied and depended on multiple factors, for example, popular apps with a high number of installations had a better response to library updates and, while it took 77 days on average for app developers to adopt version updates for advertising libraries, it took 237 days for updates of utility libraries to be adopted. We discuss practical ways to eliminate libraries with vulnerabilities and to improve the responsiveness of app developers to library updates.

CCS CONCEPTS

• **Security and privacy → Software security engineering**;

KEYWORDS

Android Security; Mobile Apps Measurement; Software Library; Mobile App Developers

ACM Reference Format:
Tatsuhiko Yasumatsu, Takuya Watanabe, Fumihiro Kanei, Eitaro Shioji, Mitsuaki Akiyama, and Tatsuya Mori. 2019. Understanding the Responsiveness of Mobile App Developers to Software Library Updates. In *Ninth ACM Conference on Data and Application Security and Privacy (CODASPY '19), March 25–27, 2019, Richardson, TX, USA.* ACM, New York, NY, USA, 12 pages. https://doi.org/10.1145/3292006.3300020

1 INTRODUCTION

The rise of mobile app marketplaces has attracted a large number of app developers who wish to publish or monetize their apps on mobile app distribution platforms. The number of applications on these platforms has dramatically increased since the first iPhone /Android was released way back in 2007/2008. As of September 2018, there are over 2.8 million apps available on the official app distribution platform for Android–Google Play [3]. Published Android apps have been installed in over 2 billion Android devices worldwide.

Modern mobile app development is highly dependent on software libraries, which enable developers to incorporate rich functionalities into their apps without requiring large coding effort, for example, installing advertisements to monetize apps, providing access to social media services such as Twitter or Facebook, and providing QR code reader functionalities. In general, mobile app developers use third-party libraries to ease the burden of the app development process.

The widespread use of software libraries has resulted in high productivity in the development of apps, however some software libraries can be piggybacked with vulnerabilities, thereby putting end users of the app at a security risk. In fact, previous studies [8, 24, 37, 43] have reported that many app vulnerabilities originate from vulnerabilities in third-party libraries. The problem is that, even if a developer of a software library has fixed a vulnerability, many app developers may not notice the update or may not adopt it immediately, leaving the vulnerable version of the library in their apps. In addition, defects found in a third-party library may lower the quality of the apps that use that library, consequently degrading the quality of the end users' experience [5, 35].

Therefore, being responsive to updates of software libraries plays a key role in maintaining the security and/or quality of mobile apps. However, it is not clear how responsive app developers are to software library updates. In particular, we are interested in the following research questions.

- *How long does it take for an app developer to adopt an update of a software library?*
- *What are the primary factors that determine their responsiveness to updates of software libraries?*

To address these research questions, we performed a longitudinal, large-scale measurement study of Android apps. We first collected 21,046 unique Android apps. For each app, we collected its previous versions, resulting in 142,611 unique application package kit (APK) files, each corresponding to a different version of an app. Note that these APK files were released between November 2008 and August 2017, that is, our measurement time window is approximately 9 years. By performing a statistical analysis on these APK files, we detected 152 different software libraries, or 1078 unique versions. For the detected libraries, we also noted their release dates. By correlating the release dates of the libraries with the detected libraries in the different versions of the apps, we can measure the time taken for an app developer to adopt an update of a library.

Our key findings are summarized as follows:

- We found an undesirable level of responsiveness by the app developers: 50% of library update adoptions were performed for more than 3 months after the release date of the library, whereas 50% of outdated libraries used in apps were retained for over 10 months.
- Security fix campaigns conducted by the app market provider can effectively reduce the number of apps with unfixed vulnerabilities; however, CVE-numbered vulnerabilities (without a security fix campaign) were prone to remain unfixed.
- The responsiveness of the app developers varied and depended on several different factors, for example, popular apps with a high number of installations had a better response to library updates. They took 77 days, on average, to adopt library version updates for advertising libraries and took 237 days to update utility libraries.

Given these observations, we discuss possible ways to eliminate vulnerable libraries and improve the responsiveness of mobile app developers.

2   DATA

In this section, we present two key data acquisition methodologies we used for our analysis: (i) extracting the version histories of apps and (ii) software library detection. Then, we provide an overview of the data we collected. Note that we adopted Android OS as our analysis target because, of the official and third-party mobile app marketplaces, it has the largest number of users and available apps.

2.1   Data Acquisition Methodologies

2.1.1   Collecting previous versions of apps.
In the Android marketplace (Google Play), a mobile device will only see the latest version of an app. However, if one specifies a previous version, it is possible to retrieve this version by sending a request via Google Play API [23]. The version that needs to be specified is called the *versionCode*, which is expressed as an integer value assigned by the app developer. App developers can version apps arbitrarily; however, *versionCode* takes any value between 1 and 2,100,000,000[1].

We collected the version histories of apps using the following procedure. First, we checked the latest version of the app. Then, we made iterative requests for previous versions by decrementing the version requested. Note that downloading one version of an app corresponds to downloading a single APK file. APK is a file format used to install Android application software. It contains the execution codes and resources required to execute the app on an Android device. To limit any harmful effects to the service, we limited our rate of requests and spent 2 months on data collection. Other ethical considerations that we took when collecting the data are discussed in Section 5.

2.1.2   Library Detection.
To analyze the responsiveness of app developers when adopting library updates, we need to know which version of a library is included in the APK. There have been several studies that have proposed methods to detect libraries included in an APK [4, 11, 36, 43]. We adopted a tool known as LibScout [4], which can detect libraries and their versions for a given APK file. LibScout constructs fingerprints from class profiles of both apps and libraries and establishes an obfuscation-resilient similarity scoring.

By detecting the library and its version from each APK in the version history of an app, we could identify the timings at which an app adopted each library update. We used this timing information to study the responsiveness of the app developers. Because there are diverse types of libraries, we manually investigated the functionalities of the detected libraries and categorized them into 10 groups, as shown in Table 1. The compiled rule of categorization is available at https://github.com/Library-Responsiveness/category.

2.2   Data Overview

App version histories were carefully collected from Google Play from July 2017 to August 2017, applying the methodologies covered in Section 2.1. Apps on Google Play were classified into 34 categories, for example, Social, News, or Games. We compiled a list of the top apps in each category. In addition, for each app listed, we checked the supplementary apps developed by the same developer and added them to the list.

As a result, we collected the version histories of 21,046 apps and, because each app history may consist of multiple APKs, our data set included 142,611 distinct APKs. Of these apps, 12,790 (134,355 APKs) had more than two versions, indicating that they had been updated at least once. We succeeded in downloading the version history of the apps in the following top-five categories: Games (2137 apps), Lifestyle (1978 apps), Personalization (1786 apps), Entertainment (1376 apps), and Education (1088 apps). The measurement window of the collected APKs spans 9 years, from November 2008 to August 2017.

---

[1]The greatest value allowed for versionCode is set to 2,100,000,000 on Google Play.

Table 1: Library categories.

Category	Description
Advertising	Ad-libraries.
Analytics	Libraries for analytics services.
AndroidDev	Android support or Google Play Services libraries.
AndroidUtil	Utility libraries that are specific to Android apps.
Extension	Extensions of Java core functions, such as IO improvement.
External	Libraries that provide access to external services other than SocialMedia.
Image	Libraries that support image processing.
Network	Libraries that support networking, such as HTTP or TLS client.
SocialMedia	Libraries that provide access to social media services.
Util	Generic utility libraries and other libraries.

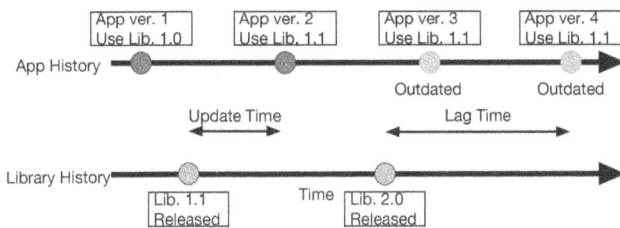

Figure 1: Example of measuring the update time and the lag time.

Applying library detection to the collected apps, we detected 152 different libraries with 1078 library versions. Apart from core Android development libraries, the most often-detected software library was Gson, which is an open-source JSON parser. Gson was used in 21,290 different APKs (12,896 apps).

3 ANALYSIS OF RESPONSIVENESS

In this section, we introduce two metrics, *update time* and *lag time*, aiming to measure the responsiveness of mobile app developers to software library updates. Using these two metrics, we then analyze the responsiveness of the mobile app developers. Finally, we perform an in-depth analysis of their responsiveness by looking at the differences between the libraries.

3.1 Metrics

To quantify the responsiveness of mobile app developers to library updates, we defined two key metrics, update time and lag time. Update time is defined as the time difference (in days) from the day the new version of the library was released to the day the app adopted the newly updated version of the library. Figure 1 illustrates an example of an update time measurement where the developer of an app adopted a version update of a library from version 1.0 to 1.1. The update time is the number of days between the release date of the library version 1.1 and the day that the next version of the app (version 2) was compiled and built. The update time measures the time needed for the app developer to adopt an update of a software library. App developers may build an APK multiple times before releasing it to Google Play. In our study, we used the build date of

the APK that was actually released to Google Play and available to end users.

The lag time is defined as the time (in days) the app used an outdated (lagged) version of the library. Library usage is considered to be lagged when the latest version of the library is not used at the time when a version of an app is built. In other words, the lag time represents the period when the app is using an outdated version of the library. Figure 1 illustrates an example of a lag time measurement where versions 3 and 4 of an app used an outdated version of the library. Note that, if the next version, which is likely version 5, updates the library to 2.0, the lagged period will not be extended. The lag time measures the time a developer continues using an outdated version of a software library. In other words, it represents the length of time for which an app developer has ignored a software library update.

We opted to use the build date of the app instead of the release date in the marketplace because we were interested in how developers respond to library updates at the time of app development. Here, the build date can be extracted from the timestamp of a file called "AndroidManifest.xml," which is given in every APK file. Leveraging the build date gives us more accurate insights into the responsiveness of the app developers. Note that the build dates and the release dates of the apps in the marketplace are fairly close. We analyzed 17,000 randomly sampled apps and found that, for more than 80%, the time differences between the build date and the release date were within 5 days, which indicates that the majority of app developers release an app to the marketplace right after they built the latest version.

Note that, while both metrics look similar, they have clear differences, that is, while the update time characterizes app developers who are responsive to software library updates, the lag time characterizes developers who are less responsive and do not maintain their libraries. More specifically, the update time measures the time taken to adopt a library update since its release, and the lag time measures how long the library used in an app was left outdated. For example, when an app developer adopts the latest library update (i.e., App ver. 2 in Figure 1), this adoption cannot be measured with the lag time because the corresponding library was not outdated (lagged) at all. Therefore, examining both the update time and the lag time will provide better insights into the responsiveness of mobile app developers.

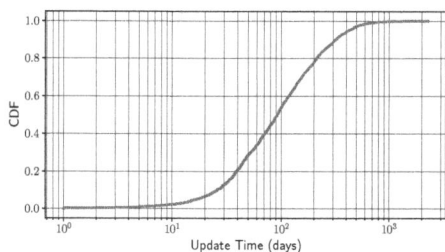

Figure 2: CDF of the update time.

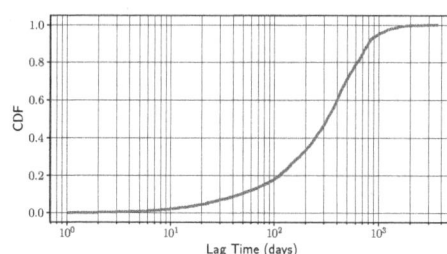

Figure 3: CDF of the lag time.

3.2 Analysis of the update time and the lag time

3.2.1 Measuring the update time and the lag time.

Measuring the update time and the lag time requires the release dates for each version of a library and the build dates for each version of an app throughout its version history. For the release dates of the libraries, we used the information included in LibScout [4]. For the build dates of the apps, we used the timestamp for "AndroidManifest.xml", a file every APK must contain. This timestamp records the time the APK was built.

Limitation: Note that recent versions of Gradle, which is the default build system for Android Studio (the IDE for developing an Android app), zero out the timestamps of files in APKs. Therefore, for APKs developed with recent versions of Gradle, we could not extract the time information. We disregarded such APKs in our analysis (except when counting the number of vulnerabilities). We observed update times that had negative values. These cases were caused primarily because of incomplete library-release-date data. Libraries with incomplete release date data were removed from our analysis. As the fraction of removed apps was 15% in total, we believe that this data cleansing will not affect the subsequent analyses.

3.2.2 Results.

Figure 2 shows the cumulative distribution of the update time analysis applied to our data. We found that approximately 50% of the library version update adoptions were performed for more than 90 days after the release of the library, that is, it took approximately 3 months for app developers to adopt library updates to succeeding app versions. Note that libraries used in apps that have never been updated by app developers will not appear in this figure. Figure 3 shows the cumulative distribution of the lag times measured from the version histories of our app data set. We found that approximately 50% of outdated usages of libraries remain for more than 300 days (10 months). The majority of this long lag time corresponds to cases where library updates were not adopted during the measurement period.

To our surprise, we found that 58.7% of the adoptions of library updates in apps did not adopt the newest versions. This indicates that app developers adopted outdated versions of the library update instead of the latest version at the time the APK was built. As Derr et al. [11] reported, Android app developers tend to search for library updates on the Internet (e.g., official web sites, blogs, or Stack Overflow) because the Android app platform does not provide

a central library marketplace such as CocoaPods for iOS. Because the information available on such web sites can become obsolete, developers are prone to adopting outdated versions of libraries.

3.3 In-depth analysis of responsiveness

Next, we studied how the responsiveness of mobile developers differs between the library categories shown in Table 1. Table 2 summarizes the results. Overall, library categories that access external services (e.g., Advertising, Social Media, and External) adopt library updates quicker than libraries that do not. Note that Network libraries are those that provide networking functionalities to clients but do not provide access to external services by themselves. Because libraries empowered with external services are prone to changes in services and/or APIs, it is natural that app developers attend to such updates so that the apps can continue to work with the external services. Specifically, advertising libraries had the shortest average update time and lag time, indicating developers' incentive to keep such libraries updated so as not to lose revenue from advertisements.

Conversely, libraries such as Extension or Util had the worst update/lag statistics. Because these libraries may not change their specifications drastically, it is natural that app developers do not adopt updates of these libraries even when newer versions become available.

To look into the responsiveness of mobile developers at a fine-grain scale, we sampled the three specific libraries as shown in Table 3. These libraries will be used for further analyses in Section 4. Figures 4 and 5 present the distributions of the average update time and lag time per app for the three libraries, respectively. The panels are sorted according to their median values. Note that Gson had the longest update/lag time. This agrees with the results shown above that the update/lag time of utility libraries tend to be longer than those of other libraries. This observation agrees with the results of Derr et al. [11], who reported that the primary motivation for app developers to adopt library updates is to make use of a new functionality. Because Gson is a parsing library, the frequency of new functionalities is less. In addition, we observed that the update/lag time for AdColony was relatively short. Again, this observation agrees with the results shown in Table 2, that is, app developers tend to adopt library updates more quickly for the advertising libraries than for other libraries.

Table 2: Statistics of the detected updates/lags for each library category.

Category	# detected updates	# detected lags	average update time (days)	average lagged time (days)
Advertising	768	2,017	77	223
SocialMedia	1,198	2,667	103	485
External	49	238	105	334
Network	681	2,937	123	487
AndroidDev	21,020	86,301	138	364
AndroidUtil	285	1582	145	482
Image	284	1,834	166	587
Analytics	50	284	199	416
Extension	295	2,276	218	566
Util	700	3,795	237	666

Table 3: The three specific libraries chosen for further analysis.

Name	Category	Description
Gson [22]	Utility	The most used library across all the categories except AndroidDev.
Facebook [13]	SocialMedia	The most used library in the SocialMedia category.
AdColony [1]	Advertising	The most used library in the Advertising category.

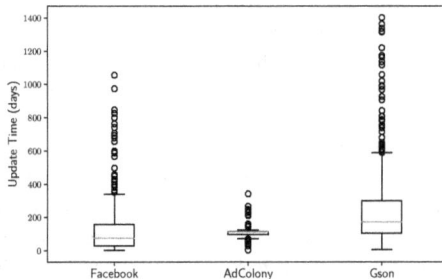

Figure 4: Distributions of the update time (box plots).

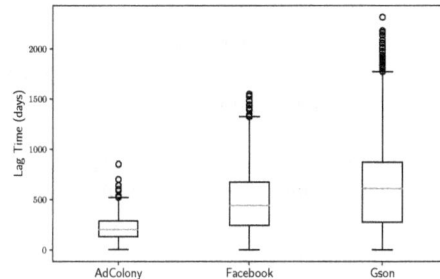

Figure 5: Distributions of the lag time (box plots).

Table 4: Statistics of vulnerable libraries.

Library	Vulnerable Versions	Vulnerable apps	Unfixed	CVE	CVSS	ASI Program
MoPub	3.10-4.3	119	8 (6.72%)	-	5.9	✓
Supersonic	5.14-6.3.4	71	10 (14.1%)	-	4.8	✓
Vungle	3.0.6-3.3.0	28	4 (14.3%)	-	9.0	✓
Facebook	3.15	54	23 (42.6%)	-	6.6	-
ApacheCC	3.2.1 / 4.0.0	34	18 (52.9%)	-	9.0	-
Dropbox	1.5.4-1.6.1	18	10 (55.6%)	CVE-2014-8889	5.3	-
OkHttp	2.1.0-2.7.4 / 3.0.0-3.1.2	1,031	653 (63.3%)	CVE-2016-2402	5.9	-
Total		1,355	726 (53.6%)			

4 FACTORS ASSOCIATED WITH THE RESPONSE TIME

In this section, we examine several factors that are likely associated with the responsiveness of developers. In particular, we study the vulnerabilities included in a library, app properties (popularity and category), library properties, developer properties, and software development conventions (semantic versioning).

4.1 Reaction to Vulnerabilities

4.1.1 Detecting Apps with Vulnerable Versions of Libraries.
We were able to decide whether a library was vulnerable by parsing the library version detected from each APK and comparing that version to a vulnerable version of the library. Table 4 summarizes the vulnerabilities [18, 21, 34, 39, 40] detected for the seven libraries found in our data set and whether they were fixed. We sampled

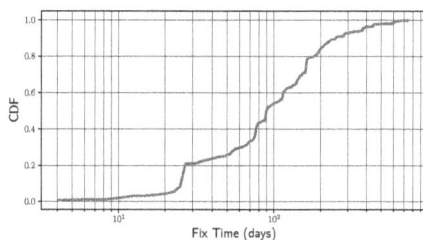

Figure 6: CDF of the fix time.

these seven libraries due to their popularity; in fact, we found that 28.3% of APK files we collected made use of one of these libraries. An app was deemed vulnerable if at least one vulnerable version of a library was featured in its history. Then each vulnerable app was classified into one of two groups: fixed apps and unfixed apps. An app was considered fixed if it is no longer vulnerable, either via updating the library or via removal of that library. If an app still had the vulnerability in its most recent version, it is considered to be unfixed.

For each vulnerability, we obtained the average number of installations for the fixed and unfixed apps. Contrary to our expectation that the fixed apps would have a larger number of installations than unfixed apps, there were three vulnerabilities (MoPub, Dropbox, and Apache CC) for which fixed apps had a lower number of installations. This result shows that even popular apps may leave vulnerabilities unfixed and expose end users to security risks. Because Google Play is known to be a supermarket [42], where a small percentage of apps contribute to most of the app downloads, the fact that even a popular app may not fix its vulnerabilities needs to be addressed.

4.1.2 Time taken to fix the vulnerabilities.
Having detected the vulnerable libraries in the apps, we can measure how long it takes for the app developers to fix a vulnerability. For apps that fixed their vulnerabilities, we measured the fix time, that is, the time difference in days from the day the very first safe version of the library was released to the day when the app that adopted a safe version of the library was built. The definition of the fix time is similar to the update time. The difference is that the measurement period starts only if the library update includes a vulnerability fix and ends when the app has adopted the fixed version of the library.

Figure 6 shows the cumulative distribution of the fix time analysis applied to the vulnerable libraries listed in Table 4. For this analysis, we excluded libraries with inaccurate release dates. The distribution shows that, for 50% of the vulnerable libraries in apps, approximately 90 days were required for the app developer to adopt library updates fixing a vulnerability. We also notice that there is a spike between 20 and 30 days. The spike corresponds to the apps developed by a single prolific developer. The developer has fixed many apps published by him/her in a short period of time. In Section 4.6, we will look into the effect of such prolific app developers who have published a large number of apps in the marketplace.

4.1.3 CVE ID.
We also studied whether the detected library vulnerabilities were assigned IDs of CVEs [33], which is a list of common identifiers for publicly known vulnerabilities. Of the libraries we investigated,

Dropbox and OkHttp had vulnerabilities with CVE IDs, indicating that these vulnerabilities had been widely announced. For each library, we measured the *unfixed rate*, which is the fraction of unfixed apps of the apps that we marked vulnerable, that is, the apps that contained the vulnerable libraries. The fourth column in Table 4 shows the results. It is surprising to see that the unfixed rates of both vulnerabilities with CVE IDs are high (Dropbox with 55.6% and OkHttp with 63.3%) and that they are the highest unfixed rates out of all the vulnerabilities we analyzed; this indicates the absence of knowledge about CVE IDs among app developers.

4.1.4 Severity of the Vulnerabilities.
Next, we studied whether the severity of the vulnerabilities prompted app developers to fix the library vulnerabilities. To quantify the severity of each vulnerability, we used the Common Vulnerability Scoring System v3.0 (CVSS) [16], which is an open framework that generates a numerical score reflecting the severity of a given vulnerability; the scores range from 0 to 10, and the vulnerability is considered more severe when the CVSS score is high. The sixth column in Table 4 presents the CVSS score for each vulnerability. For vulnerabilities with a corresponding CVE ID, we made use of a CVE database [41] to obtain the CVSS scores. For the vulnerabilities without an assigned CVE ID, we manually calculated the CVSS score, following the CVSS specifications [17].

The result indicates that there is no clear correlation between the severity of the vulnerability and the unfixed ratio. For example, both the libraries Vungle and Apache CC had severe vulnerabilities, that is, CVSS scores of 9.0. While Vungle had a low unfixed rate of 14.4%, Apache CC had a high unfixed rate of 52.9%. Therefore, the high severity of a vulnerability does not always prompt app developers to fix it, implying that even severe vulnerabilities could be left unfixed in the app market. We believe that the primary reason why many app developers fixed the vulnerability found in Vungle was because the vulnerability had been targeted by Google's App Security Improvement Program (the ASI Program).

4.1.5 App Security Improvement Campaign.
A security fix campaign conducted as a part of the ASI Program [21] has targeted several vulnerabilities found in Android apps. When a vulnerability is targeted by an ASI Program campaign, app developers that have published an app with the targeted vulnerability receive a message via email that informs them of how to fix the vulnerability. Each ASI Program campaign sets a deadline to fix the vulnerability, and after the deadline, any app with the vulnerability will not be able to be uploaded to Google Play; therefore, app developers are forced to remove such vulnerabilities. This indicates that Google Play will scan the APK file for vulnerabilities before publishing it in the market. Note that apps with targeted vulnerabilities will not be deleted from Google Play even after the deadline. The only penalty is that the developers are prohibited from uploading a new version of an app, unless that new version has fixed the vulnerability.

Of the vulnerabilities listed in Table 4, MoPub, Supersonic, and Vungle were targeted by the ASI program. We can clearly see the effectiveness of the ASI Program campaign because apps with these targeted libraries have lower unfixed rates compared to those of other vulnerabilities. For these targeted vulnerabilities, more than 85% of apps fixed the vulnerabilities during the measurement period.

4.2 App Popularity

Next, we study the relationship between the app popularity and the responsiveness of developers to library updates using the number of installations per app for the three specific libraries shown in Table 3. It is possible for a version history of an app to have more than one update time or lag time for a single library, that is, an app using a software library can update/lag it more than once, resulting in multiple update/lag times. Therefore, we calculated the mean values of the update/lag times per app. Owing to space constraints, in the following analysis, we omit the results for the update time and only show the results for the lag time.

To make the analysis clear, we also classified the apps according to the number of installations, i_a, which can be obtained from metadata provided in the marketplace. Using the 33rd percentile, I_1 and the 67th percentile, I_2 of the apps' number of installations of an app subject to our analysis, we classified the apps into the following three groups:

(1) Unpopular: $i_a < I_1$;
(2) Normal: $I_1 \leq i_a < I_2$; and
(3) Popular: $I_2 \leq i_a$;

where $I_1 = 1000$ and $I_2 = 10,000$ in the data set. Note that the number of installations published in Google Play is discretized, for example, 100, 500, and 1000.

Figure 7 shows the CDFs of the lag time for the three libraries. For each library, we analyzed how the difference in the app popularity affected the responsiveness via the lag time. First, in all three libraries, no significant difference was found between the normal and unpopular apps. For Gson and Facebook, we can see that the distributions of the lag times for popular apps are skewed toward short lag times, that is, popular apps tend to adopt a library update more quickly than normal and unpopular apps. For Gson, for example, the average lag time for popular apps with more than 10,000 downloads is 597 days, which is long but still shorter than that of apps with normal popularity, which is 684 days. Mann–Whitney U-tests between the popular and normal app lag times revealed statistically significant differences for Gson ($p < 10^{-4}$) and Facebook ($p < 0.01$). On the contrary, for AdColony, we did not find any statistically significant differences between the three popularity classes. This observation implies that even apps with few installations and low prevalence are as sensitive as popular apps when it comes to advertisement libraries.

Finally, to verify the generality of the observed tendency, we extended the study by analyzing 10 additional libraries taken from the most popular libraries. For each library, we first classified the apps into three groups—unpopular, normal, and popular—following our definition shown above. We then analyzed the lag times of the apps in each category. We aimed to test whether there were statistically significant differences in the lag times for the different popularity classes. Accordingly, we used the Mann–Whitney U-test. Table 5 summarizes the results. Of the 13 libraries, including the 3 reference libraries, 10 libraries exhibited the same tendency, that is, popular apps had shorter lag times than normal/unpopular apps with a statistically significant difference. This result positively supports our observation that popular apps tend to adopt library updates more quickly than less popular apps.

Table 5: Mann–Whitney U-tests of the lag times for apps from different popularity classes: U, unpopular; N, normal; and P, popular. The libraries presented with bold fonts had statistically significant differences between popularity classes. (top) The three reference libraries and (bottom) additional libraries.

Library	U vs. N	N vs. P
	p-value	
Gson	0.0516	**$< 10^{-4}$**
Facebook	0.0604	**< 0.01**
AdColony	0.839	0.261
OkHttp	0.233	**$< 10^{-5}$**
Nine-Old-Androids	1.00	0.33
universal-image-loader	0.696	**$< 10^{-10}$**
Picasso	**< 0.02**	0.499
Retrofit	0.119	**$< 10^{-4}$**
Bolts	0.434	**< 0.02**
okio	0.624	**$< 10^{-6}$**
Twitter4J	**< 0.03**	**< 0.02**
Apache-Commons-Lang	0.506	**< 0.01**
Apache-Commons-IO	0.454	0.148

Our findings suggest that app popularity does affect the motivation of app developers to adopt library updates. More popular apps react to new library releases more sensitively than do less popular apps.

4.3 Number of App Versions

To determine how the number of versions released for an app affects the responsiveness of the app developers, we classified the apps into three groups depending on the number of versions released. According to the number of released versions of an app, v_a, we grouped the apps as follows:

(1) Few versions: $v_a < V_1$;
(2) Medium versions: $V_1 \leq v_a < V_2$; and
(3) Many versions: $V_2 \leq v_a$;

where V_1 and V_2 are the 33rd and 67th percentiles, respectively. In our data set, the percentiles were $V_1 = 3$ and $V_2 = 8$.

In this analysis, we ignored apps that have released only one version. Figure 8 shows the distributions of the lag time for the three groups defined above. Overall, we do not see a clear unified relationship between the number of released versions for an app and the lag time. For Gson, apps with more versions had shorter lag times. For Facebook and AdColony, the relationship was opposite, that is, apps with fewer versions had shorter lag times. Therefore, we believe that the number of released app versions is not a primary factor determining the responsiveness of a developer.

4.4 App Category

To study the relationship between the app category and the responsiveness of the developers, we measured the average lag time per app for the top-five app categories in our data set, that is, Games, Education, Lifestyle, Personalization, and Entertainment. Table 6 summarizes the results using the three case study libraries shown

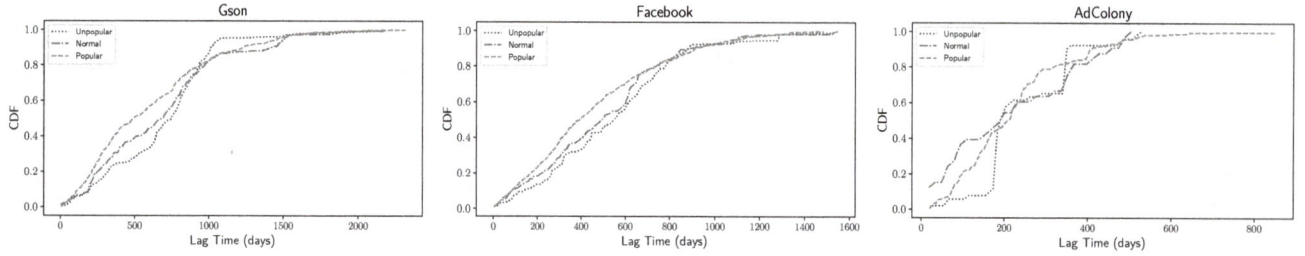

Figure 7: Popularity of apps versus the lag time per app for three libraries: Gson, Facebook, and AdColony.

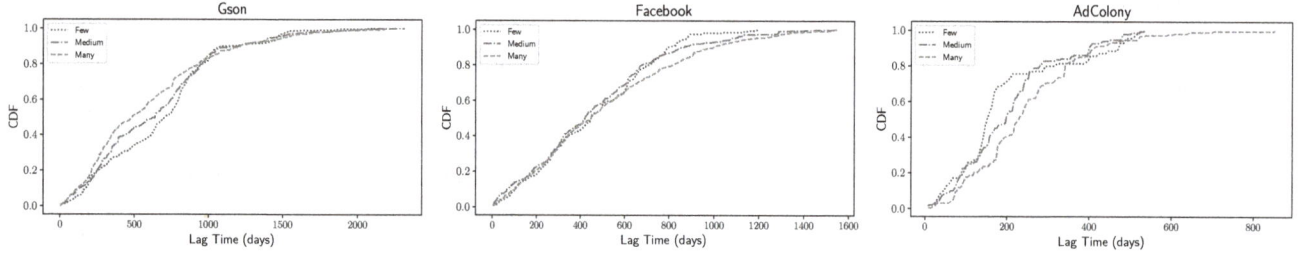

Figure 8: Number of released versions versus the lag time per app for three libraries: Gson, Facebook, and AdColony.

Table 6: Average lag time (days) for the top-five app categories in the data set.

	Gson	Facebook	AdColony
Game	772	449	259
Education	551	434	177
Lifestyle	735	560	190
Personalization	383	414	143
Entertainment	818	372	237

Table 7: Spearman's rank correlation coefficients, ρ, for the pairs (T_i, T_u) and (T_i, T_l), where T_i is the average of update interval of a library and T_u and T_l are the averages of the update and lag times for a library, respectively.

pair	ρ	p-value
(T_i, T_u)	0.465	$< 10^{-5}$
(T_i, T_l)	0.317	$< 10^{-3}$

in Table 3. While we cannot observe any unifying rule of responsiveness in the categories, we found that the responsiveness to each library is different for each app category. For example, Gson lagged for 818 days on average for Entertainment apps, whereas the lag time for the same library was much shorter for Personalization apps, with an average lag time of 383 days. As expected, these are statistically different with a significance level of $p < 10^{-9}$.

If we focus on the app categories, we see that four out of the five app categories have AdColony as the library with the fastest responsiveness. Again, this advertising library exhibited the fastest responsiveness across all the app categories. For other libraries, we do not see a clear rule with which to interpret the results, for example, in Personalization apps, Gson had the next shortest average lag time of 383 days, whereas in Entertainment apps, Facebook had the next shortest average lag time of 372 days.

4.5 Frequency of Library Updates

To understand the relationship between the library evolution speed and the responsiveness of developers to library updates, we analyzed the correlation between the average update interval of the libraries and the responsiveness of app developers to library updates. For this, we adopted the Spearman rank correlation coefficient. For each library we detected, we first measured the average length of the update intervals. Next, for each library, we analyzed apps

that were using that library, extracted their update/lag times, and took their average values. Finally, we computed the Spearman rank correlation coefficient for pairs of the average update interval of a library (T_i) and the average of the update/lag times for a library (T_u/T_l). The results are shown in Table 7. For both cases, we can see a low positive correlation. These positive correlations imply that either app developers had a tendency to keep up with a quickly evolving library or that they had a tendency to lose interest in adopting updates for slowly evolving libraries. However, because the correlations were weak, we could not derive a conclusive interpretation.

4.6 Prolific Developers

Throughout our analysis, we observed that there are a non-negligible number of prolific developers who have published many apps in the marketplace. Given this observation, we studied whether prolific developers are responsive to library updates. Figure 9 shows the CDF of the number of apps published by a developer. Our hypothesis was that prolific developers would adopt library updates more quickly than other developers. Similar to the previous analyses, we classified the apps into two groups depending on whether the developer of the app had developed five or more apps. We set the threshold, 5, as the 67th percentile of the number of apps published by a developer. If the developer of an app had developed five or

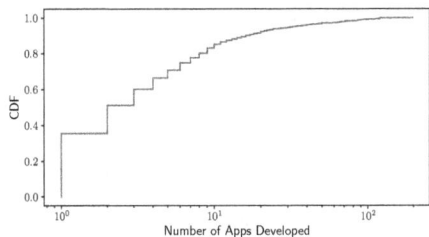

Figure 9: CDF of the number of apps published by a developer.

Table 8: Average lag time (days) for the apps developed by normal and prolific developers.

Library	Normal	Prolific	p-value
Gson	578	652	$< 10^{-5}$
Facebook	442	498	$< 10^{-3}$
AdColony	215	225	0.315

more apps, we categorized the app as an app developed by a prolific developer. If the developer of an app had developed four or fewer apps, we categorized the app as an app developed by a normal developer.

Table 8 summarizes the results. These results contradict our hypothesis, that is, for Gson and Facebook, apps that were developed by prolific developers tended to have longer lag times, indicating that prolific developers were not responsive to library updates. The average number of installations for apps developed by prolific developers was 30.7×10^4, whereas that for apps developed by normal developers was 13.2×10^5. This observation agrees with the result shown in Section 4.2 that popular apps adopt libraries more quickly than less popular apps.

4.7 Semantic Versioning

A previous study [11] reported that failures in semantic versioning are the primary *root cause* of the poor adoption of third-party library updates. Given this background, we studied how the semantic versioning strategy used by a library affects the responsiveness of developers to that library. Semantic versioning [38] is a versioning strategy for software development that consists of a set of simple rules. By following these rules, the versioning on a software update can inform software users of what type of update it was. The semantic versioning rule guides software developers to adopt the version format X.Y.Z and increment each digit following the next rules: increment X on backward-incompatible changes (MAJOR updates); increment Y if a new backward-compatible functionality is introduced (MINOR updates); and increment Z if only backward-compatible bug fixes are introduced (PATCH updates).

For the 40 libraries that we collected from the Maven repository, we used the LibScout API analysis functionality to measure how each library's updates followed or violated the semantic versioning strategy. In addition, we calculated the averages of the update time and the lag time as responsiveness measures for each library. Then, we measured the Spearman rank correlation (ρ) between the percentage of updates that followed semantic versioning and the

responsiveness measures for each library. We found no correlation between the correctness of the semantic versioning and the update time ($\rho = -0.269$). Nor did we detect any correlation between the correctness and the lag time ($\rho = -0.279$).

We further investigated problematic violations of the semantic versioning rule where the versioning of the update is indicated as MINOR or PATCH, even though the update was actually backward incompatible. This violation is problematic because the versioning tells the library user that the update does not break any backward compatibility, even though the actual change in the library breaks this compatibility, which may lead the library user to experience difficulties. For each library we measured the percentage of problematic updates and measured the Spearman correlations with the library adoption measures. Again, no correlation was found between the rate of problematic updates and the update time ($\rho = 0.190$) or the lag time ($\rho = 0.107$).

Even though further study might reveal some relationship between the semantic versioning and the responsiveness of app developers to library updates, we could not find any clear correlations between the two. Even though failures in semantic versioning could contribute to the poor responsiveness of app developers, it may not be a primary *root cause*, seeing how we found many other factors that are associated with the responsiveness of mobile app developers.

4.8 Summary

We found that the responsiveness of mobile app developers to library updates is based on several different factors. Of the possible factors we analyzed, we observed clear correlations for the following three factors: awareness of the vulnerability, app popularity, and library category. In the following, we highlight these three factors.

First, we found that the presence of CVE ID and the high severity of a vulnerability had a small impact on prompting app developers to fix them. We also found that the deployment of Google's ASI Program campaign was effective in reducing unfixed vulnerabilities; more than 85% of apps with the three libraries targeted by the ASI program fixed such the vulnerabilities. These two observations imply that explicitly letting developers be aware of the presence of vulnerabilities in their apps is a key success factor in reducing the number of unfixed vulnerabilities.

Second, popular apps were more sensitive to adopting new versions of libraries than are unpopular apps. Of the 13 libraries we studied, 10 libraries indicated that popular apps had shorter lag times than normal/unpopular apps with a statistically significant difference.

Finally, via several avenues of research, we found that advertising libraries tend to elicit better responsiveness than those in other categories of libraries. Because developers monetize their apps using advertising libraries, it is natural that they will be sensitive to changes in such libraries, which represent the source of their revenue from these apps.

5 DISCUSSION

In this section, we discuss the limitations of our work. In addition, we discuss the effective methods to eliminate vulnerable libraries and improve the responsiveness of mobile app developers. Finally, we discuss the ethical considerations we took when we performed our measurements.

5.1 Limitations

This study is a first step toward understanding the responsiveness of mobile developers in adopting updates of libraries. Our study has several limitations. One is a possible bias in our data set. Because our app data set consists of free apps from Google Play, our analysis result may not apply to paid apps or apps from other app markets such as the Apple App Store or other third-party marketplaces [27]. We note that more than 95% of Android apps published on Google Play are free apps [3]. In addition, we collected the app history, as explained in Section 2.1.1; this app collection method can collect the version history of apps but fails to collect the apps whose versionCode exceeds 40,374.

Because our library detection is based on an OSS tool LibScout, the accuracy of the study is limited by the precision of the tool. In addition, for some analyses, we based our app analysis on several case study libraries. A natural avenue for future work is to extend our analysis to libraries that we have not studied here. Now that we have undertaken basic case studies for several libraries and have obtained interesting insights into the responsiveness of app developers to library updates, it will be easier for us to extend our measurement to many other libraries that are being used in apps.

We performed in-depth app analyses in Section 3 and Section 4, using the 13 case study libraries we adopted. We note that although the number of libraries used for the analysis was limited, we have focused our case study analyses on popular libraries as explained in Table 3 and Section 4.2. Because popular libraries should have stronger effect on the entire app market, compared to unpopular libraries, analyzing popular libraries is a reasonable sampling way to understand the responsiveness of app developers in the app market.

5.2 Elimination of Vulnerable Libraries

To the best of our knowledge, we are the first to quantify the effectiveness of a market-wide security campaign (Google ASI). Vulnerabilities targeted by the ASI Program had a low unfixed rate with a maximum value of 14.3%. In addition, we demonstrated that the method of assigning CVE IDs was less effective in eliminating vulnerable libraries. Vulnerabilities with CVE IDs have a high unfixed rate with a minimum value of 55.6%, which is among the highest rates of the vulnerabilities we tested.

Given these observations, we suggest several ideas to reduce unfixed vulnerabilities in apps. One straightforward approach is to enhance a vulnerability fixing campaign similar to the ASI Program, which will encourage developers to fix vulnerabilities in their apps. Of the vulnerabilities we analyzed, four were not targeted by the ASI Program campaign. It is reasonable for a market provider (not only Google Play but also other marketplaces for other mobile platforms) to target these and other untargeted vulnerabilities to encourage app developers to fix vulnerabilities in their apps.

Another natural solution for encouraging developers to fix vulnerabilities would be to take actions to make the idea of CVE more widely understood by common Android app developers. As mentioned above, our finding imply that many app developers pay little attention to CVE; communicating the idea of CVE will help developers become aware of the existence of vulnerabilities.

Even for the severe vulnerability we found in the Facebook library, there was no official documents commenting on the vulnerability. This lack of documentation is problematic because Facebook is the most frequently used library that accesses external services. The reduced interest of library developers in announcing vulnerabilities will lessen opportunities for app developers to notice such vulnerability. Library developers must be more sensitive to security issues and let the app developers know about the vulnerabilities.

5.3 Improving Responsiveness to Library Updates

Our analysis revealed Android app developers' poor responsiveness to the updates of software libraries; the continued use of 50% of outdated libraries in apps, for more than 300 days. These poor and slow trends of library adoption may lead to various types of negative impacts on the Android ecosystem, such as security vulnerabilities or degradation in app quality.

In Section 4.2 we categorized the studied apps into three groups, popular, normal, and unpopular, depending on the number of installations. We found that popular apps adopt library updates quicker than normal or unpopular apps. Even though apps with reduced popularity are less dominant on Google Play, the apps in our data set have been installed more than 10 million times and their impact on end users is not negligible. Such observations suggest that enhancing the library responsiveness of these apps may greatly contribute to increasing the quality of the entire app market.

References [12, 15] highlight the increase and prevailing trend of citizen developers, that is, developers with lower technical skills. It is important to work toward a more sophisticated and easy-to-adopt library management system, such as an automatic library updating system, or semantic versioning with comprehensive information about the library version, to avoid confusion for such developers. However, because our analysis in Section 4.7 reveals no correlation between the semantic versioning and the library update adoption responses, in order for the semantic versioning to affect the responsiveness of app developers to library updates, the idea of semantic versioning must first be more widely recognized by developers.

A promising solution to improve the responsiveness of app developers is to set up a central library marketplace and to develop a package management tool for Android development. We observed that, when apps adopt library updates, 58.7% of apps do not adopt the latest version of the library. Because there is no central library marketplace, Android app developers tend to rely on information from the Web. However, obsolete information on web sites makes app developers prone to adopting outdated versions of libraries. As such, setting up a central market of libraries will help developers access fresh information and enhance their responsiveness to library updates. It is noteworthy that introducing a plugin to IDE such as Gradle Versions Plugin [6] could be another possible solution. Such IDE plugin is expected to automatically resolve the dependency of library updates.

5.4 Ethical considerations

Finally, we discuss the ethical considerations we took in our measurement study. We acquired all the APK files carefully so as not to violate the Acceptable Use Policy or to cause any harmful effects to the service. Accordingly, we slowly crawled the APK files and spent 2 months on the entire data collection. Our motive for of crawling the APKs was purely for research. For bona fide researchers who are interested in analyzing the data we collected, we are ready to share the data on request. Because our study exposed unfixed vulnerabilities in apps and libraries, we are following the principle of responsible disclosure and are now in the process of reporting our results to the corresponding app/library developers. The disclosures will include the app/library names and the categories of the vulnerability.

6 RELATED WORK

Mobile App Analysis. There have been several studies that have performed large-scale mobile app analyses [20, 25, 26, 32, 42, 44]. Viennot et al. [42] developed a system called PlayDrone, which efficiently crawls the official market (i.e., Google Play) and stores APK files. By collecting apps from Google Play for 47 days, McIlroy et al. [32] were able to analyze how frequently apps are updated. Ishi et al. [26] analyzed over 1.3 million Android apps collected from official and third-party marketplaces, and revealed that in the third-party marketplaces, 76% of the *cloned apps* that were originally published in the official market, were repackaged malware. Gonzalez et al. [20], examined the code reuse in both legitimate and malicious Android apps collected from various app marketplaces. Wu et al. [44] examined the relationship between the declared Android SDK versions in apps and the API calls used in the apps. They revealed that there were 1.8K Android apps that had the inconsistency between the SDK versions and API usage. Huang et al. [25] demonstrated that online malware scanning services are being used by not only legitimate users, but also by Android malware developers. Aldini et al. [2] proposed a method to detect repackaged Android apps by collecting execution traces of both genuine and repackaged apps from users.

There have been prior studies that have attempted longitudinal measurement studies of apps [9, 31, 37]. Carbundar et al. [9] crawled Google Play for 6 months and revealed that at most, 50% of apps are updated in all app categories.Taylor et al. [37] have taken snapshots of Google Play over time and investigated changes in permission and security. McDonnell et al. [31] analyzed the relationship between the core Android API stability and the API adoptions of app developers. Their results suggest that developers use fast-evolving APIs more than slow-evolving APIs.

Software Library Analysis. Software libraries play an essential role on modern software development in mobile platforms to reduce development costs and accelerate the release cycles of apps. The mainstream method of assessing mobile apps is first to detect the software libraries. There are a number of state-of-the-art library detection tools [4, 10, 29, 30, 43, 45]. LibD [29], LibRader [30], and LibScout [4] are publicly available. In particular, LibScout is the most frequently updated of these tools as of August 2018. The aim of library detection in our study was to analyze the responsiveness of app developers via changes in the libraries; therefore, we selected LibScout which can detect both the library and its version from a provided APK, as well as its release date.

Use of harmful or low quality libraries, can involve innocent host apps in security threats, or degrade the user experience of an app [5, 7, 28, 35, 43]. Li et al. [28] indicated that piggybacked apps with libraries containing malicious code could mislead security analyses. Bhoraskar et al. [7] also notes that a host app as a whole could become vulnerable if there were bugs in its libraries. Watanabe et al. [43] revealed that the majority of app vulnerabilities were attributed to third-party libraries. Bavota et al. [5] further revealed that high-rated apps are more likely to use stable APIs, whereas, Mojica et al. [35] demonstrated that the use of certain advertising libraries will lower the reputation of an app using those libraries.

Studies on App Developers. Derr et al. [11] conducted a human study on Android app developers via an online survey. They reported that many third-party libraries did not follow semantic versioning strategies, confusing app developers. However, they did not verify their finding via actual measurements over the app histories. On the contrary, we investigated the app developers' responsiveness to library updates by analyzing the version histories of the apps. Even though a further analysis may reveal the effect of semantic versioning, in our study, we did not find any correlation between the semantic versioning and the app developers' responsiveness to library updates.

Fischer et al. [14] examined if Android app developers copy security related code snippets from online discussion platform. They analyzed 1.3 million apps and revealed that 15.4% contained security related code snippets from online discussion platform.

Coarse-grained permission system may make developers prone to writing over privileged codes, resulting in insecure apps. Fratantonio et al. [19] demonstrated that providing *finer-grained* Android Internet permission management is a practical and desirable solution for the better management permission without sacrificing the usability. Also, app developers often make use of third-party services in their apps. It is known that some of such apps contain *developer credential* to authenticate themselves to the third-party server. Zhou et al. [46] analyzed Android apps collected from various markets and revealed that many developers do not protect their credentials at all, therefore it will be easy for an attacker to extract them from the apps.

7 CONCLUSION

In this paper, we report a longitudinal measurement study on the responsiveness of Android app developers to library updates. The study was based on app version histories collected from Google Play, and a static code analysis was applied to the app histories to detect which libraries were used in the apps. By comparing the app build dates and the library release dates, we were able to quantify the responsiveness of the mobile app developers.

Our findings revealed that the majority of developers were less responsive to library updates; 50% of library updates were adopted for more than 3 months after the library release date. We also studied factors that were likely associated with the responsiveness of the developers. We found that security fix campaign was effective in encouraging app developers to adopt library version updates, whereas several vulnerable libraries without such a campaign were prone to being unfixed even if the vulnerabilities were severe or had CVE IDs. We also found that unpopular apps tended to respond to library updates slowly compared to popular apps and that it is important to enhance the responsiveness, to improve the overall quality of the app market. We hope our insights in this study will motivate the market, library developers, and the app developers to improve the status quo for responses to library updates.

ACKNOWLEDGMENT

A part of this work was supported by JSPS Grant-in-Aid for Scientific Research B, Grant Number 16H02832.

REFERENCES

[1] AdColony, Inc. [n. d.]. AdColony - Elevating mobile advertising across today's hottest apps. Retrieved September 22, 2018 from https://www.adcolony.com/
[2] Alessandro Aldini, Fabio Martinelli, Andrea Saracino, and Daniele Sgandurra. [n. d.]. Detection of repackaged mobile applications through a collaborative approach. *Concurrency and Computation: Practice and Experience* 27, 11 ([n. d.]), 2818–2838.
[3] AppBrain. 2018. Google Play stats. Retrieved September 22, 2018 from http://www.appbrain.com/stats/
[4] Michael Backes, Sven Bugiel, and Erik Derr. 2016. Reliable Third-Party Library Detection in Android and Its Security Applications. In *Proc. of ACM CCS, 2016*. 356–367.
[5] Gabriele Bavota, Mario Linares Vásquez, Carlos Eduardo Bernal-Cárdenas, Massimiliano Di Penta, Rocco Oliveto, and Denys Poshyvanyk. 2015. The Impact of API Change- and Fault-Proneness on the User Ratings of Android Apps. *IEEE Transactions on Software Engineering* 41, 4 (April 2015), 384–407.
[6] Ben Manes. 2018. GitHub - Gradle Versions Plugin. Retrieved September 24, 2018 from https://github.com/ben-manes/gradle-versions-plugin
[7] Ravi Bhoraskar, Seungyeop Han, Jinseong Jeon, Tanzirul Azim, Shuo Chen, Jaeyeon Jung, Suman Nath, Rui Wang, and David Wetherall. 2014. Brahmastra: Driving Apps to Test the Security of Third-Party Components.. In *Proc. of USENIX Security, 2014*. 1021–1036.
[8] Theodore Book, Adam Pridgen, and Dan S. Wallach. 2013. Longitudinal Analysis of Android Ad Library Permissions. *CoRR* abs/1303.0857 (2013). arXiv:1303.0857 http://arxiv.org/abs/1303.0857
[9] Bogdan Carbunar and Rahul Potharaju. 2015. A longitudinal study of the Google app market. In *Proc of IEEE/ACM ASONAM, 2015*. 242–249.
[10] Kai Chen, Xueqiang Wang, Yi Chen, Peng Wang, Yeonjoon Lee, XiaoFeng Wang, Bin Ma, Aohui Wang, Yingjun Zhang, and Wei Zou. 2016. Following devil's footprints: Cross-platform analysis of potentially harmful libraries on android and ios. In *Proc. of the IEEE SP, 2016*. 357–376.
[11] Erik Derr, Sven Bugiel, Sascha Fahl, Yasemin Acar, and Michael Backes. 2017. Keep Me Updated: An Empirical Study of Third-Party Library Updatability on Android. In *Proc. of ACM CCS, 2017*. 2187–2200.
[12] Dion Hinchcliffe. 2017. The advent of the citizen developer. Retrieved September 22, 2018 from https://www.zdnet.com/article/the-advent-of-the-citizen-developer/
[13] Facebook, Inc. [n. d.]. Android SDK - Facebook for Developers. Retrieved September 22, 2018 from https://developers.facebook.com/docs/android/
[14] F. Fischer, K. Böttinger, H. Xiao, C. Stransky, Y. Acar, M. Backes, and S. Fahl. 2017. Stack Overflow Considered Harmful? The Impact of Copy amp;Paste on Android Application Security. In *Proc. of the IEEE SP, 2017*. 121–136.
[15] Fisher, Anne. 2017. How Companies Are Developing More Apps With Fewer Developers. Retrieved September 22, 2018 from http://fortune.com/2016/08/30/quickbase-coding-apps-developers/
[16] Forum of Incident Response and Security Teams. [n. d.]. Common Vulnerability Scoring System SIG. Retrieved September 22, 2018 from https://www.first.org/cvss/
[17] Forum of Incident Response and Security Teams. [n. d.]. Common Vulnerability Scoring System v3.0: Specification Document. Retrieved September 22, 2018 from https://www.first.org/cvss/specification-document
[18] The Apache Software Foundation. [n. d.]. Apache Commons Collections Security Vulnerabilities. Retrieved September 22, 2018 from https://commons.apache.org/proper/commons-collections/security-reports.html
[19] Yanick Fratantonio, Antonio Bianchi, William Robertson, Manuel Egele, Christopher Kruegel, Engin Kirda, and Giovanni Vigna. 2015. On the Security and Engineering Implications of Finer-Grained Access Controls for Android Developers and Users. In *Proc. of DIMVA, 2015*. 282–303.
[20] Hugo Gonzalez, Natalia Stakhanova, and Ali A. Ghorbani. 2016. Measuring code reuse in Android apps. In *Proc. of PST, 2016*. 187–195.

[21] Google Inc. 2018. App Security Improvement Program. https://developer.android.com/google/play/asi.html
[22] Google, Inc. 2018. GitHub - google/gson: A Java serialization/deserialization library to convert Java Objects into JSON and back. Retrieved September 22, 2018 from https://sites.google.com/site/gson/
[23] Google Play API 2012. Google Play API. Retrieved September 22, 2018 from https://github.com/egirault/googleplay-api
[24] Michael C. Grace, Wu Zhou, Xuxian Jiang, and Ahmad-Reza Sadeghi. 2012. Unsafe Exposure Analysis of Mobile In-app Advertisements. In *Proc. of ACM WISEC, 2012 (WISEC '12)*. 101–112.
[25] Heqing Huang, Cong Zheng, Junyuan Zeng, Wu Zhou, Sencun Zhu, Peng Liu, Suresh Chari, and Ce Zhang. 2016. Android malware development on public malware scanning platforms: A large-scale data-driven study. In *Proc. of IEEE Big Data, 2016*. 1090–1099.
[26] Yuta Ishii, Takuya Watanabe, Mitsuaki Akiyama, and Tatsuya Mori. 2016. Clone or Relative?: Understanding the Origins of Similar Android Apps. In *Proc. of ACM IWSPA, 2016*. 25–32.
[27] Yuta Ishii, Takuya Watanabe, Fumihiro Kanei, Yuta Takata, Eitaro Shioji, Mitsuaki Akiyama, Takeshi Yagi, Bo Sun, and Tatsuya Mori. 2017. Understanding the security management of global third-party Android marketplaces. In *Proc. of ACM WAMA, 2017*. 12–18.
[28] Li Li, Tegawendé F Bissyandé, Jacques Klein, and Yves Le Traon. 2016. An Investigation into the Use of Common Libraries in Android Apps. In *Proc. of SANER, 2016*.
[29] Menghao Li, Wei Wang, Pei Wang, Shuai Wang, Dinghao Wu, Jian Liu, Rui Xue, and Wei Huo. 2017. Libd: Scalable and precise third-party library detection in Android markets. In *Proc. of ICSE, 2017*. 335–346.
[30] Ziang Ma, Haoyu Wang, Yao Guo, and Xiangqun Chen. 2016. LibRadar: fast and accurate detection of third-party libraries in Android apps. In *Proc. of IEEE/ACM ICSE, 2016*. 653–656.
[31] Tyler McDonnell, Baishakhi Ray, and Miryung Kim. 2013. An Empirical Study of API Stability and Adoption in the Android Ecosystem. In *Proc. of IEEE ICSME, 2013*. 70–79.
[32] Stuart McIlroy, Nasir Ali, and Ahmed E Hassan. 2016. Fresh apps: an empirical study of frequently-updated mobile apps in the Google play store. *Empirical Software Engineering* 21, 3 (2016), 1346–1370.
[33] MITRE Corporation. 2018. CVE - Common Vulnerabilities and Exposures (CVE). Retrieved September 22, 2018 from https://cve.mitre.org/
[34] The Hacker News. 2014. Facebook SDK Vulnerability Puts Millions of Smart- phone Users' Accounts at Risk. https://thehackernews.com/2014/07/facebook-sdk-vulnerabilities-puts.html
[35] I. J. Mojica Ruiz, M. Nagappan, B. Adams, T. Berger, S. Dienst, and A. E. Hassan. 2014. Impact of Ad Libraries on Ratings of Android Mobile Apps. *IEEE Software* 31, 6 (Nov 2014), 86–92.
[36] Israel J Mojica Ruiz, Meiyappan Nagappan, Bram Adams, Thorsten Berger, Steffen Dienst, and Ahmed E Hassan. 2016. Analyzing ad library updates in android apps. *IEEE Software* 33, 2 (2016), 74–80.
[37] Vincent F. Taylor and Ivan Martinovic. 2017. To Update or Not to Update: Insights From a Two-Year Study of Android App Evolution. In *Proc. of ASIA CCS, 2017*. 45–57.
[38] Tom Preston-Werner. [n. d.]. Semantic Versioning 2.0.0. Retrieved September 22, 2018 from https://semver.org
[39] U.S. National Institute of Standards and Technology. 2017. CVE-2014-8889 Detail. Retrieved September 22, 2018 from https://nvd.nist.gov/vuln/detail/CVE-2014-8889
[40] U.S. National Institute of Standards and Technology. 2017. CVE-2016-2402 Detail. Retrieved September 22, 2018 from https://nvd.nist.gov/vuln/detail/CVE-2016-2402
[41] U.S. National Institute of Standards and Technology. 2018. National Vulnerability Database. Retrieved September 22, 2018 from https://nvd.nist.gov/
[42] Nicolas Viennot, Edward Garcia, and Jason Nieh. 2014. A Measurement Study of Google Play. In *Proc. of SIGMETRICS, 2014 (SIGMETRICS '14)*. 221–233.
[43] Takuya Watanabe, Mitsuaki Akiyama, Fumihiro Kanei, Eitaro Shioji, Yuta Takata, Bo Sun, Yuta Ishi, Toshiki Shibahara, Takeshi Yagi, and Tatsuya Mori. 2017. Understanding the Origins of Mobile App Vulnerabilities: A Large-scale Measurement Study of Free and Paid Apps. In *Proc. of MSR, 2017*. 14–24.
[44] Daoyuan Wu, Ximing Liu, Jiayun Xu, David Lo, and Debin Gao. 2017. Measuring the Declared SDK Versions and Their Consistency with API Calls in Android Apps. In *Proc. of WASA, 2017*. 678–690.
[45] Yuan Zhang, Jiarun Dai, Xiaohan Zhang, Sirong Huang, Zhemin Yang, Min Yang, and Hao Chen. 2018. Detecting third-party libraries in Android applications with high precision and recall. In *Proc. of SANER, 2018*. 141–152.
[46] Yajin Zhou, Lei Wu, Zhi Wang, and Xuxian Jiang. 2015. Harvesting Developer Credentials in Android Apps. In *Proc. of ACM WiSec, 2015*. Article 23, 23:1–23:12 pages.

ACMiner: Extraction and Analysis of Authorization Checks in Android's Middleware

Sigmund Albert
Gorski III
North Carolina State
University
sagorski@ncsu.edu

Benjamin Andow
North Carolina State
University
beandow@ncsu.edu

Adwait Nadkarni
William & Mary
nadkarni@cs.wm.edu

Sunil Manandhar
William & Mary
sunil@cs.wm.edu

William Enck
North Carolina State
University
whenck@ncsu.edu

Eric Bodden
Paderborn University
eric.bodden@uni-paderbo
rn.de

Alexandre Bartel
University of Luxembourg
alexandre.bartel@uni.lu

ABSTRACT

Billions of users rely on the security of the Android platform to protect phones, tablets, and many different types of consumer electronics. While Android's permission model is well studied, the *enforcement* of the protection policy has received relatively little attention. Much of this enforcement is spread across system services, taking the form of hard-coded checks within their implementations. In this paper, we propose Authorization Check Miner (ACMiner), a framework for evaluating the correctness of Android's access control enforcement through consistency analysis of authorization checks. ACMiner combines program and text analysis techniques to generate a rich set of authorization checks, mines the corresponding protection policy for each service entry point, and uses association rule mining at a service granularity to identify inconsistencies that may correspond to vulnerabilities. We used ACMiner to study the AOSP version of Android 7.1.1 to identify 28 vulnerabilities relating to missing authorization checks. In doing so, we demonstrate ACMiner's ability to help domain experts process thousands of authorization checks scattered across millions of lines of code.

ACM Reference Format:
Sigmund Albert Gorski III, Benjamin Andow, Adwait Nadkarni, Sunil Manandhar, William Enck, Eric Bodden, and Alexandre Bartel. 2019. ACMiner: Extraction and Analysis of Authorization Checks in Android's Middleware. In *Ninth ACM Conference on Data and Application Security and Privacy (CODASPY '19), March 25–27, 2019, Richardson, TX, USA*. ACM, New York, NY, USA, 12 pages. https://doi.org/10.1145/3292006.3300023

1 INTRODUCTION

Android has become the world's dominant computing platform, powering over 2 billion devices by mid-2017 [10]. Not only is Android the primary computing platform for many end-users, it also has significant use by business enterprises [33] and government

agencies [34, 37]. As a result, any security flaw in the Android platform is likely to cause significant and widespread damage, lending immense importance to evaluating the platform's security.

While Android is built on Linux, it has many differences. A key appeal of the platform is its semantically rich application programming interfaces (APIs) that provide application developers simple and convenient abstractions to access information and resources (e.g., retrieve the GPS location, record audio using the microphone, and take a picture with the camera). This functionality, along with corresponding security checks, is implemented within a collection of privileged userspace services. While most Android security research has focused on third party applications [7, 13, 15, 18, 19, 35, 36, 39], the several efforts that consider platform security highlight the need for more systematic evaluation of security and access control checks within privileged userspace services (e.g., evidence of system apps re-exposing information without security checks [25, 43], or missing checks in the Package Manager service leading to Pile-Up vulnerabilities [44]).

To date, only two prior works have attempted to evaluate the correctness of access control logic within Android's system services. Both Kratos [38] and AceDroid [2] approximate correctness through consistency measures, as previously done for evaluating correctness of security hooks in the Linux kernel [12, 29, 41]. However, these prior works have limitations. Kratos only considers a small number of manually-defined authorization checks (e.g., it excludes App Ops checks). AceDroid considers a larger set of authorization checks, but these are still largely manually defined, primarily through observation. Kratos performs coarse-grained analysis using call-graphs, leading to imprecision. AceDroid's program analysis provides better precision, but oversimplifies its access control representation, making it difficult to identify vulnerabilities within single system images.

In this paper, we propose Authorization Check Miner (ACMiner), a framework for evaluating the correctness of Android's access control enforcement through consistency analysis of authorization checks. ACMiner is based on several novel insights. First, we avoid identification of protected operations (a key challenge in the space) by considering program logic between service entry points and code that throws a SecurityException. Second, we propose a semi-automated method of discovering authorization checks. More specifically, we mine all constants and names of methods and variables that influence conditional logic leading to throwing a Security-yException. From this dataset, we identify security-relevant values (e.g., "restricted") and develop regular expressions to automatically identify those conditions during program analysis that mines policy rules from the code. Third, we use association rule mining to identify inconsistent authorization checks for entry points in the same service. Association rule mining has the added benefit of suggesting changes to make authorization checks more consistent, which is valuable when triaging results. By applying this methodology, ACMiner allows a domain expert (i.e., a developer familiar with the AOSP source code) to quickly identify missing authorization checks that allow abuse by third-party applications.

We evaluated the utility of ACMiner by applying it to the AOSP code for Android 7.1.1. Of the 4,004 total entry points to system services, ACMiner identified 1,995 with authorization checks. Of these entry points, the association rule mining identified inconsistencies in 246. We manually investigated these 246 entry points with the aid of the rules suggested by the association rule mining, which allowed us to identify 28 security vulnerabilities. ACMiner not only reduced the effort required to analyze system services (i.e., by narrowing down to only 246 entry points out of 4004), but also allowed us to rapidly triage results by suggesting solutions. Out of the 28 security vulnerabilities, 7 were in security-sensitive entry points that may be exploited from third-party applications, and an additional 12 were in security-sensitive entry points that may be exploited from system applications. The rest were in entry points with relatively low security value. All 28 vulnerabilities have been reported to Google. At the time of writing, Google has confirmed 2 of these vulnerabilities as "moderate severity."

This paper makes the following contributions:

- *We design and implement ACMiner, a framework that enables a domain expert to identify and systematically evaluate inconsistent access control enforcement in Android's system services. Our results show that this analysis is not only useful for identifying existing vulnerabilities, but also inconsistencies that may lead to vulnerabilities in the future.*

- *We combine program and text analysis techniques to generate a rich set of authorization checks used in system services. This technique is a significant improvement over prior approaches that use manually-defined authorization checks.*

- *We use ACMiner to evaluate the AOSP version of Android 7.1.1 and identify 28 vulnerabilities. All vulnerabilities have been reported to Google, which at the time of writing has classified 2 as "moderate severity."*

This paper describes how ACMiner can systematically analyze the consistency of the authorization checks in the system services. However, ACMiner may also be useful for other forms of analysis. For instance, ACMiner can aid regression testing, as it can be extended to highlight changes to the policy implementation on a semantic level. The information extracted by ACMiner can also be used to study the evolution of access control in Android, potentially discovering new vulnerabilities. Finally, since changes by OEMs have historically introduced vulnerabilities, OEMs can use ACMiner to validate their implemented checks against AOSP.

The remainder of this paper proceeds as follows. Section 2 provides background. Section 3 describes the challenges and provides

```
1   // Entry point with correct authorization checks
2   boolean hasBaseUserRestriction(String key, int userId) {
3     checkManageUsersPermission("hasBaseUserRestriction");
4     // Unique check without a SecurityException
5     if (!UserRestrictionsUtils.isValidRestriction(key))
6       return false;
7     ...}
8
9   // Entry point missing checkManageUsersPermission
10  boolean hasUserRestriction(String key, int userId) {
11    if (!UserRestrictionsUtils.isValidRestriction(key))
12      return false;
13    ...}
14
15  void checkManageUsersPermission(String message) {
16    if (!hasManageUsersPermission())
17      throw new SecurityException();}
18
19  boolean hasManageUsersPermission() {
20    int callingUid = Binder.getCallingUid();
21    return UserHandle.isSameApp(callingUid,
22        Process.SYSTEM_UID)
23      || callingUid == Process.ROOT_UID
24      || ActivityManager.checkComponentPermission(
25        "android.permission.MANAGE_USERS",
26        callingUid, -1, true) ==
27        PackageManager.PERMISSION_GRANTED;}
```

Figure 1: Vulnerability found in `UserManagerService` by our tool

an overview of ACMiner. Section 4 describes the design of AC-Miner in detail. Sections 5 and 6 describe our analysis of the system services of AOSP 7.1.1. Section 7 describes the limitations of our approach. Section 8 discusses related work. Section 9 concludes.

2 BACKGROUND AND MOTIVATION

The Android middleware is implemented using the same component abstractions as third-party applications [16]: activities, content providers, broadcast receivers, and services. In this paper, we only consider service components, which provide daemon-like functionality. Apps interface with service components via the Binder inter-process communication (IPC) mechanism, which consists of sending *parcel* objects that indicate the target interface method being called via an integer. For the most part, Android's system services use the Android Interface Description Language (AIDL) to automatically generate the code that unmarshalles these parcels. Moreover, when interfacing with system services, third party apps rely on public APIs implementing a *proxy* to construct the parcel. When the parcel is unmarshalled by the service interface, the arguments are passed to a *stub* that calls the corresponding *entry point* method in the service component.

Android uses two broad techniques to enforce access control. For coarse-grained checks (i.e., at the component level), the Activity Manager Service (AMS) enforces policy specified in application manifest files. This paper focuses on fine-grained checks (i.e., at the service entry point level), which are enforced using hard-coded logic within the service implementation. This hard-coded logic includes variants of the `checkPermission` method, Unix Identifier (UID) checks, as well as many subtle checks based on service-specific state. Prior work [2, 38] has primarily relied on manual enumeration of these checks, which is error prone. To simplify discussion in this paper, we refer to such methods that return or check Android system state as *context queries*.

Figure 1 provides a motivating example for this paper, which contains a vulnerability discovered by ACMiner. The simplified code snippet is from the User Manager Service, which provides core functionality similar to the Activity Manager and Package Manager Services. In the figure, there are two entry points: hasBaseUserRestriction and hasUserRestriction. The entry points perform very similar functionality, but have inconsistent authorization checks. Specifically, hasBaseUserRestriction throws a SecurityException if the caller does not have the proper UID or permission.

This example is particularly apropos to ACMiner, because hasUserRestriction does not call any of the context queries considered by prior work [2, 38]. It also does not throw a SecurityException. Without knowledge that isValidRestriction is an authorization check, no form of consistency analysis could have identified that hasUserRestriction has a missing check.

3 OVERVIEW

The goal of this paper is to help a domain expert quickly identify and assess the impact of incorrect access control logic in implementations of system services in Android. As with most nontrivial software systems, no ground truth specification of correctness exists. Rather, the "ground truth" resides largely within the heads of the platform developers. Prior literature has approached this type of problem by approximating correctness with consistency. The intuition is that system developers are not malicious and that they are likely to get most of the checks correct. The approach was first applied to security hook placement in the Linux kernel [12, 29, 41] and more recently the Android platform [2, 38].

Evaluating authorization check correctness via consistency analysis requires addressing the following challenges.

- *Protected Operations:* Nontrivial systems rarely have a clear specification of the functional operations that require protection by the access control system. Protected operations range from accessing a device node to reading a value from a private member variable. Axplorer [6] attempts to enumerate protected operations for Android; however, the specification is far from complete.
- *Authorization Checks:* What constitutes an authorization check is vague and imprecise. While some authorization checks are clear (e.g., those based on checkPermission and getCallingUid), many others are based on service-specific state and the corresponding authorization checks use a variety of method and variable names.
- *Consistency:* The granularity and type of consistency impacts the precision and utility of the analysis. While increasing the scope of relevant authorization checks increases the noise in the analysis, not considering all authorization checks (as in Kratos [38]) or using heuristics to determine relevancy (as in AceDroid [2]) raises the risk of not detecting vulnerabilities.

ACMiner addresses these challenges through several novel insights. First, ACMiner avoids the need to specify protected operations by considering program logic between service entry points and code that throws a SecurityException. Our intuition is that if one control flow path leads to a SecurityException, an alternate control flow path leads to a protected operation. Furthermore, the conditional logic leading to the SecurityException describes the authorization checks. However, we found that not all authorization denials lead to a SecurityException, therefore, we also include

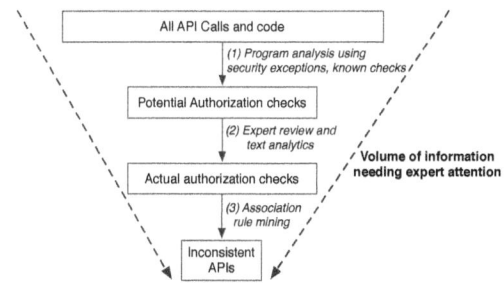

Figure 2: Overview of ACMiner. At each stage, ACMiner significantly reduces the information an expert needs to analyze.

entry points that contain known authorization checks. Second, ACMiner semi-automatically discovers new authorization checks using a combination of static program analysis and textual processing. More specifically, ACMiner identifies all of the method names, variable names, and strings that influence the conditional logic leading to a SecurityException. The security-relevant values are manually refined and used to generate regular expressions that identify a broader set of authorization checks within service implementations. Third and finally, ACMiner uses association rule mining for consistency analysis. For each entry point, ACMiner uses static program analysis to extract a set of authorization checks. Association rule mining compares the authorization check sets between entry points in the same service. The analysis produces suggestions (called "rules") of how the sets should change to make them more consistent. These rules include confidence scores that greatly aid domain experts when triaging the results. This general approach is depicted in Figure 2.

To more concretely understand how ACMiner operates, consider the discovery of the vulnerability shown in Figure 1. As a preprocessing step, ACMiner helps a domain expert semi-automatically identify authorization checks. First, ACMiner determines that the return value of isValidRestriction controls flow from the entry point hasBaseUserRestriction to a SecurityException. As such, this method name, along with many security irrelevant names are given to a domain expert. The domain expert then identifies security relevant terms (e.g. "restriction"), which ACMiner consumes as part of a regular expression. Next, ACMiner mines the policy of the User Manager Service, extracting a policy for both hasBaseUserRestriction and hasUserRestriction, with the policy for hasUserRestriction only being extracted because isValidRestriction was identified as an authorization check. For each entry point, the policy is then encoded as a set of authorization checks (e.g. isValidRestriction and ROOT_UID == getCallingUid()). Finally, ACMiner performs association rule mining to suggest set changes that make the policy more consistent. Such suggestions led us to discover the vulnerability in hasUserRestriction.

4 DESIGN

ACMiner is constructed on top of the Java static analysis framework Soot [30, 42] and has been largely parallelized so as to improve the run time of the complex analysis of Android's services. The design of ACMiner can be divided into three phases: (§4.1) Mining Authorization Checks, (§4.2) Refining Authorization Checks, and (§4.3) Inconsistency Analysis.

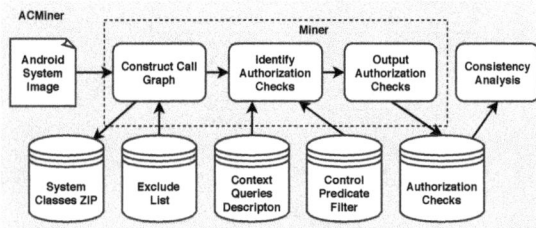

Figure 3: ACMiner's processing stages and input files.

4.1 Mining Authorization Checks

The first phase of ACMiner is mining authorization checks. This phase consist of the following program analysis challenges: (§4.1.1) Call Graph Construction, (§4.1.2) Identifying Authorization-Check Statements, and (§4.1.3) Representing Authorization Checks.

4.1.1 Call Graph Construction. Authorization checks are mined by traversing a call graph of the service implementation. ACMiner constructs call graphs using the following three steps.

Extracting Java Class Files: ACMiner extracts a *.jar* containing all the class files of the Android middleware in Soot's Jimple format from Android's *system.img*. This *.jar* containing Jimple files is then used on all subsequent runs of ACMiner. The implementation of this approach is detailed in the extended version [24].

Extracting System Services and Entry Points: Android's middleware is composed of isolated services that communicate through predefined Binder boundaries. This division allows ACMiner to analyze each service separately, by defining each service by the code reachable through its Binder entry points. ACMiner extracts system services and their entry points similar to prior work [2, 5, 38]. For implementation details, please see the extended version [24].

Reducing the Call Graph: ACMiner constructs a call graph representing all possible transitive calls from the entry points. ACMiner uses the Class Hierarchy Analysis (CHA) [11], which is guaranteed to provide an over-approximation of the actual runtime call graph. In contrast, Kratos and AceDroid use other potentially more accurate call graph builders (i.e., SPARK [32] and its WALA equivalent), which use points-to analysis to construct a less complete under-approximation of the runtime call graph. The loss of completeness occurs when constructing call graphs for libraries and other Java code without main methods. Therefore, it is important to note that unlike the prior work, ACMiner is more complete and guaranteed to include all paths containing authorization checks.

Since CHA call graphs are coarse over-approximations of the runtime call graph, ACMiner must apply heuristics to mitigate call graph bloat. When resolving targets for method invocations, CHA considers every possible implementation of the target method whose declaring type is within the type hierarchy of the call's receiver type. If the invoked method is defined in a widely used interface or superclass, the resolution may identify hundreds of targets for a single invocation. Thus, the resulting CHA call graph for the Android middleware is too large to be analyzed in a reasonable amount of time and memory [31].

To mitigate call graph bloat, we manually defined a list of classes and methods to exclude from the analysis, which become cutoff points in the call graph. We ensured that the class or method subject to exclusion did not contain, lead to, or was used in an authoriza-

tion check. While the exclude list may require revision for newer versions of AOSP or modifications made by vendors, the creation of the exclude list is a largely one-time effort. Please see the extended version [24] for a detailed description of the exclusion procedure and our website [1] for a full list of excluded classes/methods.

Finally, when analyzing an entry point, ACMiner treats all other entry points as cutoff points in the call graph. This decision further reduces call graph bloat. Unfortunately, it also introduces unsoundness into the call graph, which we discuss in Section 7.

4.1.2 Identifying Authorization Check Statements. Once ACMiner has the call graph for all entry points, the next step is to identify authorization checks. As described in Section 2, the complete set of authorization checks is unknown. ACMiner takes a two pronged approach to identifying authorization checks. First, it identifies all possible checks leading to a protected operation (this section). Second, it refines the list of possible authorization checks based on code names and string values (Section 4.2). To describe this process, we must first define a *control predicate*.

Definition 1 (*Control Predicate*). A conditional statement (i.e., an if or switch statement) whose logic authorizes access to some protected operation.

Identifying protected operations is nontrivial, as they may range from accessing a device node to returning a private member variable. However, even if we knew the protected operations, we would still need to determine which conditional statements are control predicates. ACMiner uses the key observation that Android frequently throws a SecurityException when access is denied. Therefore, ACMiner marks all conditional statements on the control flow path between entry points and the statement throwing the SecurityException as *potential* control predicates.

While throwing a SecurityException is the most common way Android denies access, it is not the only way. Some entry points deny access by returning false or even by returning empty data. Such denials are not easily identifiable. Fortunately, as shown in Figure 1, Android often groups authorization checks into methods to simplify placement. We refer to such groups of authorization checks as *context queries*.

Definition 2 (*Context Query*). A method consisting entirely of a set of *control predicates*, calls to other *context queries*, and/or whose return value is frequently used as part of a *control predicate*.

By identifying *context queries*, ACMiner can mark control predicates not on the path between a entry point and a thrown SecurityException, thereby making the authorization check mining more complete. As shown in Figure 3, ACMiner is configured with a input file that specifies context queries. Our method for defining this input is described in Section 4.2.

Using these insights, ACMiner identifies authorization checks with fairly high accuracy. The identification procedure is as follows. First, ACMiner marks all conditional statements inside a context query and the subsequent transitive callees as control predicates for the entry point. Next, ACMiner performs a backwards interprocedural control flow analysis from each statement throwing a SecurityException and each context query invocation to the entry point. During this backwards analysis, ACMiner marks all conditional statements on the path as potential control predicates. Finally, to capture control predicates that occur without a `SecurityException`, ACMiner performs a forward inter-procedural def-use analysis on the return value of a context query. During this analysis, AC-Miner marks any conditional statement that uses the return value as a potential control predicate. Note, ACMiner does not currently track the return value through fields, as this was found to be too noisy. However, ACMiner can track the return value through variable assignments, arithmetic operations, array assignments, and the passed parameters of a method invoke.

4.1.3 Representing Authorization Checks. ACMiner represents the authorization checks for each entry point as a set of context queries and control predicates. We initially represented authorization checks as boolean expressions representing the control flow decisions that lead to a thrown `SecurityException` or invoked context query. This representation would allow ACMiner to verify the existence, order, and the comparison operators of the authorization checks. However, for complex services (e.g., the Activity Manager) this representation was infeasible due to the large number of authorization checks. Additionally, we found that without more complex context-sensitive analysis, ACMiner could not extract authorization checks involving implicit flows. Therefore, we simplified our consistency analysis to only consider *the existence* of an authorization check for an entry point. This approach requires two reasonable correctness assumptions: (1) all authorization checks have been placed and ordered correctly, and (2) all control predicates have the correct comparison operator. ACMiner cannot detect violations of these assumptions.

The existence of authorization checks is easily represented as a set; however some processing is required. For each variable in a authorization check statement, ACMiner must substitute all possible values for that variable. More specifically, for each control predicates and context queries statement (i.e., conditional or method invoke statement), ACMiner must generate a list containing the product of all the possible variables and the values for each variable. To reduce redundant output, ACMiner only computes the product for context queries that do not have a return value or whose return value is not used in a control predicates.

For this expansion, ACMiner applies an inter-procedural def-use analysis to each variable used in a statement, thereby obtaining the set of all possible values for that variable from the entry point to this specific use site. It then computes the product of these sets to achieve the complete set of authorization checks for a single statement. If a variable is assigned a value from the return of a method call, ACMiner does not consider the possible return values of the method, but instead includes a reference to all the possible targets of the method call. Similarly, if a variable is assigned a value from the field of a class or an array, ACMiner includes only a reference to the field or array instead of all the possible values that may be assigned to the field or array. As such, while the list of values largely consists of constants, it may also contain references to fields, methods and arrays. The resulting combination of all the iterations of values for each control predicate and each required context query of an entry point makes up the final set of authorization checks output by ACMiner.

The resulting set has the potential to be exponentially large. To prevent this growth and to remove noise in ACMiner's output,

Table 1: Initial List of *Context Queries*

Classes	Methods
Context	enforcePermission
ContextImpl	enforceCallingPermission
ContextWrapper	enforceCallingOrSelfPermission
	checkPermission
	checkCallingPermission
	checkCallingOrSelfPermission
AccountManagerService	checkBinderPermission
LocationManagerService	checkPackageName
IActivityManager	checkPermission
ActivityManagerProxy	
ActivityManagerService	
ActivityManagerService	checkComponentPermission
ActivityManager	checkUidPermission
IPackageManager	checkUidPermission
IPackageManager$Stub$Proxy	checkPermission
PackageManagerService	

we apply several simplifications to the authorization checks (see the extended version [24]). These simplifications are designed to increase the number of authorization checks that are equivalent from a security standpoint and in no way affect the completeness of the authorization checks.

4.2 Refining Authorization Checks

The techniques in Section 4.1.2 identify *potential* control predicates; however, not all conditional statements are authorization checks. Performing consistency analysis at this point would be infeasible due to the excessive noise in the data. Therefore, ACMiner uses a one-time, semi-automated method to significantly reduce noise.

Our key observation is that Section 4.1 over approximates authorization checks on the path from entry points to a thrown `SecurityException` or context query. From this over-approximation, ACMiner can generate a list of all the strings and fields used in the conditional statements, a list of the methods whose return values are used in the conditional statements, and the methods containing the conditional statements. These values can be manually classified as authorization-related or not. The general refinement procedure is as follows: (1) a domain expert filters out values not related to authorization; (2) the refined list is translated into generalized expressions; (3) ACMiner uses the generalized expressions to automatically filter out values not related to authorization; (4) the generalized expressions are refined until the automatically generated list is close to that defined by the domain expert. While creating generalized expressions is time consuming, they can be used to analyze multiple Android builds with minimal modifications.

The specific refinement procedure is divided into two phases: (§4.2.1) identifying additional context queries, and (§4.2.2) refining control predicate identification.

4.2.1 Identifying Additional Context Queries. ACMiner uses context queries as indicators of the existence of authorization checks when no `SecurityException` is thrown. Our initial list of *context queries*, shown in Table 1, was very limited and only contained 33 methods. To expand this list we performed the following steps: (1) run ACMiner as described in Section 4.1 using the initial list of *context queries*, (2) from the marked conditional statements, generate a list of the methods containing these conditional statements and the methods whose return values are used in these conditional statements, (3) have a domain expert inspect the list and identify methods that match our definition of a context query, and add these to our list of context queries, and (4) repeat steps 1→3 until no new context queries are added to the list. For Android AOSP 7.1.1, this

```
(and (or (starts-with-package android.)
         (starts-with-package com.android.))
     (regex-name-words '^(enforce|has|check)\s
         ([a-z\s]+\s)?permission(s)?\b')
     (not (equal-package android.test))...))
```

Figure 4: Example expressions to describe context queries.

procedure took about 48 hours and increased the number of *context queries* to 620 methods.

To make this list reusable, we translate it into a set of generalized expressions that describe context queries across different Android versions. The expressions consist of regular expressions and string matches for the package, class, and name of a method, and also include conditional logic. An example expression is shown in Figure 4. Overall, we defined 49 generalized expressions to describe context queries for Android AOSP 7.1.1, which took <10 hours. The expressions enabled ACMiner to identify an additional 255 methods, resulting in a total of 875 context queries. Please see the extended version [24] for details on the translation procedure and our website [1] for the expression-list.

4.2.2 Refining Control Predicate Identification. To refine the overapproximation of authorization checks, ACMiner again uses a semi-automated method of refinement, this time for control predicates. The process begins by running ACMiner with the refined context queries from Section 4.2.1. The expert then inspects lists of strings, fields, and methods for the *potential* control predicates, removing those not related to authorization.

From our exploration, we discovered a number of different categories of control predicates. Some we were aware of such as those involving *UID*, *PID*, *GID*, *UserId*, *AppId*, and package name. However, even within these categories, we discovered new fields, methods, and contexts in which checks are performed. We also discovered previously unknown categories of control predicates including those: (1) involving SystemProperties, (2) involving flags, (3) performing permission checks using the string equals method instead of the standard check permission methods, (4) checking for specific intent strings, and (5) checking boolean fields in specific classes. Finally, we discovered that a significant amount of noise was generated by the conditional statements of loops and sanity checks such as *null* checks. Using all of the information gained from the exploration of elements related to possible *control predicates*, we defined a filter that refines control predicate and reduces the overall noise.

Overall, the exploration took about 56 hours. We defined a 41-rule filter in about 16 hours (see our website [1] for the actual filter and the extended version [24] for the specification process). The application of the filter for Android AOSP 7.1.1 reduced what ACMiner considered to be control predicates from 25808 to 3308. Such a significant reduction not only underscores the need for a filter but also makes the consistency analysis (Section 4.3) more feasible.

4.3 Consistency Analysis

The final step of ACMiner is consistency analysis of authorization checks for each entry point. In this paper, we perform consistency analysis of all entry points within a service. However, the methodology may work across multiple services, or even across different OEM firmwares. ACMiner performs consistency analysis by automatically discovering underlying correlative relationships between sets of authorization checks. Specifically, ACMiner adopts a targeted

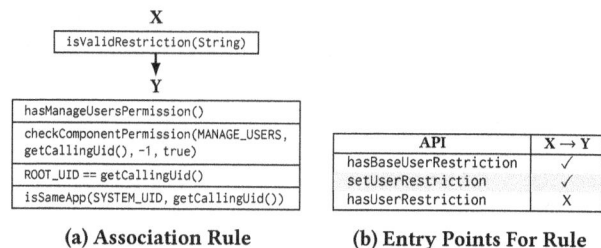

(a) Association Rule

API	$X \rightarrow Y$
hasBaseUserRestriction	✓
setUserRestriction	✓
hasUserRestriction	X

(b) Entry Points For Rule

Figure 5: (a) shows an association rule generated from the code in Figure 1 and (b) illustrates how the first 2 entry points satisfy the rule, while hasUserRestriction does not, indicating it contains one or more inconsistent authorization checks.

approach for association rule mining by using constraint-based querying. It then uses these association rules to predict whether an entry point's authorization checks are consistent. The results are presented to a domain expert for review.

Figure 5a shows an example association rule generated by ACMiner from the code in Figure 1. X and Y are sets of authorization checks found in entry points. The rule states that if an entry point has check(s) from the set X, then it must also have the check(s) in set Y. ACMiner then uses these generated rules to identify potential vulnerabilities by reporting entry points that violate the learned rules (i.e., if an entry point has all of the checks in X, but it is missing checks in Y, then a violation occurs). For instance, Figure 5b shows the three entry points that match X for the rule in Figure 5a, out of which hasUserRestriction fails to satisfy the rule (it does not contain checkManageUsersPermission). On closer inspection, we discovered that all three entry points either set or get information about user restrictions. Moreover, the functionality of hasUserRestriction is nearly identical to hasBaseUserRestriction, which suggests checkManageUsersPermission is needed. As seen in these examples, ACMiner allows an expert to only compare entry points that are close in terms of their authorization checks, which is more precise than comparing all entry points to one another.

The remainder of this section discusses ACMiner's approach to efficiently discover these association rules and how ACMiner uses them to detect inconsistencies in authorization checks.

4.3.1 Association Rule Mining. Association rule mining discovers correlative relationships between sets of authorization checks, $A = \{i_1, i_2, \cdots, i_n\}$, across a set of entry points, $E = \{t_1, t_2, \cdots, t_m\}$ where each entry point in E contains a subset of the items in A. An association rule takes the form $X \implies Y$ where X (antecedent) and Y (consequent) are sets of authorization checks and X and Y are disjoint, i.e., $X \subseteq A$ and $Y \subseteq A$ and $X \cap Y = \emptyset$.

To avoid an excessive number of association rules, ACMiner uses two statistical constraints (support and confidence) to remove candidate association rules that are less than the thresholds minimum support (*minsup*) and minimum confidence (*minconf*). Let $\alpha(I)$ represent the set of entry points in E that contain the authorization checks $I \subseteq A$, i.e., $\alpha(I) = \{t \in E \mid \forall i \in I, i \in t\}$. The support of an association rule $X \implies Y$ is the probability that a set of authorization checks $Z = X \cup Y$ appears in the set of transactions E, i.e., $\sigma(Z) = \frac{|\alpha(Z)|}{|E|}$. The confidence of an association rule is an estimate of the conditional probability of the association rule $P(Y|X)$ where

$X \implies Y$ and can be calculated as $conf(X \implies Y) = \frac{\sigma(X \cup Y)}{\sigma(X)}$.

While association rule mining has been applied to similar problems by prior work [28], the large transaction size (i.e., number of authorization checks in an entry point) in our problem domain makes general association rule mining algorithms infeasible due to their exponential complexity. Therefore, ACMiner uses two main optimizations to reduce the complexity to polynomial time.

First, ACMiner only generates a subset of the association rules called closed association rules [40]. An association rule $X \implies Y$ is closed if $X \cup Y$ is a frequent closed itemset. A frequent closed itemset is a set of authorization checks $C \subseteq A$ where the support of C is greater than *minsup* and there does not exist a superset C' that has the same support as C. C is closed iff $\beta(\alpha(C)) = C$ where $\beta(T)$ represents the largest set of common authorization checks present in the entry points T where $T \subseteq E$, i.e., $\beta(T) = \{i \in A \mid \forall t \in T, i \in t\}$. Note that only mining frequent closed itemsets is lossless, because all frequent itemsets can be generated from the set of frequent closed itemsets, as proven by Zaki and Hsiao [45]. Our proof that closed association rules also do not result in information loss can be found in the extended version [24].

Second, ACMiner generates closed association rules in a targeted manner by placing constraints on the authorization checks that appear in the antecedent of the association rule. Since the goal of consistency analysis is to predict whether an entry point's implementation of authorization checks is consistent, we are only interested in generating association rules where the antecedent of the association rule is a subset of the entry point's authorization checks (i.e., $X \subseteq A_j$ where A_j is the authorization checks of entry point e_j). For example, consider $A_j = \{i_1, i_2, i_3\}$ and we have two frequent closed itemsets $\{i_1, i_2, i_3, i_4\}$ and $\{i_5, i_6, i_7\}$. The association rule $\{i_1, i_2, i_3 \implies i_4\}$ is useful, as it could potentially hint that the authorization checks in A_j is inconsistent and should also contain i_4. However, all of the association rules from the set $\{i_5, i_6, i_7\}$ do not provide additional information on the consistency of authorization checks in A_j, as the two sets are disjoint.

Further, assuming that the authorization checks that are present within an entry point are correct, we can force the antecedent to be constant. In particular, when generating association rules from a frequent closed itemset I for an entry point A_j, we set $X = A_j \cap I$ and can generate association rules by varying the items in Y. If we reduce the authorization checks in X, then we are making the rule less relevant to the consistency of the entry point A_j while keeping X constant only produces the most relevant association rules.

4.3.2 Inconsistency Detection and Output Generation. ACMiner uses the association rules discussed in Section 4.3.1 to analyze the consistency of an entry point's authorization checks. To minimize the amount of manual effort required to verify the presence of an inconsistency, we ensure the output only contains high confidence rules by setting *minconf* to 85%. Moreover, as we want the authorization checks in the consequent of an association rule to be formed by at least 2 entry points, we set the *minsup* to $\frac{2}{|E|}$.

While generating the association rules, we mark an entry point's authorization checks as consistent if there exists a frequent closed itemset that contains the exact same authorization checks as the entry point, as this hints that the entry point's authorization checks are consistent with another entry point's authorization checks. In

particular, entry point e_j's authorization checks A_j is consistent iff $\exists C \in A \mid C = A_j \wedge \beta(\alpha(C)) \wedge \sigma(C) \geq \frac{2}{|E|}$. In contrast, we mark an entry point's authorization checks as potentially inconsistent if an association rule exists where the entry point's authorization checks are the antecedent of the rule and the consequent is not empty (i.e., $\exists X \implies Y \mid X \subseteq A_j \wedge Y \neq \emptyset$).

ACMiner outputs an HTML file for the domain expert to review for each association rule representing a potentially inconsistent entry point. The HTML file contains the set of supporting authorization checks for the association rule (i.e. the antecedent), the set of authorization checks being recommended by the association rule (i.e. the consequent), and the 3 or more entry points that contain the authorization checks of the association rule. This group of entry points can be subdivided into two sets: the target entry point and the supporting entry points. The target entry point is the entry point the association rule has identified as being inconsistent, i.e., the entry point the association rule is recommending additional authorization checks for. The supporting entry points are the 2 or more entry points where the recommended authorization checks occur. Note that the supporting authorization checks occur in both the target and the supporting entry points. To aid the review, the HTML file also contains the set of all authorization checks from the target entry point that do not occur in the supporting authorization checks and for all authorization checks, the method in the Android source code where the checks occur.

To reduce the manual effort required to confirm inconsistencies, we perform two post-processing techniques. First, we remove association rules where $|recommended\ authorization\ checks| >= 5 * |supporting\ authorization\ checks|$, since association rules that contain 100 authorization checks which imply 500 authorization checks is improbable. Second, we remove any remaining association rules that have over 100 recommended authorization checks as such association rules are unlikely to indicate inconsistencies, and the domain expert may not be able to evaluate such rules in a reasonable amount of time.

5 EVALUATION

We evaluated ACMiner by performing an empirical analysis of the system services in AOSP version 7.1.1_r1 (i.e., API 25) built for a Nexus 5X device. Our analysis was performed on a machine with an Intel Xeon E5-2620 V3 (2.40 GHz), 128 GB RAM, running Ubuntu 14.04.1 as the host OS, OpenJDK 1.8.0_141, and Python 2.7.6.

We used ACMiner to mine the authorization checks of all the entry points from this build of AOSP and perform consistency analysis, as described in Section 4. Finally, we manually analyzed the inconsistencies using a systematic methodology to identify high risk (i.e., easily exploitable) and high impact vulnerabilities, and developed proof-of-concept exploits to validate our findings. Our evaluation is guided by the following research questions:

RQ1 *Does ACMiner reduce the effort required by the domain expert in terms of the entry points that need to be analyzed?*

RQ2 *Do the inconsistencies identified by ACMiner help a domain expert in finding security vulnerabilities?*

RQ3 *What are the major causes behind inconsistencies that do not resolve to security vulnerabilities?*

RQ4 *Is ACMiner more effective than prior work at detecting vulner-*

High Impact Low Impact

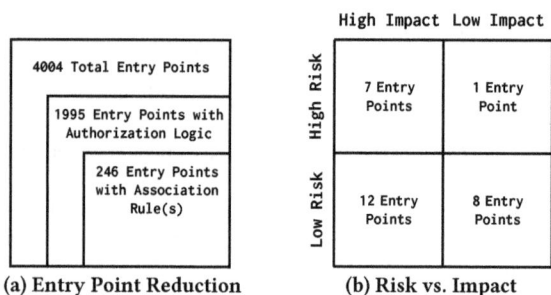

(a) Entry Point Reduction   (b) Risk vs. Impact

Figure 6: (a) shows how ACMiner is able to reduce the scope of the AOSP 7.1.1 system code a domain expert needs to evaluate and (b) breaks down the 28 vulnerabilities in terms of risk and impact.

    abilities in system services?

RQ5 *What is the time required by ACMiner to analyze all the system services in a build of Android?*

We now highlight the salient findings from our evaluation, followed by the categorization of the discovered vulnerabilities. The categorization of non-security inconsistencies, developed via a systematic manual analysis of our results, is described in Section 6.

5.1 Evaluation Highlights

As shown in Figure 6a, ACMiner reduces the total number of entry points that need to be manually analyzed down to just 246 entry points with inconsistent authorization checks, a 94% reduction (**RQ1**). As a result, ACMiner significantly enhances a domain expert's ability to evaluate the consistency of access control enforcement in the Android system by minimizing the effort required. Further, ACMiner took approximately 1 hour and 16 minutes to mine the authorization checks of all entry points from the system image of the AOSP build, and spent an additional 30 minutes producing the HTML files for the association rules that represent potentially vulnerable entry points. While ACMiner could be optimized further, time taken by ACMiner is a feasible cost, given its scalability benefits over a fully manual analysis (**RQ5**).

On manually analyzing the 246 entry points, we discovered a total of 28 entry points containing security vulnerabilities (**RQ2**). As Figure 6b illustrates, these 28 vulnerabilities were then classified in terms of their risk (i.e., the ease of exploiting a vulnerability) as well as the impact (i.e., the gravity of the consequence of an exploited vulnerability). Using this criteria, we found 7 vulnerabilities that were high risk as well as high impact, 1 vulnerability that was high risk only, 12 vulnerabilities that were high impact only, and 8 vulnerabilities that were low in terms of both risk and impact. All 28 vulnerabilities have been submitted to Google. So far, 2 of our vulnerabilities have been assigned a "moderate" Android Security Rewards (ASR) severity level, which is generally awarded to bypasses in access control mechanisms (e.g., restrictions on constrained processes, or general bypasses of privileged processes [22]). In Section 5.2, we categorize these 28 vulnerabilities according to their effect; however, we only discuss a few of these vulnerabilities in depth, due to space constraints.

ACMiner is significantly more effective than prior work at identifying inconsistent authorization checks. For instance, ACMiner is able to identify 875 unique context queries using the semi-automated approach described in Section 4.2.1, a drastic 2552% improve-ment over the original 33 context queries that encompass a majority of the context queries considered by Kratos [38]. Further, while AceDroid [2] is more comprehensive than Kratos in its identification of Android's authorization checks, it relies on a manually defined list of context queries, which is insufficient. That is, as described in Section 4.2.1, our thorough attempts at identifying context queries through manual observation alone resulted in the identification of only 620 context queries, 71% of the total context queries that ACMiner is able to find using its semi-automated approach. Thus, while AceDroid does not provide quantitative information on its set of context queries, we can certainly say that it is not as complete as ACMiner in its identification of Android's authorization checks. Indeed, the context query isValidRestriction in Figure 1 is an example of a context query that neither AceDroid nor Kratos was able to identify, and in fact, one that we missed in our manual definition of Android's authorization checks. However, through the general expressions, ACMiner was able to identify isValidRestriction as a context query and the vulnerability outlined in Figure 1. Moreover, neither AceDroid nor Kratos makes any mention of the App Ops restrictions in their definition of Android's authorization checks. Yet ACMiner is able to identify 2 vulnerabilities relating to the App Ops restrictions (see Section 5.2). While a full empirical comparison with Kratos and AceDroid is infeasible due to the lack of source code access, our evaluation demonstrates that ACMiner makes significant advancements to existing work in terms of the coverage of the authorization checks, making the consistency analysis as complete as possible (**RQ4**).

Finally, ACMiner produced 453 association rules denoting inconsistent authorization checks in 246 entry points. Some entry points had more than one inconsistency. Furthermore, while some inconsistencies were indeed valid security vulnerabilities (30/453), others were a result of irregular coding practices in Android (25/453) or indicative of ACMiner's limitations in terms of analyzing the semantics of the authorization checks (**RQ3**). The limitations identified via our analysis point to hard problems in analyzing Android's access control logic and motivate future work.

5.2 Findings

Table 2 describes the vulnerabilities discovered through our analysis of Android 7.1.1 with ACMiner. On manually analyzing the inconsistent entry points produced by ACMiner, we discovered 28 entry points that represent security vulnerabilities. While most of these entry points represent one vulnerability each, two entry points (i.e., getLastLocation and setStayOnSetting, vulnerabilities 15 and 16 in Table 2 respectively) each led us to clusters of multiple identically vulnerable entry points, as described later in this section. For simplicity, we count each cluster as a single vulnerability.

We group the vulnerabilities into the following 3 categories: (1) user separation and restrictions, (2) App Ops, (3) and pre23. This categorization is based on the subsystems affected by the vulnerabilities (e.g., App Ops), as well as the characteristics they have in common (e.g., pre23). Additionally, some vulnerabilities that are hard to classify have been categorized as (4) miscellaneous. **VC1: Multi-user Enforcement:** As shown in Table 2, a majority (i.e., 14) of the vulnerabilities affect Android's separation among users (i.e. user profiles in Android's multi-user enforcement [23]).

Table 2: Description of vulnerabilities, along with the services in which they are present

Associated Entry Point (Service)	Vulnerability Description
VC1: Multi-user Enforcement	
1. getInstalledApplications (PMS)	Missing the enforceCrossUserPermission check, allowing any app on one user profile to discover apps installed on other profiles.
2. getPackagesHoldingPermissions (PMS)	Missing enforceCrossUserPermission, allowing any app on one user profile to get sensitive permission information about other profiles.
3. hasUserRestriction (UMS)	Missing the hasManageUsersPermission check, which checks for the permission MANAGE_USERS, is missing, allowing any user to discover the restrictions on their own and other user profiles.
4. checkUriPermission (AMS)	Missing the handleIncomingUser check that verifies if a user can operate on behalf of another, allowing any user access to content provider URIs belonging to another user, so long as the app making the request has access to the content provider.
5. grantUriPermission (AMS)	Missing the handleIncomingUser check, with similar implications as checkUriPermission.
6. killPackageDependents (AMS)	Missing the handleIncomingUser check, allowing any user to kill the apps and background processes of another user.
7. setUserProvisioningState (DPMS)	Missing the enforceFullCrossUsersPermission check, enabling any user to change another user profile's state.
8. setDefaultBrowserPackageName (PMS)	Missing the enforceCrossUserPermission check, enabling any user to set the default browser of any other user.
9. updateLockTaskPackages (AMS)	Missing handleIncomingUser, enabling any user to modify the apps that may be permanently pinned to the screen in a kiosk like venue.
10. installExistingPackageAsUser (PMS)	Does not check if the target user exists, allowing any user to install apps on user profiles that may be created at a later time.
11. setApplicationHiddenSettingAsUser (PMS)	Does not check if the target user exists, allowing any user to hide apps on user profiles that may be created in the future.
12. setAlwaysOnVpnPackage (CS)	Does not check for the no_config_vpn user restriction, allowing a managed user to set its always on VPN to another application.
13. setWallpaperComponent (WPMS)	Missing the two checks isSetWallpaperAllowed and isWallpaperSupported, allowing a managed user to change their wallpaper.
14. startUpdateCredentialsSession (ACMS)	Missing checks canUserModifyAccounts and canUserModifyAccountsForType, allowing a user to trigger an update for the credentials of online accounts like Google and Facebook even when restricted.
VC2: App Ops	
15. noteProxyOperation (AOMS)	Missing the verifyIncomingUid check, which checks for a signature permission, allowing non-system apps to call this entry point.
16. getLastLocation (LMS)	A majority of the entry points in the LMS use the AppOpsManager check checkOp, which is not intended for security, instead of the security check noteOp. getLastLocation uses the correct check.
VC3: Pre23	
17. setStayOnSetting (POMS)	On systems with API 23 or above, the pre23 protection level allows any permission to be automatically granted to non-system apps built targeting the API 22 or below. This vulnerability allows non-system apps to access 6 additional entry points protected by the WRITE_SETTINGS *signature* permission, as WRITE_SETTINGS also has the pre23 protection level.
VC4: Miscellaneous	
18. unbindBackupAgent (AMS)	Missing check for if caller is performing a backup, allowing any app to disrupt the backup process of another app.
19. getPersistentApplications (PMS)	Missing system UID check, allowing any non-system app to discover what apps and services permantly run in the background.
20. logEvents (MLS)	Incorrect check for permission CONNECTIVITY_INTERNAL, should check DUMP when writing sensitive data to logs.
21. getMonitoringTypes (GHS)	Missing check checkPermission, allowing a caller access both fine and coarse levels of geofence location data.
22. getStatusOfMonitoringType (GHS)	Missing check checkPermission, with similar implications as getMonitoringTypes.
23. setApplicationEnabledSetting (PMS)	Missing isPackageDeviceAdmin check, allowing an app to disable an active administrator app.
24. setComponentEnabledSetting (PMS)	Missing isPackageDeviceAdmin check, allowing an app to disable components of an active administrator app.
25. convertFromTranslucent (AMS)	Missing check for enforceNotIsolatedCaller, allowing a isolated process to affect the transparency of windows.
26. notifyLockedProfile (AMS)	Missing check for enforceNotIsolatedCaller, allowing an isolated process to trigger a retrun to the home screen.
27. setActiveScorer (NSS)	Missing BROADCAST_NETWORK_PRIVILEGED permission check which is always paired with the SCORE_NETWORKS permission check.
28. getCompleteVoiceMailNumberForSubscriber (PSIC)	Incorrect check for permission CALL_PRIVILEGED instead of the READ_PRIVILEGED_PHONE_STATE results in coarse-grained enforcement.

AMS=ActivityManagerService; AOMS=AppOpsManagerService; CS=ConnectivityService; DPMS=DevicePolicyManagerService; LMS=LocationManagerService; PMS=PackageManagerService; POMS=PowerManagerService; UMS=UserManagerService; WPMS=WallpaperManagerService; PSIC=PhoneSubInfoController; ACMS=AccountManagerService; MLS=MetricsLoggerService; GHS=GeofenceHardwareService; NSS=NetworkScoreService

These can be further divided into four subcategories based on how they may be exploited: (1) leaking user information across users, (2) operating across users, (3) modifying user settings before a user exists, and (4) allowing users to bypass restrictions.

1. Leaking Information to Other Users: In 5 entry points (i.e., 1→5 in Table 2), the lack of checks leads to potential leaks of security-sensitive information to other users. For instance, using the vulnerable entry point getInstalledApplications in the PackageManagerService, any user can learn of the applications another user has installed, as the entry point does not enforce any checks other than checking if the user being queried exists. Similarly, the entry point hasUserRestriction in the UserManagerService, previously used as the motivating example, is not protected with the *signature* level permission MANAGE_USERS, which is present in the similar hasBaseUserRestriction entry point. This omitted authorization check allows a user to know of the restrictions placed on other users, which is security-sensitive information that should not be public. The entry points getPackagesHoldingPermissions, checkUriPermission and grantUriPermission similarly leak sensitive information.

We experimentally confirmed the existence of both the vulnerabilities in hasUserRestriction and getInstalledApplications in Android 7.1.1 as well as Android 8.1. We have submitted bug reports to Google and received "moderate" ASR severity level for

both the bugs. Further, we confirmed that the vulnerability in getPackagesHoldingPermissions was fixed in Android 8.1. As a result, we could not submit it to Google's bug program, which only considers bugs affecting the latest version of Android. All remaining vulnerabilities have been reported to Google.

2. Operating Across Users: Missing authorization checks in 4 entry points (i.e., 6→9 in Table 2) allow users to bypass multi-user restrictions and perform sensitive operations on behalf of other users. For example, we discovered that the entry point killPackageDependents takes in a *userId* as an argument but does not actually verify whether the calling user is allowed to perform operations on behalf of the supplied *userId*. This allows *any user to kill the apps and background processes of any other user*. A similar flaw in entry point setUserProvisioningState enables any user to set the state of any other user profile to states such as "managed", "unmanaged", or "finalized". Such changes may be dangerous. For instance, a user may be able to set their managed enterprise profile to unmanaged, releasing it from the administrator's control.

Fortunately, all four entry points described in this category can only be called from apps installed on the system image (i.e., are protected by authorization checks that ensure this). This indirectly mitigates some damage, by making the vulnerabilities difficult to exploit from a third-party app. However, capability leaks in privileged

```
1   /** Do a quick check for whether an application might be
2    * able to perform an operation. This is not a security
3    * check; you must use noteOp or startOp for your actual
4    * security checks, which also ensure that the given uid
5    * and package name are consistent. ... */
6   int checkOp(int op, int uid, String packageName) {...}
```

Figure 7: The comment above checkOp from the class AppOpsManager that states it should not be used as a security check.

apps may allow such vulnerabilities to be exploited by third-party apps, as prior work has demonstrated [25, 43]. All of these vulnerabilities have been reported to Google.

3. Modifying User Settings Before A User Exists: Both the entry points installExistingPackageAsUser and setApplicationHiddenSettingAsUser do not perform the authorization check exists, which verifies if a the *userId* passed into the entry points represents a valid user. Without this check, it is possible for a caller to install an app for a non-existent user or hide an app from a non-existent user. Thus, when the user for whom this change was made is actually created, these settings will already be in place. These entry points are only callable from systems apps; however, system apps may be compromised or may leak capabilities, and the *exists* check needs to be in place to prevent system apps from being tricked into allowing users to install apps in profiles that have yet to be created (e.g., installing apps in a future enterprise profile). We have submitted these vulnerabilities to Google.

4. Allowing Users to Bypass Restrictions: Vulnerabilities in entry points 12→14 from Table 2 allow a user to perform operations despite the restrictions placed on the user profile. For instance, the entry point setAlwaysOnVpnPackage does not check for the restriction no_config_vpn, allowing a managed user to set the always on VPN for the user profile to another application, effectively switching VPN connections. The entry points setWallpaperComponent and startUpdateCredentialsSession have similar vulnerabilities. All of these vulnerabilities have been reported to Google.

VC2: App Ops: ACMiner identified weaknesses related to App Ops. One such vulnerability lies in the noteProxyOperation of the AppOpsService. The entry point makes a note of an application performing some operation on behalf of some other application through IPC. However, unlike other entry points in the AppOpsService, noteProxyOperation is missing the authorization check verifyIncomingUid which includes a check for the *signature* level permission UPDATE_APP_OPS_STATS. Without verifyIncomingUid, it is possible for any non-system app to use noteProxyOperation to query the restrictions a user has placed on other apps, thus retrieving information that should not be available to non-system apps.

We discovered a set of identical vulnerabilities in App Ops through our analysis of the getLastLocation entry point in the LocationManagerService, which ACMiner pointed out as having inconsistent authorization checks. The getLastLocation entry point calls the authorization check reportLocationAccessNoThrow which performs the check noteOpNoThrow from the AppOpsManager, a wrapper for the AppOpsService. ACMiner correctly identified the use of noteOpNoThrow as an inconsistency since a majority of the entry points (9) in LocationManagerService use the authorization check checkLocationAccess which performs the check checkOp from the AppOpsManager. However, as Figure 7 shows, the comment above the checkOp method clearly states that checkOp should not be used

```
<permission android:name="android.permission.WRITE_SETTINGS"
    android:protectionLevel="signature|preinstalled|appop|pre23" />
```

Figure 8: The permission protection levels of WRITE_SETTINGS in the AndroidManifest.xml file [3]

to perform a security check. Instead, one of the various forms of noteOp should be used. This implies that all 9 entry points using the context query checkLocationAccess suffer from a vulnerability, and that the use of reportLocationAccessNoThrow in getLastLocation is actually appropriate. This instance demonstrates an interesting outcome of the use of consistency analysis in ACMiner. That is, our use of consistency analysis in ACMiner is also useful in identifying instances, where the majority of the related entry points are vulnerable. As described previously, for simplicity, we count this cluster of vulnerable entry points as a single vulnerability, which has been submitted to Google.

VC3: Pre23: ACMiner identified a group of vulnerabilities related to Android's *pre23* permission protection level. The entry point setStayOnSetting in the PowerManagerService uses the authorization check checkAndNoteWriteSettingsOperation, which checks if an app has the *signature* level permission WRITE_SETTINGS. Permissions with the *signature* protection level can only be granted to system apps (i.e., apps that were originally packaged with the system image). However, as shown in Figure 8, WRITE_SETTINGS has an additional protection level of *pre23*, which has an interesting effect on Android versions 6.0 or above (i.e., API 23 or above). It allows permissions marked as *pre23* to be granted to non-system apps that target API 22 or below [21]. Thus, as a result of the improperly defined permission protection levels for WRITE_SETTINGS, the *pre23* grants non-system apps access to a *signature* level permission.

The damage resulting from the *pre23* vulnerability is not restricted to the entry point setStayOnSetting. A simple search for the use of the permission WRITE_SETTINGS in the authorization checks ACMiner mined for all entry points in the system revealed 13 additional entry points checking for the permission WRITE_SETTINGS, 6 of which can be called from a non-system app using the *pre23* vulnerability (i.e., these 6 entry points are not protected with any other *signature* permission). Of the 6, the following 5 entry points deal with tethering and are located in the ConnectivityService: setUsbTethering, stopTethering, startTethering, tether, and untether. The last setWifiApEnabled was located in the WifiServiceImpl and allows a caller to set some WIFI access point configuration, causing the device to connect or disconnect from any WIFI access point the caller provides. These entry points are clearly more important to protect than setStayOnSetting, and an adversary may be able to do considerable damage by exploiting them. We do not count these entry points in our initial list of 28 vulnerabilities. All entry points affected by the *pre23* vulnerability have been submitted to Google.

VC4: Miscellaneous Vulnerabilities: ACMiner also identified 11 vulnerabilities related to information leaks, denial of service, disabling of administrator apps, and a mixture of other minor vulnerabilities. All of these vulnerabilities have been reported to Google.

6 NON-SECURITY INCONSISTENCIES

ACMiner identified 423 inconsistencies (i.e., rules) that did not represent vulnerabilities. Aside from the 20 rules that were caused by easily fixed bugs in ACMiner, we resolve these non-security incon-

Table 3: Non-security Inconsistencies

Type of Inconsistency	Number of Rules
1. Shortcuts to Speed-Up Access	7
2. Fixing Access Bugs	2
3. Potential Vulnerabilities	16
4. Difference in Functionality	189
5. Checks With Different Arguments	66
6. Noise in Captured Checks	53
7. Restricted to Special Callers	37
8. Semantic Groups of Checks	23
9. Equivalent Checks	10

sistencies to their likely causes, and classify them into 9 categories, shown in Table 3 (**RQ3**). The first three categories point to irregular coding practices, i.e., (1) inconsistent application of short-cuts to speed up access, (2) access bugs or discrepancies in how the permission should be used as per the documentation, or (3) inconsistent application of hard-coded checks that would potentially lead to vulnerabilities on future updates. The remaining 6 categories point to issues that could be corrected by engineering improvements to ACMiner, such as considering semantic equivalence between authorization checks, or the integration of call graph comparison and method-name comparison to mitigate the analysis of functionally different entry points. We provide additional details on all of the 9 categories in the extended version [24].

7 LIMITATIONS

While ACMiner is effective at discovering inconsistencies that lead to vulnerabilities, consistency analysis has a general limitation, i.e., it may not discover vulnerabilities that are consistent throughout code. Further, for precision, ACMiner does not handle the invocation of secondary entry points, i.e., calls to entry points from within other entry points. ACMiner omits the *ordering* of the authorization checks and hence does not identify improper operator use in *control predicates*, which we plan to explore in the future. Moreover, ACMiner's semi-automated analysis requires the participation of domain experts. However, as Section 5 demonstrates, our design significantly reduces manual effort in contrast with the manual validation of system services. As we have already analyzed AOSP version 7.1.1, only minor input is needed to analyze newer versions or vendor modifications. Finally, ACMiner shares the general choices made by Android static analysis techniques for precision, i.e., it does not consider native code, or runtime modifications (e.g., reflection, dynamic code loading, Message Handlers).

8 RELATED WORK

ACMiner addresses a problem that has conceptual origins in prior work on authorization hook validation for traditional systems. Early investigations targeted the Linux Security Modules (LSM) hook placement in the Linux kernel, using techniques such as type analysis using CQUAL [47], program dominance [48], and dynamic analysis to create authorization graphs from control flow traces [12, 29]. As the lack of ground truth is a general challenge for hook validation, prior work commonly uses consistency analysis [12, 29, 41]. Closest to our work is AutoISES [41], which infers security specifications from code bases such as the Linux kernel and Xen. However, AutoISES assumes a known set of security functions or security-specific data structures, whereas ACMiner identifies a diverse set of authorization checks in the Android middleware.

The closest to our approach is prior work on authorization

hook validation in the Android platform, i.e., Kratos [38] and AceDroid [2]. ACMiner distinguishes itself from Kratos and AceDroid through its deep analysis of Android's system services, and its significantly improved coverage of Android's authorization checks.

Kratos [38] compares a small subset of Android's authorization checks across entry points of the same system image to look for inconsistent checks between different system services. ACMiner does not analyze for consistency across services. Instead, we hypothesize that entry points within a single service are similar in purpose, and hence, analyze the consistency of the authorization checks by comparing the entry points of every system service with other entry points in the same service. Further, ACMiner's semi-automated approach for identifying authorization checks results in a 2552% improvement over Kratos' manually-curated list (Section 5).

Similarly, AceDroid [2] evaluates the consistency of the authorization checks among different vendor-modified Android images, and hence differs from ACMiner in terms of its objective. AceDroid makes key improvements over Kratos, as it considers various non-standard context queries not considered by Kratos. However, AceDroid also relies on a manually-defined list of context queries, which may produce only approximately 71% of the context queries that ACMiner is able to find (Section 5).

Finally, recent literature is rich with static and dynamic program analysis of third-party Android apps targeted at privacy infringement [13, 20, 26], malware [17, 27, 46], as well as vulnerabilities [9, 14]. As the Android platform and apps use similar programming abstractions, researchers have applied these tools and techniques to the platform code, e.g., for providing a mapping between APIs and corresponding permissions [5, 8, 18] or automatically identifies privacy-sensitive sources and sinks [4]. Moreover, prior work has also studied the platform code, to analyze OEM apps for capability leaks (e.g., Woodpecker [25] and SEFA [43]), discover privilege escalation on update vulnerabilities (e.g., Xing et al. [44]), or uncover gaps in the file access control policies in OEM firmware images (e.g., Zhou et al. [49]). While ACMiner shares a similar objective, unlike prior work, ACMiner provides an automated and systematic investigation of core platform services.

9 CONCLUSION

This paper provides an approach for the systematic and in-depth analysis of a crucial portion of Android's reference monitor, i.e., its system services. We design ACMiner, a static analysis framework that comprehensively identifies a diverse array of authorization checks used in Android's system services, and then adapts the well-founded technique of association-rule mining to detect inconsistent access control among service entry points. We discover 28 security vulnerabilities by analyzing AOSP version 7.1 using ACMiner, and demonstrate significantly higher coverage of checks than the state of the art. Our work demonstrates the feasibility of in-depth analysis of Android's system services with ACMiner, as it significantly reduces the number of entry points that must be analyzed, from over 4000 with millions of lines of code to a mere 246.

Acknowledgements: This work was supported by the Army Research Office (ARO) grant W911NF-16-1-0299 and the National Science Foundation (NSF) grants CNS-1253346 and CNS-1513690. Opinions, findings, conclusions, or recommendations in this work are those of the authors and do not reflect the views of the funders.

REFERENCES

[1] 2019. ACMiner Project Website. https://wspr.csc.ncsu.edu/acminer.
[2] Yousra Aafer, Jianjun Huang, Yi Sun, Xiangyu Zhang, Ninghui Li, and Chen Tian. 2018. AceDroid: Normalizing Diverse Android Access Control Checks for Inconsistency Detection. In *Proceedings of the ISOC Network and Distributed System Security Symposium (NDSS)*.
[3] AndroidXref. 2019. WRITE_SETTINGS permission in AndroidManifest.xml. http://androidxref.com/7.1.1_r6/xref/frameworks/base/core/res/AndroidManifest.xml#1865. Accessed Jan. 10, 2019.
[4] Steven Arzt, Siegfried Rasthofer, and Eric Bodden. 2014. A Machine-learning Approach for Classifying and Categorizing Android Sources and Sinks. In *Proceedings of the ISOC Network and Distributed Systems Symposium (NDSS)*.
[5] Kathy Wain Yee Au, Yi Fan Zhou, Zhen Huang, and David Lie. 2012. PScout: Analyzing the Android Permission Specification. In *Proceedings of the 2012 ACM conference on Computer and communications security*. 217–228.
[6] Michael Backes, Sven Bugiel, Erik Derr, Patrick D McDaniel, Damien Octeau, and Sebastian Weisgerber. 2016. On Demystifying the Android Application Framework: Re-Visiting Android Permission Specification Analysis. In *Proceedings of the USENIX Security Symposium*.
[7] Michael Backes, Sven Bugiel, Christian Hammer, Oliver Schranz, and Philipp von Styp-Rekowsky. 2015. Boxify: Full-fledged App Sandboxing for Stock Android.. In *USENIX Security Symposium*.
[8] Alexandre Bartel, Jacques Klein, Martin Monperrus, and Yves Le Traon. 2014. Static Analysis for Extracting Permission Checks of a Large Scale Framework: The Challenges And Solutions for Analyzing Android. *IEEE Transactions on Software Engineering (TSE)* 40, 6 (June 2014).
[9] Erika Chin, Adrienne Porter Felt, Kate Greenwood, and David Wagner. 2011. Analyzing Inter-Application Communication in Android. In *Proceedings of the 9th Annual International Conference on Mobile Systems, Applications, and Services*.
[10] Andrew Dalton. 2019. Android powers 2 billion devices around the world. https://www.engadget.com/2017/05/17/android-powers-2-billion-devices-around-the-world/. Accessed Jan. 10, 2019.
[11] Jeffrey Dean, David Grove, and Craig Chambers. 1995. Optimization of Object-Oriented Programs Using Static Class Hierarchy Analysis. In *Proceedings of the European Conference on Object-Oriented Programming (ECOOP)*.
[12] Antony Edwards, Trent Jaeger, and Xiaolan Zhang. 2002. Runtime Verification of Authorization Hook Placement for the Linux Security Modules Framework. In *Proceedings of the ACM Conference on Computer and Communications Security*.
[13] William Enck, Peter Gilbert, Byung-Gon Chun, Landon P. Cox, Jaeyeon Jung, Patrick McDaniel, and Anmol N. Sheth. 2010. TaintDroid: An Information-Flow Tracking System for Realtime Privacy Monitoring on Smartphones. In *Proceedings of the 9th USENIX Symposium on Operating Systems Design and Implementation*.
[14] William Enck, Damien Octeau, Patrick McDaniel, and Swarat Chaudhuri. 2011. A Study of Android Application Security. In *Proceedings of the USENIX Security Symposium*.
[15] William Enck, Machigar Ongtang, and Patrick McDaniel. 2009. On Lightweight Mobile Phone Application Certification. In *Proceedings of the 16th ACM Conference on Computer and Communications Security (CCS)*.
[16] William Enck, Machigar Ongtang, and Patrick McDaniel. 2009. Understanding Android Security. *IEEE Security & Privacy Magazine* 7, 1 (January/February 2009).
[17] Michael D. Ernst, René Just, Suzanne Millstein, Werner Dietl, Stuart Pernsteiner, Franziska Roesner, Karl Koscher, Paulo Barros, Ravi Bhoraskar, Seungyeop Han, Paul Vines, and Edward Wu. 2014. Collaborative Verification of Information Flow for a High-Assurance App Store. In *Proceedings of the ACM Conference on Computer and Communications Security (CCS)*.
[18] Adrienne Porter Felt, Erika Chin, Steve Hanna, Dawn Song, and David Wagner. 2011. Android Permissions Demystified. In *Proceedings of the ACM Conference on Computer and Communications Security (CCS)*.
[19] Adrienne Porter Felt, Helen J. Wang, Alexander Moshchuk, Steven Hanna, and Erika Chin. 2011. Permission Re-Delegation: Attacks and Defenses. In *Proceedings of the USENIX Security Symposium*.
[20] Clint Gibler, Jon Crussell, Jeremy Erickson, and Hao Chen. 2012. AndroidLeaks: Automatically Detecting Potential Privacy Leaks In Android Applications on a Large Scale. In *Proceedings of the International Conference on Trust and Trustworthy Computing (TRUST)*.
[21] Google. 2019. protectionLevel. https://developer.android.com/reference/android/R.attr#protectionLevel. Accessed Jan. 10, 2019.
[22] Google. 2019. Security Updates and Resources. https://source.android.com/security/overview/updates-resources. Accessed Jan. 10, 2019.
[23] Google. 2019. Supporting Multiple Users. https://source.android.com/devices/tech/admin/multi-user. Accessed Jan. 10, 2019.
[24] Sigmund Albert Gorski III, Benjamin Andow, Adwait Nadkarni, Sunil Manandhar, William Enck, Eric Bodden, and Alexandre Bartel. 2019. ACMiner: Extraction and Analysis of Authorization Checks in Android's Middleware. http://arxiv.org/abs/1901.03603. (Jan. 2019). arXiv:1901.03603

[25] Michael Grace, Yajin Zhou, Zhi Wang, and Xuxian Jiang. 2012. Systematic Detection of Capability Leaks in Stock Android Smartphones. In *Proceedings of the ISCO Network and Distributed System Security Symposium (NDSS)*.
[26] Peter Hornyack, Seungyeop Han, Jaeyeon Jung, Stuart Schechter, and David Wetherall. 2011. These Aren't the Droids You're Looking For: Retrofitting Android to Protect Data from Imperious Applications. In *Proceedings of the ACM Conference on Computer and Communications Security (CCS)*.
[27] Jianjun Huang, Xiangyu Zhang, Lin Tan, Peng Wang, and Bin Liang. 2014. AsDroid: Detecting Stealthy Behaviors in Android Applications by User Interface and Program Behavior Contradiction. In *Proceedings of the International Conference on Software Engineering (ICSE)*.
[28] JeeHyun Hwang, Tao Xie, Vincent Hu, and Mine Altunay. 2010. Mining likely properties of access control policies via association rule mining. *Data and Applications Security and Privacy XXIV* (2010), 193–208.
[29] Trent Jaeger, Antony Edwards, and Xiaolan Zhang. 2004. Consistency Analysis of Authorization Hook Placement in the Linux Security Modules Framework. *Transactions on Information and System Security* 7, 2 (May 2004), 175–205.
[30] Patrick Lam, Eric Bodden, Ondrej Lhoták, and Laurie Hendren. 2011. The Soot framework for Java Program Analysis: A Retrospective. In *Proceedings of the Cetus Users and Compiler Infrastructure Workshop (CETUS)*.
[31] Ond∨rej Lhoták. 2007. Comparing Call Graphs. In *Proceedings of the ACM Workshop on Program Analysis for Software Tools and Engineering (PASTE)*.
[32] Ondřej Lhoták and Laurie Hendren. 2003. Scaling Java Points-to Analysis Using SPARK. In *Proceedings of the 12th International Conference on Compiler Construction (CC 03)*. Springer Berlin Heidelberg, Warsaw, Poland, 153–169.
[33] Travis McCoy. 2019. How the World Bank is mobilizing their workforce with Android. https://www.blog.google/topics/connected-workspaces/how-world-bank-mobilizing-their-workforce-android/. Accessed Jan. 10, 2019.
[34] Mark Milian. 2019. U.S. government, military to get secure Android phones. http://www.cnn.com/2012/02/03/tech/mobile/government-android-phones/index.html. Accessed Jan. 10, 2019.
[35] Adwait Nadkarni and William Enck. 2013. Preventing Accidental Data Disclosure in Modern Operating Systems. In *Proceedings of the ACM Conference on Computer and Communications Security (CCS)*.
[36] Paul Pearce, Adrienne Porter Felt, Gabriel Nunez, and David Wagner. 2012. AdDroid: Privilege Separation for Applications and Advertisers in Android. In *Proc. of the ACM Symposium on Information, Computer and Communications Security*.
[37] Steve Ranger. 2019. The world's most secure smartphones – and why they're all Androids. http://www.zdnet.com/article/the-worlds-most-secure-smartphones-and-why-theyre-all-androids/. Accessed Jan. 10, 2019.
[38] Yuru Shao, Jason Ott, Qi Alfred Chen, Zhiyun Qian, and Z. Morley Mao. 2016. Kratos: Discovering Inconsistent Security Policy Enforcement in the Android Framework. In *Proceedings of the ISOC Network and Distributed System Security Symposium (NDSS)*.
[39] Riley Spahn, Jonathan Bell, Michael Lee, Sravan Bhamidipati, Roxana Geambasu, and Gail Kaiser. 2014. Pebbles: Fine-Grained Data Management Abstractions for Modern Operating Systems. In *Proceedings of the USENIX Operating Systems Design and Implementation (OSDI)*.
[40] Laszlo Szathmary. 2006. *Symbolic Data Mining Methods with the Coron Platform*. Ph.D. Dissertation. Université Henri Poincaré-Nancy I.
[41] Lin Tan, Xiaolan Zhang, Xiao Ma, Weiwei Xiong, and Yuanyuan Zhou. 2008. AutoISES: Automatically Inferring Security Specification and Detecting Violations. In *Proceedings of the USENIX Security Syposium*.
[42] Raja Vallée-Rai, Phong Co, Etienne Gagnon, Laurie Hendren, Patrick Lam, and Vijay Sundaresan. 1999. Soot - A Java Bytecode Optimization Framework. In *Proc. of the Conference of the Centre for Advanced Studies on Collaborative Research*.
[43] Lei Wu, Michael Grace, Yajin Zhou, Chiachih Wu, and Xuxian Jiang. 2013. The Impact of Vendor Customizations on Android Security. In *Proceedings of the ACM Conference on Computer and Communications Security (CCS)*. 623–634.
[44] Luyi Xing, Xiaorui Pan, Rui Wang, Kan Yuan, and XiaoFeng Wang. 2014. Upgrading Your Android, Elevating My Malware: Privilege Escalation through Mobile OS Updating. In *Proceedings of the IEEE Symposium on Security and Privacy*.
[45] Mohammed J Zaki and Ching-Jui Hsiao. 2002. CHARM: An Efficient Algorithm for Closed Itemset Mining. In *Proceedings of the 2002 SIAM International Conference on Data Mining*.
[46] Mu Zhang, Yue Duan, Heng Yin, and Zhiruo Zhao. 2014. Semantics-Aware Android Malware Classification Using Weighted Contextual API Dependency Graphs. In *Proceedings of the ACM Conference on Computer and Communications Security (CCS)*.
[47] Xiaolan Zhang, Antony Edwards, and Trent Jaeger. 2002. Using CQUAL for Static Analysis of Authorization Hook Placement. In *Proceedings of the USENIX Security Symposium*.
[48] Xiaolan Zhang, Trent Jaeger, and Larry Koved. 2004. Applying Static Analysis to Verifying Security Properties. In *Proceedings of the Grace Hopper Celebration of Women in Computing Conference (GHC)*.
[49] Xiaoyong Zhou, Yeonjoon Lee, Nan Zhang, Muhammad Naveed, and XiaoFeng Wang. 2014. The Peril of Fragmentation: Security Hazards in Android Device Driver Customizations. In *Proc. of the IEEE Symposium on Security and Privacy*.

REAPER: Real-time App Analysis for Augmenting the Android Permission System

Michalis Diamantaris
FORTH, Greece
diamant@ics.forth.gr

Elias P. Papadopoulos
FORTH, Greece
php@ics.forth.gr

Evangelos P. Markatos
FORTH, Greece
markatos@ics.forth.gr

Sotiris Ioannidis
FORTH, Greece
sotiris@ics.forth.gr

Jason Polakis
Univ. of Illinois at Chicago, USA
polakis@uic.edu

ABSTRACT

Android's app ecosystem relies heavily on third-party libraries as they facilitate code development and provide a steady stream of revenue for developers. However, while Android has moved towards a more fine-grained run time permission system, users currently lack the required resources for deciding whether a specific permission request is actually intended for the app itself or is requested by possibly dangerous third-party libraries.

In this paper we present Reaper, a novel dynamic analysis system that traces the permissions requested by apps in real time and distinguishes those requested by the app's core functionality from those requested by third-party libraries linked with the app. We implement a sophisticated UI automator and conduct an extensive evaluation of our system's performance and find that Reaper introduces negligible overhead, rendering it suitable both for end users (by integrating it in the OS) and for deployment as part of an official app vetting process. Our study on over 5K popular apps demonstrates the large extent to which personally identifiable information is being accessed by libraries and highlights the privacy risks that users face. We find that an impressive 65% of the permissions requested do *not* originate from the core app but are issued by linked third-party libraries, 37.3% of which are used for functionality related to ads, tracking, and analytics. Overall, Reaper enhances the functionality of Android's run time permission model without requiring OS or app modifications, and provides the necessary contextual information that can enable users to selectively deny permissions that are not part of an app's core functionality.

CCS CONCEPTS

• **Security and privacy** → **Mobile platform security**; *Mobile and wireless security*; *Access control*.

KEYWORDS

Android; dynamic analysis; permission origin; personally identifiable information; third-party libraries

ACM Reference Format:
Michalis Diamantaris, Elias P. Papadopoulos, Evangelos P. Markatos, Sotiris Ioannidis, and Jason Polakis. 2019. REAPER: Real-time App Analysis for Augmenting the Android Permission System. In *Ninth ACM Conference on Data and Application Security and Privacy (CODASPY '19), March 25–27, 2019, Richardson, TX, USA*. ACM, New York, NY, USA, 12 pages. https://doi.org/10.1145/3292006.3300027

1 INTRODUCTION

Modern smartphones have become a treasure trove of sensitive user data and personally identifiable information (PII) that is regularly collected and exfiltrated by Android applications ("apps") [36, 47, 48, 56, 63, 64]. At the same time, the limitations of Android's permission system have been explored extensively and various modifications have been proposed [31, 47, 65, 72, 75]. The privacy risks that arise from permission management are further exacerbated by the dominating role that third-party libraries have achieved in the Android app ecosystem by providing a revenue stream for developers [54]. On average, 41% of an app's code is contributed by common libraries [49]. The prevalence of libraries has serious implications, as they incentivize apps to request more permissions than needed [70] and extensively leak personal information [2, 4, 5, 52, 62].

Android has been moving toward a more fine-grained permission control system with each major revision, showing considerable improvements over the original design where users were presented with confusing blocks of information at installation time [46]. Following the introduction of the new permission system in Android 6, users can now accept or reject a permission request at run time, or revoke permissions at any time through the system's settings. However, recent work [39] demonstrated that users still do not fully grasp how permissions work and found that they are more likely to deny a permission request when given a detailed description of their personal information that will be accessed and uploaded (e.g., their actual phone number). Lin et al. [50] found that providing users with information on why a resource is being used can alleviate their privacy concerns, while in a different context Wang et al. [78] found that users perceive permissions differently when they are related to an application's core functionality.

Even though the new approach empowers users by enabling a more precise granting of permissions, apps remain a black box with hidden inner workings, thus preventing users from fully benefiting from its potential; as users cannot differentiate between permission requests needed for the core functionality of the app and requests from third-party libraries, they can not make informed decisions regarding which permissions should be granted to each app. Motivated by this rationale, we argue that a fine-grained access control permission system should notify users of the origin of a permission request and explicitly state if it is needed by the app's core functionality or an integrated third-party library.

To bridge this significant gap we present Reaper, a system for dynamically analyzing apps and inferring the origin of permission-protected calls (PPCs) through inline hooking that enables passive monitoring of the internals of the Android operating system. This requires tackling several challenges, each of which is addressed by one of the main components of our system. First, a dynamic analysis framework requires an efficient tool for traversing the graph of each app with sufficient coverage. We develop UIHarvester, an automation tool that utilizes hooks in the Android rendering process for identifying interactive elements and their properties, for traversing the app's graph without a priori knowledge of the app's functionality or visual characteristics. UIHarvester introduces negligible overhead that is 30-38 times smaller than that of Android's UI Automator, and improves coverage by ∼ 26% compared to the tool that achieved the highest coverage in a comparative study [35].

PermissionHarvester is responsible for the main functionality of Reaper, as it hooks PPCs at run time and extracts the current stacktrace. Since the permissions required by functions are not the same across all Android versions, with newer versions not requiring permissions for certain calls that access PII, our tool automatically recognizes the OS version and adjusts its functionality accordingly. Even though PPCs protect device resources, common users do not have complete knowledge of Android's documentation and internals and are mainly concerned with apps accessing personally identifiable information. As such, PermissionHarvester also monitors PII access regardless of whether the call is protected by a permission or not. Extracted stacktraces are processed for identifying the origin of calls that are protected by permissions or access PII. Our approach is not affected by encryption techniques that may attempt to hide the presence of third-party libraries and the exfiltration of PII. Furthermore, Reaper does not require any modifications to the OS and does not depend on any sort of instrumentation, thus, introducing minimal performance overhead (we only require root access). Our system can be incorporated as part of the Android Open Source Project for enriching the contextual information shown to users.

To explore the potential benefits of our system, we use Reaper to analyze over 5K popular Android apps, and find several alarming results regarding the extent of third-party libraries' use of permissions and permission-protected calls. Indicatively, our study reveals that for 90% of the apps third-parties initiate more permission protected calls than the core app itself. We find that on average 65% of used permissions are needed by third-party libraries, and 34% of the apps never issue PPCs from their core code as the requested permissions originate solely from library code. To make matters worse, when it comes to *dangerous permissions* 48-59% of the requests originate from third-party libraries. For permission-protected calls that reach PII, in 59% of the apps third-party libraries use getRunningAppProcesses(), which can lead to precise user

identification [23]. We also find many libraries accessing PII from non-permission protected calls. Finally, we explore how the origin information is augmented by accounting for the library type. We find that at least 37.3% of PPCs and 28.6% of PII accesses that originate from libraries are exclusively intended for functionality related to ads, tracking and analytics and could safely be denied by users without preventing the apps' intended functionality.

The key contributions of our work are the following:

- We develop Reaper, a **real**-time **per**mission analysis system that infers the origin of calls to permission-protected resources or non-permission-protected sensitive PII. Our system can augment Android's run time permission system by enriching the contextual information provided to users.
- We experimentally evaluate our system and find that the overhead introduced is minimal, rendering it suitable for analyzing apps at a large-scale, or integrating in user devices.
- We use Reaper to explore the interaction between libraries and Android's permission system in depth. We provide a fine-grained analysis of PPCs and PII access *by third-party libraries* in the wild. Our findings shed light on the alarming extent to which libraries dominate such calls, and motivate the need for incorporating origin information in permission requests.
- We publicly released our source code and the datasets used at http://www.reaper.gr .

2 BACKGROUND AND MOTIVATION

The incorporation of third-party libraries allows app developers to take advantage of useful existing functionality and also tap into an alternative revenue stream without the need to charge users for the app itself. While this may appear beneficial to end users as they are able to obtain apps seemingly for free, it suffers from the inherent privacy risks of the prevailing paradigm of services being free because users are the product [3] and "pay" with their personal data [54]. Not only have such libraries become prevalent (49% of apps contain at least one ad library [57]), but the risks they present [44] increase through time as they ask for increasingly more dangerous permissions [32]. This necessitates the deployment of functionality that can differentiate between permissions required by the actual app and those requested by third-party libraries. Tracing permission requests back to third-party libraries allows for enriching the contextual information presented to users.

While libraries can offer useful functionality to app developers, they may also surreptitiously add (potentially dangerous) permissions without the developer being explicitly informed. As such, users cannot rely on developers' intentions or safe practices for ensuring appropriate access to their data. Indeed, Android supports the merging of multiple manifest files, as each APK file can contain only one manifest file. While this functionality is meant to facilitate the inclusion of external libraries, it also allows third-party libraries to silently include permissions without the developer's approval. To make matters worse, developers have to explicitly and proactively include specific commands (tools:node="remove") in their manifest to prevent libraries from including specific permissions.

To verify that this occurs in practice, we conduct an exploratory experiment with popular libraries. We create a test app and separately integrate each library; after compilation we extract the final

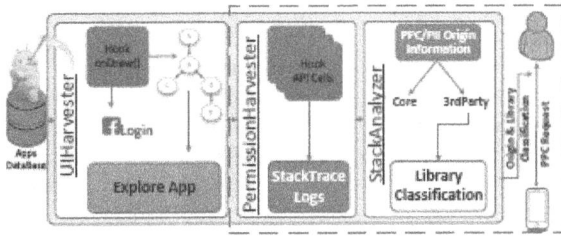

Figure 1: Overview of Reaper's architecture.

manifest file to see which permissions have been included by the libraries without any form of notification. First, we look at one of the most prevalent libraries [18], namely Google Play Services. Google offers multiple libraries and we test Firebase and GMS (which incorporate functionality for analytics, ads etc.) and find that they add six and eight permissions respectively. We investigate whether libraries also merge dangerous permissions, and find that Instabug and Paypal silently include three (read,write access to External Storage and Record Audio) and one (Camera) dangerous permissions respectively. This simple experiment highlights how Android offers functionality that can be misused by third-party libraries to silently obtain access to permissions that can affect the user's privacy or the device's normal operation. It is not meant to be exhaustive and many more libraries may be exhibiting such behavior in practice.

3 REAPER DESIGN AND IMPLEMENTATION

Reaper's primary goal is to distinguish which permissions are needed by the core functionality of the app and which by integrated third-party libraries. Many advertising and tracking companies freely provide preconfigured libraries and online tutorials on how to integrate them. Moreover, previous work [44] found that advertising libraries are prone to downloading code over HTTPS and dynamically loading and executing this code using the DexClassLoader class. Even though dynamic code loading offers useful functionality to developers, it can also be used to evade static analysis [59]. Furthermore apps may also hide their functionality through common obfuscation and encryption techniques [11, 36].

We leverage the hooking mechanism of Xposed [1] to build a dynamic analysis system that is designed to overcome the aforementioned obstacles. We require root access but do not rely on any OS modification, such as changing and recompiling the AOSP image, allowing us to apply it to any stock Android version. Figure 1 shows an overview of Reaper, which consists of three components: (i) UIHarvester (Section 3.1) a sophisticated UI automation tool for exercising apps, (ii) PermissionHarvester (Section 3.2) for hooking and monitoring the stacktrace of functions that lead to permission checks, and (iii) StackAnalyzer (Section 3.3) for analyzing stacktraces and inferring if they originate from a third-party library and of what type. If our system is adopted as part of an official app vetting process, or used by other researchers for dynamically analyzing apps, then all three components should be used, as shown in the gray box. If Reaper's functionality is integrated in the OS for augmenting the permission system, then only two of those components are required, as shown in the dotted line.

3.1 UI Harvester

A significant challenge when performing dynamic analysis on mobile apps is the traversal of the app's graph through the simulation of user interactions, without any a priori knowledge of the interactive content that will be displayed in the app. Previous work [24, 27, 33, 45, 53, 60, 61, 71, 74, 81, 85, 86], has explored the dynamic traversal of an application from different perspectives, such as achieving high traversing coverage or identifying malicious behavior. Unfortunately apart from requiring static analysis of the apk [24, 27, 45, 60, 71, 74, 81, 85], they may require some form of app instrumentation [27, 45, 60], or OS code modification [53, 61, 85], or are pinned to a specific Android version [24, 33, 85, 86].

UI Automator [21] is a useful tool available from the Android SDK that offers functionality similar to what we require; it can dump the interactable objects of the display and provide additional information about them. However, UI Automator presents two major disadvantages that render it unsuitable for our needs. First, if the app uses the WindowManager.LayoutParams.FLAG_SECURE option, UI Automator has to respect this specific flag and cannot output information about the objects being displayed. This flag is a security feature that treats the contents of the window as "secure" and prevents taking screenshots or being viewed on non secure displays [22]. This flag is not uncommon and is used to secure apps (e.g., PayPal) from side channel attacks, and can be used by apps or third-party libraries that want to evade dynamic analysis. Second, the performance overhead introduced is significant, rendering UI Automator unsuitable for a large scale analysis (details in Section 5).

To overcome the aforementioned restrictions, we developed a **plug & play** prototype that simulates user interactions, which fulfils the following design constraints:

- No requirement for a priori information on the content that will be displayed in the app.
- No requirement for decompilation or static analysis of the apk file, or access to the app's source code.
- No requirement for code modification (app or OS).
- No inefficient and ineffective random input generation approaches.
- Support for a wide range of Android versions.

Harvesting UI elements. Android renders the contents of the display based on a specific procedure, where each activity receiving focus provides the root node of the layout hierarchy and draws its layout. Drawing starts at the root node of the layout tree and is traversed in a top-down order. Android also provides the View class, which is the basic building block for UI elements. While traversing the tree each View is rendered in the appropriate region. Rendering begins with a measure pass and continues with a layout pass. The former, is responsible for the dimension specifications of each View, while in the latter each parent positions all the children based on the measurements obtained during the measure pass. After this two-step process, the onDraw() function of the Canvas is called for rendering the contents of a View object. Whenever something changes on the display, View notifies the system and, depending on the changed properties, either the invalidate() or the requestLayout() functions are called. The former calls the onDraw() for the specified object while the latter instantiates the procedure from the beginning. Since onDraw() is called last before the actual rendering, we hook it to capture the displayed elements.

Identifying interactable objects. Having access to a `View` object enables us to use every method of the `View` class [14] from the Android SDK. This allows us to detect what type of elements are contained in the `View` object (e.g., `TextView`, `Button`, `Image`), as well as the corresponding metadata such as the text displayed, the resource-id, the index, and horizontal/vertical scrolling. To identify whether the elements of the `View` object are user interactable, we use the `getImportantForAccessibility()`, `hasWindowFocus()` and `isShown()` methods on each object. Moreover, we also find the position and the coordinates of each object by using the methods `getLocationInWindow()` and `getLocationOnScreen()`.

Traversing applications. UIHarvester hooks into the `onDraw()` function and exports all the information to `logcat`. Using a Python parser we extract this information and use all the interactable objects for performing a breadth-first traversal of the app. Since we know the type of each element as well as its coordinates, we utilize the Android Debug Bridge for performing the appropriate actions (e.g., tap, swipe, keyevents, etc.). Every time a new `View` is drawn on the display (e.g., after a button is pressed), UIHarvester exports its elements. By obtaining all the `View`s that have been drawn on the display, we can recreate the app's UI graph.

Login. Many apps provide a login option for a more personalized experience, while others require users to login before using the app. Not being able to handle such cases significantly limits the coverage and usefulness of any UI automator. As such, we implement an automated login feature that leverages Facebook's SSO.

Setting a threshold. Due to the dynamic nature and content of Android apps, it is possible for UI automators to get stuck in an infinite recursion of state transitions for certain apps. A simple example is the `"back to menu"` button. We handle this case by checking whether the elements (and their properties) have already been encountered in the exact same order. A case that can not be handled by our approach is when an activity renders content that is downloaded from the web and changes between transitions. As such, we need to impose a threshold for terminating the traversal of these apps. Since our goal is to execute as many permission-protected functions as possible, we set a rule to stop the traversal when five minutes pass from when the last permission request occurred. While this could potentially result in a loss of certain requests, tracking and advertising libraries often perform their functionality either at launch time or after the user logs in [7, 55].

3.2 Permission Harvester

This is the core component of Reaper and is responsible for monitoring function calls and logging the current stacktrace for subsequent analysis. Since blindly hooking into every function call would result in an increase of the overhead without providing any additional information, we first need to identify the functions that lead to a permission request from the Android Server.

Permission mappings. The constant evolution of Android's permission system has led to many changes as well as compatibility and security issues regarding how each permission works [84]. Due to the differences between API versions, functions may lead to other permissions or may no longer be permission-protected across versions. For instance, the `getScanResults()` function from the `net.wifi.WifiManager` class only needs the `ACCESS_WIFI_STATE`

permission up to API 22. Since API 23, this method also requires access to the device's location through `ACCESS_COARSE_LOCATION` or `ACCESS_FINE_LOCATION`. The Stowaway project [41] used static analysis in Android 2.2 to determine an app's API calls, and provided a map that identifies what permissions are needed for each API call. Recently PScout [26] and AXPLORER [29], statically analyzed the Android Framework, extended the mappings for newer versions and corrected previous uncertainties. When comparing the mappings of PScout and AXPLORER, we find various differences in their results; in API 22 AXPLORER registers the function `getWifiState()` in `net.wifi.WifiManager` with the `ACCESS_WIFI_STATE` permission. On the contrary, PScout registers the same function with the `DUMP` permission. As such, it is important to dynamically validate the permission mappings as we discuss below.

Mappings selection. Our system identifies the OS version and adjusts the permission mappings, using AXPLORER's results for APIs 16 (Android v. 4.1) to 25 (v. 7.1) by hooking the appropriate functions. We excluded API 20 as AXPLORER does not provide mappings for this version. To facilitate our system's description we will refer to an example permission-protected call and the induced hooks as illustrated in Figure 2. By monitoring the PPCs ①, we can identify the corresponding permission through AXPLORER's list and the origin of the function call through the stacktrace of the current thread. The Java stacktrace holds every execution until a Binder transaction occurs, and also reveals the path and exact Java file (inside the apk) from which the call originated ②.

Validating permission mappings. To dynamically validate the mappings from previous work, we need to hook the appropriate functions of the Android Server. The `checkPermission()` and `checkpermissionWithToken()` functions (found in the class `ActivityManagerService`) grant or deny access to resources according to the app's permissions. Prior to API 22 access to these two functions is feasible by directly hooking them. Since API 22, a different entry point is needed for reaching them. To reach the methods and classes of the Android framework we hook the `systemMain()` function of the `app.ActivityThread` class. Within that hook we can monitor the permissions that each app and process request at run time by encapsulating the hooks for these functions.

Handling asynchronous calls. In Android different resources are handled by different System Services. For an app to access such information ①, a new thread of the appropriate service manager is created and this newly created thread calls the validation check mechanism ②. During this process, Android Binder is responsible for passing messages between entities, using the `onTransact()` and `execTransact()` functions. Even though the functions involved in permission validation are asynchronous calls, we know a priori the functions that will lead to a permission request ① and can call them sequentially and map each function call with the appropriate permission check that occurs on the Android Server ②. To this end we created a mock application that executes in a sequential manner all the permission-protected calls of the Android SDK.

In practice asynchronous callbacks are frequently used in Android, and a library can register its functionality, or part of it, as a callback. Even though the registered callback executes in a separate thread, the stacktrace of this newly created thread contains the origin of the embedded executed code. Since PermissionHarvester monitors the execution of PPCs independently of asynchronous

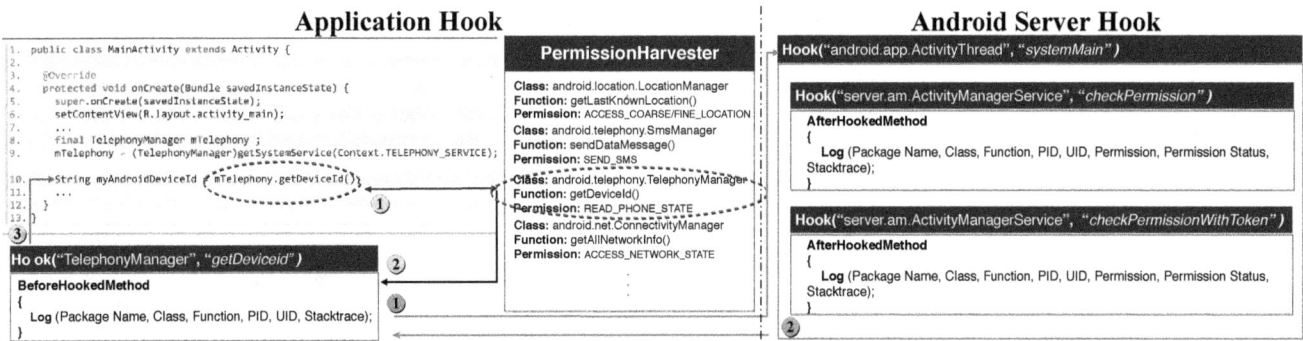

Figure 2: Application Hook is PermissionHarvester's *core hooking mechanism* that monitors PPCs and inspects stacktraces for extracting their origin. Android Server Hook is only used for validating the permission mappings.

```
0  java.lang.Thread.getStackTrace(Thread.java:580)'
1  android.location.LocationManager.getLastKnownLocation()'
2  com.appodeal.ads.an.e(SourceFile:243)'
3  com.appodeal.ads.d.b.<init>(SourceFile:180)'
4  com.appodeal.ads.d.i.a(SourceFile:295)'
5  com.appodeal.ads.d.i.a(SourceFile:105)'
6  com.appodeal.ads.d.i.doInBackground(SourceFile:37)'
7  android.os.AsyncTask$2.call(AsyncTask.java:292)'
...
13 java.lang.Thread.run(Thread.java:818)'
```

Listing 1: Example stacktrace for getLastKnownLocation(). The code that initiated the PPC through an asynchronous call belongs to "com.appodeal" package, which corresponds to the Appodeal third-party library.

calls, the StackAnalyzer component can identify the true origin of the PPC. We illustrate this process with an example of a library registering a PPC in an asynchronous callback. Listing 1 presents a callback that executes the getLastKnownLocation() function needed by the "com.appodeal" library. This library creates a subclass of an AsyncTask and overrides the method doInBackground(). Even though the code that is placed in this method is executed in a different thread, thus obscuring whether the core app or the library registered the callback, we can still successfully identify whether the executed code belongs to a third-party library.

Non-permission-protected PII leaks. It is important to note that not all PII is protected by permissions, and library developers may take extra measures to hide the presence of PII leaks and the surreptitious exfiltration of data (i.e., obfuscation, encryption and dynamic code loading). As PII can enable user tracking, it is crucial to identify the origin of such requests. Recent work [56] released an extensive list with such device characteristics that are leaked. We manually map those characteristics with their appropriate function calls and find that 8 such functions are not permission-protected. By extending Reaper to support these calls, our system is *able to identify the origin of PII leaks regardless of the call being protected by a permission or not.* While this is not part of our work's main focus, we include this information to further highlight the invasive behavior of third-party libraries in our study in Section 6.

Our approach can reveal privacy leakage without the need to perform deep packet inspection, thus, bypassing the obstacle of attempting to identify data exfiltrated in an obfuscated form, which

has stifled previous work on PII leakage. For instance, in our experiments we found two apps (com.sevideo.slideshow.videoeditor, com.fourvideo.videoshow.videoslide) that integrate the XavirAd library, which downloads a dex file from a remote server, collects PII and sends them encrypted over the network [11].

3.3 Stack Analyzer

Apart from being useful for debugging, stacktraces can be used during run time execution since they contain essential information about the current thread. We opted for this approach as it provides a straightforward solution for identifying the origin of a function. The stacktrace contains a path to the source file and has four fields of interest: the package name, the class from which the method was called, the actual method and the file name of the source code. StackAnalyzer processes the stacktraces of important calls and checks if the package name of a known third-party library exists in the path of the stacktrace's function call. Even though library code can be obfuscated (e.g., classes, functions, etc.), by default library package names remain intact since developers need to know which library to link in their app during the build process. To verify that stack inspection is effective in practice, we manually examined the package name of all the stacktraces collected from our experiments (see Section 4) and found that only 1.14% have an obfuscated package name, preventing us from identifying their origin. This is further corroborated by Wermke al. [79], who conducted an obfuscation detection analysis on 1.7 million apps from Google Play and found that even for obfuscated libraries larger scopes remain identifiable in package names (e.g., com.google.ads.*).

Third-party library package names. Li et al. [49] conducted a large scale analysis of 1.5 million apps from Google Play, in order to identify common Android libraries. Even though their approach does not handle obfuscated code, they identified 1,353 third-party libraries. LibScout [28] bypassed the limitations of obfuscated code by using a variant of Merkle trees and performing profile-matching between known third-party libraries and the contents of the apk file being tested. Since the results provided by LibScout are bound by the dataset they are trained with, it is possible for LibScout to miss some of the libraries that are integrated in the application. Indeed, during our experiments we came across such an example: AppsFlyer [15] a well known mobile tracking library. StackAnalyzer

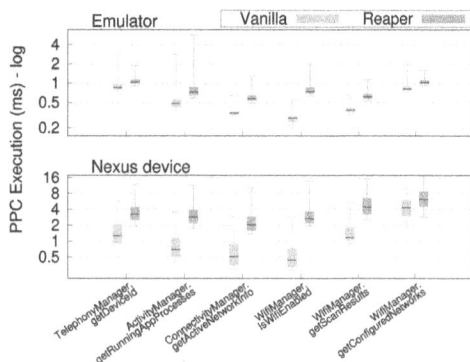

Figure 3: Performance overhead of PermissionHarvester, including the overhead for the hook.

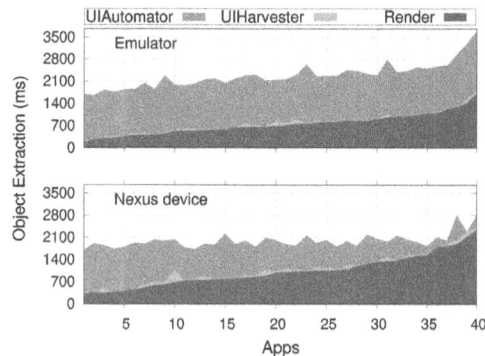

Figure 4: Performance overhead comparison between Reaper's UIHarvester and UIAutomator.

uses the combined results of both systems to create a coherent list of package names and to identify at runtime whether the stacktrace belongs to code originating from a third-party library.

Library classification. In practice, developers may use code from a third-party library that is integral to the app's functionality. By classifying the type of the library from which the permission request originates, we obtain more detailed information regarding the nature of the call and whether it can be attributed to code that is necessary for the app's intended functionality; e.g., by differentiating calls from an ad library to those from an app-development library. By disambiguating the origin of the calls Reaper further augments the contextual information presented to users and guides them towards granting "useful" permissions. Specifically, our system uses information from two sources [13, 49] to ascertain the category of the library from which each third-party call is initiated at runtime and provide that information to the user.

4 DATASET & EXPERIMENTAL SETUP

We downloaded free apps from Google Play using Raccoon [20] and performed the majority of experiments using emulators. We opted for an emulator for the ability to deploy multiple virtual machines and analyze a large amount of apps. While third-party libraries may be able to infer the presence of a virtualized execution environment and alter their behavior, previous work on app analysis has also relied on emulators [68, 69]. To make the environment look more like an actual device we installed the Google Play services and signed in with a legitimate Google account. We conduct the experiments in Android API 22, as it is the API with the most accurate permission mappings available – AXPLORER's mappings for API 23 are incomplete [17]. Overall, we selected the top 300 apps (or as many as were available) from each category, and downloaded a total of 5457 from 38 categories.

5 PERFORMANCE EVALUATION

Here we evaluate our system's performance and measure the overhead introduced by each of the main components. We also compare UIHarvester to popular tools and demonstrate the advantages of our approach. We perform experiments using both an emulator and a Google Nexus 6 device, running the AOSP image with API 22.

PermissionHarvester overhead. The same code handles every PPC. Using a mock app that individually issues six PPCs from different managers, we measure the time needed for each PPC with and without PermissionHarvester present. In the vast majority of cases the function calls tested had an execution time of less than 1ms and 4ms for the emulator and the real device respectively. Since System.currentTimeMillis() does not produce readings of less than 1ms, we used the System.nanoTime() to extract a more accurate representation of the execution time. Figure 3 presents the results from 50K executions of the app. We observe that even though the same code applies to every hooked PPC, the induced penalty varies between 0.18-0.45ms for the emulator and 1.93-3.77ms for the Nexus device. The reason for this is that each PPC can result in stacktraces of different sizes. While System.nanoTime() is significantly more accurate than System.currentTimeMillis(), it is a relatively expensive call. It depends on the underlying architecture and can take up to 100 CPU cycles while measuring with millisecond precision takes only 5-6 CPU cycles. Apart from being more expensive, it also exhibits deviation in its execution time, which is reflected in the larger deviation of getRunningProcess() and getDeviceID(). Overall, the overhead for the actual hook is 0.0075ms [6] and the remaining overhead is due to the system call required for logging the stacktrace.

UIHarvester overhead. We measure the induced overhead of UIHarvester, by checking the extra time needed to render the contents of the display. We use the "Displayed" value from logcat, which represents the time elapsed between launching an activity and drawing its contents. For this experiment we selected 40 apps of different sizes and varying loading times, and measured the time needed to launch the main activity with and without UIHarvester.

As shown in Figure 4 the penalty in the emulator is between 0.3%-21% with an average of 6.55%, and depends on the number of elements drawn in the display. In the device the penalty is 0.16%-56.59% with an average penalty of 7.8%. In the worst case, the overhead to render the contents of a heavy View is 140ms for the emulator and 386.1ms for the device, which is acceptable for fully automated dynamic analysis. We also compare to the time needed to extract information about the display using UIAutomator, which offers similar functionality. On average UIHarvester only requires 40.19ms for the emulator and 67.29ms for the device. UIAutomator

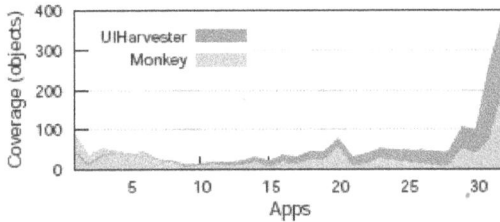

Figure 5: Comparison of interactable object coverage between Reaper's UIHarvester and Android's Monkey.

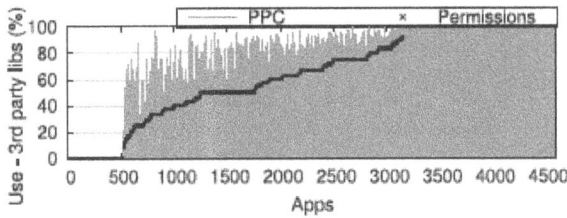

Figure 6: Per app use of permissions and PPC by libs.

Table 1: Issues that resulted in certain apps not being traversed during our experiments.

Apps Without Interaction	89
- *Addon (41), Launcher (31), Plugin (9), Theme (5), Widget (3)*	
Manual Login Required	45
Installation Failure	37
Device Specific	15
Emulator Detection	1
Root Detection	1
Malfunction / Crash	156
Total	**344**

takes over 1,546ms and 2,001ms to extract the elements respectively, resulting in a 30 to 38-fold increase. Thus our tool offers superior performance while being more effective for this study.

UIHarvester Coverage. While GUI exploration and coverage in Android can be measured using different techniques (line coverage, activities, crashes, etc.) we opted for counting the interactive elements since it can be applied to both open and closed-source apps without the need for instrumentation. Choudhary et al. [35] evaluated six input generation techniques and compared them to Android's Monkey. They found that the Monkey fuzzer was the best option, achieving a 40% coverage. To evaluate UIHarvester's coverage, we obtained the same set of apps from [35] and compared the interactive objects found by UIHarvester and Monkey; we tested the 32 apps that remain functional. Since Monkey can only perform random clicks and does not count the interactive elements, we used the technique employed in UIHarvester to extract them. For a direct comparison, we set a timeout of 5 minutes and configured the time required to generate input events to be consistent between both tools. In Figure 5 we plot the number of objects found by Monkey (averaged over three runs) and the objects found by UIHarvester. Overall, UIHarvester improves coverage by 25.98%.

Compatibility between versions. A common limitation of analysis tools is being pinned to a specific Android version. By designing Reaper to have minimum dependencies, we maintain compatibility across APIs. We verified this by analyzing ten backwards-compatible apps on the four most common Android versions [12] and found that all Reaper components remained fully functional.

6 PERMISSION ANALYSIS

We study 5457 apps in order to understand the use of PPC and access of PII by third-party libraries in practice. Our study dynamically examines the origin of such calls, enabling a fine-grained exploration of the corresponding privacy risks.

Apps without PPC. In our experiments 315 apps did not issue a PPC call during their analysis. Furthermore, we were not able to traverse an additional 344 apps and obtain a PPC stacktrace. Table 1 breaks down the numbers for the issues that resulted in this; 89 apps could not be traversed due to their type, as they do not contain launchable activities and there is no direct interaction. Out of the remaining, 45 required a manual login, 37 failed during installation, 15 apps were for a specific device brand or only available for certain CPUs/GPUs and 2 apps did not execute because of the device's environment. Also, 156 apps malfunctioned at launch time. To understand whether Reaper affects these 156 apps, we tested them without our framework, and observed that in both cases the apps remained non-functional. When executed without the Xposed framework, 155 apps continued to crash. While one app appears to be detecting Xposed, this can be trivially bypassed by renaming the Xposed package. Thus, practically, our experimental environment only prevented one app from running. To analyze apps that perform emulation or root detection, Reaper can also be used with a real device and the root requirement can be hidden using known root-hiding techniques [9]. Interestingly, certain apps that can not be traversed due to their type still perform PPCs (at launch time).

Third-party library use. In Figure 6 we explore the use of PPCs and their corresponding permissions by libraries. We observe that for 521 apps PPCs are only used by the app's core functionality, while for 1,642 apps every PPC originates from third-party libraries. While there is varying behavior in the remaining 2,635 apps, there is significant use of PPC throughout. Overall, 65.22% of the permissions requested are not from the apps' core code, but are requested by the libraries. These results verify our intuition that PPCs and their underlying permissions are heavily used by third-party libraries, with 34% of these apps never calling them from their core code. This highlights the benefit of adopting the functionality offered by Reaper for informing users about the origin of permission requests and enabling more fine-grained control.

Function and permission origin. To better understand the origin of each function, we explore their use across all apps. As shown in Figure 7, use of permission-protected functions by libraries remains high and certain functions *are never used by core functionality*. For instance, one such function that also accesses PII, is getSubscriberId() which returns the device's IMSI.

In Figure 8 we plot the 30 most used functions. We find that these typically are calls that return device specific information, such as Device-IDs, Network-Info, SSIDs, Location, Apps-installed, which

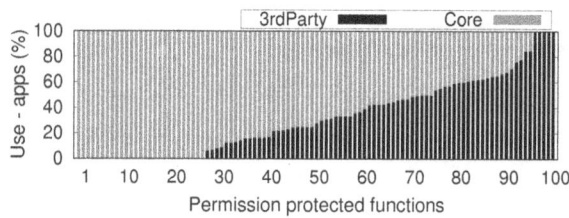

Figure 7: Origin of every permission protected function.

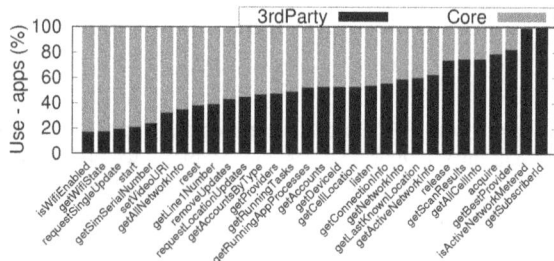

Figure 8: Breakdown for the 30 most used PPCs.

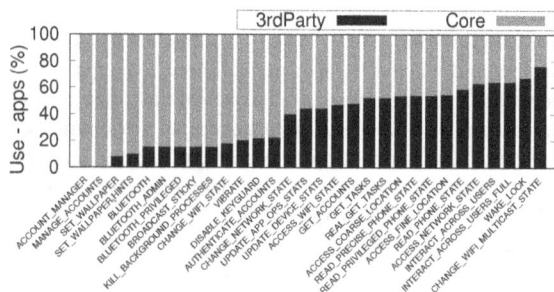

Figure 9: Breakdown for the 30 most used permissions.

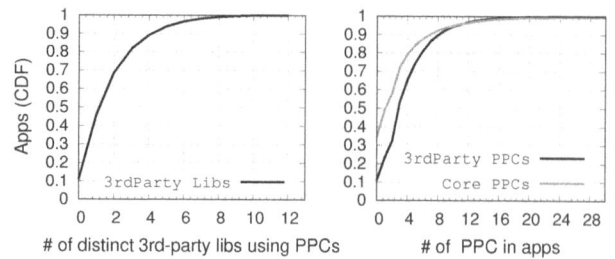

Figure 10: Distinct libraries issuing PPCs in each app, and breakdown of PPCs for third-party and core functionality.

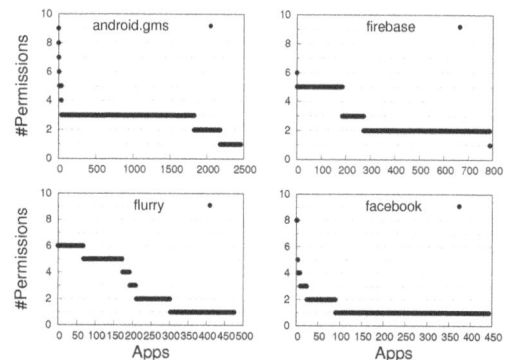

Figure 11: Number of permissions used across the apps that include the 4 most used libraries.

are considered PII and are used by advertising and tracking companies. We observe that the getSubscriberId() function which is also included in the top 30, requires the READ_PHONE_STATE permission which is one of the permissions considered dangerous by the Android developer guide. In Figure 9, we plot the 30 most used permissions. We manually mapped these permissions to their protection level from the official Android source code [19] and found that third-party libraries also use permissions that fall in different protection levels such as signature, privileged, installer, development and dangerous. The use of the four dangerous permissions (i.e., ACCESS_COARSE_LOCATION, ACCESS_FINE_LOCATION, GET_PHONE_STATE, READ_ACCOUNTS) ranges from 48% to 59% for third-party libraries. This means that for these apps *when users are presented with a dangerous permission request at run time, roughly half the time the permission does not originate from core code.*

Third-party library integration. To understand how many third-party libraries are used inside apps, we calculate the fraction of distinct third-party libraries using PPCs, as well as the total fraction of PPCs attributed to 3rd parties or core functionality. In Figure 10 (left) we observe that 30% of our dataset contains at least two distinct third-party libraries that initiate PPCs. Moreover, as

can be seen in Figure 10 (right), for 90% of the apps third parties initiate more PPCs than the app's core code.

Permission variation. We found cases where a library uses a different number of permissions across apps. In Figure 11, we select four of the most used libraries and plot the number of permissions used across all apps. One possible reason for this could be because UIHarvester was not able to reach a level of coverage that would trigger all the permission requests. However this will not always be the case since apps contain different versions of the same library, which may offer different functionality. Furthermore, libraries may also adjust according to the number of permissions granted [16].

PII access. While not our main focus, an important aspect of our analysis is exploring the extent of third-party libraries accessing PII; the origin information provided by Reaper results in a more fine-grained and precise view of PII leakage when compared to prior studies that explore apps' behaviors as a whole. We map function calls to PII based on the identifiers provided by prior work [56, 63] and the Android SDK documentation, and analyze the information provided by Reaper. Figure 12 shows all the functions that access PII, whether through a permission-protected call (blue circles) or not (red circles). The size of the circle denotes the number of apps that contain the respective library and issue the corresponding function call. Due to space constraints we only include the 13 most popular libraries. We find that third-party libraries access the non-protected calls more frequently than the permission-protected calls. As users can be fingerprinted from the information returned by these functions, it is troubling that Android

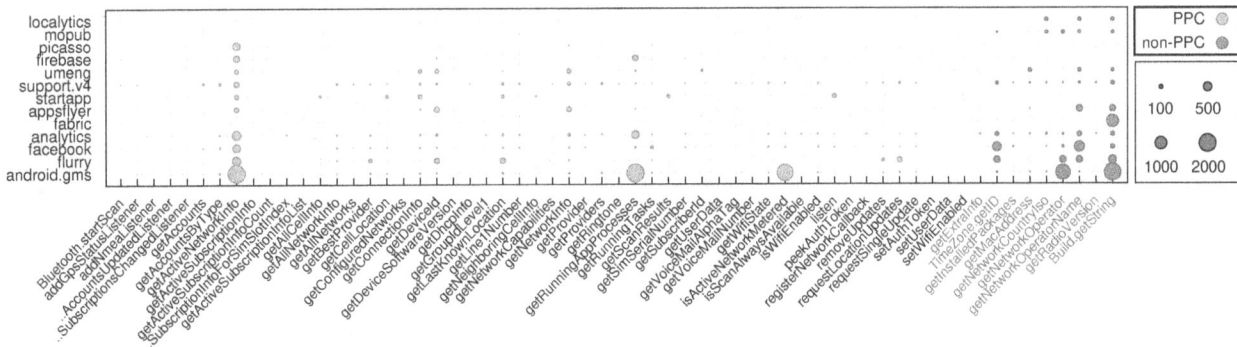

Figure 12: PII leakage from the most popular third-party libraries (sorted in descending order) broken down to the corresponding function call used. Blue circles denote PII being accessed through permission-protected calls, while the red circles indicate PII access by functions that are not permission-protected. The size of the circle denotes the number of apps in each case.

does not enforce a permission requirement. *We argue that all calls that lead to PII should be permission-protected, allowing users to manage what information can be accessed by apps and third parties.* The getRunningAppProcesses() function can also be called without the GET_TASKS permission. It returns a list of running processes and is being used by 3,218 (59%) apps. This is also a significant privacy threat, as previous work has shown that tracking companies can potentially identify users when as few as 4 apps are known [23]. Despite being discontinued for APIs $\geq$ 23, it remains active for older versions, with 66.4% of devices running APIs $\geq$ 23 [12].

Library classification. To further enrich the origin information, Reaper classifies the type of libraries initiating each monitored call, which allows our system to further disambiguate the origin of calls. In Figure 13 (left) we present the coarse-grained classification of the type of library from which each call originated. Libraries that have multiple labels are counted in all respective categories. For a subset of the libraries we also obtain fine-grained information regarding the functionality that they offer, which we present in Figure 13 (right). While we provide a coarse-grained classification of all the calls initiated by libraries in our dataset, we are not able to obtain fine-grained labels for all the libraries identified in our experiments. Specifically, we obtain labels for 84 out of the 234 libraries that issue PPC calls, and for 75 of the 203 third-party libraries that access PII. As can be seen in Figure 13 (right), analytics-based libraries are responsible for the most PPC calls and PII accesses, while ad-related libraries issue more calls when the different subcategories are aggregated. It is also evident that specific libraries that ease the app development process are very common.

Using the coarse labels, we find that 15,610 PPCs and 21,322 PII accesses originate from libraries that are *exclusively* labelled as developer libraries, indicating that they are needed for the app's core functionality and should likely be granted. On the other hand, 1,287 PPCs and 845 PII accesses originate from tracking or ad libraries, and can be safely denied. Furthermore, for libraries with multiple coarse-grained labels, we leverage the fine-grained labels and find that an additional 9,129 PPCs and 5,240 PII calls can be safely denied as they are used exclusively for analytics and advertising. Three of the most used libraries (facebook, google.gms and firebase) cannot be excluded using fine-grained labels as they cover a wide spectrum

of functionality and contain numerous labels; however, for all three we can infer which aspect of their functionality is used in each call as the respective package name (e.g., com.google.android.gms.ads) explicitly denotes it (obviously, this approach cannot be applied to untrusted or unknown libraries). As such, the stacktraces allow us to identify an additional 10,424 PPCs and 11,580 PII calls than can be denied as they are used for analytics, ads, and tracking.

Overall, out of the 55,859 distinct PPC calls Reaper would enable users to safely deny 20,840 (37.3%) PPCs without preventing apps from leveraging third-party code for core functionality. Similarly, out of 61,602 PII accesses users could safely deny 17,665 (28.6%). Thus, apart from augmenting the permission system by providing rich contextual information, Reaper can further help users by providing concrete recommendations to accept or deny a considerable number of "straightforward" permission requests. The information provided by our system can also be used to expand access control tools like XPrivacy, allowing for more fine-grained control of user data, as it can selectively block invasive calls originating from third-parties while allowing such calls required for core functionality; we consider this part of our future work. For the remaining calls, displaying the library's type and the specific permission requested can significantly improve the existing permission system and better guide users into making informed decisions based on the app's intended functionality.

Permission mapping inconsistencies. While Reaper relies on permission mappings provided by prior work, our system can be used to dynamically validate those statically generated mappings. Thus, while not part of our study's main focus, we conduct an exploratory study as more accurate mappings will further improve the main functionality of our system; we opt for API 22, since it is the most recent version with the most accurate permission mappings. We created a mock application that sequentially executes all the permission-protected calls of the Android SDK, and verified the permission of each function call based on the permission check occurring in the Android Server. The divideMessage() function exists in two different classes, and PScout and AXPLORER report different permissions for this function. Using Reaper we found that this function does not need a permission. To further verify this result, we triggered this function without declaring any permission in

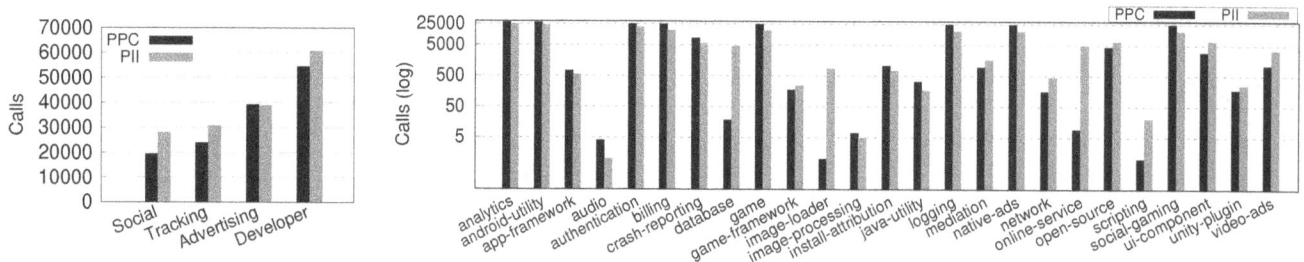

Figure 13: Coarse-grained (left) and Fine-grained (right) classification of PPCs and PII accesses initiated by libraries.

the app's manifest file and observed the same functionality without any warnings, errors, or crashes. We also manually investigated certain functions that were not mentioned in either study, and found that prior work missed sendStickyBroadcast(), which requires the BROADCAST_STICKY permission.

Interestingly, we find that functions being permission-protected also depends on the arguments provided. For example, the function getprovider() from the LocationManager class is permission-protected when provided with GPS_PROVIDER but does not need a permission for KEY_LOCATION_CHANGED. We argue that there is dire need for better documentation of the internals of Android permissions, as such scenarios can further confuse developers.

7 DISCUSSION AND LIMITATIONS

Defining origin. Reaper distinguishes core from third-party functionality based on the origin of the executed code. We compiled a list of libraries using data from [8, 28] for identifying their origin. If a library is not in the list, the corresponding stacktrace will not be flagged as third party functionality. Similarly, our library classification relies on external resources [8, 13]. As lists of libraries are extended and become more complete, Reaper's coverage will also increase. Moreover, core functionality could potentially be misclassified if a function has the same name with that of a known library. We investigated our dataset and did not find such instances.

Call mappings. Reaper maintains a permissions-to-function-calls mapping that contains the functions that should be monitored. While we have used Reaper to validate these mappings, expanding the mappings reported by prior work is out of our scope; thus, our system will not monitor PPCs missing from that list.

Native code. Android apps are written in Java or in native code. Xposed is able to hook functions written in Java, as well as native code in cases of JNI. However, we cannot hook custom native code written by developers since it is not supported by Xposed.

Kernel permissions. Certain Android permissions are regulated by the kernel. Since Pscout and AXPLORER did not conduct a native code analysis and have not created mappings for such permissions, we have not included these permissions in our study.

Graph coverage. UIHarvester may miss displayed content when apps use wrappers or webviews, as will UI Automator.

Emulators. Since apps or libraries can identify that they are being executed in a virtual environment [58], our results may present a lower bound of the privacy risks posed by libraries.

Obfuscated package names. While PPCs that originate from obfuscated package names only account for 1.14% in our study, Reaper could incorporate a static analysis tool like LibScout to reverse the obfuscated package name back to its original form.

8 RELATED WORK

A plethora of prior work has explored the Android operating system in depth. While previous studies have not explored the origin of PPCs and PII accesses and how it can be leveraged to augment the permission systems, they have explored complimentary directions including data leakage and the dynamic analysis of apps. Due to space constraints we only present the most relevant prior work, and discuss how Reaper improves upon, or compliments, that work.

Leak detection and prevention. Meng et al. [54], studied the privacy concerns that arise from in-app advertising, and found that ad publishers can identify user demographic information. Son et al. [67] studied the isolation of different Ad SDKs, and showed that the same-origin policy is not sufficient for protecting users' privacy. Ad libraries also have the potential for increased data collection through side-channels [38] . Papadopoulos et al. [56] analyzed what leaks occur while accessing the same service through the mobile app and a mobile browser, and showed that accessing a service through the app leaks more device-specific information. Agrigento [36] is a black-box differential analysis tool capable of identifying leaks even in the presence of obfuscation offering significant improvement over prior work. However, their approach cannot handle apps that use custom encryption or custom or native code for certificate checking. On the contrary, Reaper can detect when an app attempts to *access* such data, and could be used in conjunction with their system. Moreover, their differential analysis could be improved by incorporating UIHarvester for exercising apps.

FLEXDROID [65] is an extension to Android's permission system that provides dynamic, fine-grained access control for third-party libraries, and allows developers to separate permissions needed by host apps from those required by the libraries. FLEXDROID identifies the principal of the currently running code using stack inspection and, depending on the identified principal, allows or denies the request by dynamically adjusting the app's permissions according to the pre-specified permissions in the app's manifest. However, this approach presents several drawbacks compared to Reaper. The heavy instrumentation of the OS and apps presents a significant obstacle to adoption. Moreover, they require developers to incorporate specific code in the manifest to protect users, but do not provide developers with incentives to do so. On the other hand, Reaper gives control to the users.

A similar work [34] extended the AppOps manager to provide users with contextual information about the origin of permission requests. Since they do not provide enough technical details we can not compare to their approach. Moreover their library classification is done manually while Reaper does it automatically.

TaintDroid [40] and FLOWDROID [25] used dynamic and static taint analysis respectively, for detecting data leaks. PmDroid [43] uses TaintDroid to track and block sensitive data obtained through certain PPCs from being sent to ad networks, but obtains incomplete taint tracking coverage and relies on volatile domain information for identifying ad networks. VetDroid [83] extends the taint tracking logic of TaintDroid to monitor callbacks but suffers from the same coverage limitations. TAINTART [73] presented an information flow tracking system integrated inside ART that can be used for detecting data leakage. ARTist [30] is a compiler-based app instrumentation framework that can be used for intra-app taint tracking, as well as dynamic permission enforcement. ArtDroid [37] is a dynamic analysis framework for hooking virtual-method calls supporting both Java and JNI methods. Liu et al. [51] proposed PEDAL, a system that can identify libraries even when the source code is obfuscated. AdDroid [57], Aframe [82], AdSplit [66] and NativeGuard [72] proposed various techniques for separating integrated libraries from the host app. Recon [63] is a VPN-based solution that monitors network traffic to detect and blocks PII exfiltration. MockDroid [31] modified the Android OS so as to replace sensitive information with fake values. Fu et al. [42] proposed a permission policy manager that monitors each library's method invocation and tracks the execution thread tree. XPrivacy [10] is designed to prevent PII-access but does not distinguish libraries or core functionality; incorporating the origin information produced by Reaper would allow for more fine-grained access control and significantly improve the usability aspect of such tools.

Android Permission Analysis. Wijesekera et al. [80] conducted a user study to understand how often apps require access to protected resources by instrumenting the Android platform. Wang et al. [76] employed text analysis and machine learning to infer how two specific permissions are used based on a manual labelling of 622 apps. They relied on the PScout mappings and reported an accuracy of 85% and 94% for the two permissions. To overcome the obstacle of obfuscated code, they recently incorporated a dynamic analysis aspect and conducted a study on 830 apps [77]. While their approach has similarities with Reaper it presents significant limitations. They rely on a modified version of TaintDroid in Android 4.3 and only perform stack inspection at sink points (e.g., the network). Since stack inspection at this layer does not provide much information about the purpose of the permission due to multithreading, they heavily modified Dalvik to also capture the stacktrace of the parent thread. Their system also induces a slowdown of up to 47% compared to stock Android, while relying on random fuzzy testing which is inherently limited. Reaper has negligible overhead and performs stack inspection at the access level; this allows us to successfully monitor all PPCs for different Android versions, including those based on the ART compiler. Overall, while their study focuses on a different aspect of permissions, incorporating Reaper for their dynamic analysis would allow them to efficiently conduct a large

scale study and achieve higher coverage without the drawbacks of their extensive OS modification.

9 CONCLUSION

Given the ubiquitous presence of smartphones and the massive amount of sensitive information they store, it is imperative to stringently mediate access to user data. Currently, the proliferation and prevalence of third-party libraries renders them a significant privacy risk. To address this issue we developed Reaper, a novel dynamic analysis system that traces the origin of permission-protected calls and non-protected calls that access PII. Our subsequent study on over 5K of the most popular apps, revealed the extent of libraries accessing sensitive data and found that certain permission-protected calls were used exclusively by these libraries and not by the apps' core functionality. Reaper's functionality can enhance Android's fine-grained run time permission system and enable users to prevent third parties from accessing their personal data.

ACKNOWLEDGMENTS

This project has received funding from the European Research Council (ERC) under the European Union's Horizon 2020 research and innovation programme, under grant agreements, No 740787 (SMESEC), No 786669 (ReAct), No 786890 (THREAT-ARREST) and by the CEF project CertCoop, under grant agreement No. INEA/CEF/ICT/A2016/1332498. In addition, this project has received funding from the European Union's Horizon 2020 research and innovation programme under the Marie Sklodowska-Curie grant agreement No 690972 (PROTASIS). This paper reflects only the view of the authors and the funding bodies are not responsible for any use that may be made of the information it contains.

REFERENCES

[1] 2011. Xposed Framework API. https://bit.ly/2L4XmpU.
[2] 2012. Over half of 3rd party Android in-app ad libraries have privacy issues and possible security holes. https://bit.ly/2G3Vejl.
[3] 2013. Forbes - Google Users: You're The Product, Not The Customer. https://bit.ly/2G7dDM9.
[4] 2013. ThreatPost - Unnamed Android Mobile Ad Library Poses Large-Scale Risk. https://bit.ly/2G5jUrM.
[5] 2014. PC World - Researchers: Mobile users at risk from lack of HTTPS use by mobile ad libraries. https://bit.ly/2BYbzC5.
[6] 2014. Xposed Hook Overhead. https://bit.ly/2BW1HZp.
[7] 2016. MobileAppScrutinator: A Simple yet Efficient Dynamic Analysis Approach for Detecting Privacy Leaks across Mobile OSs. https://bit.ly/2RHTxcC.
[8] 2016. A repository of Android libraries. https://bit.ly/2RCf5Y1.
[9] 2016. Root Detection Evasion on iOS and Android. https://bit.ly/2rpLHZH.
[10] 2016. The ultimate privacy manager for Android. https://bit.ly/2zMdd8a.
[11] 2017. The Google Play apps that say they don't collect your data, and then do. https://bit.ly/2L0CTCu.
[12] 2018. Android Distribution between Platform versions. https://bit.ly/1kjKifB.
[13] 2018. Android library statistics. https://bit.ly/2L1S5zd.
[14] 2018. Android View Class. https://bit.ly/1ZSHM2l.
[15] 2018. AppsFlyer - Mobile App Tracking & Attribution. https://bit.ly/1lMd3oa.
[16] 2018. AppsFlyer SDK Integration - Android. https://bit.ly/2QjPzKz.
[17] 2018. Axplorer. https://bit.ly/2L2XoP3.
[18] 2018. GMS, Google's most popular apps, all in one place. https://bit.ly/2L6cdk4.
[19] 2018. Permission Protection Level. https://bit.ly/2BWzhif.
[20] 2018. Raccoon - APK downloader. https://bit.ly/1yIT4bR.
[21] 2018. UI Automator - Android's UI testing framework. https://bit.ly/2B2ze2m.
[22] 2018. Window Layout - FLAG_SECURE. https://bit.ly/2QHEoLk.
[23] Jagdish Prasad Achara, Gergely Acs, and Claude Castelluccia. 2015. On the Unicity of Smartphone Applications. In *WPES '15*.
[24] Domenico Amalfitano, Anna Rita Fasolino, Porfirio Tramontana, Salvatore De Carmine, and Atif M. Memon. 2012. Using GUI Ripping for Automated Testing of Android Applications. In *ASE '12*.

[25] Steven Arzt, Siegfried Rasthofer, Christian Fritz, Eric Bodden, Alexandre Bartel, Jacques Klein, Yves Le Traon, Damien Octeau, and Patrick McDaniel. 2014. FlowDroid: precise context, flow, field, object-sensitive and lifecycle-aware taint analysis for Android apps. In *PLDI '14*.

[26] Kathy Wain Yee Au, Yi Fan Zhou, Zhen Huang, and David Lie. 2012. PScout: Analyzing the Android Permission Specification. In *CCS '12*.

[27] Tanzirul Azim and Iulian Neamtiu. 2013. Targeted and Depth-first Exploration for Systematic Testing of Android apps. In *OOPSLA '13*.

[28] Michael Backes, Sven Bugiel, and Erik Derr. 2016. Reliable Third-Party Library Detection in Android and Its Security Applications. In *CCS '16*.

[29] Michael Backes, Sven Bugiel, Erik Derr, Patrick McDaniel, Damien Octeau, and Sebastian Weisgerber. 2016. On Demystifying the Android Application Framework: Re-Visiting Android Permission Specification Analysis. In *USENIX Security '16*.

[30] M. Backes, S. Bugiel, O. Schranz, P. v. Styp-Rekowsky, and S. Weisgerber. 2017. ARTist: The Android Runtime Instrumentation and Security Toolkit. In *EuroSP'17*.

[31] Alastair R Beresford, Andrew Rice, Nicholas Skehin, and Ripduman Sohan. 2011. Mockdroid: trading privacy for application functionality on smartphones. In *HotMobile '11*.

[32] Theodore Book, Adam Pridgen, and Dan S. Wallach. 2013. Longitudinal Analysis of Android Ad Library Permissions. In *MoST '13*.

[33] Patrick Carter, Collin Mulliner, Martina Lindorfer, William Robertson, and Engin Kirda. 2016. CuriousDroid: Automated User Interface Interaction for Android Application Analysis Sandboxes. In *FC '16*.

[34] Saksham Chitkara, Nishad Gothoskar, Suhas Harish, Jason I. Hong, and Yuvraj Agarwal. 2017. Does This App Really Need My Location?: Context-Aware Privacy Management for Smartphones. *IMWUT '17* (2017).

[35] S. R. Choudhary, A. Gorla, and A. Orso. 2015. Automated Test Input Generation for Android: Are We There Yet? (E). In *ASE '15*.

[36] Andrea Continella, Yanick Fratantonio, Martina Lindorfer, Alessandro Puccetti, Ali Zand, Christopher Kruegel, and Giovanni Vigna. 2017. Obfuscation-resilient privacy leak detection for mobile apps through differential analysis. In *NDSS '17*.

[37] Valerio Costamagna and Cong Zheng. 2016. ARTDroid: A Virtual-Method Hooking Framework on Android ART Runtime.. In *ESSoS '16*.

[38] Soteris Demetriou, Whitney Merrill, Wei Yang, Aston Zhang, and Carl A. Gunter. 2016. Free for All! Assessing User Data Exposure to Advertising Libraries on Android. In *NDSS '16*.

[39] Nicole Eling, Siegfried Rasthofer, Max Kolhagen, Eric Bodden, and Peter Buxmann. 2016. Investigating Users' Reaction to Fine-Grained Data Requests: A Market Experiment. In *HICSS '16*.

[40] William Enck, Peter Gilbert, Byung-Gon Chun, Landon P. Cox, Jaeyeon Jung, Patrick McDaniel, and Anmol N. Sheth. 2010. TaintDroid: An Information-flow Tracking System for Realtime Privacy Monitoring on Smartphones. In *OSDI'10*.

[41] Adrienne Porter Felt, Erika Chin, Steve Hanna, Dawn Song, and David Wagner. 2011. Android Permissions Demystified. In *CCS '11*.

[42] Jiaojiao Fu, Yangfan Zhou, Huan Liu, Yu Kang, and Xin Wang. 2017. Perman: Fine-Grained Permission Management for Android Applications. In *ISSRE' 17*.

[43] Xing Gao, Dachuan Liu, Haining Wang, and Kun Sun. 2015. PmDroid: Permission Supervision for Android Advertising. In *SRDS '15*.

[44] Michael C Grace, Wu Zhou, Xuxian Jiang, and Ahmad Reza Sadeghi. 2012. Unsafe exposure analysis of mobile in-app advertisements. In *WISEC '12'*.

[45] Shuai Hao, Bin Liu, Suman Nath, William G.J. Halfond, and Ramesh Govindan. 2014. PUMA: Programmable UI-automation for Large-scale Dynamic Analysis of Mobile Apps. In *MobiSys '14*.

[46] Patrick Gage Kelley, Sunny Consolvo, Lorrie Faith Cranor, Jaeyeon Jung, Norman Sadeh, and David Wetherall. 2012. A Conundrum of Permissions: Installing Applications on an Android Smartphone. In *FC'12*.

[47] Ilias Leontiadis, Christos Efstratiou, Marco Picone, and Cecilia Mascolo. 2012. Don'T Kill My Ads!: Balancing Privacy in an Ad-supported Mobile Application Market. In *HotMobile '12*.

[48] Christophe Leung, Jingjing Ren, David Choffnes, and Christo Wilson. 2016. Should You Use the App for That?: Comparing the Privacy Implications of App- and Web-based Online Services. In *IMC '16*.

[49] Li Li, Tegawendé F. Bissyandé, Jacques Klein, and Yves Le Traon. 2016. An Investigation into the Use of Common Libraries in Android Apps. In *SANER '16*.

[50] Jialiu Lin, Shahriyar Amini, Jason I. Hong, Norman Sadeh, Janne Lindqvist, and Joy Zhang. 2012. Expectation and Purpose: Understanding Users' Mental Models of Mobile App Privacy Through Crowdsourcing. In *UbiComp '12*.

[51] Bin Liu, Bin Liu, Hongxia Jin, and Ramesh Govindan. 2015. Efficient Privilege De-Escalation for Ad Libraries in Mobile Apps. In *MobiSys '15*.

[52] Xing Liu, Sencun Zhu, Wei Wang, and Jiqiang Liu. 2016. Alde: privacy risk analysis of analytics libraries in the android ecosystem. In *SecureComm '16*.

[53] Aravind Machiry, Rohan Tahiliani, and Mayur Naik. 2013. Dynodroid: An Input Generation System for Android Apps. In *ESEC/FSE '13*.

[54] Wei Meng, Ren Ding, Simon P. Chung, Steven Han, and Wenke Lee. 2016. The Price of Free: Privacy Leakage in Personalized Mobile In-Apps Ads. In *NDSS '16*.

[55] Suman Nath. 2015. MAdScope: Characterizing Mobile In-App Targeted Ads. In *MobiSys '15*.

[56] Elias P. Papadopoulos, Michalis Diamantaris, Panagiotis Papadopoulos, Thanasis Petsas, Sotiris Ioannidis, and Evangelos P. Markatos. 2017. The Long-Standing Privacy Debate: Mobile Websites vs Mobile Apps. In *WWW '17*.

[57] Paul Pearce, Adrienne Porter Felt, Gabriel Nunez, and David Wagner. 2012. AdDroid: Privilege Separation for Applications and Advertisers in Android. In *ASIACCS '12*.

[58] Thanasis Petsas, Giannis Voyatzis, Elias Athanasopoulos, Michalis Polychronakis, and Sotiris Ioannidis. 2014. Rage Against the Virtual Machine: Hindering Dynamic Analysis of Android Malware. In *EuroSec '14*.

[59] Sebastian Poeplau, Yanick Fratantonio, Antonio Bianchi, Christopher Kruegel, and Giovanni Vigna. 2014. Execute This! Analyzing Unsafe and Malicious Dynamic Code Loading in Android Applications.. In *NDSS '14*.

[60] Siegfried Rasthofer, Steven Arzt, Marc Miltenberger, and Eric Bodden. 2016. Harvesting runtime values in android applications that feature anti-analysis techniques. In *NDSS '16*.

[61] Vaibhav Rastogi, Yan Chen, and William Enck. 2013. AppsPlayground: Automatic Security Analysis of Smartphone Applications. In *CODASPY '13*.

[62] Vaibhav Rastogi, Rui Shao, Yan Chen, Xiang Pan, Shihong Zou, and Ryan Riley. 2016. Are these ads safe: Detecting hidden attacks through the mobile app-web interfaces. In *NDSS '16*.

[63] Jingjing Ren, Ashwin Rao, Martina Lindorfer, Arnaud Legout, and David Choffnes. 2016. ReCon: Revealing and Controlling PII Leaks in Mobile Network Traffic. In *MobiSys '16*.

[64] Suranga Seneviratne, Harini Kolamunna, and Aruna Seneviratne. 2015. A Measurement Study of Tracking in Paid Mobile Applications. In *WiSec '15*.

[65] Jaebaek Seo, Daehyeok Kim, Donghyun Cho, Insik Shin, and Taesoo Kim. 2016. FLEXDROID: Enforcing In-App Privilege Separation in Android. In *NDSS '16*.

[66] Shashi Shekhar, Michael Dietz, and Dan S. Wallach. 2012. AdSplit: Separating Smartphone Advertising from Applications. In *USENIX Security '12*.

[67] Sooel Son, Daehyeok Kim, and Vitaly Shmatikov. 2016. What Mobile Ads Know About Mobile Users. In *NDSS '16*.

[68] Yihang Song and Urs Hengartner. 2015. PrivacyGuard: A VPN-based Platform to Detect Information Leakage on Android Devices. In *SPSM '15*.

[69] Michael Spreitzenbarth, Felix Freiling, Florian Echtler, Thomas Schreck, and Johannes Hoffmann. 2013. Mobile-sandbox: Having a Deeper Look into Android Applications. In *SAC '13*.

[70] Ryan Stevens, Clint Gibler, Jon Crussell, Jeremy Erickson, and Hao Chen. 2012. Investigating user privacy in android ad libraries. In *MoST '12*.

[71] Ting Su, Guozhu Meng, Yuting Chen, Ke Wu, Weiming Yang, Yao Yao, Geguang Pu, Yang Liu, and Zhendong Su. 2017. Guided, Stochastic Model-based GUI Testing of Android Apps. In *ESEC/FSE '17*.

[72] Mengtao Sun and Gang Tan. 2014. NativeGuard: Protecting Android Applications from Third-party Native Libraries. In *WiSec '14*.

[73] Mingshen Sun, Tao Wei, and John Lui. 2016. Taintart: A practical multi-level information-flow tracking system for android runtime. In *CCS '16*.

[74] Kimberly Tam, Salahuddin J Khan, Aristide Fattori, and Lorenzo Cavallaro. 2015. CopperDroid: Automatic Reconstruction of Android Malware Behaviors. In *NDSS '15*.

[75] Fabo Wang, Yuqing Zhang, Kai Wang, Peng Liu, and Wenjie Wang. 2016. Stay in Your Cage! A Sound Sandbox for Third-Party Libraries on Android. In *ESORICS'16*.

[76] Haoyu Wang, Jason Hong, and Yao Guo. 2015. Using Text Mining to Infer the Purpose of Permission Use in Mobile Apps. In *UbiComp '15*.

[77] Haoyu Wang, Yuanchun Li, Yao Guo, Yuvraj Agarwal, and Jason I Hong. 2017. Understanding the Purpose of Permission Use in Mobile Apps. *TOIS '17* (2017).

[78] Na Wang, Pamela Wisniewski, Heng Xu, and Jens Grossklags. 2014. Designing the Default Privacy Settings for Facebook Applications. In *CSCW '14'*.

[79] Dominik Wermke, Nicolas Huaman, Yasemin Acar, Bradley Reaves, Patrick Traynor, and Sascha Fahl. 2018. A Large Scale Investigation of Obfuscation Use in Google Play. (2018). http://arxiv.org/abs/1801.02742

[80] Primal Wijesekera, Arjun Baokar, Ashkan Hosseini, Serge Egelman, David Wagner, and Konstantin Beznosov. 2015. Android Permissions Remystified: A Field Study on Contextual Integrity. In *USENIX Security '15*.

[81] Michelle Y Wong and David Lie. 2016. Intellidroid: A targeted input generator for the dynamic analysis of android malware. In *NDSS '16*.

[82] Xiao Zhang, Amit Ahlawat, and Wenliang Du. 2013. Aframe: Isolating advertisements from mobile applications in android. In *ACSAC '13*.

[83] Yuan Zhang, Min Yang, Bingquan Xu, Zhemin Yang, Guofei Gu, Peng Ning, X. Sean Wang, and Binyu Zang. 2013. Vetting Undesirable Behaviors in Android Apps with Permission Use Analysis. In *CCS '13*.

[84] Yury Zhauniarovich and Olga Gadyatskaya. 2016. Small changes, big changes: an updated view on the Android permission system. In *RAID '16*.

[85] Cong Zheng, Shixiong Zhu, Shuaifu Dai, Guofei Gu, Xiaorui Gong, Xinhui Han, and Wei Zou. 2012. SmartDroid: An Automatic System for Revealing UI-based Trigger Conditions in Android Applications. In *SPSM '12*.

[86] Chaoshun Zuo, Qingchuan Zhao, and Zhiqiang Lin. 2017. AUTHSCOPE: Towards Automatic Discovery of Vulnerable Authorizations in Online Services. In *CCS'17*.

Verifiable Round-Robin Scheme for Smart Homes*

Nisha Panwar, Shantanu Sharma, Guoxi Wang, Sharad Mehrotra, and Nalini Venkatasubramanian
University of California, Irvine, USA.

ABSTRACT

Advances in sensing, networking, and actuation technologies have resulted in the IoT wave that is expected to revolutionize all aspects of modern society. This paper focuses on the new challenges of privacy that arise in IoT in the context of smart homes. Specifically, the paper focuses on preventing the user's privacy via inferences through channel and in-home device activities. We propose a method for securely scheduling the devices while decoupling the device and channels activities. The proposed solution avoids any attacks that may reveal the coordinated schedule of the devices, and hence, also, assures that inferences that may compromise individual's privacy are not leaked due to device and channel level activities. Our experiments also validate the proposed approach, and consequently, an adversary cannot infer device and channel activities by just observing the network traffic.

CCS CONCEPTS

• **Security and privacy** → **Security protocols**; *Mobile and wireless security*; *Domain-specific security and privacy architectures*; Social aspects of security and privacy;

KEYWORDS

Internet of Things; smart homes; user privacy; channel and device activity; inference attacks.

ACM Reference Format:
Nisha Panwar, Shantanu Sharma, Guoxi Wang, Sharad Mehrotra, and Nalini Venkatasubramanian. 2019. Verifiable Round-Robin Scheme for Smart Homes. In *Ninth ACM Conference on Data and Application Security and Privacy (CODASPY '19), March 25–27, 2019, Richardson, TX, USA*. ACM, New York, NY, USA, 12 pages. https://doi.org/10.1145/3292006.3300043

1 INTRODUCTION

The IoT devices are quickly becoming a pervasive and integral part of modern smart homes [9]. The homeowner, typically, possesses a heterogeneous set of devices ranging from wearable devices, information/entertainment devices to smart home appliances. These devices provide comfort/assisted-living and/or improve sustainability, reduce costs, and reduce carbon footprint. For example, a Belkin Wemo switch can automatically switch lights on/off and open/close window shades based on the sunlight and time of the day. Likewise, dampers in the AC vent can be partially/fully opened/closed to modulate airflow. Other devices popular in smart homes include Nest cameras, smart door locks, Lenovo Smart Assistant, Amazon Echo, Echo dot, Echo show, Alexa, Philips-Hue Bloom/Lightstrip Plus, SteriGrip self-cleaning door handles, Unico smartbrush, Sensus Metering Systems, and Logitech Circle 2 among others.

While the emerging smart home devices provide significant benefits, the support for security in such devices is often limited to the security offered by the original equipment manufacturer (OEM). Lack of strong end-to-end architecture for security has led to devices being vulnerable to a variety of attacks. For example, McAfee Labs [1] found that the well-known Wi-Fi-enabled Wemo Insight Smart Plug has critical security vulnerability due to Universal Plug and Play (UPnP) protocol library it uses, which, due to design flaws, enable attackers to execute remote codes on this smart plug. Note that this attack is not just limited to disturbing smart plug's normal operations such as shutting it down unexpectedly, but could also use the smart plug as an entry point for a larger attack in the network. Further, [1] showed the usage of a compromised WeMo switch as a middleman to launch attacks against a TCL smart TV.

The privacy vulnerabilities introduced by smart home devices are even more challenging. IoT devices capture, store, share, and (depending upon the underlying computational architecture) outsource personal data that can lead to inferences about individual's habits, behavior, family dynamics etc. Challenges arise since privacy leakage can occur through direct data leakage, as well as, through inferences based on device actuations, interactions, and schedules. For instance, the timing of the actuation of a coffee machine, if leaked can allow an adversary to determine when a family wakes up. Likewise, locking and unlocking schedule of door locks can enable leakage of the time when no one is at home, etc. While privacy challenges from data leakage can be prevented by encrypting device data and network payloads, inferences about device actuation and schedule are significantly more complex to hide due to leakage from network traffic patterns at the channel level, at the hub/router level or at the cloud level.

For example, Figure 1 shows the channel traffic generated by three different devices. The figure clearly shows that each device generates a very distinct traffic pattern and, the adversary, having access to the channel traffic can figure out which device is activated leading to potential inferences about user's personal habits. Note that such an inference, since it is independent of the actual network payload, is not prevented by encryption.

Inferences from monitoring channel traffic can also arise due to the characteristics of the current network protocols. For instance, in the widely used 802.11 Wi-Fi protocol, while a message payload is encrypted in a password-protected network, the MAC addresses

*This material is based on research sponsored by DARPA under agreement number FA8750-16-2-0021. The U.S. Government is authorized to reproduce and distribute reprints for Governmental purposes notwithstanding any copyright notation thereon. The views and conclusions contained herein are those of the authors and should not be interpreted as necessarily representing the official policies or endorsements, either expressed or implied, of DARPA or the U.S. Government. This work is partially supported by NSF grants 1527536 and 1545071.

CODASPY '19, March 25–27, 2019, Richardson, TX, USA
© 2019 Association for Computing Machinery
ACM ISBN 978-1-4503-6099-9/19/03...$15.00
https://doi.org/10.1145/3292006.3300043

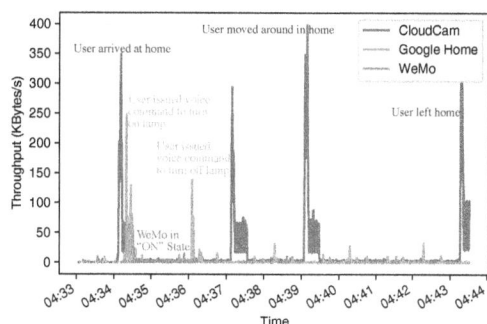

Figure 1: Channel activity for home devices.
The figure above shows the channel activity for three home devices: CloudCam, Google Home, and Belkin WeMo. The CloudCam shows a peak in the channel activity (up to 400 KB/s traffic rate) as the user enters the home, moves inside the home or exits the home. The Google Home shows a peak in the channel activity (up to 250 KB/s traffic rate) whenever a user initiated a voice command for the light bulbs to turn on/off. Similarly, a bi-state WeMo switch peaks during the on state and creates a channel activity lesser than 20 KB/s.

of both the sender and receiver are in cleartext. This is to prevent requiring every potential device on the network to have to decrypt a message just to determine if the message is intended for the device. The leakage of the sender/receiver MAC address, coupled with the fact that manufacturer's information is commonly encoded in plain-text device identifier, can lead to leakage of the identity of the device from the network traffic, which, in turn, can lead to an attack on user's privacy. For example, the MAC address of Amazon CloudCam security camera used in our experiment to transmit video footage over Wi-Fi is F0-81-73-23-CC-75. The first 3 bytes of such a MAC address (e.g., F0-81-73) can be searched in the publicly accessible IEEE Organizationally Unique Identifier (OUI) [2] dataset to find the vendor related information (e.g., Amazon device). Furthermore, by monitoring the device's traffic patterns and the fact that Amazon only manufactures a limited range of devices (e.g., Kindle, CloudCam, Echo, etc.), it is easier to infer the device type by merely overhearing the traffic.

In this paper, we study privacy leakage that may occur from device activity and network channel traffic analysis and develop protocols that can be used to prevent such leakages. We focus, in particular, on device workflows that are common in smart homes. By a device workflow, we refer to a coordinated sequence of device actuations. Device workflows may arise in a *triggered* (or *synchronized*) manner or in a *scheduled* manner. The synchronized workflows arise as a result of one device resulting in an actuation of the other. For instance, sensors determining occupancy change in a part of the building may result in HVAC controls /AC vents to be redirected to the occupied areas and to close other vents that cover areas with no occupancy. Likewise, light intensity sensors coupled with thermal sensors may detect the amount of sunlight entering the room and accordingly lower/raise the sunshades based on the homeowner's preference. A scheduled workflow, on the other hand, is scheduled actuation of a set of devices that occur at specific time intervals of each other based on a schedule. For instance, switching on a coffee machine at a specific time in the morning followed by warming of the car seats a given time interval following that, and then opening/closing of door locks following the actuation of the car seat warmer might be on a schedule. A more elaborate example

of a scheduled workflow could be a homeowner's routine related to returning. A homeowner may schedule the smart car to self-drive to home to initiate the workflow. Fifteen minutes after the start of the workflow, the heating/cooling system may start off to ensure that the home is at the comfortable temperature on arrival. Likewise, half an hour after the trip starts the oven may be set to a pre-heat and the laundry machine turns on if the load is detected.

We focus on the scheduled workflows in this paper since such workflows require hiding the identity of the devices being actuated but also their schedule. As will become clear, mechanisms to prevent leakage for scheduled workflows will also prevent leakage from triggered workflows. Furthermore, the scheduled activities can lead not just to adversary learning user's past behavior but also their future activities which can lead to more severe consequences.

The problem. This paper deals with a problem of avoiding inference attacks on the scheduled workflows in a home network. The workflows can be identified through *coupling* between the *channel* and *device activity*. Basically, there are two crucial concepts that are subject to privacy violations: workflow (i.e., the specific order of device actuation) and workflow execution (i.e., duration in which the devices coordinate, and the resulting device actuations unfold). Our problem statement considers hiding both the workflow and the execution of the workflow.

The privacy violations can occur as a result of two threats: first, overhearing the channel activity as a means to infer device activity pattern, second, accessing the device temporarily and be able to analyze the state of workflow execution. In the latter case, the adversary can read the sent/received messages or the internal state of the device. Both of the above threats may assist the adversary to predict users' activities, such as presence/absence, arrival/departure, and localization etc.

Contributions. Our contributions are twofold:

(1) A new architecture for in-home communication among the devices and the hub through passing a token carrying commands. The token passing communication model decouples the channel and device activities so that the devices interact with the hub and the other devices without revealing the communication pattern. In addition, this architecture is also useful for secure data upload from devices to the hub, while also hiding the device footprints that has generated the data.

(2) We provide an owner-defined pre-scheduling mechanism for all devices that are connected with the hub in a pre-defined topology. The proposed approach uses a single message transmission for all N devices while ensuring that the in-home communication remains peakless. The scheduling mechanism is secure against a computationally unbounded adversary and, also, verifies the delay between each device actuation.

Outline. The paper proceeds as follows: Section 2 provides the system setting, the adversarial model, security goals, and design requirements. Section 3 provides our proposed scheduling algorithm for home networks. Section 4 provides proofs of security and privacy. Finally, Section 5 provides an experimental evaluation of the approach. All notations are given in Table 1.

Notations	Meaning	Notations	Meaning
O	A homeowner	H	Hub
O_{id}	Owner's identity	H_{id}	Hub identity
D	Device	D_{id}	Device identity
O_{PK}	Owner public key	O_{SK}	Owner secret key
H_{PK}	hub public key	H_{SK}	hub secret key
D_{PK}	device public key	D_{SK}	device secret key
c_l	partially ordered l commands	m^i	puzzle message for ith device
n	modulus	a	random chosen integer
$\hat{t}$	time complexity of puzzle	t'	time to decrypt command
S	capacity of puzzle solver	S'	enhanced capacity
$Sign(O_{SK})$	Signature using secret-key O_{SK}	N	number of devices
E_k	encrypted key k	E_z	encrypted command z
k_s	static key	^nP_n	n permutations
$\phi(n)$	Euler's totient on n	b_o	overwritten data bits
b_g	device generated data bits	b_r	random data bits
p	large prime number	q	second large prime number
t_{val}	command validity time	t_{cur}	current time
t_{rcv}^i	token receiving time	t_{fwd}^i	token forwarding time
t_{beg}^H	token round beginning time at hub	t_{end}^H	token round ending time at hub
t_{diff}	allowed clock drift time	t_{com}	total computation time
$t_{com}^{\mathcal{A}}$	puzzle computation time by adversary	ϵ	negligibly small value
$\mathcal{A}$	adversary	$\hat{a}$	malicious commands
$\mathcal{T}$	token	$\mathcal{H}$	One-way hash function
Data field	data upload field	b_{toggle}	toggle bit string field
$\mathcal{R}$	partial order	$\mathcal{E}'$	partially ordered set

Table 1: Notations

2 PRELIMINARIES

This section presents the system model, the adversarial model, inference attacks on the user privacy, an overview of our proposed approach to prevent inference attacks, design requirements, and building blocks of the proposed algorithms.

2.1 The Model

Network assumptions. We consider a homeowner, O, who owns a collection of N $(D^1, D^2, \ldots, D^N)$ heterogenous smart home devices that provide different functionalities to the owner. Each device D^i has a unique identity, denoted by D_{id}^i. All devices might possess heterogeneous hardware/software underneath, and be located on different spatial (devices that are not in the line-of-sight) dimensions. These ad-hoc devices can shift in space in the smart home, and hence, might have a different set of peer devices at different time intervals. We assume that each device possesses a read-only hardware clock, and due to the ad-hoc nature of devices, we assume a clock drift within the bound t_{diff} such that two clocks cannot differ beyond the t_{diff} amount of time.

The owner initializes the devices and a controlling hub, H, using proper security mechanisms. We will list our assumptions about the underlying security mechanism below. In our model, the network is configured as a ring topology, which poses an ordering among devices, unlike the model that the current smart home devices use, where the owner communicates directly to the desired device via the hub. This ring topology could be built directly among devices and hub, if the communication protocols they use have P2P communication capability, like Zig-Bee, BLE, and Wi-Fi. Alternatively, it

could be built as an overlay on top of a star topology network, like Wi-Fi infrastructure mode. In this case, if a device tries to forward the message to the next device in the proposed ring topology, then it needs to first send the message to the hub, and the hub, then, directly forwards the message to its next device. Note that we do not discuss a failure-resilient ring topology and existing fault-tolerant schemes can be leveraged here.

The owner sends workflows to the home devices through the hub. After receiving a workflow, the device gets actuated, stores its corresponding command, and forwards the workflow received from the previous device to the next device in the topology. After executing the command, the device may generate the data (for example, Nest camera starts recording and sends data whenever motion is detected). We use the ring topology to send this data to the hub that may be stored at the hub or may be transmitted to the cloud.[1] In this paper, we use the words 'command execution' and 'workflow execution' interchangeably.

Token. In our ring topology, we circulate a token that has three fields: (*i*) command field, which carries a computational puzzle and the workflow, (*ii*) data field, which carries the data generated by devices to deliver to the hub, and (*iii*) toggle bit string, which is used to indicate which device has generated the data to the hub. Details of the token are given in Section 3.

Security assumptions. Each device, hub, and homeowner possess the corresponding signing key-pair, i.e., (D_{SK}^i, D_{PK}^i), (H_{SK}, H_{PK}), and (O_{SK}, O_{PK}), respectively. We do not assume an arbitrary behavior from the owner or the hub. The *homeowner and hub* mutually verify the identities of each other through digital signatures in order to build the trust between them. Therefore, the hub and the owner trust each other, and an adversary cannot compromise either the homeowner or the hub. Further, *the hub and devices* build their own trust that is also based on the knowledge of a certified public-private key-pair of home devices.

2.2 Adversarial Model

The devices execute user-defined commands or workflows, as mentioned previously. The adversary wishes to learn the commands or workflows and the execution of workflows based on the encrypted network traffic to infer the user privacy. This type of adversary is similar to the adversary considered in [6, 14]. Thus, the adversary has access to the secure (encrypted) messages flowing among the devices and the hub/homeowner. Further, we assume that the adversary knows the number of smart devices in the home. Based on this information, the adversary aims to learn: (*i*) the device activities, and (*ii*) coupling between the channel and the device activities. However, the adversary cannot inject any fabricated messages over the channel to assess the state of the devices.

Further, we assume that the adversary may gain a short-term physical access[2] to the device, and hence, can retrieve the device

---

[1]Recall that we are not dealing with how the data will be transmitted from the hub to the cloud without revealing anything. Our solution hides any activity within the home, i.e., how the data will be transmitted by the device to the hub without any privacy violations.

[2]For example, an inspection authority has to visit the home for a periodic inspection in the absence of the homeowner. In this case, the inspection might be related to any leakage detection, maintenance issues, insurance issues, etc. This short visit to the home for an inspection allows them to monitor and check home devices as well. However, based on our proposed solution, those inspecting authorities would not be

state or messages. The objective behind gaining a short-term access to any device is to predict the future workflows of devices to infer the user activity. Our objective is to prevent the adversary to know (*i*) which device has received the messages at which time, (*ii*) when would a device execute the command, and (*iii*) which devices have executed the command at which time[3].

Adversarial view and inference attacks. When the user wishes to execute any command at a smart home device, an adversary knows which device received the message from the user at what time due to the network traffic generated by the user. Note that this information is revealed, because in network protocols such as 802.11 MAC addresses or the device identifiers are transmitted in cleartext, and only the payload is encrypted, as mentioned in Section 1. Further, the device may also produce some data in response to the requested message, and this also reveals to the adversary which device has generated the data at what time. We refer such information as the adversarial view, denoted by AV: $AV = In_c \cup Op_d$, where In_c refers to the command given to the device at some time and Op_d refers to the data generated by the device after executing the command.

Users command	Adversarial view	
	In_c	Op_d
For D^1	$E(c_1), D^1, t_1$	No
For D^2	$E(c_2), D^2, t_2$	$E(d_2), D^2, t_3$

Table 2: Adversarial view.

For example, consider that there are two devices, say D^1 and D^2, in the home. In Table 2, the first row shows that the user transmits a command to the device D^1. Though the device D^1 receives this encrypted command, denoted by $E(c_1)$, the adversary knows that a command is received at time t_1 by the device D^1 and the device D^1 has not generated any data in response the command. The second row shows that the adversary knows the device D^2 receives an encrypted command $E(c_2)$ at time t_2 and generated encrypted data $E(d_2)$ at time t_3. Hence, simply based on the above characteristic of the arrival of a message and generation of data, the adversary can determine which device was actuated.

2.3 Preventing Inference Attacks: overview of our Approach

In order to prevent inference attacks, we develop an approach that decouples the device and channel activities. In short, the approach provides an ability to pre-schedule a set of commands for home devices, where the homeowner defines: (*a*) what should be the workflow/schedule of home devices, and (*b*) when should the devices execute a workflow. Informally, the proposed approach works as follows:

(1) The owner invokes the hub by sending an encrypted schedule or workflow of the devices. Here, the hub authenticates the owner to validate the encrypted schedule. This step provides a guarantee that no channel spoofing or message re-transmission have occurred.

---

able to analyze the current state of the devices or the activity pattern of the devices in near future.
[3]The command execution could enable the device to produce visible or auditory cues such as blinking lights or machine being activated which, in turn, may leak the state of the device. Such inferences from physical cues are outside the scope of the paper. We assume that the adversary does not have access to such device data.

(2) After a successful authentication phase, the hub creates a token ($\mathcal{T}$) to circulate the schedule to be executed by devices. This token rotates continuously in the topology. Note that in the token, device identifiers or MAC addresses are also encrypted. Further note that whenever the user wishes to transmit a schedule to devices, the immediate next round of token originated by the hub carries the encrypted schedule, and after that, the encrypted schedule is replaced by a random message to maintain the token size constant.

(3) On receiving the token, each device retrieves the encrypted schedule that carries device-specific commands. Each device must complete a computation task before executing the original command. This computation task is referred to as a puzzle throughout the paper. Then, the device must check the puzzle validity time t_{val}, by using the current time t_{cur}, and the allowed clock difference t_{diff}. If the timer has not expired yet, the device decrypts the message, executes the puzzle to retrieve the real command to be executed.

(4) As soon as a device finishes the command execution, it may generate data to be uploaded at the hub (as mentioned in Section 2.1). Now to hide which device has generated the data, each device follows a request-based approach, where a device D^i flips the ith bit inside one of the fields of the token to indicate the need to upload freshly generated data in an anonymous manner. As a result of ith bit flipping, the hub knows that the device D^i has requested the data upload, and in the next token cycle, the device D^i appends the data inside a dedicated field of the token.

Note that since a constant size token flows regularly in the topology of the home devices, an adversary observing the network traffic cannot distinguish which device has received a command at which time (due to step 2) and which devices have generated the data (due to step 4). Hence, based on this approach, the adversarial view for each round of token has the same information, which prevents inference attacks based on the devices and channel activities.

2.4 Security Goals

This section describes the security properties for preventing any inferences about the workflow and their executions from the adversary. Let us assume that an adversary knows some auxiliary information about the devices and the topology such as the number of devices and the types of devices. However, this auxiliary information does not increase the probabilistic advantage that an adversary gains over any instance of the protocol. In particular, an adversary cannot reveal the workflow or the execution time of the workflow, i.e., which devices execute the command or when does a device execute the command. The probabilistic advantage of an adversary, denoted by $Adv(\mathcal{A})$, is derived through the security properties given below.

Authentication is required during the workflow release from the homeowner to the hub. This would require a mutual authentication between the (mobile device held by the) homeowner (to dispatch the workflow) and the hub (to circulate the workflow anonymously). Note that establishing the shared secret between the homeowner and the hub is a one-time process, which is carried each time the homeowner invokes a new workflow. Here, the homeowner produces a signature, say *Sign*, on the ordered commands (c_l) in any workflow by using its secret-key O_{SK}. Thus, the hub must reject any other messages signed by a different key, say $O_{SK'}$.

$$Pr[(O_{SK}, c_l) \rightarrow Sign] \geq 1 - \epsilon$$

Note that ϵ is negligibly small and an adversary cannot produce a verifiable signature $Sign$ on c_l by using $O_{SK'}$ instead of O_{SK}.

Anonymity is required during the consistent circulation of the encrypted commands such that (*i*) no channel activity can be mapped to a device activity, and (*ii*) no inference on device activity can be mapped to the device generated data, i.e., which device is sending data at a specific time. As shown below, the probability of distinguishing two different tokens $(\mathcal{T}, \mathcal{T}')$ each carrying different messages (m^i, m^j) for different devices (i, j) is negligible.

$$Pr[\mathcal{T}(m^i)] - Pr[\mathcal{T}'(m^j)] < \epsilon$$

Similarly, the probability of distinguishing a token $\mathcal{T}$ carrying the random data b_r or carrying the overwritten data b_o, is negligibly small. Therefore, a token carrying the random data inside the data field and another token carrying the overwritten data (after data generation) inside the data field are indistinguishable, hence, solely based on the token data field no inferences can be derived.

$$Pr[\mathcal{T}(b_r)] - Pr[\mathcal{T}(b_o)] < \epsilon$$

Verifiable delay An adversary cannot infer the information about the device execution ahead of time. Let $\hat{t}_i$ be the time a device would execute even when the adversary has temporary access to the device.

$$Pr[t_{com}^{\mathcal{A}}|state] \approx Pr[t_{com}^{\mathcal{A}}]$$

The probability of an adversary finishing the computation task earlier, when it gains temporary access to the device state, is approximately same as when the adversary does not have access to the device state. In addition, an adversary cannot outpace a device that requires $\hat{t}^i$ time to complete the computation task, i.e., $Pr[t_{com}^{\mathcal{A}} < \hat{t}_i] < \epsilon$.

An adversary gaining access to the device cannot retrieve the information required for device actuation, i.e., the computational task to be executed prior to its actuation. We have described a game-theoretic approach in Section 4 that shows the overall probabilistic advantage of an adversary is negligibly small.

2.5 Challenges and Solutions

Implementing reliable ordering for device actuation is to provide a secure and self-executing state of devices at a pre-defined time for protecting the owner privacy is deceptively non-trivial. Below, we discuss the challenges we encountered and describe how we addressed them.

C1. Anonymous trigger from the hub to devices. As mentioned before, we need to mask the channel activities, device activities, and the coupling between both the channel as well as the devices. Note that in this context, the encryption techniques merely hide the meaning of the message across the channel, not the fact that to which device this message belongs to, and hence, it reveals the user activity. In addition, the solutions-based on *traffic shaping*[4], which incur excessive communication and latency overhead, also fail to decouple the device to channel activities.

| Solution. | To address this challenge, the distribution of user-commands to each device in the home network is based on a pre-defined topology, e.g., ring, where a token rotates continuously within the one directional (1-D) ring topology.[5] Thereby, channel activity remains consistent and independent of the devices actuated as a result of the workflow. In our context, the token $(\mathcal{T})$ has three fields: (*i*) command field, which contains the encrypted commands corresponding to each device, (*ii*) data field, which contains the device generated data, and, (*iii*) a toggle bit string field, which contains a N bit string, where each bit denotes a unique device in the topology. This toggle bit string is used to indicate that a device is interested in uploading the freshly generated data during upcoming token arrival at the device. Since the order of device actuation reveals crucial information about the user activity inside the home, our token-based solution guarantees a secure ordering among devices while executing the commands. In addition, the device actuation is controlled in a manner that a recipient device itself cannot pre-decode and/or pre-pone the command execution.

C2. Command execution and verifiable ordering. After masking the channel activity through a constantly rotating token, the next step is to have a verifiable ordering of command execution at each device. Each device receives a command through the token. Now, these devices can decrypt and execute the command immediately. However, it again enables the channel to device activity mapping. Therefore, the next challenge is to insert an artificial delay between a device receiving the commands, and then, executing the commands at an appropriate time, without relating to any specific channel activity. The artificial delay enables a correct execution order at each comparable or non-comparable device[6].

| Solution. | The protocol message from the homeowner to hub includes the ordered commands (c_l) that pass through a device D^i to another device D^{i+1} using the anonymous token circulation. The token is encrypted using a shared symmetric key between the hub and the devices in the topology. The recipient device D^i retrieves the encrypted command (m^i) from the command field of the token and begins with a puzzle computation. Note that the devices do not execute the commands immediately after receiving (time-locked) commands. In particular, these devices wait for a pre-defined amount of time before executing the command, such that neither the artificial delay at each device can be known by the adversary in advance, nor the devices can control this artificial delay to postpone or prepone the scheduled commands. However, this waiting period is not idle, and the devices resume on some computational task.

C3. Anonymous response from devices to the hub. Once the devices have received the commands in an anonymous manner, they may generate some data as a result of command execution. However, uploading this data immediately would reveal the device activity patterns. Clearly, this periodic channel activity (in the form of traffic) relates to a specific device that had executed the command recently. Therefore, the upstream data upload on the hub should be anonymous too.

---

[4]The traffic shaping solution keeps the constant traffic rate based on a threshold, such that any excessive traffic above the threshold is delayed through a buffer and below the threshold requires additional dummy packets.

[5]In order to leverage a continuous channel-activity as a means to hide the actual channel-activity, the ring topology is efficient as compared to star alignment. In addition, one can also use the mesh-topology with anonymous-routing that requires asymmetric-key cryptography overheads at each relay-node while sending token between a source and a destination.

[6]The comparable-devices are those that are defined under certain relative order in a workflow. The incomparable-devices are independent and are not restricted under any relative order with respect to other devices.

Solution. In our scheme, each device is required to send a request for data upload to the hub using the rotating token, which contains a toggle bit string field of size N bits, where each bit represents a unique device in the topology. The ith toggled bit indicates that the device D^i has generated the data and is ready to anonymously transmit the data by using the data field of the token. The data field is used to carry the device generated data without revealing the data and the sender of the data. The data field contains random data as long as there is no request from the devices to send the data to hub. The details of data upload phase from device to hub will be clear in step 4, given in Section 3.

2.6 Building Blocks

This section provides a brief overview of basic building blocks used to develop the proposed solution as detailed in Section 3.

RSA puzzles. The verifiable delay regarding device actuation is based on cryptographic RSA puzzles [12]. These time-bounded puzzles are useful for the applications that require security against the hardware parallelization attacks (i.e., bypassing a security solution by running a mathematical problem on different hardware in parallel) through Application Specific Integrated Circuits (ASIC). Accordingly, the puzzle solution is based on inherently sequential operations such as *modular exponentiation*. Let us assume that t' be the time to release an encrypted message. Also, a device is capable of computing S number of square operations modulo n per second. Thus, the puzzle requires sequenced exponentiations of $(a^{2^{\hat{t}}} \ mod \ n)$ where $n = pq$ is publicly known RSA modulus and $\hat{t}$, p, q and $\phi(n) = (p-1)(q-1)$ remains secret. In particular, $\hat{t} = St'$ denotes the difficulty level of the puzzle for a specific device. Therefore, the computation of this modular exponentiation operation requires either the inherently sequential execution of these operations *or* to solve the integer factorization problem.

In the proposed scheme, the RSA puzzles enable an artificial yet verifiable delay with respect to command execution. To compensate this delay an adversary must know the private key of a device and then invest the same time as the victim device was supposed to invest in, for the puzzle computation. In particular, the adversary can always lengthen the delay (which is easily detectable during the puzzle validity check), but cannot shrink the delay due to inherently sequential operations.

Order-preserving bijection. The order-preserving bijection guarantees an instance of the totally ordered set elements as derived from the partially ordered set of the same elements. In particular, the bijection provides a unique sequence of the totally ordered set elements. Let us assume there is a partial order relation $\mathcal{R} = \{\leq\}$ on set elements $\mathcal{E} = (e^1, e^2, e^3, e^4)$ such that $\mathcal{R}$ is: reflexive, i.e., $e^i \mathcal{R} e^i$; antisymmetric, i.e., if $e^i \mathcal{R} e^j$ and $e^j \mathcal{R} e^i$ then $e^i = e^j$; and transitive, i.e., if $e^i \mathcal{R} e^j$ and $e^j \mathcal{R} e^k$ then $e^i \mathcal{R} e^k$. In addition, the partially ordered set $\mathcal{E}' = ((e^1, e^2), (e^3, e^4))$ under relation $\mathcal{R} = \{\leq\}$ has a unique minimal and maximal element. Therefore, an order-preserving bijection generates a linear ordering of elements in set $\mathcal{E}'$. Essentially, this linear extension generates a permutation order of the elements in a given partially ordered set $\mathcal{E}'$. All of those permutation sequences in which e^i appears before e^j given that $(e^i \leq e^j) \in \mathcal{E}'$ are a valid candidate as per any totally ordered set element sequence. The reliable ordering of device actuation

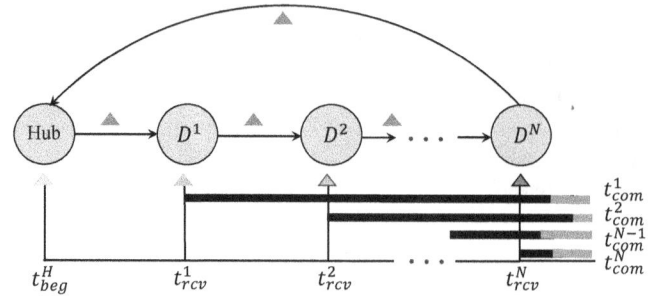

Figure 2: Device ordering on the timeline.

is guaranteed through the linear extension of the owner-defined schedule even when the application host is unavailable.

3 DECOUPLING CHANNEL ACTIVITY FROM DEVICE ACTIVITY

This section provides the details of our proposed protocol for decoupling channel activities from device activities. First, we illustrate the device-to-device interaction through an example as below:

3.1 Example

Consider N number of devices $(D^1, D^2, \ldots, D^N)$ that are connected through a hub (H), as shown in Figure 2. Let s^i_{on} (and s^i_{off}) be the on (and off) state of a device i. The owner O can create a partial ordering for devices such as $\langle (D^1, D^2, D^3), (D^4, D^5), \ldots, (D^{N-1}, D^N) \rangle$ based on their states, e.g., $\langle (s^1_{on}, s^2_{off}, s^3_{off}), (s^4_{off}, s^5_{on}), \ldots, (s^{N-1}_{off}, s^N_{on}) \rangle$ that shows the device D^1 must change its state to on, i.e., s^1_{on}, before the devices D^2 and D^3 change states to off, i.e., s^2_{off} and s^3_{off}. Similarly, the device D^4 must change its state to off, i.e., s^4_{off}, before the device D^5 changes its state to on, i.e., s^5_{on}.[7] After creating the partial order of devices, the owner sends a message to the hub that sends the message (shown in red color) to one of the devices, as shown D^1 in Figure 2. We refer to the message from the hub to devices as a token. Each device i receives the token at time t^i_{rcv}, forwards the token, and begins computation at time t^i_{com}. The bottom part shows when each device receives the token in a sequence as $(D^1, D^2, \ldots, D^{N-1}, D^N)$. Note that due to user-defined partial order of device actuation $\langle (D^1, D^2, D^3), (D^4, D^5), \ldots, (D^{N-1}, D^N) \rangle$, the devices across the partial orders are mutually incomparable[8]. In Figure 2, thick black line (for each device) shows that the device is having the token and waiting for the predefined time (given in the token) for its activation, and the green line shows when the devices start working.

3.2 Verifiable Ordering Protocol

The Section formally defines the verifiable ordering protocol and a detailed description for each step as below.

Definition 3.1 (Verifiable Ordering Protocol). The verifiable device ordering protocol is a tuple $(param, puzgen, P^i_D, P_O)$ of four polynomial-time algorithms such that:

---

[7]For the sake of simplicity this example includes the ordering between the devices and the corresponding states. However, throughout the paper, our focus is to order time intervals for devices' actuation.

[8]In case, the user finds a change in his/her schedule, then another remote command can overwrite the previous commands and the schedule workflow, correspondingly.

Algorithm 1: Algorithm for order creation.

Inputs: set of $l \in N$ devices (D^i), public keys (D^i_{PK})
Variables: $\mathcal{P}$ a puzzle, z a command.

1 **Function** $create\,(c_l, D^N)$
2 **begin**
3   **for** $\forall(i,j)\, \exists (D^i, D^j) \in H$ **do**
4         $schedule\,((D^i, D^{i+1}), (D^j, D^{j+1}))$
5   **for** $\forall(i, i+1)$ **do**
6             $z = (s_{on} \vee s_{off}) \wedge (\hat{t}_i \leq \hat{t}_{i+1})$
7             $generate\,(\mathcal{P}^i) = (n, a, \hat{t}_i, E_z, E_k)$
8             $m^i = enc(\mathcal{P}^i, D^i_{PK})$
            end for
        end for
9   **return** $c_l = ((m^i, m^{i+1}), (m^j, m^{j+1}))$ **end**

- *Public parameter generator. param*$(1^\lambda) \to (n, a)$. *param*(1^λ) initializes the prime integer factors $n = pq$ (where p and q are two large prime numbers) and random value a for the puzzle creation.
- *Puzzle generator. puzgen*$(n, a, \hat{t}, E_z, E_k) \to \mathcal{P}$. *puzgen*$(n, a, \hat{t}, E_z, E_k)$ selects the input values as target time for commands execution $\hat{t}$, encrypted command $E_z(z, k)$, encrypted key $E_k(a, \hat{t}, n, k)$ and outputs a puzzle $\mathcal{P}$ for each device.
- Follower $D^i(\mathcal{P}^i, SK) \to z(\hat{t}_i, t^i_{com}]$ completes the puzzle $\mathcal{P}^i$ and executes the command within the half-open interval, i.e., no earlier than $\hat{t}_i$ but earlier than or at t^i_{com}.
- Owner $O(\mathcal{P}, \phi(n), PK^i) \to accept(t^i_{com} \geq \hat{t}_i)$ accepts the timely command execution at each device using $\phi(n)$.

Setup and key distribution. The manufacturing authority initializes a unique identity for the owner, hub, and, home devices by using the secure identity distribution function, say $\mathtt{Init}(1^\lambda) \to identity$, where 1^λ is the security parameter that generates a unique *identity* for each entity. The certificate authority verifies that each of these devices knows the private key paired to the public key proposed for certification as: the homeowner (O_{SK}, O_{PK}), the hub (H_{SK}, H_{PK}), and i^{th} home device (D^i_{SK}, D^i_{PK}), possesses a valid key pair.

Step 1: Order creation: schedule creation at the owner. The homeowner O first creates a schedule, say *Schedule*, for device actuation. The creation of schedule is inherently specific to the preferences of the owner on a day to day basis and can include all or a subset of the home devices. The schedule creation does not require interaction with any device D^i or the hub H. Below we show a partially ordered timeline/schedule of four devices:

$$Schedule = ((D^1, D^2), (D^3, D^4))$$

Where only the elements of the same subset are comparable, e.g., D^1 with D^2, and, D^3 with D^4, based on the timeline. The owner converts this schedule to a verifiable device ordering (see Algorithm 1), before sending it to hub. The function $create(c_l, D^N)$ of Algorithm 1 converts a schedule for devices into the partially ordered sets of commands of length c_l, where $l \subseteq N$. Line 3 considers a pair[9] of devices in the topology of the hub. Line 4 creates a mutually dependent schedule for the pair of devices with temporal dependency. Lines 5 and 6 consider all of these mutually dependent

---

[9]We consider only pairs of devices, to simply demonstrate the relative ordering. However, a different subset may contain as large as the total number of devices.

Algorithm 2: Algorithm for chaining.

Inputs: set of devices (D^N), user-defined schedule $((D^i, D^{i+1}), (D^j, D^{j+1}))$

1 **Function** $chain(D^i, D^j, \mathcal{R})$ **begin**
2   **for** $\forall(i, j, \mathcal{R}) \in schedule(D^i, D^j); i\mathcal{R}j = i < j$ **do**
3         $^n P_n(D^i)$
4   **for** $\forall \{D^i\}_{n!} \wedge i\mathcal{R}j = true$ **do**
5   **return** $^n P'_n \{D^i\}^n_{i=1}$
    end for
    end

pairs, decide the state of command as $z = (s_{on} \vee s_{off})$, and then, generate a unique puzzle $\mathcal{P}^i$ for each device in Line 7. Here, the puzzle message contains a tuple of variables $(n, a, \hat{t}_i, E_z, E_k)$, where n is the product of two large prime numbers p and q, a is a random number, $\hat{t}_i$ is the time-complexity of the puzzle, E_z is the encrypted command z using key k, and E_k is the encrypted key k. Line 8 encrypts each puzzle $\mathcal{P}^i$ into a message m^i for a device D^i using the public key of the device D^i_{PK}. Line 9 returns an assembled order c_l that contains an encrypted message for each device corresponding to the mutually dependent devices in the schedule. This ends the creation of a relative order for the chosen set of devices. Next, the homeowner sends securely this order, say *Order*, to the hub, as follows:

$$Order = (O_{id}, H_{id}, c_l, Sign(\mathcal{H}, O_{SK}))$$

i.e., the homeowner sends its identity (O_{id}), the identity of the hub (H_{id}), and encrypted order of commands (c_l) along with hash digest of all three attributes.

Step 2: Token generation by the hub and token delivery to devices. On receiving the partial order of commands from the owner, the hub verifies the sender by computing a local hash digest $\mathcal{H}'$ over (O_{id}, H_{id}, c_l). Also the hub verifies the signature using O_{PK} and compares the received hash digest $\mathcal{H}$ with the locally computed hash digest $\mathcal{H}'$. If $\mathcal{H} = \mathcal{H}'$ then the hub accepts this order.

After the verification of order origination, the hub creates a token that is used for order delivery (in this step) and for data collection generated by devices (step 4). The token has three fields: command field c_l, data field, and toggle bit string b_{toggle}. Every token field has sensitive information regarding the device activity. Therefore, we assume that the token is encrypted using a shared symmetric key k_s among the devices and the controller hub.

$$\mathcal{T} = E((c_l || Data\,field || b_{toggle}), k_s)$$

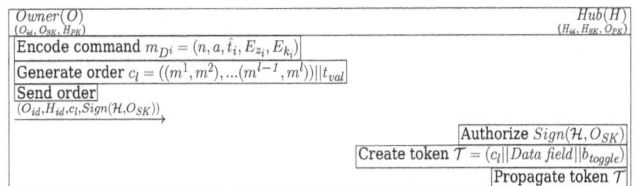

Figure 3: Order creation.

The hub, then, forwards the token among all devices in the topology even if a device was not included in the schedule, as shown in Figure 3. On receiving the token, each device decodes the corresponding command in token and forwards the token to the next

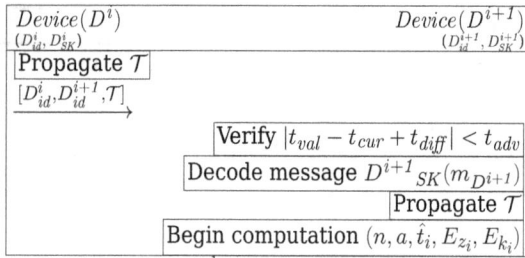

Figure 4: Token circulation.

peer device in the topology. The next peer device is chosen as per the topology underneath. Recall that the devices are connected in a pre-defined topology[10] such as in an unidirectional ring, bidirectional ring, star (fault-tolerant), grid, mesh or hybrid setting. Note that the token rotates constantly in the topology (see Figure 4).

Algorithm 2 explains the linear ordering of devices in function $chain(D^i, D^j, \mathcal{R})$. The linear ordering condition requires that each device D^i and D^j must satisfy: the exact same mutual ordering or relation $\mathcal{R} = \{\leq\}$ as in c_l. The line 2 selects each pair (i, j) of device that is paired under relation $\mathcal{R} = \{\leq\}$ in the original schedule. Line 3 enumerates all possible permutations of these devices, say $^n P_n(D^i)$ where $i \in N$. Line 4 selects one permuted order $^n P'_n$ of devices (from the total number of permutations) such that the precedence relation still holds true, i.e., $i\mathcal{R}j = true$. Finally, in line 5, the selected topological order $^n P'_n$ is returned from all possible permuted orders $^n P_n(D^i)$ of the devices.

Step 3: Order retrieval and puzzle computation at the devices. Note that the activation sequence of devices is released ahead of their actual activation; however, we need to restrict them not to execute the command before prescribed time. Thus, in this step, devices perform a pre-defined computation task (as detailed in Figure 5) to unlock and execute the owner-defined command.

It must be noted that unlocking the command is as necessary as unlocking the command within the prescribed duration, i.e., knowing the particular order of a device in the overall sequence. A device receives the computation task in the form of a puzzle as soon as the order is delivered in step 2. Subsequently, the device begins the computation task if the puzzle validity period has not expired yet. The time-bound during which a device is restricted to begin, as well as, end the computation task cannot be compressed unless the device possesses a distinguisher for the factoring problem. Therefore, the verification that the secure computation task is crucial. This can be verified through the Euler's totient as a trapdoor for factoring n inside the puzzle. Note that the value of n is public and the value of $\phi(n)$ is kept secret. Therefore, computing $\phi(n)$ from n is as hard as integer factorization. In addition, without the knowledge of $\phi(n)$ the computation time for E_k is directly dependent on $\hat{t}$ time-consuming square operations.

Algorithm 3 explains the verification of time-bounded commands in function $verify(D^i, \hat{t}_i)$. Line 3, considers all devices that are part of the current schedule. In order to verify that a specific device has executed the command within the pre-defined interval, O securely

---

[10]It must be noted that from the practical deployment aspect it is difficult to connect these smart devices in a ring topology unless the devices belong to the same OEMs, e.g., Apple HomeKit. Therefore, a star or a grid topology can be used to combat the single point of failure and device heterogeneity in the current scenario.

The puzzle messages:

$$n = pq$$
$$\hat{t} = St'$$
$$E_z = enc(z, k)$$
$$E_k = k + a^{2^{\hat{t}}} \ (mod \ n)$$

The puzzle computation ($\mathcal{P}$):

(1) Initially, $\mathcal{P}$ receives as input a secret key k and encrypt the original message z denoted as E_z. It must be noticed that each individual command corresponding to a device D^i is secured in the form of an encrypted message m_i. Furthermore, a cascaded command as a whole contains multiple messages of these types.

(2) Subsequently, $\mathcal{P}$ receives inputs as a secret key k, random number a, puzzle difficulty level $\hat{t}$, modulus n, and then generate E_k. The puzzle computation relies on the secrecy of key k used to encrypt a secret message $E_z = (z, k)$. Also, $\hat{t} = S * t'$ denotes the difficulty level of the puzzle for a specific device which can perform S number of square operations per second and t' is the time to decrypt the message using a regular encryption scheme.

(3) The puzzle $\mathcal{P}$ includes the tuple $(n, a, \hat{t}, E_z, E_k)$ for which the computation task is to be solved. Evidently, the recipient of this puzzle would have to spend at least $\hat{t}$ amount of time to complete the computation task and reveal the key k.

Figure 5: Puzzle computation.

Algorithm 3: Algorithm for delay verification.

Inputs: a puzzle ($\mathcal{P}$) with a set of public variables $(n, a, \hat{t}_i, z_i, k_i)$

1 **Function** $verify(D^i, \hat{t}_i)$
2 **begin**
3   **for** $\forall(i, j) \in schedule((D^i, D^{i+1}), (D^j, D^{j+1}))$ **do**
4   **if** $a^{2^{\hat{t}}} \ mod \ n \equiv a^{2^{\hat{t}} \ mod \ \phi(n)} \ mod \ n$ **then**
5   **if** $(t^i_{com} \leq t^{i+1}_{com}) \wedge (t^j_{com} \leq t^{j+1}_{com})$ **then**
6   return *True*
     end if
   end for
   return *False* **end**

---

pre-computes the Euler's totient $\phi(n) = (p - 1)(q - 1)$ such that p, q is discarded after computing the n and $\phi(n)$. Line 4, verifies the time bound for each of these devices, such that

$$a^{2^{\hat{t}}} \ mod \ n \equiv a^{2^{\hat{t}} \ mod \ \phi(n)} \ mod \ n$$

Line 5 compares the execution order of devices that have happened as a result of puzzle computation and returns true in line 6 if it is a total order.

Step 4: Data generation at the devices. Once the devices have completed the puzzle computation, they generate the data as a result of the command execution. These home devices are bound to upload the locally generated data to the hub. In our scheme, the token contains an anonymous data field to securely transmit the device generated data to the hub. We use bitwise (b) XOR padding to overwrite the random data in the token data field as:

Overwrite data (b_o) = *Random data* (b_r) ⊕ *Generated data* (b_g)

It is cryptographically hard to distinguish the presence of random data from the device generated data as stored inside the token. Note that our threat model does not consider the ISP or DNS level threats, therefore, devices are only assumed to securely generate and anonymously dispatch the data to the hub and combat any passive learning attacks within the physical periphery of the home. *Collision:* Our token circulation strategy and the token structure are primarily for smart home scenarios, where we assume that the single token field can accommodate the peak hour traffic. However, in case the peak hour traffic exceeds and multiple devices request for data upload, for example in a multi-tenant building, then to avoid the collision situation more data fields are required. A simple approach is to create sub-fields inside the data field such that each sub-field belongs to a unique device. Thus, each device can fairly utilize the data upload capacity in any round during the token circulation.

3.3 Time Analysis

The time spent during the token circulation and puzzle computation is directly proportional to the number of devices connected in the network. For example, token begins at time (t_{beg}^H) at the hub and completes the first round of token circulation at time (t_{end}^H). The time spent at ith device is $(t_{fwd}^i - t_{rcv}^i)$ that receive the token at time (t_{rcv}^i) and forward it to next device at time (t_{fwd}^i). Therefore, the total time spent in one round of token circulation:

$$t_{sum} = (t_{end}^H - t_{beg}^H) - (t_{fwd}^i - t_{rcv}^i)_{i=1}^N$$

Note that the token circulation time is sequenced and linear w.r.t. the number of devices. While the puzzle computation time t_{com}^i varies independently among all devices. So the puzzle computation time at ith device is $t_{com}^i \approx \hat{t}^i$. In order to optimize the puzzle computation time and still retain the verifiable guarantees on the artificial delay, we consider three type of puzzles.

- *For comparable devices:* Each pair of comparable devices in the topology requires that $\hat{t}$'s are *at least* $(N-1)(t_{fwd}^N - t_{fwd}^{N-1})$ apart. The devices forward the token before beginning the local computation task. Any two adjacent devices (D^{N-1}, D^N) that begin the computation after forwarding the token, must possess:

$$|\hat{t}^N - \hat{t}^{N-1}| \geq (N-1)(t_{fwd}^N - t_{fwd}^{N-1})$$

- *For incomparable devices:* The set of incomparable devices require that $\hat{t}$'s are *exactly* $(j-i)(t_{fwd}^j - t_{fwd}^i)$ apart. Every time a device D^i forwards a token to D^{i+1} it jumps $(t_{fwd}^{i+1} - t_{fwd}^i)$ ahead on the computation timeline with respect to next device due to token propagation delay. Therefore, in order to provide an identical time of actuation for all incomparable devices:

$$|\hat{t}^i - \hat{t}^j| = (j-i)(t_{fwd}^j - t_{fwd}^i)$$

The total number of slots required is $(N-k)+1$ where k represents the number of comparable devices. In particular, each comparable device requires a unique and non-overlapping $|\hat{t}|$ w.r.t. other comparable devices; while each incomparable device can be scheduled for an identical and overlapping $|\hat{t}|$.

Token frequency: The token frequency is a crucial attribute from the perspective of how early a user can decide the schedule for all N devices and, how many data upload requests are received during the peak hours. The frequency of token circulation can be either *fixed* or *random*. Let us assume a *fixed* slot i between any two consecutive rounds of the token circulation such that the token begins a new round at every ith unit of time. The optimal length of the slot is the same as the maximum $\hat{t}^i$ in any schedule.

$$Slot\ length = max\{\hat{t}^i\}_{i=1}^{l \in N}$$

For example, if $(\hat{t}^1, \hat{t}^2, \ldots, \hat{t}^{l-1}, \hat{t}^l)$ is the time-bound for l devices in any scheduled workflow then the slot length is same as the farthest possible device on the timeline of a scheduled workflow.

Table 3 represents the cost comparison based on mathematical operations such as encryption (E), decryption (D), signature generation and verification (S), exclusive-OR (XOR), hashing (H), scalar multiplication (M), and modular exponentiation (Me). The scheme in [6] imposes a relative overhead such that (p_m) number of masking packets are required per traffic flow in case the traffic flow is lesser than a pre-defined threshold value. Therefore, the total overhead per traffic flow is (Cp_m) where C is the communication overhead per packet. Similarly, if the traffic flow is above the threshold value then those excess packets p_m' are delayed and stored inside a queue. Therefore, the total latency per traffic flow is (Tp_m') where T is the latency overhead per packet. As shown here, that our proposed scheme requires the minimum number of operations. Further, in our approach the computational complexity at devices is variable and it depends on the required number of modular exponentiations, e.g., $\hat{t}$, as initialized by the owner.

4 SECURITY ANALYSIS

This section provides the security analysis for proposed scheme. We first model the security experiment, below, like the standard security model.

ATTACK GAME 1. *Let* I *be the order-preserving protocol between the challenger and adversary* $\mathcal{A}$ *then the attack game works as:*

- Public parameter generation: The challenger generates (n, a) using $param(1^\lambda)$.
- Puzzle generation: The challenger generates $\mathcal{P}$ using $puzgen(n, a, \hat{t}, E_k, E_z)$.
- Query phase: An adversary attempts to attack I through token query given the access to a recently generated token $\mathcal{T}'$. The adversary sends a value $\hat{t}$ to the challenger. The challenger generates the corresponding puzzle $\mathcal{P}$ and adds in c_l. The follower devices receive c_l, extract the unique puzzle, and execute the command. The challenger then sends $\mathcal{T}'$ to the adversary.
- State identification attempt: The adversary attempts to retrieve the intermediate state of the computation task and attempts to solve the puzzle earlier than device through $t_{com}^{\mathcal{A}}$ for the same $\mathcal{P}$ in $\mathcal{T}'$, such that $t_{com}^{\mathcal{A}}$ is lower than the original $\hat{t}$.

An adversary $\mathcal{A}$ wins the game, if $t_{com}^{\mathcal{A}} < \hat{t}_i$ and the owner outputs *accept*. The probabilistic advantage of the adversary, $Adv(\mathcal{A})$, for winning the game is:

$$Adv(\mathcal{A}) = Pr[t_{com}^{\mathcal{A}} < \hat{t}_i]$$

Protocol	Cost at device	Cost at hub	Cost at owner
Proposed scheme	$(2D + 1XOR + \hat{t}Me)$	$(1S + 1E + 1XOR)$	$(1S + lE + \hat{t}mod\phi(n)Me)$
Scheme [11]	$(3H + 7XOR + 1E + 1D)$	$(5H + 8XOR + 1E + 1D)$	-
Scheme [13]	$(3M + 2H + 4XOR)$	$(1H + 4XOR)$	-
Scheme [6]	-	$(Cp_m + Tp'_m)$	-

Table 3: Cost comparison between our scheme and existing schemes [6, 11, 13].

We present a sequence of games as Game 0 to Game 2. Each Game i shows that the advantage of an adversary $Pr[t^{\mathcal{A}}_{com} < \hat{t}_i]$ is negligibly small. Similarly, each subsequent game Game (i+1) is produced through previous game such that the changes in secret parameters remain indistinguishable to the adversary. Therefore, the advantage of an adversary through changes in secret parameters (i.e., transitioning from one game to another) remains negligibly small. If $Pr[\mathcal{A}(i) \to 0] - Pr[\mathcal{A}(i+1) \to 0]$ is non-negligible then that adversary can be used as a distinguisher or as a solver for the integer factorization problem in our scheme; where $Pr[\mathcal{A}(i)]$ and $Pr[\mathcal{A}(i+1)]$ represent the probability of adversary winning the Game i and Game (i+1), respectively. The Game 0 represents the original attack such that $(t^{\mathcal{A}}_{com} = \hat{t}_i)$ and the artificial delay before the command execution is kept null. The Game 1 represents the attack with enhanced t' while $(t^{\mathcal{A}}_{com} < t' \wedge \hat{t}_i)$. Similarly, the Game 2 represents the attack with general t' while $(t^{\mathcal{A}}_{com} = t')$ but $(t^{\mathcal{A}}_{com} < \hat{t}_i)$.

Game 0: [**Record attack**] Let us assume that the puzzle P_1 contains $\hat{t} = 0$ then the device must perform only one iteration to compute and decode the enciphered command. However, an adversary cannot distinguish an early puzzle such as P_1 from a delayed puzzle such as P_2 for which $\hat{t} > 0$. In the token query phase, an adversary gathers the token transcripts for a known value of $\hat{t}$.

```
Experiment Exp^{t^{A}_{com}=\hat{t}_i}_{A}
    let c_l((m^1, m^2), ..., (m^{l-1}, m^l)) ← A(T)
    generate m^i(\hat{t}) at random
    (m^k(\hat{t})) ← A(c_l((m^1, m^2), ..., (m^{l-1}, m^l)))
    if (m^k(\hat{t}) = m^i(\hat{t}))
        return 1
    else return 0
```

It is computationally hard to distinguish between encrypted commands and to identify the command that carries known $\hat{t}$ within time $t^{\mathcal{A}}_{com} = \hat{t}_i$. An adversary can distinguish the commands with the advantage

$$Adv(\mathcal{A})_{\text{Game } 0} = Pr[m^i(\hat{t}) \leftarrow c_l((m^1, m^2), ..., (m^{l-1}, m^l))] \le \epsilon$$

Game 1: [**Clone attack with lesser t'**] Let us assume that the adversary computes the puzzle in time $t^{\mathcal{A}}_{com} < t' \wedge \hat{t}_i$ where the unit time capacity t' of the adversary is slower. Therefore, the advantage of the adversary depends on the probability to compute the $\hat{t}$ square operations faster than the home device. This requires that the adversary can solve the prime factors for modulus n.

$$Adv(\mathcal{A})_{\text{Game } 1} = Pr[(p, q) \leftarrow (n)] \le \epsilon$$

Game 2: [**Clone attack with general t'**] Let us assume that the adversary can compute as fast as the home device, i.e., t'. In particular, the adversary can also perform S number of square operations per second. The probability $Pr[t' = t^{\mathcal{A}}_{com} < \hat{t}_i]$ that an adversary $\mathcal{A}$ can solve a puzzle with the difficulty level $\hat{t}$ in lesser time than

Properties	[11]	[13]	[6]	Our scheme
Upstream direction	✓	✓	✓	✓
Downstream direction	✓	✗	✓	✓
Verifiable delay	✗	✗	✗	✓
Partial ordering	✗	✗	✗	✓
Total ordering	✗	✗	✗	✓
Privacy	✗	✗	✓	✓
Passive attack resistant	✗	✗	✓	✓
Active attack resistant	✓	✓	✗	✓

Table 4: Comparison between our and existing schemes.

the home device is negligibly small. Since the adversary must compute S' number of operations for each S operations at home device where $(S' - S > \epsilon)$:

$$Adv(\mathcal{A})_{\text{Game } 2} = Pr[t^{\mathcal{A}}_{com}(S't') \leftarrow \hat{t}_i(St')] \le \epsilon$$

In this sequence of games Game 0 through Game 2 the total advantage of the adversary $Adv(\mathcal{A})$ depends on the sum of the probability to win each of these games.

$$Pr[t^{\mathcal{A}}_{com} = \hat{t}_i] + Pr[t^{\mathcal{A}}_{com} < t' \wedge \hat{t}_i] + Pr[t' = t^{\mathcal{A}}_{com} < \hat{t}_i] \le \epsilon$$

Overall, the advantage of the adversary is proportional to the availability of computational resources to solve the puzzle for all devices in parallel. Similarly, the advantage of the adversary with respect to a single puzzle and a single device are proportional to the availability of computational resources to solve the inherently sequential operations of that individual puzzle. Therefore, the total advantage of an adversary to clone the entire timeline depends on the total computational power for both, the parallel and the sequential operations to decrypt the command ahead of time.

In Table 4 a comparison is shown between our proposed scheme and the existing work. The comparison is based on the data flow direction, ordering, verification of ordering, privacy violation, and attack resistance.

5 EXPERIMENTAL EVALUATION

This section evaluates our proposed system using our prototype implementation. We describe the mock-up testing IoT application, experimental setup and overall results from our experiments.

5.1 Experiment Setup

In order to demonstrate the effectiveness and performance of our proposed architecture, we developed the prototype implementation and setup the testbed in our lab (as shown in Figure 6). This proof-of-concept prototype implements the protocols described in Section 3 and a test application with Python. In this mock-up IoT application, a device awaits and executes two types of command given by the homeowner. The "Set" command will change a variable in the program of the target device while the "Read" command will

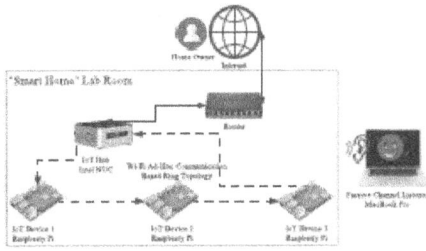

Figure 6: Experimental testbed in our lab

require the device to send the variable together with device status, e.g., RAM and CPU usages, back to the homeowner. This mock-up application is created to simulate two-way communication between the homeowner and devices. Further, note that the application runs on top of the approach, we proposed in this paper.

Figure 6 depicts the architecture and configuration of the smart home testbed. An Intel NUC system is programmed to work as the hub H that forwards information between the homeowner and smart devices. The hub H equips with two network interfaces: (*i*) Ethernet interface that has connections to receive the homeowner-defined schedule and sends the data of smart devices to the homeowner, and (*ii*) Wi-Fi interface that is used to communicate with smart home devices. Smart home device programs are deployed on three Raspberry Pis (D^1, D^2, D^3) (3rd Gen B+ Model) that are equipped with built-in Wi-Fi interface. Wi-Fi interfaces on the hub H and the devices (D^1, D^2, D^3) are configured to work in Wi-Fi ad-hoc mode [4], which enables direct device-to-device communication. All Wi-Fi interfaces are configured with pre-defined Wi-Fi channel, static IP address, and routing information to have a ring topology. A MacBook Pro with its Wi-Fi interface is deployed in a different room next to the testbed performs as an adversary, who listens and dumps all channel activities on the pre-defined channel into the pcap (packet capture) file for future analysis.

5.2 Results

Based on the testbed described above, we performed different experiments to evaluate the proposed system and the approach. We first validate our system to check whether it could prevent the adversary from learning device activity from channel activity or not. Then, we explore the performance of the proposed ring topology communication with a set of experiments.

Decoupling channel activities from device activities. To evaluate the effectiveness that our system protects against the passive channel listeners, we first defined a sequence of sample user commands, e.g., D^1: Set, D^2: Set, D^2: Read, and D^3: Read. In a one-minute experiment, these commands will be issued in 10 seconds intervals. We performed the experiment by executing the above-mentioned sequence in our proposed system and also over Wi-Fi infrastructure network without a ring topology to compare with. The channel activities are recorded by the passive channel listener laptop deployed near our testbed.

Figure 7a shows the passive adversary's view, i.e., which device receives a message from the homeowner at which time due to channel activities in the experiment. It is clear that each time the user sends a command to devices or devices send data to the user, there will be a peak in the channel activity. Thus, the adversary infers

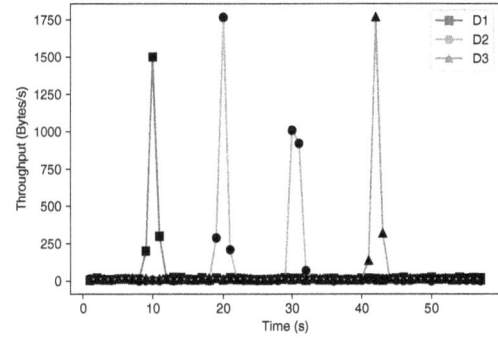

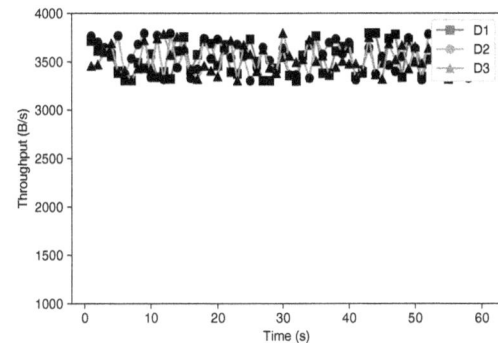

(b) Devices working with our proposed system

Figure 7: The adversarial view due to observing channel activities

the device activity and user-device interaction from channel activity. In contrast, Figure 7b shows the effectiveness of our proposed approach. Note that the channel activity patterns are completely eliminated, due to the token ring communication.

Communication latency. Instead of sending individual commands or data to/from devices or hub, the commands and data in our system are encapsulated in tokens and transmitted in a ring topology, which will incur additional communication latency. We performed experiments to evaluate the impact of increasing latency as the number of devices in the ring topology increases. Since we only have a very limited number of *real* devices, we modified our protocol to simulate the scenario that includes a large number of devices to investigate an impact on communication latency. To achieve this goal, we add a counter in each token. When the hub generates the token, it sets the counter equals to the number of devices we want to simulate in the experiments. This counter is decreased by one when each device receives and forwards the token to the next device. When the last device (D^3 in our testbed) in the ring topology receives the token, it checks the value of the current counter. If the value of the counter is more than zero, D^3 forwards the token to the first device (D^1) to extend the ring topology. If the counter number is less than or equal to zero, the last device forwards the token back to the hub to complete a single round of the token. Here, since each device will receive the same token multiple times, we also need to prevent the device from solving same puzzles and executing same commands multiple times. To do so, a unique token ID is added to each token. Thus, the device solves the puzzle and executes the command only when the device gets a new token ID.

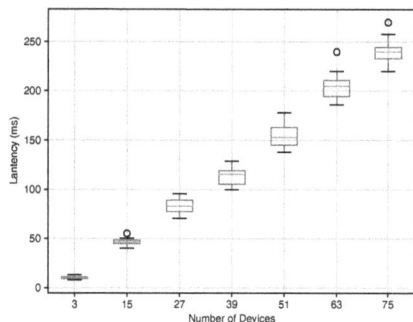

Figure 8: Impact of ring topology on the latency

Figure 8 shows that both mean and variation of the latency increase as more devices added into the ring topology. The mean of latency rises linearly at the beginning as each additional hop in the ring topology introduces more latency. After around 39 devices in the ring topology, the mean latency starts rising faster, since the length of token also increases with the growth of a number of devices. Consequently, it may take more time at devices to transmit the token to the next hop. Of course, the ring latency is not affected, when there is a few devices, since the number of commands and toggle bit strings decrease in the token as an decreasing number of devices. The variation of latency gets larger since it is more likely that the token transmission at more hops get delayed or re-transmitted because of unexpected interference or system lag at the devices.

# Devices	3	27	51	63	75
Avg. Token Len(bytes)	1807	5024	8189	9757	11305

Table 5: Average token length for ring topology size

Communication and computation overheads. It is also important to understand the additional overheads incurred due to our approach. We first measure how the length of token increases as the number of devices grows. Table 5 shows that the average token length grows linearly. We also use a USB power meter to measure the power consumption of the Raspberry Pi in different working states. Table 6 shows that our system introduces 63% more power consumption to completely eliminate the channel activity patterns of all devices.

6 RELATED WORK

There exist various IoT frameworks such as *Apple HomeKit*, *SmartThing*, *Azure IoT Suite*, *IBM Watson* IoT platform, *Brillo/Weave* platform by Google, *Calvin* IoT platform by Ericsson, *ARM mbed* IoT platform, *Kura* IoT project by Eclipse, interested readers may refer [3, 7] for more details. Overall, the smart home communication [8, 10] is a network component that executes commands based on contextual factors. To the best of our knowledge, none of the work [5, 6] highlight the significance of secure device ordering in a smart home scenario. We highlight the presence of a pattern among smart home devices such that a partial ordering on device activity is observed on daily basis. The authors in [6] have presented a privacy-preserving traffic shaping scheme to mask the channel activity and thereby the device or user activity at the ISP level. According to the scheme, if the shaped traffic rate is lower than the device traffic then the packets are queued, and if the shaped traffic rate is higher than the device traffic then the dummy packets are added to

State	Idle	IoT App w/o Ring Sys.	IoT App w/ Ring Sys.
Avg. Power	2.25W	3.03W	4.91W

Table 6: Average energy consumption of devices in different working states

cover the original traffic rate variations. However, these techniques do not avoid the inferences on device activity pattern due to the straightforward binding between the channel activity and device activity. Our scheme decouples the channel activity from the device activity such that a communication activity over the channel at any given time cannot be coupled with a specific device activity or the user activity. The recent work [11, 13] provides a security framework for home devices and guarantees message anonymity and unlinkability during the communication sessions from hub to the device. The scheme is based on authentication and one-time session key agreement in a 3-way handshake protocol. However, as mentioned, authentication and encrypted message cannot prevent the inferences over the communication activity.

7 CONCLUSION

This paper focuses on the security and privacy challenges in smart homes that facilitate the execution of multiple workflows. In particular, our solution avoids any inference attacks regarding these workflows that can reveal the user activity pattern, both in the past and the future. The primary source of these inference attacks is the ability to learn communication patterns among the smart home devices. The channel activity and the corresponding device activities are also sensitive from the user's privacy perspective. Therefore, decoupling the channel activity from the device activity is essential to hide the execution of scheduled workflows.

REFERENCES

[1] In *Insight' into Home Automation Reveals Vulnerability in Simple IoT Product*, available at URL: https://securingtomorrow.mcafee.com/mcafee-labs/insight-into-home-automation-reveals-vulnerability-in-simple-iot-product.
[2] In *IEEE OUI (Organizationally Unique Identifier)*, available at URL: http://standards-oui.ieee.org/oui.txt.
[3] M. Ammar et al. Internet of things: A survey on the security of IoT frameworks. *JISA*, 38:8 – 27, 2018.
[4] G. Anastasi et al. Wi-fi in ad hoc mode: a measurement study. In *PerCom*, pages 145–154, 2004.
[5] N. Apthorpe et al. Closing the blinds: Four strategies for protecting smart home privacy from network observers. *CoRR*, abs/1705.06809, 2017.
[6] N. Apthorpe et al. Spying on the smart home: Privacy attacks and defenses on encrypted IoT traffic. *CoRR*, abs/1708.05044, 2017.
[7] T. T. Doan et al. Towards a resilient smart home. In *IoT S&P*, pages 15–21, 2018.
[8] S. M. D'Souza et al. Time-based coordination in geo-distributed cyber-physical systems. In *HotCloud*, 2017.
[9] S. Feng et al. Smart home: Cognitive interactive people-centric internet of things. *IEEE Communications Magazine*, 55(2):34–39, 2017.
[10] D. N. Kalofonos et al. Intuisec: A framework for intuitive user interaction with smart home security using mobile devices. In *PIMRC*, pages 1–5, 2007.
[11] P. Kumar et al. Anonymous secure framework in connected smart home environments. *IEEE Trans. Information Forensics and Security*, 12(4):968–979, 2017.
[12] R. L. Rivest et al. Time-lock puzzles and timed-release crypto. Technical report, MIT/LCS/TR-684, MIT Lab for Computer Science, 1996.
[13] J. Shen et al. Secure data uploading scheme for a smart home system. *Information Sciences*, 453:186 – 197, 2018.
[14] G. J. Watson et al. Lost: Location based storage. In *ACM Workshop on Cloud Computing Security*, pages 59–70, 2012.

Dynamic Groups and Attribute-Based Access Control for Next-Generation Smart Cars

Maanak Gupta, James Benson, Farhan Patwa and Ravi Sandhu

Institute for Cyber Security (ICS),
Center for Security and Privacy Enhanced Cloud Computing (C-SPECC),
Department of Computer Science, University of Texas at San Antonio, San Antonio, Texas, USA
Email: gmaanakg@yahoo.com, {james.benson, farhan.patwa, ravi.sandhu}@utsa.edu

ABSTRACT

Smart cars are among the essential components and major drivers of future cities and connected world. The interaction among connected entities in this vehicular internet of things (IoT) domain, which also involves smart traffic infrastructure, restaurant beacons, emergency vehicles, etc., offer several real-time applications and provide safer and pleasant driving experience to consumers. With more than 100 million lines of code and hundreds of sensors, these connected vehicles (CVs) expose a large attack surface, which can be remotely compromised and exploited by malicious attackers. Security and privacy are big concerns that deter the adoption of smart cars, which if not properly addressed will have grave implications with risk to human life and limb. In this paper, we present a formalized dynamic groups and attribute-based access control (ABAC) model (referred as CV-ABAC$_G$) for smart cars ecosystem, where the model not only considers system wide attributes-based security policies but also takes into account the individual user privacy preferences for allowing or denying service notifications, alerts and operations to on-board resources. Further, we introduce a novel notion of groups in vehicular IoT, which are dynamically assigned to moving entities like connected cars, based on their current GPS coordinates, speed or other attributes, to ensure relevance of location and time sensitive notification services, to provide administrative benefits to manage large numbers of entities, and to enable attributes inheritance for fine-grained authorization policies. We present proof of concept implementation of our model in AWS cloud platform demonstrating real-world uses cases along with performance metrics.

CCS CONCEPTS

• **Security and privacy** → **Formal security models**; **Access control**; **Authorization**; *Security requirements*; *Domain-specific security and privacy architectures*;

KEYWORDS

Access Control, Smart Cars, Connected Vehicles, Internet of Things, Authorization, Attribute-Based Access Control, Amazon Web Services (AWS), Autonomous Cars, Security, Privacy, Cloud Computing

ACM Reference Format:
Maanak Gupta, James Benson, Farhan Patwa and Ravi Sandhu. 2019. Dynamic Groups and Attribute-Based Access Control for Next-Generation Smart Cars. In *Ninth ACM Conference on Data and Application Security and Privacy (CODASPY '19), March 25–27, 2019, Richardson, TX, USA*. ACM, New York, NY, USA, 12 pages. https://doi.org/10.1145/3292006.3300048

1 INTRODUCTION

Internet of Things (IoT) has become a dominant technology which has proliferated to different application domains including healthcare, homes, industry, power-grid, to make lives smarter. It is predicted [2] that the global IoT market will grow to $457 Billion by year 2020, attaining a compound annual growth rate of 28.5%. Automation is leading the world today, and with 'things' around sensing and acting on their own or with a remote user command, has given humans to have anything accessible with a finger touch. Data generated by these smart devices unleash countless business opportunities and offer customer targeted services. IoT along with 'infinite' capabilities of cloud computing are ideally matched with desirable synergy in current technology-oriented world, which has been often termed as cloud-enabled, cloud-centric or cloud-assisted IoT in literature [12, 17, 18, 38].

IoT is embraced by every industry with automobile manufacturers and transportation among the most aggressive. Vehicular IoT inherits intrinsic IoT characteristics but dynamic pairing, mobility of vehicles, real-time, location sensitivity are some features which separates it from common IoT applications. The vision of smart city incorporates intelligent transportation where connected vehicles can 'talk' to each other (V2V) and exchange information to ensure driver safety and offer location-based services. These intelligent vehicles can also interact with smart roadside infrastructure (V2I), with pedestrian on road (V2H) or send data to the cloud for processing. Basic safety messages (BSMs) are exchanged among entities using commonly used WiFi like secure and reliable Dedicated Short Range Communication (DSRC) protocol. Vehicles can receive speed limit notification and flash flood alerts on car dashboard or via seat vibration. A car will receive information about nearby parking garages, restaurant offers or remote engine monitoring by authorized mechanic with nearby repair facility and discounts updating automatically. These services will provide pleasant travel experience to drivers and unleash business potential in this intelligent transportation domain. Smart internet connected vehicles embed softwares having more than 100 million lines of code to control critical systems and functionality, with plethora of sensors and electronic control units (ECUs) on board generating huge amounts of data so these vehicles are often termed as 'datacenter on wheels'.

As vehicles get exposed to external environment and internet, they become vulnerable to cyber attacks. Common security vulnerabilities including buffer overflow, malware, privilege escalation, and trojans etc. can be exploited in connected vehicles. Other potential threats include untrustworthy or fake messages from smart objects, malicious software injection, data privacy, ECU hacking and control, and spoofing connected vehicle sensor. With broad attack surface exposed via air-bag ECU, On-Board Diagnostics (OBD) port, USB, Bluetooth, remote key, and tire-pressure monitoring system etc. these attacks have become much easier to orchestrate. In-vehicle Controller Area Network (CAN) bus also needs security to protect message exchange among ECUs. Further, communication with external networks including cellular, WiFi and insecure public networks of gas stations, toll roads, service garages, or after-market dongles are a big threat to connected vehicles security. Cyber incidents including Jeep [54] and Tesla Model X [51] hacks where engine was stopped and steering remotely controlled demonstrate security vulnerabilities. Smart car incidents have serious implications as they can even result in loss of human life.

Access control [22, 46, 47] mechanisms are widely used to restrict unauthorized access to resources and secure communication among entities. Attribute-based access control (ABAC) [35, 37] provides finer granularity and offers flexibility in distributed multi-entity communication scenarios, which considers characteristics of participating entities along with system and environment properties to determine access decision. Smart cars ecosystem involves dynamic interaction and message exchange among connected objects, which must be authorized. It is necessary that only legitimate entities are allowed to control on-board sensors, data messages and send notifications. Further, user-centric privacy requires that users can control what alerts they want to receive, what advertisements they are interested or who can access their car's sensors, etc. This paper focuses on the access control needs in connected smart cars and proposes an attribute-based access control model for connected vehicles[1] ecosystem, referred as CV-ABAC$_G$. Our solution considers the attributes of moving entities like current location, speed etc. to dynamically assign them to various groups (predefined by smart city administration), for implementing attributes-based security policies, and also incorporate user-specific privacy preferences for ensuring relevance of notifications service in constantly changing and mobile smart cars ecosystem. We implemented a prototype of our model as an external authorization engine hooked into the widely used AWS (Amazon Web Services) cloud platform [3].

Rest of the paper is organized as follows. Section 2 discusses related work and reviews the extended access control architecture (E-ACO) recently proposed for vehicular IoT environment. Section 3 highlights authorization requirements and emphasize the need of dynamic groups in smart cars applications. Section 4 presents and formalizes our proposed groups and attribute-based access control model (CV-ABAC$_G$) for connected vehicles ecosystem. Section 5 provides AWS implementation of dynamic groups assignment of entities based on attributes and discusses our external policy decision and enforcement engine along with performance metrics. Section 6 summarizes our work.

---

[1]In this paper, we use the terms smart cars and connected vehicles interchangeably which also subsumes autonomous vehicles.

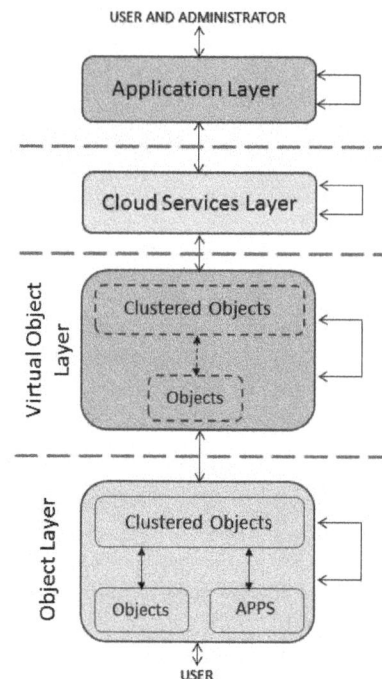

Figure 1: E-ACO Architecture [31]

2 RELATED WORK

Vehicular IoT and smart cars involve dynamic communications and data exchange which requires access controls to restrict within authorized entities. In this section, we first discuss a recently proposed extended access control architecture (E-ACO) which focuses on access control requirements in connected vehicles. We also highlight some important work done by government and private agencies to gauge cyber risks and security measures in smart vehicles.

2.1 Extended ACO Architecture

Several IoT architectures with multi-layer stack have been discussed in literature [13–15, 19, 25]. Alsehri and Sandhu [14] recently presented a general IoT architecture which includes virtual objects [42] and cloud as two middleware layers. Virtual objects resolve IoT issues of heterogeneity and connectivity whereas on-demand capabilities of cloud are in cloud service layer. Gupta and Sandhu [31, 32] extended this IoT architecture for specific vehicular IoT and connected vehicles domain. This extended access control architecture (E-ACO), shown in Figure 1, introduced clustered objects (like smart cars and traffic lights) which are objects with multiple individual sensors. Also, these clustered objects have applications (for example, lane departure or safety warning system in cars) installed on board, which is usually not the case in general IoT realm.

As shown in Figure 1, four layered E-ACO has **Object Layer** at the bottom which represents physical clustered objects and sensors along with applications installed on them. In-vehicle communication at this layer is mainly supported by Ethernet and CAN technologies, whereas communication across clustered objects is done using DSRC (used for BSM exchange in V2V communication), WiFi, or LTE etc. It should be noted that each layer in E-ACO architecture interacts within itself and with entities in adjacent layers. Therefore, object layer will interact with users at the bottom and virtual object layer above it. The **Virtual Object Layer** acts as an intermediate between cloud services and physical layer, which offers the necessary abstraction by creating cyber entities for physical objects in object layer. In particular in connected vehicles domain, where cars are moving across different terrains where internet connectivity can be an issue, it is important to have cyber entities which maintain the state of the corresponding physical object as best known and to be updated when connectivity is restored. When two sensors s_1 and s_2 across different vehicles interact with each other, the order of communication using virtual objects will follow s_1 to vs_1 (virtual entity of s_1), vs_1 to vs_2 and vs_2 to physical sensor s_2. **Cloud Services and Application Layer:** As applications use cloud services, therefore these two layers are discussed together. On-board sensors generate data which is stored and processed by cloud services, which is used by applications to offer services to end-users. Cyber entities of physical objects can be created in cloud layer which provides a persistent state information of objects. It is important to mention that central cloud may incur latency and bandwidth issues in time-sensitive applications which can be resolved by introducing edge or fog computing infrastructure.

2.2 Relevant Background

Smart cars and associated applications are still in early stages but involve some established technologies. Vehicular Ad-hoc Networks (VANETs) [11] have been discussed which support vehicle to vehicle and infrastructure communication for user services. In VANETS, moving cars and infrastructure act as network nodes to provide storage, computation and other services. This concept is further extended with the inclusion of cloud computing. Vehicular Clouds (VC) [20, 24, 43] were proposed to integrate VANETs and cloud, to offer on-the fly edge/cloud platform to cars and applications by utilizing on-board resources. VCs are relevant in smart cars real-time and location-centric applications and services, which are otherwise impractical due to latency and bandwidth issues of central cloud. Several VC architectures have been discussed including stationary, fixed infrastructure or dynamic [36, 53].

Cyber threats to connected vehicles are very serious concerns. Government agencies and private sectors are well aware of the risks involved and want to ensure that no open doors are left to orchestrate attacks before wide adoption. The US Department of Transportation (USDOT) has invested in Intelligent Transportation System (ITS) [16] which has connected vehicles as an important component with aim to reduce accidental fatalities. Cyber security is a key area and along with National Highway Traffic Safety Administration (NHTSA), it has released cyber-security guidelines [40, 41]. Security Credential Management System (SCMS) [52] is proposed as DSRC message security solution in vehicle-to-vehicle (V2V) and vehicle-to-infrastructure (V2I) communication. It uses Public Key Infrastructure (PKI)-based approach to enable trusted interaction where a certificate authority issued certificate is attached to each BSM [1] to ensure vehicle trustworthiness. US Government Accountability Office (GAO) [23] have widely discussed vulnerabilities and attack surfaces in smart vehicles, and also proposed

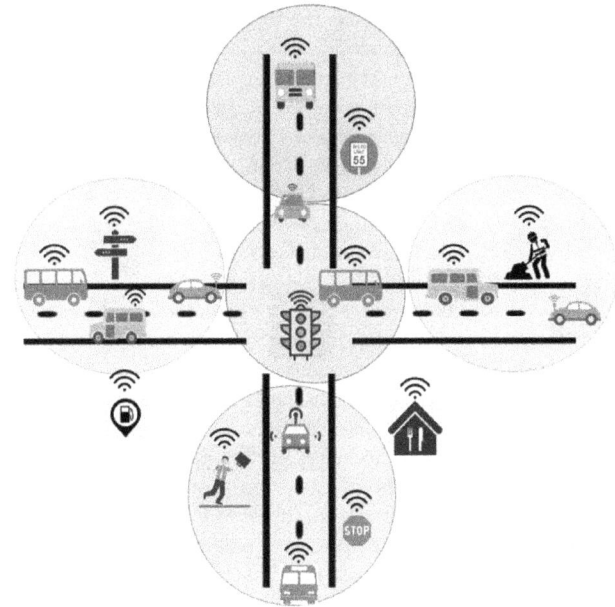

Figure 2: Smart City with Location Groups

solutions to prevent such threats. European Union Agency for Network and Information Security (ENISA) also studied critical assets and threats in smart cars together with security mechanisms to mitigate them [21]. Cooperative Intelligent Transport Systems (C-ITS) for European Union [49, 50] has defined a PKI-based trust model to ensure authenticity and integrity of vehicle messages.

Homomorphic encryption based security solutions and protocols have been extensively discussed to provide location proximity [33, 39, 55] which can help to provide location based services without sharing the exact coordinates of drivers. These approaches can be used and complement our proposed CV-ABAC$_G$ model to resolve the privacy concerns of end users.

Access controls are widely used in computer systems to restrict unauthorized access to resources. Park et al [44, 45] proposed an activity centric access control model for social networks which considers user privacy policies in access decision. CV-ABAC$_G$ model is inspired from this work besides being a pure ABAC model with dynamic groups which are pertinent in smart cars ecosystem.

3 AUTHORIZATION REQUIREMENTS IN SMART CARS

Smart cars expose the conventionally isolated car systems to external environment via internet. The dynamic and short-lived real time V2V and V2I interaction with entities in and around connected vehicle needs to ensure message confidentiality and integrity, as also protection of on-board resources from adversaries. This section provides an overview of access control requirements and underlines the need for dynamic groups in smart vehicles IoT domain.

3.1 Multi-Layer and User Privacy Preferences

Broad attack surface of connected vehicles is the first entry point to in-vehicle critical systems. We believe that two level access control policies are the minimum essential to protect the external interface and internal ECU communication. Access control for external environment will protect on-board sensors, applications and user personal data from unauthorized access by entities including vehicles, applications, masquerading remote mechanics or other adversaries. Over-the air firmware update needs to be checked and must be allowed only from authorized sources. An attacker even if successful in passing through the first check point, must be restricted at the in-vehicle level, which secures overwrite and control of critical units (engine, brakes, telematics etc.) from adversaries. Vehicles exchange BSMs which raises an important question about trust. It must be ensured that information received is correct and from a trusted party, before being used by on-vehicle applications. Applications access sensors within and outside the car, which must be authorized, for example, a lane departure warning system accessing tire sensors must be checked to prevent a spoofed application reading vehicle movements. A passenger accessing infotainment (information and entertainment) systems of the car via Bluetooth or using smartphone inside car must also be authorized.

Smart cars location-based services enable notifications and alerts to vehicles. A user must be allowed to set his personal preferences whether he wants to receive advertisements or filter out which ones are acceptable. For instance, a user may not want to receive restaurant notifications but is interested in flash-flood warnings. System wide policy, like a speed warning to all over-speeding vehicles or a policy of who can control speed of autonomous car are needed.

Data protection in cloud is critical due to frequent occurrence of data breaches. Big Data access control [26–29] is essential when user privacy has to be ensured and unauthorized disclosure is not allowed. Cross cloud trust models are needed to allow data access when mechanic application in private cloud reads data in car-manufacturer cloud. Physical tampering of vehicle OBD and sensors also require protection but is out of scope for this paper.

3.2 Relevance of Groups

Most smart cars applications and service requests from drivers are location specific and time sensitive. For example, a driver might want to get warning signals when traveling near a blind spot, in school zone or pedestrians crossing road. Further, notifications sent to drivers are short-lived and mostly pertinent around current GPS coordinates. A gas discount notification from a nearby station, an accident warning two blocks away or ice on the bridge, are some example where alerts are sent to all vehicles in the area. Therefore, we believe that dynamically categorizing connected vehicles into location groups will be helpful for scoping the vehicles to be notified instead of a general broadcast and reduce administrative overheads, since single notification for the group will trigger alerts for all its members. Also, entities present at a location have certain characteristics (like stop sign warning, speed limit, deer-threat etc.) in common, which can be inherited by being a group member. Figure 2 represents how various smart entities can be separated into different location groups defined by appropriate authorities in a smart city system. These groups are dynamically assigned to connected vehicles based on their attributes, personal preferences, interests or current GPS coordinates as further elaborated in the model and implementation section discussed later.

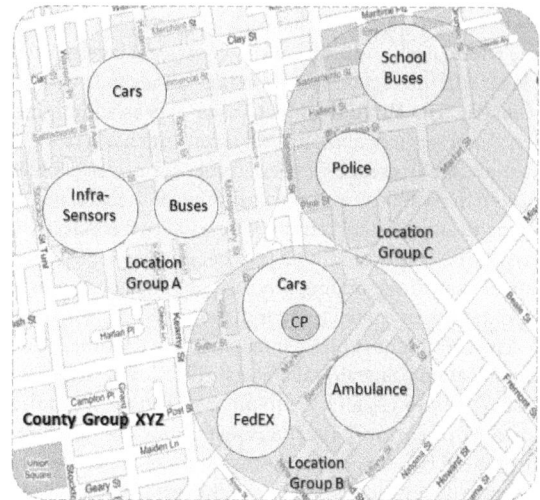

Figure 3: Representative Groups Hierarchy

Groups hierarchy can also exist, as shown in Figure 3, with subgroups within a larger parent group so as to reduce the number of vehicles to be notified. For instance, under location group, subgroups can be created for cars, buses, police vehicles or ambulances, to enable targeted alerts to ambulances or police vehicle sub-groups defined within the location group. Groups can be defined based on services, for example, a group of cars within the car parent group which take part in car-pooling (CP) service or those which want to receive gas station offers. Group hierarchy [30, 48] also enables attributes inheritance from parent to child groups.

4 ACCESS CONTROL MODEL FOR CONNECTED VEHICLES ECOSYSTEM

Dynamic communication and data exchange among entities in connected vehicles ecosystem require multi-layer access control policies, which are managed centrally and also driven by individual user preferences. Therefore, an access control model must incorporate all such user and system requirements and offer fine-grained authorization solutions. In this section, we will discuss and formally define our proposed connected vehicle attribute-based access control model with dynamic groups, which we refer as CV-ABAC$_G$.

4.1 CV-ABAC$_G$ Model Overview

The conceptual CV-ABAC$_G$ model is shown in Figure 4 with formal definitions summarized in Table 1. The basic model has following components: Sources (S), Clustered Objects (CO), Objects in clustered objects (O), Groups (G), Operations (OP), Activities (A), Authorization Policies (POL), and Attributes (ATT).

Sources (S): These entities initiate activities (explained below) on various smart objects, groups and applications in the ecosystem. A source can be a user, an application, administrator, sensor, handheld device, clustered object (such as a connected car), or a group defined in the system. For instance, in case of flash flood or deer threat warning, activity source is police or city department triggering an alert to all vehicles in the area. Similarly, car mechanic is a

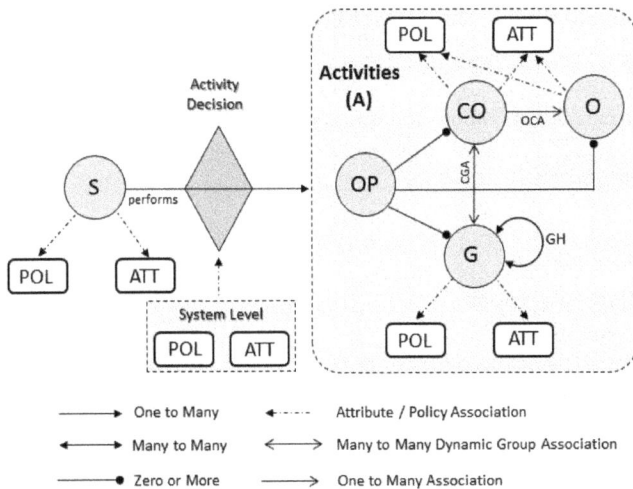

Figure 4: A Conceptual CV-ABAC$_G$ Model

source, when he tries to access data from on-board engine sensor in the car using his remote cloud based application. A restaurant or gas-station issuing coupons are also considered as source.

Clustered Objects (CO): Clustered objects are particularly relevant in case of connected vehicles, traffic lights or smart devices held by humans as they have multiple sensors and actuators. A smart car with on-board sensors, ECUs (like tire pressure, lane departure, or engine control) and applications is a clustered object. These smart entities interact and exchange data among themselves and with others such as requestor source, applications or cloud. An important reason to incorporate clustered objects is to reflect cross-vehicle and intra-vehicle communication. The fact that two smart vehicles can exchange basic safety messages (BSM) with each other shows clustered object communication.

Objects in clustered objects (O): These are individual sensors, ECUs and applications installed in clustered objects. Objects in smart cars include sensors for internal state of the vehicle, e.g., engine diagnostics, emission control, cabin monitoring system, as well as sensors for external environment such as cameras, temperature, rain, etc. Control commands can directly be issued to these objects, and data can be read remotely. Applications (like lane departure warning system) on board can also access data from these objects to provide alerts to driver or to a remote service provider.

Groups (G): A group is a logical collection of clustered objects with similar characteristics or requirements. With these groups, subset of COs can be sent relevant notification and also attributes can be assigned to group members. Some groups which can be defined smart vehicles ecosystem include location specific groups, service specific groups (like car-pooling, gas station promotions etc.) or vehicle type (a group of cars, buses etc.). Group hierarchy (GH) also exists which enables attributes and policies inheritance from parent to children groups. For simplicity, we require that a vehicle or CO can be direct member of only one group at same hierarchy level. For example, a car can be in either location A or B group and but not both. Such restriction helps in managing attributes inheritance and enhances the usability of our model.

Operations (OP): These are actions which can be performed against clustered objects, individual objects or groups. Examples include: a mechanic performing read, write or control operations on engine ECU, a restaurant triggering notifications to vehicles in location A group. Operations also include administrative actions like creating or updating attributes or policies for COs, objects and groups, which are usually performed by system/security administrators.

Activities (A): Activities encompass both operational and administrative activities which are performed by various sources in the system. An activity can have one or many atomic operations (OP) involved and will need authorization policies, which can be user privacy preferences, system defined or both, to allow or deny an activity. For example, a car pooling notification activity generated by a requestor (source) will be broadcast to all relevant vehicles in the locations nearby using location groups, however individual drivers must also receive or respond to that request based on individual preferences. A driver may not want to car-pool the requestor because of poor rating or because he is not going to the destination the requestor asked for. Therefore, an activity can involve multiple set of policies defined at different levels which must be evaluated, in car-pooling case a policy is set to determine cars to be notified and then driver personal preferences. We have primarily divided these smart car activities into following categories.

- Service Requests: These are activities initiated by entities or users (via applications). For instance, a vehicle break-down initiates a service request to other vehicles around, or a user using a smartphone initiates a car-pooling requests for a destination to cars which are available for the service.
- Administration: These activities perform administrative operations in system which include changing policies and attributes of entities or determining the group hierarchy. It also defines the scope of groups, how user privacy preferences are used, or how vehicles are determined to be a member of a group etc.
- Notifications: These are group centric activities where all members are notified for any updates about the group (like speed limit or deer threat notifications in location A) or for locations-based marketing promotions by parking lots or restaurants.
- Control and Usage: These activities include simple read, write or control operations performed remotely or within a vehicle. Over the air updates issued by manufacturer or turning on car climate control using a smart key are remote activities whereas a passenger accessing infotainment system using smartphone and on-board car applications reading car camera are local.

Authorization Policies and Attributes: CV-ABAC$_G$ model incorporates individual user privacy controls for different entities by managing authorization policies and entity attributes. A shown in Figure 4 policy of sources include personal preferences, whereas attributes reflect characteristics like name, age or gender. Policies can be defined for clustered objects, for instance, a USB can be plugged only by car owner, or which mechanic can access an on-board sensor. Attributes of a car include GPS coordinates, speed, heading direction, and vehicle size. Groups also set policies and attributes for themselves, for example, car pooling group policy of who can be its member. Similarly, system wide policies are also considered, for instance, policy to determine which groups will be sent information when a request comes from a source, or policy to

Table 1: Formal CV-ABAC$_G$ Model Definitions for Connected Vehicles Ecosystem

---

Basic Sets and Functions

– S, CO, O, G, OP are finite sets of sources, clustered objects, objects, groups and operations respectively [blue circles in Figure 4].

– A is a finite set of activities which can be performed in system.

– ATT is a finite set of attributes associated with S, CO, O, G and system-wide.

– For each attribute att in ATT, Range(att) is a finite set of atomic values.

– attType: ATT = {set, atomic}, defines attributes to be set or atomic valued.

– Each attribute att in ATT maps entities in S, CO, O, G to attribute values. Formally,

$$\text{att} : S \cup CO \cup O \cup G \cup \{\text{system-wide}\} \rightarrow \begin{cases} \text{Range(att)} \cup \{\bot\} & \text{if attType(att) = atomic} \\ 2^{\text{Range(att)}} & \text{if attType(att) = set} \end{cases}$$

– POL is a finite set of authorization policies associated with individual S, CO, O, G.

– directG : CO $\rightarrow$ G, mapping each clustered object to a system group, equivalently CGA $\subseteq$ CO $\times$ G.

– parentCO : O $\rightarrow$ CO, mapping each object to a clustered object, equivalently OCA $\subseteq$ O $\times$ CO.

– GH $\subseteq$ G $\times$ G, a partial order relation $\geq_g$ on G. Equivalently, parentG : G $\rightarrow$ 2^G, mapping group to a set of parent groups in hierarchy.

Effective Attributes of Groups, Clustered Objects and Objects (Derived Functions)

– For each attribute att in ATT such that attType(att) = set:

- effG$_{\text{att}}$: G $\rightarrow$ $2^{\text{Range(att)}}$, defined as effG$_{\text{att}}$(g$_i$) = att(g$_i$) $\cup$ ($\bigcup_{g \, \in \, \{g_j | g_i \, \geq_g \, g_j\}}$ effG$_{\text{att}}$(g)).

- effCO$_{\text{att}}$: CO $\rightarrow$ $2^{\text{Range(att)}}$, defined as effCO$_{\text{att}}$(co) = att(co) $\cup$ effG$_{\text{att}}$(directG(co)).

- effO$_{\text{att}}$: O $\rightarrow$ $2^{\text{Range(att)}}$, defined as effO$_{\text{att}}$(o) = att(o) $\cup$ effCO$_{\text{att}}$(parentCO(o)).

– For each attribute att in ATT such that attType(att) = atomic:

- effG$_{\text{att}}$: G $\rightarrow$ Range(att) $\cup$ $\{\bot\}$, defined as effG$_{\text{att}}$(g$_i$) = $\begin{cases} \text{att}(g_i) & \text{if } \forall g' \in \text{parentG}(g_i). \text{ effG}_{\text{att}}(g') = \bot \\ \text{effG}_{\text{att}}(g') & \text{if } \exists \text{ parentG}(g_i). \text{ effG}_{\text{att}}(\text{parentG}(g_i)) \neq \bot \text{ then select} \\ & \text{parent } g' \text{ with effG}_{\text{att}}(g') \neq \bot \text{ updated most recently.} \end{cases}$

- effCO$_{\text{att}}$: CO $\rightarrow$ Range(att) $\cup$ $\{\bot\}$, defined as effCO$_{\text{att}}$(co) = $\begin{cases} \text{att(co)} & \text{if effG}_{\text{att}}(\text{directG(co)}) = \bot \\ \text{effG}_{\text{att}}(\text{directG(co)}) & \text{otherwise} \end{cases}$

- effO$_{\text{att}}$: O $\rightarrow$ Range(att) $\cup$ $\{\bot\}$, defined as effO$_{\text{att}}$(o) = $\begin{cases} \text{att(o)} & \text{if effCO}_{\text{att}}(\text{parentCO(o)}) = \bot \\ \text{effCO}_{\text{att}}(\text{parentCO(o)}) & \text{otherwise} \end{cases}$

Authorization Functions (Policies)

– Authorization Function: For each op $\in$ OP, Auth$_{\text{op}}$(s : S, ob : CO $\cup$ O $\cup$ G) is a propositional logic formula returning true or false, which is defined using the following policy language:

- $\alpha ::= \alpha \wedge \alpha \mid \alpha \vee \alpha \mid (\alpha) \mid \neg\alpha \mid \exists \, x \in \text{set}.\alpha \mid \forall \, x \in \text{set}.\alpha \mid \text{set} \bigtriangleup \text{set} \mid \text{atomic} \in \text{set} \mid \text{atomic} \notin \text{set}$

- $\bigtriangleup ::= \subset \mid \subseteq \mid \nsubseteq \mid \cap \mid \cup$

- set ::= eff$_{\text{att}}$(i) | att(i)   for att $\in$ ATT, i $\in$ S $\cup$ CO $\cup$ O $\cup$ G $\cup$ {system-wide}, attType(att) = set

- atomic ::= eff$_{\text{att}}$(i) | att(i) | value   for att $\in$ ATT, i $\in$ S $\cup$ CO $\cup$ O $\cup$ G $\cup$ {system-wide}, attType(att) = atomic

---

Authorization Decision

– A source s $\in$ S is allowed to perform an activity a $\in$ A, stated as Authorization(a : A, s : S), if the required policies needed to allow the activity are included and evaluated to make final decision. These multi-layer policies must be evaluated for individual operations (op$_i$ $\in$ OP) to be performed by source s $\in$ S on relevant objects (x$_i$ $\in$ CO $\cup$ O $\cup$ G).

Formally, Authorization(a : A, s : S) $\Rightarrow$ Auth$_{\text{op}_1}$(s : S, x$_1$), Auth$_{\text{op}_2}$(s : S, x$_2$), ..., Auth$_{\text{op}_n}$(s : S, x$_3$)

---

change group hierarchy. Policies also include attributes of entities involved in an activity. A CO can inherit attributes from dynamically assigned groups which will change as the CO leaves old group and adds to new group.

It should be noted that attributes of entities change more often than system wide or individual policies. Attributes are more dynamic in nature which are added or removed with the movement of vehicles or change in surroundings, like GPS coordinates or temperature. Policies once set by administrators or users are more static

and only the attributes which comprise the policy change the outcome of a policy but the policy definition remains relatively fixed. For instance, a user policy could state that 'Send restaurant notifications only from Cheesecake factory'. In such case, only attribute name of the restaurant sending the notification will be checked and if it is equal to Cheesecake factory will be able to advertise to that user. Dynamic policies are also possible, for instance, a policy may state that police vans in locations groups A and B are notified in case of emergency, but, in case of a bigger threat this policy can be changed or overwritten with police vans in groups A, B C and

D. Our model assumes that no policies or attributes are changed during an activity evaluation.

Some activities will need multi-level policy evaluation and may include user privacy preferences. For instance, a user must be allowed to decide if he wants to share data from car sensors or whether wants to get marketing advertisements. Each activity will evaluate required system and user policies to make final decision.

4.2 Formal Definitions

As shown in Table 1, sources, clustered objects, objects and groups can be directly assigned values from the set of atomic values (denoted by Range(att)) for attribute att in set ATT. Each attribute can be a set or atomic valued, determined by attType function and based on its type, entities can be assigned a single value including null ($\perp$) for an atomic attribute, or multiple values for set-valued attribute from the attribute range. POL is the set of authorization policies defined in the system which will be defined below.

Clustered objects can be members of different groups, based on preferences and requirements. For example, a car is assigned to a location group based on its GPS coordinates. In our model, we assume that a clustered object can be directly assigned to only one group at same hierarchy level (specified by directG function). As we will discuss later that since groups inherit attributes from parent groups, assigning a clustered object to one parent group is sufficient to realize attributes inheritance. Smart cars have sensors and applications installed in them, which can also be accessed by different sources. Therefore, parentCO function determines the clustered object to which an object belongs, which is a one to many mapping i.e an object can only belong to one CO while a CO can have multiple objects. Further, group hierarchy GH (shown as self loop on G), is defined using a partial order relation on G and denoted by $\geq_g$, where $g_1 \geq_g g_2$ signifies g_1 is child group of g_2 and g_1 inherits all the attributes of g_2. Function parentG computes the set of parent groups in hierarchy for a child group.

The benefit to introduce groups is ease of administration where multiple attributes can be assigned or removed from member clustered objects with single administrative operation. Group hierarchy enables attributes inheritance from parent to child groups. Therefore, in case of set valued attributes, the effective attribute att of a group g_i (denoted by $effG_{att}(g_i)$) is the union of directly assigned values for attribute att and the effective values for att for all its parent groups in group hierarchy. This definition is well formed since $\geq_g$ is a partial order. For a maximal group g_j in this ordering, we have $effG_{att}(g_j) = att(g_j)$, giving base cases for this recursive definition. The effective attribute values of clustered object for attribute att (stated as $effCO_{att}$) will then be the directly assigned values for att and the effective attribute values of att for the group to which CO is directly assigned (by directG). Similarly, in addition to direct attributes, sensors in car can inherit attributes from the car itself (eg. make, model, location), $effO_{att}$ calculates these effective attributes of objects. For set valued attributes, union operation will be sufficient which is not true for atomic attributes. In case of groups, the most recently updated non-null attribute values in parent groups will overwrite the values of child group as defined in Table 1. For example, if the most recent value updated in one of the parent groups for Deer_Threat attribute is 'ON', this value will

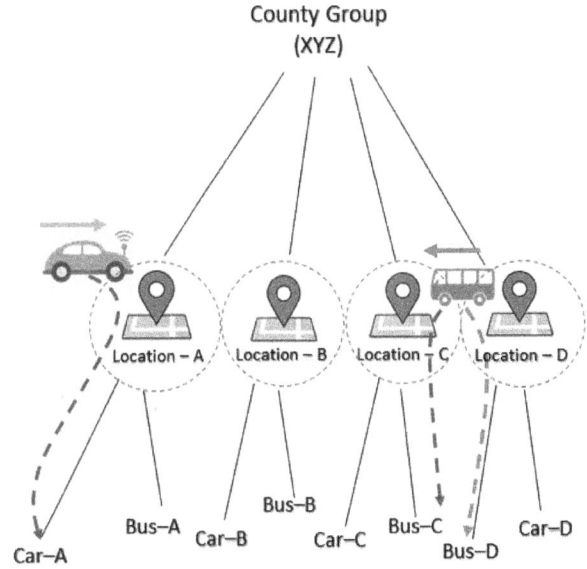

Figure 5: Groups Hierarchy in AWS

trickle to the child group. It should be noted that overwriting with the most recently updated value in groups is one of the many approaches to inherit atomic attributes, but for the dynamic nature of smart cars ecosystem, we believe this is most appropriate. Clustered object inherits non-null atomic value from its direct parent group as stated by $effCO_{att}(co) = effG_{att}(directG(co))$. In case of objects, parent clustered object will overwrite non-null atomic attributes. For atomic attributes, if the parent(s) has null value for an attribute, the entity (group, clustered object or object) will retain its directly assigned value without any overwrite.

Authorization functions are defined for each operation op $\in$ OP, which are policies defined in the system. POL is the set of all authorization functions, $Auth_{op}(s : S, ob : CO \cup O \cup G)$, which specify the conditions under which source s $\in$ S can execute operation op $\in$ OP on object ob $\in CO \cup O \cup G$. Such policies include privacy preferences set by users for individual clustered object, objects and groups or can be system wide by security administrators. The conditions can be specified as propositional logic formula using policy language defined in Table 1. Multiple policies must be satisfied before an activity is allowed to perform. Authorization function, Authorization(a : A, s : S), where an activity a $\in$ A is allowed by source s $\in$ S, specifies the system level, user privacy policies or other relevant policies returning true for an activity to succeed.

$CV\text{-}ABAC_G$ is an attribute-based access control model which satisfies fine-grained authorization needs of dynamic, location oriented and time sensitive services and applications in cloud assisted smart cars ecosystem. The model supports personalized privacy controls by utilizing individual user policies and attributes, along with dynamic groups assignment. Our model assumes that the information and attributes shared by source and object entities are trusted, for instance, location coordinates sent by a car are correct, and uses this shared information to make access and notification decisions. How to ensure that the information is from a trusted source or is correct is out of the scope of this work.

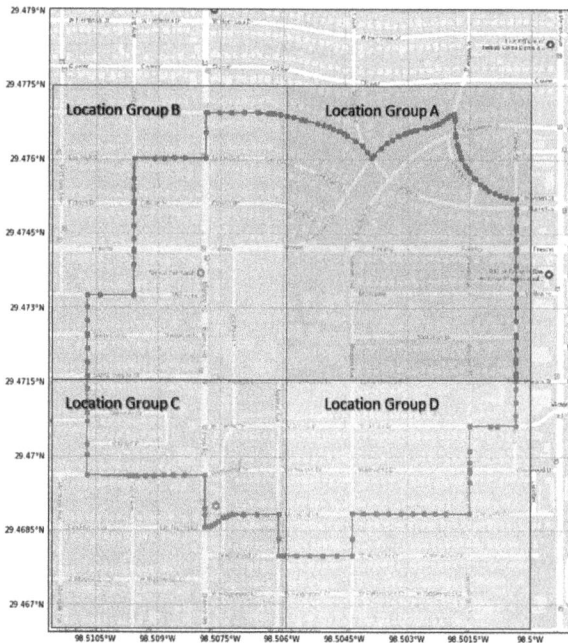

Figure 6: Vehicle GPS Coordinates and Groups Demarcation

5 CV-ABAC$_G$ ENFORCEMENT IN AWS

In this section, we present a proof of concept demonstration of CV-ABAC$_G$ model by enforcing a use case of smart cars using AWS IoT service [5]. The implementation will demonstrate how dynamic groups assignment and multi-layer authorization policies required in connected vehicle ecosystem can be realized in AWS. We have used simulations to reflect real connected smart vehicles, however, it does not undermine the plausibility, use and advantage of our proposed model as further elaborated in following discussion. It should be noted that no long term vehicle data including real-time GPS coordinates are collected in central cloud, which mitigates user privacy concerns and encourages wide adoption of the model.

5.1 Description of Use Cases

Location based alerts and notifications are important in smart cars applications and motivate our use cases. We will build upon our defined group hierarchy in AWS shown in Figure 5. Our implementation will enforce access controls and service notification relevance in following use cases:

Deer Threat Notification - Smart infrastructure in the city can sense the surrounding environment and notify group(s) regarding the change. In this use case, a motion sensor senses deers in the area and changes Deer_Threat attribute of location group to ON which in-turn sends alerts to all member vehicles in that location. Similar, implementation can be done in case of accident notification, speed limit warning or location based marketing.

Car-Pooling - A traveller needs a ride to Location-A. Using a mobile application, he sends car-pooling requests to vehicles in his vicinity which are heading to the destination location asked by the traveller. The request is received by AWS cloud, which computes location and appropriate groups based on the coordinates of the

```
('Received new coordinates from:', 'Vehicle-1')
Sun May 27 02:56:30 2018
  Location A
     Car-A : [u'Vehicle-1', u'Vehicle-2']
     Bus-A : []
  Location B
     Car-B : []
     Bus-B : [u'Vehicle-6']
  Location C
     Car-C : [u'Vehicle-3', u'Vehicle-4']
     Bus-C : []
  Location D
     Car-D : []
     Bus-D : [u'Vehicle-5']
```

Figure 7: Dynamic Groups and Vehicles in AWS

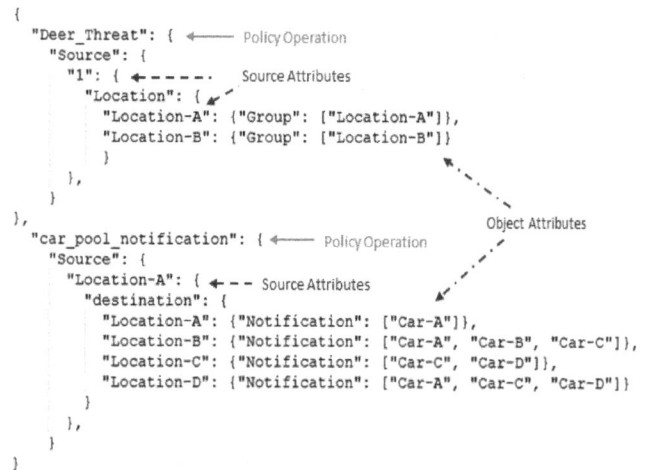

```
{
  "Deer_Threat": {        Policy Operation
    "Source": {
      "1": {              Source Attributes
        "Location": {
          "Location-A": {"Group": ["Location-A"]},
          "Location-B": {"Group": ["Location-B"]}
        }
      },
    }
  },
  "car_pool_notification": {    Policy Operation
    "Source": {
      "Location-A": {            Source Attributes
        "destination": {
          "Location-A": {"Notification": ["Car-A"]},
          "Location-B": {"Notification": ["Car-A", "Car-B", "Car-C"]},
          "Location-C": {"Notification": ["Car-C", "Car-D"]},
          "Location-D": {"Notification": ["Car-A", "Car-C", "Car-D"]}
        }
      },
    }
}
```
Object Attributes

Figure 8: Attribute Based Policies in AWS

requester, to publish notifications to nearby cars. All the members of group Car-A, B, C or D can get the request, but some cars may not want to be part of car-pooling, or do not want some requestors to join them because of ratings. User policies will be also checked before a driver is notified of likely car-pool customer.

5.2 Prototype Implementation

AWS implementation of our model in these use-cases involves two phases: administrative phase and operational phase. Administrative part involves creation of groups hierarchy, dynamic assignment of moving vehicles to different location and sub-groups, attributes inheritance from parent to child groups and to group members, and attributes modification of entities. Operational part covers how groups are used to scope down the number of vehicles who receive messages or notifications from different sources. Both these phases involve multi-layer access control polices. We created an ABAC policy decision (PDP) and enforcement point (PEP) [34], and implemented our external policy evaluation engine which is hooked with AWS to enable attribute-based authorization.

Administrative Phase: We created a group hierarchy in AWS as shown in Figure 5. In this hierarchy, County-XYZ is divided into four disjoint Location-A, B, C and D groups, with each having Car and Bus subgroups for vehicle type car or bus. We created 10

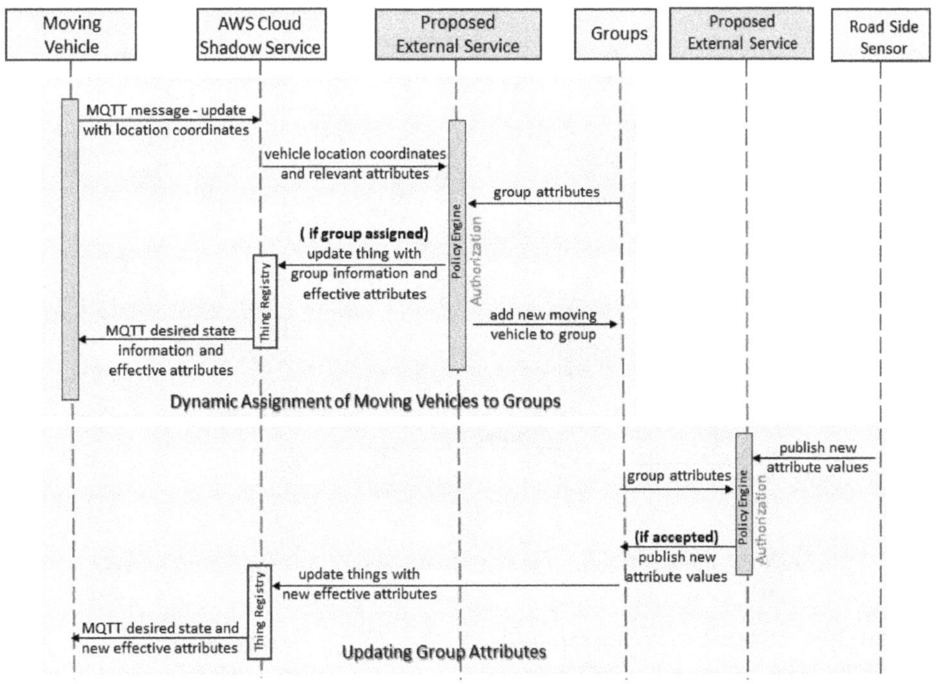

Figure 9: Sequence Diagram for Dynamic Groups and Attributes Assignment in AWS

vehicles and simulated their movement using a python script which publishes MQTT message to shadows of these vehicles with current GPS coordinates (generated using Google API [10]) iterated over green dots shown in Figure 6. The area was demarcated into four locations and a moving vehicle belongs to a subgroup in one of these groups. Assuming current location of Vehicle-1 as Location-D, and it publishes MQTT message with payload:

```
{"state": {"reported": {"Latitude": "29.4769353",
                    "Longitude":"-98.5018237"}}}
```

to AWS topic: $aws/things/Vehicle-1/shadow/update, its new location changes to Location-A and since we defined the vehicle type as car, it is assigned to Car-A group under Location-A as shown by snippet in Figure 7. Both attributes, vehicle type and current coordinates of vehicle, are used to dynamically assign groups, which is important in moving smart vehicles. These functionalities are implemented as a stand alone service (can be enforced as a Lambda service [6] function) using Boto [7] which is the AWS SDK for Python. Further, in case of deer threat notification use-case, we simulated a location-sensor which senses deers in the area and updates the attribute 'Deer_Threat' of location group to 'ON' or 'OFF', which is then notified to all members of location and its subgroups. We defined an attribute-based policy to control which sensors can change the 'Deer_Threat' attribute of location groups. As shown in Figure 8, our policy for Deer_Threat operation checks that a motion sensor with ID = '1' and current groups of Location-A can update the attribute Deer_Threat for group Location-A, and if sensor is relocated to Location-B it can update attribute for Location-B group only. This policy ensures that the sensor must be in that location group for which it is updating Deer_Threat attribute.

The complete sequence of events performed in AWS along with our stand-alone service for the administrative phase is shown in Figure 9. A moving vehicle updates its coordinates to AWS shadow service, which along with attributes of vehicles and location groups determines if the vehicle can be member of the group using our external enforcement service. If authorization policy allows vehicle to be a member of group, the vehicle and group is notified and vehicle inherits all attributes of its newly assigned group. Similarly, if attribute 'Deer_Threat' of group is allowed (by authorization policy) to be changed by the location sensor, the new values are propagated to all its members. We implemented attribute inheritance from parent to child groups through our service using update_thing_group and update_thing methods. In our use-case attributes inheritance exist from Location-A to all both subgroups Car-A and Bus-A, and to vehicles in Car-A and Bus-A. Therefore, when attribute 'Deer_Threat' is set to ON in group Location-A, its new attributes using Boto describe_thing_group command are:

```
{'Center-Latitude': '29.4745', 'Center-Longitude':
            '-98.503','Deer_Threat': 'ON'}
```

This inherits the attributes to Car-A child group whose effective attributes will now be:

```
{'Center-Latitude': '29.4745', 'Center-Longitude':
'-98.503','Deer_Threat': 'ON', 'Location': 'A'}
```

As shown in Figure 7, both Vehicle-1 and Vehicle-2 as member of Car-A, the effective attributes of Vehicle-2 are:

```
{'Center-Latitude': '29.4745', 'Center-Longitude':
'-98.503','Deer_Threat': 'ON', 'Location': 'A',
'Type': 'Car', 'VIN': '9246572903752', 'thingName':
'Vehicle-2'}
```

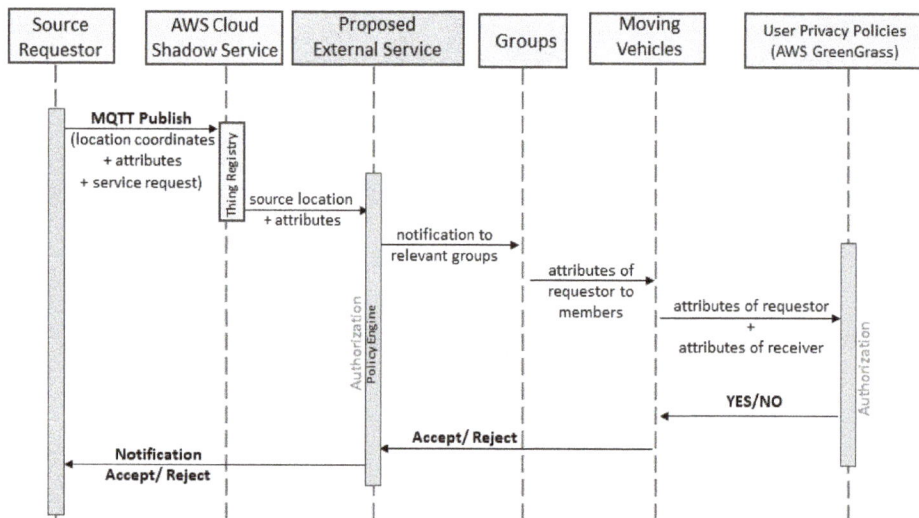

Figure 10: Sequence Diagram for Attributes Based Authorization in AWS

Operational Phase: In this phase, attribute-based policies are used to restrict service and notification activities which may require single or multi-level policies along with user preferences. In car-pooling use case, we defined policies to restrict notifications to only a subset of relevant vehicles in specific locations. We simulated requestor in AWS needing car-pool. It has attribute 'destination' with value in Location-A, B, C or D. Requestor sends current and destination location as MQTT message to AWS topic `$aws/things/Requestor/shadow/update` which based on these attributes determine subgroups to which service requests is sent.

```
{"state": {"reported": {"policy":
 "car_pool_notification", "source": "Location-A",
 "destination": "Location-B"}}}
```

The policy for `car_pool_notification` operation (shown in Figure 8) suggests that if current location of source requestor is 'Location-A' and destination location is somewhere in 'Location-A' then all members of sub-group Car-A should be notified. Similarly, if the destination attribute is Location-B, then all members of Car-A, Car-B and Car-C needs notification. In our use-case, all members of these sub-groups are notified. The policy restricts the number of vehicles which will be requested as compared to all vehicles getting irrelevant notification (as they are far from the requestor or are not vehicle type car) and illustrates the importance of location-centric smart car ecosystem. Similarly, location-based marketing can be restricted and policies can be defined to control such notifications.

User privacy policies take into effect once the subset of vehicles is calculated. These policies encapsulate user preferences, for instance, in car pooling a particular driver is not going to the destination requested by the requestor in his request or a driver do not want restaurant advertisements, therefore such notifications will not be displayed on his car dashboard. These local policies are implemented using AWS Greengrass [4] which allows to run local lambda functions on the device (in our case a connected vehicle) to enable edge computing facility, an important requirement in real-time smart car applications and enforce privacy policies. Once

Number of Requests	Policy Enforcer Execution Time (in ms)	nth Request	Cars Notified	
			With ABAC Policy	Without Policy
10	0.0501	41st	2	5
20	0.1011	42nd	3	5
30	0.1264	43rd	5	5
40	0.1630	44th	3	5
50	0.1999	45th	2	5
		46th	3	5

Figure 11: Policy Enforcement Time and Scoping

accepted by drivers, a SNS (AWS Simple Notification Service) [8] message can be triggered for requestor from accepting vehicles along with name and vehicle number. The sequence of events for car-pooling activity and multi-layer authorization policies together with user personal preferences is shown in Figure 10.

Our proposed external service to implement ABAC policy decision and evaluation helps achieve fine grained authorization needed in smart cars ecosystem. The implementation also demonstrates dynamic groups assignment based on mobile vehicle GPS coordinates and attributes along with groups based attributes inheritance which offer administrative benefits in enforcing an ABAC model. In this entire implementation, no persistent data from moving vehicles is collected or stored by the central authority hosted cloud which reaffirms its privacy preserving benefits. Note that the use-cases discussed to enforce CV-ABAC$_G$ are not real-time and can bear some latency due to the use of cloud infrastructure. Although our CV-ABAC$_G$ enforcement in AWS reflects its use for cloud based applications, we believe similar model can also be implemented in edge (or fog) systems as well to cater more real-time use-cases.

5.3 Performance Evaluation

We evaluated the performance of our proposed CV-ABAC$_G$ model in AWS and provide different metrics when no policies were used

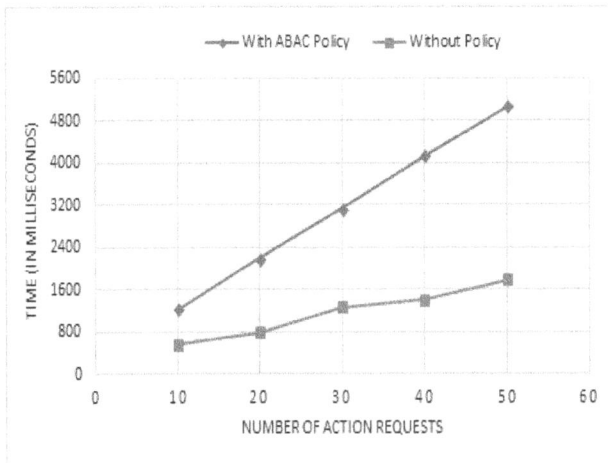

Figure 12: Performance Evaluation

against our implemented ABAC policies for the car-pooling notification use-case. As shown in Figure 11, our external policy evaluation engine has average time (in milliseconds) to decide on car-pooling service requests and provide the subset of cars which are notified. This scoping ensures the service relevance as without a policy all 5 vehicles were sent car-pool request (even when one was 20 miles away from the requestor), whereas with attribute based policies only nearby cars are notified. The performance graph shown in Figure 12 compares no policy execution time (red line) against implemented ABAC policy (blue line). Since, in our experiments the policy (shown in Figure 8) evaluated for each access requests is the same, we get a linear graph as the number of access requests increase the number of times the policy is evaluated and so its total evaluation time. Some variation in red line is because of the network latency time to access AWS cloud, although this can change based on the communication technologies used by vehicles including 3G, LTE, cellular or DSRC [9]. Clearly, this external policy engine does have some impact on the performance against no policy when used with number of vehicles. However, we believe when used in city wide scenario this time will be overshadowed by the notification time to all vehicles against a subset of vehicles provided by the policy evaluation engine. Our model and the use-case is focused to ensure service relevance to moving drivers on road which is well achieved even with a little tradeoff.

We understand that practical smart city transportation scenarios will have hundreds and thousands of moving cars (and other connected entities) associated to cloud (or fog infrastructures) and interacting. Although a detailed performance evaluation is eventually necessary by simulating large set of vehicles, we believe that our proof of concept in AWS is to showcase the practical viability and use of fine grained attribute based security policies in context of smart cars ecosystem, without the need to capture large set of data points from real world traffic scenarios spread across wide geographic area and sizable on-road moving vehicles. Such scaled setting will only stress the entire system without reflecting any change in security policy evaluation. We consider more detailed performance analysis as an extension to this work.

6 SUMMARY

This research work presents a fine-grained attribute-based access control model for time-sensitive and location-centric smart cars ecosystem. Our model introduces the novel notion of dynamic groups in relation to connected vehicles and emphasizes its relevance in this context. Besides considering system wide authorization policies, this model also supports personal preference policies for different users, which is required in today's privacy conscious world. Several real world use-cases are discussed and a proof of concept implementation of our CV-ABAC$_G$ model is shown in Amazon Web Services (AWS) cloud platform. This implementation demonstrates how moving vehicles can be dynamically assigned to location and sub-groups defined in the system based on the current GPS coordinates, vehicle-type and other attributes, besides the use of attribute based security policies in distributed and mobile connected cars ecosystem. Performance has been evaluated against time taken to determine activity access control decision when groups and ABAC policies are used against when no security policies are available. We envision to extend our model to introduce in-vehicle security and built risk aware trust-based models for smart vehicles environment. Also a more detailed evaluation and performance analysis of this model is needed to cover large set of moving vehicles, which is an enhancement to this work. Further, location privacy preserving approaches such as homomorphic encryption and other anonymity techniques can be used to complement and extend our model which can mitigate location sharing concerns without effecting its advantages and application. V2X trusted DSRC communication and privacy concerns also need further investigation, which we plan to explore as part of our future work in intelligent transportation.

ACKNOWLEDGEMENTS

This work is partially supported by NSF CREST Grant HRD-1736209, NSF grant CNS-1423481, and DoD ARL Grant W911NF-15-1-0518.

REFERENCES

[1] 2014. *Connected Vehicles and Your Privacy.* https://www.its.dot.gov/factsheets/pdf/Privacy_factsheet.pdf
[2] 2017. *2017 Roundup Of Internet Of Things Forecasts.* https://www.forbes.com/sites/louiscolumbus/2017/12/10/2017-roundup-of-internet-of-things-forecasts/#67005b6a1480 [Online; Accessed: 2018-05-03].
[3] 2018. *AWS.* https://aws.amazon.com/ [Online; Accessed: 2018-05-09].
[4] 2018. *AWS Greengrass.* https://aws.amazon.com/greengrass/ [Online; Accessed: 2018-05-27].
[5] 2018. *AWS-IoT.* https://aws.amazon.com/iot/ [Online; Accessed: 2018-05-09].
[6] 2018. *AWS Lambda.* https://aws.amazon.com/lambda/ [Online; Accessed: 2018-05-20].
[7] 2018. *AWS SDK for Python (Boto3).* https://aws.amazon.com/sdk-for-python/ [Online; Accessed: 2018-05-23].
[8] 2018. *AWS Simple Notification Service.* https://aws.amazon.com/sns/ [Online; Accessed: 2018-05-20].
[9] 2018. *DSRC.* https://en.wikipedia.org/wiki/Dedicated_short-range_communications [Online; Accessed: 2018-08-07].
[10] 2018. *Google Maps Platform.* https://cloud.google.com/maps-platform/ [Online; Accessed: 2018-05-09].
[11] 2018. *Vehicular ad hoc networks.* https://en.wikipedia.org/wiki/Vehicular_ad_hoc_network [Online; Accessed: 2018-05-30].
[12] M. Aazam and et al. 2014. Cloud of Things: Integrating Internet of Things and cloud computing and the issues involved. In *Proc. of IBCAST.* 414–419.
[13] A. Al-Fuqaha and et al. 2015. Internet of things: A survey on enabling technologies, protocols, and applications. *IEEE Comm. Surveys & Tutorials* (2015), 2347–2376.
[14] Asma Alshehri and Ravi Sandhu. 2016. Access control models for cloud-enabled internet of things: A proposed architecture and research agenda. In *Proc. of IEEE CIC.* 530–538.

[15] Luigi Atzori, Antonio Iera, and Giacomo Morabito. 2010. The internet of things: A survey. *Computer networks* 54, 15 (2010), 2787–2805.
[16] Jim Barbaresso and et al. 2014. USDOT's Intelligent Transportation Systems ITS Strategic Plan 2015- 2019. (2014).
[17] S. Bhatt, F. Patwa, and R. Sandhu. 2017. An Access Control Framework for Cloud-Enabled Wearable Internet of Things. In *Proc. of IEEE CIC*. 328–338.
[18] Smriti Bhatt, Farhan Patwa, and Ravi Sandhu. 2017. Access Control Model for AWS Internet of Things. In *Proc. of NSS*. Springer, 721–736.
[19] A. Botta, W. de Donato, V. Persico, and A. PescapÄĺ. 2014. On the Integration of Cloud Computing and Internet of Things. In *Proc. of IEEE FiCLOUD*. 23–30.
[20] Mohamed Eltoweissy and et al. 2010. Towards Autonomous Vehicular Clouds. In *Ad Hoc Networks*. Springer, 1–16.
[21] ENISA. 2017. *Cyber Security and Resilience of smart cars: Good practices and recommendations.* https://www.enisa.europa.eu/publications/cyber-security-and-resilience-of-smart-cars [Online; Accessed: 2018-01-27].
[22] David F Ferraiolo, Ravi Sandhu, Serban Gavrila, D Richard Kuhn, and Ramaswamy Chandramouli. 2001. Proposed NIST standard for role-based access control. *ACM Transactions on Information and System Security (TISSEC)* 4, 3 (2001), 224–274.
[23] US GAO. 2016, March. Vehicle Cybersecurity . *GAO-16-350* (2016, March). https://www.gao.gov/assets/680/676064.pdf
[24] M. Gerla, E. Lee, G. Pau, and U. Lee. 2014. Internet of vehicles: From intelligent grid to autonomous cars and vehicular clouds. In *Proc. of IEEE WF-IoT*. 241–246.
[25] J. Gubbi and et al. 2013. Internet of Things (IoT): A vision, architectural elements, and future directions. *Future generation computer systems* 29, 7 (2013), 1645–1660.
[26] M. Gupta and et al. 2017. Multi-Layer Authorization Framework for a Representative Hadoop Ecosystem Deployment. In *Proc. of ACM SACMAT*. 183–190.
[27] Maanak Gupta, Farhan Patwa, and Ravi Sandhu. 2017. Object-Tagged RBAC Model for the Hadoop Ecosystem. In *Proc. of DBSec*. Springer, 63–81.
[28] Maanak Gupta, Farhan Patwa, and Ravi Sandhu. 2017. POSTER: Access control model for the Hadoop Ecosystem. In *Proceedings of the 22nd ACM on Symposium on Access Control Models and Technologies*. ACM, 125–127.
[29] Maanak Gupta, Farhan Patwa, and Ravi Sandhu. 2018. An Attribute-Based Access Control Model for Secure Big Data Processing in Hadoop Ecosystem. In *Proc. of the Third ACM Workshop on Attribute-Based Access Control*. 13–24.
[30] Maanak Gupta and Ravi Sandhu. 2016. The GURA_G Administrative Model for User and Group Attribute Assignment. In *Proc. of NSS*. Springer, 318–332.
[31] Maanak Gupta and Ravi Sandhu. 2018. Authorization Framework for Secure Cloud Assisted Connected Cars and Vehicular Internet of Things. In *Proc. of ACM SACMAT*. 193–204.
[32] Maanak Gupta and Ravi Sandhu. 2018. POSTER: Access Control Needs in Smart Cars. https://www.ieee-security.org/TC/SP2018/poster-abstracts/oakland2018-paper26-poster-abstract.pdf. [Online; Accessed: 2018-10-04].
[33] Per Hallgren, Martin Ochoa, and Andrei Sabelfeld. 2015. Innercircle: A parallelizable decentralized privacy-preserving location proximity protocol. In *Privacy, Security and Trust (PST), 2015 13th Annual Conference on*. IEEE, 1–6.
[34] Vincent C Hu, David Ferraiolo, Rick Kuhn, Arthur R Friedman, Alan J Lang, Margaret M Cogdell, Adam Schnitzer, Kenneth Sandlin, Robert Miller, and Karen

Scarfone. 2014. Guide to attribute based access control (ABAC) definition and considerations. *NIST Special Publication 800-162* (2014).
[35] Vincent C Hu, D Richard Kuhn, and David F Ferraiolo. 2015. Attribute-based access control. *IEEE Computer* 2 (2015), 85–88.
[36] Rasheed Hussain and et al. 2012. Rethinking vehicular communications: Merging VANET with cloud computing. In *Proc. of IEEE CloudCom*. 606–609.
[37] Xin Jin, Ram Krishnan, and Ravi Sandhu. 2012. A unified attribute-based access control model covering DAC, MAC and RBAC. In *DBSec*. Springer, 41–55.
[38] R. Lea and M. Blackstock. 2014. City Hub: A Cloud-Based IoT Platform for Smart Cities. In *Proc. of IEEE CloudCom*. 799–804.
[39] Arvind Narayanan, Narendran Thiagarajan, Mugdha Lakhani, Michael Hamburg, Dan Boneh, et al. 2011. Location Privacy via Private Proximity Testing.. In *NDSS*, Vol. 11.
[40] NHTSA. 2016. NHTSA and Vehicle CyberSecurity. *NHTSA Report* (2016).
[41] NHTSA. 2016, October. Cybersecurity Best Practices for Modern Vehicles. *NHTSA Report No. DOT HS 812 333* (2016, October).
[42] M. Nitti and et al. 2016. The virtual object as a major element of the internet of things: a survey. *IEEE Comm. Surveys & Tutorials* (2016), 1228–1240.
[43] Stephan Olariu and et al. 2011. Taking VANET to the clouds. *International Journal of Pervasive Computing and Communications* 7, 1 (2011), 7–21.
[44] Jaehong Park, Ravi Sandhu, and Yuan Cheng. 2011. Acon: Activity-centric access control for social computing. In *Proc. of IEEE ARES*. 242–247.
[45] Jaehong Park, Ravi Sandhu, and Yuan Cheng. 2011. A user-activity-centric framework for access control in online social networks. *IEEE Internet Computing* 15, 5 (2011), 62–65.
[46] Ravi S Sandhu, Edward J Coyne, Hal L Feinstein, and Charles E Youman. 1996. Role-based access control models. *Computer* 29, 2 (1996), 38–47.
[47] Ravi S Sandhu and Pierangela Samarati. 1994. Access control: principle and practice. *IEEE communications magazine* 32, 9 (1994), 40–48.
[48] Daniel Servos and Sylvia L Osborn. 2014. HGABAC: Towards a Formal Model of Hierarchical Attribute-Based Access Control. In *International Symposium on Foundations and Practice of Security*. Springer, 187–204.
[49] European Union. 2017. *Certificate Policy for Deployment and Operation of European Cooperative Intelligent Transport Systems (C-ITS)*. https://ec.europa.eu/transport/sites/transport/files/c-its_certificate_policy_release_1.pdf
[50] European Union. 2017. *Security Policy & Governance Framework for Deployment and Operation of European Cooperative Intelligent Transport Systems (C-ITS)*. https://ec.europa.eu/transport/sites/transport/files/c-its_security_policy_release_1.pdf
[51] USAToday. 2017. *Chinese group hacks a Tesla for the second year in a row.*
[52] USDOT. 2016. *Securty Credential Management System.* https://www.its.dot.gov/resources/scms.htm [Online; Accessed: 2018-01-13].
[53] Md Whaiduzzaman and et al. 2014. A survey on vehicular cloud computing. *Journal of Network and Computer Applications* 40 (2014), 325–344.
[54] Wired. 2015. *Hackers Remotely Kill a Jeep on the Highway-With Me in It.*
[55] Ge Zhong, Ian Goldberg, and Urs Hengartner. 2007. Louis, lester and pierre: Three protocols for location privacy. In *International Workshop on Privacy Enhancing Technologies*. Springer, 62–76.

A Study of Data Store-based Home Automation

Kaushal Kafle, Kevin Moran, Sunil Manandhar, Adwait Nadkarni, Denys Poshyvanyk

William & Mary, Williamsburg, VA, USA

{kkafle,kpmoran,sunil,nadkarni,denys}@cs.wm.edu

ABSTRACT

Home automation platforms provide a new level of convenience by enabling consumers to automate various aspects of physical objects in their homes. While the convenience is beneficial, security flaws in the platforms or integrated third-party products can have serious consequences for the integrity of a user's physical environment. In this paper we perform a systematic security evaluation of two popular smart home platforms, Google's Nest platform and Philips Hue, that implement home automation "routines" (*i.e.*, trigger-action programs involving apps and devices) via manipulation of state variables in a *centralized data store*. Our semi-automated analysis examines, among other things, platform access control enforcement, the rigor of non-system enforcement procedures, and the potential for misuse of routines. This analysis results in *ten* key findings with serious security implications. For instance, we demonstrate the potential for the misuse of smart home routines in the Nest platform to perform a lateral privilege escalation, illustrate how Nest's product review system is ineffective at preventing multiple stages of this attack that it examines, and demonstrate how emerging platforms may fail to provide even bare-minimum security by allowing apps to arbitrarily add/remove other apps from the user's smart home. Our findings draw attention to the unique security challenges of platforms that execute routines via centralized data stores, and highlight the importance of enforcing security by design in emerging home automation platforms.

KEYWORDS

Smart Home; Routines; Lateral Privilege Escalation; Overprivilege

ACM Reference Format:

Kaushal Kafle, Kevin Moran, Sunil Manandhar, Adwait Nadkarni, Denys Poshyvanyk. 2019. A Study of Data Store-based Home Automation. In *Ninth ACM Conference on Data and Application Security and Privacy (CODASPY '19), March 25–27, 2019, Richardson, TX, USA.* ACM, New York, NY, USA, 12 pages. https://doi.org/10.1145/3292006.3300031

1 INTRODUCTION

Internet-connected, embedded computing objects known as *smart home products* have become extremely popular with consumers. The utility and practicality afforded by these devices has spurred tremendous market interest, with over 20 billion smart home products projected to be in use by 2020 [13]. The diversity of these

products is staggering, ranging from small physical devices with embedded computers such as smart locks and light bulbs, to full fledged appliances such as refrigerators and HVAC systems. In the modern computing landscape, smart home devices are unique as they provide an often imperceptible bridge between the digital and physical worlds by connecting physical objects to digital services via the Internet, allowing the user to conveniently automate their home. However, because many of these products are tied to the user's security or privacy (*e.g.*, door locks, cameras), it is important to understand the attack surface of such devices and platforms, in order to build practical defenses without sacrificing utility.

As the market for smart home devices has continued to mature, a new software paradigm has emerged to facilitate smart home automation via the interactions between smart home devices and the apps that control them. These interactions may be expressed as *routines*, which are sequences of app and device actions that are executed upon one or more triggers, *i.e.*, an instance of the trigger-action paradigm in the smart home. Routines are becoming the foundational unit of home automation [8, 40, 48, 49], and as a result, it is natural to characterize existing platforms based on how routines are implemented.

If we categorize available platforms based on how routines are facilitated, we observe two broad categories: (1) API-based Smart Home Managers such as Yeti [53], Yonomi [54], IFTTT [18], and Stringify [46] that allow users to chain together a diverse set of devices using third-party APIs exposed by device vendors, and (2) smart home platforms such as Google's Works with Nest [32], Samsung SmartThings [43], and Philips Hue [38] that leverage *centralized data stores* to monitor and maintain the states of IoT devices. We term these platforms as Data Store-Based (DSB) Smart Home Platforms. In DSB platforms, complex routines are executed via reads/writes to state variables in a central data store.

This paper is motivated by a key observation that while routines are supported via centralized data stores in all DSB platforms, there are differences in the manner in which routines are created, observed, and managed by the user. That is, SmartThings encourages users to take full control of creating and managing routines involving third-party apps and devices via the SmartThings app. On the contrary, in Nest, users do not have a centralized perspective of routines at all, and instead, manage routines using third-party apps/devices. This key difference may imply unique security challenges for Nest. Similarly, being a much simpler platform within this category of DSB platforms, Hue represents another unique and interesting instance of the DSB platform paradigm. While prior work has explored the security of routines enabled by a smart home manager (*i.e.*, specifically, IFTTT recipes [47]), the permission enforcement and application security in the SmartThings platform [12], and the side-effects of SmartThings SmartApps [4], there is a notable gap in current research. Namely, prior studies do not evaluate the potential fo *adversarial* misuse of routines, which are the essence of DSB platforms, and by extension, home automation.

Contributions: This paper performs a systematic security analysis b sm e b the less studied, but widely popular, data store-based smart home platforms, *i.e.*, Nest and Hue, helping to close the existing gap in prior research. In particular, we evaluate (1) the access control enforcement in the platforms themselves, (2) the robustness b b her non-system enforcement (*e.g.*, product reviews in Nest), (3) the use and mo e importantly the *misuse* of routines via manipulation of the data store by low-integ ity devices, [1] and finally, (4) the security of applications that integ ate into these platforms. To our k owledge, this paper is the first to analyze this relatively new class of smart home platforms, in particular the Nest and Hue platforms, and to provide a holistic analysis of routines, their use, and potential fo their misuse in DSB platforms. Moreover, this paper is the first to analyze the accuracy of app-defined permission prompts, which form one of the few sources of access control information for the user. Our novel findings ($\mathcal{F}_1 \rightarrow \mathcal{F}_{10}$), summarized as follows, demonstrate the unique security challenges faced by DSB platforms at the cost of seamless automation:

- **Misuse of routines** – The permission model in Nest is fine-grained and enforced according to specifications ($\mathcal{F}_1$), giving low-integrity third-party apps/devices (*e.g.*, a switch) little room for directly modifying the data store variables of high-integrity devices (*e.g.*, security cameras). However, the routines supported by Nest allow low-integrity devices/apps to indirectly modify the state of high-integrity devices, by modifying the shared variables that both hi /low integrity devices rely on ($\mathcal{F}_4$).

- **Lack of systematic defenses** – Nest does not employ transitive access cn trb enfo cement to prevent indirect modificatin b security-sensitive data store variables; instead, it relies on a product review of application artifacts before allowing API access. We discover that the product review process is insufficient and may nb prevent malicious exploitation of routines; *i.e.*, the review mandates that apps prompt the user before modifying certain variables, but does not validate *what* the prompt contain, allowing apps to deceive users into providing consent ($\mathcal{F}_5$). Moreover, permission descriptions provided by apps during authorization are also often incorrect or misleading ($\mathcal{F}_6$, $\mathcal{F}_9$), which demonstrates that malicious apps may easily find ways to gain more priv lege than necessary ($\mathcal{F}_7$), circumventing both users and the Nest product review ($\mathcal{F}_8$).

- **Lateral privilege escalation** – We find that smart home apps, particularly those that connect to Nest and have permissions to access security-sensitive data store variables, have a significantly high rate of SSL vulnerabilities ($\mathcal{F}_{10}$). We combine these SSL flaws with the findings discussed previously (specifically $\mathcal{F}_4 \rightarrow \mathcal{F}_9$) and demonstrate a novel form of a *lateral* privilege escalation attack. That is, we compromise a low-integrity app that has access to the user's Nest smart home (*e.g.*, a TP Link Kasa switch), use the com romie d app to change the state of the data store to trigger a security-sensitive routine, and indirectly chang the state of a high-integrity Nest device (*e.g.*, the Nest security camera). This

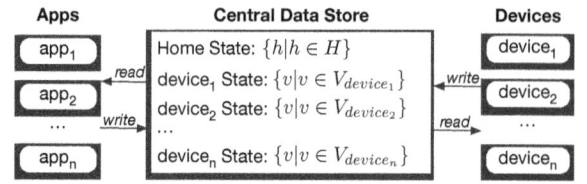

Figure 1: The general architecture of home automation platforms that leverage centralized data stores. Note that H is the universe of all home state variables, and V_{device_i} is the universe of all state variables specific to $device_i$

attack can be used to deceive the Nest Cam into determining that the user is hom when they are actually away, and prevent it from monitoring the home in the user's absence.

- **Lack of bare minimum protections** – Unlike Nest, the access control enforcement of Hue is woefully inadequate. Third-party apps that have been added to a user's Hue platform may arbitrarily add other third-party apps without user consent, despite an existing policy that the user must consent by physically pressing a button ($\mathcal{F}_2$). Making matters worse, an app may *remove* other apps integrated with the platform by exploiting unprotected data store variables in Hue ($\mathcal{F}_3$). These vulnerabilities may allow an app with seemingly useful functionality (*i.e.*, a Trojan [20]) to install malicious add-ons in a manner invisible to the user, and replace the user's integrated apps with its m licious sub titutes.

The rest of the paper is structured as follows: Section 2 describes the key attributes of DSB platforms, and provides background. Section 3 provides an overview of our analysis, and Sections 4, 5 and 6 describe our analysis of permission enforcement in Nest and Hue, security ramifications of routines, and security of smart home apps, respectively. Section 7 provides an end-to-end attack, and Section 8 describes the lessons learned. Section 9 describes the vendors' response to our findings. Section 10 describes the threats to validity. Section 11 describes the related work, and Section 12 concludes.

2 HOME AUTOMATION VIA CENTRALIZED DATA STORES

This section describes the general characteristics of data store-based platforms, *i.e.*, smart platforms that use a *centralized data store* to facilitate ru tines. Fb lowing this general descriptin , we provide background on two such platforms, namely (1) Google's "Works with Nest" [34] platform (henceforth called "Nest") and (2) the Philips Hue lighting system [37] (henceforth called "Hue"), which serve as the targets of our security analysis. While there are no official statistics on the market adoption of either Nest or Hue, the Android apps for both of the systems have over a million downloads on Google Play [16, 17], indicating significant adoption, and far-reaching security impact of our analysis.

2.1 General Characteristics

Figure 1 describes the general architecture of DSB platforms, consisting of three main components: *apps*, *devices*, and the *centralized data store*. These components generally communicate over the Internet. Additionally, a physical hub that facilitates local communication via protocols such as Zigbee or Z-wave may or may not be included in this setup (*e.g.*, the Hue Bridge); *i.e.*, in a general sense, routines are agnostic of the presence of the hub. Hence, we

---

[1]In the context of our study, we define a device as high-integrity if it is advertised as security-critical by the device vendor (*e.g.*, Nest Cam) while those that are not security-critical are referred to as low-integrity (*e.g.*, Philips Hue lamp).

exclude the hub in Figure 1. Similarly, the apps may either be Web services hosted on the cloud, or mobile apps communicating via Web services. At this juncture, we generalize apps as third-party software interacting with the data store, and provide the specifics for individual platforms in later sections.

The centralized data store facilitates communication among apps and devices via state variables. The data store exposes two types of state variables: (1) *Home* state variables that reflect the general state of the entire smart home (*e.g.*, if the user is at *home/away*, the *devices attached* to the home, the *postal code*), and (2) *Device-specific* state variables that reflect the attributes specific to particular devices (*e.g.*, if the Camera is *streaming*, the *target temperature* of the thermostat, the *battery health* of the smoke alarm).

Apps and devices communicate by reading from or writing to the state variables in the centralized data store. This model allows expressive communication, from simple state updates to indirect trigger-action routines. Consider this simple state update: the user may change the temperature of the thermostat from an app, which in turn *writes* the change to the *target temperature* variable in the data store. The thermostat device receives an update from the data store (*i.e.*, *reads* the *target temperature* state variable), and changes its target temperature accordingly. Further, as stated previously, expressive routines may also be implemented using the data store. For instance, the thermostat may change to its "economy" mode when the home's state changes to *away*. That is, the thermostat's app may detect that the user has left the smart home (*e.g.*, using Geofencing), and *write* to the home state variable *away*. The thermostat may then *read* this change, and switch to its economy mode.

A salient characteristic of DSB platforms is that they lean towards seamless home automation, by automatically interacting with devices and executing complex routines via the centralized data store. However, even within platforms that follow this model (*e.g.*, Samsung SmartThings, Nest, and Hue), our preliminary investigation led to the following *key observations* that motivate a targeted analysis of the Nest and Hue platforms and their apps:

Key Observations: We observe that both Nest and SmartThings execute routines; however, there is a key difference in how routines are managed. SmartThings allows users to create and manage routines from the SmartThings app itself, thereby providing users with a general view of all the routines executing in the home [44]. In contrast, Nest routines are generally implemented as *decentralized* third-party integrations. Third-party products that facilitate routines provide the user with the ability to view and manage them. As a result, the Nest platform does not provide the user with a *centralized view* of the routines that are in place. Due to this lack of user control, Nest smart homes may face unique security risks and challenges, which motivates this security analysis. Similarly, we observe that the Philips Hue platform may be another interesting variant of DSB platforms. That is, Hue integrates *homogeneous* devices related to lighting such as lamps and bulbs, unlike Nest and SmartThings that integrate heterogeneous devices, and represents a drastically simpler (and hence unique) variant of home automation platforms that use centralized data stores. As a result, the analysis of Hue's attack surface has potential to draw attention to other similar, homogeneous platforms, which is especially important considering the fragmentation in the smart home product ecosystem [6]. To

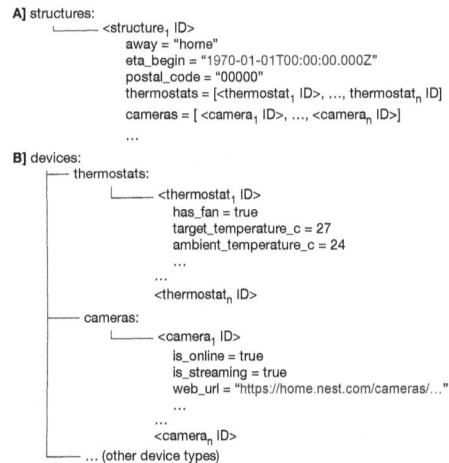

Figure 2: A simplified view of the centralized data store in Nest.

our knowledge, this paper is the first to analyze this relatively new class of smart home platforms, and specifically, Nest and Hue.

2.2 Nest Background

The *Works with Nest* platform integrates a heterogenous set of devices, including devices from Nest (*e.g.*, Nest thermostat, Nest Cam, Nest Protect) as well as from other brands (*e.g.*, Wemo and Kasa switches, Google Home, MyQ Chamberlain garage door opener) [34]. This section describes the key characteristics of Nest, *i.e.*, its data store, its access control model, and routines.

Data store composition: Figure 2 shows a simplified, conceptual view of the centralized data store in Nest. Note that the figure shows a small fraction of the true data store, *i.e.*, only enough to facilitate understanding. Nest implements the data store as a JSON-format document divided into two main top-level sections: *structures* and *devices*. A *structure* represents an entire smart home environment such as a user's home or office, and is defined by various state variables that are global across the smart home (*e.g.*, *Away* to indicate the presence or absence of the user in the structure and the *postal_code* to indicate the home's physical location). The devices are subdivided into device types (*e.g.*, thermostats, cameras, smoke detectors), and there can be many devices of a certain type, as shown in Figure 2. Each device stores its state in variables that are relevant to its type; *e.g.*, a thermostat has state variables for *humidity*, and *target_temperature_c*, whereas a camera has the variables *is_online* and *is_streaming*. Aside from these type-specific variables, devices also have certain variables in common; *e.g.*, the alphanumeric *device ID*, the *structure ID* of the structure in which the device is installed, the device's user-assigned *name*, and *battery_health*.

Access Control in Nest.: Nest treats third-party apps, Web services, and devices that want to integrate with a Nest-based smart home as "products". Each Nest user account has a specific data store assigned to it and any product that requests access to the user's data store needs to be first authorized by the user using OAuth 2.0. Nest defines read or read/write permissions for each of the variables in the data store. Additionally, some variables *e.g.*, the list of all thermostats in the structure are always *read-only*. A product that wants to register with Nest must first declare the permissions that it needs (*e.g.*, *thermostat read*, *thermostat read/write*) in the Nest developer console. When connecting a product to Nest, during the OAuth authorization phase, the user is shown the permissions requested by the product. Once the user grants the permissions, a revocable access token is generated specific to the product, the set of permissions requested, and the particular smart home to which the product is connected. This token is used for subsequent interactions with the data store.

Accessing the Nest data store.: Devices and applications that are connected to a particular smart home (*i.e.,* the user's Nest account) can update data store variables to which they have access, and also subscribe to the changes to the state of the data store. Nest uses the REST approach for these update communications, as well as for apps/devices to modify the data store. The REST endpoints can be accessed through HTTPS by any registered Nest products.

Routines in Nest: The ability of connected devices to observe and write to state variables in the centralized data store facilitates trigger-action routines. However, in Nest, the user cannot create or view routines in a centralized interface (*i.e.,* unlike SmartThings). Instead, apps may provide routines as opt-in features. For example, the Nest smoke alarm's *smoke_alarm_state* variable has three possible values, "ok", "warning", and "emergency". When this variable is changed to "warning", other smart home products (e.g., Somfy Protect [26]) can be configured to trigger and warn the user. Note that in the *Home/Away assist* section of the Nest app settings, users can view a summary of how certain variables (i.e., home or away) affect their Nest-manufactured devices; however, there is no way for users to observe the triggers/apps that change the state of the *away* variable *simultaneously* with the resultant actions, preventing them from fully understanding how routines execute in their home.

2.3 Hue Background

Unlike Nest, which is a platform for heterogeneous devices, Philips Hue deals exclusively with lighting devices such as lamps and bulbs. As a result, the centralized data store of Philips Hue supports much simpler routines. Hue implements its data store as a JSON document with sections related to (1) physical lighting devices, (2) semantic groups of these devices, and (3) global config variables (such as *whitelisted apps* and the *linkbutton*). To connect a third-party management app to a user's existing Hue system, the app identifies a Hue bridge connected to the local network, and requires the user to press a physical button on the bridge. Once this action is completed by the user, the app receives a *username* token that is stored in the *whitelisted* section of the Hue data store. Whitelisted apps can then read and modify data store variables as dictated by Hue's access control policy, which grants all authorized apps the same access regardless of their purported functionality. Our online appendix provides additional details regarding the Hue platform [1].

3 ANALYSIS OVERVIEW

This paper analyzes the security of home automation platforms that rely on centralized data stores (*i.e.,* DSB platforms). Third-party apps are the security principals on such platforms, as they are assigned specific permissions to interact with the integrated devices. That is, as described in Section 2, DSB platforms consist of (1) *third-party apps* that interact with the smart home (*i.e.,* centralized data store and devices) by acquiring (2) *platform permissions*, and execute a complex set of such interactions as (3) *trigger-action routines*. Our

analysis methodology takes these three aspects into consideration, starting with platform permissions, as follows:

A. Analysis of Platform Permissions (Section 4): We analyze the *enforcement* of platform permissions/access control to discover inconsistencies. For this analysis, we automatically build permission maps, and semi-automatically analyze them.

B. Analysis of Routines (Section 5): While analyzing permission enforcement gives us an idea of what individual devices can accomplish with a certain set of permissions, we perform an experimental analysis with real devices to identify the interdependencies among devices and apps through the shared data model, and the ramifications of such interdependencies on the user's security and privacy. Additionally, we notice that Nest does not enforce transitive access control policies to prevent dangerous side-effects of routines, but instead employs a product review process as a defense mechanism. We analyze the effectiveness of this review process using the permission prompts used by existing apps as evidence.

C. Analysis of Third-party Apps (Section 6): We analyze the permission descriptions presented by mobile apps compatible with Nest to identify over-privileged apps, or apps whose permission descriptions are inconsistent with the permission requested. We then analyze the apps for signs of SSL misuse, in order to exploit applications that possess critical permissions, which can be leveraged to indirectly exploit security critical devices in the smart home.

We combine the findings from these three analyses to demonstrate an instance of a *lateral privilege escalation* attack in a smart home (Section 7). That is, we demonstrate how an attacker can compromise a low-integrity device/app integrated into a smart home (*e.g.,* a light bulb), and use routines to perform protected operations on a high-integrity product (e.g., a security camera).

4 EVALUATING PERMISSION ENFORCEMENT

The centralized data store described in Section 2 may contain variables whose secrecy or integrity is crucial; *e.g.,* unprotected write access to the *web_url* field of the camera may allow a malicious app to launch a phishing attack, by replacing the URL in the field with an attacker-controlled one. To understand if appropriate barriers are in place to protect such sensitive variables, we perform an analysis of the permission enforcement in Nest and Hue.

Our approach is to generate and analyze the *permission map* for each platform, *i.e.,* the variables that can be accessed with each permission, and inversely, the permissions needed to access each variable of the data store. Note that while this information should ideally be available in the platform documentation, prior analysis of similar systems has demonstrated that the documentation may not always be complete or correct in this regard [10, 12].

4.1 Generating Permission Maps

We generate the permission map using automated testing as in prior work on Android [10]. We use two separate approaches for Nest and Hue, owing to their disparate access control models.

Approach for Nest: We first created a simulated home environment using the Nest Home Simulator [33], and linked our Nest user account to this simulated smart home. We then created our test Android app, and connected our test app to the simulated home (*i.e.,* our Nest user account) as described in Section 2.2. Note that the simulated smart home is virtually identical to an end-user's setup, such that real devices may be added to it. Using the simulator allows us to investigate the data store information of Nest devices (*e.g.*, the Smoke/CO detector) that we may not have installed.

In order to generate a complete view of the data store, we granted our test app all of the 15 permissions in Nest (*e.g.,Away read/write, Thermostat read*), and read all accompanying information. To build the permission map for Nest's 15 permissions, we created 15 apps, such that each app requested a single unique permission, and registered these apps to our developer account in the Nest developer console. Note that we do not test the effect of permission combinations, as our goal is to test the enforcement of individual permissions, and Nest's simple authorization logic simply provides an app with a union of the privileges of the individual permissions.

We then connected each of the 15 apps to our Nest user account using the procedure described in Section 2.2. We programmed each app to attempt to read and write each variable of the data store (*i.e.*, the previously derived *complete view*). We recorded the outcome of each access, *i.e.*, if it was successful, or an access control denial. In the cases where we experienced non-security errors writing to data store variables (*e.g.*, writing data with an incorrect type), we revised our apps and repeated the test. The outcome of this process was a permission map, *i.e.*, the mapping of each permission to the data store variables that it can read and/or write.

Approach for Hue: We followed the procedure for Hue described in Section 2.3 to get a unique token that registers our single test app with the data store of our Hue bridge. In Hue, all the variables of the data store are "readable" (*i.e.*, we verified that all the variables described in the developer documentation [38] can be read by third-party apps). Therefore, to build the permission map, we first extracted the contents of the entire data store. Then, for each subsection within the data store, our app made repeated write requests, *i.e.*, PUT calls with the payload consisting of a dummy value based on the variable type (*i.e.*, String, Boolean and Integer). All the variables that were successfully written to using this method were assigned as "writable" variables. Similarly, our app made repeated DELETE calls to the API and the variables that were successfully deleted were assigned as "writable" variables. This generated permission map applies to all third-party apps connected to Hue, since the platform provides equal privilege to all third-party apps.

4.2 Analyzing Permission Maps

The objective behind obtaining the permission map is to understand the potential for application overprivilege, by analyzing the granularity as well as the correctness of the enforcement. We analyze the permission map to identify instances of (1) *coarse-grained permissions*, *i.e.*, permissions that give the third-party app access to a set of security-sensitive resources that must ideally be protected under separate permissions, and (2) *incorrect enforcement*, *i.e.*, when an app has access to more resources (*i.e.*, state variables) than it should have given its permission set, as per the documentation; *e.g.*, apps on SmartThings may lock/unlock the door lock without the explicit permission required to do so [12].

To perform this analysis, we first identified data store variables that may be security or privacy-sensitive. This identification was performed using an open-coding methodology by one author, and separately verified by another author, for each platform. We then

performed further analysis by separately considering each such variable, and the permission(s) that allow access to it. A major consideration in our analysis is the security impact of an adversary being allowed read or read/write access to a particular resource. Moreover, our evaluation of the impact of the access control enforcement was contextualized to the platform under inspection. That is, when evaluating Nest, we took into consideration the semantic meaning and purpose of certain permissions in terms of the data store variables, as described in the documentation (*e.g.*, that the *Away read/write* permission should be required to write to the *away* variable [28]). For Hue, we only considered the security-impact of an adversary accessing data store variables. Our rationale is that the Hue platform defines the same static policy (*i.e.*, same permissions) for all third-party apps, and hence, its permission map can be simply said to consist of just one permission that provides access to a fixed set of data store variables. As a result, we judge application over-privilege in Hue by considering the impact of an adversarial third-party app reading from or writing to each of the security-sensitive variables identified in Hue's permission map.

The creation of the permission maps for both Nest and Hue requires the application of well-studied automated testing techniques, and as such, can be replicated for similar platforms, with minor changes to input data (*e.g.*, the permissions to test for). We will release our code and data to developers and platform vendors.

4.3 Permission Enforcement Findings ($\mathcal{F}_1 \rightarrow \mathcal{F}_3$)

Finding 1: The permission enforcement in Nest is fine-grained and correctly enforced, *i.e.*, as per the specification ($\mathcal{F}_1$). We observe that the Nest permission map is significantly more fine-grained, and permissions are correctly enforced, relative to the observations of prior research in similar platforms (*e.g.*, the analysis of SmartThings [12]). Some highly sensitive variables are always read-only (*e.g.*, the *web_url* where the camera feed is posted), and there are separate read and read/write permissions to access sensitive variables. Variables that control the state of the entire smart home are protected by dedicated permissions that control write privilege; *e.g.*, the *away* variable can only be written to using the *Away read/write* permission, the *ETA* variable has separate permissions for apps to read and write to it (*i.e., ETA read* and *ETA write*), and the Nest Cam can only be turned on/off via the *is_streaming* variable, using the *Camera + Images read/write* permission that controls write access to it. Moreover, since many apps need to respond to the *away* variable (*i.e.*, react when the user is home/away), device-specific read permissions (*e.g., Thermostat read, Smoke + CO read*) also allow apps to *read* the *away* variable, eliminating the need for apps to ask for higher-privileged *Away read* permission. The separate read and read/write permissions are correctly enforced, *i.e.,our generated permission map provides the same access as is defined in the Nest permission documentation [28]*. This is in contrast with findings of similar analyses of permission models in the past (*e.g.*, the Android permission model [10], SmartThings [12]), and demonstrates that the Nest platform has incorporated lessons from prior work in permission enforcement.

Finding 2: In Hue, the access control policy allows apps to bypass the user's explicit consent ($\mathcal{F}_2$). We discovered two data store variables that were not write-protected, and which have a significant part to play in controlling access to the data store and the user's smart home. First, any third-party app can write to the *linkbutton* flag. Recall from Section 2.3 that the user has to press the physical button on the Hue bridge device to authorize an app's addition to the bridge. The physical button press changes the *linkbutton* value to "true", and allows the app to be added to the *whitelist* of allowed third-party apps. However, we discovered that once installed, an app can toggle the *linkbutton* variable at will, *enabling third-party apps to add other third-party apps to the smart home without the user's consent*. This exploitable access control vulnerability can allow an app with seemingly useful functionality to install malicious add-ons by bypassing the user altogether. In our tests, we verified this attack with apps that were connected to the local network. This condition is feasible as a malicious app that needs to be added without the user's consent may not even have to pretend to work with Hue; all it needs is to be connected to the local network (*i.e.*, a game on the mobile device from one of the people present in the smart home). Note that it is also possible to remotely perform this attack, which we discuss in Section 10.

Finding 3. In Hue, third-party apps can directly modify the list of added apps, adding and revoking access without user consent ($\mathcal{F}_3$). Hue stores the authorization tokens of apps connected to the particular smart home in a *whitelist* on the Hue Bridge device. While analyzing the permission map, we discovered that not only could our third-party test app read from this list, it could also directly delete tokens from it. We experimentally confirmed this finding again, by removing *Alexa* and *Google Home* from the smart home, without the user's consent. An adversary could easily combine this vulnerability with ($\mathcal{F}_2$), to remove legitimate apps added by the user, add adversary-controlled apps (*i.e.*, by keeping the *linkbutton* "true"), all without the user's consent. More importantly, users do not get alerts when such changes are made (*i.e.*, since it is assumed that the enforcement will correctly acquire user consent). Hence, unless the user actually checks the list of integrated apps using the Hue Web app, the user would not notice these changes.

While the Nest permission model is robust in its mapping of data store variables and permissions required to access them, Section 5 demonstrates how fields disallowed by permissions may be indirectly modified via strategic misuse of routines, and describes Nest's product review guidelines to prevent the same [30]. Section 6 describes how badly written and overprivileged apps escape these review guidelines, and motivate a technical solution.

5 EVALUATING SMART HOME ROUTINES

Prior work has demonstrated that in platforms that favor application interoperability but lack transitive access control enforcement, problems such as confused deputy and application collusion may persist [5, 11, 21, 22]. Smart homes that facilitate routines are no different, but the exploitability and impact of routines on smart homes is unknown, which motivates this aspect of our study.

Recall that routines are trigger-action programs that are either triggered by a change in some variable of the data store, or whose action modifies certain variables of the data store. While both Nest and Hue share this characteristic, routines in Hue are fairly limited in scope, and their exploitation is bound to only affect the lighting of the smart home. As a result, while we provide confirmed examples of Hue routines in Section 2.3, the security evaluation described

in this section is focused on the heterogeneous Nest platform that facilitates more diverse and expressive routines.

5.1 Methodology for the Analysis of Routines

While using the simulator as described in Section 4 allows us to understand what routines are *possible* on the platform, *i.e.*, what variables might be manipulated, and what Nest devices (e.g., the Nest Cam, Nest Thermostat) are affected as a result, we performed additional experiments with real apps and devices to study existing routines in the wild. For this experiment, we extended the smart home setup previously discussed in Section 4 with real devices.

We started by collecting a list of devices that integrate with Nest from the *Works with Nest* website [34]. Using this initial list and information from the website, we purchased a set of 7 devices that possessed a set of characteristics relevant to this study, *i.e.*, devices that (1) take part in routines (*i.e.*, as advertised on the website), (2) are important for the user's security or privacy, and (3) are widely-known/popular with a large user base (*i.e.*, determined by the number of installs of the mobile client on Google Play). We obtained a final list of devices (7 real and 2 simulated) to our Nest smart home, namely, the Nest Cam (*i.e.*, a security camera), Hue light bulb, Belkin Wemo switch, the MyQ Chamberlain garage door opener, TP Link Kasa Smart Plug, Google Home, Alexa, Nest Thermostat (simulated), and the Nest Protect Smoke & CO Alarm (simulated). Some devices that may be important for security did not participate in routines at the time of the study, and hence were excluded from our final device list.

We connected these devices to our Nest smart home using the Android apps provided by device vendors, and connected a small set of smart home managers (*e.g.*, Yeti [53] and Yonomi [54]) to our Nest smart home as well. For each device, we set up and executed each individual routine as described on the Works with Nest as well as the device vendor's website, and observed the effects on the rest of the smart home (especially, security-sensitive devices). Also, we manipulated data store variables from our test app, and observed the effects on previously configured routines and devices.

5.2 Smart Home Routine Findings ($\mathcal{F}_4 \rightarrow \mathcal{F}_5$)

Finding 4. Third-party apps that do not have the permission to turn on/off the Nest Cam directly, can do so by modifying the *away* variable ($\mathcal{F}_4$). The Nest Cam is a home monitoring device, and important for the users' security. The *is_streaming* variable of the Nest Cam controls whether the camera is on (*i.e.*, streaming) or off, and can only be written to by an app with the permission *Camera r/w*. The Nest Cam provides a routine as a feature, which allows the camera to be automatically switched on when the user leaves the home (*i.e.*, when the *away* variable of the smart home is set to "away"), and switched off when the user returns (*i.e.*, when *away* is set to "home"). Leveraging this routine, third-party apps such as the Belkin Wemo switch can manipulate the *away* field, and indirectly affect the Nest Cam, without having explicit permission to do so. We tested this ability with our test app (see Section 4) as well, which could indirectly switch the camera *on* and *off* at will. This problem has serious consequences; *e.g.*, a malicious test app with the *away r/w* permission may set the variable to "home" when the user is away to prevent the camera from recording a burglary. The key problem here is that a *low-integrity device/app can trigger a change in a high-integrity device indirectly*, *i.e.*, by modifying a

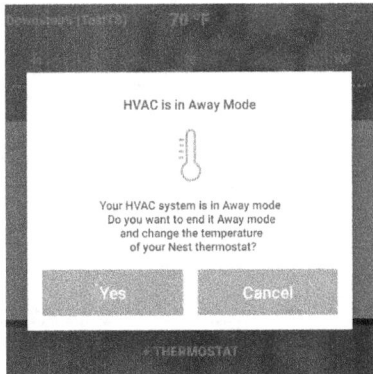

Figure 3: The *Keen Home* app asks the user to modify the thermostat's mode, but in reality, this action leads to the *entire* smart home being set to "home" mode, which affects a number of other devices.

variable it relies on, which is an instance of the well-known information flow *integrity* problem. Moreover, this is not the only instance of a high-integrity routine that relies on *away*; *e.g.*, the Nest x Yale Lock can lock automatically when the home changes to *away* mode [25], leakSMART reads the *away* state of the home and can notify the user's emergency contact when a leak occurs [24].

Nest has a basic defense to prevent such issues: application design policies that apply to apps with more than 50 users [30]. App developers are required to submit their app for a product review to the Nest team once the app reaches 50 users, and a violation of the rather strict and detailed review guidelines can result in the app being rejected from using the Nest API. One of the review policies (*i.e.*, specifically policy 5.8) states that *"Products that modify Home-/Away state automatically without user confirmation or direct user action will be rejected." [30].* Nest users may be vulnerable in spite of this defense, for two reasons. First, as attacking a smart home is an attack on a user's personal space, it is feasible to assume that most attacks that exploit routines will be targeted (*e.g.*, to perform burglaries). Assuming that the adversary can use social engineering to get the user to connect a malicious app to their Nest setup, *a targeted attack on a specific user will succeed in spite of the policy*, as the app would be developed solely for the targeted user and hence will have <50 users, and be exempt from the Nest product review. Second, it is unclear how apps are checked against this policy; our next finding demonstrates a significant omission in Nest's review.

Finding 5. Nest's product review policies dictate that the apps must prompt users before modifying *away*, but there is no official constraint on *what* the prompt may display ($\mathcal{F}_5$). Consider the example in Figure 3, which shows one such prompt by the *Keen Home* app [23] *when the user tries to change the temperature of the thermostat.* That is, when the user tries to change the temperature of the thermostat while the *away* variable is set to "away", the app requires us to change it to "home" before the thermostat temperature can be changed. This condition is entirely unnecessary to change the temperature. More importantly, it presents the prompt to the user in a way that states that the home/away modes are specific to the HVAC alone. This is in contrast to the actual functionality of these modes, in which a change to the *away* variable affects the *entire* smart home; *i.e.*, we confirmed that the Nest Cam gets turned off as well once we agree to the prompt. It is important

to note that the *Keen Home* app has passed the Nest product review, as it has well over 50 users (1K+ downloads on Google Play [15]). Therefore, this case demonstrates that the Nest product review does not consider the contents of the prompt, and a malicious app may easily misinform the user and make them trigger the *away* variable to the app's advantage. Finally, in Section 6.1 we demonstrate that this problem of misinforming the user is not just limited to *runtime in-app prompts* described in this section, but extends to application-defined *install-time permission descriptions* ($\mathcal{F}_6 \rightarrow \mathcal{F}_9$).

6 SECURITY ANALYSIS OF NEST APPS

In this Section, we investigate the privileges of apps developed to be integrated with Nest. Unlike prior work [12], we not only report the permissions requested by apps, but also analyze the information prompts displayed to the user when requesting the permission. Additionally, we analyze the rate of SSL misuse by both general smart home management apps as well as apps integrated with Nest. For this section, we do not consider the Hue platform as it has a limited ecosystem of apps as compared to Nest. We derived two datasets to perform the analyses that we describe in this section, the $\text{Apps}_{general}$ dataset, which contains 650 smart home management apps extracted from Google Play, and the Apps_{nest} dataset, which includes 39 apps that integrate into the Nest platform. Our online appendix [1] details our dataset collection methodologies.

6.1 Application Permission Descriptions

On Nest, developers provide permission descriptions that explain how an app uses a permission while registering their apps in the Nest developer console. These developer-provided descriptions are the *only* direct source of information available to the user to understand why an app requires a particular permission, *i.e.*, Nest itself only provides a short and generic permission "title" phrase that is displayed to the user along with the developer-defined description (*e.g.*, for *Thermostat read*, the Nest phrase is "See the temperature and settings on your thermostat(s)"). Owing to their significant role in the user's understanding of the permission requirements, we analyze the *correctness* of such developer-defined descriptions relative to the permissions requested.

6.1.1 Analysis Methodology. As described in Section 2, upon registering permissions at the developer console, developers are granted an OAuth URL that they can direct the user to for obtaining an access token. As a result, permissions are not encoded in the client mobile app or Web app (*i.e.*, unlike Android), which makes the task of extracting permissions difficult. However, we observe that the permissions that an app asks for are *always* displayed to the user for approval (*i.e.*, when first connecting an app to their Nest smart home using OAuth). We leverage this observation to obtain permissions dynamically, *i.e.*, by executing apps to the point of integrating them with our Nest smart home, and recording the permission prompt displayed for the user's approval. The procedure is the same for mobile as well as Web apps.

6.1.2 Nest App Findings ($\mathcal{F}_6 \rightarrow \mathcal{F}_9$). The two permissions that dominate the permission count are *Away read/write* and *Thermostat read-/write*, requested by 20 and 24 apps respectively, from the Apps_{nest} dataset. Our online appendix [1] provides the permission count for all other permissions. Our findings are as follows:

Table 1: Permission description violations discovered in Works with Nest apps

Application	Incorrect Permission Description
VC1: Requesting Read/Write instead of Read	
1. Home alerts	"**thermostat read/write**: Allows Home alerts to notify you when the Nest temperature exceeds your threshold(s)"
2. Home alerts	"**away read/write**: Allows Home Alerts to notify you when someone is in your home while in away-mode"
3. MyQ Chamberlain	"**thermostat read/write**: Allows Chamberlain to display your Nest Thermostat temperature in the MyQ app"
4. leakSMART	"**thermostat read/write**: Allows leakSMART to show Nest Thermostat room temperature and humidity. New HVAC sensor mode will notify you to shut off your thermostat if a leak is detected in your HVAC system."
5. Simplehuman Mirror	"**Camera+Images read/write**: Allow your simplehuman sensor mirror pro to capture and recreate the light your Nest Cam sees"
6. Iris by Lowe's	"**structure read/write**: View your Nest Structure names so Iris can help you pair your Nest Structures to the correct Iris Places"
7. Heatworks model 1	"**away read/write**: Allows the Heatworks MODEL 1 to be placed into vacation mode to save on power consumption while you're away"
8. Feather Controller	"**Camera+Images read/write**: Allows Feather to show you your camera and activity images. Additionally, Feather will allow you to request a snapshot."
9. Heatworks model 1	"**thermostat r/w**: Allows your Heatworks MODEL 1 water heater to go into vacation mode when your home is set to away"
VC2: Describing *Away* as a property of the thermostat alone, rather than something that affects the entire smart home	
10. Gideon	"**away read/write**: Allows Gideon to read and update the Away state of your thermostat"
11. Muzzley	"**away read/write**: Allows Muzzley to read and update the Away state of your thermostat"
12. Keen home smart vent	"**away read/write**: Allows Smart vent to read the state of your Thermostat and change the state from Away to Home"
VC3: Both VC1 and VC2	
13. WeMo	"**away read/write**: Allows your WeMo products to turn off when your Nest Thermostat is set to Away and on when set to Home."
14. IFTTT thermostat service	"**thermostat read/write**: Now you can turn on Nest Thermostat Applets that monitor when you're home, away and when the temperature changes."
VC4: Descriptions that do not relate to the permission	
15. IFTTT thermostat service	"**away read/write**: Now you can set your temperature or turn on the fan with Nest Thermostat Applets on IFTTT"
16. Life360	"**away read/write**: We need this permission to automatically turn on/off your nest system"

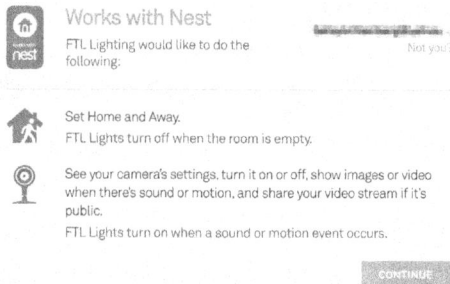

Figure 4: An example from the Nest documentation on OAuth authorization [29] that displays a permission description violation (specifically, VC1) for the *Away r/w* and *Camera + images r/w* permissions. The developer's permission description indicates that the FTL Lights only need to read data store variables, in both cases.

Finding 6. A significant number of apps provide incorrect permission descriptions, which may misinform users ($\mathcal{F}_6$). As shown in Table 1, we found a total of 15 permission description violations in 13/39 apps from the Apps$_{nest}$ dataset. We classify these incorrect descriptions into 5 violation categories (*i.e.*, VC1 → VC4), based on the specific manner in which they misinform the user, such as requesting more privileges than required for the described need (*e.g.*, read/write permissions when only reading is required), or misrepresenting the effect of the use of the permission (*e.g.*, stating *Away* as affecting only the thermostat). That is, *over 33.33% of the apps we could integrate have violating permission descriptions.*

Finding 7. In most cases of violations, apps request read/write permissions instead of read ($\mathcal{F}_7$). In 9 cases, apps request the more privileged *read/write* version of the permission, when they should have clearly requested the *read* version, as per their permission description (*i.e.*, VC1 in Table 1). For example, consider the "MyQ Chamberlain" app (Table 1, entry 3), which asks for the *thermostat read/write* permission, but whose description only suggests the need for the *thermostat read* permission, *i.e.*, "Allows Chamberlain to display your Nest Thermostat temperature in the

MyQ app". More importantly, a majority of the violations of this kind occur for the *Away read/write* and *Camera+Images read/write* permissions, which may have serious consequences if these over-privileged apps are compromised, *i.e.*, as *Away read/write* regulates control over indicating whether a user is at home or out of the house, and *Camera+Images read/write* may allow apps to turn off the Nest cam via the *is_streaming* variable. These violations exist in spite of Nest guidelines that mention the following as a *Key Point*: "*Choose 'read' permissions when your product needs to check status. Choose 'read/write' permissions to get status checks and to write data values.*" [28]. Finally, we found that the *Nest documentation may itself have incorrect instructions*, *e.g.*, the Nest's documentation on OAuth 2.0 authentication [29] shows an example permission prompt that incorrectly requests the *Away read/write* permission while only needing read access, *i.e.*, with the description "FTL Lights turn off when the room is empty", as shown in the Figure 4.

Finding 8. The Nest product review is insufficient when it comes to reviewing the correctness of permission descriptions and requests by apps ($\mathcal{F}_8$). The Nest product review suggests the following two rules, violating which may cause apps to be rejected: (1) "*3.3. Products with names, descriptions, or permissions not relevant to the functionality of the product*", and (2) "*3.5. Products that have permissions that don't match the functionality offered by the products*" [30]. Our findings demonstrate that the 16 violations discovered violate either one or both of these rules (*e.g.*, by requesting read/write permissions, when the app only requires read). The fact that the apps are still available suggests that the Nest product review may not be rigorously enforced, and as a result, may be insufficient in protecting the attacks discovered in Section 5.

Finding 9. Apps often incorrectly describe the *Away* field as a local field of the Nest thermostat, which is misleading ($\mathcal{F}_9$). One example of this kind (VC2 in Table 1) is the *Keen Home* app described in Section 5 (Table 1. entry 12), which states that it needs *Away read/write* in order to "*Allow Smart vent to read the state of your Thermostat and change the state from Away to Home*". As a result, *Keen Home* misrepresents the effect and significance of writing to the *Away* field, by making it seem like *Away* is a variable of the thermostat, instead of a field that affects numerous devices in the entire smart home. Gideon and Muzzley (entries 10 and 11 in Table 1) present a similar anomaly. Our hypothesis is that such violations occur because Nest originally started as a smart thermostat that gradually evolved into a smart home platform. Finally, in addition to misleading descriptions classified as VC1 and VC2, we discovered apps whose permission descriptions did not relate to the permissions requested at all (VC4), and apps whose descriptions satisfied both VC1 and VC2 (*i.e.*, VC3 in Table 1).

The accuracy of permission descriptions is important, as the user has no other source of information upon which to base their decision to trust an app. Nest recognizes this, and hence, makes permissions and descriptions a part of its product review. The discovery of inaccurate descriptions not only demonstrates that apps may be overprivileged, but also that Nest's design review process is incomplete, as it puts all its importance on getting the user's consent via permission prompts (*e.g.*, in Findings 5→9), but not on what information is actually shown.

6.2 Application SSL Use

The previous section demonstrated that smart home apps may be overprivileged in spite of a dedicated product review. An adversary may be able to compromise the smart home by exploiting vulnerabilities in such overprivileged apps. As a result, we decided to empirically derive an estimate of how vulnerable smart home apps are, in terms of their use of SSL APIs, which form an important portion of the apps' attack surface.

We used two datasets for this experiment, *i.e.*, the $\text{Apps}_{general}$ dataset consisting of 650 generic smart home (Android) apps crawled from Google Play, and an extended version of the Apps_{nest} dataset, *i.e.*, the $\text{Apps}_{nestExt}$ dataset, which consists of 111 Android apps built for Works with Nest devices (*i.e.*, including the ones for which we do not possess devices). We analyzed each app from both the datasets using MalloDroid [9], to discover common SSL flaws.

Finding 10. A significant percentage of general smart home management apps, as well as apps that connect to Nest have serious SSL vulnerabilities ($\mathcal{F}_{10}$). 20.61% (*i.e.*, 134/650) of the smart home apps from the $\text{Apps}_{general}$ dataset, and 19.82% (*i.e.*, 22/111) apps from the $\text{Apps}_{nestExt}$ dataset, have at least one SSL violation as flagged by MalloDroid. Specifically, in the $\text{Apps}_{nestExt}$ dataset, the most common cause of an SSL vulnerability is a broken *TrustManager* that accepts *all certificates* (*i.e.*, 20 violations), followed by a broken *HostNameVerifier* that does not verify the hostname of a valid certificate (*i.e.*, 11 violations). What is particularly worrisome is that apps such as *MyQ Chamberlain* and *Wemo* have multiple SSL vulnerabilities as well as the *Away read/write* permission, which makes their compromise especially dangerous. In the next section, we demonstrate an end-to-end attack on the Nest security camera, using one of the SSL vulnerabilities discovered from this analysis, and the Nest*Away read/write* permission.

7 LATERAL PRIVILEGE ESCALATION

While our findings from the previous sections are individually significant, we demonstrate that they can be combined to form an instance of a lateral privilege escalation attack [39], in the context of smart homes. That is, we demonstrate how *an adversary can compromise one product (device/app) integrated into a smart home, and escalate privileges to perform protected operations on another product, leveraging routines configured via the centralized data store.*

This attack is interesting in the context of smart homes, because of two core assumptions that it relies on (1) low-integrity (or non-security) smart home products may be easier to directly compromise than high-integrity devices such as the Nest Cam (*i.e.*, none of the SSL vulnerabilities in $\mathcal{F}_{10}$ were in security-sensitive apps), and (2) while low-integrity devices may not be able to directly modify the state of high-integrity devices ($\mathcal{F}_1$), they may be able to indirectly do so via *automated routines* triggered by global smart home variables ($\mathcal{F}_4$). (3) Moreover, since the low-integrity device is not being intentionally malicious, but is compromised, the product review process would not be useful, even if it was effective (which it is not, as demonstrated by $\mathcal{F}_5 \rightarrow \mathcal{F}_9$). This last point distinguishes a lateral privilege escalation from actions of malicious apps that trigger routines (*e.g.*, the "fake alarm attack" discussed in prior work [12]). These conditions make lateral privilege escalation particularly interesting in the context of smart home platforms.

Attack Scenario and Threat Model: We consider a common man-in-the-middle (MiTM) scenario, similar to the SSL-exploitation scenarios that motivate prior work [9, 41]. Consider Alice, a smart home user who has configured a security camera to record when she is away (*i.e.*, using the *away* variable in the centralized data store). Bob is an acquaintance (*e.g.*, a disgruntled employee or an ex-boyfriend) whose motive is to steal a valuable from Alice's house without being recorded by the camera. We assume that Bob also knows that Alice uses a smart switch in her home, and controls it via its app, which is integrated with Alice's smart home. Bob follows Alice, and connects to the same public network as her (*e.g.*, a coffee shop, common workplace), sniffs the access token sent by the switch's app to its server using a known SSL vulnerability in the app, and then uses the token to directly control the *away* variable. Setting the *away* to "home" confuses the security camera into thinking that Alice is at home, and it stops recording. Bob can now burglarize the house without being recorded.

The Attack: The example scenario described previously can be executed on a Nest smart home, using the Nest Cam and the TP Link Kasa switch (and the accompanying Kasa app). We compromise the SSL connection of Kasa app, which was found to contain a broken SSL TrustManager in our analysis described in Section 6. We choose Kasa app as it requests the sensitive *Away read/write* permission, and has a sizable user base (1M+ downloads on Google Play [14]). It is interesting to note that the Kasa app has also passed the Nest product review process and is advertised on the Works with Nest website [31], but can still be leveraged to perform an attack. We use *bettercap* [2] as a MiTM proxy to intercept and modify unencrypted data. Additionally, as described in the attack scenario, we assume that (1) the victim's Nest smart home has the Nest Cam and the Kasa switch installed, (2) the popular routine which triggers the Nest Cam to stop recording when the user is home is enabled, and (3) the user connects her smartphone to a network to which the attacker has access (e.g., coffee shop, office), which is a common assumption when exploiting SSL-misuse [9, 41].

The attack proceeds as follows: (1) The user utilizes the Kasa app to control the switch, while the user's mobile device is connected

Listing 1: The Kasa app's unencrypted GET request.

```
1    {"data":{"uri":"com.tplinkra.iot.authentication.impl.
         RetrieveAccountSettingRequest"},
2        "iotContext":
3            {"userContext":{"accountToken":"<anonymized
                 alphanumeric token>",
4            "app":{"appType":"Kasa_Android"},
5            "email":"<anonymized>",
6            "terminalId":"<anonymized>"}}, ...
```

to public network. (2) The attacker uses a MiTM proxy to intercept Kasa app's attempt to contact its own server, and supplies the attacker's certificate to the app during the SSL handshake, which is accepted by the Kasa app due to the faulty TrustManager. (3) The Kasa app then sends an authorization token (see Listing 1) to the MiTM proxy (*i.e.,* assuming it is the authenticated server), which is stolen by the attacker. This token authorizes a particular client app to send commands to the TP Link server. (4) Using the stolen token, the attacker instructs the TP Link server to set the smart home's *away* variable to the value "home", while the user is actually "away". This action is possible as the TP Link server (*i.e.,* Web app) has the *-Away read/write* permission for the user's Nest smart home. (5) This triggers the routine in the Nest Cam, which stops recording.

In sum, the attacker compromises a security-insensitive (i.e., low-integrity) product in the system, and uses it along with a routine to escalate privileges, *i.e.,* to modify the state of a security-sensitive (i.e., high-integrity) product. It should be noted that while this is one verified instance of a lateral privilege escalation attack on DSB smart home platforms, given the broad attack surface indicated by our findings, it is likely that similar undiscovered attacks exist.

8 LESSONS

Our findings ($\mathcal{F}_1$)→($\mathcal{F}_{10}$) demonstrate numerous gaps in the security of smart home platforms that implement routines using centralized data stores. Moreover, while many of the findings may apply to platforms such as SmartThings as well, their implications are more serious on Nest, as the user does not have a centralized perspective of the routines programmed into the smart home. We now distill the core lessons from our findings:

Lesson 1 : *Seamless automation must be accompanied by strong integrity guarantees.* It is important to note that the attack described in Section 7 may not be addressed by fixing the problem of over-privilege or via product reviews, since none of the components of the attack are overprivileged (*i.e.,* including TP Link Kasa), and our findings demonstrate that the Nest product review is insufficient ($\mathcal{F}_5$→$\mathcal{F}_9$). The attack was enabled due to the integrity-agnostic execution of routines in Nest ($\mathcal{F}_4$). To mitigate such attacks, platforms such as Nest need information flow control (IFC) enforcement that ensures strong integrity guarantees [3], and future work may explore the complex challenges of (1) specifying integrity labels for a diverse set of user devices and (2) enforcing integrity constraints without sacrificing automation. The introduction of *tiered-trust domains* in Nest (*i.e.,* via Weave) offers an encouraging start to the incorporation of integrity guarantees into smart home platforms [27].

Lesson 2: *Nest Product Reviews would benefit from at least light-weight static analysis.* Our findings demonstrate numerous violations of the Nest design policies that should have been discovered during the product review. Moreover, the review guidelines also

state that products that do not securely transmit tokens will be rejected [30], but our simple static analysis using MalloDroid discovered numerous SSL vulnerabilities in Nest apps ($\mathcal{F}_{10}$), of which one can be exploited (Section 7). We recommend the integration of light-weight tools such as MalloDroid in the review process.

Lesson 3: *The security of the smart home indirectly depends on the smart phone (apps).* Smartphone apps have been known to be susceptible to SSL misuse [9], among other security issues (*e.g.,* unprotected interfaces [5]). Thus, unprotected smartphone clients for smart home devices may enable the attacker to gain access to the smart home, and launch further attacks, as demonstrated in Section 7. Ensuring the security of smart phone apps is a hard problem, but future work may triage smartphone apps for security analyses based on the volume of smart home devices/platforms they integrate with, thereby, improving the apps that offer the widest possible attack surface to the adversary.

Lesson 4: *Popular but simpler platforms need urgent attention.* The startling gaps in the access control of Hue demonstrate that the access control of other simple (*i.e.,* homogeneous) platforms may benefit from a similar holistic security analysis ($\mathcal{F}_2$, $\mathcal{F}_3$).

9 VULNERABILITY REPORTING

We have reported the discovered vulnerabilities to Philips ($\mathcal{F}_2$, $\mathcal{F}_3$), Google ($\mathcal{F}_1$, $\mathcal{F}_4$→$\mathcal{F}_9$), and TP Link ($\mathcal{F}_{10}$). TP Link has since fixed the SSL flaw in the latest version of the app. Philips Hue is currently analyzing third party apps for the specific behavior discussed in this paper, and will eventually roll out a fix to their access control policy. We have also provided recommendations to Google on improving the safety of routines, which is a design challenge that may be hard to immediately address.

10 THREATS TO VALIDITY

1. SSL MiTM for different Android versions: Our attack described in Section 7 has been tested and is fully functional on a Nexus 7 device running Android version 4.4.2. However, we have recently observed that the MiTM proxy is blocked when intercepting connections from a Pixel 2 device running the latest version of Android (*i.e.,* 8.1.0). Our hypothesis is that the TP Link Kasa app changes its SSL API use based on the Android API version, and we are currently working on locating at what Android version (*i.e.,* between 4.4.2 and 8.1.0) the SSL component of our described attack no longer functions. However, this caveat does not change the fact that our attack is feasible under certain settings, or that third-party Android apps may often have exploitable SSL flaws [9, 36, 41]. SSL misuse is not the focal point of the lateral privilege escalation exploit we describe, which occurs primarily because of routines implemented using shared global variables in Nest ($\mathcal{F}_4$→$\mathcal{F}_6$).

2. Number of devices and apps: For the analysis in Section 6, our set of 9 devices (*i.e.,* 7 real and 2 virtual) allowed us to integrate a set of 39 apps into our Nest platform (*i.e.,* the Apps$_{nest}$ dataset), out of the around 130 "Works with" Nest apps we found. Therefore, while we cannot say that our findings ($\mathcal{F}_6$→$\mathcal{F}_9$) generalize to all the apps compatible with Nest, we can certainly say that they are valid for a significant minority (*i.e.,* over 27%).

3. Local and Remote exploits of Hue: Our exploits for the Philips Hue platform demonstrated in Section 4 ($\mathcal{F}_2$ and $\mathcal{F}_3$) can be executed from an app operating on the same local network as the Hue bridge. This is feasible, as the attacker-controlled app simply needs to be on the same network (*i.e.*, not even on the victim's device). The vulnerabilities we describe may also be remotely exploited, as access control enforcement remains the same for remote access.

11 RELATED WORK

Smart home platforms are an extension of the new modern OS paradigm, the security problems in smart home platforms are similar to prior modern OSes (*e.g.*, application over-privilege, incorrect platform enforcement). As a result, some of the same techniques may be applied in detecting such problems. For instance, in a manner similar to Felt et al.'s seminal evaluation of Android permission enforcement [10], our work uses automated testing to derive permission maps and compares the maps to the platform documentation. We also leverage lessons from prior work on SSL misuse [9, 36, 41, 45] to perform the SSL Analysis (Section 6.2) and the MiTM exploit (Section 7). The lack of transitivity in access control that we observe is similar to prior observations on Android [5, 7, 11, 21, 22]. However, the implications of intransitive enforcement are different in the smart home space, and, to our knowledge, some of the key analyses performed in this paper is novel across modern OS research (*e.g.*, exploitation of home automation routines and the ineffectiveness of Nest's product review). The novelty of this paper is rooted in using lessons learned from prior research in modern OS and application security to identify problems in popular but under-evaluated platforms such as Nest and Hue, and moreover, in demonstrating the potential misuse of home automation *routines* for performing lateral privilege escalation.

In the area of smart home security, the investigation by Fernandez et al. [12] into the SmartThings platforms and its apps is highly related to the study presented in this paper. However, our work exhibits key differences. For instance, the platforms explored in this paper (*i.e.*, Nest and Hue) are popular, and have key differences relative to SmartThings (Section 2). Moreover, while Fernandez et al. focus on application overprivilege, this work studies the utility and security of routines, and leverages routines to demonstrate the first instance of lateral privilege escalation on smart home platforms. Our analysis of permission text artifacts, product review-based defense in Nest, and SSL-misuse in apps leads to novel findings that facilitate the end-to-end attack. Finally, we demonstrate that simpler platforms (*i.e.*, Hue) fail to provide bare-minimum protections.

Aside from this closely-related work, prior work has demonstrated direct attacks on smart home platforms and applications. For instance, Sukhvir et al. attack the communication and authentication protocols in Hue and Wemo [35], Sivaraman et al. attack the home's firewall using a malicious device on the network [42], and a Veracode study demonstrated issues in a range of products such as the MyQ Garage System and Wink Relay [51]. Our work performs a holistic security evaluation of the access control enforcement in DSB platforms (*i.e.*, Nest and Hue) and their applications, and is complementary to such per-device security analysis.

Prior work has also analyzed the security of trigger-action programs. Surbatovich et al. [47] analyzed the security and privacy risks associated with IFTTT recipes, which are trigger-action programs similar to routines. The key difference is that Surbatovich et al. examines the safety of individual recipes, while our work explores routines that may be safe on their own (*e.g.*, when *home*, turn off the Nest Cam), but which may be used as gadgets by attackers to attack a high-integrity device from a low-integrity device.

In a similar vein, Celik et al. [4] presented Soteria, a static analysis system that detects side-effects of concurrent execution of Samsung's smart apps. The problem explored in our paper is broadly similar to Celik et al.'s work, *i.e.*, both papers explore problems that arise due to the lack of transitive access control in smart homes. While the techniques that underlie Soteria have advanced the state of the art for analyzing smart home products, our paper exhibits two key differences that demonstrate the novelty of our analysis. First, Soteria does not aim to address the adversarial use of routines as mechanisms to perform a lateral privilege escalation. As a result, it would not detect the attack discussed in Section 7, since the precondition for the attack is not a routine (*i.e.*, it is the exploitation of SSL vulnerability in the Kasa app, which allows us to steal the authorization token and misuse the *away* permission allocated to Kasa). Second, this paper is novel in its analysis of runtime prompts and permission descriptions on home automation platforms, and uncovers problems in how users are informed of specific sensitive automation actions ($\mathcal{F}_8 \rightarrow \mathcal{F}_9$), and how the permissions that enable such actions ($\mathcal{F}_5$) are described.

Finally, prior work has proposed novel access control enhancements, which may alleviate some of the concerns raised in this paper. ProvThings [52] provides provenance information that may allow the user to piece together evidence of some of the attacks described in this paper, but does not prevent the attacks themselves. On the contrary, ContextIoT [19] provides users with runtime prompts describing the context of sensitive data accesses, which may alert users to unintended execution of routines ($\mathcal{F}_4$), *at the cost of reducing automation*. Further, SmartAuth [50] analyzes the consistency of application descriptions with code, and may benefit the Nest product review in determining the correctness of permission descriptions.

12 CONCLUSION

Smart home platforms and devices operate in the users' physical space, hence, evaluating their security is critical. This paper evaluates the security of two such platforms, Nest and Hue, that implement home automation *routines* via centralized data stores. We systematically analyze the limitations of the access control enforced by Nest and Hue, the exploitability of routines in Nest, the robustness of Nest's product review, and the security of third-party apps that integrate with Nest. Our analysis demonstrates ten impactful findings, which we leverage to perform an end-to-end lateral privilege escalation attack in the context of the smart home. Our findings motivate more systematic and design-level defenses against attacks on the integrity of the users' smart home.

13 ACKNOWLEDGEMENTS

The authors have been supported in part by the NSF-1815336 grant and the William & Mary Summer Research Award. Any opinions, findings, and conclusions expressed herein are the authors' and do not necessarily reflect those of the sponsors.

REFERENCES

[1] 2018. Online Appendix. https://sites.google.com/view/smart-home-routines-analysis-2/home. Accessed August 27, 2018.

[2] BetterCAP. Accessed June 2018. BetterCAP stable documentation. https://www.bettercap.org/legacy///.

[3] K. J. Biba. 1977. *Integrity Considerations for Secure Computer Systems*. Technical Report MTR-3153. MITRE.

[4] Z. Berkay Celik, Patrick McDaniel, and Gang Tan. 2018. Soteria: Automated IoT Safety and Security Analysis. In *2018 USENIX Annual Technical Conference (USENIX ATC)*. 147–158.

[5] Erika Chin, Adrienne Porter Felt, Kate Greenwood, and David Wagner. 2011. Analyzing Inter-Application Communication in Android. In *Proceedings of the 9th Annual International Conference on Mobile Systems, Applications, and Services*.

[6] Ry Crist. Accessed September 2018. A smart home divided: Can it stand? https://www.cnet.com/news/a-smart-home-divided-can-it-stand/.

[7] Michael Dietz, Shashi Shekhar, Yuliy Pisetsky, Anhei Shu, and Dan S. Wallach. 2011. Quire: Lightweight Provenance for Smart Phone Operating Systems. In *Proceedings of the USENIX Security Symposium*.

[8] Engadget. Accessed June 2018. SmartThings shows off the ridiculous possibilities of its connected home system. https://www.engadget.com/2014/01/11/smartthings-labs/.

[9] Sascha Fahl, Marian Harbach, Thomas Muders, Lars Baumgärtner, Bernd Freisleben, and Matthew Smith. 2012. Why Eve and Mallory Love Android: An Analysis of Android SSL (in)Security. In *Proceedings of the 2012 ACM Conference on Computer and Communications Security*.

[10] Adrienne Porter Felt, Erika Chin, Steve Hanna, Dawn Song, and David Wagner. 2011. Android Permissions Demystified. In *Proceedings of the ACM Conference on Computer and Communications Security (CCS)*.

[11] Adrienne Porter Felt, Helen J. Wang, Alexander Moshchuk, Steven Hanna, and Erika Chin. 2011. Permission Re-Delegation: Attacks and Defenses. In *Proceedings of the USENIX Security Symposium*.

[12] Earlence Fernandes, Jaeyeon Jung, and Atul Prakash. 2016. Security analysis of emerging smart home applications. In *Security and Privacy (SP), 2016 IEEE Symposium on*. 636–654.

[13] Gartner. Accessed June 2018. Gartner Says 8.4 Billion Connected Things Will Be in Use in 2017, Up 31 Percent From 2016. https://www.gartner.com/newsroom/id/3598917.

[14] Google Play. Accessed June 2018. Kasa for Mobile. https://play.google.com/store/apps/details?id=com.tplink.kasa_android.

[15] Google Play. Accessed June 2018. Keen Home. https://play.google.com/store/apps/details?id=com.hipo.keen//.

[16] Google Play. Accessed June 2018. Nest. https://play.google.com/store/apps/details?id=com.nest.android.

[17] Google Play. Accessed June 2018. Philips Hue. https://play.google.com/store/apps/details?id=com.philips.lighting.hue2.

[18] IFTTT. Accessed June 2018. IFTTT helps your apps and devices work together. https://ifttt.com/.

[19] Yunhan Jack Jia, Qi Alfred Chen, Shiqi Wang, Amir Rahmati, Earlence Fernandes, Z Morley Mao, Atul Prakash, and Shanghai JiaoTong Unviersity. 2017. ContexIoT: Towards providing contextual integrity to appified IoT platforms. In *Proceedings of the 2017 Network and Distributed System Security Symposium (NDSS)*.

[20] Carl E. Landwehr, Alan R. Bull, John P. McDermott, and William S. Choi. 1994. A Taxonomy of Computer Program Security Flaws. *ACM Computing Surveys (CSUR)* 26, 3 (Sept. 1994).

[21] Adwait Nadkarni, Benjamin Andow, William Enck, and Somesh Jha. 2016. Practical DIFC Enforcement on Android. In *Proceedings of the 25th USENIX Security Symposium*.

[22] Adwait Nadkarni and William Enck. 2013. Preventing Accidental Data Disclosure in Modern Operating Systems. In *Proceedings of the ACM Conference on Computer and Communications Security (CCS)*.

[23] Nest. Accessed June 2018. Keen Home - Works with Nest Store. https://workswith.nest.com/company/leaksmart/leaksmart//.

[24] Nest. Accessed June 2018. LeakSmart - Works with Nest Store. https://workswith.nest.com/company/leaksmart/leaksmart//.

[25] Nest. Accessed June 2018. Nest x Yale Lock - Works with Nest Store. https://workswith.nest.com/company/yale/nest-x-yale-lock//.

[26] Nest. Accessed June 2018. Somfy Protect - Works with Nest Store. https://workswith.nest.com/company/somfy-protect-by-myfox-sas/works-with-somfy-protect//.

[27] Nest. Accessed June 2018. Weave. https://nest.com/weave/.

[28] Nest Developers. Accessed June 2018. How to Choose Permissions and Write Descriptions. https://developers.nest.com/documentation/cloud/permissions-overview.

[29] Nest Developers. Accessed June 2018. OAuth 2.0 Authentication and Authorization. https://developers.nest.com/documentation/cloud/how-to-auth.

[30] Nest Developers. Accessed June 2018. Product Review Guidelines. https://developers.nest.com/documentation/cloud/product-review-guidelines.

[31] Nest Labs. Accessed June 2018. Kasa - Works with Nest Store. https://workswith.nest.com/company/tp-link-research-america-corp/kasa.

[32] Nest Labs. Accessed June 2018. Nest Developers. https://developers.nest.com///.

[33] Nest Labs. Accessed June 2018. Nest Simulator. https://developers.nest.com/documentation/cloud/home-simulator.

[34] Nest Labs. Accessed June 2018. Works with Nest. https://nest.com/works-with-nest//.

[35] Sukhvir Notra, Muhammad Siddiqi, Hassan Habibi Gharakheili, Vijay Sivaraman, and Roksana Boreli. 2014. An experimental study of security and privacy risks with emerging household appliances. In *Proceedings of the 2014 IEEE Conference on Communications and Network Security (CNS)*. 79–84.

[36] Lucky Onwuzurike and Emiliano De Cristofaro. 2015. Danger is my middle name: experimenting with SSL vulnerabilities in Android apps. In *Proceedings of the 8th ACM Conference on Security & Privacy in Wireless and Mobile Networks*. 15.

[37] Philips. Accessed June 2018. Philips Hue: Your Personal Wireless Lighting System. https://www2.meethue.com/en-us/about-hue.

[38] Philips Hue Developers. Accessed June 2018. Philips hue API. https://developers.meethue.com/philips-hue-api.

[39] Dave Piscitello. 2016. What is Privilege Escalation. https://www.icann.org/news/blog/what-is-privilege-escalation.

[40] Popular Science. Accessed June 2018. Stop shouting at your smart home so much and set up multi-step routines. https://www.popsci.com/smart-home-routines-apple-google-amazon/.

[41] Bradley Reaves, Nolen Scaife, Adam Bates, Patrick Traynor, and Kevin R.B. Butler. 2015. Mo(bile) Money, Mo(bile) Problems: Analysis of Branchless Banking Applications in the Developing World. In *Proceedings of the 24th USENIX Security Symposium (USENIX Security 15)*. 17–32.

[42] Vijay Sivaraman, Dominic Chan, Dylan Earl, and Roksana Boreli. 2016. Smartphones attacking smart-homes. In *Proceedings of the 9th ACM Conference on Security & Privacy in Wireless and Mobile Networks*. ACM, 195–200.

[43] Smartthings Developers. Accessed June 2018. Documentation. http://developer.smartthings.com/.

[44] SmartThings Support. Accessed June 2018. Routines in the SmartThings Classic app. https://support.smartthings.com/hc/en-us/articles/205380034-Routines-in-the-SmartThings-Classic-app.

[45] David Sounthiraraj, Justin Sahs, Zhiqiang Lin, Latifur Khan, and Garrett Greenwood. 2014. SMV-Hunter: Large Scale, Automated Detection of SSL/TLS Man-in-the-Middle Vulnerabilities in Android Apps. In *Proceedings of the ISOC Network and Distributed Systems Symposium (NDSS)*.

[46] Stringify. Accessed June 2018. Stringify | Change Your Life by Connecting Everything. https://www.stringify.com//.

[47] Milijana Surbatovich, Jassim Aljuraidan, Lujo Bauer, Anupam Das, and Limin Jia. 2017. Some Recipes Can Do More Than Spoil Your Appetite: Analyzing the Security and Privacy Risks of IFTTT Recipes. In *Proceedings of the 26th International Conference on World Wide Web*. 1501–1510.

[48] TechCrunch. Accessed June 2018. Google Assistant is adding Routines and location-based reminders. https://techcrunch.com/2018/02/23/google-assistant-is-adding-routines-and-location-based-reminders/.

[49] The Verge. Accessed June 2018. You can soon activate multi-step routines in Alexa with a single command. https://www.theverge.com/2017/9/27/16375050/alexa-routines-echo-amazon-2017/.

[50] Yuan Tian, Nan Zhang, Yueh-Hsun Lin, XiaoFeng Wang, Blase Ur, XianZheng Guo, and Patrick Tague. 2017. SmartAuth: User-Centered Authorization for the Internet of Things. In *Proceedings of the 26th USENIX Security Symposium*.

[51] Veracode. 2016. The Internet of Things Poses Cybersecurity Risk. https://info.veracode.com/whitepaper-the-internet-of-things-poses-cybersecurity-risk.html.

[52] Qi Wang, Wajih Ul Hassan, Adam Bates, and Carl Gunter. 2018. Fear and Logging in the Internet of Things. In *Network and Distributed Systems Symposium*.

[53] Yeti. Accessed June 2018. Yeti - Simplify the control of your smart home. https://getyeti.co/.

[54] Yonomi. Accessed June 2018. Yonomi app - Yonomi. https://www.yonomi.co.

Detection of Threats to IoT Devices using Scalable VPN-forwarded Honeypots

Amit Tambe
Aalto University, Finland
amit.tambe@aalto.fi

Yan Lin Aung
Singapore University of Technology and Design, Singapore

Ragav Sridharan
Singapore University of Technology and Design, Singapore

Martín Ochoa
Cyxtera Technologies

Nils Ole Tippenhauer
CISPA Helmholtz Center for Information Security, Germany

Asaf Shabtai
Ben Gurion University, Israel

Yuval Elovici
Singapore University of Technology and Design, Singapore

ABSTRACT

Attacks on Internet of Things (IoT) devices, exploiting inherent vulnerabilities, have intensified over the last few years. Recent large-scale attacks, such as Persirai, Hakai, etc. corroborate concerns about the security of IoT devices. In this work, we propose an approach that allows easy integration of commercial off-the-shelf IoT devices into a general honeypot architecture. Our approach projects a small number of heterogeneous IoT devices (that are physically at one location) as many (geographically distributed) devices on the Internet, using connections to commercial and private VPN services. The goal is for those devices to be discovered and exploited by attacks on the Internet, thereby revealing unknown vulnerabilities. For detection and examination of potentially malicious traffic, we devise two analysis strategies: (1) given an outbound connection from honeypot, backtrack into network traffic to detect the corresponding attack command that caused the malicious connection and use it to download malware, (2) perform live detection of unseen URLs from HTTP requests using adaptive clustering. We show that our implementation and analysis strategies are able to detect recent large-scale attacks targeting IoT devices (IoT Reaper, Hakai, etc.) with overall low cost and maintenance effort.

CCS CONCEPTS

• **Security and privacy** → *Intrusion detection systems*; *Malware and its mitigation*;

KEYWORDS

High-Interaction IoT Honeypot; Network Traffic Analysis; Intrusion Detection; Attack Attribution; Adaptive Clustering

ACM Reference Format:
Amit Tambe, Yan Lin Aung, Ragav Sridharan, Martín Ochoa, Nils Ole Tippenhauer, Asaf Shabtai, and Yuval Elovici. 2019. Detection of Threats to IoT Devices using Scalable VPN-forwarded Honeypots. In *Ninth ACM Conference on Data and Application Security and Privacy (CODASPY '19), March 25–27, 2019, Richardson, TX, USA*. ACM, New York, NY, USA, 12 pages. https://doi.org/10.1145/3292006.3300024

1 INTRODUCTION

Internet of Things (IoT) is envisioned as a network of *things* that have physical or virtual representation in the digital world, sensing/actuation capability, a programmability feature and are uniquely identifiable [16]. IoT devices such as smart TVs or smart speakers are becoming increasingly appealing to consumers [24]. Gartner's study estimates almost 20.4 billion IoT devices to be in use by the year 2020 [25]. Due to the nature of emerging markets for IoT devices, manufacturers focus their attention mainly on the core functionalities of products and rush to introduce them in the market [27]. Security aspects of these devices are thus often neglected. Consequently, IoT devices having security vulnerabilities are launched in the market thereby exposing them to targeted exploits in large-scale attacks [5, 20, 27]. Recent large-scale attacks such as Hakai [2] and IoT Reaper [26] demonstrate the gravity of threats faced by IoT devices, exploiting multiple vulnerabilities present due to the heterogeneous nature of IoT devices. Further, exploitation of IoT devices to attack critical infrastructure has become a common attack vector, raising significant concerns for the stakeholders involved [15].

Goal – The goal of this work is to detect new attack waves targeting IoT devices, in particular, the ones leveraging 0-day vulnerabilities for specific devices. Honeypots are commonly used to learn about attacks "in the wild". By utilizing honeypots for IoT devices, we aim to detect large-scale attacks that are able to compromise a large class of IoT devices (such as Mirai that uses easy/default credentials to get shell access to a device), as well as attacks that exploit vulnerabilities in specific IoT devices (such as Persirai that uses faulty access control in specific versions of the embedded web server).

Honeypots for IoT devices can be implemented by emulating a selected set of services (e.g. Telnet [19]). As a result, attacks using services that are not emulated cannot be detected. Moreover, attackers could try to identify honeypots (e.g., by checking error handling, or detecting emulation or virtualization [19]). Additionally, due to their heterogeneous nature, reusing an already emulated IoT device to represent another device cannot guarantee replication of vulnerabilities.

Our contribution – We propose to detect novel attacks on IoT devices by leveraging real devices to build a scalable VPN-forwarded honeypot. In our work, we use real IoT devices to faithfully expose their behavior without requiring occasional enhancement of exposed environment to adapt to changing attack vectors (as in the case of emulated devices). However, using only a few real devices might not provide sufficient network traffic to gain valuable insight. On the other hand, an increasing number of real devices is neither cost-effective nor scalable. Hence, to increase the statistical chance of being attacked, we create multiple VPN tunnels, forwarding the traffic of a single physical device to several IPs worldwide. VPN tunnels are used to acquire public IP addresses and expose IoT devices on the Internet as part of our proposed honeypot. At the same time, connecting to multiple VPN servers in different countries allows devices in the honeypot to establish a geographically diverse virtual presence, which is essential for detecting large-scale attacks.

Next, we propose two live traffic analysis strategies for detection and examination of potentially malicious traffic received by honeypot. The first one starts with suspicious events that indicate potential compromises, such as anomalous communication attempts made by an IoT device in our honeypot. By backtracking into the network traffic of the device under potential attack, we can detect the malicious command issued by an attacker that caused those anomalous communication attempts. The second strategy allows live detection of potential 0-day vulnerabilities by analyzing URLs from HTTP requests. Over a period of time, the proposed honeypot framework detected several large-scale attacks targeting IoT devices (Persirai, Hakai, etc), with overall low cost and maintenance effort.

Our contributions can be summarized as follows:

- Design of a honeypot framework that incorporates commercial off-the-shelf (COTS) IoT devices for high-interaction, utilizing low-cost commercial VPN providers
- An implementation of the proposed framework, demonstrating an automated, scalable, and economical approach to integrate COTS IoT devices
- Two live traffic analysis methods to detect large-scale attacks and subsequently 0-day vulnerabilities in IoT devices using our honeypot infrastructure

The rest of this paper is organized as follows. Section 2 provides a brief background on honeypots and recent large-scale attacks targeting IoT devices. We then present the design of our honeypot framework and live traffic analysis strategies in Section 3. The implementation of the honeypot is explained in Section 4, followed by the results of evaluation of network traffic captured by the proposed honeypot in Section 5. We summarize the related work in this field in Section 6 and conclude the paper in Section 7.

2 BACKGROUND

2.1 Honeypots

A Honeypot is a closely monitored computing resource that we want to be probed, attacked, or compromised. More precisely, a honeypot is *"an information system resource whose value lies in unauthorized or illicit use of that resource"* [21]. Honeypots have traditionally been used by security researchers to present decoy systems to attract attackers and learn from their behavior. With the knowledge gained from this, researchers can then apply techniques to prevent such attacks in the future. In general, honeypots can be classified as follows:

High and Low Interaction – High interaction honeypots present real systems to attackers [17]. The main advantage of having real systems is that there is no reason to emulate anything, thus making them more convincing. These type of honeypots allow attackers to gain full access to the system enabling to gain in-depth information about attacks and therefore qualitative results on attacker behavior. A drawback, however, is their cost of implementation and maintenance due to the usage of real systems, making them difficult to scale [21]. Low interaction honeypots, on the other hand, present fully or partially simulated or emulated environments (e.g. partially implemented network stacks). They limit attackers' interaction with the honeypot and hence generate more quantitative data [21]. Their real value lies in their ease to implement, scale and maintain.

2.2 Recent large-scale IoT attacks

It is challenging to build realistic honeypots for IoT devices mainly due to their heterogeneous nature [7]. Since IoT devices are becoming more affordable, it motivates us to design a high-interaction honeypot by incorporating real IoT devices. Such a honeypot would allow detection of new threats to IoT devices while keeping pace with evolving attack vectors.

Persirai – In May 2017, TrendMicro reported a new family of IoT botnet named Persirai [1]. This malware infects cameras that are susceptible to the vulnerability CVE-2017-8225 thereby allowing unauthorized access to the credentials of vulnerable cameras [12]. The perpetrator issues a specifically crafted HTTP request to retrieve *system.ini* file containing credentials, irrespective of the strength of the password. Once the attacker gains access to credentials, the device becomes part of a botnet and scans for more IoT devices with the same vulnerability to spread the malware.

Hakai – This malware campaign was reported recently by Palo Alto Networks [2]. Hakai leverages the source code of Mirai and Gafgyt malware families and continues the recent trend of incorporating multiple exploits affecting several classes of IoT devices. Attackers get access to the device using one of the credentials from a dictionary of predefined factory-state credentials of several devices. The malware further spreads using methods similar to Mirai. However, Hakai has evolved to support several new DDoS methods that were previously unused by Mirai variants.

3 HONEYPOT FRAMEWORK AND TRAFFIC ANALYSIS METHODS

The objective of our honeypot is to attract and detect (possible 0-day) large-scale attacks on IoT devices. We start by outlining the attacker model and then identify salient features that are necessary to design and implement a high-interaction honeypot incorporating real IoT devices.

3.1 Attacker Model

We consider two types of attackers: attackers conducting attacks manually, and attackers using automated scripts to conduct large-scale attacks. In case of manual attacks, we assume the goal of the attacker is to either explore exposed devices or assess the effectiveness of exploits to be used in subsequent large-scale attacks, by first testing manually on a smaller set of devices. The attacker may interact with the devices in a variety of ways such as inspecting configuration of a printer or viewing a video on the camera. On the other hand, in case of automated attacks, the goal of the attacker is to identify as many vulnerable IoT devices as possible (of the order of thousands [13]) and exploit those to recruit in a botnet for conducting large-scale attacks. The motivation behind this is to rent such botnets on the underground market to conduct DDoS style attacks [8]. In both cases, we assume that the attacker is looking for real devices instead of emulated devices, because real IoT devices provide access to complete systems for exploitation and further proliferation using possible 0-day vulnerabilities.

3.2 Design Considerations

Stealth – The identity of a honeypot, by its nature, should stay concealed. Otherwise, it loses all of its value. When exploring IoT devices in the honeypot, an attacker conducting manual attacks may try fingerprinting those devices. The attacker may try to verify replies to executed commands, try to interact with devices like cameras by zooming, tilting, etc. It is essential, therefore, that the attacker be convinced of the devices being real and present in the actual geolocations indicated by their IP addresses. Some IoT devices (like IP cameras) could unintentionally disclose Service Set Identifiers (SSIDs) of the surrounding Wi-Fi networks through their Wi-Fi settings. Similarly, devices with microphones can capture audio, revealing inconsistencies from the purported geolocation. These need to be prevented as either can reveal the actual location of the honeypot.

Credibility and Robustness – To be credible, a honeypot needs to be realistic. For example, an IP camera will be more credible if it shows realistic visuals instead of simply displaying an empty wall. Attractive visuals closely mimicking realistic scenarios increase the value of a honeypot by making it credible. Further, a honeypot should itself be secure, not allowing attackers to take advantage of and compromise other devices within the honeypot or outside. The value of a honeypot increases if it can detect intrusion attempts and prevent the proliferation of malware.

3.3 Honeypot Features

In this section, we describe the salient features of our proposed high interaction honeypot.

Real devices – To make the honeypot credible, we use real COTS IoT devices. We note that real devices allow full access to the underlying system, thereby maximizing attack surface for attackers. An attacker trying to fingerprint real devices, by way of verifying return values of executed commands or faithful reproduction of actions like camera zoom, can be assured of their authenticity. In addition, we note that using real devices allows for easier integration of new COTS devices. To integrate a new device, we do not need to emulate anything or gain low-level access to the device. Also, we argue that novel (0-day) attacks on embedded devices (e.g. Persirai that exploits a vulnerability in the web server [11]), can only be fully observed on devices that expose this vulnerability.

Apart from using real devices, we also ensure that high interaction devices, such as IP cameras, broadcast pertinent and realistic videos, to enhance the credibility of our honeypot. The goal is to maximize the attacker's interactions with devices in the honeypot, as long as possible.

Interaction Restrictions – To prevent IoT devices from exposing SSIDs of surrounding Wi-Fi networks, wireless functionality of the devices should ideally be disabled. This can be achieved either by software or hardware means. While the software-based approach is low effort and convenient, it could be circumvented by an attacker after gaining access to the device. In order to prevent this, we prefer a hardware-based approach to prevent the attacker from turning on Wi-Fi remotely or scanning neighboring Wi-Fi networks. Similarly, devices such as IP cameras have sensors (e.g. microphones) that could leak unwanted context information of the devices (e.g. conversations in a lab setup). We need to identify a list of such IoT devices, especially with known vulnerabilities and disable their Wi-Fi chips and microphones.

Forwarding via VPN connections – The devices in our honeypot will have to be reachable via a public IP accessible by attackers. VPN providers offer such public IP addresses from servers located in various countries, thereby providing geographic diversity. Such diversity portrays the presence of a device in a different location than its actual location. IP addresses belonging to the pool of a large VPN provider could potentially be identified as such, via online service [9]. However, being heuristic in nature, such identifications are still prone to false positives [9]. In addition, we note that

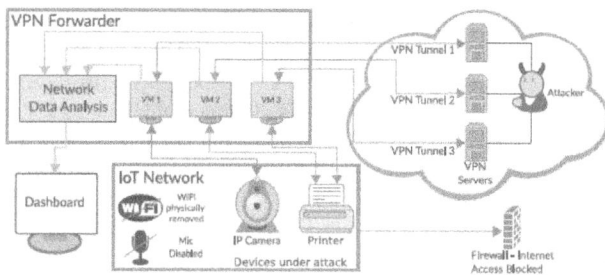

Figure 1: High level design of honeypot

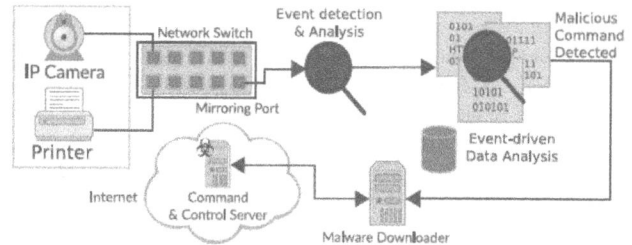

Figure 2: Steps taken during traffic analysis of outbound connections

services to identify VPN IPs usually require payment (which makes them unattractive for a careful attacker). On the other hand, even if free usage is allowed, it is usually restricted to only a small number of requests, making them impractical when conducting a large-scale attack consisting of hundreds of IPs. As result, despite the existence of such services, the efforts involved in using those services (in terms of time, cost and utility) would make it unattractive for attackers intending to conduct large-scale attacks.

Salient Attribute Extraction – Once the honeypot is deployed and starts gathering large amounts of network data, it is essential to parse and analyze traffic data efficiently. Crucial attributes of data (such as attacker location, source IP reputation, etc.) need to be extracted for data analyses. Once these attributes are extracted and stored in a database they can be reused later for data visualization.

Maintenance – Maintaining a honeypot and ensuring that it performs its intended function is a critical requirement. As the proposed honeypot scales by addition of new physical devices, maintaining it manually becomes increasingly challenging. In these circumstances, it is essential to automate the following tasks of maintenance: (1) addition and setup of new devices in the honeypot including associated VPN-forwarders and traffic capturing, (2) removal of a device and (3) periodic monitoring and logging of the health status of honeypot.

Putting it all together – Combining all these aspects, we envisage a high-level design of the proposed honeypot as shown in Figure 1. The design components include:

- Attacker – Attacker is a malicious entity targeting our honeypot. This entity could be a person attacking manually or an automated script.
- VPN Tunnels – These are public IP tunnels provided by a VPN service provider connecting attackers to VPN-forwarder.
- VPN-forwarder – These are Virtual Machines (VMs) that acquire public IPs by establishing VPN tunnels. They forward traffic back and forth between attackers on the Internet and the real IoT devices in the internal network. The VMs expose the same ports as open ports on the real devices in their factory default state to provide a credible environment.
- IoT Network – This is the VLAN that hosts all the real IoT devices that are part of the honeypot. A firewall is set up to prevent any newly initiated connections

from leaving the VLAN (for example, to prevent malware from propagating to hosts outside the VLAN). Wireless connectivity of all devices connected to this VLAN is disabled physically to prevent unintended exposure of SSIDs of neighboring wireless networks. For devices where physically disabling wireless connectivity is not possible (like motion sensor, smart plug, etc.), portable low-cost RF-enclosures can be deployed to block wireless signals from outside.

- Firewall – This blocks any outbound connections initiated from the IoT Network, thereby restricting the unintentional proliferation of malware.
- Dashboard – The dashboard component displays real-time visualization of network traffic data after performing analysis on it. It displays important data (e.g. successful logins) and other suspicious behavior (e.g. outbound connection attempts).

3.4 Network Traffic Analysis Methods

Outbound Connection Attribution. The first traffic analysis method attributes attack commands based on detection of suspicious outbound connections as shown in Figure 2.

Outbound Connection Detection – We continuously capture all network traffic flowing to and from all IoT devices in our honeypot for monitoring and analysis. In particular, we use lightweight rules to detect outbound connections from devices. Even though all unsolicited traffic to a honeypot is potentially suspicious [21], spontaneous outbound connections can be considered as potentially malicious (e.g. connections to Command and Control (C&C) servers).

Event-driven Data Analysis – Once a suspicious event such as an anomalous outbound connection attempt is detected, we deploy computationally expensive packet inspection to determine the malicious command (such as simple WGET commands in a shell, HTTP configuration change requests, etc.) that caused the outbound connection. We achieve this by backtracking in the previously captured incoming traffic.

Malware Downloading – After obtaining the malicious command that caused the outbound connection, the downloader component is triggered. It parses the obtained command and establishes a separate outbound connection to the potentially malicious server. After establishing a connection, the downloader then retrieves malware from the potential C&C server. The malware downloaded is then analyzed further.

Table 1: Details of IoT devices used in honeypot

Device	Model	Vulnerabilities (CVE)
IP Cameras		
D-Link[*]	DCS-942L	2017-7852
VStarcam[*]	C7837	2017-5674
Aztech[*]	WIP C409HD	2017-9765
Trendnet[†]	TV-IP7621C	–
Trendnet[†]	TV-IP410	Yes [4]
Sineoji[†]	PT528V	2017-9765
Other Devices		
HP Printer[*]	HP 6830	–
D-Link Router[†]	DIR-615	2017-7404
Smartthings Hub[*]	STH-ETH-200	Yes [6]
Smart Plug[*]	Belkin	Yes [23]
Motion Sensor[*]	Belkin	Yes [18]

[*] Factory state default password
[†] Modified password

Live Detection of Novel HTTP Requests. In the second analysis method, we process live network traffic and extract URLs from HTTP GET requests. The URLs are then forwarded to a customized adaptive clustering component [10] based on unsupervised learning, which we call as **HON**eypot Novel HTTP Request **AN**alyzer (HONAN). Once deployed in the honeypot, HONAN detects novel (i.e. unseen) URLs, forms clusters and raises an alarm whenever a new cluster is found.

4 IMPLEMENTATION OF VPN-FORWARDED IOT HONEYPOT

In this section, we describe the implementation of a high interaction IoT honeypot based on our proposed design.

4.1 Honeypot Implementation

Honeypot with Heterogeneous IoT Devices – The first step in implementing the proposed honeypot is selection of IoT devices that will be exposed on the Internet. We decided to include different types of IoT devices in the honeypot to provide a rich attack surface so as to detect recent threats and potential vulnerabilities in those devices. A basic query on Shodan search engine for IoT devices returns millions of results [22]. IP cameras form a majority of these results, closely followed by home routers, printers, etc. Starting with the most targeted device in recent attacks – IP cameras, we identified a list of cameras from different manufacturers, especially with known vulnerabilities, to be incorporated in our proposed honeypot. Similarly, we also identified other types of IoT devices, some of which already have known vulnerabilities. Table 1 shows a list of the real devices used in our honeypot. For some devices we retained the default factory state passwords, while for others the password was

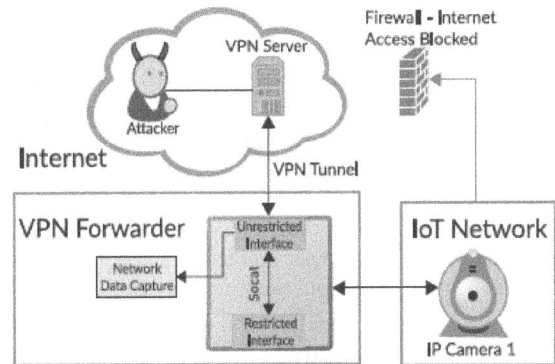

Figure 3: Implementation details for a VPN-forwarder

changed from factory default. The 'Vulnerabilities' column indicates identified vulnerabilities for those devices with the Common Vulnerabilities and Exposures (CVE) identifier (if available).

Device Preparation –Next, to prevent those devices from accidentally disclosing neighboring Wi-Fi SSIDs thereby risking exposure of the honeypot location, we disabled Wi-Fi and microphones on the IP cameras at the hardware level. For example, on D-Link DCS-942L camera, we removed the oscillator of Wi-Fi chip (MT7601U). For other devices, where removing Wi-Fi chips was not possible (such as smart plug or motion sensor), we made use of an electromagnetically shielded enclosure to prevent nearby wireless signals from reaching those devices.

As explained in the previous section, we aimed to have realistic video images to avoid early detection of the honeypot by attackers. For IP cameras, we achieved this objective in two ways: (1) by constructing a setup involving jewelery items and (2) replaying pre-recorded video of an industrial setting. This method of projecting videos does not apply to other device types (such as printer or smart plug).

VPN Provider – We chose a suitable VPN provider, by conducting latency tests for several VPN service providers. Based on the observed latencies and geographical diversity of the provider's servers, we rely on the services of 'VPN Provider1' (real name of selected VPN service provider is withheld intentionally).

VPN-forwarder – This component plays a crucial role in the implementation of the proposed honeypot by exposing the IoT device's interface on the Internet and then forwarding traffic between the attacker and real device. As shown in Figure 3, the VPN-forwarder is implemented as a virtual machine running lightweight Ubuntu operating system. It has two network interfaces:

Unrestricted Interface It has access to the Internet and establishes a VPN tunnel with VPN Provider1. It is used by attackers to gain access to devices in the honeypot.

Restricted Interface This interface connects to the isolated VLAN 'IoT Network' to which all physical devices are connected. The VLAN secures the honeypot by blocking any outbound communication. Hence, any malware that could possibly infect the honeypot is prohibited from proliferating to other hosts outside the honeypot.

The VPN-forwarder uses Socat[1] to transfer traffic from the attacker on unrestricted interface to the real device through the restricted interface, and the responses of the device back to the attacker. The network traffic going through the VPN-forwarder machine is captured using the tool TShark[2] on the unrestricted interface of the VPN-forwarder. This traffic collection happens continuously and gathered pcaps are saved on the file system of the physical host hosting the virtual machines.

Visualization and Data Analytics Dashboard – We use the dashboard to process and visualize raw data captured by honeypot. First, we continuously capture network traffic in honeypot by using TShark. To reduce processing of unwanted raw data, an automated script periodically extracts information such as HTTP credentials, HTTP URLs, geolocation information of IP addresses, etc. from the raw data Tshark's 'ek' option allows to generate JSON format output of that information, for importing into Logstash and subsequent indexing in Elasticsearch. Further, we use several custom scripts that query elasticsearch to select the data that is most pertinent (for example the number of successful logins or outbound connection attempts by IP cameras). The results of these queries are sent to Kibana component of the dashboard for visualization. Simultaneously, we also store URLs from HTTP GET requests filtered by TShark in a separate CSV file. HONAN continuously monitors this file using adaptive clustering to detect novel URLs and displays resulting clusters on a dashboard created using Shiny[3] visualization package.

Health Monitor and Framework Scalability – Building and running a honeypot also entails efforts to ensure that it runs continuously without disruption. It would be infeasible to carry out this effort manually, once the honeypot scales with addition of new devices or new VPN-forwarders. Therefore, we have prepared a script called 'Health Monitor', which runs periodically and performs a series of checks ensuring the correct functionality of the honeypot. These checks test whether: (1) VPN-forwarders are running as expected, (2) VPN connections are active, (3) TShark is capturing network traffic, and (4) end-to-end communication (from VPN-forwarders to IoT devices) is functional. The data produced by this script is logged in a database and eventually gets visualized on the Kibana dashboard to monitor the overall status of the honeypot.

Similarly, we have devised custom scripts to automate the process of addition and removal of devices to and from the honeypot. These scripts automate the task of setting up a new device including its associated VPN-forwarder, network interfaces, VPN tunnels, traffic capturing using TShark and traffic forwarding to the devices using Socat. Automating

these tasks greatly reduces manual efforts and is important for scalability.

Scalability – In order to be scalable, the proposed honeypot must be able to incorporate the increasing number of IoT devices, VPN forwarders, and public IP addresses. One single VPN forwarder virtual machine (VM) (running lightweight Ubuntu operating system) requires minimum 256MB RAM and 4GB hard disk space. Currently, we run these on a physical host with 64GB RAM and 3TB of hard disk. If we restrict the memory used by Virtual Box (our visualization software) to 60GB, then a maximum of 240 VMs could be hosted on the physical host. Therefore, one physical host can accommodate up to 240 virtual machines connecting to 240 distinct public IP addresses. If more than 240 VMs are required, an additional physical host could be integrated in our honeypot increasing the capacity of the honeypot to 480 VMs. We have prepared scripts to automate the addition of new virtual machines and collection of network traffic irrespective of the physical host they are running on. Further, all physical IoT devices in the honeypot are connected to a 24-port switch. In our configuration, four ports of the switch are utilized for – (1) incoming Internet connection, (2) mirroring port, (3) management port and (4) connection to the physical host. Thus, one switch can accommodate 20 physical IoT devices which would then be portrayed as multiple virtual devices across the Internet. Adding more than 20 physical devices is possible by incorporating another network switch.

Local Coordinating Server – Apart from the main components and tools mentioned above, we implement a local coordinating server incorporating several other tools. MySQL database is used to store most of the static data such as IP addresses of devices, public IP addresses of VPN-forwarder machines and dynamic data such as outbound connection attempts detected. The tool Socat is used to establish a bidirectional communication channel for transferring data and forwarding traffic from the attackers to the devices and back. TShark is used to capture two types of network traffic data – one between attackers and devices, and another to capture inter-device and device's outbound communication. Rsync[4] is used to transfer json files between different machines.

Running cost – The honeypot implementation makes use of a desktop machine to host all the VPN-forwarders and store captured network traffic, and a second desktop machine to host the analytics dashboard. Both these machines are a one-time investment. The most important hardware investment in the honeypot is the IoT devices. The total one-time investment of all the real devices in the honeypot is $1034. The sole recurring cost for our setup is the fees paid to the VPN service provider. These amount to $5.9 per month per IP. Thus, for our entire honeypot consisting of 44 public IP addresses, the monthly recurring cost is $259.6, making it a cost-effective approach in studying attacker behavior for threat detection. Apart from this, the Health Monitor script periodically checks for any issues in the working of

[1]https://linux.die.net/man/1/socat
[2]https://www.wireshark.org/docs/man-pages/tshark.html
[3]https://shiny.rstudio.com/
[4]https://linux.die.net/man/1/rsync

the honeypot and reports those immediately. This reduces the maintenance efforts as well. On an average, two man-hours of maintenance effort are required per week to keep the honeypot running.

4.2 Implementation of Network Traffic Analysis Methods

To implement our proposed methods for live traffic analysis, we took the following steps:

Outbound Connection Attribution

Data Capturing and Monitoring – We capture and monitor all traffic going to and from IoT devices in the honeypot. In particular, we detect traffic originating from any of the devices. To capture such traffic, it is necessary to tap into the network interface of devices in the honeypot. We achieve this by using a TP-Link switch (TL-SG1024DE) to host all real devices and use mirroring port capability of the switch. The mirroring port mirrors traffic that is generated on another port of the switch. This technique lets us capture all traffic at one place (mirroring port) without resorting to individual capturing on devices. We use TShark for capturing traffic on the mirroring port and TShark's 'ringbuffer' option to rotate captured PCAP files. Every PCAP file is parsed as soon as it is rotated by TShark.

Event Detection and Reputation Check – Next, we monitor every PCAP file for identifying (potentially) suspicious events like outbound connections. Outbound attempts are detected as attempted connections to IP addresses outside the VLAN of honeypot, specifically to public IP addresses. Outbound TCP connections are identified using TCP flags in the captured traffic (SYN flag set and ACK reset). On the other hand, outbound UDP traffic is identified as traffic originating from devices in honeypot (known source IP) and destined for VLAN outside of honeypot. Once outbound connections are detected, we obtain Autonomous System Number (ASN) information for those IP addresses. We subject those IPs to reputation check using VirusTotal, which provides an interface to many aggregated antivirus products and online scan engines. Next, we examine outbound DNS requests for potentially malicious domain names. All the data from this first round of lightweight parsing are stored in the database for further analysis.

Outbound Connection Attribution – We argue that a malicious outbound connection attempt (potentially to C&C server) is the effect of an attack command issued previously by an attacker. We, therefore, perform packet inspection of historical data, to attribute every outbound connection attempt to its corresponding attack command. We start backtracking by identifying the outbound IP, IP of the device and the protocol over which

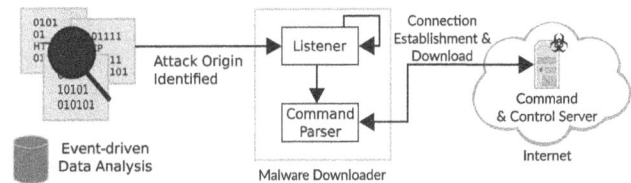

Figure 4: Detailed view of malware downloader

the device communicates, and then filtering historical PCAP data accordingly. We inspect a maximum of 30 min of historical data. This is because our goal is to detect large-scale attack campaigns that are generally short-lived. We perceive this as typical attacker behavior in such attack campaigns and therefore argue that an outbound connection would immediately follow an exploit attempt, for the attacker to maximize his advantage. We backtrack in incremental steps until we identify the packet and hence the command that caused the outbound attempt. We thus attribute an attack (exploit attempt) to an outbound connection. It may happen that some outbound connections cannot be attributed to their attack commands/exploit attempts. This can happen when an attacker tries to craft malware binary on the device manually. However, as our results in Section 5 show, we are able to attribute the high percentage of outbound connection attempts to attack commands.

Malware Downloading –Performing outbound connection attribution reveals the original attack command that caused the outbound connection. The next step is to complete this connection with the malicious server and download attack payload. Allowing this operation on the devices in honeypot poses a risk of unknown malware taking control of devices and possibly the honeypot along with neighboring networks. As such, we devise a separate component, called 'malware downloader', that runs on Ubuntu OS and performs this step of malware downloading. Figure 4 shows the steps taken by the malware downloader when downloading malware. We implemented this component for WGET and TFTP commands. It includes a listener that continuously listens for new messages (a message indicates new attack command was attributed to an outbound connection). Every new message is then parsed to extract the command and then, if required, modified (example, conversion of TFTP options from busybox to Ubuntu). The attack command is then executed to establish a connection with the potential C&C server and download malware.

Novel HTTP Request Analyzer

Implementation of HONAN, which performs unsupervised adaptive clustering of URLs is shown in Figure 5. First, network traffic from mirroring port of our honeypot is processed in real-time. Using TShark tool, timestamps

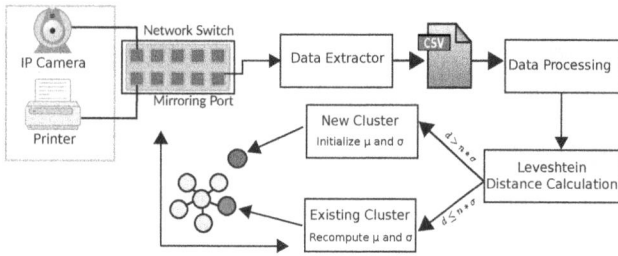

Figure 5: Implementation of adaptive clustering

and HTTP GET request URLs are extracted and stored in a CSV file. Typically, URLs consist of three parts: hostname, path and parameters. A series of regular expressions are applied on the URLs to represent them in a generic way while preserving their inherent variations.

After applying regular expressions, HONAN uses adaptive clustering to detect previously unseen URLs that can be potentially malicious. In this technique, we first calculate the distance of incoming URL with the centroids, c_μ, of existing clusters using Levenshtein distance string metric. If the distance to the closest cluster d is within a threshold of $n \times \sigma$ (σ = standard deviation of the cluster), we add the incoming URL to the closest cluster and recompute the mean, μ, and σ of that cluster. Otherwise, if $d \geq n \times \sigma$, we form a new cluster and initialize c_μ with the incoming URL and σ with a large number (50 in our case). n is a user-defined parameter which is experimentally set to 1 in our work. As more URLs get added to a cluster, μ (mean of cluster) gets updated using equation 1 and σ is updated using equation 2. Finally, to recompute cluster centroids, we calculate the mean salience value of the URLs in the cluster using Term Frequency - Inverse Document Frequency (TF-IDF) algorithm. TF-IDF scores the importance of tokens in a URL based on their occurrences within the URL and the cluster.

$$\mu = \frac{n_c \times \mu + d}{n_c + 1} \qquad (1)$$

$$\sigma = \sqrt{\left| \frac{\left(n_c * \left(\sigma^2 + \mu^2 \right) + d^2 \right)}{n_c + 1} - \mu^2 \right|} \qquad (2)$$

where n_c = number of URLs in existing cluster and d = distance to closest cluster.

5 RESULTS

Our honeypot implementation projected 12 physical IoT devices as 44 exposed devices in 15 cities across nine countries. This setup has been running for 15 months and accumulated over 365GB of network traffic data. This section presents observations from the analysis performed on the captured traffic data.

Figure 6: Geographical diversity of outbound connections from honeypot. The size of circle depicts number of connections attempted to IP addresses in that geolocation.

5.1 Live Network Traffic Analysis

When performing network traffic analysis, our goal is to detect large-scale attacks that function by compromising devices in the honeypot. To detect compromise of a physical device we utilize knowledge gained from detecting outbound connections and analyzing HTTP requests. Since IoT devices typically do not make outbound connections, we consider all outbound connections as suspicious and potentially malicious. We therefore continuously parsed traffic data for detecting outbound connections and applied our threat detection methods to detect attacker commands that caused those outbound connections. Similarly, we also considered unseen URLs detected by HONAN as suspicious.

Outbound Connections –We parsed all network traffic to detect TCP and UDP connections that were initiated by devices in the honeypot to an IP address that lies outside its VLAN. We analyzed 365GB of PCAP file data and detected over 150 million connection attempts to 4642 distinct IP addresses. Those 150 million attempts included several retries since we block outbound connections from the honeypot. We analyzed the geolocations of all those 4642 IP addresses to understand the locations of potential C&C servers and observed that connections were made to IP addresses in 109 countries. Figure. 6 shows a map representing the geographical diversity of outbound connections made by devices in the honeypot. Additionally, as part of outbound connection discovery, we also detected DNS requests made by devices and found requests to 4720 unique domains. Those also included device manufacturer domains, presumably for device software updates.

Attack Attribution – After detecting outbound connection attempts, we applied our attack attribution method. Knowing the destination IP and protocol of communication, we backtracked into PCAP traffic to attribute attack commands to corresponding outbound connections. For example, upon detecting a connection attempt to *TARGETIP* via TFTP protocol, we backtracked into PCAP traffic to detect the attack command as

```
/bin/busybox tftp -g -l dvrHelper -r dlr.arm
TARGETIP;
```

We were able to attribute attack commands for 4527 out of 4642 (97.5%) distinct IPs. This high percentage of attack attribution leads to extraction of malicious commands from PCAP traffic and downloading of malware.

Lightweight Backtracking – Backtracking performed for attack attribution was lightweight. 4018 IPs out of 4527 (89%) were attributed by backtracking between 0 to 5 seconds only. We attributed the remaining 509 IP addresses by backtracking up to 120 seconds. We were unable to attribute the remaining 105 (3%) IPs. In those cases, the attacker created malware binaries manually on the devices which caused outbound connections.

Malware Downloading – We ran the malware downloader component for a period of 45 days from 1st July 2018. In this time period, we allowed the malware downloader to execute attack commands detected from outbound connections and download potential malware. This resulted in 180 distinct files being downloaded. Those files consisted of 78 malicious binaries and 102 other text files. The 78 distinct malware binaries collected belong to multiple processor architectures, such as ARM and MIPS. The remaining text files gave further instructions to download actual malware binaries.

Novel HTTP Request Analyzer – HONAN analyzed 365GB of PCAP files captured from 11th April 2017 to 30th July 2018. We trained HONAN with URLs extracted from network traffic PCAP files captured between 11th Apr and 26th Jun 2017. We removed potential attack URLs before training and noted 2752 clusters. After training was completed, we tested HONAN with previously excluded attack URLs and found new clusters for each of those. After training and testing, we deployed HONAN on our honeypot on 31st July 2017. Since then, HONAN has identified 1259 new clusters till 30th July 2018. These new clusters included clusters representing large-scale attacks on IoT devices such as Persirai, IoT Reaper, Owari and Hakai. A malware family may utilize different HTTP request URLs to compromise multiple vulnerabilities in IoT devices (e.g., as the case with IoT Reaper). As a single attack can consist of multiple exploit URLs, it can be represented by more than one cluster. Further, after deploying HONAN, we noted new clusters that representing novel HTTP requests which did not particularly target IoT devices.

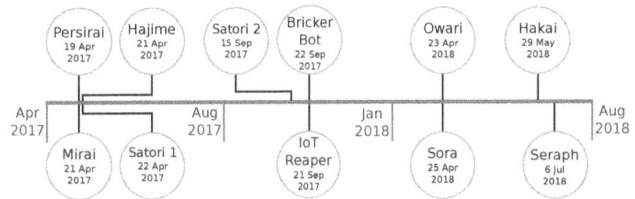

Figure 7: Timeline of malware families detected automatically (as new clusters) by our honeypot.

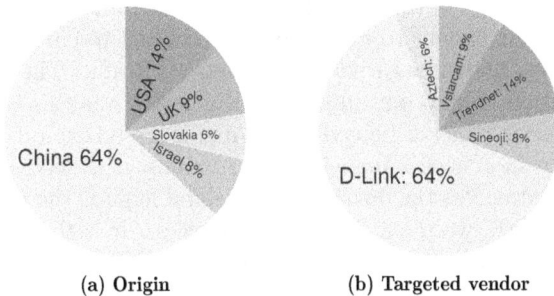

(a) Origin   (b) Targeted vendor

Figure 8: Classification of incoming traffic to honeypot

5.2 Malware Activity Detected by Honeypot

The honeypot implementation using our proposed design has been running since April 2017. Since then, we incorporated both our automated live traffic analysis methods into the honeypot. These automated methods have effectively detected several IoT malware attacks while the attack campaigns were active. Figure 7 shows the timeline of the honeypot. It depicts various malware detected by honeypot since its inception.

5.3 Honeypot Traffic Characterization

Incoming Data Classification –Continuing our automated live analysis, we analyzed 365GB of traffic received by honeypot to gather statistics on incoming traffic. We designed automated scripts to parse live network traffic to extract various pieces of information. The scripts obtained country of origin of incoming connections (to understand geographic presence of attackers), ports that received maximum traffic (to understand type of attacks), and amount of traffic received by various devices (to understand attacker preferred targets and therefore vulnerabilities in devices).

Figure. 8a shows the distribution of connections received by devices in honeypot, per country. We acknowledge that attackers can tunnel their traffic through IPs other than their own, to misrepresent their true location. We observe that majority connections originated from USA and China. We observed that 54% connections received by honeypot were on Telnet port, while HTTP ports received almost all of remaining 46% connections.

We observed that IP cameras received majority of connections in the honeypot, thereby indicating greater attacker interest in those IoT devices as compared to other devices like IP printer, smart switch, etc. We conjecture this is because several recent large-scale attacks on IoT devices target IP cameras. As shown in Figure. 8b, we note that D-Link DCS-942L IP camera received most connections among IP cameras.

Login Attempts – One of the intentions behind using real devices in the honeypot is to provide a more realistic environment to attackers as compared to emulated devices and thus garner quality network traffic. The motivation behind our automated live traffic analysis is to observe attacker behavior. For attackers to exploit devices and execute malicious instructions, it is necessary to first access the devices. A successful login is the most straightforward way to gain such access. It is therefore appropriate to analyze the collected data and search for login attempts made on the devices.

Figure. 9 shows a boxplot of login attempts per month, by attackers, via HTTP and Telnet, since the honeypot became operational in April 2017. Each box represents the range of number of login attempts in a month, while the red line inside every box represents the median for that data. Outliers are depicted as small red circles or crosses, depending on their distance from median.

We parsed the collected network traffic to detect all login attempts made by attackers. We detected attempts made via HTTP and Telnet protocols. In all 610076 HTTP requests were received from 32290 distinct public IP addresses. Of these, 86748 requests were attempts to login using HTTP authentication header, with 9877 attempts being successful. We observed over 23000 distinct credentials being used in login attempts (including several dictionary attacks). In case of single camera that had its telnet port exposed, we detected 147663 login attempts, from 4923 distinct IP addresses. Of these, 13959 attempts were successful. Thus, we detected 23836 combined successful logins over HTTP and Telnet. We further scrutinized the successful logins to distinguish those that caused outbound connections from other "benign" successful logins. We detected 5136 such logins that caused outbound connections.

Figures 9a and 9b show a comparison of total login attempts made by attackers and the successful attempts. Figure 9a shows that the number of login attempts increased steadily, as can be seen from the gradual rise in median values. Figure 9b represents successful logins and depicts many outliers. Even though all successful logins are signals for further inspection, outliers with large values are considered as excellent candidates for further probing of captured network traffic to detect

large-scale attacks. An examination of the successful credentials used by attackers reveals that either they were default factory state credentials of the devices or retrieved through exploits of commonly known vulnerabilities. We conjecture the reason being increasing number of automated scripts which assume that most IoT devices are configured with unchanged factory state credentials. Such scripts are easy for the attackers to generate and yield quick results.

Honeypot Detection – Apart from attracting attackers, maintaining stealth is also an important characteristic of a honeypot. We therefore verified whether the devices exposed by the honeypot have been detected as belonging to a honeypot, using a tool created by Shodan, called honeyscore[5]. The tool returns a score between 0.0 (not a honeypot) and 1.0 (is a honeypot) for queried IP addresses. Two out of 44 VPN-forwarders exposed by our honeypot were assigned the highest score of 0.3, none was detected as a honeypot.

5.4 Discussion

The proposed design allowed us to use few real devices and project them as multiple devices, geographically distributed around the world. Our design accommodated various kinds of IoT devices, thereby ascertaining its versatility and scalability. Based on the amount of traffic received, analysis presented and shodan honeyscores, we are certain that the honeypot was effective in attracting attackers and was realistic enough to motivate attackers to perform logins and other intrusion attempts.

However, we would like to acknowledge a few shortcomings with our design and implementation. First, a determined and skilled attacker may be able to detect our honeypot. For example, if the attacker can detect that multiple VPN-forwarders represent the same physical device, it can raise suspicion. However, the probability of an attacker discovering this is low. We observed from our collected network traffic that no attacker (single IP) discovered all VPN-forwarders representing same device.

Similarly, our real cameras currently show engaging but fabricated scenes. Though convincing and realistic at first glance, they may not fool a determined attacker for too long. Placing devices in realistic locations is an alternative. However, that may raise privacy concerns.

6 RELATED WORK

Recently, few implementations of honeypots have emerged with the goal of better understanding vulnerabilities, threats and large-scale attacks targeting IoT devices. Pa Pa et al. were the first to propose a honeypot exclusively

---

[5]https://honeyscore.shodan.io

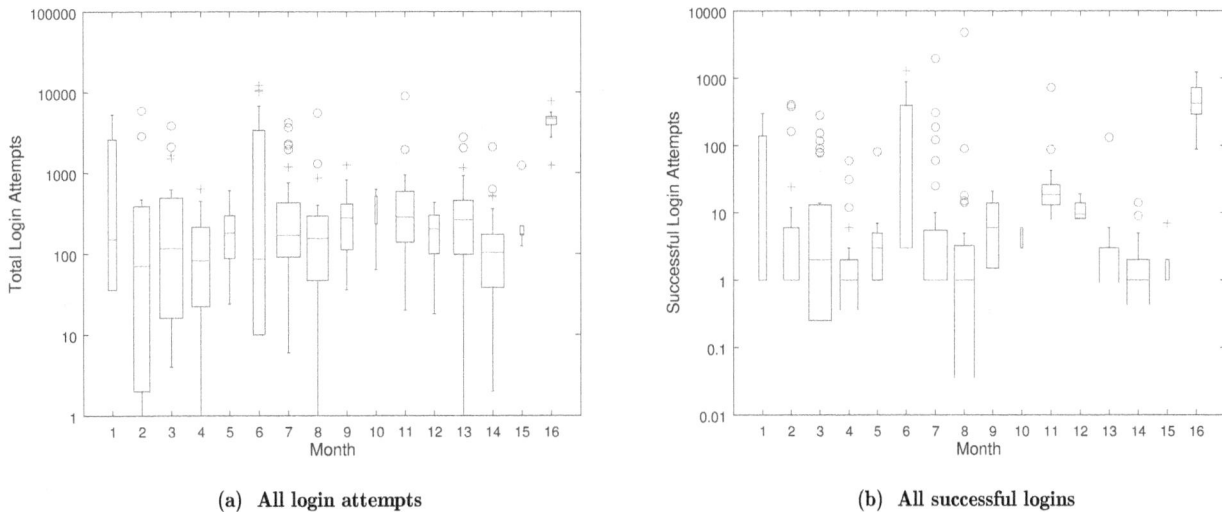

(a) **All login attempts**   (b) **All successful logins**

Figure 9: Boxplot showing comparison of all login attempts and successful logins

for IoT [19]. Their work focuses on capturing Telnet-based attacks on various IoT devices by means of a honeypot called IoTPOT. It consists of a low-interaction frontend responder cooperating with a high-interaction backend virtual environment called IoTBOX. Anirudh et al. presented a honeypot model for mitigating DoS attacks exploiting IoT devices [3]. Their model implements a low-interaction honeypot and works alongside an intrusion detection system (IDS). Their honeypot handles suspicious events detected by the IDS to avert a DoS attack. Luo et al. presented an automatic way to build an IoT honeypot called IoTCandyJar [14]. It utilizes publicly available IoT devices on the Internet to gather responses for its own requests. They applied heuristics and machine learning techniques to customize the scanning procedure for improving response logic. This extends the session longevity leading to higher chances of capturing malware. All these existing works implement honeypots for IoT devices by primarily creating virtual environment or by emulating services. Unlike previous works, Guarnizo et al. propose a high-interaction honeypot platform called SIPHON, incorporating real IoT devices [7]. They utilized cloud service providers (like Amazon AWS) to expose IoT devices on the Internet over geographically distributed IP addresses. However, such IP addresses might be identified as honeypot by the attacker as they belong to autonomous systems of cloud services. Our approach overcomes this limitation by utilizing public IP addresses assigned by VPN servers. For an attacker executing a large-scale attack with thousands of devices in his botnet, significant time and resources are required to uncover the true identity of those VPN IP addresses. Moreover, we make our honeypot stealthier by

physically disabling Wi-Fi connectivity and microphones. Disabling Wi-Fi connectivity prevents attackers from scanning neighboring SSIDs while disabling microphones prevents leakage of conversations. More importantly, we propose and implement two live traffic analysis methods to detect novel HTTP requests and attribute attacks corresponding to outbound connections. To the best of our knowledge, we are the first to propose and implement a comprehensive honeypot system that incorporates real IoT devices, performs automated live traffic analysis and captures malware.

7 CONCLUSIONS

In this work, we proposed a design for a generic honeypot framework for IoT devices by utilizing VPN connections. We collected real and high-interaction traffic of attacks by achieving low effort exposure of COTS devices on multiple IP addresses that provided geographical diversity. We implemented the proposed framework with 12 COTS devices, including IP cameras, printers, smart plugs and other smart devices. These devices were exposed on 44 IP addresses in 15 cities across nine countries. We incorporated several precautions to detect compromises and mitigate proliferation of malware. We did not instrument the COTS devices directly to detect compromise, but relied on traffic analysis instead. We proposed and implemented two live traffic analysis methods and deployed those on the traffic being captured by the honeypot.

Based on the analysis of captured traffic, we observed 5136 successful and malicious login attempts resulting in outbound connections. These connections were attempted to 4642 distinct IP addresses across 109 countries. By applying our live traffic analysis methods, we were able to attribute attack commands to 97.5% of outbound IPs. Further, by incorporating live adaptive clustering method we were able to detect several active large-scale attack campaigns such as IoT Reaper, Hakai, etc. We temporarily allowed outbound connections to be established via malware downloader component, for a period of 45 days, resulting in capture of 78 distinct malware binaries. Based on application of two automated live traffic analysis methods, our honeypot was able to effectively detect and attribute attacks to their corresponding attack commands.

REFERENCES

[1] 2017. Persirai: New Internet of Things (IoT) Botnet Targets IP Cameras. http://blog.trendmicro.com/trendlabs-security-intelligence/persirai-new-internet-things-iot-botnet-targets-ip-cameras/

[2] 2018. Unit 42 Finds New Mirai and Gafgyt IoT/Linux Botnet Campaigns - Palo Alto Networks Blog. https://researchcenter.paloaltonetworks.com/2018/07/unit42-finds-new-mirai-gafgyt-iotlinux-botnet-campaigns/. (Accessed on 08/17/2018).

[3] M Anirudh, S Arul Thileeban, and Daniel Jeswin Nallathambi. 2017. Use of honeypots for mitigating DoS attacks targeted on IoT networks. In *Proceedings of Conference on Computer, Communication and Signal Processing (ICCCSP)*. IEEE, 1–4.

[4] console cowboys. 2012. Trendnet Camera (Multiple Products) - Remote Security Bypass. https://www.exploit-db.com/exploits/36680/.

[5] Ang Cui and Salvatore J Stolfo. 2010. A quantitative analysis of the insecurity of embedded network devices: results of a wide-area scan. In *Proceedings of the Annual Computer Security Applications Conference (ACSAC)*. ACM, 97–106.

[6] Earlence Fernandes, Jaeyeon Jung, and Atul Prakash. 2016. Security analysis of emerging smart home applications. In *Security and Privacy (SP), 2016 IEEE Symposium on*. IEEE, 636–654.

[7] Juan David Guarnizo, Amit Tambe, Suman Sankar Bhunia, Martín Ochoa, Nils Ole Tippenhauer, Asaf Shabtai, and Yuval Elovici. 2017. SIPHON: Towards scalable high-interaction physical honeypots. In *Proceedings of the ACM Workshop on Cyber-Physical System Security*. ACM, ACM, 57–68.

[8] Thorsten Holz, Markus Engelberth, and Felix Freiling. 2009. Learning more about the underground economy: A case-study of keyloggers and dropzones. In *European Symposium on Research in Computer Security*. Springer, 1–18.

[9] IP Intelligence. 2018. Free Proxy / VPN / TOR / Bad IP Detection Service via API and Web Interface | IP Intelligence. https://getipintel.net/. (Accessed on 01/03/2017).

[10] Thommen George Karimpanal and Erik Wilhelm. 2017. Identification and off-policy learning of multiple objectives using adaptive clustering. *Neurocomputing* 263 (2017), 39–47.

[11] Pierre Kim. 2017. Multiple vulnerabilities found in Wireless IP Camera (P2P) WIFICAM cameras and vulnerabilities in custom http server. https://pierrekim.github.io/blog/2017-03-08-camera-goahead-0day.html#pre-auth-info-leak-goahead.

[12] Constantinos Kolias, Georgios Kambourakis, Angelos Stavrou, and Jeffrey Voas. 2017. DDoS in the IoT: Mirai and Other Botnets. *Computer* 50, 7 (2017), 80–84.

[13] Brian Krebs. 2016. KrebsOnSecurity Hit With Record DDoS. https://krebsonsecurity.com/2016/09/krebsonsecurity-hit-with-record-ddos/.

[14] Tongbo Luo, Zhaoyan Xu, Xing Jin, Yanhui Jia, and Xin Ouyang. 2017. IoTCandyJar: Towards an Intelligent-Interaction Honeypot for IoT Devices. In *Proceedings of Blackhat*.

[15] Bill Miller and Dale Rowe. 2012. A Survey SCADA of and Critical Infrastructure Incidents. In *Proceedings of the 1st Annual Conference on Research in Information Technology (RIIT '12)*. ACM, New York, NY, USA, 51–56. https://doi.org/10.1145/2380790.2380805

[16] Roberto Minerva, Abyi Biru, and Domenico Rotondi. 2015. Towards a definition of the Internet of Things (IoT). *IEEE Internet Initiative* (May 2015). http://iot.ieee.org/images/files/pdf/IEEE_IoT_Towards_Definition_Internet_of_Things_Revision1_27MAY15.pdf

[17] Iyatiti Mokube and Michele Adams. 2007. Honeypots: concepts, approaches, and challenges. In *Proceedings of the annual southeast regional conference*. ACM, 321–326.

[18] Sukhvir Notra, Muhammad Siddiqi, Hassan Habibi Gharakheili, Vijay Sivaraman, and Roksana Boreli. 2014. An experimental study of security and privacy risks with emerging household appliances. In *Communications and Network Security (CNS), 2014 IEEE Conference on*. IEEE, 79–84.

[19] Yin Minn Pa Pa, Shogo Suzuki, Katsunari Yoshioka, Tsutomu Matsumoto, Takahiro Kasama, and Christian Rossow. 2016. IoT-POT: A Novel Honeypot for Revealing Current IoT Threats. *Journal of Information Processing* 24, 3 (2016), 522–533.

[20] Mark Patton, Eric Gross, Ryan Chinn, Samantha Forbis, Leon Walker, and Hsinchun Chen. 2014. Uninvited connections: a study of vulnerable devices on the internet of things (IoT). In *Proceedings of Intelligence and Security Informatics Conference (JISIC)*. IEEE, 232–235.

[21] Niels Provos and Thorsten Holz. 2007. *Virtual honeypots: from botnet tracking to intrusion detection*. Addison-Wesley Professional.

[22] Shodan Project. 2017. Shodan. https://www.shodan.io/. (Accessed on 10/18/2017).

[23] Vijay Sivaraman, Dominic Chan, Dylan Earl, and Roksana Boreli. 2016. Smart-phones attacking smart-homes. In *Proceedings of the 9th ACM Conference on Security & Privacy in Wireless and Mobile Networks*. ACM, 195–200.

[24] Vijay Sivaraman, Hassan Habibi Gharakheili, Arun Vishwanath, Roksana Boreli, and Olivier Mehani. 2015. Network-level security and privacy control for smart-home IoT devices. In *Proceedings of Conference on Wireless and Mobile Computing, Networking and Communications (WiMob)*. IEEE, 163–167.

[25] Rob van der Meulen. 2016. Gartner Says 8.4 Billion Connected Things Will Be in Use in 2017, Up 31 Percent From 2016. http://www.gartner.com/newsroom/id/3598917.

[26] Yegenshen. 2017. IoT_reaper: A Rappid Spreading New IoT Botnet. http://blog.netlab.360.com/iot_reaper-a-rappid-spreading-new-iot-botnet-en/.

[27] Tianlong Yu, Vyas Sekar, Srinivasan Seshan, Yuvraj Agarwal, and Chenren Xu. 2015. Handling a trillion (unfixable) flaws on a billion devices: Rethinking network security for the internet-of-things. In *Proceedings of the ACM Workshop on Hot Topics in Networks*. ACM.

Deep Neural Networks Classification over Encrypted Data

Ehsan Hesamifard
University of North Texas
Denton, Texas, USA
ehsanhesamifard@my.unt.edu

Hassan Takabi
University of North Texas
Denton, Texas, USA
takabi@unt.edu

Mehdi Ghasemi
University of Saskatchewan
Saskatoon, Canda
mehdi.ghasemi@usask.ca

ABSTRACT

Deep Neural Networks (DNNs) have overtaken classic machine learning algorithms due to their superior performance in big data analysis in a broad range of applications. On the other hand, in recent years Machine Learning as a Service (MLaaS) has become more widespread in which a client uses cloud services for analyzing its data. However, the client's data may be sensitive which raises privacy concerns. In this paper, we address the issue of privacy preserving classification in a Machine Learning as a Service (MLaaS) settings and focus on convolutional neural networks (CNN). To achieve this goal, we develop new techniques to run CNNs over encrypted data. First, we design methods to approximate commonly used activation functions in CNNs (i.e. ReLU, Sigmoid, and Tanh) with low degree polynomials which is essential for a practical and efficient solution. Then, we train CNNs with approximation polynomials instead of original activation functions and implement CNNs classification over encrypted data. We evaluate the performance of our modified models at each step. The results of our experiments using several CNNs with a varying number of layers and structures are promising. When applied to the MNIST optical character recognition tasks, our approach achieved 99.25% accuracy which significantly outperforms state-of-the-art solutions and is close to the accuracy of the best non-private version. Furthermore, it can make up to 164000 predictions per hour. These results show that our approach provides accurate, efficient, and scalable privacy-preserving predictions in CNNs.

CCS CONCEPTS

• **Security and privacy** → **Cryptography**; **Privacy-preserving protocols**; **Trusted computing**; • **Computing methodologies** → *Supervised learning by classification*; • **Computer systems organization** → Neural networks;

KEYWORDS

privacy; deep learning; convolutional neural network; homomorphic encryption; classification

ACM Reference Format:
Ehsan Hesamifard, Hassan Takabi, and Mehdi Ghasemi. 2019. Deep Neural Networks Classification over Encrypted Data. In *Ninth ACM Conference on Data and Application Security and Privacy (CODASPY '19), March 25–27, 2019, Richardson, TX, USA.* ACM, New York, NY, USA, 12 pages. https://doi.org/10.1145/3292006.3300044

1 INTRODUCTION

Convolutional Neural Networks (CNNs) are one type of deep neural networks used for analyzing big data in a variety of domains. They have achieved remarkable results in applications such as image recognition, video analysis, face recognition, natural language processing, etc. On the other hand, machine learning services such as deep neural networks can be run on the Cloud where the cloud service providers' infrastructure is used for training and deploying machine learning models. Clients use these services without having any concerns about data gathering, model training and service maintenance. This is called Machine Learning as a Service (MLaaS), and several such services are currently offered including Microsoft Azure Machine Learning [29], Google Prediction API [16], GraphLab [38], and Ersatz Labs [25]. However, using these services requires sharing data with the service provider which might be privacy sensitive and not acceptable from the data owner prospective. In this paper, we propose an approach based on Homomorphic Encryption (HE) schemes for preserving the privacy of clients' data in MLaaS settings.

In recent years, several studies have investigated preserving the privacy of sensitive data in different machine learning algorithms such as linear regression [31], linear classifiers [5, 17], decision trees [1, 5] or neural networks [8, 14]. Some of the these works discuss privacy-preserving machine learning in classical machine learning algorithms ([1, 5, 17]). Recently, there are a few work that focus on Deep Neural Networks ([14, 31, 33]). However, most of these efforts are based on Secure Multiparty Computation (SMC) which has a huge communication overhead [31, 33]. They also require the client to be available for running the protocol and have a weak security model. Similar to our approach, [14] and [8] are based on Homomorphic Encryption schemes. However, their proposed solutions are limited to specific models and [8] does not provide any results over encrypted data. In contrast, we propose a general solution that can be applied to any CNN and is more accurate and more efficient.

The basic idea of our proposed approach is running deep neural network algorithms on the encrypted data by taking the advantage of Homomorphic Encryption schemes. The server provides the machine service without revealing the trained model and the clients receive the classification service without revealing their data and risking their privacy. To allow accurate predictions, we propose using CNNs which are extensively used in machine learning community for a wide variety of tasks [20, 24]. In particular, we focus on the classification phase of CNNs and main components of our approach are CNNs and HE schemes.

Recent advances in Fully Homomorphic Encryption (FHE) enable a limited set of operations to be performed on encrypted data [6, 15]. This allows us to apply deep neural network algorithms directly to encrypted data and return encrypted results without compromising security and privacy. However, due to a number of constraints associated with these cryptographic schemes, designing practical efficient solutions to run deep neural network models on the encrypted data is challenging. The most notable shortcoming is the allowed operations over encrypted values which is limited to addition and multiplication. On the other hand, the computation performed on the sensitive data by CNNs is very complex and makes it hard to support efficiently by HE schemes. Convolutional neural network models cannot simply support encrypted values without modification. Consequently, we need to adopt CNNs within these limitations. For example, activation functions -nonlinear part of network- such as Rectified Linear Unit (ReLU) ($max(x, 0)$) and Sigmoid ($\frac{1}{1+e^{-x}}$) cannot be performed over encrypted data. We have to replace them with HE-friendly functions such as polynomials that only use addition and multiplication.

In order to have efficient and practical solutions for computations over encrypted data, we typically need to use Leveled HE (LHE) schemes instead of FHE (see section 2.2). However, LHE schemes only support a limited number of operations over encrypted data. Therefore, a solution that builds upon LHE schemes has to be restricted to computing low-degree polynomials. We propose a general approximation method for different activation functions with low degree polynomials (Sigmoid, ReLU and Tanh functions) and adopt them within limitations of HE schemes.

1.1 Threat Model and Problem Statement

In this paper, we focus on the CNN, one of the most popular deep learning algorithms. We assume that the training phase is done on the plaintext data and a model has already been built and trained by the server. We consider a client-server model where the server owns the training data and the server uses this data to build a model and provide prediction service to the client. The client owns the unseen data and needs to preserve the privacy of its data while using prediction service provided by the server.

Threat Model: The server owns the model, and the structure of the model and its parameters are sensitive information from server's prospective. The client owns the unseen instances, and the feature values and result of classification are sensitive information from client's prospective. Unlike the SMC-based solutions, the server does not share any information about the model with another party and the model remains on the server side. The client sends encrypted input to the server, the server performs an inference on the encrypted data, and the client gets the encrypted prediction. Hence, the server cannot access the input data or the prediction at anytime.

Problem: *Privacy-preserving Classification on Deep Convolutional Neural Networks*

The client has a previously unseen feature vector x and the server has an already trained deep CNN model w. The server runs a classifier C over x using the model w to output a prediction $C(x, w)$. To do this, the client sends an encrypted input to the server, the server performs encrypted inference, and the client gets the encrypted

prediction. The server must not learn anything about the input data or the prediction and the client must not learn information about the trained model w.

A practical solution to this problem for real-world applications should be both **accurate** (the prediction performance should be close to the prediction performance of the plaintext) and **efficient** (the running time to obtain the prediction result should be low).

1.2 Contributions

In this paper, we design and evaluate a *privacy-preserving classification for convolutional neural networks*. Our goal is to adopt convolutional neural networks within practical limitations of HE while keeping accuracy as close as possible to the original model.

The most common activation functions used in CNNs are ReLU, Sigmoid, and Tanh. In order to achieve our goal, these functions should be replaced by HE friendly functions such as low-degree polynomials.

- We investigate several methods for approximating commonly used activation functions in CNNs (i.e. ReLU, Sigmoid, and Tanh) with the low-degree polynomials to find the best approximation.
- We provide a formal approach to polynomial approximation of activation functions that improves the methods proposed in the literature and calculates the coefficients of the polynomial approximation more accurately.
- We analyze the relation between the performance of the model which is trained based on the polynomials and the error of the polynomials, the interval of approximation and the architecture of the network.
- We utilize the generated approximation polynomials in CNNs and analyze the performance of the modified algorithms.
- We implement the CNNs with the polynomial approximations as the activation functions over encrypted data and report the results for two of the widely used datasets in deep learning MNIST and CIFAR-10.
- We will open-source our implementation which could become a useful benchmark for similar efforts in the community.

The rest of this paper is organized as follows: In Section 2, we provide a brief overview of the structure of deep CNNs and HE schemes. In Section 3, we briefly describe our theoretical foundation and propose a solution for polynomial approximation. Section 4 provides experimental results for CNN models over encrypted datasets followed by a discussion. In Section 5, we review related work. In Section 6, we conclude the paper and discuss future work.

2 OVERVIEW AND BACKGROUND INFORMATION

In this section, we briefly describe deep CNNs and modifications that are required for adopting them with HE schemes. We also introduce HE schemes briefly, along with their strengths and weaknesses, which should be considered while using them for secure computation protocols.

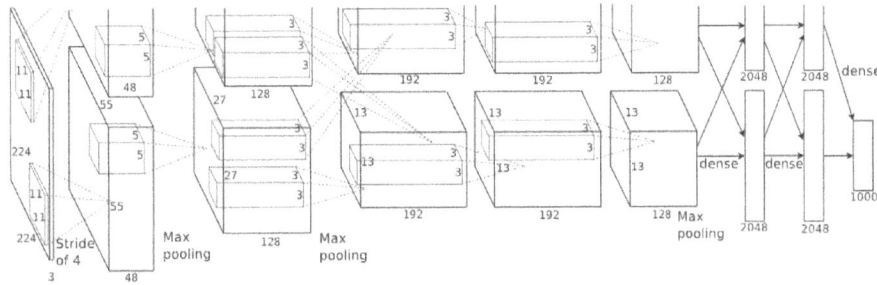

Figure 1: Different Layers in a Convolutional Neural Network

2.1 Convolutional Neural Networks (CNNs / ConvNets)

Convolutional Neural Networks (CNNs / ConvNets) are a specific type of feed-forward neural networks in which the connectivity pattern between its neurons is inspired by the organization of the animal visual cortex. They have proven to be very effective in areas such as image recognition and classification. CNNs commonly use several distinct kinds of layers as shown in Figure 1 described in the followings.[1]

The first layer in a CNN is a set of filters arranged in a *Convolutional Layer*. The idea behind using convolutional layers is learning features from the data. We convolve the pixels in the image and calculate the dot product of the filter values and related values in the neighbor of the pixel. This step only includes addition and multiplication and we can use the same computation over the encrypted data.

An *activation layer* is a non-linear function. There are several activation functions in practice including ReLU, Sigmoid and Tanh functions. We should find replacements for these functions that only include addition and multiplication operations.

A *pooling layer* is for sub-sampling from the data and reduces its size. Two of the most popular pooling layers are *max pooling* and *average pooling*. We cannot use max pooling because of the lack of the max operation over the encrypted data. We use a scaled-up version of average pooling as proposed in [14], calculate the summation of values without dividing it by the number of values.

Fully connected layer has the same structure like hidden layers in classic neural networks, a stack of neurons connected to all neurons in the previous layer. The output of each neuron is the dot product of two vectors: output of neurons in the previous layers and the related weight for each neuron.

There are different ways to use the above-mentioned layers in a CNN for training a model. However, there is a common pattern for creating a CNN, $[[Convolutional \rightarrow Activation]^n \rightarrow AveragePooling]^n$. We can use this more than one times. Then, we have one or more fully connected layers and the CNN ends with an output layer. The size of the output layer is the number of classes in the dataset.

2.2 Homomorphic Encryption

Homomorphic encryption (HE) schemes preserve the structure of the message space such that we can perform operations like addition and multiplication over the ciphertext space. Similar to other types of encryption schemes, an HE scheme has three main functions, *Gen*, *Enc*, and *Dec*, for key generation, encryption, and decryption, respectively. However, an HE scheme also has an evaluation function, *Eval*. Suppose we have a set of plaintext messages $\{m_i\}_1^n$ and relative ciphertexts $\{c_i\}_1^n$. Now, consider a circuit C. The evaluation function processes the public key pk, a set of ciphertexts $\{c_i\}_1^n$ and a circuit C such that

$$Dec(sk, Eval(pk, C, c_1, \cdots, c_n)) = C(m_1, \cdots, m_n)$$

where the sk is the secret key. HE was first introduced in 1978 by Rivest et al. [34]. Other researchers followed to introduce several other HE schemes [32]. However, most of these encryption schemes have some constraints. Some of them, such as the Paillier cryptosystem [32], only support one operation (addition). If the encryption scheme only supports one operation, it is called Somewhat Homomorphic Encryption (SHE).

The idea behind encryption function *Enc* is to add a small value, called *noise*, to m for encrypting. Therefore, each ciphertext has a small amount of noise. When we add two ciphertexts c_1 and c_2, the result is also a ciphertext, but with noise that has grown. The *Dec* function works correctly if this amount is less than a threshold. This threshold leads to a bound on the number of computations that can be performed over encrypted data. If an entity wants to decrease the noise, it should decrypt and encrypt the ciphertext. For decryption, it needs the secret key sk. For years, the community was trying to find out if there is a way to decrease the noise without having the secret key. This question was answered in 2009 when the first Fully Homomorphic Encryption (FHE) scheme was designed by Gentry [15]. An FHE scheme is an HE scheme that supports circuits with arbitrary depth. In his dissertation, Gentry introduced a technique for handling an arbitrary depth of computations, called *bootstrapping*. In bootstrapping technique, the amount of noise is decreased without needing to access the sk [15]. However, it has a huge computational cost and is a very slow process. This limitation makes FHE impractical for actual use.

Recent advances in HE have led to a faster HE scheme: Leveled Homomorphic Encryption (LHE). LHE schemes do not support the bootstrapping step, so they only allow circuits with depth less than a specific threshold. If we know the number of operations before starting the computations, we can use LHE instead of FHE. The performance of LHE schemes is further improved using Single-Instruction-Multiple-Data (SIMD) techniques. Halevi et al. in [18]

---
[1]Figure 1 adopted from [24]

use this technique to create a batch of ciphertexts. So, one single ciphertext has been replaced with an array of ciphertexts in computations. There are also other implementations of HE schemes, such as Simple Encrypted Arithmetic Library (SEAL) [30], PALISADE Lattice Cryptography Library [35] and Homomorphic Encryption for Arithmetic of Approximate Numbers (HEAAN) [10].

Despite the advantages of HE schemes, they have some limitations. The first limitation is operations that an HE scheme supports, i.e. addition and multiplication. We cannot run any other operations like division or exponential function over ciphertexts. The second important limitation is related to the noise. If the HE scheme does not support bootstrapping, the noise accumulates in the ciphertext during computations and we cannot reduce the noise without having access to the secret key. The amount of added noise to the ciphertext depends on the type of operation. Multiplication increases noise much more than addition. If the amount of noise passes a threshold, the decryption function does not work correctly. Therefore, we should always keep track of the number of operations over ciphertext to make sure that it is less than the predefined threshold. The third limitation is about the message space (integer domain). Before encrypting feature values or model parameters, we need to convert them to integers. The fourth limitation is the ciphertext size. The size of the message increases considerably by encryption and it depends on the security level of the HE scheme.

In summary, only a limited number of additions and multiplications can be performed efficiently over the encrypted data and therefore complex functions such as activation functions used in CNNs are not compatible with HE schemes.

3 THE PROPOSED PRIVACY-PRESERVING CLASSIFICATION FOR CONVOLUTIONAL NEURAL NETWORKS

Since our goal is to adopt a CNN to work within HE constraints, our focus is on operations inside the neurons. Besides activation functions inside the neurons, all other operations in a neural network are addition and multiplication, so they can be implemented over encrypted data. It is not practical within current HE schemes to use activation functions within HE schemes. Hence, we should find compatible replacement functions in order to operate over encrypted data.

The basic idea of our solution to this problem is to approximate the non-compatible functions with a compatible form so they can be implemented using HE. In general, most functions including activation functions used in CNNs, can be approximated with polynomials which are implemented using only addition and multiplication operations. Hence, we aim to approximate the activation functions with polynomials and replace them with these polynomials when operating over encrypted data. We investigate polynomial approximation of activation functions commonly used in CNNs, namely ReLU, Sigmoid, and Tanh and choose the one that approximates each activation function the best.

3.1 Activation Functions and Homomorphic Encryption

A variety of activation functions has been proposed by researchers to address the issue of non-compatible activation functions. Polynomial of degree 2 has been used to substitute the Sigmoid function in CNNs [14] and polynomial of degree 3 has been used to estimate the natural logarithm function [37]. Using square function as the activation function needs some modification in the model training phase.

There are also other approaches such as polynomial approximation of activation functions or simulation of activation functions' structure. Chabanne et al. [8] used Taylor series for approximating the Sigmoid function with polynomials. In their experiment, 99.73% of values are in the interval [−3, 3] therefore, they approximate the Sigmoid function over this interval with different degrees (2, 4 and 6). However, the Taylor series can only give a good approximation in the neighborhood of a certain point and outside that, the neighborhood error of the approximation is high [21, 22]. Also, it requires a high degree polynomial (5 or 7) for achieving an acceptable performance. Kim et al. proposed an approximation method by minimizing the mean square error [21, 22]. They approximated the Sigmoid function on the interval [−8, 8] with different degrees (3 and 7). Crawford et al. proposed using a look-up table for implementing non-compatible functions like the Sigmoid function over encrypted values [12].

Replacing the activation function with an adopted form is a challenge not only in HE scheme based solutions, but also in Secure Multiparty Computation (SMC). Implementing exponential function (Sigmoid) or the max function (ReLU) needs heavy computations and communications in SMC based solutions.

secureml and Zhang proposed approximating the Sigmoid function with piece-wise linear activation functions as well as numerical approximation with polynomials [31] . Based on the provided results, they concluded that low degree polynomials (2 or 3) have a low accuracy and computation cost while, high degree polynomials (10) have a high accuracy and computation cost (because of the number of multiplications). However, for the back-propagation step, instead of using the derivative of the new activation function, the authors suggested to use the derivative of the ReLU function. Liu et. al also used a piece-wise linear activation function for approximating the activation functions such as the Sigmoid function [27].

These approaches enable us to work on certain problems, but there is no generic solution to this problem yet. Generally, we can approximate activation functions with polynomials from different degrees. The higher degree polynomials provide a more accurate approximation and, when they replace the activation function in a CNN, lead to a better performance in the trained model. However, when operations are performed over encrypted data, a higher degree polynomial results in very slow computations. Therefore, a solution that builds upon HE schemes should be restricted to computing low-degree polynomials in order to be practical [39]. We need to find a trade-off between the degree of the polynomial approximation and the performance of the model. In the following, we first provide the theoretical foundation and prove that it is possible to find the lowest degree polynomial approximation of a function within a certain error range. Next, we propose a solution for the polynomial approximation of several activation functions (i.e. ReLU, Sigmoid, Tanh). Then, we train CNN models using these polynomials and compare the performance with the models with the original activation functions.

3.2 Polynomial Approximation: Theoretical Foundation

Among continuous functions, perhaps polynomials are the most well behaved and easiest to compute. Thus, it is no surprise that mathematicians tend to approximate other functions by polynomials. Materials in this section are mainly folklore knowledge in numerical analysis and Hilbert spaces. For more details on the subject, refer to [3, 40].

Let us denote the family of all continuous real valued functions on a non-empty compact space X by $C(X)$. Since linear combination and product of polynomials are also polynomials, we assume that A is closed under addition, scalar multiplication and product and a non-zero constant function belongs to A (This actually implies that A contains all constant functions). [*Stone–Weierstrass*] Theorem. Every element of $C(X)$ can be approximated by elements of A if and only if for every $x \neq y \in X$, there exists $p \in A$ such that $p(x) \neq p(y)$. Despite the strong and important implications of the Stone-Weierstrass theorem, it leaves computational details out and does not give a specific algorithm to generate an estimator for f with elements of A, given an error tolerance ϵ. We address this issue here.

Let μ be a finite measure on X and for $f, g \in C(X)$ define $\langle f, g \rangle = \int_X f g d\mu$. Different choices of μ gives different systems of orthogonal polynomials. Two of the most popular measures are $d\mu = dx$ and $d\mu = \frac{dx}{\sqrt{1-x^2}}$. By using $d\mu = dx$ on $[-1, 1]$, the generated polynomials are called Legendre polynomials and by using $d\mu = \frac{dx}{\sqrt{1-x^2}}$ on $[-1, 1]$ the generated polynomials called Chebyshev polynomials.

These two polynomial sets have different applications in approximation theory. For example, the nodes we use in polynomial interpolation are the roots of the Chebyshev polynomials and the Legendre polynomials are the coefficient of the Taylor series [3, 40].

3.3 Polynomial Approximation: ReLU

Several methods have been proposed in the literature for polynomial approximation including Taylor series, Chebyshev polynomials, etc. [3, 40]. We first try these approaches for finding the best approximation for the ReLU function and then present our proposed approach that provides better approximation than all these methods. We investigate the following methods for approximating the ReLU function:

(1) Numerical approximation
(2) Taylor series
(3) Standard Chebyshev polynomials
(4) Modified Chebyshev polynomials
(5) Our approach based on the derivative of ReLU function

Due to space limits, we do not provide detailed results for all these methods and only explain our conclusion for each method.

(1) Numerical analysis: For this method, we generate a set of points from ReLU function and give this set of inputs to the approximation function and a constant degree for the activation function. We experimented with polynomials of degree 3 to 13 and for lower degree polynomials, the accuracy drops considerably. For achieving a good accuracy, we have to increase the degree, which makes it inefficient when we are working with encrypted data. Our investigation showed that the method 1 is not a good approach for approximating the ReLU function.

(2) Taylor series: In this method, we use Taylor series [3, 40], a popular method for approximating functions. We used different degrees for approximating the ReLU function and trained the model using polynomials of different degrees. Two main issues make this method inefficient. The first issue is the high degree of polynomial approximation, although lower than the method 1, is still too high to be used with HE schemes. The more important issue is the interval of the approximation. The basic idea of Taylor series is to approximate a function in a neighbor of a point. For the points that are not included in the input interval, the approximation error is much higher than points included in this interval. For example, in the MNIST dataset, pixel values are integers in the interval $[0, 255]$ and this method cannot cover this interval. If we can approximate the ReLU function in a large interval, we can avoid using extra layers and this can be done using Chebyshev polynomials [40] as explained below.

(3) Standard Chebyshev polynomials: Chebyshev polynomials are not as popular as the previous methods (i.e., 1 and 2). However, they have a specific feature that makes them more suitable for our problem. In this method, we approximate a function in an interval instead of a small neighborhood of a point. HE schemes are over integers with message space $\mathbb{Z}$; therefore, we extend the interval to be able to cover integers. In the standard Chebyshev polynomials, we use $d\mu = \frac{dx}{\sqrt{1-x^2}}$ as the standard norm. We approximate the ReLU function with this method and train the model based on that. As shown in Table 1, the accuracy is much better than methods 1 and 2, however, it is still not a good performance in comparison with the original activation function. One way to improve the accuracy and find better approximation is to modify the measure function based on the structure of the ReLU function, which is done in the next method.

(4) Modified Chebyshev polynomials: In order to simulate the structure of ReLU function, we changed the standard norm used in Chebyshev polynomials to $e^{\left(\frac{-1}{(1e-5+(x)^2)}\right)}$ and were able to achieve much better results compared to all the previous methods. The idea behind this method is that the measure for Chebyshev polynomials mainly concentrates at the endpoints of the interval which causes interpolation at mostly initial and end points with two singularities at both ends. Conversely, the second measure evens out through the whole real line and puts zero weight at the center. This behavior causes less oscillation in the resulting approximation and hence more similarities of derivatives with Sigmoid function. However, this improvement in performance is still not good enough.

Let us look at why the accuracy drops significantly in the above methods. Our goal is to approximate the ReLU function, however, note the derivative of the ReLU function is more important than the structure of the ReLU function. Therefore, we changed our approach to the problem and focused on approximating the derivative

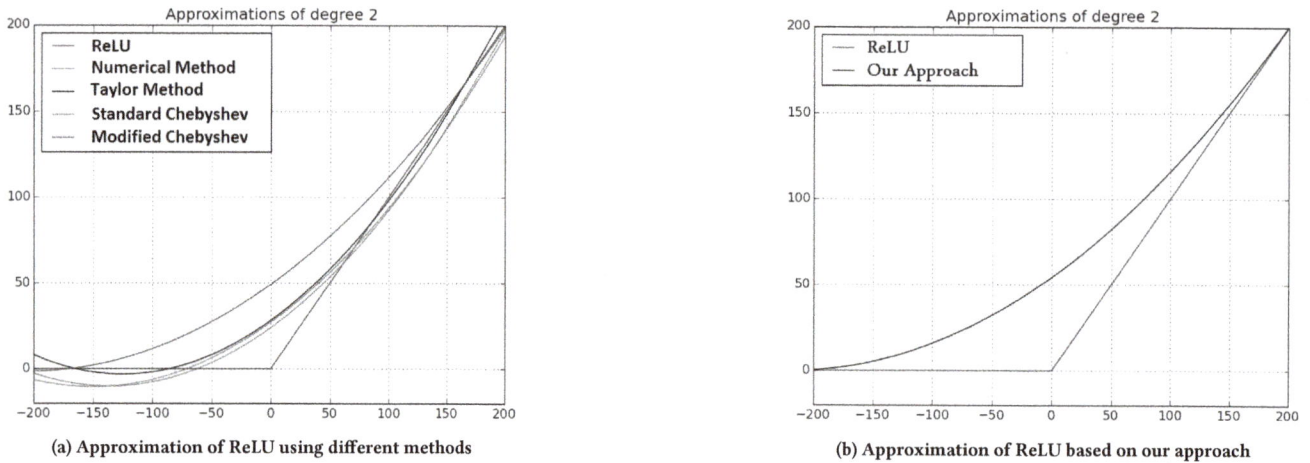

(a) Approximation of ReLU using different methods

(b) Approximation of ReLU based on our approach

Figure 2: Polynomial Approximation of ReLU

Table 1: Performance of the trained CNN using Different Approximation Methods

Method	Accuracy
Numerical analysis	56.87%
Taylor series	40.28%
Standard Chebyshev	68.98%
Modified Chebyshev	88.53%
Our Approach	98.52%

of the ReLU function instead of approximating the ReLU function as explained below. **(5) Our approach based on the derivative of ReLU function:** All the above methods are based on simulating the activation function with polynomials. In this method, however, we use another approach and consider the derivative of the activation function because of its impact on the error calculation and updating the weights. Therefore, instead of simulating the activation function, we simulate the derivative of the activation function. The derivative of ReLU function is like a Step function and is non-differentiable in point 0. If the function is continuous and infinitely derivative, we can approximate it more accurately than a non-continuous or non-infinitely differentiable function. Instead of approximating the ReLU function, we simulate the structure of derivation of the ReLU function, a Step function. The Sigmoid function is a bounded, continuous and infinitely differentiable function; it also has a structure like the derivative of the ReLU function in large intervals. We approximate the Sigmoid function with the polynomial, calculate the integral of the polynomial, and use it as the activation function. As shown in Table 1, this method achieves the best approximation of the ReLU function and we will use this method for approximation in this paper.

Figure 2a shows the structure of the functions generated by all the above approximation methods in comparison with the ReLU function whereas Figure 2b shows only the last method in comparison with the ReLU function. These two figures show that the

last method simulates the structure of the ReLU function considerably better than other methods. In Figure 2a, for some values less than zero, the structure of the polynomial goes up and down. This behavior has an impact on the performance of the model that is trained based on these polynomials. However, in Figure 2b, the structure of the function is almost the same as the ReLU function, and for this reason, we expect to have a performance close to the ReLU function. We try to keep the degree of the polynomial as low as possible; therefore, we only work with degree 2 and degree 3 polynomials.

3.4 Polynomial Approximation: Sigmoid and Tanh

In addition to the ReLU function, we also approximate two other popular activation functions: Sigmoid and Tanh. Approximating these two functions is more straightforward compared with the ReLU, because they are infinitely derivative. In this paper, we experiment with polynomial approximations of the Sigmoid function and the Tanh function over a symmetric interval $[-l, l]$ using two different orthogonal systems of polynomials. As the first choice, we consider Chebyshev polynomials on the stretched interval, which come from the measure $d\mu = \dfrac{dx}{l\sqrt{1-(x/l)^2}}$.

The measure for Chebyshev polynomials mainly concentrates at the endpoints of the interval. The second measure, conversely, evens out through the whole real line and puts zero weight at the center. This behavior causes less oscillation in the resulting approximation and hence more similarities of derivatives with Sigmoid function. Now that we have found polynomial approximations, the next step is training CNN models using these polynomials and comparing the performance of these models with the original models.

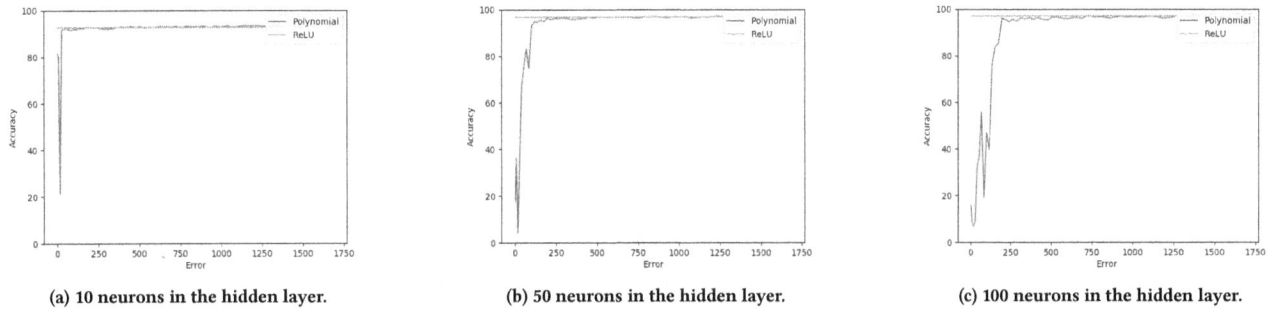

(a) 10 neurons in the hidden layer.

(b) 50 neurons in the hidden layer.

(c) 100 neurons in the hidden layer.

Figure 3: Performance of polynomials for different architectures and approximation errors.

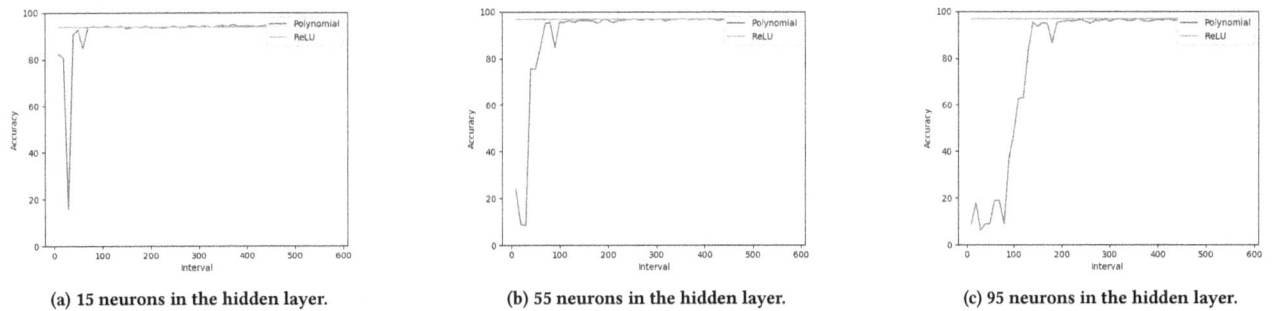

(a) 15 neurons in the hidden layer.

(b) 55 neurons in the hidden layer.

(c) 95 neurons in the hidden layer.

Figure 4: Performance of training with polynomials for different architectures and intervals.

3.5 Training based on Approximation Polynomials

In this section, we discuss the relation between the approximation interval and error with the model performance. First, we approximate the ReLU function over different intervals. We start from [-10,10] interval and go up to [-590, 590] with a 10 unit increment in each step, calling it $\mathcal{P} = \{p_i\}_1^{58}$. The approximation interval must be symmetric. Then, we consider a neural network with only one hidden layer, and increase the number of neurons from 1 to 100, calling it $\{Arc_i\}_1^{100}$. Finally, we train a model for each polynomial and each architecture up to 50 epochs.

The standard deviations of accuracy values were high (12%) due to randomized initial weights. To solve this problem, we run the experiment again using fixed initial weights. The new standard deviations are less than 3% which makes our results more reliable. Initially, we trained each model up to 50 epochs to reach a stable performance. Instead of this approach which is time consuming, we decided to use another method which is more efficient in terms of the performance and the running time. In this new method, first, we train a model up to 50 epochs based on the ReLU function. Then, we use the trained model's weights as the initial weights inputs and train our models using polynomials, see Algorithm 1. The accuracy of these new models is higher. Also, we only need to train up to 5 epochs to reach a stable performance. So, the running time is much lower compared to the training for 50 epochs.

We define the error between the polynomial and the ReLU function based on the $L2$-norm. As the Figure 3 shows, higher error values do not result in a lower accuracy. The reason is that the structure of the polynomial is similar to the ReLU function. This gives a good enough accuracy even though the error of the approximation increases.

The accuracy of the model decreases by increasing the number of neurons for a fixed interval. To improve the accuracy, we need to approximate the activation function over a larger interval. Note that for a larger approximation interval, the model performance for a small number of neurons is almost the same as the original form of the activation function. Figure 4 shows a similar trend, the approximation interval and the number of neurons. It clearly shows that as the number of neurons increases from 15 to 95, the accuracy over the smaller intervals is deteriorating. In conclusion, for training the model, we need to choose the initial weights properly in order to get a higher performance and a lower running time. For choosing the best polynomial, we need to approximate the activation function over a large interval to cover all values for calculations.

3.6 CNN Models with Polynomial Activation Function

In order to evaluate the effectiveness of different approximation methods, we use a CNN and the MNIST dataset [26] for our experiments. The MNIST dataset consists of 60,000 images of handwritten digits. Each image is a 28x28 pixel array, where the value of each

Input: $\mathcal{P} = \{p_i\}_{i=1}^{i=58}$, MNIST
Output: $\mathcal{A}$

$\mathcal{M} \leftarrow \{\}$;
$\mathcal{A} \leftarrow \{\}$;
CreateModel *CreateModel(nomNeu, actFunc)*:
    Create neural network m with *nomNeu* neurons in the
        hidden layer and the ReLU function.;
    return M;
for *nomNeus* $\leftarrow$ 1 **to** 100 **do**
    $m_{neurons} \leftarrow$ CreateModel(*nomNeu, ReLU*);
    Train model m_{nomNeu} up to 50 epochs;
    Save model m_{nomNeu};
    Add m_{nomNeu} to the Array $\mathcal{M}$;
end
for *polyIndex* $\leftarrow$ 1 **to** 58 **do**
    for *nomNeu* $\leftarrow$ 1 **to** 100 **do**
        $m_{ReLU} \leftarrow$ *nomNeu*th of $\mathcal{M}$;
        $m \leftarrow$ CreateModel(*nomNeu*, $p_{polyInd}$);
        Initial weights of $m \leftarrow m_{ReLU}$;
        Train model m up to 5 epochs;
        $a \leftarrow$ Accuracy of m;
        Add the accuracy value a to $\mathcal{A}$;
    end
end
return $\mathcal{A}$;

Algorithm 1: Training based on Polynomials

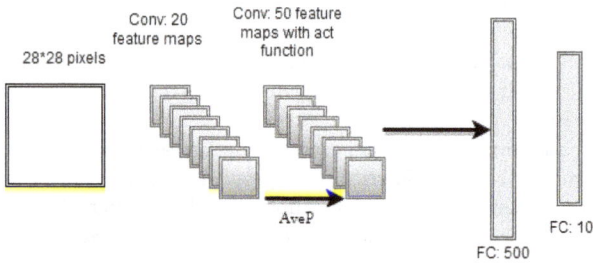

Figure 5: CNN Model (AveP stands for Average Pooling).

pixel is a positive integer in the range $[0, 255]$. We used the training part of this dataset, consisting of 50,000 images, to train the CNN and the remaining 10,000 images for testing.

The architecture of the CNN we use is shown in Figure 5. This CNN has similar architecture to the light CNN used in [8]. This will allow us to provide direct comparison with those works. We train the CNN using Keras library [11] on the MNIST dataset. We train different models using each approximation method discussed above. We use polynomials of degree 2 to replace the ReLU function in the first four methods and a polynomial of degree 3 for the last method. Table 1 shows the accuracy of the trained model using each approximation method. As we can see, different approximation

methods result in widely different accuracy values and as expected, our proposed method based on the derivative of the ReLU achieves the best accuracy among all the methods. In the rest of this paper, we only use this method for approximation of the ReLU function, and whenever approximation method is mentioned, it refers to the last method.

We train the model based on a CNN structure similar to the one used in [8]. We were able to achieve 98.52% accuracy while their accuracy was 97.95%. The main difference comes from the polynomial approximation method used; the proposed approach in [8] is based on Taylor series to approximate the ReLU function whereas we used our proposed method based on the derivative of the ReLU. These results show that our polynomial approximates the ReLU function better. However, both results are still far from the state-of-the-art digit recognition problem (99.77%). This is due to small size and simple architecture of the CNN used here. We use larger and more complex CNNs with more layers that are able to achieve accuracy much closer to the state-of-the-art as explained in Section 3.6. To ensure that the polynomial approximation is independent of the structure of the CNN and works well with different CNN structures, we change the structure of the CNN and train models based on the new one.

The accuracy of the model based on this CNN with the polynomial of degree 3 as the activation function is 98.38% and close to the first structure. This shows that the behavior of the polynomial approximation of the ReLU function is robust against the changes in the structure. In addition, to analyze the relationship between the degree of the polynomial and the performance of the model, we change the degree of the polynomial from 3 to 8 and calculate the accuracy of the model. As expected, the higher degree polynomials result in higher performance and we were able to achieve 99.21% accuracy. Next, we implement several CNNs with more layers and structures that are more complex to improve the performance of the model and get closer to the state-of-the-art. We implement each model in Keras library [11] and measure the performance to find a relationship between the depth of the CNN and the accuracy of the model.

In order to provide a comparison, we use a CNN with a similar structure to the one used in [8]. However, we start with a simpler CNN and gradually add layers to the CNN to check how the performance of the model changes as the number of layers increases and the model becomes more complex. First, we implement a CNN with 3 convolutional layers. The accuracy of the trained model is 99.10% which is very close to the same CNN with the ReLU as activation function, 99.15%. Next, we add an activation function to the first convolutional layer and the accuracy increases to 99.16%. We then add two more convolutional layers to the CNN and train the new model. The accuracy of the trained model increases to 99.29%. We go one step further and add an activation function after each convolutional layer. The accuracy for this CNN is 99.32%. Finally, we try the same structure as the deep CNN used in [8]. Therefore, we design our CNN, shown in Figure 6, to have the same depth as the deep CNN used in [8], shown in Figure 6, the accuracy is 99.52% which is very close to the accuracy of the same CNN that uses the ReLU function, 99.56%. Our accuracy is higher than both methods in [14] (98.95%) and [8] (99.30%) over plaintext for a CNN with the same structure. We also train CNNs with Sigmoid and

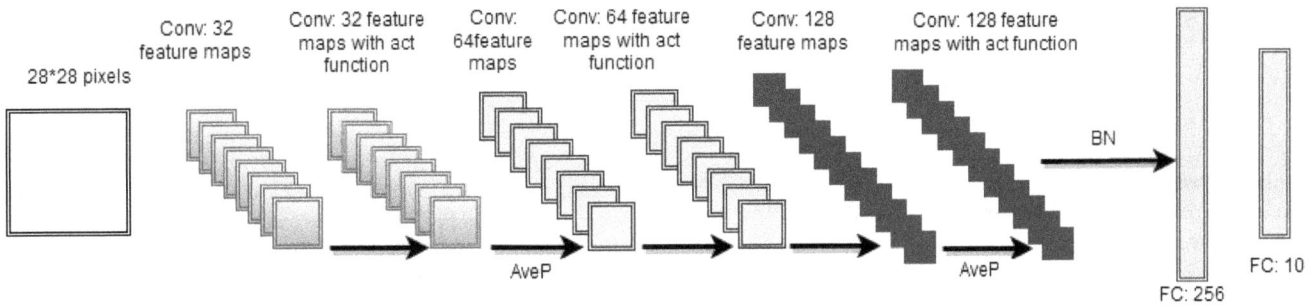

Figure 6: CNN Model (AveP stands for Average Pooling).

Table 2: Network Accuracy using different Activation Functions and their Replacement Polynomials.

Activation Function	Original Model	Polynomial Model
ReLU	99.56%	99.52%
Sigmoid	98.85%	98.94%
Tanh	97.27%	98.15%

Tanh as activation functions. To provide a comparison, we use the CNN model and only change the activation functions to Sigmoid and Tanh instead of the ReLU function. The results are shown in Table 2.

3.7 Parameter Tuning

When we build a model in machine learning, we need to tune the hyper-parameters after finalizing the architecture of the network. For a CNN, different hyper-parameters should be tuned, including number of hidden layers and units, dropout, weight initialization, learning rate, momentum, number of epochs, batch Size and etc. In our experiments, we only tune two parameters: learning rate and momentum. We use 200 as the batch size and 0.5 for the dropout. We use 250 as threshold for the number of epochs. For weight initialization, we run experiments several times with different weights and report the average accuracy. We tune a CNN with two convolutional layers and one fully connected layer (similar to the CNN proposed in [14]) for training over the MNIST dataset. We approximate the ReLU with our polynomial approximation and use it as an activation in the architecture of the CNN.

Two common methods for tuning hyper parameters are grid search and randomized search, see [4]. In our case, we tune only two parameters and we use grid search method which is more accurate compared to random search. In this method, we define one set for each parameter and then, train models for all pairs of these two parameters up to a constant number of epochs. Random search is more useful when we want to tune a high number of parameters, because it's not practical to use grid search in this situation, see [4]. Tuning parameters affects the performance of the model, especially for polynomial based architectures (see Table 3). For example, while the accuracy of the original model is 98.94%, the accuracy would drop to 98.35% without parameter tuning. After tuning the parameters, the accuracy of the model based on the polynomial is the same as the original model, 98.94%.

4 EXPERIMENTAL RESULTS: DEEP CONVOLUTIONAL NEURAL NETWORK OVER ENCRYPTED DATA

In this section, we present results of implementing adapted version of CNNs (ReLU is replaced with polynomial approximation) over encrypted data. We train the models using plaintext data and measure the accuracy of the built model for classification of encrypted data. We used HELib [18] for implementation and all computations were run on a computer with 16GB RAM, Intel Xeon E5-2640, 2.4GHz and Ubuntu 16.04. We use the CNN models trained in the earlier section. We give encrypted inputs to the trained networks and measure the accuracy of the outputs. We implement the CNN Model (Figure 5). Thanks to the SIMD feature in the HELib, in each round of classification, we can classify a batch of encrypted images. We measure the running time for encryption and sending data from the client to the server. We also measure the running time for classifying this encrypted batch as well as the amount of data transferred in the process.

First, the encryption scheme is initiated in the client side $k = 80$ as the security level. Then, the input images were encrypted. As the HELib supports SIMD operations, the images were encrypted in batches. So, for each batch of images -each having the size of 28×28 pixels- we obtained one set of ciphertext representation of size 28×28. Then, the encrypted images along with the encryption parameters and the public key were sent to the server side, where the server runs the CNN over the encrypted data. In our experiments, we classify a batch of ciphertext with size 8192 (the same batch size used in [14]) and provide the running time for classification. Table 4 shows the breakdown of the time it takes to apply our solution to the MNIST dataset using the CNN Model of Figure 5. We also provide the time required for encryption, transferring and decryption time as shown in Table 5. Our approach is much faster than [14] and the running time for classifying of a batch input is 2.68 seconds.

4.1 Comparison with the state-of-the-art Solutions

In this section, we compare our results with the state-of-the-art privacy-preserving classification of neural networks. This includes approaches based on the HE as well as secure multi-party computation (SMC) as shown in Table 6. The two closest works to our approach are CryptoNets [14] and [8]. CryptoNets uses HE and

Table 3: Performance of the model for different approaches based on the model from [14]

Model with ReLU	Tuned Model with ReLU	Polynomial	Tuned Polynomial
98.87%	98.94%	98.35%	98.94%

Table 4: Breakdown of Running Time (seconds) of CNN Model (Figure 5) over Encrypted MNIST Dataset for one batch input.

Layer	Time
Convolutional layer	13.08
Average Pooling Layer	7.63
Convolutional layer	77.64
Activation layer	9.76
Average Pooling Layer	6.54
2 Fully Connected	34.32

Table 5: The performance of our solution (seconds)

Layer	Our Approach	CryptoNets [14]
Encryption	62.8	122
Network Communication	320	570
Decryption	3.9	5

implements a CNN with two convolutional layers and two fully connected layers. It assumes Sigmoid is used as the activation function and replaces the max pooling with scaled mean-pooling and the activation function with square function. As can be seen in Table 6, our approach significantly outperforms CryptoNets in all aspects. Note that to provide a fair comparison; we use machines with similar configuration (Intel Xeon E5-1620 CPU running at 3.5GHz with 16GB of RAM in CryptoNets and Intel Xeon E5-2640, 2.4GHz with 16GB RAM in our case) for the experiments.

Chabanne et al. [8] use Taylor series for approximating the ReLU function and use batch normalization layers for improving the performance of the model. They do not provide any results over the encrypted data. Therefore, we cannot provide comparison w.r.t to the performance measures (e.g., running time, amount of data transferred, and number of predictions) over encrypted data but our approach provides much better accuracy. Our approach achieves 99.52% accuracy over plaintext data and the accuracy of our model after implementing over encrypted data is 99.25%. This is because we need transfer network's parameters from real numbers to integers. DeepSecure [36] and SecureML [31] are two recent works based on SMC techniques. Darvish et al. [36] present DeepSecure that enables distributed clients (data owners) and cloud servers, to jointly evaluate a deep learning network on their private assets. It uses Yao's Garbled Circuit (GC) protocol to securely perform deep learning. They perform experiments on MNIST dataset and report the results. As shown in Table 6, our approach significantly outperforms DeepSecure in all aspects.

Note that in [36], authors provide the communication and computation overhead for one instance, and the proposed protocol classifies one instance at each prediction round. Our approach, on the other hand, can classify a batch of instances in each round with size 8192 or larger. To provide a fair comparison, we extrapolate the

running time and number of communications reported accordingly. secureml and Zhang [31] present SecureML that aims to develop privacy-preserving training and classification of neural networks using SMC techniques. In their proposed approach, a data owner shares the data with two servers and the servers run the machine learning algorithm using two-party computation (2PC) technique. However, they can only implement a very simple neural network with 2 hidden layers with 128 neurons in each layer, without any convolutional layers and as shown in Table 6, the accuracy is very low. Implementing a CNN with their approach is not practical and hence we cannot provide comparison w.r.t to CNNs.

To provide a comparison, we implemented the same neural network (2 hidden layers with 128 neurons in each layer and without any convolutional layers) using our approach. They report 14 seconds as the running time for 100 instances, and the running time of our approach is 12 seconds. It is also worth noting that by increasing the size of the batch input, the running time increases sub-linearly in [31] whereas in our solution, the running time remains the same for larger sizes of the batch input. This is because of the SIMD feature in HELib which results in the same computation cost for one ciphertext and an array of ciphertexts (see [18]). Additionally, unlike [31] our solution does not need any communications between the client and the server for providing privacy-preserving predictions.

Generally, the SMC-based solutions have a big shortcoming, which is the very large number of communications since we need interactions between client and server for each operation. For example, DeepSecure has a huge communication cost of 722GB for a relatively small network (CNN Model of Figure 5) whereas CryptoNets's communication cost is 595.5MB and ours is only 336.7MB for the same network. In addition, since the client participates in the computations, information about the model could possibly leak. For example, the client can learn information such as the number of layers in the CNN, the structure of each layer and the activation functions.

4.2 CIFAR-10 Results

To further show the applicability of our proposed approach for more complicated network architectures, we use CIFAR-10 [23], one of the widely used benchmark dataset for deep learning, to train a CNN and implement it over encrypted data. The CIFAR-10 dataset consists of 60000 32×32 color images categorized in 10 classes, with 6000 images per class. There are 50000 training and 10000 test images. We train a CNN using CIFAR-10 dataset and we achieved 91.5% accuracy with polynomials as the activation functions whereas the accuracy with the original activation function is 94.2%. However, because of the high number of layers, we cannot implement this deep network over the encrypted data.

HELib only supports integer values as the plaintext domain. Therefore, we need to transfer all real values (feature values and network weights) to integers. The challenge is that the length of

Table 6: Comparison with the state-of-the-art Solutions

Dataset	Criteria	Our Approach	[14]	[36]*	[31]*	[9]*	[27]*	[33]*
MNIST	Accuracy	99.25%	99%	99%	93.4%	99%	99%	99%
	Running Time (s)	320	570	6328	759	41779	76349	12095
	Data Transfer	436.7MB	595.5MB	6479GB	N/A	4104GB	5386GB	86GB
	# of predictions/hour	163840	51739	379	738	706	386	1333

*: The values are extrapolated.

integer values grows during calculations. For solving this issue, we need to use different models and combine their predictions. However, by increasing the depth of algorithm, it's not computationally efficient because it requires using a large number of models. An alternative solution is using libraries that support fixed point arithmetic. By using these libraries, we can implement deeper CNNs over encrypted data which is a part of future work.

Additional Datasets: We used MNIST to be able to provide a comparison with related work which only reports results on the MNIST. Additionally, we reported results on CIFAR-10 for the first time. Our solution is independent of the dataset and can be applied to other datasets such as CIFAR-100 and ImageNet. However, these datasets usually require GPU for efficient implementation and take a very long time to train. This is left to our future work.

5 RELATED WORK

Graepel et al. propose a solution for preserving privacy of data while training based on somewhat HE scheme [17]. They proposed division-free Linear Mean and Fisher's Linear Discriminate (FLD) algorithms to adapt to limitations of HE algorithms. They focus on simple classifiers such as the linear means classifier, and do not consider algorithms that are more complex. In addition, in their approach, the client can learn the model, and they consider a weak security model. Bost et al. consider privacy-preserving classification for for three different machine learning algorithms, namely Hyperplane Decision, Naive Bayes, and Decision trees [5]. They propose use a combination of three homomorphic systems (Quadratic Residuosity, Piallier, and BGV schemes), and garbled circuits to preserve privacy of data. Their approach is based on SMC and HE, considers only classical machine learning algorithms and is only efficient for small data sets. Our proposed approach is based only on HE, focuses on the deep learning algorithms, and is efficient for large datasets.

Xie et al. discuss theoretical aspects of polynomial approximation of activation functions (the Sigmoid function) for implementing neural networks in the encrypted domain [39]. Building on this work, Dowlin et al. present CryptoNets, a neural network classifier on encrypted data [14]. Chabanne et al. improve the accuracy of CryptoNets by combining the ideas of Cryptonets' solution with the batch normalization principle [8]. These two are the closest to our work and were discussed in section 4.1.

There is a series of works based on the Secure Multiparty Computation, [9, 19, 27, 31, 33, 36]. secureml and Zhang propose a solution for privacy preserving machine learning based on SMC and SMC/HE techniques for training and classification steps [31]. Client(s) secretly shares their data with two non-trusted non-colluded servers to run a 2PC protocol. Three different algorithms considered in this paper: linear regression, logistic regression and neural network.

Rouhani et. al propose a solution for preserving the classification in neural networks based on Yao's Garbled Circuit [36]. Based on their protocol, the privacy of both DL parameters and input data is preserved while classifying a new instance. The proposed approach is suitable for low rate classification requests from clients when one client needs to dynamically analyze the data.

Chandran et. al design a framework for transferring a CNN model to a new structure that preserves the privacy of data during classification step [9]. Liu et. al propose a method for transferring a neural network to an *oblivious neural network* [27]. The new structure preserves the privacy of client's data and server's model for the classification step. They consider a client-server model, the client owns the data and the server owns the model. MiniONN transforms any "common" neural network model into an oblivious neural network without affecting the performance.

Riazi et. al addressed the privacy-preserving classification in machine learning [33]. They design a framework based on the SMC, the proposed framework built upon ABY [13] by improving the performance of implemented modules integrating sequential GCs or fixed-point arithmetic. Juvekar et. al propose a hybrid solution based on HE and SMC [19]. They design GAZELLE, a framework that equipped with fast homomorphic encryption operations which supports SIMD. Their framework optimizes the performance by switching from HE to GC or vice versa to reach low latency for preserving the privacy of data while classifying client's instance.

Aslett et al. use HE schemes for preserving privacy of data by implementing statistical machine learning over encrypted data and implement extremely random forests and Naive Bayes classifiers over 20 datasets [1]. In these algorithms, the majority of operations are addition and multiplication and they show that performing algorithms over encrypted data without any multi-party computation or communication is practical. They also analyze HE tools for use in statistical machine learning [2]. Shortell et al. use the Taylor expansion of $ln(x)$ to estimate the natural logarithm function by a polynomial of degree 5 [37]. Livni et al. analyzed the performance of polynomial as an activation function in neural networks [28] over interval $[-1, 1]$ while the message space of HE schemes is integers. Our method is able to generate the polynomial approximation for an arbitrary interval.

There are also a few recent work that look at privacy issues in training phase, specifically for back-propagation algorithm [7, 41]. Bu et al. propose a privacy-preserving back-propagation algorithm based on BGV encryption scheme on cloud [7]. Their proposed algorithm offloads the expensive operations to the cloud and uses

BGV to protect the privacy of the data during the learning process. Zhang et al. also propose using BGV encryption scheme to support the secure computation of the high-order back-propagation algorithm efficiently for deep computation model training on cloud [41]. In their approach, to avoid a multiplicative depth too big, after each iteration the updated weights are sent to the parties to be decrypted and re-encrypted. Thus, the communication complexity of the solution is very high. Unlike these papers, our focus is on privacy-preserving classification problem.

6 CONCLUSION AND FUTURE WORK

In this paper, we developed a new solution for preserving privacy of data in deep neural networks by implementing CNN algorithms over encrypted data. In order to implement the deep neural networks within limitations of HE schemes, we introduced new techniques to approximate the activation functions with the low degree polynomials. We then used these approximation polynomials to train several deep CNNs with the polynomial approximation as the activation function over the encrypted data and measured the accuracy of the trained models. Our results show that polynomials if chosen carefully, are the suitable replacements for activation functions to adopt deep neural networks within the HE schemes. We were able to achieve 99.25% accuracy and make close to 164000 predictions per hour when we applied our approach to the MNIST dataset. These results show that our proposed approach provides efficient, accurate, and scalable privacy-preserving predictions and significantly outperforms the state-of-the-art solutions.

For future work, we plan to implement models that are more complex over GPU and study privacy-preserving training of deep neural networks in addition to the classification.

REFERENCES

[1] Louis J. M. Aslett, Pedro M. Esperança, and Chris C. Holmes. 2015. Encrypted statistical machine learning: new privacy preserving methods. *CoRR* (2015).
[2] L. J. M. Aslett, P. M. Esperança, and C. C. Holmes. 2015. *A review of homomorphic encryption and software tools for encrypted statistical machine learning*. Technical Report. University of Oxford.
[3] K. Atkinson and W. Han. 2009. *Theoretical Numerical Analysis: A Functional Analysis Framework*. Springer New York.
[4] James Bergstra and Yoshua Bengio. 2012. Random Search for Hyper-parameter Optimization. *J. Mach. Learn. Res.* 13 (Feb. 2012), 281–305. http://dl.acm.org/citation.cfm?id=2188385.2188395
[5] Raphael Bost, Raluca Ada Popa, Stephen Tu, and Shafi Goldwasser. 2015. Machine Learning Classification over Encrypted Data. In *22nd Annual Network and Distributed System Security Symposium, NDSS, San Diego, California, USA*.
[6] Zvika Brakerski, Craig Gentry, and Vinod Vaikuntanathan. 2012. (Leveled) Fully Homomorphic Encryption Without Bootstrapping. In *Proceedings of the 3rd Innovations in Theoretical Computer Science Conference (ITCS '12)*. ACM, New York, NY, USA, 309–325.
[7] Fanyu Bu, Yu Ma, Zhikui Chen, and Han Xu. 2015. Privacy Preserving Back-Propagation Based on BGV on Cloud. In *17th IEEE International Conference on High Performance Computing and Communications, HPCC 2015, 7th IEEE International Symposiumon Cyberspace Safety and Security, CSS 2015, and 12th IEEE International Conference on Embedded Software and Systems, ICESS 2015, New York, NY, USA, August 24-26, 2015*. 1791–1795.
[8] Hervé Chabanne, Amaury de Wargny, Jonathan Milgram, Constance Morel, and Emmanuel Prouff. 2017. Privacy-Preserving Classification on Deep Neural Network. Cryptology ePrint Archive, Report 2017/035.
[9] Nishanth Chandran, Divya Gupta, Aseem Rastogi, Rahul Sharma, and Shardul Tripathi. 2017. EzPC: Programmable, Efficient, and Scalable Secure Two-Party Computation. *IACR Cryptology ePrint Archive* 2017 (2017), 1109.
[10] Jung Hee Cheon, Andrey Kim, Miran Kim, and Yongsoo Song. 2016. Homomorphic Encryption for Arithmetic of Approximate Numbers. Cryptology ePrint Archive, Report 2016/421. https://eprint.iacr.org/2016/421.
[11] François Chollet et al. 2017. Keras. https://github.com/fchollet/keras.

[12] Jack L.H. Crawford, Craig Gentry, Shai Halevi, Daniel Platt, and Victor Shoup. 2018. Doing Real Work with FHE: The Case of Logistic Regression. Cryptology ePrint Archive, Report 2018/202. (2018). https://eprint.iacr.org/2018/202.
[13] Daniel Demmler, Thomas Schneider, and Michael Zohner. 2015. ABY - A Framework for Efficient Mixed-Protocol Secure Two-Party Computation. In *22nd Annual Network and Distributed System Security Symposium, NDSS 2015, San Diego, California, USA, February 8-11, 2015*.
[14] Nathan Dowlin, Ran Gilad-Bachrach, Kim Laine, Kristin Lauter Michael Naehrig, and John Wernsing. 2016. *CryptoNets: Applying Neural Networks to Encrypted Data with High Throughput and Accuracy*. Technical Report MSR-TR-2016-3.
[15] Craig Gentry. 2009. *A Fully Homomorphic Encryption Scheme*. Ph.D. Dissertation. Stanford, CA, USA. Advisor(s) Boneh, Dan. AAI3382729.
[16] Google. 2017. Google Prediction API. (2017). https://cloud.google.com/prediction/
[17] Thore Graepel, Kristin Lauter, and Michael Naehrig. 2013. ML Confidential: Machine Learning on Encrypted Data. In *Proceedings of the 15th International Conference on Information Security and Cryptology (ICISC'12)*. Springer-Verlag.
[18] Shai Halevi and Victor Shoup. 2014. Algorithms in HElib. In *Advances in Cryptology - CRYPTO - 34th Annual Cryptology Conference, CA, USA, Proceedings*.
[19] Chiraag Juvekar, Vinod Vaikuntanathan, and Anantha Chandrakasan. 2018. Gazelle: A Low Latency Framework for Secure Neural Network Inference. *CoRR* abs/1801.05507 (2018). arXiv:1801.05507 http://arxiv.org/abs/1801.05507
[20] Nal Kalchbrenner, Edward Grefenstette, and Phil Blunsom. 2014. A Convolutional Neural Network for Modelling Sentences. *CoRR* abs/1404.2188 (2014).
[21] Andrey Kim, Yongsoo Song, Miran Kim, Keewoo Lee, and Jung Hee Cheon. 2018. Logistic Regression Model Training based on the Approximate Homomorphic Encryption. Cryptology ePrint Archive, Report 2018/254. (2018). https://eprint.iacr.org/2018/254.
[22] Miran Kim, Yongsoo Song, Shuang Wang, Yuhou Xia, and Xiaoqian Jiang. 2018. Secure Logistic Regression Based on Homomorphic Encryption: Design and Evaluation. Cryptology ePrint Archive, Report 2018/074. (2018). https://eprint.iacr.org/2018/074.
[23] Alex Krizhevsky, Vinod Nair, and Geoffrey Hinton. 2019. CIFAR-10 (Canadian Institute for Advanced Research). (2019). www.cs.toronto.edu/~kriz/cifar.html
[24] Alex Krizhevsky, Ilya Sutskever, and Geoffrey E Hinton. 2012. ImageNet Classification with Deep Convolutional Neural Networks. In *Advances in Neural Information Processing Systems 25*, F. Pereira, C. J. C. Burges, L. Bottou, and K. Q. Weinberger (Eds.). Curran Associates, Inc.
[25] Ersatz Labs. 2017. Ersatz. (2017). http://www.ersatzlabs.com/
[26] Yann LeCun and Corinna Cortes. 2010. MNIST handwritten digit database. (2010). http://yann.lecun.com/exdb/mnist/
[27] Jian Liu, Mika Juuti, Yao Lu, and N. Asokan. 2017. Oblivious Neural Network Predictions via MiniONN Transformations. In *Proceedings of the 2017 ACM SIGSAC Conference on Computer and Communications Security (CCS '17)*. ACM, New York, NY, USA, 619–631.
[28] Roi Livni, Shai Shalev-Shwartz, and Ohad Shamir. 2014. On the Computational Efficiency of Training Neural Networks. *CoRR* (2014).
[29] Microsft. 2017. Microsoft Azure Machine Learning. (2017). https://azure.microsoft.com/en-us/services/machine-learning/
[30] Microsft. 2018. Simple encrypted arithmetic library - SEAL. (2018). https://sealcrypto.org
[31] P. Mohassel and Y. Zhang. 2017. SecureML: A System for Scalable Privacy-Preserving Machine Learning. In *IEEE Symposium on Security and Privacy (SP)*.
[32] Pascal Paillier. 1999. Public-key Cryptosystems Based on Composite Degree Residuosity Classes. In *17th International Conference on Theory and Application of Cryptographic Techniques (EUROCRYPT'99)*. Springer-Verlag, Berlin, Heidelberg.
[33] M. Sadegh Riazi, Christian Weinert, Oleksandr Tkachenko, Ebrahim M. Songhori, Thomas Schneider, and Farinaz Koushanfar. 2018. Chameleon: A Hybrid Secure Computation Framework for Machine Learning Applications. *CoRR* abs/1801.03239 (2018). arXiv:1801.03239 http://arxiv.org/abs/1801.03239
[34] R.L. Rivest, L. Adleman, and M.L. Dertouzos. 1978. On data banks and privacy homomorphisms. In *Foundations on Secure Computation, Academia Press*.
[35] Kurt Rohloff. accessed August 2018. The PALISADE lattice cryptography library. Retrieved from https://git.njit.edu/palisade/PALISADE.
[36] Bita Darvish Rouhani, M. Sadegh Riazi, and Farinaz Koushanfar. 2017. DeepSecure: Scalable Provably-Secure Deep Learning. *CoRR* abs/1705.08963 (2017).
[37] Thomas Shortell and Ali Shokoufandeh. 2015. Secure Signal Processing Using Fully Homomorphic Encryption. In *Advanced Concepts for Intelligent Vision Systems - 16th International Conference, ACIVS, Italy, Proceedings*.
[38] Turi. 2017. GraphLab. (2017). http://www.select.cs.cmu.edu/code/graphlab/
[39] Pengtao Xie, Misha Bilenko, Tom Finley, Ran Gilad-Bachrach, Kristin E. Lauter, and Michael Naehrig. 2014. Crypto-Nets: Neural Networks over Encrypted Data. *CoRR* (2014).
[40] Yuan Xu. 2001. Orthogonal Polynomials of Several Variables. *Encyclopedia of Mathematics and its Applications* 81 (2001).
[41] Q. Zhang, L. T. Yang, and Z. Chen. 2016. Privacy Preserving Deep Computation Model on Cloud for Big Data Feature Learning. *IEEE Trans. Comput.* 65, 5 (May 2016).

Attribute Compartmentation and Greedy UCC Discovery for High-Dimensional Data Anonymisation

Nikolai J. Podlesny, Anne V.D.M. Kayem, Christoph Meinel
Hasso-Plattner-Institute, University of Potsdam
Potsdam, Germany
Nikolai.Podlesny@hpi.de,Anne.Kayem@hpi.de,Christoph.Meinel@hpi.de

ABSTRACT

High-dimensional data is particularly useful for data analytics research. In the healthcare domain, for instance, high-dimensional data analytics has been used successfully for drug discovery. Yet, in order to adhere to privacy legislation, data analytics service providers must guarantee anonymity for data owners. In the context of high-dimensional data, ensuring privacy is challenging because increased data dimensionality must be matched by an exponential growth in the size of the data to avoid sparse datasets. Syntactically, anonymising sparse datasets with methods that rely of statistical significance, makes obtaining sound and reliable results, a challenge. As such, strong privacy is only achievable at the cost of high information loss, rendering the data unusable for data analytics. In this paper, we make two contributions to addressing this problem from both the privacy and information loss perspectives. First, we show that by identifying dependencies between attribute subsets we can eliminate privacy violating attributes from the anonymised dataset. Second, to minimise information loss, we employ a greedy search algorithm to determine and eliminate maximal partial unique attribute combinations. Thus, one only needs to find the minimal set of identifying attributes to prevent re-identification. Experiments on a health cloud based on the SAP HANA platform using a semi-synthetic medical history dataset comprised of 109 attributes, demonstrate the effectiveness of our approach.

ACM Reference format:
Nikolai J. Podlesny, Anne V.D.M. Kayem, Christoph Meinel. 2019. Attribute Compartmentation and Greedy UCC Discovery for High-Dimensional Data Anonymisation. In *Proceedings of Ninth ACM Conference on Data and Application Security and Privacy, Richardson, TX, USA, March 25–27, 2019 (CODASPY '19), 11 pages.*
https://doi.org/10.1145/3292006.3300019

1 INTRODUCTION

Analysing high-dimensional data can make a meaningful contribution in fields such as medicine, environmental monitoring, agriculture, and smart home monitoring. In making the data available for analytics, it is important to also consider privacy in terms of protecting sensitive personal data from exposure. One approach

to doing so is to anonymise the data before it is shared. In areas such as medical data analytics, for performance reasons, it makes sense to generate a single anonymised dataset that can be applied to multiple use-cases.

Semantic data anonymisation algorithms, like differential privacy, fall short in this respect because they are designed to handle pre-defined use-cases where knowledge of the composition of the required dataset is known apriori [3, 5, 8, 9]. Furthermore, semantically anonymised datasets are use-case specific or reliant on runtime specifications. Pre-processing, for anonymisation, large high-dimensional datasets on a per-query basis impacts negatively on performance. In addition, postponing data anonymisation to runtime can enable colluding users to run multiple complimentary queries to return datasets that when combined, provide information to enable partial or even complete de-anonymisation of the original dataset [3, 5, 8, 9, 20]. Kifer et al. [20] address this problem with "non-interactive" differential privacy by proposing statistical evaluation apriori of user queries to identify and prevent collusions, but the performance issue in high-dimensional settings remains. From the use-case perspective therefore, syntactic rather than semantic data anonymisation algorithms are favoured for big high-dimensional medical data anonymisation for contexts where re-usability of anonymised data is performance efficient.

Problem Statement: However, effectively syntactically anonymising multi-attribute high-dimensional datasets composed from distributed data sources is a challenging problem. As Aggarwal et al. [1] have shown, increased data dimensionality results in sparse datasets that yield unreliable results when the supporting data fails to grow exponentially with dimensionality. This is due primarily to the data transformation approaches such as, (*generalisation, suppression,* and *perturbation*), that syntactic anonymisation algorithms use [1]. These data transformation approaches incur high information loss levels to achieve high privacy, resulting in data that is not usable for data analytics, which is undesirable. Therefore, in order to apply syntactic data anonymisation to big high-dimensional data in a privacy-preserving and performance efficient manner, a data transformation technique that removes the risk of de-anonymisation while maintaining high data utility, is required.

Contribution: In this paper, we propose a novel data transformation technique, which we term *attribute compartmentation*. *Attribute compartmentation* enables use-case agnostic syntactic data anonymisation, in the sense that *compartmentation* is neither confined to use-cases of the anonymised datasets nor is it contingent on runtime specifications. In *compartmentation*, data transformation occurs in two steps. In the first step, dependencies between subsets of quasi-identifier attributes are identified to eliminate privacy violating attributes. This is done by separating, instead of altering the values of the privacy violating attributes, from the dataset. The result is a significant drop in information loss. The second step, minimises the number of separated attributes by identifying the minimal set of attributes required to prevent re-identification. In order to minimise attribute separation, a greed search algorithm is used to determine maximal partial unique attribute combinations for elimination. De-anonymisation is prevented simply by obtaining the minimal set of identifying attributes required to prevent re-identification, since no unique tuples remain in the anonymised dataset. Experiments on a health cloud based on the SAP HANA platform using a semi-synthetic medical history dataset comprised of 109 attributes, demonstrate the effectiveness of our approach in comparison to standard data transformation techniques which guarantee privacy like suppression, generalisation and perturbation.

The rest of the paper is structured as follows. We discuss related work with respect to data anonymisation in Section 2. In Section 3, we formulate first and second class identifiers for the anonymisation process. The notion of *compartmentation* and the greedy search optimization is presented in Section 4. In Section 5, we address and discuss results of our experiments and closing we offer conclusions and possibilities for future work in Section 6.

2 RELATED WORK

k-anonymity [35], l-diversity [25], and t-closeness [23] have been explored extensively with respect to protecting against disclosures of sensitive personal data from publicly shared anonymised datasets. To provide strong privacy guarantees with data anonymisation, these syntactic anonymisation algorithms rely on a variety of transformation techniques like *suppression*, *generalisation*, and *perturbation*. These methods of data transformation for anonymisation can be classified into two categories namely, *randomisation* and *generalisation*.

Randomization algorithms modify data veracity by eliminating strong connections between the data and an individual. This may be achieved by either statistical shifting, permutations, or noise injections [8, 18]. The superordinate concept of differential privacy summarizes a variety of statistical techniques deciding at runtime of a query if and how much alternation is needed. One technique is the exponential mechanism that releases (statistical) information about a dataset devoiding to reveal individual data entries [26]. Its accuracy, however, is strongly correlated to the data distribution [41]. Perturbation through controlled random distribution-dependent noise additions for each query result is an instance of exponential mechanisms that is known as a Laplace mechanism [10, 21] and can be implemented very efficiently [15]. While geometric mechanisms are discretized versions of the former one [14], Liu et al. generalizes the Laplace mechanism to a Gaussian approach known as a generalized Gaussian (GG) mechanism [24]. The matrix mechanism introduces a query strategy which promises higher accuracy based on correlated noise distributions relying on either Gaussian or Laplace mechanisms [22]. Since these anonymisation approaches are runtime and use case specific, as mentioned before, applying them to large high-dimensional data is impractical performance-wise.

Generalisation denominates the family of data transformation techniques for syntactic anonymisation, and includes techniques that modify data values in accordance to a hierarchical model where each value progressively loses uniqueness as one moves upwards in the hierarchy. Generalisation algorithms have been proven effective especially with k-anonymity, l-diversity, and t-closeness. In k-anonymity each tuple in the dataset is classified with at least $k-1$ similar data records, to limit distinguishability. The $k-1$ nearest neighbors are selected based on similar describing attributes enforced by generalisation and suppression [35]. While such an approach is vulnerable to homogeneity and background knowledge attacks [25], l-diversity extends the concept by considering the granularity of sensitive data representations to ensure a diversity of a factor of l for each quasi-identifier within a given equivalence class (usually a size of k). t-closeness, handles skewness and background knowledge attacks by considering the relative distributions of sensitive values both in the entire dataset and in individual equivalence classes [23]. In all three anonymisation algorithms, and their extensions [2, 28], generalisation and suppression are used to support transforming the data [13]. However, as Aggrawal et al.[1] have shown, applying generalisation and suppress to high-dimensional data results in high information loss thereby rendering the data useless for data analytics. Wong et al. [42] propose by distributing all tuples non-uniformly the same QID in a partition for achieving k-anonymity (*non-homogeneous generalisation*) to decrease information loss. Meanwhile Tassa et al. [36] suggest an approach of reducing the information loss that is caused by generalising the database entries with k-concealment. Both contributions however deteriorate the NP-hardness in the field of high-dimensional application fields.

Perturbation corresponds to the alternation of the actual value to the closest similar findable value. This includes the effect of introducing an aggregated value or using a close by value that is adopted in the way that just one value needs modification instead of multiple ones to build clusters. Under these circumstances, finding such a value can take longer, due to the effect of having to iteratively recheck the newly created value(s) which consequently impacts negatively on performance.

In the data mining field, a variety of ideas exist as well to deal with privacy related constraints in publishing anonymised datasets. Those ideas include clustering [39], regression models [12], and naive Bayes classification [40] but simultaneous strongly focused on highly use-case specific applications with well-defined privacy constraints. This is the case particularly when combining several distributed data sources to guarantee privacy in each partition [43].

Therefore, a syntactic data transformation approach that ensures low information loss and high privacy of high- dimensional datasets is needed in order to anonymise high- dimensional data syntactically. We present a solution to this problem in the next section.

3 EXACT DISCOVERY OF COMPROMISING IDENTIFIERS

In this section, we present our proposed *attribute compartmentation* approach to transforming high-dimensional data for syntactic data anonymisation. Our compartmentation scheme works in two steps.

In the first step, we pre-process the data to eliminate 1st class identifiers. 1st class identifiers are essentially standalone attributes such as (user) IDs, phone numbers, credit card numbers, or digital fingerprints. Identifying 1st class identifiers is a useful first step in removing privacy violating attributes from the dataset. As a second step, we identify 2nd class identifiers that are basically attribute combinations that qualify as quasi-identifiers. Identifying 2nd class identifiers is important in finding dependencies that can be used for re-identification. However, to avoid high information loss from attribute suppressions to break the dependencies, we employ a greedy search algorithm to determine maximal partial unique attribute combinations for elimination. In this way, one only needs to find the minimal set of identifying attributes to prevent re-identification. In the following we provide more details on how to select 1st class and 2nd class identifiers, as well as how maximal partial unique attribute combinations are retrieved.

3.1 Notation and Definitions

We build on previous work to capture the concept of anonymity in relation to our proposed *compartmentation* approach to transforming data for anonymity [32].

Definition 3.1. Feature
An attribute or attribute combination forming new single attributes that describe an entity (row, record, user, patient) e through $f(e_{index}) = x_i$ is called a feature, where $x_i \in X = \{x_1, .., x_m\}, 1 \leq i \leq m$ and X is the set of possible feature values. Additionally, a feature set is denoted as $F = \{f_1, ..., f_n\}$.

Exemplarily, this can be a patient's weight and height, or combined the BMI serving as feature or describing attribute. We draw on the definition of a *Feature*, to define *Self-Contained Anonymity* which formalizes the idea of anonymity of individual records or a dataset, as follows:

Definition 3.2. Self-contained Anonymity
Let E be a set of entities. A snapshot S of E is said to be self-containing anonymous or sanitized, if no family $\mathcal{F} = \{F_1, .., F_m\}$ of feature sets uniquely identifies one original entity or row (k-anonymity for $k=1$).

Like Manolis Terrovitis et al. [37], this work does not distinguish between sensitive and non-sensitive attributes for several reasons: First, from previously presented de-anonymisation attacks (background knowledge, homogeneity, similarity, ..) sensitive attributes alone are not the only basis for the success of these attacks. Second, defining an exhaustive set of sensitive and non-sensitive attributes is impractical for high-dimensional datasets where user behaviours exhibit unique patterns that increase with the volumes of data collected on the individual. For instance, in medical datasets behaviour patterns like medical adherence, and/or drug intake patterns increase in uniqueness as the data points collected grow to several hundred attributes per patient.

We now present the method of identifying 1st class identifiers in our use-case agnostic anonymisation scheme that uses *compartmentation* to detach attribute relations instead of altering their values as is the case with data transformation approaches such as generalisation, suppression, and perturbation.

3.2 Identifying 1st Class Identifiers

We do not distinguish between sensitive and non-sensitive attributes because classifications of sensitive and non-sensitive attributes are the primary enabler for de-anonymisation attacks based on the semantics of the anonymised dataset. However, we do separate standalone identifier (1st class identifier) from attribute combinations forming an 2nd class identifier like behavior patterns such as medical adherence, or drug intake pattern uniqueness increases with available data points since they must be processed differently.

Transforming 1st class identifiers reduces the number of attribute combination which are needed to be processed afterwards. Treatment occurs as debarment or exclusion from the original dataset. This reduces the information loss, time complexity, and ensures data anonymity. Examples of potential 1st class identifiers for health datasets and that we use in our experiments, include the US Health Insurance Portability and Accountability Act (HIPAA)[1] which provides a list of 18 attributes based on their high cardinality.

We identify 1st class identifiers on the basis of attribute cardinality and entropy. More formally, we define a 1st class identifier as follows:

Definition 3.3. 1st class identifiers
Let F be a set of features $F = \{f_1, ..., f_n\}$, where each feature is a function $f_i : E \longrightarrow A$ mapping the set of entities $E = \{e_1, ..., e_m\}$ to a set A of realizations of f_i. A feature f_i is called a 1st class identifier, if the function f_i is injective, i.e. for all $e_j, e_k \in E$: $f_i(e_j) = f_i(e_k) \implies e_j = e_k$.

Meaning, an attribute like a genome or password hashes, which in general is not an identifier, could be an identifier in a given dataset if it includes a unique value across the dataset and therefore identifies a single entity with some given genome.

Furthermore, we define cardinality and entropy as follows:

Definition 3.4. Cardinality
The cardinality $c \in Q$ of a column or an attribute is:

$$c = \frac{\text{Number of unique entries}}{\text{Total number of entries}}$$

Definition 3.5. Entropy (Kullback-Leibler Divergence)
Let p and q denote discrete probability distributions. The Kullback-Leibler divergence or relative entropy e of p with respect to q is:

$$e = \sum_i p(i) \cdot \log(\frac{p(i)}{q(i)})$$

By removing 1st class identifiers either HIPAA or any other, no bijective linkages from the dataset to the original entities remain. Certainly, it is still possible to combine several attributes for re-identification. Therefore, we must identify and remove these attribute combinations in the following section.

3.3 Identifying 2nd Class Identifiers

We use 2nd class identifier candidates as attribute combinations as a further evaluation step to ensure self-contained data anonymity. Correspondingly, the goal is to find sets of attribute value candidates that are being unique throughout the entire dataset and therefore violate the anonymity. More formally, we define 2nd class identifiers as follows:

---

[1]http://www.dhcs.ca.gov/dataandstats/data/Pages/ListofHIPAAIdentifiers.aspx

Definition 3.6. 2nd class identifier

Let $F = \{f_1, .., f_n\}$ be a set of all features and $B := \mathcal{P}(F) = \{B_1, .., B_k\}$ its power set, i.e. the set of all possible feature combinations. A set of selected features $B_i \in B$, is called a 2nd class identifier, if B_i identifies at least one entity uniquely and all features $f_j \in B_i$ are not 1st class identifiers.

A 2nd class identifier is a collection of attributes (columns) that uniquely identifies at least one entity (row). As differentiation towards quasi-identifiers, 2nd class identifier can be consisted of any attribute combination within the dataset (not selective ones).

Example 3.7. Imagine a dataset describing medical adherence and the drug intake behavior of patients. While it is self-explanatory that a patient ID is a 1st class identifier, the combination of last name and birthday or first name, age and street name might be a possible 2nd class identifiers for selective patient records. The restriction to selective patient records is important in this context, since most patient records might be identifiable through last name and birthday while that does not have to apply to all given records (maximal partial UCC).

Identifying 2nd class identifiers is similar to finding primary key candidates or rather (maximal partial) unique column combinations (mpUCC) in the data profiling field. It may not be a primary key directly, but rather a mpUCC candidate with less than k-rows in its group. The smaller k, the stronger the candidate serves as standalone identifier. Unique column combinations (UCC) are tuples of columns which act as identifier across the entire dataset. Maximal partial UCC, however, can be understood as identifiers for (at least) one specific row. This implies the search for UCC for each specific row (maximal partial). For this purpose, all possible combinations of columns must be evaluated which sums up to:

$$C(n, r) = \binom{n}{r} = \frac{n!}{(r!(n-r)!)} \tag{1}$$

where n is the population of attributes and r the subset of n. When considering 2nd class identifiers of all lengths, r must equal all possible lengths of subsets of attributes. This can be expressed using the following equation:

$$C_2(n) = \sum_{r=1}^{n} \binom{n}{r} = \sum_{r=1}^{n} \frac{n!}{(r!(n-r)!)} = 2^n - 1 \tag{2}$$

For each column combination, a SQL *GROUP BY* statement on the dataset for the particular combination can be applied. If there is just one row represented for one value group after counting the number of entries for each group, the combination under review may serve as mpUCC (see Algorithm 1). Such group statements are highly efficient in modern in-memory platforms like SAP HANA or AWS Redshift, since reverted indices and column-wise storage supersede the necessity for these operations to step through the entire dataset.

4 ATTRIBUTE COMPARTMENTATION

After identifying the 2nd class identifiers that violate the definition of anonymity 3.1, we may classify the identifiers that adhere to anonymity. Existing research focuses on sophisticated statistical approaches which are highly use case sensitive [41]. Standard use case

---

Algorithm 1: Evaluating 2nd class identifier candidates

1 <u>find 2nd class identifiers</u> (*combination, df*);
   Input   : DataFrame *df* as table of data,
            Set *combination* as list of colnames forming a
            candidate
   Output: *True* if a 2nd class identifier is present,
             False if no 2nd class identifier is present
2 *// counting unique rows for a given combination;*
3 coverage = (SELECT COUNT(*) FROM df GROUP BY
   combination HAVING COUNT(combination)=1);
4 *// if there are any, this combination serves as a 2nd class
   identifier;*
5 **if** *coverage > 0* **then**
6 | return True;
7 **else**
8 | return False;
9 **end**

---

agnostic data transformation measures such as *local suppression, global generalisation, perturbation* [35] and separating the attributes along with other attributes can be used to support attribute *compartmentation* which we define as follows:

Definition 4.1. Compartmentation as admissible family of feature sets

Let $Q = \{Q_1, .., Q_n\}$ be a set of 2nd class identifiers and denote with $F \subset Q$ a feature set (a set of quasi-identifiers). A family $\mathcal{F} = \{F_1, .., F_m\}$ of feature sets, $F_i \subset Q, 1 \leq i \leq m$, is called admissible, if:
$\forall\, F_i, F_j \in \mathcal{F}, i \neq j : \bar{Q} = F_i \cup F_j$ is k-anonymous set of features for given data $(k < 1)$

Basically, *compartmentation* separates all attributes forming 2nd class identifiers in different pools. All other attributes from the original dataset are duplicated included in the split pools without the possibility to rejoin to the original dataset. It is important to distinguish *compartmentation* from partitioning, since partitions are intuitively disjoint (disjoint and distinct) from one another while compartments are intended to overlap. *Compartmentation* includes finding the best compartment with as few partitions as possible. Each supplemental compartment implies an additional partial redundancy of the original dataset. Therefore, all for compartmentation marked column combinations (mpmUCCs) will be projected to a graph (see Figure 1a), and the graph representation will be inversed like delineated in Figure 1b. Now, the graph represents all allowed combinations. By finding maximal cliques in this graph, the result will present us all potential and best compressed compartments which can be used to split the original dataset in parts not violating the earlier introduced anonymisation criteria (see Figure 1c). After separating the original dataset depending on the necessity of each row in its corresponding compartments, those separations can be stored either as independent datasets or joined using a FULL OUTER JOIN.

(a) Graph containing 2nd class identifiers

(b) Complemented graph illustrating all allowed attribute combinations

● AGE, WEIGHT, DRUG
○ GENDER, WEIGHT, DRUG
● AGE, DATE
◐ ZIP, DATE
● GENDER, DATE

(c) Max cliques in completed graph representing compartments with lowest redundancy

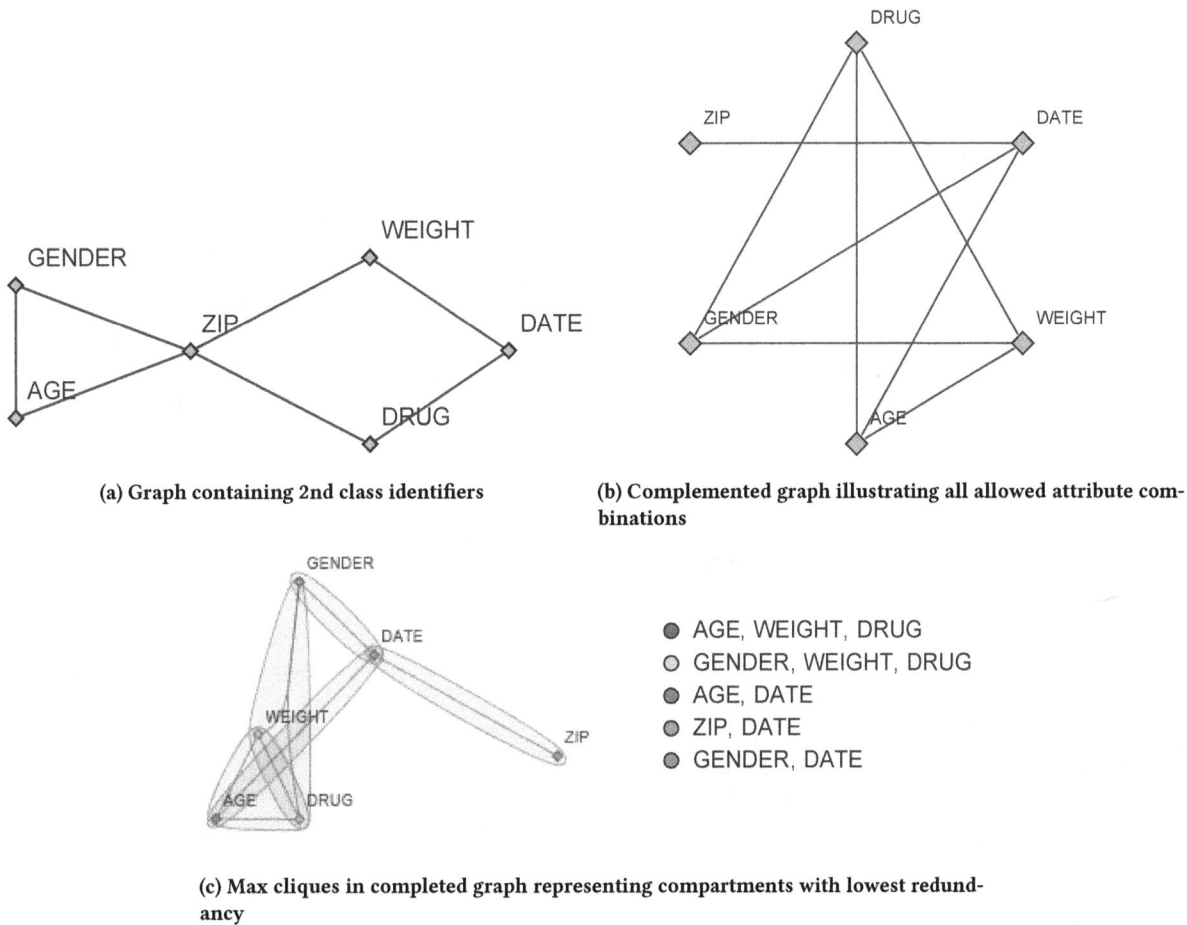

Figure 1: Steps for creating attribute compartments

4.1 Minimal 2nd Class Identifier Set

Even without the maximal partial criteria and just considering unique column combination, we note that identifying 2nd class identifiers is a NP-complete problem similar to the hidden subgroup problem (HSP) [19]. In fact, following Bläsius et al. assessment, the problem is W[2]-complete which is not a fixed parameter tractable problem (FPT) [4]. Such classification implies the absence of an exact solution better than polynomial time complexity due to its exponential nature in the attribute combination growth [4, 17, 27]. For comparison, other W[2]-complete problems are the "short multi-tape Turing machine acceptance" problem [17, 27] or to decide whether a given graph contains a dominating set with size k. As such in this subsection we look at how to optimize identifying 2nd class identifiers. As delineated in Figure 2, assessing 2^n combinations of attributes is not scalable to large datasets. Instead of searching for all possible combinations with all lengths for each row – hereinafter referred to as maximal partial unique column combinations (mpUCC) – the search may be limited to unique minimal column combinations (mpmUCC) [31]. Accordingly to Papenbrock et al., all mpUCC can be derived from mpmUCC [31].

Conveniently, it is sufficient to identify the minimal 2nd class identifier to prevent re-identification (see Figure 2). Therefore, a *minimal 2nd class identifier* is defined in the following way.

Definition 4.2. Minimal 2nd class identifier
A 2nd class identifier $B_i \in \mathcal{P}(F)$ is called minimal, if there is no combination of features $B_j \subset B_i$ that is also a 2nd class identifier.

Example 4.3. Imagine a dataset describing the drug intake behavior and medical adherence of patients. After identifying the first name, age and street name as 2nd class identifier tuple, it is obvious that any additional attribute to this tuple is still a 2nd class identifier. A minimal 2nd class identifier, however, contains just the minimal number of attributes in the tuple which are needed to serve as quasi identifier or maximal partial minimal UCC.

This implies, that the search in one branch of the search tree can be stopped immediately when a minimal 2nd class identifier is found since all super-sets can be neglected. Analogue to Papenbrock et al.'s [31] work of handling maximal partial UCCs, such shortcut improves computation time dramatically. First testing corroborates that most mpmUCCs appear in the first third of the search tree but at most in the first half. Given the *symmetry of the binomial coefficient*, this still requires to process and evaluate $\frac{2^n}{2} = 2^{n-1}$

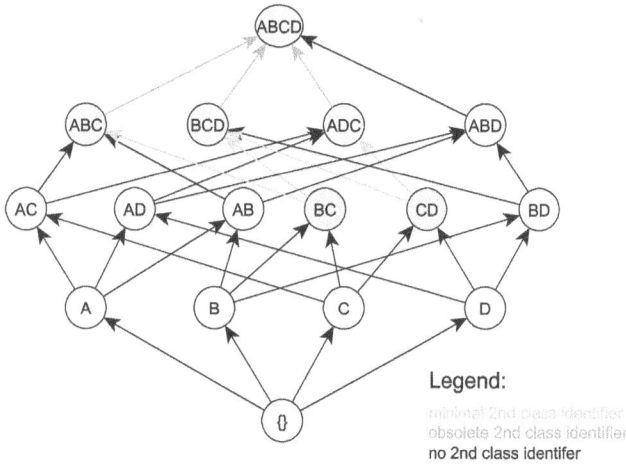

Figure 2: Maximal partial minimal unique column combin-ations combinations tree

combinations. The combination distribution and symmetry of the binomial coefficients can be depicted by arranging the binomial coefficients to form a Pascal's triangle where each Pascal's triangle level corresponds to a n value. By reducing layers and the number of combinations, an exponential growth is still present.

4.2 Greedy Search Optimization

We evaluated the option of clustering similar columns based on their relative entropy or cardinality by means of the k-means clustering algorithm [16] to reduce the set of combinations a priori. By using representatives of each cluster, their results could be projected to all other cluster members. Yet, this does not effectively consider all existing representative combinations in regards to possible tuple lengths and therefore does not identify even half of the existing 2nd class identifiers. One might think that creating overlapping groups of columns, where the overlapping columns are those with a high entropy or cardinality, could overcome this. But similar to the representative approach, there are combinations of columns which are not be represented in the groups, so this is not a trustworthy method of detecting 2nd class identifiers.

We observed that to support the exact search for mpUCCs we need to reduce the risk of compromise for each identifier type. Thus, we filter column combinations by evaluating cardinality based features like the sum of their cardinality (see Figure 3a), the mean cardinality (see Figure 3c), its mean value (see Figure 3b) or the number of elements per tuple (see Figure 3d) against given thresholds (see Algorithm 2). Given the observed distribution of tuple sizes regarding their elements expressed one may observe: The more tuples exist, the more we can filter given a static threshold. If no combination candidates are left for assessment after filtering

- while the tuple length under examination is incomplete with regard to the re-arranging of the binomial coefficients, or
- while not all tree branches are covered by the already found minimal 2nd class identifiers,

one may decrease these thresholds successively. Having found a mpmUCC, it is crucial to review its direct neighbors. Only if neither the parent or sibling neighbor is an (minimal) identifier, one may exit the inspection for this branch.

Algorithm 2: Filter 2nd class identifier candidates

---

1 filter 2nd class identifier candidate
  (combination, quasiIdentifiers, crmAttributes, thresholds);
  Input : Array *quasiIdentifiers* as list of already identified
             quasi identifiers,
             Set *combination* as tuple of attributes
             forming a candidate,
             Dictionary *thresholds* defining the thresholds
             for filtering
  Output: *True* if the 2nd class identifier candidate is to be
             evaluated,
             False if the 2nd class identifier can be
             skipped
2 // check if combination is a superset of already identified 2nd
  class identifiers;
3 **for** *quasiIdentifier in quasiIdentifiers* **do**
4   **if** *set(combination).issuperset(quasiIdentifier)* **then**
5   return False;
6   **end**
7 **end**
8 // filter based on configured thresholds;
9 **if** *MeasureSummedCardinality(combination) <*
  thresholds['minCardinalityToBeConsidered'] **then**
10   return *False*;
11 **end**
12 **if** *MeasureMeanCardinality(combination) <*
  thresholds['overallMinMeanCardinality'] **then**
13   return *False*;
14 **end**
15 **if** *MeasureMeanCardinality(combination) <*
  thresholds['minMeanCardinality'] & length(combination) >
  thresholds['minLengthForMinMeanCardinality'] **then**
16   return *False*;
17 **end**
18 return *True*;

This procedure is exact and not heuristic and turns out to perform very well against all existing approaches, as we will show in Section 5, since almost 98.5% of all attribute combinations can be trustworthy skipped. Through this incremental and iterative procedure, the worst-case runtime remains but the effective runtime drops significantly allowing us to process easily datasets of 100 entity describing attributes in a few seconds on common hardware. When keeping enterprise hardware resource in mind, several factors of 100 attributes may be easily processed.

5 EVALUATION

In order to evaluate *compartmentation* we study its impact on data anonymisation using several common precision metrics which we

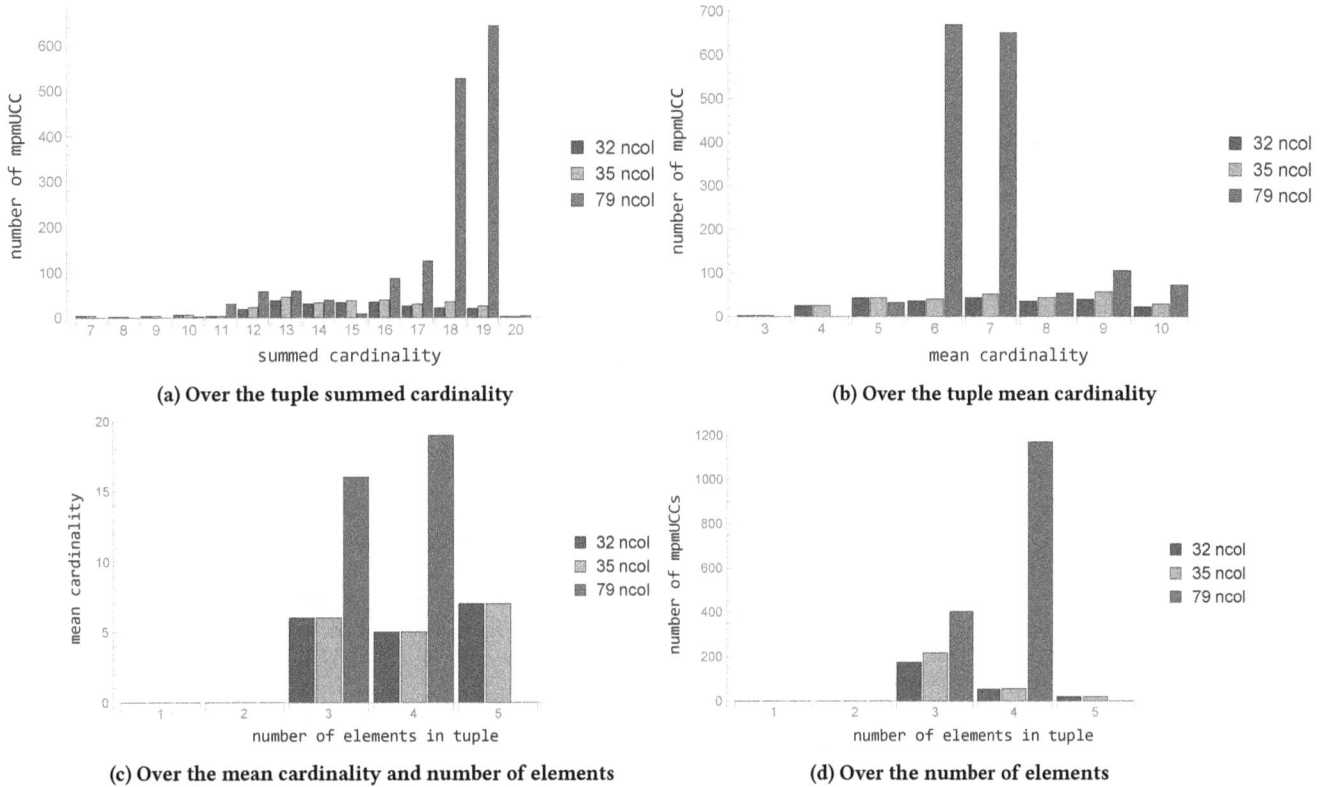

(a) Over the tuple summed cardinality

(b) Over the tuple mean cardinality

(c) Over the mean cardinality and number of elements

(d) Over the number of elements

Figure 3: Appearances of 2nd class identifier (mpmUCCs)

briefly outline in the evaluation setup, followed by a discussion of our results, and an in-depth use case study. For the comparison, we selected established anonymization techniques like local suppression, generalisation and perturbation that have an exact and not heuristic nature similar to the novel approach. A more detailed elaboration of local suppression and global generalisation besides the one from Section 2 is available in Latanya Sweeney [35], N. Li et al. [23] and Ashwin Machanavajjhala et al. [25] work.

5.1 Setup & Metrics

The data quality is determined based on three factors illustrated in Table 1. Unique values are awarded by one point, duplicates, less than one point depending on the number of duplicates. Falsified values, which include any alternation from the original value, are penalized by some function measuring their distance from the original value.

Table 1: Weighting of values for the data score

Value Condition	Score	Comment
is unique	$+1$	
is duplicated	$+\tanh(1/x)$	x = duplication amount
is falsified	$-\frac{distance}{original\ value}$	only for numeric values

The algorithm complexity is expressed in Big-O notation while additionally the data size of the sanitized dataset is evaluated. It is

noteworthy, that *compartmentation* includes redundancy of data. *Classification accuracy* as a precision metric [30], representing how often records are correctly categorized in comparison to the others, may not be illustrated in depth, since every record value in the novel approach of attribute compartmentation is not altered resulting in an absolute low utility preservation and therefore this metric will be without meaning. The experiments were conducted on a machine equipped with 16x Intel(R) Xeon(R) CPU E5-2697 v3 @ 2.60GHz and 32,94 GB RAM using an enriched dataset with 109 attributes and 1M rows. We have taken real world data from multiple sources and enriched those with fake profile data in close adjustment with real world data distributions to ensure a fair evaluation set which can be unanonymously published for reasons of confirmability and traceability without endangering single entities through their personally identifiable information.

These real-world data include CRM data, blood type distribution, disease details and disease-disease relations, drug as well as SNP and genome data and relations. The sources ranges from different datasets as part of publications [33, 34, 44], as well as official government websites like medicare.gov[2], US Food & Drug Administration[3], NY health data[4], Centers for Medicare & Medicaid Services[5] and

---

[2]https://www.medicare.gov/download/downloaddb.asp
[3]https://www.fda.gov/drugs/informationondrugs/ucm142438.htm
[4]https://health.data.ny.gov/browse?limitTo=datasets&sortBy=alpha
[5]https://www.cms.gov/Medicare/Coding/ICD9ProviderDiagnosticCodes/codes.html

many more. A complete list of all data sources and its composition is publicly available at github.com[6].

5.2 Analysis

The evaluation of 1st class identifier takes $O(n)$ time where n is the number of columns, since each column has to be checked. In terms of 2nd class identifiers, different (exact) identification approaches are delineated in Figure 4. As mentioned before, analysing every case requires the exact assessment without improvements takes nearly $O(2^n)$ time, while only evaluating minimal 2nd class identifiers (mpmUCC) results in $O(2^{n-1})$ time. Our search optimization by cardinality based filtering of candidates clearly outperforms all other approaches. Depending on the readers interpretation, the time complexity is exponential with a stretching factor of 0.0889926. Bearing in mind the classification of this search as W[2] complete

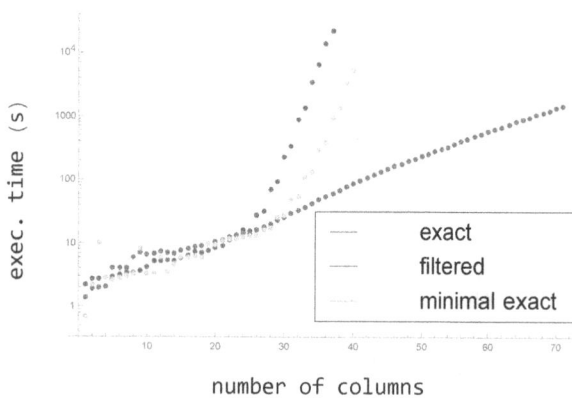

Figure 4: Identification

[4], one can conclude that there might be no better algorithm than $O(f(k) * poly(n))$ where $f(k)$ is any function of size k of the solving function and $poly(n)$ is a polynomial of input size n. Figure 5c shows the number of values needed to be altered to achieve anonymity for each transformation over the number of columns. The *distortion rate* delineated in Figure 5d can be derivated hereof representing the percentage of changes made in terms of transforming the original dataset. However, since *attribute compartmentation* does not alter individual values, its distortion rate is 0 by default. The more values need individual transformation, the slower the method may perform and the worse the data score. This is also visualized in Figure 5a. The faster a higher data score is accomplished, the less data quality loss can be denoted. Finally, the time complexity for each separate treatment is documented in Figure 5b, where generalisation unsurprisingly describes an exponential increase through its iterative nature. The uncompressed data sizes of the sanitized datasets are depicted in Figure 6a, where compartmentation increases much quicker than the other approaches. This correlates with the number of compartments which are necessary for separating attributes in 2nd class identifiers efficiently to disallow their combined usage as identifier. John W Moon and Leo Moser showed that for every n-vertex graph $3^{n/3}$ maximal cliques exist [29]. This can be

---

[6]https://github.com/jaSunny/MA-enriched-Health-Data

elucidated through the increasing possibilities in assembling (maximal) cliques as compartments in the way that their amount does not necessarily have to increase. The Bron–Kerbosch algorithm introduced by Coen Bron and Joep Kerbosch [6] can be used to find those maximal cliques in $O(3^{n/3})$ [38], wherefore the time complexity of *compartmentation* also corresponds to $O(3^{n/3}) = O(1.4422^n)$. Further, the practical time complexity has been reported to be faster [7, 11]. Given the setting of an in-memory application using dictionary encoding like SAP HANA, a redundancy of factor 20 or 30 can be apathetically neglected like Figure 6b delineates.

5.3 Discussion

In terms of time complexity, local suppression clearly wins while compartmentation still outperforms generalisation (see Figure 5b). However, we note that suppression also results in high levels of information loss which we want to avoid. Both perturbation and suppression describe a linear growth whilst generalisation and compartmentation an exponential one. This is not surprising, since suppression, perturbation and compartmentation do not have the need to re-valuate their treatments but generalisation given its recursive approach leads to significant increase in execution time. Figure 5c depicts the number of modified attribute values, where the total amount increases exponentially with the size of columns yet the number of modified data for generalisation, suppression and perturbation results in linear growth in the number of columns per modified values. Compartmentation does not modify attribute values and is therefore not represented. Even though the association between attributes is removed in compartmentation, the sanitized dataset still keeps most of their cardinality resulting in a very good increase of the data score (see Table I) expressing the quality of the data basis (see Figure 5a). The data quality of suppression and perturbation grows linear with the number of columns, while the quality accretion of perturbation is fairly constant. In fact, the data quality of suppression is also fairly constant. It is further interesting, that the data score of both generalisation and compartmentation is exponential while generalisation is much steeper, however, given the exponential increase in computation time we cannot compare the results over the full length of available columns. The data size after the transformation for the given approaches is quite similar (see Figure 6a), yet compartmentation stands out. This is due to the consciously introduced redundancy of columns within various compartments. After applying dictionary encoding this data size can be reduced efficiently (see Figure 6b). As a matter of fact, first testing reveals a redundancy factor of 30 compartments for 70 given attributes which implies carrying up to 30 indices for one actual data value, which carries no significant weight regarding the compressed data size. It is noteworthy, that the number of compartments does not grow exponentially, since the more 2nd class identifiers are present, different combinations of maximal cliques are possible thereby avoiding the necessity of increasing the number of existing cliques correspondingly (see Figure 6c).

6 CONCLUSIONS

We conclude with a summary the main contributions of this paper, and offer some suggestions for future work.

(a) Data score

(b) Exec. time

(c) Data value alteration

(d) Distortion rate

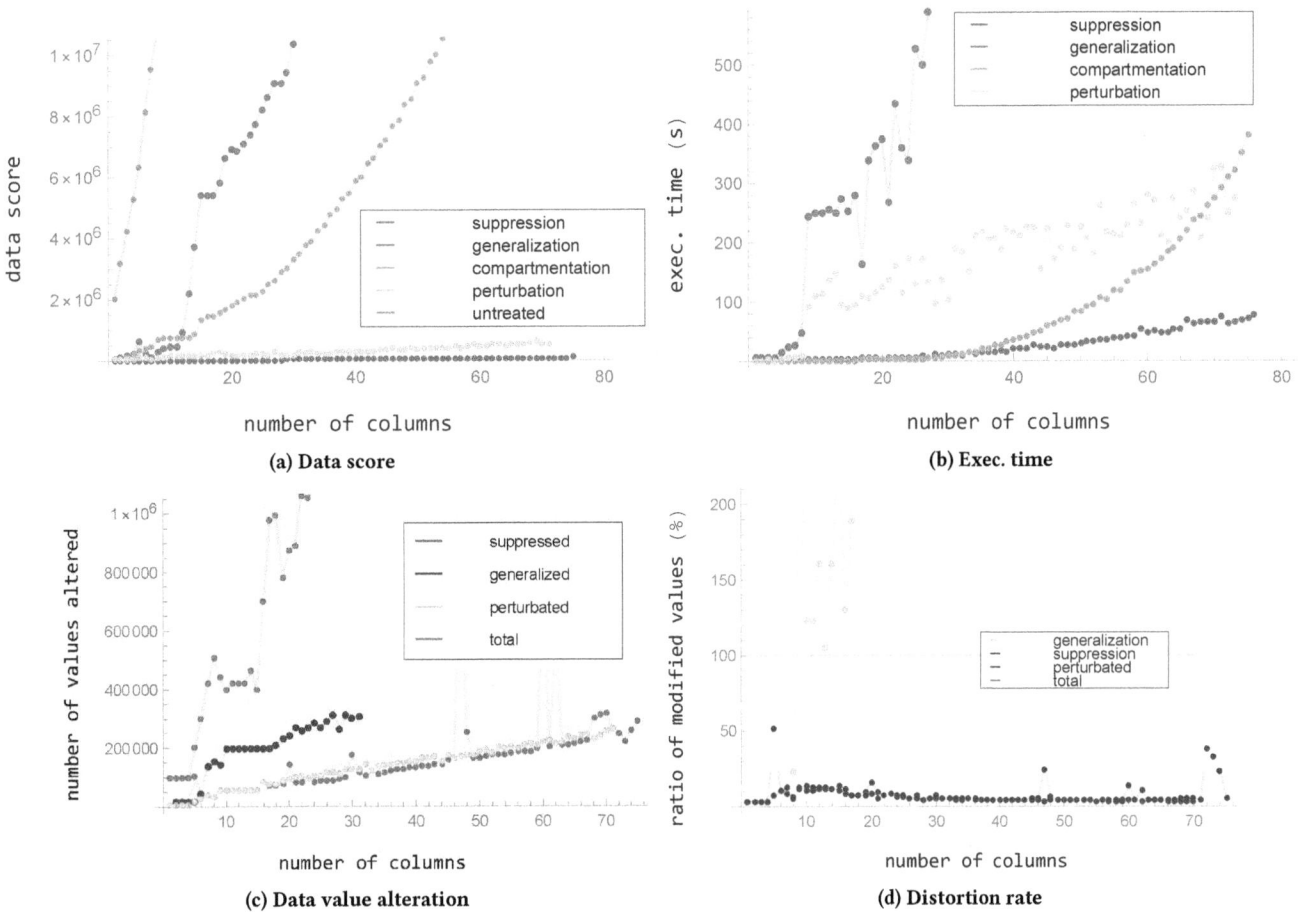

Figure 5: Analysis evaluation results

In this work, we presented a novel *compartmentation* approach to data transformation in syntactic data anonymisation algorithms. *Compartmentation* is based on an overlapping partitioning technique and attribute separation to break quasi-identifiers, instead of altering the actual data values as is the case in *generalisation* and/or *suppression*. In terms of time complexity, compartmentation is faster than *generalisation*, with a worst-case time complexity of $O(3^{n/3}) = O(1.4422^n)$ in comparison to $O(2^n)$ where n is the number of attributes in the high-dimensional dataset. Compartmentation, also significantly outperforms suppression and perturbation, in terms of information utility and privacy. The W[2]-complete search for unique column combinations as quasi-identifiers, that endanger complete anonymity of a dataset, requires exponential and thus impractical computational efforts. By incrementally considering only selected combinations, this task was complanated such that the complexity only increases reasonably. Hereby, high-dimensional datasets can be processed much quicker. Since no unique attribute tuples remain, we believe self-contained anonymity can be guaranteed. An optimal composition process was evaluated based on several metrics to limit increasing data quality loss (information loss) with increasing attributes in a dataset. Additional storage costs were a consequence of the compartmentation approach, but

could be met by leveraging modern in-memory platforms and its dictionary encoding.

We have made the source code and detailed implementation documentation publicly available[7] [8].

Future work could evaluate the gains of using graphics processing units (GPU) instead of the central processing units (CPU) for the search of 2nd class identifiers (mpmUCCs). Also, deeper insights in the effect of decoupling attributes is desirable especially for more diverse use cases besides the mentioned ones.

REFERENCES

[1] AGGARWAL, C. C. On k-anonymity and the curse of dimensionality. In *Proceedings of the 31st International Conference on Very Large Data Bases* (2005), VLDB '05, VLDB Endowment, pp. 901–909.
[2] BAYARDO, R. J., AND AGRAWAL, R. Data privacy through optimal k-anonymization. In *Data Engineering, 2005. ICDE 2005. Proceedings. 21st International Conference on* (2005), IEEE, pp. 217–228.
[3] BHASKAR, R., LAXMAN, S., SMITH, A., AND THAKURTA, A. Discovering frequent patterns in sensitive data. In *Proceedings of the 16th ACM SIGKDD international conference on Knowledge discovery and data mining* (2010), ACM, pp. 503–512.
[4] BLÄSIUS, T., FRIEDRICH, T., AND SCHIRNECK, M. The parameterized complexity of dependency detection in relational databases. In *LIPIcs-Leibniz International*

[7]https://github.com/jaSunny/MA-Anonymization-ETL
[8]https://github.com/jaSunny/MA-enriched-Health-Data

(a) Data size (uncompressed)

(b) Data size (compressed)

(c) Compartments over ncols

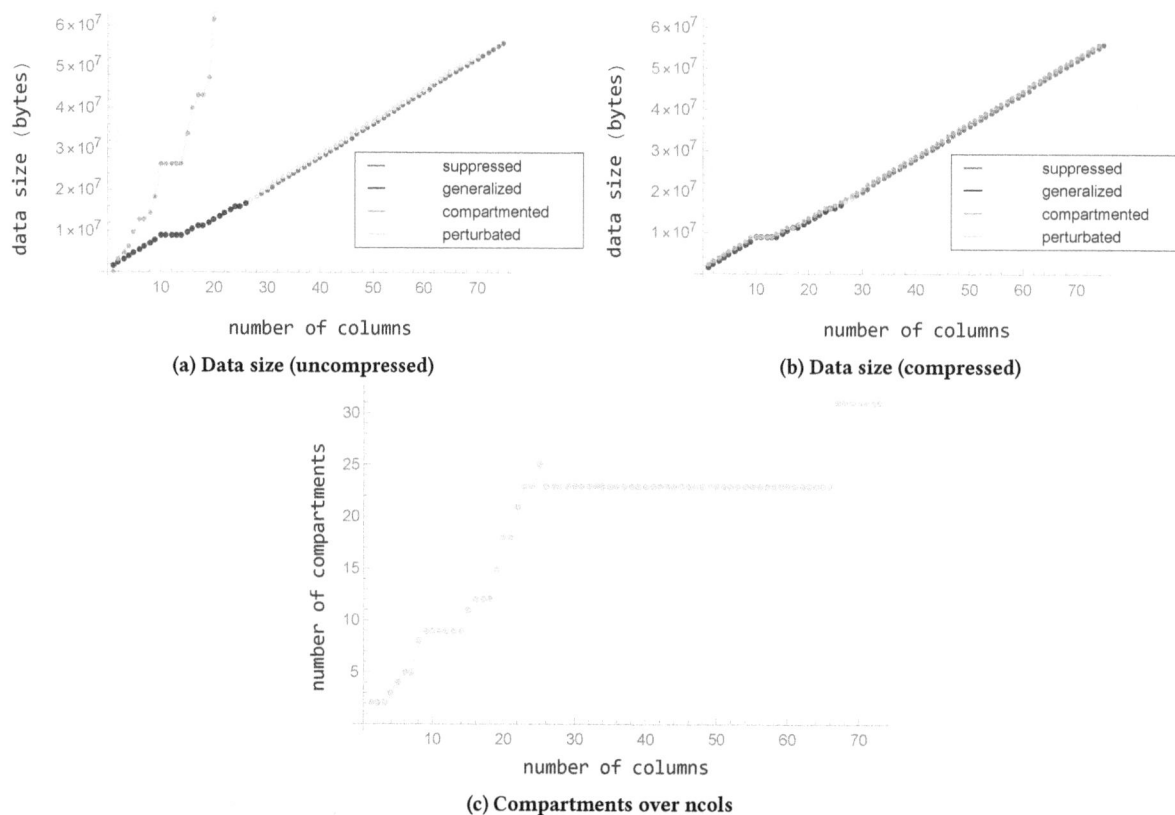

Figure 6: Anonymised dataset characteristics

Proceedings in Informatics (2017), Schloss Dagstuhl-Leibniz-Zentrum fuer Informatik.

[5] BONOMI, L., AND XIONG, L. Mining frequent patterns with differential privacy. *Proceedings of the VLDB Endowment 6*, 12 (2013), 1422–1427.

[6] BRON, C., AND KERBOSCH, J. Algorithm 457: finding all cliques of an undirected graph. *Communications of the ACM 16*, 9 (1973), 575–577.

[7] CAZALS, F., AND KARANDE, C. A note on the problem of reporting maximal cliques. *Theoretical Computer Science 407*, 1-3 (2008), 564–568.

[8] DWORK, C. Differential privacy: A survey of results. In *International Conference on Theory and Applications of Models of Computation* (2008), Springer, pp. 1–19.

[9] DWORK, C. Differential privacy. In *Encyclopedia of Cryptography and Security.* Springer, 2011, pp. 338–340.

[10] DWORK, C., MCSHERRY, F., NISSIM, K., AND SMITH, A. Calibrating noise to sensitivity in private data analysis. In *Theory of Cryptography Conference* (2006), Springer.

[11] EPPSTEIN, D., LÖFFLER, M., AND STRASH, D. Listing all maximal cliques in large sparse real-world graphs. *Journal of Experimental Algorithmics (JEA) 18* (2013), 3–1.

[12] FIENBERG, S. E., AND JIN, J. Privacy-preserving data sharing in high dimensional regression and classification settings. *Journal of Privacy and Confidentiality* (2012).

[13] FREDJ, F. B., LAMMARI, N., AND COMYN-WATTIAU, I. Abstracting anonymization techniques: A prerequisite for selecting a generalization algorithm. *Procedia Computer Science 60* (2015), 206–215.

[14] GHOSH, A., ROUGHGARDEN, T., AND SUNDARARAJAN, M. Universally utility-maximizing privacy mechanisms. *SIAM Journal on Computing 41*, 6 (2012), 1673–1693.

[15] HARDT, M., LIGETT, K., AND MCSHERRY, F. A simple and practical algorithm for differentially private data release. In *Advances in Neural Information Processing Systems* (2012), pp. 2339–2347.

[16] HARTIGAN, J. A., AND WONG, M. A. Algorithm as 136: A k-means clustering algorithm. *Journal of the Royal Statistical Society. Series C (Applied Statistics) 28*, 1 (1979), 100–108.

[17] IBARRA, O. H. Reversal-bounded multicounter machines and their decision

[18] ISLAM, M. Z., AND BRANKOVIC, L. Privacy preserving data mining: A noise addition framework using a novel clustering technique. *Knowledge-Based Systems 24*, 8 (2011).

[19] KARP, R. M. Reducibility among combinatorial problems. In *Complexity of computer computations.* Springer, 1972, pp. 85–103.

[20] KIFER, D., AND MACHANAVAJJHALA, A. No free lunch in data privacy. In *Proceedings of the 2011 ACM SIGMOD International Conference on Management of Data* (New York, NY, USA, 2011), SIGMOD '11, ACM, pp. 193–204.

[21] KOUFOGIANNIS, F., HAN, S., AND PAPPAS, G. J. Optimality of the laplace mechanism in differential privacy. *arXiv preprint arXiv:1504.00065* (2015).

[22] LI, C., MIKLAU, G., HAY, M., MCGREGOR, A., AND RASTOGI, V. The matrix mechanism: optimizing linear counting queries under differential privacy. *The VLDB Journal 24*, 6 (2015), 757–781.

[23] LI, N., LI, T., AND VENKATASUBRAMANIAN, S. t-closeness: Privacy beyond k-anonymity and l-diversity. In *2007 IEEE 23rd ICDE* (April 2007), pp. 106–115.

[24] LIU, F. Generalized gaussian mechanism for differential privacy. *arXiv preprint arXiv:1602.06028* (2016).

[25] MACHANAVAJJHALA, A., KIFER, D., GEHRKE, J., AND VENKITASUBRAMANIAM, M. l-diversity: Privacy beyond k-anonymity. *ACM Transactions on Knowledge Discovery from Data (TKDD) 1*, 1 (2007), 3.

[26] MCSHERRY, F., AND TALWAR, K. Mechanism design via differential privacy. In *Foundations of Computer Science, 2007. FOCS'07. 48th Annual IEEE Symposium on* (2007), IEEE, pp. 94–103.

[27] MEYER, A. R., AND STOCKMEYER, L. J. The equivalence problem for regular expressions with squaring requires exponential space. In *SWAT (FOCS)* (1972), pp. 125–129.

[28] MEYERSON, A., AND WILLIAMS, R. On the complexity of optimal k-anonymity. In *Proceedings of the twenty-third ACM SIGMOD-SIGACT-SIGART symposium on Principles of database systems* (2004), ACM, pp. 223–228.

[29] MOON, J. W., AND MOSER, L. On cliques in graphs. *Israel journal of Mathematics 3*, 1 (1965), 23–28.

[30] NERGIZ, M. E., AND CLIFTON, C. Thoughts on k-anonymization. *Data & Knowledge Engineering 63*, 3 (2007), 622–645.

problems. *Journal of the ACM (JACM) 25*, 1 (1978), 116–133.

[31] PAPENBROCK, T., AND NAUMANN, F. A hybrid approach for efficient unique column combination discovery. *Proc. der Fachtagung Business, Technologie und Web* (2017).

[32] PODLESNY, N. J., KAYEM, A., VON SCHORLEMER, S., AND UFLACKER, M. Minimising information loss on anonymized high dimensional data with greedy in-memory processing. In *International Conference on Database and Expert Systems Applications* (2018), Springer.

[33] RZHETSKY, A., WAJNGURT, D., PARK, N., AND ZHENG, T. Probing genetic overlap among complex human phenotypes. *Proceedings of the National Academy of Sciences 104*, 28 (2007), 11694–11699.

[34] SUTHRAM, S., DUDLEY, J. T., CHIANG, A. P., CHEN, R., HASTIE, T. J., AND BUTTE, A. J. Network-based elucidation of human disease similarities reveals common functional modules enriched for pluripotent drug targets. *PLoS computational biology* (2010).

[35] SWEENEY, L. Achieving k-anonymity privacy protection using generalization and suppression. *International Journal of Uncertainty, Fuzziness and Knowledge-Based Systems 10*, 05 (2002), 571–588.

[36] TASSA, T., MAZZA, A., AND GIONIS, A. k-concealment: An alternative model of k-type anonymity. *Trans. Data Privacy 5*, 1 (2012), 189–222.

[37] TERROVITIS, M., MAMOULIS, N., AND KALNIS, P. Privacy-preserving anonymization of set-valued data. *Proceedings of the VLDB Endowment 1*, 1 (2008), 115–125.

[38] TOMITA, E., TANAKA, A., AND TAKAHASHI, H. The worst-case time complexity for generating all maximal cliques and computational experiments. *Theoretical Computer Science 363*, 1 (2006), 28–42.

[39] VAIDYA, J., AND CLIFTON, C. Privacy-preserving k-means clustering over vertically partitioned data. In *Proceedings of the ninth ACM SIGKDD international conference on Knowledge discovery and data mining* (2003), ACM, pp. 206–215.

[40] VAIDYA, J., KANTARCIOĞLU, M., AND CLIFTON, C. Privacy-preserving naive bayes classification. *The VLDB Journal—The International Journal on Very Large Data Bases 17*, 4 (2008), 879–898.

[41] WASSERMAN, L., AND ZHOU, S. A statistical framework for differential privacy. *Journal of the American Statistical Association 105*, 489 (2010), 375–389.

[42] WONG, W. K., MAMOULIS, N., AND CHEUNG, D. W. L. Non-homogeneous generalization in privacy preserving data publishing. In *Proceedings of the 2010 ACM SIGMOD International Conference on Management of data* (2010), ACM, pp. 747–758.

[43] ZHANG, B., DAVE, V., MOHAMMED, N., AND HASAN, M. A. Feature selection for classification under anonymity constraint. *arXiv preprint arXiv:1512.07158* (2015).

[44] ZHOU, X., MENCHE, J., BARABÁSI, A.-L., AND SHARMA, A. Human symptoms-disease network. *Nature communications 5* (2014), 4212.

APPENDIX: DATA ATTRIBUTES

Table 2: Attributes considered as behavior data describing an entity in the data set, $1 \le \{m, n, i, j\} \le 10$

Attribute	Type
BloodType	String
$Disease_n$	String
$DiseaseDate_n$	Date
$Drug_m$	String
$DrugDate_m$	Date
SNP_i	String
Gen_j	String

Table 3: Attributes considered as CRM describing an entity in the data set

Attribute	Type
ID	Integer
GivenName	String
Surname	String
Gender	Boolean
NameSet	String
Title	String
StreetAddress	String
City	String
State	String
StateFull	String
ZipCode	Integer
Country	String
EmailAddress	String
Username	String
Password	String
TelephoneNumber	String
TelephoneCountryCode	String
Birthday	Date
Age	Integer
NationalID	Integer
Color	String
Occupation	String
Company	String
Kilograms	Integer
Centimeters	Integer

CURIE: Policy-based Secure Data Exchange

Z. Berkay Celik
SIIS Laboratory, Department of CSE
The Pennsylvania State University
zbc102@cse.psu.edu

Abbas Acar, Hidayet Aksu
CPS Security Lab, Department of ECE
Florida International University
aacar001,haksu@fiu.edu

Ryan Sheatsley
SIIS Laboratory, Department of CSE
The Pennsylvania State University
rms5643@cse.psu.edu

Patrick McDaniel
SIIS Laboratory, Department of CSE
The Pennsylvania State University
mcdaniel@cse.psu.edu

A. Selcuk Uluagac
CPS Security Lab, Department of ECE
Florida International University
suluagac@fiu.edu

ABSTRACT

Data sharing among partners—users, companies, organizations—is crucial for the advancement of collaborative machine learning in many domains such as healthcare, finance, and security. Sharing through secure computation and other means allow these partners to perform privacy-preserving computations on their private data in controlled ways. However, in reality, there exist complex relationships among members (partners). Politics, regulations, interest, trust, data demands and needs prevent members from sharing their complete data. Thus, there is a need for a mechanism to meet these conflicting relationships on data sharing. This paper presents CURIE[1], an approach to exchange data among members who have complex relationships. A novel policy language, CPL, that allows members to define the specifications of data exchange requirements is introduced. With CPL, members can easily assert who and what to exchange through their local policies and negotiate a global sharing agreement. The agreement is implemented in a distributed privacy-preserving model that guarantees sharing among members will comply with the policy as negotiated. The use of CURIE is validated through an example healthcare application built on recently introduced secure multi-party computation and differential privacy frameworks, and policy and performance trade-offs are explored.

CCS CONCEPTS

• **Information systems** → **Data exchange**; • **Security and privacy** → *Economics of security and privacy.*

KEYWORDS

Collaborative learning; policy language; secure data exchange

1 INTRODUCTION

Inter-organizational data sharing is crucial to the advancement of many domains including security, health care, and finance. Previous works have shown the benefit of data sharing within distributed,

---

[1]Our paper named after Marie Curie. She is physicist and chemist who conducted pioneering research in health care and won Nobel prize twice.

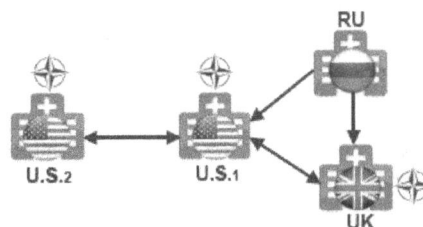

Figure 1: An illustration of data exchange requirements of countries learning a predictive model on their shared data. Arrows show the data requirements of countries.

collaborative, and federated learning [5, 12, 37]. Privacy-preserving machine learning offers data sharing among multiple members while avoiding the risks of disclosing the sensitive data (e.g., healthcare records, personally identifiable information) [14]. For example, secure multiparty computation enables multiple members, each with its training dataset, to collaboratively learn a shared predictive model without revealing their datasets [31]. These approaches solve the privacy concerns of members during model computation, yet do not consider the complex relationships such as regulations, competitive advantage, data sovereignty, and jurisdiction among members on private data sharing. Members want to be able to articulate and enforce their conflicting requirements on data sharing.

To illustrate such complex data sharing requirements, consider health care organizations that collaborate for a joint prediction model of diagnosis of patients experiencing blood clots (see Figure 1). Members wish to dictate their needs through their legal and political limitations as follows: $U.S._1$ is able to share its complete data for nation-wide members ($U.S._2$) [3, 23], yet it is obliged to share the data of patients deployed in NATO countries with NATO members (UK) [17]. However, $U.S._1$ wishes to acquire all patient data from other countries. UK is able to share and acquire complete data from NATO members, yet it desires to acquire only data of certain race groups from $U.S_1$ to increase its data diversity. RU wishes to share and acquire complete data from all members, yet members limit their data share to Russian citizens who live in their countries. Such complex data sharing requirements also commonly occur today in non-healthcare systems [28, 38]. For instance, National Security Agency has varying restrictions on how human intelligence is shared with other countries; financial companies share data based on trust, and competition among each other.

This paper presents a policy-based data exchange approach, called CURIE, that allows secure data exchange among members that have such complex relationships. Members specify their requirements on data exchange using a policy language (CPL). The requirements defined with the use of CPL form the local data exchange policies of members. Local policies are defined separately for data sharing and data acquisition policies. This property allows asymmetric relations on data exchange. For example, a member does not necessarily have to acquire the data that the other members dictate to share. By using these two policies, members specify statements of who to share/acquire and what to share/acquire. The statements are defined using *conditional* and *selection* expressions. Selections allow members to filter data and limit the data to be exchanged, whereas conditional expressions allow members to define logical statements. Another advanced property of CPL is predefined *data-dependent conditionals* for calculating the statistical metrics between member's data. For instance, members can define a conditional to compute the intersection size of data columns without disclosing their data. This allows members to define content-dependent conditional data exchange in their policies.

Once members have defined their local policies, they negotiate a sharing agreement. The guarantee provided by Curie is that all data exchanged among members will respect the agreement. The agreement is executed in a multi-party privacy-preserving prediction model enhanced with optional differential privacy guarantees. In this work, we make the following contributions:

- We introduce Curie, an approach for secure data exchange among members that have complex relationships. Curie includes CPL policy language allowing members to define complex specifications of data exchange requirements, negotiate an agreement, and execute agreements in a multi-party predictive model that policies respect the negotiated policy.
- We validate Curie through an example of real healthcare application used to prescribe warfarin dosage. A privacy-preserving joint dose model among medical institutions is compiled with the use of various data exchange policies while protecting the privacy of members' healthcare records.
- We show Curie incurs low overhead and policies are effective at improving the dose accuracy of medical institutions.

We begin in the next section by defining the analysis task and outlining the security and attacker models.

2 PROBLEM SCOPE AND ATTACKER MODEL

Problem Scope. We introduce Curie Policy Language (CPL) to express data exchange requirements of distributed members. Unlike the programming languages used for writing secure multiparty computation (MPC) [24, 33] and the frameworks designed for privacy-preserving machine learning (ML) [7, 14, 29, 31, 32], CPL is a policy language in a Backus Normal Form (BNF) notation to express the conflicting relationships of members on data sharing. Members can express data exchange requirements using the conditionals, selections, and secure pairwise data-dependent statistics. Curie then enforces the policy agreements in a shared predictive model through an MPC protocol that ensures members comply with the policies as negotiated.

We integrate Curie into 24 medical institutions. Without deployment of Curie, institutions compute warfarin dosage of a patient using a model computed on their local patient records. Curie allows institutions to construct various consortia wherein each member defines a data exchange policy for other members via CPL. This

Figure 2: Curie data exchange process in a collaborative learning setting. The dashed boxes show data remains confidential.

enables institutions to acquire the patient records based on regulations as well as the records that they need to improve the accuracy of their dose predictions. Curie implements a privacy-preserving dose model through homomorphic encryption (HE) to enforce the policy agreements of the members. We note that a centralized party in HE cannot provide a privacy-preserving model on negotiated data [39]. However, Curie implements a novel protocol that allows institutions to perform local computations by aggregating the intermediate results of the dose model. Additionally, Curie implements an optional differential private (DP) mechanism that allows institutions to perform differentially-private (DP) secure dose model. DP guarantees that no information leaks on the targeted individual (i.e., patient) with high confidence from the released dose model.

Threat Model. We consider a semi-honest adversary model. That is, members in a consortium runs the protocol exactly as specified, yet they try to learn the dataset inputs of the other members as much as possible from their views of the protocol. Additionally, we consider non-adaptive adversary wherein members cannot modify inputs of their dataset once the protocol on shared data is initiated.

3 ORGANIZATIONAL DATA EXCHANGE

Depicted in Figure 2, Curie includes two independent parts: policy management and multiparty secure computation.

Policy Management. We define a *consortium* that is a group made up of two or more members–individuals, companies or governments (ⓐ). Members of a consortium aim to compute a predictive model m over their confidential data in a secure manner. For instance, data may be curated from medical history of patients or financial reports of companies with the objective of building an ML model. Moreover, each member wants to enforce a set of local constraints toward other consortium members to control their requirements on how and with whom they share their confidential data. These constraints define a member's interest, trust, regulations and data demands, and also impacts the accuracy of a model m. Thus, there is a need for connecting data needs of members to the privacy-preserving models. In Curie, each member of a consortium defines a *local policy* (ⓑ). The local policy of a member dictates the requirements of data exchange as follows:

(1) The member wishes to specify with whom to share and acquire data (*partnership requirement*).
(2) The member wishes to define what data to share and acquire (*sharing and acquisition requirement*).

In this, the member wishes to refine its sharing and acquisition requirements to express the following:

(1) The member wishes to dictate a set of conditions to restrict data sharing and select which data to be acquired (*conditional selective share and acquisition*); and

(2) The member wishes to dictate conditionals based on the other member's data (*data-dependent conditionals*).

The policy of members need not be-nor are likely to be-symmetric. Local policy is defined with requirements for sharing and acquisition that is tailored to each partner member in the consortium–thus allowing each pairwise sharing to be unique. Here, the local policies are used to negotiate pairwise sharing within the consortium. To illustrate how members negotiate an agreement, consider the consortium of three members in Figure 3.

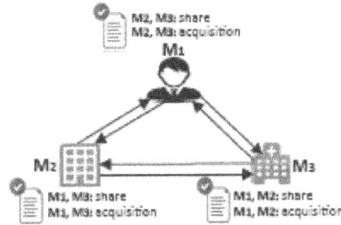

Figure 3: An example consortium of three members.

Each member initiates pairwise policy negotiations with other members to reconcile contradictions between acquisition and share policies (❶). A member starts the negotiation by sending a request message including the acquisition policy defined for a member. When a member receives the acquisition policy, it reconciles the received acquisition policy with its share policy specified for that member. Three negotiation outcomes are possible: the acquisition policy is entirely satisfied, partially satisfied with the intersection of acquisition and share policies or is an empty set. A member completes its negotiations after all of its acquisition policies for interested parties are negotiated.

Computations on Negotiated Data. Once members negotiate their policies (❷), CURIE provides a multiparty data exchange device using secure multi-party computation techniques enhanced with (optional) differential privacy guarantees. This device ensures data and individual privacy. The guarantee provided by CURIE is that all computations among members will respect their policies.

To ensure data privacy, CURIE includes cryptographic primitives such as Homomorphic Encryption (HE) and garbled circuits from the secure multi-party computation literature that allows members to perform computations on negotiated data with no disclosed data from any single member. At the end of the secure computation, all of the parties obtain a final predictive model based on their policy negotiations. To ensure the privacy of the individuals in the dataset, which the final model is computed on, CURIE integrates Differential Privacy (DP). DP protects against an attacker who tries to extract a particular individual's data in the dataset from the final computed model at the end of the secure computation protocol.

4 CURIE POLICY DESCRIPTION LANGUAGE

We now illustrate the format and semantics of the CURIE Policy Language (CPL). A BNF description of CPL is presented in Appendix A. Turning to the example consortium in Figure 3 established with three members, each member defines its requirements for other members on a dataset having the columns of age, race, genotype, and weight (see Table 1). The criteria defined by members are used throughout to construct their local policies.

Consortia member: M_1	
M_2-	desires to acquire complete data of users who are older than 25
M_2-	shares its complete data
M_3-	desires to acquire Asian users such that the Jaccard similarity of its age column and M_3's age column is greater than 0.3
M_3-	shares its complete data
Consortia member: M_2	
M_1-	desires to acquire complete data
M_1-	limits its share to EU and NATO citizen users if M_1 is both NATO and EU member and located in North America. Otherwise, it shares only White users
M_3-	desires to acquire complete data if M_3 is a NATO member
M_3-	shares its complete data
Consortia member: M_3	
M_1-	desires to acquire complete data of users having genotype 'A/A'
M_1-	share complete data if intersection size of its and M_1's genotype column is less than 10. Otherwise, it shares data of users that weigh more than 100 pounds
M_2-	desires to acquire complete data
M_2-	shares complete data if M_2 is EU member and its data size is greater than 1K

Table 1: An example of member's data exchange requirements.

Share and Acquisition Clauses. CURIE policies are collections of clauses. The collection of clauses for partners defines the local policy of a member. The clauses allow each member to dictate a member specific policy for each other member. Clauses have the following structure:

⟨clause tag⟩ : ⟨members⟩ : ⟨conditionals⟩ :: ⟨selections⟩;

Clause tags are reference names for policy entries. *Share* and *acquire* are two reserved tags. Those clauses are comprised of three parts. The first part, *members*, defines a list of members with whom to share and acquire. This can be a single member or a comma-separated list of members. An empty member entry matches all members. The second part, *conditionals*, is a list of conditions controlling when this clause will be executed. A condition is a Boolean function which expresses whether the share or acquire is allowed or not. For instance, a member may define a condition where the data size is greater than a specific value. Only if all conditions listed in conditionals are true, then this clause is executed. Last part, *selections*, states what to share or acquire. It can be a list of filters on a member's data. For instance, a member may define a filter on a column of a dataset to limit acquisition to a subset of the dataset. More complex selections can be assigned using member defined sub-clauses. A sub-clause has the following structure:

⟨tag⟩ : ⟨conditionals⟩ :: ⟨selections⟩;

where *tag* is the name of sub-clause; conditionals is, as explained above, a list of conditions stating whether this clause will be executed; selections is a list of filters or a reference to a new sub-clause. Complex data selection can be addressed with nested sub-clauses.

CPL allows members to define multiple clauses. For instance, a member may share a distinct subset of data for different conditions. CPL evaluates multiple clauses in a top-down order. When conditionals of a clause evaluate to false, it moves to the next clause until a clause is matched or it reaches end of the policy file.

Conditionals and Selections. We present the use of conditionals and selections through policies with examples. Their format and semantics are detailed. Consider an example of two members, M_1 and M_2, within a consortium. They define their local policies as:

```
@M₁ acquire : M₂ : :: s₁ ;
       share : M₂ : :: ;
@M₂ acquire : M₁ : :: ;
       share : M₁ : c₁, c₂ :: fine-select ;
       fine-select : c₃ :: s₂ ;
       fine-select : :: s₃ ;
```

where c_1, c_2 and c_3 are conditionals, s_1, s_2 and s_3 are selections and fine-select is a tag defined by M_2.

The acquire clause of M_1 states that data is requested from M_2 after it applies s_1 selection (e.g., age > 25) to its data. In contrast, its share clause allows complete share of its data if M_2 requests. On the other hand, the acquisition clause of M_1 dictates requesting complete data from M_2. However, M_2 allows data sharing if the acquisition clause issued by M_1 holds $c_1 \wedge c_2$ conditions (e.g., is both NATO and EU member). Then, M_2 delegates selection to member-defined fine-select sub-clauses. fine-select states that if the request satisfies the c_3 condition (located in North America) then the request is met with the data that is selected by the s_2 selection (e.g., limits share of its data to NATO and EU member country citizens). Otherwise, it shares data that is specified by selection s_3 (White users).

CPL supports selections through filters. A filter contains zero or more operations over data inputs describing the share and acquisition criteria to be enforced. Operations are defined as keywords or symbols such as <, >, =, *in*, *like*, and so on. Selections and filters are defined in CPL as follows:

⟨selections⟩ ::= <filters> | <tag>
      <filters> ::= <filter> [',' <filters>]
      <filter> ::= <var> <operation> <value> | ''

Selections are executed when conditionals evaluated to be true. Conditionals can be consortium and dataset-specific. For instance, a member may require other members to be in a particular country or to be in an alliance such as NATO and to have their dataset size greater than a particular value. Such conditionals do not require any data exchange between members to be evaluated. However, members may want to incorporate a relation between their data and other member's data into their policies as detailed next.

Data-dependent Conditionals. A member's decision on whether to share or to acquire data can depend on other member's data. Simply put, one example of a data-dependent conditional among two members could be whether the intersection size of the two sets (e.g., a specific column of a dataset) is not too high. Considering such knowledge, a member can make a conditional decision about share or acquisition of that data. For instance, consider a list of private IP addresses used for blacklisting the domains. If a member knows that the intersection size is close to zero, then the member may dictate an acquire clause to request complete features from that member based on IP addresses [18].

CPL defines an evaluate keyword for data-dependent conditionals through functions on data. Data-dependent conditionals take the following form:

⟨conditionals⟩ ::= <var>'='<value> [',' <conditionals>]
      | 'evaluate' '(' <data_ref> ',' <alg_arg> ',' <thshold_-arg> ')' [',' <conditionals>] | ''

A member that uses the data-dependent conditionals defines a reference data (data_ref) required for a such computation, an algorithm (alg_arg) and a threshold (thshold_arg) that is compared with the output of the computation. CPL includes four algorithms for data-dependent conditionals (see Table 2). To be brief, intersection size measures the size of the overlap between two sets; Jaccard index is a statistic measure of similarity between sets; Pearson correlation is a statistical measure of how much two sets are linearly dependent; and Cosine similarity is a measure of similarity between two vectors. Each algorithm is based on a different assumption about the underlying reference data. However, central to all of them is to privately (without leaking any sensitive data) measure a relation

Pairwise alg.	Output	Private protocol	Proof
Intersection size	$\|\mathcal{D}_i \cap \mathcal{D}_j\|$	Intersection cardinality	[11]
Jaccard index	$(\|\mathcal{D}_i \cap \mathcal{D}_j\|)/(\|\mathcal{D}_i \cup \mathcal{D}_j\|)$	Jaccard similarity	[6]
Pearson correlation	$(COV(\mathcal{D}_i, \mathcal{D}_j))/(\sigma_{\mathcal{D}_i} \sigma_{\mathcal{D}_j})$	Garbled circuits	[25]
Cosine similarity	$(\mathcal{D}_i \mathcal{D}_j)/(\|\mathcal{D}_i\| \|\mathcal{D}_j\|)$	Garbled circuits	[25]

Table 2: CPL data-dependent conditional algorithms. Two members of a consortium use the conditionals to compute the pairwise statistics. The members then use the output of the algorithm to determine whether to acquire or share data from another party. ($\mathcal{D}_i$ and $\mathcal{D}_j$ are the inputs of a dataset, and σ is std. deviation).

between two members' data to offer an effective data exchange. We note that these algorithms are found to be effective in capturing input relations in datasets [18, 19].

Data-dependent conditionals are implemented through private protocols (as defined in Table 2). These protocols are implemented with the cryptographic tools of garbled circuits and private functions. Protocols preserve the confidentiality of data. That is, each member gets the output indicated in Table 2 without revealing their sensitive data in plain text. After the private protocol terminates, the output of the algorithm is compared with a threshold value set by the requester. If the output is below the threshold value, the conditional is evaluated to true. Turning to above example M_3 joins the consortium. M_1 and M_2 extend their local policies for M_3:

@M_1 acquire : M_3 : evaluate(local data, 'Jaccard', 0.3) :: race=Asian;
   share : M_3 : :: ;
@M_2 acquire : M_3 : M_3 in \$NATO :: ;
   share : M_3 : :: ;
@M_3 acquire : M_1 : :: Genotype = 'A/A' ;
   share : M_1 : evaluate(local data,'intersection size', 10) :: ;
   share : M_1 : :: weight>150 ;
   acquire : M_2 : :: ;
   share : M_2 : M_2 in \$EU, size(data)> 1K :: ;

The acquire clause of M_1 defines a data-dependent conditional for M_3. It defines a Jaccard measure on its local data through evaluate keyword and sets its threshold value equal to 0.3. M_3 agrees to share its local data with M_1 if intersection size of its local data is less then 10. Otherwise, it consults the next share clause defined for M_1 which states that an individual's weight greater than 150 pounds will be shared. All other share and acquire clauses are trivial. Members agree to share and acquire complete data based on data size (data size > 1K), alliance membership (e.g., NATO or EU member) and inputs (e.g., genotype).

Putting pieces together, CPL allows members independently define a data exchange policy with share and acquire clauses. The policies are dictated through conditionals and selections. This allows members to dictate policies in complex and asymmetric relationships. Defined in Section 3, CPL provides members to dictate partnership, share, acquisition, and data-dependent conditionals.

Policy Negotiation and Conflicts. Data exchange between members is governed by matching share and acquire clauses in each member's respective policies. Both share and acquire clauses state conditions and selections on the data exchanged. Consider two example local policies with a share clause @m_2 ($share : m_1 : c_1 :: s_1$) and matching acquire clause @m_1 ($acquire : m_2 : c_2 : s_2$). CURIE's negotiation algorithm respects both autonomy of the data owner and the needs of the requester. It conservatively negotiates share

Policy ID	Consortium Name	Policy Definition	Acquisition Policy	Share Policy
P.1	Single Source	Each member uses its local patient dataset to learn warfarin dose model.	✗	✗
P.2	Nation-wide	Members in the same country establish a consortium based on state and country laws.	✓	✓
P.3	Regional	Members in the same continent establish a consortium.	✓	✓
P.4	NATO-EU	NATO and EU members establish a consortium independently based on their mutual agreements.	✓	✓
P.5	Global	Members exchange their complete data to build the warfarin dose model.	✓	✓

Table 3: Consortia constructed among members. Acquisition and share policies of members for each consortium are studied in Section 6.

and acquire clauses such that it will return the *intersection* of respective data sets in resulting policy assignment. The resolved policy in this example is $share : m_1 : c_1 \wedge c_2 :: s_1 \wedge s_2$ which states that the data exchange from m_2 to m_1 is subject to both c_1 and c_2 conditionals and resulting sharing has s_1 and s_2 selections on m_2's data. This authoritative negotiation makes sure no member's data is shared beyond its explicit intent, regardless how the other members' policies are defined. This is because negotiation fulfilling the criteria for each clause is based on the union of logical expressions defined in two policies. Each member runs the negotiation algorithm for members found in their member list. After all members terminate their negotiations, the negotiated policy is enforced in computations.

5 DEPLOYMENT OF CURIE

To validate CURIE in a real application, we integrated CURIE into 24 medical institutions. Each institution wants to compute a warfarin dose model on the distributed dataset without disclosing the patient health-care records. Without deployment of CURIE, institutions compute warfarin dosage of a patient using a model computed on their local patient data. CURIE first enables institutions to negotiate their data exchange requirements through CPL. In this, CURIE allows members to construct various consortia wherein each member defines a data exchange policy for other members. The next step is to compute a privacy-preserving dose model such that each party does not learn any information about the patient's records of other medical institutions and respects the policy negotiated. CURIE implements a secure dose protocol through homomorphic encryption (HE) to enforce the policy agreements of the members. We next present the deployment of CURIE to institutions (Section 5.1) and integration of policy agreements in warfarin dose model (Section 5.2).

5.1 Deployment Setup

Warfarin- known as the brand name Coumadin is a widely prescribed (over 20 million times each year in the United States) anticoagulant medication. It is mainly used to treat (or prevent) blood clots (thrombosis) in veins or arteries. Taking high-dose warfarin causes thin blood which may result in intracranial and extracranial bleeding. Taking low doses causes thick blood which may result in embolism and stroke. Current clinical practices suggest a *fixed* initial dose of 5 or 10 mg/day. Patients regularly have a blood test to check how long it takes for blood to clot (international normalized ratio (INR)). Based on the INR, subsequent doses are adjusted to maintain the patient's INR at the desired level. Therefore, it is important to predict the proper warfarin dose for the patients.

Consortium Members. 24 medical institutions from nine countries and four continents individually collected the largest patient data for predicting *personalized* warfarin dose (see Appendix D for details of members involved in the study). Members collect 68

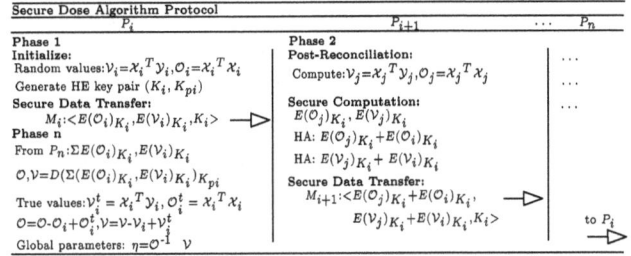

Figure 4: Secure dose algorithm protocol: Member (P_i) starts the protocol, the procedures and message flow among members are highlighted in boldface. At the final phase, P_i is able to compute the dose model coefficients from the negotiated data.

inputs from patients' genotypic, demographic, background information, yet a long study concluded that eight inputs are sufficient for proper prescriptions [26].

Warfarin Dose Prediction Model. To determine the proper personalized warfarin dosage, a long line of work concluded with an algorithm of an ordinary linear regression model [26]. The model is a function $f : X \rightarrow Y$ that aim at predicting targets of warfarin dose $y \in Y$ given a set of patient inputs $x \in X$. We represent the patient dataset of each member $\mathcal{D}_i = \{(x_i, y_i)\}_{i=1}^{n}$, and a loss function $\ell : Y \times Y \rightarrow [0, \infty)$. The loss function penalizes deviations between true dose and predictions. Learning is then searching for a dose model f minimizing the average loss:

$$\mathcal{L}(\mathcal{D}, f) = \frac{1}{n} \sum_{i=1}^{n} \ell(f(x_i), y_i). \tag{1}$$

The dose model reduces to minimizing the average loss $\mathcal{L}(\mathcal{D}, f)$ with respect to the parameters of the model f. The model is linear, i.e., $f(x) = \alpha^\top x + \beta$, and the loss function is the squared loss $\ell(f(x), y) = (f(x) - y)^2$. The dose model gives as well or better results than other more complex numerical methods and outperforms fixed-dose approach[2] [26]. We re-implemented the algorithm in Python by direct translation from the authors' implementation and found that the accuracy of our implementation has no statistically significant difference.

Consortia and Member Policies. We define consortia among medical institutions that they state partnerships for data exchange. Table 3 summarizes the consortia. The consortia are defined based on statute and regulations between members, as well as regional, and national partnerships are studied based on their countries [3, 17, 23, 34]. For example, NATO allied medical support doctrine allows strategic relationships that are otherwise not obtainable by non-NATO members. Each member in a consortium exchanges data with

---

[2]The model has been released online http://www.warfarindosing.org to help doctors and other clinicians for predicting ideal dose of warfarin.

other members based on its CPL policy. Various acquisition and share policies of CPL are studied via conditionals and selections in Section 6. We note that policy construction is a subjective enterprise. Depending on the nature and constraints of a given environment, any number of policies are appropriate. Such is the promise of policy defined behavior; alternate interpretations leading to other application requirements can be addressed through CPL.

5.2 Privacy-preserving Dose Prediction Model

The computation of *local dose* model of a medical institution is straightforward: a member calculates the dose model through Equation 2 with the use of patient data collected locally. To implement a privacy-preserving dose model among consortia members of medical institutions, we define the dose prediction formula stated in Equation 1 in a matrix form by minimizing with maximum likelihood estimation:

$$\beta = (X^{\mathsf{T}} X)^{-1} X^{\mathsf{T}} \mathcal{Y}, \qquad (2)$$

where X is the input matrix, $\mathcal{Y}$ is the dose matrix, and β is the coefficients of the dose model.

CURIE allows members to collaboratively learn a dose model without disclosing their patient records and guarantees data sharing complies with the policy as negotiated. As shown in Equation 3, each member translates its negotiated data into neutral input matrices [41]. Particularly, patient samples to be exchanged by each member are computed as an input matrix $X_0, \ldots, X_n$ and dose matrix $\mathcal{Y}_0, \ldots, \mathcal{Y}_n$. The transformation defines each member's *local statistics* $O_i = X^{\mathsf{T}} X$ and $\mathcal{V}_i = X^{\mathsf{T}} \mathcal{Y}$. Local statistics is the output of the negotiation of each member in a consortium. The aggregation of the local statistics corresponds to a *negotiated dataset* which is the exact amount that a member negotiates to obtain from other members in a consortium. CURIE constructs the dose algorithm of the negotiated dataset as a concatenation of members' local statistics as follows:

$$X^{\mathsf{T}} X = \left[X_1^{\mathsf{T}} | \ldots | X_n^{\mathsf{T}} \right] \left[X_1 | \ldots | X_n \right]^{\mathsf{T}} = \sum_{i=1}^{n} X_i^{\mathsf{T}} X_i = \sum_{i=1}^{n} \mathcal{V}_i = \mathcal{V}$$

$$X^{\mathsf{T}} \mathcal{Y} = \left[X_1^{\mathsf{T}} | \ldots | X_n^{\mathsf{T}} \right] \left[\mathcal{Y}_1 | \ldots | X_n \right]^{\mathsf{T}} = \sum_{i=1}^{n} X_i^{\mathsf{T}} \mathcal{Y}_i = \sum_{i=1}^{n} O_i = O \quad (3)$$

In Equation 3, a member computes model coefficients using the sum of other members local statistics. The local statistics includes $m \times m$ constant matrices where m is the number inputs (independent of number of dataset size). Using this observation, a party computes the coefficients of the negotiated dataset:

$$\eta^{(negotiated)} = (X^{\mathsf{T}} X)^{-1} X^{\mathsf{T}} \mathcal{Y} = O^{-1} \mathcal{V} \qquad (4)$$

In Equation 4, while the accuracy objective of the dose model is guaranteed using the coefficients obtained from the sum of local statistics, the exchange of clear statistics among parties may leak information about members' data. A member can infer knowledge about the distribution of each input of other members from matrices of O_i and $\mathcal{V}_i$ [14]. Furthermore, an adversary may sniff data traffic to control and modify exchanged messages. To solve these problems, we use homomorphic encryption (HE) that allows computation on ciphertexts [2]. HE allows members to perform the computation of joint of function without requiring additional communication complexity other than the data exchange. We note that HE itself

cannot preserve the confidentiality of data from multiple parties in centralized settings [40]. However, CURIE implements a distributed privacy-preserving multi-party dose model, as shown in Figure 4.

To illustrate, we consider an example session of n members authorized for data exchange in a consortium. In this example, a ring topology is used for secure group communication (i.e., P_i talks to P_{i+1}, and similarly P_n talks to P_i). P_1 initially generates a pair of encryption keys using the homomorphic cryptosystem and broadcasts the public key to the members in its member list. P_1 then generates random $\mathcal{V}_i, O_i$ and encrypts them $E(O_i)_{K_i}$ and $E(\mathcal{V}_i)_{K_i}$ using its public key K_i. It starts the session by sending them to the next member in the ring. When next member receives the encrypted message, it adds its local $\mathcal{V}_i$ and O_i matrices through homomorphic addition to the output of its policy reconciliation for P_1 and passes to the next member. Remaining members take the similar steps. Secure computation executes one round per member in which the computation for the particular member visits other members. This allows CURIE to enforce HE on shared data of a particular member in each round uses and does not suffer insecurities associated with centralized HE constructions [40].

At the final stage of the protocol, P_1 receives the sum statistics of O_i and $\mathcal{V}_i$ from P_n. P_1 decrypts the sum of the statistics using its private key and then subtracts the initial random values of $\mathcal{V}_i$, O_i and adds its true values used for computation of the local dose model coefficients. The final result O and $\mathcal{V}$ is the coefficients of the dose model that respects P_1's policy negotiations. Other consortium members similarly start the protocol and compute the coefficients. We present the security analysis of the dose protocol in Appendix C, and show its differentially-private extension in Appendix B.

6 EVALUATION

This section details the operation of the CURIE through policies. We show how flexible data exchange policies are implemented and operated. We focus on the following questions:

(1) What are the performance trade-offs in configuring CPL?
(2) Can members reliably use CURIE to integrate various policies?
(3) Do members improve the accuracy of dose predictions with the use of CPL?

The answers to the first two questions are addressed in Section 6.1, and the last question is answered in Section 6.2. As detailed throughout, CURIE allows 50 members to compute the privacy-preserving model using 5K data samples with 40 inputs in less than a minute. We also show how an algorithm with flexible data exchange policies can improve–often substantially–the accuracy of the warfarin dose model accuracy.

Experimental Setup. The experiments were performed on a cluster of machines with 32 GB of maximum memory and 16-core Intel Xeon CPU at 1.90 GHz, where we use one core to get a lower bound estimate. Each member is simulated in a server that stores its data. Secure computation protocols of CURIE are implemented using the open-source HElib library [4]. We set the security parameter of HElib as 128 bits. Multiplication level is optimized per member to increase the number of allowed homomorphic operations without decryption failure and to reduce the computation time.

We validate the accuracy of dose model in various consortia defined in Table 3 with members defining different data exchange policies. The dataset used in our experiments contains 5700 patient records from 21 members. Dose model accuracy of each member

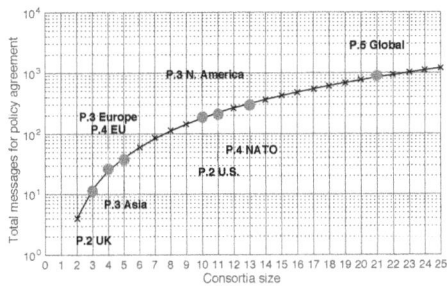

Figure 5: CPL negotiation cost - Costs associated with a number of varying members in a consortium. Each member defines asymmetric share and acquisition policy for other members. The number of members in warfarin consortia is marked with red circles.

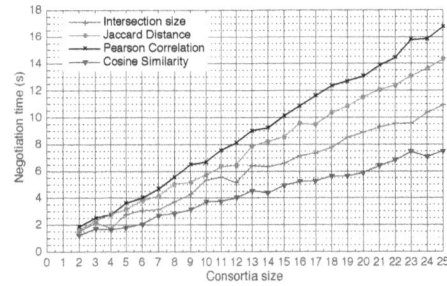

Figure 6: CPL selections and data-dependent conditional costs - Costs associated with varying members and algorithms. All consortia members agree on policy including a different data-dependent conditional and selections over one input of having 200 samples.

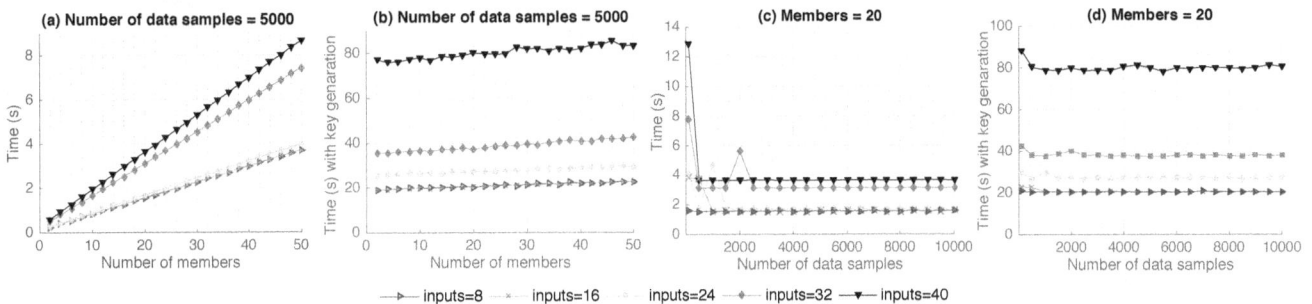

Figure 7: CPL performance on privacy-preserving and differential private protocol - All members define an asymmetric share and acquisition policy through selections and conditionals. The agreements of CPL policies between consortia members are studied with the different number of consortia members, data samples, and input size. (Std. dev. of ten runs is ± 3.6 and ± 0.3 sec. with and without homomorphic key generation.)

is validated with Mean Absolute Percentage Error (MAPE). MAPE measures the percentage of how far predicted dosages are away from true dosage. Lower values indicate better quality of treatment.

6.1   Performance Evaluation

We present the costs associated with various CURIE mechanisms. We illustrate the cost of the CPL in policy negotiations, in the use of data-dependent conditionals, and in the dose algorithm.

6.1.1   CPL Benchmarks. Our first set of experiments characterize the policy construction and negotiation costs. Various consortia and policies are instrumented to analyze the overhead of the number of messages and time required to compute the CPL selections and data-dependent conditionals. All the costs not specific to the policies are excluded in measurements (e.g., network latency). The benchmark results are summarized in Figure 5 and 6 and discussed below.

Figure 5 shows the number of messages for policy construction required for different consortia size. The number of members in warfarin study is also labeled. For instance, NATO consortium has 13 members; ten members from U.S. and three from UK. The experiments illustrate the upper bound results wherein each member defines a different share and acquisition policy for other members (i.e., asymmetric relations). In this, each member sends acquisition policy request to consortium members. After a member gets the acquisition request, it reconciles with its share policy and output of negotiation message is returned. The number of messages associated with varying number of selections and conditionals dictated

by the members does not require any additional messages. For instance, the acquisition request of a member includes arguments when conditionals are defined (e.g., reference data and a threshold value for data-dependent conditionals such as pairwise Jaccard distance), and the result is returned with the negotiation output message. However, the use of the selections and data-dependent conditionals brings additional processing cost as detailed next.

Figure 6 shows the costs associated with the use of CPL selection and data-dependent conditionals. All the members dictate data-dependent conditionals and selections on a single input. The members input size for the data-dependent conditional computations is set to 200 real values. This is the average number of inputs found in members' dataset. Since selections and conditionals reconcile contradictions between acquisition and share policies, they do not require any additional computation overhead and yield a processing time of milliseconds. However, the time associated with varying data-dependent conditionals depend on the protocol of associated secure pairwise algorithm. In our experiments, cosine similarity and intersection size exhibited shorter computation time than Pearson correlation and Jaccard distance. Overall, we found that 25 members compute the metrics less than 18 seconds. Note that the results serve as an upper bound that all members define a set of selections and a data-dependent conditional on one input.

6.1.2   Dose Model Benchmarks. Our second series of experiments characterize the impact of CPL on the average time of computing privacy-preserving dose model with varying number of members and dataset sizes. Though the warfarin study includes eight inputs,

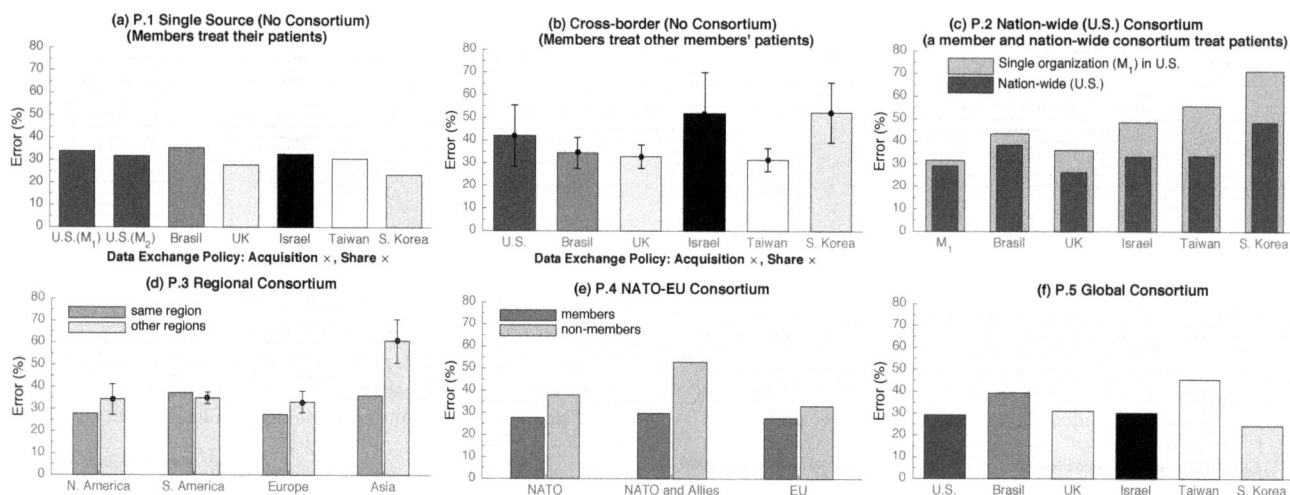

Figure 8: The implication of policies on model accuracy - errors are validated in various consortia through data exchange policies. Figure 6(c-f): The local acquisition policies of members comply with the sharing policy within a consortium (i.e., members acquire complete data of the consortia members. Std. devs. of errors are within %5, if not illustrated).

evaluations are repeated with the input size of 8, 16, 24, 32, and 40 through various dataset sample sizes for completeness. The input and sample size together represents the total dataset shared for a member as a result of the policy agreements. Our experiments show that 80% of computation overhead is attributed to HE key generation. The cost of the differential privacy takes microseconds, as the members can calculate the (optional) differential private algorithm model at the end of the secure dose protocol. Computations are instrumented to classify the overheads incurred by key generation, encryption, decryption, and evaluation. We next present the costs with and without key generation to study the impact of the number of members and data size.

Figure 7 (a-b) presents the computation cost with varying number of members. Each member's dataset includes 5000 data samples which acquired as a result of the policy negotiations. Figure 7 (a) presents the cost of the total computation time excluding HE key generation. There is a linear increase in time with the growing number of members. This is the fundamental cost of encryption and evaluation operations dominated by matrix encryption and addition. To profile the generation of key cost, in Figure 7 (b), we conducted similar experiments. Each input size cost increases because of the key generation overhead. The increase is quadratic as a number of slots (plaintext elements) are set to square of input size not to lose any data during input conversion. It is important to note that the cost is independent of the member size because a member generates the key only once in a computation of a consortium. We note that the time overhead of key generation is not a limiting factor as members may generate keys before a consortium is established.

In Figure 7 (c-d), we show the costs associated with different data samples. The number of members in a consortium is set to 20. Similar to the previous experiments, the key generation dominates the computation costs. Our experiments also reported no relationship between the cost and number of samples. That is, even though the size of the data samples increases, the overhead is amortized over the operations on the local statistics of the computations (which is the square matrix of the input size in the warfarin dataset); thus

the time of computing dose algorithm converges to the number of dataset inputs. This explains the similar trends observed in plots.

6.2 Effectiveness of Policies

We validate the performance of privacy-preserving dose model quantitatively and qualitatively. For the warfarin study, these are translated to the following questions: How do policies impact the accuracy of members' warfarin dose prediction? (Section 6.2.1), and Does policies help to prevent the adverse impacts of dose errors on patient health? (Section 6.2.2).

6.2.1 Implications of CPL on Model Accuracy. In our first set of experiments, we validate how well a member prescribe warfarin dose for its local patients and patient's of the consortium members without using CPL. These results are used as a baseline for comparison of varying consortia and data exchange policies throughout. Figure 8 (a) sought to identify the local algorithm errors (**P.1**). The errors significantly differ between countries and for the members of the same country (depicted as M_1 and M_2 in the U.S.). The low results are due to having homogeneous data; all the inputs in these countries have similar traits. For instance, similar age and ethnicity found in a dataset produce over-fitted computation results for its local patients. These findings are validated with use of local algorithms for treatment of other countries' patients. As illustrated in Figure 8 (b), the dose errors yield significantly high for particular countries' patients. The results indicate that improvements in dose predictions of local patients and members' patients lay in the creation of data exchange policies to increase the patient diversity.

The next experiments measure the impact of CPL in nation-wide (**P.2**), regional (**P.3**), NATO-EU (**P.4**) and global (**P.5**) consortia. Each member creates a local acquisition policy to acquire the complete data of consortia members (i.e., the acquisition policy of a consortium member complies with the share policy of the requested member). We make three major observations. First, varying partnerships yield different dose accuracy. For instance, members of nation-wide consortium get better dose accuracy than their local results. This result is validated through nationwide consortia

Member	Agreement of policy negotiations
U.S.	(Race="Asian")∨(EVALUATE(age))∨(height <160) ∨(weight <65)∨(CYP2C9 IN (2*/*2, 2*/*3)∨(Amiodarone="Y")∨(Enzyme="Y")
Brasil	(Race="Asian")∨(height <165)∨(CYP2C9 IN (2*/*2, 2*/*3)∨EVALUATE (Amiodarone)∨(Enzyme="Y")
UK	(Race≠"White")∨(age BETWEEN 20-29 AND >80)∨(height<165)∨(60<weight <100)∨EVALUATE(CYP2C9)∨(Amiodarone="Y"), (Enzyme="Y")
Israel	(Race≠ "White")∨(height <160cm)∨(weight <60)∨(CYP2C9=3*/*3)∨(Amiodarone="Y")∨(Enzyme Inducer ="Y")
Taiwan	(Race=All)∨(age BETWEEN 20-29)∨(height >170)∨(weight >65)∨(CYP2C9 IN (1*/*2, 2*/*2, 2*/*3, 3*/*3)∨(VK0RC1="G/G")∨(Amiodarone="Y")∨(Enzyme="Y")
S. Korea	(Race=All)∨ (age BETWEEN 20-29)∨(height >165)∨(weight >60)∨(CYP2C9 IN (1*/*2, 2*/*2, 2*/*3, 3*/*3)∨(VK0RC1="G/G")∨(Amiodarone="Y")∨(Enzyme="Y")

Table 4: An exploration of CPL policies in the global consortium (illustrated as a plain language): Each member defines asymmetric local policy based on its data diversity. The agreement of share and acquisition policies are depicted as a policy clause in a single row. The agreement result of each member for other members is not presented for brevity.

and a single member (M_1) in United States (see Figure 8 (c)). Second, supporting previous findings, all regional (excluding Asia) and NATO-EU policies decrease the error for both treatment of their patients and the other countries' patients (see Figure 8 (d-e)). However, Asia consortium results in unexpected dose errors for the treatment of other regions' patients. This is because nation-wide, regional, and NATO-EU policies include patient population having different characteristics; thus the data obtained through policy negotiations better generalize to the dosages. In contrast, Asia collaboration lacks large enough White and Black groups. Third, the global consortium results in higher dose errors when evaluated for particular countries such as Brazil and Taiwan (see Figure 8 (f)). To conclude, while CPL is effective in reducing dose error of a member, the results highlight the need for the systematic use of CPL through selections and conditionals to obtain better results.

In these experiments, each member dictates a different acquisition policy based on its racial groups. Members aim at having an ideal patient population uniformity. To do so, each member defines a local acquisition policy and negotiates it with other members. Each member sets its share policy to conditionals of being in the same consortium and data size greater than 200; thus, the policy of each member is asymmetric. Table 4 shows the simplified notation of the policy agreements in the global consortium. For instance, a member having a small number of white patients defines selections to solely acquire that group and a member having large enough patients for all genotypes sets data-dependent conditionals to obtain patient inputs that are not similar in its data samples (e.g., acquires different genotypes). Figure 9 presents a subset of results on dose errors per patient race. The errors of the other races yield similar for each member. The results without CPL conditionals and selections are plotted as a dashed line for comparison. We find that members can improve the dose accuracy with the use of policies. We note that the use of different data-dependent conditionals defined in evaluate does not result in statistically significant accuracy gain.

6.2.2 *Implications of CPL on Patient Health.* We examine the impact of the dose errors found in the previous section to better quantify the effectiveness of policies on patient health.

To identify the adverse effects of warfarin, we use a clinical study to evaluate the clinical relevance of prediction errors [9] and a medical guide to identify the consequences of over- and under-prescriptions [16]. We define errors that are inside and outside of the warfarin safety window, and the under- or over prescriptions. We consider weekly errors for each patient because using weekly values eliminates the errors posed by the initial (daily) dose. The weekly dose is in the safety window if an estimated dose falls within 20% of its corresponding clinically-deduced value [26, 27].

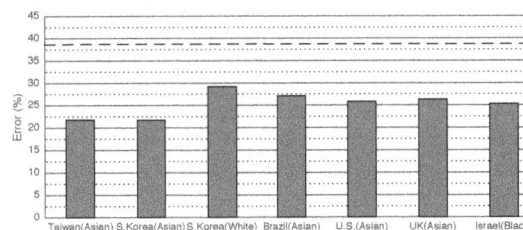

Figure 9: Dose accuracy of members using CPL policies defined in Table 4. Members construct a model per race after they reconcile the policies. The dashed line is the average error found without the use of conditionals and selections in policies.

Consortium	U	SW	O	Selections	Conditionals
Single Source	37.7%	43.4%	18.8%	✗	✗
Nation-wide	18.9%	52.3%	28.8%	✓	✓
NATO	19.3%	51.5%	29.2%	✓	✓
Regional	19%	51.3%	29.7%	✓	✓
Global	21.2%	46.8%	32%	✓	✓

Table 5: Impact of policies on health-related risks: Results are from a global consortium patients using policy agreement of a member located in the U.S. The member uses the policy defined in Table 4. (U: Under-prescription, SW: Safety Window, O: Over-prescription)

The deviations falling outside of the safety window is an under- or over prescriptions, and cause health-related risks.

Table 5 presents the percentage of patients falls in safety window, over- and -under prescriptions with varying policies of a member. We find that use of CPL increases the number of patients in the safety window. For instance, a member has 43.4% patient with using its local data (single source model), and the member increases the percentage of patients in a safety window with varying consortia and policies, for instance, it is 52.4% in the nation-wide consortium. We conclude that CPL might be useful in preventing errors that introduce health-related risks.

7 LIMITATIONS AND DISCUSSION

One requirement for correctly interpreting the CPL policies is a shared schema for solving the compatibility issues among members. For instance, members may interpret the data columns (e.g., column names and types) differently or may not have the information about consortium members (e.g., membership status of an alliance). CPL implements a shared schema describing column names, their types, and explanations of data fields as well as consortium-specific information. Members can negotiate the schema similar to the policy negotiations and revise the schema based on the schema of a negotiation initiator.

CPL provides a set of data-dependent statistical functions (e.g., cosine similarity) to compute pairwise statistics among member's local data. However, there might be a need for other functions that help members decide their data exchange policies. For example, data exchange among finance companies may require calculating the similarity between data distributions. Future work will investigate the integration of different data-dependent statistics into CPL.

Lastly, we did not focus much on the reasons of policy impacts on the prediction success of the dose algorithm and its adverse outcomes on patient health over time. While our evaluation results showed that members could express both complex relations and constraints on the data exchange through CPL policies, members require establishing true partnerships to improve the prediction model accuracy. While this explanation matches both our intuition and the experimental results, a further domain-specific formal analysis is needed. We plan to pursue this in future work.

8 RELATED WORK

Policy has been used in several contexts as a vehicle for representing configuration of secure groups [30], network management [35], threat mitigation [18], access control [13], and data retrieval systems [15]. These approaches define a schema for their target problem and do not consider the challenges in secure data exchange. In contrast, Curie defines a formal policy language to dictate the data exchange requirements of members and enforces the agreement in collaborative ML settings.

On the other hand, secure computation on sensitive proprietary data has recently attracted attention. Federated learning [20, 37], anonymization [14], multi-site statistical models [10], secure multiparty computation [28], and secure and differentially-private multiparty computation [1] have started to shed light on this issue. Such techniques have been used both for training and classification phases in deep learning [36], clustering [22], and decision trees [8]. To allow programmers to develop such applications, secure computation programming frameworks and languages are designed for general purposes [7, 14, 24, 32, 33]. However, these approaches do not consider complex relationships among members and assume members share their all data or nothing. We view our efforts in this paper to be complementary to much of these works. CPL can be integrated into these frameworks to establish partnerships and manage data exchange policies before a computation starts.

9 CONCLUSIONS

We presented Curie which provides a novel policy language called CPL to define the specifications of data exchange requirements securely for use in collaborative learning settings. Members can assert who and what to exchange separately for data sharing and data acquisition policies. This allows members to efficiently dictate their policies in complex and asymmetric relationships through selections, conditionals, and pairwise data-dependent statistics. We validated Curie in an example real-world healthcare application through varying policies of consortia members. A secure multiparty and (optional) differentially-private model is implemented to illustrate the policy/performance trade-offs. Curie allowed 50 different members to efficiently compute a privacy-preserving model

using 5K data samples with 40 inputs in less than a minute. We also showed how an algorithm with effective use of data exchange policies could improve the accuracy of the dose prediction model.

Future work will investigate the use of Curie in other collaborative learning settings exploring different statistics for data-dependent conditionals and explore its performance trade-offs by integrating it into other off-the-shelf secure computation frameworks.

ACKNOWLEDGMENT

Research was sponsored by the Army Research Laboratory and was accomplished under Cooperative Agreement Number W911NF-13-2-0045 (ARL Cyber Security CRA). This work is also partially supported by US National Science Foundation (NSF) under the grant numbers NSF-CNS-1718116 and NSF-CAREER-CNS-1453647. The statements made herein are solely the responsibility of the authors. The views and conclusions contained in this document are those of the authors and should not be interpreted as representing the official policies, either expressed or implied, of the Army Research Laboratory or the U.S. Government. The U.S. Government is authorized to reproduce and distribute reprints for Government purposes notwithstanding any copyright notation here on.

REFERENCES

[1] Abbas Acar et al. 2017. Achieving Secure and Differentially Private Computations in Multiparty Settings. In *IEEE Privacy-Aware Computing (PAC)*.

[2] Abbas Acar, Hidayet Aksu, A. Selcuk Uluagac, and Mauro Conti. 2017. A Survey on Homomorphic Encryption Schemes: Theory and Implementation. *CoRR* abs/1704.03578 (2017). arXiv:1704.03578 http://arxiv.org/abs/1704.03578

[3] American Recovery and Reinvestment Act of 2009. 2017. https://en.wikipedia.org/wiki/American_Recovery_and_Reinvestment_Act_of_2009. [Online; accessed 01-June-2018].

[4] An Implementation of Homomorphic Encryption. 2017. https://github.com/shaih/HElib. [Online; accessed 01-January-2017].

[5] Rohan Anil, Gabriel Pereyra, Alexandre Passos, Robert Ormandi, George E Dahl, and Geoffrey E Hinton. 2018. Large scale distributed neural network training through online distillation. *arXiv preprint arXiv:1804.03235* (2018).

[6] Carlo Blundo et al. 2013. EsPRESSo: Efficient Privacy-preserving Evaluation of Sample Set Similarity. In *Data Privacy Management Security*.

[7] Dan Bogdanov et al. 2016. Rmind: a Tool for Cryptographically Secure Statistical Analysis. *IEEE Transactions on Dependable and Secure Computing* (2016).

[8] Raphael Bost, Raluca Ada Popa, Stephen Tu, and Shafi Goldwasser. 2015. Machine Learning Classification over Encrypted Data. In *NDSS*.

[9] Z. Berkay Celik, David Lopez-Paz, and Patrick McDaniel. 2016. Patient-Driven Privacy Control through Generalized Distillation. *IEEE Symposium on Privacy-Aware Computing* (2016).

[10] Fida K Dankar. 2015. Privacy Preserving Linear Regression on Distributed Databases. *Transactions on Data Privacy* (2015).

[11] Emiliano De Cristofaro, Paolo Gasti, and Gene Tsudik. 2012. Fast and Private Computation of Cardinality of Set Intersection and Union. In *Cryptology and Network Security*.

[12] Jeffrey Dean, Greg Corrado, Rajat Monga, Kai Chen, Matthieu Devin, Mark Mao, Andrew Senior, Paul Tucker, Ke Yang, Quoc V Le, et al. 2012. Large scale distributed deep networks. In *NIPS*.

[13] Li Duan, Yang Zhang, Chen, et al. 2016. Automated Policy Combination for Secure Data Sharing in Cross-Organizational Collaborations. *IEEE Access* (2016).

[14] Khaled El Emam et al. 2013. A Secure Dist. Logistic Regression Protocol for the Detection of Rare Adverse Drug Events. *American Medical Informatics* (2013).

[15] Eslam Elnikety et al. 2016. Thoth: Comprehensive Policy Compliance in Data Retrieval Systems. In *USENIX Security*.

[16] U.S. Food and Drug Administration. 2017. Medication guide, Caumadin (warfarin sodium). http://www.fda.gov. [Online; accessed 01-June-2018].

[17] NATO Standard Allied Joint Doctrine for Medical Support. 2017. http://www.nato.int. [Online; accessed 01-June-2018].

[18] Julien Freudiger, Emiliano De Cristofaro, and Alejandro E Brito. 2015. Controlled Data Sharing for Collaborative Predictive Blacklisting. In *DIMVA*.

[19] Roberto Garrido-Pelaz et al. 2016. Shall We Collaborate?: A model to Analyse the Benefits of Information Sharing. In *ACM Workshop on Information Sharing and Collaborative Security*.

[20] Robin C Geyer, Tassilo Klein, and Moin Nabi. 2017. Differentially Private Federated Learning: A Client Level Perspective. *arXiv preprint arXiv:1712.07557* (2017).

[21] Oded Goldreich. 2009. *Foundations of Cryptography: Basic Applications.* Cambridge university press.
[22] Thore Graepel, Kristin Lauter, and Michael Naehrig. 2012. ML Confidential: Machine Learning on Encrypted Data. In *Information Security and Cryptology.*
[23] Health Information Technology for Economic and Clinical Health Act. 2017. https://en.wikipedia.org. [Online; accessed 01-June-2018].
[24] Wilko Henecka et al. 2010. TASTY: Tool for Automating Secure Two-party Computations. In *ACM CCS.*
[25] Yan Huang et al. 2011. Faster Secure Two-Party Computation Using Garbled Circuits. In *USENIX Security Symposium.*
[26] International Warfarin Pharmacogenetics Consortium. 2009. Estimation of the Warfarin Dose with Clinical and Pharmacogenetic Data. *The New England Journal of Medicine* (2009).
[27] Stephen E Kimmel et al. 2013. A pharmacogenetic versus a Clinical Algorithm for Warfarin Dosing. *New England Journal of Medicine* (2013).
[28] Yehuda Lindell and Benny Pinkas. 2009. Secure Multiparty Computation for Privacypreserving Data Mining. *Journal of Privacy and Confidentiality* (2009).
[29] Chang Liu et al. 2015. Oblivm: A programming Framework for Secure Computation. In *Security and Privacy.*
[30] Patrick McDaniel and Atul Prakash. 2006. Methods and Limitations of Security Policy Reconciliation. *ACM TISSEC* (2006).
[31] Payman Mohassel and Yupeng Zhang. 2017. SecureML: A system for scalable privacy-preserving machine learning. In *Security and Privacy (SP).*
[32] Olga Ohrimenko et al. 2016. Oblivious Multi-Party Machine Learning on Trusted Processors. In *USENIX Security Symposium.*
[33] Aseem Rastogi et al. 2014. Wysteria: A programming language for generic, mixed-mode multiparty computations. In *IEEE Security and Privacy (SP).*
[34] European Commission Report. 2017. Overview of the National Laws on Electronic Health Records in the EU Member States. http://ec.europa.eu. [Online; accessed 01-June-2018].
[35] Ana C Riekstin et al. 2016. Orchestration of Energy efficiency Capabilities in Networks. *Journal of Network and Computer Applications* (2016).
[36] Reza Shokri et al. 2015. Privacy-preserving Deep Learning. In *ACM CCS.*
[37] Virginia Smith, Chao-Kai Chiang, Maziar Sanjabi, and Ameet S Talwalkar. 2017. Federated Multi-Task Learning. In *NIPS.*
[38] Daniel J Solove and Paul M Schwartz. 2015. *Information Privacy Law.* Aspen.
[39] Marten Van Dijk and Ari Juels. 2010. On the Impossibility of Cryptography Alone for Privacy-preserving Cloud Computing. *HotSec* (2010).
[40] Marten Van Dijk and Ari Juels. 2010. On the Impossibility of Cryptography Alone for Privacy-preserving Cloud Computing. In *USENIX Hot Topics in Security.*
[41] Fang-Jing Wu, Yu-Fen Kao, et al. 2011. From Wireless Sensor Networks Towards Cyber Physical Systems. *Pervasive and Mobile Computing* (2011).
[42] Xi Wu et al. 2015. Revisiting Differentially Private Regression: Lessons from Learning Theory and their Consequences. *arXiv:1512.06388* (2015).
[43] Jun Zhang et al. 2012. Functional Mechanism: Regression Analysis under Differential Privacy. *VLDB* (2012).

A CURIE POLICY LANGUAGE

This section presents the Backus Naur Form of Curie data exchange policy language.

⟨curie_policy⟩	::=	⟨statements⟩
⟨statements⟩	::=	⟨statement⟩ ';' [⟨statements⟩]
⟨statement⟩	::=	⟨share_clause⟩
	|	⟨acquire_clause⟩
	|	⟨attribute⟩
	|	⟨sub_clause⟩

; share clauses defined as follows:

⟨share_clause⟩	::=	'share' ':' [⟨members⟩] ':' [⟨conditionals⟩] ': :' ⟨selections⟩

; acquisition clauses defined as follows:

⟨acquire_clause⟩	::=	'acquire' ':' [⟨members⟩] ':' [⟨conditionals⟩] ': :' ⟨selections⟩

; attributes are defined as follows:

⟨attribute⟩	::=	⟨identifier⟩ ':=' '<' ⟨value⟩ '>'
	|	⟨identifier⟩ ':=' '<' ⟨value_list⟩ '>'

; user defined sub-clauses defined as follows:

⟨sub_clause⟩	::=	⟨tag⟩ ':' [⟨conditionals⟩] ': :' ⟨selections⟩

; conditionals including data-dependent functions defined as follows:

⟨conditionals⟩	::=	⟨var⟩'='⟨value⟩ [',' ⟨conditionals⟩]
	|	'evaluate' '(' ⟨data_ref⟩ ',' ⟨alg_arg⟩ ',' ⟨threshold_arg⟩ ')' [',' ⟨conditionals⟩] | ''
⟨selections⟩	::=	⟨filters⟩
	|	⟨tag⟩

⟨filters⟩	::=	⟨filter⟩ [',' ⟨filters⟩]
⟨filter⟩	::=	⟨var⟩ ⟨operation⟩ ⟨value⟩ | ''
⟨data_ref⟩	::=	'&' ⟨identifier⟩
⟨alg_arg⟩	::=	⟨algorithms⟩
⟨algorithms⟩	::=	'Intersection size'
	|	'Jaccard index'
	|	'Pearson correlation'
	|	'Cosine similarity'
⟨threshold_arg⟩	::=	⟨floating_point_number⟩
⟨operation⟩	::=	'=' | '<' | '>' | '!=' | in |
⟨value_list⟩	::=	'{' ⟨value⟩ '}' [',' ⟨value_list⟩]
⟨members⟩	::=	⟨member⟩ [',' ⟨members⟩]
⟨member⟩	::=	⟨identifier⟩ | ''

; for completeness, trivial items defined as follows:

⟨identifier⟩	::=	⟨word⟩
⟨var⟩	::=	'$' ⟨identifier⟩
⟨value⟩	::=	⟨string⟩
⟨tag⟩	::=	⟨word⟩
⟨string⟩	::=	'"' ⟨stringchars⟩ '"'
⟨stringchars⟩	::=	⟨stringletter⟩ [⟨stringchars⟩]
⟨stringletter⟩	::=	0x10 | 0x13|0x20| ... | 0x7F
⟨word⟩	::=	⟨char⟩ [⟨word⟩]
⟨char⟩	::=	⟨letter⟩ | ⟨digit⟩
⟨letter⟩	::=	'A' | 'B' | ... | 'Z' | 'a' | 'b' | ... | 'z' | 0x80 | 0x81 | ... | 0xFF
⟨digit⟩	::=	'0' | '1' | ... | '9'
⟨floating_point_number⟩	::=	⟨decimal_number⟩ '.' [⟨decimal_number⟩]
⟨decimal_number⟩	::=	⟨digit⟩ [⟨decimal_number⟩]

B DIFFERENTIALLY-PRIVATE DOSE ALGORITHM

We presented how members compute a privacy-preserving dose model on negotiated data through their policies. In this section, we consider individual privacy that allows a member to guarantee no information leakage on the targeted individual (i.e., patient) involved in the computation. Specifically, while members compute a secure dose model using the data obtained as a result of their policy negotiations, they also ensure that an adversary cannot infer whether any particular individual is included in computations to build the dose algorithm. In warfarin study, this corresponds to a differentially-private secure dose algorithm on shared data.

To implement a differentially-private secure algorithm, we use a functional mechanism technique [42, 43]. The technique accepts a dataset ($\mathcal{D}$), an objective function ($f_\mathcal{D}(\eta)$), and a privacy budget (ϵ) as an input and returns ϵ-differentially-private coefficients $\widetilde{\eta}$ of an algorithm. The intuition behind the functional mechanism is perturbing the objective function of the optimization problem. Perturbation includes both sensitivity analysis and Laplacian noise insertion as opposed to perturbing the results via differentially-private synthetic data generation.

To inter-operate the functional mechanism with the secure dose protocol, members convert each column from [min, max] to [-1,1] before negotiation starts. This processing ensures that sufficient noise is added to the objective function on negotiated data. Then, members proceed with the protocol. At the final stage of the secure algorithm protocol, a member gets clear statistics of $O = X^\mathsf{T}X$ and $\mathcal{V} = X^\mathsf{T}\mathcal{Y}$ and input dimension d that is the size of O or $\mathcal{V}$. These statistics are the exact quantities that are minimized in the objective of the functional mechanism [43]. Using these statistics, a member

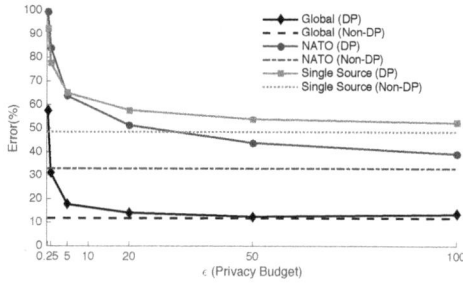

Figure 1: Non-private secure algorithm (Non-DP) vs. differentially-private secure algorithm (DP) performance of a member in U.S. measured against various policies depicted in Figure 8.

may (optionally) compute ϵ-differential private secure algorithm without any additional data exchange and computational overhead.

Differential Privacy Results. To protect individual privacy in secure dose algorithm, members may compute the differentially-private secure algorithm on their negotiated data. This section presents the results of using the differential-private secure algorithm (DP) instead of using secure dose algorithm (Non-DP). To establish a baseline performance, we constructed non-private secure algorithms of a member. We then build the differential-private secure algorithm for different privacy budgets ($\epsilon = 0.25, 1, 5, 20, 50$ and 100). Finally, we compare the results of two algorithms through different policies of a member. Figure 1 shows the results of a member in the U.S. that applies both algorithms to predict the dosage. The algorithms are constructed for the single source, NATO, and global consortia. In this, the member dictates acquisition policy for complete data and other members complies with their share policy. The average error over 100 distinct model for each budget value is reported. The use of DP degrades the accuracy as the ϵ value increases. For instance, the accuracy improvement obtained through NATO policy over single source degrades with the privacy budget less than or equal to 20. We note that other consortia and policies with use of selections and conditionals show similar effect on the dose accuracy.

C ANALYSIS OF THE DOSE ALGORITHM

We present security and privacy guarantees of the dose algorithm provided to all members through the share of encrypted integrated statistics, ($O_i = X^\mathsf{T}X$ and $\mathcal{V}_i = X^\mathsf{T}\mathcal{Y}$ matrices). Since all data exchange among parties is encrypted through the use of HE, the security of the algorithm against any adversary outside the authorized parties is based on the underlying HE cryptosystem.

An adversary not involving session initiator. Assume for now that a session initiator does not collude with other parties. Loosely speaking, since all computations are performed on the encrypted data, none of the parties learn anything about other parties' input.

We consider a party P_{i+1} in Figure 4. The party P_{i+1} has the public key generated by the session initiator K_i, the encryption of local statistics of previous parties $M_i = (E(O_i)_K, E(\mathcal{V}_i)_K)$. Its input is $(\mathcal{V}_{i+1}, O_{i+1})$ and its output is $M_{i+1} = (E(O_i + O_{i+1}), E(\mathcal{V}_i + \mathcal{V}_{i+1}))$. A simulator S selects random values for its own inputs $(\mathcal{V}'_{i+1}, O'_{i+1})$ and encrypts them using the public key published by the session initiator. Then, the simulator S performs the homomorphic operation on the received message M_i and outputs $M'_{i+1} = (E(O_i + O'_{i+1})_K, E(\mathcal{V}_i + \mathcal{V}'_{i+1})_K)$. Here, we assume the underlying HE is

semantically secure. Therefore, the output of the simulator M'_{i+1} is computationally indistinguishable from output of the real execution of the protocol M_{i+1} for every input pairs. Therefore, using the definition in [21] the protocol privately computes the function in the presence of one semi-honest corrupted party. The extension to multi-corrupted semi-honest adversaries is straightforward as the only difference is the view of a subset of parties having many encrypted messages. Since the semantic security of the underlying HE is hold for any pair of these many encrypted messages, no information leaks about the corresponding plaintexts.

Adversary involving session initiator. We consider the case when the session initiator is corrupted. The corrupted parties including session initiator can infer the input of an honest party if the predecessor (previous party) and successor (next party) of an honest party are both corrupted. We consider the possible cases for data leakage: (1) *2-party:* The session initiator is corrupted, and another party is honest. In this case, predecessor and successor of the honest party are both the corrupted session initiator. Therefore, the input of honest party is learned by the corrupted party, (2) *3-party:* A corrupted session initiator is either predecessor or successor; thus it can learn inputs of the one of the honest party only if another party is corrupted, and (3) *n-party (n > 3):* To learn an honest party's input, at least two parties must be corrupted and placed in previous and next of the honest party.

While the individual raw data of members does not leak, the risk of inappropriate disclosures from local summary statistics exists in some extreme cases [14]. Consider the exchange of plain matrix $V_i = X^\mathsf{T}Y$ among two parties; a party may use the extreme values found in V_i to identify particular patients. For instance, in dose algorithm, taking inducers such as Rifadin and Dilantin could indicate high dose prescriptions. If the values of V_i are high, then a party may infer a patient that takes enzyme inducers and the presence of high dosage warfarin intake. Similarly, exchange of $O_i = X^\mathsf{T}X$ may leak information about the number of observations and represent the number of 0s or 1s in a column. For instance, for the former first entry in the matrix, $X^\mathsf{T}X$, gives the total number of patients. For the latter, $(X^\mathsf{T}X)_{j,j}$ gives the number of 1s in the column. This type information lets a party infer knowledge, particularly when binary inputs (e.g., use of the medicine) are used.

D CURIE DEPLOYMENT DETAILS

We use a dataset collected by the International Warfarin Pharmacogenetics Consortium (IWPC), to date the most comprehensive database containing patient data collected from 24 medical institutions from 9 countries [26]. The dataset does not include the name of the medical institutions, yet there is a separate ethnicity dataset provided for identifying the genomic impacts of the algorithm. We use the race (reported by patients) and race categories (defined by the Office of Management and Budget) to predict the country of a patient[3]. For instance, we consider a medical institution with a high number of Japanese race is located in Japan. We use subsets of patient records that have no missing inputs for accurate evaluation. We split the dataset into two cohorts: training cohort is used to learn the algorithm, and validation cohort is used to assign dose to the new patients based on the consortia and data exchange policies.

---

[3]The authors indicated via personal communication that they cannot provide the exact name of the institutions due to the privacy concerns.

Result-Based Detection of Insider Threats to Relational Databases

Asmaa Sallam and Elisa Bertino
Department of Computer Sciences, Purdue University
West Lafayette, IN 47906
{asallam,bertino}@purdue.edu

ABSTRACT

Insiders misuse of resources is a real threat to organizations. According to recent security reports, data has been the most vulnerable to attacks by insiders, especially data located in databases and corporate file servers. Although anomaly detection is an effective technique for flagging early signs of insider attacks, modern techniques for the detection of anomalies in database access are not able to detect several sophisticated data misuse scenarios such as attempts to track data updates and the aggregation of data by an insider that exceeds his/her need to perform job functions. In such scenarios, if the insider does not have prior knowledge of the distribution of the target data, many of his/her queries may extract no data or small amounts of data. Therefore, monitoring the total size of data retrieved by each user and comparing it to normal levels will either result in low anomaly detection accuracy or long time to anomaly detection. In this paper, we propose anomaly detection techniques designed to detect data aggregation and attempts to track data updates. Our techniques infer the normal rates of tables references and tuples retrievals from past database access logs. User queries are then analyzed to detect queries that lead to exceeding the normal data access rates. We evaluated the proposed techniques on the query logs of a real database. The results of the evaluation indicate that when the system configuration parameters are adequately selected and sufficient data is available for training, our techniques have low false alarm generation rate and high anomaly detection accuracy.

KEYWORDS

Insider Threats, Data Analytics for Security, Relational Databases, Anomaly Detection, Temporal Attacks

ACM Reference format:
Asmaa Sallam and Elisa Bertino. 2019. Result-Based Detection of Insider Threats to Relational Databases. In *Proceedings of Ninth ACM Conference on Data and Application Security and Privacy, Richardson, TX, USA, March 25–27, 2019 (CODASPY '19),* 11 pages.
https://doi.org/10.1145/3292006.3300039

1 INTRODUCTION

The detection and response to threats from trusted and authorized users are particularly challenging [6] as it is often difficult to determine when activities by such users are strictly related to their job functions. As data is considered a core asset of many organizations, data has been the most vulnerable to insider attacks, especially confidential business information such as financial, customer and employee data, and sensitive personal information [16, 17].

According to recent security reports, changes in users access patterns are considered important indicators of insider attacks [6]. Intrusion detection and prevention systems, log management, and security and event management (SIEM) are thus the most widely used controls by companies to detect and analyze insider attacks [17]. A security event detected by these controls composes an early indicator of malicious intents. Therefore, analysis of events and collecting data from different sources are useful in inferring the relationships between different security events, differentiating between negligent or unintentional and malicious threats, and preparing responses to malicious acts [18].

Anomaly detection (AD) in database (DB) access is a prominent technique for the detection of insider threats to DBs [2]. An AD system builds models based on log analysis and checks user behavior against these models to detect and flag abnormalities. Modern AD techniques for DB protection against insider threats are capable of the detection of changes in the patterns of access to the DB entities [4, 7], query execution frequencies [9, 12], and sizes of data retrieved by single queries [14, 15] and sequences of queries [5, 13]. However, they are unable to track data access frequencies; as a result, the following temporal data misuse scenarios cannot be detected.

(1) *Data aggregation.* The execution of a single query that extracts a large data-set from the DB can easily be flagged as anomalous if the normal sizes of result-sets of queries by the issuer or other users in his/her role are smaller than the size of the data retrieved by the query [13–15]. To hide his/her tracks, a malicious insider may try to aggregate data of interest over time by issuing a sequence of queries; each of which extracts portions of the target data-set. This approach is referred to as data aggregation [6] and can be the first step of a data ex-filtration attack on a DB [3]. AD will fail to detect this misuse scenario if each query is inspected individually. Tracking the aggregate sizes of result-sets of queries will rather be effective in this case [13].

However, if the insider does not have prior knowledge on the distribution of the target data, many of his/her queries may result in retrieving no data or small amounts of data; therefore, the approach that relies on tracking aggregate sizes of result-sets of queries will also have limited detection accuracy or long time to AD. A better approach would be to track the users' rates of referencing the DB tables.

(2) *Attempts to track data updates.* A malicious insider may execute one or more queries repeatedly across a (short or long) temporal interval aiming at tracking updates to the data tuples read by the queries. These queries are considered legitimate if the insider has permissions to read from the DB entities referenced by the queries. However, the insider's behavior is anomalous when the access rates to the tuples retrieved by the queries are compared to the normal access rates by the insider or the users who belong to his/her role.

In this paper, we present AD techniques for DB access monitoring that aim at the detection of the misuse scenarios described above. Our techniques capture the normal data access rates from past logs of user activity during a training phase. This information is used to build profiles that describe the data access patterns of the DB users. After the training is complete, our techniques inspect queries executed against the monitored DB in order to track the users' rates of referencing the DB tables and tuples. An increase in a user's data access rates beyond the normal levels is flagged as anomalous to indicate that the behavior of the user is suspicious and requires further analysis.

Our techniques inspect each user query in two main steps. The first step is referred to as preliminary inspection and aims at detecting anomalies in the rates of referencing the DB tables. Preliminary inspection of a query is performed before the query execution and is designed to be fast by only requiring parsing queries in order to extract their syntactic features.

The second step for query inspection aims at detecting anomalies in the rates of tuples retrievals and is referred to as deep inspection. Deep inspection of a query checks the raw data tuples retrieved by the query and thus requires the execution of the query against the monitored DB. Since the execution of a query for the purpose of AD only is not a suitable approach, we introduce an architecture that supports the inspection of the rows in queries result-sets before returning them to the issuers.

We implemented the proposed techniques and developed a proof of concept prototype of the architecture that shows that our techniques can be employed as part of database management systems (DBMSs) that return query result-sets in the form of pipe-lines of rows. We evaluated the proposed techniques using the query logs of a real DB. We present and discuss the results of the evaluation, which indicate that our techniques can accurately detect anomalies in data access rates and produce few false alarms. Based on the results of the evaluation, we draw conclusions on approaches for choosing the system configuration parameters and for estimating the risk degrees of queries and user activities [11].

The remainder of this paper is organized as follows. We discuss the architecture in which the proposed techniques can be deployed in Section 2. In Sections 3 and 4, we present detailed algorithms for the proposed techniques and the data structures that support their implementation. We describe our approach for the experimental evaluation of the proposed techniques and discuss the results of the evaluation in Section 5. In Section 6, we compare our work with the related work. Section 7 concludes the paper and discusses potential future work.

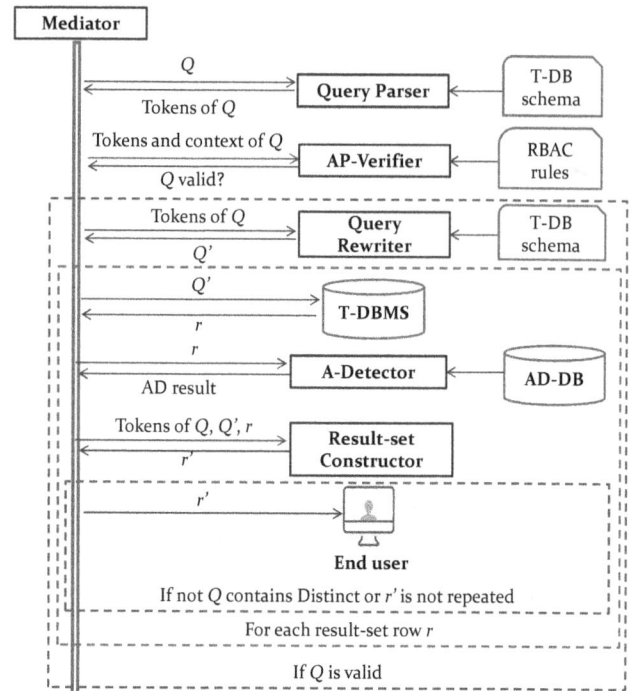

Figure 1: Steps for the inspection of a new user query (Q)

2 ARCHITECTURE

The AD techniques we propose can be employed by any organization that uses a DBMS to manage data. We refer to the monitored DB and the DBMS that manages it as the target DB (T-DB) and the target DBMS (T-DBMS) respectively as they are the target of insiders misuse.

The proposed techniques operate in two phases: training and detection. During the training phase, a Profiler module is fed with past logs of the T-DBMS in order to capture the T-DB users' access patterns and build profiles of the users accordingly. The Profiler executes the training queries on a copy of the T-DB, referred to as the training DB. The training DB also stores temporal data that characterize references to the T-DB tables and tuples. A copy of the T-DB is thus required at the start of training and is used to setup the training DB.

Since most modern DB systems employ role-based access control (RBAC) to manage users access privileges, we assume that each user query has associated role information that indicates the role activated by the user at the time of query execution. Based on RBAC, it is valid to assume common behavior of users belonging to the same role. The Profiler thus combines individual user profiles to form roles profiles, which are smaller in number and can thus be better managed.

The training is done once offline and transparently to the T-DBMS users. The detection phase starts after the training is complete. The communication between the T-DBMS and its users during the detection phase is established through the use of a Mediator component. The Mediator executes queries on behalf of the T-DB users and is thus responsible for logging users interactions with the T-DBMS in addition to the AD results.

The Mediator communicates with the different system components to detect anomalies in the users behaviors based on the select queries executed by the users. The Mediator employs an SQL parser to extract the syntactic features of each select query, which characterize the tables and attributes referenced in the query, in order to prepare it for inspection. The Mediator thus has access to a copy of the schema of the T-DB. It is the job of the Mediator to monitor other types of queries that lead to changes to the T-DB schema and data.

Given an input select query, the Mediator first verifies that the issuer has the necessary privileges to access the DB entities referenced in the query. For this purpose, the Mediator employs an Access Privileges Verifier component (AP-Verifier), which refers to the RBAC rules of the T-DBMS to decide whether the query is allowed by its issuer. The Mediator generates an error and stops the execution of the query if it does not match the RBAC rules. Otherwise, the Mediator sends the query to a Query Rewriter component, which performs modifications to the query string that are necessary for the extraction of additional information on the data retrieved by the query.

The mediator then executes the modified query at the T-DBMS on behalf of the query issuer and establishes a connection with an A-Detector component, which performs the actual inspection of the query. The Mediator sends the query to the A-Detector and relays the rows of the result-set of the query from the T-DBMS to the A-Detector. The A-Detector stores user tracking data and parts of the T-DB data in a DB referred to as the AD-DB and uses this DB for query inspection.

Based on the result of the inspection and the rules of the AD response policies, the Mediator chooses whether to relay the rows of the result-set to the issuer. The Mediator employs a Result-set Constructor component to modify each result-set row to match the original input query and present the row in the format accepted by the issuing user application. The Mediator also removes any duplicate rows that are added due to the modifications made to the query before its execution.

The execution of queries on commercial DBMSs follows a pipelined approach in which the rows of the result-sets are presented as a pipeline rather than as a bulk. This approach is useful for the proper application of our techniques as the inspection of the tuples in the output of a query at the A-Detector can be performed in parallel to the execution of the query at the T-DBMS.

Figure 1 shows the interactions between the system components for the purpose of the inspection of a new user query. Table 1 contains the list of acronyms used throughout the paper.

3 TRAINING PHASE

The purpose of training is to measure the expected number of references by the users of each role to the T-DB tables and tuples during tracking intervals of different lengths and store this information in roles profiles. The profile of a role consists of two sets of records. The first set represents the expected rates for referencing the T-DB tables in queries, while the second set represents the expected rates

Table 1: Acronyms

Acronym	Description
AD	Anomaly detection
DB	Database
DBMS	Database management system
QRM	Query replication multiple
FPR	False-positive error rate
FNR	False-negative error rate

Table 2: Data access rates

t	l_i	n
Emps	2	1
Emps	3	2
Emps	4	2

of tuples retrievals. Table 2 shows an example record set. The attribute t refers to the name of a T-DB table, l_i refers to the length of tracking intervals and n refers to the number of expected references to t or to the tuples of t within a time interval of length equal to l_i. The lengths of time intervals are measured in terms of the system resolution (L_{res}).

Our approach for computing the rates of retrievals of the T-DB tuples is to not distinguish between retrievals of a tuple by the same user if the time-stamps of the retrievals are within an interval of length equal to L_{res}. We made this choice based on our experiments on a real DB referenced by an application program. We noticed that the program may read the same tuple multiple times by different queries as part of the program's flow. A tuple may also be read several times by the same query as a result of a primary-key-foreign-key relationship between tables joined by the query. This resolution assumption complies with our initial goal to detect attempts for tracking data updates as tuples are unlikely to change within short time intervals. Reading the same tuple multiple times within a short time interval thus does not convey additional information to a malicious insider.

On the other hand, the resolution concept does not apply to tables references as multiple references to the same table within a short time interval that return no data or small amounts of data can convey important information on the distribution of the data stored in the table. The main design goal of our techniques is to detect this case.

During the training phase, the Profiler processes the T-DBMS logs in two main steps: organizing logs and building profiles in order to form roles profiles. In the rest of this section, we discuss details on the two training steps.

3.1 Organizing Logs

The Profiler organizes the training logs by partitioning their queries into roles sub-logs and users sub-logs. Users sub-logs contain sufficient data that allows the Profiler to process them individually and sequentially in the profiles building step.

Table 3: Example Training Data

(a) Role sub-log

Query	uid	Timestamp
SELECT * FROM Emps WHERE name = 'Lucas Isaac'	1001	6/1/17 9:15:35:010
UPDATE Emps SET salary = salary + 500 WHERE name = 'Lucas Isaac'	1002	6/1/17 9:30:48:123
SELECT * FROM Emps WHERE name = 'John Blake'	1001	6/1/17 9:50:52:820
SELECT * FROM Emps WHERE name = 'John Blake'	1002	6/1/17 9:55:00:010
SELECT * FROM Emps WHERE name = 'John Blake'	1002	6/1/17 9:58:00:020

(b) A user sub-log (uid = 1001)

Query	Timestamp
SELECT * FROM Emps WHERE name = 'Lucas Isaac'	6/1/17 9:15:35:010
UPDATE Emps SET salary = salary + 500 WHERE name = 'Lucas Isaac'	6/1/17 9:30:48:123
SELECT * FROM Emps WHERE name = 'John Blake'	6/1/17 9:50:52:820

Definition 3.1. The sub-log of a role r contains all select queries issued by the users activating the role r at the time of executing the queries in addition to all other types of queries present in the logs. Queries in a role sub-log are ordered chronologically.

Definition 3.2. The sub-log of a user u who belongs to a role r contains all select queries in r's sub-log that are executed by u in addition to all other types of queries present in the logs. Queries in a user sub-log are ordered chronologically.

Tables 3a and 3b show an example role sub-log and one of the corresponding users sub-logs respectively. The logs contain queries that reference the table *Emps* (short for employees), which has the schema: *Emps(eid, name, position, salary)*.

3.2 Building Profiles

The Profiler computes the data access rates for each role based on the sub-logs of its users. For this purpose, the Profiler references the training DB to execute queries and record access time information. The training DB is initialized before processing each user sub-log to restore the initial state of the T-DB at the start time of the logs.

The training DB contains intermediate tracking information. The access rates to tables are stored in a training DB table named: *tables-references*. A record in *tables-references* contains four attributes:

(1) *table-name*: the name of a T-DB table,
(2) *ats* (short for *access-time-series*): a time-series that stores the references made by the user whose sub-log is currently being processed to the table with the name *table-name*,
(3) *ats-start*: the time-stamp of the start of *ats*, and

(4) *sums*: a list that contains the sums of entries in *ats* that lie within tracking intervals of different lengths.

Other tables in the training DB correspond to the T-DB tables. A table t_{train} that corresponds to the T-DB table t contains all the attributes of t and the attributes *ats*, *ats-start* and *sums* that are similar to the temporal attributes of *tables-references*.

Given a user sub-log, the Profiler scans its queries and directly executes all statements on the training DB except select statements. When a select query is encountered, the Profiler composes and executes a modified version of the query against the training DB by replacing the projection-list of the original query with the list of primary-keys of the tables referenced in the query. This information is used to identify the raw tuples retrieved by the query. For example, if the original query is:

SELECT name
FROM Emps
WHERE salary >= 60,000,

the modified version of the query will be:

SELECT eid
FROM Emps
WHERE salary >= 60,000.

The Profiler then scans the result-set values in the primary-key attributes of each table and updates the time-series that correspond to each value. The Profiler also records the time-stamp of the query in *tables-references*.

To maintain the training DB time-series and record references to the T-DB tables and tuples, the Profiler employs a sliding-window algorithm. When the time-stamp of a training query does not fall within the interval initially-represented by a time-series stored in a training DB tuple, the time interval that the time-series represents should be updated, i.e., the time-series entries should be shifted and older entries should be discarded. To avoid recomputing the number of references that lie within the shifted interval, the sliding-window algorithm is used to maintain the sum of references encoded in the part of the interval that is not discarded. Samples of the sums of references encoded in discarded time-series in *tables-references* and other training tables are recorded in the training DB. Table 4 shows the steps for maintaining a time-series based on the time-stamps of queries that reference the table or tuple that the time-series represents.

Recording references to tuples by aggregate select queries is performed differently based on the type of the aggregate functions of the queries as follows.

(1) *TOP n queries.* A TOP n query selects the first n rows only from the result-set of a similar query that does not contain the TOP n function. Given a TOP n training query, the Profiler modifies the query by removing the aggregate function from the query and adding the primary key attributes of the tables referenced by the query to the query's projection list as previously explained for non-aggregate queries. The Profiler then executes the query, observes the output rows in its result-set, records the original query's time-stamp in the time-series of the corresponding T-DB tuples and stops the execution of the query after n rows are observed.

Table 4: Maintenance of time-series ($L_{res} = 20$ mins, $L_i = \{2,3\}, L_s = 3$)

Query Time	ats				sums	Sample Sums
9:01	8:02	8:22 0	8:42 0	9:02 1	{1,1}	{}
9:50	8:02	8:22 0	8:42 0	9:02 1	{1,2}	$\{(l_i = 2) => \{1,1\}, (l_i = 3) => \{1,1,1\}\}$
10:01	8:02	8:22 0	8:42 0	9:02 1	{1,2}	$\{(l_i = 2) => \{1,1\}, (l_i = 3) => \{1,1,1\}\}$
10:03	8:02	8:22 0	8:42 0	9:02 1	{2,2}	$\{(l_i = 2) => \{1,1,1\}, (l_i = 3) => \{1,1,1,2\}\}$

Table 5: Data in the T-DB table *Emps*

eid	name	position	salary
1	Lucas Isaac	JD1	50,000
2	John Blake	JD2	62,000
3	Jamie Adam	JD2	65,000
4	Joseph King	SD1	80,000

(2) *MAX and MIN queries.* The Profiler executes the original MIN and MAX queries and then executes additional queries to extract the primary-keys of the tuples referenced by the original queries. For example, given the query:

SELECT MAX(salary)
FROM Emps,

the profiler executes the query as is and observes the output value of the MAX function; in this query case, the result is equal to 80,000 based on the T-DB data shown in Table 5. The Profiler then records the time-stamp of the original training query in the time-series of tuples that correspond to the rows of the result-set of the query:

SELECT eid
FROM Emps
WHERE salary = 80,000.

(3) *Other aggregate functions, e.g., COUNT, SUM, AVG, and STDEV.* The Profiler discards all types of aggregate queries other than TOP *n*, MAX and MIN queries as they present data to the issuer that may have been computed based on a large number of values of the T-DB attributes; marking the tuples that contain these values as read will be inadequate as the attributes of these rows may not be contributing much to the results of the original queries.

After processing the sub-logs of all the users of one role (*rl*), the Profiler computes the threshold levels to be stored in *rl*'s profile. Since the training data may contain anomalies, the maximum values of the sample sums of time-series are inadequate measures of the threshold levels. Alternatively, given a list of values that represents the sample sums of the time-series of references to a table *t* or the tuples of a table *t* by the users of *rl* during time intervals of length *l*, the Profiler considers the p_{upper} percentile of the values as the threshold level for referencing *t* or the tuples of *t* and stores this information in record-sets similar to the ones shown in Table 2. In addition to removing previous anomalous references to tables

and tuples from the training data, using the p_{upper} percentiles as thresholds is also beneficial in eliminating the effect of variations in training references rates on the accuracy of computation of the training thresholds.

The default value of p_{upper} is 95%. This values is suitable in both cases:

(1) *A training log that contains no anomalies.* Considering that the training sums are based on queries executed by multiple users, the proper value of the threshold and values close to it are repeated towards the end of the training sums list. Accordingly, discarding 5% of the values at the end of a list will not lead to major reduction in the threshold value.

(2) *A training log that contains anomalies.* In this case, discarding 5% of the values of a list will be sufficient to eliminate the anomalies without affecting the proper value of the threshold as discussed in the first case.

Algorithm 1 shows parts of the training phase algorithms. Algorithm 1 references the configuration parameters listed in Table 6. Procedure *record-tuples-retrievals* describes the steps followed by the Profiler for processing a list of primary-key values of a table that are part of the result-set of a training select query. For each primary-key value in the input list, the procedure extracts the training DB tuple (*r*) that corresponds to the primary-key value (line 3), finds the bucket that corresponds to the query execution time in the time-series stored in *r* (line 4) and updates this time-series to include the query execution time if necessary (lines 5:16). Time-series related to the T-DB tables and stored in *tables-references* are updated in an approach similar to *record-tuples-retrievals* except that the concept of resolution employed in *record-tuples-retrievals*:12 does not apply in case of tables.

4 DETECTION PHASE

During the detection phase, the A-Detector tracks the access rates of the users to the T-DB tables and tuples and flags an anomaly if any of the thresholds captured during the training phase is exceeded. The A-Detector performs the inspection of each input select query in two main steps: preliminary inspection and deep inspection. The goal of preliminary query inspection is to check if the thresholds on tables references rates have been exceeded, while the goal of deep inspection is to check if the thresholds on tuples retrievals rates have been exceeded.

The A-Detector uses the AD-DB to store information on references to the tables and tuples by the T-DB users for the purpose

Table 6: Configuration parameters

Name	Description	Default
L_{res}	Resolution	1 hour
N_i	Number of tracking intervals lengths	1
L_i	An array of length equal to N_i that stores the lengths of the tracking intervals	{6}
L_s	Length of time-series in the training and AD DBs	10
p_{upper}	Upper percentile (used for choosing training thresholds)	95%

Algorithm 1 Training Phase Algorithms

1: **procedure** RECORD-TUPLES-RETRIEVALS(t: name of a T-DB table, PK: list of values of the primary-key of t, $query$-$time$: the time of execution of a query that retrieves the tuples identified by the values in PK)
2:     **for each** $pk \in PK$ **do**
3:         $r \leftarrow$ read-tuple(t, pk)
4:         $index \leftarrow \dfrac{query\text{-}time - r.ats\text{-}start}{L_{res}}$
5:         **while** $index >= L_s$ **do**
6:             $index\text{-}\text{-}$
7:             **for** $i = 0 : N_i - 1$ **do**
8:                 $first \leftarrow r.ats[L_s - L_i[i]]$
9:                 record-sum$(t, L_i[i], r.sums[i])$
10:                $r.sums[i] \leftarrow r.sums[i] - first$
11:             $r.ats\text{-}start \leftarrow r.ats\text{-}start + L_{res}$
12:         **if** $r.ats[index] == 0$ **then**
13:             $r.ats[index]\text{++}$
14:             **for** $i = 0 : N_i - 1$ **do**
15:                 **if** $index >= L_s - L_i[i]$ **then**
16:                     $r.sums[i]\text{++}$

---

of query inspection. References to the T-DB tables are stored in a table named *tables-references*. Each table t in the T-DB has two corresponding tables in the AD-DB: *t-PK* and *t-tuples-retrievals*, which store the primary-key values of t and the time-stamps of tuples retrievals respectively. The time-stamps of user queries are stored in an approach similar to the organization of time-stamps in the training DB.

The schema of the AD-DB is shown in Figure 2. Tables 7 and 8 show the AD-DB tables that correspond to the T-DB table *Emps* shown in Table 5. The time-series in *Emps-tuples-retrievals* correspond to the log queries in Table 3a.

Preliminary inspection of an input query requires parsing the query only in order to extract its range-tables, i.e., the tables referenced in the query. The A-Detector records the time-stamp of the query in the time-series in the AD-DB table *tables-references* and returns the result of the preliminary inspection to the Mediator. Since the tuples retrieved by the input query cannot be located based on the query's result-set individually, deep inspection of an input query requires the execution of a modified version of the query against the T-DB. The Mediator composes a new query by adding the primary-keys of the query's range-tables to the projection-list

of the query to extract raw tuple information from the T-DB. For example, if the original query is:

    SELECT name
    FROM Emps
    WHERE salary >= 60,000,

the modified version of the query will be:

    SELECT eid, name
    FROM Emps
    WHERE salary >= 60,000.

The Mediator then executes the modified query against the T-DB, observes the output rows in the result-set and relays them to the A-Detector.

Given one result-set row of a query under inspection, the A-Detector finds the values of the primary-keys of each range-table, checks if any of the thresholds on the retrievals of tuples from the table has been exceeded by the issuer, and records the time-stamp of the new retrieval in the AD-DB. The A-Detector responds to the Mediator with the result of AD, which in-turn updates the tuple to match the original input query.

It is to be noted that the approaches for extracting the raw tuples retrieved by training queries and queries under inspection are different. The original projection-list of a query under inspection is retained because the values of the projection-list attributes are relayed to the query issuer after performing AD; these values are not useful in the case of a training query. However, the modifications made to queries under inspection not only change the result-sets rows, but may also result in adding more rows to the result-sets. Tables 9a and 9b illustrate the differences between the result-set of an example query that has the syntax:

    SELECT DISTINCT position
    FROM Emps
    WHERE salary >= 60,000

and the result-set of its modified version that has the syntax:

    SELECT DISTINCT eid, position
    FROM Emps
    WHERE salary >= 60,000.

It is the job of the Mediator to detect and discard added rows. For this purpose, when given a select distinct query, the Mediator uses a hash-table session variable to record the combined values of the attributes of rows sent to the user as part of the result of the query, searches for each row in the query's result-set and drops rows that are found in the hash-table.

Algorithm 2 shows parts of the detection phase algorithms. Procedure *check-tuples-retrievals* in Algorithm 2 shows the steps for the inspection of the primary-key values of a range-table of an input query. The algorithm flags an anomaly if the retrievals of one or more tuples are found to be anomalous. Other approaches for estimating risk degrees for queries and user activities are discussed in Section 5.3. The algorithm for checking the rates of referencing a range-table of an input query is similar to Procedure *check-tuples-retrievals*; the main difference between the two algorithms is that the use of resolution in *check-tuples-retrievals*:15 has to be omitted in case of checking tables references.

Table 7:		
Emps-PK		

seq	eid
0	1
1	2
2	3
3	4

Table 8: *Emps-tuples-retrievals*
($L_{res} = 20$ *mins*, $L_i = \{2,3\}$, $L_s = 3$)

seq	uid	ats	ats-start	sums
0	1001	{0,0,1}	6/1/17 8:16:00:000	{1,1}
1	1001	{0,0,1}	6/1/17 8:51:00:000	{1,1}
1	1002	{0,1,1}	6/1/17 9:16:00:000	{2,2}

Table 9: Result-sets of an example query and its modified version

(a) Result-set of the original query		(b) Result-set of the modified version	
position		**eid**	**position**
JD2		2	JD2
SD1		3	JD2
		4	SD1

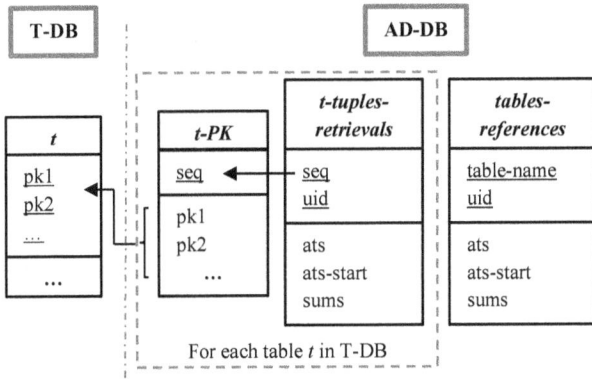

Figure 2: Detection phase data-structures

5 EXPERIMENTAL EVALUATION

We now present the results of experiments for the evaluation of the proposed techniques. The data-set used in experimentation [19] is a real SQL Server DB that contains 71 data tables and the logs of queries executed by the users of an application program that references the DB. The query logs cover a time period of length equal to 3 days and contain 16 user sessions and about 6,000 select queries; each conforms with one of 220 query templates. The main metrics considered in the evaluation are the false-positive error rates (FPRs) and false-negative error rates (FNRs).

5.1 False-Positive Errors

We assumed that the query logs contain no anomalies and thus considered the anomalies flagged by the A-Detector when inspecting any of the log queries as false-positive errors. We set the default

---

Algorithm 2 Detection Phase Algorithms

1: **procedure** CHECK-TUPLES-RETRIEVALS(*query-time*: the time of execution of the input query q, u: the name identifier of the issuer of q, rl: the name identifier of the role activated by u at the time of executing q, r: a row in the result-set of q, T: range-tables of q)
2:      $result \leftarrow$ NORMAL
3:      **for each** $t \in T$ **do**
4:        $thr_t \leftarrow$ get-tuples-retrievals-threshold(rl, t)
5:        $PK_t \leftarrow$ get-table-PK(r, t)
6:        $r_{AD} \leftarrow$ get-AD-tuple(u, t, PK_t)
7:        $index \leftarrow \frac{query\text{-}time - r_{AD}.ats\text{-}start}{L_{res}}$
8:        **while** $index >= L_s$ **do**
9:          **for** $i = 0 : N_i - 1$ **do**
10:            $first \leftarrow r_{AD}.ats[L_s - L_i[i]]$
11:            $sums[i] = sums[i] - first$
12:          remove-first($r_{AD}.ats$)
13:          $index\text{-}\text{-}$
14:          $r_{AD}.ats\text{-}start \leftarrow r_{AD}.ats\text{-}start + L_{res}$
15:        **if** $r_{AD}.ats[index] == 0$ **then**
16:        $r_{AD}.ats[index]$++
17:        **for** $i = 0 : N_i - 1$ **do**
18:          **if** $index >= L_s - L_i[i]$ **then**
19:          $r_{AD}.sums[i]$++
20:          **if** $r_{AD}.sums[i] > thr_t[i]$ **then**
21:            $result \leftarrow$ ANOMALOUS
22:      **return** $result$

---

value of p_{upper} to 95%; therefore, only 5% of the training sample sums related to a table or to the tuples of a table are discarded when computing the reference threshold related to the table or to its tuples.

We measured the effect of the following factors on the rate of the false-positive errors produced by preliminary and deep inspection.

(1) *Size of the training data.*

To generate training data-sets of different sizes, we chose p_t% of the total available training data for building profiles and the most recent 20% of the log queries for model evaluation. We measured the FPRs for p_t equal to 10, 20 ... 80.

Figures 3(a) and 4(a) show the percentages of queries flagged as anomalous by preliminary inspection and deep inspection respectively for the different values of p_t. The error rates are computed as the average error rates produced as a result of using different tracking intervals lengths, which range between 2 and 8 hours. Preliminary inspection considers a query anomalous if one or more tables of the query's range-tables are flagged as anomalous as a result of the inspection of the query. Deep inspection considers a query anomalous if one or more tuples retrieved by the query are flagged as anomalous. Figure 4(b) compares the percentage of the number of tuples flagged as anomalous by deep inspection to the number of queries flagged as anomalous by the same method if one or more of the references to the tuples read by the queries were found to be anomalous. The result proves that using more data for training produces a more accurate AD model and thus reduces the false-positive errors. Using 30% of the training data was sufficient for capturing accurate tables references thresholds and producing an accurate model for preliminary inspection. However, deep inspection required more data to produce an accurate model as deep inspection captures more information on data access rates. To better understand the changes that occur to the characteristics of the training data when its size changes, we computed two statistical metrics for each of the training data-sets. These are the average number of references to the T-DB tables per hour and the average number of tuples retrieved per hour. Significant changes in the values of both metrics occur when the size of the training data-set changes. The values of the first metric stabilizes for training data-sets of sizes equal to or bigger than 30% of the total evaluation data-set as shown in Figures 3(b) and 3(c). The result thus explains why smaller training data-sets lead to more false-positive errors by preliminary inspection. However, the average number of tuples retrieved per hour was not suitable for describing the characteristics of the training data and none of the two metrics could be used to find the size of data that is suitable for training the deep inspection model.

In the rest of our experiments, we chose the default size of the training and evaluation queries to be 80% and 20% of the available queries, respectively. We were thus able to rule out the effect of insufficient training data on the accuracy of the AD model.

(2) *Length of the tracking intervals.*

Figures 3(d) and 4(c) show the average FPRs produced by preliminary inspection and deep inspection respectively for various lengths of the tracking intervals, which range between 2 and 8 hours.

We observed that both preliminary inspection and deep inspection produce low error rates when the length of the tracking intervals is equal to 4 hours or more. These values are related to the lengths of the training sessions, which range between 2.5 and 5.5 hours. We can thus conclude that as the length of the tracking intervals is closer to the lengths of user sessions, more accurate thresholds on the rates of tables references and tuples retrievals can be captured.

(3) *The number of tracking intervals lengths.*

We observed from some of our experiments that the errors in AD are not produced consistently when the length of the tracking intervals changes. Therefore, we chose to measure the accuracy of AD when multiple tracking intervals lengths, which range between 2 and 8 hours, are used. The A-Detector ignores an anomaly related to a table or tuple if it is flagged based on one tracking intervals length only.

The result indicates major reductions in the false-positive errors produced by deep inspection as a result of using multiple tracking intervals lengths. On the other hand, we did not observe reductions in the false-positive errors produced by preliminary inspection. In both cases, we observed no increase in the FNRs.

(4) *Percentile (p_{upper}) used in computing training thresholds.*

Figure 3(e) compares the FPRs produced by preliminary inspection when the value of p_{upper} is set to 75% and 95%. Using a higher value for p_{upper} consistently leads to less false positive errors as it enables for higher values for the training thresholds. This result also applies to deep inspection as shown in Figure 4(d).

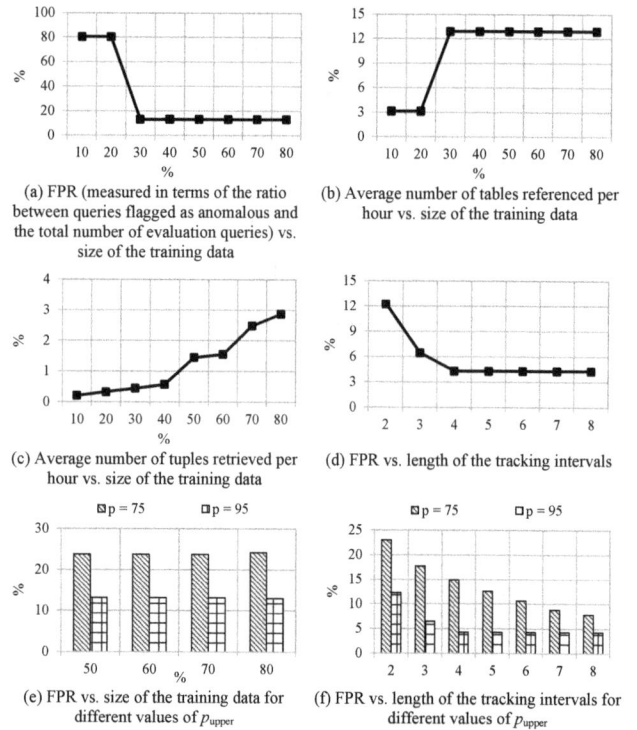

(a) FPR (measured in terms of the ratio between queries flagged as anomalous and the total number of evaluation queries) vs. size of the training data

(b) Average number of tables referenced per hour vs. size of the training data

(c) Average number of tuples retrieved per hour vs. size of the training data

(d) FPR vs. length of the tracking intervals

(e) FPR vs. size of the training data for different values of p_{upper}

(f) FPR vs. length of the tracking intervals for different values of p_{upper}

Figure 3: False-positive errors by preliminary inspection

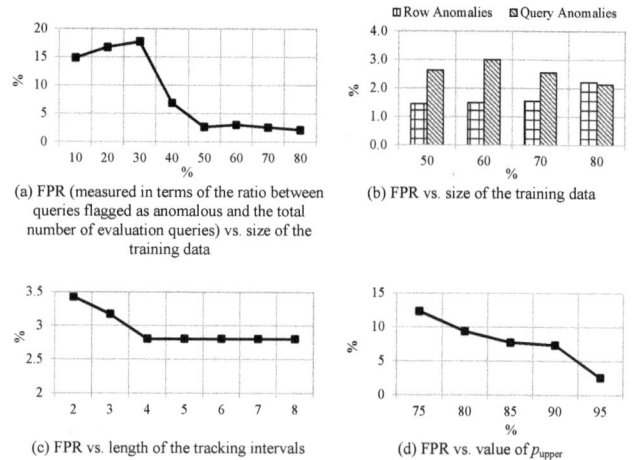

(a) FPR (measured in terms of the ratio between queries flagged as anomalous and the total number of evaluation queries) vs. size of the training data

(b) FPR vs. size of the training data

(c) FPR vs. length of the tracking intervals

(d) FPR vs. value of p_{upper}

Figure 4: False-positive errors by deep inspection

5.2 False-Negative Errors

Since the query logs contain no anomalies, we replicated the evaluation queries to add anomalies to the original log in order to measure the FNRs. We refer to the number of times a query is replicated as the query replication multiple (QRM).

Based on the results of our experiments for measuring the false-positive errors, we chose the default value of the length of the tracking intervals to be equal to 6 hours. This length is guaranteed to produce low FPRs; we can thus rule out the effect of the choice of the length of the tracking intervals on the FNRs.

For each replicated query or group of replicated queries that lie within the same tracking interval, preliminary inspection is expected to flag an anomaly for each table referenced in the queries. However, in case of deep inspection, replicated queries that lie within the same time bucket are not expected to produce anomalies due to the use of the resolution concept. Replicating a query and setting its execution time-stamp to be at least one bucket away from the original query is expected to produce anomalies within one tracking interval of the original query. Our approach to measuring the FNRs is thus to consider each tuple retrieved by the replicated queries individually rather than considering queries that are flagged as anomalous. If no anomalies are flagged for one of these tuples, we count this error as one false-negative error.

We considered the effect of the following factors on the FNRs.

(1) *Number of query replications.*

We measured the FNRs for values of the QRM that range between 1 and 3. We set the distance between a query and its i-th replica to $i * 20\%$ the length of the tracking intervals; in this case, replicated queries will not belong to the same bucket as the original query or any other replica.

Figures 5(a) and 6(a) show the average FNRs produced by preliminary inspection and deep inspection respectively for different values of the QRM. The result indicates that the accuracy of AD increases as the number of references to the same table or tuple increases, i.e., when the thresholds are expected to be reached. The accuracy of deep inspection is lower than preliminary inspection. The FNR becomes constant for higher values of the QRM; that is because if the threshold associated with a table is met, all succeeding references to this table within the same tracking interval will be considered anomalous. In general, there is 87% probability that the first anomalous reference to a table is detected and 98.8% probability that the second anomalous retrieval of a tuple is detected.

The time to AD is an important metric to consider in the evaluation. We considered two units for measuring the time to AD. The first unit is the number of anomalous references to a table or tuple that are considered normal before a related anomaly is flagged. Although it is intuitive to use this unit for measuring the time to AD, the values for this unit for references to tables cannot be easily interpreted as they depend on the training thresholds and the time of the anomalous reference within the tracking interval that includes the reference.

The second unit for measuring the time to AD resolves the problems associated with the first unit by considering the length of the tracking intervals in the computation. The time required to detect an anomaly related to a table is computed as the ratio between the number of anomalous references to the table that are considered normal before the anomaly is flagged and the threshold of reference to the table. It is to be noted that the second unit is not suitable for measuring the time to the detection of anomalies related to tuples because of two reasons: (1) the number of references to the tuples of a table during one tracking interval is different from the threshold that is related to the table and stored in the profiles because the resolution concept

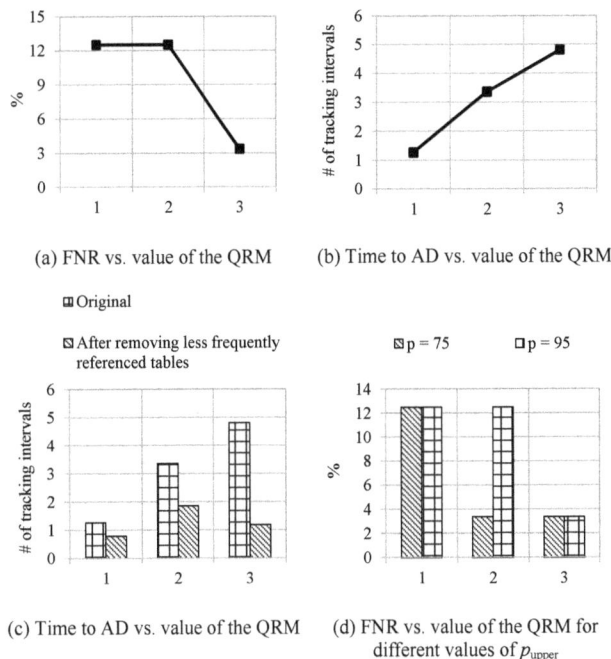

(a) FNR vs. value of the QRM   (b) Time to AD vs. value of the QRM

□ Original

▨ After removing less frequently referenced tables   ▨ p = 75   □ p = 95

(c) Time to AD vs. value of the QRM   (d) FNR vs. value of the QRM for different values of p_{upper}

Figure 5: False-negative errors by preliminary inspection

is used, and (2) a tuple is not as frequently referenced as a table and it is thus useful to consider each reference to a tuple rather than considering all number of references to it during a tracking interval.

Figures 5(b) and 6(b) show the time required by preliminary inspection and deep inspection to detect anomalies. The average time required to detect anomalies in references to tables is high and is equal to 5 times the length of the tracking intervals when the value of the QRM is equal to 3. When considering the individual tables for computing the time to AD, we observed that the time to the detection of anomalies related to tables that are less-referenced in the training logs is longer. We then removed the anomalies related to these tables and recomputed the time to AD. Figure 5(c) compares the time to AD before and after removing less frequently referenced tables. Considering the results in Figures 5(a) and 5(c), we can conclude that, on average, the third anomalous reference to a frequently-referenced table can be detected after a time interval of length equal to the length of the tracking intervals.

(2) *Percentile (p_{upper}) used in computing training thresholds..*

In contrast to FPRs, using a smaller value for p_{upper}, which leads to stricter training thresholds, results in less FNRs in case of both preliminary and deep inspection as shown in Figures 5(d) and 6(c) and in less time to AD in case of deep inspection as shown in Figure 6(d).

5.3 Concluding Remarks

The results of the experimental evaluation indicate that our techniques have low error rates only when sufficient data is available for

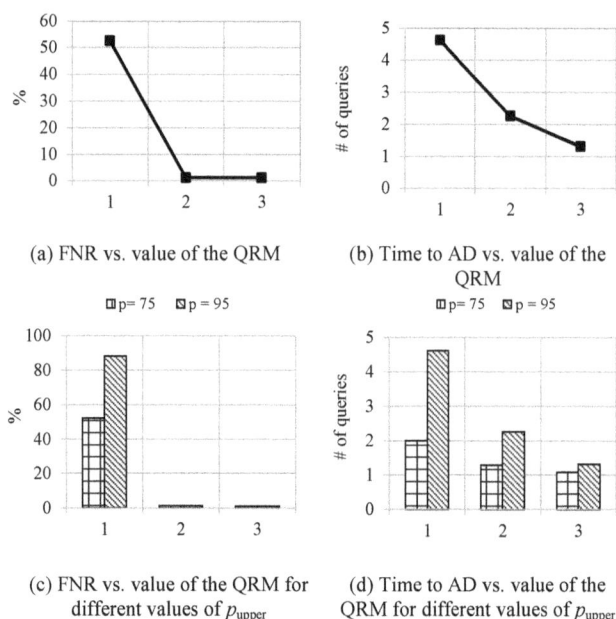

(a) FNR vs. value of the QRM

(b) Time to AD vs. value of the QRM

(c) FNR vs. value of the QRM for different values of p_{upper}

(d) Time to AD vs. value of the QRM for different values of p_{upper}

Figure 6: False-negative errors by deep inspection

training and the configuration parameters are selected adequately. A few remarks must be made on the results of the evaluation.

- The instability of the values of the statistical metrics described in Section 5.1 for small training data-sets indicates that these data-sets are insufficient for producing an adequate model. The procedure described for evaluation can thus be used before employing the proposed AD techniques to detect insufficient training data. Changes in the values of the metrics can be automatically detected using the statistical methods employed in level-shift outlier detection (LSO) [10], which is mainly used for the detection of changes (also referred to as break-points) in time-series.

- The proper length of the tracking intervals for the detection of anomalies in tables and tuples references rates is related to the lengths of user sessions. Since sessions lengths are expected to vary depending on the start time of the sessions, it is important to consider the time-stamps of user queries in AD. The data-set we used for evaluation does not contain such variations; therefore, considering the time-stamps of user queries is part of our future work.

- The rates of the false-negative errors produced by preliminary inspection depend on the values of the thresholds captured during training and the variations in the rates of tables references. It is thus important to adopt other techniques for the detection of such variations. For example, one could adopt the outlier detection techniques by Kamra et al. [7] for capturing the syntactic features of normal queries and ruling out outliers in the training data for the detection of queries that are not frequently executed.

- Computing a degree of risk for each flagged anomaly is useful in eliminating false-positive errors and automating the response to detected anomalies. The degree of risk of references to tables can be easily computed based on the difference between the

training thresholds and the actual users access rates. However, different approaches can be used for computing the degree of risk of anomalous tuples retrievals, e.g., the degree of risk of the individual who repeatedly retrieves multiple T-DB tuples and the degree of risk of anomalous query sequences that reference the different tables.

- Using multiple tracking intervals lengths is extremely useful in eliminating false positive errors. This approach, combined with computing risk degrees of detected anomalies that take into account multiple tracking intervals lengths, helps achieve high detection accuracy.

6 RELATED WORK

The detection of insider threats to DBs has been widely addressed by past research. The existing solutions can be categorized according to the strategy for threat detection into signature-based solutions and user behavior analytics.

Signature-based solutions, also referred to as misuse detection, define a black list that contains the set of patterns that describe the different misuse scenarios. While being effective in the detection of different types of attacks, e.g., SQL injection, signature-based solutions fail to account for unknown threats. On the other hand, user behavior analytics, also referred to as AD solutions, automatically learn the expected access patterns and flag users behaviors that deviate from the expected patterns as potential threats. The existing AD solutions follow different algorithmic approaches and rely on features that can be one or more of four types: contextual, syntactic, result-based, and temporal.

Kamra et al. [4, 7] propose modeling normal queries in the form of records that encode the syntactic features of queries and have different degrees of granularity. They use machine learning (classification for role-based AD and clustering for user-based AD) to detect changes in command types and references to the DB entities.

Sallam et al. [14, 15] propose adding data-centric features that describe the selectivities of the tables referenced in queries to the triplet representation introduced in [4]. The added features are useful in the detection of anomalous queries that access data-sets that are larger than normal. In their paper [12], Sallam et al. consider the queries temporal features represented by the time-stamps of execution of queries to detect periodic queries and track the frequencies of their execution. They present novel AD algorithms that infer the relationships between periodic queries that are issued together and rely on computing the auto-correlation of time-series to detect periodic queries and the expected time of their execution.

Mathew et al. [8] assume that the data in result-sets of queries should statistically comply with that of the training queries. They thus propose modeling queries based on statistics on their result-sets and using different machine learning algorithms to detect anomalies. Although useful in the detection of some misuse scenarios, the syntax-based approach allows more flexibility in matching queries under inspection to the training queries.

Constante et al. [5] propose using user-editable histograms to represent the aggregate syntactic, data-centric, temporal and contextual features of normal queries. Their techniques compute anomaly scores for transactions and transaction sets based on histograms probabilities and flag an anomaly when an anomaly score is higher than a configuration threshold. Their approach combines the advantages of both the syntactic [7] and data-centric [8] approaches.

Mazzawi et al. [9] propose modeling user activity patterns in a probabilistic approach and consider queries syntactic, temporal, and contextual features. They propose analyzing the activities by each user during time frames in order to compute two anomaly scores that describe the consistency of the user's activities with the history of previous activities by the user and activities by the other DB users. An alarm is raised when an anomaly score exceeds a configuration threshold. The proposed solutions have been integrated into Guardium [1], the SIEM tool by IBM.

Sallam et al. [13] also propose techniques for the detection of data aggregation threats by monitoring the sizes of data retrieved by queries and sequences of queries during user sessions. They use different clustering and outlier detection algorithms to evaluate each session periodically and at its end in order to take into account the dependencies between the sizes of aggregate data retrieved from the different tables and the sessions lengths. The proposed techniques are only effective when the queries are guaranteed to retrieve data from the monitored DB as discussed earlier; however, they cannot detect attempts for inferring the distribution of the target data that can be part of data aggregation threats.

The techniques described in this paper differ significantly from the related work as none of the existing AD solutions considers the detection of the misuse scenarios discussed in this paper. We rely on syntactic, data-centric and temporal features to represent user activities and present novel algorithms for AD. We provide implementation details and thorough evaluation of the proposed techniques, which prove that our solutions are effective and can be part of a working DB system.

7 FUTURE WORK

We plan to extend the work presented in this paper by developing techniques for the automatic detection and application of changes in the users access patterns to the profiles during the detection phase. We also plan to add an initialization step to the training phase during which the Profiler selects portions of the log that are representative of the current access patterns of the T-DBMS users before performing the actual profile creation. The initialization step is crucial because using the complete log of accesses by the users of a role for building the profile of the role is inadequate if the log represents a long time period of accesses during which the users access patterns may have changed.

REFERENCES

[1] 2018. IBM Security Guardium family. https://www.ibm.com/security/data-security/guardium/. (2018). Accessed: 2018-5-20.

[2] Elisa Bertino. 2012. *Data Protection from Insider Threats. Synthesis Lectures on Data Management.* Morgan and Claypool Publishers.

[3] Elisa Bertino and Gabriel Ghinita. 2011. Towards Mechanisms for Detection and Prevention of Data Exfiltration by Insiders: Keynote Talk Paper. In *Proceedings of the 6th ACM Symposium on Information, Computer and Communications Security (ASIACCS '11).* ACM, New York, NY, USA, 10–19. https://doi.org/10.1145/1966913.1966916

[4] Elisa Bertino, Ashish Kamra, Evimaria Terzi, and Athena Vakali. 2005. Intrusion Detection in RBAC-administered Databases. In *Proceedings of the 21st Annual Computer Security Applications Conference (ACSAC '05).* IEEE Computer Society, 170–182. https://doi.org/10.1109/CSAC.2005.33

[5] Elisa Costante, Sokratis Vavilis, Sandro Etalle, Jerry den Hartog, Milan Petković, and Nicola Zannone. 2017. A white-box anomaly-based framework for database leakage detection. *Journal of Information Security and Applications* 32 (2017), 27 – 46. https://doi.org/10.1016/j.jisa.2016.10.001

[6] Software Engineering Institute. 2015. *Analytic Approaches to Detect Insider Threats.* Technical Report. Software Engineering Institute, Carnegie Mellon University, Pittsburgh, PA. http://resources.sei.cmu.edu/library/asset-view.cfm?assetid=451065, accessed 10-28-2016.

[7] Ashish Kamra, Evimaria Terzi, and Elisa Bertino. 2008. Detecting Anomalous Access Patterns in Relational Databases. *The VLDB Journal* 17, 5 (Aug. 2008), 1063–1077. https://doi.org/10.1007/s00778-007-0051-4

[8] Sunu Mathew, Michalis Petropoulos, Hung Q. Ngo, and Shambhu Upadhyaya. 2010. A Data-centric Approach to Insider Attack Detection in Database Systems. In *Proceedings of the 13th International Conference on Recent Advances in Intrusion Detection (RAID'10).* Springer-Verlag, 382–401. http://dl.acm.org/citation.cfm?id=1894166.1894192

[9] H. Mazzawi, G. Dalal, D. Rozenblatz, L. Ein-Dorx, M. Niniox, and O. Lavi. 2017. Anomaly Detection in Large Databases Using Behavioral Patterning. In *2017 IEEE 33rd International Conference on Data Engineering (ICDE).* 1140–1149. https://doi.org/10.1109/ICDE.2017.158

[10] Tsay Ruey S. 1988. Outliers, level shifts, and variance changes in time series. *Journal of Forecasting* 7, 1 (1988), 1–20. https://doi.org/10.1002/for.3980070102 arXiv:https://onlinelibrary.wiley.com/doi/pdf/10.1002/for.3980070102

[11] Malek Ben Salem, Shlomo Hershkop, and Salvatore J. Stolfo. 2008. *A Survey of Insider Attack Detection Research.* Springer US, 69–90. https://doi.org/10.1007/978-0-387-77322-3_5

[12] Asmaa Sallam and Elisa Bertino. 2017. Detection of Temporal Insider Threats to Relational Databases. In *2017 IEEE 3rd International Conference on Collaboration and Internet Computing (CIC),* Vol. 00. 406–415. https://doi.org/10.1109/CIC.2017.00058

[13] Asmaa Sallam and Elisa Bertino. 2018. Detection of Temporal Data Ex-filtration Threats to Relational Databases. In *Proceedings of the 4th IEEE International Conference on Collaboration and Internet Computing (CIC '18).* IEEE, Philadelphia, PA, USA, 10.

[14] Asmaa Sallam, Daren Fadolalkarim, Elisa Bertino, and Qian Xiao. 2016. Data and syntax centric anomaly detection for relational databases. *Wiley Interdisciplinary Reviews: Data Mining and Knowledge Discovery* 6, 6 (2016), 231–239. https://doi.org/10.1002/widm.1195

[15] Asmaa Sallam, Qian Xiao, Elisa Bertino, and Daren Fadolalkarim. 2016. Anomaly Detection Techniques for Database Protection Against Insider Threats. In *2016 IEEE International Conference on Information Reuse and Integration, IRI 2016, Pittsburgh, PA, USA, July 28-30.*

[16] Holger Schulze. 2016. *Insider Threat Spotlight Report.* Technical Report. Information Security Community on LinkedIn. http://www.infosecbuddy.com/wp-content/uploads/2016/07/Insider-Threat-Report-2016.pdf.

[17] Holger Schulze. 2018. *2018 Insider Threat Report.* Technical Report. Cybersecurity Insiders. https://www.cybersecurity-insiders.com/ninety-percent-organizations-vulnerable-insider-threats-according-new-cybersecurity-report/.

[18] Dtex systems. 2018. *Insider Threat Intelligence Report.* Technical Report. Dtex systems. https://dtexsystems.com/.

[19] Qingsong Yao, Aijun An, and Xiangji Huang. 2005. Finding and Analyzing Database User Sessions. In *Proceedings of the 10th International Conference on Database Systems for Advanced Applications (DASFAA'05).* Springer-Verlag, Berlin, Heidelberg, 851–862. https://doi.org/10.1007/11408079_77

PrivStream: Differentially Private Event Detection on Data Streams

Maryam Fanaeepour
Duke University
Department of Computer Science
maryam@cs.duke.edu

Ashwin Machanavajjhala
Duke University
Department of Computer Science
ashwin@sc.duke.edu

ABSTRACT

Event monitoring and detection in real-time systems is crucial. Protecting users' data while reporting an event in almost real-time will increase the level of this challenge. In this work, we adopt the strong notion of differential privacy to private stream counting for event detection with the aim of minimizing false positive and false negative rates as our utility metrics.

CCS CONCEPTS

• **Information systems** → **Data streams**; • **Security and privacy** → **Privacy-preserving protocols**; **Data anonymization and sanitization**; • **Theory of computation** → *Theory of database privacy and security.*

KEYWORDS

Data Stream, Differential Privacy, Event Detection, Real-time Analytics

ACM Reference Format:
Maryam Fanaeepour and Ashwin Machanavajjhala. 2019. PrivStream: Differentially Private Event Detection on Data Streams. In *Ninth ACM Conference on Data and Application Security and Privacy (CODASPY '19), March 25–27, 2019, Richardson, TX, USA.* ACM, New York, NY, USA, 3 pages. https://doi.org/10.1145/3292006.3302379

1 INTRODUCTION

Today is the era of fast data stream generation coming from various sources such as sensor data, the Internet of Things, telecommunication data, social media, health care, epidemics & disasters and so on. In the settings of data streaming which is continuously generated data, real-time event analytics and query response is vital, in scenarios such as real-time fraud analysis and detection such as in Uber [1], improving traffic safety and efficiency, *e.g.*, TFL London Transport Management System[2], time sensitive health care monitoring. This indeed triggers privacy concerns for the individuals sharing their information. One of the governance challenges in these applications is the ownership of the data, and how rights and obligations will be respected and forced. According to an Accenture study, 57

[1]https://eng.uber.com/fraud-prevention-team-profile/
[2]https://wso2.com/blogs/thesource/2017/10/a-smarter-transport-management-system-for-london-with-the-help-of-wso2/

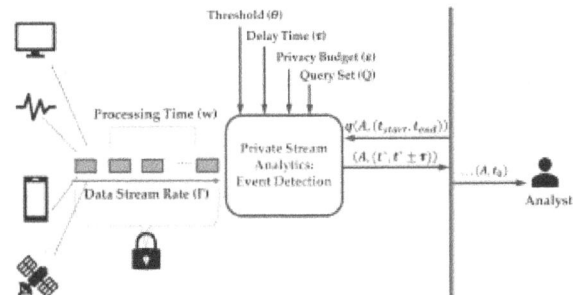

Figure 1: Data flow in private streaming for event detection.

percent of respondents were willing to share information if they are assured their data would not be sold or shared. 56 percent of consumers wanted guarantees that data protection safeguards were in place before they would share information [7].

Consider a scenario for an event detection, where a system analyst wants to start collecting evidence, keep monitoring the system, and tracking some functions *e.g.*, aggregates. At the time that aggregate satisfies some conditions, the analyst wants to be notified so that they can fix the system and start monitoring again. Which aggregates and what conditions does an analyst want to track? What is the window time that data can be processed? What is the delay measure? What is the privacy budget? These are the questions that need to be addressed.

One use-case to consider is the occupancy level for specific rooms in a building. An event of interest is when a room's occupancy meets a defined threshold, then an alert needs to be sent to the system. However, due to privacy reasons, individuals' data can not be touched. The goal in this paper is to design algorithms that not only analyze the data streams in real-time for the purpose of *event detection*, the events' privacy can also be guaranteed through the strong notion of differential privacy (DP) framework [4].

There are works in the setting of private streaming [1, 3, 5] outputting accumulated sum of counts for the continual monitoring stream data. There is also a work that reports counts using a data dependant approach that uses the data distribution to provide a better utility [2]. There has also been some attempts using local differential privacy [9] to sanitize the data on the user side before sharing it with a service provider, but the goal in this work is to design differentially private algorithms for an event detection system that receives the flow of data stream, and event queries. Figure 1 illustrates the data flow for event detection in a private stream analytics system.

We introduce a query type for event monitoring that can vary in determined time period for running queries and defined predicates to apply (see Section 2). Our proposed algorithms aim to minimize the *false positive* (FP) and *false negative* (FN) rates as our utility metrics depending on the error bounds, to guarantee that w.h.p. an event is detected. To address the challenge of utility in real-time analytics, we propose the notion of time delay to be able to have some level of certainty before reporting an event with privacy guarantee, minimizing FP and FN both at the same time. We also discuss approaches to run event queries in parallel reducing the privacy budget used.

2 PRIVATE EVENT DETECTION OVER DATA STREAMS

2.1 Definitions

The goal in this work to preserve *event-level DP* defined as follows.

Definition 2.1 (event-level ϵ-differential privacy [3, 5]). A randomized mechanism $\mathcal{M}$, that takes as input an arbitrary size of stream prefix, is considered to preserve *event-level ϵ-differential privacy* for $\epsilon > 0$, if for all adjacent stream prefixes S_t, S'_t, all timestamps t and all possible set of outputs $\mathcal{O} \subseteq Range(\mathcal{M})$, the following holds $P(\mathcal{M}(S_t) \in \mathcal{O}) \leq \exp(\epsilon) \cdot P(\mathcal{M}(S'_t) \in \mathcal{O})$.

A mechanism that protects any single event preserves event-level privacy.

2.2 Event Detection

As shown in Figure 1, there is a set of event query monitoring the data stream for certain events, A_i, and our system is outputting Yes/No. A query takes stream of input over a window of time and computes a function, considering a specific event, *e.g.*, whether $q(A_i) \geq \theta$ to then output True or False based on the threshold. The input to our event detection algorithms are as follows (*cf.* Figure 1).

- A query q or a set of queries Q, which includes:
  - Events of interest, A_i
  - Processing window of time $w = (t_{start}, t_{end})$
- Condition threshold θ
- Privacy budget ϵ
- Time Delay τ

In the setting of *event detection*, various queries could be considered based on the defined events and determined time window: $q(A_i, w)$. The focus of this paper is on queries in the form of Query 1 as follows. They are counting how many times the defined predicate becomes True on an incoming stream, and once the number of met condition reach the threshold report an event.

Query 1: Aggregate function (*e.g.*, Count) on a time window starting from time zero, up until now or a specified end time $w = (0, t)$ and with predicates $q(A_i) \geq$ or $\leq \theta$;

Event Time vs Report Time (Time Delay τ): The time an event occurs vs the time that is reported is crucial in real-time analytics. To this end, we define a delay parameter to measure the accuracy of a reported event, whether it is reported within a time delay.

What are the mistakes that a system can make? A system outputs an alert even though the condition has not been met yet (system reports the condition is true before an event occurs); or a system notifies an analyst after the condition has been met; or the condition is true but the system does not notify at all.

2.3 Evaluation Metrics

We consider the following metrics to evaluate solutions to our problem.

(1) **Utility**: The two error measures that we consider are *false positive)* (FP) and *false negative* (FN) rates with considering time delay τ. FP(τ) happens when the time of detection is τ time units before the actual time t^* the event occurs. FN(τ) happens when the time of detection is τ time units after the actual time the event occurs (or does not report the event). We use FP and FN to denote FP(0) and FN(0) respectively.

(2) **Privacy**: Mechanisms should achieve *event-level ϵ-differential privacy*, at some ϵ in their release of output.

2.4 Problem Statement

We wish to address Problem 1 based on Query 1 (*cf.* Section 2.2).

PROBLEM 1. *Given an input of data streams, let A be a set of events, $\{A_1, A_2, ..., A_d\}$, that our system is monitoring over time window $(0, t)$. Consider an event query or a sequence of queries $\big(q(A_1), (0, t)\big), \big(q(A_2), (0, t)\big), \cdots$, that are outputting Yes/No for queries in the type of Query 1: $q(A_i) \geq \theta$; Given a bounded privacy budget ϵ, and a defined threshold θ, our goal is to design an algorithm that privately releases $(A_1, t'_1), (A_2, t'_2), \cdots$ [within a specified time delay τ], that w.h.p. detects an event or a series of events in real-time with regard to the evaluation metrics.*

3 BINARY MECHANISM FOR EVENT DETECTION

Our baseline approach is adopted from Binary Mechanism [1, 5] proposed to save the amount of privacy budget used. We call this algorithm as *Binary Mechanism for Event Detection*. The input to Binary Mechanism (BM) is a time upper bound T; a privacy parameter ϵ; and a stream $\sigma\{0, 1\}^T$ (*i.e.*, sequence of $q_i(t)$ in the time period of $(0, T)$. BM outputs estimate of count at each point of time. Here, we call BM and then check if a condition for an event query meets a threshold given the computed error bound for BM. Algorithm 1 runs a single event query to notify an analyst when an event occurs.

Algorithm 1: Binary Mechanism for Event Detection

Input : Data Streams S; Query of interest $q(A, (0, T))$; Threshold θ; Privacy budget ϵ; Error bound α

Output : Detected time for an event of interest

/* Estimate the count of q calling **BM**, that estimates $\hat{q}$ at each point of time $t \in (0, T)$ as $\hat{q}(t)$ */

1 **BM** (T, ϵ, q)

2 **if** $\hat{q}(t) + \alpha \geq \theta$ **then**

3 $\quad$ $t_0 \leftarrow t$ // t_0 as the time that event is detected using noisy counts

4 $\quad$ Report event A at time t_0

THEOREM 3.1. *Algorithm 1 achieves $T\epsilon$-differential privacy.*

THEOREM 3.2 (UTILITY). *For confidence level $\delta \in (0,1)$ and $t \in [T]$, Algorithm 1 is (α, δ)-accurate w.h.p. at least $1 - \delta$: when $\alpha = -\left(\sqrt{8\log 2/\delta} \cdot \log T \sqrt{\log t} \log 1/\delta\right)/\epsilon$ then it ensures that $P(FP) < \delta$; when $\alpha = +\left(\sqrt{8\log 2/\delta} \cdot \log T \sqrt{\log t} \log 1/\delta\right)/\epsilon$ then $P(FN) < \delta$.*

PROOF. The final error bound follows by applying Theorem 3.6 [1], and the fact that the scale of the Laplace mechanism is the same. Then according to Corollary 2.9 [1], the sum of our random variables is at most $(\sqrt{\log t} \cdot \lambda \cdot \log 1/\delta)/\epsilon$: $\alpha = O(1/\epsilon \cdot \log T \cdot \sqrt{\log t} \cdot \log 1/\delta)$, where the constant is $\sqrt{8\log 2/\delta}$. □

4 PRIVATE STREAM COUNTING MECHANISM FOR EVENT DETECTION USING SVT

Algorithm 1 reports estimated count at each point of time, and as a result consumes unnecessary privacy budget. In the case of event detection, the only time that an estimated count needs to be considered but not reported is when it meets a certain threshold. To improve Algorithm 1, we use sparse vector technique (SVT) [8] as described in Algorithm 2. For the case of event monitoring and detection, we only need to report the event once, and then the privacy budget gets refreshed as the system analyst needs to take an action. Therefore, the cut-off point parameter c is 1, and no need to keep track of it. As a result, the Laplace parameter for the next step to add noise to c will be $2\Delta/\epsilon_2$ instead of $2c\Delta/\epsilon_2$. In addition, it is suggested to apply Δ/ϵ_2 instead of $2\Delta/\epsilon_2$, when the original query function is monotonic. In terms of budget allocation for each separate privacy budget, we could do $1 : 1$ or as suggested by authors in [8] $1 : (c)^{2/3}$ for monotonic case, which will be again $1 : 1$ in our case as c is 1.

Algorithm 2: Private Stream Counting Mechanism for Event Detection using SVT

Input : Data Streams S; Query of interest $q(A, (0, T))$; Threshold θ; Privacy budget ϵ; Error Bound α

Output : Detected time for an event of interest

```
// Initialize the privacy budget
```
1 $\epsilon_1 = \epsilon_2 = \epsilon/2$
2 $\hat{\theta} = \theta + Lap(1/\epsilon_1)$
3 **for** $t \in (0, T)$ **do**
4   **if** $q(t) + \alpha + Lap(1/\epsilon_2) \geq \hat{\theta}$ **then**
5        $t_0 \longleftarrow t$ // t_0 as the time that event is detected using noisy counts
6   Report event A at time t_0

THEOREM 4.1. *Algorithm 2 achieves ϵ-differential privacy [8].*

THEOREM 4.2 (UTILITY). *For confidence level $\delta \in (0,1)$, Algorithm 2 is (α, δ)-accurate, w.h.p. at least $1 - \delta$, when $\alpha = -\left(\frac{8(\log t + \log(2/\delta))}{\epsilon}\right)$ then Algorithm 2 guarantees that $P(FP) < \delta$; when $\alpha = +\left(\frac{8(\log t + \log(2/\delta))}{\epsilon}\right)$ then $P(FN) < \delta$.*

PROOF. Proof follows by similar ways in Theorem 3.24 [6]. □

Comparing the error bounds for Algorithms 1 and 2, Algorithm 2 provides a smaller bound and as a result a better utility.

FP or FN with time delay τ. Ideally we wish to have a bound on both FP and FN at the same time, therefore we consider the utility metric with the notion of time delay.

THEOREM 4.3 (UTILITY WITH TIME DELAY τ). *For confidence level $\delta \in (0,1)$ and $t \in [T]$, a DP algorithm is (α, δ)-accurate w.h.p. at least $1-\delta$, such that we can guarantee that $P(FP) < \delta$ when an event is detected at time $t_0 < t^* - \tau$, given the true event occurs at t^*, and $P(FN) < \delta$ when an event is detected at time $t_0 > t^* + \tau$. If we define a function of time for data stream rate, $\Gamma(\tau)$ for the increases in $q(t)$, i.e., in τ time, $q(t)$ increases by $\Gamma(\tau)$ w.h.p. δ. Then we will have the following changes in our decision rules:*
(a) if $\hat{q}(t) - (\alpha - \Gamma(\tau)) \geq \theta \Rightarrow P(FP$ with delay$) < 2\delta$
(b) if $\hat{q}(t) + (\alpha - \Gamma(\tau)) \geq \theta \Rightarrow P(FN$ with delay$) < 2\delta$
If we set α to be equal to $\Gamma(\tau)$ then both rules become the same and we will have a bound on both FP and FN at the same time.

REMARK 1. *If we are to run a set of event queries, in the worst case, it will follow the sequential mechanism and provides $d\epsilon$-DP, d as the number of queries. However, our algorithm could perform better if event queries are in the form of vector presentation. Then, for the BM we can assume that if we have a set of queries represented as a workload matrix w, then the sensitivity of a workload, which is represented as a matrix of 0 and 1's, is the maximum column norm, each column is one entry for every possible value for the domain. A column with the largest number of 1's determines the largest sensitivity, then our algorithm achieves $max(\Delta_i)\epsilon$-DP. Therefore, we only need to scale the BM to the max sensitivity of the workload.*

5 CONCLUDING REMARKS

In this work, we propose private stream counting algorithms for event detection using binary mechanism and sparse vector technique. This is an initiation for differentially private event detection aiming for minimizing false positive rate and/or false negative rate, depending on which metrics users decide to apply.

Acknowledgements: This work was supported by the National Science Foundation under grants 1253327, 1408982; and by DARPA and SPAWAR under contract N66001-15-C-4067.

REFERENCES
[1] T.-H. Hubert Chan, Elaine Shi, and Dawn Song. 2010. Private and Continual Release of Statistics. In *ICALP*. 405–417.
[2] Yan Chen, Ashwin Machanavajjhala, Michael Hay, and Gerome Miklau. 2017. PeGaSus: Data-Adaptive Differentially Private Stream Processing. In *CCS*. 1375–1388.
[3] Cynthia Dwork. 2010. Differential Privacy in New Settings. In *SODA*. 174–183.
[4] Cynthia Dwork, Frank McSherry, Kobbi Nissim, and Adam Smith. 2006. Calibrating Noise to Sensitivity in Private Data Analysis. In *TCC'06*. 265–284.
[5] Cynthia Dwork, Moni Naor, Toniann Pitassi, and Guy N. Rothblum. 2010. Differential privacy under continual observation. In *STOC*. 715–724.
[6] Cynthia Dwork and Aaron Roth. 2014. The Algorithmic Foundations of Differential Privacy. *Foundations and Trends in Theoretical Computer Science* 9, 3-4 (2014), 211–407.
[7] Priya Keshav and Jason R. Baron. 2018. INSIGHT: The Internet of Things and Information Governance: What You Need To Know To Manage Data Streaming From Everywhere. https://www.bna.com/insight-internet-things-n73014476349/
[8] Min Lyu, Dong Su, and Ninghui Li. 2017. Understanding the Sparse Vector Technique for Differential Privacy. *PVLDB* 10, 6 (2017), 637–648.
[9] Do Le Quoc, Martin Beck, Pramod Bhatotia, Ruichuan Chen, Christof Fetzer, and Thorsten Strufe. 2017. PrivApprox: Privacy-Preserving Stream Analytics. In *USENIX*. 659–672.

Custom-made Anonymization by Data Analysis Program Provided by Recipient

Wakana Maeda
FUJITSU LABORATORIES LTD.
maeda.wakana@fujitsu.com

Yuji Yamaoka
FUJITSU LABORATORIES LTD.
yamaoka.yuji@fujitsu.com

ABSTRACT

Anonymization is a method used in privacy-preserving data publishing. Previous studies show that anonymization based on the request of a data recipient, the priority of attributes, helps to maintain data utility. However, it is difficult for recipients to generate requests because they can not know which attribute important without data analysis. To address this issue, we propose a framework for performing custom-made anonymization by data analysis program provided by recipient. This enables the recipient to generate a request after creating a program and performing an indirect analysis of an original dataset by the program. Moreover, we describe an inference attack model for this framework and propose a secure method for restraining such an attack.

ACM Reference Format:
Wakana Maeda and Yuji Yamaoka. 2019. Custom-made Anonymization by Data Analysis Program Provided by Recipient. In *Ninth ACM Conference on Data and Application Security and Privacy (CODASPY '19), March 25–27, 2019, Richardson, TX, USA*. ACM, New York, NY, USA, 3 pages. https://doi.org/10.1145/3292006.3302380

1 INTRODUCTION

To the effective utilization of personal data with preserving data privacy, research in privacy-preserving data publishing (PPDP) has progressed [1] . A PPDP model consists of a data provider (DP) and a data recipient (DR), where the DP anonymizes personal data and provides it, which the DR receives and uses. Anonymization serves to hide the identity of record owners when sensitive data must be retained for data analysis and the DR wants to minimize any reduction in data utility.

Previous studies show that anonymization based on the request of a DR, the priority of attributes, helps to maintain data utility [4, 6]. Tian [4] proposed a framework using a request that is utility specification that indicates a priority of attributes to be maintained. Xiong [6] used a request with attributes prioritized by weighting.

However, it is often difficult for the DR to determine the priority of attributes in advance. For example, in machine learning, although it is necessary to select features to improve prediction accuracy, the DR can not know which feature is important without data analysis. There is also a remote execution method [5], where the DR analyzes an original dataset indirectly. It is used in the provision of government statistical data. In this method, the DR submits an aggregation

program and obtains an aggregated result that is generated based on microdata. However, in the process of aggregation, much of the information contained in the microdata is lost. Therefore, if the DR wants to perform a detailed analysis or make accurate predictions, microdata has higher flexibility and availability [2].

In this paper, we propose a framework for performing custom-made anonymization by data analysis program provided by recipient. This framework enables the DR to generate a request for anonymization after indirect analysis of an original dataset using a program created by the DR. Then, the DP generates an anonymized dataset based on the request and provides it for the DR.

In addition, we describe an inference attack model for this framework and propose a secure method for restraining such an attack. Via a request, an adversary can embed information and use it to infer data about a specified individual in an anonymized dataset. As countermeasures, we use two approaches. First, we use datasets constructed from multiple samples, so that the DP will obtain different requests by a submitted program. Several of them might be the same. The DP then selects the request that has the maximum frequency. Because the datasets to be analyzed are prevented from including specific individuals, we can make it difficult for a malicious request to be selected and thereby reduce the probability of a successful attack. Second, to prevent a malicious program from outputting different requests for each dataset, we set a maximum number of request types that any one program can output. If the target request of an adversary is the most frequent, it will be used in the anonymization step. We prevent this from occurring.

In the rest of this paper, we define our terms (section 2) and propose our framework (section 3). Then, we define an inference attack model (section 4) and propose a method for restraining such an attack (section 5). Finally, we summarize the above (section 6).

2 PRELIMINARIES
2.1 Data Definition

An original dataset D is personal data, and D' is an anonymized dataset from D. These datasets consist of records from each individual in j attributes: QI and SA. The **QI** (quasi-Identifier) is a set of attributes, which has the potential to reveal the private information

	(a)				(b)			
	Quasi-identifier			Sensitive	Quasi-identifier			Sensitive
name	gender	age	occupation	Income	gender	age	occupation	Income
Alice	male	31	teacher	4M	male	31	teacher	4M
Bob	male	31	teacher	4M	male	31	teacher	4M
Carol	female	33	teacher	4M	female	-	teacher	4M
Dave	female	34	teacher	4M	female	-	teacher	4M

Table 1: (a): Original dataset, (b): 2-anonymized dataset by cell supression.

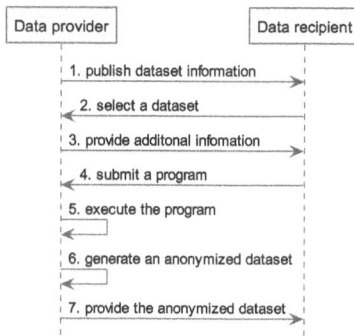

Figure 1: Sequence diagram of our framework

of individuals by joining with other QI attributes. The **SA** (sensitive attribute) is an attribute that is unknown to an adversary. Hence, the adversary wants to identify the SA value of the target individual. The **equivalence class** e_x denotes a group of records having the same QI values. The size of an equivalence class means the number of records that belong to e_x, let it be $|e_x|$.

For example, in (a) of the Table 1, a combination of QI {male, 31, teacher} comprises one equivalence class, and {Female, 33, teacher } is another. {Female, 34, teacher } is a third.

The DP transforms dataset D into anonymized dataset D'. Let A_j be an attribute of QI or SA, and let $a_{S,i}$ be an SA value. Moreover, let Y_{e_x} be the set of SA values in e_x.

2.2 Anonymization

To preserve privacy, We use k-anonymization [3]. It causes a dataset to satisfy k-anonymity, where the size of every equivalence class is greater or equal to pre-defined k value.

For simplification, we use cell suppression [7] to anonymize a dataset, whereby cells are deleted so that the dataset will satisfy k-anonymity. For example, in Table 1, (b) shows the result for achieving a 2-anonymized dataset from (a) using cell suppression. Two cells specific to "age" are suppressed in the records of Carol and Dave, but not in other records.

2.3 Transformation Request

In this paper, we use the format of utility specification [4] for the transformation request (TR). [1] The DR generates a TR to set a priority of attributes, with the intent of maintaining the original values as much as possible. The TR is a list of priority-ordered attributes; for example, $TR = [A_1, ..., A_j]$.

3 CUSTOM-MADE ANONYMIZATION FRAMEWORK

We propose a framework for performing custom-made anonymization by data analysis program provided by recipient. Figure 1 shows a sequence diagram of our framework. [2] The program processes input data, which the DR freely wrote for data preprocessing and analysis. It then generates and outputs TR based on the result.

Step 1: The DP publishes dataset information, which includes an explanation of the attributes. Step 2: The DR selects a dataset, and

[1] For simplicity, in this paper, we allow the specifying of attribute only.
[2] The sequence of procedures can be performed only once for each original dataset.

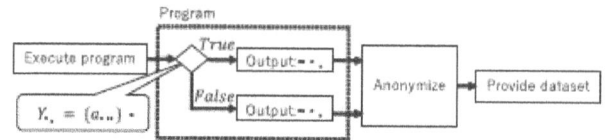

Figure 2: Process of embedding target information into an anonymized dataset by a submitted program. If $Y_{e_x} = \{a_{S,t}\}$ then TR_1 is outputted, otherwise TR_2. On this basis, the DP generates an anonymized dataset, in which the target information is embedded.

informs the DP that a dataset is required. Step 3: The DP provides additional information, e.g., test data for program creation. Step 4: The DR creates and submits a program that contains the desired function, analyzes the original dataset, and generates TR. Step 5: The DP executes the program, using the original dataset as input data, and the program generates TR as output data. Step 6: The DP generates an anonymized dataset based on the TR. Step 7: The DP provides the anonymized dataset for the DR.

4 INFERENCE ATTACK MODEL

In this section, we describe an attack model for our framework. We assume that the DP has D that includes the specific individual X. Let e_x be the equivalence class of X, and its size $|e_x| = 1$. Moreover, let $a_{S,t}$ be the SA value of X, and let $Y_{e_x} = a_{S,t}$.

The adversary's intent is to determine whether D includes the record of X and, if so, identify the SA value of X. The adversary can submit a program that generates TR and then receives the anonymized dataset D' based on the TR.

By creating a program that generates a malicious TR, the adversary can embed target information in the anonymized dataset D', like steganography. Figure 2 shows the process of using a program to embed target information into D'. The adversary submits a program that generates a malicious TR based on the presence of X and its SA value. For example, the program outputs $TR_1 = [A1, A2, ...]$ if $Y_{e_x} = \{a_{S,1}\}$, $TR_2 = [A2, A1, ...]$ otherwise. The DP executes the program and generates D' based on the outputted TR, then provides this for the adversary.

The adversary can then infer the SA value of X by judging the condition based on the received D'. For example, when cell suppression enables one to know the priority order of attributes based on the number of remaining cells of every attribute, from which the TR can be inferred. Concretely, if the attribute with the maximum number of remaining cells is A_1, then TR_1 is outputted, otherwise TR_2, etc. TR_1 is outputted when $Y_{e_x} = \{a_{S,1}\}$, therefore, the adversary can infer that the SA value of X is $a_{S,1}$. In this way, the adversary can embed target information in the anonymized dataset and can succeed in this inference attack to obtain the SA value of a specific individual.

5 METHOD FOR RESTRAINING INFERENCE ATTACK

To restrain inference attacks, we propose a secure method that improves Step 5 in section 3. We define CTR as a candidate TR. Only one of the multiple $CTRs$ is selected as TR. Let CTR_{target} be the CTR that embeds target information on the specific individual X, such that $|e_x| = 1$ in an original dataset D. Moreover, let CTR_{others} be other $CTRs$ and $|CTR|$ be the frequency of CTR. This method uses the following two approaches to restrain inference attacks.

1: A submitted program is executed for multiple partial datasets sampled from an original dataset D, and the CTR with the maximum frequency is selected as TR. Using the original dataset includes the record of X, the program necessarily outputs CTR_{target}. However, using sampled datasets, CTR_{target} is not necessarily generated; they may not contain the record of X. In this way, it is possible to restrain the generation and selection of CTR_{target} and reduce the probability of a successful attack.

2: The number of CTR types is limited. An adversary might create a program that outputs many different $CTRs$ such that CTR_{target} will have the frequency. Therefore, we set a maximum allowable number of CTR types. Let this maximum number be m. If the number of CTR types is more than m, the process ends and an anonymized data is not generated. For example, suppose that five partial datasets are used. Then, let $|CTR_{target}| = 2$. If a different CTR is outputted for each of the remaining three partial datasets, the CTR with the maximum frequency is CTR_{target}. However, if $m = 3$, the process ends because the total number of CTR types combined with CTR_{target} is more than m. Thus, the adversary cannot receive anonymized data and cannot attack.

5.1 Algorithm

Algorithm 1 outlines the process used in our secure method. Let s be sampling rate and n be the frequency of sampling. Moreover, let G be a submitted program that outputs CTR_h and T be the number of CTR types.

Algorithm 1

Require: s: sampling rate, D: original dataset,
   G: submitted program, m: maximum number of CTR types
Ensure: $R[0]$: TR
1: **for** $i = 0$ to n **do**
2:   $P[i] \leftarrow Sampling(D, s)$
3:   $C[i] \leftarrow Execute(P[i], G)$
4:   $T \leftarrow Size(Set(C))$
5:   **if** $T < m$ **then**
6:     $R \leftarrow CountMax(C)$
7:     **if** $Size(R) == 1$ **then**
8:       **return** $R[0]$
9: **exit**

The "for" statement calls two functions, "Sampling" and "Execute." "Sampling" performs sampling with s from D and obtains a partial dataset, which is inserted into $P[i]$. "Execute" obtains CTR_h by executing G with $P[i]$ as input data, which is inserted into $C[i]$.

Next, this algorithm checks the number of CTR types and the number of $CTRs$ with the maximum frequency. T is obtained by using two functions, "Set" and "Size." "Set" converts a list into a set, and "Size" obtains the number of elements. Moreover, The first "if" statement checks that T is less than m. If the condition is satisfied, a list R of the most frequent $CTRs$ is obtained from C by "CountMax" that obtains a list of the most frequent elements. The final "if" statement checks whether the size of R is 1 or not. If the condition

is satisfied, the first element of the R is returned. If any one of these conditions is not satisfied, the process ends.

5.2 How to restrain inference attack

In this section, we demonstrate how this method restrains the inference attack. Let r_X be the record of a specific individual X. Moreover, Let $f(0 \leq f \leq n)$ be the number of partial datasets including r_X, and $N - f$ be the number of partial datasets not including r_X. For example, if only $P[1]$ and $P[2]$ include r_X, $f = 2$. Moreover, let CTR_{max} be the CTR that has the maximum frequency and is outputted from the partial datasets not including r_X.

In the attack model, the adversary submits a program that outputs CTR_{target} if the SA value set of equivalence class e_x is $Y_{e_x} = \{a_{S,1}\}$ in $P[i]$, otherwise $CTR_1, ..., CTR_h$ are randomly outputted. We consider the frequency of CTR_{max} in the following.

Case1: Where $f < |CTR_{max}| \leq N - f$, the CTR with the maximum frequency is CTR_{max}. Then, CTR_{target} is not outputted as TR. Therefore, the adversary cannot attack.

Case2: Where $|CTR_{max}| = f$, the CTR with the maximum frequency is two, CTR_{target} and CTR_{max}. Then, the process ends. Therefore, the adversary cannot attack.

Case3: Where $|CTR_{max}| < f$, the CTR with the maximum frequency is CTR_{target}. The minimum value of $T = t + 1$ when CTR_{target} is the CTR with the maximum frequency. Where q, t and u are integers, t can be obtained using Formula (1) below. When $m < T$, the process ends and the adversary cannot attack.

$$N - f = qt + u \qquad (1 \leq q < f, u < q, 1 \leq t) \tag{1}$$

6 CONCLUSION

In this paper, we proposed a framework for performing custom-made anonymization by data analysis program provided by recipient. This framework enables a recipient to generate a request for data anonymization after creating a program and performing an indirect analysis of an original dataset by the program. Moreover, we described an inference attack model for this framework and proposed a secure method for restraining such an attack. In future work, we will conduct an experiment to reveal how our secure method affects the generation of a request.

REFERENCES

[1] Benjamin C. M. Fung, Ke Wang, Rui Chen, and Philip S. Yu. 2010. Privacy-preserving Data Publishing: A Survey of Recent Developments. *Comput. Surveys* 42, 4, Article 14 (2010), 14:1–14:53 pages.
[2] Pierangela Samarati. 2001. Protecting respondents identities in microdata release. *IEEE transactions on Knowledge and Data Engineering* 13, 6 (2001), 1010–1027.
[3] Latanya Sweeney. 2002. k-anonymity: A model for protecting privacy. *International Journal of Uncertainty, Fuzziness and Knowledge-Based Systems* 10, 05 (2002), 557–570.
[4] Hongwei Tian and Weining Zhang. 2013. Privacy-Preserving Data Publishing Based on Utility Specification. In *Social Computing (SocialCom), 2013 International Conference on*. IEEE, 114–121.
[5] D Trewin, A Andersen, T Beridze, L Biggeri, I Fellegi, and T Toczynski. 2007. Managing statistical confidentiality and microdata access: Principles and guidelines of good practice. *Geneva, UNECE/CES* (2007).
[6] Li Xiong and Kumudhavalli Rangachari. 2008. Towards application-oriented data anonymization. In *First SIAM International Workshop on Practical Privacy-Preserving Data Mining, Atlanta, US*. 1–10.
[7] Yuji Yamaoka and Kouichi Itoh. 2017. k-presence-secrecy: Practical privacy model as extension of k-anonymity. *IEICE TRANSACTIONS on Information and Systems* 100, 4 (2017), 730–740.

ABACaaS: Attribute-Based Access Control as a Service

Augustee Meshram
IIT Kharagpur
West Bengal
augusteebenoxide360@iitkgp.ac.in

Saptarshi Das
IIT Kharagpur
West Bengal
saptarshidas13@iitkgp.ac.in

Shamik Sural
IIT Kharagpur
West Bengal
shamik@cse.iitkgp.ernet.in

Jaideep Vaidya
Rutgers University
New Jersey
jsvaidya@business.rutgers.edu

Vijayalakshmi Atluri
Rutgers University
New Jersey
atluri@rutgers.edu

ABSTRACT

In recent years, Attribute-Based Access Control (ABAC) has emerged as the desired access control model in scenarios involving sharing of resources across multiple domains. This necessitates organizations using traditional access control models to use ABAC. However, *ab initio* deployment of ABAC is both cost and time intensive. In this paper, we present ABACaaS - a cloud service that enables any organization to integrate ABAC into their own environment irrespective of the platform they operate in. We show both SaaS as well as PaaS instances of ABACaaS along with results on its performance.

CCS CONCEPTS

• **Security and privacy** → **Access control**; • **Networks** → *Cloud computing*.

KEYWORDS

Attribute-Based Access Control, Cloud service, Red Hat OpenShift

ACM Reference Format:
Augustee Meshram, Saptarshi Das, Shamik Sural, Jaideep Vaidya, and Vijayalakshmi Atluri. 2019. ABACaaS: Attribute-Based Access Control as a Service. In *Ninth ACM Conference on Data and Application Security and Privacy (CODASPY '19), March 25–27, 2019, Richardson, TX, USA*. ACM, New York, NY, USA, 3 pages. https://doi.org/10.1145/3292006.3302381

1 INTRODUCTION

Over the last few decades, various access control models have been designed to protect organizational resources from unauthorized accesses. While contemporary models like Role-Based Access Control (RBAC) [1] is competent in providing secure access to resources pertaining to a single organization, it has severe limitations in scenarios that require inter-organizational resource sharing. RBAC is based on the notion of a predefined set of roles and access decisions are based on the roles assigned to a given user and the operations that the role is authorized to perform. RBAC suffers from the problem of role-explosion, which occurs when there are numerous roles, leading to potential leakage of rights if the roles

are not properly assigned to users. Of late, ABAC [2] is emerging as the desired access control model due to a significant rise in the number of dynamic platforms like cloud and fog computing, IoT, e-commerce, mobile computing, etc., in which, sharing of resources across entities is quintessential.

However, *ab-initio* deployment of ABAC in an organization is both time and resource consuming [3]. In this context, we propose a service that is seamlessly supported in platform-based cloud applications or be used as a software service. The service enables an application developer to integrate ABAC into her application.

While numerous applications have been developed and deployed as cloud services during the last few years, only a few of them aim to provide access control as a service. Calero et al. [4] propose a model that supports multi-tenancy, role-based access control, and path based object hierarchies. Wu et al. [5] present a cloud service called Access Control as a Service (ACaaS), which supports multiple access control models as pluggable modules in cloud services. Additionally, they design and implement RBAC for Amazon Web Services using ACaaS. Although their service is capable of supporting several access control models including RBAC on various cloud platforms, it does not consider ABAC, as provided by ABACaaS. Jin [6] shows the implementation of ABAC for applications on cloud, but it does not provide ABAC as a service to various organizations.

2 PRELIMINARIES

In this section, we first discuss the various components of an ABAC system and present formal notations for representing them. Next, we briefly describe the features provided by the Red Hat OpenShift container platform on which our proposed service is built.

2.1 Components of ABAC

ABAC comprises a set of users ($\mathcal{U}$), a set of resources ($\mathcal{R}$), a set of environmental conditions ($\mathcal{E}$). It also has a set of user attributes ($\mathcal{UA}$) that a user of the system possesses. A user can have multiple attribute values for the same attribute. Similarly, $\mathcal{RA}$ and $\mathcal{EA}$ are the set of resource attributes and the set of environmental attributes, respectively. A function of the following form is defined: $\mathcal{FS} : \mathcal{U} \times \mathcal{UA} \rightarrow \{k | k \text{ is a user attribute value}\}$. It represents the value for each attribute for each user. Likewise, the functions $\mathcal{FR}$ and $\mathcal{FE}$ are defined for resource and environment attributes, respectively. $\mathcal{OP}$ is a set of operations that can be performed on the resources. Finally, a set of access control rules together form the organizational ABAC policy ($\mathcal{P}$). Each rule $p \in \mathcal{P}$ is represented as a 4-tuple $\langle UC, RC, EC, op \rangle$, where UC, RC and EC represent a

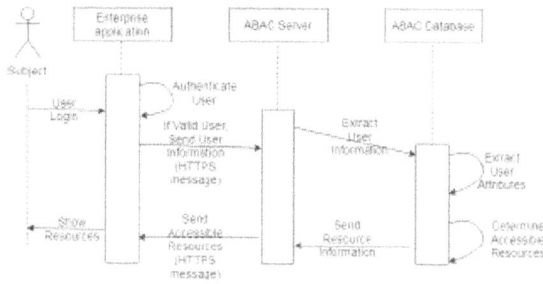

Figure 1: Service sequence flow for ABACaaS

set of user, resource and environment attribute key-value pairs, respectively, while *op* is an operation.

2.2 OpenShift Container Platform

OpenShift is a Platform as a Service (PaaS) [7] product from Red Hat that is used for container-based software deployment and management.It enables organizations to create, host and deploy applications. PaaS saves the developers from the complexities of handling the infrastructure side of the cloud, e.g., setting up, managing and maintaining the servers and the databases. The clients can use any platform such as PHP, ruby, python, etc., to create their applications in OpenShift. Permanent data storage is also provided.

2.3 Software as a Service (SaaS)

SaaS [7] is a software distribution model where a third-party service provider hosts its own application and makes it available to the clients over the Internet which can be accessed using a client interface like a web browser. The client need not manage the underlying cloud infrastructure like the network, servers, operating system, etc., which is handled by the SaaS service provider.

3 IMPLEMENTATION OF ABACaaS

In this section, we first discuss the exigency of ABACaaS followed by its functional details. Finally, we present an illustrative example of how ABACaaS is instantiated as PaaS and SaaS services.

3.1 Requirements of ABACaaS

Every organization attempting to migrate to ABAC can have its own individual needs and requirements which are very different from that of others. ABACaaS is designed to cater to such diverse needs of clients. Organizations can decide to choose all or a subset of features provided by ABACaaS. They can also adopt an incremental approach by initially deploying ABAC with limited functionality and then enriching it gradually over a period of time.

3.2 ABACaaS Functionality

First, ABACaaS involves the assignment of attributes to users and resources. The application security administrator ensures that the attributes are stored and maintained in the database provided by our service. ABACaaS inherently permits the administrators of different organizations to specify their own names for user attributes,

resource attributes, and their associated key-value pairs. The authorization rules that affect the access decisions are also flexibly defined. Then the security administrator registers the employees of the organization and the organizational resources into the service database. Next, the attributes which are associated with the users and the resources are specified. It is ensured that only the permitted attributes are assigned to users and resources. Then the key-value pairs are determined to define the values each attribute can have.

Once all the key-value pairs are specified, those associated with each user and resource are entered in the service. Finally, the authorization rules are specified. After the attributes, key-values pairs and the rules have been added, the service operates as illustrated in Figure 1. The steps involved in ABACaaS are as follows.

- An application user first logs into her system. Authentication is done locally.
- Once authenticated, the user-id of the person logging into the system is passed to ABACaaS.
- Attributes of the user are identified by mapping the user to her unique identity stored in ABACaaS.
- ABACaaS next determines the resources accessible by the user using the ABAC rules maintained in its database.
- The access decision made by ABACaaS is sent back to the client application. The user can only access those resources that are permitted to it by ABACaaS.

Secure transfer of information between the user application and ABACaaS is ensured by using HTTPS messages. The client application sends user information using HTTPS messages as JavaScript Object Notification (JSON) encoded data to ABACaaS. This data is received by ABACaaS and decoded to determine the permitted resources. Finally, the accessible resources are also sent back as JSON encoded data to the client application. The client application then decodes the data and depending on the nature of the application, the appropriate resources are made accessible to the user.

3.3 Illustrative Example

We now illustrate the steps required to integrate ABACaaS service into a client application.

3.3.1 ABACaaS as a PaaS service. To instantiate ABACaaS as a PaaS service, Red Hat OpenShift is used. For integrating the service, the OpenShift container platform is installed and a project (client application) is created that will use the ABACaaS service. Next, a database (MySQL) is added to the created project. The username and password can be chosen at user discretion. The created database is integrated into the project for use by the ABACaaS service.

Next, the ABACaaS service is downloaded from GitHub repository. Once the repository is added, it becomes part of the project and deployed on its own private IP address. Next, the ABACaaS service is connected to the database which can be done by configuring the OpenShift environmental variables. This allows the service to act as if it is embedded into the application. Now, ABACaaS becomes a part of the OpenShift container platform which can be used in the current as well as new projects in the client organization.

3.3.2 Implementation as a SaaS service. Consider that a client organization *X* wishes to use ABACaaS in its application *App1*. To use the service, *X* registers with ABACaaS and is provided a user-name,

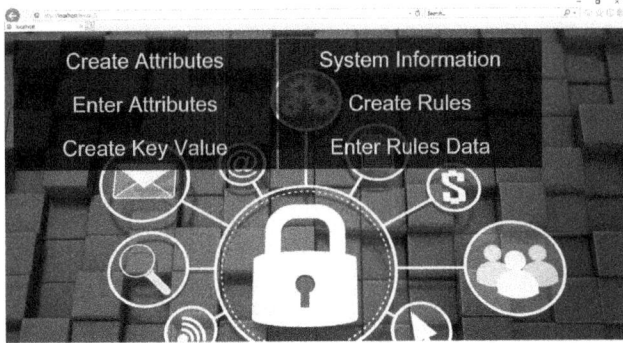

Figure 2: ABACaaS menu

Test_Report.pdf Final_Report1.docx Monthly_Evaluation Yearly_Evaluation

Figure 3: Accessible resources

which is subsequently used to uniquely identify the client. Once registered, the next task is to provide rules for access control, which is done by the security administrator of *App1*. The administrator gets a menu as shown in Figure 2 that lists the set of information to be provided for proper setting up of the rules. The administrator enters the users who will use the application and also the application resources that need to be protected. Next, the attributes of users and resources are specified. Finally, the ABAC rules are entered. Now, the ABAC instance maintained by ABACaaS as a SaaS service can be used by the application *App1*.

Let *Alice* be a user of *App1* deployed in organization *X*. For using *App1*, she enters her user-name and password, which are stored in the ABACaaS database maintained specifically for *App1* of *X*. Once authenticated, the user-name is sent to the ABAC service using HTTPS messages. If *Alice* is identified as a valid user and mapped to the database of the ABACaaS service, the attributes associated with *Alice* are determined and then, the rules are checked to obtain the resources accessible by *Alice*. The list of resources is sent back to *App1* as shown in Figure 3.

4 EXPERIMENTAL RESULTS

In the absence of any publicly available data set, the performance of ABACaaS was evaluated on a number of synthetically generated data sets comprising sets of users, resources, user to user attribute assignments and resource to resource attribute assignments. ABACaaS was implemented in PHP 5.6 on a 2.5 GHz Intel i7 machine having 16 GB of RAM. MySql 5.7.19 was used to create the database for ABACaaS and Apache Tomcat server 3.0.6 was used for the SaaS implementation. We present the results obtained using number of users ($|\mathcal{U}|$), number of resources ($|\mathcal{R}|$), number of rules ($|\mathcal{P}|$) and execution time ($\mathcal{T}$) (in msec). While evaluating the service, we consider the following scenarios: (i) variation in $|\mathcal{U}|$ and $|\mathcal{R}|$ when $|\mathcal{P}|$ is fixed (ii) variation in $|\mathcal{U}|$ and $|\mathcal{P}|$ when $|\mathcal{R}|$ is fixed.

Table 1 shows that if the number of rules is fixed, execution time increases marginally with the number of users and resources. It takes more time for execution if the number of users and resources

Table 1: Variation of $\mathcal{T}$ (in msec) with $|\mathcal{U}|$ and $|\mathcal{R}|$

$|\mathcal{R}|$ \ $|\mathcal{U}|$	100	200	500	800	1000
100	1.02	1.81	2.92	4.75	5.31
200	2.91	3.92	4.72	6.73	9.75
500	6.96	7.5	8.3	9.92	11.52
800	7.9	8.25	11.06	13.32	14.42
1000	10.22	16.1	16.87	17.16	17.37

Table 2: Variation of $\mathcal{T}$ (in msec) with $|\mathcal{P}|$ and $|\mathcal{U}|$

$|\mathcal{U}|$ \ $|\mathcal{P}|$	10	25	50	100
100	3.05	5.11	6.93	8.16
500	6.31	6.95	8.11	11.13
1000	7.03	8.31	10.81	13.61

is large, whereas, the execution time is comparatively less if one of the parameters, either the number of users or resources is small as compared to the other. This variation occurs as more users and resources result in more number of possible access requests which need to be resolved by ABACaaS.

Table 2 shows that the execution time increases very slowly with the number of rules and users. The number of resources is kept constant at 500. In the presence of more rules, each access request needs to be evaluated against all the rules, which increases the execution time. If the number of users is increased, the execution time increases further. Similar to Table 1, the increase in execution time of ABACaaS is due to an increase in the number of possible access requests with the number of users.

5 CONCLUSION AND FUTURE DIRECTIONS

In this paper, we presented a novel cloud service model for Attribute-Based Access Control referred as ABACaaS. It is all-inclusive and can be seamlessly integrated into any client application irrespective of its platform. We have also shown that ABACaaS can be used both as a PaaS and a SaaS service. It reduces the deployment time and cost of setting up an ABAC infrastructure in any organization, thereby making ABAC easily implementable. In the future, we plan to provide more fine-grained access control by introducing concepts like attribute value hierarchy and environment conditions.

REFERENCES

[1] R. Sandhu, E. J. Coyne, H. L. Feinstein, and C. E. Youman: Role-Based Access Control Models. IEEE Computer 29, 2, 38–47 (1996)
[2] V. C. Hu, D. Ferraiolo, R. Kuhn, A. Schnitzer, K. Sandlin, R. Miller, and K. Scarfon: Guide to Attribute Based Access Control (ABAC) Definition and Considerations. NIST Special Publication (2014)
[3] D. Servos, and S. L. Osborn: Current Research and Open Problems in Attribute-Based Access Control. ACM Comput. Surv., 65:1–65:45 (2017)
[4] J. M. Alcaraz Calero, N. Edwards, J. Kirschnick, L. Wilcock, and M. Wray: Toward a Multi-Tenancy Authorization System for Cloud Services. IEEE Security and Privacy, 48–55 (2010)
[5] R. Wu, X. Zhang, G-J. Ahn, H. Sharifi, and H. Xie: ACaaS: Access Control as a Service for IaaS Cloud. International Conference on Social Computing, 423–428 (2013)
[6] X. Jin: Attribute-Based Access Control Models and Implementation in cloud Infrastructure as a Service. Ph.D. Thesis, The University of Texas, (2014)
[7] NIST definition for SaaS, PaaS, IaaS, https://cloudinfosec.wordpress.com/2013/05/04/nist-definition-for-saas-paas-iaas/

Toward Efficient Spammers Gathering in Twitter Social Networks

Yihe Zhang
University of Louisiana at Lafayette,
Lafayette, LA, USA

Hao Zhang
Oracle Corp.,
Redwood Shores, CA, USA

Xu Yuan
University of Louisiana at Lafayette,
Lafayette, LA, USA

ABSTRACT

This paper introduces a novel system, named pseudo-honeypot, for efficient spammers gathering. Different from the manual setup in the honeypot, the pseudo-honeypot takes advantage of Twitter users' diversity and selects accounts with the attributes of having the higher potentials of attracting spammers, as the parasitic bodies. By harnessing a set of normal accounts possessing these attributes and monitoring their streaming posts and behavioral patterns, the pseudo-honeypot can gather the tweets that are far more likely of including spammer activities, while removing the risks of being recognized by smart spammers. It substantially advances the honeypot-based solutions in attribute availability, deployment flexibility, network scalability, and system portability. We present the system design and implementation of pseudo-honeypot (including node selection, monitoring, feature extraction, and learning-based classification) in Twitter networks. Through experiments, we demonstrate its effectiveness in term of spammer gathering.

CCS CONCEPTS

• **Information systems** → **Spam detection**.

KEYWORDS

Spammers gathering; Honeypot; Pseudo-honeypot

ACM Reference Format:
Yihe Zhang, Hao Zhang, and Xu Yuan. 2019. Toward Efficient Spammers Gathering in Twitter Social Networks. In *Ninth ACM Conference on Data and Application Security and Privacy (CODASPY '19), March 25–27, 2019, Richardson, TX, USA.* ACM, New York, NY, USA, 3 pages. https://doi.org/10.1145/3292006.3302382

1 INTRODUCTION

Spammers have been pervasively annoying normal users since the inception of online social networks. By creating fake accounts or comprising benign ones, spammers can initialize social relationships or send unsolicited requests/messages, and then spread harm to the social users. There has been some efforts [1, 7] on exploiting the effective mechanisms to capture spammers. However, most of existing solutions are time-consuming and low efficient as they filter spams (or spammers) from a large set of blindly collected network contents (or accounts), but can only detect a small portion of spammers. The honeypot is proposed as an promising solution

by manually creating accounts as lures for spammers [3, 4, 6, 8]. However, such category of solutions has the essential drawbacks on deployment flexibility, attribute variability, and network scalability, as it involves the considerable human overhead.

In this paper, we aim to propose a novel system, called pseudo-honeypot, for efficient spammer gathering. Instead of creating artificial accounts commonly used in honeypot-based solutions, we allow the pseudo-honeypot to take a normal user as the parasitic body and harness such a user to monitor spammer activities. Through this way, pseudo-honeypot can take advantage of users' diversity in Twitter social networks and utilize them as the key resources to attract spammers. By carefully identifying the attributes that are more likely of attracting spammers, we can select a set of accounts that possess such attributes to be served as the pseudo-honeypot nodes. Pseudo-honeypot can harness these users and monitor their streaming posts/behavioral patterns transparently. From this point of view, the pseudo-honeypot can perform the similar functions as the honeypot in terms of attracting and trapping spammers but has much richer diversity. The existing Twitter's API enables us to harness the selected pseudo-honeypot and monitor the associated accounts transparently, whereas Twitter API's privacy policy terms will be strictly followed by us. Subsequently, we extract the features that can reflect spammer's behaviors and leverage the machine learning classifier to identify each collected tweet as spam or non-spam intelligently and automatically. To validate the performance of our system, we create a pseudo-honeypot network with 1000 nodes and deploy them into Twitter social networks for spammer capturing. During a 500-hour experiment, we collect $1,227,708$ tweets posted by $476,345$ unique users which count as 1.3% of total active Twitter users, in which we capture a total of $371,981$ spams and $53,857$ spammers.

2 SYSTEM DESIGN OF PSEUDO-HONEYPOT

Our goal is to develop an efficient and effective mechanism to collect Twitter social network contents that are far more likely of including spammers' activities so as to detect and remove them. As user diversity provides abundant resources, we propose a novel framework called pseudo-honeypot by utilizing such diversity to attract and trap spammers. Our solution screens a set of normal users that possess attributes of meeting spammer's tastes. By constructing on the top of these users that may suffer spammy behaviors, pseudo-honeypots can collect the tweets that have a higher probability of including spammers' activities. Notably, to comply with the Twitter privacy policy, the pseudo-honeypot is not allowed to affect the activities of normal users or make any change to their posts or behavioral patterns. By harnessing these accounts, pseudo-honeypot can monitor public streaming posts and behavioral patterns crossing these accounts in a real-time manner while keep invisible to

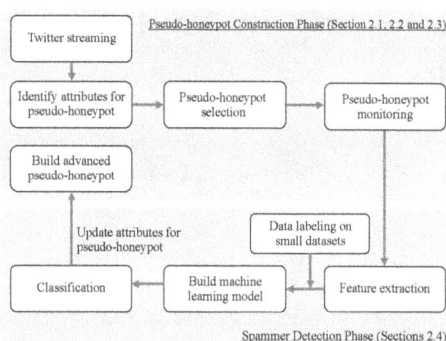

Figure 1: The system design of the pseudo-honeypot.

them. After obtaining the streaming data, we design a spam detector to extract features reflecting spammer's behaviors and leverage machine learning-based approaches to classify spams/spammers. Figure 1 shows the system design of Pseudo-honeypot.

2.1 Attribute-based Pseudo-honeypot Selection

The key challenge of building pseudo-honeypot network is to select the effective attributes that have the high potential of attracting spammers. Here, we take the reverse engineering strategy. That is, we first select a large pool of prevalent attributes that have been widely studied in previous research and use them to select accounts serving as pseudo-honeypot nodes while creating a sampling pseudo-honeypot system. After running it for a period of time, we examine all attributes and refine the top ones that have the highest probability of capturing spammers. Then, we utilize the refined attributes to advise our design of a highly effective pseudo-honeypot system. As a start point, we mainly concentrate on a set of prevalent hashtag-based and trending-based attributes [5, 8], i.e., *entertainment, business, tech, education, environment, social, trending-up topics, trending-down topics, popular tweets,* and *no-trend topics.*

2.2 Constructing Pseudo-honeypot

We use hashtag-based and trending-based attributes to select a set of accounts with each account possessing at least one attribute. The pseudo-honeypot takes these types of accounts as parasitic bodies to monitor their posted tweets and behavioral patterns, thus are more likely of capturing spammers. Note here, the Twitter APIs (e.g., Streaming API) that are available for developers enable the pseudo-honeypot to monitor user accounts activities (only public information) while keeping invisible to them so as to follow Twitter's privacy policy Through this way, we have constructed the pseudo-honeypot that can perform similar functions as the honeypot in terms of attracting spammers without manually creating user accounts. Obviously, such pseudo-honeypot has salient advantages in the attribute availability, deployment flexibility, network scalability, while has no chance to be recognized by spammers when comparing to the traditional honeypot.

2.3 Pseudo-honeypot Monitoring

With the constructed pseudo-honeypot network, we can start to monitor tweets and users' behavioral patterns. In this stage, we collect only the direct interactive behaviors instead of all streaming

passing through the associated accounts to reduce the processing workload of the pseudo-honeypot network. In particular, we collect the "mentions" behaviors from the selected accounts as the "mention" activities are proactive behaviors that spammers commonly use to attract user's attention and interact with victims.

2.4 Pseduo-Honeypot Spam Detector

It is unrealistic to perform manual checking among all collected tweets. Here, we employ machine learning-based classifier for pseudo-honeypot spam detector so as to automatically classify the collected data as spams or not. Our detector includes three components. First, we extract a rich set of features from account profiles, tweet contents, and users behaviors that can reflect tweets' characteristics. Next, we manually label a ground truth dataset for training to cover a majority types of spammers. In the end, we employ the machine learning algorithms to classify the collected tweets and users.

3 SYSTEM EVALUATION

In this section, we implement the pseudo-honeypot system and use experimental results to demonstrate the advances of our system in gathering spammers.

3.1 System Implementation

Our system is implemented by selecting a set of accounts that include the attributes as discussed in Section 2.1. For hashtag-based attributes, we select the top 10 hashtags (from [2]) in each attribute and identify 10 accounts associated with each hashtag to serve as the pseudo-honeypot nodes. For example, in *entertainment*, we collect the top 10 popular hashtags and then select 10 user accounts for each hashtag. Hence, there is a total of 100 pseudo-honeypot nodes in *entertainment* attribute. Similarly, we also select 100 pseudo-honeypot nodes for *business, tech, education, environment,* and *social,* respectively. In total, we have 600 pseudo-honeypot nodes in the hashtag-based category. For the trending-based category, we select the top 10 topics that are satisfying each attribute from [2] and then identify 10 user accounts for each topic to serve as the pseudo-honeypot nodes. For the *non-trending* topic, we randomly select 100 pseudo-honeypot nodes that are not posting tweets with the topics in [2]. Thus, there is a total of 400 pseudo-honeypot nodes under the trending-based category. Overall, we have created a pseudo-honeypot network with 1000 nodes with the construction time less than 1 *min.* Such low time cost outperforms the traditional honeypot-based solution, which requires considerable human efforts to create and configure honeypots.

Our experiment is conducted with a total of 500 hours to evaluate the performance of the constructed pseudo-honeypot system. Within this period, we collected a total of $1,227,708$ mention behavioral tweets which associated with a total amount of $476,345$ unique accounts.

3.2 Ground Truth Labeling

We create a 100-node pseudo-honeypot network by randomly selecting attributes from hashtag-based and trending-based categories, and then run 300 hours to collect tweets to serve as the ground truth training dataset. We manually label a total of $1,290$

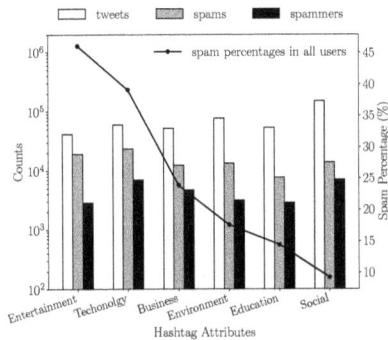

Figure 2: The number of collected tweets, classified spams and spammers as well as the ratio of spammers over total users in each hashtag-based attribute.

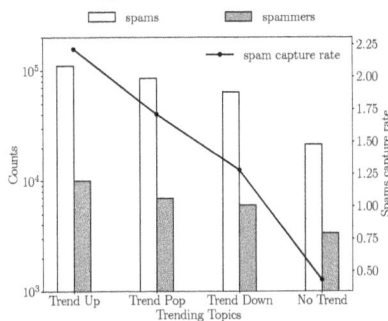

Figure 3: The number of collected tweets, classified spams and spammers as well as the ratio of spams over tweets in each trending-based attribute.

spams and 5, 517 non-spams by checking suspended accounts from Twitter and clustering the tweets to serve as the ground truth data.

3.3   Effectiveness of Pseudo-honeypot

We take *Random Forest* as our machine learning classifier to equip our pseudo-honeypot detector and perform classification in the all 500-hour collected tweets. There is a total of 371, 981 tweets that are identified as spams and all remains are classified as non-spams. The 371, 981 spams are associated with 53, 857 unique accounts, so we have classified a total of 53, 857 spammers. This result significantly outperforms the prominent honeypot solutions from Stringhini *et.al.* [6] , Lee *et.al.* [4], Yang *et.al.* [8], and Yang *et.al.* [8]'s advanced system, which gathered spammers of 15,857 in 11 months, 36,000 in 7 months, 1,159 in 5 months, and 17,336 in 10 days, respectively.

Figure 2 shows the total number of collected tweets, classified spams, and spammers under various hashtag-based attributes. This figure shows that *social, technology,* and *business* are top three attributes in our pseudo-honeypot system capturing most spammers with the values of 7, 030, 6, 913 and 4, 692, respectively. In this figure, the solid line represents the spam's ratio (i.e., the garnered spams over the total tweets) associated with each attribute. We can see *entertainment* has the highest spam ratio of 46.07% while *social, technology,* and *business* are 9.21%, 39.10%, and 23.86%, respectively.

Figure 3 shows the total number of classified spams and spammers in various trending-based attributes. This figure shows the number of spammers captured by our pseudo-honeypots with the attributes of *trending up, popular, trending down,* and *no trending*

topic are 10, 013, 6, 951, 6, 029, and 3, 362, respectively. The spam capture rate (the number of spams captured per pseudo-honeypot per hour) of these four trending attributes are 2.21, 1.71, 1.28, and 0.43, respectively. Thus, the tweets with *trending up* and *popular* attributes have more potential of attracting spam messages. The spam ratios of *trending up, popular,* and *trending down* are all located between 12.4% to 13.5% which is much higher than *no trending topic* 6.79%.

3.4   Advanced Pseudo-honeypot System

We use results from Figures 2 and 3 as guidelines to design the advanced pseudo-honeypot system by taking into account the top five most effective (highest spam capture rate) attributes in term of gathering spams, i.e., *trending up, popular, trending down, technology* and *entertainment*. These five attributes are used to select pseudo-honeypot nodes, where 10 users accounts are selected of possessing each attribute. With such a 50-node pseudo-honeypot network, we run a total of 50 hours and gather 2, 301 spammers. The efficiency of spammers gathering is 0.92 spammers per honeypot per hour. However, in Stringhini *et.al.* [6] , Lee *et.al.* [4], Yang *et.al.* [8], Yang *et.al.* [8]'s advanced system, the efficiencies are only 0.0067, 0.12, 0.0034, and 0.087, respectively. This demonstrates the advantages of pseudo-honeypot system over the state-of-the-art honeypot-based solutions.

4   CONCLUSION

In this paper, we proposed pseudo-honeypot as a novel solution for spammers gathering in Twitter social networks. By taking advantage of user diversity, the proposed pseudo-honeypot system can substantially improve the deployment flexibility and enrich the feature availability while removing the risk of being recognized by spammers, when comparing the prominent honeypot-based solutions. We presented the system design of pseudo-honeypot and implement it in the Twitter social network for spammer gathering. Through conducting the experimental analysis on gathered data, we validated the effectiveness of the pseudo-honeypot system in spammers gathering.

REFERENCES

[1] Weiling Chen, Chai Kiat Yeo, Chiew Tong Lau, and Bu Sung Lee. 2017. A study on real-time low-quality content detection on Twitter from the users' perspective. *PLOS ONE* 12, 8 (08 2017), 1–22.
[2] LOGIKA Corporation. 2018. Hashtag analytics for your brand, business, product, service, event or blog. (2018). http://www.hashtags.org
[3] Kyumin Lee, James Caverlee, and Steve Webb. 2010. Uncovering Social Spammers: Social Honeypots + Machine Learning. In *Proceedings of the ACM SIGIR Conference on Research and Development in Information Retrieval.* 435–442.
[4] Kyumin Lee, Brian David Eoff, and James Caverlee. 2011. Seven months with the devils: A long-term study of content polluters on twitter. In *Proceedings of the ICWSM.* 185–192.
[5] Surendra Sedhai and Aixin Sun. 2015. Hspam14: A collection of 14 million tweets for hashtag-oriented spam research. In *Proceedings of the ACM SIGIR Conference on Research and Development in Information Retrieval.* 223–232.
[6] Gianluca Stringhini, Christopher Kruegel, and Giovanni Vigna. 2010. Detecting spammers on social networks. In *Proceedings of the Annual Computer Security Applications Conference (ACSAC).*
[7] Kurt Thomas, Chris Grier, Dawn Song, and Vern Paxson. 2011. Suspended accounts in retrospect: An analysis of twitter spam. In *Proceedings of the ACM SIGCOMM conference on Internet Measurement.* 243–258.
[8] Chao Yang, Jialong Zhang, and Guofei Gu. 2014. A taste of tweets: Reverse engineering Twitter spammers. In *Proceedings of the Annual Computer Security Applications Conference (ACSAC).* 86–95.

Large Scale PoC Experiment with 57,000 people to Accumulate Patterns for Lifestyle Authentication

Ryosuke Kobayashi
Mitsubishi Electric Information Systems Corporation
4-13-23 Shibaura, Minato-ku, Tokyo, 108-0023
Japan
kobayashi.ryousuke@sict.i.u-tokyo.ac.jp

Nobuyuki Saji
INFOCORPUS Inc.
3-5-1 Shimomeguro, Meguro-ku, Tokyo, 153-0064
Japan
saji.nobuyuki@yamagula.ic.i.u-tokyo.ac.jp

Nobuo Shigeta
The University of Tokyo
7-3-1 Hongo, Bunkyo-ku, Tokyo, 113-8656
Japan
shigeta@yamagula.ic.i.u-tokyo.ac.jp

Rie Shigetomi Yamaguchi
The University of Tokyo
7-3-1 Hongo, Bunkyo-ku, Tokyo, 113-8656
Japan
yamaguchi.rie@i.u-tokyo.ac.jp

ABSTRACT

The spread of ICT has made it possible for people to use various online services via the Internet. User authentication technique is important for using online services in order to confirm that the user is legitimate. There are already some authentication methods, but several problems have been pointed out in them. We focused attention on lifestyle authentication as a new individual authentication method, that utilizes human behavior information. Then, we conducted a large scale PoC experiment in order to collect human behavior information, and we succeeded in gathering data of about 57,000 people. By analyzing the collected data, we found that human behavior is patterned. In this paper, we introduce the large scale PoC experiment and the analysis result of human behavior.

KEYWORDS

Lifestyle Authentication; Human Behavior; IoT; Smartphone

ACM Reference Format:
Ryosuke Kobayashi, Nobuyuki Saji, Nobuo Shigeta, and Rie Shigetomi Yamaguchi. 2019. Large Scale PoC Experiment with 57,000 people to Accumulate Patterns for Lifestyle Authentication. In *Ninth ACM Conference on Data and Application Security and Privacy (CODASPY '19), March 25–27, 2019, Richardson, TX, USA.* ACM, New York, NY, USA, 3 pages. https://doi.org/10.1145/3292006.3302383

1 INTRODUCTION

In recent years, ICT (Information and Communication Technology) has great influence on our lives. People can access various useful services through the Internet such as EC (Electronic Commerce) and SNS (Social Networking Service). One factor of this change lies wide acceptance of smartphones. The penetration rate of smartphones in many countries exceeds 60%, and it is increasing every year [7]. People can access online services easily by using their smartphones.

The popularization of online services has made user authentication techniques important. Service providers have to confirm whether the user of the service is a legitimate person or not. If the user is not legitimate and malicious, the genuine user and the service providers may be damaged. However, the service providers cannot directly confirm the user because he/she is on the network destination. Therefore, they verify the user with user authentication techniques.

Passwords or fingerprint are often used as authentication factors. These information include users' characteristics, so useful for user authentication. What kind of these authentication factors to enter is determined for each services by the service providers, not the users. However, some users cannot enter certain authentication information determined by the service providers. For example, some users who have impaired eyesight may not be able to enter their passwords. They cannot use the services because they are not verified to be legitimate. Online services are inconvenient for them, and as the number of the services increase in the future, they feel increasingly inconvenient. The point is that it makes it more convenient if the type of authentication factor is determined by the user. Therefore, it is important to develop user authentication methods utilizing new authentication factors.

We propose *Lifestyle Authentication* using human behavior information as a new user authentication method. Recently, it has become the IoT (Internet of Things) era when various things are connected to the Internet and a variety of data are automatically collected via the Internet. The data includes lifelogs which are the life behavioral information of a user recorded on an electronic medium. Lifestyle authentication utilizes the lifelogs. Users do not need to input authentication information because the lifelogs are automatically collected, and the number of authentication factors will increase because of the diversity. Thus, the lifestyle authentication is expected to be a convenient method for users.

We conducted a large scale PoC experiment to gather large amount of behavior information because they are necessary in order to promote research on lifestyle authentication. The experiment is called MITHRA Project and we succeeded in gathering data of about 57,000 people. The collected data includes location information, Wi-Fi information, application usage, and so on. By analyzing the data, we found that they have users' characteristics.

2 LIFESTYLE AUTHENTICATION

In this section, we explain the overview of lifestyle authentication and some existing research on user authentication utilizing lifelogs.

2.1 Overview

Lifestyle authentication is a new user authentication method utilizing human's lifestyle and its attribute. Lifestyle means humans ordinary behavior in their life. The lifestyle habit is considered to have repetitive property each day. Lifestyle authentication utilize the user characteristics obtained from the habituation of the lifestyle property.

Human behavior information can be easily acquired from IoT sensors around a user. Most of people have their smartphones and some sensors are installed in the devices. Users simply have normal life with their smartphones, and their behavior information are collected unconsciously and automatically. The data collected in the way is applied to lifestyle authentication.

2.2 Related Work

There have been some studies on personal authentication methods utilizing lifestyle patterns. Tang et al. [6] and Kobayashi et al. [3] proposed to utilize information that can be captured by smartphone sensors. Tang et al. used location information captured by GPS and Kobayashi et al. used Wi-Fi information captured by Wi-Fi sensors. Susuki et al. [5] used wearable device sensors instead of smartphone for data collection. They proposed an authentication method utilizing activity information. Authentication methods using content posted on SNS, rather than information obtained by sensors, have also been investigated. Sultana et al. [4] argued that social interactions possess unique behavioral patterns of individuals. They analyzed online social context given by 241 Twitter users and concluded that social behavioral biometric features have properties such as uniqueness, stability, and recognition accuracy for a set of frequent and non-frequent online social networking users. Fridman et al. [1] conducted an authentication experiment using multiple factors. They combined four biometric behavioral modalities: text entered via soft keyboard, application usage, websites visited, and physical location of the device.

3 MITHRA PROJECT

The Social ICT Research Center (SICT) at the University of Tokyo conducted a large scale PoC (Proof of Concept) experiment for data collection from January 11th to April 26th in 2017. The project is named Multi-factor Identification/auTHentication ReseArch (MITHRA) project. The experimental participants were recruited through the Internet, etc., and the total number of the participants reached 57,046. All participants agreed to provide their data before participating in the MITHRA project and were able to start to participate at a time of their choosing during the experimental period. Additionally, they were able to decline the experiment at any time.

The MITHRA project was reviewed by the Ethics Review Committee of the Graduate School of Information Science and Technology for approximately half a year and was considered to be exempt. We asked participants to reveal only their email addresses as personally identifiable information and did not ask for account names or home addresses. We collected the email addresses to provide a means for participants to opt out. In addition to information such as location and application usage, all participants provided informed consent to participate in the project. We stored all information in an encrypted format. Moreover, when using the information, personally identifiable information was separated and stored in a key locker.

3.1 Data Collection Method

MITHRA project collected data in four different ways. These collection methods are described in this section.

First is *MITHRA application* for smartphones. It is a data logger application and was created for this experiment. The application runs in background and gather information every five minutes which includes location, Wi-Fi, IP address, os version, and the smartphone's model name. 16,027 participants installed the MITHRA application.

Second is *Shufoo!* which is a flyer application for smartphones released by TOPPAN PRINTING CO., LTD. Shufoo! users could participants in this project by agreeing to provide their application usage history. The number of Shufoo! participants was 33,338.

Third is *MangaOne* which is a comic application for smartphones that was released by Shogakukan Inc. MangaONE users could participate in this project by agreeing to provide their application usage history. The number of MangaONE participants was 7,584.

Last is *Activity Meters*. In this way, experiment participants were recruited directly rather than through the Internet because the participants had to receive an activity meter. 97 participants wore the activity meters for the experiment period.

4 ANALYSIS RESULT

We describe some examples of analysis results of behavior information in this section.

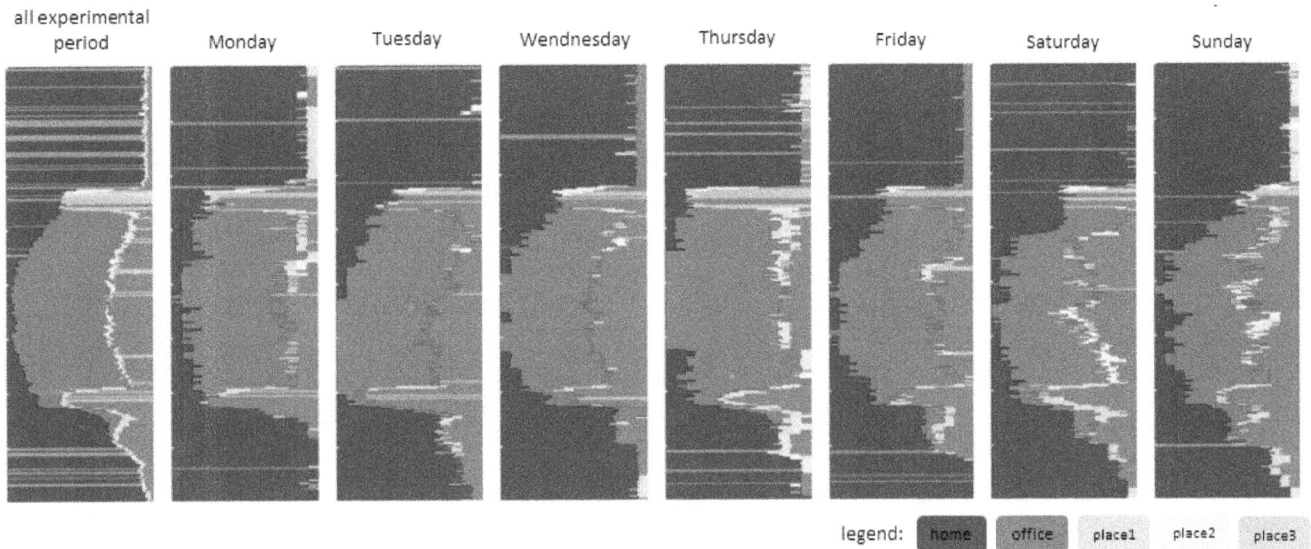

Figure 1: Location Information of One User for Each Day of the Week

4.1 Location Analysis

Figure 1 shows the location information of one user for each day of the week. We set five location area as *home, office, place1, place2, place3* in order of the staying time during the experiment period. Note that *home* and *office* were guessed from the analysis results and were not inquired to the user. The vertical axis of the figure represents from 0 o'clock to 24 o'clock of one day and the horizontal axis represents of staying time for each area. We found from the figure that the user stayed the same area at the same time regardless of the day of the week. In other words, the location information represents the habit of the user.

4.2 Application for Wi-Fi Authentication

We applied the Wi-Fi information gathered in the MITHRA project to the existing authentication method [2]. The data applied were those of 100 users randomly selected from the experiment subjects who participated it over 60 days. The evaluation items are TAR (True Acceptance Rate) and FAR (False Acceptance Rate). Table 1 shows the maximum, average, and minimum value of the results of 100 persons.

Table 1: Max, Mean, and Min of TAR and FAR

	Max	Mean	Min
TAR	1.000	0.932	0.033
FAR	0.002	0.000	0.000

As a result of experiments, we were able to obtain high authentication accuracy. In other words, the Wi-Fi information represents the habits of the users.

5 CONCLUSION

In this paper, we discussed the necessity of new authentication methods utilizing new factors, and focused on lifestyle authentication. To promote research on lifestyle authentication, we conducted a large scale PoC experiment and succeeded in collecting behavior information of about 57,000 people. By analyzing this data, we showed some examples that human habitability appears in behavior information.

ACKNOWLEDGMENTS

We would like to thank Mitsubishi UFJ NICOS Co., Ltd., TOPPAN PRINTING CO., LTD. and Shogakukan Inc. for a grant that made it possible to complete this work.

REFERENCES

[1] Lex Fridman, Steven Weber, Rachel Greenstadt, and Moshe Kam. 2017. Active authentication on mobile devices via stylometry, application usage, web browsing, and GPS location. *IEEE Systems Journal* 11, 2 (2017), 513–521.

[2] Ryosuke Kobayashi and Rie Shigetomi Yamaguchi. 2015. A Behavior Authentication Method Using Wi-Fi BSSIDs around Smartphone Carried by a User. In *Computing and Networking (CANDAR), 2015 Third International Symposium on*. IEEE, 463–469.

[3] Ryosuke Kobayashi and Rie Shigetomi Yamaguchi. 2016. One hour term authentication for Wi-Fi information captured by smartphone sensors. In *Information Theory and Its Applications (ISITA), 2016 International Symposium on*. IEEE, 330–334.

[4] Madeena Sultana, Padma Polash Paul, and Marina L Gavrilova. 2017. User recognition from social behavior in computer-mediated social context. *IEEE Transactions on Human-Machine Systems* 47, 3 (2017), 356–367.

[5] Hiroya Susuki and Rie Shigetomi Yamaguchi. 2015. Cost-Effective Modeling for Authentication and Its Application to Activity Tracker. In *International Workshop on Information Security Applications*. Springer, 373–385.

[6] Yujin Tang, Nakazato Hidenori, and Yoshiyori Urano. 2010. User authentication on smart phones using a data mining method. In *Information Society (i-Society), 2010 International Conference on*. IEEE, 173–178.

[7] Zenith. 2018. Smartphone penetration to reach 66% in 2018. https://www.zenithmedia.com/smartphone-penetration-reach-66-2018/.

Scaling Cryptographic Techniques by Exploiting Data Sensitivity at a Public Cloud*

Sharad Mehrotra,[1] Shantanu Sharma,[1] Jeffrey D. Ullman[2]

[1] University of California, Irvine, USA. [2] Stanford University, USA.

ABSTRACT

Despite extensive research on cryptography, secure and efficient query processing over outsourced data remains an open challenge. This poster continues along the emerging trend in secure data processing that recognizes that the entire dataset may not be sensitive, and hence, non-sensitivity of data can be exploited to overcome some of the limitations of existing encryption-based approaches. In particular, this poster outlines a new secure keyword search approach, called *query keyword binning* (QB) that allows non-sensitive parts of the data to be outsourced in clear-text while guaranteeing that no information is leaked by joint processing of non-sensitive data (in clear-text) and sensitive data (in encrypted form). QB improves the performance of and strengthens the security of the underlying cryptographic technique by preventing size, frequency-count, and workload-skew attacks.

CCS CONCEPTS

• **Security and privacy → Database and storage security.**

KEYWORDS

Cryptographic techniques; scalability.

ACM Reference Format:

Sharad Mehrotra, Shantanu Sharma, Jeffrey D. Ullman. 2019. Scaling Cryptographic Techniques by Exploiting Data Sensitivity at a Public Cloud. In *Ninth ACM Conference on Data and Application Security and Privacy (CODASPY '19), March 25–27, 2019, Richardson, TX, USA.* ACM, NY, NY. 3 pages. DOI: https://doi.org/10.1145/3292006.3302384

1 INTRODUCTION

The numerous benefits of public clouds (*e.g.*, no cost of purchasing, installing, running, maintaining data management systems) impose significant security and privacy concerns related to sensitive data storage (*e.g.*, sensitive client information, credit card, social security numbers, and medical records) or the query execution. Such concerns are not a new revelation – indeed, they were identified as

*The approach sketched in this poster may be found in details in its ICDE 2019 conference version [16]. This material is based on research sponsored by DARPA under agreement number FA8750-16-2-0021. The U.S. Government is authorized to reproduce and distribute reprints for Governmental purposes notwithstanding any copyright notation thereon. The views and conclusions contained herein are those of the authors and should not be interpreted as necessarily representing the official policies or endorsements, either expressed or implied, of DARPA or the U.S. Government. This work is partially supported by NSF grants 1527536 and 1545071.

Techniques	Time	Preventing attacks		
		Size	Workload-Skew	Access-patterns
Deterministic encryption	$1.43x$			
Non-deterministic encryption [18]	$2.1x$			
DSSE [14]	$3281x$			✓
SGX [5]	$6724x$			✓
Full-retrieval	$11135x$	✓	✓	✓
Homomorphic Encryption with ORAM	$> 11135x$			✓

Table 1: Comparing different cryptographic techniques in terms of time (for selection queries over TPC-H data) and attacks. x is the time to search a predicate in cleartext. ✓ indicates a technique is not vulnerable to a given attack.

a key impediment for organizations adopting the database-as-as-service model in early work on data outsourcing [13]. Since then, security/confidentiality challenge has been extensively studied in both the cryptography and database literature, which has resulted in many techniques to achieve *data privacy, query privacy,* and *inference prevention*. Existing work on secure data/query outsourcing may loosely be classified into the following three categories:

(1) **Encryption based techniques.** *E.g.*, order-preserving encryption [1], deterministic encryption, homomorphic encryption [10], bucketization [13], searchable encryption [22].

(2) **Secret-sharing [20] based techniques.** *E.g.*, distributed point function [11], function secret-sharing [4], accumulating-automata [7, 8], and others [9].

(3) **Trusted hardware-based techniques.** They are either based on a secure coprocessor (*e.g.*, [2]) or Intel SGX [5], which allows decrypting data in a secure area and perform some computations (*e.g.*, Opaque [24]).

Existing solutions suffer from several limitations. First, cryptographic approaches that prevent leakage, *e.g.*, fully homomorphic encryption coupled with ORAM, simply do not scale to large data sets and complex queries for them to be of practical value. Most of the above-mentioned techniques are not developed to deal with a large amount of data and the corresponding overheads of such techniques can be very high (see Table 1 comparing the time taken for TPC-H selection queries under different cryptographic solutions; note that none of the above-mentioned techniques are completely secure against each attack mentioned in the table, except the full retrieval of the database from the public cloud to the trusted private side). Second, systems such as CryptDB [19] have tried to take a more practical approach by allowing users to explore the tradeoffs between the system functionality and the security it offers. Unfortunately, precisely characterizing the security offered by such systems given the underlying cryptographic approaches have turned out to be extremely difficult. For instance, [15, 17] show that when order-preserving and deterministic encryption techniques are used together, on a dataset in which the entropy of the values is not high enough, an attacker might be able to construct the entire plaintext by doing a frequency analysis of the encrypted data. Third,

	EId	FirstName	LastName	SSN	Office#	Department
t_1	E101	Adam	Smith	111	1	Defense
t_2	E259	John	Williams	222	2	Design
t_3	E199	Eve	Smith	333	2	Design
t_4	E259	John	Williams	222	6	Defense
t_5	E152	Clark	Cook	444	1	Defense
t_6	E254	David	Watts	555	4	Design
t_7	E159	Lisa	Ross	666	2	Defense
t_8	E152	Clark	Cook	444	3	Design

Figure 1: A relation: *Employee.*

mechanisms based on secret-sharing [20] are potentially more scalable; however, splitting data amongst multiple non-colluding cloud operators incurs significant communication overheads and can only support a limited set of selection and aggregation queries efficiently. Finally, SGX-based solutions also leak information during a query execution due to different attacks on SGX (*e.g.,* cache-line, branch shadowing, and page-fault attacks [12, 23]) and are significantly slower when overcoming these attacks using ORAM-based computations or emerging architectures such as T-SGX [21] or Sanctum [6].

While the race to develop cryptographic solutions that (*i*) are efficient, (*ii*) support complex SQL queries, (*iii*) offer provable security from the application's perspective is ongoing, this poster outlines a different (but complementary) approach to secure data processing by partitioning a computation over the public cloud based on the data classification into sensitive and non-sensitive data. We focus on an approach for situations when only part of the data is sensitive, while the remainder (that may consist of the majority) is non-sensitive. In particular, we consider a **partitioned computation model** that exploits such a classification of data into sensitive/non-sensitive subsets to develop efficient data processing solutions with **provable security guarantees**. Partitioned computing potentially provides significant benefits by (*i*) avoiding (expensive) cryptographic operations on non-sensitive data, and, (*ii*) allowing query processing on non-sensitive data to exploit indices.

2 PARTITIONED COMPUTATIONS

Let R be a relation that is partitioned into two sub-relations, $R_e \supseteq R_s$ and $R_p \subseteq R_{ns}$, such that $R = R_e \cup R_p$. The relation R_e contains all the sensitive tuples (denoted by R_s) of the relation R and will be stored in encrypted form in the cloud. The relation R_p refer to the sub-relation of R that will be stored in plaintext on the cloud. Naturally, R_p does not contain any sensitive tuples. For the remainder of the poster, we will assume that $R_e = R_s$ and $R_p = R_{ns}$. A partition computation strategy splits the execution of Q into two independent sub-queries: Q_s: a query to be executed on $E(R_e)$ and Q_{ns}: a query to be executed on R_{ns}. The final results are computed (using a query Q_{merge}) by appropriately merging the results of the two sub-queries at the trusted database (DB) owner side (or in the cloud, if a trusted component, *e.g.,* Intel SGX, is available for such a merge operation). In particular, the query Q on a relation R is partitioned, as follows: $Q(R) = Q_{merge}\Big(Q_s(R_s), Q_{ns}(R_{ns})\Big)$.

Let us illustrate partitioned computations through an example.

Example: Consider an *Employee* relation, see Figure 1. In this relation, the attribute *SSN* is sensitive, and furthermore, all tuples of employees for the *Department* = "Defense" are sensitive. In such a case, the *Employee* relation may be stored as the following three relations: (*i*) *Employee1* with attributes *EId* and *SSN* (see Figure 2a); (*ii*) *Employee2* with attributes *EId, FirstName, LastName, Office#,* and *Department,* where *Department* = "Defense" (see Figure 2b); and

EId	SSN
E101	111
E259	222
E199	333
E152	444
E254	555
E159	666

(a) A sensitive relation: *Employee1.*

	EId	FirstName	LastName	Office	Dept
t_1	E101	Adam	Smith	1	Defense
t_4	E259	John	Williams	6	Defense
t_5	E152	Clark	Cook	1	Defense
t_7	E159	Lisa	Ross	2	Defense

(b) A sensitive relation: *Employee2.*

	EId	FirstName	LastName	Office	Dept
t_2	E259	John	Williams	2	Design
t_3	E199	Eve	Smith	2	Design
t_6	E254	David	Watts	4	Design
t_8	E152	Clark	Cook	3	Design

(c) A non-sensitive relation: *Employee3.*

Figure 2: Three relations obtained from *Employee* **relation.**

(*iii*) *Employee3* with attributes *EId, FirstName, LastName, Office#,* and *Department,* where *Department* <> "Defense" (see Figure 2c). Since the relations *Employee1* and *Employee2* (Figures 2a and 2b) contain only sensitive data, these two relations are encrypted before outsourcing, while *Employee3* (Figure 2c), which contains only non-sensitive data, is outsourced in clear-text. We assume that the sensitive data is strongly encrypted such that the property of *ciphertext indistinguishability* (*i.e.,* an adversary cannot distinguish pairs of ciphertexts) is achieved. Thus, the two occurrences of E152 have two different ciphertexts.

Consider a query Q: SELECT FirstName, LastName, Office#, Department from Employee where FirstName = ''John''. In partitioned computation, the query Q is partitioned into two sub-queries: Q_s that executes on Employee2, and Q_{ns} that executes on Employee3. Q_s will retrieve the tuple t_4 while Q_{ns} will retrieve the tuple t_2. Q_{merge} in this example is simply a union operator. Note that the execution of the query Q will also retrieve the same tuples.

Inference Attack in Partitioned Computations. Partitioned computations, if performed naively, could lead to inferences about sensitive data from non-sensitive data. To see this, consider following three queries on the *Employee2* and *Employee3* relations: (*i*) retrieve tuples of the employee Eid = E259, (*ii*) retrieve tuples of the employee Eid = E101, and (*iii*) retrieve tuples of the employee Eid = E199. We consider an *honest-but-curious* adversarial cloud that returns the correct answers to the queries but wishes to know information about the encrypted sensitive tables, *Employee1* and *Employee2*. Table 2 shows what does the adversary learn after executing the above three queries assuming that the tuple retrieving cryptographic approaches are not hiding access-patterns. During the execution, the adversary gains complete knowledge of non-sensitive tuples returned, and furthermore, knowledge about which encrypted tuples are returned as a result of Q_s ($E(t_i)$ in the table refers to the encrypted tuple t_i).

Partitioned Data Security. In order to prevent such above-mentioned inference attack, we need a new security definition. Informally, partitioned

Query value	Returned tuples/Adversarial view	
	Employee2	Employee3
E259	$E(t_4)$	t_2
E101	$E(t_1)$	null
E199	null	t_3

Table 2: Queries and returned tuples.

data security requires us to ensure that: (*i*) The posterior probability that a sensitive record and a non-sensitive record are related (e.g., encode the same value) remains identical to the prior probability before query execution, and (*ii*) The posterior probability about the distribution (relative frequency) of sensitive values remains identical to the prior probability.

3 QUERY BINNING

Query binning (QB) is related to bucketization, which is studied in past [13]. While bucketization was carried over the data in [13], QB performs bucketization on queries. In general, one may ask more queries than original query while adding overhead but it prevents the above-mentioned inference attack. We provide QB under some assumptions and settings, given below.[1]

Problem Setup. We assume the following two entities in our model: (i) A database (DB) owner: who splits each relation R in the database having attributes R_s and R_{ns} containing all sensitive and non-sensitive tuples, respectively. (ii) A public cloud: The DB owner outsources the relation R_{ns} to a public cloud. The tuples in R_s are encrypted using any existing mechanism before outsourcing to the same public cloud. However, in the approach, we use non-deterministic encryption, i.e., the cipher representation of two occurrences of an identical value has different representations.

DB Owner Assumptions. In our setting, the DB owner stores some (limited) metadata such as searchable values and their frequency counts, which are used for appropriate query formulation. The DB owner is assumed to have sufficient storage for such metadata, and also computational capabilities to perform encryption and decryption. The size of metadata is significantly smaller than the size of the original data.

Assumptions for QB. We develop QB initially under the assumption that queries are only on a single attribute, say A. The QB approach takes as inputs: (i) the set of data values (of the attribute A) that are sensitive along with their counts, and (ii) the set of data values (of the attribute A) that are non-sensitive, along with their counts. The QB returns a partition of attribute values that form the query bins for both the sensitive as well as for the non-sensitive parts of the query.

The Approach. We develop an efficient approach to execute selection queries securely (preventing the information leakage as shown above) by appropriately partitioning the query at a public cloud, where sensitive data is cryptographically secure while non-sensitive data stays in cleartext. For answering a selection query, naturally, we use any existing cryptographic technique on sensitive data and a simple search on the cleartext non-sensitive data.

Informally, QB distributes attribute values in a matrix, where rows are sensitive bins, and columns are non-sensitive bins. For example, suppose there are 16 values, say $0, 1, \ldots, 15$, and assume all the values have sensitive and associated non-sensitive tuples. Now, the DB owner arranges 16 values in a 4×4 matrix, as follows:

In this example, we have four sensitive bins: SB_0 {11,2,5,14}, SB_1 {10,3,8,7}, SB_2 {0,15,6,4}, SB_3 {13,1,12,9}, and four non-sensitive bins: NSB_0 {11,10,0,13}, NSB_1 {2,3,15,1}, NSB_2 {5,8,6,12}, NSB_3 {14,7,4,9}. When a query arrives for a value, say 1, the DB owner searches for the tuples containing values 2,3,15,1 (viz. NSB_1) on the non-sensitive data and values in SB_3 (viz., 13,1,12,9) on the sensitive data using the cryptographic mechanism integrated into QB. While the adversary learns that the query corresponds to one of the four values in NSB_1, since query values in SB_3 are encrypted, the adversary does not learn

	NSB_0	NSB_1	NSB_2	NSB_3
SB_0	11	2	5	14
SB_1	10	3	8	7
SB_2	0	15	6	4
SB_3	13	1	12	9

any sensitive value or a non-sensitive value that is identical to a clear-text sensitive value.

Based on QB, for answering the above-mentioned three queries, given in §2, QB creates two sets or bins on sensitive parts: sensitive bin 1, denoted by SB_1, contains {E101, E259}, sensitive bin 2, denoted by SB_2, contains {E152, E159}, and two sets/bins on non-sensitive parts: non-sensitive bin 1, denoted by NSB_1, contains {E259, E254}, non-sensitive bin 2, denoted by NSB_2, contains {E199, E152}. Table 3 shows that when answering a query using QB, the adversary cannot learn which employee works only in defense, design, or in both.

Evaluation. Table 4 shows the time taken when using QB with SGX-based Opaque and MPC-based Jana at different levels of sensitivity. Without using QB for answering a simple selection query, Opaque [24] took 89 seconds on a dataset of size 700MB (TPC-H LineItem table having 6M tuples) and Jana [3] took 1051 seconds on a dataset of size 116MB (1M tuples), while the time to execute the same query on cleartext data of size 700MB took only 0.0002 seconds.

Query value	Returned tuples/Adversarial view	
	Employee1	Employee2
E259	$E(t_4), E(t_1)$	t_2, t_6
E101	$E(t_4), E(t_1)$	t_3, t_8
E199	$E(t_4), E(t_1)$	t_3, t_8

Table 3: Queries and returned tuples when following QB.

Technique	1%	5%	20%	40%	60%
SGX-based Opaque [24]	11	15	26	42	59
MPC-based Jana [3]	22	80	270	505	749

Table 4: Time (in seconds) when mixing QB with Opaque and Jana at different levels of sensitivity.

REFERENCES

[1] Rakesh Agrawal et al. 2004. Order-Preserving Encryption for Numeric Data. In SIGMOD. 563–574.
[2] Arvind Arasu et al. 2013. Orthogonal Security with Cipherbase. In CIDR.
[3] David W. Archer et al. 2018. From Keys to Databases - Real-World Applications of Secure Multi-Party Computation. Comput. J. 61, 12 (2018), 1749–1771.
[4] Elette Boyle et al. 2015. Function Secret Sharing. In EUROCRYPT.
[5] Victor Costan et al. 2016. Intel SGX Explained. IACR Cryptology ePrint Archive (2016).
[6] Victor Costan et al. 2016. Sanctum: Minimal Hardware Extensions for Strong Software Isolation. In USENIX Security. 857–874.
[7] Shlomi Dolev et al. 2015. Accumulating Automata and Cascaded Equations Automata for Communicationless Information Theoretically Secure Multi-Party Computation: Extended Abstract. In SCC@ASIACCS. 21–29.
[8] Shlomi Dolev et al. 2016. Private and Secure Secret Shared MapReduce. In DBSec. 151–160.
[9] Fatih Emekçi et al. 2014. Dividing secrets to secure data outsourcing. Inf. Sci. 263 (2014), 198–210.
[10] Craig Gentry. 2009. A fully homomorphic encryption scheme. Ph.D. Dissertation.
[11] Niv Gilboa et al. 2014. Distributed Point Functions and Their Applications. In EUROCRYPT. 640–658.
[12] Johannes Götzfried et al. 2017. Cache Attacks on Intel SGX. In EUROSEC. 2:1–2:6.
[13] Hakan Hacigümüs et al. 2002. Providing Database as a Service. In SIGMOD. 29–38.
[14] Yuval Ishai et al. 2016. Private Large-Scale Databases with Distributed Searchable Symmetric Encryption. In RSA. 90–107.
[15] Georgios Kellaris et al. 2016. Generic Attacks on Secure Outsourced Databases. In CCS. 1329–1340.
[16] Sharad Mehrotra et al. 2019. Partitioned Data Security on Outsourced Sensitive and Non-sensitive Data. In ICDE. Also as a technical report at Department of Computer Science, UC, Irvine, http://isg.ics.uci.edu/pubs/tr/partitioned.pdf.
[17] Muhammad Naveed et al. 2015. Inference Attacks on Property-Preserving Encrypted Databases. In SIGSAC. 644–655. https://doi.org/10.1145/2810103.2813651
[18] Rishabh Poddar et al. 2016. Arx: A Strongly Encrypted Database System. IACR Cryptology ePrint Archive (2016). http://eprint.iacr.org/2016/591
[19] Raluca A. Popa et al. 2012. CryptDB: processing queries on an encrypted database. Commun. ACM 55, 9 (2012), 103–111. https://doi.org/10.1145/2330667.2330691
[20] Adi Shamir. 1979. How to Share a Secret. Commun. ACM 22 (1979), 612–613.
[21] Ming-Wei Shih et al. 2017. T-SGX: Eradicating Controlled-Channel Attacks Against Enclave Programs. In NDSS.
[22] Dawn Xiaodong Song et al. 2000. Practical Techniques for Searches on Encrypted Data. In IEEE SP. 44–55. https://doi.org/10.1109/SECPRI.2000.848445
[23] Wenhao Wang et al. 2017. Leaky Cauldron on the Dark Land: Understanding Memory Side-Channel Hazards in SGX. In CCS. 2421–2434.
[24] Wenting Zheng et al. 2017. Opaque: An Oblivious and Encrypted Distributed Analytics Platform. In NSDI. 283–298.

[1]These assumptions are made primarily for ease of the exposition and relaxed in [16].

Parameter Tuning and Confidence Limits of Malware Clustering

Houtan Faridi
Department of Computer Science
University of Houston, TX
hfaridi@uh.edu

Srivathsan Srinivasagopalan
Alienvault Inc
Austin, TX
ssrinivasagopalan@alienvault.com

Rakesh Verma
Department of Computer Science
University of Houston, TX
rverma@uh.edu

ABSTRACT

The growing number of new malware and the sophisticated obfuscation techniques used by malware authors are causing major problems in identifying, managing, and releasing anti-malware products to the consumers. Clustering malware variants based on their behavior has the potential to ease this problem of scale and conveniently lend itself to better, faster, and efficient prioritization of malware analysis. In this paper, we cluster real-world malware and expand on commonly used algorithms through fine grained testing. Results of top performing algorithms are discussed.

1 INTRODUCTION

Today, anti-virus vendors are being overwhelmed by the number of malware that have to be processed every day.[1] This makes it challenging for anti-virus vendors to detect zero-day attacks and release updates in a reasonable time-frame to prevent infection and propagation. To alleviate this problem, clustering of malware has been proposed, which could help in understanding the general behavior of the clusters and their members. Furthermore, from each cluster, the salient features can be identified and might help in signature generation. Behavior and arrival patterns of certain variants could be predicted by monitoring their prevalence and occurrence over several cycles.

1.1 Problem Statement

Given a set of files, each representing a malicious program's behavior, can we cluster those files in such a way that the resulting clusters represent variants of each kind of malware?

1.2 Contributions

We provide a detailed study of clustering malware based on behavioral characteristics. Multiple sets of HTTP features with different distance metrics are used on a real-world dataset. Our study incorporates some less often used techniques in this area: Affinity Propagation and Bootstrapping. We build upon the work of Faridi *et al.* [7] by performing bootstraps and granular parameter testing.

Table 1: Top V-Measure Confidence Interval for Bootstrap Runs

Algorithm	Upper	Mean	Lower
Hierarchical	0.925	0.917	0.910
Spectral	0.919	0.895	0.871
DBSCAN	0.853	0.840	0.829

Table 2: Top V-Measure Attained on Each Bootstrap Run

Algorithm	1st Run	2nd Run	3rd Run	Original Run
Hierarchical	0.914	0.913	0.922	0.921
Spectral	0.875	0.911	0.900	0.893
DBSCAN	0.845	0.841	0.846	0.829

Table 3: Samples Per Reference Cluster Statistics

Statistic	Samples
Mean	60.35
St-dev	119.03
Var	14168.90
Median	14.5
Mode	3
Max cluster size	772
Min cluster size	1

2 DATASET AND PREPROCESSING

The given input data is sufficiently preprocessed to ensure that the clustering algorithms are able to distinguish the files to arrive at a good set of clusters. The dataset and preprocessing steps are as follows.

2.1 Dataset

The dataset consisted of information extracted from 5,673 malicious samples from an industry partner. Each sample was run through Cuckoo sandbox [1] for three minutes to get its behavioral information. The output of Cuckoo sandbox is a JSON file that contains a wealth of information about the dynamic behaviors of a given sample.

We also use a set of ground-truth reference clusters for measuring cluster quality. These reference clusters consisted of groups of malware that triggered specific Suricata rules[2] to generate an alert. Malware which triggered the same Suricata signatures were grouped in the same clusters. This ground-truth consisted of 94 clusters of various sizes ranging from one to 772 malicious samples. The general statistics of the ground-truth can be seen in Table 3.

Previous works in malware clustering often employ VirusTotal's [2] majority voting to construct reference clusters. This method involves building reference clusters based on labels retrieved by a majority of anti-virus scanners on VirusTotal. Any samples that do not produce a clear majority in their VirusTotal labeling are discarded. This method can be problematic as clustering only malware which share common anti-virus signatures could lead to clustering samples that are inherently easy to distinguish [10]. Furthermore,

---

[1] Approximately 400,000 new malware are registered every day [3]

[2] Suricata is a free and open source network threat detection engine.

this method significantly reduces the number of usable samples as most anti-virus labels do not follow similar standards [4].

2.2 Feature Extraction

To produce a feature representation for each malicious sample, a set of HTTP features were extracted from the behavioral JSON files generated for each sample. These HTTP features included the host, path, user-agent, and entire URI of all HTTP requests sent and received by the malware, as well as the body and data of non-encrypted HTTP requests. This extracted HTTP request information was a set of long strings used to represent a malicious file's intent.

2.3 Similarity Construction

From these string representations of samples, a normalized TF-IDF matrix is generated.[3] Distance matrices are generated that compute pair-wise dissimilarity of vectors. The distance functions used include Cosine, Braycurtis [5], Minkowski, and Chebyshev (L_∞ metric). Another set of matrices were generated via the plain feature text using Jaccard distance [6], Normalized Compression distance [7], SSDeep Fuzzy Hashing [9], and several forms of Locality Sensitive Hashing [11].

3 CLUSTERING ALGORITHMS

We employed density based, hierarchical, prototype-based, and dimensionality reducing clustering methods through the use of DB-SCAN, Agglomerative hierarchical clustering, Affinity Propagation, and Spectral clustering . Furthermore, we used several distance metrics while running each clustering algorithm along with variations in hyper-parameter values. All results are evaluated against the ground-truth reference clusters using Homogeneity, Completeness, and V-Measure [12] verification metrics.

4 RESULTS AND DISCUSSION

The focus of our experiments was to achieve very good cluster quality. Essentially, the experiments were centered around the use of different clustering algorithms with a tunable set of distance metrics and behavioral features. All experiments were run on a server using Intel Xeon processors running at 2.20 GHz. The code was run in a parallelized mode (used all 8 cores) whenever possible.

4.1 Affinity Propagation

To further test the viability of Affinity Propagation, we performed multiple runs of this algorithm using a series of damping factors. Initially a range of values from 0.5 to 0.9 in increments of 0.1 were tested. The graph of the top performing distance metrics, shown in Figure 1, displayed a spike at a damping factor of 0.8 with a general increase towards 0.9. This prompted testing of damping values of 0.75, 0.85, and 0.95. Unexpectedly, values of 0.75 and 0.85 produced dramatic dips for some distance metrics including Normalized Compression distance which attained the best results with a V-Measure of 0.792. Jaccard distance also presented an interesting result with its best performance coming at damping factors of 0.5 and 0.95

---

[3]Before this matrix is produced, all features not found in at least 2 samples are dropped to reduce features which do not provide reliable information.

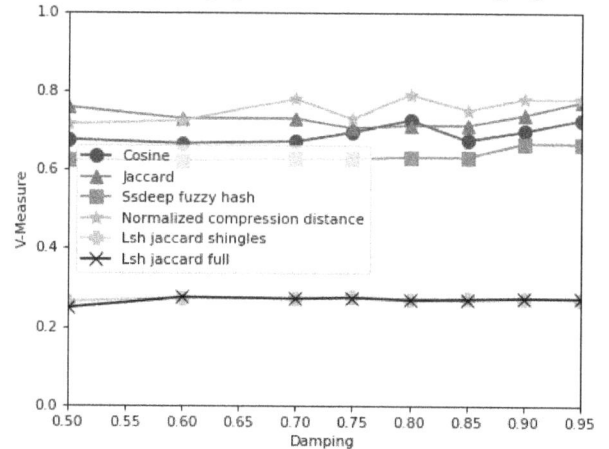

Figure 1: Affinity Propagation V-Measure vs Damping Factor

with decreased performance in between. Affinity Propagation saw a significant increase in performance compared to its original run [7]. The best performance results are presented in Table 4.

4.2 Bootstrap

Bootstrap sampling [8] was used to produce a confidence interval on the results of the top three algorithms from Faridi *et al.* [7]. To do this, each run produced a random sample set with replacement that was the same size as the original population. Three bootstrap runs produced along with the initial run from Faridi *et al.* were used to construct a 95% confidence interval on the results, shown in Table 1, with z-scores of 1.116. This table represents a rough model of the performance range each of the top scoring algorithms can expect to receive when given varying data. The max scores attained for each algorithm on every run is displayed in Table 2. Each run produced varied rankings among top scoring distance metrics and parameters, however the relative performance of the algorithms remained constant.

4.3 Hierarchical

Hierarchical clustering produced several of the highest scoring results [7] using different cutoff methods. However, the highest score produced using distance thresholds was attained at the max threshold of 0.75. We further tested the performance of hierarchical clustering across distance thresholds ranging from 0.7 up to 0.95 in increments of 0.05. Initially the best results were produced on a distance threshold of 0.95. This prompted further testing with distance thresholds of 0.96 - 0.99. Figure 2 shows maximum V-measure of 0.923 is achieved at a distance threshold of 0.96. This increased performance places hierarchical clustering via distance threshold as the best performing algorithm, beating the previous best algorithm [7]. The top resulting scores of Hierarchical clustering are shown in Table 5. While several distance metric exhibited improved performance at higher thresholds, other metrics saw a decrease in performance. Furthermore, several distance metrics including Cosine, Cityblock, Euclidean, Minkowski, and Chebyshev produce similar results and seemed to be relatively unaffected by changes in

Table 4: Top Affinity Propagation Results

Measure	Damping	Clusters	VM.	Homo.	Comp.	Time (sec)
NCD	0.8	507	**0.792**	**0.977**	**0.666**	2927.21
NCD	0.7	679	0.780	0.977	0.649	2927.21
NCD	0.9	510	0.780	0.977	0.649	2927.21
Jaccard	0.5	581	0.773	0.976	0.638	2964.81

Table 5: Top Hierarchical Clustering Results

Measure	Distance	Linkage	Clusters	VM.	Homo.	Comp.	Time (sec)
Braycurtis	0.96	Average	105	**0.923**	0.909	0.938	188.11
Braycurtis	0.95	Average	131	0.919	0.918	0.920	188.75
Braycurtis	0.9	Weighted	140	0.914	0.933	0.896	188.75
Cosine	0.95	Average	265	0.900	0.950	0.856	188.75

Figure 2: Hierarchical Clustering V-Measure vs Distance Threshold Across Average Linkage

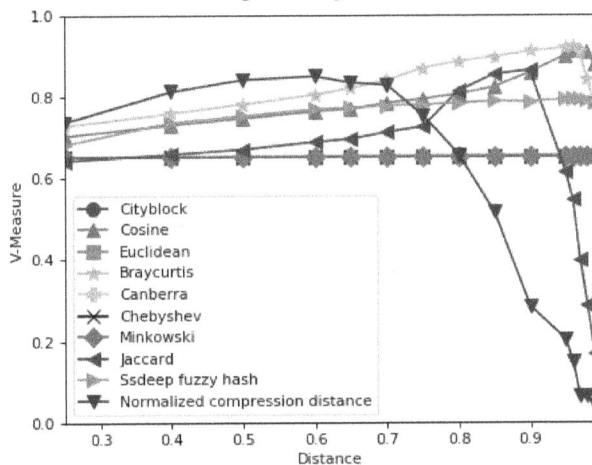

Figure 3: Hierarchical Clustering Max V-Measure on each Linkage

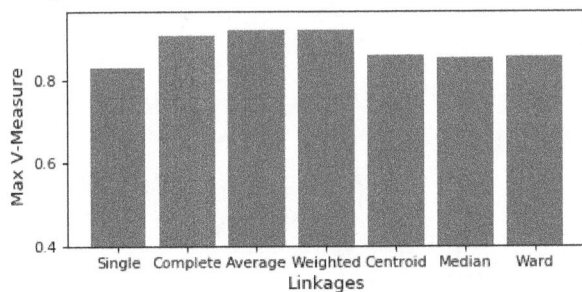

distance thresholds. The max V-Measure produced by each linkage method can also be seen in Figure 3.

5 CONCLUSION

Building upon previous implementations, we have shown that both Hierarchical clustering and Affinity Propagation can produce significantly better results in classifying malware through hyper parameter tuning. We have also produced a confidence interval for the top performing algorithms to simulate how performance might vary across different sample sets.

ACKNOWLEDGEMENTS

This research was supported in part by NSF grants CNS 1319212, DGE 1433817, and DUE 1356705. This material is also based upon work supported by, or in part by, the U. S. Army Research Laboratory and the U. S. Army Research Office under contract/grant number W911NF-16-1-0422.

REFERENCES

[1] 2018. Cuckoo Sandbox. Retrieved November 26, 2018 from cuckoosandbox.org
[2] 2019. VirusTotal. Retrieved January 11, 2019 from virustotal.com
[3] Ferri Abolhassan. 2017. *Cyber Security. Simply. Make It Happen.: Leveraging Digitization Through IT Security* (1st ed.). Springer Publishing Company, Incorporated.
[4] Michael Bailey, Jon Oberheide, Jon Andersen, Z Morley Mao, Farnam Jahanian, and Jose Nazario. 2007. Automated classification and analysis of internet malware. In *International Workshop on Recent Advances in Intrusion Detection*. Springer, 178–197.
[5] J Roger Bray and John T Curtis. 1957. An ordination of the upland forest communities of southern Wisconsin. *Ecological monographs* 27, 4 (1957), 325–349.
[6] Andrei Z Broder, Steven C Glassman, Mark S Manasse, and Geoffrey Zweig. 1997. Syntactic clustering of the web. *Computer Networks and ISDN Systems* 29, 8 (1997), 1157–1166.
[7] Houtan Faridi, Srivathsan Srinivasagopalan, and Rakesh Verma. 2018. Performance Evaluation of Features and Clustering Algorithms for Malware. *IEEE ICDMW (ADMiS)* (2018).
[8] Joseph Felsenstein. 1985. Confidence limits on phylogenies: an approach using the bootstrap. *Evolution* 39, 4 (1985), 783–791.
[9] Jesse Kornblum. 2006. Identifying almost identical files using context triggered piecewise hashing. *Digital investigation* 3 (2006), 91–97.
[10] Peng Li, Limin Liu, Debin Gao, and Michael K Reiter. 2010. On challenges in evaluating malware clustering. In *International Workshop on Recent Advances in Intrusion Detection*. Springer, 238–255.
[11] Anand Rajaraman and Jeffrey David Ullman. 2011. *Mining of Massive Datasets*. Cambridge U. Press, New York, NY.
[12] Andrew Rosenberg and Julia Hirschberg. 2007. V-Measure: A Conditional Entropy-Based External Cluster Evaluation Measure. In *Proceedings of the 2007 Joint Conference on Empirical Methods in Natural Language Processing and Computational Natural Language Learning(EMNLP-CoNLL)*. 410–420.

Specification and Analysis of ABAC Policies
via the Category-Based Metamodel

Maribel Fernández
King's College London, UK

Ian Mackie
École Polytechnique, France

Bhavani Thuraisingham
University of Texas at Dallas, USA

ABSTRACT

The Attribute-Based Access Control (ABAC) model is one of the most powerful access control models in use. It subsumes popular models, such as the Role-Based Access Control (RBAC) model, and can also enforce dynamic policies where authorisations depend on values of user, resource or environment attributes. However, in its general form, ABAC does not lend itself well to some operations, such as review queries, and ABAC policies are in general more difficult to specify and analyse than simpler RBAC policies. In this paper we propose a formal specification of ABAC in the category-based metamodel of access control, which adds structure to ABAC policies, making them easier to design and understand. We provide an axiomatic and an operational semantics for ABAC policies, and show how to use them to analyse policies and evaluate review queries.

CCS CONCEPTS

• **Security and privacy** → **Formal security models**; **Access control**; **Logic and verification**;

KEYWORDS

Access Control Policy, Attribute-Based Access Control, Category-Based Access Control, Policy Analysis

ACM Reference Format:
Maribel Fernández, Ian Mackie, and Bhavani Thuraisingham. 2019. Specification and Analysis of ABAC Policies, via the Category-Based Metamodel. In *Ninth ACM Conference on Data and Application Security and Privacy (CO-DASPY '19), March 25–27, 2019, Richardson, TX, USA.* ACM, New York, NY, USA, 12 pages. https://doi.org/10.1145/3292006.3300033

1 INTRODUCTION

This paper presents techniques to define and analyse Attribute-Based Access Control (ABAC) policies [39], with the aim of facilitating policy specification and verification tasks for security administrators.

Access control is a fundamental concept in computer security. Access control systems protect resources from unauthorised users by enforcing policies that restrict the operations that each user is allowed to perform. Different kinds of access control models are in use, from simple access control lists (used, e.g., in file systems),

to sophisticated models such as ABAC [26, 29, 39], where access to resources is controlled by evaluating rules against the attributes of the user and the object involved in the access request, as well as relevant attributes from the environment.

ABAC is one of the most powerful access control models in use. It subsumes the popular Role-Based Access Control (RBAC) model [23, 25, 34, 35], where users are authorised or denied access depending on their role. It also subsumes *dynamic* models, such as the time-location extension of RBAC [18], where users' rights may depend on the location and time of the access request, and RB-RBAC [2], where the role assignment is based on a set of rules. ABAC is able to implement dynamic models thanks to the use of user, object and environment attributes in the decision process to grant or deny access requests: access decisions can change if attribute values change, without administrator intervention. The downside, as mentioned in [26], is that ABAC systems are more costly to implement and maintain than simpler access control models such as RBAC (although there are extensions of ABAC, such as HGABAC [37], and enumerated versions of ABAC, such as LaBAC [15] and PM [24], which simplify these tasks). Since policy rules governing access to resources are based on attribute values, it may be difficult to know, for example, which users have access to a specific resource at a given time. This kind of capability is important within the context of "before the fact audits" [26]. For example, specifying the combination of attribute values that is needed for each pair action-resource, a crucial task in ABAC, has to be done each time a new resource is added.

To address these issues, in this paper we propose a formal model of ABAC using the *category-based metamodel of access control* (CBAC) [7], based on the ideas sketched in [21]. Formal specifications of access control models are essential to be able to analyse and prove properties of policies, and given the complexities and scope involved in the definition of policies, automated reasoning techniques are needed [9, 10]. Previous efforts have used logic programming, theorem provers, purpose-built logics (see, for instance, [17, 38, 39]), as well as functional and rewriting-based approaches (see, for example, [4, 14, 36]). In this paper, we follow Barker's approach [7], where access control models are defined as instances of the CBAC metamodel, thus inheriting its formal semantics and reasoning techniques [7, 11]. In particular, by axiomatising ABAC in the CBAC metamodel, we directly derive a rewrite-based operational semantics for query evaluation, and techniques to analyse policies, including policy review queries. Using standard rewriting tools, rewrite-based policies can be verified to ensure, for example, that each access request has a unique answer [12, 14, 36].

The CBAC metamodel [7] identifies a core set of principles of access control. Key in the CBAC metamodel is the notion of a category: permissions are assigned to categories of users, rather than to individual users. A category is a class of entities that share some properties. Classic types of groupings used in access control, like a role, a security clearance, a discrete measure of trust, etc., are particular instances of the more general notion of category. The classification of entities into categories can be static (as in the case of roles, which can only be updated by the administrator) or can be defined in terms of dynamic parameters (e.g., an airline may categorise clients in terms of the miles travelled, which can be automatically updated each time a user validates new airmiles). Since categories can be application dependent, CBAC is extremely expressive: most of the existing access control models can be defined as instances of the CBAC metamodel by selecting appropriate sets of entities and relationships and specifying adequate notions of categories (see [7, 11]). To formalise ABAC, we use a notion of category based on user, resource and environment attributes. For example, a policy can give a permission to perform an action (e.g., download) on a resource (e.g., a film) to users in the age category "16+" but not in the category "child". In this way, permissions change in a dynamic and autonomous way (e.g., when a user's age changes); we give more detailed examples in Section 3. The use of categories in the formalisation of ABAC adds structure to ABAC policies, so that policies are easier to design and maintain. For example, if a new resource is added to the system (e.g., a new film that is suitable for audiences over 16), it is sufficient to assign it to the "16+" category to automatically restrict it to users older than 16. Also as a direct byproduct of the CBAC formalisation of ABAC, review queries become easier to evaluate, and simple systems such as RBAC can be directly implemented as instances of ABAC without additional costs. We illustrate these features in Section 4.

Summarising, our main contributions are:

- an axiomatic definition of the general ABAC model, which we call C-ABAC, following [21];
- a rewrite-based operational semantics for C-ABAC policies based on the rewriting semantics of the CBAC metamodel [11];
- a simple mechanism to specify hierarchical RBAC policies and enumerated versions of ABAC in C-ABAC, which follows directly from the additional structure achieved by incorporating categories in ABAC;
- a technique to answer review queries and to prove properties of C-ABAC policies, in particular *totality and consistency* of policies, based on termination and confluence properties of the underlying rewriting system.

Overview: We recall the definition of the CBAC metamodel in Section 2. Section 3 presents C-ABAC and examples of application. The expressive power of C-ABAC is illustrated in Section 4. We give an operational semantics of C-ABAC in Section 5, and discuss analysis techniques in Section 6. Section 7 discusses related work and Section 8 concludes.

2 PRELIMINARIES: THE CBAC METAMODEL

In this section we recall the main concepts underlying the category-based access control metamodel [7]. We assume familiarity with basic notions on first-order logic and term rewriting systems [6].

The CBAC metamodel is a logical framework designed to facilitate the definition of access control models. It consist of a family $\mathcal{E}$ of sets of **entities**, which are classified into **categories**, a family

$\mathcal{R}el$ of **relationships between entities**, and a set $\mathcal{A}x$ of **axioms** that specify the properties that the model must satisfy.

The metamodel includes the following generic sets of entities in addition to application-dependent entities: a countable set C of categories, denoted $c_0, c_1, \ldots$; a countable set $\mathcal{P}$ of principals, denoted $p_0, p_1, \ldots$ (we assume that principals that request access to resources are pre-authenticated); a countable set $\mathcal{A}$ of named *actions*, denoted $a_0, a_1, \ldots$; a countable set $\mathcal{R}$ of *resource identifiers*, denoted $r_0, r_1, \ldots$; a finite set $\mathcal{A}uth$ of possible *answers* to access requests (e.g., {grant, deny, undetermined}) and a countable set $\mathcal{S}$ of *situational identifiers* to denote contextual information.

Informally, a category is any of several distinct classes or groups to which entities may be assigned. Formally, the assignment of entities to categories is specified by means of relationships, which can be defined extensionally (as a table) or intentionally (e.g., the actual set of tuples in a relationship may be obtained by executing a program). The metamodel includes the following generic relationships, in addition to application-dependent ones:

- *Principal-Category Assignment*, $\mathcal{PCA} \subseteq \mathcal{P} \times C$, which assigns categories to each principal: $(p, c) \in \mathcal{PCA}$ iff the principal $p \in \mathcal{P}$ is assigned to the category $c \in C$;
- *Permission-category assignment*: $\mathcal{ARCA} \subseteq \mathcal{A} \times \mathcal{R} \times C$, such that $(a, r, c) \in \mathcal{ARCA}$ iff the action $a \in \mathcal{A}$ on resource $r \in \mathcal{R}$ can be performed by principals assigned to the category $c \in C$.
- *Authorisations*, $\mathcal{PAR} \subseteq \mathcal{P} \times \mathcal{A} \times \mathcal{R}$, such that $(p, a, r) \in \mathcal{PAR}$ iff the principal $p \in \mathcal{P}$ is allowed to perform the action $a \in \mathcal{A}$ on the resource $r \in \mathcal{R}$. A relation defining prohibitions is also included.

Additional relations can also be considered, depending on the application domain. For example, it is possible to include in the metamodel a reflexive-transitive relation $\subseteq$ between categories if a hierarchy of categories exists in the application domain. If $c \subseteq c'$ we say that c is above c'; for example manager $\subseteq$ employee.

Authorisations are directly deduced from the previous relations using the **core axiom** defined below (to deal with prohibitions, a second axiom is added, we refer to [12] for details). Below we assume that there exists a relationship $\subseteq$ between categories (this can simply be equality, set inclusion, or be application-dependent).

$(a1)$ $\quad \forall p \in \mathcal{P}, \ \forall a \in \mathcal{A}, \ \forall r \in \mathcal{R},$
$\quad \exists c, c' \in C, ((p, c) \in \mathcal{PCA} \ \land \ c \subseteq c' \ \land \ (a, r, c') \in \mathcal{ARCA})$
$\qquad\qquad\qquad\qquad\qquad \Leftrightarrow (p, a, r) \in \mathcal{PAR}$

Given a specification of $\mathcal{E}$ and $\mathcal{R}el$, and a set $\mathcal{A}x$ of axioms defining an access control model M, a **policy** is a tuple $\langle E, Rel \rangle$ that defines the contents of $\mathcal{E}$ and $\mathcal{R}el$ such that E, R satisfy all the axioms in $\mathcal{A}x$.

Operationally, axiom $(a1)$ can be realised through a set of functions defined by rewrite rules, as shown in [11]. We recall the definition of the function par(P, A, R) below; it relies on functions pca, which returns the list of categories of a principal, and arca, which returns a list of permissions assigned to a category.

$(b1)$ $\quad$ par$(P, A, R) \quad \rightarrow \quad$ *if* $(A, R) \in$ arca*(contain(pca(P)))
$\qquad\qquad\qquad\qquad\qquad$ *then* grant *else* deny

As the function name suggests, contain computes the set of categories that contain any of the categories given in the list pca(P).

The function $\in$ is a membership operator on lists, grant and deny are answers, and arca* generalises the function arca to take into account lists of categories (we use nil and cons as list constructors):

$$\text{arca}^*(\text{nil}) \rightarrow \text{nil} \quad \text{arca}^*(\text{cons}(C, L)) \rightarrow \text{append}(\text{arca}(C), \text{arca}^*(L))$$

An access request by a principal p to perform the action a on the resource r can then be evaluated simply by rewriting the term $\text{par}(p, a, r)$ to normal form.

The axiom $(a1)$, and its algebraic version $(b1)$, state that a request by a principal p to perform the action a on a resource r is authorised if and only if p belongs to a category c such that for some category below c (e.g., c itself) the action a is authorised on r, otherwise the request is denied. There are other alternatives, e.g., considering *undetermined* as answer if there is not enough information to grant the request. We end this section with an example from [11]:

Example 2.1. Consider the following scenario:

> Employees in a company are classified as Managers, Senior Managers or Senior Executives. Any Senior Executive is permitted to read the personal information, including salary, stored in an employee's file, provided the employee is a Manager in a profitable branch. To be a Senior Executive, a principal must be registered as a senior manager and must be a member of the company's executive board.

To represent this policy we use categories Manager, Senior_mng, Senior_exec, and define pca as follows:

$$\text{pca}(P) \quad \rightarrow \quad \textit{if } P \in \text{Senior\_mng\_register}$$
$$\textit{then } (\textit{if } P \in \text{Exec\_board} \quad \textit{then } [\text{Senior\_exec}]$$
$$\textit{else } [\text{Senior\_mng}])$$
$$\textit{else } [\text{Manager}]$$

The specification of the arca function, which assigns to senior executives the permission to read managers' salaries in profitable branches, is given below. The auxiliary function profbranch returns the list of branches that are profitable. The function managers returns the list of managers of the branches in the input parameter. We omit the definition of the function zip-read, which, given a list $L = [l_1, \ldots, l_n]$, returns a list of pairs $[(\text{read}, l_1), \ldots, (\text{read}, l_n)]$.

$$\text{arca}(\text{Senior\_exec}) \quad \rightarrow \quad \text{zip-read}(\text{managers}(\text{profbranch}))$$
$$\text{profbranch} \quad \rightarrow \quad [(b_1, \ldots, b_m)]$$

3 AN AXIOMATIC SPECIFICATION OF THE ABAC MODEL: C-ABAC

In this section we present a formal definition of ABAC using the CBAC metamodel [7]. To define an access control model as an instance of CBAC, we need to specify the relevant entities together with appropriate categories, relationships and axioms. In the case of ABAC, categories will be defined on the basis of user, resource and environment attributes. The resulting model is called C-ABAC.

3.1 C-ABAC Definition

We start by defining the relevant set $\mathcal{E}$ of entities in C-ABAC: In addition to the generic sets $\mathcal{P}$, $\mathcal{A}$, $\mathcal{R}$, C mentioned in Section 2, $\mathcal{E}$ will include a countable set $\mathcal{E}nv$ of environment entities (e.g., networks, channels, etc.) and a set $\mathcal{A}t$ of *attributes*, ranging over

values $\mathcal{V}$. The precise set $\mathcal{A}t$ of attributes that is admitted is application specific, and in most examples values will be numbers, Booleans, strings, lists and sets, but more sophisticated types can be used. In general, attributes will be represented by functions that return appropriate values. For example, the function representing the attribute *age* should not return negative numbers. We consider also a set *Cond* of Boolean expressions involving attributes and values, which will be used to define categories: the expressions will specify the acceptable ranges of attribute values required by each category (we give examples below).

The set $\mathcal{A}t$ will be partitioned into *principal attributes, resource attributes, environment attributes* and, if required, also administrative attributes, session attributes, etc. Due to space restrictions, in this paper we do not consider the notion of a session; sessions could be included in the model by adding another set of entities and a relation between principals and their activated sessions.

The following relationships are included in $\mathcal{R}el$ in C-ABAC (the notation X^* denotes a sequence of 0 or more elements in X, as usual).

- *Principal-Attribute Assignment*, $\mathcal{P}\mathcal{A}t\mathcal{A} \subseteq \mathcal{P} \times (\mathcal{A}t \times \mathcal{V})^*$, which defines the attributes of each principal.
  $(p, (a_1, v_1), \ldots, (a_n, v_n)) \in \mathcal{P}\mathcal{A}t\mathcal{A}$ iff principal $p \in \mathcal{P}$ has attributes $a_1, \ldots, a_n$ with values $v_1, \ldots, v_n$. At each point in time, there is at most one tuple in $\mathcal{P}\mathcal{A}t\mathcal{A}$ for each principal (since we assume attributes are computed by functions, which by definition return at most one result); we denote by l_p the list of attribute-values in p's tuple.
- *Resource-Attribute Assignment*, $\mathcal{R}\mathcal{A}t\mathcal{A} \subseteq \mathcal{R} \times (\mathcal{A}t \times \mathcal{V})^*$, which defines the attributes of each resource:
  $(r, (a_1, v_1), \ldots, (a_n, v_n)) \in \mathcal{R}\mathcal{A}t\mathcal{A}$ iff resource $r \in \mathcal{R}$ has attributes $a_1, \ldots, a_n$ with values $v_1, \ldots, v_n$. At each point in time, there is at most one tuple in $\mathcal{R}\mathcal{A}t\mathcal{A}$ for each resource; we denote by l_r the list of attribute-values in r's tuple.
- *Environment-Attribute Assignment*, $\mathcal{E}\mathcal{A}t\mathcal{A} \subseteq \mathcal{E}nv \times (\mathcal{A}t \times \mathcal{V})^*$, which defines the relevant environmental attributes:
  $(e, (a_1, v_1), \ldots, (a_n, v_n)) \in \mathcal{E}\mathcal{A}t\mathcal{A}$ iff the environment entity e has attributes $a_1, \ldots, a_n$ have values $v_1, \ldots, v_n$; again, there is at most one tuple for each environment entity at any given point in time, and we denote by l_e the list of attribute-values in e's tuple.
- *Category-Attribute Assignment*, $C\mathcal{A}t\mathcal{A} \subseteq C \times Cond$, which defines the attribute values required in each category:
  $(c, cond) \in C\mathcal{A}t\mathcal{A}$ iff category $c \in C$ requires attribute values satisfying the Boolean condition $cond \in Cond$; we say that c **is defined by** $cond$. We write $\Gamma \vdash cond$ if Γ specifies attributes and values that satisfy $cond$.
  An additional reflexive-transitive relation $\subseteq$ between categories is included in $\mathcal{R}el$ to define a hierarchical version of ABAC (it can simply be equality). We assume $\subseteq$ is compatible with the conditions defining categories, i.e., $c \subseteq c'$ means that the defining condition for c implies that of c':

$(c0)$ $\forall c, c' \in C, \forall \Gamma,$
$(\exists (c, d), (c', d') \in C\mathcal{A}t\mathcal{A}, \Gamma \vdash d \Rightarrow \Gamma \vdash d') \Leftrightarrow (c \subseteq c')$

The relationships defined in C-ABAC are abstract, in the sense that they do not necessarily map to tables. An implementation could use tables or implement them via functional maps for example.

We adopt the $\mathcal{PCA}$ relationship of CBAC (see Section 2), and add a relationship $\mathcal{RCA}$ to categorise resources. The permissions relation $\mathcal{ARCA}$ is then generalised accordingly in order to deal with categories of resources as well as categories of principals. Thus, in C-ABAC the set $\mathcal{Rel}$ includes:

- *Principal-Category Assignment, $\mathcal{PCA} \subseteq \mathcal{P} \times C$,* which assigns categories to each principal: $(p, c) \in \mathcal{PCA}$ iff the principal $p \in \mathcal{P}$ is in the category $c \in C$;
- *Resource-Category Assignment, $\mathcal{RCA} \subseteq \mathcal{R} \times C$,* which assigns categories to each resource in the system: $(r, c) \in \mathcal{RCA}$ iff the resource $r \in \mathcal{R}$ is in the category $c \in C$;
- *Permissions, $\mathcal{ARCA} \subseteq \mathcal{A} \times C_R \times C_P$,* which assigns permitted actions to categories of principals and resources;
- *Authorisations, $\mathcal{PAR} \subseteq \mathcal{P} \times \mathcal{A} \times \mathcal{R}$,* such that $(p, a, r) \in \mathcal{PAR}$ iff the principal $p \in \mathcal{P}$ can perform the action $a \in \mathcal{A}$ on the resource $r \in \mathcal{R}$. A relation defining prohibitions can also be defined, omitted here due to space constraints.

Since in ABAC the categories of principals and resources are computed on the basis of attribute values, which may vary in time, the relations $\mathcal{PCA}$ and $\mathcal{RCA}$ are dynamic (the tuples in the relation can vary with time). The following axioms state that an entity belongs to a category c if its attribute values satisfy c's definition.

Definition 3.1 (Categorisation Axioms).

$(c1) \quad \forall p \in \mathcal{P}, \forall c \in C, ((p, c) \in \mathcal{PCA} \Leftrightarrow$
$\quad \exists (p, l_p) \in \mathcal{PAtA}, \exists (c, d) \in \mathcal{CAtA}, (l_p, \mathcal{RAtA}, \mathcal{EAtA} \vdash d))$
$(c2) \quad \forall r \in \mathcal{R}, \forall c \in C, ((r, c) \in \mathcal{RCA} \Leftrightarrow$
$\quad \exists (r, l_r) \in \mathcal{RAtA}, \exists (c, d) \in \mathcal{CAtA}, (l_r, \mathcal{PAtA}, \mathcal{EAtA} \vdash d))$

Example 3.2. Assume that principals' rights depend on age. We define a category *child* for ages 0 to 17 by including the tuple $(child, age \in [0, \ldots, 17])$ in $\mathcal{CAtA}$, and a category *adult* with defining condition $age \geq 18$. Then, a principal p aged 17, i.e., p such that $(p, \ldots, (age, 17), \ldots) \in \mathcal{PAtA}$, is classified as a child: $(p, child) \in \mathcal{PCA}$ according to axiom $(c1)$. However, when p reaches 18, p will automatically move to the adult category, i.e., at that point in time $(p, child) \notin \mathcal{PCA}$.

Similarly, suppose a film (resource) f has been labelled as suitable for all publics, i.e. $(f, [\ldots, classification = unrestricted, \ldots]) \in \mathcal{RAtA}$. We define categories of films based on the film's classification, e.g., a category *AllPublic* for films classified as unrestricted: $(AllPublic, classification = unrestricted) \in \mathcal{CAtA}$. Then we will derive $(f, AllPublic) \in \mathcal{RCA}$, according to axiom $(c2)$.

Note that a principal (resp. resource) could belong to many different categories at a given time. The set $\mathcal{Ax}$ of logical axioms that governs C-ABAC includes the following core axiom, which specifies how authorisations are derived.

Definition 3.3 (Authorisation Axiom).

$(c3) \quad \forall p \in \mathcal{P}, \forall a \in \mathcal{A}, \forall r \in \mathcal{R},$
$\quad (\exists c_p \in C, \exists c_p' \in C, \exists c_r \in C, \exists c_r' \in C,$
$\quad (p, c_p) \in \mathcal{PCA} \wedge (r, c_r) \in \mathcal{RCA}$
$\quad \wedge c_p \subseteq c_p' \wedge c_r \subseteq c_r' \wedge (a, c_r', c_p') \in \mathcal{ARCA})$
$\quad \Leftrightarrow (p, a, r) \in \mathcal{PAR}$

Based on this axiom, it is possible to deduce that if a principal p is in the category c_p (that is, $(p, c_p) \in \mathcal{PCA}$), a resource r is in the category c_r (that is, $(r, c_r) \in \mathcal{RCA}$), and the category c_p is permitted to perform the action a on resource category c_r (that is, $(a, c_r, c_p) \in \mathcal{ARCA}$) then p is authorised to perform a on r (that is, $(p, a, r) \in \mathcal{PAR}$). If a hierarchy of principal and resource categories is used, this axiom allows us to derive inherited authorisations. For categories of principals, $c \subseteq c'$ denotes that principals in c are "senior to" principals in c' from an authorisation point of view. For example, *manager $\subseteq$ employee*. For categories of resources, $c \subseteq c'$ can also be understood as an inheritance relation: for example, *public $\subseteq$ secret* means that actions available for secret documents can also apply to public ones.

Example 3.4. Following from Example 3.2, assume the category *All* has no age restriction (i.e., it is defined by $age \geq 0$), *child $\subseteq$ All, adult $\subseteq$ All*. Assume $(download, All, AllPublic) \in \mathcal{ARCA}$. Then, if p is a child, i.e. $(p, child) \in \mathcal{PCA}$, and a film f is categorised as suitable for all publics, i.e., $(f, AllPublic) \in \mathcal{RCA}$, then p will be authorised to view f since $(p, download, f) \in \mathcal{PAR}$ according to axiom $(c3)$.

Additional axioms can be included in C-ABAC in order to specify prohibitions and obligations in the style of CBAC [12].

3.2 Examples of Application

We discuss two scenarios to illustrate the applicability of C-ABAC.

Example 3.5 (Airline). Consider an airline with clients (anybody who lands in the airline website is considered to be a potential client), passengers (who have made a booking, independently of the ticket status), club members (passengers are invited to register as club members to earn points and benefit from a range of services), and employees, who are classified as crew or land staff. Clients, passengers and employees have specific rights and the airline needs a policy to control their actions. For example, passengers should be allowed to modify their bookings and issue boarding passes for their flights but not others'; land staff have access to airport facilities; crew can use first-class lounges, as well as club members who have obtained a specified minimum number of points or passengers who have bought a first-class ticket for a flight departing within 4 hours; club members can use their points to upgrade their tickets, buy products, etc.

To specify the security policy using C-ABAC, we start by defining the set of entities and attributes, and the relevant categories.

Principals: The set of attributes for principals includes generic attributes such as ID, name, date of birth, address, email address, mobile phone number, and specific attributes, such as attributes related to the principal's browsing habits, club membership, etc. Principals will be categorised using their attributes: for example, to be a club member, the principal must have a club membership number. Each principal will be represented by a tuple in the relation $\mathcal{PAtA}$, which will be used to categorise principals into the categories specified below. For each category, a tuple should be present in the relation $\mathcal{CAtA}$ specifying the condition the attributes should satisfy, so that the assignment of principals to categories (relation $\mathcal{PCA}$) can be derived as specified by axiom (c1).

The set of categories of principals includes:

- *client*: default category for website visitors. The attributes of principals in this category hold information related to their connection, browser, previous visits (if known), etc.
- *passenger*: to be in this category, a principal must have a valid booking, that is, $(p, passenger) \in \mathcal{PCA}$ if there exists a booking where the owner attribute has value p. Since passengers who have bought a first-class ticket have additional rights if their flight is within 4 hours, we define a subcategory *first-class* $\subseteq$ *passenger*, with a defining condition based on the ownership of a first-class ticket and a constraint on time (environment attribute, see below).
- *club*: this category is defined by a membership condition, that is, to be categorised as *club*, p must be a member of the airline club. Principals in this category have attributes that relate to their club membership, such as club-member number, number of points collected, etc. Since club members have different kinds of benefits depending on their number of points, we define subcategories within *club*. For example, *Gold, Silver, Bronze* (with appropriate conditions on the value of the attribute collected-points) such that *Gold* $\subseteq$ *Silver* $\subseteq$ *Bronze* $\subseteq$ *club* to ensure that *Gold* members have all the privileges of the category *Silver*, who have all the privileges of the category *Bronze*, etc.
- Similarly, we define a category *employee* with subcategories *crew, land*, etc., and include in the hierarchical relation the pairs *crew* $\subseteq$ *employee*, *land* $\subseteq$ *employee*, etc.
- Other categories of principals can be considered, such as members of clubs of partner airlines, travel agents, etc.

Resources: The set of resources includes bookings, tickets, airport facilities (such as the first-class lounge), etc. In C-ABAC, resources are categorised (relation $\mathcal{RCA}$) on the basis of their attributes, specified in the relation $\mathcal{RAtA}$, see axiom (c2). For example, each time a booking is made, a tuple is added to the relation $\mathcal{RAtA}$ to store the booking's attributes. The defining condition for the resource category *booking* is simple: All bookings belong to category *booking*. Similarly for category *ticket*. Additional categories of resources are defined to deal with *boarding pass*, *product* and *facility*, with sub-categories (defined using the hierarchical relation $\subseteq$) to distinguish various kinds of products that passengers can buy, and different kinds of airport facilities (e.g. *office* $\subseteq$ *facility*, *FirstclassLounge* $\subseteq$ *facility*).

Environment: Relevant environmental attributes in $\mathcal{EAtA}$ include time, location, connection attributes for website visitors, etc.

Policy: Once $\mathcal{PAtA}$, $\mathcal{RAtA}$ and $\mathcal{EAtA}$ are defined and $\mathcal{PCA}$ and $\mathcal{RCA}$ derived using the relevant axioms, it remains only to define the relation $\mathcal{ARCA}$, which specifies the permissions associated with each category. Then authorisations (relation $\mathcal{PAR}$) are derived using axiom (c3). For example, in this simple scenario we could specify that principals in the categories *Gold, crew* and *first-class* are allowed to access the first-class lounges by including $(access, FirstclassLounge, Gold)$, $(access, FirstclassLounge, crew)$ and $(access, FirstclassLounge, first-class)$ in $\mathcal{ARCA}$. Then, by axiom (c3), a principal p who has collected the number of points necessary to be in the *Gold* category will be authorised to access a first-class lounge, since $(p, access, FirstclassLounge) \in \mathcal{PAR}$.

Example 3.6 (File Sharing: Exam Preparation System). Assume a department in a university needs a web-based application to manage the exam preparation process using a file-sharing system with the following features: lecturers should be able to upload files (containing the draft or final version of the examination paper for their modules); internal and external examiners should be able to read draft examination papers and upload comments on the papers, but are not allowed to copy draft exam files into their own space to avoid accidental information leakage; based on the comments received on the draft of the exam paper, lecturers should prepare and upload the final version; the exam coordinator, who has overall responsibility for the process, should be allowed to see the draft and final versions of all the exam papers but should not copy them; and the examination secretary should be allowed to make three copies of the final version of each examination paper (but only during normal office hours and with a local connection), one copy for the Central Examination Office (to be printed and distributed to students in the examination hall), another copy for the Central Archival Service, and the third to be kept in the departmental archive. The three copies made by the secretary should not be copied any further, but can be read on demand (for example, for auditing purposes).

To deal with these requirements, we can use a security type system for file sharing [3], which permits to control the number of copies that can be made for each file by assigning it a type NC (read but no copy), LC^n (maximum n copies) or UC (unrestricted copy). However, this type system does not allow us to control who is making the copies, or to specify different security types for different kinds of users. To specify the required restrictions, we propose to use security types as part of a C-ABAC policy, as follows.

Principals: The set of principals includes lecturers, examiners, coordinators and administrative staff. We categorise them according to their role in the exam preparation process. We assume principals have attributes: role with values lecturer, coordinator, admin, internal-examiner, external-examiner, etc., and additional attributes describing for example the modules taught, modules for which the lecturer is an internal examiner, etc. Thus, if p is the lecturer in charge of the Foundations of Computing (FC) module, and is an internal examiner for Computer Systems (CS) and for Formal Languages (FL), then p's tuple in $\mathcal{PAtA}$ will include:

$$[\ldots, (role, \{lecturer, internal-examiner\}), (module\text{-}taught, \{FC\}),$$
$$(module\text{-}examined, \{CS, FL\}), \ldots].$$

We define the set of categories accordingly:

$$C = \{lecturer, coordinator, internal\text{-}examiner, \\ external\text{-}examiner, admin, deptAd, central, archive, \ldots\}$$
$$deptAd \subseteq admin, \; central \subseteq admin, \; archive \subseteq admin$$

All the categories have defining conditions based on the attribute *role*, but the condition defining the department admin category deptAd involves also environment attributes: to be categorised as deptAd, a principal must have the admin role, a local connection and be within normal office hours.

We can also specify subcategories for lecturers and internal examiners according to the module they are responsible for. For example, lecturer-FC is a subcategory of lecturer (i.e., lecturer-FC $\subseteq$ lecturer) that includes only the lecturers in charge of the module FC, and similarly, internal-examiner-CS is a subcategory of internal-examiner that includes all the internal examiners for the module *CS*. We assume that the coordinator and external examiners must check all the papers so we do not divide these categories into subcategories. The conditions defining these categories are simple conjunctions of membership tests (e.g., $(p, \text{lecturer-FC}) \in \mathcal{PCA}$ if lecturer $\in$ *role(p)* and $FC \in$ *module-taught(p)*).

Resources: The set of resources consists of exam files, each with a set of attributes that specify the module (e.g., *FC*, *CS*, etc.), status (e.g., *draft* or *final*), the names of the lecturers in charge of the module, the names of the internal and external examiners, etc. Based on the values of the attributes module and status, specified in the relation $\mathcal{RAtA}$ for each exam file, we define a category exam with subcategories draft and final, which in turn have one subcategory for each module. The categories are defined by membership conditions, for example, to be in the category draft-FC, a file must have the value *FC* in the module attribute and the value *draft* in the status attribute.

Environment: Environmental attributes include time and connection, since access to certain resources (for instance to create copies of the final version of exam papers), depends on the values of these two attributes.

Policy: After defining the relations $\mathcal{PAtA}$, $\mathcal{RAtA}$ and $\mathcal{EAtA}$, from which $\mathcal{PCA}$ and $\mathcal{RCA}$ are derived, it remains only to specify the permissions for each category via the relation $\mathcal{ARCA}$. For example, since principals in the category lecturer-FC are allowed to upload files in the category draft-FC and final-FC, we include in $\mathcal{ARCA}$ the tuples $(\text{upload}, \text{lecturer-FC}, \text{draft-FC})$ and $(\text{upload}, \text{lecturer-FC}, \text{final-FC})$. Similarly, we add in $\mathcal{ARCA}$ tuples to define the rights of examiners and coordinator: for example, since external examiners can read (but not copy) the exam drafts, we need a tuple $(NC, \text{external-examiner}, \text{draft})$, and since the coordinator can read (but not copy) both draft and final versions of all the exam files, we include the tuple $(NC, \text{coordinator}, \text{exam})$. To restrict the departmental administrative staff to make only three copies of final exam papers, we add a tuple $(LC^3, \text{deptAD}, \text{final}) \in \mathcal{ARCA}$. The security type system we are using enforces the type conditions, ensuring that a file with type LC^3 cannot be further copied after 3 copies have been made, and none of the copies made can be copied.

4 EXPRESSIVE POWER OF C-ABAC

In this section we give encodings of standard ABAC models and we also show that the traditional Hierarchical RBAC model can be *directly* represented in C-ABAC.

4.1 Representing ABAC policies in C-ABAC

According to Hu et al. [26], *an ABAC policy is a set of rules that protect objects by defining the privileges available to subjects; the administrator or owner of a resource creates a rule to protect each resource using relevant attributes*. It is a requirement of ABAC that "Every object in the system must have at least one policy that defines the access rules for the allowable subjects, operations and environment conditions to the object" [26]. There are two main methods to define ABAC policies. The conventional method uses logical formulas to define the rules that protect resources: a policy grants access if the formula is evaluated to be true using the current

values of the requesting user, requested object and environment. Another method is to enumerate the values of attributes that grant access to a resource, in the style of the Policy Machine [24]. For example, LaBAC [15] follows this approach.

Encoding ABAC policies defined by logical formulas. In C-ABAC, the rules that protect each resource are defined by means of category definitions (which consist of Boolean expressions), together with the $\mathcal{ARCA}$ relation, which specifies permissions for categories. Thus, to represent ABAC policies where rules are defined directly for each resource in terms of logical formulas it is sufficient to consider singleton resource categories. More precisely, for each ABAC rule with condition *cond* that grants the action *a* on a resource *r*, we define a category of principals c_p with condition *cond* and a category c_r containing only *r*, and add to $\mathcal{ARCA}$ the tuple (a, c_r, c_p). In this way we can simulate in C-ABAC a version of ABAC where access control specifications apply to individual entities. Dually, we can see C-ABAC as a particular case of ABAC, since a C-ABAC policy satisfies the requirement to have a set of rules protecting each resource: using $\mathcal{ARCA}$ and the category definitions we can derive a set of rules for each resource.

Encoding Enumerated ABAC policies. Enumerated ABAC policies can also be defined directly within C-ABAC. We recall that in Policy Machine (PM) [24] enumerated ABAC policies are defined using one user attribute, one object attribute and a set of actions. A privilege in PM is defined by a triple (ua_i, OP, oa_i) where ua_i and oa_i are values of user and object attributes, respectively, and OP is a set of operations. Despite its simplicity, this idea is very powerful: traditional models such as RBAC and MAC can be easily encoded (however, not all the ABAC policies that can be defined using logical formulas can be defined by enumeration, in particular because logical formulas can include negation). PM deals not only with authorisation but also with prohibitions and obligations. LaBAC (Label-Based Access Control) is a family of enumerated ABAC models with a formal semantics, which can be seen as a simplified version of PM focusing on authorisations. Indeed, Biswas et al. [15] provide an encoding of a reduced version of PM, which deals only with assignment of attributes and definition of privileges, in LaBAC. We now give an encoding of Hierarchical LaBAC in C-ABAC.

LaBAC uses one user label, called *uLabel*, and one object label, called *oLabel*. These labels are special set-valued attributes: $uLabel : U \rightarrow \mathcal{P}(UL)$ maps a user from a set U to one or more values from a set UL, and $oLabel : O \rightarrow \mathcal{P}(UL)$ maps objects from a set O to one or more values from a set OL. Values are assigned by an administrator, and it is assumed that values are partially ordered, that is, UL and OL admit a partial ordering. A LaBAC policy is comprised of a subset of all tuples in $UL \times OL$. For each action *a*, there must be one policy, denoted $Policy_a$, where $Policy_a \subseteq UL \times OL$. The authorisation function grants an access request from a user *u* to perform the action *a* on the object *o* if and only if there exists $ul \in uLabel(u)$ and $ol \in oLabel(o)$ such that $(ul, ol) \in Policy_a$.

Hierarchical LaBAC introduces a user-label hierarchy and object-label hierarchy, expressed via orderings $\geq_{UL}$ on UL and $\geq_{OL}$ on OL with the following semantics: $ul_i \geq_{UL} ul_j$ means that ul_i is senior to ul_j and users assigned to *uLabel* value ul_i should be able to exercise all the privileges of users whose *uLabel* value is ul_j. In the object hierarchy, it is the other way around: if $ol_i \geq_{OL} ol_j$ then objects assigned a value ol_j inherit the authorisations of objects assigned a value ol_i. Hierarchical LaBAC is characterised as follows:

The authorisation function grants an access request from a user u to perform the action a on the object o if and only if there exists $ul_i \in uLabel(u)$ and $ol_j \in oLabel(o)$ such that $(ul, ol) \in Policy_a$, $ul_i \geq_{UL} ul$ and $ol \geq_{OL} ol_j$.

We encode a Hierarchical LaBAC policy in C-ABAC as follows:

(1) The sets $\mathcal{P}$ of principals and $\mathcal{R}$ of resources in the C-ABAC policy are the sets U (users) and O (objects) in the LaBAC policy. For each principal (resp. resource), an attribute $uLabel$ (resp. $oLabel$) is defined, such that $(p, (uLabel, v)) \in \mathcal{PAtA} \Leftrightarrow uLabel(p) = v$, and similarly $(r, (oLabel, v)) \in \mathcal{RAtA} \Leftrightarrow oLabel(r) = v$.

(2) We define a category of principals associated with each value of $uLabel$ and a category of resources associated with each value of $oLabel$, with a membership condition based on the attribute's value, so that, for example, a user u with $uLabel = v$ belongs to the category c_v. The hierarchical relation between values in UL in LaBAC is mapped directly to the hierarchical relation between categories of principals; for resources, we use the inverse, i.e., $ol_i \geq ol_j$ in OL is translated as $c_{ol_j} \subseteq c_{ol_i}$.

(3) Finally, the relation $\mathcal{ARCA}$ is defined as follows: $(a, c_r, c_p) \in \mathcal{ARCA}$ if and only if $(c_p, c_v) \in Policy_a$.

PROPOSITION 4.1 (CORRECTNESS OF THE LaBAC ENCODING). *Given a Hierarchical LaBAC policy, an access request by principal u to perform the action a on object o is granted if and only if in the translated C-ABAC policy $(u, a, o) \in \mathcal{PAR}$.*

PROOF. According to the LaBAC specification given above, a request by u to perform a on o is granted if and only if there exists $ul_i \in uLabel(u)$ and $ol_j \in oLabel(o)$ such that $(ul, ol) \in Policy_a$, $ul_i \geq_{UL} ul$ and $ol \geq_{OL} ol_j$.

According to the encoding, the LaBAC policy assigns a value ul_i to u if and only if in the C-ABAC policy u is in category c_{ul_i}, i.e., $(u, c_{ul_i}) \in \mathcal{PCA}$, since $(u, (uLabel, ul_i)) \in \mathcal{PAtA}$ (axiom (c1)). Similarly, o is in category c_{ol_j} if and only if $oLabel(o) = ol_j$.

Note that the authorisation relation in the C-ABAC policy is obtained by axiom (c3), where the inheritance between categories of principals is the same as in LaBAC, but for objects it is not. This is the reason why in the translation, we have encoded LaBAC's partial ordering on OL using the inverse. Now, since $\mathcal{ARCA}$ contains the same tuples as the LaBAC policy, and the partial orderings used in axiom (c3) for categories coincide with the ones used by the authorisation relation in LaBAC, it follows that the LaBAC policy grants the request by u to perform a on o if and only if $(u, a, o) \in \mathcal{PAR}$ according to axiom (c3). □

4.2 Encoding Hierarchical RBAC

ABAC can encode a range of access control models, including RBAC (see, e.g., [15, 29]). In RBAC, principals are assigned a role by the administrator, who also specifies the actions authorised for each role. However, in ABAC the dual point of view is adopted: ABAC rules put the focus on resources (at least one rule should be defined for each resource) whereas RBAC puts the focus on principal's roles. For this reason, the translation from RBAC to ABAC is not direct (the situation is even more complicated in the case of ANSI

Hierarchical RBAC policies, which include a role hierarchy). C-ABAC allows us to encode in a *direct* way the ANSI Hierarchical RBAC model as shown below. We first recall the characterisation of ANSI Hierarchical RBAC:

A request from a principal p to perform an action a on the resource r results on grant or deny depending on whether the permission (a, r) is associated with p's role or one of its subordinate roles.

In terms of C-ABAC primitives, hierarchical RBAC can be expressed by axiom (c3) assuming principals are assigned a role attribute, categories of principals are limited to roles and categories of resources are limited to singleton sets (i.e., each resource has its own category). More precisely, we translate an RBAC policy into a C-ABAC policy as follows:

(1) The sets of principals and resources in the C-ABAC policy are the same as in the given RBAC policy. Each principal has an attribute role, with a value of type set.

(2) The set of categories coincides with the set of roles. The role hierarchy maps directly to the category hierarchy $\subseteq$.

(3) The relation $\mathcal{PAtA}$ specifies the roles for each principal: $r_1, \ldots, r_n$ are the roles of p in the RBAC policy if and only if $(p, (role, \{r_1, \ldots, r_n\})) \in \mathcal{PAtA}$.

(4) Since there is a bijection between categories of resources and resources, we simply assume that $\mathcal{RAtA}$ contains a list of resource IDs.

(5) Finally, the relation $\mathcal{ARCA}$ is defined as follows: $(a, r, r_i) \in \mathcal{ARCA}$ if and only if the role r_i has the permission (a, r).

PROPOSITION 4.2 (CORRECTNESS OF THE RBAC ENCODING). *Given a Hierarchical RBAC policy, an access request by principal p to perform the action a on resource r is granted if and only if in the translated C-ABAC policy $(p, a, r) \in \mathcal{PAR}$.*

PROOF. According to the RBAC specification given above, a request by p to perform a on r is granted if and only if (a, r) is in the list of permissions associated with p's roles or subordinate roles.

According to the encoding, the RBAC policy assigns the roles $r_1, \ldots r_n$ to p if and only if in the translated C-ABAC policy, $(p, (role, \{r_1, \ldots, r_n\})) \in \mathcal{PAtA}$. By axiom (c1), the relation $\mathcal{PCA}$ contains the tuples (p, r_i) $(1 \leq i \leq n)$.

Since the role hierarchy coincides with the hierarchy on categories, and $(a, r, r_i) \in \mathcal{ARCA}$ if and only if the role r_i has the permission (a, r), it follows that the RBAC policy grants the request by p to perform a on r if and only if $(p, a, r) \in \mathcal{PAR})$ according to axiom (c3). □

Extensions of RBAC that take into account location and time constraints, and more general models, such as the Event-Based Access Control model or the Action-Status Access Control model [8, 13], have already been shown to be instances of CBAC and are also expressible in C-ABAC. The encoding above could also be used for dynamic versions of RBAC where role assignment is based on attribute values [2, 32]. C-ABAC also allows us to encode powerful extensions of ABAC such as HGABAC [37], discussed next.

4.3 Hierarchical Groups in C-ABAC

To highlight the flexibility of C-ABAC, we show how to define a hierarchical version of ABAC where attribute values are assigned to users and resources either directly or by allocating them to groups, as in HGABAC [37]. Groups have a predefined set of attributes and values, and the idea is that users can in this way "inherit" the values of the attributes from their group and use them to get access to resources. Here we consider a restricted version of HGABAC without sessions: the basic elements are users, objects, operations and additionally, *user groups* and *object groups*. Each user and object group is defined by a name and a list of members. Moreover, there is a hierarchical relation between groups, so that if an entity e is a member of a group g, and group g' is a *parent* of g, then e is also a member of g'.

The relation UAA defines for each user a set of attributes and values, while OAA assigns attributes and values to objects. In addition, $UGAA$ and $OGAA$ assign attributes and values to user groups and object groups, respectively.

Permissions are defined, as in all ABAC models, on the basis of the values of attributes of users, objects and environment, but in this case, not only the attributes and values assigned directly to users and objects (i.e., in UAA and OAA) are used, but also the attributes and values of their groups (obtained via $UGAA$ and $OGAA$). A *policy string*, defines for each operation on a resource, a Boolean condition that the attributes of user, object and environment must satisfy for the operation to be authorised. A *permission* is a pairing of a policy string and an operation, written (ps, a).

The function *effective* returns the set of attributes and values assigned directly to a user, object or group, or inherited via the group membership. Thus, for every user, object or group x, *effective*(x) returns the full list of attributes and values associated with x.

The authorisation function is characterised as follows:

A request from a user u to perform an action a on an object o is granted if and only if there exists a permission (ps, a), such that ps is satisfied by the effective attributes of u and o and the values of any required environment attributes.

To represent HGABAC in C-ABAC, users in HGABAC are mapped to principals and objects to resources, and for every directly assigned attribute, we define the same attribute in $\mathcal{PAtA}$ for users or $\mathcal{RAtA}$ for resources. In addition, we introduce an attribute $groupP$ for principals and an attribute $groupR$ for resources. These attributes have values of type set of tuples, defining all the groups to which the principal or resource is allocated (taking into account the *parent* relation), together with the attributes of the group. For example, if in the HGABAC policy, u belongs to the groups $ug_1, \ldots, ug_n$ (either as a member, or via the parent relation between groups), and the group ug_i $(1 \le i \le n)$ has attributes $a_{i1} \ldots a_{ij_i}$ with values $v_{i1}, \ldots, v_{ij_i}$ in $UGAA$, then in the translated C-ABAC policy,

$$groupP(u) = \{(ug_i, (a_{i1}, v_{i1}), \ldots, (a_{ij_i}, v_{ij_i})) \mid i \in \{1, \ldots, n\}\}.$$

The attribute $groupR$ for resources is defined in a similar way.

With these definitions, the relations $\mathcal{PAtA}$ and $\mathcal{RAtA}$ provide all the values of attributes assigned directly or indirectly to principals and resources. Thus, we can state the following result:

PROPOSITION 4.3. *For each principal u, there is a tuple*

$$(u, (a_1, v_1), \ldots, (a_m, v_m),$$
$$(groupP, \{(ug_i, (a_{i1}, v_{i1}), \ldots, (a_{ij_i}, v_{ij_i})) \mid i \in \{1, \ldots, n\}\}))$$

in $\mathcal{PAtA}$ if and only if in the HGABAC policy

$$effective(u) = \{(a_1, v_1), \ldots, (a_m, v_m)\} \cup$$
$$\{(a_{i1}, v_{i1}), \ldots, (a_{ij_i}, v_{ij_i}) \mid i \in \{1, \ldots, n\}\}.$$

For each resource o, there is a tuple

$$(o, (a_1, v_1), \ldots, (a_m, v_m),$$
$$(groupR, \{(og_i, (a_{i1}, v_{i1}), \ldots, (a_{ij_i}, v_{ij_i})) \mid i \in \{1, \ldots, n\}\}))$$

in $\mathcal{RAtA}$ if and only if in the HGABAC policy

$$effective(o) = \{(a_1, v_1), \ldots, (a_m, v_m)\} \cup$$
$$\{(a_{i1}, v_{i1}), \ldots, (a_{ij_i}, v_{ij_i}) \mid i \in \{1, \ldots, n\}\}.$$

It remains to define the encoding of HGABAC's notion of permission in C-ABAC. Since in a permission (ps, a), a is an action on a resource r and the condition ps is a Boolean formula on attributes, we can use it to define a category. Let c be a category of resources with defining condition ps. For each user u, we define a singleton category c_u, and include in $\mathcal{ARCA}$ the tuple (a, c, c_u). Then, by axioms (c1) and (c2) in C-ABAC, the formulas evaluated to categorise entities in C-ABAC coincide with the formulas evaluated in HGABAC. It follows that the relation $\mathcal{PAR}$ in C-ABAC computes the same authorisations as HGABAC since the values of attributes used to check the formulas coincide by Proposition 4.3.

The encoding of groups within $\mathcal{PAtA}$ and $\mathcal{RAtA}$ produces a space explosion if using tables. To avoid it, $\mathcal{PAtA}$ and $\mathcal{RAtA}$ should be implemented using pointers or functions instead of expanding the group definitions. An explicit axiomatisation of groups in the metamodel (adding user groups and object groups as entities and UGAA and OGAA as relationships, with additional axioms to model their properties) would also be possible but is out of the scope of this paper.

4.4 Policy maintenance

Maintaining access control policies is a particularly challenging task, due to the complexity of policies and the fact that small changes may have costly implications. Depending on the access control model used, adapting a policy to changes in principals or resources might require the intervention of the administrator to manually make updates, or the whole system might need to be re-programmed and re-compiled.

RBAC has many advantages due to its simplicity. RBAC policies are easy to understand, but not well-suited to dynamic scenarios where principals do not have specific pre-defined roles or where principals' roles change often. In this case, policy maintenance becomes a costly task due to the need to perform multiple manual updates. Compared with RBAC, ABAC policies may be more difficult to understand (since the rules that protect resources may, in the general case, have arbitrary structure and use complex logical formulas), but ABAC policies can automatically adapt to role changes, simplifying the tasks for administrators. There are however certain changes, such as adding new resources, which still require administrator intervention.

Let us compare the operations required in RBAC, ABAC and C-ABAC to deal with an additional resource:

Adding a resource in an RBAC system requires not only a change in the resource table but also changes in role permissions in order to authorise principals in specific roles to access the new resource; however, no programming or recompilation is required.

Adding a new resource in ABAC implies considering which conditions on attribute values (for principals, environment and the resource itself) are needed, and adding to the policy appropriate rules (which, depending on the system, may require recompilation).

C-ABAC can be seen as an intermediate approach between RBAC and ABAC, combining features of both access control models. For static environments, an RBAC-style policy can be directly defined in C-ABAC by using categories as roles, as discussed in Section 4.2. For dynamic environments, conditions on attribute values can be used to derive authorisations, as in ABAC systems. Adding a new resource in a C-ABAC system is a simple operation if the resource belongs to one of the existing categories: the administrator simply adds a tuple in $\mathcal{RAtA}$ to specify the resource attributes. No changes in permissions are needed (unlike RBAC, which requires updates in role permissions), and no new rules are required (unlike ABAC, which requires new rules): the new resource will be automatically categorised in the existing category, and access requests to this resource will be dealt with using the existing policy rules. If a new resource category is needed, then it should be added to $\mathcal{CAtA}$, together with the defining condition.

Having to define categories may seem a burden in some cases: compared with plain ABAC, C-ABAC involves an additional step that must be carried out at policy-design time, to link attribute values and categories. However, by associating access restrictions with categories rather than with individual users or resources, policies can be more concise, easier to design and easier to maintain, in particular when a policy has to deal with many resources of the same kind or many users with the same privileges.

5 OPERATIONAL SEMANTICS

The axiomatic specification of C-ABAC within the Category-Based metamodel gives a precise account of the authorisations, but cannot be directly executed. In this section, we translate the axioms defining C-ABAC into a set of functions to evaluate access requests, following the metamodel's operational semantics (see Section 2).

The set of authorisations is defined by the relation $\mathcal{PAR}$, which is derived from $\mathcal{PCA}$, $\mathcal{RCA}$ and $\mathcal{ARCA}$ (see axiom (c3) in Section 3). We model the relations $\mathcal{PCA}$, $\mathcal{RCA}$ and $\mathcal{ARCA}$ with functions pca, rca and arca, respectively. The function pca (resp. rca) returns the list of categories to which the principal (resp. resource) belongs and arca returns a list of permissions for each category. These functions are application dependent, and rely on the definition of functions to compute attribute values for principals and resources, implementing the relations $\mathcal{PAtA}$, $\mathcal{RAtA}$ and $\mathcal{EAtA}$. We assume below that pca and rca have been correctly defined according to axioms (c1) and (c2), satisfying the compatibility property (c0) if $\subseteq$ is used. Below we define a function par generalising the rule (b1) given in Section 2.

Definition 5.1. The rewrite-based specification of the axiom (c3) given in Section 3 is given by the rewrite rule:

$$(c3') \quad \text{par}(P, A, R) \quad \rightarrow \quad \begin{array}{l} \textit{if } zip(A, \text{contain}(\text{rca}(R))) \cap \\ \quad \text{arca}^*(\text{contain}(\text{pca}(P))) \neq \emptyset \\ \textit{then } \text{grant } \textit{else } \text{deny} \end{array}$$

where the function *zip* takes an action A and a list of categories and returns a list of pairs as follows:

$$\begin{array}{rcl} zip(A, nil) & \rightarrow & nil \\ zip(A, cons(C, L)) & \rightarrow & cons((A, C), zip(A, L)) \end{array}$$

The function contain computes the set of categories that contain any of the categories given in a list of categories (i.e., contain implements the hierarchical relation between categories) and $\cap$ computes the intersection of two lists. The function arca* is a generalised version of the previously mentioned function arca to take into account lists of categories instead of a single category (see Section 2). We assume that the answers are only grant or deny; a more general version of axiom (c3) could be defined, for instance, to produce undefined when none of the categories of the resource is in the list of permissions for the categories of the principal issuing the request.

Now, to evaluate an access request by a principal p to perform the action a on the resource r we rewrite the term par(p, a, r) to normal form.

PROPOSITION 5.2. *The rewrite-based definition of* par *(Def. 5.1) is a correct realisation of the C-ABAC axioms:* par$(p, a, r) \rightarrow^*$ grant *if and only if* $(p, a, r) \in \mathcal{PAR}$.

PROOF. Using the rules given in Definition 5.1, the normal form of arca*(contain(pca(p))) is a list containing the elements in arca(c) for each c in pca(p). Similarly, contain(rca(r)) returns the list of all the categories to which the resource r belongs. Thus, par$(p, a, r) \rightarrow^*$ grant if and only if (a, c_r) is in arca(c) for some c in pca(p). By assumption, $(a, c_r) \in$ arca(c) iff $(a, c_r, c) \in \mathcal{ARCA}$, and $c \in$ pca(p) iff $(p, c) \in \mathcal{PCA}$. Therefore par$(p, a, r) \rightarrow^*$ grant iff $(a, c_r, c) \in \mathcal{ARCA}$ and $(p, c) \in \mathcal{PCA}$, iff $(p, a, r) \in \mathcal{PAR}$. □

6 ANALYSIS OF ABAC POLICIES

Access control systems are usually a critical part of software systems, and as such it is crucial that they ensure the right level of security. This motivated the development of tools and technologies to analyse policies (see, e.g., [9]). In this section we consider standard queries in ABAC policies and show how they can be answered using the C-ABAC specification. According to the basic policy analysis model defined in [9], analysis queries are classified as *policy metadata queries*, *policy content queries* and *policy effect queries*. Policy metadata queries concern metadata information about the policy; examples of information that can be retrieved with metadata queries are the author and date of creation of the policy. Using the C-ABAC model we propose in this paper, metadata information can be stored as attributes of an environment entity 'metadata'.

Policy content queries (sometimes called policy review queries) directly examine the content of policies, and policy effect queries are queries about the outcome the policy will produce in various situations. More precisely, policy effect queries relate to the authorisations and prohibitions specified by the policy, and usually mention principals, actions and resources. Property verification queries are a particular case of policy effect queries. Policy content queries and policy effect queries are the traditional administrator queries in access control systems. We discuss them below.

Policy content queries. Policy content queries are important for ABAC administrators because they help review the capabilities associated with principals and their attributes, and the access control entries associated with resources and their attributes. Specifically, these queries allow administrators to perform "before the fact audits", that is, to know what access each individual has before the requests are made. As highlighted in [26], before the fact audit is often necessary to demonstrate compliance to specific regulations, but is not easy to perform for ABAC policies. One of the main difficulties is the use of arbitrary logical formula in rules, whose satisfiability is an NP problem (enumerated ABAC does not use formulas but policies are not as expressive). Although C-ABAC also uses logical formulas, it limits its use to the definition of categories. The structure provided by categories in C-ABAC can help implement policy content queries, as shown below.

We consider the following policy content queries in ABAC, which aim at obtaining information about the policy at the time the query is issued.[1]

(1) Are all the resources accessible (in terms of principals and permissions)?
(2) Which principals are authorised to perform a given operation on a resource?
(3) For a given principal, what are the associated permissions?

In C-ABAC, in addition to the above, there are category-related queries, such as:

(4) Are all the principals associated with at least one category? Are all the resources associated with at least one category?
(5) Are there permissions associated with each category?
(6) For a given category of principals, who are the associated principals? For a given category of resources, which resources are in this category?
(7) To which categories belongs a given principal? To which categories belongs a given resource?
(8) For a given category, what are the associated permissions?

Following [9], if for a given policy there is a principal not assigned to any category, or a category without associated permissions, or a resource which is not accessible, we say that the policy is *ineffective*. It is unlikely that a policy is intentionally written to behave in this way; the analysis should try to identify ineffectiveness. We show how this can be done using the framework defined in the previous sections.

Given a C-ABAC policy $\langle E, Rel \rangle$, the queries above can be formalised and answered in the following way, where we assume that attribute values (i.e., the relations $\mathcal{PAtA}$, $\mathcal{RAtA}$, $\mathcal{EAtA}$ in Rel) and $\mathcal{ARCA} \in Rel$ can be computed in polynomial time (a standard assumption, always satisfied if relations are defined as tables storing attribute values).

(1) All the resources are accessible if and only if for each resource r there is at least one category c_r (see Q 4) such that
  • r satisfies the condition defining c_r;
  • there is a tuple $(a, c_r, c_p) \in \mathcal{ARCA}$ involving c_r;
  • there is at least one principal whose attributes satisfy the condition defining the category c_p (see Q 6).
(2) We can answer in terms of categories, that is, we check in which categories the resource is (as above) and then we retrieve from $\mathcal{ARCA}$ all the tuples (a, c_r, c_p) that involve those categories, and project on the third component. We can also enumerate the principals, by performing a further

step: for each existing principal in $\mathcal{PAtA}$, check which ones have attributes that satisfy c_p.

(3) To answer this query, we need to retrieve the categories to which the principal belongs (see Q 7), then retrieve from $\mathcal{ARCA}$ the tuples involving those categories and project on the first two elements. In this way, we obtain a set of pairs (a, c_r) defining all the actions that the principal can do on categories of resources. We can enumerate the actual resources by obtaining for each c_r the list of members (see Q 6).
(4) For each principal p, we can compute the set of categories to which p belongs by evaluating the conditions in each category definition using the values of p's attributes, specified in $\mathcal{PAtA}$. Similarly, for each resource r, we can compute the set of categories to which r belongs by evaluating the conditions in each category definition using the values of r's attributes, specified in $\mathcal{RAtA}$.
(5) To retrieve the set of permissions associated with a category c, we simply need to extract from $\mathcal{ARCA}$ all the tuples involving c.
(6) To retrieve the set of principals that belong to a category c_p (resp. the set of resources that belong to c_r), we check for each tuple in $\mathcal{PAtA}$ (resp. $\mathcal{RAtA}$) whether the tuple satisfies the formula defining the category.
(7) To retrieve the set of categories to which a principal p (resp. a resource r) belongs, we check which of the conditions defining the categories are satisfied by the tuple associated to p in $\mathcal{PAtA}$ (resp. r in $\mathcal{RAtA}$).
(8) For a given category c, the associated permissions are computed simply by extracting from $\mathcal{ARCA}$ the tuples involving c, and projecting on the other two components.

Note that from a complexity point of view, these queries only require to check whether given attribute values satisfy a formula, which is polynomial. Thus, we obtain the following result.

PROPOSITION 6.1. *The queries Q1-Q8 listed above can be answered in polynomial time with respect to the size of the policy (assuming the basic relations $\mathcal{PAtA}$, $\mathcal{RAtA}$ and $\mathcal{ARCA}$ can be computed in polynomial time).*

An interesting query if a hierarchy of categories is used is whether the category definitions are compatible with $\subseteq$ (axiom c0). The implementation of this check depends on the language used to define category conditions. A similar analysis has been made for Dynamic RBAC, see [5] where SMT solvers are used to check this property.

A further interesting query is: Which values of attributes allow a principal to access to a particular resource? To answer this query we need to solve a satisfiability problem, which, depending on the language used to specify the conditions could be exponential or even undecidable. However, in C-ABAC there is another way to answer this query, which does not involve solving logical formulas: we can find the categories $c_1, \ldots, c_n$ of principals that are allowed access to the resource (by retrieving from $\mathcal{ARCA}$ the tuples associated with the resource category), and then retrieve the definitions ($cond_i$) of those categories, i.e., instead of answering this query by enumerating the attribute values, we can answer "Those values that categorise the principal as $c_1, \ldots, c_n$, that is, those values that satisfy at least one of the conditions $cond_i$".

---

[1]If a policy is static (e.g., in the case of an RBAC policy) then the answer does not depend on time.

Policy effect queries. Policy effect queries relate to specific properties of the policy and are usually stated in terms of authorisations, prohibitions and their interactions. Typical queries relate to the *totality* and *consistency* of the policy. A policy is total if every access request receives an answer. It is consistent if there is a unique answer for each request (this ensures that the same request cannot be both authorised and prohibited by the policy). More precisely, we are interested in the following properties of ABAC policies:

Totality: Each access request from a valid principal p to perform a valid action a on a resource r receives an answer.

Consistency: For any $p \in \mathcal{P}$, $a \in \mathcal{A}$, $r \in \mathcal{R}$, at most one result is possible for an authorisation request $par(p, a, r)$.

Soundness and Completeness: For any $p \in \mathcal{P}$, $a \in \mathcal{A}$, $r \in \mathcal{R}$, an access request by p to perform the action a on r is granted if and only if p has the attribute values required for the permission (a, r).

Totality and consistency can be proved, for policies defined as term rewriting systems, by checking that the rewrite relation is confluent and terminating. Termination ensures that all access requests produce a result (e.g. a result that is not grant or deny is interpreted as undetermined) and confluence ensures that this result is unique. The soundness and completeness of a policy can be checked by analysing the normal forms of access requests, using tools like CiME [19], see [14].

Confluence and termination of rewriting are undecidable properties in general, but there are several results available that provide sufficient conditions for these properties to hold. For example, to prove termination, a C-ABAC policy can be considered as a *hierarchical* rewrite system, where the basis includes the set of constants identifying the main entities in the model as well as the set of auxiliary data structures (such as booleans, lists) and functions on these data structures. The next level in the hierarchy contains the parameter functions of the model, namely pca, rca, arca, arca*,contain. Finally the last level of the hierarchy consists of the definition of the function par. Several sufficient conditions for termination of rewrite systems defined as a hierarchical union of rules are available (see e.g. [20]). Sufficient conditions for confluence include orthogonality (where rules are left-linear and without superpositions) [31], and for systems that terminate, absence of critical pairs [33].

7 RELATED WORK

Several general models and languages for access control have been described in the literature. For example, the GTRBAC model [30] and ASL [28] aim at providing a general framework for the definition of policies. In GTRBAC, the focus is on the notion of a role; in ASL, users, groups and roles are admitted in the language. ABLP logic [1] also provides a formal framework for reasoning about access control, with a focus on language constructs for formulating policies and axioms and inference rules for defining a system for proof, e.g., for proving authorised forms of access. In contrast, the CBAC metamodel is based on abstracting, from the generalities of access control models, the common aspects of access control from which core functions are identified. Most of the existing access control models have been shown to be instances of the metamodel, using different concepts to specify principal-category assignments, such as roles, events, actions or histories [13]. In this paper, we

have used attribute values to specify category assignments, obtaining the C-ABAC model. Using CBAC to formalise ABAC was first suggested in [21], but attributes were not formalised and no comparisons with other ABAC models were provided.

Previous formalisations of ABAC have also used logic: Wang et al [39] use stratified logic programming with constraints over sets to define rules specifying conditions on user attributes for each action. $ABAC_\alpha$ [29] formalises the essential components of ABAC using propositional logic to define authorisations, and includes a constraint language to deal with attribute changes. There are also logic-based formalisations of enumerated ABAC, for example, the family of LaBAC models [15] is specified using first-order logic, including constraints on attribute values and constraints on relations. C-ABAC, being an instance of the category-based metamodel, introduces structure in ABAC via the categorisation of entities. This structure facilitates some kinds of review queries, but introduces an extra step in the policy design phase and in the evaluation of access requests. In its current version, C-ABAC does not deal with constraints; these could be added as axioms in future extensions.

C-ABAC is a hybrid version of ABAC, in that it uses relations as in enumerated ABAC, but they are specified by logical formulas. Categories could also be seen as a form of attribute-reduction [16] by considering categories as attributes; however, by separating the notions of category and attribute C-ABAC adds structure to policies, which permits to avoid some conflicts and circular definitions.

Kuhn et al [32] compare RBAC and ABAC and conclude that a combination of both can take advantage of their strengths; they classify combinations as Attribute-centric, Role-centric, or using Dynamic roles. C-ABAC is in the third class: it can be seen as a dynamic version of RBAC, where roles (represented by categories), are defined by Boolean formulas on attribute values, and in addition the same idea of categorisation is applied also to resources. There are several existing extensions of RBAC that incorporate attribute evaluation: Huang et al [27] add environment conditions to user-role and role-permission assignments and propose to use rule schemas to define these assignments, to facilitate the specification of policies with large number of users or resources; however, this makes it harder to review policies as different rules can give different permissions to the same roles, thus losing RBAC's structuring features. Al-Kahtani and Sandhu [2] consider systems with a large number of users, where manual assignment of users to roles is not feasible, and propose the use of attributes to perform automatic assignment to roles, whereas in the EDAC model [22], attributes such as time are used by a front-end module to assign roles to users. C-ABAC can be seen as a formalisation of the essential components of EDAC, including categories for resources as well as categories for users (not to be confused with EDAC resource roles, which correspond to categories of principals). However, C-ABAC lacks support for the sophisticated attribute management operations of practical models such as EDAC (attribute management is abstracted in the relations $\mathcal{PAtA}$, $\mathcal{RAtA}$ and $\mathcal{EAtA}$).

8 CONCLUSIONS

ABAC is a powerful access control model, which is well-suited for open systems where users are not known in advance. In this paper we have provided an axiomatisation of ABAC in first-order logic, using the CBAC metamodel. In the resulting C-ABAC model, authorisations are derived from user, object and environment attributes by means of a process of categorisation. We have shown that ABAC policies can be represented in C-ABAC, and conversely, given a C-ABAC policy it is possible to expand the category definitions and permission assignments into a set of ABAC rules. Thus, C-ABAC does not increase the expressive power of ABAC, but can be seen as providing a structured representation of ABAC policies, which could have advantages from the point of view of policy maintenance. Regarding the main existing approaches to specify ABAC policies (via logical formulas and via enumerated relations), C-ABAC can be seen as a middle point, where policies are defined by relations in the style of enumerated ABAC, but the relations are defined via logical formulas involving conditions on attribute values. A visual representation of C-ABAC policies could be obtained by using the graph representation of CBAC policies described in [4].

Several important aspects of ABAC policies have not been covered in this paper, such as the definition of sessions, the axiomatisation of prohibitions and obligations, the specification of constraints such as separation of duties, and the management of combinations of policies. In future work we will address these aspects using the techniques available in the CBAC metamodel [12].

REFERENCES

[1] M. Abadi, M. Burrows, B. W. Lampson, and G. D. Plotkin. 1993. A Calculus for Access Control in Distributed Systems. *ACM Trans. Program. Lang. Syst.* 15, 4 (1993), 706–734.
[2] M. A. Al-Kahtani and R. S. Sandhu. 2002. A Model for Attribute-Based User-Role Assignment. In *18th Annual Computer Security Applications Conference (ACSAC 2002), 9-13 December 2002, Las Vegas, NV, USA.* 353–362. https://doi.org/10.1109/CSAC.2002.1176307
[3] R. Alsowail and I. Mackie. 2017. Controlling File Access with Types. *Electr. Notes Theor. Comput. Sci.* 332 (2017), 3–20. https://doi.org/10.1016/j.entcs.2017.04.002
[4] S. Alves and M. Fernández. 2017. A graph-based framework for the analysis of access control policies. *Theor. Comput. Sci.* 685 (2017), 3–22. https://doi.org/10.1016/j.tcs.2016.10.018
[5] A. Armando and S. Ranise. 2012. Automated and Efficient Analysis of Role-Based Access Control with Attributes. In *Data and Applications Security and Privacy XXVI - 26th Annual IFIP WG 11.3 Conference, DBSec 2012, Paris, France, July 11-13,2012. Proceedings.* 25–40. https://doi.org/10.1007/978-3-642-31540-4_3
[6] F. Baader and T. Nipkow. 1998. *Term Rewriting and All That.* Cambridge University Press.
[7] S. Barker. 2009. The next 700 access control models or a unifying meta-model?. In *SACMAT 2009, 14th ACM Symposium on Access Control Models and Technologies, Stresa, Italy, June 3-5, 2009, Proceedings.* ACM Press, 187–196.
[8] S. Barker, M. J. Sergot, and D. Wijesekera. 2008. Status-Based Access Control. *ACM Trans. Inf. Syst. Secur.* 12, 1 (2008), 1:1–1:47. https://doi.org/10.1145/1410234.1410235
[9] E. Bertino, C. Brodie, S. B. Calo, L. F. Cranor, C-M. Karat, J. Karat, N. Li, D. Lin, J. Lobo, Q. Ni, P. Rao, and X. Wang. 2009. Analysis of privacy and security policies. *IBM Journal of Research and Development* 53, 2 (2009), 3. https://doi.org/10.1147/JRD.2009.5429045
[10] E. Bertino, B. Catania, E. Ferrari, and P. Perlasca. 2003. A logical framework for reasoning about access control models. *ACM Trans. Inf. Syst. Secur.* 6, 1 (2003), 71–127.
[11] C. Bertolissi and M. Fernández. 2010. Category-based authorisation models: operational semantics and expressive power. In *Proc. of Int. Symposium on Engineering Secure Software and Systems, ESSOS 2010, Pisa (Lecture Notes in Computer Science).* Springer, 140–156.
[12] C. Bertolissi and M. Fernández. 2014. A metamodel of access control for distributed environments: Applications and properties. *Inf. Comput.* 238 (2014), 187–207. https://doi.org/10.1016/j.ic.2014.07.009
[13] C. Bertolissi, M. Fernández, and S. Barker. 2007. Dynamic Event-Based Access Control as Term Rewriting. In *Data and Applications Security XXI. Proceedings of DBSEC 2007 (Lecture Notes in Computer Science).* Springer-Verlag.
[14] C. Bertolissi and W. Uttha. 2013. Automated analysis of rule-based access control policies. In *Proceedings of the 7th Workshop on Programming languages meets program verification, PLPV 2013, Rome, Italy, January 22, 2013.* 47–56. https://doi.org/10.1145/2428116.2428125
[15] P. Biswas, R. Sandhu, and R. Krishnan. 2016. Label-Based Access Control: An ABAC Model with Enumerated Authorization Policy. In *Proceedings of the 2016 ACM International Workshop on Attribute Based Access Control, ABAC@CODASPY 2016, New Orleans, Louisiana, USA, March 11, 2016.* 1–12. https://doi.org/10.1145/2875491.2875498
[16] P. Biswas, R. Sandhu, and R. Krishnan. 2017. Attribute Transformation for Attribute-Based Access Control. In *Proceedings of the 2nd ACM Workshop on Attribute-Based Access Control, ABAC@CODASPY 2017, Scottsdale, Arizona, USA, March 24, 2017.* 1–8. https://doi.org/10.1145/3041048.3041052
[17] P. A. Bonatti and P. Samarati. 2003. Logics for Authorization and Security.. In *Logics for Emerging Applications of Databases*, J. Chomicki, R. van der Meyden, and G. Saake (Eds.). Springer, 277–323.
[18] S. M. Chandran and J. B. D. Joshi. 2005. LoT-RBAC: A Location and Time-Based RBAC Model. In *Proc. of WISE 2005, 6th International Conference on Web Information Systems Engineering, NY, USA, 2005 (Lecture Notes in Computer Science).* Springer, 361–375.
[19] É. Contejean, A. Paskevich, X. Urbain, P. Courtieu, O. Pons, and J. Forest. 2010. A3PAT, an approach for certified automated termination proofs. In *Proc. of the 2010 ACM SIGPLAN workshop on Partial evaluation and program manipulation (PEPM '10).* ACM, New York, NY, USA, 63–72.
[20] M. Fernández and J.-P. Jouannaud. 1995. Modular Termination of Term Rewriting Systems Revisited. In *Recent Trends in Data Type Specification. Proc. 10th. Workshop on Specification of Abstract Data Types (ADT'94) (Lecture Notes in Computer Science).* Santa Margherita, Italy.
[21] M. Fernández and B. Thuraisingham. 2018. A Category-Based Model for ABAC. In *Proceedings of the Third ACM Workshop on Attribute-Based Access Control, CODASPY.* ACM Press, 32–34.
[22] Richard Fernandez. 2006. Enterprise Dynamic Access Control Version 2 Overview. US Space and Naval Warfare Systems Center.
[23] D. Ferraiolo, R. Kuhn, and R. Chandramouli. 2003. *Role-Based Access Control.* Artech House.
[24] D. F. Ferraiolo, V. Atluri, and S. I. Gavrila. 2011. The Policy Machine: A novel architecture and framework for access control policy specification and enforcement. *Journal of Systems Architecture - Embedded Systems Design* 57, 4 (2011), 412–424. https://doi.org/10.1016/j.sysarc.2010.04.005
[25] D. F. Ferraiolo, R. S. Sandhu, S. I. Gavrila, D. Richard Kuhn, and R. Chandramouli. 2001. Proposed NIST standard for role-based access control. *ACM TISSEC* 4, 3 (2001), 224–274.
[26] V. C. Hu, D. Ferraiolo, R. Kuhn, A. Schnitzer, K. Sandlin, R. Miller, and K. Scarfone. 2014. Guide to Attribute Based Access Control (ABAC) Definitions and Considerations. NIST Special Publication 800-162.
[27] J. Huang, D. M. Nicol, R. Bobba, and J. Ho Huh. 2012. A framework integrating attribute-based policies into role-based access control. In *17th ACM Symposium on Access Control Models and Technologies, SACMAT '12, Newark, NJ, USA - June 20 - 22, 2012.* 187–196. https://doi.org/10.1145/2295136.2295170
[28] S. Jajodia, P. Samarati, M. Sapino, and V.S. Subrahmaninan. 2001. Flexible Support for Multiple Access Control Policies. *ACM TODS* 26, 2 (2001), 214–260.
[29] X. Jin, R. Krishnan, and R.S. Sandhu. 2012. A unified attribute-based access control model covering DAC, MAC and RBAC. In *DBSec 2012.* Springer, 42–55.
[30] J. Joshi, E. Bertino, U. Latif, and A. Ghafoor. 2005. A Generalized Temporal Role-Based Access Control Model. *IEEE Trans. Knowl. Data Eng.* 17, 1 (2005), 4–23.
[31] J.-W. Klop, V. van Oostrom, and F. van Raamsdonk. 1993. Combinatory Reduction Systems, introduction and survey. *Theoretical Computer Science* 121 (1993), 279–308.
[32] D. Richard Kuhn, Edward J. Coyne, and Timothy R. Weil. 2010. Adding Attributes to Role-Based Access Control. *IEEE Computer* 43, 6 (2010), 79–81. https://doi.org/10.1109/MC.2010.155
[33] M.H.A. Newman. 1942. On theories with a combinatorial definition of equivalence. *Annals of Mathematics* 43, 2 (1942), 223–243.
[34] R. Sandhu, E. Coyne, H. Feinstein, and C. Youman. 1996. Role-Based Access Control Models. *IEEE Computer* 29, 2 (1996), 38–47.
[35] R. Sandhu, D. Ferraiolo, and R. Kuhn. 2000. The NIST Model for RRole-based Access Control: Towards a Unified Standard. In *Proc. 4th ACM Workshop on Role-Based Access Control.* 47–61.
[36] A. Santana de Oliveira. 2008. *Réécriture et Modularité pour les Politiques de Sécurité.* Ph.D. Dissertation. Université Henri Poincaré, Nancy, France.
[37] D. Servos and S. L. Osborn. 2014. HGABAC: Towards a Formal Model of Hierarchical Attribute-Based Access Control. In *Foundations and Practice of Security - 7th International Symposium, FPS 2014, Montreal, QC, Canada, November 3-5, 2014. Revised Selected Papers.* 187–204. https://doi.org/10.1007/978-3-319-17040-4_12
[38] K. Sohr, M. Drouineaud, G-J Ahn, and M. Gogolla. 2008. Analyzing and Managing Role-Based Access Control Policies. *IEEE Trans. Knowl. Data Eng.* 20, 7 (2008), 924–939. https://doi.org/10.1109/TKDE.2008.28
[39] L. Wang, D. Wijesekera, and S. Jajodia. 2004. A logic-based framework for attribute based access control.. In *Proceedings of Formal methods in security engineering (FMSE).* 45–55.

Results in Workflow Resiliency

Complexity, New Formulation, and ASP Encoding

Philip W.L. Fong
University of Calgary
pwlfong@ucalgary.ca

ABSTRACT

First proposed by Wang and Li in 2007, workflow resiliency is a policy analysis for ensuring that, even when an adversarial environment removes a subset of workers from service, a workflow can still be instantiated to satisfy all the security constraints. Wang and Li proposed three notions of workflow resiliency: static, decremental, and dynamic resiliency. While decremental and dynamic resiliency are both PSPACE-complete, Wang and Li did not provide a matching lower and upper bound for the complexity of static resiliency.

The present work begins with proving that static resiliency is Π_2^p-complete, thereby bridging a long-standing complexity gap in the literature. In addition, a fourth notion of workflow resiliency, one-shot resiliency, is proposed and shown to remain in the third level of the polynomial hierarchy. This shows that sophisticated notions of workflow resiliency need not be PSPACE-complete. Lastly, we demonstrate how to reduce static and one-shot resiliency to Answer Set Programming (ASP), a modern constraint-solving technology that can be used for solving reasoning tasks in the lower levels of the polynomial hierarchy. In summary, this work demonstrates the value of focusing on notions of workflow resiliency that reside in the lower levels of the polynomial hierarchy.

CCS CONCEPTS

• **Security and privacy** → **Access control**.

KEYWORDS

Availability; Workflow authorization model; Workflow resiliency; Static resiliency; One-shot resiliency; Answer set programming

ACM Reference Format:
Philip W.L. Fong. 2019. Results in Workflow Resiliency: Complexity, New Formulation, and ASP Encoding. In *Ninth ACM Conference on Data and Application Security and Privacy (CODASPY '19), March 25–27, 2019, Richardson, TX, USA*. ACM, New York, NY, USA, 12 pages. https://doi.org/10.1145/3292006.3300038

1 INTRODUCTION

Confidentiality, integrity, and availability are three essential goals of security. This paper is about availability considerations in workflow authorization models.

A workflow is an application-level abstraction of a business process. Access control in a workflow application is captured in a workflow authorization model [1, 3, 7, 37, 38], the main idea of which is to realize the Principle of Least Privilege [35] through permission abstraction [2]. Instead of granting permissions directly to users, permissions are granted to the steps of a workflow. When a user is assigned to perform a step in the workflow, the permissions are then made available to the user. Two additional access control features are typically found in a workflow authorization model. First, qualification requirements can be imposed on each workflow step. An example is to require that the "Prepare Budget" step be carried out by an "Account Clerk," while the "Account Review" step be carried out by an "Account Manager" (example taken from [40]). This is typically framed in terms of roles in an underlying Role-Based Access Control (RBAC) model. Second, further security constraints may be imposed across steps to prevent abuse. A classical example would be separation-of-duty constraints: e.g., the "Create Payment" step and the "Approve Payment" step must be carried out by two distinct users (example taken from [15]). Recent works in workflow authorization models have considered arbitrary binary constraints, thereby introducing into workflow authorization models an element of Relationship-Based Access Control (ReBAC) [25, 39, 40].

As permissions are now encapsulated in workflow steps, we want to make sure that the workflow can actually be executed, or else the situation amounts to a denial of service. In other words, one must ensure that it is possible to assign users to workflow steps, so that all qualification requirements and security constraints are satisfied. This notion of availability has been known in the literature as the ***workflow satisfiability problem (WSP)*** [3, 7, 15, 40]. WSP can be used as a policy analysis to help the workflow developer debug her formulation, so that the latter is not overly constrained.

A major landmark in the study of the WSP has been the work of Wang and Li [39, 40], who first introduced into the literature the application of Fixed Parameter Tractable (FPT) algorithms [21] to solve WSP. Subsequently, major breakthroughs in the design of FPT algorithms for WSP have been invented by the research group at Royal Holloway University of London, including kernelization algorithms [8, 14, 15], exploitation of problem symmetry in pattern-based algorithms [5, 6], and novel problem formulations [9, 12],

A second major contribution of Wang and Li's work is the introduction of an advanced notion of availability that is stronger than workflow satisfiability. That notion is workflow resiliency [39, 40], the subject of this paper. The idea is to anticipate catastrophes that may remove users from service. One would like to ensure that, even if the adversarial environment has taken away a certain number of users, the workflow is still satisfiable by the remaining personnel. More specifically, Wang and Li proposed three different notions of workflow resiliency, namely, static, decremental, and dynamic resiliency. While decremental and dynamic resiliency have been shown to be PSPACE-complete, Wang and Li did not provide a matching upper and lower bound for the complexity of static resiliency: static resiliency is in Π_2^p and is NP-hard. Whether static resiliency is Π_2^p-complete has remained an open problem since the notion was first conceived a decade ago. Bridging this complexity gap is the first motivation of this work.

The last few years have witnessed a renewed interest in the study of workflow resiliency [10, 29–31]. Two lines of research have been representative. The first is the work of Mace *et al.* [29–31], who argue that it is more important to assess to what (quantitative) degree of resiliency a workflow enjoys, rather than to test if the workflow is resilient or not (binary). The goal is to offer guidance to the workflow developer in terms of refining the formulation of the business process.

While Mace *et al.*'s approach is valuable, it is the position of this paper that deep insights of the workflow can be gained by evaluating the workflow against multiple and incomparable notions of workflow resiliency: e.g., statically resilient for a budget of t_1 and decrementally resilient for a budget of t_2, where $t_2 < t_1$. In fact, each notion of workflow resiliency captures a family of attack scenarios. Confirming that a workflow is resilient in terms of several incomparable notions of resiliency offers deep insight into the formulation of the workflow. We therefore need a good number of notions of workflow resiliency, rather than just a few. More than that, we need notions of workflow resiliency that are not computationally prohibitive to test. Unfortunately, a pessimistic reader of Wang and Li may come to the conclusion that static resiliency is an exception rather than a rule, and that most notions of workflow resiliency are PSPACE-complete. This pessimism is understandable as the notions of workflow resiliency proposed by Wang and Li are formulated in terms of strategic games. If resiliency is fundamentally a PSPACE-complete phenomenon, then hoping for an efficient solution may be unrealistic. A second motivation of this work is to demonstrate that there are indeed useful notions of workflow resiliency that are not as prohibitive as decremental and dynamic resiliency.

A second line of recent work in workflow resiliency is that of Crampton *et al.* [10], who devised a first FPT algorithm for deciding dynamic resiliency. The parameter they used was $k + t$, where k is the number of steps in the workflow, and t is the number of users that the adversary can remove. While k is universally accepted to be a small parameter in the literature [15, 40], t is not. For example, if t is a fixed fraction of the number of users (e.g., 5% of the user population), it already grows much faster than is acceptable for an FPT algorithm. It is the position of this paper that parameterizing the problem using t is not fruitful (see §8, however, for an example of adversary models in which such a parameterization could make sense). In this light, non-FPT approaches are still valuable when t is not a small parameter. The formulation of algorithmic solutions

for workflow resiliency without assuming a small t is the third motivation of this work.

This paper has three contributions:

(1) In §3, static resiliency is proven to be Π_2^p-complete, thereby bridging the long-standing complexity gap in the work of Wang and Li [39, 40]. This result also provides the intellectual justification for the third contribution below.

(2) In §4, we dispel the pessimistic interpretation of Wang and Li's work by formulating a new notion of workflow resiliency, one-shot resiliency, which is more sophisticated than static resiliency, and nevertheless remains in the third level of the polynomial hierarchy (Σ_3^p-complete). This means that useful notions of workflow resiliency can be formulated without flirting with PSPACE-completeness.

(3) We advocate the use of Answer Set Programming (ASP) [22, 23], a modern constraint-solving technology, for deciding static and one-shot resiliency. ASP has been shown to be particularly fitted for reasoning problems in the lower levels of the polynomial hierarchy [4, 19, 20, 34]. In §6, we demonstrate the feasibility of this approach by presenting ASP encodings of static and one-shot resiliency. These reductions employ an encoding technique known as the model saturation technique [19, 20]. This solution approach does not require the parameter t to be small.

2 BACKGROUND: WORKFLOW SATISFIABILITY AND RESILIENCY

This section provides a brief introduction to workflow satisfiability and resiliency, in order to prepare the reader to understand the rest of this paper. All the materials presented in this section have already appeared in previous work (particularly [39, 40]).

2.1 Workflow Satisfiability

A workflow is the abstract representation of a business process.

Definition 2.1. A **workflow** $(S, \leq)$ is a partial ordering of steps. For steps $s_1, s_2 \in S$, we write $s_1 < s_2$ whenever $s_1 \leq s_2$ but $s_1 \neq s_2$.

Steps are tasks to be executed by users, and the partial ordering expresses the causal dependencies among steps. If two steps are ordered by $<$, then they must be executed in that order; otherwise, they can interleave in any arbitrary manner.

When a workflow is executed, users are assigned to the steps, sometimes in an incremental manner.

Definition 2.2. Given a workflow $(S, \leq)$ and a set U of users, a **partial plan** is a function $\theta : T \rightarrow U$ such that (a) the domain T is a subset of S, and (b) θ is **causally closed**: that is, for every $s_1, s_2 \in S$, if $s_1 \in T$ and $s_2 < s_1$, then $s_2 \in T$. A partial plan θ is also called a **plan** when $dom(\theta) = S$.

Security constraints, such as seperation of duty, may be imposed on a workflow in order to prevent abuse.

Definition 2.3 (in the style of [5, 6]). A **workflow authorization policy** W is a 5-tuple $(S, \leq, U, A, C)$, where the components are defined as follows:

- $(S, \leq)$ is a workflow.

- U is a set of users.
- $A \subseteq S \times U$ is the **step authorization policy**, which lists for each step those users who are qualified to carry out the step.
- C is a set of **constraints**. Each constraint has the form (T, Θ). The set $T \subseteq S$ specifies the steps constrained by the constraint. The component Θ is a set of partial plans, each with T as its domain. The set Θ specifies the combinations of assignments that are permitted by the constraint.

The following definition specifies when a (partial) plan satisfies the requirements imposed by a workflow authorization policy.

Definition 2.4. Suppose θ is a partial plan for the workflow authorization policy $W = (S, \leq, U, A, C)$. We say that θ is **valid** if and only if the following conditions hold:

- For every step $s \in S$, $(s, \theta(s)) \in A$.
- For every constraint $(T, \Theta) \in C$, if $T \subseteq dom(\theta)$, then there exists $\theta' \in \Theta$ such that for every $s \in T$, $\theta(s) = \theta(s)'$.

A plan is valid if and only if it is valid as a partial plan.

The following are some examples of constraints. Following [39, 40], we focus mostly on entailment constraints, including the generalization by [14, 15]. Our ASP encodings of §6 can easily handle the cardinality constraints of [14, 15] as well.

Example 2.5. Suppose S is a set of steps, and U is a set of users.

- Suppose S_1 and S_2 are non-empty subsets of S, and $\rho \subseteq U \times U$ is a binary relation. We write $ent(\rho, S_1, S_2)$ to denote the **entailment constraint** (T, Θ) for which $T = T_1 \cup T_2$, and $\Theta = \{\theta \in U^T \mid \exists s_1 \in T_1, s_2 \in T_2 . (\theta(s_1), \theta(s_2)) \in \rho\}$.
- Crampton *et al.* classify entailment constraints in to various types [14, 15]. A **type-1** entailment constraint is one in which both step sets are singleton sets. We overload notation and write $ent(\rho, s_1, s_2)$ to denote $ent(\rho, \{s_1\}, \{s_2\})$. A **type-2** entailment constraint is one in which exactly one of the two step sets is a singleton set. A **type-3** entailment constraint is one in which neither of the step sets is a singleton set.
- The **separation-of-duty constraint** $sod(s_1, s_2)$ is the type-1 entailment constraint $ent(\neq, s_1, s_2)$. Similarly, the **binding-of-duty constraint** $bod(s_1, s_2)$ is defined to be $ent(=, s_1, s_2)$.

When one formulates a workflow authorization policy, one must ensure that the constraints are not overly restrictive to the point that no valid plan exists.

Definition 2.6. A workflow authorization policy W is **satisfiable** if and only if at least one valid plan exists. *WSP* is the language of workflow authorization policies that are satisfiable.

THEOREM 2.7 ([39, 40]). *WSP is NP-complete.*

Even though *WSP* is theoretically intractable, previous work has demonstrated that it can be decided with moderate efficiency by apply modern *SAT* solving technologies [40], and with even greater efficiency by Fixed-Parameter Tractable algorithms [5, 6, 15, 40].

2.2 Workflow Resiliency

For mission critical business processes, a degree of availability higher than workflow satisfiability is often desired. The basic idea is to anticipate catastrophic events, which may render some users

unavailable for duty. The goal is to ensure that there is enough redundancy in human resources so that the workflow can execute to completion even when accidents occur.

The first notion of workflow resiliency models a workflow that runs for a very short period of time (e.g., in minutes). Some users become unavailable prior to workflow execution. Due to the short duration of the workflow, no further users are removed from service.

Definition 2.8 (Static Resiliency [39, 40]). A workflow authorization policy $W = (S, \leq, U, A, C)$ is **statically resilient** for an integer budget $t \geq 0$ if and only if, for every subset Δ of U that has size t or less, there is a valid plan $\theta : S \to (U \setminus \Delta)$ that does not assign the users in Δ.

Workflow resiliency is typically described in terms of two-person games: Player 1 attempts to construct a valid plan, while Player 2, who models the adversarial environment, counters Player 1 by removing users from service. Static resiliency can thus be modelled by a two-person game that is played in one round: Player 2 first removes up to t users, and then Player 1 constructs a valid plan with the remaining users. A workflow authorization policy is statically resilient when Player 1 can win no matter how Player 2 plays.

The next notion of workflow resiliency models the situation in which the workflow runs for a moderately long time (e.g., within a day). During the execution of the workflow, more and more users become unavailable.

Definition 2.9 (Decremental Resiliency [39, 40]). A workflow authorization policy $W = (S, \leq, U, A, C)$ is **decrementally resilient** for integer budget $t \geq 0$ if and only if Player 1 can win the **decremental resiliency game** no matter how Player 2 plays.

The decremental resiliency game is a two-player game that proceeds in rounds. At any time, the configuration of the game is a pair (Δ, θ), where $\Delta \subseteq U$, and θ is a partial plan. In the initial configuration, both Δ and θ are $\emptyset$.

Each round begins by Player 2 choosing some users from U to be added to Δ, so long as $|\Delta| \leq t$. (A legitimate special case is when no user is chosen. Also, users added to Δ remain there until the end of the game.) Next, Player 1 extends θ by assigning a user from $U \setminus \Delta$ to a not-yet-assigned step.

Player 2 wins right away if $U \setminus \Delta$ becomes empty, or if θ becomes invalid. Player 1 wins if θ is eventually turned into a valid plan (i.e., every step is assigned a user).

The third notion of workflow resiliency models situations in which the workflow runs for an extended period of time (e.g., in days). Once an accident occurs to remove some users from service, they return to work before the next accident has a chance to occur.

Definition 2.10 (Dynamic resiliency [39, 40]). A workflow authorization policy $W = (S, \leq, U, A, C)$ is **dynamically resilient** for integer budget $t \geq 0$ if and only if Player 1 can win the **dynamic resiliency game** no matter how Player 2 plays.

The dynamic resiliency game is a two-player game that proceeds in rounds. At any time, the configuration of the game is a partial plan θ. Initially, θ is $\emptyset$.

Each round begins by Player 2 choosing a subset Δ of U such that $|\Delta| \leq t$. Next, Player 1 extends θ by assigning a member of $U \setminus \Delta$ to a not-yet-assigned step.

Player 2 wins right away if $\Delta = U$, or if θ becomes invalid. Player 1 wins if θ is eventually turned into a valid plan.

We write *SRCP* for the language of pairs (W, t) for which W is statically resilient for a budget t. Similarly, we write *CRCP* and *DRCP* for the respective language of decremental and dynamic resiliency.

The three notions of resiliency are totally ordered in terms of how demanding they are.

THEOREM 2.11 ([39, 40]). *DRCP* $\subset$ *CRCP* $\subset$ *SRCP*.

Note the proper set inclusion in the statement above. While *SRCP* is the least demanding notion of resiliency among the three, its computational complexity is also the least intimidating.

THEOREM 2.12 ([39, 40]). *DRCP and CRCP are* PSPACE*-complete. SRCP is in* Π_2^p, *and is* NP*-hard.*

Note that the upper and lower bound for *SRCP* do not match. Since the publication of Wang and Li's works a decade ago, whether *SRCP* is Π_2^p-complete has remained an open problem. The starting point of the present work is to provide an affirmative answer to this problem.

3 STATIC RESILIENCY REVISITED

The first main contribution of this work is the following result:

THEOREM 3.1. *SRCP is* Π_2^p*-hard.*

In addition to providing a matching lower bound for Wang and Li's upper bound (Theorem 2.12), this result has practical implications for the choice of solution strategy for *SRCP*. Π_2^p-completeness implies that it is unlikely one can employ *SAT*-solving technologies to solve *SRCP*. One is now driven to employ constraint-solving technologies that are designed for problems in the second level of the polynomial hierarchy. As we shall see in §5, one such technology is Answer-Set Programming.

PROOF. We sketch a polynomial-time Karp reduction from the Π_2^p-complete problem, **Dynamic Hamiltonian Circuit (DHC)** [26, 36], to *SRCP*.

Problem: *DHC* [26]
Instance: A simple graph[1] $G = (V, E)$, and an edge set $B \subseteq E$.
Question: Is it the case that for every $D \subseteq B$ with $|D| \leq |B|/2$, G_D has a Hamilton cycle?
Remark: The graph G_D is defined to be $(V, E \setminus D)$.

The proposed reduction takes as input an instance of *DHC*, which consists of a graph $G = (V, E)$ and a set $B \subseteq E$. The reduction returns an instance of *SRCP* consisting of a budget $t = |B|/2$ and a workflow authorization policy $(S, \leq, U, A, C)$:

(1) $S = SV \cup SE$ is a set of $2N$ steps, where $N = |V|$:

$$SV = \{sv_1, sv_2, \ldots, sv_N\}$$
$$SE = \{se_1, se_2, \ldots, se_N\}$$

These steps model a Hamiltonian cycle: each step in *SV* models a vertex in the Hamiltonian cycle, and each step in *SE* corresponds to an edge in the Hamiltonian cycle.

(2) The partial order $\leq$ is simply the equality relation (=). In other words, steps can be executed in any order.

(3) $U = UV \cup UE$ is the set of users defined as follows:

$$UV = \bigcup_{v \in V} UV_v$$
$$UE = \bigcup_{e \in E} UE_e$$

$$UV_v = \{(v, 1), (v, 2), \ldots, (v, t + 1)\} \qquad \text{for } v \in V \qquad (1)$$
$$UE_e = \{(e, 1), (e, 2), \ldots, (e, t + 1)\} \qquad \text{for } e \in E \setminus B \qquad (2)$$
$$UE_e = \{(e, 1)\} \qquad \text{for } e \in B \qquad (3)$$

Intuitively, the users represent vertices and edges in graph G. A plan, which assigns users to steps, effectively identifies vertices and edges that participate in the Hamiltonian cycle. All vertices and those edges *not* in B have $t + 1$ copies (see (1) and (2)). That means the adversary cannot make these vertices and edges unavailable by removing t users. There are, however, only one copy of those edges in B (see (3)). The adversary can prevent these edges from participating in the Hamiltonian cycle.

(4) The step authorization policy A ensures that users representing vertices are assigned to steps representing vertices, and the same for edges.

$$A = (SV \times UV) \cup (SE \times UE)$$

(5) The constraint set $C = C_{cir} \cup C_{ham}$ is made up of two types of constraint. Intuitively, the constraints in C_{cir} ensure that each valid plan identifies a circuit of size $N = |V|$, while the constraints in C_{ham} ensure that the identified circuit is Hamiltonian.

(a) C_{cir} is a set of type-1 entailment constraints induced by the binary relation *incident*. For every edge $e \in E$ connecting vertices $u, v \in V$, define a binary relation $incident_e \subseteq U \times U$:

$$incident_e = (UE_e \times UV_u) \cup (UE_e \times UV_v)$$

In other words, $incident_e$ relates a user representing e to a user representing one of the two vertices connected by e. Now, *incident* is defined as follows:

$$incident = \bigcup_{e \in E} incident_e$$

We also write $incident^{-1}$ to represent the converse[2] of *incident*. In short, $incident^{-1}$ relates a user representing a vertex to a user representing an edge that has that vertex as one of its two ends. Now, define $C_{cir} = C_1 \cup C_2 \cup C_3$:

$$C_1 = \{\text{ent}(incident^{-1}, sv_i, se_i) \mid 1 \leq i \leq N\}$$
$$C_2 = \{\text{ent}(incident, se_i, sv_{i+1}) \mid 1 \leq i \leq N - 1\}$$
$$C_3 = \{\text{ent}(incident, se_N, sv_1)\}$$

The overall effect of the constraints in C_{cir} is that a valid plan identifies a circuit in the graph.

(b) C_{ham} contains type-1 entailment constraints that are specified using the binary relation $distinct \subseteq U \times U$:

$$distinct = \{((u, i), (v, j)) \in UV \times UV \mid u \neq v\}$$

---

[1] An undirected graph is **simple** if it contains neither loops nor multi-edges.

[2] The converse of $R \subseteq X \times Y$ is the relation $\{(y, x) \in Y \times X \mid (x, y) \in R\}$.

Intuitively, two users are related by *distinct* whenever they represent two distinct vertices. C_{ham} can now be defined as follows:

$$C_{ham} = \{\text{ent}(distinct, sv_i, sv_j) \mid 1 \le i < j \le N\}$$

Effectively, C_{ham} ensures that any circuit identified by a valid plan passes through pairwise distinct vertices: i.e., the circuit is a Hamiltonian cycle.

It is obvious that the reduction can be computed in time polynomial to the size of the *DHC* instance. Observe also the following:

(1) There is a one-to-one correspondence between a valid plan of W and a Hamiltonian cycle in G.

(2) For every choice of $D \subseteq B$ with $|D| \le |B|/2$, there is a corresponding set of no more than t users from $\bigcup_{e \in B} UE_e$ that the adversary can remove.

(3) When the adversary removes t users from U, no more than t of them belong $\bigcup_{e \in B} UE_e$. These latter users correspond to a choice of $D \subseteq B$ with $|D| \le |B|/2$.

Consequently, the input instance (G, B) belongs to *DHC* if and only if the output instance (W, t) belongs to *SRCP*. □

The reduction above employs only type-1 entailment constraints, meaning that type-1 entailment is all that is required to drive the complexity of *SRCP* to the second level of the polynomial hierarchy.

4 ONE-SHOT RESILIENCY

An impression that one may get from reading [39, 40] is that, with static resiliency as an exception, other notions of workflow resiliency (such as decremental and dynamic resiliency) are largely PSPACE-complete because of their game-based definition. The goal of this section is to dispel this false impression. We do so by proposing a notion of workflow resiliency that is more sophisticated than static resiliency, and yet remains in the lower levels of the polynomial hierarchy.

4.1 Problem Definition

One-shot resiliency is a generalization of static resiliency and a specialization of decremental resiliency. Rather than removing users at the beginning of the game, as in static resiliency, the adversary of one-shot resiliency may wait till a more opportune time, and then remove users in the middle of the game. Yet, unlike decremental resiliency, in which the adversary may "strike" multiple times, the adversary in one-shot resiliency may only strike at most once.

Definition 4.1 (One-shot Resiliency). A workflow authorization policy $W = (S, \le, U, A, C)$ is **one-shot resilient** for integer budget $t \ge 0$ if and only if Player 1 can win the **one-shot resiliency game** no matter how Player 2 plays.

The one-shot resiliency game is a two-player game that proceeds in rounds. At any time, the configuration of the game is a pair (Δ, θ), where $\Delta \subseteq U$, and θ is a partial plan. Initially, Δ and θ are both $\emptyset$.

Each round begins by Player 2 opting to either **pass** or **strike**, with the restriction that Player 2 must pass in all future rounds after it has struck in a round. If Player 2 chooses to strike, then it further selects no more than t users from U to be placed in Δ. No action is required of Player 2 if it passes. Next, Player 1 extends θ

by assigning a member of $U \setminus \Delta$ to a not-yet-assigned step, so that θ remains causally closed.

Player 2 wins right away if $U \setminus \Delta = \emptyset$, or if θ becomes invalid. Player 1 wins if θ is eventually extended to a valid plan.

One-shot resiliency models situations in which the workflow runs for a moderate length of time (as in decremental resiliency), but a catastrophe is a truly rare event. The latter either does not occur, or else it occurs only once. The effect of the catastrophe is irreversible during the execution of the workflow, as in the cases of static and decremental resiliency (i.e., removed users do not return to the game).

We write *ORCP* to denote the language containing pairs (W, t) so that W is one-shot resilient for budget t.

THEOREM 4.2. *CRCP $\subset$ ORCP $\subset$ SRCP.*

PROOF. The inclusion relationships are obvious as one-shot resiliency is by definition no more stringent than decremental resiliency and no less stringent than static resiliency. What is not obvious is whether the inclusion relationships are proper.

To see that the inclusion of *ORCP* in *SRCP* is proper, consider a budget $t = 1$ and a workflow authorization policy W composed of 3 steps ordered as follows: $s_1 \prec s_2$ and $s_1 \prec s_3$. Users a, b, c and d are authorized for s_1; only users a and b are authorized for s_2; only users c and d are authorized for s_3. We impose $sod(s_i, s_j)$ for every unordered pair of steps $\{s_i, s_j\}$. One can check that (W, t) is in *SRCP* but not in *ORCP*. To see this, note that Player 2 can win by striking in round 2, but can never win by striking in round 1.

To see that the inclusion of *CRCP* in *ORCP* is proper, consider a budget $t = 2$ and a workflow authorization policy W composed of totally-ordered steps $s_1 \prec s_2 \prec s_3$, such that the users in $U = \{a, b, c\}$ are authorized for all steps. In addition, the entailment constraints $\text{ent}(R, s_1, s_2)$ and $\text{ent}(R, s_2, s_3)$ are imposed in W, so that the binary relation R is defined as follows:

$$(x, y) \in R \text{ iff } x = a \vee x = y \tag{4}$$

(W, t) is in *ORCP* but not in *CRCP*. To see the latter, observe that Player 2 can win by first removing user a in round 1, and then removing in round 2 the same user that Player 1 assigns to s_1. □

Even though it is defined in terms of a strategic game, one-shot resiliency remains in the third level of the polynomial hierarchy.

THEOREM 4.3. *ORCP is Σ_3^p-complete.*

A proof of this result will be given in §4.2 and §4.3. This result provides the intellectual justification for deciding one-shot resiliency through a reduction to first-order Answer-Set Programming with bounded predicate arities (§6)

4.2 Membership in Σ_3^p

We begin the proof of Σ_3^p-completeness by arguing that *ORCP* is in Σ_3^p. This argument turns out to be anything but trivial, and it sheds light on the problem structure of *ORCP*: there is a short encoding of a winning strategy for Player 1. This insight will be used in our ASP encoding of *ORCP* in §6.

Suppose W is a workflow authorization policy W. We construct a decision tree $\mathcal{T}_W$ that captures the "moves" of Player 1. A sequence

---

Algorithm 1: A non-deterministic algorithm for deciding *ORCP*.

Input: a workflow authorization plan $W = (S, \leq, U, A, C)$.

Input: an integer budget $t \geq 0$.

Output: a boolean value indicating if W is one-shot resilient for budget t.

Remarks: This algorithm is equipped with an *SRCP* oracle.

1 Guess a functional sequence
$$\pi = (s_1, u_1) \cdot (s_2, u_1) \cdot \ldots \cdot (s_{|S|}, u_{|S|});$$

2 **if** θ_π *is not a valid plan* **then return** *false*;

3 $W_0 \leftarrow W$;

4 **for** *i from* 1 *to* $|S|$ **do**

5   **if** $(W_{i-1}, t) \notin SRCP$ **then return** *false*;

6     $W_i \leftarrow project(W_{i-1}, s_i, u_i)$;

7 **return** *true*;

$\tau \in (S \times U)^*$ is **functional** if and only if no step appears more than once in τ. Every functional sequence represents a function θ_τ that maps steps to users. When θ_τ is a valid partial plan, we call τ a **play** of Player 1. Each play represents a legitimate sequence of "moves" that Player 1 can make (without losing). The decision tree $\mathcal{T}_W$ is constructed as follows: (a) tree nodes are plays; (b) a play τ is the parent of another play π whenever $\pi = \tau \cdot (s, u)$ (i.e., π is obtained from τ by assigning a user to an additional step). In $\mathcal{T}_W$, the empty sequence ϵ is the root of the tree, and a play π is a descendent of another play τ whenever τ is a prefix of π. A play τ is called a **terminus** whenever θ_τ is a valid plan (i.e., every step is assigned). W is satisfiable if and only if $\mathcal{T}_W$ has at least one terminus.

Suppose t is the budget for Player 2. A **strike** of Player 2 is a pair of the form (τ, Δ), where τ is a play, $dom(\theta_\tau) \neq S$, $\Delta \subseteq U$, and $|\Delta| \leq t$. The play τ is the **trigger** of the strike. Intuitively, a strike is a rule that tells Player 2 to remove the users in Δ immediately after Player 1 has made the moves in τ. A strike (τ, Δ) **invalidates** a terminus π when (a) π is a descendent of τ in $\mathcal{T}_W$, and (b) no user from Δ is assigned by π after the moves in τ. A strike is **successful** if and only if it invalidates every terminus that is a descendent of its trigger. A set $\mathcal{S}$ of successful strikes is a **strategy** for Player 2 if the strikes are pairwise **independent**: two strikes are independent whenever they have distinct triggers that are not descendents of each other. The requirement of independence ensures that Player 2 strikes at most once during a game play. A strategy $\mathcal{S}$ of Player 2 is a **winning strategy** if and only if every terminus of $\mathcal{T}_W$ is invalidated by a strike in $\mathcal{S}$. A strategy $\mathcal{S}'$ **subsumes** another strategy $\mathcal{S}$ if and only if (a) every terminus that $\mathcal{S}$ invalidates is also invalidated by $\mathcal{S}'$, and (a) $\mathcal{S}'$ invalidates at least one terminus that $\mathcal{S}$ does not invalidate. A strategy $\mathcal{S}$ is **maximal** if and only if there it is not subsumed by any other strategy.

Suppose W is one-shot resilient for budget t. Consider a maximal strategy $\mathcal{S}$ for Player 2. Since $\mathcal{S}$ cannot be a winning strategy, there is at least one terminus π that is not invalidated by any strike in $\mathcal{S}$. Here is the crux of the present argument: No strike can invalidate π, or else we can construct another strategy $\mathcal{S}'$ that subsumes $\mathcal{S}$, thereby contradicting the maximality of $\mathcal{S}$. The play π can be seen as a succinct representation of a winning strategy for Player 1.

LEMMA 4.4. $(W, t) \in ORCP$ if and only if there is a sequence π of assignments such that (a) θ_π is a valid plan, and (b) for every play τ that is a prefix of π (i.e., τ is an ancestor of π in $\mathcal{T}_W$), no strike with trigger τ can be successful.

The idea of Lemma 4.4 can be translated into a non-deterministic algorithm for deciding *ORCP*, as depicted in Algorithm 1. The algorithm begins by guessing a play π that corresponds to a valid plan θ_π, and then check that no prefix τ of π can trigger a successful strike. An insight is that this latter check can be achieved by invoking an *SRCP* oracle against the "remaining workflow" after the assignments in τ are committed. This notion of the "remaining workflow" is formalized in the following definition, which defines the notation used in line 6.

Definition 4.5. Suppose $W = (S, \leq, U, A, C)$ is a workflow authorization policy, and $\{(s, u)\}$ is a valid partial plan for W. Then $project(W, s, u)$ is the workflow authorization plan $(S', \leq', U', A', C')$ such that:

$$S' = S \setminus \{s\}$$
$$\leq' = (\leq) \cap (S' \times S')$$
$$U' = U$$
$$A' = A \cap (S' \times U')$$

and C' is defined as follows:

$$C' = \{(T, \Theta) \mid (T, \Theta) \in C, s \notin T\} \cup$$
$$\{(T \setminus \{s\}, \Theta\langle s, u\rangle) \mid (T, \Theta) \in C, s \in T, |T| > 1\}$$

where the notation $\Theta\langle s, u\rangle$ is defined below:

$$\Theta\langle s, u\rangle = \{\theta \setminus \{(s, u)\} \mid \theta \in \Theta, (s, u) \in \theta\}$$

Intuitively, $\Theta\langle s, u\rangle$ selects those partial plans in Θ that are consistent with the assignment of u to s, and then eliminates the pair (s, u) from those selected partial plans.

Since *SRCP* is Π_2^p-complete, Algorithm 1 depends on an $\mathrm{NP}^{\mathrm{NP}}$ oracle. In addition, Algorithm 1 runs in non-deterministic polynomial time. Therefore, *ORCP* belongs to Σ_3^p.

4.3 Σ_3^p-hardness

To demonstrate that *ORCP* is hard for Σ_3^p, we present a polynomial-time Karp reduction from *SUCCINCT-k-RADIUS* to *ORCP*. The problem *SUCCINCT-k-RADIUS* is known to be Σ_3^p-complete for every $k \geq 2$ [24, 36].

The **radius** of a directed graph $G = (V, E)$ is the smallest k such that there exists a vertex $u \in V$ such that every vertex $v \in V$ is reachable from u by some directed path of length no greater than k. (We consider u reachable from itself by a directed path of length zero.) Deciding if G has a radius no greater than k is not hard if G is represented as, say, an access control matrix or adjacency lists. What causes the problem to become intractable is when G is specified using a **succinct representation**. In such a representation, the adjacency matrix of G is specified through a boolean circuit. Suppose V has a size of 2^n for some $n \geq 1$, then vertices can be identified by bit vectors of length n. The adjacency matrix of G can now be represented by a boolean circuit BC_G that takes two size-n bit vectors $\vec{x}$ and $\vec{y}$ as input, and returns a one-bit value to indicate if there is a directed edge from vertex $\vec{x}$ to vertex $\vec{y}$. Formulated in this way, deciding if the radius of G is bounded by k is Σ_3^p-complete.

Problem: *SUCCINCT-k-RADIUS* [24]
Instance: A boolean circuit BC_G that succinctly represents a directed graph G
Question: Is the radius of G no greater than k?

Given BC_G, one can construct a boolean circuit $BC_{reach}(\vec{x}, \vec{y}; \vec{z}^1, \vec{z}^2, \ldots, \vec{z}^{k-1})$, which takes $k + 1$ size-n bit vectors as input, and returns 1 if and only if vertex $\vec{y}$ is reachable from vertex $\vec{x}$ by a directed path of length no more than k, and that directed path visits intermediate vertices $\vec{z}^1, \vec{z}^2$, etc in that order.

$$BC_{reach}(\vec{x}, \vec{y}; \vec{z}^1, \vec{z}^2, \ldots, \vec{z}^{k-1}) = BC_=(\vec{x}, \vec{y}) \vee BC_G(\vec{x}, \vec{y}) \vee$$
$$BC_{walk}(\vec{x}, \vec{y}; \vec{z}^1) \vee \ldots \vee BC_{walk}(\vec{x}, \vec{y}; \vec{z}^1, \ldots, \vec{z}^{k-1})$$

The circuit $BC_=(\vec{x}, \vec{y})$ tests if $\vec{x}$ and $\vec{y}$ are identical bit vectors. The circuit BC_{walk} is defined as follows:

$$BC_{walk}(\vec{x}, \vec{y}; \vec{z}^1, \vec{z}^2, \ldots, \vec{z}^i) =$$
$$BC_G(\vec{x}, \vec{z}^1) \wedge BC_G(\vec{z}^1, \vec{z}^2) \wedge \ldots \wedge BC_G(\vec{z}^i, \vec{y})$$

Note that BC_{reach} has a size that is $O(k^2)$ times the size of BC_G.

One can now check if G has a radius no greater than k by checking the following:

$$\exists \vec{x} . \forall \vec{y} . \exists \vec{z}^1, \vec{z}^2, \ldots, \vec{z}^{k-1} . BC_{reach}(\vec{x}, \vec{y}; \vec{z}^1, \vec{z}^2, \ldots \vec{z}^{k-1}) = 1 \quad (5)$$

Our goal is now to encode (5) using an *ORCP* instance.

Our reduction takes as input an instance of *SUCCINCT-k-RADIUS* consisting of a boolean circuit BC_G, where G has 2^n vertices, and constructs an instance of *ORCP* consisting of a budget $t = n$ and a workflow authorization policy $W = (S, \leq, U, A, C)$:

(1) The steps in S are "placeholders" for boolean values representing the input and output bits of BC_{reach}, as well as the intermediate values computed by the gates in BC_{reach}.
   - $S = S_x \cup S_y \cup S_z \cup S_{gate} \cup S_{out}$.
   - $S_x = \{x_1, \ldots, x_n\}$ and $S_y = \{y_1, \ldots, y_n\}$ contain one step for each bit of $\vec{x}$ and $\vec{y}$.
   - $S_z = \{z_1^1, \ldots, z_n^1, z_1^2, \ldots, z_n^2, \ldots, z_1^{k-1}, \ldots, z_n^{k-1}\}$ contains one step for each bit in $\vec{z}^1, \vec{z}^2, \ldots, \vec{z}^{k-1}$, for a total of $n \times (k-1)$ steps.
   - S_{gate} contains one step each gate in BC_{reach}. Intuitively, these steps represent the output bits of the gates.
   - $S_{out} = \{out\}$ contains exactly one step representing the output bit of BC_{reach}.
(2) $\leq$ orders the steps in S_x first, then S_y, followed by S_z, and then S_{gate}, and lastly S_{out}.
(3) Users represent the two boolean values (true and false). A plan can thus be interpreted as an assignment of boolean values to the the input, output, and gates of the boolean circuit BC_{reach}. Although there are only two boolean values, there are multiple copies for each.

$$U = U_{bool} \cup U_\star$$
$$U_{bool} = U_\perp \cup U_\top$$
$$U_\perp = \{(\perp, 1), (\perp, 2), \ldots, (\perp, n + 1)\}$$
$$U_\top = \{(\top, 1), (\top, 2), \ldots, (\top, n + 1)\}$$
$$U_\star = \{(f, 1), (t, 2), (f, 3), (t, 4), \ldots, (f, 2n - 1), (t, 2n)\}$$

There are two variants of boolean values, the $\top/\perp$-variant (U_{bool}), and the t/f-variant ($U_\star$). "True" is represented by $\top$- and t-users, and "false" is represented by $\perp$- and f-users. Each boolean value of the $\top/\perp$-variant has $n + 1$ copies (i.e., more than the budget $t = n$). There are, however, only n copies of each boolean value of the t/f-variant

(4) The step authorization policy A describes what type of boolean values can be assigned to each step.

$$A = ((S_x \cup S_z \cup S_{gate}) \times U_{bool}) \cup$$
$$(S_{out} \times U_\top) \cup (S_y \times U_\star)$$

Essentially, boolean values of the $\top/\perp$-variant can be assigned to steps representing $\vec{x}$, $\vec{z}^i$, and the circuit gates. The output of the entire boolean circuit is forced to be true, as only $\top$-values can be assigned. Only boolean values of the t/f-variant can be assigned to steps representing $\vec{y}$.

(5) $C = C_{order} \cup C_{gate} \cup C_{out}$ contains three types of constraint.:
   (a) Constraints in C_{gate} encode the computation performed by the gates in BC_{reach}. For example, suppose step $s \in S_{gate}$ corresponds to an AND gate, which in turn takes its two input bits from the output of the gates represented by steps $s_1, s_2 \in S_{gate}$. Then we formulate a constraint $(\{s, s_1, s_2\}, \Theta_{and})$, so that Θ_{and} contains all partial plans θ such that $\theta(s)$ is a user representing "true" if and only if both $\theta(s_1)$ and $\theta(s_2)$ are users represent "true." Similar constraints can be formulated for OR gates and NOT gates.
   (b) C_{out} contains exactly one type-1 entailment constraint $ent(equal, out, s)$, where $s \in S_{gate}$ represents the gate that computes the overall output of BC_{reach}, and $equal \subseteq U \times U$ is a binary relation such that $(u_1, u_2) \in equal$ whenever u_1 and u_2 both represent the same boolean value. Since $out \in S_{out}$ can only be assigned $\top$-users, this constraint forces BC_{reach} to output "true."
   (c) C_{order} contains a type-1 entailment constraints $ent(order, y_i, y_{i+1})$ for every pair of steps $y_i, y_{i+1} \in S_y$. The binary relation $order \subseteq U_\star \times U_\star$ is defined in such a way that $((b_1, j_1), (b_2, j_2)) \in order$ if and only if $j_1 < j_2$. These constraints forces a linearization of the t/f truth values when they are assigned to $\vec{y}$.

The encoding of the boolean circuit BC_{reach} is straightforward to understand. We explain here how the quantification structure ($\exists$-$\forall$-$\exists$) of formula (5) is captured by the reduction. There are $n + 1$ copies of each boolean value of the $\top/\perp$-variant, but the budget of Player 2 is only $t = n$. No matter which t users are removed by Player 2, Player 1 can freely assign any boolean values of the $\top/\perp$-variant to the steps representing the bit vectors $\vec{x}$ and $\vec{z}^i$. That is not the case for $\vec{y}$. If Player 2 strikes before the steps in S_y are assigned, and it also removes $t = n$ users of the t/f-variant, then there are only n such t/f values left to be assigned to the n steps in S_y. In addition, the constraints in C_{order} requires that the remaining t/f-users are assigned to the S_y in "sorted order" of their indices. This means that the remaining n boolean values of the t/f-variant are now linearized into a bit vector when they are assigned to $\vec{y}$. In this way, Player 2 can dictate the value of $\vec{y}$. To maximize its control, Player 2 will (a) strike before any of the S_y-steps are assigned, (b) strike after all the S_x-steps are assigned so as to maximize its knowledge of $\vec{x}$, and (c) remove only users from $U_\star$ (since removing users of the $\top/\bot$-variant has no effect on the decisions of Player 1). The overall effect is that Player 1 will first pick $\vec{x}$, then Player 2 picks $\vec{y}$, and after that Player 1 picks the $\vec{z}^i$'s. This captures exactly the quantification structure of the formula in (5).

Now that we know *SRCP* and *ORCP* are respectively complete problems in the second and third level of the polynomial hierarchy, we propose in the following a solution approach for these two problems.

5 BACKGROUND: ANSWER-SET PROGRAMMING

Answer-Set Programming (ASP) is a declarative programming paradigm [22]. It is essentially Datalog with disjunction and default negation, defined over a stable model semantics. Over the last decades, ASP implementations have become increasingly competitive in efficiency. A notable example of a mature ASP implementation is the Potassco project [33], which is the ASP solver used in this work. Due to such progress in ASP implementation technologies, reasoning tasks at the lower levels of the polynomial hierarchy have now been regularly encoded in ASP (e.g., [4, 34]). To these computational problems, ASP plays a role analogous to what *SAT* is for the NP-complete problems.

We offer here a brief introduction to the stable model semantics of propositional ASP. This prepares the reader to understand how the **model saturation technique** [20] works in the encodings of §6.

We begin with the abstract syntax of *propositional* ASP. An ASP program P is a finite set of **rules**. A rule r has the following form:

$$a_1 \vee \ldots \vee a_n \,\text{:-}\, b_1, \ldots, b_k, \text{not}\, b_{k+1}, \ldots, \text{not}\, b_m$$

Here, the a_i's and b_i's are atoms (i.e., propositional symbols), and at most one of m or n can be zero. The **head** of r, written $H(r)$, is the set $\{a_1, \ldots, a_n\}$, and the **body** of r is $B(r) = \{b_1, \ldots, b_k, \text{not}\, b_{k+1}, \ldots, \text{not}\, b_m\}$. We write $B^+(r)$ for $\{b_1, \ldots, b_k\}$, and $B^-(r)$ for $\{b_{k+1}, \ldots, b_m\}$. A rule with $m = 0$ is a **fact** (in which case we omit the ":-"). A rule with $n = 0$ is an **integrity constraint**. Intuitively, a rule asserts that one of the head atom holds if the body, read as a conjunction of literals, holds. A fact asserts a (disjunctive) condition unconditionally. An integrity constraint asserts that the body does not hold.

Unlike Prolog, whose semantics is defined procedurally, ASP is purely declarative. The semantics of ASP is defined in terms of stable models [23]. An interpretation I of program P is a set of atoms. I is a **model** of P if and only if, for every $r \in P$, $H(r) \cap I \neq \emptyset$ when $B^+(r) \subseteq I$ and $B^-(r) \cap I = \emptyset$. Not every model is stable though. To arrive at the definition of a stable model, we need to define the **reduct of** P **relative to** I:

$$P^I = \{H(r)\,\text{:-}\,B^+(r) \mid r \in P,\, B^-(r) \cap I = \emptyset\}$$

SRCP	ORCP	Fact	
ignored		step(s).	for each $s \in S$
		before(s_1, s_2).	whenever $s_1 < s_2$
		user(u).	for each $u \in U$
		auth(s, u).	for each $(s, u) \in A$
	ignored	sod(s_1, s_2).	for each sod(s_1, s_2) $\in C$

Figure 1: Instance-specific facts used in the ASP encoding of *SRCP* **and** *ORCP*. **The predicate** before/2 **is ignored in the** *SRCP* **encoding, while** sod/2 **is ignored in the** *ORCP* **encoding.**

An interpretation I is a **stable model** of P if and only if I is a $\subseteq$-minimal model of P^I. In other words, an I cannot be a stable model of P if P^I has a model I' that is a proper subset of I. This requirement of minimality is crucial for understanding how the model saturation technique [20] works in the ASP encodings of §6.

The definition of stable models can be extended to first-order programs through the use of Hebrand interpretations [19]. The minimality requirement for the models of the reduct carries to the first-order case.

Checking the existence of stable models in the presence of disjunction and default negation is Σ_2^p-complete for propositional ASP [20], and Σ_3^p-complete for first-order ASP with bounded predicate arities [19]. The complexity results presented in §3 and §4 grant us the rational justification for employing ASP technologies to solve *SRCP* and *ORCP*.

6 ASP ENCODING OF *SRCP* AND *ORCP*

ASP is a natural constraint solving technology for tackling problems in the lower levels of the polynomial hierarchy. Solving *SRCP* and *ORCP* using ASP does not require us to assume that t is a small parameter (an assumption made in [10]). This section demonstrates the feasibility of this solution approach by presenting ASP encodings of *SRCP* and *ORCP* instances.

The presentation below uses the concrete syntax of logic programs supported by the Potassco collection of ASP solving tools [33]. We do so to ensure realism: our encoding is literally executable. This, however, does not affect the generality of our encoding, as every Potassco-specific syntax employed by our encoding can be reduced to pure ASP [22, Chapter 2].

In this section, only separation-of-duty constraints are encoded. The encoding can be extended readily to accommodate binding-of-duty, cardinality, and entailment constraints [14, 15]. The focus here is not so much on the encoding of various constraint types in ASP, but on using ASP to express the quantification structure of *SRCP* and *ORCP*.

6.1 Encoding Static Resiliency

We present a Karp reduction from the *complement* of *SRCP* to propositional ASP satisfiability (i.e., existence of stable models) [20]. Given a workflow authorization policy $W = (S, \leq, U, A, C)$ and a budget $t \geq 0$, the pair (W, t) belongs to the complement of *SRCP* if and only if there exists a subset Δ of no more than t users such that every plan that does not assign users from Δ will fail to satisfy W. Given (W, t), our Karp reduction will generate a

```
1    % Generate Player 2's strike
2    { removed(U) : user(U) } t.

3    % Generate Player 1's assignment
4    avail(S, U) :- auth(S, U), not removed(U).
5    assign(S, U) : avail(S, U) :- step(S).

6    % Test separation-of-duty constraints
7    violation :-
8       sod(S1, S2), assign(S1, U), assign(S2, U).

9    % Model saturation
10   assign(S, U) :- violation, avail(S, U).

11   % Reject unsaturated models
12   :- not violation.
```

Figure 2: Rules common to all instances in the ASP encoding of *SRCP*.

corresponding ASP program P. If P is unsatisfiable (has no stable model), then W is statically resilient for budget t. Conversely, if P is satisfiable (has at least one stable model), then every stable model encodes a subset Δ of users that can be removed by the adversarial environment to render W unsatisfiable.

Our ASP encoding is **uniform** [22, Chapter 3] in the sense that every instance of *SRCP* can be reduced to a logic program P that can be "factorized" into two parts, a part P_C containing rules that are common to all instances of *SRCP*, and an instance-specific part P_I, such that $P = P_C \cup P_I$.

Suppose we have been given an *SRCP* instance consisting of a workflow authorization policy $W = (S, \leq, U, A, C)$ and a budget $t \geq 0$. The instance-specific part of the ASP encoding consists of the facts in Fig. 1, which describe the components S, $<$, U, A, and C of W. The rules common to all instances of *SRCP* are listed in Fig. 2.

The rules on lines 2, 4, and 5 in Fig. 2 are responsible for generating interpretations that serve as candidates for stable models.

Line 2 is a **choice rule** that models the choice of Player 2. Specifically, it generates up to t ground atoms of the remove/2 predicate in a model candidate. These facts represent the set Δ of users removed by Player 2.

Line 4 specifies when a user u is available for assignment to a step s, given the choice of Δ by Player 2. Line 5 is a shorthand that asserts, for each step s, the following disjunction:

$$\text{assign}(s,\ u_1) \lor \ldots \lor \text{assign}(s,\ u_m).$$

where $u_1, \ldots, u_m$ are the users identified by predicate avail/2 to be available for assignment to s.

The cumulating effect of the model generation rules (lines 2, 4, and 5) is that an interpretation $I_{\Delta, \theta}$ will be generated as a model candidate for each user set Δ of size t or less, and for each plan θ that both complies with the step authorization policy and assigns only users from $U \setminus \Delta$. Each model candidate $I_{\Delta, \theta}$ contains, on top of the instance-specific facts in Fig. 1, the following ground atoms:

- removed(u) for each $u \in \Delta$

- avail(s, u) whenever u is available for assignment to s
- assign(s, u) whenever $\theta(s) = u$

There are now two cases:

Case 1: θ *is valid.* Neither lines 7–8 nor line 10 will be "triggered." But line 12 will reject $I_{\Delta, \theta}$.

Case 2: θ *is not valid.* Then lines 7–8 will detect this case, and introduce the proposition violation into the interpretation under consideration. Moreover, the interpretation will then be **saturated** by line 10: all possible ground atoms of predicate assign/2 will be added to the interpretation. In short, model candidate $I_{\Delta, \theta}$ will be "converted" to a superset $I_{\Delta, *}$, which contains, on top of the ground atoms in $I_{\Delta, \theta}$, the following ground atoms:

- violation
- assign(s, u) for every u available for assignment to s

Suppose $(W, t) \in SRCP$. For every choice of Δ, there exists at least one valid plan θ_0 that does not assign users from Δ. Note that the model candidate I_{Δ, θ_0} will not be saturated, and thus it will be rejected by line 12. Not only that, the saturated model $I_{\Delta, *}$ is not a minimal model for $P^{I_{\Delta, *}}$, because its proper subset I_{Δ, θ_0} is also a model for $P^{I_{\Delta, *}}$. Consequently, no stable model exists for the program P.

Conversely, suppose $(W, t) \notin SRCP$. Then there is a Δ_0 such that every plan θ that does not assign users from Δ_0 is invalid. This means that Case 1 above never holds for this choice of Δ_0. This also means that every model candidate $I_{\Delta_0, \theta}$ is converted into a saturated model $I_{\Delta_0, *}$. As none of the interpretations $I_{\Delta_\star, \theta}$ is a model for $P^{I_{\Delta_\star, *}}$, $I_{\Delta_\star, *}$ is the minimal model for $P^{I_{\Delta_\star, *}}$. The program P has at least one stable model.

We have thus demonstrated that it is feasible to use ASP for encoding *SRCP*. The key is to use an advanced ASP programming technique known as model saturation [20] to encode the quantification structure (i.e., ∃-∀) of *SRCP*'s complement. We now examine an extension of this technique for encoding *ORCP*.

6.2 Encoding One-shot Resiliency

We present below a Karp reduction from *ORCP* to the satisfiability problem of first-order ASP with bounded predicate arities [19]. The crux in designing an ASP encoding of *ORCP* lies in capturing the quantification structure of Σ_3^p (i.e., ∃-∀-∃). To this end, we employ the advanced adaption of model saturation as found in the proof of Lemma 6 and Lemma 7 in [19].

Unlike the encoding in §6.1, the ASP encoding of *ORCP* presented here is not uniform. It cannot be factorized into an instance-specific set of facts and a set of of rules that are common to all instances. More specifically, *ORCP* is encoded using the instance-specific facts in Fig. 1 and the rules in Fig. 3. Note that lines 18–20 of Fig. 3 are only examples. Each *ORCP* instance will have a different formulation of those lines, depending on what constraints are in C.

Our ASP encoding of *ORCP* basically follows the idea of Lemma 4.4, and thus Fig. 3 could be seen as an ASP variant of Algorithm 1:

(1) The logic program "guesses" a functional sequence τ that encodes the strategy of Player 1.
(2) Then model saturation is employed for capturing the universal quantification of Player 2's strikes.

```
1:  % Generate a plan as part of Player 1's strategy
2:  1 { assign(S, U) : auth(S, U) } 1 :- step(S).

3:  % Generate a total ordering of steps as part of
4:  % Player 1's strategy
5:  order(X, Y); order(Y, X) :-
6:      step(X), step(Y), X != Y.
7:  order(X, Y) :- before(X, Y).
8:  order(X, Z) :- order(X, Y), order(Y, Z).

9:  % Generate strike point of Player 2
10: post(S); pre(S) :- step(S).
11: post(S2) :- post(S1), order(S1, S2).

12: % Generate strike set of Player 2
13: removed(U); preserved(U) :- user(U).

14: % Available assignments for Player 1
15: avail(S, U) :- pre(S), assign(S, U).
16: avail(S, U) :- post(S), auth(S, U), preserved(U).

17: % Detect satisfiability
18: sat :-
19:     avail(1, U1), avail(2, U2), ..., avail(9, U9),
20:     U2 != U7, U3 != U4, ..., U8 != U9.

21: % Player 2 loses if it removes more than t users
22: sat :- t+1 { removed(U) : user(U) }.

23: % Model saturation
24: pre(S) :- sat, step(S).
25: post(S) :- sat, step(S).
26: removed(U) :- sat, user(U).
27: preserved(U) :- sat, user(U).
28: avail(S, U) :- sat, auth(S, U).

29: % Reject unsaturated models
30: :- not sat.
```

Figure 3: ASP encoding of *ORCP*. Note that the rule on lines 18–20 are instance specific. This encoding also assumes the instance-specific facts in Fig. 1.

(3) Lastly, testing whether a prefix π of τ can be extended to a terminus is performed without model generation rules.

Generating Player 1's strategy. The first part of Player 1's strategy is a plan, which is represented by the predicate assign/2. Using a choice rule, line 2 generates, for each step s, exactly one fact of the form assign(s, u) if user u is authorized to execute step s.

The second part of Player 1's strategy is a total ordering of steps. This is represented by the predicate order/2, which is generated by lines 5–8. More specifically, lines 5–6 generate, for every pair of distinct steps X and Y, either order(X, Y) or order(Y, X).

Line 7 ensures that the generated ordering honors the ordering constraints of the workflow, and line 8 ensures transitivity.

Generating Player 2's strike. The strike of Player 2 is generated by lines 9–13. There are two parts to the strike. The first part is a subset Δ of users to be removed. Line 13 is a shorthand that asserts, for each user u, the disjunction below:

$$removed(u) \lor preserved(u).$$

The alert reader will notice that no constraint on the size of Δ is placed here. As we shall see, the size is controlled by having Player 2 loses the game if it picks more than t users in Δ (see line 22).

The second part of Player 2's strike is the choice of a round to launch the strike. This choice is generated by lines 10–11. More specifically, every step is labelled as either "pre-strike" or "post-strike" by line 10. A pre-strike step is one that is ordered before the launch point according to the total ordering chosen by Player 1 above; otherwise, the step is post-strike. Line 11 ensures that post-strike steps are never ordered before pre-strike steps.

Testing if a prefix of Player 1's strategy can be extended to a terminus. Lines 14–20 check whether, after the strike chosen by Player 2, the assignments made prior to the strike by Player 1 can be extended to a valid plan. This section can be further divided into two subsections: (a) lines 15–16, and (b) lines 18–20.

Lines 15–16 determine which user s is available for assignment to which step s after the strike. For pre-strike steps, the assignment is fixed according to Player 1's strategy (line 15). For post-strike steps, authorized users who have not been removed by the strike are available (line 16).

Then comes lines 18–20, which mark the interpretation by the marker proposition sat whenever the workflow authorization policy is found to be satisfiable (given Player 1's strategy and Player 2's strike). This is the part of the encoding that has been inspired by the proof of Lemma 7 in [19]. The main feature of this section is that satisfiability is checked without model generation rules (e.g., choice rules and disjunctive rules). Instead, a single rule is used. This rule, however, is instance specific: a different rule of this form will have to be formulated for each *ORCP* instance. The rule considers all possible user assignments to the steps (line 19), and then checks the SOD constraints inline (line 20). By encoding the nested existential quantification without model generation rules, we can reuse the model saturation technique to encode the outer existential-universal quantifications.

Other mechanics. Line 22 ensures that Player 2 plays according to the budget. If Player 2 removes more than t users, then Player 1 wins: i.e., the workflow authorization policy is considered satisfied.

If the workflow authorization policy is satisfiable (i.e., the proposition sat is part of the model), then lines 24–28 will saturate the model by producing all possible ground atoms that can ever be asserted as a result of Player 2's choice. Finally, line 30 rejects unsaturated models. Using an argument analogous to the one in §6.1, one can demonstrate that a stable model exists if and only if Player 1 has a winning strategy.

7 RELATED WORK

The notion of resiliency was introduced into the study of access control by Li *et al.*, originally in the context of RBAC rather than in workflow authorization models [27, 28]. Significant recent advances have been achieved in employing parameterized complexity analysis to facilitate the design of efficient algorithms for the Resiliency Checking Problem (RCP) [13]. In particular, the efficient FPT algorithms designed for WSP is employed as subroutines for solving RCP. There is also interest in formulating "resiliency"-variants of combinatorial problems in general [11]. A form of resiliency checking problem has also been defined for Relationship-Based Access Control (ReBAC), in the context of policy negotiation performed among co-owners of the a resource [32]. ReBAC resiliency checking was shown to be complete for Π_2^p. That result, however, is significantly different from Theorem 3.1 of the present paper. First, ReBAC resiliency is about an adversary who can remove relationship edges in an underlying social graph, whereas the adversary of workflow resiliency removes users. Second, the hardness proof of [32] involves a reduction from the Graph Consistency problem, and is therefore fundamentally different from the one presented in this paper. In general, the nature of RCP is different from workflow resiliency, as the latter contains an element of dynamism, allowing the adversarial environment to remove users as the workflow is executing.

The idea of workflow resiliency was first introduced by Wang and Li [39, 40]. The present paper bridges the complexity gap of static resiliency that existed since the first conception of the idea a decade ago.

Two notable lines of recent research explore new directions in the study of workflow resiliency. Mace *et al.* [29–31] pointed out that simply knowing whether a workflow is resilient or not is not sufficient. The real interest of the workflow developer is to receive feedback from the policy analysis in order to repair the workflow. They proposed a quantitative model of resiliency in response to this need. The idea is to build a probabilistic adversary model, and then formulate a Markov Decision Process to capture how users are removed over time. While the insight of their perspective is acknowledged, it is the position of this paper that multiple notions of resiliency are needed in order to provide insights into the workflow engineering process. The proposal of one-shot resiliency is partly motivated by this consideration.

A second recent work on workflow resiliency is the FPT algorithm of Crampton *et al.* for deciding dynamic resiliency [10]. Unfortunately, the parameter they used involves the budget t of the adversary, which is not universally considered small. It is therefore necessary to consider solution approaches that do not assume a small t. The proposal of ASP as a solution approaches for static and one-shot resiliency in the present work is a response to this challenge.

Kahn and Fong proposed *workflow feasibility* as a dual notion of workflow resiliency [25]. The idea is based whether the current protection state can be repaired to make the workflow satisfiable. Feasibility checking is also defined for ReBAC [32], and shown to be complete for Σ_2^p.

8 CONCLUSION AND FUTURE WORK

We proved that static resiliency is complete for Π_2^p, thereby solving a problem that has been open for more than a decade since Wang and Li first proposed the notion of workflow resiliency [39, 40].

We have also demonstrated that useful notions of workflow resiliency need not be PSPACE-hard. The fact that we can define a notion of workflow resiliency (one-shot resiliency) that remains in the lower levels of the polynomial hierarchy (Σ_3^p) implies that the lower complexity of static resiliency is not an exception.

The completeness of *SRCP* and *ORCP* in the second and third level of the polynomial hierarchy also suggests that Answer-Set Programming is a natural choice of constraint-solving technology for solving the two problems (without having to assume that t is a small parameter). We have demonstrated the feasibility of this approach by presenting ASP encodings of *SRCP* and *ORCP*. These encodings involve the application of the model saturation technique [20] and its advanced adaptation [19].

A number of research directions are suggested below:

(1) It is unlikely that the ASP encodings of *SRCP* and *ORCP* presented in §6 are the most efficient ones. Since the encodings are formulated mainly for demonstration of feasibility, they are optimized for brevity. It is well-known that the efficiency of ASP programs can benefit from advanced optimization techniques [22]. A natural follow-up work is to explore these optimization techniques, and empirically benchmark the performance of ASP-based solutions for *SRCP* and *ORCP*. A promising direction is to combine the pattern-based technique of [5, 6] with ASP-solving.

(2) The proposal of *ORCP* affirms the possibility for defining alternative notions of workflow resiliency beyond the three advanced by Wang and Li. *ORCP* not only avoids the PSPACE-completeness of *CRCP* and *DRCP*, but also admits encoding in first-order ASP with bounded predicate arities. An interesting research direction is to explore if there are other useful formulations of workflow resiliency that also reside in the lower levels of the polynomial hierarchy.

(3) The source of complexity for PSPACE-complete notions of workflow resiliency (i.e., *CRCP* and *DRCP*) is that the adversary model is overly powerful. An open question is whether there are alternative adversary models for workflow resiliency that involve a less powerful adversary and still lead to useful notions of availability for workflow authorization models. (In some sense, the quantitative model of Mace *et al.* could be seen as an alternative adversary model [29–31].) The existing adversary model is framed in terms of a budget t, and a flexible consumption schedule of this budget. Alternative adversary models can envision a different way in which the adversarial environment interacts with workflow execution. Consider, for example, a *small-accidents* variant of decremental resiliency, in which at most one user may be removed in each round. The assumption that $k + t$ is small now makes a lot of sense in this adversary model, and the FPT algorithm of [10] is genuinely reasonable in this model. Creative deviation from the adversary model of Wang and Li is therefore a promising research direction.

(4) FPT-reductions to *SAT* may be possible for some notions of workflow resiliency. It is now a standard problem-solving technique to seek FPT reductions of hard problems to *SAT*, so as to exploit the efficiency of *SAT*-solving technologies

[17, 18]. Bounded Model Checking is often cited as an example of this approach. An even more general approach is to consider FPT algorithms that query a *SAT*-solver multiple times (i.e., FPT Turing reductions) [16]. An open question is whether static and one-shot resiliency can be solved via FPT reductions to *SAT*, and if not, whether there are other useful notions of workflow resiliency that can be solved in this way.

ACKNOWLEDGMENTS

This work is supported in part by an NSERC Discovery Grant (RGPIN-2014-06611) and a Canada Research Chair (950-229712).

REFERENCES

[1] Vijayalakshmi Atluri and Wei-kuang Huang. 1996. An Authorization Model for Workflows. In *Proceedings of the 4th European Symposium on Research in Computer Security (ESORICS'96)*. Rome, Italy, 44–64. http://dl.acm.org/citation.cfm?id=646646.699195

[2] Robert W. Baldwin. 1990. Naming and Grouping Privileges to Simplify Security Management in Large Databases. In *Proceedings of the 1990 IEEE Symposium on Security and Privacy (S&P'90)*. Oakland, CA, USA, 116–132.

[3] Elisa Bertino, Elena Ferrari, and Vijay Atluri. 1999. The specification and enforcement of authorization constraints in workflow management systems. *ACM Transactions on Information and System Security* 18, 1 (Feb. 1999), 65–104. https://doi.org/10.1145/300830.300837

[4] Gerhard Brewka, Martin Diller, Georg Heissenberger, Thomas Linsbichler, and Stefan Woltran. 2017. Solving Advanced Argumentation Problems with Answer-Set Programming. In *Proceedings of the 31st AAAI Conference on Artificial Intelligence (AAAI'2017)*. San Francisco, CA, USA, 1077–1083.

[5] David Cohen, Jason Crampton, Andrei Gagarin, Gregory Gutin, and Mark Jones. 2014. Iterative Plan Construction for the Workflow Satisfiability Problem. *Journal of Artificial Intelligence Research* 51 (2014), 555–577.

[6] D. Cohen, J. Crampton, A. Gagarin, G. Gutin, and M. Jones. 2016. Algorithms for the workflow satisfiability problem engineered for counting constraints. *Journal of Combinatorial Optimization* 32, 1 (July 2016), 3–24.

[7] Jason Crampton. 2005. A reference monitor for workflow systems with constrained task execution. In *Proceedings of the tenth ACM symposium on Access control models and technologies (SACMAT'05)*. Stockholm, Sweden, 38–47. https://doi.org/10.1145/1063979.1063986

[8] Jason Crampton and Gregory Gutin. 2013. Constraint Expressions and Workflow Satisfiability. In *Proceedings of the 18th ACM Symposium on Access Control Models and Technologies (SACMAT'2013)*. Amsterdam, The Netherlands, 73–84.

[9] Jason Crampton, Gregory Gutin, and Daniel Karapetyan. 2015. Valued Workflow Satisfiability Problem. In *Proceedings of the 20th ACM Symposium on Access Control Models and Technologies (SACMAT'2015)*. Vienna, Astria, 3–13.

[10] Jason Crampton, Gregory Gutin, Daniel Karapetyan, and Rémi Watrigant. 2017. The bi-objective workflow satisfiability problem and workflow resiliency. *Journal of Computer Security* 25, 1 (2017), 83–115.

[11] Jason Crampton, Gregory Gutin, Martin Koutecký, and Rémi Watrigant. 2017. Parameterized Resiliency Problems via Integer Linear Programming. In *Proceedings of the 10th International Conference on Algorithms and Complexity (CIAC'2017) (LNCS)*, Vol. 10236. Athens, Greece, 164–176.

[12] Jason Crampton, Gregory Gutin, and Rémi Watrigant. [n. d.]. On the Satisfiability of Workflows with Release Points. In *Proceedings of the 22nd ACM Symposium on Access Control Models and Technologies (SACMAT'2017)*. Indianapolis, IN, USA, 207–217.

[13] Jason Crampton, Gregory Gutin, and Rémi Watrigant. 2016. Resiliency Policies in Access Control Revisited. In *Proceedings of the 21st ACM Symposium on Access Control Models and Technologies (SACMAT'2016)*. Shanghai, China, 101–111.

[14] Jason Crampton, Gregory Gutin, and Anders Yeo. 2012. On the parameterized complexity of the workflow satisfiability problem. In *Proceedings of the 2012 ACM Conference on Computer and Communications Security (CCS'2012)*. Raleigh, North Carolina, USA, 857–868.

[15] Jason Crampton, Gregory Gutin, and Anders Yeo. 2013. On the Parameterized Complexity and Kernelization of the Workflow Satisfiability Problem. *ACM Transactions on Information and System Security* 16, 1 (June 2013), 4:1–31.

[16] Ronald de Haan and Stefan Szeider. 2014. Fixed-Parameter Tractable Reductions to SAT. In *Proceedings of the 17th International Conference on Theory and Applications of Satisfiability Testing (SAT'2014) (LNCS)*, Vol. 8561. Springer, Vienna, Austria, 85–102.

[17] Ronald de Haan and Stefan Szeider. 2014. The Parameterized Complexity of Reasoning Problems Beyond NP. Vienna, Austria, 82–91.

[18] Ronald de Haan and Stefan Szeider. 2017. Parameterized complexity classes beyond para-NP. *J. Comput. System Sci.* 87 (2017), 16–57.

[19] Thomas Eiter, Wolfgang Faber, Michael Fink, and Stefan Woltran. 2007. Complexity Results for Answer Set Programming with Bounded Predicate Arities and Implications. *Annals of Mathematics and Artificial Intelligence* 51, 2 (2007), 123–165.

[20] Thomas Eiter and Georg Gottlob. 1995. On the Computational Cost of Disjunctive Logic Programming: Propositional Case. *Annals of Mathematics and Artificial Intelligence* 15 (1995), 289–323.

[21] Rodney G. Downey Michael R. Fellows. 2013. *Fundamentals of Parameterized Complexity*. Springer.

[22] Martin Gebser, Roland Kaminski, Benjamin Kaufmann, and Torsten Schaub. 2013. *Answer Set Solving in Practice*. Morgan and Claypool Publishers.

[23] Michael Gelfond and Vladimir Lifschitz. 1988. The Stable Model Semantics for Logic Programming. In *Proceedings of the Fifth International Conference and Symposium on Logic Programming (ICLP)*. Seattle, WA, USA, 1070–1080.

[24] Edith Hemaspaandra, Lane A. Hemaspaandra, Till Tantau, and Osamu Watanabe. 2010. On the complexity of kings. *Theoretical Computer Science* 411 (2010), 783–798.

[25] Arif Akram Khan and Philip W. L. Fong. 2012. Satisfiability and Feasibility in a Relationship-based Workflow Authorization Model. In *Proceedings of the 17th European Symposium on Research in Computer Security (ESORICS'2012) (LNCS)*, Vol. 7459. Springer, Pisa, Italy, 109–126.

[26] Ker-I Ko and Chih-Long Lin. 1995. On the Complexity of Min-Max Optimization Problems and Their Approximation. In *Minimax and Applications*, Ding-Zhu Du and Panos M. Pardalos (Eds.). Springer, 219–239.

[27] Ninghui Li, Mahesh Tripunitara, and Qihua Wang. 2006. Resiliency Policies in Access Control. In *Proceedings of the 13th ACM Conference on Computer and Communications Security (CCS'2006)*. Alexandria, VA, USA, 113–123.

[28] Ninghui Li, Qihua Wang, and Mahesh Tripunitara. 2009. Resiliency Policies in Access Control. *ACM Transactions on Information and System Security* 12, 4 (April 2009), 1–34.

[29] John C. Mace, Charles Morisset, and Aad van Moorsel. 2014. Quantitative Workflow Resiliency. In *Proceedings of the 19th European Symposium on Research in Computer Security (ESORICS'2014) (LNCS)*, Vol. 8712. Wroclaw, Poland, 344–361.

[30] John C. Mace, Charles Morisset, and Aad van Moorsel. 2015. Impact of Policy Design on Workflow Resiliency Computation Time. In *Proceedings of the 12th International Conference on Quantitative Evaluation of Systems (QEST'2015) (LNCS)*, Vol. 9259. Madrid, Spain, 244–259.

[31] John C. Mace, Charles Morisset, and Aad van Moorsel. 2015. Resiliency Variance in Workflows with Choice. In *Proceedings of the 7th International Workshop on Software Engineering for Resilient Systems (SERENE'2015) (LNCS)*, Vol. 9274. Paris, France, 128–143.

[32] Pooya Mehregan and Philip W. L. Fong. 2016. Policy Negotiation for Co-owned Resources in Relationship-Based Access Control. In *Proceedings of the 21st ACM Symposium on Access Control Models and Technologies (SACMAT'2016)*. Shanghai, China, 125–136.

[33] Potassco [n. d.]. Potassco, the Potsdam Answer Set Solving Collection. https://potassco.org/

[34] Chiaki Sakama and Tjitze Rienstra. 2017. Representing Argumentation Frameworks in Answer Set Programming. *Fundamenta Informaticae* 155 (2017), 261–292.

[35] Jerry H. Saltzer and Mike D. Schroeder. 1975. The protection of information in computer systems. *Proc. IEEE* 63, 9 (Sept. 1975), 1278–1308.

[36] Marcus Schaefer and Christopher Umans. 2002. Completeness in the polynomial-time hierarchy: A compendium. *SIGACT News* 33, 3 (Sept. 2002), 32–49.

[37] Kaijun Tan, Jason Crampton, and Carl A. Gunter. 2004. The Consistency of Task-Based Authorization Constraints in Workflow Systems. In *Proceedings of the 17th IEEE Workshop on Computer Security Foundations (CSFW'04)*. IEEE Computer Society, Washington, DC, USA, 155–169. https://doi.org/10.1109/CSFW.2004.22

[38] Roshan K. Thomas and Ravi S. Sandhu. 1998. Task-Based Authorization Controls (TBAC): A Family of Models for Active and Enterprise-Oriented Authorization Management. In *Proceedings of the 11th IFIP WG11.3 Working Conference on Database and Application Security (DAS'98)*. Lake Tahoe, California, USA, 166–181. http://dl.acm.org/citation.cfm?id=646115.679940

[39] Qihua Wang and Ninghui Li. 2007. Satisfiability and Resiliency in Workflow Systems. In *Proceedings of the 12th European Symposium on Research in Computer Security (ESORICS'2007) (LNCS)*, Vol. 4734. Springer, Dresden, Germany, 90–105.

[40] Qihua Wang and Ninghui Li. 2010. Satisfiability and Resiliency in Workflow Authorization Systems. *ACM Transactions on Information and System Security* 13, 4 (Dec. 2010), 40:1–35.

Efficient and Precise Information Flow Control for Machine Code through Demand-Driven Secure Multi-Execution

Tobias Pfeffer
Technische Universität Berlin
Berlin, Germany
tobias.pfeffer@tu-berlin.de

Thomas Göthel
Technische Universität Berlin
Berlin, Germany
thomas.goethel@tu-berlin.de

Sabine Glesner
Technische Universität Berlin
Berlin, Germany
sabine.glesner@tu-berlin.de

ABSTRACT

Dynamic Information Flow Control (IFC) systems, like No-Sensitive-Upgrade or Permissive-Upgrade, can guarantee Termination-Insensitive Non-Interference, but reject valid programs due to their inability to track implicit flows. More advanced multi-execution based approaches, like Shadow Execution and Secure Multi-Execution, are precise and guarantee Termination-Sensitive Non-Interference, but require additional resources or, in the case of Faceted Evaluation, deep changes to the execution semantics. In this paper, we propose a novel efficient and precise Information Flow Control system for machine code through *Demand-Driven Secure Multi-Execution*. Our key idea is to use lightweight single-execution monitoring as long as the execution is *secretless* and fork multiple copies *on-demand* when necessary. We present the first Secure Multi-Execution implementation for legacy code in Unix-based environments and show that our demand-driven optimization drastically reduces the run-time overhead for `cat` and `sha256sum`. Our results indicate that further acceleration is possible through improved static analyses, making multi-execution based IFC systems applicable to machine code.

CCS CONCEPTS

• **Security and privacy** → **Information flow control**; **Software and application security**;

KEYWORDS

Information Flow Control; Machine Code; Multi-Execution

ACM Reference Format:
Tobias Pfeffer, Thomas Göthel, and Sabine Glesner. 2019. Efficient and Precise Information Flow Control for, Machine Code through Demand-Driven Secure Multi-Execution. In *Ninth ACM Conference on Data and Application Security and Privacy (CODASPY '19), March 25–27, 2019, Richardson, TX, USA*. ACM, New York, NY, USA, 12 pages. https://doi.org/10.1145/3292006.3300040

1 INTRODUCTION

Automatic data processing has become an important backbone of modern society. Because of the intrinsic value of data, it is often vital that its confidentiality is preserved during processing. This security requirement is usually expressed in the form of Hypersafety Protperties [8], such as Non-Interference [10]. Following these definitions, a program is considered confidential, if all executions that agree on inputs with low security classification also agree on output events on low-security channels. This implies that high-security inputs do not interfere with low-security outputs. If this is the case, an outside observer with low security clearance cannot gain knowledge about the high-security data. Unfortunately, such hypersafety properties require computationally complex enforcement algorithms. Proving that a program is non-interferent requires a proof of behavioral equivalence, which is known to be Π_2-hard [12].

Since two diverging executions with equal low inputs are sufficient to refute Non-Interference [27], static enforcement approaches usually aim to falsify confidentiality [6]. For unstructured languages such as binary code that lacks type information and relies heavily on pointers, these static approaches have proven to be hard in practice [18]. Due to the complexities of binary code, they must sacrifice precision for efficiency [26]. Consequently, the resulting over-approximation falsely prevents benign executions.

Under these circumstances, dynamic enforcement techniques have gained traction [23]. Unfortunately, single-execution enforcement techniques, such as No-Sensitive-Upgrade [1, 30] or Permissive-Upgrade [2], are incapable of tracking implicit flows. This drives the need for multi-execution enforcement, such as Secure Multi-Execution (SME) [9]. SME enforces Non-Interference by executing a program multiple times, once for each layer in the security-level lattice. Each execution is responsible for the creation of outputs that match the security level of the execution. Where inputs of higher security levels are required, the executions are provided dummy values. The method is secure by design; since executions with low security clearance do not get access to classified information, they cannot leak these to low-security outputs. If scheduled correctly, it is also transparent [29] and timing-sensitive [14]. Unfortunately, running the whole system multiple times creates intolerable overhead. Multi-Faceted evaluation of a single execution with has been proposed to simulate SME in a more efficient manner [3]. This, however, requires changes to the language semantics, which in the case of machine code would imply changes to the underlying hardware. These requirements have so far impeded the applicability of Secure Multi-Execution to machine code.

With our work, we aim to create a precise and efficient Non-Interference enforcement method for low-level languages such as binary code. To achieve precise enforcement, we use Secure Multi-Execution. To increase the efficiency, we aim to use expensive enforcement only where necessary. The key idea of our work is to use lightweight single-execution monitoring as long as the execution is *secretless*. This allows us to quickly skip over provably benign sections of the code and use the Secure Multi-Execution *on-demand*.

We address various challenges to achieve this goal. First, we introduce a definition of a *secretless run* and prove that it implies Progress-Sensitive Non-Interference on deterministic programs. Second, we use this 1-safety property to build a combination of single- and multi-execution monitoring, called *Demand-Driven Secure Multi-Execution*[1]. Third, we present the first implementation of Secure Multi-Execution and our Demand-Driven augmentation for machine code. Fourth, we evaluate our prototypical implementation using real-world applications and show that our augmentation drastically reduces the run-time overhead of Non-Interference enforcement.

The rest of the paper is structured as follows. In Section 2, we give a short background on machine code, Non-Interference and Secure Multi-Execution. We then compare our approach to related work. In Section 4, we define secretless execution, prove that it implies Non-Interference and outline how it can be used to speed up multi-execution enforcement. We then present our implementation for machine code and various design choices in Section 5. The results of the evaluation of our approach are presented in Section 6. Finally, we conclude our work in Section 7.

2 BACKGROUND

In this section, we describe the semantics of our machine code language, introduce Non-Interference and Secure Multi-Execution as an enforcement approach and provide definitions necessary for the rest of the paper. We then provide a small example to illustrate the necessity for multi-execution enforcement. We use the example again to illustrate our improvements in Section 4.

2.1 Machine Code

Machine code is usually provided in compiled form and without high-level specifications. Compiled machine code differs from high-level languages in two key aspects. The use of unrestricted pointers to access values in memory and the use of a computed goto instruction to model control-flow.

Figure 1 gives the semantics of our model of machine code. We use four different instructions. A program state s is described by the code Σ, the mapping of memory addresses to values μ, the current program counter pc, and the current instruction ι. While real machine code usually uses many

---

[1]A term taken from recent work on Faceted Secure Multi-Execution by Schmitz et al. [24]

$$[\text{EVAL}] \frac{\mu \vdash e \Downarrow x \qquad \mu' = \mu[v \mapsto x] \qquad \iota = \Sigma[pc+1]}{\Sigma, \mu, pc, v := e \xrightarrow{\bullet} \Sigma, \mu', pc+1, \iota}$$

$$[\text{GOTO}] \frac{\mu \vdash e \Downarrow x \qquad \iota = \Sigma[x]}{\Sigma, \mu, pc, \texttt{goto } e \xrightarrow{\bullet} \Sigma, \mu, x, \iota}$$

$$[\text{OUTPUT}] \frac{v = \mu[x] \qquad \iota = \Sigma[pc+1]}{\Sigma, \mu, pc, \texttt{out}(c, x) \xrightarrow{c!v} \Sigma, \mu, pc+1, \iota}$$

$$[\text{INPUT}] \frac{\mu' = \mu[x \mapsto v] \qquad \iota = \Sigma[pc+1]}{\Sigma, \mu, pc, \texttt{in}(c, x) \xrightarrow{c?v} \Sigma, \mu', pc+1, \iota}$$

Figure 1: Machine Code Semantics

different instructions to execute arbitrary expressions, we use a single instruction, called [EVAL]. The [EVAL] instruction evaluates the expression operand e under the current μ to a value x, denoted $\mu \vdash e \Downarrow x$. The result x is then stored in the memory location specified by the operand v. A single [EVAL] instruction can be used to read from memory, modify the value, and store the result at another memory location. To model non-sequential control flow, the [GOTO] instruction evaluates an expression e and sets the result as the new program counter. Every transition from a state s to a state s' creates a discrete event that is observable from a black-box perspective. The set of labels is given by

$$a := \bullet \mid c?v \mid c!v$$

where c denotes the channel and v denotes the value. The above mentioned instructions all describe internal behavior of the program, denoted by creating a $\bullet$ event. Output is produced through the [OUTPUT] instruction, which emits a $c!v$ event. Input is received through the [INPUT] instruction, signaled by a $c?v$ event.

Programs written in our machine language behave deterministically if the storage μ behaves deterministically. Deterministic programs are defined as follows.

Definition 2.1. Let $\mathsf{S}(s_0)$ denote the set of states reachable from s_0. s_0 is *deterministic* iff $\forall s \in \mathsf{S}(s_0)$.

(1) $\forall s_1, s_2, a \centerdot s \xrightarrow{a} s_1 \wedge s \xrightarrow{a} s_2 \implies s_1 = s_2$, and
(2) $\forall a_1, a_2 \centerdot s \xrightarrow{a_1} \wedge s \xrightarrow{a_2} \wedge a_1 \neq a_2 \implies \exists c, v_1, v_2 \centerdot a_1 = c?v_1 \wedge a_2 = c?v_2$.

The storage μ is deterministic, iff $\forall e, v_1, v_2 \centerdot \mu \vdash e \Downarrow v_1 \wedge \mu \vdash e \Downarrow v_2 \implies v_1 = v_2$ and $\forall x, v_1, v_2 \centerdot \mu[x] = v_1 \wedge \mu[x] = v_2 \implies v_1 = v_2$. We omit the proof that the machine language is deterministic.

2.2 Progress-Sensitive Non-Interference

For the definition of Non-Interference, we use the notation and results from Rafnsson and Sabelfeld [22] and only present necessary definitions here. For more detailed information, we refer the reader to the original paper.

We write $s \xrightarrow{a} s'$ if s transitions to s' with event a, and $s \xrightarrow{\bar{a}}$ if s transitions to some state with a (possibly infinite) trace (list) of events $\bar{a}$. Input is obtained from an environment e, modeled as a mapping of channels to the stream of provided inputs on that channel. An execution trace $\bar{a}$ is consistent with an environment e, written $e \models \bar{a}$, iff the list of inputs in $\bar{a}$ is a prefix of the list of inputs in e. This implies that $\forall \bar{a}, e, n.e \models \bar{a} \wedge \bar{a}(n) = c?v \implies e(c)[n] = v$.

We assume a complete lattice $(\mathcal{L}, \sqsubseteq)$ of security levels, ranged over by ℓ. We further assume that each channel is labeled with a security label provided by $\pi(c)$. The lowest security level is given by the infimum $\sqcap \mathcal{L}$ of $\mathcal{L}$.

For the definition of Non-Interference, we need to express that two traces agree on their events. This is done using progress-sensitive ℓ-equivalence.

Definition 2.2. Two traces $\bar{a}_1$ and $\bar{a}_2$ are *progress-sensitive ℓ-equivalent*, written $\bar{a}_1 \approx_\ell \bar{a}_2$, iff $\bar{a}_1 \restriction_{\ell,\bullet} = \bar{a}_2 \restriction_{\ell,\bullet}$, where $\restriction_{\ell,\bullet}$ removes all events on channels with security classification strictly higher than ℓ and all $\bullet$ events.

Because the $\bullet$ events are removed before comparison, this equivalence does not take timing into account. Progress-sensitive ℓ-equivalence can be transferred to environments.

Definition 2.3. $e_1 \approx_\ell e_2$ iff $\forall c . \pi(c) \sqsubseteq \ell \implies e_1(c) \approx_\ell e_2(c)$.

This is sufficient to give a definition of *Progress-Sensitive Non-Interference* (PSNI).

Definition 2.4. $s \in$ PSNI iff $\forall \ell, e_1, e_2 . e_1 \approx_\ell e_2 \implies \forall \bar{a}_1 . e_1 \models s \xrightarrow{\bar{a}_1} \implies \exists \bar{a}_2 . e_2 \models s \xrightarrow{\bar{a}_2} \wedge \bar{a}_1 \approx_\ell \bar{a}_2$

Progress-Sensitive Non-Interference is enforced by Secure Multi-Execution. Secure Multi-Execution was originally introduced by Devriese and Piessens [9]. It works by running multiple executions of the same program, once for every level in the security lattice. Each execution is responsible for output at its classification level and has access to information with equal or lower classification. As a consequence, Secure Multi-Execution is secure by design, as outputs on low-security channels have been produced by executions that are not aware of classified information. For the exact semantics and proof of soundness and transparency, we refer the reader to the works by Devrise and Piessens [9] or Rafnsson and Sabelfeld [22].

2.3 Example

To illustrate the complexity of Non-Interference enforcement for machine code, we use the example given in Figure 2. The example uses two channels, L and H, where $\pi(L) \sqsubset \pi(H)$.

In the example, a value is read from the low-security input channel into the variable x. This value is used in a possibly complex computation to calculate z. Then, sensitive information is read in from the high-security channel into variably y. Using this information as an offset into a memory location addressed by z, a value from memory is loaded and written into y. This value is emitted on a low-security channel and subsequently used to divert the control flow, creating an implicit channel. If line 7 is executed, a constant 0 is emitted. At line 8, the information stored in y is overwritten

```
1    in(L,  x)
2    z := f(x)
3    in(H,  y)
4    y := z[y]
5    out(L,  y)
6    goto 7 + y
7    out(L,  0)
8    y := 0
9    out(L,  y)
```

Figure 2: Possibly interferent code

with 0 and emitted on the low-security channel. According to the definition above, the program is non-interferent if the values emitted on the low-security channel are equal for all environment with equal low-inputs. Intuitively, this seems not to be the case in the example, since the value emitted on the low-security channel depends on the value received from the high-security channel. However, it may be that the value loaded from location $z[y]$ is the same for any value in y's range. Hence, to verify Non-Interference, static analysis would have to prove that for *every* possible value for z, $z[y]$ evaluates to the same value, independently of y. As all runs of the program have to be evaluated, non-interference is a hyperproperty [8]. The a solution can be approximated statically using safe Value-Set Analysis, as proposed in [4], or Taint Analysis [25]. However, due to the approximate nature, secure programs may be rejected as interfering. Dynamic approaches to analyze a single execution have the same problem, as they do not know about alternative outcomes. This is a known limitation in regards to the implicit channel created by using y to divert the control flow [3]. A point of criticism is that such a scenario may be considered unlikely. Yet, since there is no feasible and precise way to statically prove its absence, it cannot correctly be proven that it hasn't been added to some benign code with malicious intent.

To illustrate how Secure Multi-Execution enforces Non-Interference, consider the runs depicted in Figure 3. We assume that the secret input contains one bit of information and that the value at memory location $z[0]$ is 0 and the value at memory location $z[1]$ is 1. Assuming the high-security execution receives a 0 from the high-channel and the dummy value is 1. Note that comparison of the traces refutes non-interference, as the events they produce are not low-equivalent. However, due to Secure Multi-Execution semantics, outputs on low-channels from the high-execution are skipped. Hence, to a low-observer the trace behaves as if the high-information was 1, while in fact it was 0. The low-observer thus does not gain knowledge about the actual high-information.

3 RELATED WORK

The observation that Non-Interference is a Hypersafety Property has direct consequences on its enforcement. It follows

$$s_1^H \xrightarrow{L?x} s_2^H \xrightarrow{\bullet} s_3^H \xrightarrow{H?0} s_4^H \xrightarrow{\bullet} s_5^H \xrightarrow[\cancel{L!0}]{\bullet} s_6^H \xrightarrow{\bullet} s_7^H \xrightarrow[\cancel{L!0}]{\bullet} s_8^H \xrightarrow{\bullet} s_9^H \xrightarrow{L!0}$$

$$s_1^L \xrightarrow{L?x} s_2^L \xrightarrow{\bullet} s_3^L \xrightarrow{H?1} s_4^L \xrightarrow{\bullet} s_5^L \xrightarrow{L!1} s_6^L \xrightarrow{\bullet} s_8^L \xrightarrow{\bullet} s_9^L \xrightarrow{L!0}$$

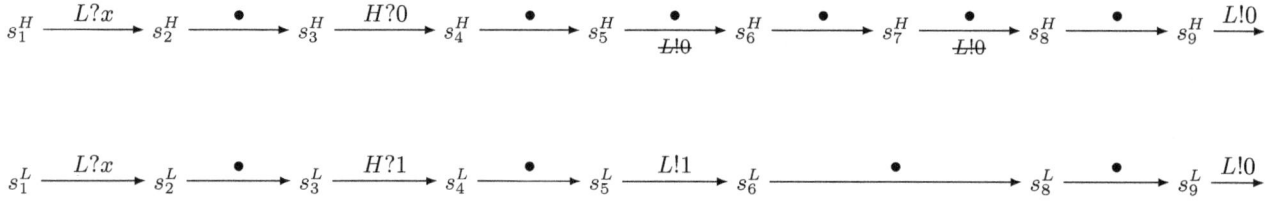

Figure 3: SME enforcement of Figure 2

that single-execution monitoring techniques like No-Sensitive-Upgrade [1, 30] or Permissive-Upgrade [2] are incapable of enforcing Non-Interference precisely. Consequently, multi-execution based approaches have been proposed in the form of Shadow Execution (SE) [7] and Secure Multi-Execution (SME) [9].

These techniques enforce Non-Interference by running multiple copies of a program, one for each security level in the security lattice. Each execution is responsible for outputs on channels with equivalent security classification. To compute these, each execution has access to input channels of equivalent or lower security classification. Where input from channels with higher security classification is needed, dummy values are provided instead. Unfortunately, due to the requirement to create one execution per security level, multi-execution typically comes with severely heightened resource requirements. To alleviate this, Austin and Flanagan proposed the use of Multiple Facets (MF) [3] to simulate multi-execution with less overhead. Instead of running multiple executions that compute one value each, they propose to simulate one execution on multiple, *faceted* values. The key benefit is that in any case where these values are equivalent for multiple executions, they can be collapsed to a single value, avoiding wasteful recalculations. Evaluation of faceted values must be supported by the target language and, thus, requires changes to the language semantics. In the case of machine code, the language semantics are determined by the underlying hardware architecture and thus cannot be changed with ease. However, the observation that recalculation of equivalent values is unnecessary wasteful, inspired the technique presented in this paper.

With regard to machine code, some approaches exist that leverage binary analysis frameworks for this cause. Most notably Balliu et al. [5], who use symbolic execution to create symbolic observation trees for confidentiality verification. Their approach is not fully automatic, as user input is needed to annotate loops with invariants. Also, the approach does not scale and has only been evaluated on binaries with a size of up to 80 lines of code. Other approaches for Non-Interference verification, such as the work by Milushev et al. [20], are usually targeted at source code, which is not available in our scenario. Multi-execution is also used to thwart memory-corruption based attacks, often in the form of Multi-Variant Execution. In this scenario, a program is in multiple, artificially diversified variants. For example, the GHUMVEE, MvArmor and VARAN frameworks use memory

layout diversification to defend programs against code-reuse attacks [13, 16, 28]. This is different from our approach, where programs are executed without artificial diversity.

Addionally, multi-execution has been used for confidentiality analysis by Kwon et al. [17]. Their system infers causality through dual-execution of a program, practically using a form of self-composition. Consequently, it cannot be used to repair interfering executions at run time. Additionally, the proposed analysis requires structured code, for example, in the form of source code or LLVM's structured intermediate representation.

4 DEMAND-DRIVEN SECURE MULTI-EXECUTION

The goal of our work is to reduce the run-time overhead of Secure Multi-Execution based Non-Interference enforcement for unstructured low-level languages such as binary code. The key idea of our work is to use a 1-safety property, called *secretless execution*, that implies Hypersafety Non-Interference for parts of the code. The reasoning behind our approach is that enforcing a 1-safety property is significantly less complex than enforcing Hypersafety. This allows us to use single-execution monitoring for benign parts of the code, reducing the overall resource requirements.

Reconsider the Secure Multi-Execution enforced run of the example depicted in Figure 3. Note that, while the unaltered traces are not low-equivalent, they still contain low-equivalent subtraces. Assuming that Secure Multi-Execution is used from the beginning, both executions start in the same state s_1. Since both have access to the same low-input and the program is deterministic, they will both be in the same states s_2 and s_3 after the next steps. Because they get different classified input, the executions diverge after s_3. However, after the information in y is overwritten in line 8, the executions will have converged again. Hence, they will end up in the same state s_9.

We call the parts where the two executions are in the same state *secretless*, as neither knows about a secret that the other is unaware of. As long as the multi-execution is in a secretless state, Non-Interference is implied as both executions behave equally. We use this observation to collapse the multi-execution to save resources, as depicted in Figure 4. The resulting enforcement uses Secure Multi-Execution *on-demand* and enforces *secretless execution* otherwise.

In the following, we give definitions for these intuitive observations and prove that secretless execution in fact implies

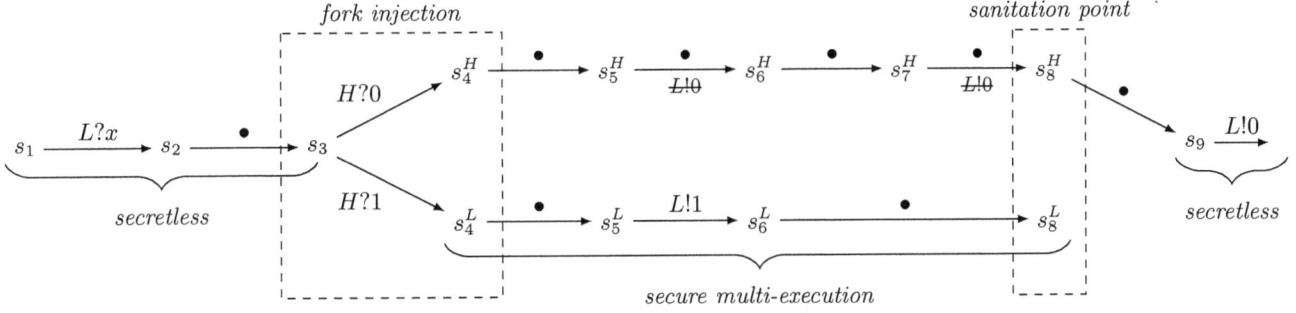

Figure 4: Demand-Driven SME enforcement of Figure 2

Non-Interference. We then discuss the practicality of convergence as a criterion to collapse multi-execution. In the next section, we describe our first implementation of the resulting *Demand-Driven Secure Multi-Execution* engine for machine code.

4.1 Secretless Execution

Our key idea to reduce the overhead of Non-Interference enforcement is to use a lightweight 1-safety enforcement method where possible. To achieve this, we introduce *secretless execution*. If a deterministic program is executed without knowledge about secret inputs, it is naturally non-interferent and does not require expensive Secure Multi-Execution enforcement. At the same time, proving that an execution has no knowledge about secret inputs can be done with lightweight execution monitoring. In the following, we give a definition of *secretless execution* and prove that it implies Progress-Sensitive Non-Interference (PSNI) for deterministic programs.

Any input from a channel with higher-security classification than the observer, must be considered secret to that observer. Hence, an execution without any secrets cannot obtain input from channels that are secret to any observer. This is the case for executions that either receive no input at all or only input from the channels with the lowest security classification. The lowest security classification is given by $\sqcap \mathcal{L}$. Thus, we define secretless execution as follows.

Definition 4.1. A trace $\bar{a}$ is *secretless* iff
$\forall i \in \mathbb{N}.\, 0 \le i \le |\bar{a}| \wedge \bar{a}(i) = c?v \implies \pi(c) = \sqcap \mathcal{L}$.

Since $\sqcap \mathcal{L}$ is the lowest security classification, any inputs on channels with this classification as visible to all observers. Hence, if two environments are ℓ-equivalent for any security level, they must also be equivalent for inputs from channels with the lowest security level.

LEMMA 4.2. $\ell, e_1, e_2 \,.\, \exists \ell \,.\, e_1 \approx_\ell e_2 \implies e_1 \approx_{\sqcap \mathcal{L}} e_2$.

PROOF. Using the definition of $e_1 \approx_\ell e_2$ and of the infimum, we get that $\forall c \,.\, \pi(c) \sqsubseteq \ell \implies e_1(c) \approx_\ell e_2(c)$ implies $\forall c \,.\, \pi(c) = \sqcap \mathcal{L} \implies e_1(c) \approx_\ell e_2(c)$. Hence, $\forall c \,.\, \pi(c) \sqsubseteq \sqcap \mathcal{L} \implies e_1(c) \approx_{\sqcap \mathcal{L}} e_2(c)$, which is $e_1 \approx_{\sqcap \mathcal{L}} e_2$. □

This observation allows us to prove that no multi-execution enforcement is necessary for secretless runs of deterministic programs.

THEOREM 4.3. All secretless runs *of deterministic programs satisfy* PSNI.

PROOF. We need to proof that $\forall s, \ell, e_1, e_2 \,.\, e_1 \approx_\ell e_2 \implies \forall \bar{a}_1.e_1 \models s \xrightarrow{\bar{a}_1} \implies \exists \bar{a}_2.e_2 \models s \xrightarrow{\bar{a}_2} \wedge \bar{a}_1 \approx_\ell \bar{a}_2$, where $\bar{a}_1$ and $\bar{a}_2$ are *secretless* runs and s is a deterministic program. We do this by showing that in fact $\bar{a}_1 = \bar{a}_2$. Proof by induction in $n = |\bar{a}_1|$.

$n = 0$: Then $\bar{a}_1(n) = \epsilon = \bar{a}_2(n)$. Both runs are in the same initial state s.

$n + 1$: Assume that $e_1 \models s \xrightarrow{\bar{a}_1(n+1)} s_1$ and $e_2 \models s \xrightarrow{\bar{a}_2(n+1)} s_2$ and $\bar{a}_i(n+1) = a_i$. Case distinction over the equivalence of the created actions:

$a_1 = a_2$: Then also $s_1 = s_2$, because s is deterministic.

$a_1 \ne a_2$: Then, $\exists c, v_1, v_2 \,.\, a_1 = c?v_1 \wedge a_2 = c?v_2 \wedge v_1 \ne v_2$, because s is deterministic. Because $\bar{a}_1$ and $\bar{a}_2$ are *secretless* runs, we get $\exists v_1, v_2 \,.\, a_1 = \sqcap \mathcal{L}?v_1 \wedge a_2 = \sqcap \mathcal{L}?v_2 \wedge v_1 \ne v_2$. Because the traces are consistent with the environments e_1 and e_2, it follows that $v_1 = e_1(\sqcap \mathcal{L})[n + 1]$ and $v_2 = e_2(\sqcap \mathcal{L})[n + 1]$. Using Lemma 4.2 and $e_1 \approx_\ell e_2$, we get that $e_1 \approx_{\sqcap \mathcal{L}} e_2$ and, thus, $v_1 = v_2$. This contradicts that $a_1 \ne a_2$, proving that this case cannot occur for secretless runs of deterministic programs.

Because $\bar{a}_1 = \bar{a}_2$ holds for $n = 0$ and because for every $n + 1$ it holds that $\bar{a}_1(n + 1) = \bar{a}_2(n + 1)$, we get that $\bar{a}_1 = \bar{a}_2$. As $\bar{a}_1 = \bar{a}_2 \implies \bar{a}_1 \approx_\ell \bar{a}_2$, all *secretless runs* of deterministic programs satisfy PSNI. □

This result allows us to use lightweight *secretless execution monitoring* instead of Secure Multi-Execution for parts of the program. We do this by creating a single-execution detector that is satisfied as long as no input is received from classified channels.

Definition 4.4. δ is a *detector for secretlessness*, iff

$$\delta(a) = \begin{cases} \bot & ,a = c?v \wedge c \sqsupset \sqcap \mathcal{L} \\ \top & ,\text{otherwise} \end{cases}$$

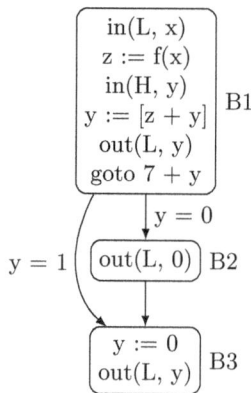

Figure 5: Recovered CFG of the running example

Once the detector returns bottom, we switch to Secure Multi-Execution semantics to ensure precise enforcement of Non-Interference in the presence of classified information. A problem that remains it that, once we switched to SME semantics, we can no longer use lightweight monitoring. We solve this problem by using static analysis to determine where multiple executions of the code can be collapsed. The result is a description of *critical sections* that restrict multi-execution enforcement to parts of the code.

4.2 Critical Section Analysis

Using our secretless execution detection only at the beginning of the execution would imply that any reduction of the execution overhead is determined by the earliest occurrence of secret input. Once we have performed the switched to SME semantics, the single-execution based detector is of no further use. However, our proof that secretless execution implies Non-Interference only requires that the initial state s for both executions is equal. If this is the case and both environments are still ℓ-equivalent, PSNI is again implied until information on a classified channel is received. This implies that multi-execution can safely be collapsed into a single-execution once all execution have converged.

Unfortunately, while this result shows that reducing multiple executions to a single execution is valid in certain scenarios, it is practically infeasible to check for convergence of all executions after every execution step. Consider a situation where some executions have taken different paths, resulting in diverging program counters. Until their program counters converge, the various states cannot be equivalent. Thus, the multi-execution cannot be collapsed. However, if all executions are advanced at roughly the same pace (e.g., using round-robin scheduling), one copy may overtake the others. As a result, they will never meet at the same location. Additionally, equivalence of the whole states is hard to validate and at the same time unlikely. Equivalence of the states implies equivalence of their memory mappings, which would have to be validated by expensive memory comparison. As long as classified information resides in memory, the memory is unlikely to converge. Consequently, we consider

convergence validation after each execution step impractical. Instead, we propose to use information gathered through static analysis to i) identify locations where the control-flow of multiple executions converges and ii) analyze the impact of differences in their respective memory states.

Control-Flow Recovery. Identification of locations were the control-flow converges, requires knowledge of the Control-Flow Graph (CFG). Unfortunately, the control-flow paths in machine code are concealed due to the indirect [GOTO] commands. We solve this by static recovery of the CFG of the machine code program. For example, the recovered CFG of our example can be seen in Figure 5. This additional information allows for the identification of promising states. In our example, convergence can be checked when both executions entered B3, but can be skipped in B2 as potentially only one execution reaches this location. Hence, a barrier synchronization on B2 may never terminate, a barrier synchronization on B3 must.

Note that infinite blocking at a barrier synchronization may introduce a termination channel. Consider a situation where the unclassified execution waits at a barrier shortly before emitting a message on the unclassified channel. The classified execution is stuck in an endless loop, due to the specific value of the classified information. An observer with low security clearance may infer from the absence of message on the unclassified channel, that the classified information has caused the program to get stuck and thus infer the specific value. As has been propsed by Schmitz et al. [24], this problem can be solved by removing the barrier after a certain time-out. All executions are then advanced as usual, removing the termination-channel. While this optimization decreases the number of convergence checks by selecting promising code locations, the availability of the CFG also enables further optimization.

Live Memory Analysis. State convergence, as described above, is a sufficient condition for Non-Interference, but it is not necessary. That is because varieties that persist in a set of states must not necessarily influence observable behavior. Reconsider the example from Section 2.3. Static analysis can show that all outputs after line 7 use values defined in line 8. Hence, with regard to the output in line 9, any divergence in memory apart from location y does not have an effect on the output.

If the executions converge for a subset of the memory that entails all values that influence the future output behavior, the dead part of memory can be ignored in the state comparison. Unfortunately, this puts us in the undesirable position of statically enforcing a Hyperproperty again. To determine the part of memory that influences future output behavior is equivalent to non-interference verification and behavior equivalence checking. As argued above, doing it precisely on machine code is infeasible. Fortunately, as the memory partition is only used to increase performance but has no impact on the soundness of the multi-execution enforcement, perfect precision is not necessary here. As long as the memory partition is a safe over-approximation of the actually used memory subset, using it to guide Demand-Driven Secure Multi-Execution enforcement is also safe. Calculating a safe over-approximation of used memory for a given statement can be done in various ways, e.g. using Value-Set Analysis [4] or Taint-Analysis [25]. We give details on our implementation in Section 5.3.

Combined, these analyses provide a description of potential *sanitation points*, where executions may be collapsed. These consist of a code location and a set of memory locations, describing the live subset of memory at that state. Once all executions have reached the sanitation point, equivalence of the live part of memory is validated. If this is the case, we continue secretless execution monitoring to save additional resources. Finally, in the presence of the CFG of the machine code, static analysis can also reduce some of the monitoring work. Usually, the secretless execution monitor intercepts all observable events and checks whether these are input events using a classified channel. Given the CFG, we can pre-determine all locations where input events can occur and thus reduce the number of intercepted events. An additional effect is that we can combine input locations with sanitation points to create *critical sections*. These encompass all runs from an entry location to potential exit locations that require multi-execution enforcement. Thus, this effectively partitions all possible runs into benign and critical sections.

In the next section, we describe our implementation of our Demand-Driven Secure Multi-Execution enforcement method for machine code as described above. We then evaluate our prototype to show that our approach significantly reduces the run-time overhead for real-world binaries.

5 IMPLEMENTATION

To evaluate the increase in efficiency of our approach, we designed and developed a prototype capable of running Unix-style binary programs both under traditional SME semantics and under our optimized approach. Our implementation consists of a simple execution monitor that enforces *secretless* execution, an SME-based enforcement module, and a static analysis back-end to determine critical sections. An overview of the system architecture is given in Figure 6. First, the static analysis component is used to determine critical sections in the code. This is done by recovery of the CFG and subsequent Taint Analysis. The description of critical sections consists of an entry location and an exit location. The entry location provides a hint to the secretless execution monitor when to expect input events. This way, unnecessary interception of benign events can be minimized. The exit location defines the sanitation point for this critical section. If the end of the critical section is reached during secretless execution, we continue the execution unmonitored until the next critical section entry is reached. This means that for all parts of the code where the static analysis can prove that they are secretless, we omit using run-time monitoring. If the secretless execution monitor detects input from classified channels, we switch to Secure-Multi Execution defense using our fork injection technique. If the Secure Multi-Execution

enforcement is aborted, we simply detach from the replica and kill the process. Execution continues in single-execution mode with the primary process. In the following, we present each component and provide details about our design decisions for their development. Where multiple solutions exist, we usually chose the solution with the lowest performance overhead.

Naturally, due to the complexity of building SME systems in general and the specific challenges of machine language, our prototype currently has some limitations. As we require deterministic memory, we currently do not support concurrent executions, shared memory etc. Also, our classification implementation currently only supports a two-level lattice ($\{(L, H)\}$). In the future, we plan to provide solutions to these problems and extend the functionality of our framework.

5.1 Secretless Execution Monitor

Our secretless execution monitor enforces the PSNI based on the policy introduced in Section 4.1. Because secretless execution is a 1-safety policy, the execution monitor analyzes a single trace. The goal is to intercept all input events and validate the security level of the according channel for a given security classification.

In Unix-like systems, input is delivered to a program through the kernel. To signal the kernel that input is required, the program executes a `syscall` instruction with appropriate arguments. For our prototype, we focus on the `read` system call that is used to read a number of bytes from a file descriptor into a buffer that resides in program memory. Interception of system calls can be achieved through the Unix-native `ptrace` framework. Using the PTRACE_SYSCALL request, execution will only be stopped when a system call occurs. This allows for skipping over benign instructions. The system call arguments can be inferred from the register state of the paused process.

The `read` system call uses a file descriptor (FD) as the source argument. These are symbolic values that may be reused for various real sources during execution. Therefore, they do not uniquely describe a single channel. To overcome this problem, we use a mixture of two techniques: We use information from `procfs` when entering a critical section and then trace FD handling internally. By intercepting all `open` and `close` system calls, a record of currently open FDs and their real source can be managed by the monitor. As this results in additional pauses of the execution, which leads to heightened overhead, we only use it when the monitor is attached. Upon attachment, the real source of a file descriptor are resolved through the `procfs`. The `procfs` reflects currently opened FDs and their sources and thus provides an up-to-date record. The classification for our implementation is based on file locations in the system. This allows us to classify individual files as well as file directories. The execution monitor compares the real source location of a `read` system call with a given classification. Should the location of the real source be black-listed, we consider this to be classified input. Once such a situation occurs, the execution monitor

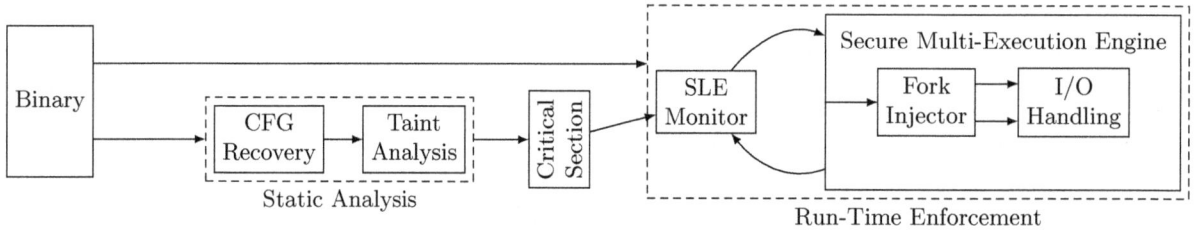

Figure 6: System architecture

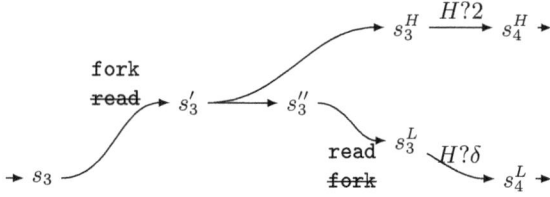

Figure 7: Fork injection

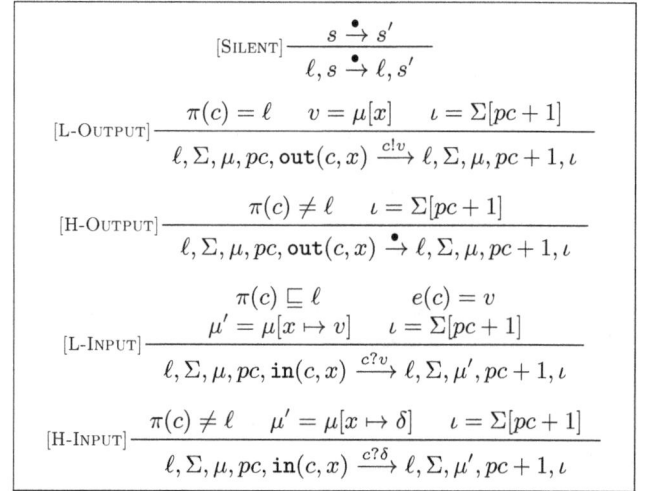

Figure 8: Local SME Semantics

detects secret input, which violates the secretless execution policy. Consequently, further execution may not necessarily satisfy PSNI and must thus be secured by multi-execution.

5.2 Secure Multi-Execution Engine

Our SME engine is invoked by the secretless execution monitor, once a **read** from a classified source occurred. The goal of the SME engine is to enforce PSNI using multi-execution. Due to the characteristics of machine code and our demand-driven optimization, implementation of SME for our approach is not trivial. In the following, we address the biggest challenges and present our solutions.

Fork Injection. Unlike traditional SME and Multi-Variant Execution implementations, our engine is not started alongside its targets. Hence, the SME engine must be capable to create a copy of the current execution at run-time. The fastest and simplest mechanism to duplicate a running process we discovered, uses the **fork** mechanism intended to spawn new threads in a Unix-like environment. This, essentially, creates a second process that is running on the same code. Unfortunately, the **fork** needs to be executed in the context of the running process. To overcome this problem, we developed the *Fork Injection* method shown in Figure 7.

Due to the architecture of our system, our SME engine will always be initiated by the secretless execution monitor when the process is about to enter a **read** system call. Since the functionality of a system call is defined by an identifier value stored in a register, it can easily be altered using **ptrace**. For the fork injection, we first backup the identifier and argument values of the original system call. Then, we exchange the identifier for the **fork** ID. The system call is executed and the forked process is connected to our enforcement engine using **ptrace**. Since we replace the original **read** system call, this would effectively suppress an output event. To mask

this, we rewind the program counter in the stored process context before executing the system call. When returning from the system call, the altered program counter is loaded and both processes continue from the original system call location, repeating the actual **read**. The copies are identified by unique PIDs and equipped with a security level ℓ in the monitor.

I/O Handling. Switching to SME semantics for the forked copies requires changes to I/O handling of each copy, described in Figure 8 While Rafnsson and Sabelfeld have provided a definition of SME that is purely black-box [22], we provide the localized semantics in the style of the original work of Devrise and Piessens here [9]. This illustrates the impact of Secure Multi-Execution on the machine code semantics.

Note that all •-emitting instructions are not affected by SME enforcement. As these internal steps do not create observable output events, they are irrelevant for PSNI. The semantics of [OUTPUT] is changed to ensure that each execution emits output events only for their respective security level. Output on other channels is masked as an internal transition. Input is provided to all execution with equal or higher security level. In cases where input is requested from classified sources, dummy values are provided, denoted by δ.

As mentioned above, on Unix-like systems, [INPUT] and [OUTPUT] are realized in the kernel and accessed through system calls. Therefore, their semantics is not defined by the hardware, but by coder in the kernel. Through the interception mechanism of `ptrace`, the changes described above can be realized without changing either hardware or kernel code. For example, if output on channels that the execution is not responsible for is requested, the system call is skipped.

Dummy Values. A general challenge of secure multi-execution exists in the choice of the dummy values. As Rafnsson and Sabelfeld note, the wrong choice of values may lead to executions crashing [22]. Technically, it is possible to change the input read into a buffer using `ptrace`. However, this approach is very slow for large inputs and should be avoided. Instead, we provide a dummy source through a valid file descriptor. By opening the dummy source before forking child processes, the attached file descriptor remains valid in the child executions. Providing dummy values then only requires a single change of the file descriptor argument in `read` system calls. Additionally, the real source can be any kind of stream. Random dummy values can be provided by opening `/dev/urandom`, the read can be re-targeted to another existing file, etc. We discuss the use of infinite streams in the evaluation.

Asynchronous Input. Another problem arises with shared input. Since we fork multiple copies from a single execution, the copies inherit open file descriptors from the child. Unfortunately, these file descriptors are connected to the same file description, meaning that the cursor position is shared as well. If multiple copies read from the same channel at different times, a race-condition occurs where the first to perform a read receives the first part of the information in the channel and later copies receive the rest. A possible solution to this problem is to use barrier synchronization on inputs, where all executions join up and received input is shared[2]. However, since the multiple copies may have diverged due to different classified information, they may not all arrive at the same input location. Hence, we opted for a different approach. To unshare the cursor positions, we create a copy of the cursor for all executions in the SME engine and keep track of alterations to it by observation of the I/O behaviors. We then replace any request to `read` from a source with the `pread` variant, where the cursor location can be provided by our monitor. This allows us to handle input requests from all copies independently.

Scheduling. For our implementation, we schedule both copies in parallel to make use of multi-core architectures. The executions are handled individually in the monitor, as soon as they request interaction with the kernel.

Since multi-execution of the program and management of the copies requires additional resources, running of the SME engine inadvertently creates a performance overhead. However, if secretless continuation can be assured, we can stop the multi-execution and downgrade to lightweight execution

monitoring again. We describe our approach to finding critical sections using static analysis in the following section.

5.3 Static Analysis

As described in Section 4.2, critical section analysis requires the Control-Flow Graph (CFG) of the program, as well as live memory analysis. Both is notoriously hard to do on machine code, which is why we currently depend on a combination of automated and manual reverse engineering of the code.

Recovery of the CFG from programs written in machine code requires precise resolution of indirect control-flow targets. Various techniques have been proposed, e.g. Value-Set Analysis [15], cofibered domains [19], Symbolic Execution [26], and extracting CFI-information [21]. Unfortunately, these approaches are usually stand-alone implementations and are not trivially combinable with further analyses.

Live memory analysis suffers from the same difficulties. Hence, statically calculating the effect of input locations on output locations is also very hard. If both explicit and implicit information flows should be covered precisely, the problem reduces to proving behavioral equivalence for the whole program. Fortunately, as described in Section 4.2, in the case of our approach, an imprecise analysis is sufficient, provided that it is sound. This allows for the usage of well-researched over-approximate information flow analysis, such as Taint Analysis [25]. If a sufficiently strict taint policy is used (one that includes program counter and memory address tainting), Taint Analysis can produce sound may-analyses for information flow. As a consequence, if sound static Taint Analysis returns a negative result for an input-output pair, it can be concluded that any variance introduced at the input cannot affect the observable behavior at the output location. In combination with the CFG, this information is sufficient to determine the last affected output location with regard to an input location. This can be used to statically determine *critical sections* in the code that *may* be interferent. More importantly, every part of the code that is outside of these critical sections is provably benign and can therefore be omitted from multi-execution enforcement under all conditions.

For our prototype, we use a combination of manual inspection using `IDA Pro` and automated Taint Analysis using the BAP-based Saluki Framework [11]. The creation of a fully automated critical section analysis is left for future work.

6 EVALUATION

We evaluated our approach using our prototype and two real-world binaries from the `coreutils` package, `cat` and `sha256sum`. Both programs are single-threaded and receive all significant input through a `read` system call. `Cat` echos the received inputs on `stdout`, `sha256sum` collects the input in a heap structure, calculates the SHA-256 sum and prints the result to `stdout`. In both cases, this core functionality takes up a small portion of the code, while the rest is dedicated to advanced features and error handling. The fact that the time spend in the critical section depends on the input, allows us to

---

[2]this strategy is also called record and replay [28]

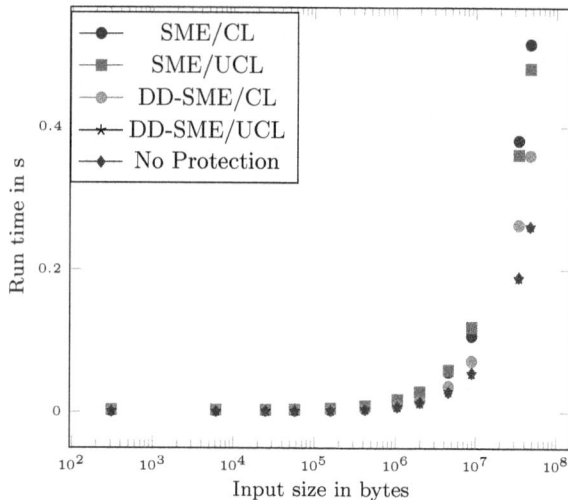

Figure 9: Sha256sum **run time comparison**

measure the change in the speedup for executions that spend more time in the critical section (using larger input files) or less (using smaller input files). Additionally, we compare runs where the input file is in a classified location (CL) versus runs where the input file is not (UCL). As both `cat` and `sha256sum` keep reading input until it is depleted, using an infinite stream as the dummy source (e.g. `/dev/urandom`) would lead to non-termination of the lower copy. Hence, throughout all measurements, we have used the same file as input and dummy source, to ensure deterministic behavior. We describe the two case studies in more detail in the following sections. All tests where performed on an Intel® Core™ i7-5600U CPU @ 2.60GHz machine with four physical cores. To account for the overhead produced by using `ptrace`, we have run the unprotected execution in trace mode as well, without intercepting any events. Hence, the unprotected runtimes are higher than normal.

6.1 Sha256Sum

`Sha256sum` computes the SHA-256 hashes for a given file. To achieve this, `sha256sum` repeatedly reads from the input file and stores the information in an allocated memory region and calculates the hash. Once all information has been processed, the result is written to `stdout`. Static analysis shows that the information received from the file does not effect future outputs, because the last output prints the path of the file but no contents. As a consequence, the critical section reaches from the `read` system call till the location after the `write`.

Figure 9 shows our run-time measurements for various input sizes. Naturally, the unprotected run is always the fastest, as it consists of a single execution only. However, Demand-Driven Secure multi-Execution is nearly equivalent, if no reads from classified channels occur. This is the result of running the secretless execution monitor only within critical sections, which in this case only requires one `read` system call to be intercepted. This can be seen more clearly, when

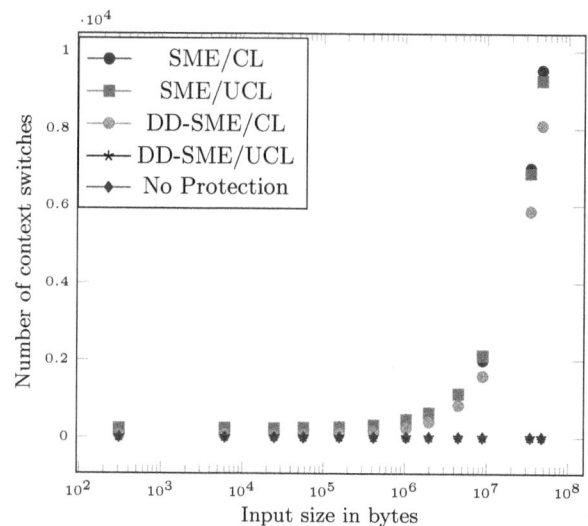

Figure 10: Sha256sum **context switches**

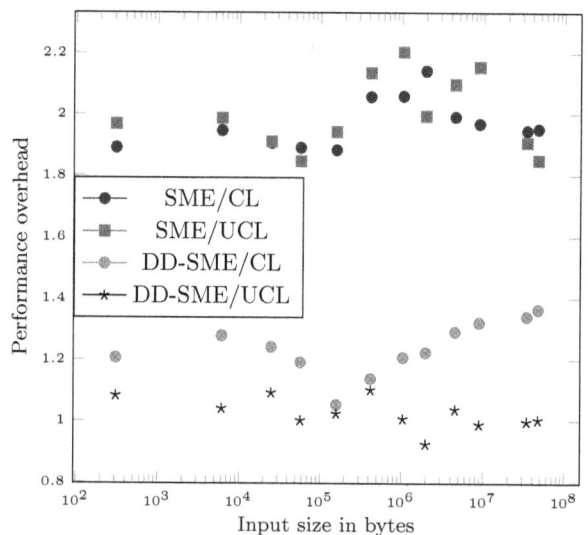

Figure 11: Sha256sum **effective overhead**

comparing the number of context switches performed during execution. Figure 10 shows that the number of switches for unclassified runs of Demand-Driven Secure Multi-Execution are nearly identical with unprotected execution. Both figures also show that traditional Secure Multi-Execution does not benefit from unclassified runs, as it does not validate secretlessness.

Figure 11 gives the overheads of traditional SME and Demand-Driven SME compared to unprotected execution. As can be seed, traditional SME and DD-SME are clearly separated. While traditional SME comes with an overhead between 50% and 250%, our demand-driven optimization reduces the overhead to between 10% to 50%. As the time spent in the critical section is dependent on the input size,

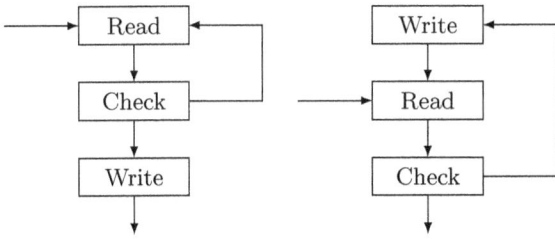

Figure 12: Input/Output loop of sha256sum and cat

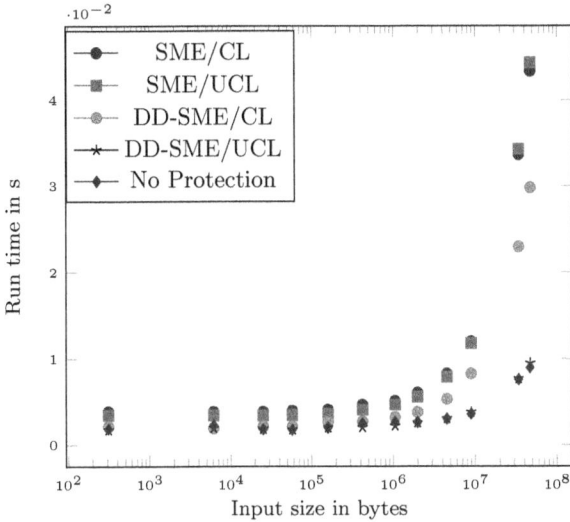

Figure 13: Cat run time comparison

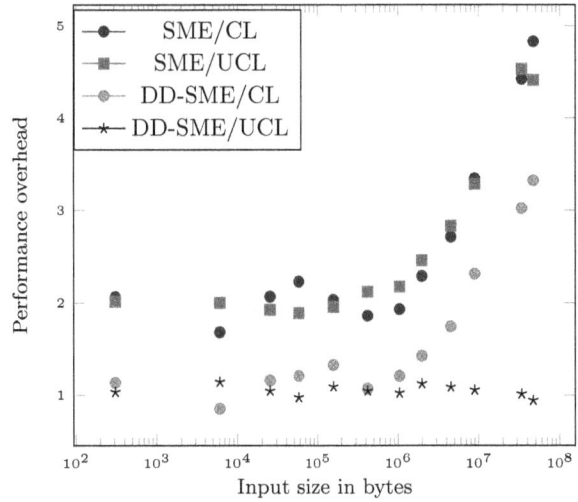

Figure 14: Cat effective overhead

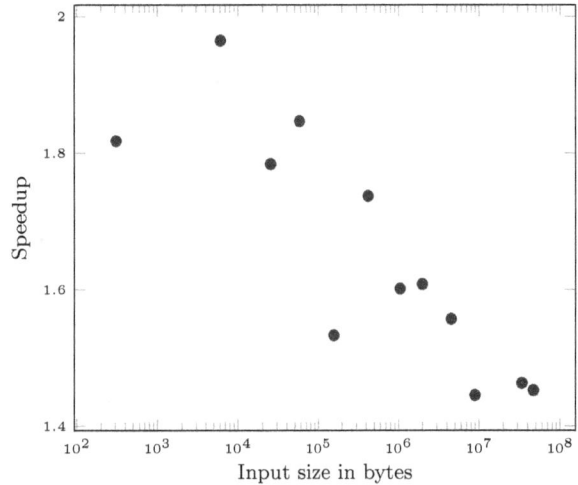

Figure 15: DD-SME speedup for cat

larger inputs lead to a slight reduction in the speedup of our approach. At the same time, the impact of the fixed portion of the monitoring overhead of traditional SME is reduced, leading to a decrease in overhead. For increasingly large inputs, overhead of the two approaches would naturally converge, as DD-SME becomes traditional SME if the whole program is considered critical.

6.2 Cat

Cat echoes the contents of a file to the standard output. It is similar to sha256sum in its core structure, with one significant exception. Unlike sha256sum, cat processes each input chunk directly, instead of collecting it in memory. This leads to an I/O loop (depicted in Figure 12) where the last write occurs before the last read. Therefore, a critical section starting in the location of read and ending in the location of write would never be left. Hence, we manually moved the beginning of the critical section to before entering the I/O loop.

A comparison of the run times is given in Figure 13. Here, the difference between unprotected runs and protected runs is more distinct. This is because cat does not process received data, but simply echoes it. Hence, unprotected runs are much faster and the monitoring overhead becomes more prominent.

This impacts the overheads, as depicted in Figure 14. For cat, the overhead of traditional secure multi-execution ranges from 80% to 400%. The overhead of Demand-Driven SME ranges from 10% to 250%. The diminishing effect of our on-demand optimization can be seen in Figure 15. However, this also shows that even for very large input data (i.e., a lot of time spend in the critical section) our approach still achieves a significant speedup above a factor of 1.4.

7 CONCLUSION

In this paper, we have presented an efficient and precise method to enforce Progress-Sensitive Non-Interference on programs written in machine code through *Demand-Driven Secure Multi-Execution*. While Secure Multi-Execution is known to precisely enforce Non-Interference, it usually imposes an intolerable overhead on the execution. Our key idea to reduce this overhead is to use expensive enforcement only where necessary. To achieve this, we have defined *secretless execution* and proven that this 1-safety policy implies 2-safety Non-Interference. This allows us to use a simpler execution monitoring approach for large parts of the execution. Secure multi-execution is only used *on-demand*, i.e., whenever the execution becomes aware of secret information. We continue with efficient secretless execution monitoring, once the states converge with respect to live memory. To evaluate our approach, we are the first to have implemented a secure multi-execution engine for x86 binaries on Unix-style systems. Furthermore, we have augmented our SME engine with secretless execution monitoring, resulting in a Demand-Driven Secure Multi-Execution engine. Our evaluation on representative corutils binaries shows that DD-SME is applicable to machine code and that our augmentation leads to a significant improvement in the performance overhead.

Our research opens a lot of promising directions for future work. While our prototype shows that DD-SME can be used for legacy code, we currently only support a limited set of features. Future extensions of our approach should integrate concurrent programs, shared memory support etc. Additionally, our approach is currently limited to small security lattices, where most information comes from channels with the lowest security level. It remains to show how secretless execution can be used to collapse multiple executions in the presence of information with intermediate classification. Also, our static analysis pass to determine critical sections still requires human interaction. Automating this phase promises interesting new insights into static information flow analysis.

REFERENCES

[1] Thomas H Austin and Cormac Flanagan. 2009. Efficient purely-dynamic information flow analysis. In *Proceedings of the ACM SIGPLAN Fourth Workshop on Programming Languages and Analysis for Security*. ACM, 113–124.

[2] Thomas H Austin and Cormac Flanagan. 2010. Permissive dynamic information flow analysis. In *Proceedings of the 5th ACM SIGPLAN Workshop on Programming Languages and Analysis for Security*. ACM, 3.

[3] Thomas H Austin and Cormac Flanagan. 2012. Multiple facets for dynamic information flow. In *ACM Sigplan Notices*, Vol. 47. ACM, 165–178.

[4] Gogul Balakrishnan and Thomas Reps. 2004. Analyzing memory accesses in x86 executables. In *International conference on compiler construction*. Springer, 5–23.

[5] Musard Balliu, Mads Dam, and Roberto Guanciale. 2014. Automating Information Flow Analysis of Low Level Code. In *Proceedings of the 2014 ACM SIGSAC Conference on Computer and Communications Security (CCS '14)*. ACM, New York, NY, USA, 1080–1091. https://doi.org/10.1145/2660267.2660322

[6] Gilles Barthe, Pedro R D'Argenio, and Tamara Rezk. 2004. Secure information flow by self-composition. In *Computer Security Foundations Workshop, 2004. Proceedings. 17th IEEE*. IEEE, 100–114.

[7] R. Capizzi, A. Longo, V. N. Venkatakrishnan, and A. P. Sistla. 2008. Preventing Information Leaks through Shadow Executions. In *2008 Annual Computer Security Applications Conference (ACSAC)*. 322–331. https://doi.org/10.1109/ACSAC.2008.50

[8] Michael R Clarkson and Fred B Schneider. 2010. Hyperproperties. *Journal of Computer Security* 18, 6 (2010), 1157–1210.

[9] Dominique Devriese and Frank Piessens. 2010. Noninterference through secure multi-execution. In *Security and Privacy (SP), 2010 IEEE Symposium on*. IEEE, 109–124.

[10] Joseph A Goguen and José Meseguer. 1982. Security policies and security models. In *Security and Privacy, 1982 IEEE Symposium on*. IEEE, 11–11.

[11] Ivan Gotovchits, Rijnard van Tonder, and David Brumley. 2018. Saluki: finding taint-style vulnerabilities with static property checking.

[12] Kevin W Hamlen, Greg Morrisett, and Fred B Schneider. 2006. Computability classes for enforcement mechanisms. *ACM Transactions on Programming Languages and Systems (TOPLAS)* 28, 1 (2006), 175–205.

[13] Petr Hosek and Cristian Cadar. 2015. VARAN the Unbelievable: An Efficient N-version Execution Framework. *SIGPLAN Not.* 50, 4 (March 2015), 339–353. https://doi.org/10.1145/2775054.2694390

[14] Vineeth Kashyap, Ben Wiedermann, and Ben Hardekopf. 2011. Timing-and termination-sensitive secure information flow: Exploring a new approach. In *Security and Privacy (SP), 2011 IEEE Symposium on*. IEEE, 413–428.

[15] Johannes Kinder. 2010. *Static Analysis of x86 Executables*. Ph.D. Dissertation. Technische Universität Darmstadt.

[16] Koen Koning, Herbert Bos, and Cristiano Giuffrida. 2016. Secure and efficient multi-variant execution using hardware-assisted process virtualization. In *Dependable Systems and Networks (DSN), 2016 46th Annual IEEE/IFIP International Conference on*. IEEE, 431–442.

[17] Yonghwi Kwon, Dohyeong Kim, William Nick Sumner, Kyungtae Kim, Brendan Saltaformaggio, Xiangyu Zhang, and Dongyan Xu. 2016. LDX: Causality Inference by Lightweight Dual Execution. In *Proceedings of the Twenty-First International Conference on Architectural Support for Programming Languages and Operating Systems (ASPLOS '16)*. ACM, New York, NY, USA, 503–515. https://doi.org/10.1145/2872362.2872395

[18] Xiaozhu Meng and B Miller. 2015. *Binary code is not easy*. Technical Report. Tech. rep., Computer Sciences Department, University of Wisconsin, Madison.

[19] Bogdan Mihaila. 2015. *Adaptable Static Analysis of Executables for proving the Absence of Vulnerabilities*. Ph.D. Dissertation. München, Technische Universität München, Diss., 2015.

[20] Dimiter Milushev, Wim Beck, and Dave Clarke. 2012. Noninterference via Symbolic Execution. *FMOODS/FORTE* 7273 (2012), 152–168.

[21] Tobias Pfeffer, Paula Herber, Lucas Druschke, and Sabine Glesner. 2018. Efficient and Safe Control Flow Recovery Using a Restricted Intermediate Language. In *VSC Track on Validation of Safety critical Collaboration systems at the IEEE International Conference on Enabling Technologies: Infrastructure for Collaborative Enterprises (WETICE 2018, to appear)*. IEEE Computer Society.

[22] Willard Rafnsson and Andrei Sabelfeld. 2016. Secure multi-execution: Fine-grained, declassification-aware, and transparent. *Journal of Computer Security* 24, 1 (2016), 39–90.

[23] Andrei Sabelfeld and Alejandro Russo. 2009. From Dynamic to Static and Back: Riding the Roller Coaster of Information-Flow Control Research.. In *Ershov Memorial Conference*, Vol. 5947. Springer, 352–365.

[24] Thomas Schmitz, Maximilian Algehed, Cormac Flanagan, and Alejandro Russo. 2018. Faceted Secure Multi Execution. (2018).

[25] Edward J Schwartz, Thanassis Avgerinos, and David Brumley. 2010. All you ever wanted to know about dynamic taint analysis and forward symbolic execution (but might have been afraid to ask). In *Security and privacy (SP), 2010 IEEE symposium on*. IEEE, 317–331.

[26] Yan Shoshitaishvili, Ruoyu Wang, Christopher Salls, Nick Stephens, Mario Polino, Andrew Dutcher, John Grosen, Siji Feng, Christophe Hauser, Christopher Kruegel, and Giovanni Vigna. 2016. SoK: (State of) The Art of War: Offensive Techniques in Binary Analysis. In *IEEE Symposium on Security and Privacy*.

[27] Tachio Terauchi and Alexander Aiken. 2005. Secure information flow as a safety problem. In *SAS*, Vol. 3672. Springer, 352–367.

[28] Stijn Volckaert, Bart Coppens, and Bjorn De Sutter. 2015. Cloning your Gadgets: Complete ROP Attack Immunity with Multi-Variant Execution. (2015).

[29] D. Zanarini, M. Jaskelioff, and A. Russo. 2013. Precise Enforcement of Confidentiality for Reactive Systems. In *2013 IEEE 26th Computer Security Foundations Symposium*. 18–32. https://doi.org/10.1109/CSF.2013.9

[30] Stephan Arthur Zdancewic and Andrew Myers. 2002. *Programming languages for information security*. Cornell University.

PoLPer: Process-Aware Restriction of Over-Privileged Setuid Calls in Legacy Applications

Yuseok Jeon
Purdue

Junghwan Rhee
NEC Laboratories America

Chung Hwan Kim
NEC Laboratories America

Zhichun Li
NEC Laboratories America

Mathias Payer
EPFL and Purdue

Byoungyoung Lee
Seoul National and Purdue

Zhenyu Wu
NEC Laboratories America

ABSTRACT

setuid system calls enable critical functions such as user authentications and modular privileged components. Such operations must only be executed after careful validation. However, current systems do not perform rigorous checks, allowing exploitation of privileges through memory corruption vulnerabilities in privileged programs. As a solution, understanding which setuid system calls can be invoked in what context of a process allows precise enforcement of least privileges. We propose a novel comprehensive method to systematically extract and enforce least privilege of setuid system calls to prevent misuse. Our approach learns the required process contexts of setuid system calls along multiple dimensions: process hierarchy, call stack, and parameter in a process-aware way. Every setuid system call is then restricted to the per-process context by our kernel-level context enforcer. Previous approaches without process-awareness are too coarse-grained to control setuid system calls, resulting in over-privilege. Our method reduces available privileges even for identical code depending on whether it is run by a parent or a child process. We present our prototype called PoLPer which systematically discovers only required setuid system calls and effectively prevents real-world exploits targeting vulnerabilities of the setuid family of system calls in popular desktop and server software at near zero overhead.

CCS CONCEPTS

• **Security and privacy** → **Systems security; Software and application security**;

KEYWORDS

Setuid system calls, Least Privilege Principle, Process hierarchy

ACM Reference Format:
Yuseok Jeon, Junghwan Rhee, Chung Hwan Kim, Zhichun Li, Mathias Payer, Byoungyoung Lee, and Zhenyu Wu. 2019. PoLPer: Process-Aware Restriction of Over-Privileged Setuid Calls in Legacy Applications . In *Ninth ACM Conference on Data and Application Security and Privacy (CODASPY '19), March 25–27, 2019, Richardson, TX, USA.* ACM, New York, NY, USA, 12 pages. https://doi.org/10.1145/3292006.3300028

1 INTRODUCTION

The setuid family of system calls[1] is a well-established mechanism in major operating systems to manage privileges in applications [11]. The setuid system calls enable critical security functions such as user authentication and modular privileged components. The code invoking setuid calls, namely *privilege sensitive code*, provides *a conceptual security gateway* for privileged operations. However, if privilege sensitive code is misused or fails to perform rigorous checks, this code can lead to a disastrous system breach by allowing unintended privileges (e.g., a root shell spawned by an attacker). As such, privilege sensitive code essentially forms the foundational principle of least privilege [48].

In an ideal deployment with the principle of least privilege (PoLP), a certain entity is granted with a privilege only when needed, and de-privileged otherwise. Specifically, the system must be compartmentalized so that a privileged operation can only be executed after careful checking of the context. On one hand, compartmentalization [21, 23] reduces the amount of code that may execute setuid calls. And, on the other hand, it enables a strict interface on how privileged operations can be reached. For instance, Qmail [5] uses separate modules under separate user IDs where each ID has only limited access to a subset of resources. The highest privilege (e.g., root) is contained in a very small restricted module to prevent its misuse. As another example, secure computing mode (seccomp) [49] is a security facility in the Linux kernel allowing a process to make a one-way transition in a secure state; for instance, a system call is restricted on certain parameters or entirely after a state transition.

In addition, the principle of least privilege requires different modules to interact through clearly defined channels. That is, a module may only request services from other modules using a well-defined API. If the principle of least privilege is enforced correctly, vulnerable modules are unprivileged (e.g., rendering engines in a browser or audio/video decoding modules in media players). Thus, adversaries must not only hijack the control flow or manipulate the data flow but also launch *confused deputy attacks* [22] to circumvent least privilege. In particular, attackers must launch confused deputy attacks to confuse the trusted module through the exposed API, such that their hijacked unprivileged context can be escalated to a higher privilege context which is suitable to perform malicious actions.

Although the principle of least privilege raises the security bar significantly, it is challenging to enforce on legacy applications that

---

[1]The setuid family includes system calls that set user ID (UID) and group ID (GID) in Unix-like operating systems, such as setuid, seteuid, setgid, and setegid. We also use *setuid calls* to refer to these system calls herein.

```
sudo
static char * sudo_askpass(...) {
...
if ((pid = fork()) == -1) ...
if (pid == 0) {
    {(void) setuid(ROOT_UID);}
    if (setgid(user_details.gid)) { ...
    if (setuid(user_details.uid)) { ...
    ... execl(askpass, askpass, ...);
    _exit(255);
}
zero_bytes(&sa, sizeo...
sigemptyset(&sa.sa_...
sa.sa_flags = SA_INTE...
sa.sa_handler = SIG_IGN;
(void) sigaction(SIGPIPE, &sa, ...);
```
Privilege sensitive code

Child Process			Parent Process		
Process Hierarchy Context: 1			Process Hierarchy Context: 0		
Privilege Operation	Data Context	Call Context	Privilege Operation	Data Context	Call Context
setuid	0	C1	∅	∅	∅
setgid	1000	C2	∅	∅	∅
setuid	1000	C3	∅	∅	∅
∅	∅	∅	∅	∅	∅
∅	∅	∅	∅	∅	∅
∅	∅	∅	∅	∅	∅
∅	∅	∅	∅	∅	∅
∅	∅	∅	∅	∅	∅
∅	∅	∅	∅	∅	∅

```
sshd
pid_t subprocess(...) {
...
switch ((pid = fork())) {
case 0:
    ...
    if (setresgid(pw->pw_gid,...)) { ...
    if (setresuid(pw->pw_uid,...)) { ...
    ... execve(av[0], av, child_env);
    _exit(127);
}
default:
break;
}
close(p[1]);
```
Privilege sensitive code

Child Process		Parent Process	
Process Hierarchy Context: 1		Process Hierarchy Context: 0	
Privilege Operation	Data Context	Privilege Operation	Data Context
setresgid	1000,1000,1000	∅	∅
setresuid	1000,1000,1000	∅	∅
∅	∅	∅	∅
∅	∅	∅	∅
∅	∅	∅	∅
∅	∅	∅	∅
∅	∅	∅	∅
∅	∅	∅	∅

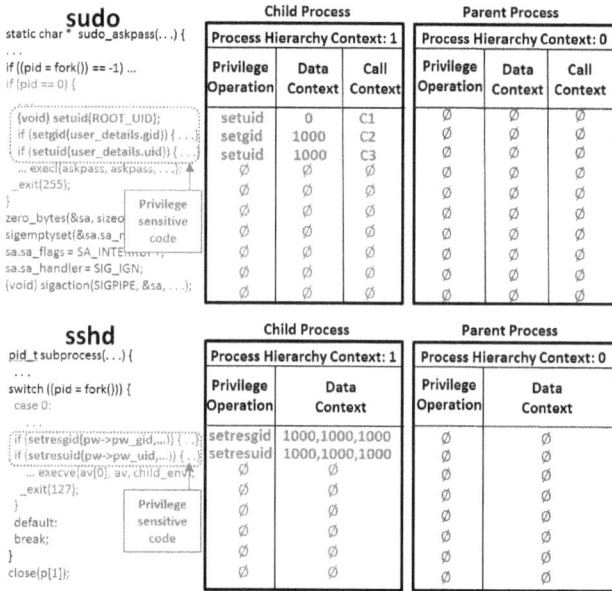

Figure 1: Automatically extracted multiple process contexts of setuid calls in sudo and sshd. PoLPer prevents any unnecessary setuid calls for the parent process while they are allowed for a child process. PoLPer enforces only required setuid calls based on *process context*.

are already deployed widely. Many legacy applications are monolithic and do not follow a modular design. Moreover, many existing techniques (including compartmentalization and seccomp) require re-design of software to adopt them, hindering their wide adoption by legacy software in practice. As a result, *legacy applications allow large parts of the program to run over-privileged (the superset of all required privileges)* instead of separating it into compartments/communicating modules with different sets of privileges.

In particular, such modules often run in separate processes but their least privileges are not properly enforced. For instance, Figure 1 shows monolithic code examples of setuid system calls for more than one process. In this example, it is assumed that a child process is temporarily privileged and then de-privileged using setuid syscalls while a parent process runs without privilege changes (which is usually the case in multi-process based service daemons such as Apache and Nginx web servers). This privilege switch for a child process is enabled by privilege sensitive code, which is shown in red color in Figure 1. However, since privilege sensitive code is shared by the parent and its child process, the same code can be exploited by the parent process. More specifically, if the attacker can manipulate the control flow of the parent process, such privilege sensitive code can be abused to launch privilege escalation attacks [7, 46]. Hence, many legacy programs using setuid calls have been an active target by many shell code [16], ROP attacks [34, 47], and non-control data attacks [24, 27].

In this paper, we propose PoLPer [2] to defend against adversaries exploiting such *an over-privilege*. Based on our study (Table 2 in Section 5.2) many popular programs use setuid system calls with

---

[2] PoLPer represents **P**rinciple **o**f **L**east **P**rivilege Enforce**r**.

distinct patterns in parent or child processes. Therefore, a policy control in the program level causes over-provision of privileges in run-time states. This problem is currently not addressed by existing work to the best of our knowledge, and it poses a high risk for privilege exploitation. PoLPer provides a novel mechanism to recognize and apply this *process-aware policy to restrict current over-privileges of legacy software without any change in code with negligible run-time overhead.*

Specifically, our approach systematically extracts and enforces only required setuid calls following the least privilege principle. In particular, it analyzes multiple comprehensive contexts of required setuid calls regarding the type of a process, data values, and call stack contexts. This is achieved by static program analysis and training of the run-time contexts of setuid calls for each process. The context details are as follows: **Process Hierarchy Context:** In Figure 1, given identical code, different portions of code are executed at run-time depending on the process' role inside a program. The setuid calls marked in red are made by a child process while the parent process marked in blue does not run this code, shown as empty sets in the parent process table. Therefore, the setuid calls invoked by the red code should be restricted to the child process only. This can only be done by recognizing processes' hierarchical contexts (i.e., whether it is a parent or a child process). Our work proposes a new technique to observe this context for multiple run-time context checks. **Process Data and Call Contexts:** Once the process context is recognized, our approach hardens the execution of setuid system calls by learning and enforcing only necessary contexts in data parameters and call stack, which are indexed by a process hierarchy meaning that the profiles of contexts are individualized per process.

Contributions: We present PoLPer with the following contributions:

- **Dividing setuid execution profiles of a program with process hierarchy context:** Multiple processes and threads share the same code for execution. However, processes may have different requirements of setuid calls depending on their logic. It is crucial to divide program's execution contexts of a whole program level into a finer-grained process level to prevent over-privilege of setuid calls. We solve this problem by learning and run-time monitoring with a process hierarchy context.

- **Automated extraction of process-aware setuid contexts:** We present an automated approach to extract process-aware contexts of setuid calls from a program using static analysis and dynamic training. Data context and call contexts of setuid calls are indexed with a process hierarchy context to individualize each process behavior.

- **Efficient and practical hardening of setuid calls using restriction on process context:** We propose a practical approach to harden data context and call context of setuid calls individualized per process. It tightens previously over-provisioned privileges due to the failure of distinction on processes and effectively prevents security exploits and bugs with minimal overhead. In the benchmarks of multiple commonly used client and server software, the performance overhead of our system is under 0.54%.

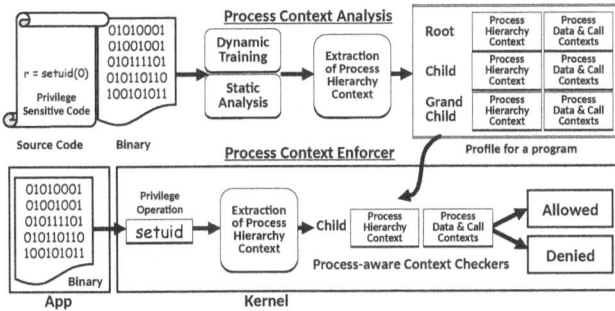

Figure 2: Architecture of PoLPer.

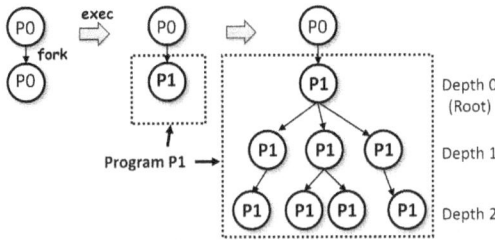

Figure 3: Example of process hierarchy context.

2 THREAT MODEL

We assume a strong adversary who can compromise any program in user space, including privileged programs with setuid calls, using a non-administrative user account. For example, the adversary has a login to a user account using a stolen password and hijacks the control flow of a privileged program by exploiting software vulnerabilities. The adversary can also manipulate the privileged program's code and data in either disk or process memory.

However, based on the wide availability of code injection prevention [37, 53] and file-based [31] integrity checkers, naïve manipulation in file or code injection would be easily detectable. Thus we assume that the binary file and code integrity of the privileged program, user-level libraries, system libraries, the operating system, and PoLPer can be verified. The operating system and the run-time enforcer of PoLPer inside the kernel space are part of the trusted computing base, and thus cannot be altered by the adversary.

In our usage model, a user is either a software developer who can provide a default policy for the program or a system administrator who can customize the policy based on an environmental context on the deployed system. This model is reasonable as seen in major security tools like AppArmor or SELinux that take a similar approach to deploy policies for various software. Therefore, we assume that PoLPer has access to the program binary (source code is optional) along with its workload regarding setuid calls in normal usages before its deployment and any adversarial attempt. Also if its source code is optionally available, PoLPer further improves the precision of policies. Because an administrator handles the program before its installation, this prior access is reasonable. This paper focuses on software written in C/C++ and compiled to native binary code.

3 DESIGN OF POLPER

3.1 Architecture

In this section, we present the architecture of PoLPer. Our goal is to enforce only required privileges for the setuid calls of application code, which are essentially the setuid calls identified in the program code and specified by developers. There are multiple aspects in how this family of system calls is used. First, there can be more than one process involved in program execution. In many server programs, the executed part of code and corresponding roles of processes are different even though they share the exact same code image. Differentiating such roles is *essential* to achieve least privileges (i.e., we prohibit a setuid call and a potential exploitation to a worker process which does not require a setuid call). We achieve this aspect with our novel *process hierarchy context*. Second, setuid family calls have different behaviors and risks depending on the input parameters (e.g., a nobody account vs. the root account) and process. Therefore, the values of parameters passed to privilege operations must be carefully inspected and restricted based on the required values profiled for each process. We extract this aspect, called *process data context*, from the program code with static analysis and dynamic training. Lastly. setuid calls should be inspected in a fine-grained way regarding which privilege sensitive code can invoke them in what specific call contexts in each process. Therefore, we learn and enforce the detailed call stack patterns of setuid system calls given each process and this aspect is called *process call context*.

Figure 2 presents the architecture of PoLPer regarding how it learns and enforces data and call contexts *indexed by* each process' context. In the first process context analysis stage, given a program, its code and run-time execution is analyzed using static analysis and dynamic training to extract the process contexts of setuid calls. In the second stage, the process context enforcement, the extracted contexts are loaded into the OS kernel. Whenever the program calls any setuid system calls, its process hierarchy, data, and call contexts are cross-checked if the call complies with the extracted contexts. Any violating call is detected and prevented as a misuse of seuid system calls.

In this paper, we focus on setuid family calls as one instance of privilege operations because of their prevalence in major legacy software and corresponding attacks. We note that our system can be easily extended to apply our techniques to other operations such as capabilities as future work.

3.2 Extraction of Process Hierarchy Context

Process Behavior Role: Programs that leverage multiple processes and/or threads often leverage different units of execution to decompose functionalities. Each class of processes/threads executes a specific behavior, restricted to a subset of the code although the entire code image is shared across all processes and threads. For example, popular server programs such as sshd and apache use child processes as workers while the parent process manages a pool of workers and distributes the workload. To describe such different characteristics of a set of processes/threads inside the same program, we use the term *process behavior role*.

Such different behavior roles imply that the capability to run setuid calls are over-provisioned due to the inability to apply individualized policies for processes. Unrestricted capabilities to run `setuid` calls pose the risk that such code can be exploited through a vulnerability.

Inferring Process Behavior Role with a Process Hierarchy Context: We infer a process' behavior role using the hierarchical position of it relative to other processes. As process creation system calls (e.g., `fork/clone`) are invoked, the processes and threads inside a program form parent and child relationships, resulting in a process tree where the root is the first process of the program (Figure 3). We use the hierarchical distance between the process and the root process in the tree to infer its behavior role. We call this distance the process hierarchy context.

Our key intuition is that a process usually exhibits a different role depending on where it is located within a process hierarchy tree. Thus, we differentiate the process' behavior role using the relative distance from the root (i.e., depth), which becomes our metric to systematically infer and capture a process behavior role.

In Figure 3 the root of a program is the oldest parent process whose parent's program image is different from its program image. This may not be determined at the program creation time because, in many OSes (e.g., Unix variants like Linux), the first process of a program is a child clone of a program invoker. Later, its program image is replaced using another system call such as exec. Thus our algorithm determines this distance or depth at a program image replacement call (e.g., exec) and caches its result for run-time usage. The depth increases when a process forks/clones a child process/thread.

PoLPer uses process states in an operating system kernel. A process node represents a process state (e.g., a `task_struct` in Linux). When a `setuid` call is invoked, PoLPer determines the current process node (i.e., the current process in OS). Given a process node, our algorithm follows the reference for its parent until it reaches the root process of the program, whose parent has a different program image and has the depth 0. Then its depth is calculated as the distance of a traversal to the root process. If there is more than one role in the same depth, this scheme determines them as one combined role.

Given our evaluation, we found that this scheme is effective to distinguish a process behavior role at minimal run-time cost. However, in complex software, it is possible in some rare cases that multiple processes with the same depth can play different roles. Our current policy over-approximates this situation as combined process behavior. PoLPer can improve the precision by using additional program contexts, such as the call stacks of the origin process during fork and the child.

3.3 Extraction of Process Data Context

`setuid` system calls use parameters to represent various information involved to change a privilege in each process context. Given the logic and the context where a program makes a transition of privilege from one to another, the parameters will have corresponding particular values.

The patterns of parameters are learned with the process hierarchy context to differentiate unique parameter behavior of each process role. We use a hybrid approach combining dynamic and static analyses for the advantages of both approaches.

Learning Process Data Context using Dynamic Training: Our dynamic and static analyses have different contributions to capturing data context. The dynamic analysis captures crucial information including process hierarchy context and concrete values from outside of a program such as the values from files, network, or OS. The static analysis can further contribute to the patterns by discovering possible data flows systematically.

The same environment and input for `setuid` system calls are used for dynamic and static analyses. Our dynamic analysis starts with the program binary under the account assumed in the execution environment. When one of `setuid` family system call is invoked, it traps to our analysis module. Our module records concrete parameter values along with the process hierarchy context and call context at the `setuid` call.

Enhancing Data Context using Static Analysis: If source code is available, static analysis systematically discovers over-approximated potential data contexts. Combined with dynamic results, it further improves learning which will be presented in Section 5.2. Our analysis discovers data contexts with the following details. After the analysis, the result is associated with the profile from dynamic training.

- **Constant Values:** We found many instances of constant values in the `setuid` calls of evaluated programs where the parameter values are exactly determined in the code. For instance, some code always invokes a `setuid` call to set the `root` privilege. Then our analyses find the constant value corresponding to the root. These invariant cases are effective for tightly restricting the parameter.

- **Symbolic Values:** We also found that some parameters can be determined systematically by certain API calls. For instance, getuid system API obtains the current user ID from OS. A frequent use case invokes this API first, followed by a `setuid` call based on the returned value. Essentially there is a strict data flow from the source using a symbolic value, *the current user ID*, to the `setuid` call. Thus when this program is running under a certain account, we can have a specific value for the parameter given the context of the account. We first determine this case from static analysis, and then it is checked by accessing the user ID in the OS state (e.g., `task_struct`).

- **External Values:** There are other cases where these parameters are derived from various other constants or variables, an input, or OS. We use dynamic training to determine concrete values given in our execution environment. Technically it would be feasible to determine the source of such variables using advanced program analysis techniques (e.g., system level information tracking) as a future improvement.

We use the UniSan framework [36] as our basis of context-sensitive data flow analysis and extended various functionalities such as the coverage of global scope. The following steps show a high-level description on how our Algorithm 1 works.

- *Line 1:* The input for this analysis is a set of setuid system calls and program code. We select 8 `setuid` system calls in Linux in this work.

- *Line 2-5:* Static analysis first determines the list of call sites for a setuid call p, which is one of the supported set of setuid system calls shown as P. For each call site s of p, data flow analysis is performed.

Algorithm 1 Static data context extraction.

```
C : Code
P : Set of setuid family system calls
F : Profile of data context
 1: function EXTRACTDC(C, P)
 2:    for p ∈ P do
 3:        S = Find all call sites of p in C
 4:        for s ∈ S do
 5:            F[p, s] = OnSetUIDCall(p, s)
 6:        end for
 7:    end for
 8: end function
 9: function ONSETUIDCALL(p, s)
10:    res = []
11:    R = Get a parameter list in the invoca-
       tion
12:    for r in R do
13:        if r is a constant then
14:            res[r] = (Static, val(r))
15:        end if
16:        if r is a return from a function F
       then
17:            res[r] = (Dynamic, return(F))
18:        else
19:            V is all variables and constants

20:            success, matches    =
           FindReachableDataFlow(V, r)
21:            if success == True then
22:                out = []
23:                for m ∈ matches do
24:                    [type, val or F] = m
25:                    switch type do
26:                        case Const
27:                            out  =  out  ∪
                      (Static, val)
28:                            break
29:                        case Function
30:                            out  =  out  ∪
                      (Dynamic, return(F))
31:                            break
32:                end for
33:                res[r] = out
34:            else
35:                res[r] = (Dynamic, Null)
36:            end if
37:        end if
38:    end forreturn res
39: end function
```

- *Line 9-11:* For each privilege sensitive code *s* calling a setuid function *p*, a list of its parameters in the invocation is obtained.
- *Line 13-15:* If a parameter is a constant value, the analysis stops and records the value.
- *Line 16-17:* If a parameter is a return value from a function F (e.g., getuid()), this case is handled as a symbolic variable.
- *Line 18-20:* If a parameter *r* is a variable, an inter-procedural data flow analysis is performed to find the source of the value. To find the sources, it first obtains a set of all variables and constants, denoted as *V*. And then, it checks whether any item *v* reaches *r*.
- *Line 21-33:* When one or more constant or variable is used for the parameter *r*, possible values are stored in the profile. If the source that *r*'s value is from is a constant (Line 26-28), the corresponding value is stored. If it is returned from a function, its value is determined in dynamic training (Line 29-31).
- *Line 34-35:* If no variable or constant can reach a parameter *r*, it could be due to limitation of static analysis. Then its concrete value is determined in dynamic training.

3.4 Extraction of Process Call Context

A call stack at a setuid system call can identify a specific code location and call context how the setuid call is made. By being recorded together with the process hierarchy context this information can represent specific patterns of setuid calls in each process role.

We leverage dynamic analysis for high accuracy call context (i.e., call stack). Static analysis may be able to determine the call context as well. However, if the call stack involves dynamically linked library code, which may have internal function calls within the library, dynamic analysis provides higher accuracy.

3.5 Run-time Enforcement of Process Contexts

This section presents how to detect execution anomalies based on the process contexts of setuid family system calls.

When a program executes, any invocation of a setuid call is captured by the system call interposition layer. The process hierarchy context and process contexts are collected and compared with the profile that was previously extracted from the program to determine whether they are part of known behavior.

Any unknown behavior is denied returning a failure code and logging of this violation incident (to be exported to a system administrator). Upon a denied attempt, this detailed log showing program internal states will help the developer and an administrator to understand how (process hierarchy context, call context) and with what parameters (data context) this application was about to be exploited but protected.

4 IMPLEMENTATION

In this section, we present the technical details in the implementation of PoLPer. There are two major components: process context analyzer and enforcer.

Process Context Analyzer: Our static data flow analysis is implemented by extending UniSan [36], which is based on the LLVM framework [35]. UniSan is designed for eliminating information leak vulnerabilities in OS kernels caused by uninitialized data reads. We use its functionalities to track data flow for identifying the data context in this paper. Our major extensions are three-fold: (1) checking reachability from an object allocation site to privilege operation calls, (2) collecting possible store values (e.g., foo = getuid();) during tracking data flow, and (3) tracking global objects (UniSan only track heap and stack objects) since the parameters may have values derived from global objects. Dynamic training is performed by using process context enforcer to be explained next with a permissive learning mode which records process contexts on setuid system calls.

Process Context Enforcer: This component residing in the OS kernel intercepts an invocation of a setuid family system call and inspects the run-time states. We implemented this component using Kprobes [29], a kernel-based probing mechanism which can dynamically hook any kernel routine. Note that Kprobes avoids any instrumentation or modification inside software binary or in the user space. Thus it provides a near-native speed of execution of the program code without intrusively instrumenting the application.

PoLPer inserts Kprobes hooks on the entry points of setuid family system calls. When any setuid system call is invoked, PoLPer takes a control through Kprobes and extracts process hierarchy, data, and call contexts. When this module is used for dynamic analysis in a learning mode, the extracted contexts are temporarily stored in kernel heap, then it is stored in a file as a profile for the program. When it is used for the enforcement, the extracted run-time contexts are verified whether they comply with the profile.

When PoLPer inspects the process hierarchy, data parameters, and the call stack on setuid calls, we applied multiple optimization code to keep the run-time overhead minimal.

5 EVALUATION

In this section, we evaluate PoLPer in multiple aspects: (1) detection of real-world exploits, (2) multi-context extraction, (3) performance evaluation, and (4) case studies.

Experimental Setting: All evaluations were performed on Ubuntu Linux 14.04.5 LTS with a quad-core 3.40GHz CPU (Intel i7-6700), 1TB HDD, and 16GB RAM. Note that we chose the old OS version to evaluate real exploit case studies in situ. Our design and implementation have no restriction to support other Linux operating system distributions.

Evaluation Target Programs: We have tested PoLPer with the following real-world desktop and server programs: Ping, Sudo, AccountsService, Upstart, Telnet, Shadow, SSH, Wireshark, Apache, and Nginx. These are common selected applications which use setuid system calls with a varying size and complexity from small utility programs (e.g., Ping) to larger server programs like Apache. As described in our threat model, this work focuses on the software written in C/C++, and compiled to a native binary.

5.1 Detection of Real-world Security Exploits

We evaluate the effectiveness of PoLPer using real-world exploits as illustrated in Table 1. The first column shows exploit patterns. The following columns present the details of attack exploits regarding the name of the software that is being attacked, the exploit name, and the privilege operations exploited. A comparison between PoLPer and other approaches follows. CFI (control flow integrity), NCI (non-control data integrity), DFI (data flow integrity) respectively refer to the approaches that detect control flow manipulation [3], non-control data manipulation [12], and the manipulation of both [10][3]. Note although DEP [37, 53] has been widely deployed to prevent stack smashing attacks, it has not been successful due to the ROP attacks which can easily disable DEP and transfer control to the shell code using mprotect in Linux and VirtualProtect in Windows [1, 2].

PoLPer uses Process Data Contexts (P-DC) and Process Call Contexts (P-CC) determined using process hierarchy contexts at run-time to detect each exploit. For all cases, PoLPer detects them by using process contexts, while only one of CFI or NCI is able to detect each attack. Data flow integrity (DFI) approach can detect both of control data and non-control data manipulation but with a significant overhead [10]. PoLPer can detect these exploits with negligible overhead (see Section 5.3). In all cases, the contexts of privilege sensitive operations are extracted and enforced while identifying the process hierarchy context at run-time. PoLPer can complement DEP, CFI, NCI when they fail depending on the exploit type and it offers efficient prevention comparable to DFI with much low overhead to be presented.

The top two cases use data-oriented programming to manipulate data without changing the control flow of a program where control flow integrity (CFI) cannot detect them. The following cases involve a change in its call stack where a setuid system call is called. CFI, DFI, and PoLPer (P-CC) are able to detect the attacks while NCI could not detect them.

Ground Truth Validation: As a ground truth validation, we manually examined the source code to locate relevant setuid family calls of 1~25 function call instances in only 10 minutes~1 hour due to a small well-defined scope of privilege functions. In our environment set up and the workload given, we did not face false positives or false negatives, and manual code examination also found our analyses properly cover the code relevant to our experiments.

---

[3]Regarding [10], this approach can detect both control data (e.g., function pointers and return addresses) manipulation and non-control data manipulation.

5.2 Extraction of Process Contexts

Next, we evaluate the details of PoLPer regarding the extraction of multiple contexts.

Extraction of Process Hierarchy Context: Table 2 presents the process hierarchy context extracted from dynamic training. We cover 8 setuid family system calls in Linux shown in column headers for the programs shown in the row headers. seteuid and setegid columns are omitted since they are replaced with setresuid and setresgid calls. Column D_0, D_1, D_2 respectively show the process hierarchy information of depth 0, 1, and 2 (i.e., the root, a child of the root, a grandchild of the root). Inside each column, there are two sub-columns, P and I. P shows the number of process instances and I shows the average number of setuid call invocation per a process.

This table illustrates *process-aware* privilege operations under various process depths (depth 0~2). This new context of process hierarchy enables more concise and stricter contexts for each individual depth by avoiding the merge of the contexts for all depths. At run-time each process is restricted only using the contexts of its depth.

Reduction of Rules: Each context of a process is described as an enforcement policy rule. Process hierarchy context enables the reduction of run-time complexity by checking only the rules associated to each process depth. Table 3 shows this runtime cost reduction. The reduction ratio of enforcement rules (shown as Rule cut) is calculated as $\frac{\text{Process aware rules}}{\text{Non-process aware rules}} = \frac{\sum_{n=1}^{N} |D_i| n_i}{N |\cup_{i=1}^{N} D_i|}$ where D_i is a set of distinct rules for a depth i, n_i is a number of processes for a depth i, and N is the sum of n_i. In general the programs with multiple processes have high percentage of rule reduction. Overall there is *48.92% reduction of the rules on average*.

Extraction of Static Data Context: Table 4 shows data contexts systematically extracted from source code. For each setuid system call, our static analysis determines where the parameters come from. The sources of parameters are shown as four notations. If the parameter comes from a function call (e.g., setuid(getuid())), it is shown as F. The parameter coming from a constant (e.g., setuid(0)) is counted as C. When the parameter is determined from a data flow analysis which eventually derives it from a constant or a function, it is shown as V (e.g., int uid = 0; setuid(uid)). If the static analysis cannot determine the source of a parameter, it is indicated as N. Since several programs have complex code/data structures and initialize values using the values from a file (e.g., /etc/passwd), this N case is supported by dynamic data context analysis. Note this is an implementation issue of static analysis which can be improved by advancing the scalability of data flow analysis or with advanced system-wide analyses.

Extraction of Dynamic Process Data and Call Context: The run-time data context and call context in our dynamic analysis are shown in Table 5. Column C represents the diversity of call contexts for each privilege operation and Column D shows the average number of distinct parameters per each context. For instance, if C is 1, there is only one particular way to call a privilege operation inside the program. If only one value is used for its parameter, D would be 1. For the same reason as Table 2, setuid and setegid columns are omitted due to their replacement by other operations.

Exploit Pattern	Vul. Program	Exploit Name (EDB)	Setuid Syscall Exploited	Detected				
				PoLPer		CFI	NCI	DFI
				P-DC	P-CC			
Modify Setuid Parameters	Sudo	(N/A)	setuid	✓	✗	✗	✓	✓
	Wu_ftpd	(N/A)	seteuid	✓	✗	✗	✓	✓
Run privilege operation (e.g., setuid(0)) before running a shell	Overlayfs	37292-2015	setresuid, setresgid	✗	✓	✓	✗	✓
	Overlayfs	39230-2016	setresuid	✗	✓	✓	✗	✓
	Glibc	209-2000	setuid, setgid	✗	✓	✓	✗	✓
	Mkdir	20554-2001	setuid, setgid	✗	✓	✓	✗	✓
	KApplication	19981-2000	setuid, setregid	✗	✓	✓	✗	✓
	Suid_dumpable	2006-2006	setuid, setgid	✗	✓	✓	✗	✓
	Execve/ptrace	20720-2001	setuid	✗	✓	✓	✗	✓
	Splitvt	20013-2000	setuid	✗	✓	✓	✗	✓
	Openmovieeditor	2338-2006	setuid, setgid	✗	✓	✓	✗	✓
	Traceroute	178-2000	setuid, setgid	✗	✓	✓	✗	✓
	VMWare	19371-1999	setuid	✗	✓	✓	✗	✓
	Su	(N/A)	setuid	✗	✓	✓	✗	✓

Table 1: Evaluation of security exploit analysis. This table presents the effectiveness of PoLPer for real-world exploits. P-DC and P-CC respectively represent data contexts and call contexts by process hierarchy context.

	Setuid						Setreuid						Setresuid						Setgid						Setregid						Setresgid					
	D_0		D_1		D_2		D_0		D_1		D_2		D_0		D_1		D_2		D_0		D_1		D_2		D_0		D_1		D_2		D_0		D_1		D_2	
	P	I	P	I	P	I	P	I	P	I	P	I	P	I	P	I	P	I	P	I	P	I	P	I	P	I	P	I	P	I	P	I	P	I	P	I
Ping	1	1	-	-	-	-	-	-	-	-	-	-	-	-	-	-	-	-	-	-	-	-	-	-	-	-	-	-	-	-	-	-	-	-	-	-
Sudo	2	1	1	1	-	-	-	-	-	-	-	-	5	10	2	1	-	-	-	-	3	1	-	-	-	-	-	-	-	-	5	9	-	-	-	-
Xterm	11	1	7	1	-	-	-	-	-	-	-	-	-	-	-	-	-	-	-	-	7	1	-	-	-	-	-	-	-	-	7	1	-	-	-	-
Cron	-	-	-	-	1	1	-	-	-	-	-	-	-	-	-	-	-	-	-	-	-	-	1	1	-	-	-	-	-	-	-	-	-	-	-	-
Telinit	2	1	-	-	-	-	-	-	-	-	-	-	-	-	-	-	-	-	-	-	-	-	-	-	-	-	-	-	-	-	-	-	-	-	-	-
Telnet-Login	1	1	1	1	-	-	-	-	-	-	-	-	-	-	-	-	-	-	-	-	1	1	-	-	-	-	-	-	-	-	-	-	-	-	-	-
Login	-	-	1	1	-	-	-	-	-	-	-	-	-	-	-	-	-	-	1	1	-	-	-	-	-	-	-	-	-	-	-	-	-	-	-	-
SSH & SCP	-	-	-	-	5	1	-	-	2	3	-	-	-	-	2	3	5	2	-	-	-	-	5	1	-	-	2	5	-	-	-	-	2	6	5	2
WireShark	-	-	-	-	-	-	-	-	-	-	-	-	1	1	-	-	-	-	-	-	-	-	-	-	-	-	-	-	-	-	1	1	-	-	-	-
Apache	-	-	1	1	-	-	-	-	-	-	-	-	-	-	-	-	-	-	-	-	1	1	-	-	-	-	-	-	-	-	-	-	-	-	-	-
Nginx	-	-	1	1	-	-	-	-	-	-	-	-	-	-	-	-	-	-	-	-	1	1	-	-	-	-	-	-	-	-	-	-	-	-	-	-

Table 2: Extracted process hierarchy context. This table presents setuid syscalls and the process hierarchy (column head) for each application (row head). P is a number of process instances and I is an average number of setuid calls per process called. D_0 is the root, D_n is a nth child of D_0. It illustrates PoLPer's novel capability to learn and detect *process-aware* contexts.

Programs	Non-process aware rules	Process aware rules	Rule Cut (%)
Ping	1	1	0
Sudo	352	196	44
Xterm	576	296	49
Cron	2	2	0
Telinit	4	4	0
Telnet-Login	6	3	50
Login	4	2	50
SSH & SCP	182	88	52
WireShark	2	2	0
Apache	2	2	0
Nginx	2	2	0

Table 3: Reduction of rules due to process-aware restriction using process hierarchy contexts.

Ground Truth Validation: We performed a ground truth validation using manual analysis of the source and confirmed that the process hierarchy, call, and data contexts from our static and dynamic analyses correspond to the application behavior in our test bed's configurations and workloads.

5.3 Performance Impact

We evaluated the performance impact of PoLPer in two aspects: the run-time overhead caused by the inspection of an individual setuid call, and end-to-end performance of applications.

Micro-benchmark: This benchmark measures the cost of the inspection of a setuid family system call which includes (1) an interposition of a system call, (2) getting its process hierarchy depth, its parameter(s), and call stack information, and (3) retrieving and comparing the run-time values with the PoLPer's profile.

Note that all data types used by setuid family system calls have well-defined sizes (e.g., integers) and do not use complex data types such as strings, arrays, or pointers. Therefore, data contexts are efficiently checked without any uncertainty of overhead.

Figure 4 depicts the overhead of PoLPer's inspection of a setuid system call. This graph shows the run-time overhead of a setuid call verification with a varying size of call contexts and data contexts. The X-axis represents the number of call context and the Y-axis indicates verification time in microseconds. The complexity of inspection due to different data context size is shown by different graphs. As the size of data context (e.g., parameters) increases from 1 to 10 (shown as d1 to d10), inspection time of a system call increases. Also, a higher number of call contexts causes higher overhead.

Program	Setuid				Seteuid				Setreuid				Setresuid				Setgid				Setegid				Setregid				Setresgid			
	F	V	C	N	F	V	C	N	F	V	C	N	F	V	C	N	F	V	C	N	F	V	C	N	F	V	C	N	F	V	C	N
Ping	1	-	-	-	-	-	-	-	-	-	-	-	-	-	-	-	-	-	-	-	-	-	-	-	-	-	-	-	-	-	-	-
Sudo	-	-	3	1	-	-	3	3	-	-	-	1	-	-	-	-	-	-	-	2	-	-	-	2	-	-	-	-	-	-	-	-
Xterm	-	1	-	4	2	-	1	-	-	-	-	-	-	-	-	-	-	1	-	3	-	2	-	-	-	-	-	-	-	-	-	-
Cron	1	1	-	1	2	-	1	1	1	-	-	-	-	-	-	-	-	-	-	1	-	-	-	-	-	-	-	-	-	-	-	-
Telinit	3	-	-	-	-	-	-	-	-	-	-	-	-	-	-	-	-	-	-	-	-	-	-	-	-	-	-	-	-	-	-	-
Telnet-Login	-	-	1	-	-	-	-	-	-	-	-	-	-	-	-	-	-	-	-	1	-	-	-	-	-	-	-	-	-	-	-	-
Login	1	-	4	-	-	-	-	-	-	-	-	-	-	-	1	-	1	-	-	-	-	-	-	-	-	-	-	-	-	-	-	1
SSH & SCP	2	-	-	-	2	5	1	3	-	-	-	1	-	-	-	3	2	-	-	2	3	-	-	-	-	-	-	-	1	-	-	2
WireShark	-	-	-	-	-	-	-	-	-	-	-	-	-	1	-	-	-	-	-	-	-	-	-	-	-	-	-	-	-	1	-	-
Apache	-	-	-	4	-	-	-	-	-	-	-	-	-	-	-	-	-	-	-	3	-	-	-	-	-	-	-	-	-	-	-	-
Nginx	-	-	-	1	-	-	-	-	-	-	-	-	-	-	-	-	-	-	-	1	-	-	-	-	-	-	-	-	-	-	-	-

Table 4: Extracted static data context. This table presents the number of parameters extracted using source code analysis. Sources of parameters: function calls (*F*), constants (*C*), variables (*V*), and others (*N*).

Program	Setuid						Setreuid						Setresuid						Setgid						Setregid						Setresgid					
	D_0		D_1		D_2		D_0		D_1		D_2		D_0		D_1		D_2		D_0		D_1		D_2		D_0		D_1		D_2		D_0		D_1		D_2	
	C	D	C	D	C	D	C	D	C	D	C	D	C	D	C	D	C	D	C	D	C	D	C	D	C	D	C	D	C	D	C	D	C	D	C	D
Ping	1	1	-	-	-	-	-	-	-	-	-	-	-	-	-	-	-	-	-	-	-	-	-	-	-	-	-	-	-	-	-	-	-	-	-	-
Sudo	2	1	1	2	-	-	-	-	-	-	-	-	9	1	2	2	-	-	-	-	3	2	-	-	-	-	-	-	-	-	7	3	-	-	-	-
Xterm	11	1	7	1	-	-	-	-	-	-	-	-	-	-	-	-	-	-	-	-	7	1	-	-	-	-	-	-	-	-	7	1	-	-	-	-
Cron	-	-	-	-	1	1	-	-	-	-	-	-	-	-	-	-	-	-	-	-	1	1	-	-	-	-	-	-	-	-	-	-	-	-	-	-
Telinit	2	1	-	-	-	-	-	-	-	-	-	-	-	-	-	-	-	-	-	-	-	-	-	-	-	-	-	-	-	-	-	-	-	-	-	-
Telnet-Login	1	1	1	1	-	-	-	-	-	-	-	-	-	-	-	-	-	-	1	1	1	1	-	-	-	-	-	-	-	-	-	-	-	-	-	-
Login	-	-	1	1	-	-	-	-	-	-	-	-	-	-	-	-	-	-	1	1	1	1	-	-	-	-	-	-	-	-	-	-	-	-	-	-
SSH & SCP	-	-	-	-	3	1	-	-	2	2	-	-	-	-	2	2	3	1	-	-	-	-	3	1	-	-	2	2	-	-	-	-	2	1	3	1
WireShark	-	-	-	-	-	-	-	-	-	-	-	-	1	1	-	-	-	-	-	-	-	-	-	-	-	-	-	-	-	-	1	1	-	-	-	-
Apache	-	-	1	1	-	-	-	-	-	-	-	-	-	-	-	-	-	-	1	1	-	-	-	-	-	-	-	-	-	-	-	-	-	-	-	-
Nginx	-	-	1	1	-	-	-	-	-	-	-	-	-	-	-	-	-	-	1	1	-	-	-	-	-	-	-	-	-	-	-	-	-	-	-	-

Table 5: Dynamic process data and call contexts indexed by process hierarchy context. Process hierarchy depth (D_x), a number of call contexts (*C*), and an average number of parameters (*D*) for each depth (e.g., D_0: root, D_1: a child, D_2: a grand child).

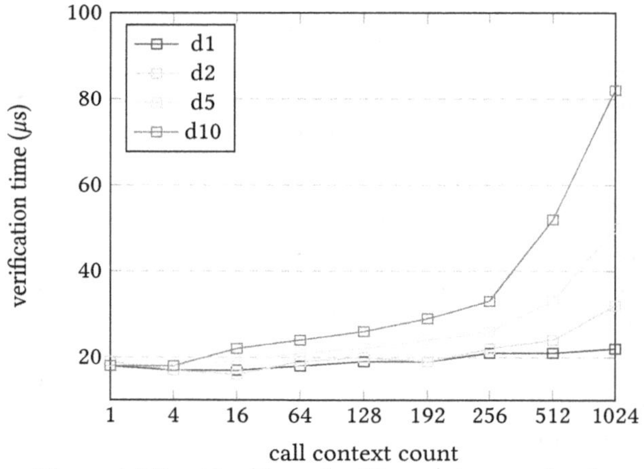

Figure 4: Micro-benchmark of inspection overhead.
(Plot of verification time (μs) versus call context count (1, 4, 16, 64, 128, 192, 256, 512, 1024); legend: d1, d2, d5, d10.)

Program	Base (s)	PoLPer (s)	$|I|$	Overhead (%)
Ping (s20121221)	9.0019	9.0039	1	0.02
Nginx (1.4.6)	11.522	11.539	0	0.14
Apache (2.4.7)	18.250	18.286	0	0.1
Telnet (0.17-36)	1.001	1.004	5	0.29
SCP (6.6.1p1)	0.1656	0.1665	28	0.54

Table 6: End-to-end benchmarks.

If there is one call context with one data context for a setuid call, its verification takes 18 μs. As the number of call and the size of data context are increased, the overhead increases as well. These cases are simulations of extreme situations with a lot of call contexts and data contexts for setuid system calls showing how PoLPer will work in challenging cases. Real-world programs typically have only a small number of call contexts and data contexts as described in Section 5.2. Therefore, real-world overhead is typically insignificant as presented next.

End-to-end benchmarks: We performed another set of experiments to measure the overhead of PoLPer in the end-to-end performance of application software. A list of benchmarked software was selected based on the popularity of server and client software which have privilege sensitive code invoking setuid system calls. The selection includes from small utility programs such as ping to large server programs (e.g., Nginx and Apache). Based on our study of these desktop and server software, the overhead is typically not strongly dependent on the workload because generally the setuid calls are not used per each workload but per an initialization of software. Table 6 shows the data. The column $|I|$ shows the number of setuid calls.

Overall the performance impact of setuid inspection is very marginal. First, we tested ping where each try sends 10 packets repeated 10 times and overhead was 0.02%. Ping has one setuid call verified. Nginx and Apache servers are tested by using Apache Bench (normally used for measuring of HTTP web servers). To measure overhead, we repeated 100K HTTP GET requests 10 times with concurrency of up to 100 requests to the localhost. There was no overhead other than measurement errors since Nginx and Apache do not have setuid calls verified during the benchmark workload. Login/logout behavior was tested with telnet. This workload triggered 5 `setuid` call verifications. We repeated this process 10 times to get an average performance number (0.29%). Another popular software for login/logout is SSH, which is tested with SCP as another selection because they share authentication logic. SCP was measured by downloading a 1KB file 10 times from a local directory. During this process, there were 28 verifications of `setuid` calls which caused overhead of 0.54%.

5.4 Case Study: A Real-world Data-oriented Attack

We leverage a vulnerability in `sudo` to show how PoLPer detects and prevents exploitation. Hu et al. [24] proposed an approach to constructing data-oriented attacks automatically and showed an attack on sudo using its format string vulnerability (CVE-2012-0809). This attack changes `ud.uid` to the root ID value using the format string vulnerability in the `sudo_debug` function as shown in Figure 5.

PoLPer detects this attack using a data context shown in Table 7. `ud.uid` should be initialized by `getuid()`, which has an expected value of 1000. This exploit is detected because it sets zero to `ud.uid`.

```
struct user_details {
    uid_t uid;
    ...
} ud_details;
//in get_user_info()
ud.uid = getuid();
//in sudo_debug()
vfprintf(...);
//in sudo_askpass()
setuid(ud.uid);
```

Figure 5: Sudo code example.

Depth	1				
Priv. Op.	setuid				
Parameter	(Profile) 1000 (from getuid()), -1, -1				
	(Exploit) 0 (root shell), -1, -1				
Call Stack	#	Inode	Offset	File	Function
	21	158023	0x32 + 0xb75f7b44	../libc.so.6	-
	20	10171	0x8053080	../bin/sudo	sudo_askpass
	...				
	3	10171	0x804f4af	../bin/sudo	main
	2	158023	0xf3 + 54653	../libc.so.6	-
	1	10171	0x8049dd1	../bin/sudo	-

Table 7: Process-aware detection of the sudo exploit.

5.5 Case Study: Process-aware Detection of a Data-oriented Attack

In Figure 6, we present an example of data modification attack that highlights the unique capability of process-aware detection that can distinguish the abnormality of the attack. In this example, `setuid` call sets a user ID from a variable `uid` determined inside an if-else statement. Based on code analyses both non-root-id (from `getuid`)

```
int change_privilege(int uid) {
    ...
    return setuid(uid);
}

void vulnerable_function() {
    int uid;
    char buffer[10];
    int pid = fork();

    if (pid == 0) { //child process area
        uid = getuid();
        ...
        strcpy(buffer, argv[1]); // manipulate uid
        (buffer overflow)
        change_privilege(uid);
        non_root_works();
    } else { //parent process area
        uid = root_id;
        change_prvilege(uid);
        root_works();
    }
    ...
}
```

Figure 6: Process-aware exploit example.

Non-process-aware (parent/child)		Process-aware (parent)	
Priv. Op.	setuid	Depth	0
Parameter		Priv. Op.	setuid
Profile	root_id non-root-id	Parameter	
Exploit	root_id	Profile	root_id

(child)	
Depth	1
Priv. Op.	setuid
Parameter	
Profile	non-root-id
Exploit	root_id

Table 8: Comparison of non-process-aware and process-aware enforcement.

and root_id should be permitted because they are used respectively by a child and a parent process.

When an adversary manipulates the `uid` using a buffer overflow in the `strcpy` function to obtain the root_id and a corresponding root shell in a child process, a non-process-aware approach cannot block this attack because both root and non-root-id are legitimate as shown in Table 8. In contrast, PoLPer will prevent this exploit attempt because it distinguishes the `setuid` parameters in parent and child processes at run-time and enforces that only non-root-id is allowed in a child process. This case highlights a unique strength of process-aware detection.

6 DISCUSSION

Extended Support for Other Privilege Operations: This work focuses on the protection of setuid family system calls in Linux as these system calls are commonly leveraged for privilege escalation attacks. Privileged processes can bypass kernel permission checks and it is hard to control their privileges in a fine-grained way. Therefore, from Linux kernel version 2.2, privileges were divided into several categories according to *capabilities* [8].

Although capabilities were designed to remedy the problems of setuid family system calls, many popular legacy programs do not adopt them. Therefore, the vulnerability and problems of setuid calls still remain.

Conceptually, capabilities are also privileges and PoLPer can be extended to cover these sensitive operations as a future work — this extension is pure engineering effort and orthogonal to the conceptual work presented in this paper.

Analysis Coverage: In general, the focus of our code analysis is small relative to the full size of the application since setuid system calls are a small subset of all available code and can, therefore, be evaluated by enumerating all call sites of setuid calls. As a ground truth validation for our evaluations, we manually examined the source code of the applications evaluated and we found setuid family calls of 1~25 function call instances only in 10 minutes~1 hour due to a small well-defined scope of privilege functions. Manual code examination confirmed that our combined static and dynamic analyses achieve complete coverage relevant to our environment and the workload giving no false positives in experiments.

Based on our experiments, this is reasonable as in many programs setuid calls are used for the initialization of services which are common across workloads. For example, many client programs (e.g., ping, sudo, su) and server programs (e.g., Apache, Nginx) follow this pattern. Another set of programs (e.g., ssh, scp) exhibits complete coverage by having commonly used functions in every transaction which cannot be missed by either of our analyses.

However, if the software is written in a way which uses frequent setuid calls with diverse patterns in complex software structures, it may cause high complexity in the static and dynamic analyses to achieve complete contexts. As a complementary analysis method, fuzzing framework such as AFL [58] could help to further improve the coverage of static and dynamic analyses if needed for such complicated programs.

Mimicry Attacks and Manipulation of Call Contexts: For a mimicry attack where a system call sequence may fall within the original program's pattern, our approach will validate data parameters, and call stacks with process hierarchy contexts on setuid calls beyond a system call sequence. A combination of these contexts will significantly raise the bar to make a meaningful attack or maintaining its control without a detection. As another possible attack, a fake stack on the memory can be easily determined by PoLPer because it has complete knowledge on the process' stack memory. Misleading the view of stack walking via the manipulation of the ebp register can be easily caught because our approach uses stack layout from .eh_frame which verifies the register values and stack consistency in the unwinding steps similar to [20]. As a worst-case scenario, even though the adversary managed to bypass control flow integrity check, our approach applies multiple context checks on the data, process as well. Thus it would be considerably challenging to evade all of them. PoLPer can be further improved to be resilient to advanced stack attacks by combining with several known techniques such as a shadow stack [15] and Control-flow Enforcement Technology (CET) [26].

Address Space Layout Randomization: The kernel component of PoLPer uses information regarding memory layout including individual library addresses and therefore supports ASLR as we record not absolute addresses but files and offsets.

Generalization of Model: As we described in Section 2, our usage model of PoLPer is that system administrator customizes the policy based on an environmental context on the deployed system. This is a similar model used in major security tools like AppArmor or SELinux to deploy policies. On the deployment of a new software, this model is updated along with the installation via a new training. We are expecting that updating rules for new applications would not be different from already tested applications. This is because PoLPer is based on the general program behavior of setuid system calls such as process hierarchy, call stack, and parameters, which are orthogonal to the types of applications. Also, PoLPer did not have any particular assumptions about the target applications. When a new user is added into the system (e.g., adduser), which is another case to change an environmental context, PoLPer requires to update the model as well to handle a new user. Since a user ID is easily recognizable in the rule sets, it is straightforward to extend data flow check to use an ID template, therefore, including or excluding users. Our future work on this ID generalization will further improve the convenience and usability of PoLPer.

7 RELATED WORK

In this section, we discuss the approaches related to PoLPer and how PoLPer is differentiated from them. Table 9 provides a comparison between PoLPer and other works that are most closely related.

The principle of least privilege [48] means enforcing minimal privileges that allow the user/module to perform an intended role. The principle of least privilege is mainly achieved by separating the system into isolated compartments or using other techniques such as setuid system calls [11], Linux capabilities [8]. Qmail [5] has a software architecture that follows this principle (separating modules run into separate user IDs). Approaches such as JIGSAW [56], WatchIT [50], program compartmentalization [21, 23], SMV [23], SOAAP [21], Minion [30] follow this principle to reduce unnecessary privileges. PoLPer also follows this principle with a focus on the setuid system calls. The necessary privilege is extracted from the source code and dynamic training and enforced at run-time.

Several approaches [11, 17, 28] have investigated the status of setuid system calls and identified their semantic inconsistency. This problem occurred with human errors because they were insufficiently documented and poorly designed. Authors proposed more stable high-level APIs instead of low-level setuid system calls [11, 17] or migration of setuid policies from user-space programs to the kernel [28] as remedies.

Another line of work [19, 32, 38] models system call behavior during run-time. These approaches only rely on run-time behavior, unlike PoLPer. Additionally, they are based on process insensitive context. Therefore their detection policies do not differentiate

Approaches	Overhead	PA	KE	CF	DM	NS	NM	NK	PV	DA	SA	Main Techniques
CFI [3, 39–42]	1~15%	✗	✓/✗	✓	✗	✓/✗	✗	✓/✗	✓	✓	✓	Analyze and enforce control flow integrity
DFI [4, 10, 52]	7~103%	✗	✓/✗	✓/✗	✓	✓/✗	✗	✓/✗	✓	✓/✗	✓	Analyze and enforce data flow integrity
Kruegel et al. [32]	0~58%	✗	✗[1]	✗	✓	✓	✓	✓	✗	✓	✗	Analyze arguments of system call for detection
Feng et al. [19]	0~250%	✗	✗[1]	✓	✗	✓	✓	✓	✗	✓	✗	Analyze call stack of system call for detection
Mutz et al. [38]	0~100%	✗	✗[1]	✓	✓	✓	✓	✓	✗	✓	✗	Analyze call stack and arguments of system call for detection
Setuid [11, 17]	-[2]	✗	✗[3]	-[4]	-[4]	✓	✓	✓	-[4]	✗	✗	Identify semantic inconsistency of priv. operations
Protego [28]	0~7.4%	✗	✓	-[5]	-[5]	✗	✗	✗	-[5]	-	-	Migrate setuid policies from user space to kernel
Seccomp [49]	2%	✗	✓	✗	✓	✗	✗	✗	✓	✗	✗	Filter system calls based on predefined rule
Linux Capabilities [8]	-[2]	✗	✓	✗	✗	✓[7]	✓[7]	✗	✓	✗	✗	Divide the power of superuser into pieces
PoLPer	0~0.54%	✓	✓	✓	✓	✓[6]	✓	✓	✓	✓	✓	Extract and enforce the least priv. in multi contexts

Table 9: Comparison of PoLPer and related approaches. PA: process-aware policy granularity, KE: kernel-space enforcement, CF: control flow exploit detection, DM : Data modification exploit detection, NS: No source code required, NM: No modification on software, NK: Independent to kernel, interfaces and services, PV: Prevention of attacks, DA: Dynamic analysis, SA: Static analysis, [1]: Use a monitoring service or user level implementation without enforcement, [2]: No evaluation on performance, [3]: only interfaces are presented for semantic correction, [4]: These approaches do not detect attacks, [5]: Removes setuid related attacks with the cost of redesign of interfaces and software, [6]: Higher accuracy if source code is available. [7]: Linux capabilities can be used as OS policy configuration without modifying or involving software logic.

distinct requirement of setuid calls in each process causing over-approximated policies.

Policy enforcement approaches [45, 55, 57] create system call execution policies through the inspection of system call properties. These approaches are based on mandatory access control systems such as AppArmor [44], Seccomp [49], and SELinux [51]. They pose several limitations such as coarse-grained program level policies, and non-trivial overhead. In contrast, PoLPer creates process context sensitive profiles which help to reduce the number of policies and thus lower overhead. PoLPer transparently restricts setuid system calls using a comprehensive combination of process sensitive execution contexts without any modification on the protected software.

Code-reuse attacks, such as ROP [47], are advanced attack mechanisms that bypass conventional defense mechanisms, such as data execution prevention (DEP) [37, 53]. The main goal of CFI [3] is to prevent code-reuse attacks by restricting the execution of a program to only follow the correct known control flow. Although the conceptual design of CFI has been sound from its beginning, there have been issues to be addressed in accuracy and efficient enforcement of CFI in practice. Niu et al. [40, 42] achieve a high precision of CFG leveraging both static analysis and dynamic points-to analysis. There have been highly practical CFI mechanisms based on binary analysis and hardware-assisted control transfer monitoring [54, 60, 61]. Another line of work aims to address detecting ROP attacks [13, 43], while others focus on CFI challenges in C++ programs [6, 59]. Despite these research efforts, many others have reported weaknesses of the existing CFI mechanisms [9, 14, 18]. Compared to CFI, PoLPer focuses on detecting process-aware multiple context misuses on setuid calls. Regarding control flow, PoLPer checks the backward function call level control flow using call stack. While CFI focuses solely on the control flow of a program, PoLPer can prevent data modification exploit that does not make any change in the control flow by using multiple process-aware contexts including data contexts and call contexts.

Since exploits corrupt both control data (e.g., function pointer, jump targets, and return address) and non-control data (e.g., the arguments of privilege operations) mitigations must protect both

angles. While CFI [3] and CPI [33] protect against the manipulation of control data, they cannot protect against other data modifications. With the rise of automatic synthesis of non-control data attacks [12, 24, 25, 27], data-flow must be protected as well. Current fine-grained solutions are either not yet practical because of coverage issues (e.g., KENALI [52] is only designed for OS kernels) and overhead issues (e.g., DFI [10]'s overhead is 104% since it handles all control and non-control data manipulation).

For the detection and prevention of privilege operation attacks (e.g., privilege escalation) based on the manipulation of control and non-control data, practical data flow integrity checking solutions are needed. PoLPer provides coarse-grained data context integrity (both control and non-control) on the scope of setuid calls with negligible overhead.

8 CONCLUSION

PoLPer systematically extracts only the required contexts of setuid calls from programs to discover the distinct demand of privilege operation of each process. PoLPer transparently enforces these *process-aware* characteristics using a comprehensive combination of process contexts so that unnecessary contexts of setuid calls are tightly restricted in legacy software without any change. Our evaluation presents that PoLPer can prevent real-world exploits based on state-of-the-art attack techniques manipulating data context or control context of setuid system calls effectively and efficiently with near zero overhead in the end-to-end performance in various desktop and server programs.

ACKNOWLEDGMENTS

The first author worked on this project during an internship at NEC Laboratories America, Princeton. We would like to thank the anonymous reviewers for their detailed and constructive comments. This work was supported by NSF awards #1801601, #1513783, and ONR award N00014-17-1-2513. Any opinions, findings, and conclusions or recommendations expressed in this material are those of the authors and do not necessarily reflect the views of our sponsors.

REFERENCES

[1] Online; accessed 22-Sept-2018. Bypassing non-executable memory, ASLR and stack canaries on x86-64 Linux. https://www.antoniobarresi.com/security/exploitdev/2014/05/03/64bitexploitation/.

[2] Online; accessed 22-Sept-2018. Defeating DEP with ROP. https://samsclass.info/127/proj/rop.htm.

[3] Martín Abadi, Mihai Budiu, Úlfar Erlingsson, and Jay Ligatti. 2009. Control-flow Integrity Principles, Implementations, and Applications. *ACM Trans. Inf. Syst. Secur.*

[4] Periklis Akritidis, Cristian Cadar, Costin Raiciu, Manuel Costa, and Miguel Castro. 2008. Preventing memory error exploits with WIT. In *Proceedings of S&P'08*.

[5] Daniel J Bernstein. 2007. Some thoughts on security after ten years of qmail 1.0. In *Proceedings of CSAW'07*.

[6] Dimitar Bounov, Rami Gökhan Kici, and Sorin Lerner. 2016. Protecting C++ Dynamic Dispatch Through VTable Interleaving. In *Proceedings of NDSS'16*.

[7] Scott Brookes and Stephen Taylor. 2016. Containing a Confused Deputy on x86: A Survey of Privilege Escalation Mitigation Techniques. *International Journal of Advanced Computer Science and Applications*.

[8] Linux capabilities. Online; accessed 23-Sep-2018. http://man7.org/linux/man-pages/man7/capabilities.7.html.

[9] Nicolas Carlini, Antonio Barresi, Mathias Payer, David Wagner, and Thomas R. Gross. 2015. Control-flow Bending: On the Effectiveness of Control-flow Integrity. In *Proceedings of SEC'15*.

[10] Miguel Castro, Manuel Costa, and Tim Harris. 2006. Securing software by enforcing data-flow integrity. In *Proceedings of OSDI'06*.

[11] Hao Chen, David Wagner, and Drew Dean. 2002. Setuid Demystified. In *Proceedings of SEC'02*.

[12] Shuo Chen, Jun Xu, Emre Can Sezer, Prachi Gauriar, and Ravishankar K Iyer. 2005. Non-Control-Data Attacks Are Realistic Threats. In *Proceedings of SEC'05*.

[13] Yueqiang Cheng, Zongwei Zhou, Yu Miao, Xuhua Ding, and Huijie Robert Deng. 2014. ROPecker: A generic and practical approach for defending against rop attacks. In *Proceedings of NDSS'14*.

[14] Mauro Conti, Stephen Crane, Lucas Davi, Michael Franz, Per Larsen, Marco Negro, Christopher Liebchen, Mohaned Qunaibit, and Ahmad-Reza Sadeghi. 2015. Losing Control: On the Effectiveness of Control-Flow Integrity Under Stack Attacks. In *Proceedings of CCS'15*.

[15] Thurston HY Dang, Petros Maniatis, and David Wagner. 2015. The performance cost of shadow stacks and stack canaries. In *Proceedings of ASIACCS'15*.

[16] Shellcodes database for study cases. Online; accessed 23-Sep-2018. http://shell-storm.org/shellcode/.

[17] Mark S Dittmer and Mahesh V Tripunitara. 2014. The UNIX process identity crisis: A standards-driven approach to setuid. In *Proceedings of CCS'14*.

[18] Isaac Evans, Fan Long, Ulziibayar Otgonbaatar, Howard Shrobe, Martin Rinard, Hamed Okhravi, and Stelios Sidiroglou-Douskos. 2015. Control Jujutsu: On the Weaknesses of Fine-Grained Control Flow Integrity. In *Proceedings of CCS'15*.

[19] Henry Hanping Feng, Oleg M Kolesnikov, Prahlad Fogla, Wenke Lee, and Weibo Gong. 2003. Anomaly detection using call stack information. In *Proceedings of S&P'03*.

[20] Yangchun Fu, Junghwan Rhee, Zhiqiang Lin, Zhichun Li, Hui Zhang, and Guofei Jiang. 2016. Detecting Stack Layout Corruptions with Robust Stack Unwinding. In *Proceedings of RAID'16*.

[21] Khilan Gudka, Robert N.M. Watson, Jonathan Anderson, David Chis nall, Brooks Davis, Ben Laurie, Ilias Marinos, Pe ter G. Neumann, and Alex Richardson. 2015. Clean Application Compartmentalization with SOAAP. In *Proceedings of CCS'15*.

[22] Norm Hardy. 1988. The Confused Deputy:(or why capabilities might have been invented). In *Proceedings of SIGOPS'88*.

[23] terry ching-hsiang Hsu, kevin hoffman, patrick eugster, and mathias payer. 2016. enforcing least privilege memory views for multithreaded applications. In *proceedings of CCS'16*.

[24] Hong Hu, Zheng Leong Chua, Sendroiu Adrian, Prateek Saxena, and Zhenkai Liang. 2015. Automatic Generation of Data-Oriented Exploits.. In *Proceedings of SEC'15*.

[25] Hong Hu, Shweta Shinde, Sendroiu Adrian, Zheng Leong Chua, Prateek Saxena, and Zhenkai Liang. 2016. Data-oriented programming: On the expressiveness of non-control data attacks. In *Proceedings of S&P'16*.

[26] Intel. Online; accessed 23-Sep-2018. Control-flow enforcement technology (CET) preview. https://software.intel.com/sites/default/files/managed/4d/2a/control-flow-enforcement-technology-preview.pdf.

[27] Kyriakos Ispoglou, Bader AlBassam, Trent Jaeger, and Mathias Payer. [n. d.]. Block Oriented Programming: Automating Data-Only Attacks. In *Proceedings of CCS'18*.

[28] Bhushan Jain, Chia-Che Tsai, Jitin John, and Donald E Porter. 2014. Practical Techniques to Obviate Setuid-to-root Binaries. In *Proceedings of EuroSys'14*.

[29] Jim Keniston. Online; accessed 23-Sep-2018. Kernel Probes. https://elixir.free-electrons.com/linux/v4.0/source/Documentation/kprobes.txt.

[30] Chung Hwan Kim, Taegyu Kim, Hongjun Choi, Zhongshu Gu, Byoungyoung Lee, Xiangyu Zhang, and Dongyan Xu. 2018. Securing Real-Time Microcontroller Systems through Customized Memory View Switching. In *Proceedings of NDSS'18*.

[31] Gene H Kim and Eugene H Spafford. 1994. The design and implementation of tripwire: A file system integrity checker. In *Proceedings of CCS'94*.

[32] Christopher Kruegel, Darren Mutz, Fredrik Valeur, and Giovanni Vigna. 2003. On the detection of anomalous system call arguments. In *Proceedings of ESORICS'03*.

[33] Volodymyr Kuznetsov, László Szekeres, Mathias Payer, George Candea, R Sekar, and Dawn Song. 2014. Code-Pointer Integrity. In *Proceedings of OSDI'14*.

[34] Long Le. 2010. Payload Already Inside: Data Reuse for ROP Exploits. (2010).

[35] LLVM. Online; accessed 23-Sep-2018. The LLVM Compiler Infrastructure Project. http://llvm.org/.

[36] Kangjie Lu, Chengyu Song, Taesoo Kim, and Wenke Lee. 2016. UniSan: Proactive kernel memory initialization to eliminate data leakages. In *Proceedings of CCS'16*.

[37] Microsoft. Online; accessed 23-Sep-2018. Data Execution Prevention (DEP). https://msdn.microsoft.com/en-us/library/windows/desktop/aa366553(v=vs.85).aspx.

[38] Darren Mutz, William Robertson, Giovanni Vigna, and Richard Kemmerer. 2007. Exploiting execution context for the detection of anomalous system calls. In *Proceedings of RAID'07*.

[39] Ben Niu and Gang Tan. 2013. Monitor Integrity Protection with Space Efficiency and Separate Compilation. In *Proceedings of CCS'13*.

[40] Ben Niu and Gang Tan. 2014. Modular Control-flow Integrity. In *Proceedings of PLDI'14*.

[41] Ben Niu and Gang Tan. 2014. RockJIT: Securing Just-In-Time Compilation Using Modular Control-Flow Integrity. In *Proceedings of CCS'14*.

[42] Ben Niu and Gang Tan. 2015. Per-input control-flow integrity. In *Proceedings of CCS'15*.

[43] Vasilis Pappas, Michalis Polychronakis, and Angelos D. Keromytis. 2013. Transparent ROP Exploit Mitigation Using Indirect Branch Tracing. In *Proceedings of SEC'13*.

[44] AppArmor Project. Online; accessed 23-Sep-2018. http://wiki.apparmor.net/index.php/Main_Page.

[45] Niels Provos. 2003. Improving Host Security with System Call Policies.. In *Proceedings of SEC'03*.

[46] Mohammed Rangwala, Ping Zhang, Xukai Zou, and Feng Li. 2014. A taxonomy of privilege escalation attacks in android applications. *International Journal of Security and Networks* (2014).

[47] Ryan Roemer, Erik Buchanan, Hovav Shacham, and Stefan Savage. 2012. Return-Oriented Programming: Systems, Languages, and Applications. *ACM Trans. Inf. Syst. Secur.* 15, 1, Article 2 (March 2012), 34 pages. https://doi.org/10.1145/2133375.2133377

[48] Jerome H. Saltzer. 1974. Protection and the Control of Information Sharing in Multics. *Comm. ACM*.

[49] Seccomp. Online; accessed 23-Sep-2018. SECure COMPuting with filters. https://www.kernel.org/doc/Documentation/prctl/seccomp_filter.txt.

[50] Noam Shalev, Idit Keidar, Yaron Weinsberg, Yosef Moatti, and Elad Ben-Yehuda. 2017. WatchIT: Who Watches Your IT Guy?. In *Proceedings of SOSP'17*.

[51] Stephen Smalley, Chris Vance, and Wayne Salamon. 2001. Implementing SELinux as a Linux security module. *NAI Labs Report*.

[52] Chengyu Song, Byoungyoung Lee, Kangjie Lu, William Harris, Taesoo Kim, and Wenke Lee. 2016. Enforcing Kernel Security Invariants with Data Flow Integrity. In *Proceedings of NDSS'16*.

[53] PaX Team. Online; accessed 23-Sep-2018. Pax: the Linux kernel patch for least privilege protection. https://en.wikipedia.org/wiki/PaX.

[54] Victor Van der Veen, Dennis Andriesse, Enes Göktaş, Ben Gras, Lionel Sambuc, Asia Slowinska, Herbert Bos, and Cristiano Giuffrida. 2015. Practical Context-Sensitive CFI. In *Proceedings of CCS'15*.

[55] Jeffrey A Vaughan and Andrew D Hilton. 2010. Paladin: Helping Programs Help Themselves with Internal System Call Interposition.

[56] Hayawardh Vijayakumar, Xinyang Ge, Mathias Payer, and Trent Jaeger. 2014. JIGSAW: Protecting Resource Access by Inferring Programmer Expectations. In *Proceedings of SEC'14*.

[57] David Wagner and R Dean. 2001. Intrusion detection via static analysis. In *Proceedings of S&P'01*.

[58] M. Zalewski. Online; accessed 23-Sep-2018. American Fuzzy Lop. http://lcamtuf.coredump.cx/afl/.

[59] Chao Zhang, Dawn Xiaodong Song, Scott A. Carr, Mathias Payer, Tongxin Li, Yu Ding, and Chengyu Song. 2016. VTrust: Regaining Trust on Virtual Calls. In *Proceedings of NDSS'16*.

[60] Chao Zhang, Tao Wei, Zhaofeng Chen, Lei Duan, Laszlo Szekeres, Stephen Mc-Camant, Dawn Song, and Wei Zou. 2013. Practical Control Flow Integrity and Randomization for Binary Executables. In *Proceedings of S&P'13*.

[61] Mingwei Zhang and R. Sekar. 2013. Control Flow Integrity for COTS Binaries. In *Proceedings of SEC'13*.

Extracting Secrets from Encrypted Virtual Machines

Mathias Morbitzer*
Fraunhofer AISEC
Garching near Munich, Germany
morbitzer@aisec.fraunhofer.de

Manuel Huber*
Fraunhofer AISEC
Garching near Munich, Germany
manuel.huber@aisec.fraunhofer.de

Julian Horsch
Fraunhofer AISEC
Garching near Munich, Germany
julian.horsch@aisec.fraunhofer.de

ABSTRACT

AMD SEV is a hardware extension for main memory encryption on multi-tenant systems. SEV uses an on-chip coprocessor, the AMD Secure Processor, to transparently encrypt virtual machine memory with individual, ephemeral keys never leaving the coprocessor. The goal is to protect the confidentiality of the tenants' memory from a malicious or compromised hypervisor and from memory attacks, for instance via cold boot or DMA. The SEVered attack has shown that it is nevertheless possible for a hypervisor to extract memory in plaintext from SEV-encrypted virtual machines without access to their encryption keys. However, the encryption impedes traditional virtual machine introspection techniques from locating secrets in memory prior to extraction. This can require the extraction of large amounts of memory to retrieve specific secrets and thus result in a time-consuming, obvious attack. We present an approach that allows a malicious hypervisor quick identification and theft of secrets, such as TLS, SSH or FDE keys, from encrypted virtual machines on current SEV hardware. We first observe activities of a virtual machine from within the hypervisor in order to infer the memory regions most likely to contain the secrets. Then, we systematically extract those memory regions and analyze their contents on-the-fly. This allows for the efficient retrieval of targeted secrets, strongly increasing the chances of a fast, robust and stealthy theft.

CCS CONCEPTS

• Security and privacy → Virtualization and security.

KEYWORDS

AMD SEV; virtual machine encryption; virtual machine introspection; memory extraction; data confidentiality

ACM Reference Format:
Mathias Morbitzer, Manuel Huber, and Julian Horsch. 2019. Extracting Secrets from Encrypted Virtual Machines. In *Ninth ACM Conference on Data and Application Security and Privacy (CODASPY '19), March 25–27, 2019, Richardson, TX, USA.* ACM, New York, NY, USA, 10 pages. https://doi.org/10.1145/3292006.3300022

*Both authors contributed equally to the work.

1 INTRODUCTION

On common multi-tenant systems, the confidentiality of sensitive Virtual Machine (VM) data depends on both the Hypervisor's (HV) integrity and on the operator's trustworthiness. Unfortunately, these strong requirements are prone to getting infringed by different attack vectors. Examples are attacks by other tenants exploiting software-level vulnerabilities to escape their sandboxed VMs [15, 21, 23], attackers with physical access conducting a memory attack, e.g., via Direct Memory Access (DMA) [3, 4, 7] or cold boot [10], or simply a malicious operator using the HV to read the VM's memory. In order to protect the VM's memory in such scenarios, AMD introduced Secure Encrypted Virtualization (SEV) [2, 6] on recent server systems. SEV is a hardware extension for main memory encryption on a per-VM granularity. With SEV enabled, AMD's Secure Processor (SP) transparently encrypts the main memory of each VM with individual SP-bound keys. The goal is to protect VMs from memory attacks and from a malicious or compromised HV. To attest tenants that their VMs' memory is indeed encrypted, SEV includes a cryptographic protocol to verify VM encryption on an SEV-enabled platform.

SEVered [16] is a recent attack on AMD SEV, which showed that it is nevertheless possible for a HV to extract plaintext contents from SEV-encrypted VMs. SEVered exploits SEV's missing integrity protection for VM memory pages, previously discovered by [11, 17], to modify the memory mapping of a non-colluding service inside a VM. The modification causes the service to access and return an arbitrary portion of plaintext memory when serving requests. This allows an attacker in the HV to extract all the VM's main memory in plaintext by repeatedly requesting the same resource and changing its mapping. However, the encryption prevents the attacker from locating the VM's most valuable resources in memory prior to extraction, such as keys for Transport Layer Security (TLS), Secure Shell (SSH) or Full Disk Encryption (FDE). In the worst case, extracting those secrets requires a full dump of the VM's memory. This can take a significant amount of time, depending on the size of the attacker-controlled resource and throughput of the service. For example, an extraction speed of about 80 KB/s was reached with web servers providing a resource covering exactly one memory page. In this scenario, it takes more than 7 hours and requires 524,288 requests to extract all memory contents of a VM with 2 GB of main memory. During this time, other clients requesting the same resource also receive arbitrary contents, making full memory extraction conspicuous.

In this paper, we show that it is possible to overcome these downsides and present an approach that makes HVs capable of quickly locating and extracting specific secrets from SEV-enabled VMs. Our approach has two phases, the *observation* and the *retrieval* phase. In the observation phase, we exploit the fact that the HV is able to observe certain events triggered by VMs. These *observable events* can, for instance, be page faults which the HV handles but also I/O events like network traffic or disk writes. We observe and combine such events to identify a minimal set of VM memory pages likely to contain the targeted secrets. Second, in the retrieval phase, we iteratively extract and analyze the identified set of pages on the fly until we find the targeted secret. For this phase, we use the SEVered attack, but could potentially leverage other vectors allowing memory extraction from SEV-encrypted VMs.

Our targeted extraction approach offers an inconspicuous, reliable and efficient method to steal various secrets from encrypted VMs. We demonstrate the potential of our approach by extracting TLS and SSH keys from a VM's user space memory, and FDE keys stored in the VM's kernel space. We conduct our experiments on an SEV-enabled EPYC processor, running Apache and nginx web servers as well as the OpenSSH server. To show that our approach can cope with real-world scenarios where VMs can be under varying levels of load, we base our experiments on a load model in which multiple independent clients concurrently access the VM's services during our attack.

2   AMD SEV AND THE SEVERED ATTACK

This section provides background information on AMD SEV, the Second Level Address Translation (SLAT) concepts of HVs, and the SEVered attack.

SEV. The AMD SEV technology allows for the transparent encryption of main memory of individual VMs. SEV primarily targets server systems and builds on the AMD Secure Memory Encryption (SME) technology, which provides transparent full main memory encryption. While the goal of SME is to protect systems against physical attacks on the main memory, SEV tries to additionally protect memory of individual VMs against attacks from other VMs and from a malicious HV. The SEV encryption is executed by a hardware AES engine located in the memory controller. The keys for the encryption are created and managed by an additional component, the AMD SP. All keys are ephemeral and never exposed to software on the main CPU. In contrast to SME, SEV uses different keys for each VM and for the HV. Additionally, a VM running on an SEV-protected system can request encryption and receive proof that its memory contents are being encrypted, which establishes trust between its owner and the remote operator. While SME was first integrated into AMD's Ryzen CPUs, SEV was introduced onto the market with the EPYC processor family. The mainline Linux kernel provides necessary software-level support for SEV.

SLAT. AMD SEV integrates with the existing AMD hardware virtualization technologies marketed as AMD-V. An integral component of hardware virtualization is an additional address translation, often named *nested paging* or SLAT [1]. While non-virtualized systems simply translate virtual addresses directly to physical addresses, a hardware-virtualized system distinguishes between three different types of addresses. When the VM accesses a Guest Virtual Address (GVA), the guest-controlled first level translation translates the address to a Guest Physical Address (GPA). The GPA is then translated to a Host Physical Address (HPA) using the second-level translation controlled by the HV. SLAT is completely transparent to the VM. This allows running multiple VMs that use the same GPA

space while separating them in physical memory. With SEV enabled, the first level translation from GVA to GPA in the encrypted VM is non-accessible to the HV. But the HV is still responsible for managing physical memory for its VMs and is therefore able to restrict access and change second-level mappings from GPAs to HPAs. Since there is no integrity protection in SEV, the HV can use SLAT to transparently switch a GPA to HPA mapping to a different HPA page belonging to the same VM.

SEVered. The SEVered attack [16] enables a malicious or compromised HV to extract the full memory of SEV-encrypted VMs in plaintext by exploiting SEV's missing integrity protection. SEVered requires a (non-colluding) service in the targeted VM, e.g., a web server, offering a remotely accessible resource. The first step of SEVered is to identify the HPAs, i.e., the physical pages, at which the accessible resource is located in the VM's encrypted memory. The number of pages containing (parts of) the resource depends on the size of the resource as well as on the page size. The knowledge about the resource's location allows SEVered to modify the VM's GPA to HPA mappings to point to arbitrary other HPAs of the VM instead of to the service's resource. The modified mapping causes the service to access different memory pages instead of the real resource when handling requests. In the second step, SEVered repeatedly requests the resource while remapping the memory (using the SLAT feature). This leads to the iterative extraction of an encrypted VM's full memory contents. The throughput of SEVered depends on the service and on the amount of pages that can be extracted at once. Our attack uses SEVered for the extraction of main memory from SEV-encrypted VMs. Like SEVered, our attack neither requires breaking SEV's cryptographic primitives, nor control over the SP. Likewise, our attack requires control over the HV, i.e., a malicious administrator or a compromise of the HV. We refer to [16] for further information about SEVered.

3   FINDING AND EXTRACTING SECRETS

Our concept for the targeted extraction of secrets from SEV-encrypted VMs has two phases: In the first phase, we start our attack by *observing* the page accesses of the targeted VM in the HV until an event occurs which indicates the VM's recent use of the targeted secret. In the second phase, we *search* the VM's memory for the secret by systematically extracting and analyzing the set of observed pages accesses. This section describes both phases in detail.

3.1   Observation Phase

The goal of the observation phase is to narrow down the set of VM memory pages possibly containing the targeted secret. We start the phase at an arbitrary point in time by tracking the VM's page accesses in the HV until observing the end of a particular *activity*. This activity *must* make use of the targeted secret *at least once*. The start of the activity, denoted by $Activity_{Start}$, does not need to be observable by the HV. In contrast, the end of an activity, called $Activity_{End}$, *must* be a HV-observable event. This event indicates that the VM *recently* used the secret one or multiple times, denoted by $Use_1..Use_n$. As soon as we observe $Activity_{End}$, we stop tracking, denoted by $Tracking_{End}$. We do not actively attempt to trigger $Activity_{Start}$ in order to interfere as little as possible.

To start page access tracking, denoted by $Tracking_{Start}$, the HV invalidates all the target VM's GPA to HPA mappings. As a consequence, each of the VM's page accesses causes an observable event, a SLAT page fault. For each SLAT page fault, we record the GPA as well as the time and type of the page access (read, write, execute) in a list and re-validate the mapping. The re-validation *clears* the page from tracking. This means that each accessed page triggers exactly one page fault and that we track the page *exactly once*, namely the first time it is accessed after $Tracking_{Start}$. The tracking enforces that accesses to the secret will inevitably be recorded. Note that the secret can be contained in a single page or span over multiple pages and can have multiple occurrences on different pages.

An example for an activity is a TLS handshake as part of a request to a web server. The server uses the targeted secret, in this case its TLS private key, to authenticate itself to a client during the handshake. The HV can observe $Activity_{End}$ by monitoring network traffic, waiting for the packet the VM sends to complete the handshake.

Figure 1 depicts an attack scenario with the target VM and the HV in the upper and lower box, respectively. The illustration shows the start and end of a VM's activity along with events triggered by the activity, such as $Use_1..Use_n$. The vertical arrows crossing the upper and lower box represent the events observable from the HV. These are, for instance, SLAT page faults, network packets or disk I/O. Some of the vertical arrows do not cross the boundary of the VM. These are events not observable by the HV, for example, page faults handled by the VM or possibly $Activity_{Start}$. Some of the events may be related to concurrent activities, and multiple other activities may potentially make use of the secret as well, cases which are not depicted in Figure 1. The illustration emphasizes that $Tracking_{End}$ concludes the observation phase right after $Activity_{End}$.

When starting tracking between Use_n and $Activity_{End}$, we do not observe any of the page accesses to the secret. This means that we are unable to find the secret in the later search phase, requiring to repeat the attack. This is why we call the timespan between Use_n and $Activity_{End}$ the *critical window*. The critical window size is an important factor regarding the quality of the attack. The smaller the critical window the higher the probability that the attack succeeds. Further, a small critical window means quick termination of page access tracking after Use_n. This causes Use_n to be tracked *at the very end* of the phase, and likely only a few more pages to be tracked after Use_n. We evaluate the critical window size for different scenarios with various levels of load in Section 5.

It is *not* necessary to synchronize the start of the observation phase with a possibly non-observable $Activity_{Start}$. If $Tracking_{Start}$ takes place *long before* $Activity_{Start}$, the observation phase might take longer, but since every page is tracked only once, this does not lead to a persistent performance impact. On the other hand, if $Tracking_{Start}$ takes place *after* $Activity_{Start}$ (but not inside the critical window), the tracking period will be shorter and likely output less tracked page accesses.

To conclude, the result of the observation phase is a list of pages in which the page with the targeted secret is contained at least once as long as $Tracking_{Start}$ is not inside the critical window. The set of pages in the list is significantly smaller than the whole set of the VM's pages.

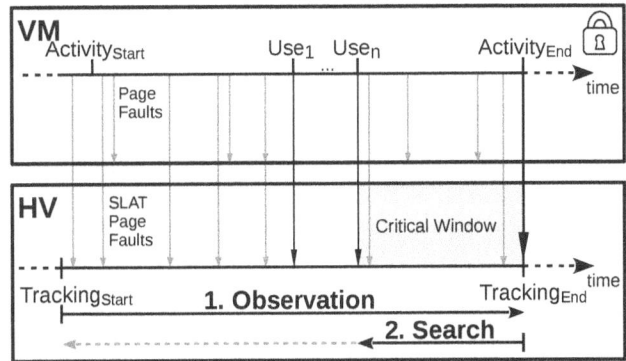

Figure 1: A HV first observing an activity inside an encrypted VM and then searching for the targeted secret. The vertical lines crossing the VM boundary into the HV box depict the events observable outside the VM.

3.2 Search Phase

The goal of the search phase is to extract the targeted secret from the VM's memory as quickly as possible, i.e., with a minimal number of memory requests. The input to the search phase is the list of tracked pages acquired during the observation phase. It is unknown which of the page accesses in the list correspond to $Use_1..Use_n$. The naive extraction of all pages in the list would still require a fairly high number of memory requests to find the secret. In the following, we describe our approach for a more efficient extraction.

The search phase starts right after $Tracking_{End}$, as depicted at the bottom of Figure 1. We know that $Activity_{End}$ indicates *recent* use of the secret. This means that Use_n must have occurred shortly before $Tracking_{End}$. For this reason, we consecutively extract the tracked pages *in backward order* until we find the secret. We thus start the extraction with the *most recently* tracked pages. This backward search is shown by the arrow directed to the left at the bottom of Figure 1. We analyze extracted memory chunks for the presence of the secret *on the fly* to be able to terminate the extraction procedure as early as possible. On the fly means we search the latest extracted memory chunk for the secret while we request the next chunk. When finding the secret in the chunk, we terminate the search phase, otherwise we request another chunk. The actual analysis is specific to the targeted secret and described in Section 4 for different secrets.

We propose an optional *preprocessing* step before the extraction to further minimize the number of memory requests. Preprocessing *filters* page accesses from the list, which *cannot* represent a use of the secret, and *prioritizes* accesses that are *likely* to represent a use. The ability to filter and prioritize depends on the use case, in particular, on the specific activity and secret. In most cases, the secret is a data structure on a page in non-executable memory, allowing to filter all execute-accesses from our list. The page is likely to be read, but may also be written during an activity. Depending on the use case, it is also possible that the secret resides in a read-only area, or represents confidential code. The information about this can often be acquired prior to the attack. A further possibility for preprocessing is to conduct a representative offline access pattern analysis for the activity to observe the expected timing of $Use_1..Use_n$. An offline analysis is more representative the more the hardware platform and the software configuration inside the VM resemble the attack target. With the gained timing information, an attacker can further filter or re-prioritize pages in the list.

Extracting the secret from the encrypted VM using SEVered requires the secret to remain at the same location during the attack. This means that the secret must not be erased or moved to a different HPA by the VM's kernel before the search phase terminates. We show that the secrets we chose for extraction always fulfilled this requirement and investigate preprocessing possibilities as part of our evaluation in Section 5.

4 KEY EXTRACTION SCENARIOS

In the following, we describe the application of our concept for the extraction of targeted secrets at the example of private keys and symmetric FDE keys. We focus on the aspects from Section 3 that are specific for the type of secret. These aspects are the activities with their events and the on the fly analysis.

4.1 Private Keys

For the extraction of private keys, we focus on the example of web server TLS keys. These keys are resources located in a VM's user space and highly sensitive. Web servers use these keys to establish authenticated TLS channels with clients. An attacker can make use of a stolen private key for identity spoofing and deceive clients for fraud or data exfiltration.

Events. $Activity_{Start}$ is the start of a TLS handshake. The handshake can be part of an HTTPS request or be directly triggered by a client. Use_i represents a server's use of the TLS key for its authentication during the handshake. The exact moment of use depends on the key exchange method. For instance, in case of an Elliptic-Curve Diffie-Hellman Ephemeral (ECDHE)-based key exchange algorithm, this is the moment of signing curve parameters. For an RSA-based key exchange, this moment is the decryption of the premaster secret encrypted by the client with the server's public key. $Activity_{End}$ happens when the VM sends the client a specific network packet during the handshake. We observe these packets with network monitoring tools. The *change cipher spec* packet is an indicator independent of the specific key exchange algorithm. Depending on the algorithm, packets sent earlier may be usable indicators as well. Note that we can also observe or even trigger $Activity_{Start}$ ourselves in this scenario. We discuss this aspect in Section 6.

On the fly analysis. The public key and its length are part of the server's certificate and known in advance. When using RSA, the private components of the key are the factors p or q of known length dividing the modulus of the public key. For every extraction request we make, we traverse the extracted chunk of memory and check if it contains a contiguous bit sequence that divides the modulus without remainder. If so, we found either p or q and can instantly determine the other factor. Otherwise, we request the next chunk of memory. Analyzing a chunk this way usually takes less time than memory extraction with SEVered, see Section 5.

The same approach can be used for extracting SSH private keys. In the SSH scenario, the SSH server must also use its private key for authentication during the SSH handshake when establishing a session. We evaluate the extraction of TLS and SSH keys using the Apache, nginx and OpenSSH servers in Section 5.

4.2 FDE Keys

The normal approach when using SEV is to first perform an attestation of the platform. The attestation proves to the tenant that the VM has been started with SEV enabled. After a successful attestation, the tenant provides the FDE key in encrypted form to the VM [2]. This protects the key from eavesdropping adversaries in the network and from being read by the HV. Thereafter, the FDE key is present in the VM's memory and can be extracted with our approach. The FDE key is particularly important, because it allows attackers to decrypt the VM's persistent storage gaining access to further valuable secrets.

Events. The corresponding activity is a disk I/O operation. The trigger for $Activity_{Start}$ is not observable by the HV and unlike in the TLS key scenario, $Activity_{Start}$ can have many different triggers. The trigger can, for instance, be data uploaded to a service, a request to a web server being logged, or an operation of the VM's OS involving disk I/O. The event Use_i is the VM's use of the FDE key to en- or decrypt disk content to be read or written. We observe $Activity_{End}$ by monitoring the VM's disk image file in the HV.

On the fly analysis. We can be sure that we found the secret as soon as we are able to successfully decrypt the VM's persistent storage. Traversing extracted memory chunks and naively trying each possible sequence as key leads to an inefficient approach. Our goal is thus to first identify key candidates in extracted memory chunks. For this purpose, we search the extracted memory for characteristics specific to FDE keys based on the following two criteria.

First, the FDE key is stored in the VM's kernel in a specific data structure. This structure has various fields, some of which must have certain value ranges, for instance, kernel addresses pointing to other kernel objects. Our first criterion for a key candidate is thus the identification of possible FDE key structures in extracted memory chunks.

Our second criterion is based on the statistical properties of the FDE key. Because FDE is usually AES-based, the kernel derives round keys from the FDE key and keeps them in *AES key schedules* in memory. The round keys have common statistical properties that can be identified with linear complexity. The first-round key is the AES key itself. We use aeskeyfind [5] to search memory chunks for AES key schedules. Note that candidates that turn out to be false positives are possibly symmetric keys used for other purposes and might also be valuable secrets. The traversal of memory chunks based on these two criteria takes considerably less time than the extraction of memory with SEVered, see Section 5.

We evaluate the FDE key extraction scenario as part of the following section.

5 IMPLEMENTATION AND EVALUATION

In the following, we first define performance indicators and then present our prototype and test setup. Based on that, we evaluate the extraction of TLS, FDE and SSH keys, as discussed in Section 4. In the final part of our evaluation, we present strategies for optimization with preprocessing and summarize our results.

5.1 Performance Indicators

The key factors we investigate are the *success probability* and the *attack time*.

Success Probability. As discussed in Section 3, the critical window size is the factor determining the success probability of our attack. The smaller the critical window, the smaller the probability that the observation phase ends without having tracked the access to the secret. In our evaluation, we present the success probability for the tested scenarios and provide an upper bound on the size of the critical window. We call the upper bound the *reaction time* of our attack. The reaction time is the sum of the critical window (the time frame between Use_n and $Activity_{End}$) and the time our prototype requires to detect $Activity_{End}$ and stop tracking (the time frame between $Activity_{End}$ and $Tracking_{End}$).

Attack Time. We divide the total attack time of a full attack into its three components: the time required to setup SEVered prior to extraction, the duration of the observation phase and the duration of the search phase.

Setup of SEVered. The time required to setup SEVered is evaluated in [16] and is thus not subject of our evaluation. Setting up SEVered usually takes less than 20 seconds, depending on the load of the VM. After setting up SEVered once, we can arbitrarily extract the victim VM's memory and repeat our attack when necessary.

Observation phase. The main factor for the duration of the observation phase is the frequency of the targeted activity. For instance, a web server under high load will often make TLS handshakes while SSH logins generally occur less frequently.

Search phase. The duration of the search phase is mainly determined by the amount of memory that has to be extracted until the secret is found. This is driven by the number of pages we track within the reaction time frame. The reaction time not only provides an upper bound on the critical window, but also serves as indicator for the expected number of tracked pages.

In our evaluation, we investigate the number of pages that have to be extracted, and the duration of the observation and search phase. We call the combined duration of both phases the *attack time*.

5.2 Prototype and Test Setup

We implemented our prototype including the functionality required for SEVered based on Kernel-based Virtual Machine (KVM). To start and stop page tracking and change mappings, we extended the KVM API with additional calls, in particular, with *KVM system ioctls* [19]. This allows us to launch the attack from user space by communicating with the KVM kernel module. For page access tracking in KVM we used the technique from [9, 16]. While tracking is active, we record all tracked pages in a list in kernel memory.

Upon the call to stop tracking, KVM returns the list of tracked pages to user space.

We ran KVM on Debian with a page size of 4 KB using an SEV-enabled Linux kernel in version 4.18.13 and QEMU 3.0.50. We used an AMD EPYC 7251 processor with full support for SEV. We created a victim VM with 2 GB of memory and one of the four available CPU cores. We deployed Apache 2.4.25-3 and nginx 1.10.3-1 for the TLS key scenarios, and OpenSSH 7.4 for the SSH scenario in the VM. The FDE scenario is independent of a service, because the FDE key is a kernel resource exclusively used by the OS. We deployed eleven different web resources on each web server. We used 4096-bit private keys for TLS and SSH and a 256-bit symmetric FDE key for storage encryption with AES-XTS. As target for memory extraction with SEVered, we used a page-sized web resource served by nginx.

To capture the handshake messages for the TLS and SSH key scenarios, we used tcpdump with libpcap, a library for network packet capturing. For TLS, we captured the *change cipher spec* packet the services send to conclude a TLS handshake (filter tcp[37] == 0x04). For SSH, we captured the *new keys* message, which concludes the SSH handshake (filter tcp[37] == 0x15). We patched libpcap to execute a system call for $Tracking_{Start}$ the moment packet capturing begins, and a call for $Tracking_{End}$ the moment the filtered packet is captured. This tight interconnection minimizes the reaction time. To monitor disk I/O events of the VM in the FDE key scenario, we used the tool inotifywait to observe *inotify* events. In particular, the *notify* option allows to detect disk writes on the VM's disk image file. We modified inotifywait to issue the calls for $Tracking_{Start}$ right before starting to watch events and for $Tracking_{End}$ as soon as an inotify event is identified.

In real-world scenarios, a tenant's VM can show higher or less activity depending on the load caused by its clients. To simulate this behavior, we executed all our tests based on a *load model* with various *load levels*, representing low to high load. In our model, a load level of nine, for instance, refers to nine requests per second to the VM. We randomly alternate between the services for each request. With a probability of $\frac{300}{301}$, we make a request to one of the resources offered by one of the two web servers with equal probability. With a probability of $\frac{1}{301}$, we initiate an SSH login with a user remaining logged in for two minutes. Compared to the number of web server requests, we execute only few SSH logins, as these usually happen less frequently than requests to a web server. The average duration of the observation phase thus lies in the range of a few seconds to a few hundreds of milliseconds for the web servers and in the range of a few minutes to tens of seconds for SSH. Note that sshd forks a new process for each new SSH connection. When the session terminates, the process exits and purges its SSH key. This means that the search time must be less than two minutes to extract the SSH key before the forked process exits.

We conducted 2,000 independent iterations of our attack for each of the four scenarios on four load levels: level *1*, *9*, *17*, and *25*. We started our attacks at random points in time while the VM processed requests according to the specific load level of our model. As an initial preprocessing step before the search phase, we filtered all execute-accesses. In our scenarios, all secrets are data structures located on non-executable memory pages.

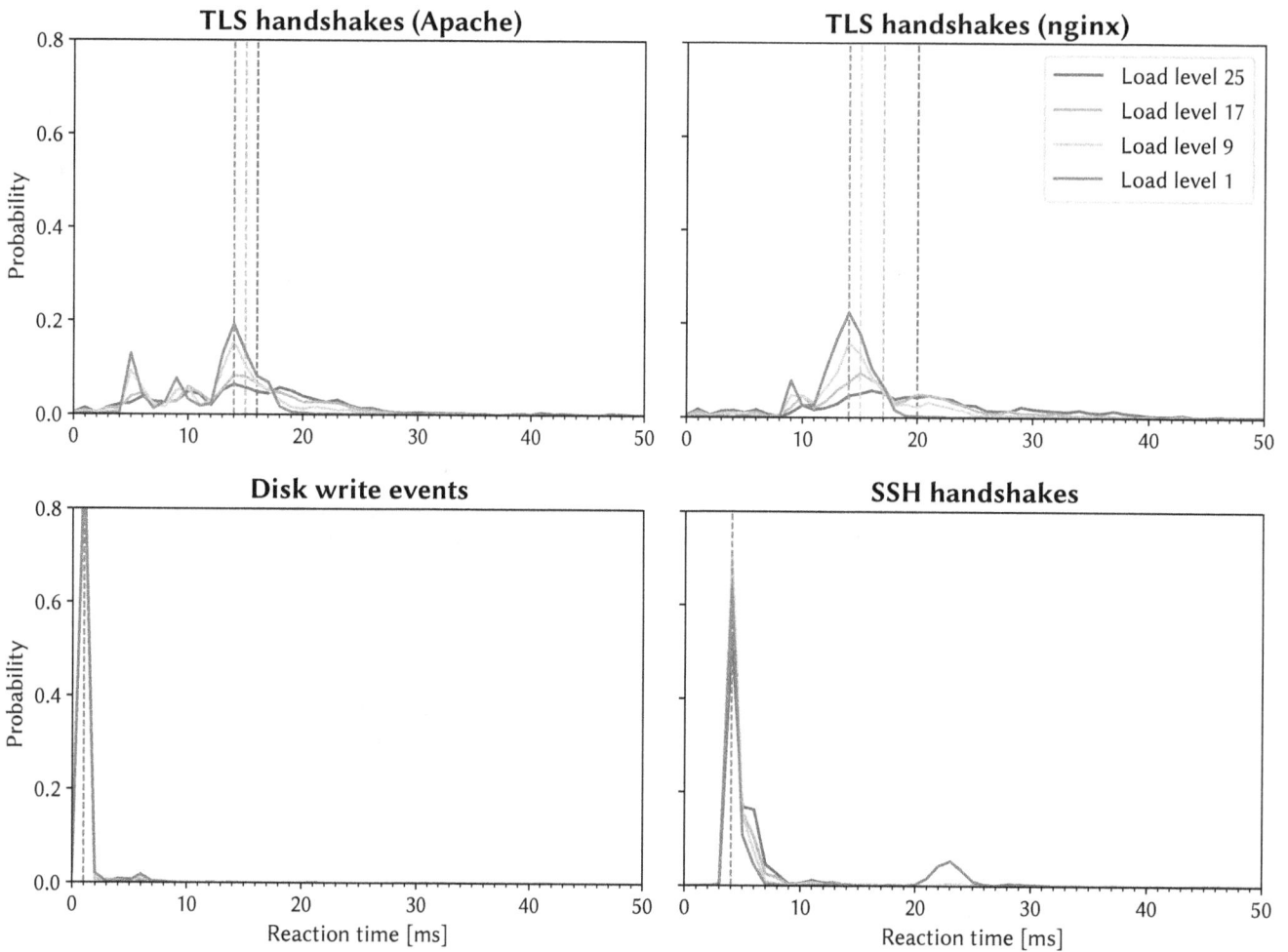

Figure 2: Distribution of the reaction times for all scenarios and load levels. The X-axes show discretized time steps of one millisecond and the Y-axes are normalized to one.

5.3 Success Probability and Reaction Time

In this part, we investigate the success probability and reaction times. The four diagrams in Figure 2 illustrate the distribution of measured reaction times for each scenario. The four graphs in each diagram represent the four load levels. The X-axes are discretized in steps of one millisecond, and the Y-axes are normalized to one. The vertical dashed lines show the median reaction times over all repetitions for each level, providing an upper bound on the median critical window size.

The results for Apache and nginx TLS handshakes are depicted in the top row of Figure 2. Both diagrams show a clear peak for the two lower load levels, indicating a reliable reaction time when the VM is not under high load. For the lowest load level, we can even observe that the reaction time never exceeded 21 milliseconds with Apache and 22 milliseconds with nginx. For higher load levels, more concurrent activities are executed by the VM, and the measurements are more dispersed over time. Consequently, it becomes likely that more pages have to be extracted in the search phase until the secret is found. This led to a maximum reaction time of around

50 milliseconds for both nginx and Apache in rare cases. However, the median reaction time increased to about only 20 milliseconds for nginx, and to about 16 milliseconds for Apache. As the reaction time is an upper bound for the critical window, the latter is smaller than tens of milliseconds for both Apache and nginx. We achieved a very high success rate of around 99.99% for both web servers on all load levels, meaning that we started tracking inside the critical window only in a few cases. The high success rate indicates that the upper bound we measured is a very conservative estimate. This comes from the fact that our prototype requires some time to actually stop tracking and (especially for the TLS scenarios) to recognize $Activity_{End}$. Note that if $Tracking_{Start}$ occurs inside the critical window of a TLS handshake, we still have the chance to observe Use_i of other handshakes being concurrently processed on higher load levels where lots of handshakes are made each second. The critical window can thus be even smaller on higher load levels.

The bottom left diagram in Figure 2 for disk write events shows that our implementation achieved an extremely fast reaction time of one millisecond in the median for each load level. Only in a few

Table 1: Statistics for the median length of the observation and search phases, and for the median number of extracted pages with the median absolute deviation for the different scenarios and load levels.

Use Case	Load Level	Median Page No	MAD Page No	Median Time Observ.	Median Time Search
TLS (nginx)	1	102	5	1.46s	17.72s
	9	116	19	0.37s	15.48s
	17	165	69	0.32s	18.61s
	25	301	160	0.31s	32.71s
TLS (Apache)	1	128	21	1.42s	21.90s
	9	137	40	0.37s	17.95s
	17	154	80	0.33s	17.44s
	25	171	109	0.32s	18.65s
FDE	1	70	8	2.43s	12.24s
	9	71	9	2.15s	9.34s
	17	70	8	2.08s	7.84s
	25	69	9	2.04s	7.37s
SSH	1	7	1	193.36s	1.33s
	9	7	1	27.23s	0.97s
	17	7	1	16.19s	0.83s
	25	7	1	14.41s	0.80s

cases, we encountered a slightly higher reaction time. In contrast to the TLS key scenarios, the behavior was generally independent of the load level. In the TLS key scenarios, the network packets must first be sent by the VM to the network interface, on which the HV executes more time-consuming network packet capturing. The interception of disk write events is less complex and introduces less delay. The success rate for FDE key extraction was about 99.99%, indicating a very small critical window, as confirmed by the upper bound in the graph.

The bottom right diagram in Figure 2 shows that the reaction time for SSH handshakes was four milliseconds in the median and mostly independent of the load level. We encountered only a few samples going up to about 30 milliseconds. As for the TLS scenario, this indicates a small upper bound on the critical window and a possibly quick extraction. Accordingly, our attack had a success rate of 99.98%.

5.4 Attack Time

This part investigates the attack times for each scenario. Table 1 summarizes the relevant statistics for the median number of pages to be extracted and the median attack time for every scenario and load level. For both Apache and nginx, the median number of pages to be extracted until finding the TLS key increased between low and high load levels. We measured an increase of the median from 102 to 301 pages (i.e., 408 to 1,204 KB of memory) for nginx, and from 128 to 171 pages (i.e., 512 to 684 KB of memory) for Apache. Additionally, the Median Absolute Deviation (MAD) increased from 5 to 160 from low to high load for nginx, respectively from 21 to 109

for Apache. The median number of extracted pages was particularly small compared to the median number of total tracked pages, which was for both cases between 1,691 and 2,085 (not listed in Table 1). The median duration of the search phase was between about 15.5 and 32.7 seconds for nginx, and between about 17.5 and 22 seconds for Apache. We measured an average extraction time of around 123 milliseconds for a single page with our SEVered implementation and setup. We measured this time to fluctuate quite frequently in the scale of a few tens of milliseconds. This is why a higher median number of extracted pages did not affect the duration of the search phase in a clearly linear way. The on the fly analysis for a single memory page took about 50 milliseconds. This means that the page extraction performance is the limiting factor of our attack. The higher the load, the less time we required for the observation phase, which ranged from 1.46 to 0.31 seconds in case of nginx, for instance. This is because the probability of quickly observing $Activity_{End}$ increases with a high frequency of requests. To summarize, we measured an attack time between about 16 and 33 seconds in the median for the web services.

For the FDE key scenario, the amount of pages that had to be extracted was very small and mostly independent of the load level. Accordingly, the median number of extracted pages was between 69 and 71 for the different load levels (i.e., 276 to 284 KB of memory) As in the TLS key scenario, this number is small compared to the median number of total tracked pages, which was between 2,526 and 3,433. The overall duration of the search phase was between about 7.4 and 12.3 seconds. The on the fly analysis for a single memory page took only about 2 milliseconds on average. We mostly identified the key as part of the AES key schedule, and only occasionally by the kernel data structure, see Section 4. We measured a slightly decreasing observation time from 2.43 to 2.04 seconds. This indicates that the VM's OS is regularly writing pages to disk, in our case mostly regardless of the load level. In sum, the attack time was between less than 9.5 and 14.7 seconds in the median.

In the SSH scenario, we merely had to extract seven pages in the median with a MAD of one. This is a particularly small number, especially compared to the median number of 10,102 to 11,094 total tracked pages, omitted from Table 1. We measured a median duration of the search phase of about 0.80 to 1.33 seconds. This means that the attack works reliably assuming that the SSH connection lasts at least 1.33 seconds. Similar to the TLS key scenario, the on the fly analysis of a memory page took about 50 milliseconds. With our load model, the observation time of about 14 to 194 seconds was comparably high for the SSH scenario. This is another reason why the number of extracted pages was especially low for the SSH case. In long observation phases, we already tracked a high number of pages before Use_n, making it very unlikely that many pages are tracked within in the reaction time frame at the end of the activity.

5.5 Optimization with Preprocessing

As discussed in Section 3, preprocessing with prioritization and filtering is an optional optimization before the search phase. Preprocessing usually requires a priori knowledge about the use case and behavior of the VM, which may not always be available. This behavior may also vary between different hard- and software configurations. For our evaluation, we already used the knowledge that all secrets are data structures located on non-executable memory pages. This allowed us to filter execute-accesses from the list of tracked pages. The amount of pages to be extracted was thereby reduced by about 22% on average over all samples.

Use_n was a read-access in 96% of our attacks for the TLS handshakes and in 93% a write-access for the SSH handshakes. For disk write events, Use_n was always a read-access. Whether the page containing the secret is tracked as read- or write-access depends on the other data located within the page. The type of access thus cannot be predetermined with certainty. Filtering of write-accesses could significantly reduce the attack time, but could also reduce the success probability. Also, prioritizing the extraction of read-accesses over write-accesses in the list would boost the attack in most cases, but could also introduce costly outliers.

Another possibility for prioritization is knowledge about the reaction time, as shown in Figure 2. The graphs for the two web server scenarios show that the reaction time was rarely less than eight milliseconds before $Tracking_{End}$. Re-arranging these early accesses further back in the list of tracked pages can thus reduce the amount of pages to be extracted until the secret is found. The same observation can be made for the SSH scenario, where Use_n never happened less than three milliseconds before $Tracking_{End}$. However, in this case the number of pages to be extracted is already so small that further optimization may not be required.

The reaction times in Figure 2 can also help to determine a good criterion for restarting the attack when a secret has not been found after a certain number of extracted pages. For instance, page accesses tracked later than 30 milliseconds before $Tracking_{End}$ are likely exceeding the reaction time frame and thus unlikely to be a candidate for Use_n. This can be used as a criterion to detect that $Tracking_{Start}$ was inside the critical window and to restart the attack from the observation phase.

5.6 Summary

For all evaluated scenarios, both performance indicators are very promising. We found that the critical window was very small in all cases. $Tracking_{Start}$ was thus inside the critical window only in a few cases, resulting in a very high success probability throughout all scenarios and load levels. The most important factor for the attack time, the duration of the search phase, was also very small. Extracting all memory from our VM with 2 GB of main memory would take more than 7 hours with SEVered [16]. Assuming that a key can reside not only on one but on several pages, the naive extraction would require several hours on average to find the key. Our approach can extract secrets faster by several orders of magnitude.

In cases when $Tracking_{Start}$ is inside the critical window, the attack fails and we extract all tracked pages without finding the secret. In such cases, we have to repeat both the observation and search phase. To avoid a lengthy extraction of all tracked pages in unsuccessful attempts, the search can be canceled early when the likelihood of finding the secret drops, according to our evaluated distribution. For the following search phase, all pages extracted in the previous attempts can then be excluded from extraction given that the secret does not change its location. In sum, our results have shown that our prototype is able to quickly and reliably extract different sensitive secrets and performs well even under high load.

6 DISCUSSION

In the following, we discuss further important aspects of our attack and possible countermeasures:

Overhead. The overhead caused by the tracking itself is limited, because each accessed page only triggers a SLAT page fault once. We neither detected perceivable effects like delays in response times in the HV nor inside the VM. The host system and VM remained stable even on the highest load level. We measured only a small additional delay of web and SSH server responses when tracking was active.

Low Memory. When the VM is low on memory, its kernel might try to free memory by swapping out pages, by unmapping file-backed pages, or by killing processes. A page containing the secret might then be re-used by another process or by the kernel during our attack. In such a case, we are still able to extract the memory contents of the page, but its contents might have already been overwritten. We did not encounter such cases in our tests.

Triggering Activities. In our concept, we start tracking at an undefined point in time and do not actively trigger activities to interfere as little as possible with the VM's normal operation. Our concept worked well in our evaluated scenarios, because we extracted frequently used secrets. In the SSH scenario, however, the key may be used rather infrequently. This is, for instance, the case when an administrator logs in to a web server for maintenance only from time to time. When a secret is rarely used but the attacker requires the observation phase to be as short as possible, the attacker can consider the active triggering of an activity. In the SSH scenario, an attacker can actively start a login procedure without a user account. SSH servers use their key for server authentication and wait for the user to authenticate with a default timeout of two minutes. An attacker can thus initiate a login and extract the SSH key before the session timeout without waiting for a legitimate user to login. Note that active triggering might increase the probability of the attack being detected and might not always be possible.

Portability. We expect that our approach can be transferred to other scenarios and configurations than evaluated. Our approach does not depend on specific service or library versions. Furthermore, our approach is not tied to a specific SEV processor and mostly independent of the VM's performance and OS. Our approach can also be leveraged to extract other types of memory, such as confidential code, documents or images. The performance of our approach can differ on systems with other hard- and software configurations. However, we expect the performance to vary only slightly assuming that $Tracking_{End}$ can be observed quickly. We ran several tests in which we assigned our VM more memory, multiple cores and in which we configured the web servers to utilize a high number of worker processes. The performance indicators remained coherent with our evaluation results in all runs.

Countermeasures. A countermeasure against our attack is to prevent the SEVered attack [16], which we rely on for memory extraction. Further, our attack relies on targeted secrets to remain at their memory location during our attack. Purging secrets in memory after use would cause the search phase to fail. We found TLS and FDE keys to always remain at their memory location in our tests. However, in case of SSH keys, the processes forked by the SSH daemon for initiating new SSH connections purge their private key when a session terminates and then exit. This means that an SSH session must remain open until the secret is extracted. This, for instance, requires a user to remain logged in or a login attempt to remain pending over the time of the search phase, which is less than 1.5 seconds in our case.

Systematically purging all sorts of secrets from main memory after use would require adapting existing software. For some secrets, purging might not be feasible. An example is the FDE key, which is constantly required for disk I/O. A more promising solution is to relocate the most valuable secrets from main memory to dedicated hardware. Since SEVered can only extract contents from main memory, storing secrets in hardware would prevent them from being extracted by a malicious HV. This can, for example, be realized using Hardware Security Modules (HSMs). Additionally, hardware-based disk encryption can be used to protect the FDE key.

7 RELATED WORK

While there are established Virtual Machine Introspection (VMI) frameworks [14, 18, 20] for data analysis and extraction on unencrypted VMs, the systematic extraction of memory from encrypted VMs has not been subject to extensive study. On AMD SEV platforms, the SP protects page encryption and the corresponding keys from the HV. This makes it infeasible to directly read memory contents from SEV-enabled VMs as long as the SP cannot be compromised [13]. Payer [17] early discussed the missing integrity protection on AMD SEV platforms. By remapping memory in the HV, this can be used to extract memory without compromising the SP, as done by the SEVered attack [16]. While SEVered allows the extraction of data, it does not provide concepts for quickly extracting specific secrets.

Buhren et al. presented an attack [11] to gain remote code execution with user privileges on an SEV-enabled VM. Their approach exploits memory remapping to modify the control flow of an SSH service. The first step is an off-line tracing of the system call sequences performed during an SSH login on a comparable, unencrypted VM. The goal of this analysis is to determine the behavior of a VM accessing the login information of the SSH session, the *credentials data structure*. The next step is to wait for a victim user to login to the SSH service. With the information gained in the off-line analysis, they identify the memory page containing the user's login information. They then try to illicitly login by remapping the valid user's credential data structure to the one the SSH service creates during the illicit login attempt. This allows the attacker to re-use the victim user's login information. In their evaluation, they achieved a success rate of around 23%. The low rate was primarily caused by the fact that the SSH service may store the *credentials data structure* at different offsets within the page. As a condition for a successful attack, the SSH service must have stored both the victim user's and attacker's credentials data structures at the same page offset. Besides being quite invasive, this approach requires access to a comparable VM, detailed analysis of the SSH service, user interaction, and data being incidentally stored at specific offsets.

The attack described in [8] follows the same goal of gaining remote code execution on an SEV-encrypted VM, but does not exploit remapping. Instead, the authors describe a *ciphertext block move* attack, which also exploits the missing integrity protection. The authors argue that it is possible to move memory contents in physical memory. This is because the HPA is not part of the AES-based encryption scheme itself but is incorporated into the encryption result in a later step with a reversible physical address-based tweak algorithm that uses static parameters. After reversing the tweak, ciphertext can be moved and the tweak re-applied with the target HPA. The authors describe a method that moves the pages to exploit an SSH process. Both the approaches in [11] and [8] were, to the best of our knowledge, not confirmed on real SEV hardware. The *ciphertext block move* attack could possibly be leveraged for the memory extraction as an alternative to the remapping in SEVered.

On the side of defenses, Fidelius [22] is a software-based extension to SEV. This extension is a privileged module separate from the HV that restricts the HV from accessing specific critical resources with *non-bypassable memory isolation*, for instance, to prevent replay attacks. The authors provide a VM lifecycle concept that describes how to start Fidelius and provide tenants proof that the system runs Fidelius in addition to SEV. This requires trusting the Fidelius module instead of the operating HV.

Intel announced the implementation of its own hardware-based memory encryption approach called Multi-Key Total Memory Encryption (MKTME) [12]. According to our understanding of the specification, MKTME does not protect from a malicious or compromised HV, but only from memory attacks from outside. The HV remains, for instance, capable of enabling or disabling the encryption, or to handle the sharing of memory with other VMs.

8 CONCLUSION

We presented an approach for the efficient extraction of secrets from SEV-encrypted VMs. Compared to time-consuming, naive memory extraction, our two-phased approach exfiltrates secrets unobtrusively and quickly with a high success probability. In the first phase, we track the page accesses of an encrypted VM until detecting an event indicating that the VM recently accessed the secret. In the second phase, we leverage an existing attack for memory extraction to systematically retrieve the tracked pages and simultaneously analyze their contents to quickly identify the secret. We presented various use cases for highly sensitive secrets usually found in VMs in cloud scenarios. We performed an evaluation for these cases on a fully SEV-enabled EPYC processor with varying levels of load, usually caused by independent clients not involved in the attack. Our results show that we are able to extract TLS keys after a handshake in less than 15.5 seconds in the median on lower load levels and in no more than about 32.7 seconds in the median on our highest evaluated load level. The extraction of the FDE key after a disk write event took between less than 7.4 seconds and 12.3 seconds in the median. The extraction phase for SSH keys after an SSH handshake took about 0.8 to 1.35 seconds in the median. We expect that our approach can be used for the extraction of further types of secrets, which we are going to investigate in future work.

ACKNOWLEDGMENTS

This work has been partially funded in the project CAR-BITS.de by the German Federal Ministry for Economic Affairs and Energy under the reference 01MD16004B. We would like to thank Michael Velten for the implementation of the tool that searches extracted memory dumps for the private components of public key moduli, see Section 4.

REFERENCES

[1] Advanced Micro Devices. 2008. Nested Paging. http://developer.amd.com/wordpress/media/2012/10/NPT-WP-1%201-final-TM.pdf.

[2] Advanced Micro Devices. 2018. Secure Encrypted Virtualization API Version 0.16. http://support.amd.com/TechDocs/55766_SEV-KM%20API_Specification.pdf.

[3] Michael Becher, Maximillian Dornseif, and Christian N Klein. 2005. FireWire: All Your Memory Are Belong To Us. *Proceedings of CanSecWest.*

[4] Adam Boileau. 2006. Hit by a bus: Physical access attacks with Firewire. *Presentation, Ruxcon.*

[5] Center for Information Technology Policy at Princeton University. 2008. Memory Research Project Source Code. https://citp.princeton.edu/research/memory/code/.

[6] David Kaplan. 2017. Protecting VM Register State with SEV-ES. White Paper.

[7] Christophe Devine and Guillaume Vissian. 2009. Compromission physique par le bus PCI. *Proceedings of SSTIC.*

[8] Zhao-Hui Du, Zhiwei Ying, Zhenke Ma, Yufei Mai, Phoebe Wang, Jesse Liu, and Jesse Fang. 2017. Secure Encrypted Virtualization is Unsecure. arXiv:cs.CR/1712.05090 https://arxiv.org/abs/1712.05090

[9] Xiao Guangrong. 2016. [PATCH v3 00/11] KVM: x86: Track Guest Page Access. http://www.mail-archive.com/linux-kernel@vger.kernel.org/msg1076006.html.

[10] J. Alex Halderman, Seth D. Schoen, Nadia Heninger, William Clarkson, William Paul, Joseph A. Calandrino, Ariel J. Feldman, Jacob Appelbaum, and Edward W. Felten. 2009. Lest We Remember: Cold-boot Attacks on Encryption Keys. *Commun. ACM* 52, 5 (May 2009), 91–98. https://doi.org/10.1145/1506409.1506429

[11] Felicitas Hetzelt and Robert Buhren. 2017. Security Analysis of Encrypted Virtual Machines. In *Proceedings of the 13th ACM SIGPLAN/SIGOPS International Conference on Virtual Execution Environments (VEE '17).* ACM, New York, NY, USA, 129–142. https://doi.org/10.1145/3050748.3050763

[12] Intel. 2017. Intel Architecture Memory Encryption Technologies Specification. https://software.intel.com/sites/default/files/managed/a5/16/Multi-Key-Total-Memory-Encryption-Spec.pdf.

[13] CTS Labs. 2018. *Severe Security Advisory on AMD Processors.* Technical Report.

[14] LibVMI Project. 2015. LibVMI Virtual Machine Introspection. http://libvmi.com/.

[15] Microsoft. 2017. Microsoft Security Bulletin MS17-008 - Critical. https://technet.microsoft.com/en-us/library/security/ms17-008.aspx.

[16] Mathias Morbitzer, Manuel Huber, Julian Horsch, and Sascha Wessel. 2018. SEVered: Subverting AMD's Virtual Machine Encryption. In *Proceedings of the 11th European Workshop on Systems Security (EuroSec'18).* ACM, New York, NY, USA, Article 1, 6 pages. https://doi.org/10.1145/3193111.3193112

[17] Mathias Payer. 2016. AMD SEV Attack Surface: a Tale of too Much Trust. https://nebelwelt.net/blog/20160922-AMD-SEV-attack-surface.html.

[18] Rekall Forensics. 2018. Rekall. http://www.rekall-forensic.com/.

[19] The Linux Kernel Organization. 2018. The Definitive KVM (Kernel-based Virtual Machine) API Documentation. https://www.kernel.org/doc/Documentation/virtual/kvm/api.txt.

[20] The Volatility Foundation. 2018. Open Source Memory Forensics. https://www.volatilityfoundation.org/.

[21] VMware. 2017. VMSA-2017-0006: VMware ESXi, Workstation and Fusion Updates Address Critical and Moderate Security Issues. https://www.vmware.com/security/advisories/VMSA-2017-0006.html.

[22] Yuming Wu, Yutao Liu, Ruifeng Liu, Haibo Chen, Binyu Zang, and Haibing Guan. 2018. Comprehensive VM Protection Against Untrusted Hypervisor Through Retrofitted AMD Memory Encryption. In *2018 IEEE International Symposium on High Performance Computer Architecture (HPCA).* 441–453. https://doi.org/10.1109/HPCA.2018.00045

[23] Xenproject.org Security Team. 2017. x86: Broken Check in memory_exchange() Permits PV Guest Breakout. https://xenbits.xen.org/xsa/advisory-212.html.

Careful-Packing: A Practical and Scalable Anti-Tampering Software Protection enforced by Trusted Computing

Flavio Toffalini
Singapore University of Technology and Design
ST Electronics-SUTD Cyber Security Laboratory
flavio_toffalini@myemail.sutd.edu.sg

Martín Ochoa
Cyxtera Technologies
ST Electronics-SUTD Cyber Security Laboratory
martin.ochoa@cyxtera.com

Sun Jun
Singapore University of Technology and Design
ST Electronics-SUTD Cyber Security Laboratory
sunjun@sutd.edu.sg

Jianying Zhou
Singapore University of Technology and Design
jianying_zhou@sutd.edu.sg

ABSTRACT

Ensuring the correct behaviour of an application is a critical security issue. One of the most popular ways to modify the intended behaviour of a program is to tamper its binary. Several solutions have been proposed to solve this problem, including trusted computing and anti-tampering techniques. Both can substantially increase security, and yet both have limitations. In this work, we propose an approach which combines trusted computing technologies and anti-tampering techniques, and that synergistically overcomes some of their inherent limitations. In our approach critical software regions are protected by leveraging on trusted computing technologies and cryptographic packing, without introducing additional software layers. To illustrate our approach we implemented a secure monitor which collects user activities, such as keyboard and mouse events for insider attack detection. We show how our solution provides a strong anti-tampering guarantee with a low overhead: around 10 lines of code added to the entire application, an average execution time overhead of 5.7% and only 300KB of memory allocated for the trusted module.

ACM Reference Format:
Flavio Toffalini, Martín Ochoa, Sun Jun, and Jianying Zhou. 2019. Careful-Packing: A Practical and Scalable Anti-Tampering Software Protection enforced by Trusted Computing. In *Ninth ACM Conference on Data and Application Security and Privacy (CODASPY '19), March 25–27, 2019, Richardson, TX, USA.* ACM, New York, NY, USA, 12 pages. https://doi.org/10.1145/3292006.3300029

1 INTRODUCTION

The widespread of commercial software and of potential security threats makes it necessary to develop systematic protection mechanisms. For instance, a customer could attempt to use a program without paying the license fee [38], a player might cheat in a videogame [21], or an anti-virus software can be sabotaged [31] by malware. To achieve these goals, a common strategy is to edit the binary code of such software in order to alter its logic. These threats are often referred to as Man-At-The-End attackers (MATE) [3]. Both academic researchers and commercial companies have spent an extensive effort against MATE threats [5, 12, 16, 18, 50, 53]. The goal of the defending mechanisms is to guarantee that an attack cannot change the software logic to some extent. It is possible to achieve this goal in different ways, *e.g.*, through anti-tampering techniques [36] or through trusted computing technologies [20].

Anti-tampering techniques allow a software to inspect itself and check whether its code has been modified. We refer to those techniques as *self-checking*, which literally read the binary code of the protected software by using special functions called *checkers*. The checkers compute a digital fingerprint of the software bytecode and verify whether that fingerprint matches a pre-computed value [36]. On the other hand, trusted computing technologies provide dedicated hardware so that the software can be executed in secure containers which are physically separated from the rest of the system. Those containers are composed of memory regions that cannot be directly read/written by other processes (either from kernel-space or from user-space). Trusted computing technologies are further reinforced against physical attacks such as flashing BIOS/firmware, page swap, or page cache attacks [13].

However, both anti-tampering and trusted computing have limitations. On the one hand, purely software-based anti-tampering techniques are not completely secure, since the defending mechanisms reside in an untrusted memory region and a determined attacker can identify and disarm such defenses. It is possible to harden anti-tampering techniques by using a combination of additional approaches [6, 10, 11, 51] that raise the bar for the attackers but that do not fundamentally address the problem [22]. On the other hand, trusted computing technologies, which provide higher security guarantees than purely software-based solutions, often have practical limitations, e.g., software within a secure container cannot directly interact with the hosting operating system (OS); and the secure container often has size limitations [7]. Previous works studied solutions that move part of the OS functionality inside a trusted region [4, 7, 47], but they introduce further complexity for employing a secure interaction with the rest of the world (*e.g.*, networking, file system). Other authors suggested protecting only portions of the code [30, 41]. However, these approaches do not address critical limitations such as the interaction with the underlying OS, or the limited amount of memory. Limited memory makes it unsustainable to deploy all processes in dedicated trusted containers. For instance, machines featured with Intel Software Guard eXtension (SGX) [40] provide only a few hundred megabytes that must be shared among all the running trusted containers. If we consider processes such as Skype or Firefox, which require around 100MB each, we need multiple trusted containers for each process to protect. Therefore, this approach does not scale for multiple parallel processes. The introduction of SGX 2.0 allows modifying the size of a single trusted container but it does not modify the maximum memory available for trusted containers.

Our proposal overcomes the limitations of both pure anti-tampering and trusted computing by combining both approaches. We extend hardware security features of trusted computing over untrusted memory regions by using a minimal (possibly fixed) amount of code. To achieve this, we harden anti-tampering functionality (*e.g.*, checkers) by moving them in trusted components, while critical code segments (which invoke the checkers stored within a trusted module) are protected by cryptographic packing. As a result, we keep the majority of the software outside of the secure container, this leads to three advantages: (i) we avoid further sophistication in communicating with the OS, (ii) we maximize the number of trusted containers issued contemporaneously, and (iii) we also maximise the number of processes protected.

Realizing our idea in practice is non-trivial. Besides the self-checking functionalities, we need to carefully design other phases of our approach such as installation, boot, and response. The installation phase must guarantee that the program is installed properly, while the boot phase should validate that the program starts untampered. Both phases require us to solve the attestation problem. The third phase, the response, is the mechanism which allows a program to react against an attack once it has been detected. Moreover, trusted computing technologies, such as SGX, do not offer stand-alone threads that can run independently of insecure code. Instead, protected functionality needs to be called from (potentially) insecure code regions. As a result, such technologies do not provide *availability* guarantees. Therefore, one design aspect of our solution is to cope with and mitigate *denial of service* threats.

As a proof-of-concept, we implemented a monitoring application which integrates our approach. For this example, we opted for SGX as a trusted module. The application is an agent which traces user's events (*i.e.*, mouse movements and keystrokes) and stores the data in a central server. We developed the monitoring agent in C++ and we deployed it in a Windows environment. In our implementation, we designed the checkers to monitor those functions dedicated to collect data from the OS, while the response was implemented as a digital fingerprint which represents the status of the client (*i.e.*, client secure, client tampered).

To evaluate our approach, we systematically analyze which attacks can be performed against our approach and we show that, with the user monitoring application, our solution provides better protection than previous approaches. We measure the overhead of our approach in terms of Lines of Code (LoC), execution time, and trusted memory allocated. We show that fewer than 10 LoC are required to integrate our approach, while the trusted container

requires around 300 LoC. Furthermore, the overhead in terms of execution time is negligible, i.e., on average 5.7% *w.r.t.* the original program. During our experiment, we managed to run and protect up to 90 instances at the same time.

Problem Statement: The research question we are addressing in this work is thus: Is it possible to extend trusted computing security guarantees to untrusted memory regions without moving the code entirely within a trusted module?

Contributions: In summary, the contributions of this paper are: (**a**) We propose a new technique to extend trusted computing over untrusted zones minimizing the amount of code to store within a trusted module. (**b**) We propose a technique to mitigate *denial-of-service* problems in trusted computing technologies. (**c**) We propose an algorithm for achieving a secure installation and boot phase.

Organization. We provide background on SGX and software protection in Section 2. Then, we discuss the threat model in Section 3 and describe our approach and the technical challenges in Section 4. After that, we explain our implementation in Section 5, while we perform an evaluation of our approach in Section 6. Finally, we provide a discussion about related works in Section 7 and conclude in Section 8.

2 BACKGROUND

In the following, we recap some notions of Intel Software Guard eXtension (SGX) [40] and of anti-tampering techniques.

2.1 Software Guard eXtention Overview

Although our approach is not bounded to one particular trusted computing technology, we have chosen to develop our first proof-of-concept prototype based on Intel Software Guard eXtension (SGX) [40].

At the core of SGX are *enclaves*. An enclave is a memory region located in the user-space which contains trusted functions. A system can host multiple enclaves at the same time, each of which has a dedicated set of pages (4kB each) in DRAM. Each enclave has direct access only to its own page set and it cannot read/write pages belonged to other enclaves. Processes in neither the user-space nor the kernel-space can direct access to an enclave's pages. Figure 1 shows the SGX memory structure. This is achieved by using a *Processor Reserved Memory* layout (PRM), which reserves a subset of DRAM pages only for enclaves instantiations. The system assigns some pages of PRM to a specific enclave, this association is maintained thanks to the *Enclave Page Cache* (EPC). Finally, SGX keeps track of the status of each page assigned by a specific table called the Enclave Page Cache Map (EPCM).

SGX provides a gateway mechanism for calling trusted functions in the enclaves, which is implemented by a dedicated instruction (*ECALL*). All trusted functions are enumerated at the compilation time. Then, a process calling a trusted function will provide a pointer to the enclave along with the number of the function to call. The passage of parameters from the untrusted zone to the trusted one is implemented through a proxy mechanism: SGX provides a set of functions for moving parameters into the enclave, and also for retrieving the return values. SGX also allows pointer parameters that

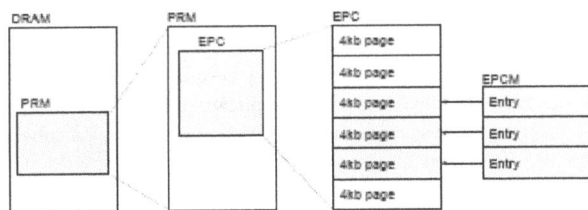

Figure 1: Intel Software Guard eXecution Memory Structure

allow a trusted function to directly read/write untrusted memory regions.

To export data outside an enclave, SGX provides a mechanism called *sealing*. Sealing works by encrypting a buffer of bytes before it leaves the trusted memory region. Through sealing, an enclave can encrypt a secret (*i.e.,* a variable) such that only the enclave itself can read it again. It is also possible to encrypt a secret such that two or more enclaves can read it. To achieve it, SGX provides an attestation process which guarantees the identification of an enclave and the hardware in which it is deployed. Sealing is used when an enclave needs to store its state in a non-volatile storage, or else when an enclave needs to share information with another one inside the same machine or over a network.

It is possible to implement multi-threading computation in SGX, *i.e.,* trusted functions, which belong to the same enclave, can be called simultaneously by threads. We refer to parallel trusted function as *trusted threads*, while the normal threads are called *untrusted threads*. The number of secure threads is statically defined at compilation time, and each (trusted) thread status is maintained by structures (TCS) within the enclave, SGX also provides secure synchronization mechanisms (*i.e.,* locks). Moreover, it is possible to use policies that guarantee an *untrusted* thread to be always bounded to the same *trusted thread*. This feature allows us to extend our approach to multi-threading programs.

As introduced before, enclaves suffer from *denial-of-service, e.g.,* a malicious OS might avoid execution of the trusted functions. In this work, we show how our approach can mitigate these limitations.

2.2 Anti-Tampering Techniques

We say that a program P is tamper-resistant if P is designed such that an attacker would have difficulties to modify P's code. There are several strategies for achieving this goal [36]. In this work, we focus on *self-checking*. These techniques work at bytecode level, and they are structured such that the software can read its own bytecode in order to find anomalies and then reacts accordingly. We call *checkers* those sections of the software which check the software status, and *responses* those which react to the checkers' requests.

A checker's duties include reading a portion of the software's bytecode and verifying whether that code matches specific expectations. That is, the checker computes a hash code of the bytecode using a hashing function and compares the hash value with a pre-computed value. Once a mismatch is found, the software might adopt different reactions, *e.g.,* it can emit an alarm or restore the un-tampered code.

To prevent the checkers from being disabled by an attacker, they typically spread over the code and/or triggered randomly during the execution. Checkers, hash functions, and hash values can be prone to attack; therefore, an anti-tampering protection must be designed for protecting itself. This is achievable by using different techniques, *e.g.,* through obfuscation techniques [6], or a network of checkers (which communicate with each other so that if one checker is disabled/tampered, other checkers become aware of the attack).

3 THREAT MODEL

In a tampering attack, the goal of an attacker is to edit the code of a victim program [12]. This goal can be achieved in different ways. One way is to change the bytecode of a program before its execution, this is called *off-line* tampering. That is, the attacker first analyzes the binary of the program and then disables/removes the anti-tampering mechanisms. The challenge for an attacker is thus to remove the anti-tampering mechanism without compromising the program logic. Using tools such as debuggers or analyzers, the attacker can deduce how the anti-tampering protection works and disable it accordingly. To cope with *off-line* attacks, it is possible to adopt anti-tampering mechanisms based on digital fingerprint mechanisms. They employ a cryptographic fingerprint of software (*e.g.,* signature, hash, checksum) to validate software status before the execution [2, 33]. Besides *off-line* attacks, there are the so-called *on-line* attacks. In this category, the attacker aims to edit the code during the execution of the victim program. Such attacks can be performed either from the kernel-space or from the user-space. The key to such attacks is to synchronize the attacker and the victim process such that the victim code is edited in a way unnoticed by the anti-tampering mechanism.

In our scenario, an attacker can compromise the victim logic (*i.e.,* the bytecode) by using both *off-line* and *on-line* approaches. We also consider acceptable to steal the victim software, or a piece of, as long as this keeps the environment unaltered. A suitable example for our scenario is represented by distributed anti-viruses. This software is composed by a client-server infrastructure and they are commonly used in companies. In particular, the clients report the status of their host machine to a central server, and the server stores the reports and eventually notifies an intrusion. In our example, it is possible to mount a set of attacks that will be easily detected. For instance, if a client is disabled, the central server will detect the anomaly, similarly if an unauthorized client is installed. If an attacker manages to steal a copy of the client software, it may be possible to run a tampered client in a controlled environment made ah-hoc, however, as long as the attacker cannot run such client in the original infrastructure, there is not effective damage for the companies. A tampered client becomes really dangerous when the attacker manages to run such client in the corporate environment in order to allow illicit activities. In this case, the attack has to happen such that the central server does not recognize the anomaly.

The attacker model we consider works at user-space level; therefore, we assume the kernel is healthy. Having a healthy kernel is acceptable in corporate scenarios where the machines are constantly checked. Moreover, a user-space threat (*e.g.,* user-space malware, spyware) is generally simpler to mount than one at kernel-space.

Even though we assume having a trusted kernel, and we could have instantiated our approach on the kernel itself, we opted to implement our PoC by using SGX in order to raise the bar for attackers that have compromised the kernel, as we will discuss in the following sections. We also assume the machines are not virtualized, this avoids the attacker to use VMX features [49]. Moreover, we assume the task scheduler is trusted, this is crucial to avoid a perfect synchronization of two processes (see Section 6.5).

To sum up, the adversary we face has the following properties: (i) he can analyze and change the binary *off-line*; (ii) he can change the *on-line* memory of a victim process at runtime; (iii) he cannot tamper with the task scheduler; (iv) he cannot virtualize the victim machine.

4 DESIGN

Our *anti-tampering technique* is an extension of the classic *self-checking* mechanism. In the following, we describe how we improve upon existing techniques with trusted computing technologies. We start with a description of the problem addressed and then analyze limitations of existing approaches before explaining how our idea can help to limit the attacking surface of existing approaches.

4.1 Challenges

In our model, a program's execution can be described as a triplet (M, b, i) where M represents the state of the program (*i.e.*, memory), b is the sequence of instruction to execute (*i.e.*, code section) and i denotes the next instruction to execute (*i.e.*, instruction pointer). For simplicity, we focus on sequential and deterministic programs, whose instructions are executed step-by-step; however, in Section 4 we will discuss also multi-threading scenarios. Each step of the program can be represented as follows:

$$(M, b, i) \rightarrow (M', b', j),$$

where M' is the updated memory status, b' is the updated instruction sequence, and $\rightarrow$ is the small-step semantics of the program. From a software security point of view, a program should satisfy the following properties: (i) the next instruction j must be decided uniquely by the program logic (*i.e.*, M and the current instruction at i); (ii) the program state M' must be determined according to the previous program state M, and the instruction executed i; (iii) instructions b must not change during the program execution (*i.e.*, $b = b'$). Note that we assume that the application code is not dynamically generated, and that input and output operations happen through writing/reading operation in the memory.

Property (i) is related to the control flow integrity problem [29], which is guaranteed neither by anti-tampering techniques [36] nor by trusted computing [28]. But it is tackled by tools such as [32, 46] and discussed in previous works [1, 14, 37, 52, 54].

Property (ii) can be guaranteed by moving only sensitive data inside a trusted module and using *get()\set()* functions for interacting with them. This was already implemented by Joshua et al. [30] in their Glamdring tool. Such a solution is prone to space constraint because it keeps data within the trusted module (*i.e.*, an enclave).

Property (iii) can be implemented by moving all code inside trusted modules, which was the first approach employed [4, 7, 47].

However, simply moving all code into the trusted module has two problems. First, a trusted module has a limited amount of memory available, and therefore only certain critical sections can be executed securely. Second, the application needs access to other OS layers to interact with the environment (network, peripherals). Our approach aims to address these limitations.

A naive *anti-tampering* mechanism is to run a *checker* function over the entire code b right before executing any instruction. This is described as follows:

$$(M, b, i) \rightarrow check(b) \rightarrow (M', b', j),$$

where the *check()* function verifies the integrity of the code b. This approach verifies the integrity of the entire application code at each step. However, this is inefficient since a program must read its entire code at each step. Furthermore, we must protect the *checker* function throughout the program.

In order to address space and efficiency constraints, as suggested in [9, 43, 44], we may consider only certain parts of the program to be sensitive, which are referred to as *critical sections* (CS) hereafter. CSs include delicate parts of the software such as license checking in commercial products. We could thus focus on protecting only the critical part of the program and checking a block of instructions instead of the entire program (*i.e.*, CSs). That is, instead of checking every instruction in every step, we check only the CSs. Therefore, the function check() is executed when we encounter an instruction starting a CS. This is illustrated as follows:

$$(M, b, i) \xrightarrow{\text{if } i \in \text{CS}} check(CS) \rightarrow (M', b', j)$$
$$(M, b, i) \xrightarrow{\text{else}} (M', b', j),$$

where $i \in$ CS means the instruction i is the beginning of a critical section CS and *check(CS)* checks the critical section CS.

Intuitively, even though the above idea improves the efficiency of the anti-tampering mechanism, it is still subject to attacks. Firstly, it is subject to just-in-time patch & repair. That is, an attacker could synchronize its actions to change the victim code right after the checking and restore the original code before the checker is executed again. To conduct such an attack (without having to compromise the task scheduler), the attacker and the software to be protected must run as concurrent processes, and the attack must time its actions according to the task scheduler. We argue that this attack is practically very challenging to carry out. In Section 6.5, we discuss the feasibility of such attacks in more depth. Secondly, an attacker may compromise the anti-tampering mechanisms (*i.e.*, modify the checkers and responses). Defenses against these attacks already exist. For instance, one may employ code obfuscation on *checkers* and *responses* so that the attacker would not identify them; or design the *checkers* and *responses* such that they are strongly interconnected with the application code [8] so it is challenging to compromise the anti-tampering mechanisms without compromising the application logic; or move part of the code (*e.g.*, checkers and responses) to the server [51]. These approaches are however prone to a similar threat, *i.e.*, all of them allocate their detection system in untrusted zones, and therefore, with enough time any attacker can understand and disarm these systems.

4.2 Anti-Tampering based on Trusted Computing

In this section, we will present the technical solutions to realize our approach in a real system. To achieve this, we require a trusted module to harden anti-tampering techniques. For the sake of coherence with our proof-of-concept implementation (see Section 5), we use the Intel Software Guard eXtension (SGX) [40] terminology. However, it is possible to use other trusted modules (see Section 6.6).

Unlike previous solutions that simple "hide" checking functions by adopting obfuscation or anti-reversing techniques [6, 10, 11, 51], we store code relevant to the anti-tampering mechanism in a trusted module (i.e., an enclave), through which we monitor and react to attacks conducted on the untrusted memory region. Saving anti-tampering mechanisms within trusted containers is significantly different from previous purely software-based solutions since an attacker cannot directly tamper with them. This is illustrated in Figure 2, which presents an overview of our technique. In detail, a given application is divided into two zones: an untrusted zone (on the left side) and a trusted zone (on the right side). The untrusted zone contains the entire application code, whereas the trusted zone contains all functions and global variables employed by our anti-tampering technique, such as *checkers* and *responses* (shown in blue). The untrusted zone is further divided into different regions: the CSs which we aim to protect (shown in red), the non-sensitive blocks (shown in pale yellow) and the code for calling the trusted functions in the trusted zone (shown in green). We also included three labels (i.e., a, b, and c) to identify specific regions that will be used ahead in the discussion. By using this structure, we can check the status of the untrusted zone by being inside the trusted zone.

Critical Section Definition. A CS is any continuous region of code which is surrounded by two instructions, respectively labeled as *CS_Begin* and *CS_End*, and that satisfies the following rules:

(1) *CS_Begin* and *CS_End* must be in the same function.
(2) For each program execution, *CS_Begin* is always executed before *CS_End*.
(3) Every execution path from a *CS_Begin* must reach only the corresponding *CS_End*.
(4) Every execution path which connects *CS_Begin* and a *CS_End* must not encounter other *CS_Begin* instructions.
(5) A CS cannot contain try/catch blocks
(6) We consider function calls from within a CS as atomic, i.e., we do not consider the called function as a part of the CS.
(7) The loops contained by a CS must be bounded to a known constant.

Points (2) and (3) can be implemented by using a forward analysis [34] of all possible branches from *CS_Begin* to *CS_End*, and considering all function calls as atomic operations. We also desire that a CS contains only unwinding loops to minimize the time in which a CS is plain. The other points are simply static patterns. The above rules are implemented by static analysis at compilation time. If a CS does not satisfy one of those requirements, the compilation process is interrupted. Therefore, we assume having only valid CSs at runtime.

In order to maintain the application stable, and to reduce the attacker surface, we desire that at most one CS remains decrypted

(plain) during each thread execution. This is achieved by introducing a global variable, called *plain_cs*, within the trusted zone (as illustrated in Figure 2-c). The variable *plain_cs* indicates which CS is currently decrypted. Also, as we will illustrate later, the value of *plain_cs* is updated by encrypt() and decrypt() functions. For sake of simplicity, we describe the following techniques by considering only single-thread programs. While we extend our approaches to multi-threading programs at the end of this section.

Overcoming Denial of Service Issues. Even if a trusted function is protected from being tampered with, usually trusted computing components do not provide availability guarantees, in the sense that the code in the trusted zone must be invoked externally. We overcome this limitation by employing *packing* [48], a technique which is often used by malware to hide its functionality, combined with a heartbeat [18]. Our intuition is to force the untrusted zone to call trusted functions in order to execute application logic. This configuration is depicted in Figure 2-a. In the beginning, CSs are encrypted (red shape). Therefore an attacker cannot directly change CSs' content, and the code cannot be executed unless unpacked. Each CS is surrounded by calls to two functions, which are called decrypt() and encrypt(). In our design, decrypt() and encrypt() functions has the role of *checkers*. Those functions take a CS identification (e.g., CS address) as an input, then they apply cryptographic operations to the CS by using a private key. The private key is stored inside the trusted module (see Figure 2-c). The first call (green shape) points to the decrypt() function which performs three operations: (i) it decrypts the CS, (ii) it sets *plain_cs* to CS, and (iii) it performs a hash of the code to check the CS integrity. Once this checker is executed, the CS contains plain assembly code that can be processed. As a result, the untrusted zone *must* call the checker in order to execute the CS's code. After the CS, a second call (green shape) points to the encrypt() function which performs three operations: (i) it encrypts the CS, (ii) it sets *plain_cs* to *NULL*, and (iii) it performs a hash of the code to check the CS integrity. Note that decrypt() and encrypt() are considered as atomic. These functions are used as primitive to build more sophisticated mechanisms later. We illustrate the runtime packing algorithm in Figure 3. In the beginning, the CS is encrypted (i.e., $E[CS]$) while the decrypt() function is executed (Figure 3-1). After the decryption phase, the CS is plain (white color) and it is normally executed (Figure 3-2). Finally, the encrypt() function is executed and the CS gets encrypted again (Figure 3-3).

Together with the packing mechanism already explained, we employ a parallel heartbeat as a response, which is depicted in Figure 2-c. The heartbeat is implemented by calling a response() function which resides within the trusted zone. The response's duty is to select a random CS and validate its hash value along with its respective decrypt and encrypt function calls, the outcome of this check is an encrypted packet shipped to a server that validates the application status. The heartbeat does not prevent software tampering, it is a *responsive* strategy to alert a central system about an attack. To implement a heartbeat, it is possible to adopt different strategies, e.g., we can set a dedicated thread which is risen according to a time series, or else we can merge the heartbeat with a communication channel between the client and the server (as we opted in our proof-of-concept application).

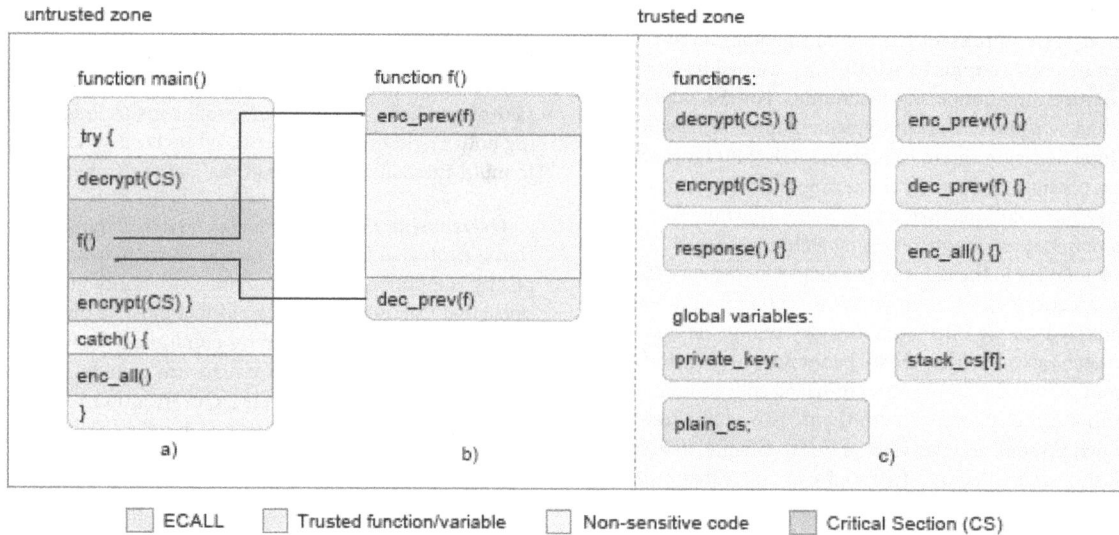

Figure 2: An overview of our schema for single-thread applications, the memory is split in trusted and untrusted zones. The trusted zone contains all methods required for our technique, while in the untrusted zone we show the interaction of those methods with the CSs.

Function Calls and Recursions. Since we allow a CS to host function calls, a CS might remain plain after a call. This potentially increases the attacker surface. To mitigate this issue, we desire that a CS is encrypted once the control leaves the CS itself, and decrypted again right after. This is achieved by introducing two new functions, namely enc_prev(f) and dec_prev(f), which are handled by the trusted module, as described in Figure 2-b. At compilation time, we instrument all functions that are directly called from within a CS by adding a function call toward enc_prev(f) in their preamble, and toward dec_prev(f) for each of its exit point (*i.e.,* return operation). Both enc_prev(f) and dec_prev(f) functions require a parameter f, this parameter identifies which is the function that calls enc_prev(f) and dec_prev(f). Since several CSs can call the same function f, we introduce a stack for each function f to handle these cases, as depicted in Figure 2-c. These stacks are global variable inside the trusted module, we identify the stack for the function f as follows:

$$stack\_cs[f] = stack<CS>().$$

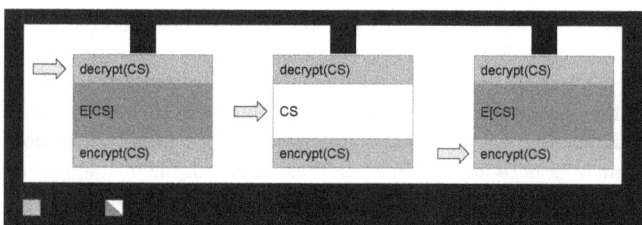

Figure 3: Packing mechanism of our schema.

The enc_prev(f), dec_prev(f) functions and the stack_cs[f] interact through each other in the following way. Once enc_prev(f) is called, it identifies whether the control comes from a CS by checking the global variable *plain_cs*. If it is the case, the function performs two operations: (i) it pushes *plain_cs* in stack[f], and (ii) it calls encrypt(plain_cs). Therefore, after calling enc_prev(f) the system reaches this status: (i) the outer CS is encrypted (and thus protected), (ii) *plain_cs* is set to *NULL*, and (iii) the thread is ready to handle a new CS. Similarly, once the control leaves the function f, the epilogue calls dec_prev(f). This function performs two operations: (i) it pops the last CS from stack[f] into *plain_cs*, and (ii) it restores the previous CS status by calling decrypt(plain_cs). As a result, the control can safe pass to the outer CS. In the opposite scenario, once the control enters in the function f and the *plain_cs* is set to *NULL*, it means that the function f was not called by a CS; and therefore, enc_prev(f) and dec_prev(f) do nothing. Stacks allow us to handle recursions, if the function f is repetitively called, we trace all previous CSs.

Exceptions within Critical Section. We can handle exceptions from within a CS by introducing a new function, namely enc_all(), which is handled by the trusted module, as described in Figure 2-c. This function is an alias for encrypt(plain_cs). That is, we wrap any CS with a try/catch block at compilation time, as described in Figure 2-a. The exception block is made such that (i) to catch all exceptions, (ii) to run enc_all(), (iii) to throw the exception again. In this way, we restore the anti-tampering mechanism as soon as an exception appears. Thus, after an exception, we encrypt all the plain CSs and the application can continue normally. Note that the *response* function has to be extended in order to protect the *catch* block, or else, an attacker might raise an exception in order force a CS to be plain[1].

Multi-threading programs. We can extend the previous techniques in order to handle parallel computation, this is possible because some trusted computing technologies allow multi-threading programming, like SGX (see Section 2.1). To achieve multi-threading, we maintain a *plain_cs* and a stack_cs[f] for each thread. Moreover, we introduce a counter for each CS. These global variables represent the number of threads which are executing a CS in a specific moment. In the beginning, the CSs' counters are set to *zero*. Then, they are increased and decreased by decrypt() and encrypt() functions respectively.

Ensuring a Secure Booting Phase. Our approach requires that the program has a secure booting phase, which means having the following assumptions for the *encrypt, decrypt* and *response*: the key for crypto algorithms must be loaded in a secure way together with a table which describes where the CSs are located (*i.e.,* their address and length) with their hash values. We refer to this table as *block table*. We assume a trusted loading of this information by adopting SGX sealing and attestation mechanisms. Those mechanisms ensure to store information on a disk or to establish a secure channel with other enclaves within the same machine (*i.e.,* local) or with a remote one (*i.e.,* remote) in a trusted way. Details on sealing and attestation are discussed in Section 2.1.

5 IMPLEMENTATION

In this section, we describe a proof-of-concept implementation of our anti-tampering technique, whose architecture is depicted in Figure 4. The application is composed by a central server that handles a set of clients which are spread over a network. Each client is a monitoring application that traces user's activities (*i.e.,* keystrokes and mouse traces) and sends the data to the central server. As a trusted module, we opted for the Intel Software Guard eXtension (SGX) [40], however, it is possible to use other solutions that involves the kernel (*e.g.,* TPM [26]). We deployed the architecture in a Windows environment. Through this application we describe the specific technical solutions we adopted for the client, and how we implemented installation phase, boot phase, and response.

5.1 Client

We describe the internal structure of the client in order to clarify some practical implementation strategies. We developed this application in C++ and we deployed it on Windows machines. For sake of simplicity, we did not implement Address Space Layout Randomization (ASLR) [45], however, it is possible to deduct the right address offset by employing a Drawbridge system [39].

Software Architecture. The client is formed by three modules: the main program, and two dynamic linked libraries (DLL) namely untrusted DLL and trusted DLL. This architecture is depicted in Figure 5, the application communicates with the untrusted DLL to call the functions described in Section 4. The untrusted DLL works together with the trusted DLL (*i.e.,* the enclave) to handle the whole anti-tampering technique. We choose this architecture to

simplify the integration of our anti-tampering system. In this way, the developer can focus on the main program and integrate the anti-tampering system later. Each component of the architecture is described as follows:

- **Application:** this is the client that we aim to enforce. Natively, it contains all the functionalities for collecting information from the underline OS and ship them to the server.
- **Untrusted DLL:** this contains the untrusted functions for interacting with the enclave. Also, it keeps track of the status of the enclave (*i.e.,* enclave pointer) and exposes routines procedures.
- **Trusted DLL (enclave):** this is the enclave. It contains the trusted functions described in Section 4 (*e.g.,* checkers, response) along with some extra routine functions (*i.e.,* installation and boot).

Critical Section Definition. Since this client is a monitoring agent, we identify as CSs those functions used to collect the information issued by the OS: PAKeyStroked, which collects keystroked, and its twin PAMouseMovement, which collects mouse events. These functions are callback risen by the OS along with the relative event information. For sake of simplicity, we trust in argument passed by the OS. The main duties of these functions are: (i) collecting the data, (ii) crafting a packet with the data collected, (iii) signing the

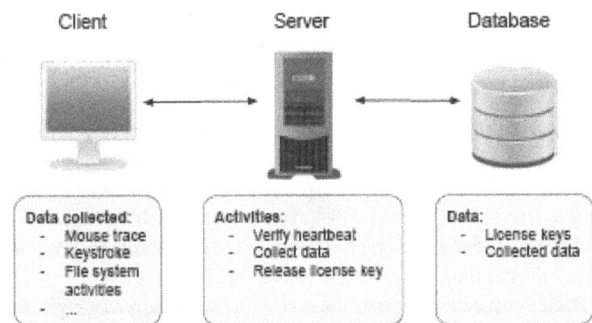

Figure 4: The architecture of proof-of-concept program. The client is a monitoring agent which collects user's activities, the server handles clients, and the database stores collect data and license keys.

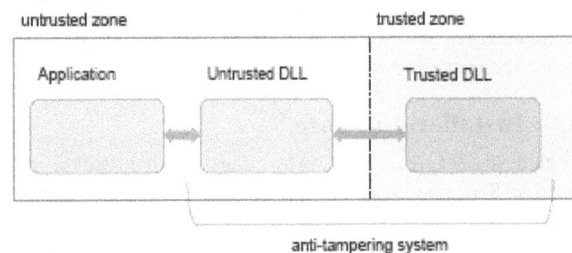

Figure 5: The software organization of the client.

---

[1]We do not deal with runtime attacks to exception handlers, such as SEH, since they do not belong to anti-tampering problems.

packet, and finally (iv) shipping it to the server. Since in our implementation we required only integrity, we implemented a digital fingerprint.

Packaging Algorithm. The packaging algorithm adopted is an AES-GCM encryption schema [55] between the assembly code and the license key. SGX natively provides an implementation of this algorithm [25].

Heartbeat. The heartbeat is implemented as a digital fingerprint which is used on all packets exchanged between client and server, our strategy allows the server to validate client status by testing the digital fingerprint itself and also for mitigating *denial-of-service*.

The digital fingerprint is created by feeding a *sha256* function with the concatenation of the message to sign, the license key, and a special byte called *check byte*, which can have two values (*safe*, or *corrupted*) according to the status of the program. The digital fingerprint algorithm randomly selects a CS and sets the *check byte* accordingly. Then, the server verifies the digital fingerprint by guessing the *check byte* value used at the client side. That is, the server crafts the two digital fingerprints by using the two possible values of the *check byte*. If one of the generated digital fingerprints matches the original one, the server can infer the status of the client (*i.e.*, it is healthy or tampered). Otherwise, that means the message was corrupted, or it was originated by the wrong machine. This simple heartbeat implementation allows the sever to identify *denial-of-service* at client side. If an attacker switches off the monitor agent, the communication will be immediately affected.

In our implementation, we adopted semaphores in order to avoid conflicts with checking functions, and we added timestamps to exchanged packets for avoiding replay attacks.

Block Table. Packaging and heartbeat functions require the coordinates of all CSs (start address, size, and hash-value) along with the license key for running. This information can be handled mainly in two ways: a) the client loads the entire table in the enclave memory; b) the client loads the entire table in the untrusted zone and adds a digital fingerprint to guarantee entries integrity.

Both approaches have pro and cons. The first approach guarantees also confidentiality at the table. Moreover, since the table is stored in the enclave, all trusted functions can retrieve the entries faster. On the other hand, if the table is too large the enclave might be overloaded. The second approach is lighter in term of memory consumption because it keeps all rows within the untrusted zone. However, in this case, the algorithm results slowly because it has to inspect the untrusted zone to retrieve the entries and to verify their integrity. In our implementation, we opted for the second option where each entry is protected by using the license key and stored within the untrusted memory region.

5.2 Installation Phase

We achieve a secure installation by using an authentication protocol based on SGX remote attestation, the entire protocol is depicted in Figure 6. In this scenario, the server has a database which contains all license keys, all the CSs, and the block table of each client. On the other side, each client is only formed by the program to protect, with the encrypted CSs already replaced, and its enclave, which contains *checkers*, *responses*, and *installation* routines.

Licensing System The goal of the installation phase is to deliver the correct *license key* to the respective client in a secure fashion. To achieve this, each client instance uses a different *private key* to decrypt its CSs. The *private key* is directly derived from the *license key*. That is, each client instance requires its own *license key* to work properly. In the following paragraph, we exploit this fact to authenticate a client to the server.

Installation Procedure In this phase, the aim of the client is to perform a remote attestation with the server, this latter then verifies client's identity and releases the relative license key and the block table, which allows the client to run properly. In order to establish a remote attestation, the enclave is signed by a certification authority and the server is awarded for the certificates shared with clients.

In the beginning, the client and the server follow the remote attestation mechanism described by Intel in [24] (Figure 6-0). After this, both entities can rely on a secure end-to-end channel. Also, this allows the server to obtain the client measurement, which is a cryptographic hash that probes the client enclave version and the client hardware. This information is used by the server to bind client identity and license key. Once the channel is created, the client sends an installation request to the server (Figure 6-I), the request is an encrypted CS which is randomly taken from the client itself. The server receives the installation requests, and it verifies which license key belongs to the CSs. Then, the server binds the client measurements with the license key, and it releases this latter to the client along with the block table (Figure 6-II). When the enclave receives the license key and the block table, it will seal all in the client machine. At this point, only the client can read these information through SGX sealing process (Figure 6-III). Even if a malicious client forces a signed enclave to send an installation request with a CS to the server, the retrieved license key will be sealed on the machine, and only the signed enclave can read it.

At this point, the installation phase is concluded: the server has the information about the location of the client and the key license and block table are securely stored on the client machine.

6 EVALUATION

We evaluated our technique from different perspectives. At first, we quantify the overhead in terms of Lines of Code (LoC), execution time (microbenchmark), and memory required by our enclave. Then, we discuss the impact of several security threats to the infrastructure proposed. Finally, we perform an empirical evaluation of the likelihood to accomplish a just-in-time attack.

6.1 Lines-of-Code Overhead

A useful metric to measure the impact of our technique is the amount of code added to the original program, this is illustrated in Table 1. Looking at the table, it is possible to notice that the majority part of the code is contained in the main program (96, 5%). The Untrusted and Trusted DLL, which implement our anti-tampering technique, require respectively 2, 0% and 1, 5% of the code. Within the main program, each CS contains only two lines of code, one for calling `decrypt()` function and another for calling `encrypt()` function. We remark that through our technique it is possible to protect an indefinite number of CSs by using always the same amount of code in the enclave.

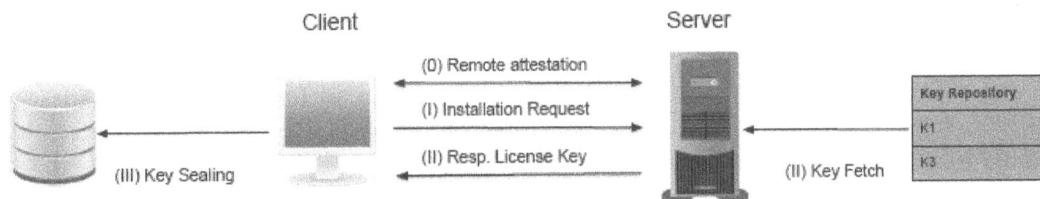

Figure 6: Secure installation protocol between client and server.

Table 1: Number of LoC for each module

Module	LoC	Perc.
Main program	12175	96,5%
Untrusted DLL	248	2,0%
Trusted DLL	186	1,5%

6.2 Microbenchmark Measurements

In these experiments, we perform a set of microbenchmark to measure the overhead in time introduced by our technique. As a use case, we measure the execution time of the CSs in our proof-of-concept monitoring agent (see Section 5). At first, we briefly introduce the experiment setup. Then, we measure the execution time of the CSs with and without our anti-tampering technique. Finally, we measure the execution time of the CSs in case of multiple instances. All execution times are measured in milliseconds.

User-Simulator Bot. For performing the following tests, we developed a user-simulator bot which mimics the standard user activity by stroking keys and moving the cursor. The bot is a Python script which is based on the *PyWin32* library. Since we aim at measuring the monitoring agent's performances, we designed a very basic user-simulator's behavior. The user-simulator generates keystrokes on a text program (*i.e.,* notepad) and randomly moves the mouse around the screen. Keystroke frequency is around 100 words per minute, while mouse speed is around 500 pixel per second. This bot allows us to easily repeat the experiments.

Single Instance Microbenchmark. We measure the impact of our anti-tampering technique to the performances of the CSs in our proof-of-concept monitoring agent. In this experiment, we performed 5 exercises, each of one is composed by two runs, namely with and without the anti-tampering technique. For each run, we traced the CS's execution time. The outcome of the experiment is plotted in Figure 7. In the plot, each bar represents the average elapsed time for a run and each pair of bars represents a single exercise. More precisely, orange bars mean runs with the anti-tampering technique active, while blue bars mean runs without. Looking at the graph, we can see that functions require on average between 2ms and 2.4ms for being executed. It is also evident that with the anti-tampering technique the performances are slightly degraded. On average, the delta time is 0.12ms, with a peak of 0.34ms for the second instance. Also, time overhead is less than 6% on average, with a peak of 16.61% in the second instance. This

peak depends on the system status at execution time. According to our experiments, we conclude that the performances degradation is negligible after the introduction of our anti-tampering system.

Multiple Instances. We empirically investigate whether our approach can be deployed over multiple processes at the same time. We performed this test by running a different number of instances of our proof-of-concept monitoring agent and then measuring the average execution time of their CSs.

The outcome of the experiment is depicted in Figure 8. The plot shows the average execution time of the CS on the y-axis (expressed in milliseconds), while the number of instances is indicated on the x-axis (from 10 to 90). Looking at the plot, it is possible to notice that the average execution time grows linearly *w.r.t.* the number of instances. The average execution time is around 5ms in case of 10 parallel instances, while it degrades to 11ms in case of 90. This means that the performances get only halved after decupling the number of instances; therefore, our technique results scalable.

6.3 Enclave Size Considerations

In our proof-of-concept monitoring agent, we used an enclave that occupies at around 300*KB*. As we stated, in our approach the enclave size does not depend by the size of the software to protect. This allows us to estimate the number of processes we can protect at the same time. In a common machine SGX featured (*e.g.,* Dell XPS 13 9370), we can dedicate at most 128*MB* for enclaves. If we

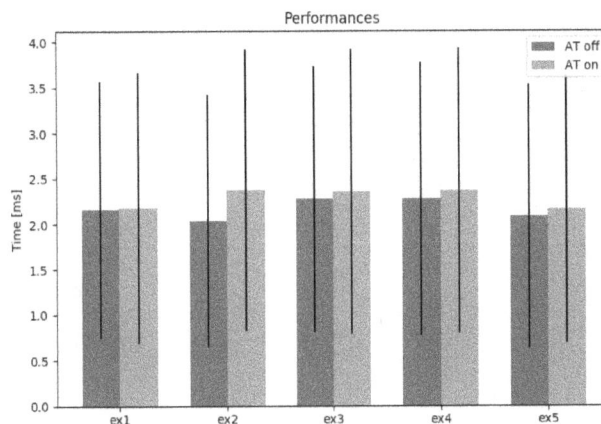

Figure 7: Average response time with and without anti-tampering technique

consider the enclave used in our proof-of-concept, we can roughly estimate at around 400 enclaves contemporaneously loaded that will protect the same number of processes.

6.4 Threat Mitigation

We explain how our approach mitigates threats according to the attacker model described in Section 3.

Protection of checkers and responses. In our approach, the functions for anti-tampering mechanisms (*e.g.*, *checker* and *response*) reside in a trusted module. Since we assume trusted computing guarantees hardware isolation, those functions are protected by design.

Protection against disarm. An attacker can always disarm a function by removing its invocation. Moreover, SGX is prone to *denial-of-service attacks* due to its nature (see Section 2.1). We protect trusted invocations by adopting the packaging tactic discussed in Section 4. The software contains parts of code which are encrypted and they need checkers action for being executed properly.

Just-in-time Patch & Repair Mitigation. After a *decryption* function is run, the CS is plain and ready to be executed. At this moment, there is a chance for the attacker to replace the code within a CS and restore it before the next *encryption*. This is called just-in-time patch & repair attack.

Assuming the attacker cannot directly tamper with the task scheduler (as described in Section 3), it is still possible to perform attacks from the user-space [19]. However, those attacks are not strong enough to bypass our defense for mainly three reasons: (i) they are tailored for specific contexts (*e.g.*, single core, OS version), (ii) they aim at slowing down a process and not to achieve a perfect synchronization between adversary and victim, (iii) modern OSs mount task schedulers which are designed to resist (or at least mitigate) such attacks [27]. To achieve an *on-line* tampering, as introduced in Section 3, an attacker must replace a CS code such that encrypt() and decrypt() functions do not notice the replacement. This means that a single error will be detected by the server.

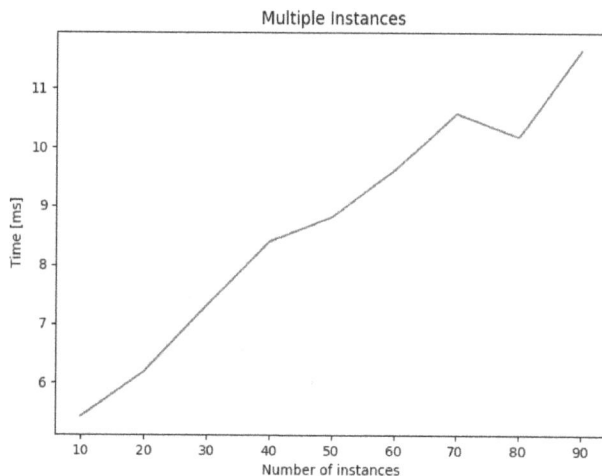

Figure 8: Average response time with multiple instances

None of the attacks from user-space can achieve such precision. An alternative approach is to adopt virtualization to debug a process step-by-step at runtime, but this contradicts the assumptions of our threat model (*i.e.*, the original infrastructure is not altered). We, however, try to estimate the likelihood that this attack might happen by performing an empirical experiment which will be described in Section 6.5.

Reverse Engineering. An attacker may attempt to reverse the application code in order to extract the plain code hidden in the encrypted blocks, and then build a new executable which does not contain any checker. The new executable is therefore prone to any manipulation. This goal can be achieved by using debuggers and/or analyzers. Even though the literature contains several anti-debugging techniques and most of them can be enforced by using our anti-tampering technique, we assume that an attacker can bypass all of them. However, an attacker cannot debug the software inside the trusted zone, which is true for SGX enclaves compiled in release mode [23]. The best an attacker can do is debugging the code within the untrusted memory region and considering the enclave as a black box. After applying these considerations, we can state an attacker can manage to dump the plain code after that *decryption* functions are called, and even make a new custom application. However, this attack is still coherent with our threat model (see Section 3) because the new application cannot work into the original infrastructure (*i.e.*, the heartbeat cannot work properly) and therefore it is useless. For instance, in the implementation presented in Section 5, the monitoring agent can work properly only if the software contains all the functions employed by our technique along with the original CSs. If this is not respected (*i.e.*, by removing checkers) the application cannot emit a correct heartbeat, and therefore the attack is not considered accomplished.

6.5 Study of Just-in-Time Patch & Repair Attack

In this experiment, we investigate the likelihood of a just-in-time patch & repair attack in a real context. Here, the attacker's goal is to temporarily replace the bytecode within a CS such that the injected code is executed but the system cannot realize the attack. The setup is formed by a victim process (*i.e.*, our agent) and an attacker process. Also, we consider a trusted task scheduler, and that each process is executed on a dedicated core. Both attacker and victim are written in C++ and developed for Windows, the experiments were run on a Windows 10 machine with 16GB RAM and Intel® Core™ i7-7500 2, 70GHz processor.

The victim process is formed by an infinite loop which continuously updates an internal variable through a CS. This latter is enforced by self-checking mechanisms. Moreover, the victim process contains a checker to validate the status of the program. If the internal status is set wrongly, that will be logged. The attacker process, instead, is a concurrent process which can edit the victim process at runtime. Attacker's goal is to replace the victim CS such that the internal variable of the victim process will contain an incongruent value. We attempted the attack for 10.000 times, but the self-checking mechanism managed to detect all attacks. Therefore, we consider that this kind of attack is not practical in case of a trusted task scheduler.

6.6 Discussion

We have shown how to implement our technique by means of a case study involving a monitor agent, however there are few aspects to note about the validity of our evaluation effort. First, although the application code is protected, an attacker can still analyze and change variable values at runtime, thus potentially harming its normal execution. Note that our approach could be extended in order to mitigate this issue by using cryptographic hashes to validate the integrity of certain critical variables. Moreover, our design and implementation requires a healthy kernel, otherwise it would be possible to mount attacks such as the just-in-time patch and repair attack we discussed previously (by manipulating the scheduler). We believe that even with a compromised kernel mounting those attacks would require significant effort, but we leave a more thorough investigation for future work. Other aspects, such as an evaluation of applying our technique a different granularities (such as basic-block level), or extending protection to *PLT, GOT,* and *exception table* are also left for future work.

7 RELATED WORK

We considered works which deal with to Intel Software Guard eXtension (SGX) [40] and anti-tampering techniques.

Anti-tampering techniques Morang et al. [35], Ghost et al. [18], and Dewan et al. [15], base their anti-tampering techniques on hyper-visor level. In all works, authors rely trustiness on the hyper-visor, while we propose a *self-checking* mechanism which is built on top of a trusted module. Feng et al. [17] propose an anti-cheating mechanism for video-games. In their approach, they simulating client logic on a server to identify inconsistencies. Unlike them, we spot client anomalies by using a *self-checking* system.

Viticchié et al. [51] developed an anti-tampering mechanism which is based on a remote attestation. Here, the client is moved to a trusted server. Their approach is substantially different than ours because they do not rely on a trusted module. Also, their mechanism forces an application to be partially moved to a server, while we do not alter client structure.

Commercial anti-tampering solutions for video-games, such as [16, 50], perform a software signature which communicates with a trusted server; however, they do not consider trusted computing for improving software protection.

Software protection by using SGX The first strategy for protecting applications by using SGX was moving the whole code inside an enclave. This was proposed by Baumann et al. [7], and by Tsai et al. [47] after. They respectively developed Haven (for Windows) and Graphene (for Linux), which are tools that allow one to execute legacy applications inside an enclave. Their attacker model is the Iago attacker, which consider the host OS as malicious, while our attacker model aims at modifying code at runtime from user-space. These tools contain a micro-kernel inside an enclave that communicates through a Drawbridge system with the host OS [39]. A spin in this direction was proposed by Seo et al. [42], who extend the project Graphene by adding Address Space Layout Randomization (ASLR) features. Arnautov et al. [4], instead, deployed previous approaches to Docker containers in their tool SCONE. All these systems have a common approach: they run the whole application in an enclave. However, they need to introduce

some compromise: Haven and Graphene need specific libraries for the OS. Moreover, they limit applications' features (*e.g.,* Haven does not allow graphical interfaces, SCONE do not support fork() operations), also, they limit application size because of the enclave limitation. Our approach, instead ,can protect a vast code surface exploiting few code lines in the enclave without any additional library or limitation in term of features.

Another approach for SGX technology is to move into enclave only those parts of the application which are considered secure-sensitive. This approach was adopted by Schuster et al. [41], who combined MapReduce framework and SGX enclaves to perform big data analysis. In this work, authors define ad-hoc enclave for their application. This approach was then automatized by Joshua et al.[30], who proposed a tool (Glamdring) that moves critical sections (and variables) into automatically generated enclaves. Our approach is different because we protect critical sections without moving them inside enclaves.

8 CONCLUSION

In this work, we presented a novel anti-tampering technique which leverages trusted computing technologies. We achieved this by adopting a packing strategy that is similar to the one used by malware to hide its functionality. Our approach forces a program to call trusted functions in order to be executed properly (by unpacking a piece of software from a trusted container).

We implemented a proof-of-concept prototype of our technique by using Intel Software Guard eXtension (SGX) [40] technology. We illustrated our approach by protecting an agent that was designed to collect user's event and ship them to a central server. Through this implementation, we showed how our architecture can guarantee further security properties such as a secure installation and a continuous client monitoring.

Using our prototype, we measured the overhead in terms of lines of code (less than 10 lines), execution time (on average 5.7% more), and space required for the trusted container (300*KB*). In sum, our approach results in a scalable and practical software protection solution.

ACKNOWLEDGMENTS

This research was supported by ST Engineering Electronics and National Research Foundation, Prime Minister's Office Singapore, under Corporate Laboratory @ University Scheme (Programme Title: STEE Infosec - SUTD Corporate Laboratory). This work was also partly supported by SUTD start-up research grant SRG-ISTD-2017-124.

REFERENCES

[1] Martín Abadi, Mihai Budiu, Ulfar Erlingsson, and Jay Ligatti. 2005. Control-flow integrity. In *Proceedings of the 12th ACM conference on Computer and communications security*. ACM, 340–353.
[2] Tigist Abera, N. Asokan, Lucas Davi, Jan-Erik Ekberg, Thomas Nyman, Andrew Paverd, Ahmad-Reza Sadeghi, and Gene Tsudik. 2016. C-FLAT: Control-Flow Attestation for Embedded Systems Software. In *Proceedings of the 2016 ACM SIGSAC Conference on Computer and Communications Security (CCS '16)*. ACM, New York, NY, USA, 743–754. https://doi.org/10.1145/2976749.2978358
[3] Adnan Akhunzada, Mehdi Sookhak, Nor Badrul Anuar, Abdullah Gani, Ejaz Ahmed, Muhammad Shiraz, Steven Furnell, Amir Hayat, and Muhammad Khurram Khan. 2015. Man-At-The-End attacks: Analysis, taxonomy, human aspects, motivation and future directions. *Journal of Network and Computer Applications* 48 (2015), 44 – 57. https://doi.org/10.1016/j.jnca.2014.10.009

[4] Sergei Arnautov, Bohdan Trach, Franz Gregor, Thomas Knauth, Andre Martin, Christian Priebe, Joshua Lind, Divya Muthukumaran, Dan O'Keeffe, Mark Stillwell, et al. 2016. SCONE: Secure Linux Containers with Intel SGX.. In *OSDI*. 689–703.

[5] Sebastian Banescu, Mohsen Ahmadvand, Alexander Pretschner, Robert Shield, and Chris Hamilton. 2017. Detecting Patching of Executables without System Calls. In *Proceedings of the Seventh ACM on Conference on Data and Application Security and Privacy*. ACM, 185–196.

[6] Sebastian Banescu and Alexander Pretschner. 2017. A tutorial on software obfuscation. *Advances in Computers* (2017).

[7] Andrew Baumann, Marcus Peinado, and Galen Hunt. 2015. Shielding applications from an untrusted cloud with haven. *ACM Transactions on Computer Systems (TOCS)* 33, 3 (2015), 8.

[8] Philippe Biondi and Fabrice Desclaux. 2006. Silver needle in the Skype. *Black Hat Europe* 6 (2006), 25–47.

[9] David Brumley and Dawn Song. 2004. Privtrans: Automatically partitioning programs for privilege separation. In *USENIX Security Symposium*. 57–72.

[10] Hoi Chang and Mikhail J Atallah. 2001. Protecting software code by guards. In *Digital Rights Management Workshop*, Vol. 2320. Springer, 160–175.

[11] Ping Chen, Christophe Huygens, Lieven Desmet, and Wouter Joosen. 2016. Advanced or not? A comparative study of the use of anti-debugging and anti-VM techniques in generic and targeted malware. In *IFIP International Information Security and Privacy Conference*. Springer, 323–336.

[12] Christian S. Collberg and Clark Thomborson. 2002. Watermarking, tamper-proofing, and obfuscation-tools for software protection. *IEEE Transactions on software engineering* 28, 8 (2002), 735–746.

[13] Victor Costan and Srinivas Devadas. 2016. Intel SGX Explained. *IACR Cryptology ePrint Archive* 2016 (2016), 86.

[14] Lucas Davi, Ahmad-Reza Sadeghi, Daniel Lehmann, and Fabian Monrose. 2014. Stitching the Gadgets: On the Ineffectiveness of Coarse-Grained Control-Flow Integrity Protection.. In *USENIX Security Symposium*, Vol. 2014.

[15] Prashant Dewan, David Durham, Hormuzd Khosravi, Men Long, and Gayathri Nagabhushan. 2008. A Hypervisor-based System for Protecting Software Runtime Memory and Persistent Storage. In *Proceedings of the 2008 Spring Simulation Multiconference (SpringSim '08)*. Society for Computer Simulation International, San Diego, CA, USA, 828–835. http://dl.acm.org/citation.cfm?id=1400549.1400685

[16] Evenbalance. 2017. PunkBuster. http://www.evenbalance.com/pbsetup.php Last visit on 13 Nov 2017.

[17] Wu-chang Feng, Ed Kaiser, and Travis Schluessler. 2008. Stealth Measurements for Cheat Detection in On-line Games. In *Proceedings of the 7th ACM SIGCOMM Workshop on Network and System Support for Games (NetGames '08)*. ACM, New York, NY, USA, 15–20. https://doi.org/10.1145/1517494.1517497

[18] Sudeep Ghosh, Jason D Hiser, and Jack W Davidson. 2010. A secure and robust approach to software tamper resistance. In *International Workshop on Information Hiding*. Springer, 33–47.

[19] D. Gullasch, E. Bangerter, and S. Krenn. 2011. Cache Games – Bringing Access-Based Cache Attacks on AES to Practice. In *2011 IEEE Symposium on Security and Privacy*. 490–505. https://doi.org/10.1109/SP.2011.22

[20] Walter Allen Helbig Sr. 1998. Trusted computer system. US Patent 5,841,868.

[21] G Hoglund. 2006. Hacking world of warcraft: An exercise in advanced rootkit design. *Black Hat* (2006).

[22] Bill Horne, Lesley Matheson, Casey Sheehan, and Robert E Tarjan. 2001. Dynamic self-checking techniques for improved tamper resistance. In *ACM Workshop on Digital Rights Management*. Springer, 141–159.

[23] Intel. 2016. Intel SGX: Debug, Production, Pre-release what's the difference? https://software.intel.com/en-us/blogs/2016/01/07/intel-sgx-debug-production-prelease-whats-the-difference Last visit on 30 Nov 2017.

[24] Intel. 2016. Remote (Inter-Platform) Attestation. https://software.intel.com/en-us/node/702984 Last visit on 6 Dec 2017.

[25] Intel. 2018. Rijndael AES-GCM encryption API. https://software.intel.com/en-us/node/709139 Last visit on 10 Mar 2017.

[26] ISO. 2015. ISO/IEC 11889-1:2015. https://www.iso.org/standard/66510.html Last visit 13 Nov 2017.

[27] Kernel.org. 2018. CFS Scheduler. https://www.kernel.org/doc/Documentation/scheduler/sched-design-CFS.txt Last visit on 20 Aug 2018.

[28] Jaehyuk Lee, Jinsoo Jang, Yeongjin Jang, Nohyun Kwak, Yeseul Choi, Changho Choi, Taesoo Kim, Marcus Peinado, and Brent Byunghoon Kang. 2017. Hacking in darkness: Return-oriented programming against secure enclaves. In *USENIX Security*. 523–539.

[29] J. Li, X. Tong, F. Zhang, and J. Ma. 2018. Fine-CFI: Fine-Grained Control-Flow Integrity for Operating System Kernels. *IEEE Transactions on Information Forensics and Security* 13, 6 (June 2018), 1535–1550. https://doi.org/10.1109/TIFS.2018.

2797932

[30] Joshua Lind, Christian Priebe, Divya Muthukumaran, Dan OâĂŹKeeffe, Pierre-Louis Aublin, Florian Kelbert, Tobias Reiher, David Goltzsche, David Eyers, Rüdiger Kapitza, et al. 2017. Glamdring: Automatic application partitioning for Intel SGX. In *Proceedings of the USENIX Annual Technical Conference (ATC)*. 24.

[31] Cybellum Technologies LTD. 2017. Double Agent. https://github.com/Cybellum/DoubleAgent Laste visit 15 Nov 2017.

[32] Microsoft. 2015. Control Flow Guard (CFG). https://msdn.microsoft.com/en-us/library/windows/desktop/mt637065(v=vs.85).aspx Last visit on 28 Nov 2017.

[33] Microsoft. 2017. Driver Signing. https://docs.microsoft.com/en-us/windows-hardware/drivers/install/driver-signing Last visit on 02 Mar 2018.

[34] Anders Møller and Michael I Schwartzbach. 2012. Static program analysis.

[35] B. Morgan, ÅĹ. Alata, V. Nicomette, M. KÃćaniche, and G. Averlant. 2015. Design and Implementation of a Hardware Assisted Security Architecture for Software Integrity Monitoring. In *2015 IEEE 21st Pacific Rim International Symposium on Dependable Computing (PRDC)*. 189–198. https://doi.org/10.1109/PRDC.2015.46

[36] Jasvir Nagra and Christian Collberg. 2009. *Surreptitious software: obfuscation, watermarking, and tamperproofing for software protection*. Pearson Education.

[37] Kaan Onarlioglu, Leyla Bilge, Andrea Lanzi, Davide Balzarotti, and Engin Kirda. 2010. G-Free: defeating return-oriented programming through gadget-less binaries. In *Proceedings of the 26th Annual Computer Security Applications Conference*. ACM, 49–58.

[38] onhax.me. 2017. Bypass license in Android. https://onhax.me/bypass-license-verification-failed Last visit on 15 Nov 2017.

[39] Donald E Porter, Silas Boyd-Wickizer, Jon Howell, Reuben Olinsky, and Galen C Hunt. 2011. Rethinking the library OS from the top down. In *ACM SIGPLAN Notices*, Vol. 46. ACM, 291–304.

[40] Carlos Rozas. 2013. Intel® Software Guard Extensions (Intel® SGX). (2013).

[41] Felix Schuster, Manuel Costa, Cédric Fournet, Christos Gkantsidis, Marcus Peinado, Gloria Mainar-Ruiz, and Mark Russinovich. 2015. VC3: Trustworthy data analytics in the cloud using SGX. In *Security and Privacy (SP), 2015 IEEE Symposium on*. IEEE, 38–54.

[42] Jaebaek Seo, Byounyoung Lee, Seongmin Kim, Ming-Wei Shih, Insik Shin, Dongsu Han, and Taesoo Kim. 2017. SGX-Shield: Enabling address space layout randomization for SGX programs. In *Proceedings of the 2017 Annual Network and Distributed System Security Symposium (NDSS), San Diego, CA*.

[43] Lenin Singaravelu, Calton Pu, Hermann Härtig, and Christian Helmuth. 2006. Reducing TCB complexity for security-sensitive applications: Three case studies. In *ACM SIGOPS Operating Systems Review*, Vol. 40. ACM, 161–174.

[44] Scott F Smith and Mark Thober. 2006. Refactoring programs to secure information flows. In *Proceedings of the 2006 workshop on Programming languages and analysis for security*. ACM, 75–84.

[45] Kevin Z Snow, Fabian Monrose, Lucas Davi, Alexandra Dmitrienko, Christopher Liebchen, and Ahmad-Reza Sadeghi. 2013. Just-in-time code reuse: On the effectiveness of fine-grained address space layout randomization. In *Security and Privacy (SP), 2013 IEEE Symposium on*. IEEE, 574–588.

[46] Caroline Tice, Tom Roeder, Peter Collingbourne, Stephen Checkoway, Úlfar Erlingsson, Luis Lozano, and Geoff Pike. 2014. Enforcing Forward-Edge Control-Flow Integrity in GCC & LLVM.. In *USENIX Security Symposium*. 941–955.

[47] Chia-Che Tsai, Donald E Porter, and Mona Vij. 2017. Graphene-SGX: A practical library OS for unmodified applications on SGX. In *Proceedings of the 2017 USENIX Annual Technical Conference, Santa Clara, CA*.

[48] Xabier Ugarte-Pedrero, Davide Balzarotti, Igor Santos, and Pablo G Bringas. 2016. Rambo: Run-time packer analysis with multiple branch observation. In *Detection of Intrusions and Malware, and Vulnerability Assessment*. Springer, 186–206.

[49] Rich Uhlig, Gil Neiger, Dion Rodgers, Amy L Santoni, Fernando CM Martins, Andrew V Anderson, Steven M Bennett, Alain Kagi, Felix H Leung, and Larry Smith. 2005. Intel virtualization technology. *Computer* 38, 5 (2005), 48–56.

[50] Valve. 2017. Valve Anti-Cheat System (VAC). https://support.steampowered.com/kb_article.php?p_faqid=370 Last visit 13 Nov 2017.

[51] Alessio Viticchié, Cataldo Basile, Andrea Avancini, Mariano Ceccato, Bert Abrath, and Bart Coppens. 2016. Reactive Attestation: Automatic Detection and Reaction to Software Tampering Attacks. In *Proceedings of the 2016 ACM Workshop on Software PROtection*. ACM, 73–84.

[52] Zhi Wang and Xuxian Jiang. 2010. Hypersafe: A lightweight approach to provide lifetime hypervisor control-flow integrity. In *Security and Privacy (SP), 2010 IEEE Symposium on*. IEEE, 380–395.

[53] Windows. 2012. Windows Media DRM 10 (Janus). http://www.samsung.com/ca/support/skp/faq/20189 Last visit on 15 Nov 2017.

[54] Mingwei Zhang and R Sekar. 2013. Control Flow Integrity for COTS Binaries.. In *USENIX Security Symposium*. 337–352.

[55] Gang Zhou, Harald Michalik, and Laszlo Hinsenkamp. 2007. Efficient and high-throughput implementations of AES-GCM on FPGAs. In *Field-Programmable Technology, 2007. ICFPT 2007. International Conference on*. IEEE, 185–192.

Behind Enemy Lines: Exploring Trusted Data Stream Processing on Untrusted Systems

Cory Thoma
University of Pittsburgh, PA
corythoma@cs.pitt.edu

Adam J. Lee
University of Pittsburgh, PA
adamlee@cs.pitt.edu

Alexandros Labrinidis
University of Pittsburgh, PA
labrinid@cs.pitt.edu

ABSTRACT

Data Stream Processing Systems (DSPSs) execute long-running, continuous queries over transient streaming data, often making use of outsourced, third-party computational platforms. However, third-party outsourcing can lead to unwanted violations of data providers' access controls or privacy policies, as data potentially flows through untrusted infrastructure. To address these types of violations, data providers can elect to use stream processing techniques based upon computation-enabling encryption. Unfortunately, this class of solutions can leak information about underlying plaintext values, reduce the possible set of queries that can be executed, and come with detrimental performance overheads.

To alleviate the concerns with cryptographically-enforced access controls in DSPSs, we have developed Sanctuary, a DSPS that makes use of Intel's Software Guard Extensions (SGX) to protect data being processed on untrusted infrastructure. We show that Sanctuary can execute *arbitrary* queries while leaking no more information than an idealized Trusted Infrastructure system. At the same time, an extensive evaluation shows that the overheads associated with stream processing in Sanctuary are comparable to its computation-enabling encryption counterparts for many queries.

ACM Reference Format:
Cory Thoma, Adam J. Lee, and Alexandros Labrinidis. 2019. Behind Enemy Lines: Exploring Trusted Data Stream Processing on Untrusted Systems. In *Proceedings of Ninth ACM Conference on Data and Application Security and Privacy (CODASPY '19)*. ACM, New York, NY, USA, 12 pages. https://doi.org/10.1145/3292006.3300021

1 INTRODUCTION

Data Stream Processing Systems (DSPS) have been proposed to execute long-running continuous queries (CQs) over large volumes of fast moving, transient data. DSPSs have applications in a variety of domains such as medical device monitoring, social media, and wearable/mobile devices. Often, DSPSs make use of outsourced third-party computational platforms, such as Microsoft Azure or Amazon EC2, to reduce the overall monetary cost of maintaining the DSPS and to allow for hardware flexibility and service scalability. Such use of a third-party system, however, may violate the confidentiality constraints and access controls of data providers by permitting an unauthorized third-party to view their data.

To address this issue, data providers often specify access controls to limit the disclosure of their sensitive data. These access controls

can be enforced by either trusting the DSPS (and its underlying infrastructure) to abide by the specified policies, or through cryptographic mechanisms. The use of a DSPS for enforcement requires that the data provider have some level of established trust with not only the DSPS, but also with the platform on which the DSPS is executing (e.g., Amazon EC2), which may often not be the case. Naive use of cryptography requires the decryption of information prior to query processing, and thus eliminates the possibility of in-network processing on untrusted infrastructure. Fortunately, recent work such as PolyStream [35] and Streamforce [3] makes use of computation-enabling cryptographic techniques. Computation-enabling cryptographic schemes allow some level of query execution to be processed directly on encrypted data (e.g., an order-preserving cryptographic scheme will allow a user to execute an arbitrary range query on a protected data stream). Such solutions can allow for third-party systems to be utilized for processing since data is again protected, and the underlying DSPS framework can remain unchanged.

Unfortunately, these systems are limited in the scope of what *types* of query operators can be supported. For instance, without prior collaboration between data providers, data consumers cannot execute an arbitrary join query over streams emitted by two or more data providers, as each provider will be encrypting their streams using a different key. Moreover, the operations available to consumers are dictated by *how* data providers encrypt their data. For example, if a data provider does not encrypt using an order-preserving encryption scheme, consumers will not be able to execute range queries over encrypted data. As a result, supporting a rich—albeit still limited—collection of operations requires a data provider to encrypt its data in multiple ways (once for each type of operations to be enabled), resulting in increased data transmission overheads.

The use of computation-enabling encryption further has the side effect of leaking peripheral information about a data stream. For instance, a deterministic encryption scheme retains the equality property of the underlying data, which permits a querier to test the equality of two values. This, however, also allows outside observers to learn a distribution of the underlying values. Similarly, the use order-preserving encryption allows outside observers to learn the distribution and relative ordering of underlying values. A data provider can opt out of any given computation-enabling encryption scheme if they deem that the information leaked is too excessive, but this limits the scope of queries that can be executed.

To help alleviate these types of concerns, we explore the use of Intel's Software Guard Extensions (SGX) for securely executing arbitrary data stream queries on third-party systems while minimizing peripheral leakage of information. Our prototype system, Sanctuary, handles only encrypted data and makes use of SGX enclaves to process arbitrary operations over this data in a manner that prevents the exposure of underlying plaintext characteristics. In developing Sanctuary, we make the following contributions:

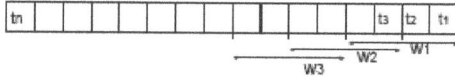

Figure 1: Sliding window with a length of 4 tuples and a slide of 2 tuples.

- We develop Sanctuary, a Data Stream Processing System that utilizes SGX enclaves to support the execution of arbitrary streaming relational operations over sensitive data on untrusted third-party infrastructure.
- SGX enclaves have access to a limited memory (128 MB). Often, stateful operators will require more memory than what an enclave can provide. To this end, we present algorithms for stateful relational operators used by Sanctuary that are designed for the memory-limited enclave environment.
- We provide a detailed analysis of the information that can be gathered by an adversary when using Sanctuary. We show that Sanctuary can achieve a greater level of data protection when compared to state-of-the-art cryptographically-enforced access controls, and further show Sanctuary to be near ideal in terms of information leakage when compared to a baseline system.
- Finally, we carry out an in-depth evaluation of each relational streaming operation in Sanctuary and compare it to similar relational streaming operations for both unprotected (i.e., plaintext) data, and different computation-enabling encryption techniques [3, 35]. We further include enclave-enabled operators as part of larger query networks and evaluate the overheads associated with their use.

The remainder of this paper is organized as follows. We overview SGX and related work in Section 2. We describe the Sanctuary architecture and threat model in Section 3. We detail the challenges in enclave-enabled relational streaming operators and the overheads associated with them in Section 4. We present enclave-enabled limited memory streaming operators used by Sanctuary in Section 5. We provide a detailed discussion on information leakage in Section 6 and evaluate operations and queries that use SGX enclaves in Section 7. Finally, we conclude in Section 8.

2 BACKGROUND AND RELATED WORK

Here, we overview related work and describe Intel's SGX at a level that is sufficient to fully understand the remainder of the paper.

2.1 Data Streaming Systems

Data Stream Processing Systems (DSPSs) either operate on a single machine [1, 4], or are distributed over a cluster or wide-area-network of machines [2, 10, 21, 34]. In a distributed environment (DDSPSs), continuous queries can place individual streaming operations on different, sometimes geographically distant, compute nodes to reduce the network overheads [7, 15, 27, 30], total monetary cost [27], or computational cost of the query [19, 33]. Given the nature of a DSPS, outsourcing computation is desirable to help allocate or re-allocate appropriate resources for each streaming query. However, this may lead to a potential violation of a data provider's access controls.

In this paper, we assume a common streaming model (as assumed in [23, 24, 35]) where data providers distribute data through third-party cloud computing systems. Data consumers place streaming operators onto the cloud system for data processing.

Data streaming operators can broadly be classified into two types: stateless and stateful. *Stateless* operators execute on one

tuple of a data stream at a time, without any knowledge of prior tuples, to produce a result (e.g., filter out all values over a certain threshold). *Stateful* operators require some knowledge of prior or concurrent tuples in order to produce a result. Typically, these operators keep this information in a *window* that defines a length of time or a number of tuples that are used to compute a result. For instance, a querier may wish to know the average stock price over the last *five minutes*, which requires the streaming operator to keep a window for the last five minutes worth of tuples. In addition to this window, a querier can elect to use a *slide* to form a *sliding window*. A slide simply defines how often the querier desires to receive a window's result. For instance, consider Figure 1. A querier requests the average stock price for the last four tuples but wants the latest average reported *every two tuples* (i.e., a window of 4 with a slide of 2 tuples) (the moving brackets labeled w1, w2, and w3) to yield a finer granularity for their application.

2.2 Access Controls in DDSPSs

To address the privacy and access control concerns of a data provider, several systems and algorithms have been proposed. These systems can be broadly characterized into two groups: *trusted third-party* and *untrusted third-party* access control enforcement. In a trusted third-party access control enforcement environment, data providers specify access controls and allow an outsourced third-party to enforce these access controls. Systems such as FENCE [23, 24] enforce access controls by adding special streaming operators that enforce access controls by filtering tuples that are not permitted to be accessed by a querier. Other systems rewrite queries or alter streaming operators [11–13, 25], while others focus on protecting a single system, such as Borealis [22]. This class of solutions exposes provider data to the infrastructure itself, and must trust the infrastructure to correctly enforce provider access control policies.

Systems that do not trust third-party access control enforcement will rely on cryptographically-enforced access controls. Rather than forcing a querier to process data only after it has been decrypted, systems like PolyStream [35] and Streamforce [3] allow the data provider to use specialized computation-enabling encryption techniques to enable third-party computation for a querier *directly on encrypted data*. These systems, however, limit the expressiveness and accessibility of a queriers' potential query. In Streamforce, a querier may only access *integer* data via a *view-like* format, (i.e., only allowing filtering and aggregations on numeric data). PolyStream supports a richer set of query operations than Streamforce, but cannot support join or complex user-defined functions over streams from multiple providers. Furthermore, these systems also leak information about the underlying plaintext values, such as equality, relative partial ordering, or relationships between groups of tuples (i.e., the encrypted aggregate of some encrypted data).

To help overcome these limitations and provide an alternate avenue for untrusted third-party computation, in this paper, we enable a querier to employ remote SGX enclaves to ensure private computation and to restore expressiveness by allowing for *any* streaming operation to execute on the third-party system.

2.3 SGX

*Overview:*Intel's Software Guard Extensions (SGX) [16] are a set of architectural enhancements to recent Intel processors that provide developers with the ability to create a trusted environment within an untrusted machine. An enclave is given exclusive use of a core of the CPU while it is executing, meaning that no other processes can access on-chip storage, as enforced by the CPU. Further, when the enclave is either finished processing or the CPU has an interrupt, all data is encrypted and written to memory so that no other process can access the plaintext data. An enclave, therefore, offers a developer the opportunity to trust the computation of a third party device in terms of confidentiality (sensitive data values cannot be observed outside of the enclave) and integrity (attempted modifications to protected data or instructions will be detected). SGX also supports the use of remote attestation processes to ensure the integrity of an enclave being staged onto a remote machine.

There are certain aspects of SGX enclave use that a developer must consider. Each interrupt to the SGX-enabled core causes the CPU to encrypt and write data out to unprotected memory, and each further startup causes that data to be brought back into the CPU and decrypted. These *context switches* can cause the overall enclave execution to slow down and can negatively impact performance. Developers need to be cognizant of these types of overheads when making use of enclave technology. Further, enclave memory is limited to at most 128 MB at any given time. Any large-scale, in-memory processes will be severely hindered by this cap and will require the developer to manage swapping to (encrypted) non-enclave memory on-the-fly. The remainder of this paper is devoted to exploring the use SGX enclaves for streaming application, with a focus on exploring algorithms that work with the above issues with SGX enclaves to allow data consumers to make use of third-party computation platforms that provide SGX-enabled CPUs.

SGX for Data Protection: Current work in SGX-enabled computation has focused on many different areas, from securing ZooKeeper data [9]; to managing transactions, or enterprise rights management privately [18]; to segregating linux containers [6]. Secure-Stream [17] is a system that explores the use of Intel's SGX as a way to execute Map-Reduce streaming applications. Further, VC3 [31] builds a Map-Reduce engine on top of SGX hardware that allows for attestation of code and data on a powerful adversary. In Sanctuary we focus on streaming relational data operators and the challenges associated with windowed operators and memory limitations.

Opaque [37] augments SQL operators so that their memory accesses are hidden and operate within an SGX enclave. Similarly, EnclaveDB [29] provides SQL operators that execute with an SGX enclave. Finally, SGX-BigMatrix [32] provides a high level language that can be used to provide secure, enclave-enabled computations. Sanctuary is complementary to these previous works, as it is designed to enable enclave-protected, real-time relational stream processing with the goal of overcoming the limitations of state-of-the-art cryptographic stream processing systems while also providing enhanced security (cf. Section 6).

3 ARCHITECTURE AND THREAT MODEL

This section overviews the architecture, system model, and threat model assumed by Sanctuary.

3.1 Architecture and System Model

The architecture and system model assumed by Sanctuary are presented in Figure 2. We assume queries are specified in a declarative language like the Continuous Query Language (CQL) [5]. The Sanctuary optimizer (which is/can be run locally on the querier's trusted machine) transforms the query into a set of streaming operators that will need to be ordered and placed in the query network. The

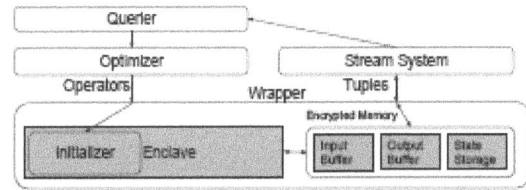

Figure 2: Architecture of an SGX-enabled stream processing system (with a single SGX-enabled core on a single node).

optimizer in Sanctuary may decide to place an operation in an SGX enclave and will use the initializer (which can either operate as part of the streaming operator's code base or even within an enclave) to do so. The work of the initializer is detailed in Section 3.3. We assume that all encryption keys between the data provider and the consumer are transmitted off-line (as described in Section 3.3).

Once the initializer and optimizer have finished executing, all operations are placed and the query may execute. As encrypted data arrives, it is placed into a non-enclave memory Input Buffer. Once the enclave occupies the CPU-core, data will be read from this buffer, decrypted (with the key provided to the initializer during the enclave provisioning step), processed, and encrypted results are stored in the non-enclave memory Output Buffer to be further propagated through the query network. If state must be kept when the enclave does not occupy the CPU, it is encrypted and stored in the State Storage non-enclave memory buffer.

In this paper, we assume that all relevant data arrives encrypted. Individual data packets are represented as *tuples* with *fields* for each piece of information within a data tuple. Tuples can be represented by a *schema* that describes each field (e.g., {ID(int), name(string), heartrate(int), date(dateTime)} or something similar). A schema can also be described using a *key-value* approach.

3.2 Threat Model

Sanctuary is designed to execute operators on an *untrusted* computational platform. We assume that the untrusted party is *honest-but-curious* (an assumption also made in [35], [3], and [28]). An honest-but-curious adversary is one that will not maliciously alter, drop, or add data but will rather try to learn information about the victim by reading and understanding their data. This follows from our system model: it is expected that third-party service providers are attempting to earn money and be successful by providing a cloud computing service. Maliciously altering, dropping, or adding data will result in lost customers and a negative reputation, ultimately causing them to lose money. We further assume that the SGX hardware itself remains uncompromised; i.e., it is patched against side-channel attacks such as Spectre [20] and Foreshadow [36]. As we later detail, Sanctuary is data oblivious with respect to its use of cryptographic keys, which are unlikely to be leaked via side-channel attacks. We further detail how Sanctuary is *not* data oblivious in terms of the data being processed in Section 6.

Sanctuary aims to prevent third-party service providers and adversaries observing the network from being able to obtain or infer the underlying plaintext data produced and transmitted by a data provider. Moreover, Sanctuary allows for data to be fully encrypted during transit to prevent inference of the underlying plaintext values. Finally, Sanctuary aims at limiting the leakage of ancillary data (e.g., tuple value distributions, orderings, etc.) to the service provider and third-parties observing the system.

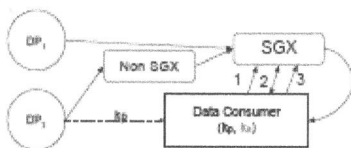

Figure 3: An example scenario of Sanctuary query deployment.

3.3 Deployment Model

Processing a query in Sanctuary involves three main steps: ensuring that the data consumer has the necessary cryptographic keys to decrypt all relevant streams; generating and deploying standard or enclave-based data stream operators; and executing the running query. We will describe each of these phases using Figure 3 as a simple example. This query involves two streams: an unencrypted stream originated by $DP1$, and an encrypted stream originated by $DP2$. In this query, a standard selection operator is first applied to the unencrypted data stream. The resulting stream is then joined to the encrypted stream using SGX-enabled operator.

Key acquisition. In order for a data consumer to access an encrypted data stream, they must have access to the cryptographic key (or keys) used to encrypt the stream. For simplicity, in Figure 3, we assume that a single key, k_p, is used to encrypt the stream originated by $DP2$. In Sanctuary, key management is handled either in an offline manner, or online using a mechanism such as Fence [24] or Polystream [35]. Once a data consumer is able to decrypt streaming data, they are in a position to leverage the ability of Sanctuary to deploy SGX-enabled query operators.

Query deployment. Sanctuary is developed on top of the Apache Storm [34] infrastructure (cf. Section 7 for details). Plaintext relational operators are deployed as Storm bolts in the typical manner. The deployment of SGX-enabled operators is a multi-step process, as shown in Figure 3. First, Sanctuary will create an SGX enclave capable of executing the desired streaming operator (cf. Sections 4 and 5 for details). Next, this enclave is deployed to the Storm infrastructure (arrow 1). SGX remote attestation is then used to ensure the integrity of this operator as it is instantiated within Storm (bidirectional arrow 2). This process results in the derivation of a session key k_s that can be used to communicate securely between the data consumer and the enclave. Finally, k_s is used to encrypt and transmit the data stream key k_p to the operator enclave (arrow 3). At this point, the query network is ready to receive input tuples.

Query execution. In steady state, unencrypted tuples from $DP1$ and processed by the selection operator as in a standard DSMS. Encrypted tuples flowing from $DP2$ into the enclave-based join operator are decrypted using k_p and joined with the output of the selection operator. All result tuples are encrypted with k_s and forwarded to the data consumer.

4 STATELESS OPERATORS

In this section we briefly describe common DSPS stateless operators supported by Sanctuary and discuss how these operators must be altered to execute within an SGX enclave.

4.1 Stateless Operator Overview

Stateless operators interact with the enclave in a manner depicted in Figure 4. Operators are sent to the untrusted third-party by the data consumer. As data arrives from the data providers, it is decrypted, processed, re-encrypted, and finally sent to the data

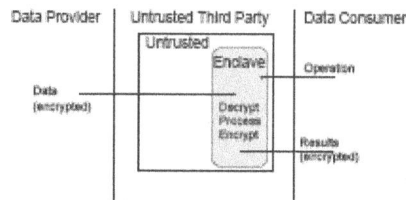

Figure 4: Stateless operator interaction with the enclave.

consumer. This decryption key is provided at the initialization of the enclave as part of the operation itself. There are three common stateless operators used in DSPSs: Filter, Projection, and Map. Given the straightforward nature of these operators, the only changes needed for execution within an enclave are the decryption of input tuples and the (potential) re-encryption of output tuples with a constant overhead (explored further in Section 7).

Filter: The filter operation simply verifies that a particular field matches a desired expression for range or equality (e.g., $x = y$, $x > y$, etc.). A filter must store *the predicate* (i.e., the constant comparator as described by the data consumer's query), the field to compare the predicate too (i.e., the "name" field, or a field identified by its placement in the tuple), and the operator code itself within the enclave, which reduces the overall enclave capacity. Processing a tuple will likely require a decryption (of at least the required field) and may require a re-encryption, depending upon whether the result must be transmitted in ciphertext or plaintext.

Projection: The projection operation reduces the size of a tuple by filtering out a specific set of fields to be passed along. The only information required to be saved in the enclave for a filter operation is the set of field identifiers (e.g., field name or placement within the tuple) to be preserved in the resulting tuple. It is likely that the tuple will not need to be decrypted, as no value is being checked. However, if fields are identified by a key-value type of system (i.e., fields may appear in any order in a given tuple), then a decryption of the entire tuple is required.

Map: Similar to the projection operation, a mapping operation reduces the size of a tuple by performing a function on several fields. For instance, a mapping operation may take fields for *revenue* and *expenses* and produce one field called *profit*. A mapping operator will have to decrypt the desired fields required to preform its function, and may need to encrypt the resulting field if the result needs to passed further down the operator network.

4.2 Enclave vs. Non-Enclave CPU Contention

Recall from Section 2 that when a program requests enclave operations, the CPU will halt all other processes and load the enclave-enabled program, as well as any data that is associated with the program itself. Similarly, whenever the enclave-enabled program completes its task within the enclave, it must write back any instance data, its code, CPU memory, and its metadata back to encrypted memory so that the CPU can preform other tasks and maintain the proper separation between enclave and non-enclave processes. This context-switching adds a processing overhead to the overall operator execution for every switch that is required. Specifically, entering an enclave will have a cost c_{enter} and exiting has a cost of c_{exit}. Each cost is dependent on the machine, workload, and other processes on the CPU and can vary with every entry and exit. The best way to mitigate this context-switching cost is to reduce the number of entries into and exits from the enclave.

Some context switching is unavoidable, but a streaming operation can mitigate the negative impact of context switching by simply reducing the number of calls into the enclave by batching data tuples. Rather than calling the enclave and paying c_{enter} and c_{exit} for *every* data tuple received, data tuples can be batched so that a single c_{enter} and c_{exit} is incurred and amortized over all n tuples in a batch. In a data stream, batching may add considerable latency to a query since results are delayed until a batch has been filled. In Section 7 we explore the benefits of batching.

5 STATEFUL OPERATIONS

When an operation is required to consider multiple tuples in order to execute a query, it is considered to be stateful. In this section, we overview the common stateful operators used by Sanctuary, and detail the challenges associated with implementing this class of operations within an enclave. We further propose three algorithms for executing stateful operations inside an SGX enclave.

5.1 Operators

There are two main types of stateful operations in a DSPS: joins an aggregations. This section overviews those operations and classifies the different types of each.

Joins: In a streaming system, a join operation compares two or more different streams in a given window and returns a set of data tuples comprised of data from each stream based upon some join condition. The specified period for comparing each stream is called the *window* which can be expressed either in time or in number of data tuples. A join must keep state on all data tuples that are within the current window for all streams in the join. For example, if a data consumer requests "all tuples where streamA.id = streamB.id for the last 10 minutes", all tuples in streamA and streamB that were timestamped within the last 10 minutes must be stored to compare with new tuples within the window.

Streaming join algorithms can be designed to either 1.) consider all possible pairs of join tuples, or 2.) consider a smaller set of tuples in each stream by using some auxiliary data structure. The *nested loop join* (NLJ) is a join algorithm that must consider all of the tuples in each stream's state by attempting to join every data tuple in one stream with every data tuple in the other. In practice, such a join algorithm is undesirable because of the overheads incurred. However, looping over all tuples avoids the leakage of positional information regarding the specific tuples being joined. *Hash joins* use an auxiliary hashing structure to reduce the number of tuples that need to be compared, reducing the overhead for the join algorithm, but potentially leak information about underlying data.

Distributive and Algebraic Aggregation: An aggregation is *distributive* if the input can be distributed to many partitions where a partial aggregation is processed, followed by a final aggregation of the partials (e.g., a sum can be broken down into smaller sums, with a final sum of the partials generating the overall result). *Algebraic* aggregations are those that can be represented as an algebraic function of two or more distributive aggregations (e.g., average can be calculated by a summation and a count). Distributive and algebraic aggregates have a constant memory overhead.

Holistic Aggregation: An aggregation is holistic if there is no constant bound on the memory required for partial or final aggregation. For instance, the *median* operation is holistic because there is no way to determine the size of the resulting set of median

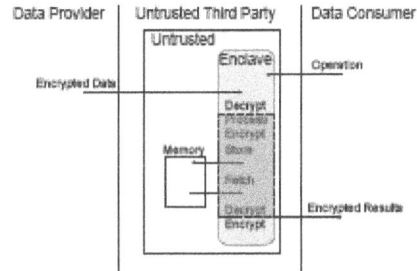

Figure 5: Stateful operator interaction with the enclave.

values. A window in a holistic aggregate is treated in the same manner as in the distributive or algebraic aggregations.

5.2 Issues with Stateful operators and Enclaves

Stateful operators cannot be directly implemented in an enclave environment without alteration. Specifically, there are two main concerns when implementing a stateful operation on an enclave: *memory limitations* of the enclave and *update costs* associated with auxiliary data structures that may be required.

Memory Limitations: Recall from Section 2 that an enclave is limited to just 128 MB of memory, which is further reduced by the need to store operator code o and meta-data m within the enclave. Stateful operations must make use of this limited memory to store each operation's windows of tuples. Windows can be of a nondeterministic size w (e.g., the last 10 minutes saw 10k tuples, but the next 10 minutes may see 13k tuples) and may not fit into enclave memory. Any stateful algorithm will therefore have to consider swapping between (encrypted) non-enclave memory and enclave memory.

In addition to the window itself, some operations (e.g., hash joins) maintain auxiliary structures. Such structures will vary in size s across operators and will likely need to be kept (at least in part) in enclave memory, further reducing the available memory. Therefore, the total capacity for storing data tuples in an enclave with $enclaveSize = 128MB$ and n operators each with w_s windows (that can vary in size, 0 for stateless operations) is fixed at:

$$capacity = enclaveSize - (m + (\Sigma_0^n (o + s + \Sigma_0^{w_s} w))). \quad (1)$$

Update Cost Overhead: In a traditional DSPS, removing tuples from or adding tuples to a window in relatively straightforward: one simply checks the timestamp for each tuple as new tuples are added, and removes or dereferences those that have expired. The use of an SGX enclave presents a new challenge with regards to updating the state of a stateful operator. Specifically, when the state of an operator is encrypted in non-enclave memory, the timestamp and most recent tuple information may not be available without either trusting the third-party service to remove expired tuples or leaking some temporal information about the tuples. We can calculate the cost c_{up} of an update by simply multiplying the number of tuples being updated n_{up} by the time it takes to execute that update l_{up}. This cost is added to the overall latency for stateful operators.

5.3 Enclave-Enabled Stateful Operators

We now introduce three algorithms for stateful streaming operations that can execute within an SGX enclave: Nested Loop Join (NLJ), Hash Join (HJ), and generic aggregation (AGG). All algorithms follow the structure depicted in Figure 5. Data consumers use SGX's remote attestation capabilities to ensure that their stateful operator

---

Algorithm 1 $enclaveNestedLoopJoin(Array\{tuple\}batch)$

```
 1: Array[tuple] batchSide          ▷ Stored tuples from the same stream as the tuples in batch
 2: Array[tuple] otherBuffer                    ▷ Stored tuples from the other stream
 3: int maxJoinSetSize                          ▷ Available in-enclave memory.
 4: Object metadata                             ▷ Storage describing the operator.
 5: for t ∈ batch do
 6:    batchSide.add(t)
 7:    enclave.decrypt(t)
 8: for i = 0; i ≤ ⌈otherBuffer/maxJoinSetSize⌉; i + + do
 9:    if i! = ⌈otherBuffer[i]/maxJoinSetSize⌉ then
10:       segment_tuple = memGet(i * maxJoinSetSize, (i * maxJoinSetSize) + maxJoinSetSize)
11:    else
12:       segment = memGet(i * maxJoinSetSize, otherBuffer.size)
13:    for l ∈ segment do
14:       if l.timeStamp < currentTime − window then
15:          evict(otherBuffer.getiAllMatchingValues(l.value))
16:       enclave.decrypt(l)
17:       for s ∈ batch do
18:          if l[metadata.joinField] ⋈ s[metadata.joinField] then
19:             emit(enclave.encrypt(join(l, s)))
```

Algorithm 2 $hashJoin(Array\{tuple\}batch)$

```
 1: Map[String, Array[tuple]] batchSideHash
 2: Map[String, Array[tuple]] otherHash
 3: Array[tuple] batchSideBuffer            ▷ Stored tuples from batch's corresponding stream.
 4: Array[tuple] otherBuffer                         ▷ Stored tuples from the other stream.
 5: int maxJoinSetSize                               ▷ Available in-enclave memory.
 6: Object metadata                                  ▷ Storage describing the operator.
 7: for t ∈ batch_tuple do
 8:    enclave.decrypt(t)
 9:    if otherHash.get(t.value)! = null then
10:       int jSize = otherBuffer(otherHash.get(t.value)).size
11:       for i = 0; i ≤ ⌈jSize/maxJoinSetSize⌉; i + + do
12:          if i! = ⌈jSize/maxJoinSetSize⌉ then
13:             matchSet = memGet(otherBuffer, i * maxJoinSetSize, (i * maxJoinSetSize) +
          maxJoinSetSize)
14:          else
15:             matchSet = memGet(otherBuffer, i * maxJoinSetSize, otherBuffer.size)
16:          for r ∈ matchSet do
17:             enclave.decrypt(r)
18:             if r.timeStamp < currentTime − window then
19:                evict(otherHash.get(r.value).get(r))
20:             else if t[metadata.joinField] ⋈ r[metadata.joinField] then
21:                emit(enclave.encrypt(join(t, r)))
22:    if t.value ∈ batchSideHash then
23:       batchSideBuffer[batchSideHash.get(t.value)].add(t)
24:    else
25:       batchSideHash.put(t)
26:       batchSideBuffer.extendByOne()
27:       batchSideHash.get(t) = batchSideBuffer.size − 1
28:       batchSideBuffer[batchSideBuffer.size − 1] = newArray()
29:       batchSideBuffer[batchSideBuffer.size − 1].add(t)
```

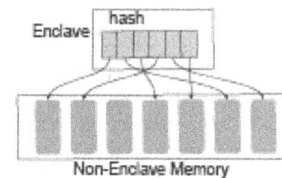

Figure 6: Use hashing to split a window in non-enclave memory.

enclaves have been appropriately provisioned to the remote infrastructure. As (encrypted) data is received by the enclave from a data provider, it is decrypted and processed. Once processed, it is either discarded (aggregation) or stored in untrusted, encrypted memory. Tuples can be brought back into enclave memory as needed (e.g., to be joined with new tuples) or the partial aggregate to which it contributed can be brought into memory (e.g., the sum for the slides affected by the tuple is brought in to sum new tuples to). This process of fetching and storing continues until all new data is processed. Note that these alrorithms are deisgned to work in *any* memory limited environment, but are more well suited for the SGX use-case as they aim at avoiding costs associated with CPU context switching.

5.3.1 Join Algorithms. **Nested Loop Join:** We first overview our Nested Loop Join (NLJ) in Algorithm 1. The enclave sets up two spaces in non-enclave memory to represent the windows for each stream. When new data for a stream enters the enclave, the window for the other stream is loaded into enclave memory. If the entire window does not fit, it is segmented (lines 8–12). The *memGet* function simply takes two indices, maps them to registers in memory, and fetches the values. Each segment is then compared and joined to the new tuples being processed (lines 13–19), any joined results are emitted to the next operation or data consumer. In addition to being compared to new tuples, a tuple being brought in from non-enclave memory is also evicted if its timestamp no longer fits within the window (line 14). Finally, all new tuples are added to the end of their window without bringing that state into memory. To implement such an operator, Sanctuary need only the field names from each stream, as well as the slide and window. Sanctuary simply submits the operator with this metadata to a remote system as a function and then verifies it via remote attestation. Whenever the query is ready to be executed, Sanctuary simply executes the function.

A Nested Loop Join is not generally desirable, given that it must compare every tuple in one window with every tuple in the other (or at the very least compare new tuples from each window with the other one). This does, however, offer a nice confidentiality guarantee in an enclave setting, as it does not reveal the relationship between any *specific* tuples in non-enclave memory with new tuples being processed (discussed further in the next section), since every tuple is compared against all buffered tuples.

Hash Join: Algorithm 2 details our Hash Join (HJ) algorithm. Within the enclave memory, a hash structure it maintained for each stream in the join. For every unique key in the join predicate (e.g., each name in a "name" field that has been processed), an entry is made into the hash structure where the key is the predicate, and the value is a space in non-enclave memory where the actual tuples are held, as pictured in Figure 6.

The process of operating on a new tuple is simple. It is first decrypted (Line 8) and then the tuple's join predicate value is hashed to see if there exists at least one match in the other stream (Line 9). If so, the entire set of tuples in the hash entry, or the *matching set* (i.e., the segment of all tuples with the same hash key) is brought into the enclave by enclave-memory sized segments (Lines 10–15). Once all matching tuples are joined to the new tuple, the new tuple is added to its originating stream's hash with its corresponding entry. If the tuple's predicate did not exist in the stream's hash, a new entry is created and the tuple is added to the endpoint for the pointer stored in the hash (Lines 22–29). Note that if the internal hash structures(s) run out of memory, a secondary hash is created in non-enclave memory that will absorb some hash values (i.e., all non-matching predicates are sent to a second hash to be checked). This adds one extra memory operation and one extra hash operation to fetch the desired hash-value. This is not included in Algorithm 2 for simplicity. Similar to the requirements for Nested Loop Join, Sanctuary only requires the fields needed to preform the join, as well as the window and slide. The user may also specify some memory specifications for how they prefer to handle allocation of enclave memory.

Updates in the HJ algorithm are a bit more complicated. A tuple is only removed from a set referred to by a hash entry if that entry is brought into enclave memory. The benefit of this approach is rather straightforward in that updates are handled in an ad-hoc, on-the-fly manner without requiring any extra loads from memory. The obvious drawback is that some data may linger around for a while if its predicate is not matched by the other stream. We leave garbage collecting expired tuples to future work.

5.3.2 Generic Aggregation.
Our generic aggregation algorithm (AGG) can handle distributive, algebraic, and holistic aggregations. There are two main memory structures for an aggregation: storage for internal partial aggregations, and the final aggregation step. For distributive and algebraic operations, the state needed for storing the partial results during a window is deterministic and can be provisioned accordingly. To accommodate for holistic operations, we assume that the size of the returned result is non-deterministic for all aggregations. In a memory limited environment, this means that results for each window of the aggregation may need to be stored in non-enclave memory. Further, in a holistic aggregation, these results may vary in size depending on the data and the window.

To accommodate for all three types of aggregation operations, we adopt an approach similar to the hash join approach. Each slide (or window in the case where there is no slide) gets an entry in an in enclave memory array. This entry (potentially) points to a hash table kept in non-enclave memory. For distributive and algebraic aggregation, this hash table may contain only one entry and may fit in enclave memory. For holistic aggregations, this hash table may contain many entries that need updating (e.g., the total sales for each company in a given stream for a given window).

Algorithm 3 details our aggregation algorithm. Each slide is given an index in an array that is stored in enclave memory. Every time a new tuple is received (or a batch of tuples), the algorithm loops through this array. If an entry has expired (based on checking the time inside a designated hash entry (Line 7) it is brought into memory (Lines 8–18) where each entry is emitted (Line 15) and cleared (Line 16) so that the hash may be reused.

For non-expired slides, they are similarly brought into memory, but instead of being emitted, they are aggregated with each tuple in the batch (Line 24). If the entry already exists in the hash for the batched value, it is aggregated to the matching value (Lines 25- 26). The function *genAgMemHelp* takes the array that the hash refers to, the current index, and the maximum size of the buffer, and fills that buffer with values from the encrypted memory by converting the index into a starting and ending register. Once all of the hash has been brought into enclave memory, if any new tuples remain (e.g., a new company has entered the stream that was not yet encountered during this window), they are simply added to the hash as the first entry for that value (Line 28- 30).

Again, to make use of this operator, Sanctuary simply needs the field to aggregate, the type of aggregation, and the window and slide information. The user may also specify the allocation of memory here as well, but Sanctuary handles the bulk of the load by allowing a user to just specify the most basic of information and doing the submission, attestation, and execution for them.

State updates in AGG are simple in that they only require that a slide expire for state to be reset. An adversary can only gain information on how many entries are in a hash table and how many

slides are in a window based on what is stored in non-enclave memory. This is no different than in distributive or algebraic operations directly on encrypted data, as the length of the slide can be determined by the rate at which results are produced, and the size of the result set is equivalent to the size of the hash table in AGG.

Algorithm 3 $aggregate(Array\{tuple\}newBatch,$
$\quad\quad\quad int\ window,\ int\ slide,\ int\ maxBufferSize)$

1: Takes: $aggregate(Array[tuple]newBatch,\ int\ window,\ int\ maxBufferSize)$
2: Array[Array[tuple]] $slideArray$ ▷ Stores current slides in the window
3: Map[String, Array[tuple]] $hash$
4: int $maxBufferSize$ ▷ Available in-enclave memory.
5: **for** $hash \in slideArray$ **do**
6:     ▷ If the hashed aggregates are now greater than the window length, emit them as results.
7:     **if** $earliestTime(newBatch) \leq (hash.get(startTime)) + slide$ **then**
8:         **for** $i = 0; i < \lceil hash.size/maxBufferSize\rceil; i + +$ **do**
9:             Map[String, Array[tuple]] $currentHash$
10:             **if** $i < \lceil hash.size/maxBufferSize\rceil$ **then**
11:                 $currentHash = genAgMemHelp(slideArray.indexOf(hash),\ i,\ maxBufferSize)$
12:             **else**
13:                 $currentHash = genAgMemHelp(slideArray.indexOf(hash),\ i,\ hash.size)$
14:             **for** $j = 0; j < currentHash.size; j + +$ **do**
15:                 $emit(currentHash.get(j))$
16:                 $currentHash.get(j).clear$
17:         ▷ Otherwise aggregate the new batch into each slide.
18:     **else**
19:         **for** $i = 0; i < \lceil hash.size/maxBufferSize\rceil; i + +$ **do**
20:             **if** $i < \lceil hash.size/maxBufferSize\rceil$ **then**
21:                 $currentHash = genAgMemHelp(slideArray.indexOf(hash),\ i,\ maxBufferSize)$
22:             **else**
23:                 $currentHash = genAgMemHelp(slideArray.indexOf(hash),\ i,\ hash.size)$
24:             **for** $t \in newBatch$ **do**
25:                 **if** $t.group \in keys(currentHash)$ **then**
26:                     $aggregate(t.value,\ currentHash.get(t.group))$
27:                     $newBatch.remove(t)$
28:             **if** $i = \lceil hash.size/maxBufferSize\rceil$ && $newBatch.size > 0$ **then**
29:                 **for** $t \in newBatch$ **do**
30:                   $currentHash.put(t.group) = t.value$
31:             $memOut(hashArray.indexOf(hash),\ i,\ currentHash)$

---

6 SECURITY ANALYSIS

We now detail the information that an adversary can learn by observing the execution of queries within Sanctuary. To contextualize this analysis, we compare directly to two alternative DSMS approaches.

6.1 Comparison Framework

Below are the three system models (including Sanctuary) within which we will compare information leakage:

- **Sanctuary**: In this system model (cf. Section 3) we assume that our adversary is the third-party computational infrastructure hosting a query comprised of the SGX-enabled streaming operators described in this paper. As such, the adversary can observe all (encrypted) traffic flowing between operators, as well the encrypted traffic flowing between the enclave and non-enclave portions of an individual operator. To upper-bound information leakage, we assume one operator per enclave.

- **Cryptographic**: In this system model, we assume that our adversary is a third-party computational platform hosting a query comprised of cryptographic streaming operators. I.e., data streams are encrypted using computation-enabling encryption as in [3, 28, 35]. As such, the adversary can observe all (encrypted) traffic flowing in and between operators.

- **Trusted Infrastructure**: As a baseline for comparison, we consider a trusted third-party computational platform capable of processing standard streaming operators over plaintext tuples (e.g., [23, 24]). This is effectively the *optimal* approach in terms

Table 1: Level of leakage for the various approaches (S = Selectivity, TM = tuple matching, VO = tuple ordering, VD = value distribution, SM = segment matching, W = Window)

Operator		Sanctuary	Cryptographic Data	Trusted Infrastructure
Filter	Equality	S	S, TM, VD	S
	Range	S	S, TM, VO, VD	S
Project		∅	∅	∅
Join		S, SM, W	*Not Supported*	S
Aggregation		W	W	W

of minimizing leakages with our current threat model. We assume that all streaming tuples are encrypted (e.g., using TLS) while in the network. Our adversary is *not* the computational infrastructure, but rather an entity capable of monitoring all communications between nodes in the system. To upper-bound information leakage, we assume one operator per node.

The Sanctuary and cryptographic models are meant to provide a level playing field for comparing the approach presented in this paper with the current state-of-the-art by considering streaming computations that execute on an untrusted infrastructure. The latter Trusted Infrastructure model serves as a basis of comparison for considering what information can be learned by an outside observer who is watching data being processed on a trusted platform. We now examine the types of leakages exhibited by each type of operator considered in this paper, within each of the above system models.

6.2 Properties

To understand the leakage of information in various DDSMS deployment models, we first identify types of leakage. In this section, we use the notation $E_{DET}(k, v_i)$ (resp. $E_{OPE}(k, v_i)$ or $E_{CCA}(k, v_i)$) to denote the deterministic (resp. order-preserving or CCA-secure) encryption of a tuple v_i using the key k. We use the notation $E(k, v_i)$ in situations where the specific type of encryption used is immaterial.

- **Tuple Matching (TM):** Given a set of input tuples $S^{in} = \{t_1^{in}, \ldots, t_i^{in}\}$ and a set of output tuples $S^{out} = \{t_1^{out}, \ldots, t_j^{out}\}$, compute the matching $M = \{\forall t^{out} \in S^{out} : (t^{in}, t^{out}) | t^{in} = E(k, v^{in}) \wedge t^{out} = E(k, v^{out}) \wedge v^{in} = v^{out}\}$.
- **Value Ordering (VO):** Given a set of tuples $S = \{t_1 = E(k, v_1), t_2 = E(k, v_2) \ldots, t_i = E(k, v_i)\}$, compute an ordering $t_1', t_2', \ldots, t_i'$ such that $v_1' \le v_2' \le \ldots \le v_i'$.
- **Value Distribution (VD):** Given a set of tuples $S = \{t_1 = E(k, v_1), t_2 = E(k, v_2) \ldots, t_i = E(k, v_i)\}$, compute the frequency distribution $\hat{v}_1 = \text{count}(v_1, S), \hat{v}_2 = \text{count}(v_2, S), \ldots, \hat{v}_i = \text{count}(v_i, S)$. Note $\hat{v}_i$ does not necessarily reveal the value v_i.
- **Segment Match (SM):** Given an input tuple t and a segmented window $w = \{ms_1, \ldots, ms_k\}$, identify the matching segments ms_i within which t can complete a join.

In addition, we will explore whether the selectivity (S) of a given predicate or the window size (W) of an operation can be inferred.

6.3 Leakage Comparison

We now examine the information that can be inferred by an adversary when observing the execution of each of the above systems. We consider the streaming relational operators described in this paper, and summarize our results in Table 1.

Select/Filter. Each selection operator takes as input a stream $S^{in} = t_1^{in}, \ldots, t_i^{in}$, applies a filter f, and produces as output a stream $S^{out} = t_1^{out}, \ldots, t_j^{out}$. In each system considered, the adversary can compute the selectivity of f by comparing the cardinality of S^{in} and S^{out} over some window. In both the Sanctuary and Trusted Infrastructure models, all tuples are encrypted using CCA-secure cryptography (i.e., $t_i = E_{CCA}(k, v_i)$). As such, the values v_i comprising the input and output streams are protected.

In the Cryptographic model, equality filtering is enabled by the use of deterministic encryption (i.e., $t_i = E_{DET}(k, v_i)$). As a result, $E_{DET}(k, v_i) = E_{DET}(k, v_j)$ if and only if $v_i = v_j$. This enables the adversary to infer a distribution of values over the encrypted tuples in S^{in} irrespective of the filter f. Further, the adversary can infer exactly which tuples t_i^{in} match the predicate f, as these tuples appear unmodified in S^{out}. For range filtering, order-preserving encryption must be employed (i.e., $t_i = E_{OPE}(k, v_i)$) so that $E_{OPE}(k, v_i) \le E_{OPE}(k, v_j)$ if and only $v_i \le v_j$. This enables the adversary to determine an ordering over tuples appearing in S^{in} and S^{out}.

Projection. For all three frameworks, a projection simply removes fields from *every* tuple and therefore always has a 100% selectivity. Since input and output values are encrypted, tuple values, distributions, and orderings remain hidden in all cases.

Join. A join operator takes as input two streams $S_1^{in} = t_{11}^{in}, \ldots, t_{i1}^{in}$ and $S_1^{in} = t_{12}^{in}, \ldots, t_{j2}^{in}$, applies a join predicate p, and produces an output stream $S^{out} = t_1^{out}, \ldots, t_k^{out}$ that joins S_1^{in} and S_2^{in} using p over some (time- or tuple-based) window W. Given that S_1^{in} and S_2^{in} are typically encrypted with different keys, no existing cryptographic DDSMS supports join operations over streaming data.

In both the Sanctuary and Trusted Infrastructure models, input tuples are encrypted using randomized encryption (i.e., $t_{ij}^{in} = E_{CCA}(k_j, v_i)$), thereby preventing the inference of tuple values, distributions, and orderings. In both cases, the adversary can easily compute the selectivity of p by comparing the cardinality of S_1^{in}, S_2^{in}, and S^{out} over some time window. In Sanctuary, the adversary has the ability to monitor the enclave's accesses to non-enclave memory. Recall that given enclave memory limitations, a join window $w_i^1 \in S_1^{in}$ is managed as a set of matching segments $w_i^1 = \{ms_{i1}^1, \ldots, ms_{ik}^1\}$ each of which fits into enclave memory. By monitoring the eviction rate from these segments, the adversary can infer the window size used by the join. Further, as new tuples arrive, auxiliary data structures are used to retrieve only the segments that will join with the incoming tuples, thereby leaking the segments that incoming tuples match to.

Aggregation. During aggregation, a sliding window of tuples is combined to produce a single output tuple. In the Cryptographic and Trusted Infrastructure models, the adversary can infer the window size, W, used for the aggregation operation by counting the number of tuples $E(k, v_i)$ consumed by the operator prior to emitting each output tuple. Likewise, in Sanctuary, the adversary can infer the W by watching the transition of encrypted tuples between enclave and non-enclave memory. In all cases, the use of randomized encryption prevents the inference of tuple values, ordering, and distribution.

Summary: Sanctuary leaks the same minimal information as the Trusted Infrastructure system for all operations excepting the join, which can be mitigated if the join state fits in enclave memory. Further, Sanctuary not only leaks the same or less information as cryptographic DDSMS systems, but also enables arbitrary join operations, the lack of which is a severe limitation of existing cryptographic systems.

7 EVALUATION

In this section, we explore the efficiency of Sanctuary operations in a real streaming system. Specifically, we benchmark each operation in comparison to Trusted Infrastructure approaches under different experimental conditions. We then use SGX-enabled operations within the context of deployed streaming queries to evaluate the impact of enclave-based operations on query performance.

7.1 Configuration

Our evaluation framework builds upon the Apache Storm infrastructure [34] to manage the network topology and deliver tuples. Our work can be trivially deployed over any DSPS. Storm uses two main computational components called *spouts* (provide data) and *bolts* (execute on it). For this work, we use bolts to emulate a node. This implies that a single bolt has access to one SGX-enabled CPU. We use Storm to emulate the temporal aspect of real-time data stream processing since it can be configured to guarantee in-order tuple delivery, and spouts can emit tuples at a given timestamp (to better control input rate). All experiments were executed on a machine using the Windows 10 operating system with a dual core Intel i5-6200 CPU (2.30 GHz) and 4 GB of ram.

Datasets: To better explore the tradeoffs in size, speed, and selectivity of data, we will use two different types of data-sources. The first type is synthetically-generated data that is purposefully created to test the boundaries for each SGX-enabled operation as well as its alternatives. Each evaluation that alters this data will describe, in detail, how it is generated and used. The second set of data is the 2015 DEBS Grand Challenge dataset [14] consisting of tuples that describe an instance of a taxi ride (i.e., the start time, taxi driver ID, cab ID, end time, fare, distance, etc.).

Comparison Approaches: For each operator or algorithm we test, we will compare it to the same operation executed over *plaintext* and also in a DSPS using *computation-enabled encryption*. We will use three different encryption techniques for comparison: 1.) Deterministic Encryption (DET, which uses AES in CBC mode with padding, see [35] and [28]) for equality operations, 2.) Order Preserving Encryption (OPE, which uses the Boldyreva et. al [8] technique) for range operations, and 3.) Homomorphic Encryption (HOM, using the Paillier technique [26]) for aggregate operations.

7.2 Micro Benchmark: Stateless Operations

For stateless operators, there is no state to keep track of, tuples are simply fed directly to the enclave and processed in *batches*, with batched results being returned. All results are based on the average processing time for 10,000 tuples. For batch execution, the results are based on the average of 10 runs for each batch size.

7.2.1 Filter. **Configuration:** Given that the time to decrypt a field depends on the size of the field, we evaluate the processing time for different sized fields. We further evaluate enclave batching by including five different batch sizes (1, 1K, 10K, 100K, 1M) and their overheads. We compare Sanctuary to a plaintext system as well as one that uses order-preserving encryption.

Results: Sanctuary filters will incur roughly 2x-4x overall execution time versus plaintext approaches (but leak less information), and 1.5x-3x overall execution time versus computation-enabling

encryption. Note that most of the overhead is due to context switching between trusted and untrusted code in the CPU. To this end, using larger batch sizes reduces this overhead, and most execution times are under 10ms overall. Moreover, Sanctuary operations are similarly impacted by the size of the underlying ciphertext.

7.2.2 In-Memory Aggregation. Here, we evaluate Sanctuary summation operations against a HOM computation-enabling cryptographic operation. Since a HOM summation is done through multiplication, processing on encrypted data requires greater overhead.

Configuration: We use a summation operation to evaluate an in-memory aggregation within the enclave. For simplicity, we assume no window semantics (meaning the final aggregation is simply inclusive of all tuples) to better understand the underlying operation. We will use a windowed query in Section 7.4 to evaluate performance on an actual streaming query. Again, we include five batching sizes and compare to a plaintext non-enclave summation, and we use a HOM computation-enabled encryption scheme.

Results (Figure 8): Batching for an in-memory aggregation algorithm has a similar impact as the filter operation. However, when using the Paillier homomorphic encryption scheme, computing a sum requires multiplication which comes at a greater cost. This is evident from the HOM line in Figure 8 being the most costly line. Even in the case where there is a batch size of one, the enclave-enabled in-memory aggregation operation can outperform its encrypted counterpart. Since both the HOM-encrypted processing and the Sanctuary enabled operation provide an adversary with the same level of information, Sanctuary becomes a desirable choice when considered in conjunction with the performance advantages.

7.3 Micro Benchmark: Stateful Operations

This section explores the overheads required for the security advantages of the memory-limited algorithms presented in Section 5. Recall from Section 5 that there are five factors that can influence the overhead of a memory-limited operation; 1.) Batch Size, 2.) Enclave Memory Structure Size 3.) Operator State Size, 4.) Window Size, and 5.) Update Cost. We reduce all arbitrary units of size measurement (e.g., tuple, enclave memory) to megabytes for simplicity when making comparisons. We evaluate each of the four algorithms presented in Section 5 based on the tradeoffs below:

- **Batch Size vs. Enclave Memory Size**: Given the limited memory of an enclave, there exists an inherent tradeoff between the batch size of incoming tuples and the enclave memory available for bringing operator state into the enclave for processing.
- **Operator State Size vs. Enclave Memory Size**: Stateful operations require a comparison or computation over some amount of internal state. Given the limitation on the internal enclave memory available for operator state, there is a tradeoff that can affect the execution time (or the latency) of the operation.
- **Window Size vs. Update Cost**: When a tuple expires or is introduced to the state of the operation, there is an associated update cost. For larger windows (either by definition or through high-bandwidth streams), these updates can come with a greater overhead, affecting the overall performance of an operation.

Each experiment depicts the average of seven runs with the lowest and highest removed to ensure that background tasks are weighted similarly as the CPU is shared by other processes.

7.3.1 Symmetric Hash Join. **Configuration:** Each tuple contains two fields: a *comparator* (8 Bytes) and a *payload* (92 Bytes). Joined

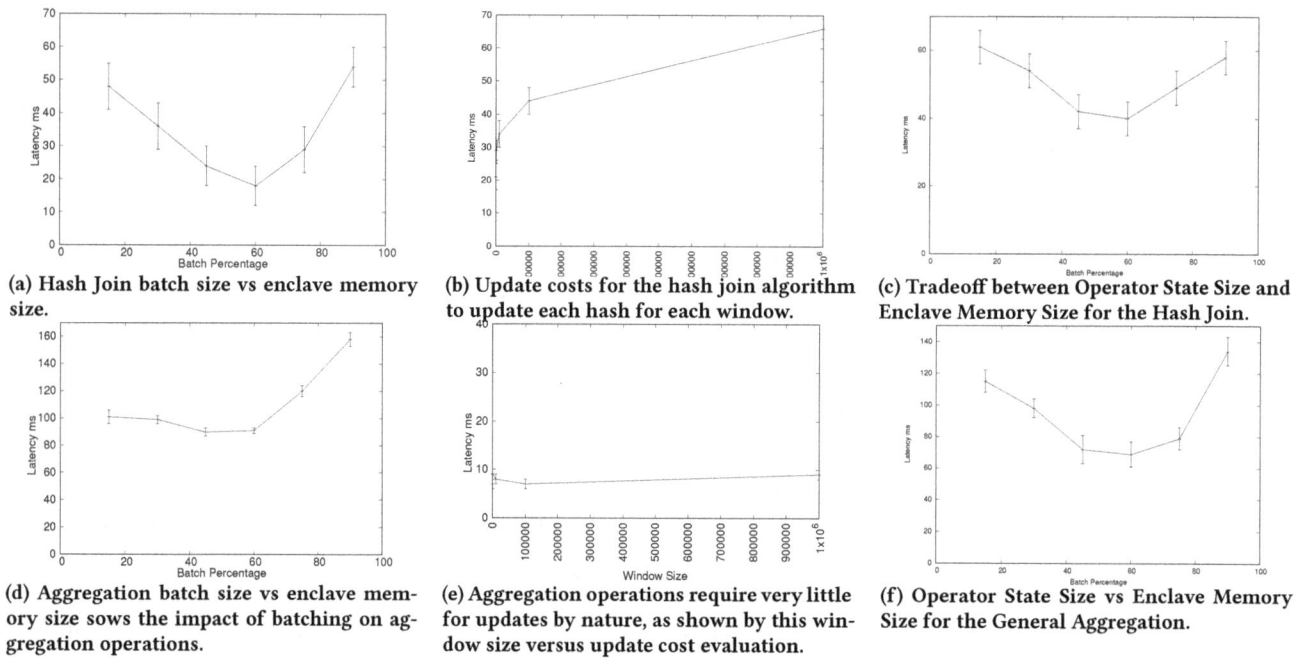

(a) Hash Join batch size vs enclave memory size.

(b) Update costs for the hash join algorithm to update each hash for each window.

(c) Tradeoff between Operator State Size and Enclave Memory Size for the Hash Join.

(d) Aggregation batch size vs enclave memory size sows the impact of batching on aggregation operations.

(e) Aggregation operations require very little for updates by nature, as shown by this window size versus update cost evaluation.

(f) Operator State Size vs Enclave Memory Size for the General Aggregation.

Figure 7: Results for the the common evaluation for the three stateful operations from Section 5

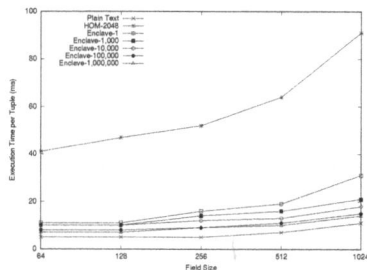

Figure 8: Execution time for in memory aggregation operation for non-enclave and enclave-enabled operations.

tuples are combined into 184 Byte payloads. Comparator fields are uniformly selected from a range of integers from 1-256. After metadata, the internal enclave memory is roughly 122 MB, of which all is available for buffers and state comparisons.

Results (Figure 7a) Batch Size vs Enclave Memory Size: For this experiment, we evaluate the batch size versus the available enclave memory. Specifically, we hold the window size constant at 100 MB with an input rate of 10 MB/s. We reserve 30% of the enclave memory to be given to the internal hash for tracking non-enclave memory. We see the tradeoff between batching and freed enclave memory maximize at roughly 60%.

Results (Figure 7b) Window Size vs. Update Cost: For this experiment, we fix the batching to enclave memory ratio at 50% each. We adjust the window size from 10MB to 100 MB and hold an input of 10 MB/s. We again allocate 30% of enclave memory to the internal hash. Recall that an update to the external structure to expire a tuple will only occur when that value is joined (Lines 18- 19 in Algorithm 2). Note here that each data tuple must be hashed, brought into memory, compared, then evicted, which all adds to a higher latency compared to a plaintext system.

Results (Figure 7c) Operator State Size vs. Enclave Memory Size: Here, we fix the batch size at 30% of enclave memory. We then tradeoff internal state size with free memory size. We hold the input rate at 10 MB/s as usual with a window size of 100 MB. This tradeoff exhibits similar behavior to all of the others. Giving more memory to the hash for each stream yields the best results with a 60% ratio. It is important to note, however, that for a join that has a very low selectivity (i.e., one in which the two streams rarely join), the enclave memory will not be filled since there is insufficient data with which it can be filled. This means an enclave will only employ external memory when the join is highly selective.

7.3.2 General Windowed Aggregation. We evaluate the general windowed aggregate operation using the four costs from the previous section and the update cost. We also evaluate the impact on an operation's overhead based on the size and number of slides.

Configuration: We use the same data as in Section 7.3.1, but focus on a portion of the payload for aggregation operations (16 B integers) that is symmetrically encrypted. The 16 B integers are uniformly generated from 1-30,000 and used in a summation aggregation operation across 250 different groups. We use a window that can be divided into 10 slides for all experiments.

Results (Figure 7d) Batch Size vs Enclave Memory Size: This experiment is set up exactly like the SHJ Batch Size vs Enclave Memory Size experiment, with 30% allocated to a possible internal hash structured. Note that we no longer see a profound benefit from greater batching (gaining only 10ms), and we see a far greater increase in latency after about 40% to 60% batch allocation due to the consistent size of the hash structures storing each slide. No matter what we batch, every tuple must be aggregated to the same segmentation size of non-enclave memory, meaning that the relative effects of batching are reduced, since the cost of bringing non-enclave memory into the enclave is normalized.

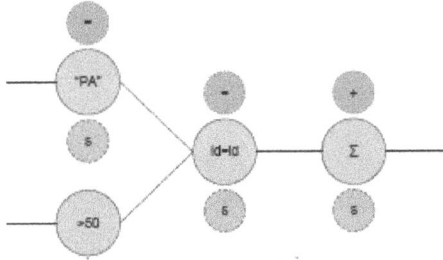

Figure 9: Example continuous query. The operations in the red dotted circles execute on computation-enabling encrypted tuples ("=" for deterministic, "+" for homomorphic), the blue dashed circles represent non memory-limited enclave-enabled operations, and the green solid circles represent plaintext operations.

Results (Figure 7e) Window Size vs. Update Cost: This experiment is similarly set up the same as SHJ Window Size vs. Update Cost, but with slides dividing the window size by 1 t Larger windows do not cause significant increases in update cost as one might expect with larger slides due to the consistent slide size for each hash brought into memory. More specifically, this consistency can be attributed to the uniform group size of 250. If we remove this uniformity and increase the number of groups (not included as a figure), we see that the greater the number of groups, the larger the update cost, especially with a greatly segmented hash table.

Results (Figure 7f) Operator State Size vs. Enclave Memory Size: This experiment is configured exactly like the SHJ Operator State Size vs. Enclave Memory Size experiment with the internal operator structure representing a cache of some hash tables. Similar to what we saw in the Batch Size vs Enclave Memory vs. Operator State Size evaluation for this aggregation, giving more memory to caching is advantageous up to about 60%.

7.4 Macro Benchmark

Here, we chose a query to execute on streaming data with varying conditions. We break the query evaluation into two different environments. The first environment illustrates the effectiveness of an enclave-enabled operation when all of the state fits into enclave memory. The second uses operations where state does not fit in memory. For each query, we compare to 1.) a plaintext version (i.e., no enclave) and 2.) a version where operators are compared with a computation-enabling encryption version. We further test by altering the input rate, selectivity, and size of the data tuples.

7.4.1 Non Memory-Limited Query.
The query we use to evaluate the operations that fit entirely in enclave memory is intended to test each of the operation types (i.e., join, aggregation, and a stateless operation) on a real system. The query (below) aims to get the total profit for all companies whose profit margin is more than $500. The query is presented below in SQL and graphically in Figure 9:

```
SELECT SUM(t.sales) FROM t JOIN o
WHERE t.id = o.id AND t.state = "PA"
   AND o.profitMargin > 500
GROUP BY t.company EVERY 30s UPDATE 5s
```

There are two filter operations (the "=" in Figure 9), a join (the "id=id" in Figure 9), and an aggregate-group by operation (the "+" in Figure 9). The encrypted versions of the operations are presented in dotted red circles in Figure 9.

Results: In this experiment, we wish to evaluate the overhead of introducing Sanctuary and SGX-enabled operators into the normal query processing pipeline. When evaluating a streaming query, one must consider the effects of input rate, selectivity, and tuple size on the responsiveness of the system. In this section, we explore changes in input rate and selectivity since tuple size was explored through micro-benchmarking. For each result, we evaluate a completely plaintext set of operations, a set of operations using only computation-enabling encryption, and then queries where each of the operator types (the summation, the join, and a filter) are all placed on an enclave using one of the algorithms from Section 5.

Selectivity (Figure 10a): Here, we change the overall selectivity and inspect the result. To change the selectivity, we simply increase the selectivities of each of the filters and the join incrementally to reach the desired selectivity (.1-.9) while maintaining an input rate of 1,000 tuples/s. As you can see from Figure 10a, a decrease in selectivity generally causes an increase in individual tuple latency, regardless of the operator type. Note that latency here includes the window time for each tuple. An increase in latency signifies that operators have difficulty processing data within a given window. Given that all of the operator state fits into memory, the effects of increasing selectivity was equally beneficial for all operators.

Input Rate (Figure 10b): We evaluate the input rate by increasing from 500 to 2,500 tuples/s (kept sufficiently slow so that we can evaluate scenarios wherein the input rate does not cause the memory capacity to be exceeded) and inspecting the latency. Similarly to the selectivity result, we notice from Figure 10b no significant difference between each operator type with increased throughput. We also notice that latency was within 15% of plaintext, and 7% of computation-enabling cryptosystems for SGX-enabled operators.

7.4.2 Memory-Limited Query.
For our memory-limited query, we simply re-use the query above, but with a drastically increased workload to force the utilization of non-enclave memory.

Selectivity (Figure 10c): For this experiment, we increase the input rate to 20,000 tuples/s (where only roughly 10,000 tuples can fit into memory. We otherwise keep the same configuration as the non-memory-limited version above. Notice from Figure 10c that selectivity has a greater impact on latency in this scenario. Specifically, when more results are filtered, less state is kept, and therefore SGX operators benefit (especially the join operation) since less state is needed to compute the final result, with fewer iterations to non-enclave memory. Specifically, a join performs up to 2.5x faster on data with very low selectivity versus very high, and an aggregation can perform up to 2x faster.

Input Rate (Figure 11): We generate input rates from 10,000 to 50,000 tuples/s to explore the impact on throughput of SGX-enabled operations. We can immediately see from Figure 11 that higher input rates negatively affect latency across the board, but more noticeably for SGX operations. This is expected since it will increase the state being stored in non-enclave memory, and therefore increase the overall processing time per tuple. In some instances we see the join operation increasing latency as much as 78% for large input rates, and as much as 31% for aggregations versus plaintext, and 58% for joins and 2% for aggregations versus a computation-enabling encryption operation. Note that this increase in throughput allows a user to have near-minimal leakage when compared to the encrypted version, and also allows for third-party joins to be executed.

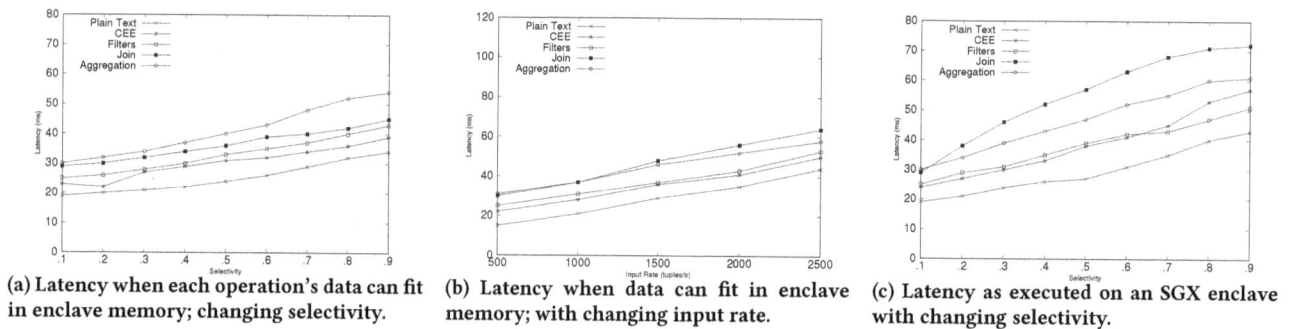

(a) Latency when each operation's data can fit in enclave memory; changing selectivity.

(b) Latency when data can fit in enclave memory; with changing input rate.

(c) Latency as executed on an SGX enclave with changing selectivity.

Figure 10: Changes in latency as changing input selectivity and input rate.

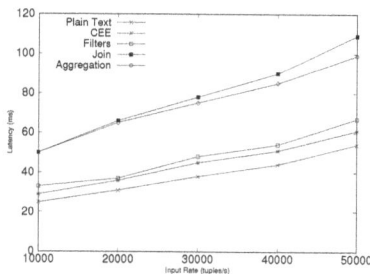

Figure 11: Latency of each operation type as executed on an SGX enclave with changing input rate.

8 CONCLUSION

The current state-of-the-art access control enforcement systems for Data Stream Management Systems either rely on trusted third-party systems to enforce controls, or use some form of computation-enabling encryption that limits query expressiveness, increases data transmission overheads, and can leak information about underlying plaintext values. In this paper, we introduce Sanctuary to implement and evaluate and a method for using Intel's SGX as a trusted computing base for executing streaming operations on untrusted cloud providers. In doing so, we are able to overcome the limitations of the state-of-the-art computation-enabling systems by allowing for *any* query to be executed on an untrusted machine while maintaining *near-Trusted Infrastructure* level information leakage. Moreover, we discuss and resolve issues related to enclave memory size limitations by introducing memory-aware, stateful streaming operators. Finally, we demonstrate that the use of enclave-based processing in a streaming environment incurs only modest overheads when compared to the state-of-the-art systems.

Acknowledgements. This work was supported in part by the National Science Foundation (CNS–1253204 and CNS–1704139).

REFERENCES

[1] Daniel Abadi et al. 2003. Aurora: a new model and architecture for data stream management. *VLDB* 12, 2 (2003), 120–139.
[2] D.J. Abadi et al. 2005. The design of the borealis stream processing engine. In *CIDR*.
[3] Dinh Tien Tuan Anh and Anwitaman Datta. 2014. Streamforce: outsourcing access control enforcement for stream data to the clouds. In *ACM CODASPY*.
[4] Arvind Arasu et al. 2004. Stream: The stanford data stream management system. *Book chapter* (2004).
[5] Arvind Arasu et al. 2006. The CQL continuous query language: semantic foundations and query execution. *The VLDB Journal* 15, 2 (2006), 121–142.
[6] Sergei Arnautov et al. 2016. SCONE: Secure linux containers with Intel SGX. In *12th USENIX OSDI*.
[7] Nathan Backman, Rodrigo Fonseca, and Uğur Çetintemel. 2012. Managing parallelism for stream processing in the cloud. In *HOTCDP*. ACM, 1–5.

[8] Alexandra Boldyreva et al. 2009. Order-preserving symmetric encryption. In *Eurocrypt*. Springer, 224–241.
[9] Stefan Brenner et al. 2016. SecureKeeper: Confidential ZooKeeper using Intel SGX. In *Middleware*.
[10] Paris Carbone et al. 2015. Apache flink: Stream and batch processing in a single engine. *Data Engineering* (2015), 28.
[11] Barbara Carminati et al. 2007. Enforcing access control over data streams. In *ACM SACMAT*. 21–30.
[12] Barbara Carminati et al. 2007. Specifying access control policies on data streams. In *DASFAA*. Springer, 410–421.
[13] Barbara Carminati et al. 2010. A framework to enforce access control over data streams. *ACM TISSEC* 13, 3 (2010), 28.
[14] Debs Grand Challenge. 2014. DEBS Grand Challenge. http://dl.acm.org/citation.cfm?id=2772598. (2014).
[15] Andreas Chatzistergiou and Stratis D Viglas. 2014. Fast heuristics for near-optimal task allocation in data stream processing over clusters. In *CIKM*. ACM.
[16] Victor Costan and Srinivas Devadas. 2016. Intel SGX Explained. *IACR Cryptology ePrint Archive* 2016 (2016), 86.
[17] Aurélien Havet et al. 2017. SecureStreams: A Reactive Middleware Framework for Secure Data Stream Processing. In *DEBS*. ACM, 124–133.
[18] Matthew Hoekstra et al. 2013. Using innovative instructions to create trustworthy software solutions.. In *HASP@ ISCA*. 11.
[19] Yuanqiang Huang et al. 2011. Operator placement with QoS constraints for distributed stream processing. In *CNSM*. IEEE, 1–7.
[20] Paul Kocher, Daniel Genkin, et al. 2018. Spectre attacks: Exploiting speculative execution. *arXiv preprint arXiv:1801.01203* (2018).
[21] Sanjeev Kulkarni et al. 2015. Twitter Heron: Stream Processing at Scale. In *SIGMOD*. ACM, 239–250.
[22] Wolfgang Lindner and Jörg Meier. 2006. Securing the borealis data stream engine. In *IEEE IDEAS*. 137–147.
[23] Rima Nehme et al. 2008. A security punctuation framework for enforcing access control on streaming data. In *ICDE*. 406–415.
[24] Rimma V Nehme et al. 2013. FENCE: Continuous access control enforcement in dynamic data stream environments. In *ACM CODASPY*. 243–254.
[25] Wee Siong Ng et al. 2012. Privacy preservation in streaming data collection. In *ICPADS*. 810–815.
[26] Pascal Paillier. 1999. Public Key Cryptosystems Based on Composite Degree Residuosity Classes. *Advances in Cryptography - EURPCRYPT'99* 1562 (1999).
[27] Peter Pietzuch et al. 2006. Network-aware operator placement for stream-processing systems. In *ICDE*. IEEE, 49–49.
[28] Raluca Popa et al. 2011. Cryptdb: protecting confidentiality with encrypted query processing. In *ACM SOSP*. 85–100.
[29] Christian Priebe, Kapil Vaswani, and Manuel Costa. 2018. EnclaveDB: A Secure Database using SGX. In *EnclaveDB: A Secure Database using SGX*. IEEE, 0.
[30] Stamatia Rizou et al. 2010. Solving the multi-operator placement problem in large-scale operator networks. In *ICCCN*. IEEE, 1–6.
[31] Felix Schuster, Manuel Costa, et al. 2015. VC3: Trustworthy data analytics in the cloud using SGX. In *SP*. IEEE, 38–54.
[32] Fahad Shaon, Murat Kantarcioglu, et al. 2017. SGX-BigMatrix: A Practical Encrypted Data Analytic Framework With Trusted Processors. In *SIGSAC*. ACM, 1211–1228.
[33] Utkarsh Srivastava, Kamesh Munagala, and Jennifer Widom. 2005. Operator placement for in-network stream query processing. In *SIGMOD*. ACM, 250–258.
[34] StormProject. 2014. Storm: Distributed and Fault-Tolerant Realtime Computation. http://storm.incubator.apache.org/documentation/Home.html. (2014).
[35] Cory Thoma et al. 2016. PolyStream: Cryptographically Enforced Access Controls for Outsourced Data Stream Processing. In *SACMAT*, Vol. 21. 12.
[36] Jo Van Bulck, Marina Minkin, et al. 2018. Foreshadow: Extracting the Keys to the Intel {SGX} Kingdom with Transient Out-of-Order Execution. In *27th {USENIX} Security Symposium ({USENIX} Security 18)*. 991–1008.
[37] Wenting Zheng, Ankur Dave, Jethro G Beekman, et al. 2017. Opaque: An Oblivious and Encrypted Distributed Analytics Platform.. In *NSDI*. 283–298.

A Practical Intel SGX Setting for Linux Containers in the Cloud

Dave (Jing) Tian
University of Florida
daveti@ufl.edu

Joseph I. Choi
University of Florida
choijoseph007@ufl.edu

Grant Hernandez
University of Florida
grant.hernandez@ufl.edu

Patrick Traynor
University of Florida
traynor@ufl.edu

Kevin R. B. Butler
University of Florida
butler@ufl.edu

ABSTRACT

With close to native performance, Linux containers are becoming the de facto platform for cloud computing. While various solutions have been proposed to secure applications and containers in the cloud environment by leveraging Intel SGX, most cloud operators do not yet offer SGX as a service. This is likely due to a number of security, scalability, and usability concerns coming from both cloud providers and users. Cloud operators worry about the security guarantees of unofficial SDKs, limited support for remote attestation within containers, limited physical memory for the Enclave Page Cache (EPC) making it difficult to support hundreds of enclaves, and potential DoS attacks against EPC by malicious users. Meanwhile, end users need to worry about careful program partitioning to reduce the TCB and adapting legacy applications to use SGX.

We note that most of these concerns are the result of an incomplete infrastructure, from the OS to the application layer. We address these concerns with *lxcsgx*, which allows SGX applications to run inside containers while also: enabling SGX remote attestation for containerized applications, enforcing EPC memory usage control on a per-container basis, providing a general software TPM using SGX to augment legacy applications, and supporting partitioning with a GCC plugin. We then retrofit Nginx/OpenSSL and Memcached using the software TPM and SGX partitioning to defend against known and potential attacks. Thanks to the small EPC footprint of each enclave, we are able to run up to 100 containerized Memcached instances without EPC swapping. Our evaluation shows the overhead introduced by *lxcsgx* is less than 6.9% for simple SGX applications, 9.5% for Nginx/OpenSSL, and 20.9% for containerized Memcached.

CCS CONCEPTS

• **Security and privacy** → **Trusted computing**; **Virtualization and security**; *Operating systems security*.

KEYWORDS

Cloud; Containers; Security; SGX

ACM Reference Format:
Dave (Jing) Tian, Joseph I. Choi, Grant Hernandez, Patrick Traynor, and Kevin R. B. Butler. 2019. A Practical Intel SGX Setting for Linux Containers in the Cloud. In *Ninth ACM Conference on Data and Application Security and Privacy (CODASPY '19), March 25–27, 2019, Richardson, TX, USA*. ACM, New York, NY, USA, 12 pages. https://doi.org/10.1145/3292006.3300030

1 INTRODUCTION

In the past few years, solutions such as Linux Containers (LXC) and Docker have provided compelling alternatives to heavyweight solutions such as virtual machine monitors running guest operating systems. Container mechanisms provide *OS-level virtualization*, where multiple isolated systems can be run under the same operating system kernel. Cloud computing providers, in particular, stand to gain from containers, as their substantially lighter use of computing resources allows far greater density of deployments per physical machine and drives down infrastructure costs. However, a significant concern with this approach is the extent to which *separation* between containers is possible. Specifically, because containers share a common OS kernel, any vulnerability that exploits the kernel would affect all other containers on the system.

Intel Software Guard Extensions (SGX) [22] provides a compelling new way to establish guarantees of trustworthy execution and platform integrity. SGX preserves the confidentiality and integrity of sensitive data in *enclaves*, secure regions of memory that are protected from unauthorized access by higher privileged processes and system software. Unfortunately, while there has been a surge of research into providing SGX-enabled security guarantees within cloud environments, including Haven [5], Graphene-SGX [59, 60], SCONE [3], and Panoply [54], these have not been adopted to-date by most cloud providers. This may be due to a number of security, scalability, and usability concerns from both cloud providers and users: cloud operators worry about the security guarantee of unofficial SDKs (current solutions that integrate SGX do not interface with the official SDK provided by Intel), limited support for remote attestation within containers, limited physical memory for Enclave Page Cache (EPC) making it difficult to support hundreds of enclaves, and potential denial-of-service attacks against EPC by malicious users; meanwhile, end users need to carefully partition SGX programs to reduce the TCB and face the challenge of rewriting legacy applications to make use of SGX. Solutions such as Haven, Graphene-SGX, and SCONE do offer convenience by removing this need to partition, but come at the cost of an increased TCB that includes all of an application's insensitive components. While Panoply places different parts of application logic into separate enclaves, the creation of and communication with multiple enclaves per application increases EPC memory consumption.

In particular, when deploying SGX in a cloud environment, we believe the following issues must be addressed:

(1) *Limited support for remote attestation:* A critically important feature of SGX is its ability to attest to the identity and integrity of SGX applications to third parties (e.g., cloud users), but neither Haven nor SCONE provides native support for CPU remote attestation.

(2) *SGX application security:* Solutions that involve placing entire applications within a secure enclave, such as Haven, Graphene-SGX, and SCONE, do not necessarily guarantee security, as they can dramatically expand the TCB and may contain vulnerabilities from within either applications or libraries, such as the Heartbleed [9] bug within OpenSSL.

(3) *Limited EPC memory:* The current maximum EPC size is 128 MB, with approximately 90 MB left for users after accounting for enclave management [28]. While EPC page swapping is supported on Linux, it leads to a considerable performance hit. A cloud operator has a vested interest in minimizing the memory footprint of enclaves, which would allow the supporting of many users and reducing of performance degradation (due to swapping) at the same time. The EPC limit also implies cloud providers need to protect the EPC from (malicious) overconsumption, a factor not considered by existing solutions. SGXv2 even allows dynamic EPC page allocation during the enclave runtime, exacerbating EPC memory consumption.[1]

(4) *Support for legacy applications:* To reduce the TCB inside enclaves, Intel [21, 23] mandates program partitioning. Unfortunately, this makes programming for SGX non-trivial.[2]

We note that most of the concerns surrounding adoption of SGX-supported containers in the cloud are the result of an incomplete infrastructure, from the OS to the application layer. We address these concerns through our development of *lxcsgx*, a platform fully enabling Intel SGX deployment for Linux Containers (LXC) in the cloud environment. Unlike past solutions, we pay particular attention to the practical deployment concerns in a cloud environment mentioned above. In so doing, our contributions include:

- Enabling SGX remote attestation for containerized applications. Compared to native host attestations, the overhead is 6.9% and 4.9% for containerized local and remote attestations.

- Enforcing EPC memory usage control per container in the Linux kernel to prevent (malicious) overuse of resources.

- Implementing a GCC plugin to assist program partitioning to reduce the TCB in the enclave and better support scalability.

- Implementing a software TPM using SGX, providing a fast hardware TPM replacement as well as socket APIs for legacy applications, which can access the TPM functionality in an attestable enclave instead of being fully refactored for SGX. The speed of TPM operations ranges from 10 to 280 μs.

- Retrofitting and evaluating Nginx/OpenSSL and Memcached using SGX based on *lxcsgx*. Compared to original native applications, the overhead is less than 9.5% for Nginx/OpenSSL and 20.9% for containerized Memcached.

Outline. The remainder of this paper is structured as follows: Section 2 further motivates our work on *lxcsgx*; Section 3 describes the design and implementation of *lxcsgx*; Section 4 shows how to retrofit applications by leveraging *lxcsgx*; Section 5 evaluates the performance of *lxcsgx* and the applications built atop it. Finally we discuss takeaways from our work in Section 6, while contrasting it against the existing literature in Section 7, and conclude in Section 8.

2 MOTIVATION

Solutions allowing an entire application to run within an SGX enclave without any modifications, such as Graphene-SGX and SCONE, ease the integration of SGX with existing (legacy) applications. However, these approaches tend to bloat both TCB and enclave size, miss key features such as remote attestation, and ignore hardware constraints on EPC size (instead totally relying on EPC page swapping). We examine limitations of these solutions to further motivate our work.

2.1 Why could unofficial SDKs be problematic?

We observe that some cloud providers (e.g., IBM and Azure [48]) had SGX-capable servers available as early as 2017, but they did not officially support SGX applications until recently. We speculate that concern over unofficial SDKs was a contributing factor to the holdup.

Solutions built on customized software stacks or unofficial/homemade SDKs, such as Haven and SCONE, cannot provide native support for remote attestation.[3] Remote attestation requires Intel's Quoting Enclave (QE), which leverages Intel Enhanced Privacy ID (EPID) [32] and is part of the Intel SGX software stack. The missing remote attestation is critical, because it provides cloud users with a guarantee that the desired enclave has the right measurement and is running on a genuine Intel CPU with SGX enabled (rather than a software emulator).[4] Without such a guarantee, it is impossible to reason about the security of the SGX-supported cloud platform.[5]

Runtime libraries within the enclave impose security concerns as well. Software Grand Exposure [7] and Cachezoom [40] have shown that traditional crypto libraries inside the enclave, such as the OpenSSL used by Graphene-SGX and Panoply, are still vulnerable to cache-based side channel attacks. Intel Integrated Performance Primitives (IPP, built into the Intel SGX SDK) appears more secure due to its usage of AES-NI [30]. Similarly, putting glibc or musl[6] into the enclave naively, as Graphene-SGX and SCONE do, might still be a vulnerable practice due to the insecure functions included (e.g., strcpy). In contrast, all "dangerous" functions are removed from Intel's trusted C library, and "sensitive" functions are implemented using hardware instructions (e.g., RDRAND for rand).

---

[1] We provide further discussion on why SGXv2 is not a panacea in Section 6.
[2] The Intel SGX SDK Developer Manual v1.9 has 320 pages.

[3] Haven's attestation is emulated and requires trust in the cloud provider.
[4] SCONE provides only local attestation, which does not give the latter guarantee. Haven, while not strictly a container environment, does not support remote attestation either.
[5] With regard to the recent Foreshadow [61] attack, which leverages out-of-order execution to extract a SGX-enabled machine's private attestation key and allows an adversary to forge valid attestation responses, Intel has released microcode updates [27]. As stated by Van Bulck et al. [61], Foreshadow exploits an implementation bug and does not invalidate the architectural design of Intel SGX.
[6] https://www.musl-libc.org/

Compared to other SGX software stacks, the official Intel SGX SDK seems to be the most secure open-source solution, designed for security and with defenses against Spectre attacks [34]. Azure also exclusively supports the Intel SGX SDK in its cloud environment [48]. While other libraries may provide alternative means for attestation and hardening against attacks, reliance on them consequently alters the SGX trust model. In the remainder of the paper, we assume the official Intel SGX SDK to be deployed in the cloud environment.

2.2 Why is program partitioning preferred?

Program partitioning requires application developers to figure out the most security-sensitive parts of the code, and transform them to use SGX. Though cumbersome, this methodology may be the best security practice to reduce the attack surface via reducing the TCB in the enclave. Because syscalls are not allowed inside the enclave, any SGX solution that does not require program partitioning instead relies on an additional middle layer (e.g., LibOS) to emulate these syscalls; this practice might bloat the TCB depending on the coverage of the emulation. Furthermore, as explicitly mentioned in the SGX Developer Manual [24]), putting vulnerable code into enclaves does not suddenly make the code secure.

The other benefit of program partitioning comes from the potentially small EPC memory consumption in both loading time and runtime. The binary size of Drawbridge LibOS used by Haven is over 200 MB, which is even beyond the maximum 128 MB EPC memory limitation. While TCB size does not directly determine the memory consumption, they are related. For example, a partitioned OpenSSL library in Panoply takes around 6 MB of EPC memory, whereas an unmodified library takes 65 MB in Graphene. To assist with program partitioning, *lxcsgx* contains a GCC plugin *gccsgx*, which supports security level tagging in the source file and lightweight tainting analysis based on the tagging.

2.3 Why is EPC memory control important?

Supporting many users with only 128 MB EPC memory on a single server imposes fundamental challenges to cloud providers. A simple memory leakage bug in SGX applications can exhaust the limited EPC resource and cause the SGX kernel driver [25] to swap out enclaves of other users. Even worse, a malicious user could launch DoS attacks against the EPC memory or conceal cache attacks in the enclave [52]. The result of these attacks are performance degradations [45] and security breaches. The situation gets worse for KVM SGX [26], Intel's SGX virtualization on KVM solution. KVM SGX does not support EPC oversubscription, meaning a VM cannot be created if the virtual EPC requested is beyond the physical EPC limit. Unlike any existing SGX solutions, *lxcsgx* recognizes the importance of EPC memory protection, and enforces EPC memory usage control per container.

2.4 Why is a software TPM crucial?

Programming SGX applications using the Intel SGX SDK is not easy. It requires application developers to have a deep understanding of security concerns specific to the application, as well as of the SDK APIs. Moreover, as shown in later sections, even a simple enclave implementation may take 1 MB of EPC memory. This means a single server can support no more than 100 users at the same time.[7] As a

Haven	Graphene	SCONE	Panoply	*tpmsgx*
209	64.7	>4.0	5.9	1.1

Table 1: Enclave size (MB) for Nginx/OpenSSL in different SGX solutions.

result, EPC page swapping will eventually happen when a new user needs to create an enclave, impacting performance and security by introducing page faults. Unfortunately, unlike a typical shared library such as glibc, an enclave cannot be shared by different processes to reduce EPC memory consumption. Each process needs to allocate a new virtual address region to load the same enclave, which maps into different EPC pages. By design, EPC pages are not shared.

We observe that the desired SGX functionalities are usually shared among a number of applications; these include crypto operations, random number generation, and secure storage. Therefore, it is possible to have this general platform service create a single enclave that serves many different applications at the same time. This cloud service can provide user-friendly APIs, and reduce the EPC memory consumption by avoiding user enclave creation. We instantiate this service as a software TPM[8] using SGX (*tpmsgx*). As a core component of *lxcsgx*, it provides common crypto implementations based on the Intel SGX SDK, and a typical socket API for application developers. As we will later demonstrate, we transform Nginx/OpenSSL to use *tpmsgx* for crypto operations during the SSL/TLS handshake. Table 1 shows how much *tpmsgx* helps to reduce the EPC memory consumption by reducing the enclave size, compared to other SGX solutions.[9]

We summarize and compare the various features of existing SGX solutions and *lxcsgx* in Table 2. We also separately list *tpmsgx* in the table, because it can be used independently of the other components of *lxcsgx*. We believe *lxcsgx* provides an SGX solution that considers practical deployment issues for containers in a cloud environment.

3 DESIGN AND IMPLEMENTATION

Intel SGX provides a means to improve the security of applications via runtime integrity and confidentiality. We investigate how to properly intertwine Linux containers and SGX in a cloud environment through our *lxcsgx* architecture, shown in Figure 1. We choose to focus on LXC, but *lxcsgx* can be extended to support Docker as well.[10] Although the components of *lxcsgx* may appear to be loosely coupled, they share a unified goal and work together under a common platform infrastructure to facilitate SGX use within cloud environments. We fully describe the design and implementation of each component in this section; we also discuss the considerations made for balancing practical architectural limitations and the programming paradigm of SGX with respect to security, scalability, and usability.

3.1 Threat Model and Trust Model

We consider a cooperative cloud environment, where each server supports hundreds of Linux containers. This number is reasonable [33] for deployment due to the lightweight nature of containers compared to VMs, and is particularly apt for microservice-based environments.

---

[7] Recall that the actual EPC memory left for users is around 90 MB.

[8] While simply plugging in a TPM does not necessarily make a legacy application secure, we hope the familiarity of a TPM, along with the provided software APIs for interfacing with it, will ease the process of supporting legacy applications.
[9] Please note that the number for SCONE is conservative, since OpenSSL is not included.
[10] Docker is descended from LXC and, while different, shares many of the same principles.

Solution	Container Support	Remote Attestation	EPC Control	TCB (LoC)	Enclave Size (MB)	Software Stack	Overhead	FOSS
Haven [5]	N/A	N	N	>1.0M	209	Simulation	<54%	N
Graphene-SGX [59, 60]	N/A	Y	N	1.3M	58.5+App	Custom	50% (avg)	Y
SCONE [3]	Docker	N	N	>187K	2.5+App	Custom	<40%	N
Panoply [54]	N/A	Y	N	140K	PartitionDep	Custom	24% (avg)	Y
lxcsgx	LXC	Y	Y	119K	PartitionDep	Intel	<20%	Y
tpmsgx	LXC	Y	N	2K	1.1	Intel	<10%	Y

Table 2: Comparison among existing SGX solutions versus *lxcsgx* and *tpmsgx*

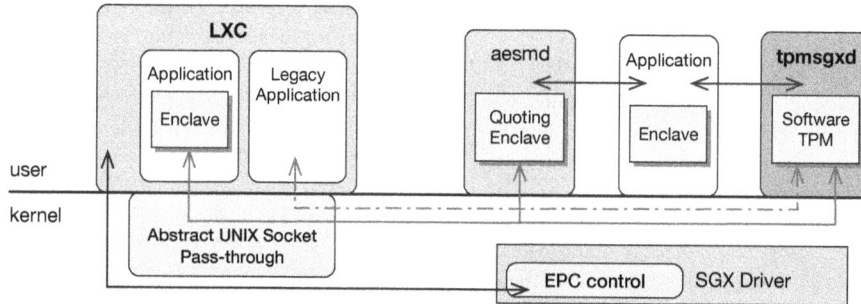

Figure 1: *lxcsgx*'s design enables containerized applications to communicate out from LXC via an abstract UNIX socket. This gives applications within a container access to Intel's *aesmd* and our software TPM (*tpmsgxd*), all while the SGX driver monitors each LXC container's EPC usage. *tpmsgxd* is also available to applications outside a container.

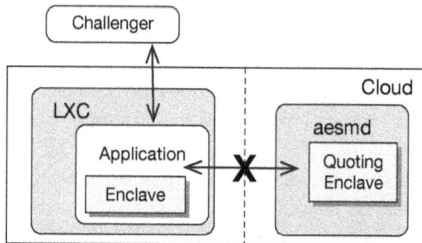

Figure 2: Where there was previously no path between an application in LXC and *aesmd*, our abstract UNIX socket pass-through enables this path and thus attestation.

We expect that the cloud service provider attempts to uphold its contract with customers (e.g., through timely system patching to fix bugs and isolating containers using kernel features). However, we do not necessarily trust the cloud provider, which may be interested in breaking the confidentiality of hosted containers unbeknownst to its customers. Malicious cloud providers may also actively try to compromise the confidentiality and integrity of hosted containers.

The TCB of *lxcsgx* comprises SGX-enabled CPUs and code/data loaded into enclaves. Neither the Linux kernel nor the LXC programs running on the cloud server are trusted, although we expect them to provide certain basic functionality (e.g., starting the system and containers). We do not consider DoS attacks launched by ring-0 attackers (e.g., to prevent users from using Intel SGX). Additionally, we do not consider controlled-channel attacks from ring-0 attackers or side-channel attacks from ring-3 attackers. These attacks [7, 52, 62, 65] are orthogonal to the problem *lxcsgx* is trying to solve and have been well considered in the literature [6, 14, 31, 38, 53, 63].

3.2 Remote Attestation for LXC Applications

When challenger and attester applications are both running within the same container, local (intra-platform) attestation may be achieved by the two applications communicating with each other and exchanging the enclave measurement [2]. However, when the challenger is

running in a different container or on a different physical machine, remote (inter-platform) attestation is needed, where the remote challenger is provided a proof, or *quote*, of the desired enclave. Getting a quote requires the attester to communicate with the Quoting Enclave (QE) [2, 32], provided by Intel SGX SDK as daemon process *aesmd* running on the native machine. Due to the use of an abstract UNIX socket by *aesmd*, and the inability of LXC/Docker to mount a non file-backend socket, remote attestation for containerized applications does not simply work out-of-the-box, as shown in Figure 2.

The simplest solution would be to make the network namespace of the container the same as that of the native host (e.g., by bridging the container's network interface card (NIC) to one in the host machine). However, this configuration breaks network isolation between containers and the host, meaning it cannot be used in a cloud environment. Another potential solution would be to run *aesmd* inside containers. Unfortunately, this does not work either because the SGX kernel driver cannot be installed inside containers. Furthermore, the driver only supports one *aesmd*/QE given a platform. Even in the absence of these limitations, cloud providers might not wish to duplicate all the SGX platform services per container, which both runs up against disk quotas and wastes EPC memory.

Linux kernel implementation. While it is easier to modify the Intel SGX SDK directly,[11] we add a new feature to the Linux kernel to support abstract UNIX socket pass-through for Linux containers.[12] We believe this to be a missing feature for both the Linux kernel and LXC. We modify the *connect()* syscall for UNIX sockets. We add a new directory under /proc called *lxcsgx*, and add an entry *sgx_sock*, which accepts inputs from user space (e.g., the container process) specifying the abstract UNIX socket to be passed through. When applications write into /proc/lxcsgx/sgx_sock, the kernel retrieves the PID and network namespace of the application, along with the abstract socket name, storing these together in the kernel space as

---

[11] Intel actually did this in the recent versions, downgrading the abstract UNIX socket to a traditional one, whose pass-through is supported both by the Linux kernel and LXC.
[12] Open-source kernel changes can be verified by the community and Linux maintainers.

a record indexed by network namespace. For a connection request using an abstract UNIX socket, the original network namespace checks will reject the request unless both source and destination sockets share a namespace. We extend these checks for abstract socket pass-through by looking to see if a pass-through record exists with the source and destination abstract sockets.

LXC implementation. To enable LXC to use the abstract UNIX socket pass-through feature provided by the kernel, we add a new configuration to LXC named *lxcsgx.sgx.sock*. Requests are passed to the kernel using */proc/lxcsgx/sgx_sock*. For example, to support remote attestation, setting "*lxcsgx.sgx.sock = sgx_aesm_socket_base*" is sufficient to let the kernel pass the connection request from the container to *aesmd* outside the container. After mounting the SGX driver using *lxc.mount.entry*, we are able to support remote attestation of SGX applications running inside containers.

3.3 Controlling EPC Memory Usage

To prevent EPC memory from being (maliciously) exhausted by certain users or containers, we count the number of EPC pages allocated per container, rejecting further allocation requests if the EPC quota of the requesting container is exceeded. However, finding the corresponding container that is responsible for each EPC allocation request is non-trivial, because containers are transparent to the underlying Linux kernel, which only sees processes. One possible solution is to trace the Parent PID (PPID) all the way back to the container process (i.e., *lxc-start*) if the given process belongs to a container. Unfortunately, this method has $O(n)$ complexity, and does not work if the process is not directly forked by the container process (e.g., if running applications using *lxc-attach*). Instead, we use the network namespace as a unique identifier for containers, since it is shared by all applications running inside the container. In most cases, containers are configured with different virtual NICs (veth in LXC), and thus have different network namespaces. When one network namespace is shared by multiple containers, the EPC control will be applied to every container within the namespace.

SGX kernel driver implementation. The SGX kernel driver is responsible for EPC memory management, including allocation, swapping, and reclaiming. To access EPC control from user space, we add another two entries under the */proc/lxcsgx* directory, named *epc_control* and *epc_limit*. The former is used to enable/disable EPC control globally on the machine, while the latter is used by containers to pass the EPC control information to the kernel. Each EPC control record saved in the kernel contains network namespace, PID of the record creator, EPC usage limit (number of 4K pages), a flag to activate/deactivate this record, and the current usage of EPC memory of the container. Upon each attempted EPC page allocation (EADD), we find the PID of the requesting process using the enclave owner information maintained by the SGX driver. Given the PID, we find the corresponding network namespace and retrieve the EPC control record. If the record is activated and the requested EPC usage is within the limit, allocation is permitted and usage count increased. Similarly, for EPC page deallocation, we reduce the current usage count of the corresponding EPC control record.

LXC implementation. To leverage the EPC control mechanism, another two new configurations (*lxc.sgx.epc.limit* and *lxc.sgx.epc.control*) are added into LXC. For example, "*lxc.sgx.epc.limit = 1000*" is used to

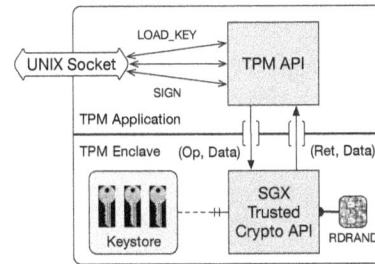

Figure 3: The architecture of *tpmsgxd*. The TPM APIs are exposed via a UNIX socket. The whole software TPM implementation is self-contained, running inside the enclave.

set the maximum EPC memory usage to be 1000 pages for the container, while "*lxc.sgx.epc.control = 1*" is used to activate the EPC control for this container. The container writes into */proc/lxcsgx/epc_limit* to add the EPC record into the kernel during startup. System administrators may also apply commands to the */proc* entries to modify EPC control records in the kernel as needed.

3.4 *tpmsgx*: A Software TPM Using SGX

To reduce the learning curve of SGX programming and free the users from creating their own enclaves, we design a software TPM using SGX, *tpmsgx*, as a general platform service providing a socket API for applications not written with SGX in mind. The whole design of *tpmsgx* is grounded in the functionality and security features provided by TPM; we focus on application-facing functionality and not on additional features (such as measured boot and system attestation) that are built upon TPM. We summarize the differences among (hardware) TPM, fTPM [47],[13] and *tpmsgx* in Table 3. Unlike low-speed TPM chips with fixed firmware installed, *tpmsgx* enjoys both CPU speed and flexible implementations, with the SGX-enabled CPU becoming the hardware root of trust. This also means the security of *tpmsgx* is heavily dependent on the code in the enclave.[14] We build upon Intel IPP within the SDK to provide common TPM functionality in *tpmsgx*, including random number generation, hashing, symmetric/asymmetric crypto primitives, and secure storage.

An issue with using SGX as a TPM is the lack of persistent storage. The data (keys) saved in the enclave will be lost after a reboot. This can be solved with CPU sealing, which encrypts data to the disk using a sealing key generated by the EGETKEY instruction based on different sealing policies [2]. For instance, the sealing can bind to the measurement of the enclave, so only the enclave with the same measurement can unseal the data (similarly to TPM sealing using PCRs). Compared to TPM-based attestation, *tpmsgx* also supports SGX attestation, which not only provides a trusted measurement of the implementation to the challenger, but also establishes a secure channel with the remote party thanks to the key exchange which occurs during the remote attestation procedure. Since the cloud provider is not trusted in our threat model, we expect *tpmsgx* to be auditable (e.g., open source), and customers can use SGX attestation to retrieve the measurement of the *tpmsgx* running within the cloud environment and verify it is as expected, thus establishing trust.

---

[13] An alternative TPM implementation built atop ARM TrustZone.
[14] Again, putting the entire OpenSSL/GnuTLS inside an enclave to use its functionality for *tpmsgx* might be a bad idea, due to their large attacking surfaces [15, 16].

Solution	Trust Anchor	Implementation	CPU Mode	Software Stack	Secure Storage	RT Integrity	Secure Channel	Speed*
TPM [58]	TPM	Hardware	Ring-0	TSS	NVM	N/A	N/A	10-400ms [57]
fTPM [47]	TrustZone	Firmware	Secure World	OP-TEE	eMMC RPMB	N/A	N/A	10-200ms
tpmsgx	SGX	Software	Ring-3	Intel SGX SDK	Sealing	Y	Y	15-280μs

Table 3: Comparison between *tpmsgx* and other TPM technologies. Note that the speed column provides a timing range of different TPM commands, such as RNG, key generation, quote, etc.

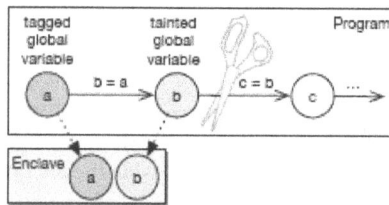

Figure 4: Given a set of tagged global variables (e.g., a), *gccsgx* identifies intermediate tainted variables (e.g., b). These global variables (e.g., a and b) constitute a minimal TCB for the enclave. The same process applies to tagged functions.

Software TPM implementation. *tpmsgx* is implemented as a daemon process *tpmsgxd* running on the native host (similarly to *aesmd*). It uses an abstract UNIX socket to receive requests from either native applications or containerized ones. Figure 3 summarizes its interface and components. Applications use the socket API to access TPM functionalities inside *tpmsgxd*. When remote attestation is enabled, an AES128 shared secret is established between the *tpmsgx* enclave and the requesting application. All responses from *tpmsgxd* are encrypted using AES128-GCM before leaving the enclave. *tpmsgx* provides the operations listed below:

- Random number generation using RDRAND.
- Loading of AES128 symmetric or ECC256 private keys.
- ECC256 key generation.
- AES128-GCM encryption/decryption.
- DH key exchange.
- SHA256 hashing.[15]
- ECDSA signing and verification.

LXC implementation. For applications running inside containers to use *tpmsgx*, we add another new configuration into LXC, named *lxc.sgx.tpm.sock*. Similarly to *lxc.sgx.sock*, "*lxc.sgx. tpm.sock = tpmsgxd_sock_base*" enables communication between the containerized applications and the *tpmsgxd*, with the help of the abstract UNIX socket pass-through feature in the kernel.

3.5 *gccsgx*: A SGX Program Partitioning Helper

Retrofitting legacy applications using SGX is challenging. Developers need to find and place security-sensitive parts of their program into an enclave while minimizing TCB, making it as small as possible to reduce the attack surface. We design *gccsgx* based on GCC to help facilitate SGX program partitioning by finding a minimal TCB for the enclave using static tainting analysis. We first add a new attribute in GCC – *SGX_ENCLAVE()*, allowing developers to tag global variables or functions considered security-sensitive within the application. We design the attribute to model multilevel security (MLS) labels supporting different security levels, such as top-secret

or confidential, for two purposes. Given the EPC quota in a cloud environment, developers can decide whether or not to include code or data with lower security levels based on the resulting enclave binary size and runtime memory consumption. The tainting analysis may also taint the code or data with a different security level from what it was tagged as. By keeping the tagged level unchanged and providing a tainting level at the same time, we are able to reveal intrinsic connections within the program and catch potential mistakes made in security analysis for program partitioning.

To find a minimal TCB for the enclave, we consider global variables and functions which are directly tagged and intermediately tainted, as shown in Figure 4. This is a tradeoff between an actual minimal TCB, which only includes tagged components, and a complete minimal TCB, which incorporates everything along the tainting paths.[16] We do not consider implicit flows in *gccsgx*.

Glamdring [35] may be used instead if a complete minimal TCB is desired. To use Glamdring, developers first annotate input and output variables in the source code that contain sensitive data. Starting with the annotated inputs, Glamdring performs static dataflow analysis to track the propagation of sensitive data through the application. Using these annotations, Glamdring performs static backward slicing to identify functions that annotated outputs depend on. All security-sensitive functions identified by the above two processes are placed inside the enclave. Glamdring is compatible with our *lxcsgx* architecture, but we choose *gccsgx*; by not fully propagating taint, *gccsgx* produces a smaller TCB than approaches targeting completeness.

We assume developers would find most obvious places to tag after a security analysis, and *gccsgx* extends the minimal TCB with minimal taint propagation. Note that once this security-sensitive data/code is inside the enclave, the original tainting path will be broken. For instance, variable *c* in Figure 4 cannot get the value of *b* until an ECall is explicitly defined to grant access permission. We leave the choice to developers to determine if an ECall should be made or that part of code/data should be inside the enclave as well.[17]

Implementation. We implement *gccsgx* as a GCC 4.8.4 plugin using the GCC Python Plugin interface [37]. We implement three security levels for the *SGX_ENCLAVE()* attribute: "top-secret", "secret", and "confidential."[18] To handle memory aliasing, we require the "-O" optimization during compilation, as *gccsgx* hooks right after the "alias" GCC pass, which performs structural alias analysis, points-to and escape analysis, and flow-sensitive/insensitive analysis [18]. Example output from *gccsgx* is provided below. For example, tainting analysis may raise the tagged security level, such as *var1*, or find missing components during initial tagging, such as *var3* and *fun3*.

---

[15]Even though SHA256 is not a keyed operation, SHA256 is often used in security-sensitive contexts (e.g., hashing of raw data by the SGX SDK to produce signatures).

[16] It is possible that a large part of an application needs to be put inside the enclave as a result of high taint propagation.

[17] *gccsgx* only identifies the minimal TCB and does not perform enclave code generation, so we must ultimately rely on the developer to make decisions like these.

[18]Note that these labels are only used by tainting, rather than for policy control or privilege separation.

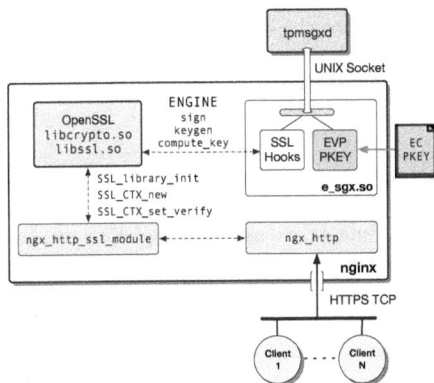

Figure 5: Relationship of *tpmsgxd*, *sgxengine* (e_sgx.so), and Nginx. HTTPS connections are routed through Nginx which communicates with OpenSSL to establish a TLS session.

```
********************
Global vars:
var1[test.c:14]: tagged["confidential"], tainted["secret"]
var2[test.c:25]: tagged["secret"], tainted["N/A"]
var3[test.c:17]: tagged["N/A"], tainted["confidential"]
--------------------
Functions:
fun1[test1.c:9]: tagged["secret"], tainted["N/A"]
fun2[test1.c:10]: tagged["confidential"], tainted["N/A"]
fun3[test1.c:33]: tagged["N/A"], tainted["secret"]
********************
```

4 APPLICATION CASE STUDY

We now consider how *lxcsgx* can support containerized applications. We examine Nginx/OpenSSL (a web server providing HTTPS services) and Memcached (a key-value in-memory database). Each application leverages different components of *lxcsgx*, based on different threat models and tradeoffs. Both run inside LXC containers.

4.1 Hardening Nginx/OpenSSL

Nginx [55] is a popular open-source web server that touts high performance and scalability. It embeds the OpenSSL [44] library to handle all low-level details for the web server, such as crypto operations. In order to provide authenticity to remote users via HTTPS, the web server requires a server certificate and private key to be generated. This certificate is signed by a Certificate Authority (CA) in order to create a chain of trust from a well-known issuer to the website. The server's private key is an important component in running HTTPS. This key is loaded upon Nginx boot from the file system and passed into the OpenSSL library for signing. During an SSL/TLS handshake, the private key is used to sign data, and the client verifies the signature using the server's public key (available in the server certificate). The security of the private key is essential; if compromised, an attacker can impersonate the web server.

A major bug found in OpenSSL in 2014 called Heartbleed [67] allowed remote attackers to leak random ranges of server memory, some of which were discovered to contain cookies, HTTP request bodies, passwords, and server private keys. Unless a web server was using a physical TPM for all TLS signing operations, the private key would have to be in memory at some point during Nginx's lifetime. For most cloud users running on remote hosting, placing private keys in a physical TPM may be difficult or impossible to coordinate

with their cloud providers. The low speed of TPM also interferes with the scalability of Nginx [41]. In response, software-only solutions have attempted to partition server private keys away from the Nginx process and OpenSSL library [56]. Unfortunately, these solutions merely place the private key in a different process/service on the same machine, while requiring changes to Nginx and OpenSSL.

This is a typical use case of *tpmsgx*, where legacy applications need a trusted execution environment for crypto operations, and yet developers do not need to accommodate a new programming paradigm. Leveraging *tpmsgx*, we develop an OpenSSL ENGINE called *sgxengine*, a pluggable module that allows hooking of key cryptographic operations. This ENGINE talks to *tpmsgxd*, transferring and translating function calls dealing with the private key into the TPM enclave, as shown in Figure 5. With all functionality pushed into the SGX-based TPM, the ***private key never has to be loaded into Nginx/OpenSSL memory***. As we show in later sections, our solution achieves security and scalability at the same time.

Implementation. OpenSSL started to support the ENGINE API from version 0.9.6 onwards. Thus we choose OpenSSL 1.1.0c as the testing base. For Nginx, we choose 1.11.9, and slightly patch it to force the usage of our OpenSSL ENGINE. Note that we do not modify OpenSSL itself. In the *sgxengine*, we set the default private key loading function of OpenSSL to the one provided by *tpmsgx*. We then do a one-time load of the private key into the TPM and receive a key-id back for future reference. To guarantee that this key only stays inside the enclave memory, we fake the PKEY structure that is returned to OpenSSL so that we don't break the ENGINE API.

We configure Nginx to use the strongest cipher suite, ECDHE-ECDSA-AES128-GCM-SHA256, also known as NSA Suite B [49] combination 1, supporting TLSv1.2 connections. The *sgxengine* is essentially a hooked implementation of EC_KEY_METHOD in OpenSSL. This covers key generation, shared key computation, and signing, which are mapped into EC key generation, ECDH shared secret computation, and ECDSA signing in *tpmsgx*. During TLS session key generation, the real public key and a fake private key are returned to OpenSSL, while the real private key stays only inside the enclave memory. All future TLS operations that would normally use the private key in OpenSSL are now routed to and handled by *tpmsgx*.

One ENGINE API limitation we discovered was how the design of signing in OpenSSL differs from that in Intel SGX SDK. The signing function in OpenSSL expects the message digest, while the SGX SDK receives the raw data and performs hashing internally. We opt to not change any source code within OpenSSL or Intel SGX SDK. Therefore, we hook the SHA256 digest functions in the *sgxengine* to record the raw data of digest for future transfer to *tpmsgx*.

4.2 Securing Memcached Credentials

Memcached [17] is a key-value store used to alleviate the load from web databases by first attempting to handle queries from RAM before forwarding them to the database. While Graphene-SGX [60] and Glamdring [35] have tried to secure the database by putting the whole application or a portion of it into the enclave, we consider user credential protection as an alternative. Starting from 2014 [19], Memcached supports the Simple Authentication and Security Layer (SASL) [42] which requires clients to supply a username and password before a connection. During authentication, the supplied credentials are checked against an internal SASL password database containing plaintext entries, which are loaded from disk into memory.

Unfortunately, due to remote code execution vulnerabilities [10–12], attackers could not only change the data saved in the memory, but also steal user credentials. Ironically, one of the vulnerabilities lies in the SASL authentication [12]. Ideally, SASL should be used only as a way to provide an authentication protocol for receiving the input from the client and sending back the authentication result. Even if the SASL layer is compromised, the sensitive information saved in Memcached should not be leaked to its third-party libraries. We achieve this security goal by retrofitting the authentication part of Memcached using SGX. We find the security-sensitive code and data with the help of *gccsgx*, and put them into the enclave, preventing credential leakage to the untrusted code.

Implementation. As the first step in security analysis, We first pinpoint the global variable *memcached_sasl_pwdb*, which refers to the database holding credentials. We then tag this variable as an enclave candidate with security level "top-secret", and enable *gccsgx* for GCC in the Makefile. The output of *gccsgx* is shown below:

```
********************
Global vars:
memcached_sasl_pwdb[sasl_defs.c:37]: tagged["top-secret"], tainted
    ["N/A"]
--------------------
Functions:
init_sasl[sasl_defs.c:170]: tagged["N/A"], tainted["top-secret"]
sasl_log[sasl_defs.c:122]: tagged["N/A"], tainted["N/A"]
sasl_server_userdb_checkpass[sasl_defs.c:40]: tagged["N/A"],
    tainted["top-secret"]
********************
```

Even though we have not tagged any functions, there are two functions tainted by the tagged global variable, these being *init_sasl* and *sasl_server_userdb_checkpass*. We manually verified that this result of *gccsgx* is correct (e.g., no memory aliasing for the tagged global variable). The tainted functions, together with the global variable, need to be placed in the enclave. We also provide an interface for *sasl_server_userdb_checkpass* function in EDL, making this function accessible to the untrusted part of the program as an ECall. We will later demonstrate the running of 100 containers with SASL-enabled Memcached at the same time without introducing EPC page swapping, thanks to the limited TCB and EPC memory consumption as the result of program partitioning.

5 EVALUATION

All evaluation is done on a machine with a 4-core SGX-enabled CPU and 8 GB memory. The machine is running Ubuntu 14.04 LTS, with Linux kernel 4.2.8, LXC 2.0.0, GCC 4.8.4, Intel SGX SDK 1.7, and Intel SGX driver 1.0.[19] In evaluating our case study applications, we use Nginx 1.11.9, OpenSSL 1.1.0c, and Memcached 1.4.33. Our Linux container instances also use the template for Ubuntu 14.04 LTS on amd64. All containers are created with abstract UNIX socket pass-through and EPC control enabled. The socket pass-through is configured with *aesmd* and *tpmsgxd*; the EPC limit is set to 1000K pages (4MB) for each container, making sure all tests run to completion without being throttled. Both *aesmd* and *tpmsgxd* run on the native host, as shown in Figure 1. We consider three running environments:

(1) *Stock*: stock kernel + original SGX driver.
(2) *lxcsgx*: *lxcsgx* kernel + SGX driver with EPC control.
(3) *LXC*: container running atop the *lxcsgx* environment.

Unless stated otherwise, assume all cases are repeated 100 times.

Simple SGX Applications. To measure the general overhead of enclave creation, local attestation, and remote attestation in each of our three environments, we use the SampleEnclave, LocalAttestation, and RemoteAttestation applications contained in the Intel SGX SDK. Our results are displayed in Figure 6(a). In all testing cases, the stock kernel has the best performance, followed first by our *lxcsgx* kernel, with added overhead from EPC control, and then LXC, which is slowed down by both the socket pass-through and EPC control in the container environment. The overhead introduced by *lxcsgx* and LXC is fairly small compared to the stock setting, ranging from 0.6% to 4.6% and 4.9% to 6.9%, respectively. In fact, since EPC control is enforced only during the initialization phase,[20] the overhead of *lxcsgx* and LXC will be amortized once the application reaches a stable state.

tpmsgx. To measure the performance of our software TPM, we run *tpmsgxd* on the host machine and our benchmark tool in all environments to time eight TPM commands, including: generating a 16-byte random number, loading an AES 128-bit key, encrypting/decrypting 32-byte data using AES128-GCM, generating an ECC256 key pair, computing DH key exchange based on ECC256, and signing/verifying 32-byte data or a 64-byte signature using ECDSA. We repeat all test cases with remote attestation enabled to establish a secure channel between the benchmarking tool and *tpmsgxd*, measuring the overhead due to the extra encryption/decryption. The results are shown in Figure 6(b).

Random number generation, key loading, and encryption/decryption commands return a response to the client in less than 15 μs. When remote attestation is enabled, the response is slower due to the internal encryption before the result leaves the enclave. However, the response is still within 23 μs. Key loading has the lowest overhead with remote attestation enabled. Whereas other TPM commands return at least 16 bytes of data to be encrypted, key loading just returns a 4-byte key handle. Crypto operations involving ECC256 are slow compared to the first group of TPM commands, ranging from 200 μs to 280 μs. The overhead of remote attestation is not obvious anymore, as the operations themselves take most of the computation cycles. Since we run the same command 100 times, the overhead introduced by the SGX enclave creation, EPC control, and abstract socket pass-through in both *lxcsgx* and LXC environments are amortized, achieving close performance to the stock environment.

Nginx/OpenSSL. To measure the overhead introduced by *sgxengine* communicating with *tpmsgx* in Nginx, we configure Nginx to use NSA Suite B [49] combination 1[21] as the only cipher supported in the SSL/TLS handshake, and we compare against the original Nginx running on the native host. We use the OpenSSL client tool (*s_client*) to establish a HTTPS connection, and measure the connection setup

---

[19] No fundamental changes were made to the driver since the tested version (e.g., still no EPC control), but incremental changes to SGX added support for SGXv2 instructions.

[20] SGXv1 does not support dynamic allocation of more EPC pages to applications after enclave build time [64]. Our EPC control is also applicable to SGXv2; the only difference is that EPC control will be additionally enforced whenever more pages are allocated.
[21] AES with 128-bit key in GCM mode, ECDH using the 256-bit prime, modulus curve P-256 [DSS], TLS PRF with SHA-256 [SHS].

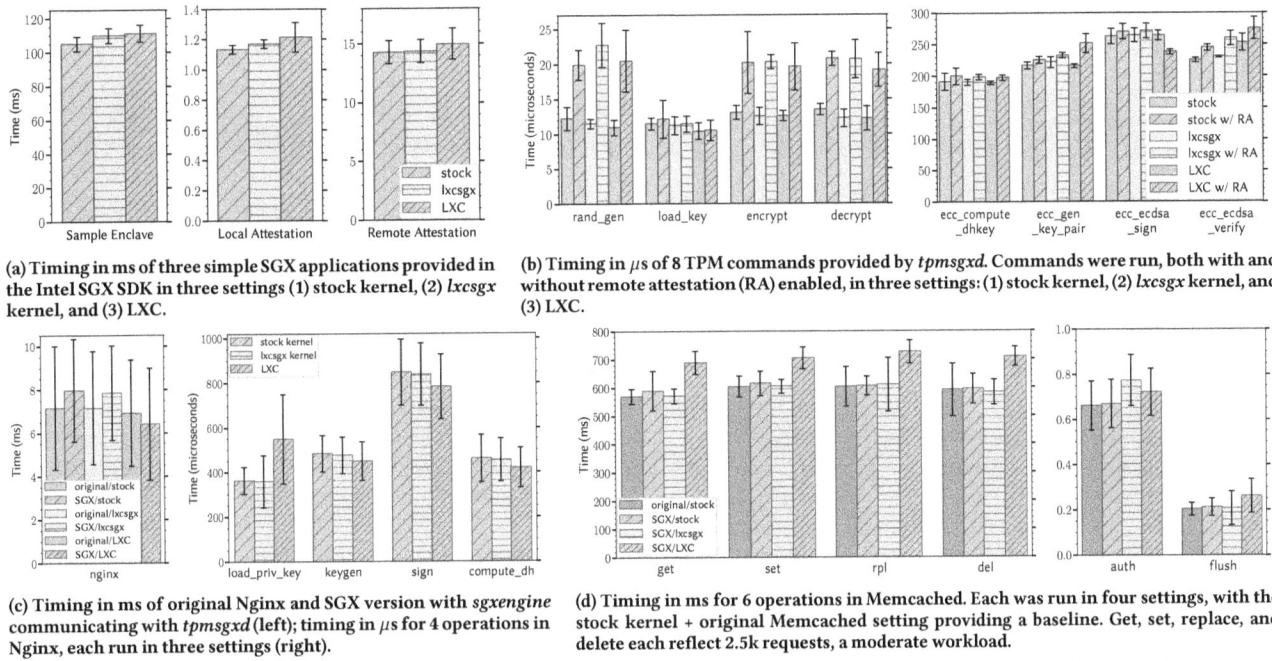

(a) Timing in ms of three simple SGX applications provided in the Intel SGX SDK in three settings (1) stock kernel, (2) *lxcsgx* kernel, and (3) LXC.

(b) Timing in μs of 8 TPM commands provided by *tpmsgxd*. Commands were run, both with and without remote attestation (RA) enabled, in three settings: (1) stock kernel, (2) *lxcsgx* kernel, and (3) LXC.

(c) Timing in ms of original Nginx and SGX version with *sgxengine* communicating with *tpmsgxd* (left); timing in μs for 4 operations in Nginx, each run in three settings (right).

(d) Timing in ms for 6 operations in Memcached. Each was run in four settings, with the stock kernel + original Memcached setting providing a baseline. Get, set, replace, and delete each reflect 2.5k requests, a moderate workload.

Figure 6: Our evaluation results for (a) simple SGX applications, (b) *tpmsgx*, and (c) Nginx, and (d) Memcached.

time. As shown in Figure 6(c)-L, the introduced overhead is less than 1 *ms* for all three SGX environments. Comparing to the raw Nginx performance, **the overhead introduced by *lxcsgx*, *tpmsgx*, and *sgxengine* together is less than 9.5%, which is much lower than Graphene-SGX (50%), SCONE (20%), and Panoply (24%).**[22]

To understand the overhead caused by *tpmsgx* in the *sgxengine*, we measure the time taken for key loading, ECDSA signing, key generation, and DH key computation, hooked by *sgxengine*, as shown in Figure 6(c)-R. The slowest operation is ECDSA signing, which still takes less than 0.9 *ms*. Besides key loading, all operations exhibit similar performance regardless of environment. If we compare this benchmark with the *tpmsgx* benchmark, we see a big portion of the overhead resulting from socket communication and OpenSSL rather than the software TPM itself (e.g., around 0.5 *ms* for signing). Interestingly, key loading is particularly slow in the LXC environment. We suspect this is related with the container rootfs being mounted under the native rootfs, complicating file accesses in the kernel.

Memcached. To measure the overhead introduced by performing the SASL authentication of Memcached in SGX, we use python-binary-memcached [50] as a client to benchmark the Memcached server with SASL authentication support. In each run, we set/get/re-place/delete 2.5K entries and perform 1 authentication and 1 flush operation. We use stock kernel + unmodified Memcached environment as a baseline, comparing it against our SGX-version of Memcached under the three environments.

As shown in Figure 6(d), all SGX-enabled environments except LXC show comparative performance with the baseline, with overhead ranging from 0.3% to 3.5%. This is reasonable, since most of the

Compilation	Min	Avg	Max	Stdev
Memcached	0.59	0.67	0.78	0.06
GCC w/ *gccsgx*	36.49	36.55	36.66	0.05
OpenSSL	32.61	33.08	33.48	0.27
GCC w/ *gccsgx*	693.22	695.73	707.86	4.11

Table 4: Memcached and OpenSSL compilation time in seconds using GCC both w/o and w/ *gccsgx*.

operations are pure database manipulations, which do not involve SGX. However, the LXC environment does show some overhead compared to the other configurations, ranging from 16.7% to 20.9%. We suspect this may be due to its intrinsic resource constraints, such as default quotas on CPU/memory, and networking overhead introduced by containers. The authentication operation captures the overhead of using SGX enclave to hold the SASL credentials and check against the password. With *lxcsgx* enabled, native host and LXC environments show an overhead of 9.1% to 17.1% relative to the stock kernel. Nevertheless, **the maximum overhead is less than 0.2 ms per authentication**.

gccsgx. To measure the overhead of the GCC plugin during the compilation, we compile Memcached and OpenSSL using GCC, both without and with *gccsgx* enabled for 10 times each, as shown in Table 4. For Memcached, a normal compilation takes less than 1 second to finish. With *gccsgx* enabled, compilation takes around 36 seconds even though we are performing a lightweight static tainting analysis. The overhead compared to normal compilation is around 55x. This slowdown may be the result of Python implementation of the plugin, the number of global variables contained in the program, and the fact that *gccsgx* processes each function three times across the different compilation phases to pass the tainting information. OpenSSL compilation with *gccsgx* takes around 11 min, introducing

---

[22]Panoply did not evaluate Nginx. The number we reference is an average overhead for applications they tested.

Application	Peak Stack	Peak Heap	Enclave Size
SampleEnclave	11 KB	12 KB	439 KB
LocalAttestation	3*6 KB	3*16 KB	3*1.1 MB
RemoteAttestation	3 KB	16 KB	1.0 MB
tpmsgx	2 KB	12 KB	1.1 MB
Memcached	2 KB	4 KB	130 KB

Table 5: EPC memory consumption for all applications we tested. Note that LocalAttestation creates 3 enclaves.

Application	EADD	EREMOVE	EPC Pages Used
aesmd	4574	4123	451
LXC/Memcached	75911	52458	23453
Total	80485	56581	23904

Table 6: Number of SGX instructions and EPC pages allocated/reclaimed by the SGX kernel driver with 100 LXC/Memcached instances. Total EPC consumption is around 96 MB.

an overhead of around 21x compared to the normal build. Fortunately, this overhead is just a one-time effort during partitioning.

Through *gccsgx*, we offer a lightweight alternative for partitioning SGX programs. Unlike the Glamdring [35] approach, we further reduce the TCB via minimal taint propagation based on tagged global variables and functions. We believe the plugin would be faster than Glamdring with respect to analysis time; unfortunately, as Glamdring is not open-source, we were unable to compare *gccsgx* with it.

EPC memory consumption. The EPC memory consumption of an application includes the static enclave size and the dynamic memory allocation. We measure static enclave size by looking at the size of the enclave image generated during the SGX build. We measure dynamic memory consumption using sgx-gdb provided by Intel SGX SDK with memory measurement enabled in application enclaves. The results are shown in Table 5. Most applications use 1 MB or less of EPC memory per enclave, thanks to program partitioning. The enclave binary itself appears to be responsible for most of the EPC consumption due to static linking against extra libraries, such as trusted C/C++ runtime and crypto. To support more keys generated or loaded into *tpmsgx*, we need to increase the heap size of the enclave, which is configurable during the SGX build. If we assume AES 128-bit keys, each EPC page (4KB) can hold around 256 keys. This means 1 MB EPC memory could support 65536 TLS connections at the same time. Note that these numbers are conservative. Actual runtime consumption is higher due to extra memory needed for enclave management and buffers holding data from untrusted memory.

We create and start 100 LXC containers with SASL-enabled Memcached running inside. We record the number of SGX instructions issued by the SGX kernel driver, to inspect the actual runtime EPC page consumption from the kernel, rather than counting what is visible in the user-space. The SGXv1 instructions we focus on are EADD, which adds a page into an uninitialized enclave, and EREMOVE, which removes a page from the EPC. As shown in Table 6, there are around 24K EPC pages used in total. Most of these are requested by the 100 containers.[23] Therefore, the actual EPC memory consumption is $24K*4KB=96MB$ in total. Each container consumes less than 1 MB EPC at runtime. Although EPC memory consumption is application-dependent, given a reasonable security analysis and program partitioning, having 1 MB EPC memory usage might be practical for many applications.

---

[23]We ignore the impact of other platform software, such as *aesmd*.

6 DISCUSSION

Abstract UNIX socket pass-through in *lxcsgx* may open a new attack vector on the host. However, mounting an abstract UNIX socket into a container should be more secure than mounting a traditional UNIX socket, which has well-known exploitations (20 CVEs [13]) due to its use of the file backend. The abstract UNIX socket is designed to solve known vulnerabilities in traditional UNIX sockets. Moreover, abstract UNIX sockets are still under the control of SELinux [36], which could also limit the impact of exploiting *aesmd* or *tpmsgxd*.

The EPC memory consumption control in *lxcsgx* currently only works for containers rather than normal processes running on the native host machine, although it can easily be extended to support EPC control per process. Since SGXv1 does not support adding more EPC pages after the enclave is initialized [64], the final EPC memory consumption is constrained by the static configuration of the enclave (determined by the user), and EPC quote (determined by the cloud provider). For SGXv2, EPC control is the only defense against (malicious) EPC memory oversubscription, because enclaves can request more EPC pages during the runtime, breaking the limit in the static configuration.[24] A future work for EPC control is to merge it into the *cgroups* [39] subsystem in the Linux kernel as a new resource controller, providing a more general group-wide policy control.

While fTPM [47] makes fair points on why ARM TrustZone [1] is the superior software TPM candidate, use of SGX comes with its own advantages. Since *tpmsgx* just relies on enclave code running at ring-3, extending or bug fixing for *tpmsgx* is much like normal user-space programming. This upgrade flexibility is important, as demonstrated when RSA encryption keys were exposed by a recent firmware bug found in Infineon TPMs [43]. The fix required hardware OEMs to change their own BIOS/UEFI to update the TPM firmware. *tpmsgx* is also very fast, running at CPU speed with a small software stack.

One limitation of *tpmsgx* lies in the persistent storage (sealing), since we could not stop the cloud provider from deleting the sealed data. As we consider a cooperative cloud environment, we assume the cloud provider would not erase user data in reality because doing so is in violation of the service contract with the end users. However, rolling back the old sealed data is possible since old data can still be unsealed by *tpmsgx*. A potential solution is to use the monotonic counter and trusted time features of Intel Management Engine (ME) to defend against these rollback attacks [29]. DoS attacks against *tpmgsx* are also possible when some containers issue a large number of requests. A potential solution is to add request rate control per container within *tpmsgx*, throttling requests from certain containers if the sending rate exceeds certain limits.

Automatic program partitioning is a hard problem that has been an active research topic for years. Being a lightweight static tainting analysis plugin for GCC, *gccsgx* cannot automatically generate compiler-ready code partitions, but it gives a framework for assisting with this problem that is quite challenging to do in a completely manual fashion. Developers still need to write in EDL to define ECalls and OCalls, which bridge the normal application and the enclave implementation. Nevertheless, *gccsgx* is designed to seamlessly work with the current build system (rather than requiring another toolchain,

---

[24] SGXv2's max-heap and max-stack parameters [64] only reserve the address space. Developers may specify a large number (e.g., 1 GB) for these limits to make sure the address space is large enough for future EPC expansion, in which case actual EPC page allocation remains unrestricted.

such as LLVM used by Glamdring [35]), to help facilitate program partitioning and to provide a minimum TCB option following the lightweight tainting analysis. For fully automatic SGX program partitioning with sound tainting analysis, one can refer to Glamdring, which can also be integrated into the *lxcsgx* infrastructure.

7 RELATED WORK

Intel SGX. Haven [5] is the first attempt to protect user applications from an untrusted cloud environment using SGX, by putting the unmodified application and a LibOS together into the enclave. Subsequently, VC^3 [51] tries to secure MapReduce computations in an untrusted cloud environment. Both Haven and VC^3 are based on an SGX emulator rather than real SGX hardware. Graphene-SGX is an extension of Graphene LibOS [59, 60] to support SGX. Similarly to Haven, Graphene-SGX relies on LibLinux to run the application inside the enclave without changes. Note that these solutions focus on easing SGX adoption for legacy applications but, unlike *lxcsgx*, downplay or ignore the potential impact of a large TCB inside the enclave and limited EPC memory available in a system

To reduce the TCB in the enclave, SCONE [3] replaces the LibOS with a shim layer, and supports running a whole Docker container inside the enclave. Ryoan [20] alternatively uses NaCl [66] to build an application sandbox within the enclave. While these solutions have a thinner middleware layer than LibOS approaches, putting the whole application into the enclave may still bloat the TCB, introducing a large attack surface as a result. Panoply [54] further reduces the TCB by partitioning programs and putting part of the application logic (namely "micron") into the enclave. Each application may depend on interaction with many microns; the creation and communication of multiple microns per application come at the cost of EPC memory consumption and performance degradation. Our solution instead keeps with the standard partitioning practice for SGX applications.

Eleos [45] notices issues caused by the limited EPC memory, and proposes a user-space memory allocator for EPC to reduce EPC page faults that result from EPC page swapping. We believe Eleos can be integrated into *lxcsgx* to improve the performance of SGX applications in general by reducing their EPC memory requirements. To automate the program partitioning using Intel SGX SDK, Glamdring [35] applies heavyweight data-flow analysis and backward slicing to find security sensitive code and data, as well as source-level transformation to generate compiler-ready code. It requires the LLVM toolchain rather than GCC, and the compilation overhead is not clear. In cases where a minimal, yet complete, TCB is desired, Glamdring may be integrated into *lxcsgx* as a substitute for our partitioning using *gccsgx*.

TPM. As the cornerstone of Trusted Computing, TPM [58] provides a hardware root of trust for software stacks. TPM 2.0 [4] even includes different specifications for PC client, mobile, and automotive systems. Unfortunately, these TPM chips are well-known to be slow and hard to patch or fix. Software TPM solutions instead try to provide better performance and/or extend more functionalities. vTPM [46] virtualizes TPM in the Xen environment, by having slave vTPMs in domains and a master vTPM in domain 0, which serializes the communication between vTPMs and the hardware TPM. cTPM [8] extends the TPM commands for cross-device applications by sharing an additional root key with the cloud. fTPM [47] implements

a software TPM using TrustZone [1], which is available on mobile platforms. Nevertheless, due to their dependency on a hardware TPM or on running inside TrustZone's secure world, these solutions are still slow when compared to native application speed. Patching or upgrading is still challenging since most of these implementations are in the form of firmware. To the best of our knowledge, *tpmsgx* is the first software TPM solution to use SGX, achieving CPU speed and enabling normal user-space programming.

8 CONCLUSION

We design and implement *lxcsgx*, providing a practical Intel SGX setting for Linux containers in the cloud environment. This includes an infrastructure that supports remote attestation and EPC memory control for containers, a software TPM that can be more easily allow legacy application to leverage SGX, and a GCC plugin to assist with program partitioning. We retrofit different applications using the software TPM or program partitioning to use SGX, while reducing the TCB and EPC memory consumption at the same time. The evaluation shows reasonable overhead ranging from 6.9% to 20.9%, which is the lowest when compared to that of previous SGX solutions.

ACKNOWLEDGMENTS

This work was supported in part by the US National Science Foundation under grant numbers CNS-1642973, CNS-1540217, and CNS-1815883; and by Intel Corporation. Any opinions, findings, and conclusions or recommendations expressed in this material are those of the authors and do not necessarily reflect the views of the National Science Foundation or Intel Corporation.

REFERENCES

[1] Tiago Alves, Don Felton, et al. 2004. TrustZone: Integrated Hardware and Software Security. *ARM White Paper* 3, 4 (2004), 18–24.
[2] Ittai Anati, Shay Gueron, Simon Johnson, and Vincent Scarlata. 2013. Innovative Technology for CPU Based Attestation and Sealing. In *Proceedings of the 2nd International Workshop on Hardware and Architectural Support for Security and Privacy (HASP)*.
[3] Sergei Arnautov, Bohdan Trach, Franz Gregor, Thomas Knauth, Andre Martin, Christian Priebe, Joshua Lind, Divya Muthukumaran, Daniel O'Keeffe, Mark L Stillwell, and Others. 2016. SCONE: Secure Linux Containers with Intel SGX. In *Proceedings of the 12th USENIX Symposium on Operating Systems Design and Implementation (OSDI)*.
[4] Will Arthur and David Challener. 2015. *A Practical Guide to TPM 2.0: Using the Trusted Platform Module in the New Age of Security*. Apress.
[5] Andrew Baumann, Marcus Peinado, and Galen Hunt. 2015. Shielding Applications from an Untrusted Cloud with Haven. *ACM Transactions on Computer Systems (TOCS)* 33, 3 (2015), 8.
[6] Jethro Beekman. 2017. On the recent side-channel attacks on Intel SGX. https://jbeekman.nl/blog/2017/03/sgx-side-channel-attacks/ Accessed.
[7] Ferdinand Brasser, Urs Müller, Alexandra Dmitrienko, Kari Kostiainen, Srdjan Capkun, and Ahmad-Reza Sadeghi. 2017. Software Grand Exposure: SGX Cache Attacks Are Practical. In *Proceedings of the 11th USENIX Workshop on Offensive Technologies (WOOT)*.
[8] Chen Chen, Himanshu Raj, Stefan Saroiu, and Alec Wolman. 2014. cTPM: A Cloud TPM for Cross-Device Trusted Applications. In *Proceedings of the 11th USENIX Symposium on Networked Systems Design and Implementation (NSDI)*.
[9] Common Vulnerabilities and Exposures. 2016. CVE-2014-0160. https://cve.mitre.org/cgi-bin/cvename.cgi?name=CVE-2014-0160.
[10] Common Vulnerabilities and Exposures. 2016. CVE-2016-8704. https://cve.mitre.org/cgi-bin/cvename.cgi?name=CVE-2016-8704.
[11] Common Vulnerabilities and Exposures. 2016. CVE-2016-8705. https://cve.mitre.org/cgi-bin/cvename.cgi?name=CVE-2016-8705.
[12] Common Vulnerabilities and Exposures. 2016. CVE-2016-8706. https://cve.mitre.org/cgi-bin/cvename.cgi?name=CVE-2016-8706.
[13] Common Vulnerabilities and Exposures. 2017. UNIX Socket Vulnerabilities. https://cve.mitre.org/cgi-bin/cvekey.cgi?keyword=unix+socket+vulnerability Accessed.

[14] Victor Costan, Ilia Lebedev, and Srinivas Devadas. 2016. Sanctum: Minimal Hardware Extensions for Strong Software Isolation. In *Proceedings of the 25th USENIX Security Symposium*.

[15] CVE Details. 2017. GNU/TLS Vulnerability Statistics. https://www.cvedetails.com/product/4433/GNU-Gnutls.html?vendor_id=72 Accessed.

[16] CVE Details. 2017. OpenSSL Vulnerability Statistics. http://www.cvedetails.com/product/383/Openssl-Openssl.html?vendor_id=217 Accessed.

[17] Brad Fitzpatrick. 2004. Distributed Caching with Memcached. *Linux Journal* 2004, 124 (2004), 5.

[18] Free Software Foundation, Inc. 2017. GNU Compiler Collection (GCC) Internals. https://gcc.gnu.org/onlinedocs/gccint/ Accessed.

[19] Patrick Galbraith. 2017. SASL memcached now available! https://blog.couchbase.com/sasl-memcached-now-available/ Accessed.

[20] Tyler Hunt, Zhiting Zhu, Yuanzhong Xu, Simon Peter, and Emmett Witchel. 2016. Ryoan: A Distributed Sandbox for Untrusted Computation on Secret Data. In *Proceedings of the 12th USENIX Symposium on Operating Systems Design and Implementation (OSDI)*.

[21] Intel Corporation. 2016. Intel Software Guard Extensions for Linux OS. https://01.org/intel-softwareguard-extensions.

[22] Intel Corporation. 2016. Intel Software Guard Extensions (Intel SGX). https://software.intel.com/en-us/sgx.

[23] Intel Corporation. 2016. Intel Software Guard Extensions (Intel SGX) SDK. https://software.intel.com/sgx-sdk.

[24] Intel Corporation. 2016. Intel® Software Guard Extensions SDK for Linux* OS Developer Reference . https://download.01.org/intel-sgx/linux-1.7/docs/Intel_SGX_SDK_Developer_Reference_Linux_1.7_Open_Source.pdf.

[25] Intel Corporation. 2016. Linux SGX Driver. https://github.com/01org/linux-sgx-driver.

[26] Intel Corporation. 2017. KVM SGX. https://github.com/intel/kvm-sgx.

[27] Intel Corporation. 2018. Intel-SA-00161: Q3 2018 Speculative Execution Side Channel Update. https://www.intel.com/content/www/us/en/security-center/advisory/intel-sa-00161.html.

[28] Intel Developer Zone. 2017. SGX - is HeapMaxSize necessary? https://software.intel.com/en-us/forums/intel-software-guard-extensions-intel-sgx/topic/607004#comment-1857071 Accessed.

[29] Intel Developer Zone. 2017. SGX enclaves. https://software.intel.com/en-us/forums/intel-software-guard-extensions-intel-sgx/topic/670388 Accessed.

[30] Gorka Irazoqui, Kai Cong, Xiaofei Guo, Hareesh Khattri, Arun Kanuparthi, Thomas Eisenbarth, and Berk Sunar. 2017. Did we learn from LLC Side Channel Attacks? A Cache Leakage Detection Tool for Crypto Libraries. *arXiv preprint arXiv:1709.01552* (2017).

[31] Seo Jaebaek, Lee Byoungyoung, Kim Sungmin, Shih Ming-Wei, Shin Insik, Han Dongsu, and Kim Taesoo. 2017. T-SGX: Eradicating Controlled-Channel Attacks Against Enclave Programs. In *Proceedings of the Network and Distributed System Security Symposium (NDSS)*.

[32] Simon Johnson, Vincent Scarlata, Carlos Rozas, Ernie Brickell, and Frank Mckeen. 2016. Intel® Software Guard Extensions: EPID Provisioning and Attestation Services. *White Paper* (March 2016).

[33] Dustin Kirkland. 2015. How many containers can you run on your machine? https://blog.ubuntu.com/2015/06/11/how-many-containers-can-you-run-on-your-machine.

[34] Paul Kocher, Daniel Genkin, Daniel Gruss, Werner Haas, Mike Hamburg, Moritz Lipp, Stefan Mangard, Thomas Prescher, Michael Schwarz, and Yuval Yarom. 2018. Spectre Attacks: Exploiting Speculative Execution. *arXiv preprint arXiv:1801.01203* (2018).

[35] Joshua Lind, Christian Priebe, Divya Muthukumaran, Dan O'Keeffe, Pierre-Louis Aublin, Florian Kelbert, Tobias Reiher, David Goltzsche, David Eyers, Rüdiger Kapitza, et al. 2017. Glamdring: Automatic Application Partitioning for Intel SGX. In *Proceedings of the 2017 USENIX Annual Technical Conference (ATC)*.

[36] Peter Loscocco and Stephen Smalley. 2001. Meeting Critical Security Objectives with Security-Enhanced Linux. In *Proceedings of the Ottawa Linux Symposium*.

[37] David Malcolm. 2017. GCC plugin that embeds CPython inside the compiler. https://github.com/davidmalcolm/gcc-python-plugin Accessed.

[38] Sinisa Matetic, Mansoor Ahmed, Kari Kostiainen, Aritra Dhar, David Sommer, Arthur Gervais, Ari Juels, and Srdjan Capkun. 2017. ROTE: Rollback Protection for Trusted Execution. In *Proceedings of the 26th USENIX Security Symposium*.

[39] Paul Menage. 2016. CGROUPS. https://www.kernel.org/doc/Documentation/cgroup-v1/cgroups.txt.

[40] Ahmad Moghimi, Gorka Irazoqui, and Thomas Eisenbarth. 2017. CacheZoom: How SGX Amplifies the Power of Cache Attacks. In *Proceedings of the Conference on Cryptographic Hardware and Embedded Systems (CHES)*.

[41] Thomas Moyer, Kevin Butler, Joshua Schiffman, Patrick McDaniel, and Trent Jaeger. 2009. Scalable Web Content Attestation. In *Proceedings of the Annual Computer Security Applications Conference (ACSAC)*.

[42] John G Myers. 1997. Simple Authentication and Security Layer (SASL). (1997).

[43] Matus Nemec, Marek Sys, Petr Svenda, Dusan Klinec, and Vashek Matyas. 2017. The Return of Coppersmith's Attack: Practical Factorization of Widely Used RSA Moduli. In *Proceedings of the ACM SIGSAC Conference on Computer and Communications Security (CCS)*.

[44] OpenSSL. 2017. OpenSSL- Cryptography and SSL/TLS Toolkit. https://www.openssl.org/.

[45] Meni Orenbach, Pavel Lifshits, Marina Minkin, and Mark Silberstein. 2017. Eleos: ExitLess OS Services for SGX Enclaves. In *Proceedings of the 12th European Conference on Computer Systems (EuroSys)*. 238–253.

[46] Ronald Perez, Reiner Sailer, Leendert van Doorn, et al. 2006. vTPM: Virtualizing the Trusted Platform Module. In *Proceedings of the 15th USENIX Security Symposium*.

[47] Himanshu Raj, Stefan Saroiu, Alec Wolman, Ronald Aigner, Jeremiah Cox, Paul England, Chris Fenner, Kinshuman Kinshumann, Jork Loeser, Dennis Mattoon, et al. 2016. fTPM: A Software-Only Implementation of a TPM Chip. In *Proceedings of the 25th USENIX Security Symposium*.

[48] Mark Russinovich. 2018. Azure confidential computing. https://azure.microsoft.com/en-us/blog/azure-confidential-computing/.

[49] Margaret Salter and Russ Housley. 2012. *Suite B Profile for Transport Layer Security (TLS)*. Technical Report. RFC 6460.

[50] Jayson Santos. 2017. python-binary-memcached. https://github.com/jaysonsantos/python-binary-memcached.

[51] Felix Schuster, Manuel Costa, Cédric Fournet, Christos Gkantsidis, Marcus Peinado, Gloria Mainar-Ruiz, and Mark Russinovich. 2015. VC3: Trustworthy Data Analytics in the Cloud using SGX. In *Proceedings of the IEEE Symposium on Security and Privacy (IEEE S&P)*.

[52] Michael Schwarz, Samuel Weiser, Daniel Gruss, Clémentine Maurice, and Stefan Mangard. 2017. Malware Guard Extension: Using SGX to Conceal Cache Attacks. In *Proceedings of the Conference on Detection of Intrusions and Malware & Vulnerability Assessment (DIMVA)*.

[53] Jaebaek Seo, Byounyoung Lee, Seongmin Kim, Ming-Wei Shih, Insik Shin, Dongsu Han, and Taesoo Kim. 2017. SGX-Shield: Enabling Address Space Layout Randomization for SGX Programs. In *Proceedings of the Network and Distributed System Security Symposium (NDSS)*.

[54] Shweta Shinde, Dat Le Tien, Shruti Tople, and Prateek Saxena. 2017. Panoply: Low-TCB Linux Applications With SGX Enclaves. In *Proceedings of the 24th Network and Distributed System Security Symposium (NDSS)*.

[55] Igor Sysoev. 2017. NGINX. https://nginx.org/en/ Accessed.

[56] The H2O project. 2017. Privilege separation engine for OpenSSL / LibreSSL. https://github.com/h2o/neverbleed Accessed.

[57] Dave (Jing) Tian, Kevin R. B. Butler, Joseph I. Choi, Patrick McDaniel, and Padma Krishnaswamy. 2017. Securing ARP/NDP From the Ground Up. *IEEE Transactions on Information Forensics and Security (TIFS)* 12, 9 (2017), 2131–2143.

[58] Trusted Computing Group. 2011. Trusted Platform Module Main Specification, version 1.2, revision 116. https://linuxcontainers.org/.

[59] Chia-Che Tsai, Kumar Saurabh Arora, Nehal Bandi, Bhushan Jain, William Jannen, Jitin John, Harry A Kalodner, Vrushali Kulkarni, Daniela Oliveira, and Donald E Porter. 2014. Cooperation and Security Isolation of Library OSes for Multi-Process Applications. In *Proceedings of the Ninth European Conference on Computer Systems (EuroSys)*.

[60] Chia-Che Tsai, Donald E Porter, and Mona Vij. 2017. Graphene-SGX: A Practical Library OS for Unmodified Applications on SGX. In *Proceedings of the USENIX Annual Technical Conference (ATC)*.

[61] Jo Van Bulck, Minkin Marina, Ofir Weisse, Daniel Genkin, Baris Kasikci, Frank Piessens, Mark Silberstein, Thomas F. Wenisch, Yuval Yarom, and Raoul Strackx. 2018. Foreshadow: Extracting the Keys to the Intel SGX Kingdom with Transient Out-of-Order Execution. In *Proceedings of the 27th USENIX Security Symposium*.

[62] Wenhao Wang, Guoxing Chen, Xiaorui Pan, Yinqian Zhang, XiaoFeng Wang, Vincent Bindschaedler, Haixu Tang, and Carl A. Gunter. 2017. Leaky Cauldron on the Dark Land: Understanding Memory Side-Channel Hazards in SGX. In *Proceedings of the ACM Conference on Computer and Communications Security (CCS)*.

[63] Nico Weichbrodt, Anil Kurmus, Peter Pietzuch, and Rüdiger Kapitza. 2016. Async-Shock: Exploiting Synchronisation Bugs in Intel SGX Enclaves. In *Proceedings of the European Symposium on Research in Computer Security (ESORICS)*.

[64] Bin Cedric Xing, Mark Shanahan, and Rebekah Leslie-Hurd. 2016. Intel® Software Guard Extensions (Intel® SGX) Software Support for Dynamic Memory Allocation Inside an Enclave. In *Proceedings of the Conference on Hardware and Architectural Support for Security and Privacy (HASP)*.

[65] Yuanzhong Xu, Weidong Cui, and Marcus Peinado. 2015. Controlled-Channel Attacks: Deterministic Side Channels for Untrusted Operating Systems. In *Proceedings of the IEEE Symposium on Security and Privacy (IEEE S&P)*.

[66] Bennet Yee, David Sehr, Gregory Dardyk, J Bradley Chen, Robert Muth, Tavis Ormandy, Shiki Okasaka, Neha Narula, and Nicholas Fullagar. 2009. Native Client: A Sandbox for Portable, Untrusted x86 Native Code. In *Proceedings of the 30th IEEE Symposium on Security and Privacy (IEEE S&P)*.

[67] Liang Zhang, David Choffnes, Dave Levin, Tudor Dumitras, Alan Mislove, Aaron Schulman, and Christo Wilson. 2014. Analysis of SSL Certificate Reissues and Revocations in the Wake of Heartbleed. In *Proceedings of the Internet Measurement Conference (IMC)*.

Limitless HTTP in an HTTPS World: Inferring the Semantics of the HTTPS Protocol without Decryption

Blake Anderson
Cisco
blake.anderson@cisco.com

Andrew Chi
University of North Carolina
achi@cs.unc.edu

Scott Dunlop
Cisco
scdunlop@cisco.com

David McGrew
Cisco
mcgrew@cisco.com

ABSTRACT

We present new analytic techniques for inferring HTTP semantics from passive observations of HTTPS that can infer the value of important fields including the status-code, Content-Type, and Server, and the presence or absence of several additional HTTP header fields, e.g., Cookie and Referer. Our goals are to improve the understanding of the confidentiality limitations of HTTPS, and to explore benign uses of traffic analysis that could replace HTTPS interception and static private keys in some scenarios. We found that our techniques increase the efficacy of malware detection, but they do not enable more powerful website fingerprinting attacks against Tor. Our broader set of results raises concerns about the confidentiality goals of TLS relative to a user's expectation of privacy, warranting future research.

We apply our methods to the semantics of both HTTP/1.1 and HTTP/2 on data collected from automated runs of Firefox 58.0, Chrome 63.0, and Tor Browser 7.0.11 in a lab setting, and from applications running in a malware sandbox. We obtain ground truth plaintext for a diverse set of applications from the malware sandbox by extracting the key material needed for decryption from RAM post-execution. We developed an iterative approach to simultaneously solve several multi-class (field values) and binary (field presence) classification problems, and we show that our inference algorithm achieves an unweighted F_1 score greater than 0.900 for most HTTP fields examined.

CCS CONCEPTS

• Security and privacy → **Web protocol security**; *Cryptanalysis and other attacks*;

KEYWORDS

Transport Layer Security; Network Traffic Analysis; Machine Learning; Malware Detection; Website Fingerprinting

ACM Reference Format:

Blake Anderson, Andrew Chi, Scott Dunlop, and David McGrew. 2019. Limitless HTTP in an HTTPS World: Inferring the Semantics of the HTTPS Protocol without Decryption. In *Ninth ACM Conference on Data and Application Security and Privacy (CODASPY '19), March 25–27, 2019, Richardson, TX, USA.* ACM, New York, NY, USA, 12 pages. https://doi.org/10.1145/3292006.3300025

1 INTRODUCTION

HTTPS, or HTTP-over-TLS, encrypts HTTP requests and responses, and is foundational to internet security. In this paper, we show that it is possible to infer the HTTP method, status-code, and header fields without decrypting the connection. Inferring HTTP protocol semantics from observations of HTTPS connections aims to provide "Limitless HTTP in an HTTPS World", to adapt an ironic phrase[1]. A primary goal for TLS is confidentiality [9, 30]; our work explores places where it fails due to the gap between theory and practice. Semantic security [14, 15] requires that an attacker has negligible advantage in guessing any plaintext value, but the cryptographic algorithms in TLS only meet the lesser goal of indistinguishability of the plaintext from messages of the same size. A cipher meeting the lesser goal fails at semantic security when applied to the message space consisting of the strings YES and NO. While our proposed methods cannot undo encryption entirely, they can often recover detailed information about the underlying HTTP protocol plaintext, which raises questions about what goals for HTTPS are most appropriate and achievable. Many users would reject a hypothetical variant of HTTPS that left the method, content-type, and status codes unencrypted 98% of the time, yet our analysis produces essentially the same outcome on standard HTTPS implementations.

We frame the HTTP inference problem as a number of disjoint multi-class and binary classification problems. The multi-class classifiers model field values, e.g., nginx-1.13 for the Server field and text/html for the Content-Type field. The binary classifiers model the presence or absence of a field, e.g., the presence of the Cookie and Referer fields in an HTTP request. We designed classifiers for the method and status-code fields as well as HTTP headers that were well-represented in both our HTTP/1.1 and HTTP/2 datasets and exhibited a reasonable level of diversity, i.e., the majority class label appeared in less than 80% of the decrypted sessions. Many of these values are correlated with other values in the same HTTP transaction or other transactions in the same TLS connection, e.g.,

---

[1]Michael Scott's unwittingly incongruous slogan from *The Office*, "Limitless Paper in a Paperless World".

text/css and text/javascript objects are often transferred using the same TLS connection. Using this intuition, we developed an iterative classification strategy that utilizes the inferences of related transactions predicted during the previous iteration.

The HTTP inference experiments use data collected from Firefox 58.0, Chrome 63.0, Tor Browser 7.0.11, and data collected from a malware sandbox over a two-week period. We designed two sets of experiments where we segmented the training and testing datasets based on the TLS server_name extension and the collection week, which reflects how these methods would be used in practice and highlights the importance of maintaining a current, representative training dataset. A malware sandbox service generated the malware data through automated runs of submitted samples, and we generated the browser data daily by collecting all connections after initiating a connection to each website in the Alexa top-1,000 list.

The experiments tested optimistic and more realistic deployments of our techniques. In the optimistic deployment, the week-based splitting of the Firefox, Chrome, and Tor datasets into training and testing sets resulted in some overfitting. We believe these experiments are still informative because inferences capturing the purpose of common connections with high efficacy are valuable, and our data collection strategy captured dynamic content directly loaded by the target website, e.g., news stories, and indirectly loaded by the target website, e.g., referred advertising sites, resulting in a more temporally diverse dataset than one would expect. The dataset splitting based on the server_name reflected a setting where the model must generalize to unseen connections.

As with all traffic analysis research, our results have implications for both attackers and defenders; we touch on both sides of this dichotomy throughout this paper, and examine two popular research areas that embody the moral tension of our results. The first, malware detection, has become increasingly important with the rise of encrypted traffic, and malware's predictable use of encryption to obfuscate its network behavior [1, 3]. The second, website fingerprinting, has serious privacy implications, which the literature examines in the context of the Tor protocol [26, 39]. Our techniques did not improve the performance of website fingerprinting, which we attribute to Tor's use of fixed-length cells and multiplexing. On the other hand, we found that inferring the HTTP protocol semantics improved the detection of TLS encrypted malware communication. We attribute this increase in performance to the differences in the distributions of HTTP header fields, e.g., requested Content-Type and Server fields, and the presentation of these learned concepts to the malware classifier.

HTTPS traffic is often subject to interception to detect and block malicious content [11] and to passive monitoring using static private keys [16]. Benign traffic analysis offers an alternative that better respects the principle of least privilege. Green et al. [16] cite application troubleshooting and performance analysis as major motivations for passive HTTPS monitoring, and those use cases can directly leverage our HTTP inferences, without third-party decryption or key escrow. Similarly, benign traffic analysis may allow some network administrators to avoid the use of TLS termination proxies and the associated security issues [11, 34]. This approach has many advantages over actively probing servers. Specifically, active probes have difficulty accounting for all possible client configurations, the server and associated software need to be active during the scan,

and the probes will not necessarily exercise problematic server options. For example, 3.2% of the HTTP/2 connections we observed used multiple web servers within the same connection, and this behavior was often dependent on the requested URI. These connections typically included proxy servers, servers providing static and dynamic content, and servers processing client data, e.g., YouTube's YouTube Frontend Proxy/sffe/ESF stack.

To implement the algorithms outlined in this paper, we assume the adversary or defender to have several capabilities. First, they need the ability to perform passive monitoring of the target network's traffic. Second, they need to have a large, diverse, and current corpus of training data correlating the encrypted traffic patterns observable on a network with the underlying HTTP transactions. Third, the adversary or defender needs to have the computational power to execute many classifiers per observed TLS connection.

We make the following novel contributions:

(1) We describe the first framework to infer an extensive set of HTTP/1.1 and HTTP/2 protocol semantics inside of TLS and Tor encrypted tunnels without performing decryption.
(2) We test our algorithms on datasets based on Firefox 58.0, Chrome 63.0, Tor Browser 7.0.11, and data collected from a malware sandbox. We show that we can reliably infer the semantics of HTTP messages on all datasets except for Tor.
(3) We apply our methods to TLS encrypted malware detection and Tor website fingerprinting. We show that first modeling the semantics of encrypted HTTP messages has the potential to improve malware detection, but fails to improve website fingerprinting due to Tor's implemented defenses.

2 BACKGROUND

2.1 Relevant Protocols

The data and analysis of this paper revolves around making inferences relative to 4 main protocols: HTTP/1.1 [12, 13], HTTP/2 [4], TLS 1.2 [9], and Tor [10]. Other Transport Layer Security (TLS) versions, such as TLS 1.3 [30], did appear in our data, but represented less than 5% of connections.

HTTP is the prominent protocol to facilitate data transfer on the World Wide Web. HTTP/1.1 [12, 13] and HTTP/2 [4] are the most popular versions of the HTTP protocol, and as shown in Table 1, their representation was roughly equal in our datasets. HTTP/1.1 is a stateless protocol that enables the exchange of requests and responses between a client and server. An HTTP/1.1 request begins with a request-line specifying the method, request-target, and HTTP-version of the request, and a response begins with a status-line specifying the HTTP-version, status-code, and reason-phrase. Following the request-line or status-line, there is a potentially unordered, case-insensitive list of header fields with their associated values. In this paper, we make inferences on the request-line's method, the status-line's status-code, and many of the headers fields and values, such as Referer, Server, and Content-Type. HTTP/1.1 supports pipelining, where a client can send 2 or more requests before receiving the server's response, and the server will then send a series of responses in the same order as they were requested.

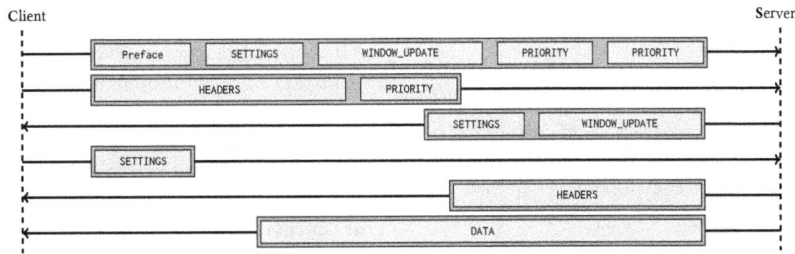

Figure 1: Firefox 58.0 HTTP/2 connection to google.com inside of a TLS encrypted tunnel. The gray boxes indicate a single TLS application_data record, and the light blue boxes indicate HTTP/2 frames.

HTTP/2 [4] was introduced to solve some of HTTP/1.1's shortcomings, e.g., by introducing multiplexing and header compression. HTTP/2 can multiplex multiple streams over a single HTTP/2 connection by using various frames to communicate the state of different streams. Figure 1 illustrates the creation of an HTTP/2 connection inside of a TLS tunnel. The dark gray boxes represent TLS application_data records, and the light blue boxes represent HTTP/2 frames. The client begins an HTTP/2 connection by sending a fixed set of bytes indicating the connection is HTTP/2 immediately followed by a SETTINGS frame containing the parameters related to the client's HTTP/2 configuration. The client can send additional frames at this point, and in Figure 1, the client sends a WINDOW_UPDATE frame for flow control management, a set of PRIORITY frames defining the priority of the multiple streams in the connection, a HEADERS frame containing the request header fields and values, and finally another PRIORITY frame. The server must begin an HTTP/2 connection by sending a SETTINGS frame. After an additional exchange of SETTINGS frames, the server sends a HEADERS frame containing the response header fields and values, and finally a DATA frame containing the requested data. The header fields are compressed using HPACK [28]. Our goal is to identify HEADERS frames and the values they contain.

TLS is increasingly securing HTTP/1.1 requests and responses, and browser vendors have stated that they will not implement HTTP/2 without encryption. The TLS handshake begins with the exchange of client_hello and server_hello records that establish the cryptographic parameters needed to encrypt and authenticate data. The client and server can also negotiate the application layer protocol with these messages by using the application_layer_protocol_negotiation extension, where the values http/1.1 and h2 reasonably refer to HTTP/1.1 and HTTP/2. After establishing a set of shared keys, the client and server each send change_cipher_spec and finished records designating the end of the TLS handshake, and can now send encrypted application_data records containing application layer data. The dark gray boxes in Figure 1 represent application_data records.

Tor securely transmits and anonymizes TCP-based application layer protocols, e.g., HTTP, using a combination of TLS, its own encryption protocol, and an overlay network [10]. The client creates a Tor connection by first negotiating a TLS handshake with a Tor entry node. After performing a Tor handshake, the client then constructs a circuit by sending a CREATE2 cell to the first onion router in the chain, where a cell is the basic unit of communication similar to an HTTP/2 frame. The onion router responds with a CREATED2

cell with the information needed to derive a pair of 128-bit AES keys to encrypt outgoing messages and decrypt incoming messages. The client sends an RELAY_EXTEND2 cell to extend the circuit to an additional onion router, and will follow the same key establishment protocol with the contents of the returned RELAY_EXTENDED2 cell. After repeating this process multiple times, The 128-bit AES keys of each onion router in the circuit's path sequentially encrypt the RELAY_DATA cells. The contents of RELAY_DATA cells carry the relevant application layer data, e.g., TLS records needed to perform an additional TLS handshake, and are null padded so that they always contain 514 bytes.

2.2 Inferences on Encrypted Traffic

Inferring the content and intent of encrypted traffic has a rich history in the academic literature. While not directly targeting encrypted traffic, previous work has applied protocol-agnostic network threat detection to encrypted communication with reasonable results. These methods rely on data features such as the number of packets sent and periodicity of connections [17, 32]. Other methods have used features specific to the TLS protocol to correlate the application's identity, server's identity, and behavior of the interaction to improve detection [1].

Website fingerprinting is another well-studied encrypted traffic inference goal [20, 26, 27, 38, 39]. This problem is typically framed as the adversary attempting to identify connections to a small list of censored websites over the Tor network by leveraging side channel information such as the size of packet bursts and unique packet sizes [38]. Tor, especially when used with pluggable transports, makes website fingerprinting significantly more difficult, but the reliable detection of Tor pluggable transports has been demonstrated [37].

Previous work has also studied direct inferences on the body of encrypted HTTP messages. One example of this class of attacks includes inferring the video a user is watching over popular streaming services [29, 31]. Keyword fingerprinting is a recent attack that identifies individual queries sent to web applications, e.g., a search query to Google, over Tor [25]. Inferring the size of an encrypted resource is well known [36], and has recently been used to identify users based on the unique, dynamic content the web server sends them [35].

In contrast to previous work that makes inferences on the HTTP body, we introduce methods that infer the HTTP protocol semantics, thus understanding the protocol machinery of HTTP transactions inside of a TLS encrypted tunnel. Our results may provide value

Dataset Name	TLS Connections	HTTP/1.1 TX's	HTTP/2 TX's
firefox_h	61,091	72,828	132,685
chrome_h	379,734	515,022	561,666
tor_h	6,067	50,799	0
malware_h	86,083	182,498	14,734
enterprise_m	171,542	–	–
malware_m	73,936	–	–
tor_open_w	5,000	54,079	0
tor_censor_w	2,500	31,707	0

Table 1: The HTTP protocol semantics classification experiments use datasets ending with _h (Section 4), the malware classification experiments use datasets ending with _m (Section 5.1), and the website fingerprinting experiments use datasets ending with _w (Section 5.2).

for many of the goals described in this section, either directly or indirectly as a means to normalize data features.

3 DATA

Throughout this paper, we use a combination of data sources collected from automated runs in Linux-based virtual machines, a commercial malware analysis sandbox, and a real enterprise network. The Linux-based VMs used CentOS 7 running on VMware ESXi. The malware analysis sandbox executed tens-of-thousands of unique binaries each day under Windows 7 and 10, where we restricted our analysis to convicted samples that used TLS to communicate. The enterprise network had roughly 3,500 unique internal IP addresses per day. With the notable exception of the data collected from the enterprise network, we also collected the key material necessary to decrypt the connections in all datasets. This allowed us to correlate the decrypted HTTP transactions with the observable data features. A summary of the datasets is given in Table 1, where the HTTP inference experiments use datasets ending with _h (Section 4), the malware classification experiments use datasets ending with _m (Section 5.1), and the website fingerprinting experiments use datasets ending with _w (Section 5.2).

3.1 HTTP Inferences Data

To collect the ground truth for the application layer requests and responses, the Linux-based VMs contacted each site in the Alexa top-1,000 using Chrome 63.0, Firefox 58.0, and Tor Browser 7.0.11. We repeated this data collection each day for two weeks in December 2017. We collected two weeks of malware data from a commercial malware analysis sandbox during October 2017. We used varying approaches to collect the key material necessary to decrypt the connections for each dataset as explained in each subsection. When a given network connection failed or decryption of that connection failed, we discarded the sample resulting in different datasets sizes. Session decryption failures occurred due to occasional key extraction problems, e.g., the encryption keys were not in memory during the memory snapshots for Tor. This occurred uniformly at random and thus unlikely to introduce bias.

3.1.1 Firefox 58.0 and Chrome 63.0. Both Firefox 58.0 and Chrome 63.0 support the export of TLS 1.0-1.3 master secrets through the SSLKEYLOGFILE environment variable. To prepare data collection for a given browser and site pair, we set the SSLKEYLOGFILE environment variable and begin collecting the network traffic with tcpdump. Then we launch the specified browser and site pair in private mode using the Xvfb virtual window environment, and allow the process to run for 15 seconds. After 15 seconds, all associated processes are killed, and we store the packet capture and master secrets for additional processing as described in Section 3.1.5.

For Firefox, we decrypted a total of 31,175 HTTP/1.1 and 29,916 HTTP/2 connections. For Chrome, we decrypted a total of 242,036 HTTP/1.1 and 137,698 HTTP/2 connections. We omitted browser-dependent connections from our results, e.g., pocket recommendations in Firefox.

3.1.2 Tor Browser 7.0.11. We follow a similar structure to the Firefox/Chrome data collection for Tor Browser, except that Tor Browser 7.0.11 explicitly prevents the export of its key material due to security concerns. For this reason, instead of setting the environment variable, we take memory snapshots of the tor and firefox processes every 3 seconds after the first second. The information in /proc/<pid>/maps and /proc/<pid>/mem is used to associate the correct memory to the process. The memory dumps are then processed as described in Section 3.1.4 to extract the key material.

We decrypted a total of 6,067 TLS-Tor connections and 50,799 HTTP/1.1 transactions. If the decryption of the Tor tunnel or one of the underlying streams failed, we discarded the sample. The difference in the number of connections between the Tor dataset and the Firefox/Chrome datasets was due to Tor multiplexing many unique streams over a single connection.

3.1.3 Malware Sandbox. The malware analysis sandbox executes each sample in either a Windows 7 or Windows 10 virtual machine for 5 minutes. After the 5 minute window, the packet capture was stored and the virtual machine's full memory snapshot was analyzed as described in Section 3.1.4. We decided against man-in-the-middle or other more intrusive means to collect the key material to avoid contaminating the behavior of the malware. This decision did result in fewer decrypted TLS connections than total TLS connections because the TLS library could zeroize the memory containing the key material. That being said, we were still able to decrypt ~80% of the TLS connections.

For the malware dataset, we decrypted a total of 82,177 HTTP/1.1 and 3,906 HTTP/2 connections. We omitted browser-dependent and VM-dependent connections from our results, e.g., connections to ieonline.microsoft.com. We did not perform any other filtering besides these obvious filters, i.e., we did not attempt to distinguish between legitimate malicious traffic and benign CDN connections.

This dataset is significantly more heterogeneous than the previous datasets due to the malware samples not being restricted to a single TLS library or a prescribed set of websites. ~70% of the malware samples used the Schannel library provided by the operating system, with the remaining samples using a variety of alternatives.

3.1.4 Extracting the Key Material. To decrypt the packet capture from a convicted malware sample (Section 3.1.3) or a Tor instance (Section 3.1.2), we extracted key material from the memory snapshot taken in the final moments of the malware's execution or from a series of snapshots during the lifetime of the Tor process. Prior work on scanning RAM for key material exists [18, 19, 21], but prior techniques were neither sufficiently lightweight nor general enough to directly integrate into the commercial malware analysis sandbox. The production use case required fully automated forensic analysis of a previously unknown executable, under strict CPU and time constraints. Our approach instead leveraged the fact that malware primarily uses established TLS libraries, especially ones built into the targeted platform [3].

The cornerstone of key extraction is the fact that TLS libraries tend to nest the master secret in a predictable data structure, e.g., for OpenSSL:

```
struct ssl_session_st {
  int ssl_version;
  unsigned int key_arg_length;
  unsigned char key_arg[8];
  int master_key_length;
  unsigned char master_key[48];
  unsigned int session_id_length;
  unsigned char session_id[32];
  ...
```

In memory, this data structure appears as:

```
03 03 00 00 00 00 00 00 00 00 00 00 00 00 00 00
30 00 00 00 44 0E 70 5C 1C 22 45 07 6C 1C ED 0D
E3 74 DF E2 C9 71 AF 41 2C 0B E6 AF 70 32 6E C3
A3 2C A0 E6 3A 7A FF 0E F3 70 A2 8A 88 52 B2 2D
D1 B3 F6 F2 20 00 00 00 CD 31 58 BF DF 97 B0 F8
C0 86 BA 48 47 93 B0 A5 BA C1 5B 4B 35 37 7F 98
```

where the leading 0x0303 indicates TLS 1.2, and the 48-byte master secret is highlighted. It was therefore straightforward to write a regular expression that yielded all OpenSSL master secrets in memory within seconds (BoringSSL and Microsoft Schannel were similar). Mozilla NSS allocated the TLS master secret as a standalone 48-byte buffer, which could reside anywhere on the heap with no guaranteed context. However, we discovered that in practice NSS consistently allocated the TLS master secret directly adjacent to a predictable data structure: the struct that carried the pointer to the master secret. This held true across multiple operating systems and platforms, and we were able to extract NSS master secrets reliably using regular expressions. We were able to extract the Tor 128-bit AES keys in a similar manner. We used the following regular expressions to extract TLS master secrets and AES keys:

```
BoringSSL : (\x02\x00|[\x00-\x03]\x03)\x00\x00(?=.{2}.{2}
            \x30\x00\x00\x00(.{48})[\x00-\x20]\x00\x00\x00)
       NSS : \x11\x00\x00\x00(?=(.{8}\x30\x00\x00\x00
            |.{4}.{8}\x30\x00\x00\x00.{4})(.{48}))
   OpenSSL : (\x02\x00|[\x00-\x03]\x03)\x00\x00(?=.{4}.{8}
            \x30\x00\x00\x00(.{48})[\x00-\x20]\x00\x00\x00)
  Schannel : \x35\x6c\x73\x73(?=(\x02\x00|[\x00-\x03]\x03)
            \x00\x00(.{4}.{8}.{4})(.{48}))
   Tor-AES : \x11\x01\x00\x00\x00\x00\x00\x00(?=.{16}.{16})
```

3.1.5 Decrypting the sessions.
We wrote a custom tool to decrypt a packet capture given a file containing the extracted key material. Our tool supports the decryption of SSL 2.0-TLS 1.3, 200+ cipher suites, and can parse the HTTP/1.x, HTTP/2, and Tor application layer protocols. For Tor traffic, it can also decrypt the underlying RELAY and RELAY_EARLY cells. If a decrypted stream contains a TLS session, the tool will in turn decrypt the stream and extract the resulting application layer data. The results of the decryption program are stored in JSON for convenient manipulation by the machine learning preprocessors.

Browsers that support exporting the TLS key material through the SSLKEYLOGFILE environment variable adhere to the NSS key log format, which associates the TLS client_random to a TLS master secret. The Tor and malware datasets do not support this functionality, and we were forced to create a new format that omitted the client_random. In this case, we brute force the decryption by attempting to decrypt a connection with all of the extracted keys. For TLS 1.2, this involves decrypting the small finished message, which is relatively efficient. We attempt all master secrets until the message is properly decoded. For the Tor RELAY cells, we again try all available AES keys, making sure to not disrupt the state of the previous onion layer's stream cipher in the case of a decryption failure. Once we properly decrypt the RELAY cell by identifying a valid relay command and recognized field, we add the cipher to the circuit's cipher list and return the decrypted data.

3.2 Malware Classification

For the malware classification experiments, we used malware data from the same malware analysis sandbox as above collected in November and December, 2017. We collected enterprise network data during the same period, and uniformly sampled this data to avoid severe class imbalance.

We collected the packet captures for each malware run, but ignored the key material. We processed each packet capture to extract the encrypted data in a similar format to the previous section, but did not use the decryption feature. We were able to associate the hash of the process initiating the TLS connection with the 5-tuple of the connection, and discarded any connections that were not initiated by executables that were flagged as malware. We further cleaned the dataset by discarding popular CDNs and analytics sites such as gstatic.com and google-analytics.com. This may have been overly aggressive, but after manually inspecting the decrypted contents of several hundred of these samples, we concluded that they are much more likely to be benign. Finally, we kept the number of unique TLS server_name values to a maximum of 50 uniformly at random samples per month to avoid skewing our results towards the performance on popular domains. Post-filtering, we had 34,872 and 39,064 malicious TLS connections for November and December, respectively.

For the benign dataset, we collected TLS connections from a real enterprise network using our tools during November and December, 2017. We did not have access to any key material in this case, and obviously did not perform decryption. We filtered this data with freely available IP blacklists. For the reasons described above, we only allowed a maximum of 50 unique TLS server_name values per month, chosen uniformly at random, in the enterprise data. The mean number of unique server_name values per month was

~5, which was increased by an order of magnitude to maintain some information about prevalence. After uniformly sampling and filtering, we had 87,016 and 84,526 benign TLS connections for November and December, respectively.

3.3 Website Fingerprinting

We aimed to emulate the standard website fingerprinting open world experiment [26, 39]. The data was collected in a similar fashion to what was described in Section 3.1.2, but with different website lists. While we did extract the key material, we did not use the decrypted data to train the website fingerprinting algorithms.

We used Tor Browser 7.0.11 to connect to each site in a list of 50 censored websites. We repeated this cycle until we were able to collect data from 50 successful connections for each censored website. We performed this data collection during the second week of January 2017.

During the second week of January 2017, we also used our Tor Browser data collection strategy while connecting to each site in the Alexa top-10k. We excluded any samples that failed to decrypt and sites that appeared in the list of monitored sites. Similar to previous work, we took the top 5,000 sites that remained.

4 INFERRING HTTP PROTOCOL SEMANTICS

Our framework to infer various attributes of HTTP in encrypted network connections relies heavily on the labeled data of Section 3. Given that data, it is possible to make a number of interesting inferences on encrypted HTTP transactions without having to perform decryption. We used a standard random forest classifier with 100 trees for all experiments because they have been shown to be a superior choice for network traffic analysis tasks [2]. While alternative machine learning methods could prove to be more performant, these investigations are neither the focus nor in scope for this paper.

We report both the raw accuracy and the unweighted F_1 score for each problem. As explained in Section 4.2, several of the inference problems are posed as multi-class classification, and the unweighted F_1 score provides a better representation of the classifier's performance on the minority classes. It is defined as the unweighted mean of the $F_1(L_i)$ scores for each label L_i in the multi-class problem, where $F_1(L_i)$ is defined as:

$$F_1(L_i) = 2 \times \frac{\text{precision}_i \times \text{recall}_i}{\text{precision}_i + \text{recall}_i} \qquad (1)$$

For all results in this section, we segment the two weeks of data described in Section 3.1 into training and testing datasets using two different criteria. For the first set of experiments, we use the first week of data for training and the second week of data for testing. For the second set of experiments, we segment the data into training and testing datasets based on the TLS server_name extension, and report results averaged over 10 random splits. Table 3 provides a summary of all inference results.

4.1 Data Features

We use two categories of data features to classify HTTP protocol semantics: features that are dependent on the location (relative to the surrounding TLS records) of the target TLS record containing

the HTTP request or response, and features derived from all packets in a connection. For the location-specific feature set, we analyze the current, preceding 5, and following 5 TLS records. For each TLS record, we extract:

(1) The number of packets
(2) The number of packets with the TCP PUSH flag set
(3) The average packet size in bytes
(4) The type code of the TLS record
(5) The TLS record size in bytes
(6) The direction of the TLS record

We treat the counts and sizes as real-valued features, the TLS type code as a categorical feature, and the direction as a categorical feature where 0 indicates client → server, 1 indicates server → client, and 2 indicates no TLS record. All features except direction are set to 0 if a TLS record does not exist, e.g., features related to the following 5 TLS records when the target TLS record ends the connection. We ignored timing-based features because we found them to be unreliable.

For the connection-dependent features, we extracted the number of packets, number of packets with the TCP PUSH flag set, and the average packet size separately for each direction of the connection. We also extracted the sizes in bytes of the first 100 TLS records, where we define the size to be negative if the server sent the record. This array was null padded. Finally, we computed the connection's total duration in seconds. We represented all of these values as real-valued features.

Each sample for the classification problems discussed in this section is composed of 174 data features: 66 record-dependent features, 6 features extracted from each of the 11 TLS records analyzed, and 108 connection-dependent features. The Tor experiments are the exception because we omit the connection-dependent features. We found these features to be unreliable in the Tor HTTP inference task, which is not surprising considering the number of unique TLS connections multiplexed over a single Tor tunnel.

4.2 Inferred HTTP Protocol Semantics

Before we can infer the values contained within an HTTP request or response, we need to be able to identify which TLS records contain a request or response. In our results, this problem is labeled "message-type", and it is a binary classification problem where the labels indicate if a TLS record contains at least one HTTP request or response. We chose this approach because it lets us ignore many of the complexities associated with HTTP/2 frame types and Tor cell types.

For HTTP requests, we study two multi-class classification problems: the method and Content-Type fields, and three binary classification problems: the Cookie, Referer, and Origin fields. For the binary classification problems, we are attempting to determine if the field key appears one or more times in the HTTP request.

For HTTP responses, we study three multi-class classification problems: the status-code, Content-Type, and Server fields, and four binary classification problems: the Etag, Via, Accept-Ranges, and Set-Cookie fields.

We focused on this set of problems because they frequently appeared in both the HTTP/1.1 and HTTP/2 datasets and they exhibited a reasonable level of diversity. As one would expect, our

Problem	HTTP/1.1 Label Set	HTTP/2 Label Set
method (req)	GET, POST, OPTIONS HEAD, PUT	GET, POST, OPTIONS HEAD
Cont-Type (req)	json, plain	json, plain
status-code (resp)	100, 200, 204, 206, 302 303, 301, 304, 307, 404	200, 204, 206, 301, 302 303, 304, 307, 404
Cont-Type (resp)	html, javascript, image video, css, octet, json font, plain	html, javascript, image video, css, octet, json font, plain, protobuf
Server (resp)	nginx-1.13/1.12/1.11/1.10 nginx-1.8/1.7/1.4, Apache cloudflare-nginx, nginx AmazonS3, NetDNA/2.2 IIS-7.5/8.5, jetty-9.4/9.0 openresty, Coyote/1.1	nginx-1.13/1.12/1.11/1.10 nginx-1.6/1.4/1.3, nginx cloudflare-nginx, Apache Coyote/1.1, IIS/8.5, sffe Golfe2, UploadServer gws, Dreamlab, Tengine Akamai, cafe, Google, GSE Dreamlab, Tengine, ESF AmazonS3, NetDNA/2.2

Table 2: Label sets for the multi-class HTTP protocol semantics inference experiments. For HTTP/1.1, there are 5 method, 2 request Content-Type, 10 status-code, 9 response Content-Type, and 18 Server labels. For HTTP/2, there are 4 method, 2 request Content-Type, 9 status-code, 10 response Content-Type, and 25 Server labels.

data collection strategy biased the problem selection towards HTTP response fields. As explained in Section 6, we believe the approach outlined in this paper would translate to a larger set of request-related problems if appropriate training data were available.

4.2.1 Multi-Class Labels. Table 2 lists the labels for all multi-class classification problems. There are some instances of ambiguity in the HTTP request and response field values. For example, the "application/octet" value for the response Content-Type field can be used for multiple file types, and the "nginx" value for the Server field can map to multiple version. For our experiments, we take the field value as is and do not attempt to relabel samples.

4.3 Iterative Classification

Many of the inference goals outlined in the previous section are dependent on each other, e.g., the value of the response Content-Type is correlated with the Server value, and a response Content-Type is correlated with other response Content-Type's in the same TLS connection. We incorporate this information by using an iterative classification framework.

Given a TLS connection, we first determine the application layer protocol (alp) through the TLS application_layer_protocol_negotiation extension. If this extension is absent, we use a classifier based on the first 20 TLS record lengths to classify the connection as either HTTP/1.1 or HTTP/2. Given alp and the data features described in Section 4.1, we use a binary classifier to identify each TLS application_data record containing HTTP

Algorithm 1 Iterative HTTP Protocol Semantics Inference

```
1:  procedure ITERATIVE_SEMANTICS_CLASSIFY
2:    given:
3:        conn := features describing connection
4:      alp ← application_layer_protocol(conn)
5:      recs ← classify_message_types(conn, alp)
6:    for rec ∈ recs do:
7:        if rec.type ≠ Headers then:
8:            continue
9:        get_record_features(rec, alp)
10:       classify_semantics(rec, alp)
11:   while not converged do:
12:       for rec ∈ recs do:
13:           if rec.type ≠ Headers then:
14:               continue
15:           get_record_features(rec, alp)
16:           get_inferred_features(rec, alp)
17:           classify_semantics(rec, alp)
```

header fields. In this section (but not Section 5), we discard connections with inaccurately labeled TLS records, e.g., we classify an HTTP/2 HEADERS frame as a DATA frame. Although this process resulted in a <1% reduction in the total number of samples classified, this process is important to note while interpreting this section's results.

For each TLS record identified as containing HTTP header fields, we extract the Section 4.1 data features and then apply the classifiers related to the request semantics for client records and the response semantics for server records. At this point, we associate the original record's data features with the classifier outputs for all records containing HTTP header fields in the same connection excluding the target classification problem in the target record. This enhanced feature set has length 68 for HTTP/1.1 and length 74 for HTTP/2. The subcomponents of the enhanced feature vector correspond to the sum of all other predicted outputs from the previous iteration after the algorithm translates the predicted outputs to an indicator vector. For example, if there is a connection with 7 HTTP requests and the Referer field was present in 4 out of the 6 non-target requests, then the subcomponent of the enhanced feature vector related to the Referer field would be [2, 4]. Given the enhanced features, we classify the HTTP protocol semantics using the TLS record's data features and the inferences from the previous iteration. We consider the algorithm converged when no predicted outputs change value. In our experiments, the iterative algorithm typically converged in two and at most four iterations.

Algorithm 1 summarizes the iterative classification procedure. It uses multiple, intermediate classifiers, each of which requires training. These classifiers infer the application layer protocol, the TLS records that contain the protocol semantics of HTTP requests and responses, the HTTP protocol semantics given only the target record's features, and the HTTP protocol semantics given all features. When classifying an unseen test sample, Algorithm 1 needs two classifiers per inference.

Tor necessitates a minor exception to the iterative algorithm due to the large number of unique TLS connections multiplexed over a single TLS/Tor connection. Instead of using all inferred HTTP values within a connection for the enhanced feature vector, we only

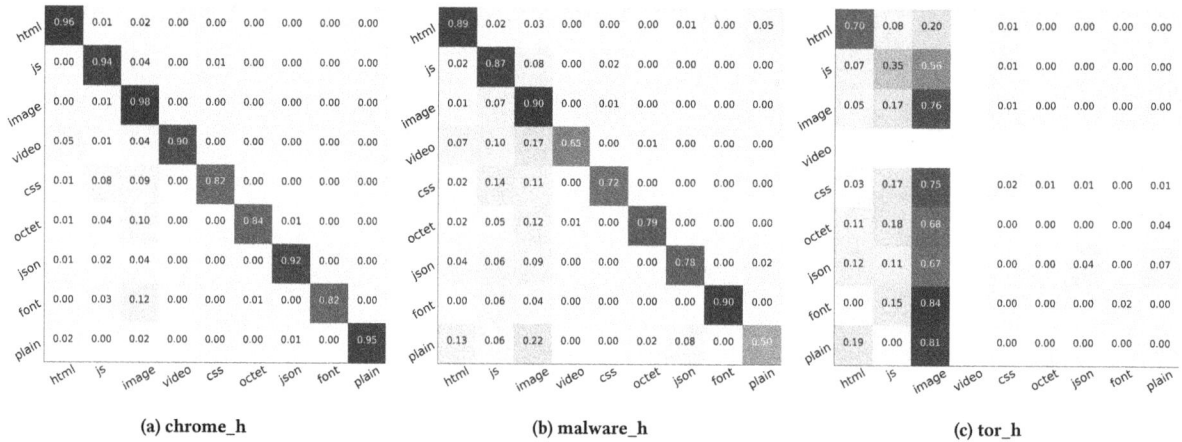

(a) chrome_h (b) malware_h (c) tor_h

Figure 2: Confusion matrices for the HTTP/1.1 response Content-Type header field value on the chrome_h, malware_h, and tor_h datasets. We left matrix elements blank if there were no relevant labels in a particular dataset.

use the predicted outputs of the preceding and following five HTTP transactions in the Tor connection.

4.4 HTTP/1.1 Results

There were a total of 72,828, 515,022, 182,498, and 50,799 HTTP/1.1 transactions in firefox_h, chrome_h, malware_h, and tor_h, respectively. This gave an average of ~2.1 to ~8.4 HTTP/1.1 transactions per TLS connection depending on the dataset, with Tor being a significant outlier. We ran two sets of experiments where we constructed the training and testing datasets using time-based and server_name-based splits.

Table 3 provides the full set of results for each classification problem. We identified TLS records containing HTTP header fields with an F_1 score of ~0.99 for both experiments and all datasets except for tor_h, which had a score of ~0.87. This experiment highlights the relative difficulty that the multiplexing facilitated by the Tor protocol poses for traffic analysis relative to standalone TLS.

Most of the other HTTP/1.1 experiments followed a similar pattern with the tor_h results being significantly worse. We effectively modeled several of the binary classification problems for the tor_h dataset, with the Cookie and Referer request fields having an F_1 score over 0.75. The response fields performed noticeably worse due to the multiplexing behavior of Tor.

For the other datasets, we achieved surprisingly competitive results across the majority of the problems. We were even able to effectively model many of the problems based on malware_h, which had a much greater diversity of TLS clients and less overlap in sites visited in the training and testing datasets. Figure 2 shows the full confusion matrices for the HTTP/1.1 response Content-Type header field value for chrome_h, malware_h, and tor_h using the time-based dataset construction. For this problem, we achieved unweighted F_1 scores of 0.919, 0.770, and 0.236 for the chrome_h, malware_h, and tor_h datasets. There was some overfitting to the majority class, image, which had roughly twice as many samples in each dataset than the next most represented class. Despite minor

overfitting in chrome_h and malware_h, Figure 2 demonstrates the feasibility of this approach to infer the value of the HTTP/1.1 response Content-Type header field value in an encrypted TLS tunnel.

The server_name-based dataset splitting experiments were comparatively worse, but not overly so. For example, both the method and status-code had comparable results. For details on the other classification problems, we refer the reader to Table 3.

4.5 HTTP/2 Results

There were a total of 132,685, 561,666, and 14,734 HTTP/2 transactions in firefox_h, chrome_h, and malware_h, respectively. This gave an average of ~4 HTTP/2 transactions per TLS connection across the datasets. We performed the experiments in this section following the same structure as the HTTP/1.1 experiments. There were no HTTP/2 transactions in tor_h, which was a result of the Tor Firefox process only being configured to advertise http/1.1.

Similar to HTTP/1.1, Table 3 also provides the full set of HTTP/2 results. We were able to identify TLS records containing HTTP header fields with an F_1 score of ~0.98 for all datasets. We expected this slight drop in performance due to the more advanced flow control mechanisms implemented by HTTP/2. In our datasets, ~55% of the TLS-HTTP/2 connections employed some form of pipelining or multiplexing. Only ~15% of the TLS-HTTP/1.1 connections employed pipelining.

The malware_h HTTP/2 results were worse than the malware_h HTTP/1.1 results for most problems, but we attribute this to having significantly less data in the case of HTTP/2. Both chrome_h and firefox_h had mostly comparable performance to the HTTP/1.1 experiments. Compared to the HTTP/1.1 results, the iterative algorithm performed exceptionally well on some problems: request method, request status-code, request Origin, response Server, and response Set-Cookie. In these cases, the iterative algorithm improved its performance by effectively leveraging HTTP/2's greater number of HTTP transactions per TLS connection.

Problem	Dataset	HTTP/1.1				HTTP/2			
		Time-Based Split		SNI-Based Split		Time-Based Split		SNI-Based Split	
		F_1 Score	Acc	F_1 Score	Acc	F_1 Score	Acc	F_1 Score	Acc
message-type	firefox_h	0.996	0.996	0.995	0.996	0.987	0.991	0.981	0.990
	chrome_h	0.991	0.993	0.989	0.991	0.986	0.986	0.982	0.984
	malware_h	0.995	0.996	0.995	0.996	0.981	0.989	0.979	0.986
	tor_h	0.869	0.878	0.845	0.848				
method	firefox_h	0.943	0.995	0.956	0.961	0.989	0.997	0.877	0.993
	chrome_h	0.978	0.998	0.947	0.957	0.936	0.999	0.913	0.993
	malware_h	0.705	0.996	0.831	0.981	0.687	0.985	0.807	0.987
	tor_h	0.846	0.965	0.865	0.973				
Content-Type	firefox_h	0.967	0.978	0.909	0.933	0.982	0.985	0.933	0.956
	chrome_h	0.977	0.993	0.874	0.875	0.998	0.998	0.842	0.864
	malware_h	0.888	0.900	0.853	0.862	0.711	0.887	0.811	0.890
	tor_h	0.836	0.904	0.659	0.864				
Cookie (b)	firefox_h	0.967	0.974	0.882	0.892	0.941	0.948	0.832	0.867
	chrome_h	0.977	0.977	0.929	0.934	0.953	0.958	0.856	0.941
	malware_h	0.916	0.918	0.876	0.876	0.898	0.913	0.850	0.861
	tor_h	0.756	0.823	0.657	0.740				
Referer (b)	firefox_h	0.969	0.989	0.942	0.964	0.950	0.987	0.830	0.941
	chrome_h	0.978	0.995	0.891	0.891	0.933	0.991	0.932	0.948
	malware_h	0.928	0.935	0.850	0.850	0.907	0.907	0.828	0.863
	tor_h	0.885	0.905	0.832	0.848				
Origin (b)	firefox_h	0.973	0.990	0.958	0.958	0.952	0.989	0.882	0.961
	chrome_h	0.985	0.995	0.924	0.924	0.969	0.991	0.866	0.956
	malware_h	0.960	0.991	0.983	0.989	0.953	0.994	0.890	0.914
	tor_h	0.510	0.955	0.638	0.956				
status-code	firefox_h	0.856	0.989	0.926	0.942	0.820	0.993	0.919	0.993
	chrome_h	0.922	0.992	0.917	0.933	0.848	0.990	0.895	0.944
	malware_h	0.684	0.962	0.738	0.894	0.829	0.960	0.943	0.955
	tor_h								
Content-Type	firefox_h	0.848	0.923	0.751	0.854	0.766	0.825	0.628	0.754
	chrome_h	0.919	0.957	0.807	0.874	0.880	0.917	0.678	0.792
	malware_h	0.770	0.866	0.594	0.811	0.711	0.887	0.594	0.894
	tor_h	0.236	0.556	0.301	0.580				
Server	firefox_h	0.916	0.969	0.785	0.892	0.948	0.985	0.778	0.883
	chrome_h	0.977	0.986	0.842	0.893	0.953	0.988	0.765	0.879
	malware_h	0.814	0.943	0.685	0.954	0.910	0.924	0.726	0.935
	tor_h	0.153	0.406	0.228	0.452				
Etag (b)	firefox_h	0.958	0.958	0.874	0.883	0.909	0.909	0.707	0.708
	chrome_h	0.969	0.975	0.922	0.922	0.954	0.959	0.865	0.871
	malware_h	0.897	0.927	0.864	0.864	0.878	0.943	0.843	0.866
	tor_h	0.676	0.703	0.660	0.691				
Via (b)	firefox_h	0.975	0.976	0.921	0.921	0.934	0.961	0.898	0.904
	chrome_h	0.964	0.987	0.858	0.915	0.960	0.979	0.932	0.942
	malware_h	0.836	0.975	0.930	0.966	0.732	0.979	0.690	0.896
	tor_h	0.547	0.859	0.533	0.835				
Accept-Ranges (b)	firefox_h	0.956	0.956	0.883	0.884	0.909	0.911	0.823	0.824
	chrome_h	0.975	0.980	0.930	0.930	0.954	0.956	0.805	0.823
	malware_h	0.929	0.940	0.797	0.800	0.947	0.959	0.847	0.873
	tor_h	0.673	0.680	0.690	0.695				
Set-Cookie (b)	firefox_h	0.964	0.987	0.903	0.937	0.920	0.968	0.934	0.951
	chrome_h	0.987	0.988	0.909	0.910	0.956	0.978	0.932	0.945
	malware_h	0.880	0.953	0.874	0.901	0.895	0.959	0.814	0.947
	tor_h	0.604	0.861	0.534	0.855				

Table 3: Summary of the HTTP protocol semantics inference results.

5 USE CASES

We now examine two possible applications of our techniques: improved malware detection and website fingerprinting. Our goal in this section is to test the feasibility of using the inferences introduced in this paper to improve the performance of these use cases; we did not attempt to demonstrate hyper-optimized results. We used the full two weeks of the previous datasets to train the classifiers needed to perform our iterative HTTP protocol semantics inferences. We then used the trained classifiers and Algorithm 1 to enrich the samples related to the two use cases. If available, we did **not** make use of any decrypted data features for samples in this section. firefox_h, chrome_h, and malware_h were used to train the classifiers needed for Section 5.1, and tor_h was used to train the classifiers needed for Section 5.2.

5.1 Malware Detection

As described in Section 3.2, we used enterprise_m and malware_m from Table 1 to test if first inferring the semantics of encrypted HTTP transactions can improve malware detection. We used the November data for training and the December data for testing. We explored two feature sets for this problem. The standard feature set included the 108 connection-dependent features described in Section 4.1. In the standard set, we also used TLS-specific features:

(1) Binary features for the 100 most commonly offered cipher suites
(2) Binary features for the 25 most commonly advertised TLS extensions (including GREASE extensions [5], which we treated as a single feature)
(3) A categorical feature for the selected cipher suite

There were 234 total features for the standard set. The enhanced set included all 234 features of the standard set, and the features representing the predicted values from Algorithm 1 and described in Section 4.3. In total, there were either 302 features for HTTP/1.1 TLS connections or 308 features for HTTP/2 TLS connections. We trained a standard random forest model as described in Section 4 to classify the test samples.

As Table 4 demonstrates, applying the iterative HTTP protocol semantics classifier and learning an intermediate representation of the HTTP transactions within the encrypted TLS tunnel significantly helped the performance of the classifier. The header inferences increased the F_1 score from 0.951 to 0.979, and had similar impacts to precision and recall. These results are a notable improvement over previous results on malware TLS detection [3], which relied on additional data features such as server certificates to obtain higher accuracy. Because TLS 1.3 obfuscates certificates [30], network operators need new techniques to address this use case.

Table 5 lists the ten most importance features for classification in the standard and enriched feature sets. We generated this ranking by computing the Gini feature importance [7]. From the standard feature set, the first TLS record length corresponding to the client_hello was informative. The seventh and eighth TLS record lengths were also informative because the enterprise dataset contained more examples of session resumption. From the enriched feature set, HTTP fields aimed at tracking and keeping state were among the most useful, e.g., Set-Cookie and Referer. The method and status-code were also in the top 10 due to malware being

Feature Set	F_1 Score	Precision	Recall	Acc
Standard	0.951	0.951	0.915	0.958
Enriched	0.979	0.984	0.959	0.982

Table 4: Malware classification results using a standard feature set and an enriched feature set that takes advantage of HTTP protocol semantics inferences.

Rank	Standard	Enriched
1	8th Record Length	8th Record Length
2	1st Record Length	HTTP: Set-Cookie
3	# Out Bytes	# Out Bytes
4	# Out Records	1st Record Length
5	Offered Cipher Suite: DHE_DSS_WITH_ AES_256_CBC_SHA	HTTP: Referer
6	# In Records	HTTP: Content-Type
7	# In Bytes	# In Records
8	Advertised Extension: channel_id	HTTP: status-code
9	Duration	# Out Packets
10	7th Record Length	HTTP: method

Table 5: The 10 most important features for classifying malware with the standard and enhanced features sets.

more likely to perform a GET request with a resulting 404 status code.

The performance of the enriched feature set would still yield too many false positives on a real network, but it is only looking at data features related to a single TLS session. A more comprehensive network monitoring architecture that correlates multiple connections and independent data sources could easily incorporate our techniques.

5.2 Website Fingerprinting

We used tor_open_w and tor_censor_w from Table 1 in our website fingerprinting experiments. Similar to previous work on website fingerprinting [38], tor_censor_w contained 50 samples per monitored site from a list of 50 sites currently blocked in some countries pertaining to information dissemination (e.g., twitter.com), covert communication (e.g., torproject.org), and pornographic imagery. tor_open_w contained 5,000 non-monitored samples, where each sample is a unique connection to a website in the Alexa top-10k. We contacted these sites in order, and selected the first 5,000 sites that properly decrypted and did not have any HTTP requests to a monitored site.

We based the feature set in this experiment on the features used by Wang et al. [38], which included total packet count, unique packet lengths, several counts related to burst patterns, and the lengths of the first 20 packets. A more detailed description of these features is provided by Wang et al. [38]. We took advantage of Wang et al.'s k-NN classifier and hyperparameter learning algorithms with

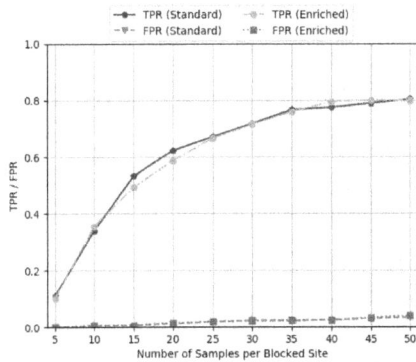

Figure 3: Website fingerprinting learning curve as we adjust the number of samples per blocked site.

k_{reco} fixed to the suggested value of 5 [38]. We used 10-fold CV, ensuring non-monitored sites were not in the training and testing sets simultaneously.

Figure 3 provides the results of this experiment as we adjust the number of unique samples per monitored site from 5 to 50 in increments of 5. The introduction of the header inferences seem to be strictly adding noise that the weight adjustment algorithm of Wang et al. effectively filters. In Section 6, we provide some references that may increase the power of this attack.

6 DISCUSSION

We have shown that it is possible to infer HTTP protocol semantics within encrypted TLS tunnels, but our results depend on the existence of a rich source of labeled data correlating the encrypted traffic patterns observable on a network with the underlying HTTP transactions. The results based on malware_h and the server_name-based split were the closest to a real-world scenario where the testing dataset consisted of many different applications visiting servers unseen in training. Table 6 shows the performance of our algorithm when training on chrome_h and testing on firefox_h, and as expected, the results are worse. One observation we made was the difference by the two browsers in utilizing HTTP/1.1 pipelining: 10% of TLS-HTTP/1.1 Chrome connections used pipelining versus 25% for Firefox. In many of these cases, Chrome would create multiple TLS connections instead of pipelining the requests. Undoubtedly, additional fundamental differences would limit the model's transferability between browsers and even operating systems. A deployable system would need to first recognize the operating system and application, which can be accomplished by readily available tools [8, 23], and then apply the relevant HTTP protocol semantics models to the data features extracted from the encrypted tunnel. This would require curating an extensive dataset, which is a reasonable burden for a well-funded department.

Our results indicated that the Tor protocol provides a suitable defense for entities wishing to defend against the methods of this paper. The fixed-length Tor cells and multiplexing many distinct TLS connections over a single TLS-Tor connection reduces the signal in many of our chosen features. This can be seen to a lesser extent in Table 3 with respect to HTTP/2 over TLS due to HTTP/2's greater

Problem	F_1 Score	Accuracy
method	0.717	0.971
Content-Type	0.790	0.841
status-code	0.492	0.869
Content-Type	0.400	0.421
Server	0.741	0.830

Table 6: HTTP/1.1 semantics inference results when training with chrome_h and testing with firefox_h.

use of pipelining and multiplexing in our datasets. Multiplexing communication to different origins over a single HTTP/2 connection has been recently proposed [6, 24], which would most likely degrade our results even further. Wang and Goldberg put forward several algorithms to properly segment and de-noise Tor streams [39]. Preprocessing tor_h with Wang and Goldberg's methods may increase the efficacy of our algorithms, and their techniques may also have applications to future implementations of HTTP/2. We leave these investigations for future work.

In the context of malware detection, our results on Tor demonstrated that malware employing common evasion strategies [10, 22, 40] should be able to mislead our HTTP protocol semantics inferences, resulting in the addition of noisy data features to the malware classifier. These evasion strategies can be detected [37]. Although these detection methods are not specific to malware communication, they can inform the malware classifier to avoid using the inferred HTTP data features. From an adversarial point-of-view, it is also important to note that the feature importances given in Table 5 are not static, and the relative importance of any particular feature is likely to change over time. However, with continual training, malware classifiers will be able to take advantage of the insights provided by the HTTP inferences presented in this paper.

Our paper's intended purpose is to highlight a fundamental, novel framework that has many potential applications. While we leave developing these applications to future work, we believe our techniques can be applied to de-anonymizing a NAT'd user's browsing history by using the presence of the Referer/Origin/Cookie fields together with timestamps. Our techniques can also identify transmitted file sizes at a much higher resolution by annotating each TLS record with the HTTP/2 frame types it contains, and discarding TLS records that do not contain relevant DATA frames. An organization could leverage a known set of sensitive file sizes correlated with endpoints, and use the methods presented in this paper to identify out-of-policy file movements. Finally, for maintenance and debugging of servers on a network, our method is superior to active scanning, which can be inefficient and ineffective due to limited client configurations and imperfect information about the client's request and server's response.

7 ETHICAL CONSIDERATIONS

We collected the majority of our data in a lab environment, and this data did not contain sensitive information. The Tor data collection adhered to the ethical Tor research guidelines [33]. The data collection for the malware detection experiments did contain highly confidential and sensitive data. We followed all institutional procedures, and obtained the appropriate authorizations. While collecting the data, we anonymized all IP addresses and enterprise user names via deterministic encryption.

8 CONCLUSIONS

In this paper, we have shown that it is possible to infer many of the underlying HTTP protocol features without needing to compromise the encryption that secures the HTTPS protocol. Our framework can correctly identify HTTP/1.1 and HTTP/2 records transmitted over HTTPS with F_1 scores of ~0.99 and ~0.98, respectively. Once the HTTP records are identified, our system uses multi-class classification to identify the value of several fields, e.g., `Content-Type`, and binary classification to identify the presence or absence of additional fields, e.g., `Cookie`. We have demonstrated competitive results on datasets composed of hundreds-of-thousands of encrypted HTTP transactions taken from Firefox 58.0, Chrome 63.0, and a malware analysis sandbox. We also applied our techniques to Tor Browser 7.0.11, but achieved significantly lower accuracies, suggesting that the Tor protocol is robust against these methods.

Inferences on the semantics of HTTP have intrinsic value that both attackers and defenders can use. For example, network administrators can use these inferences to passively monitor dynamic, complex networks to ensure a proper security posture and perform debugging without the need of TLS termination proxies, and attackers can use these inferences to de-anonymize a NAT'd user's browsing history. Given our broader set of results and the increasing sophistication of network traffic analysis techniques, future research is needed to evaluate the confidentiality goals of TLS with respect to users' expectations of privacy.

REFERENCES

[1] Blake Anderson and David McGrew. 2016. Identifying Encrypted Malware Traffic with Contextual Flow Data. In *ACM Workshop on Artificial Intelligence and Security (AISec)*. 35–46.
[2] Blake Anderson and David McGrew. 2017. Machine Learning for Encrypted Malware Traffic Classification: Accounting for Noisy Labels and Non-Stationarity. In *ACM SIGKDD International Conference on Knowledge Discovery in Data Mining (KDD)*. 1723–1732.
[3] Blake Anderson, Subharthi Paul, and David McGrew. 2017. Deciphering Malware's Use of TLS (without Decryption). *Journal of Computer Virology and Hacking Techniques* (2017), 1–17.
[4] Mike Belshe, Roberto Peon, and Martin Thomson. 2015. Hypertext Transfer Protocol Version 2 (HTTP/2). RFC 7540 (Proposed Standard). http://www.ietf.org/rfc/rfc7540.txt.
[5] David Benjamin. 2017. Applying GREASE to TLS Extensibility. Internet-Draft (Informational). https://www.ietf.org/archive/id/draft-ietf-tls-grease-00.txt.
[6] Mike Bishop, Nick Sullivan, and Martin Thomson. 2017. Secondary Certificate Authentication in HTTP/2. Internet-Draft (Standards Track). https://tools.ietf.org/html/draft-bishop-httpbis-http2-additional-certs-05.
[7] Leo Breiman, Jerome Friedman, Charles J Stone, and Richard A Olshen. 1984. *Classification and Regression Trees*. CRC press.
[8] Lee Brotherston. 2015. Stealthier Attacks and Smarter Defending with TLS Fingerprinting. *DerbyCon* (2015).
[9] Tim Dierks and Eric Rescorla. 2008. The Transport Layer Security (TLS) Protocol Version 1.2. RFC 5246 (Proposed Standard). http://www.ietf.org/rfc/rfc5246.txt.
[10] Roger Dingledine and Nick Mathewson. 2017. Tor Protocol Specification. https://gitweb.torproject.org/torspec.git/tree/tor-spec.txt.
[11] Zakir Durumeric, Zane Ma, Drew Springall, Richard Barnes, Nick Sullivan, Elie Bursztein, Michael Bailey, J Alex Halderman, and Vern Paxson. 2017. The Security Impact of HTTPS Interception. In *Network and Distributed System Security Symposium (NDSS)*.
[12] Roy Fielding and Julian Reschke. 2014. Hypertext Transfer Protocol (HTTP/1.1): Message Syntax and Routing. RFC 7230 (Proposed Standard). http://www.ietf.org/rfc/rfc7230.txt.
[13] Roy Fielding and Julian Reschke. 2014. Hypertext Transfer Protocol (HTTP/1.1): Semantics and Content. RFC 7231 (Proposed Standard). http://www.ietf.org/rfc/rfc7231.txt.
[14] Shafi Goldwasser and Silvio Micali. 1982. Probabilistic Encryption & How to Play Mental Poker Keeping Secret All Partial Information. In *ACM Symposium on Theory of Computing (STOC)*. ACM, 365–377.
[15] Shafi Goldwasser and Silvio Micali. 1984. Probabilistic Encryption. *J. Comput. Syst. Sci.* 28, 2 (1984), 270–299.
[16] M. Green, R. Droms, R. Housley, P. Turner, and S. Fenter. 2018. Data Center use of Static Diffie-Hellman in TLS 1.3. Work in Progress. https://tools.ietf.org/id/draft-green-tls-static-dh-in-tls13-01.txt.
[17] Guofei Gu, Roberto Perdisci, Junjie Zhang, and Wenke Lee. 2008. BotMiner: Clustering Analysis of Network Traffic for Protocol-and Structure-Independent Botnet Detection. In *USENIX Security Symposium*. 139–154.
[18] J Alex Halderman, Seth D Schoen, Nadia Heninger, William Clarkson, William Paul, Joseph A Calandrino, Ariel J Feldman, Jacob Appelbaum, and Edward W Felten. 2009. Lest We Remember: Cold-Boot Attacks on Encryption Keys. *Commun. ACM* 52, 5 (2009), 91–98.
[19] Jake Kambic. 2016. Cunning with CNG: Soliciting Secrets from Schannel. (2016). Black Hat USA.
[20] Marc Liberatore and Brian Neil Levine. 2006. Inferring the Source of Encrypted HTTP Connections. In *Proceedings of the Thirteenth ACM Conference on Computer and Communications Security (CCS)*. 255–263.
[21] Michael Hale Ligh, Andrew Case, Jamie Levy, and Aaron Walters. 2014. *The Art of Memory Forensics: Detecting Malware and Threats in Windows, Linux, and Mac Memory*. John Wiley & Sons.
[22] Xiapu Luo, Peng Zhou, Edmond WW Chan, Wenke Lee, Rocky KC Chang, and Roberto Perdisci. 2011. HTTPOS: Sealing Information Leaks with Browser-Side Obfuscation of Encrypted Flows. In *Network and Distributed System Security Symposium (NDSS)*.
[23] Marek Majkowski. [n. d.]. SSL Fingerprinting for p0f. https://idea.popcount.org/2012-06-17-ssl-fingerprinting-for-p0f/.
[24] Mark Nottingham and Erik Nygren. 2017. The ORIGIN HTTP/2 Frame. Internet-Draft (Standards Track). https://tools.ietf.org/html/draft-ietf-httpbis-origin-frame-06.
[25] Se Eun Oh, Shuai Li, and Nicholas Hopper. 2017. Fingerprinting Keywords in Search Queries over Tor. *Proceedings of Privacy Enhancing Technologies (PETS)* 2017 (2017), 251–270.
[26] Andriy Panchenko, Fabian Lanze, Jan Pennekamp, Thomas Engel, Andreas Zinnen, Martin Henze, and Klaus Wehrle. 2016. Website Fingerprinting at Internet Scale. In *Network and Distributed System Security Symposium (NDSS)*.
[27] Andriy Panchenko, Lukas Niessen, Andreas Zinnen, and Thomas Engel. 2011. Website Fingerprinting in Onion Routing Based Anonymization Networks. In *Proceedings of the Tenth annual ACM Workshop on Privacy in the Electronic Society (WPES)*. 103–114.
[28] Roberto Peon and Herve Ruellan. 2015. HPACK: Header Compression for HTTP/2. RFC 7541 (Proposed Standard). http://www.ietf.org/rfc/rfc7541.txt.
[29] Andrew Reed and Michael Kranch. 2017. Identifying HTTPS-Protected Netflix Videos in Real-Time. In *Proceedings of the Seventh ACM on Conference on Data and Application Security and Privacy (CODASPY)*. 361–368.
[30] Eric Rescorla. 2018. The Transport Layer Security (TLS) Protocol Version 1.3. RFC 8446 (Proposed Standard). http://www.ietf.org/rfc/rfc8446.txt.
[31] Roei Schuster, Vitaly Shmatikov, and Eran Tromer. 2017. Beauty and the Burst: Remote Identification of Encrypted Video Streams. (2017), 1357–1374.
[32] Florian Tegeler, Xiaoming Fu, Giovanni Vigna, and Christopher Kruegel. 2012. Botfinder: Finding Bots in Network Traffic without Deep Packet Inspection. In *ACM International Conference on Emerging Networking Experiments and Technologies (Co-NEXT)*. 349–360.
[33] The Tor Project. [n. d.]. Ethical Tor Research: Guidelines. https://blog.torproject.org/ethical-tor-research-guidelines. Accessed: 2018-01-15.
[34] US-CERT. 2017. HTTPS Interception Weakens TLS Security. https://www.us-cert.gov/ncas/alerts/TA17-075A.
[35] Tom Van Goethem, Mathy Vanhoef, Frank Piessens, and Wouter Joosen. 2016. Request and Conquer: Exposing Cross-Origin Resource Size. In *USENIX Security Symposium*. 447–462.
[36] David Wagner and Bruce Schneier. 1996. Analysis of the SSL 3.0 protocol. In *The Second USENIX Workshop on Electronic Commerce Proceedings*. 29–40.
[37] Liang Wang, Kevin P. Dyer, Aditya Akella, Thomas Ristenpart, and Thomas Shrimpton. 2015. Seeing Through Network-Protocol Obfuscation. In *Proceedings of the Twenty-Second ACM Conference on Computer and Communications Security (CCS)*. 57–69.
[38] Tao Wang, Xiang Cai, Rishab Nithyanand, Rob Johnson, and Ian Goldberg. 2014. Effective Attacks and Provable Defenses for Website Fingerprinting.. In *USENIX Security Symposium*. 143–157.
[39] Tao Wang and Ian Goldberg. 2016. On Realistically Attacking Tor with Website Fingerprinting. *Proceedings of Privacy Enhancing Technologies (PETS)* (2016), 21–36.
[40] Charles Wright, Scott Coull, and Fabian Monrose. 2009. Traffic Morphing: An Efficient Defense Against Statistical Traffic Analysis. In *Network and Distributed System Security Symposium (NDSS)*.

Client Diversity Factor in HTTPS Webpage Fingerprinting*

Hasan Faik Alan
Department of Computer Science
UNC - Chapel Hill, NC, USA
alan@cs.unc.edu

Jasleen Kaur
Department of Computer Science
UNC - Chapel Hill, NC, USA
jasleen@cs.unc.edu

ABSTRACT

Webpage fingerprinting methods infer the webpages visited in a traffic trace and are serious threats to the privacy of web users. Prior work evaluates webpage fingerprinting methods using traffic samples from a single client and does not consider the client diversity factor—webpages can be visited using different browsers, operating systems and devices. In this paper, we study the impact of client diversity on HTTPS webpage fingerprinting. First, we evaluate 5 prominent fingerprinting methods using traffic samples from 19 different clients. We show that the best performing methods overfit to the traffic patterns of a single client and do not generalize when they are evaluated using the samples from a different client (even if the clients use the same browser and operating system and only differ in device). Then, we investigate the traffic patterns of the clients and find differences in the HTTP messages generated, servers communicated and implementation of HTTP/2 across the clients. Finally, we show that the robustness of the methods can be increased by training them using the samples from a diverse set of clients. This study informs the community towards a realistic threat model for HTTPS webpage fingerprinting and presents an analysis of modern HTTPS traffic.

ACM Reference format:
Hasan Faik Alan and Jasleen Kaur. 2019. Client Diversity Factor in HTTPS Webpage Fingerprinting. In *Proceedings of Ninth ACM Conference on Data and Application Security and Privacy, Richardson, TX, USA, March 25–27, 2019 (CODASPY '19),* 12 pages.
https://doi.org/10.1145/3292006.3300045

1 INTRODUCTION

Traffic analysis, which infers information from the observation of traffic flows [1], is a fairly diverse field—both in terms of the *granularity* of information inferred (such as protocols, application types, user interests, websites, and webpages) as well as in terms of the *privacy-enhancing technology* used for transmitting the observed traffic (such as HTTPS, SSH, VPN, and Tor) [2–9]. The keywords *webpages* and *HTTPS* help set the specific context for this paper—we focus on the problem of HTTPS traffic analysis for the purpose of fingerprinting the webpages being visited, with an emphasis on the *diversity of client platforms* (different browsers, operating systems and devices that can be used to visit webpages).

While there have been numerous studies on fingerprinting web traffic [4–12], our focus differs from most in three key aspects. First, a majority of work in this area studies web traffic sent over tunnels using SSH, VPN or Tor—there is surprisingly scarce work on HTTPS traffic, which is the most commonly-used privacy setting. This is perhaps due to an implicit belief that fingerprinting analysis conducted for more private VPN or Tor traffic should also translate to less private HTTPS traffic.[1] Second, most prior work is focused on fingerprinting *websites* (and not individual webpages within a website), and considers just the landing pages of different websites. In HTTPS traffic, the website domain is often retrievable from the Server Name Indication (SNI) extension of TLS [4, 13]—fingerprinting webpages within a given website, however, is challenging due to similarity of webpages within a website [5]. Third, and most relevantly to the motivation of this study, evaluations in prior HTTPS webpage fingerprinting studies were performed using webpage traffic samples from the same client platform [4, 5]. Specifically, Miller et al. collected traffic traces of webpage visits using Firefox 22 browser in a virtual machine running Linux 12.04 OS [5]. Similarly, Gonzalez et al. used Firefox browser on a PC [4]. This observation leads us to question the robustness of such fingerprinting methods in the real world, given the diversity of client platforms as well as the influence of these platforms on webpage content and traffic [14, 15].

In this paper, our main objective is to examine how client diversity impacts HTTPS webpage fingerprinting. Our first major innovation is that we evaluate 5 prominent webpage fingerprinting methods from the traffic analysis literature using webpage traffic samples collected from 19 different clients—we consider 6 different browsers (Chrome, Firefox, Edge, IE, Opera and Safari), 5 different operating systems (Android, Ubuntu, Windows 10, Windows 7 and macOS), and 6 different devices (see Table 2). We show that all 5 webpage fingerprinting methods perform the best when the samples from the same client are used for training and test—this is the scenario studied in prior work. However, the performance of the methods decreases dramatically when they are tested with the samples from a client that is different than the one used for training—the accuracy of the best performing method decreases from 94% to 55% (when the clients use the same browser but different operating systems) and to 27% (when the clients use different operating systems and browsers). Even when the training and test clients use the same browser and operating system and only differ in device, the best performing method achieves only 57% accuracy.

*This material is based upon work supported by the National Science Foundation under Grant No. CNS-1526268.

[1]In this paper, we show that this is not true—features and classifiers that work well for Tor traffic do not work well in the HTTPS context.

This finding implies that evaluation of the fingerprinting methods using the samples from the *same* client may overestimate the success of a webpage fingerprinting adversary in the real world.

Next, we investigate the traffic patterns of the 19 clients. We find differences in the HTTP messages generated, HTTP/2 implementation configuration, and the servers communicated with across the 19 clients. Particularly, we find that the User-Agent string lengths of the clients differ significantly, which causes outgoing packet sizes to vary greatly across the clients. We hypothesize that this is a significant factor to help explain our findings above—when samples from only one client are used for training, fingerprinting methods may over-fit to features derived from the outgoing packet sizes. This leads to very high fingerprinting accuracy when the same client is used for testing, but very low accuracy when different clients are used.

Finally, we search for a method that is robust to the impact of client diversity. First, we observe a significant increase in the accuracy of the methods when they are trained using samples from 18 different clients and tested using samples from the remaining one client. Then, we search for the main source of improvement in the accuracies. We find that it is necessary to use traffic samples from the browser of the test client during training; however, using samples of the same browser from different client devices is even more effective in increasing the robustness of fingerprinting methods.

In the rest of this paper, we summarize problem formulation in Section 2, data collection in Section 3, and our evaluations in Section 4. We investigate differences across clients in Section 5 and search for a robust model in Section 6. We summarize related work in Section 7 and our conclusions in Section 8.

2 PROBLEM FORMULATION

2.1 Importance of HTTPS Traffic Analysis

HyperText Transfer Protocol (HTTP) is used between a web browser (e.g., Google Chrome) and a web server when a webpage is visited [16]. HTTP messages are not encrypted and their integrity is not ensured. Thus, HTTP traffic is vulnerable to eavesdropping and tampering. Given the security concerns with HTTP, browsers (e.g., Chrome and Firefox) and organizations (e.g., Let's Encrypt[2]) promote HTTPS (HTTP over TLS) which verifies the identity of a website, encrypts HTTP messages and ensures data integrity. Indeed, these efforts led to the rapid adoption of HTTPS [17].

Despite the encryption of HTTP messages, HTTPS does not provide ultimate privacy when a webpage is visited. Even though the webpage URL (e.g., https://www.plannedparenthood.org/learn/abortion) is carried in an encrypted HTTP message, identity of the visited website (e.g., www.plannedparenthood.org) is often revealed (through the IP addresses of the servers, DNS queries and/or the server name in the SNI extension of TLS) [4]. More alarmingly, Miller et al. (2014) showed that the URLs of the webpages visited *within* a website can also be predicted with high accuracy using machine learning and features based on network packet sizes [5]. This finding is alarming since more fine-grained confidential information about users (e.g., health conditions and financial status) can be learned by determining the webpages visited compared to just determining the websites visited. For example, determining that a

user is reading about abortion or reading about filing a bankruptcy gives more granular information than just determining that the user is browsing a health or a finance website. Such information can be used for mass surveillance, targeted advertising or disclosure of sensitive information in a targeted attack scenario that may result in severe consequences, such as embarrassment or financial loss of a web user. Thus, the extent of HTTPS traffic analysis should be studied, HTTPS protocol should be improved towards a more robust privacy enhancing technology (if necessary[3]), and the web users should be informed accordingly.

2.2 HTTPS Webpage Fingerprinting (Threat Model)

In this paper, we consider a scenario in which a user visits a webpage within an HTTPS website and an adversary eavesdropping on the HTTPS traffic of the user tries to predict the URL of the visited webpage. We assume that the user do not use any privacy enhancing technology, such as a DNS proxy, VPN or Tor. Furthermore, we assume an HTTPS only web in which the websites enforce TLS encrypted connections and the adversary cannot decrypt the payloads.[4] However, the adversary has access to the information in the TCP/IP and TLS headers, which are transmitted in cleartext, such as the IP addresses, port numbers and server names, as well as the side channel information, such as the packet size and timing. The adversary can use such information and build a statistical model to fingerprint webpages based on their traffic patterns (e.g., number of packets sent to a specific server IP address). Furthermore, server IP addresses, DNS queries and/or the server name in the SNI extension of TLS often reveal the visited website—possibly allowing the adversary to narrow down the visited webpages to those within certain websites. Entities that can employ webpage fingerprinting methods include Internet Service Providers, Network Administrators or anyone who can eavesdrop on the HTTPS traffic of a user (e.g., an adversary who sniffs the network traffic of a public WiFi connection).

2.3 HTTPS Webpage Fingerprinting as a Machine Learning Problem

We study HTTPS webpage fingerprinting problem using the same supervised machine learning setting as in prior work [4, 5]. Specifically, the machine learning setting consists of two main phases namely the data collection and evaluation. In the data collection phase, webpage URLs are visited in a browser using a browser automation script and the network traffic of each visit is captured using a tool such as tcpdump. In the evaluation phase, the dataset is split into training and test samples. A supervised machine learning method, such as Multinomial Logistic Regression or Support Vector Machines (SVMs), is trained using the features extracted from the traffic traces of training samples. For example, a commonly used

---

[3]While prior work achieved high accuracy in HTTPS webpage fingerprinting [4, 5], it is not clear whether such accuracies can be achieved in the real world when several factors, which are often not studied in prior work, are considered. In this work, we mainly focus on one such factor namely client diversity and discuss other factors throughout the paper.
[4]If HTTPS is not used or it is compromised, the adversary can simply inspect the packet payloads and identify the webpages visited (and much more, such as online banking login credentials) from the clear text in the payloads—a technique known as deep packet inspection.

[2]https://letsencrypt.org/

feature extraction process is to consider each unique packet size as a feature and to count how many times each packet size occurs in a traffic trace [6].[5] During training, the label of each sample (i.e., webpage URL) is also provided and the machine learning method is expected to learn a function that maps input features to the provided labels. During test, the method predicts the labels of the test samples and is evaluated using its accuracy—how many samples out of all the test samples it labels correctly.

The webpage fingerprinting methods in the traffic analysis literature, such as Liberatore and Levine [6], BoG [5], CUMUL [8], K-Fingerprinting [18], and Wfin [9] mainly differ in the features they extract from network traffic and the machine learning methods they use. We give the details of such methods in Section 4.1 before we evaluate them.

2.4 State of the Art

To the best of our knowledge, there is only limited prominent work that studies webpage fingerprinting using HTTPS traffic [4, 5]. Miller et al. study traffic traces of around 600 webpages selected using a random walk from each of 10 prominent websites [5]. They design and evaluate a fairly elaborate fingerprinting method (termed as Bag of Gaussians) as well as a Hidden Markov Model (HMM) of likely browsing sequences. The researchers achieve 76% - 96% fingerprinting accuracy across the 10 websites—compared to around 60% when they use the methods from previous studies on SSH [6] and Tor traffic analysis [19, 20].

In a somewhat related work, Gonzalez et al. show that knowing the hostname of a visited website, which is already leaked in HTTPS traffic, is enough for user profiling purposes if the content of the website is homogeneous as in the case of the websites in the games and sports categories [4]. If the content of a website is heterogeneous, the researchers use the CUMUL method [8], which was originally proposed for Tor traffic analysis, to classify traffic traces of first-level webpages[6] within that website. The researchers achieve 13% - 97% classification accuracy across the websites.

The most signification distinction of our work from the above is that prior work has evaluated HTTPS fingerprinting methods using webpage traffic samples collected from the same client platform (e.g., Firefox browser in a virtual machine running Linux 12.04 OS in Miller et al.[5]). In this paper, we investigate the robustness of such methods to client diversity—how do the webpage fingerprinting methods perform when they are evaluated with traffic samples from different browsers, operating systems, and devices?

3 DATA

We study the same 10 websites targeted by Miller et al. [5]. We crawled these websites using a breadth-first crawling algorithm. Table 1 summarizes the results of the crawls.

We randomly select 50 webpages from each of 7 out of 10 websites—3 websites did not yield consistent webpages across all clients.[7] We

Table 1: Websites studied.

Host	Finished Crawling	URLs from Crawl
www.aclu.org	No	25182
www.bankofamerica.com	Yes	861
healthy.kaiserpermanente.org	No	19173
www.legalzoom.com	Yes	5260
www.mayoclinic.org	No	13266
www.netflix.com	No	127487
www.plannedparenthood.org	Yes	23260
investor.vanguard.com	Yes	477
www.wellsfargo.com	Yes	5436
www.youtube.com	No	29534

then visit each of these webpages 28 times using each of 19 different clients (i.e., a total of 50x7x28x19 = 186,200 webpage visits) and capture the network traffic of each visit—this dataset was collected during the period 5 - 14 July 2018.

Client Platforms Browser, OS and device type of each client are given in Table 2. We used four different Android devices, one Mac mini and three different virtual machines (with Ubuntu 18.04 LTS, Windows 10 and Windows 7 operating systems). In each operating system except Android OS, we considered multiple browsers. For example, in Windows 10, we used 5 different browsers namely Chrome, Firefox, Edge, IE and Opera. Note that some browsers are not available in all operating systems—Safari and Edge are only available in macOS and Windows 10, respectively. Furthermore, we excluded Opera in Windows 7 as it crashed frequently during data collection. In Android devices, we used only Chrome as, to the best of our knowledge, only Chrome has a driver to automate webpage visits in Android OS.[8]

Traffic Capture We used the Selenium browser automation framework[9] and tcpdump[10] to capture the network traffic of webpage visits. For each webpage visit, a new instance of a web browser (i.e., a browser without any user data) was used. Webpage URLs from all of the websites were visited in a round-robin manner 28 times in each of the 19 clients.

4 IMPACT OF CLIENT DIVERSITY

In this section, we evaluate the impact of client diversity on the accuracy of prominent webpage fingerprinting methods from the traffic analysis literature. First, we summarize the webpage fingerprinting methods we evaluate. Then, we describe our evaluation methodology. Finally, we discuss the results.

4.1 Fingerprinting Methods

Liberatore and Levine (LL) (2006) [6] uses only the packet size counts as features and Naive Bayes classifier for classification. LL method was introduced to fingerprint the visits to the landing pages

---

[5]Incoming and outgoing packets are considered separately. For example, with a maximum packet size of 1500 bytes, a sample is represented as a vector of 3000 elements—each element corresponds to a packet size with a direction and the value of each element is how many times a packet with that size and direction occurs in the traffic trace of the sample.

[6]Webpages that are linked from the landing page of a website.

[7]Netflix directed all webpage URLS to the same sign-in page; Youtube and Kaiser Permanente webpages were redirected to URLs from hostnames that we never visit in other clients—Kaiser Permanente webpages often reported an HTTP error in the

---

Android clients. To achieve a balanced dataset for supervised machine learning, we wanted to select an equal number of samples for each webpage from each client. Thus, we excluded these three websites and found that we have at least 28 samples from 50 webpages in each of the remaining 7 websites for each of the 19 clients.

[8]While any app can be automated using Android adb utility, we are not aware of a method to determine whether a webpage is loaded in other browser apps (e.g. Firefox)—the driver of Chrome provides such events.

[9]https://www.seleniumhq.org/

[10]http://www.tcpdump.org/

Table 2: Browser, OS and device type of the clients used for webpage visits. User-Agent strings of the clients are given in Table 3.

ID	Browser	OS	Device
1	Chrome (67.0.3396.87)	Android 4.4.2	SM-T230NU
2	Chrome (67.0.3396.87)	Android 4.4.4	GT-I9195I
3	Chrome (67.0.3396.87)	Android 6.0.1	Nexus 5
4	Chrome (67.0.3396.87)	Android 6.0.1	Nexus 7
5	Chrome (67.0.3396.99)	Ubuntu 18.04 LTS	vm
6	Chrome (67.0.3396.99)	Windows 10	vm
7	Chrome (67.0.3396.99)	Windows 7	vm
8	Chrome (67.0.3396.99)	macOS 10.13.5	Mac mini
9	Edge (42.17134.1.0)	Windows 10	vm
10	Firefox (61.0)	Ubuntu 18.04 LTS	vm
11	Firefox (61.0)	Windows 10	vm
12	Firefox (61.0)	Windows 7	vm
13	Firefox (61.0)	macOS 10.13.5	Mac mini
14	IE (11)	Windows 10	vm
15	IE (11)	Windows 7	vm
16	Opera (67.0.3396.87)	Ubuntu 18.04 LTS	vm
17	Opera (67.0.3396.87)	Windows 10	vm
18	Opera (67.0.3396.87)	macOS 10.13.5	Mac mini
19	Safari (13605.2.8)	macOS 10.13.5	Mac mini

of websites in an SSH proxy channel. Miller et al. [5] considered LL as a baseline method that uses low level packet inspection and evaluated it in the context of HTTPS webpage fingerprinting.

Bag-of-Gaussians (BoG) (2014) [5] uses features based on clustering pairs of incoming and outgoing burst sizes according to the second level domain names of the servers as well as features based on packet size counts.[11] BoG uses logistic regression with L2 regularization for classification. Miller et al.[5] showed that BoG achieves substantially greater accuracy in HTTPS webpage fingerprinting compared to the methods introduced by Liberatore and Levine [6], Panchenko et al. [19] and Wang et al. [20]. The researchers also showed that a Hidden Markov Model can be used to model a sequence of webpage visits within a website, that can augment fingerprinting methods quite successfully.

CUMUL (2016) [8] uses 100 points sampled from a cumulative representation of packet sizes as well as the number of incoming/outgoing packets and the sum of incoming/outgoing packet sizes as features. CUMUL uses SVM with RBF kernel for classification. Panchenko et al. [8] introduced CUMUL for fingerprinting webpages visited in Tor network traffic. Gonzalez et al. [4] used CUMUL for HTTPS webpage fingerprinting.

K-fingerprinting (KFP) (2016) [18] uses 175 traffic features, such as the statistics based on the number of packets and packet timings. KFP uses Random Forest Classifier for classification. The authors of the method evaluated KFP in fingerprinting hidden services in Tor network traffic as well as in fingerprinting encrypted Web traffic.

Wfin (2018) [9] Yan and Kaur identified 40 most important traffic feature categories in web traffic analysis, such as unique packet size, packet size count, and preposition of first 300 incoming packets, and introduced the Wfin method. Wfin uses Extra-Trees classifier for classification. The researchers showed that features used in Wfin yield similar performance as features used in the LL method but perform better than features from the CUMUL and KFP methods in classifying traffic traces of landing pages of 2,000 websites.

Packet Size Counts (PS), Incoming Packet Size Counts (IPS), and Outgoing Packet Size Counts (OPS) Most methods in the traffic analysis literature include packet size counts in their feature set.[12] To have a baseline view of the webpage fingerprinting accuracy achievable using only packet size counts, we evaluate three methods that just use packet size counts and differ in the direction of the packets used: both incoming and outgoing packet size counts (PS), only incoming packet size counts (IPS), and only outgoing packet size counts (OPS). We use Random Forest Classifier for classification with these methods. Note that PS differs from LL only in the choice of classifier.

4.2 Evaluation Methodology

We evaluate the webpage fingerprinting methods detailed in Section 4.1, using our dataset described in Section 3. We consider five different scenarios—the training and test samples are from: (i) the same client (Scenario 1), (ii) the same browser, same OS but different device (Scenario 2)[13], (iii) the same browser but different OS (Scenario 3), (iv) the same OS but different browser (Scenario 4), and (v) different browser and different OS (Scenario 5). Note that we have 19 clients, 7 websites, 50 webpages from each website, and 28 samples from each webpage in our dataset. We perform a total of 20,216 evaluations (19 x 19 train/test client pairs x 8 methods x 7 websites). In this setting, an evaluation is a classification problem with 50 classes—given a traffic trace classify it as a trace of one of the 50 webpages within a website. When a client is used for training, we use the first 21 samples of each webpage from that client for training and use the remaining 7 samples when the client is considered for test—a total of 1050 training samples (i.e., 50 webpages x 21 samples) and 350 test samples are used in each evaluation.

4.3 Results

For each of the five different scenarios, Figure 1 plots the accuracy of each method (i.e., percent of the test traffic trace samples that are labeled with the correct webpage URL) for each website averaged over all training and test pairs of client platforms considered in that scenario. Figure 2 plots the accuracy in each scenario, when averaged across all websites and client pairs (and makes it easier to compare the overall performance of the methods across different scenarios). We observe that:

(1) All webpage fingerprinting methods perform their best in Scenario 1 when the training and test samples are from the same client. Recall that this is the scenario in which evaluations in all prior work are conducted. In this scenario,

---

[11]Burst size is defined as the total bytes in contiguous packets transmitted in one direction.

[12]We formulate HTTPS webpage fingerprinting as a machine learning problem in Section 2.3 and describe an example method that uses packet size counts as features.
[13]Note that we have only two clients namely client 3 and 4 that have the same browser and same OS but different devices.

(a) Scenario 1 (Same Client)

(b) Scenario 2 (Same Browser, Same OS, Different Device)

(c) Scenario 3 (Same Browser, Different OS)

(d) Scenario 4 (Different Browser, Same OS)

(e) Scenario 5 (Different Browser, Different OS)

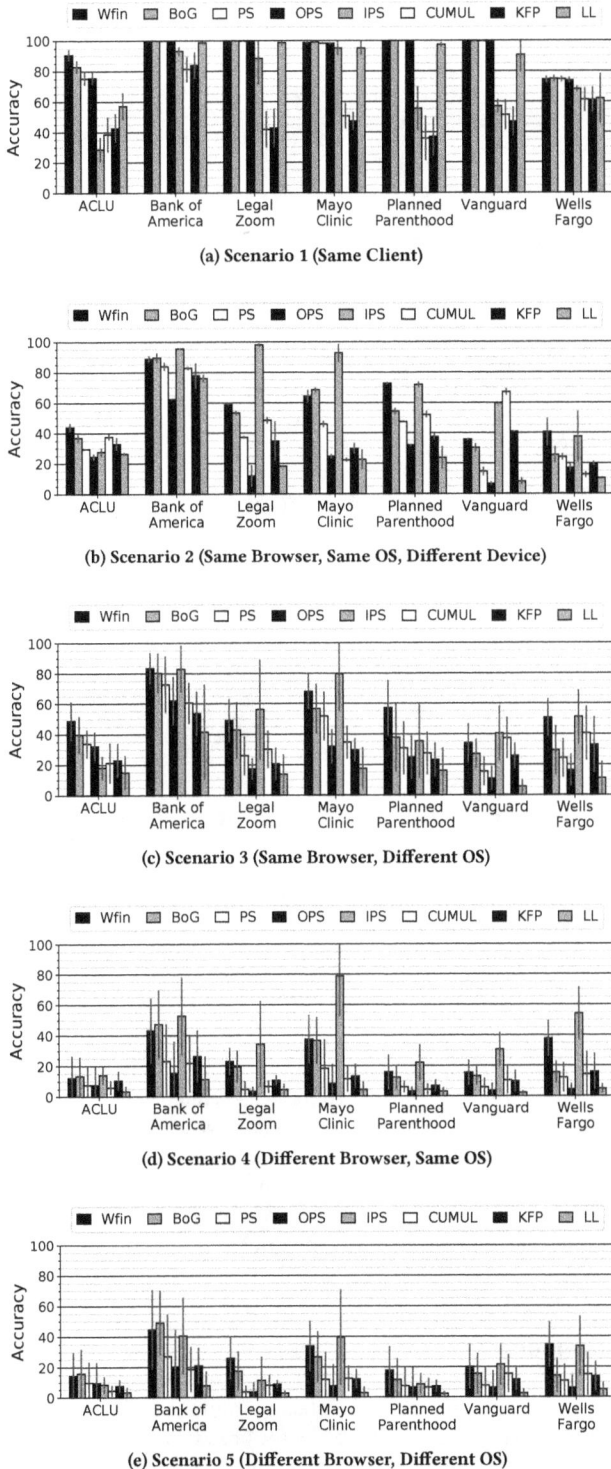

Figure 1: Performance of webpage fingerprinting methods in five different scenarios in which the training and test clients are varied.

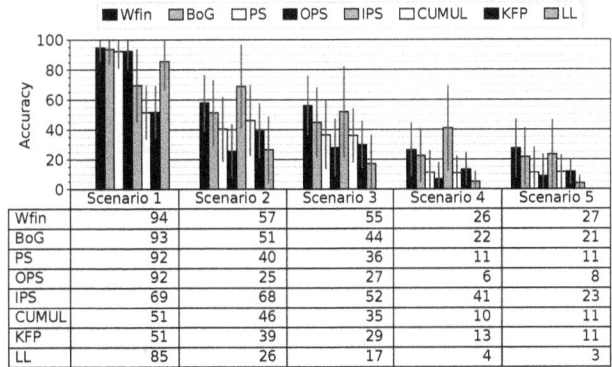

	Scenario 1	Scenario 2	Scenario 3	Scenario 4	Scenario 5
Wfin	94	57	55	26	27
BoG	93	51	44	22	21
PS	92	40	36	11	11
OPS	92	25	27	6	8
IPS	69	68	52	41	23
CUMUL	51	46	35	10	11
KFP	51	39	29	13	11
LL	85	26	17	4	3

Figure 2: Accuracy of each method in each scenario.

the best performing methods are able to classify the traffic traces of webpages within most of the websites with high accuracy. However, as reported in prior work, the traffic traces of webpages within some websites can be classified with lower accuracy than others [4, 5]—e.g., lower accuracies are observed in ACLU and Wells Fargo websites in Figure 1a.

(2) Compared to Scenario 1, the accuracies decrease significantly in Scenario 2 when the training and test samples are from the same browser, same OS but different device (Figure 1b). The accuracies of the Wfin and BoG methods, averaged cross all websites, drop from 94% and 93% to 57% and 51%, respectively (Figure 2).
   Even lower accuracies are observed in Scenario 3, when samples from the same browser but different OS are used for evaluation (Figure 1c and 2).

(3) The lowest accuracies are observed in Scenarios 4 and 5 (when samples from different browsers are used)—see Figures 1d and 1e. Compared to Scenario 1, the accuracies of the Wfin and BoG methods in Scenario 4, averaged across all websites, decrease from 94% and 93% to around 26% and 22%, respectively (Figure 2).
   In a real world setting, Scenarios 2, 3, 4 or 5 are much more likely to occur than Scenario 1, if an adversary does not consider the impact of client diversity (and trains a webpage fingerprinting method using traffic samples from only a single client). Thus, *prior evaluations of fingerprinting methods using samples from the same client may significantly overestimate the success of a webpage fingerprinting adversary.*

(4) While the OPS method, which uses only the outgoing packet size counts as features, performs comparable to the best performing methods in Scenario 1, it is outperformed in other scenarios. On the other hand, the IPS method, which uses only the incoming packet size counts, is one of the best performing methods in Scenarios 2, 3, 4 and 5.

Note that features based on outgoing packet size are used in nearly all of the fingerprinting methods—indeed, IPS is the only method included in our evaluations that does not use any feature based on outgoing packet size. Our results suggest that the presence of features based on outgoing packet size may lead to "over-fitting" when evaluations consider only a single client platform.

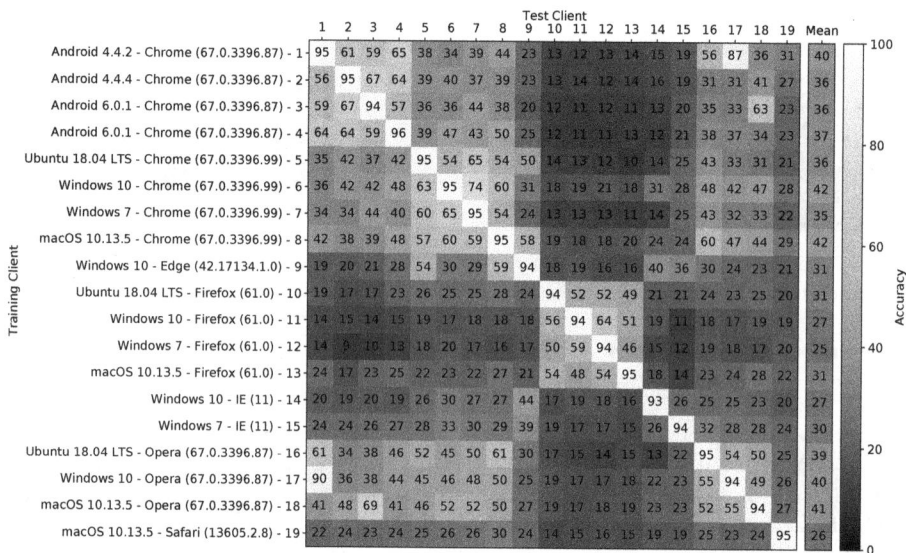

Figure 3: Accuracy of the Wfin method when the training and test clients are varied (19x19 training and test client pairs). Note that the highest accuracies are achieved when the samples from the same client are used for training and test.

In Figure 3, we plot the webpage fingerprinting accuracy (averaged across the 7 websites) of the Wfin method as a matrix for all 19x19 pairs of training and test client platforms. We find that Wfin performs better on average, when a Chrome client is used for training and Opera client is used for test (and vice versa) (e.g., using one of the clients 1-8 for training and 16-18 for test) compared to using any other client pair with different browsers. Note that the Chrome and Opera browsers are both based on the open source Chromium browser project[14]—we hypothesize that they generate similar network traffic patterns. We also find that Wfin achieves a significantly high accuracy when client 17 (Windows 10 - Opera) is used for training and client 1 (Android-Chrome) is used for test (and vice versa); and Wfin achieves the lowest accuracies when client 14 (Windows 10 - IE), 15 (Windows 7 - IE) or 19 (macOS - Safari) is used in an evaluation.

Figure 3 reports accuracy averaged across the 7 websites. We select the row for training client 8 (that gives the highest average accuracy across all test clients in Figure 3), and plot in Figure 4 the *per-website* accuracy of the Wfin method when only samples from client 8 are used for training. As before, we observe that the highest accuracies are achieved when the training and the test clients are the same. Significantly lower accuracies are observed when the browsers of the training and test clients are different (e.g., when clients 10-15 are used for test). We further investigate plausible causes of client differences in the next section.

5 CLIENT DIFFERENCES

Using data collected in 2014, prior work has shown that when different client platforms are used to access the *landing* page of popular websites, the resulting download may differ in both content as well as traffic [14, 21]. Our results so far suggest that this may be

[14]https://www.chromium.org/

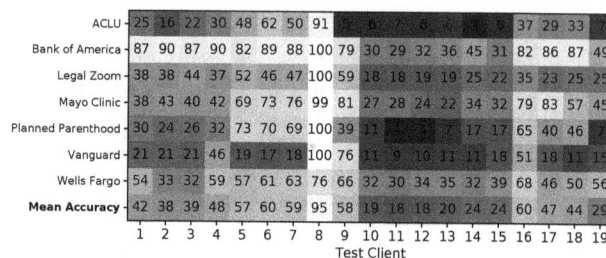

Figure 4: Accuracy of the Wfin method for each test client and website when client 8 is used for training.

true even for modern download traffic generated when webpages within websites are visited. In this section, we identify three major differences across client platforms that cause variations in web traffic patterns—these are mostly factors that influence the outgoing packet sizes in web traffic (which is likely to be a significant influence on our results in Section 4.3) .

5.1 HTTP Messages

Background When a webpage URL is entered to the address bar of a browser, the browser sends an HTTP request message to a server. The server interprets the request and returns an HTTP response. The response message is parsed by the browser and additional requests are sent and responses are received if other web resources, such as CSS, image and video files, are need to be loaded. An example HTTP message that requests the landing page of Bank of America website is given in Figure 5.

Methodology Browser developer tools provide detailed information about each HTTP message generated during a webpage visit.

Table 3: User-Agent strings of the clients.

ID	User Agent	Length
1	Mozilla/5.0 (Linux; Android 4.4.2; SM-T230NU Build/KOT49H) AppleWebKit/537.36 (KHTML, like Gecko) Chrome/67.0.3396.87 Safari/537.36	131
2	Mozilla/5.0 (Linux; Android 4.4.4; GT-I9195I Build/KTU84P) AppleWebKit/537.36 (KHTML, like Gecko) Chrome/67.0.3396.87 Mobile Safari/537.36	138
3	Mozilla/5.0 (Linux; Android 6.0.1; Nexus 5 Build/M4B30Z) AppleWebKit/537.36 (KHTML, like Gecko) Chrome/67.0.3396.87 Mobile Safari/537.36	136
4	Mozilla/5.0 (Linux; Android 6.0.1; Nexus 7 Build/MOB30X) AppleWebKit/537.36 (KHTML, like Gecko) Chrome/67.0.3396.87 Safari/537.36	129
5	Mozilla/5.0 (X11; Linux x86_64) AppleWebKit/537.36 (KHTML, like Gecko) Chrome/67.0.3396.99 Safari/537.36	104
6	Mozilla/5.0 (Windows NT 10.0; Win64; x64) AppleWebKit/537.36 (KHTML, like Gecko) Chrome/67.0.3396.99 Safari/537.36	114
7	Mozilla/5.0 (Windows NT 6.1; Win64; x64) AppleWebKit/537.36 (KHTML, like Gecko) Chrome/67.0.3396.99 Safari/537.36	113
8	Mozilla/5.0 (Macintosh; Intel Mac OS X 10_13_5) AppleWebKit/537.36 (KHTML, like Gecko) Chrome/67.0.3396.99 Safari/537.36	120
9	Mozilla/5.0 (Windows NT 10.0; Win64; x64) AppleWebKit/537.36 (KHTML, like Gecko) Chrome/64.0.3282.140 Safari/537.36 Edge/17.17134	129
10	Mozilla/5.0 (X11; Linux x86_64; rv:61.0) Gecko/20100101 Firefox/61.0	68
11	Mozilla/5.0 (Windows NT 10.0; Win64; x64; rv:61.0) Gecko/20100101 Firefox/61.0	78
12	Mozilla/5.0 (Windows NT 6.1; Win64; x64; rv:61.0) Gecko/20100101 Firefox/61.0	77
13	Mozilla/5.0 (Macintosh; Intel Mac OS X 10.13; rv:61.0) Gecko/20100101 Firefox/61.0	82
14	Mozilla/5.0 (Windows NT 10.0; WOW64; Trident/7.0; .NET4.0C; .NET4.0E; rv:11.0) like Gecko	89
15	Mozilla/5.0 (Windows NT 6.1; WOW64; Trident/7.0; SLCC2; .NET CLR 2.0.50727; .NET CLR 3.5.30729; .NET CLR 3.0.30729; Media Center PC 6.0; .NET4.0C; .NET4.0E; rv:11.0) like Gecko	176
16	Mozilla/5.0 (X11; Linux x86_64) AppleWebKit/537.36 (KHTML, like Gecko) Chrome/67.0.3396.87 Safari/537.36 OPR/54.0.2952.41	121
17	Mozilla/5.0 (Windows NT 10.0; Win64; x64) AppleWebKit/537.36 (KHTML, like Gecko) Chrome/67.0.3396.87 Safari/537.36 OPR/54.0.2952.41	131
18	Mozilla/5.0 (Macintosh; Intel Mac OS X 10_13_5) AppleWebKit/537.36 (KHTML, like Gecko) Chrome/67.0.3396.87 Safari/537.36 OPR/54.0.2952.41	137
19	Mozilla/5.0 (Macintosh; Intel Mac OS X 10_13_5) AppleWebKit/605.1.15 (KHTML, like Gecko) Version/11.1.1 Safari/605.1.15	119

```
GET / HTTP/1.1
Host: www.bankofamerica.com
Connection: keep-alive
Upgrade-Insecure-Requests: 1
User-Agent: Mozilla/5.0 (Windows NT 10.0; Win64;
    x64) AppleWebKit/537.36 (KHTML, like Gecko)
    Chrome/67.0.3396.99 Safari/537.36
Accept: text/html,application/xhtml+xml,
    application/xml;q=0.9,image/webp,
    image/apng,*/*;q=0.8
Accept-Encoding: gzip, deflate, br
Accept-Language: en-US,en;q=0.9
```

Figure 5: An HTTP request for www.bankofamerica.com, generated by the Chrome browser running on Windows 10 OS (i.e., client 6 in Table 2).

All browsers we use provide such a tool—we use these to investigate the differences in the HTTP messages generated by different clients.[15]

Results We find several practices that result in differences (and similarities) in the size of packets that carry HTTP requests from different clients:

- Clients use User-Agent strings that significantly differ in length (see Table 3 for a complete list of User-Agent strings used by the clients). For example, client 10 (Ubuntu - Firefox) and client 15 (Windows 7 - IE) have user agent strings that are 68 and 176 characters long, respectively.
- Different browsers may use different header fields (e.g., IE browser does not use "Upgrade-Insecure-Requests" header field whereas other browsers do[16]). Further, HTTP header field values may differ across different browsers (e.g., Chrome

and Opera include "image/webp,image/apng" string in their default Accept value whereas other browsers do not[17]).
- Browsers use the same headers across different operating systems (e.g., Chrome on Windows 10 and Chrome on macOS generate the same headers and only differ in the User-Agent string).
- Clients that use Chrome or Opera browser (i.e., clients 1-8 and 16-18) use the same HTTP header fields and only differ in the User-Agent string. Of these, coincidentally, client 1 (Android - Chrome) and client 17 (Windows 10 - Opera) have user agent strings with the same length (131 characters). Thus, client 1 and 17 are expected to generate HTTP messages with the same length when the same URL is requested. Indeed, in our preliminary evaluation we found that when this client pair is used for evaluation, a significantly high accuracy is achieved (see Figure 3).[18]

Our observations in this section show that HTTP request sizes can differ across different client platforms, primarily due to user agent strings but also due to other header fields. Furthermore, client pairs that generate HTTP requests of the same size for a given webpage yield high fingerprinting accuracies when used for training and testing against each other.

5.1.1 User Specific Browser Configuration. Note that the HTTP request headers may change according to the configuration of a browser. For example, if a user specifies French as an additional language preference in Chrome settings, "fr;q=0.8" string will be added to the value of Accept-Language field in Figure 5; or if a user specifies sending a "do not track" request, "DNT: 1" string will be included in each HTTP request. These changes will practically have

---

[15]We use the Chrome remote debugging tool to investigate the HTTP headers generated by the Android clients.

[16]Indeed, IE is the only major browser that does not use this header field: https://developer.mozilla.org/en-US/docs/Web/HTTP/Headers/Upgrade-Insecure-Requests

[17]Note that the value of Accept field may change according to the type of resource requested (e.g., CSS, image or video): https://developer.mozilla.org/en-US/docs/Web/HTTP/Content_negotiation/List_of_default_Accept_values

[18]Note that client 4 (Android - Chrome) and client 9 (Windows 10 - Edge) also have user agent strings with the same length (129 characters long). However, these clients use different values for Accept-Language and Accept fields—Edge uses "en-US" and "text/html, application/xhtml+xml, application/xml; q=0.9, */*; q=0.8", respectively. The Chrome values for these fields are given in Figure 5.

the same impact we observed due to the variations in the length of User-Agent string across different clients. Thus, user specific browser configuration should also be considered as a part of client diversity for webpage fingerprinting purposes.

5.2 HTTP/2 Implementation

Background HTTP/2 is an optimized alternative to HTTP/1.1 [22]. HTTP/1.1 allows only one request to be outstanding at a time on a given TCP connection, suffers from head-of-line blocking, and repeats HTTP headers in each request. HTTP/2 addresses these issues and introduces several other features: request and response multiplexing over a single TCP connection, compression of HTTP header fields, request prioritization, server push and flow control. The basic HTTP/2 protocol unit is a binary *frame*. Each HTTP request/response is associated with its own *stream*. Naturally, the network traffic footprint differs when a webpage is visited over HTTP/2 versus HTTP/1.1.

Major browsers and servers support both HTTP/1.1 and HTTP/2 [23]—a client and a server negotiate which protocol to use during the TLS handshake (selected protocol is revealed in clear text). Figure 6 shows the average number of HTTP/2 and HTTP/1.1 connections used by each client during a webpage visit in our dataset. Note that three of the Windows clients (9, 14 and 17) generate more HTTP/2 connections compared to other clients whereas IE 11 on Windows 7 (client 15) does not use HTTP/2.

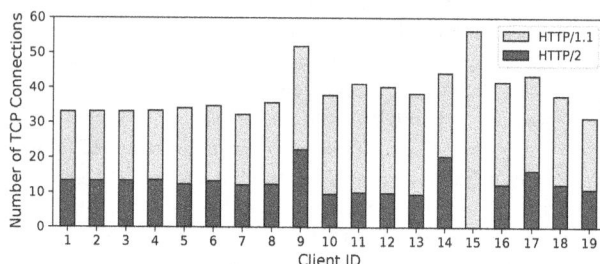

Figure 6: Average number of HTTP/2 and HTTP/1.1 connections used by each client during a webpage visit in our dataset. We have 9800 webpage visit samples (7 websites x 50 webpages x 28 samples) from each client.

Methodology Since HTTP/2 is used over TLS, HTTP/2 traffic analysis requires decryption of TLS connections. Chrome, Opera and Firefox browsers allow to generate an SSL key log file which can be used to decrypt the TLS connections whereas other browsers (IE, Edge and Safari) do not.[19] During the data collection we generated an SSL key log file for each visit performed in Chrome, Opera and Firefox browsers. After the data collection, we used tshark[20] to decrypt the TLS connections and decode the HTTP/2 frames.

Results Figure 7 shows the average number of HTTP/2 frames from each frame type generated by Chrome, Firefox and Opera browsers during a webpage visit in our dataset. We find several

---

[19]https://wiki.wireshark.org/SSL
[20]https://www.wireshark.org/docs/man-pages/tshark.html

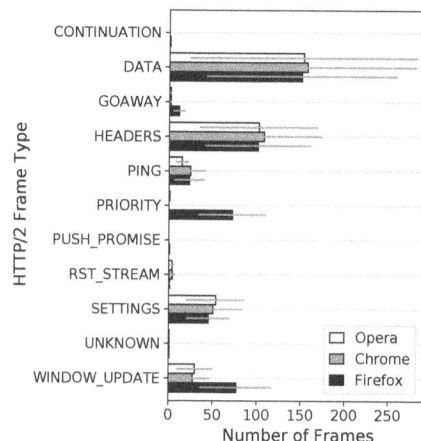

Figure 7: Average number of HTTP/2 frames from each frame type generated by Chrome, Firefox and Opera browsers during a webpage visit in our dataset.

practices that are likely to change the size of packets carrying HTTP/2 frames:

- On average, Chrome and Opera browsers generate similar number of frames. This is likely due to the fact that both Chrome and Opera are based on the Chromium open source project, and hence share the same HTTP/2 implementation.
- Firefox generates more WINDOW_ UPDATE and PRIORITY frames than Chrome or Opera. Further analysis of Firefox traffic traces reveals that WINDOW_UPDATE and HEADER frames are often found in the same network packet. A WINDOW_UPDATE frame is 13 bytes long.[21]. Thus, even if Chrome and Firefox browsers generate the same HTTP/2 HEADERS frames, most packets that contain a Firefox HEADERS frame will have 13 more bytes due to the WINDOW_ UPDATE frame in the same packet compared to the corresponding CHROME packets—significantly changing the outgoing packet sizes generated by the two browsers.
- Unlike the Chromium browsers, Firefox sends multiple PRIORITY frames in the same packet that contains the connection preface string.[22]

Our analysis in this section shows that different browsers differ in several aspects of their HTTP/2 implementations, resulting in differences in the number of packets generated as well as size of packets.

5.3 Client Specific Connections

When a webpage is visited, browsers often communicate with multiple servers to load web resources, such as HTML, CSS and image files, as well as communicate with tracking and advertisement servers. Figure 8 shows the total number of TCP connections from each client to 14 domains—we selected the domain names of the 7 websites we study and 7 additional domain names to illustrate

---

[21]9-octet frame header + 4 octet payload [22].
[22]The client and server send a preface string to establish the initial settings of HTTP/2: https://tools.ietf.org/html/rfc7540#section-3.5.

the similarities and differences in the domains communicated by different clients.

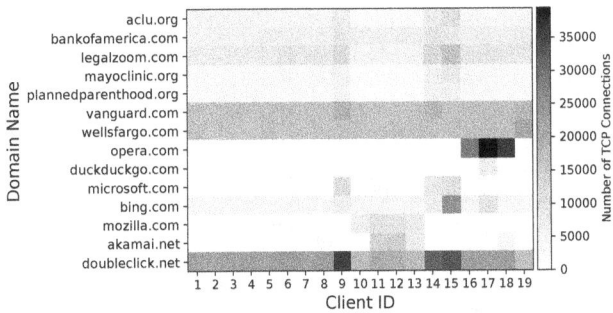

Figure 8: Total number of TCP connections from each client to 14 selected domain names in our dataset.

Similar to the observations in prior work [21], we find that some clients communicate with certain domain names significantly more than others, mainly due to browser specific communication: Opera browser (i.e., clients 16, 17 and 18) communicates with "opera.com", IE and Edge browsers (i.e., clients 9, 14 and 15) communicate with "microsoft.com" and Firefox browser (i.e., clients 11, 12 and 13) communicates with "mozilla.com". Furthermore, client 17 (Windows 10 - Opera) is the only client that communicates with "duckduckgo.com". The client specific connections significantly change the traffic features of a webpage across the clients, such as the number of incoming and outgoing packets—such features are used by several fingerprinting methods (e.g., Wfin, CUMUL and K-fingerprinting).

6 SEARCH FOR A ROBUST METHOD

In this section, we investigate whether a webpage fingerprinting method that is robust to the traffic variations across different clients can be trained through diversification of training samples.

Diversification of Training Samples We consider a scenario where a webpage fingerprinting entity, that is aware of the impact of client diversity and has sufficient computational resources, collects traffic samples from a diverse set of clients but does not consider a specific client during training—and the test samples are from that specific client. This scenario can be studied using one of the clients in our dataset as a test client and using the remaining 18 clients for training the webpage fingerprinting methods—we perform 19 such evaluations in each website with each method. As in our evaluation methodology in Section 4.2, we use the first 21 samples of a webpage from a client when the client is considered for training and use the remaining 7 samples when the client is used for test. Note that this scenario is rich in training data since we use 18 clients x 21 samples = 378 samples for each webpage during training (compared to the scenarios in Section 4 where we use only 21 samples from a single client for each webpage). Figure 9 plots the average accuracy of each method in each website in this scenario.

We observe a significant increase in the accuracy of Wfin and BoG methods compared to the scenarios in Section 4 where we evaluate the methods using samples from two different clients (Scenarios 2, 3, 4 and 5). For example, Wfin achieves around 35%

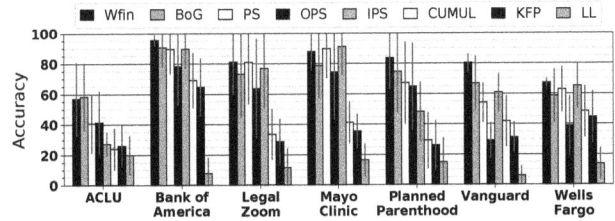

Figure 9: Webpage fingerprinting accuracy when samples from one client are used for test and samples from the remaining 18 clients are used for training—19 such evaluations are performed with each method in each website.

accuracy in Vanguard in Scenario 2 (Figure 1b) whereas it achieves around 80% in present scenario for the same website (Figure 9).[23]

However, the fingerprinting accuracy of all methods is still lower than that achieved in Scenario 1 (Figure 1a)—even when significantly more training samples that are collected from multiple diverse clients are used. This further supports our hypothesis that when samples from only one client are used to evaluate fingerprinting methods (which is true for all prior work on HTTPS webpage fingerprinting), the fingerprinting accuracy may be significantly exaggerated (due to overfitting to specific packet sizes).

Figure 10a plots the accuracy of the Wfin method observed with each of the 19 test clients used in this scenario for each website. Compared to Figure 4, where we evaluate this method using training samples from only the single client 8, we observe higher and more uniform accuracies across the 19 test clients and the 7 websites.

While we find that the methods perform better when they are trained using more samples from a diverse set of clients, compared to when they are trained using less samples from a single client, the main source of the improvement is not clear. Is it the diverse samples from different browsers? Is it the samples of the same browser from different clients or is it simply using more training samples? In order to answer these, we consider several other scenarios and evaluate the accuracy of the Wfin method, one of the best performing methods.

Samples From Just 6 Clients That Represent Different Browsers Figure 10b plots the accuracy of the Wfin method when the method is trained using samples from 6 different clients namely 6, 9, 10, 15, 16 and 19—these are clients that use the browsers Chrome, Edge, Firefox, IE, Opera, and Safari, respectively. Note that samples from all 6 browsers in our dataset are used during training, and 126 training samples (6 clients x 21 samples) are used for each webpage. We observe lower accuracies compared to Figure 10a where we train using samples from 18 different clients. However, compared to Figure 4, we observe much higher and more uniform accuracies for all websites and all test clients. It may be tempting to conclude that the 6 diverse clients represented in the training data are contributing to the performance improvement—however, it is important to

---

[23]Note that the average accuracy of some methods, such as PS, IPS and CUMUL, are lower in Figure 9 for some websites, compared to Figure 1b—in Figure 1b, we use only two test clients that use the same browser and OS but differ in device (clients 3 and 4), whereas in Figure 9 we average the accuracy over 19 test clients. When only the accuracies achieved in the two test clients used in Figure 1b are averaged, all methods achieve a higher accuracy when samples from 18 clients are used for training.

	1	2	3	4	5	6	7	8	9	10	11	12	13	14	15	16	17	18	19
aCLU	76	71	54	57	85	71	80	74	17	64	55	63	59	9	8	77	68	71	26
Bank of America	100	98	97	98	91	96	97	99	96	94	97	97	95	90	84	94	98	98	93
Legal Zoom	98	98	97	98	98	95	95	99	83	60	72	78	55	37	41	95	96	92	53
Mayo Clinic	90	90	88	91	94	93	95	96	84	88	93	96	89	72	42	93	97	95	85
Planned Parenthood	97	96	97	94	93	93	99	94	86	86	80	96	83	50	42	91	96	90	27
Vanguard	87	85	79	87	81	80	83	84	82	85	85	86	77	68	76	75	82	75	67
Wells Fargo	68	67	67	68	69	69	69	68	69	68	69	64	63	58	70	65	68		67
Mean Accuracy	88	86	83	85	87	85	89	88	74	78	79	84	75	56	50	85	86	84	60

Test Client ID

(a) When samples from one client are used for test and the samples from the remaining 18 clients are used for training.

	1	2	3	4	5	6	7	8	9	10	11	12	13	14	15	16	17	18	19
aCLU	62	57	35	60	82	T	71	66	T	T	59	58	50	9	T	T	49	45	T
Bank of America	94	94	93	96	93	T	97	97	T	T	94	91	91	86	T	T	88	93	T
Legal Zoom	73	59	60	78	88	T	81	78	T	T	49	51	41	37	T	T	77	68	T
Mayo Clinic	61	48	57	47	93	T	91	94	T	T	92	92	85	78	T	T	88	80	T
Planned Parenthood	67	48	57	54	87	T	94	91	T	T	59	58	69	54	T	T	71	77	T
Vanguard	72	79	67	78	78	T	84	86	T	T	77	69	73	65	T	T	70	76	T
Wells Fargo	64	39	41	69	84	T	70	69	T	T	66	68	62	52	T	T	57	61	T
Mean Accuracy	70	61	59	65	84	T	84	83	T	T	71	70	67	55	T	T	71	71	T

Test Client ID

(b) When samples from clients 6, 9, 10, 15, 16 and 19 are used for training. "T" indicates that a client is used for training.

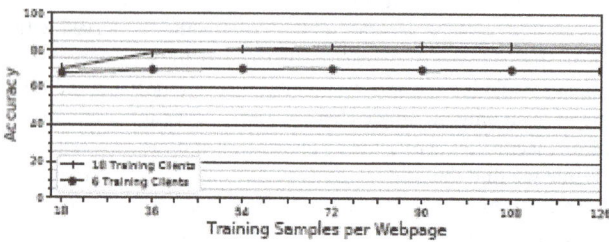

(c) Effect of increasing the number of training samples per webpage.

	1	2	3	4	5	6	7	8	9	10	11	12	13	14	15	16	17	18	19
aCLU	75	77	61	84	85	74	67	76	n/a	69	57	63	60	n/a	n/a	77	72	66	n/a
Bank of America	96	97	97	98	92	94	97	95	n/a	93	96	98	95	n/a	n/a	91	94	95	n/a
Legal Zoom	96	100	98	99	95	96	98	98	n/a	71	70	78	63	n/a	n/a	79	83	81	n/a
Mayo Clinic	91	91	93	93	73	95	97	97	n/a	93	96	97	91	n/a	n/a	82	93	84	n/a
Planned Parenthood	89	95	91	93	93	91	97	93	n/a	84	73	93	81	n/a	n/a	81	92	90	n/a
Vanguard	80	87	80	86	82	78	82	75	n/a	80	85	85	72	n/a	n/a	62	65	46	n/a
Wells Fargo	65	65	64	66	69	63	68	64	n/a	66	67	69	59	n/a	n/a	66	64	66	n/a
Mean Accuracy	85	87	83	88	84	84	87	85	n/a	79	78	83	74	n/a	n/a	77	80	75	n/a

Test Client ID

(d) The clients are grouped into those that use the same browser (client ID ranges are given in parentheses): Chrome (1-8), Firefox(10-13) and Opera(16-18). One client in a group is used for test and the remaining clients in the group are used for training. "n/a" indicates that a client is not considered in this scenario.

Figure 10: Accuracy of the Wfin method in each website for each test client in different scenarios where the training samples are varied. The same 350 test samples from a test client (50 webpages within a website x 7 test samples) are used in each evaluation.

remember that the number of training samples is quite different for the evaluations summarized in each of Figures 4, 10a, and 10b. We isolate the impact of number of training samples next.

Effect of Number of Training Samples Figure 10c plots the effect of increasing the number of training samples per webpage in the scenarios of Figures 10a and 10b—for both scenarios, Figure 10c reports the average accuracy achieved for the 13 test clients that are evaluated in Figure 10b (i.e., 13 test clients x 7 websites = 91 evaluations are performed to calculate each accuracy point). Equal number of training samples are used from each of the training clients. The x-axis represents the number of training samples used per webpage—for example, when 36 samples are used per webpage, 2 samples are used from each of 18 training clients (and 6 samples are used from each of 6 training clients). We observe a significant increase in the accuracy when more samples are used from each of 18 clients—when 90 samples are used per webpage (5 samples from each of 18 clients) the accuracy increases to around 82% compared to around 70% when only 18 samples per webpage are used. However, the accuracy gain seems to saturate after 72 samples.

In the scenario using just 6 training clients, the performance gains are only slight when more samples are used from each client. Note that the 6 training clients use different browsers whereas among the 18 clients, there are multiple clients that use the same browser. We hypothesize that with 18 different training clients, Wfin mainly benefits from the larger number of samples of the same browser across different clients. We test this next.

Samples From the Same Browser Across Different Clients We divide clients into groups that use the same browser—we create 3 groups corresponding to Chrome, Firefox, and Opera. We then use one client from a group for test and the remaining clients to train the Wfin method. In order to remove the influence of number of training samples, we use around 21 samples from each webpage for training and take equal number of samples from each training client—we take 3 samples from each of 7 training clients in Chrome group, take 7 samples from each of 3 training clients in Firefox group, and take 11 samples from each of 2 training clients in Opera group. Since we have less than 3 clients that use IE, Edge and Safari browsers, we do not consider the corresponding clients here.

Figure 10d plots the accuracy observed. We observe higher and more uniform accuracies across the test clients compared to Figure 10b. The accuracies are also similar to those in Figure 10a. Note that in this scenario, we use significantly less training samples for each webpage compared to Figure 10b (21 versus 126 samples), and use similar number of training samples as the scenario in Figure 4 (in which we use 21 samples from a single client). We find that using samples of the same browser from different clients for training increases the robustness of the methods more (Figure 10d) compared to using samples from clients that use different browsers (Figure 10b). This experiment also shows that if the browser of a test client can be identified [24], a robust fingerprinting method can be trained by using samples from a diverse set of clients that use the same browser.

Based on the evaluations in this section, we conclude that:

- Even though the samples from the test clients are not considered in the evaluations during training, machine learning methods are able to capture the variations in the traffic features across the diverse set of training clients and are now more robust to the traffic variations compared to when they are trained with samples from a single client (Figure 4).

- Significant browser differences (Section 5) necessitate that the training phase includes samples from the browser of the test client (even if the samples from the OS and device of the test client are not included).

7 RELATED WORK

Web traffic analysis research has been quite active for two decades.

HTTPS Cheng and Avnur (1998) performed the first webpage fingerprinting study in the traffic analysis literature [25]. They studied a single website and showed that most of the webpages have distinct HTML sizes which allows the visits to be identified in a traffic trace. Using HTTPS server logs, George Danezis investigated how much information can be inferred from HTTPS requests and whether a Hidden Markov Model can be used to find the most plausible explanation for the observed resource sizes [26].

In 2014, Miller et al. performed the first systematic HTTPS webpage fingerprinting study [5]. In 2016, Gonzalez et al. evaluated a method from the Tor traffic analysis domain in HTTPS webpage fingerprinting. These are discussed in Section 2.4.

Encrypted Web Proxy After the HTTPS study of Cheng and Avnur, a growing body of the traffic analysis literature investigated the feasibility of using webpage fingerprinting techniques for the web traffic protected by privacy enhancing technologies (PETs) such as SSH, VPN and Tor. One common property of these technologies is that they all use proxy tunnels to transmit web traffic and hide the identities of the web servers communicated by a client. Thus, an adversary has to consider that a client may visit any webpage on the web—the webpages cannot be narrowed down to those that are served from a single server.

Sun et al. were the first to consider such a proxy tunnel scenario [27]. They studied a scenario where a web user can visit 111,884 webpages and an adversary is interested in determining whether the user visits one of the 2191 target webpages. They argued that even though the false positive rate (i.e., the rate of predicting a visit to a webpage even though the webpage is not visited) may increase when all the webpages on the Web is considered, their methodology can be used for pruning the possibilities for a more sophisticated method. Similarly, Andrew Hintz showed that object sizes can be used to reveal the webpages visited in an encrypted web proxy named SafeWeb [28].

SSH Proxy Tunnel Bissias et al. [10] and Liberatore and Levine [6] investigated whether packet sizes can be used for fingerprinting webpages visited in an SSH proxy tunnel. Bissias et al. used cross correlation to measure similarities between packet size and inter-arrival time traces [10]. Similarly, Liberatore and Levine modeled a webpage as a multiset of packet sizes (with direction) and experimented with Jaccard Similarity and Naive Bayes classifier [6].

Anonymized NetFlow Records Coull et al. [29] and Yen et al. [24] studied fingerprinting webpages in anonymized NetFlow records (when only flow level information is available and the IP addresses are anonymized using consistent pseudonyms). Coull et al. considered the issues of network locality (collecting training and test data in different networks), browser caching, and browsing session parsing [29]. Yen et al. [24] first studied fingerprinting browsers in anonymized NetFlow records. The researchers then studied classifying traffic traces of landing pages of 52 websites as an application of browser fingerprinting. They showed that identifying the browser that generated a traffic trace first and then using a webpage fingerprinting method that was trained using the samples from that browser leads to an increase in the precision and recall (from around 25% and 5% to 32% and 15%, respectively) compared to using a generic fingerprinting method that was trained using samples from several browsers.

HTTP Maciá-Fernández et al. showed that the webpages visited within HTTP websites can be identified by matching the unique root and object file sizes of the webpages with the object sizes extracted from a traffic trace [30].

Tor Herrmann et al. investigated the feasibility of using webpage fingerprinting techniques against various other privacy enhancing technologies such as VPN and Tor and evaluated a variant of the method introduced by Liberatore and Levine [6] in this context [11]. Even though they reported less than 3% traffic trace classification accuracy for Tor, two years later Panchenko et al. [19] introduced a new set of features and used Support Vector Machines for classification and increased the accuracy to 55% in the same dataset. Since then, traffic analysis of Tor has been an active research area, with innovations mainly in the traffic features extracted and the supervised machine learning methods employed.

Notably, Cai et al. were the first to show that a sequence of webpage visits within a website can be modeled using a Hidden Markov Model to increase the accuracy of identifying a visit to a website [12]. Wang et al. [31] introduced a novel method that uses k-Nearest Neighbor to monitor the visits to 100 webpages from an open set of 5000 webpages. Hayes and Danezis used 150 different traffic features and Random Forest Classifier for fingerprinting 30 Tor hidden services [18]. Yan and Kaur [9] have shown that when an exhaustive feature selection methodology is used to find informative features, an accuracy around 92% can be achieved in classifying Tor traffic traces of landing pages of 100 websites.

Recent studies have questioned the assumptions made in the Tor traffic analysis domain [8, 32]. Panchenko et al. showed that when large number of webpages are considered, the state-of-the-art traffic analysis methods fail to identify the visited webpages in Tor network traffic. Juarez et al. [32] showed that variables such as the change of a website over time, multitab browsing, browser version, and the number of webpages considered can significantly affect the accuracy of traffic analysis methods in practice.

VPN Feghhi and Leith showed that the timing of the outgoing packets in an encrypted tunnel (e.g. VPN) can be used to predict the webpages visited [7].

Other Traffic Analysis Studies Chen et al. demonstrated that health records, tax information, investment secrets, and search queries can be leaked in network traffic due to user interactions such as keystrokes or mouse clicks [33]. Trevisan et al. showed that IP addresses and hostnames can be used to identify the traffic of popular web services, such as facebook.com, google.com and whatsapp.net [34]. Sanders and Kaur showed that anonymized TCP/IP headers can be used to classify webpage traffic traces using several different labeling schemes, such as type of content, video vs. non-video, and mobile vs. non-mobile [35].

8   CONCLUSION

In this paper, we focus on the impact of client diversity on HTTPS webpage fingerprinting. Our analysis informs us about the differences across clients, reveals the adverse effect of client diversity on the performance of prominent webpage fingerprinting methods, and suggests using samples from a diverse set of clients for training a robust webpage fingerprinting method—even if the browser and OS of the test client are known.

Limitations   While our dataset and analysis is an important step, there are several other factors—including thousands of webpages within a modern website, browser caching [5], browsing session parsing [29], multitab browsing [32], and user specific webpage content—that are expected to have a compounding adverse effect on the performance of the fingerprinting methods in the real world. We consider lack of large scale, labeled, and diverse webpage traffic trace datasets, as well as the difficulty of simulating real user webpage visits in laboratory conditions, as a major obstacle for a realistic evaluation of the webpage fingerprinting methods.

Client Diversity as a Dataset Bias Problem   In the computer vision literature, dataset bias is a well known problem—object recognition methods trained using one dataset do not generalize in other datasets [36]. In future work, methods that explicitly model dataset bias (introduced by a specific web client) can be studied to approximate an unbiased traffic trace of a webpage visit (find features that are robust in webpage visits across clients) [37].

Implications for Other Traffic Analysis Studies   While we focus on prior work on HTTPS webpage fingerprinting [4, 5], most prior traffic analysis studies in other settings were also performed using traffic samples from the same client [6, 7, 9, 11, 18, 25, 27, 30]. We hypothesize that the adverse effect of client diversity can also be observed in these settings. Future traffic analysis studies should collect traffic samples from a diverse set of clients to evaluate the robustness of proposed methods.

Our dataset and code have been made publicly available.[24]

REFERENCES

[1] Cooper A. et al. Privacy considerations for internet protocols. RFC 6973, RFC Editor, July 2013.
[2] T. Karagiannis et al. Blinc: multilevel traffic classification in the dark. In *ACM SIGCOMM Computer Communication Review*, volume 35, pages 229–240. ACM, 2005.
[3] W. Pan et al. Wenc: Https encrypted traffic classification using weighted ensemble learning and markov chain. In *Trustcom/BigDataSE/ICESS, 2017 IEEE*, pages 50–57. IEEE, 2017.
[4] R. Gonzalez et al. User profiling in the time of https. In *Proceedings of the 2016 ACM on Internet Measurement Conference*, pages 373–379. ACM, 2016.
[5] B. Miller et al. I know why you went to the clinic: Risks and realization of https traffic analysis. In *International Symposium on Privacy Enhancing Technologies Symposium*, pages 143–163. Springer, 2014.
[6] Marc Liberatore and Brian Neil Levine. Inferring the source of encrypted http connections. In *Proceedings of the 13th ACM conference on Computer and communications security*, pages 255–263. ACM, 2006.

[7] S. Feghhi et al. A web traffic analysis attack using only timing information. *IEEE Transactions on Information Forensics and Security*, 11(8):1747–1759, 2016.
[8] A. Panchenko et al. Website fingerprinting at internet scale. In *NDSS*, 2016.
[9] Junhua Yan and Jasleen Kaur. Feature selection for website fingerprinting. *Proceedings on Privacy Enhancing Technologies*, 4:200–219, 2018.
[10] G. Bissias et al. Privacy vulnerabilities in encrypted http streams. In *International Workshop on Privacy Enhancing Technologies*, pages 1–11. Springer, 2005.
[11] D. Herrmann et al. Website fingerprinting: attacking popular privacy enhancing technologies with the multinomial naïve-bayes classifier. In *Proceedings of the 2009 ACM workshop on Cloud computing security*, pages 31–42. ACM, 2009.
[12] X. Cai et al. Touching from a distance: Website fingerprinting attacks and defenses. In *Proceedings of the 2012 ACM conference on Computer and communications security*, pages 605–616. ACM, 2012.
[13] E Nygren. Reaching toward universal tls sni, 2017. URL https://blogs.akamai.com/2017/03/reaching-toward-universal-tls-sni.html.
[14] S. Sanders et al. The influence of client platform on web page content: Measurements, analysis, and implications. In *International Conference on Web Information Systems Engineering*, pages 1–16. Springer, 2015.
[15] Sean Sanders. *Techniques for the Analysis of Modern Web Page Traffic using Anonymized TCP/IP Headers*. PhD thesis, University of North Carolina at Chapel Hill, 2017.
[16] T. Berners-Lee et al. Hypertext transfer protocol – http/1.0. RFC 1945, RFC Editor, May 1996. URL http://www.rfc-editor.org/rfc/rfc1945.txt. http://www.rfc-editor.org/rfc/rfc1945.txt.
[17] A. Felt et al. Measuring https adoption on the web. In *26th USENIX Security Symposium*, pages 1323–1338, 2017.
[18] Jamie Hayes and George Danezis. k-fingerprinting: A robust scalable website fingerprinting technique. In *USENIX Security Symposium*, pages 1187–1203, 2016.
[19] A. Panchenko et al. Website fingerprinting in onion routing based anonymization networks. In *Proceedings of the 10th annual ACM workshop on Privacy in the electronic society*, pages 103–114. ACM, 2011.
[20] Tao Wang and Ian Goldberg. Improved website fingerprinting on tor. In *Proceedings of the 12th ACM workshop on Workshop on privacy in the electronic society*, pages 201–212. ACM, 2013.
[21] Sean Sanders and Jasleen Kaur. On the variation in web page download traffic across different client types. In *Network Protocols (ICNP), 2014 IEEE 22nd International Conference on*, pages 495–497. IEEE, 2014.
[22] M. Belshe et al. Hypertext transfer protocol version 2 (http/2). RFC 7540, RFC Editor, May 2015. URL http://www.rfc-editor.org/rfc/rfc7540.txt. http://www.rfc-editor.org/rfc/rfc7540.txt.
[23] M. Varvello et al. Is the web HTTP/2 yet? In *Passive and Active Measurements Conference (PAM)*, 2016.
[24] T. Yen et al. Browser fingerprinting from coarse traffic summaries: Techniques and implications. In *International Conference on Detection of Intrusions and Malware, and Vulnerability Assessment*, pages 157–175. Springer, 2009.
[25] H. Cheng et al. Traffic analysis of ssl encrypted web browsing. *URL citeseer. ist. psu. edu/656522. html*, 1998.
[26] George Danezis. Traffic analysis of the http protocol over tls, 2009.
[27] Q. Sun et al. Statistical identification of encrypted web browsing traffic. In *Security and Privacy, 2002. Proceedings. 2002 IEEE Symposium on*, pages 19–30. IEEE, 2002.
[28] Andrew Hintz. Fingerprinting websites using traffic analysis. In *International Workshop on Privacy Enhancing Technologies*, pages 171–178. Springer, 2002.
[29] S. Coull et al. On web browsing privacy in anonymized netflows. In *USENIX Security Symposium*, pages 339–352, 2007.
[30] G. Maciá-Fernández et al. Isp-enabled behavioral ad targeting without deep packet inspection. In *INFOCOM, 2010 Proceedings IEEE*, pages 1–9. IEEE, 2010.
[31] Tao Wang, Xiang Cai, Rishab Nithyanand, Rob Johnson, and Ian Goldberg. Effective attacks and provable defenses for website fingerprinting. In *USENIX Security Symposium*, pages 143–157, 2014.
[32] M. Juarez et al. A critical evaluation of website fingerprinting attacks. In *Proceedings of the 2014 ACM SIGSAC Conference on Computer and Communications Security*, pages 263–274. ACM, 2014.
[33] S. Chen et al. Side-channel leaks in web applications: A reality today, a challenge tomorrow. In *Security and Privacy (SP), 2010 IEEE Symposium on*, pages 191–206. IEEE, 2010.
[34] M. Trevisan et al. Towards web service classification using addresses and dns. In *Wireless Communications and Mobile Computing Conference (IWCMC), 2016 International*, pages 38–43. IEEE, 2016.
[35] Sean Sanders and Jasleen Kaur. Can web pages be classified using anonymized tcp/ip headers? In *Computer Communications (INFOCOM), 2015 IEEE Conference on*, pages 2272–2280. IEEE, 2015.
[36] Antonio Torralba and Alexei A Efros. Unbiased look at dataset bias. In *Computer Vision and Pattern Recognition (CVPR), 2011 IEEE Conference on*, pages 1521–1528. IEEE, 2011.
[37] A. Khosla et al. Undoing the damage of dataset bias. In *European Conference on Computer Vision*, pages 158–171. Springer, 2012.

---

[24]https://github.com/hfalan/codaspy19

Adversarial Authorship Attribution in Open-Source Projects

Alina Matyukhina
Canadian Institute for
Cybersecurity, University
of New Brunswick

Natalia Stakhanova
Department of Computer
Science, University of
Saskatchewan

Mila Dalla Preda
Dipartimento di
Informatica, University of
Verona

Celine Perley
Canadian Institute for
Cybersecurity, University
of New Brunswick

ABSTRACT

Open-source software is open to anyone by design, whether it is a community of developers, hackers or malicious users. Authors of open-source software typically hide their identity through nicknames and avatars. However, they have no protection against authorship attribution techniques that are able to create software author profiles just by analyzing software characteristics.

In this paper we present an author imitation attack that allows to deceive current authorship attribution systems and mimic a coding style of a target developer. Withing this context we explore the potential of the existing attribution techniques to be deceived. Our results show that we are able to imitate the coding style of the developers based on the data collected from the popular source code repository, GitHub. To subvert author imitation attack, we propose a novel author obfuscation approach that allows us to hide the coding style of the author. Unlike existing obfuscation tools, this new obfuscation technique uses transformations that preserve code readability. We assess the effectiveness of our attacks on several datasets produced by actual developers from GitHub, and participants of the GoogleCodeJam competition. Throughout our experiments we show that the author hiding can be achieved by making sensible transformations which significantly reduce the likelihood of identifying the author's style to 0% by current authorship attribution systems.

CCS CONCEPTS

• Security and privacy → Software security engineering;

KEYWORDS

Authorship attribution; obfuscation; imitation; open-source software; adversarial; attacks

ACM Reference Format:
Alina Matyukhina, Natalia Stakhanova, Mila Dalla Preda, and Celine Perley. 2019. Adversarial Authorship Attribution in Open-Source Projects. In *Ninth ACM Conference on Data and Application Security and Privacy (CODASPY '19), March 25–27, 2019, Richardson, TX, USA*. ACM, New York, NY, USA, 12 pages. https://doi.org/10.1145/3292006.3300032

1 INTRODUCTION

Consider the following scenario. Alice is an open source software developer. She contributes to different projects and typically stores her code on GitHub repository. Bob is a professional exploit developer who wants to hide his illegal activities and implicate Alice. To do this, he collects samples of Alice's code and mimics her coding style. A sample of Bob's malware ends up in the hands of law enforcement agency, where the analysis shows that a malware is written by Alice. This unfortunate scenario is possible due to the recent advances in software authorship attribution field that focuses on identification of the developer's style. In this work we explore adversarial side of software attribution and show how an adversary can confuse these techniques and conceal his identity.

The study of authorship attribution (also known as stylometry) comes from the literary domain where it is typically used for identifying the author of a disputed text based on the author's unique linguistic style (e.g., use of verbs, vocabulary, sentence length). The main premise of stylometric techniques lies in the assumption that authors unconsciously tend to use the same linguistic patterns. These patterns uniquely characterize the author's works and consequently, allow one to differentiate him/her among others.

Drawing an analogy between an author and a software developer, software authorship attribution aims to identify who wrote a program given its source or binary code. Applications of software authorship attribution are wide and include software forensics - where the analyst wants to determine the author of a suspicious program given a set of potential adversaries, plagiarism detection - where the analyst wants to identify illicit code reuse, programmer de-anonymization - where the analyst is interested in finding information on an anonymous programmer, and in general any scenario where software ownership needs to be determined. Traditionally, authorship attribution studies relied on a large set of samples to generate accurate representation of an author's style. A recent study by Dauber et al. [13] showed that this is no longer necessary and even small, and incomplete code fragments can be used to identify the developers of samples with up to 99% accuracy.

In this work, we propose an author imitation attack on authorship attribution techniques. *Author imitation* attack identifies a developer (the victim) and transforms the attacker's source code to a version that mimics the victim's coding style, while retaining the functionality of the original code. The attack success is measured by its ability to deter existing attribution techniques from recognizing this code as attacker's code and by its ability to imitate the victim author's style. The author imitation task can be considered as an extension of the authorship attribution task to a real-world scenario. Existing authorship attribution research assumes that authors are honest and do not attempt to disguise their coding style. We challenge this basic assumption and explore existing authorship methodologies in adversarial setting.

Within this context, we investigate four existing source code attribution techniques introduced by Ding et al. [14], Caliskan et al. [11], Burrows et al. [8], and Kothari et al. [19]. We explore their accuracy and their potential to be deceived by author imitation attack. Through our experiments we show that all these techniques are susceptible to author imitation and we are able to successfully imitate 73.48% of the authors on GoogleCodeJam and 68.1% of the authors on GitHub.

Finally, to subvert author imitation attack, we introduce an author hiding method and a novel coding style obfuscation approach- *author obfuscation*. The idea of author obfuscation is to allow authors to preserve the readability of their source code, while removing identifying stylistic features that can be leveraged for code attribution. Code obfuscation, common in software development, typically aims to disguise the appearance of the code making it difficult to understand and reverse engineer the code. In contrast, the proposed author obfuscation hides the original author's style by leaving the source code visible, readable and understandable. Our experiments show the effectiveness of author hiding. Indeed, we are able to reduce the accuracy of the Ding et al. attribution system from 73.84% of correctly classified authors to 1.08% by using only layout, lexical, syntactic transformations on the GoogleCodeJam dataset. We are also able to decrease the accuracy of the Caliskan et al. attribution system from 80.92% to 27.96% on the GitHub dataset. The attribution accuracy of Burrows et al. and Kothari et al. systems were decreased to 0% on the GitHub dataset. By adding control-flow obfuscation we were able further reduced the performance of Caliskan et al., Ding et al., Burrows et al. and Kothari et al. systems to 0%. Our results demonstrate that it is possible to successfully attack current authorship attribution systems with transformations which preserve readability of the code.

The rest of this paper is organized as follows. Section 2 analyses the existing attribution techniques. The author imitation attack is introduced in Section 3. The author hiding attack is presented in Section 4. The author obfuscation transformations and the evaluation of proposed attacks are described in Section 5. We conclude our work in Section 6.

2 BACKGROUND AND RELATED WORK

Authorship attribution, also known as stylometry, is a well known research subject in the literary domain. The recent interest in applying attribution techniques to software code raised a number of questions. One of them is the selection of characteristics (i.e., features) indicative of an author (i.e., software developer). Although the process of feature selection is one of the most crucial aspects of attribution, there is no guide to assist in the selection of the optimal set of features. As a result, the majority of studies venture to use features that prove to be most helpful in particular contexts. The earliest work in software forensics by Spafford and Weber [27] focused on a combination of features reflecting data structures and algorithms, compiler and system information, programming skill and system knowledge, choice of system calls, errors, choice of programming language, use of language features, comment style, variable names, spelling and grammar. Sallis et al. [26] extended this work by using additional features, such as cyclomatic complexity of the control flow and layout conventions. Krsul et al. [20], Kilgour et al. [17] and Ding et al. [14] introduced a broad classification of features according to their relevance for programming layout, programming style, programming structure, and linguistic metrics. Trivial source code obfuscation techniques can obscure part of these features, leading to a significant decrease in attribution accuracy.

A granular approach might be more effective in understanding what groups of features are beneficial in attribution and resistant to different kinds of obfuscation techniques. In this work, we classify the features into the following groups: layout, lexical, syntactic, control-flow, data-flow. Figure 1 shows such classification. These groups build on each other starting with simple and easily extractable features to more advanced ones focusing on the inner logic and structure of the program.

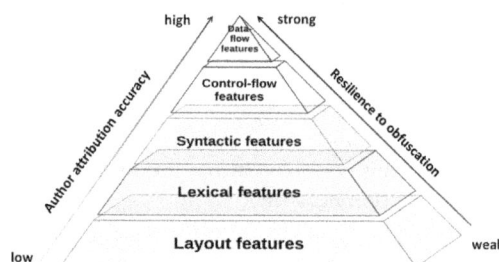

Figure 1: Feature selection levels in software authorship attribution

Layout features refer to format or layout metrics [9] that characterise the form and the shape of the code. Layout features include the length of a line of code, the number of spaces in a line of code, and the frequency of characters (underscores, semicolons, and commas) in a line of code. For the following discussion, we group these metrics as follows:

metrics that measure indentation, placement of comments, the use of white space (tab), placing of the braces.

Lexical features can be divided into programming style metrics, programming structure metrics and n-grams. Programming style metrics include character preferences, construct preferences, statistical distribution of variable lengths, and capitalisation. Programming structure metrics are assumed to be related to the programming experience and ability of a developer. For example, such metrics include the statistical distribution of lines of code per function, the ratio of keywords per line of code, the relative frequency of use of complex branching constructs and so on. A popular feature extraction technique is using n-grams to extract the frequency of sequences of n-characters from the source code.

Syntactic features are good features for authorship identification in natural language [18]. A parse tree is a convenient way to determine the syntactic structure of a sentence [23]. Baayen et al. [5] are the first to extract rewrite-rule frequencies from the parse tree for the purpose of authorship identification.

Recently, syntactic features have shown significant success also in source code authorship [4, 11]. These features represent the code structure and are invariant to changes in source code layout. Moreover, these features often describe properties of the language dependent AST (abstract syntax tree) such as code length, nesting levels, branching. AST does not include layout elements, such as unessential punctuation and delimiters (braces, semicolons, parentheses, etc.). Caliskan et al. [11, 12] investigated syntactic features to de-anonymize authors of C/C++ both at the source code and binary code level. They published the Code Stylometry Feature Set which includes layout, lexical and syntactic features. They have already achieved 94%, 96.83% and 97.67% accuracy with 1,600, 250 and 62 class authors respectively. Recently Alsulami et al. [4] proposed Long Short-Term Memory (LSTM) and Bidirectional Long Short-Term Memory (BiLSTM) models to automatically extract relevant features from the AST representation of programmers' source code.

Control-flow features have been used in binary code attribution [3] and are not typical for source code attribution. These features are derived from control flow graph (CFG) that describes the order in which the code statements are executed as well as conditions that need to be met for a particular path of execution. Statements and predicates are represented by nodes, which are connected by directed edges to indicate the transfer of control. In binary authorship analysis graphlets (3-node subgraphs of the CFG) and supergraphlets (obtained by collapsing and merging neighbour nodes of the CFG) are used to identify the author of the code [3].

Data-flow features may indicate the author's preference in resolving a particular task through the selection of algorithms, certain data structures. These features are derived from the program dependence graph (PDG) that determines all the statements and predicates of a program that affect the value of a variable at a specific program point. It was introduced by Ferrante et al. [15] and it was originally used for program slicing [30]. In binary authorship analysis, Alrabaee

et al. [3] used API data structures for this task. For binary code representation, authors analyzed the dependence between the different registers that are often accessed regardless of complexity of functions.

The arrows in Figure 1 represent our observations of feature selection influence on the authorship attribution accuracy and their strength of obfuscation. Layout features are associated with layout of programs and thus are fragile and easily alterable, for example by a code formatter. Lexical features are also related to the layout of code but are more difficult to change. Layout and lexical features alone are still less accurate (67.2% by [14]), than when used in combination with syntactic features (92.83% by [11]). Most of these features do not survive the compilation process. On the other hand, control-flow and data-flow features that retain programming ability and the experience of the programmer, are considered to provide a stronger evidence of developer's style. The existing source code attribution techniques only employ the combination of layout, lexical and syntactic features. In this work we focus on author imitation and hiding attacks at the layout, lexical, syntactic and control-flow levels.

3 AUTHOR IMITATION

The majority of previous studies show that we can successfully identify a software developer of a program. The question that naturally arises from this situation is whether it is possible to mimic someone else's coding style to avoid being detected as an author of our own software. In other words, can we pretend to be someone else?

Author imitation attack aims at deceiving existing authorship attribution techniques. The flow of the attack is shown in Figure 2 and includes three steps: (1) collecting victim's source code samples, (2) recognizing the victim's coding style, (3) imitating the victim's coding style. The pseudocode for this attack is given in Algorithm 1.

The attack starts with identifying a victim and retrieving samples of his/her source code $V_s = (s_1, s_2, ..., s_n)$. Typically, authors of open-source software hide their identity through nicknames and avatars. However, many GitHub accounts leave personal developer's information open, essentially allowing an attacker targeting a particular person collect the victim's source code samples.

Once the samples are collected, the second step is to analyze them and identify the victim's coding style. The strategy is to apply a set of transformations $M_{i,j}(A)$ to the set of source code samples $A = (t_1, t_2, ..., t_k)$ until the difference between the original victim style V and the modified attacker style is negligible.

The set of transformations $M_{i,j}$ is defined on the major feature levels i given in Figure 1, e.g., layout ($i = 1$), lexical ($i = 2$), syntactic ($i = 3$), control-flow ($i = 4$), data-flow ($i = 5$). The particular transformation j for each of the feature levels can vary. An example set of possible transformations is given in Table 2.

The distance between the feature vector extracted from the original source code of victim V and the feature vector

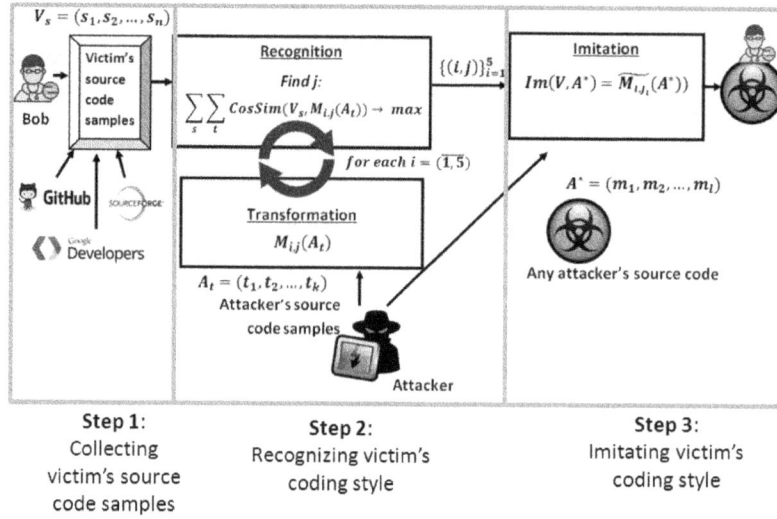

Figure 2: An overview of author imitation attack

extracted from the modified source code of A is determined based on cosine similarity[1], a widely implemented metric in information retrieval that models data as a vector of features and measures the similarity between vectors based on cosine value.

Definition 3.1 (Cosine similarity for author imitation attack). In authorship attribution, a source code can be represented as a vector of features whose dimension p depends on the considered feature set. Feature's value can refer to term frequency, average, log, or anything else depending on the features used.

Let $\vec{s_n} = \overrightarrow{(s_{n,1}, s_{n,2}, ..., s_{n,p})}$ denote the feature vector of the n-th source code of victim V, and let $\vec{t_k} = \overrightarrow{(t_{k,1}, t_{k,2}, ..., t_{k,p})}$ denote the feature vector of the k-th source code of attacker A, where $s_{n,h}$ and $t_{k,h}$ with $h \in \overline{(1, p)}$ are float numbers indicating the value of a particular feature. The cosine similarity between $\vec{s_n}$ and $\vec{t_k}$ is defined as follows:

$$CosSim(\vec{s_n}, \vec{t_k}) = \frac{\vec{s_n} \cdot \vec{t_k}}{||\vec{s_n}|| \cdot ||\vec{t_k}||} = \frac{\sqrt{\sum_{h=1}^{p} s_{n,h} \cdot t_{k,h}}}{\sqrt{\sum_{h=1}^{p} (s_{n,h})^2} \cdot \sqrt{\sum_{h=1}^{p} (t_{k,h})^2}}$$

Similarity is measured in the range 0 to 1. $CosSim = 1$ if two vectors are similar, $CosSim = 0$ if two vectors are different.

The code transformations $M_{i,j}$ that produce the maximum similarity, i.e. $CosSim(V_s, M_{i,j}(A_t)) \to max$, are the ones that the attacker should use to transform the original code in order to obtain a semantically equivalent code that mimics the victim's coding style. Note that these transformations should be calculated once per victim and can be applied on any of attacker's programs.

---

[1]For our analysis we experimented with a variety of similarity measures including Euclidean distance, Cosine distance, Minkovski distance, Jaccard distance, and Manhattan distance. Since Cosine similarity outperformed all other metrics, we employ it in our work.

Finally, to imitate the victim V, the attacker recursively applies the transformations identified in the previous step to A^*, i.e., $Im(V, A^*) = \widetilde{M_{i,j_i}}(A^*)$.

Algorithm 1 Author imitation attack

Input: $V_s = (s_1, s_2, ..., s_n)$ -victim's source code samples;
 $A_t = (t_1, t_2, ..., t_k)$ -attacker's source code samples;
 $A^* = (m_1, m_2, ..., m_l)$ -attacker's any source codes
Output: $Im(V, A^*)$ -attacker's source codes A^* with imitated victim's V coding style
 # precomputation part
 for all $i = 1$ to 5 **do**
  for all j **do**
   apply transformation M_{ij} to each A_t
   compute $\theta(i,j) = \sum_s \sum_t CosSim(\vec{V_s}, M_{ij}\vec{(A_t)})$
  end for
  take j such that $\theta(i,j)$ is maximum
 end for
 return pairs $(i, j_i)_{i=1}^{5}$ and their correspondent transformations M_i, j_i
 # main part
 for all A^* **do**
 apply i transformations M_i, j_i to attacker's source code A^* recursively: $Im(V, A^*) = \widetilde{M_{i,j_i}}(A^*)$, where $\widetilde{M_{i,j_i}}(A^*)$ is a recursive function such as: $\widetilde{M_{i+2,j_{i+2}}}(A^*) = \widetilde{M_{i+1,j_{i+1}}}(\widetilde{M_{i,j_i}}(A^*))$
 end for
 return $Im(V, A^*)$

Complexity. The attack described in Algorithm 1 consists of a precomputation step and a main phase. In the precomputation step the algorithm searches for the code transformations that once applied to the attacker's source code samples transform the attacker's coding style into the victim's coding stile. The complexity of this step depends on the number of specific transformations defined for each of the five feature levels. It should be noted that these transformations only need to be determined once per victim. The main phase consists of applying selected transformations to an attacker's source code. The time complexity of this phase grows linearly as the size of the attacker's code increases.

4 AUTHOR HIDING

To subvert author imitation attack, we propose a method that manipulates the source code to hide author's coding style while preserving code readability. The goal of author hiding is to prevent its detection by authorship attribution systems.

The author imitation attack applies transformations to the attacker's source code in order to imitate the victim's style. The most effective imitation can be generated when the distance between the source code feature vector of the victim and the modified source code feature vector of the attacker is negligible, i.e., transformations produce the maximum similarity between the two vectors.

Intuitively, to make author imitation attack unsuccessful, we should convert the original author's style to more generic less personalized version of it while fully retaining the functionality of code, i.e., these transformations should produce minimal similarity between the feature vector of the original and modified author source code. The pseudocode of author hiding is given in Algorithm 2.

In this work, we look at transformations at the layout, lexical, syntactic levels as features from these levels are commonly explored by attribution studies. Specifically, we classify all the transformations into the following groups: comment, brackets, spaces, lines, names, AST leaves, loops, and conditional statements. These transformations are low-cost and can be applied on any software with no computational overhead.

We additionally explore control flow transformation i.e. control-flow flatenning [29]. Control-flow flatenning rearranges code basic blocks (e.g., method body, loops, and conditional branch instructions) to make them appear to have the same set of predecessors and successors. Although a modified program flow is harder to follow, it is still readable for a human analyzer (Figure 3), which makes it suitable to use for our hiding approach. McCabe's complexity metric of such transformation is increased by a factor 2 to 5, which was shown by [21].

5 EVALUATION

Data. For our analysis, we collected two datasets from open source repositories. The majority of the existing attribution studies leverage programs developed during Google-CodeJam, an annual international coding competition hosted by Google. During this competition, the contestants are presented with several programming problems and need to provide solutions to these problems within a limited time frame. We follow this practice and collect source code written in the Java programming language from the GoogleCode-Jam held in 2015. Our GoogleCodeJam dataset contains 558 source code files from 62 programmers. Each program has on average 74 lines of source code. Although GoogleCode-Jam is commonly used in studies, it has seen its share of criticism [12, 13, 22]. Specifically, the researchers argue that

---

Algorithm 2 Author hiding

Input: $V_s = (s_1, s_2, ..., s_n)$ - author's V source code samples;
$V^* = (v_1, v_2, ..., v_n)$ - code, which author V wants to hide
Output: $Hide(V^*)$ - source code without author's V style
  # precomputation
  for all $i = 1$ to 5 **do**
    for all j **do**
      apply transformation M_{ij} to each V_s
      compute $\theta(i, j) = \sum_s CosSim(\vec{V_s}, M_{ij}(\vec{V_s}))$
    end for
    take j such that $\theta(i, j)$ minimum
  end for
  return pairs $(i, j_i)_{i=1}^{5}$ and their correspondent transformations M_i, j_i
  # hiding
  for all V^* **do**
    apply i transformations M_i, j_i to author's source code V^* recursively:
    $Hide(V^*) = \widetilde{M_{i,j_i}}(V^*)$, where $\widetilde{M_{i,j_i}}(V^*)$ is a recursive function such as: $\widetilde{M_{i+2,j_{i+2}}}(V^*) = M_{i+1,j_{i+1}}(\widetilde{M_{i,j_i}}(V^*))$
  end for
  return $Hide(V^*)$

---

competition setup gives little flexibility to participants resulting in somewhat artificial and constrained program code. The length of the code in GoogleCodeJam dataset is much smaller when compared with real-world programming solutions, which creates bias by making it easier to attribute programs and consequently leading to higher attribution accuracy.

To ensure the reliability of our analysis, we created second dataset with code samples from the popular open-source repository Github. Github is an online collaboration and sharing platform for programmers. Compared to the Google-CodeJam dataset, the programs are typically more complex, can include third-party libraries and use source code from other authors. As a result, performing authorship attribution on GitHub data is more challenging. We crawled the GitHub in April 2018. Although it is difficult to guarantee a sole authorship of any code posted online, we took reasonable precautions. We filtered repositories that were marked as forks, as these are typically copies of other authors' repositories and so do not constitute original work. An additional check for multiple-author repositories was performed by examining the commit logs: if there were more than one unique name and email address combination, the repository was excluded. We further removed code from "lib" and "ext" folders and duplicate files. Overall, our final GitHub dataset included 558 source code files from 62 programmers with 303 lines of code per program on average. To understand what were the semantics of the programs in the GitHub dataset, we used a combination of automated and manual techniques. The projects in GitHub come with project description and README. We used Latent Dirichlet Allocation (LDA) [7] to analyze this textual description. By specifying a set of documents, LDA recognizes a set of topics where each topic is represented as probability of generating different words. Using existing domain names for categorization of GitHub projects [24], our final collection contains Application (352), Database (0), CodeAnalyzer (32), MiddleWare (0), Library (11), Framework (132), Other (31).

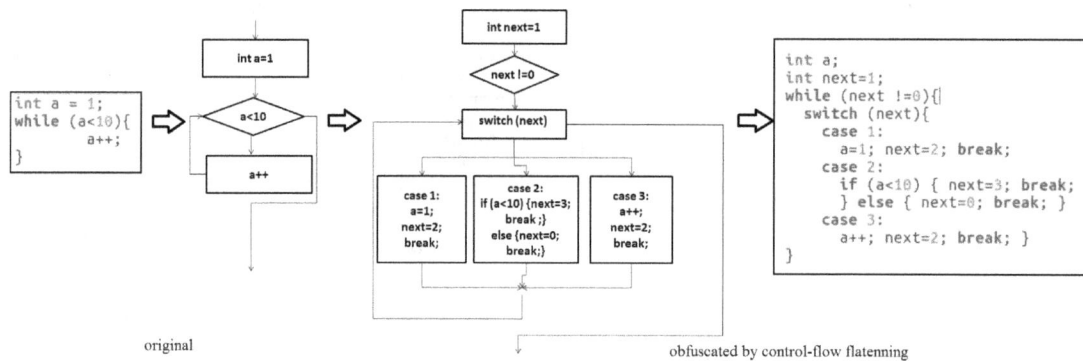

Figure 3: Control-flow flatenning obfuscation

Features. In spite of the wealth of attribution studies in the literary domain, throughout the years only a few source code attribution techniques were proposed. The majority of these studies experiment with diverse sets of features that capture developers' stylistic traits. These feature sets often range in size and level of analysis which makes it difficult to compare them. Burrows et al. [10] suggested grouping attribution systems by the type of features used in analysis: strings of n tokens/bytes (n-grams) or software metrics.

In this work we aim at exploring the accuracy of four prominent attribution systems from both categories and their potential to be attacked. In particular, we investigate the Ding et al. [14] and Caliskan et al. [11] systems that use feature sets based on software metrics, and the Burrows et al. [8] and Kothari et al. [19] attribution approaches based on n-grams features.

The study conducted by Ding et al. [14] is state-of-art research in Java source code attribution. The feature set and the obtained results serve as a reference for many studies [10]. Ding et al. collected and analysed 56 features and considered two datasets containing samples of 46 authors; the highest classification accuracy they obtained is 67.2%. Although not all features contributed to this result, the authors never provided the final subset or ranking of features. This was corrected by the follow-up study by Burrows et al. [10] that summarized previous classification techniques, and provided a final feature set of 56 metrics from the Ding et al. study. In our work, we use this feature set and refer to it as *Ding features*.

Another feature set that we explore is the one recently proposed by Caliskan et al. [11]. The study experimented with syntactic features (specifically, features derived from the AST) in an attribution context and published the Code Stylometry Feature Set. The results significantly outperformed all previously proposed attribution methods. For convenience we refer to this set as *Caliskan features*. With the dataset containing 250 authors and 9 samples per author, the study reported an attribution accuracy of 96.83%. Another dataset with 62 authors with 9 samples per author gave them an accuracy of 97.67% with Random Forest classification.

To give a fine granularity to our analysis, we created one more feature set. The Code Stylometry Feature Set (CSFS) analysed by Caliskan et al. [11] also includes term frequency of word unigrams. The authors tokenized the source file to obtain the number of occurrences of each token. Since these features constitute a significant portion of the original CSFS set (nearly half of the whole feature set), we consider them separately and refer to these features as *TFunigrams*. TFunigrams consist of term frequency of variable names, methods, classes, strings, comments, import names, etc. For each of the datasets we parsed the source codes to extract necessary sets of features. Since the study of Caliskan et al. [11] considers C++ and Python source code, we reimplemented their attribution model for Java source code. To produce AST, we use the external JavaParser library [28]. We created a parser to extract all the AST features specified in the Caliskan feature set. Following their method we reduced the total size and sparsity of the feature vector, by retaining only those features that individually have non-zero information gain. Information gain considers the difference between the entropy of the distribution classes and the entropy of conditional distribution of classes [31].

The study by Burrows et al. [8] uses indexed n-grams of tokens extracted from the parsed program source code. Their study identifies 6-grams as the most accurate n-gram size. In their follow up study [10], they explored normalised counts of n-gram occurrences as features with machine learning classifiers. Since the number of features to process increases exponentially for n-grams of features, they truncate the feature space to the most commonly occurring n-grams. In our work we use this feature set and refer to it as *Burrows features*.

Kothari et al [19] consider two sets of metrics. The first set of metrics consists of layout metrics, for example, distributions of leading spaces, line length, etc. The second metric set measures occurrences of byte-level n-grams. The n-gram length $n = 4$ is derived empirically. They use entropy to identify the fifty most discerning metrics for each author. In our work we use this feature set and refer to it as *Kothari features*. Burrows et al. [10] in their analysis of several attribution

Feature set	Number of authors	Samples/ author	L O C	Total number	Selected features	Layout	Lexical	Syntactic	Random Forest	Naive Bayes	J48	IBk
Original work												
Ding features	76	6	250	56	56	16	40	0	-	64.05%	66.17%	39.75%
Caliskan features	62	9	70	-	-	6	-	-	97.67%	-	-	-
Burrows features	76	6	250	-	1000	0	1000	0	-	73.24%	56.61%	37.01%
Kothari features	76	6	250	-	168	-	-	0	-	67.45%	74.70%	49.26%
GoogleCodeJam data set												
Ding features	62	9	74	56	56	16	40	0	**73.84%**	58.42%	59.86%	51.25%
Caliskan features	62	9	74	38630	607	6	187	414	**97.31%**	95.88%	91.03%	97.13%
TFunigrams features	62	9	74	20544	190	0	190	0	**96.95%**	95.69%	90.5%	93.01%
Burrows features	62	9	74	54267	1000	0	1000	0	**73.29%**	58.96%	64.87%	70.25%
Kothari features	62	9	74	34308	147	0	147	0	**86.56%**	79.92%	70.96%	81.99%
GitHub data set												
Ding features	62	9	303	56	56	16	40	0	**67.25%**	57.11%	54.62%	52.14%
Caliskan features	62	9	303	224478	687	5	203	479	**80.92%**	74.56%	78.12%	79.56%
TFunigrams features	62	9	303	87229	199	0	199	0	**75.08%**	67.79%	69.93%	66.01%
Burrows features	62	9	303	230735	1000	0	1000	0	**69.56%**	61.23%	66.34%	65.67%
Kothari features	62	9	303	116517	325	0	325	0	**80.23%**	72.78%	77.54%	79.52%

Table 1: The details of our datasets and feature sets employed by previous studies.

studies identified the Kothari features as the best in terms of classification accuracy; therefore the authors claimed that the n-gram approaches are more effective than the ones utilizing software metrics (note that at that time the work by Caliskan et al. [11] was not published yet). Since these studies work with source code developed with different programming languages (Java[14], C++, Python [11], and C, C++, Java [10]), in our work we bring everything to a common enumerator and employ Java programming language source code.

Table 1 shows statistics for the extracted features: number of authors, number of samples per author, average samples size in lines of code (LOC), the total number of features, the number of selected features, the number of layout, lexical, syntactic features on different datasets and original classification accuracy results reported by authors.

Classification. The previous approaches to source code authorship attribution employ various classification algorithms for attribution analysis while providing no justification of their algorithm's selection. Caliskan et al. [11] utilized Random Forest classifier, Burrows et al. [10] used Naive Bayes, Decision Tree, k-nearest neighbour classification, neural network, regression analysis, support vector machine, and voting feature interval.

For our analysis we employ Weka 3.8.2 platform [16]. Since our datasets do not have extensively large number of instances, we use the Weka implementation of Random Forest (RandomForest), Naive Bayes (NaiveBayes), J48 decision tree implementation of ID3 and IBk implementation of k-nearest neighbour algorithm. Since Burrows et al. [10] retained default parameters, for proper comparison we follow the same practice and do not change configuration for NaiveBayes, J48, IBk. For RandomForest algorithm, we chose 300 as the number of trees following the configuration used by Caliskan et al. [11]. All our experiments are performed with 9 fold cross validation.

5.1 Evaluation of existing authorship attribution methods

The results reported in Table 1 allow us to compare different authorship attribution methods on the GoogleCodeJam and GitHub datasets. The results that we obtain with the Caliskan feature set for the Java programs from GoogleCodeJam are similar to the ones originally obtained for C/C++ programs (97.31%) by Caliskan et al. [11].

Interestingly, the accuracy of this technique drops significantly (80.92%) on the GitHub dataset even though the number of features used in the analysis is 5.8 times bigger compared to the GoogleCodeJam dataset. We observe the same tendency with the TFunigrams feature set (that represents a significant amount of the Caliskan feature set) for which we have an accuracy of 96.95% on the GoogleCodeJam dataset and of 75.08% on the GitHub dataset. For the rest of the feature sets, Ding, Burrows and Kothari, the accuracy varies depending on the employed classification algorithm.

The difference in classification accuracy might be caused by the size of the source code in the dataset. The work of Caliskan et al. [11] considers only the GoogleCodeJam dataset, where each sample has on average 70 lines of code, while in real-world applications the programs are typically much larger. Indeed, the average number of lines of the samples in our GitHub dataset is 303 (4 times larger than the ones in the GoogleCodeJam considered by [11]).

An interesting observation came from the nature of the GoogleCodeJam competition that essentially forces authors to reuse their code written for previous tasks. As a result individual authors' style is derived from a set of very similar programs which significantly simplifies the attribution task.

The Code Stylometry Feature Set developed by Caliskan et al. was reported to "significantly outperform" other methods [11]. Yet our analysis does not agree with this; for example, with Kothari features we were able to achieve very similar results on Github data (80.23%) with a significantly smaller number of features. Since the Code Stylometry Feature Set of Caliskan et al. was designed solely based on the experiments on the GoogleCodeJam data, its suitability for real-world attribution is not definitive.

These results show that applying the attribution methods on different datasets leads to significantly different classification rates. Yet the majority of studies in attribution domain tend to only use the GoogleCodeJam data [3, 11, 25]. In spite of GoogleCodeJam data criticisms, an alternate dataset does not readily exist. We offer GitHub data to research community in the hope of diversifying and strengthening experiments in this field[2].

Our results in Table 1 show that RandomForest classifier performs the best for both datasets. For this reason we use the RandomForest classifier in the rest of our experiments.

5.2 Author imitation evaluation

For the evaluation of the author imitation attack, we consider the features sets and datasets detailed in Table 1. We focus on layout (comments, brackets, spaces, lines), lexical (names), syntactic (AST leaves), control-flow feature groups in this analysis. Specific transformations that are considered for these groups are given in Table 2.

Type	Name
Comments	1. Transform all comments to Block comments; 2. Transform all comments to Javadoc comments; 3. Transform all comments to Line comments; 4. Transform all comments to pure comment lines 5. Delete all inline comments; 6. Delete all pure comment lines; 7. Delete all comments; 8. Add pure comments on each line; 9. Add inline comments on each line; 10. Add pure comments on each line and one inline comments
Brackets	1. Transform all brackets to Allman style; 2. Transform all brackets to Java style; 3. Transform all brackets to Kernighan and Ritche style; 4. Transform all brackets to Stroustup style; 5. Transform all brackets to Whitesmith style; 6. Transform all brackets to VTK (Visualization toolkit) style; 7. Transform all brackets to Banner style; 8. Transform all brackets to GNU style; 9. Transform all brackets to Linux style; 10. Transform all brackets to Horstmann style; 11. Transform all brackets to "One True Brace Style"; 12. Transform all brackets to Google style; 13. Transform all brackets to Mozilla style; 14. Transform all brackets to Pico style; 15. Transform all brackets to Lisp style
Spaces	1. Indent using (from 2 to 20) number of spaces per indent; 2. Indent using tabs for indentation and spaces for continuation line alignment; 3. Indent using all tab characters, if possible;4. Indent using mix of tabs and spaces; 5. Insert space padding around operators; 6. Insert space padding after only commas; 7. Insert space padding around parenthesis on both outside and the inside; 8. Insert space padding around parenthesis on the outside only; 9. Insert space padding around parenthesis on the inside only; 10. Insert space padding between 'if', 'for', 'while'; 11. Remove extra space padding around parenthesis; 12. Remove all space/tabs padding
Lines	1. Delete empty lines within a function or method; 2. Delete all emty lines; 3. Write each statement in one line; 4. Write several statements in one line; 5. Write one declaration per line; 6. Write several declarations in one line; 7. Add emty line after each nonempty line
Names	1. Change all names on extremely short name identifiers (one-two characters); 2. Use dictionary to change names to long names (8-10 characters); 3. Change the first letter in identifiers to uppercase; 4. Change the first letter to lowcase; 5. The first sign is underscore/dollarsign
AST leaves	1. Copy and insert all comments from imitated author; 2. To imitate the author B, change all name identifiers (methods names, variable names, class names) to the same names used in author B' source code; 3. All names are unigue for every author (use different dictionaries to change the names); 4. Use the same dictionary to change names for every author
Control-flow	1. Change "for" to "while" loop 2. Change "while" to "for" loop 3. Change "else if" to "switch case" 4. Change "switch case" to "else if" 5. Control-flow flatenning (for author hiding only)

Table 2: Applied transformations

The idea of the evaluation is simple: we consider each author in our dataset as a potential victim and we mount an author imitation attack on the chosen victim from all

---

[2]https://cyberlab.usask.ca/authorattribution.html

other authors (aka attackers). If the attack is successful, all attackers should be recognized as the chosen victim author.

The methodology of the evaluation of the attack is presented in Algorithm 3.

Let n be the number of authors in the dataset $A_1, A_2, ..., A_n$, for every author we collect m samples of code: $s(A_1)$, $s(A_2)$, ..., $s(A_n)$ and extract feature vectors from every source code: $\overrightarrow{s(A_1)}, \overrightarrow{s(A_2)}, ..., \overrightarrow{s(A_n)}$. In the transformation, recognition and imitation steps, we use only feature vectors of source code that belongs to the testing set. We then apply Algorithm 1 to imitate each author in the dataset.

Specifically, we take one author (victim V), e.g. $V = A_1$, leaving the remaining $n - 1$ authors $A^* = (A_2, A_3, ..., A_n)$ to represent adversaries who want to imitate the victim's style. After applying Algorithm 1, we obtain $n - 1$ samples of attackers' source code with the imitated victim's style: $Im(V, A^*) = Im(A_1, A_2), ..., Im(A_1, A_n)$. We use a similar method to imitate each author/victim in the dataset: $A_2, ...A_n$.

Algorithm 3 Imitation attack evaluation

Input: Dataset of n authors A_w with their source code samples $s(A_w)$, where $w \in \overrightarrow{(1, n)}$, k-number of folds for cross-validation method
Output: accuracy of correctly classified authors ξ
  # precomputation
  for all w **do**
    find feature vectors $\overrightarrow{s(A_w)}$ extracted from each source code samples $s(A_w)$ by using any known authorship attribution feature extraction methods (i.e. [10], [11], etc.)
    return feature vectors $\overrightarrow{s(A_w)}$
  end for
  # main part
  for all k **do**
    divide dataset on training and testing set:
    $TRAIN = (\overrightarrow{s_{i,k}(A_1)}, \overrightarrow{s_{i,k}(A_2)}, ..., \overrightarrow{s_{i,k}(A_n)})$
    $TEST = (\overrightarrow{s_{j,k}(A_1)}, \overrightarrow{s_{j,k}(A_2)}, ..., \overrightarrow{s_{j,k}(A_n)})$
    apply imitation attack on every author n's source code from TEST set to get $TEST_{Im}$
    $fold(k) = NN(TRAIN, TEST_{Im})$
  end for

$$TEST_{Im} = \begin{pmatrix} \overrightarrow{A_1} & Im(A_1, A_2) & Im(A_1, A_3) & ... & \overline{Im(A_1, A_n)} \\ \overline{Im(A_2, A_1)} & \overrightarrow{A_2} & Im(A_2, A_3) & ... & \overline{Im(A_2, A_n)} \\ \overline{Im(A_n, A_1)} & Im(A_n, A_2) & Im(A_n, A_3) & ... & \overrightarrow{A_n} \end{pmatrix}$$

$$\xi = \sum_k fold(k)/k$$

At the end we move feature vectors from $Im(A_i, A_j)$ to the testing set $TEST_{Im}$, so that we have $m_2 * n * n$ feature vectors in the testing set $TEST_{Im}$. The evaluation then proceeds to classification to find the closest match among all authors for a given source code. In an ideal situation, we expect the closest match to be the imitated author. The accuracy is calculated as an average attribution rate after k fold cross validation. This approach allows us to test the author imitation attack on different scenarios, using different n coding styles for imitation and n styles to be imitated.

We employ all or nothing approach. Consider an example: we have 3 authors in the dataset: A_1, A_2, A_3, with 5 samples each. Take A_1 - if all A_2 and A_3 samples (i.e. all 10 samples) were attributed to A_1, then accuracy of imitating A_1 is 100%. Take A_2 - if all samples from A_3 were recognized as A_2,

Dataset	Ding features	Caliskan features	Burrows features	Kothari features	TFunigrams features
GCJ	53.4%	73.48%	100%	99.8%	100%
GitHub	40.86%	68.1%	100%	97.85%	100%

Table 3: Percentage of successfully imitated authors

but one sample from A_1 was still attributed to A_1, this means that only one author (A_3) was successfully imitating A_1, hence the accuracy is 50%. Take A_3 - if all samples from A_1 were recognized as A_3, and only 3 samples from A_2 were recognized as A_3, the accuracy of imitation of A_3 is 50%. Finally, we average the results across all authors: $(100+50+50)/3 = 66.67\%$ the accuracy after author imitation attack.

Table 3 presents the result of our evaluation. With Ding features we could imitate 40.86% of the Github authors and 53.4% of the GoogleCodeJam (GCJ). This result is expected as Ding's set is very small, only 56 features, thus they do not use any feature selection algorithm. With transformations from Table 2 we were able to imitate 32 features of 56. The rest of features are dependent to data-flow for example Java's primitive and user-defined types, fields, methods, generic parameters, and exceptions.

Using Caliskan features, more than half of the authors in Github dataset (68.1%) and in GoogleCodeJam (73.48%) are imitated successfully.

Better results were obtained with features of TFunigrams, and Burrows features: 100% for Github users and 100% for GoogleCodeJam. Since all features in this set are lexical, and require only undergo transformation, the result is nearly perfect, i.e., we are able to successfully mount an imitation attack on all users.

5.3 Author hiding evaluation

To evade author imitation attack, one could possibly use code formatting to produce a more generic less personal version of code. Alsulami at al. [4] stated that "Modern IDEs format source code file content based on particular formatting conventions. This results in consistent coding style across all source code written using the same development tools. This reduces the confidence of using format features to identify the authors of source code." Indeed, many software development standards dictate formatting style that developers have to adhere to. We hypothesize that the use of a particular style alone is not sufficient to avoid attribution. Figure 4 shows our preliminary experiments with several different types of formatting: Beautify, Java Code Convention, PrettyPrinter using the Eclipse Code Formatter. It indicates that attribution accuracy does not produce significant change after using such formatting tools. We could still attribute nearly half of the authors with the Ding feature set and more than 70% of the authors with other feature sets. After manual analysis of our data, we found that near 80% authors in our datasets were already following Java Code Convention.

Our goal is to offer a source code obfuscation technique that preserves the readability of the code and misleads existing

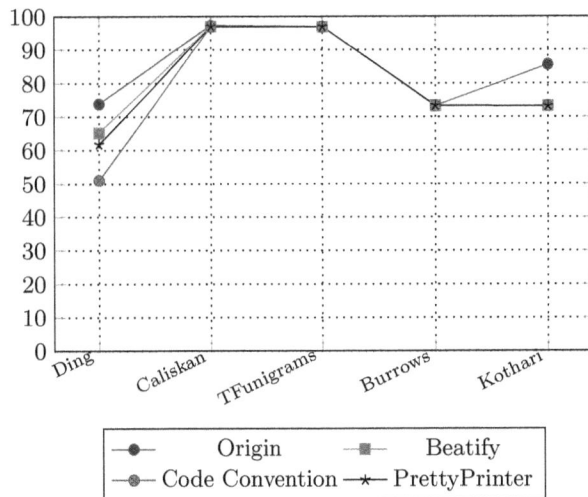

Figure 4: Percentage of correctly classified authors after using the following formatting: Beatify, Code Convention and PrettyPrinter on original source code

authorship attribution tools. We have seen that the existing methods for authorship attribution leverage layout and lexical features (Ding and Kothari) or layout and lexical, syntactic (Caliskan) or just lexical features (Burrows and TFunigrams).

In addition to these features, we also look at transforming control flow of a program. Although specific transformation can vary depending on the goal of the analysis, in this study we experimented with the transformations specified in Table 2.

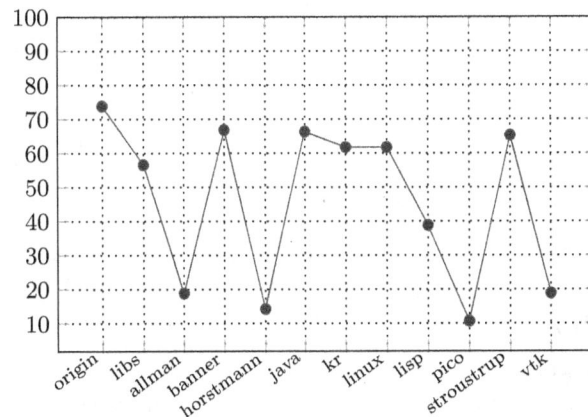

Figure 5: Percentage of correctly classified authors after brackets transformation for Google Code Jam dataset

For example, in the group brackets, we explore all possible styles of curly brackets (parentheses) that a developer can use. Figure 5 shows the results of experiments with only transformation of brackets in the code. We use 11 different styles of brackets. By changing the bracket style to pico (the most rarely used by developers), we are able to reduce the attribution rate for the Ding feature set from 73.84% to 11.29%. The worst result is obtained with Java style (66.84%), this implies that most authors in our dataset use Java style. When considering the Caliskan feature set, the accuracy results do not change much and are still around 97%. This is due to the fact that the layout features make up only 1% of the Caliskan set after information gain feature selection.

We define "HideByCosine" obfuscation as following:

Definition 5.1 ("HideByCosine" obfuscation). Let $P \rightarrow P'$ be a transformation of a source program P into a target program P'. In order for $P \rightarrow P'$ to be a "HideByCosine" obfuscation the following steps should be applied:

- Apply a set of transformations T on program P
- Select those transformations so that $CosSim(\vec{a}, \vec{b}) \rightarrow min$, where $\vec{a}$ is the feature vector of the original program and $\vec{b}$ is the feature vector of the modified program.

The setup of our experiment for "HideByCosine" is similar to that of an imitation attack; we train RandomForest classifier on the non-obfuscated code and test it on the obfuscated one.

The results of the evaluation process for "HideByCosine" are reported in Table 5. When using only layout, lexical, syntactic and control-flow obfuscation we are able to achieve 1.43% attribution rate after applying author hiding attack for the Ding feature set. The transformations are unique for each author. With the Caliskan feature set we drop accuracy from 97.31% to 39.43% for the GoogleCodeJam dataset and from 80.92% to 27.96% for the GitHub dataset. This is due to the fact that the Caliskan et al. system uses information gain to select the most informative features, most of which are term frequency of unigrams and leaves (near 87% for GoogleCodeJam and GitHub) which can be easily obfuscated by name obfuscation. Table 4 shows the statistics of Caliskan features after information gain feature selection. The next group is AST nodes and AST node bigrams features (two AST nodes that are connected to each other), which only represent 12%, and are part of control-flow features. A portion of them can be obfuscated with simple transformations, e.g., changing "for" to "while" loops, and "else if" to "switch case", and do not guarantee author style's hiding. Therefore we applied control-flow flatenning (+CFF) on the top. After such transformations 0% of authors can be successfully attributed by Caliskan et al. and Ding et al. attribution systems.

Note that our result differs from what what reported in the Caliskan et al. work. [11]. The authors claimed that their method is resistant to simple obfuscation such as provided by Stunnix [1] with the reported accuracy of 98.89%, and to more sophisticated obfuscation (such as function virtualization by Tigress obfuscator [2]) with 67.22% on GoogleCodeJam data. Our results showed significantly lower accuracy. This is due to two facts. First, the authors used a much smaller dataset with only 20 authors making the task of attribution easier. Second, the experimental setup offered by their study assumed that

Features	Layout	Lexical		Syntactic		All
		unigrams	non-unigrams	leaves	non-leaves	
GCJ						
Original	6	20544	20	17393	667	38630
After info-gain	6	187	0	342	72	607
GitHub						
Original	6	87229	20	136415	808	224478
After info-gain	5	197	6	405	76	689

Table 4: Effect of information gain feature selection using Caliskan et al. [11] approach

the adversary is manipulating the training data and thus training of the classifiers is performed on selected and already obfuscated features.

We however followed a more realistic scenario commonly used in adversarial machine learning, i.e., the adversary aims to evade detection by manipulating test samples only [6]. We thus trained the RandomForest classifier on non-obfuscated code and tested it on obfuscated samples (imitated samples in the case of imitation attack). We were able to hide the coding style of the author with lexical and syntactic features and decrease the attribution accuracy dramatically to 39.43% for GoogCodeJam and to 30.29% for GitHub. After adding control-flow flatenning, no authors were recognized correctly.

Generalization of author hiding method for any author style. The proposed author hiding method "HideBy-Cosine" requires that every time authors want to hide their identity they should first identify the code transformations that generate the most distinctive style with respect to their own style. The goal now is to define transformations which will be unique for all authors. We are doing this by considering one transformation from each group given in Table 2. We transform the source code of all authors by using this transformation and then perform classification again. In this way, for example, we are able to identify the bracket styles that are used the least in a considered dataset and then modify each author's brackets style by using this type of brackets. This gives us the opportunity to find an unique anonymous style that hides the coding style of all the authors in the dataset. We refer to this obfuscation methods as "MaxiCode" and "MiniCode". The methodolody of finding such transformations presents in Algorithm 4.

Algorithm 4 Author hiding "MaxiCode" or "MiniCode"

Input: Dataset V_s with number of authors s and number of source code samples m for each author; List of possible transformations T
Output: Set of transformations T_k

for all V_s **do**
    apply each transformation T_k untill authorship attribution will fail identify all authors s in V_s
end for
return T_k

After applying such algorithm to our datasets, we define "MaxiCode" obfuscation as following:

Definition 5.2 ("MaxiCode" obfuscation). Let $P \rightarrow P'$ be a transformation of a source program P into a target program P'. In order for $P \rightarrow P'$ to be a "MaxiCode" obfuscation the following transformations should be applied to original program P: Comments (add pure line comments on each line); Brackets (transform all brackets to pico style); Spaces (indent using all tab characters, if possible); Lines (add empty line after each nonempty); Names and AST leaves: (use dictionary to change all names to long names (8-10 characters), the first sign is underscore, all names are unique for every author); Control-flow (change "while" to "for", change "else if" to "switch case")

One of the obvious concerns with this method is the size of source code since this transformation almost triples the code size. This makes this transformation impractical to use for developers in open-source projects. A possible solution is to shrink the code instead of expanding it; we refer to this method as "Minicode".

Definition 5.3 ("MiniCode" obfuscation). Let $P \rightarrow P'$ be a transformation of a source program P into a target program P'. In order for $P \rightarrow P'$ to be a "MiniCode" obfuscation the following transformations should be applied to original program P: Comments (no comments); Brackets (transform all brackets to pico style); Spaces (remove all spaces or tabs padding); Lines (delete all empty lines; write several statements in one line); Names and AST leaves (change all names on extremely short name indentifiers, the first sign is underscore, all names are unique for every author); Control-flow (change "for" to "while", change "switch case" to "else if")

The difference between "HideByCosine" method and "Maxi-Code" ("MiniCode") method that we proposed is that the first one is more about modifying the individual author's style to the most dissimilar one; thus for every author the method identifies different transformations, while the second method is about finding an unique style that protects the style of all authors. The main advantage of using the obfuscation "MiniCode" or "MaxiCode" for author hiding is that authors do not need to make any precomputations beforehand.

Table 5 shows how the accuracy of attribution changes after applying the "MiniCode" approach to each feature set. This transformation decreases the size of the program by almost 8 times, while still preserving readability. After Mini-Code obfuscation, the Kothari feature set achieves 1.88% attribution accuracy (GoogleCodeJam dataset) and 0% accuracy (GitHub). As the Kothari feature set is composed of layout and lexical features, they can be obfuscated by our transformations. As expected, Burrows and TFunigrams give us 0% attribution, since these are n-grams features and can be easily obfuscated by transformations in Table 2. After applying control-flow flatenning (+CFF) on the top of MiniCode and MaxiCode obfuscation 0% of authors can be successfully attributed by Caliskan et al., Ding et al., and Kothari et al. attribution systems.

Author Hiding	GoogleCodeJam data set				
	Ding	Caliskan	Burrows	Kothari	TFunigrams
Origin	73.84%	97.31%	73.29%	85.56%	96.95%
HideByCosine	1.08%	39.43%	0%	1%	0%
MaxiCode	4.12%	41.04%	0%	1.97%	0%
MiniCode	4.28%	43.90%	0%	1.88%	0%
HideByCosine+CFF	0%	0%	0%	0%	0%
MaxiCode+CFF	0%	0%	0%	0%	0%
MiniCode+CFF	0%	0%	0%	0%	0%
Author Hiding	GitHub data set				
	Ding	Caliskan	Burrows	Kothari	TFunigrams
Origin	67.25%	80.92%	69.56%	80.23%	75.08%
HideByCosine	0%	27.96%	0%	0%	0%
MaxiCode	2.37%	28.67%	0%	0%	0%
MiniCode	2.49%	30.29%	0%	0%	0%
HideByCosine+CFF	0%	0%	0%	0%	0%
MaxiCode+CFF	0%	0%	0%	0%	0%
MiniCode+CFF	0%	0%	0%	0%	0%

Table 5: Results of author hiding methods on both datasets

6 CONCLUSION

In this paper, we explored the accuracy of attribution using currently existing authorship attribution techniques in the presence of deception. We introduced an author imitation attack and investigated its feasibility on real-world software repositories. We used low-cost and easily implementable obfuscation techniques.

Also, we proposed several author hiding attacking techniques: "HideByCosine", "MaxiCode" and "MiniCode". The first method, "HideByCosine", works individually with each author by obfuscating source code to a style that is the most different from that of the the user. This method has better performance with respect to the other two. The other two methods work by finding one style which is unique for all authors. "MaxiCode" modifies the source code by extending it which triples its size. In the meantime, "Minicode" significantly reduces the size of the code making it almost 7 times smaller. In addition we applied control-flow flatenning on the top of this techniques to be able fully hide the coding style of the author, which gives 0% attribution at the end.

With both author imitation and author hiding methods we could significantly decrease the accuracy of current authorship attribution techniques.

REFERENCES

[1] 2014. Stunnix. Retrieved November 2014 from http://www.stunnix.com/prod/cxxo/
[2] 2014. Tigress. http://tigress.cs.arizona.edu
[3] Saed Alrabaee, Noman Saleem, Stere Preda, Lingyu Wang, and Mourad Debbabi. 2014. Oba2: An onion approach to binary code authorship attribution. *Digital Investigation* 11 (2014), S94–S103.
[4] Bander Alsulami, Edwin Dauber, Richard Harang, Spiros Mancoridis, and Rachel Greenstadt. 2017. Source Code Authorship Attribution Using Long Short-Term Memory Based Networks. In *European Symposium on Research in Computer Security*. Springer, 65–82.
[5] Harald Baayen, Hans Van Halteren, and Fiona Tweedie. 1996. Outside the cave of shadows: Using syntactic annotation to enhance authorship attribution. *Literary and Linguistic Computing* 11, 3 (1996), 121–132.
[6] Battista Biggio, Igino Corona, Davide Maiorca, Blaine Nelson, Nedim Šrndić, Pavel Laskov, Giorgio Giacinto, and Fabio Roli. 2013. Evasion attacks against machine learning at test time. In *Joint European conference on machine learning and knowledge discovery in databases*. Springer, 387–402.
[7] David M Blei, Andrew Y Ng, and Michael I Jordan. 2003. Latent dirichlet allocation. *Journal of machine Learning research* 3,

Jan (2003), 993–1022.

[8] Steven Burrows and Seyed MM Tahaghoghi. 2007. Source code authorship attribution using n-grams. In *Proceedings of the Twelth Australasian Document Computing Symposium, Melbourne, Australia, RMIT University*. Citeseer, 32–39.

[9] Steven Burrows, Alexandra L Uitdenbogerd, and Andrew Turpin. 2009. Application of information retrieval techniques for source code authorship attribution. In *International Conference on Database Systems for Advanced Applications*. Springer, 699–713.

[10] Steven Burrows, Alexandra L Uitdenbogerd, and Andrew Turpin. 2014. Comparing techniques for authorship attribution of source code. *Software: Practice and Experience* 44, 1 (2014), 1–32.

[11] Aylin Caliskan-Islam, Richard Harang, Andrew Liu, Arvind Narayanan, Clare Voss, Fabian Yamaguchi, and Rachel Greenstadt. 2015. De-anonymizing programmers via code stylometry. In *24th USENIX Security Symposium (USENIX Security), Washington, DC*.

[12] Aylin Caliskan-Islam, Fabian Yamaguchi, Edwin Dauber, Richard Harang, Konrad Rieck, Rachel Greenstadt, and Arvind Narayanan. 2015. When coding style survives compilation: De-anonymizing programmers from executable binaries. *arXiv preprint arXiv:1512.08546* (2015).

[13] Edwin Dauber, Aylin Caliskan-Islam, Richard Harang, and Rachel Greenstadt. 2017. Git Blame Who?: Stylistic Authorship Attribution of Small, Incomplete Source Code Fragments. *arXiv preprint arXiv:1701.05681* (2017).

[14] Haibiao Ding and Mansur H Samadzadeh. 2004. Extraction of Java program fingerprints for software authorship identification. *Journal of Systems and Software* 72, 1 (2004), 49–57.

[15] Jeanne Ferrante, Karl J Ottenstein, and Joe D Warren. 1987. The program dependence graph and its use in optimization. *ACM Transactions on Programming Languages and Systems (TOPLAS)* 9, 3 (1987), 319–349.

[16] Mark Hall, Eibe Frank, Geoffrey Holmes, Bernhard Pfahringer, Peter Reutemann, and Ian H Witten. 2009. The WEKA data mining software: an update. *ACM SIGKDD explorations newsletter* 11, 1 (2009), 10–18.

[17] RI Kilgour, AR Gray, PJ Sallis, and SG MacDonell. 1998. A fuzzy logic approach to computer software source code authorship analysis. (1998).

[18] Sangkyum Kim, Hyungsul Kim, Tim Weninger, Jiawei Han, and Hyun Duk Kim. 2011. Authorship classification: a discriminative syntactic tree mining approach. In *Proceedings of the 34th international ACM SIGIR conference on Research and development in Information Retrieval*. ACM, 455–464.

[19] Jay Kothari, Maxim Shevertalov, Edward Stehle, and Spiros Mancoridis. 2007. A probabilistic approach to source code authorship identification. In *Information Technology, 2007. ITNG'07. Fourth International Conference on*. IEEE, 243–248.

[20] Ivan Krsul and Eugene H Spafford. 1997. Authorship analysis: Identifying the author of a program. *Computers & Security* 16, 3 (1997), 233–257.

[21] Thomas J McCabe. 1976. A complexity measure. *IEEE Transactions on software Engineering* 4 (1976), 308–320.

[22] Xiaozhu Meng and Barton P Miller. [n. d.]. Binary Code Multi-Author Identification in Multi-Toolchain Scenarios. ([n. d.]).

[23] Arvind Narayanan, Hristo Paskov, Neil Zhenqiang Gong, John Bethencourt, Emil Stefanov, Eui Chul Richard Shin, and Dawn Song. 2012. On the feasibility of internet-scale author identification. In *Security and Privacy (SP), 2012 IEEE Symposium on*. IEEE, 300–314.

[24] Baishakhi Ray, Daryl Posnett, Vladimir Filkov, and Premkumar Devanbu. 2014. A large scale study of programming languages and code quality in github. In *Proceedings of the 22nd ACM SIGSOFT International Symposium on Foundations of Software Engineering*. ACM, 155–165.

[25] Nathan Rosenblum, Xiaojin Zhu, and Barton Miller. 2011. Who wrote this code? identifying the authors of program binaries. *Computer Security–ESORICS 2011* (2011), 172–189.

[26] Philip Sallis, Asbjorn Aakjaer, and Stephen MacDonell. 1996. Software forensics: old methods for a new science. In *Software Engineering: Education and Practice, 1996. Proceedings. International Conference*. IEEE, 481–485.

[27] Eugene H Spafford and Stephen A Weeber. 1993. Software forensics: Can we track code to its authors? *Computers & Security* 12, 6 (1993), 585–595.

[28] Danny van Bruggen. 2017. JavaParser. Retrieved November 15, 2017 from https://javaparser.org/index.html

[29] Chenxi Wang and John Knight. 2001. *A security architecture for survivability mechanisms*. University of Virginia.

[30] Mark Weiser. 1981. Program slicing. In *Proceedings of the 5th international conference on Software engineering*. IEEE Press, 439–449.

[31] Ian H Witten, Eibe Frank, Mark A Hall, and Christopher J Pal. 2016. *Data Mining: Practical machine learning tools and techniques*. Morgan Kaufmann.

Understanding and Detecting Private Interactions in Underground Forums

Zhibo Sun[1], Carlos E. Rubio-Medrano[1], Ziming Zhao[2], Tiffany Bao[1]
Adam Doupé[1], Gail-Joon Ahn[1,3]
[1] Arizona State University
{zhibo.sun,crubiome,tbao,doupe,gahn}@asu.edu
[2] Rochester Institute of Technology
zhao@mail.rit.edu

ABSTRACT

The studies on underground forums and marketplaces have significantly advanced our understandings of cybercrime workflows and underground economies. Researchers of underground economies have conducted comprehensive studies on public interactions. However, little research focuses on private interactions. The lack of the investigation on private interactions may cause misunderstandings on underground economies, as users in underground forums and marketplaces tend to share the minimal amount of information in public interactions and resort to private messages for follow-up conversations.

In this paper, we propose methods to investigate the underground private interactions and we analyze a recently leaked dataset from Nulled.io. We present analyses on the contents and purposes of private messages. In addition, we design machine learning-based models that only use the publicly available information to detect if two underground users privately communicate with each other. Finally, we perform adversarial analysis to evaluate the robustness of the detector to different types of attacks.

CCS CONCEPTS

• **Security and privacy** → **Social network security and privacy**; • **Information systems** → *Deep web*.

KEYWORDS

Underground forums, private interaction analysis, private interaction detection

ACM Reference Format:
Zhibo Sun[1], Carlos E. Rubio-Medrano[1], Ziming Zhao[2], Tiffany Bao[1], Adam Doupé[1], Gail-Joon Ahn[1,3]. 2019. Understanding and Detecting Private Interactions in Underground Forums. In *Ninth ACM Conference on Data and Application Security and Privacy (CODASPY '19), March 25–27, 2019, Richardson, TX, USA.* ACM, New York, NY, USA, 12 pages. https://doi.org/10.1145/3292006.3300036

---

[3]Dr. Gail-Joon Ahn is also affiliated with Samsung Research.

---

1 INTRODUCTION

Underground forums and marketplaces have been the rendezvous sites for cybercriminals of all kinds to exchange information and sell illegal products and services. Given the important roles these sites play in the cybercrime ecosystem, a considerable amount of research effort has been invested in studying the organizational structures of their users [2, 46, 49], their social dynamics, such as how users gain and lose trust [1, 35], the goods and services sold [13, 17, 44, 47], and how such sites assist specific forms of cybercrimes [21, 43]. These studies have significantly advanced our understandings of the underground economies and have guided law enforcement agencies and affected businesses in how to respond cybercrimes [44].

Nevertheless, the research community has only been looking at the tip of the iceberg of underground forums and marketplaces in that *we have only investigated posts and threads that are publicly available to all registered users or even anyone on Internet.* However, due to the nature of underground forums and marketplaces, their users tend to share a very small amount of information in public interactions and resort to private messages for follow-up conversations. Hence, analyzing private messages can disclose a wealth of information, such as the illicit financial flow, narrowing down the suspects who commit the crime, etc., while our community is not even aware of what sort of information we could glean from private messages.

In this paper, we investigate private messages in underground forums by analyzing the leaked dataset of Nulled.io. Nulled.io is a popular underground forum where users discuss hacking, exploits, monetization methods, etc. The released forum dataset includes public and private messages from Jan 14, 2015 to May 6, 2016, which makes it an excellent sample for comparing the similarities and differences between public and private interactions.

To study the private messages of Nulled.io, we develop a semi-automatic approach to categorize private messages into content and purpose categories, to compare how private messages are different from public posts. We present the artifacts discovered via our analysis of private messages, such as the payment methods, contact information, etc. Our analyses show that the content and purpose distributions in private messages *are different from* their public counterparts and that there is much more sensitive information, such as the users' contact information and Bitcoin addresses in private messages than in public posts. In the meantime, private exchanged information is not always undisclosed in public.

In addition, we analyze who are more likely to be contacted in private messages by studying public interactions of recipients, users who receive the initial message in a private thread, to understand how they behave differently from other users. We compare public and private interactions of recipients to study the relationships between their public and private activities. Also, we analyze different types of public posting methods, such as creating a post and replying to a post, and study which type of posting method is more likely to attract private interactions.

We also design various machine learning-based approaches to *detect private interactions* in underground forums based solely on public information. In essence, our approach uses publicly available information to uncover hidden connections between users. The evaluation results indicate that our approach effectively detects private interactions with 94% accuracy. Additionally, we perform adversarial analysis to evaluate the robustness of the detector to different types of attacks. Our analyses indicate that our detection has a considerable effective robustness to multiple types of evasion attacks. Also, our evaluations indicate that poisoning attacks performed by the administrators cannot prevent the private interactions from the detector effectively.

The contributions of this paper are summarized as follows:

- We analyze private messages in the underground forum in terms of different types of discussed content and purpose to compare how private messages are different from public posts. Also, we manually analyze the most popular artifacts in private messages.
- We study the public activities of private message recipients to understand how they behave differently from general users. Also, we analyze the relationship between public and private interactions of private message recipients.
- By considering the characteristics of underground forums and leveraging findings from previous studies and carefully selected features, we can effectively detect private interactions from public information.
- We present an adversarial analysis against our detector to understand the robustness of our detection algorithm.

2 MOTIVATING EXAMPLE AND DATA OVERVIEW

There are many studies on analyzing user interactions in public social networks [7, 8, 26, 31], most of which focus on public interactions that can be accessed by anyone, such as likes, reposts, shares, replies or tagging pictures. Similar public interactions are also utilized to analyze the social dynamics of underground forum users [33, 46, 49]. However, private messages on underground forums have been largely overlooked. In this section, we present a motivating example that sheds light on what may be discovered in private messages. We also discuss the dataset that is used in this paper and how we preprocess the raw data.

2.1 Motivating Example

As a motivating example, as shown in Figure 1, a vendor of Nulled.io tries to sell cracked accounts in a public post. However, the public post does not include any detailed information that is needed to finish a transaction, such as the payment or delivery methods. In contrast, corresponding private messages from the same vendor is

```
Vendor: Selling HideMyAss VPN premium accounts. Type of accounts:
    monthly membership with auto renew. Price is $5 BTC. Do not
    change the password/email of the account. I am not responsible
    if you get banned for breaking the TOS of HMA, make sure to
    read it first. All sales are final.
```

Figure 1: A public post in which a vendor is selling cracked accounts

```
Buyer: I want to buy one hide my ass account with bitcoin can I?
    Thanks
Vendor: Sure, price is $5 BTC. Ready to send BTC over? BTW i can
    give you 3 accounts for $12 BTC, that is a current deal. :)
Buyer: No I want only one thanks. Yes, I'm ready please sen me your
    btc address.
Vendor: Sure, send btc to: <BTCADDRESS>
Buyer: Sent.
Vendor: <USERNAME>:<PASSWORD>. Enjoy :)
Vendor: BTW can you leave a vouch in my sales thread? Thanks in
    advance. :)
Buyer: Thank you too. Feedback sent :)
```

Figure 2: Private messages exchanged between the same vendor in Figure 1 and a buyer. The bitcoin address, username, and password have been redacted.

shown in Figure 2, and these message comprise much more detailed information. To anonymize users' identities, we use "Buyer" and "Vendor" to represent their user IDs in the forum. We also use "BTCADDRESS," "USERNAME," and "PASSWORD" to represent the vendor's Bitcoin address and the cracked account login credentials.

The private messages in Figure 2 show that a user contacts the vendor to buy a cracked account of *HideMyAss*, which is a VPN service provider and its original service price is $11.99/month. Besides the advertised price ($5/account), the vendor offers a deal ($12 for 3 accounts) to the buyer as well. Also, the vendor's Bitcoin address is disclosed in the private messages. As the vendor asks the buyer to vouch for the transaction on the public post, we find the buyer leaves *"Bought from him, all was great :) Account is working"* in the original public thread. Therefore, private messages can reveal much useful information undisclosed in public posts. In the meantime, as shown in Figure 2, private interactions is a crucial step to fulfill the trading in the underground forums. Hence, detecting private interaction can help disclose hidden connections between users, and potentially reveal the goods trading flow.

2.2 Data Overview and Preprocessing

In this paper, we use a dataset from Nulled.io, a very popular hacker forum where users mainly discuss hacking, exploits, and monetization methods. We do not claim this forum represents all underground forums, but it can provide insights into user activities in underground forums. We obtained this dataset from an unknown third party who made it publicly available. Ethically, we do not attempt to identify users in our analyses, and use expressive words to represent corresponding sensitive information, such as "Vendor" and "BTCADDRESS" shown in Figure 1 and Figure 2 to represent seller's user ID and Bitcoin address. Moreover, using leaked and publicly available datasets is an acceptable practice in the study of the underground ecosystem [2, 35].

This dataset has a wealth of information. In particular, it has 599,085 member profiles, including email address, the date of joining the forum, IP address, membership, etc. It has 3,495,596 public posts from Jan 14, 2015, to May 6, 2016, which belong to 121,499 different public post threads. There are also 673,157 user login logs, which contain access time, user ID, and location.

In addition, this dataset has 800,593 private messages, which belong to 404,355 private message threads. These messages have contents, sending time, sender ID, receiver ID, etc. Our preliminary analysis shows that 70.9% of these threads are started by the system or moderators to welcome a new user or to send warning notifications. We exclude those threads from further analysis. As a result, there are 512,227 private messages that belong to 117,708 private message threads and 43,518 user pairs who had private interactions.

To preprocess text data, we retrieved the raw data of public and private messages directly from the forum's database. We used an HTML parser (Beautiful Soup) to remove all these tags. Next, we used a sentence splitter from NLTK (Natural Language Toolkit) to divide the text content into sentences. We also used lemmatizers in NLTK to reduce inflectional forms to a common base form. For example, after this step, "took," "taken," and "takes" will be changed to "take". We also removed all the stop words in the NLTK stop word list from the raw data and punctuation marks from the messages.

3 PRIVATE AND PUBLIC MESSAGE ANALYSIS

In this section, we study the private and public messages from the dumped database for the website Nulled.io. Our goals are: (1) to understand *what* users discuss in private messages, (2) *why* users use private messages, and (3) *how* private message discussions are different from public interactions.

3.1 Content and Purpose

We first investigate the difference between public and private threads in terms of the content and purpose of the communication. Content is the topic the thread is discussing, and purpose is the high-level goal of the thread.

The challenge inherent in answering this question is to recognize the content and purpose for a large number of messages from the database. To solve this challenge, we apply an approach for text topic classification [19, 37]. Specifically, we first explore contents and purposes by manually labeling a subset of the data, and we train a machine learning model to label messages with contents and purposes. To create the manually labeled data, we randomly select 1,000 public and 1,000 private threads from the dump dataset. We then used support vector machines (SVM) for training. To preserve ordering information, we extracted 1-gram, 2-gram, and 3-gram sequences from each thread. We ignored all sequences that appeared in more than 80% of the threads to remove the most frequent ones (as these are used in so many disparate threads and would provide very limited information on the content and purpose). As a result, each thread was represented as a 66,959-dimensional term frequency-inverse document frequency feature vector. We randomly selected 20% of the labeled threads and utilized grid search and five-fold cross-validation to tune the SVM model parameters. We trained

Table 1: Content and Purpose Categories of Public and Private Threads

	Labeled as	Refined Categories	Public Threads	Private Threads
Content	Bitcoin, Card, Amazon, Money	Monetization	1.7%	0.6%
	Password, Data, Account	Stolen Credential	21.7%	34.6%
	Program, IP, App, Rat, Experience, Hacking, SEO, VPN, Service, Script, Configure Setting, Bot, Website, Proxy, Botnet, Server, Cracking Guide	Hacking-related	48.9%	37.4%
	Video, Story, Tip, Photo, Game, Self Introduction, Device, Rule, Movie, People, Ban, Threads, N/A	Other	27.8%	27.3%
Purpose	Buying, Selling	Trading	13.4%	33.2%
	Sharing	Sharing	48.3%	2.5%
	Help-seeking, Help-offering	Supporting	27.7%	49.5%
	Greeting, Arguing, N/A	Other	10.6%	15.2%

separate classifiers for the purpose and content categories. With the optimized parameters, our SVM classifiers have around 0.84 F1 scores on the labeled dataset. In the end, we used the SVM classifiers with tuned parameters to classify all public and private threads.

The content and purposes are shown in Table 1. If we cannot label a thread based on the text content, such as a thread with the untranslatable language content, then the interaction purpose and content of this thread will be labeled as *N/A*, We categorize contents to four general classes: monetization (e.g., introducing approaches to making money or transferring the money), stolen credential (e.g., stolen account credentials, cracked account credentials, or compromised data), hacking-related (e.g., hacking services, hacking technique support, and hacking tutorials) and other. We also categorize purposes to the following four general classes: trading (e.g., selling and buying), sharing (e.g., giving away materials or things for free), supporting (e.g., seeking or providing help) and other.

Table 1 shows the content and purpose statistics in public and private threads. In terms of content, we find hacking, miscellany, and monetization are mentioned more frequently in public than in private, whereas stolen credential is mentioned more frequently in private than in public. This is likely because stolen credential is more valuable, and people would prefer to keep it private. However, monetization is also valuable, yet monetization is discussed less in private than in public. Our manual analysis indicates one possible reason of such change is that many of the posters of monetization threads request users to contact them through third-party messengers, such as Skype, or directly access their shopping websites.

In terms of purpose, we notice that more public threads aim to share information while more private threads aim to trade, support, greet, or argue, which is aligned with previous findings [39]. Moreover, we find that public sharing is associated with private trading: 96.6% of users who engage in trading public threads also have sharing public interaction purposes. We believe that this is because a user who publicly shares goods implies that they have more goods, and buyers tend to privately contact the original poster for questions and trading. In a sense, this is a form of advertising. For example, one user often shares many login credentials of cracked game accounts in his/her public posts. Many users privately contact the sharer for trading, such as *"Hey i'd like to buy a lvl 30, i hope it would be possible for me to change the email as well."*

3.2 Artifacts

Based on the content labeling model in Section 3.1, we analyze the popular artifacts in public and private threads. We study login credentials, proxies, contact methods (e.g., email and Skype), and payment methods, and we have the following observations:

Most users constantly keep their personal contacts either in public or in private. For example, among all the email contacts found in private threads, only 1.9% of the email contacts appear in both public and private threads. Also, users tend to keep their Skype ID secret until the end of the trading. We notice that only 41.1% of Skype-mentioned private threads include Skype IDs.The analysis shows that many users who engage in Skype-mentioned private threads cannot reach initial deals before exchanging Skype IDs or they prefer to use the built-in private messaging function of the forum.

In addition, we notice that privately exchanged goods are also disclosed in public. For example, only 64.2% and 40.2% of privately exchanged credentials and proxies, which are most frequently exchanged in public, are never discussed in public.

Forum administrators also host multiple payment accounts. Those accounts are used to collect the administrative fee such as account upgrading and tested products purchasing. We found 7 payment accounts, and 6 of them are found from private threads. This implies that one should establish private interaction with the administrators to investigate the financial status of the underground forum.

Previous research has conducted per-user analysis, based on the fact that duplicated users are typically not allowed in the underground forum. However, we observe that 37 out of 1,165 PayPal accounts are used by multiple users, which implies that duplicated users exist in the underground forum. Our manual analysis indicates that these forum accounts likely to belong to the same person, because these users are performing the same business, clearly leaving the same private contact information, such as Skype IDs. Also, we notice that these users, who have multiple accounts linked by the same PayPal account, have used precautions to avoid being identified by the forum's Duplicated-Account detection system: they use different IP addresses when logging into their different user accounts. They also take care to use email addresses and usernames that are very different from their other accounts. Additionally, we notice that nearly 86% of such multiple-linked accounts are identified from the private threads, therefore demonstrating the importance of private messages to understanding an underground marketplace.

3.3 Private Message Recipients Behavior

A *private message recipient* is a user that is initially contacted in a private thread. As private messages can contain more security sensitive contents and purposes, studying private message recipients will help us understand how private interactions are initiated. In this subsection, we study two questions:

- What is the difference in the public activities of private message recipients and other users? Specifically, what is the difference in

Table 2: Number of Recipients in Different Public and Private Interaction Categories

		# Users in Public	# Recipients in Public	# Recipients in Private
Content	Monetization (a)	25,448 (4.2%)	6,524 (38.4%)	26 (0.2%)
	Stolen Credential (b)	93,645 (15.6%)	13,571 (79.8%)	6,817 (40.1%)
	Hacking-related (c)	279,148 (46.6%)	16,481 (97.0%)	7,221 (42.5%)
	a ∧ b	18,679 (3.1%)	6,222 (36.6%)	22 (0.1%)
	a ∧ c	24,509 (4.1%)	6,498 (38.2%)	23 (0.1%)
	b ∧ c	81,824 (13.7%)	13,387 (78.8%)	5,096 (30.0%)
	a ∧ b ∧ c	18,463 (3.1%)	6,203 (36.5%)	21 (0.1%)
	Total	291,692	16,672	8,944
Purpose	Trading (d)	32,988 (5.5%)	9,823 (57.8%)	6,983 (41.1%)
	Sharing (e)	288,403 (48.1%)	16,501 (97.1%)	541 (3.2%)
	Supporting (f)	92,091 (15.4%)	14,224 (83.7%)	8,151 (48.0%)
	d ∧ e	31,867 (5.3%)	9,697 (57.1%)	471 (2.8%)
	d ∧ f	24,021 (4.0%)	8,946 (52.6%)	5,629 (33.1%)
	e ∧ f	84,121 (14.0%)	14,090 (82.9%)	495 (2.9%)
	d ∧ e ∧ f	23,837 (4.0%)	8,916 (52.5%)	450 (2.6%)
	Total	297,310	16,731	9,530

public security messages, posts, and replies, and private security posts and replies?
- How do private message recipients behave in public as compared to in private?

To answer these questions, we take advantage of messages with content and purpose labels (§ 3.1). We divide the messages into two groups by whether its author is a private message recipient or not. For each group, we calculate the proportion of users involved in the messages with different content and different purposes. In our dataset, there are 43,518 user pairs who have private interactions, and 16,997 users are `recipients`. The statistic results of this analysis are shown in Table 2.

What is the difference in the public activities of private message recipients and other users? We study the differences in three different aspects: (1) security messages, (2) content-specific and purpose-specific messages, and (3) posts and replies. Security messages are messages with security-related content or purposes. As we stated in Table 1, in this paper we consider monetization, stolen credential, and hacking as security-related contents, and we consider trading, sharing, and supporting as security-related purposes. Content-specific and purpose-specific messages are labeled with one or multiple content or purposes from the above categories. Posts and replies are two types of messages in public thread. Posts are the messages initializing new threads, while replies are messages posted as follow-ups to existing threads.

- **Security messages.** Column # Recipients in Public and column # Users in Public shows the difference of public activities between private message recipients and other users. Private message recipients are more involved in security-related messages. For example, 98.1% of the private message recipients have discussed monetization, stolen credential, or hacking-related topics, whereas 48.6% of the other users have discussed this content. This difference also implies that users involved in more security-related activities will be more likely to be contacted privately.
- **Content-specific and purpose-specific messages.** In particular, we study the difference in posts and replies with specific contents and purposes. Table 2 shows the number of unique private message recipients that post/reply a message in a specific topic or purpose, as well as the number of unique recipients

that are contacted for the same topic and purpose. For stolen credential, hacking, trading, and supporting, more than 50% of the recipients are contacted with the same content/purpose after posting. However, for monetization and sharing, few recipients are contacted after posting.

- **Posts and replies.** We compare the total number of the unique authors to that of unique private message recipients, as shown in Table 3. Based on these results, we observe that a majority of post authors are also private message recipients. For example, 906 out of 1,296 (69.9%) authors that post monetization messages become recipients. However, many fewer authors are contacted due to their replies. Among 24,152 unique authors that reply to monetization messages, only 5,618 (23.2%) are recipients that are privately contacted by other users. This implies that to attract the other users for private interaction, one should post security messages rather than reply to existing threads.

In addition, we notice from Table 3 that there are more repliers than posters in all the categories. Our results show that most of posters never reply in his/her created thread, which indicates that repliers cannot receive any help from posters by replying to their posts. Especially, many initial posts explicitly request users to privately contact the post's creator. Because of this results, we are interested in the reasons for publicly *replying* to posts. Our manual analysis indicates one possible reason: posters attempts to have a lower *leecher* value. Because many users attempt to take advantage of the underground forum resources without making contributions, the underground forum assigns a *leecher* value to each user, which is used to quantify a user's contribution, where a lower value is better. This value is rated by the system automatically based on various metrics, such as the number of threads a user created, the number of replies a user obtained, etc. If a user has a high *leecher* value, then many of his/her activities will be restricted, such as private message limits, being unable to access particular types of post, etc. To lower the *leecher* value, a user needs his/her posts to have more replies, which imply that more users are interested in his/her posts. Therefore, most of the posters use a feature of the forum to hide essential content from the post, and this content is only revealed when other users reply to the post. This also explains why the text content of most of the replies are meaningless, such as *"thx", "ty"*.

How do private message recipients behave in public as compared to in private? Column # Recipients in Public and column # Recipients in Private show the difference of private message recipients' activities between public messages and private messages. Interestingly, we find that private message recipients discuss *less* about security in private than in public. While 98.5% of the recipients message publicly for trading, sharing, and supporting, only 56.1% of them message privately with similar purposes. Instead, these recipients use private threads for other purposes, such as to argue for reviews in public threads.

Posting is more likely than replying in having similar content or purpose in both public and private interactions. As shown in Table 4, column # Recipient-posterin Public and column # Recipient-posterin Both Public and Private shows the difference of private message recipient-posters' activities between public and private messages. In general, 6,807 out of 10,205 (66.7%) recipient-posters

Table 3: Poster and Replier Statistics Based on Their Public Thread Contents and Interaction Purposes

		# Recipient-posters	# Posters	# Recipient-repliers	# Repliers
Content	Monetization (a)	906	1,296	5,618	24,152
	Stolen Credential (b)	5,277	8,491	8,294	85,154
	Hacking-related (c)	8,576	21,172	7,905	257,976
	$a \wedge b$	631	699	2,888	14,219
	$a \wedge c$	735	914	2,065	17,087
	$b \wedge c$	3,739	4,937	4,424	63,666
	$a \wedge b \wedge c$	551	596	1,339	10,625
Purpose	Trading (d)	4,100	6,093	5,723	26,895
	Sharing (e)	7,741	17,684	8,760	270,719
	Supporting (f)	6,609	16,558	7,615	75,533
	$d \wedge e$	2,685	3,260	2,895	20,671
	$d \wedge f$	2,500	3,112	3,035	14,404
	$e \wedge f$	4,367	6,846	4,763	61,429
	$d \wedge e \wedge f$	1,935	2,215	1,849	11,696

Table 4: Number of Recipient-posters and Recipient-repliers in Different Public and Private Interaction Categories

		# Recipient-posters in Public	# Recipient-posters in Both Public and Private	# Recipient-repliers in Public	# Recipient-repliers in Both Public and Private
Content	Monetization (a)	906	6	5,618	14
	Stolen Credential (b)	5,277	3,397	8,294	2,900
	Hacking-related (c)	8,576	4,836	7,905	2,301
	$a \wedge b$	631	5	2,888	5
	$a \wedge c$	735	6	2,065	4
	$b \wedge c$	3,739	2,287	4,424	732
	$a \wedge b \wedge c$	551	5	1,339	3
	Total	10,205	6,807	13,779	4,477
Purpose	Trading (d)	4,100	2,860	5,723	2,557
	Sharing (e)	7,741	405	8,760	133
	Supporting (f)	6,609	4,454	7,615	3,088
	$d \wedge e$	2,685	269	2,895	43
	$d \wedge f$	2,500	1,863	3,035	862
	$e \wedge f$	4,367	313	4,763	47
	$d \wedge e \wedge f$	1,935	228	1,849	21
	Total	10,833	7,464	13,254	4,847

have similar security related content in both public and private, while it is only 32.5% for recipient-repliers.

4 DETECTING PRIVATE INTERACTIONS IN UNDERGROUND FORUMS

In this section, we study the *detection* of private interactions by using two users' publicly available information in underground forums. Because users trade illicit goods or services through private interactions, detection of these private interactions helps to identify illegal activities, trace goods flows, and disclose hidden connections.

4.1 Approach Overview

We apply machine learning methods to detect private interactions. We first train machine learning models with constructed user pair instances. Then, we apply the trained models on the testing data and evaluate based on precision, recall, F1 score, and accuracy.

Data Selection. In the Nulled.io dataset, there are much more user pairs that do not have private interactions than whose who have. For all of the 599,085 users, only 43,518 user pairs ever have private interactions. We randomly sub-sample user pairs of non-private interaction to avoid the common problems of an imbalanced dataset, such as the bias towards the majority class [10]. Also, we adopt data pruning and cross-field validation in sub-sampling five times to train each classifier.

Feature Extraction. Based on our observations (described in previous sections), we synthesize three categories of features for the private interaction detection: (1) features from a user's profile, (2) features from a user's public activities, and (3) features from a user pair, as shown in Table 5. The features are from *publicly available and objective information* of a user pair. We choose these features under the following considerations. First, as users try to hide their real identities in the underground forum, they may provide fake or incomplete information. Second, unlike public social networks, underground forums only need users to provide a small amount of profile information, and much of the information is hidden from the public. Also, only a small percentage of users have private interactions, and users typically have a different focus when privately interaction compared to their public interactions.

Training. We use Naive Bayesian (NB), Logistic Regression (LR), Support Vector Machine (SVM), K-Nearest Neighbors (KNN), AdaBoost, Multi-Layer Perceptron (MLP), and Random Forest (RF) to detect private interactions in the underground forum. Table 6 shows the best performance configurations of each classifier.

4.2 Testing Results

4.2.1 Detection Performance of Private Interactions of Overall Users.
We used five-fold cross-validation in our experiments, and all features were normalized. Table 7 shows the detection performance of each classifier. The precision is the fraction of correctly identified private interaction instances among all of the detected private interaction instances. The recall indicates the percentage of private interaction instances are correctly identified. The F1 score is used to measure the overall performance while considering both the precision and recall.

As shown in Table 7, the algorithms can effectively detect private interactions. Most of the algorithms can achieve higher than 0.85 in precision and 0.92 in the recall. In particular, ensemble algorithms, AdaBoost, and RF, and the neural network algorithm, MLP, have the highest F1 score. In the meantime, MLP has the best performance on precision. Additionally, RF outperforms other algorithms on overall accuracy and recall. As AdaBoost, MLP, and RF have at least one of the best measurement performances, we focus on these three algorithms in the rest of the paper.

Figure 3 depicts the ROC curves of detecting private interactions by using the three algorithms. In general, all of the algorithms have a high true positive rate (TPR) and low false positive rate (FPR). In particular, RF and MLP outperform Adaboost. Additionally, we observe that, with 10% FPR, MLP can achieve more than 95.5% TPR and RF has less than 4% false negative rate (FNR).

4.2.2 Detection Performance of Private Interactions of Publicly Active Users. As shown in Figure 4, the top 10% of privately active users engage in 80% of the total private interactions, and users who are in the top 10% publicly active engage in nearly 90% of total private interactions. To detect private interactions of top publicly active users, we constructed multiple experimental subsets from the dataset containing private interaction user pairs that consisted of users who were top n of publicly active (where n is set to 5%,

10%, and 15%). We used the same number of user pairs of non-private interactions and user pairs with private interactions to form balanced subsets.

Table 8 shows the detection performance results using AdaBoost, MLP, and RF. "PI Coverage" in Table 8 indicates the percentage of private interactions involving the users who are in the top n% of publicly active users. Note that 79.2% of private interactions attribute to the top 5% of publicly active users. As clearly shown in Table 8, the classifiers have better performance in detecting private interactions for the top n% of publicly active users.

Figure 5 shows the ROC curves of detecting private interactions of users pairs that contain the top 5% of publicly active users. Different from overall detection performance, Adaboost has a better performance than MLP. Moreover, the algorithms have a higher TPR in Figure 5 than in Figure 3 at the same FPR.

5 ADVERSARIAL ANALYSIS

In Section 4, we show that our approach can effectively detect private interactions in the underground forum. In this section, we perform adversarial attacks analysis to evaluate the robustness of our detection technique.

Because many users prefer to discuss and exchange illicit detailed information in private, in order to escape detections they may *intentionally change their public behaviors* in the underground forums. Also, to maintain the underground forums normal operations, to protect and attract users, administrators of underground forums could perform actions to prevent their users' private interactions from being detected. Therefore, it is crucial to evaluate the robustness of our detector in different adversarial scenarios. Because the adversarial attack purpose is to escape the detection, we only consider users pairs who have private interactions and measure the accuracy of successfully detected private interaction given different adversarial attack scenarios.

In this section, we analyze two scenarios: (1) The *evasion attack*, where users in underground forums adjust their behaviors and hide in other users to escape detection, and (2) The *poisoning attack*, where administrators of underground forums generate fake avatars and manipulate their activities to poison the data to prevent their users' private interactions from being detected.

5.1 Evasion Attack

Evasion attacks refer to adversaries in underground forums that adjust their behaviors to hide in the crowd to escape detection. By analyzing the features we used in the detector, we notice that some of them can be modified if adversaries intentionally change their behaviors in the underground forum. We have marked each feature as changeable, unchangeable, or partial changeable in Table 5. *Membership* and *Banned* are partially changeable features because their statuses are not fully controlled by the users. For example, a user can change his/her behaviors in the underground forum to be banned, but recover his unbanned status from banned is decided by the administrators. Also, *Leecher* in the *Reputation* can be changed by adversaries depending on how much the contribution the user makes to the underground forum. However, *Reputation* and *Like* are rated by other people that are not controlled by the adversary.

Table 5: Features Used in the Detector

	Feature Name	Explanation
Profile Features	Membership [P]	To create a generic approach, we categorize memberships into five classes: (1) Basic membership, such as *Member*; (2) Upgraded membership, such as *Royal*; (3) Limited membership, such as *Banned*; (4) Fee-based membership, such as *VIP*; (5) Staff, such as *Administrator*.
	JoinDate [u]	The time of joining the forum
	LastVisit [u]	The time of the last visit
	Views [u]	The number of views on the user's profile. A user's profile includes user's basic information, reputation values, and activity history.
	Reputation [c,u]	Many forums use multiple types of reputation values to show a user's contributions, honors, and trustworthiness. For example, the Nulled.io forum uses three such values, which are: leecher, like, and reputation, to indicate the user's contributions, honors, and trustworthiness, respectively.
	Banned [P]	A user's status: This is used to show if a user's account is banned in the forum. When a user violates the forum policy, such as creating duplicated accounts and spamming, then the staff members may ban his/her account.
Activity Features	Posts [c]	The number of a user's public posts.
	Threads [c]	The number of public threads a user engages in. This feature shows a user's public activities on different public threads.
	Topics [c]	The number of public threads initiated by a user. This feature indicates how often a user opens new public post topics in an underground forum.
	ThreadViews [u]	The number of views on a user's public threads. This feature indicates the popularity of a user's public threads.
	Subforums [c]	The number of subforums a user is involved in. The underground forum has several subforums for different themes, and the post threads must be published in the corresponding subforum. This feature indicates the number of general themes a user is interested in.
	Friends [c]	The number of users who publicly interact with the user. This feature shows the degree centrality of a user in an underground forum network, which is formed by users' public interactions.
Interaction Features	Interactions [c]	The number of this user pair's public interactions.
	CommonTopics [c]	he number of public threads that have both users' posts. This feature shows how often these two users are interested in the same public post topics.
	CommonSubforums [c]	The number of subforums that both users are involved in. This feature indicates how often these two users are interested in the same general themes in an underground forum.
	CommonFriends [c]	The number of users who publicly interact with both users. This feature reveals the number of direct neighbors shared by these two users in an underground forum interaction network.

[c] Changeable Feature
[P] Partial Changeable Feature
[u] Unchangeable Feature

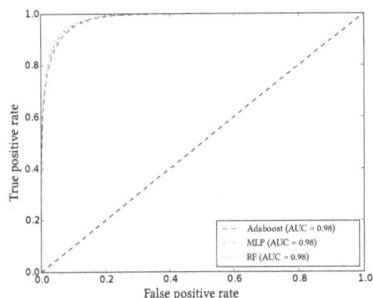

Figure 3: ROC curves of detection of overall user pairs

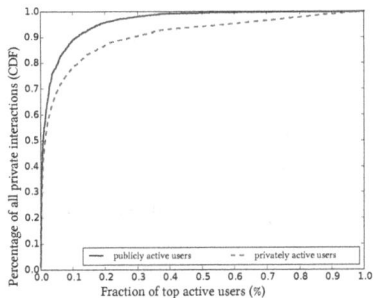

Figure 4: The growth of private interactions over the fraction of top active users

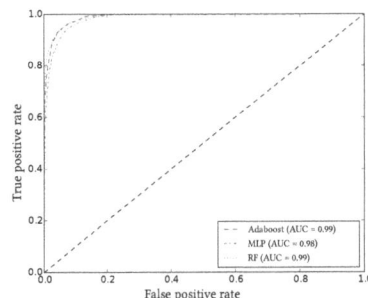

Figure 5: ROC curves of detection of user pairs that contain top 5% of publicly active users

Table 6: Classifier Configurations

Algorithm	Configurations
NB	alpha = 0.001; fit_prior = "True"
LR	C = 10; solver = "liblinear"
SVM	kernel = "rbf"; C = 100; gamma = 0.01
KNN	n_neighbors = 11; weights = "distance"; algorithm = "ball_tree"
AdaBoost	n_estimators = 250; learning_rate = 1; algorithm = "SAMME.R"
MLP	activation = "logistic"; solver = "adam"; learning_rate = "adaptive"; hidden_layer_sizes = (150,)
RF	n_estimators = 250; max_features = "sqrt"

In the evasion attack, we focus on two main situations: adversaries modify their changeable features without a strategy and with a strategy. We leave as future work the more delicate adversarial machine learning schemes on our model, as well as the assessment of the robustness of the detector against more sophisticated data evasion attacks.

Table 7: Detection Performance in the Underground Forum

Algorithm	Precision	Recall	F1 Score	Accuracy
NB	0.85	0.80	0.82	0.82
LR	0.85	0.92	0.88	0.88
SVM	0.90	0.93	0.92	0.91
KNN	0.87	0.94	0.90	0.89
AdaBoost	0.91	0.94	**0.93**	0.92
MLP	**0.93**	0.94	**0.93**	0.93
RF	0.92	**0.96**	**0.93**	**0.94**

5.1.1 Non-strategic Attack. In the non-strategic attack, adversaries do not know what features are used in the detector, and they attempt to assign random values to all changeable features by adjusting their activities. In this situation, we consider two kinds of attacks: (1) single-user attack, where one user does not want his/her private interactions to be detected, and (2) two-user attack, where two users try to prevent their private interactions from being detected. **Single-user Non-strategic Attack.** In this attack, the adversary does not consider a specific private contact user, so this user only

Table 8: Detection Performance of User Pairs Containing Top *n*% of Publicly Active Users

Top N	Performance	AdaBoost	MLP	RF	PI Coverage
5%	Precision	**0.94**	0.93	0.92	
	Recall	0.97	0.95	**0.98**	79.2%
	F1 Score	**0.95**	0.94	**0.95**	
10%	Precision	**0.94**	0.93	0.93	
	Recall	0.96	0.95	**0.97**	88.9%
	F1 Score	**0.95**	0.94	**0.95**	
15%	Precision	**0.93**	0.92	0.92	
	Recall	0.96	0.94	**0.97**	93.1%
	F1 Score	**0.95**	0.93	**0.95**	

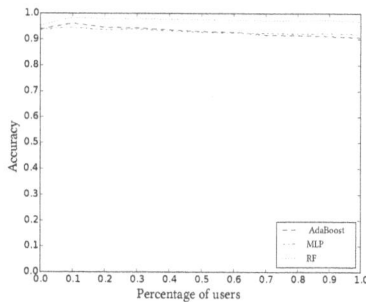

Figure 6: Detector performance on the single-user non-strategic attack

modifies his/her changeable profile and activity features to random values. To evaluate the robustness of the detector to this attack, we randomize the value of each changeable feature within a reasonable scope, which are determined by sampling from a subset of users.

It is worth pointing out that changing an adversary's activity feature values can influence his/her interaction feature values with other users. For example, the number of common topics between two users is impacted if one of the users changes his/her *Topics* value. Because the user can delete posts from topics and make new posts in new topics, or just delete or make new posts, it is difficult to know how the change impacts the number of common topics between the users. Therefore, we use Equation 1 to adjust the interaction feature values in each of the instances.

$$InteractionVal' = ChangeableVal' \times \frac{InteractionVal}{ChangeableVal} \quad (1)$$

In this example, *InteractionVal'* is the adjusted number of *CommonTopics*. *ChangeableVal'* is the randomly generated number of *Topics*. *InteractionVal* is the original number of *CommonTopics*, and *ChangeableVal* is the original number of *Topics*. To have fair results, we perform the evaluation 1,000 times, and the average results are shown in Figure 6.

Figure 6 shows the performance of private interaction detection when an adversary modifies his/her changeable information without a strategy by observing differing percentages of other users. As shown in Figure 6, our detector is robust to this kind of attack and RF outperforms other algorithms. We notice that the successful evasion rate decreases when considering a larger percentage of users.

Two-user Non-strategic Attack. In this attack, two adversaries have clear private contact targets and try to avoid detection of their private interactions. Therefore, there are three methods to perform this attack: (1) both adversaries change their changeable features in their profiles and activities, and keep the interaction features the same, (2) both adversaries modify their changeable features, and (3) both adversaries only modify their changeable interaction features. To simulate this attack, we randomize the value within a reasonable scope by sampling from a subset of users. Note that interaction features and their corresponding activity features have a relationship that constrains the randomly generated values—e.g., in the first method of this attack, as *CommonTopics* value is not changed, both adversaries' new *Topics* values should be between *CommonTopics* and maximum *Topics* value of a subset of users.

Figure 7 shows the detector performance on the two-user non-strategic attack with different methods by sampling different percentage of users. As shown in Figure 7, the detector is robust against the two-user non-strategic attack, with more than 80% accuracy in general. Also, RF outperforms other algorithms in all methods; modifying the interaction feature values can impact the RF performance. Additionally, in the two-user attack, adversaries only need to consider 10% of users' information to obtain their considerable evasion rate.

In summary: the detector is robust to the non-strategic evasion attacks, and two-user non-strategic attacks are more challenging to the detector than single-user non-strategic attacks. In addition, RF always outperforms other algorithms in our evaluations.

5.1.2 Strategic Attack. Since many publications discuss machine learning based detectors, such as [3, 6, 27], and the publicly available information in the underground forum is limited, it is possible for adversaries to guess the potential features used in the detector. Therefore, to hide themselves in the crowd, adversaries are motivated to assign specific values to a minimum number of features. In this section, we assume adversaries already know the changeable features and the value scope of each feature. In this situation, we still consider the aforementioned two kinds of attacks: (1) single-user attack and (2) two-user attack.

Single-user Strategic Attack. In this attack, an adversary does not consider a specific private contact user, so this adversary only modifies changeable features in his/her profile and activity. To evaluate the robustness of the detector, an adversary only assigns a specific value to one feature at a time. We also adopt the same approach to adjust interaction feature values (Equation 1).

Figure 8 shows the detector performance when a user performs a single-user strategic attack in terms of different algorithms. The x-axis shows within a reasonable value range of a feature, the value that will be assigned to the feature. The y-axis indicates the accuracy of successfully detected private interactions. As shown in Figure 8, the detector with RF has the most robustness (the lowest accuracy is 83.3%) to the single-user strategic attack and the MLP is the least robust one with only 32.2% accuracy. Additionally, *Friends*, *Topics*, and *Leecher* impact the detector more significantly than other features. Compared with the single-user non-strategic attack, this attack can increase the adversaries chance to evade detection.

Two-user Strategic Attack. In this attack, adversaries assign a specific value to one type of their changeable features at a time.

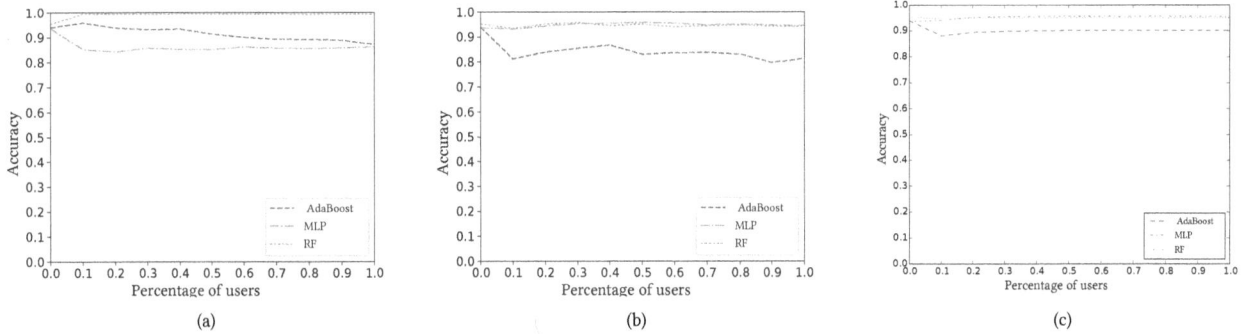

Figure 7: Detector performance on different two-user non-strategic attack methods

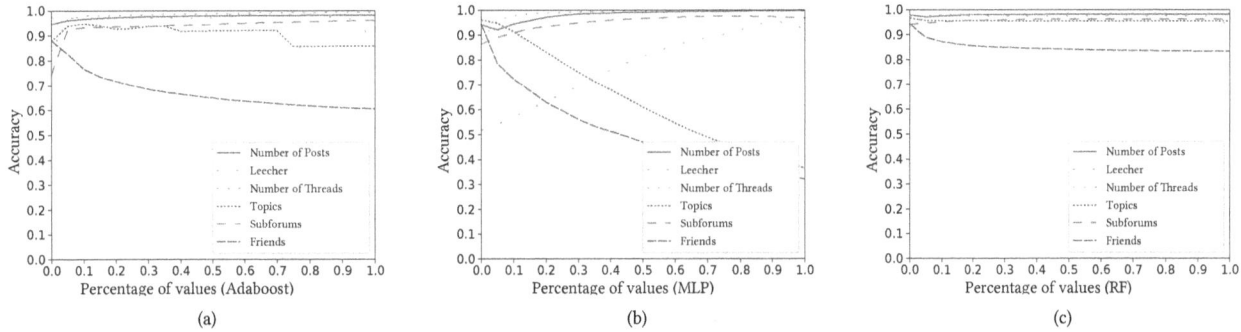

Figure 8: Detector performance on the single-user strategic attack

For example, both users modify their *Topics* features, while keeping other feature values unchanged. As explained previously, interaction features and their corresponding activity features have a relationship that constrains the value scope.

Figure 9 shows the detector performance when two adversaries perform a strategic attack in terms of different algorithms. The x-axis shows within a reasonable value range of a feature, the value that will be assigned to the feature. The y-axis indicates the accuracy of successfully detected private interactions. As shown in Figure 9, RF is the most robust algorithm in the detector, and its lowest accuracy is 91.2%. In contrast, MLP has the worst performance that is 3.9% accuracy. Also, to our surprise, interaction features do not impact the detection performance significantly, as the lowest accuracy are obtained when modifying *Friends, Topic,* and *Leecher* in Adaboost and MLP based detectors, as shown in Figure 9(a) and Figure 9(b). Although *Interactions* is more influential than other features in Figure 9(c), the detector still has more than 90% accuracy. Comparing this attack with the single-user strategic attack, although the two-user strategic attack has the lowest accuracy in MLP, frequently the single user strategic attack is more challenging to our detector.

In summary: strategic attacks have a higher chance to evade detection than non-strategic attacks. Additionally, single-user attacks are more challenging than two-user attacks in the strategic

Table 9: Detection Performance with Unchangeable Features

Algorithm	Precision	Recall	F1 Score	Accuracy
AdaBoost	0.84	0.86	0.85	0.85
MLP	0.84	0.91	0.88	0.87
RF	**0.85**	**0.94**	**0.89**	**0.89**

attacks. Also, interaction features are less influential than profile and activity features.

5.1.3 Counter Evasion Attack. To counter the evasion attack, we evaluate our detector robustness with *only using unchangeable features*. The new evaluation indicates that the detector still has considerable performance, shown in Table 9.

Figure 10 depicts the ROC curves of detecting private interactions by using unchangeable features. In general, using unchangeable features has worse performance than using all features by comparing this ROC curves with Figure 3 and Figure 5. In particular, all algorithms can have more than 0.90 TPR with 0.18 FPR. Also, RF outperforms another two algorithms.

5.2 Poisoning Attack

To make underground forums operate properly, attract more users, and protect their users' privacies, administrators of such underground forums need to take actions to help prevent their users'

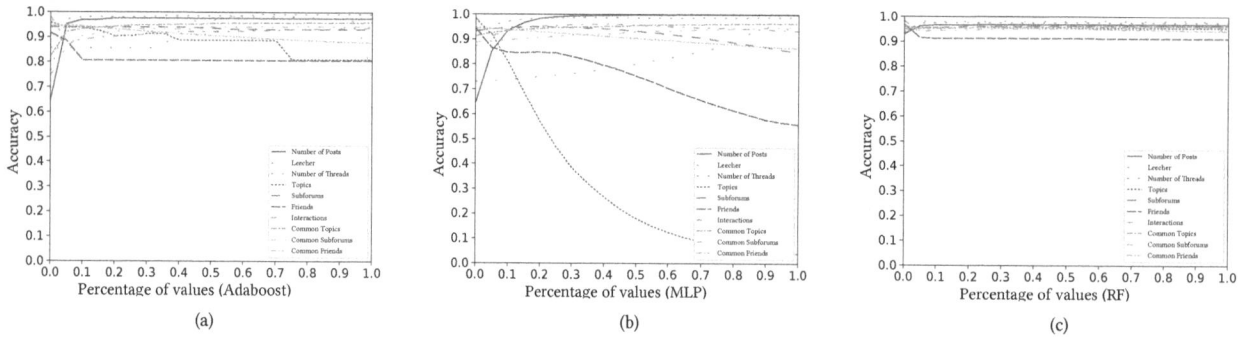

Figure 9: Detector performance on the two-user strategic attack

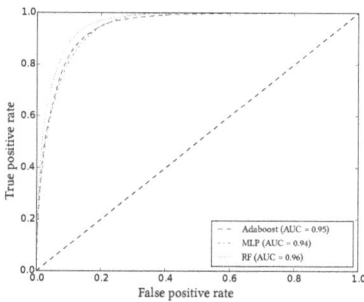

Figure 10: ROC curves of detection by using unchangeable features

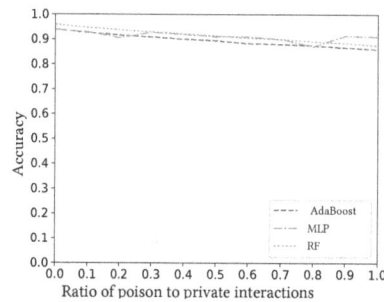

Figure 11: Detector performance on the random poisoning attack

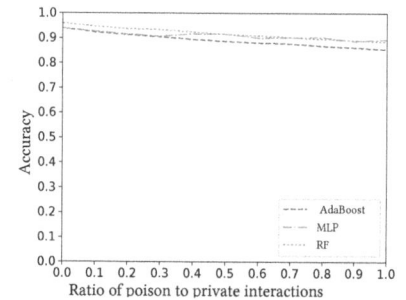

Figure 12: Detector performance on the normal-user-based poisoning attack

private interactions from being detected. As administrators have fully control of the underground forums, they can generate fake avatars and manipulate their activities to make false private interaction samples to pollute the data.

By considering the approach to create fake avatars, there are two types of poisoning attacks: (1) the *random poisoning attack*, where all individual feature values of the fake avatars are generated randomly within a reasonable scope based on all users' information, and interaction feature values of fake avatars are generated based on their individual features. (2) The *normal-user-based poisoning attack*, where administrators find out all normal users, who never have private interactions from the database, and create fake avatars by using normal users' information: while constructing the false samples, the interaction feature values are randomly generated that are within reasonable scope based on two randomly selected fake avatars.

Note that we *do not* construct false samples between fake avatars and real users while considering practical situations. Letting a fake avatar privately contact a real user will provide a bad experience to the user because it means that the user has strange private messages with unknown people. This could lead the user to feel that his/her account is stolen.

To evaluate the robustness of the detector to this attack, we first split the clean dataset into training and testing datasets. Secondly, we generate different numbers of false private interaction samples

and then mix them with real training dataset. Finally, we build our detector based on the polluted training dataset and apply the testing dataset to evaluate the detector performance.

Figure 11 and Figure 12 show the detector performance when administrators perform two types of poisoning attacks by injecting different numbers of false private interaction samples. The x-axis shows the ratio of false samples to the real private interactions, and the y-axis indicates the accuracy of successfully detected private interactions in the testing dataset.

As shown in Figure 11 and Figure 12, the detector is robust to both types of poisoning attacks, and the performances are very similar. In general, MLP outperforms other algorithms in the poisoning attack with the lowest 0.91 accuracy in random poisoning attack and 0.89 accuracy in normal-user-based poisoning attack. Additionally, injecting more false private interaction samples will decrease the detector performance, but the influence is limited. In the meantime, by comparing the detection performance in the different poisoning attacks, the normal-user-based poisoning attack is more challenging to the detector.

6 DISCUSSION

In this section, we explore the limitations of the data analysis and private interaction detection approaches, and we present the direction of our future work.

In this paper, we use Nulled.io as the subject in our study. Although Nulled.io is one of the most popular underground forums and can be representative for the security research for private interactions, a single forum may be insufficient for data analysis and private interaction detection. We will look for and investigate more data for future work.

For data analysis, we group messages into different categories in terms of contents and purposes. The categories are generated manually based on 1000 samples of public and private message in respective. Due to the limit of samples, the categories may not be complete. In the future, we will look into approaches towards complete categories for both content and purposes. Moreover, we label messages by applying SVM with supervised classification. However, the SVM model may be imprecise in labeling messages. Data labeling is known to be open in data analysis research. We leave more accurate labeling as future work.

For private interaction detection, we test the robustness of the detection model against adversarial machine learning attacks such as data evasion and data poisoning attacks. For both types of the attack, we consider hard-coded strategies for data generation. One future direction is to test our detection model on more sophisticated adversarial machine learning techniques [5, 12, 48]. Also, we will explore more robust machine learning models for private interaction detection, such as to apply the machine unlearning technique [9] to the current model.

7 RELATED WORK

Analysis and measurement of underground forums and marketplaces. Research efforts have been invested in understanding the organizational structure and social activities of underground forums and marketplaces [2, 35, 46]. Motoyama et al. studied six underground forums for understanding what the products and services were exchanged [35]. Also, researchers tried to identify anonymous authors of texts in underground forums by analyzing their writing styles [2]. Zhao et al. analyzed social dynamics relevant to net-centric attacks to discover adversarial evidence [46]. Additionally, Hao et al. analyzed the reshipping service from underground forums to show how cybercriminals monetize stolen credit cards and the relationships between different actors who are involved in this scam activities [20]. Also, Thomas et al. investigated web services that create and trade fraudulent accounts by cybercriminals in underground markets [44]. Even though Radianti et al. pointed out that users in underground forums and marketplaces prefer to discuss details in private communication channels [39], private messages in the underground society have been largely overlooked.

Messaging in online social networks. People like to post diverse types of message to share their status, moods, opinions, etc., in online social networks. The motivations and purposes of messaging in online social networks have been studied [25, 29, 34]. In the meantime, researchers also investigate how the personality and motivations related to the communications in online social networks [40, 42]. Also, many works are conducted to analyze the text contents from different aspects, such as extracting and categorizing topics [28, 34, 36], analyzing the text to discover the social structure [15, 32] and showing users' sentiments [22, 24, 30, 38].

However, in underground forums, the messages are full of leetspeak, cyber jargons, and users' motivations are different from using public online social networks. In the meantime, users prefer to show their actual purposes in private messages instead of public posts.

Link prediction in online social networks. Link prediction, which has been widely used to suggest friends in online social networks [4, 11, 14, 27, 41, 45], inspires us to design our private interaction detection algorithms because the private interaction is a kind of hidden link between users in the underground forum. Even though they share similarities, link prediction in public social networks and private interaction detection in underground forums are fundamentally different: 1) most link prediction approaches are based on network topology analysis [16]. They assume if two users have shared friends it is highly possible they have or should have a direct connection. However, in underground forums, users do their best to hide their real identities. Hence, the connection between users in the underground forum is not based on the real-world identities, but the anonymous public interactions and 2) in public social networks, users usually use their real identities and profile information [18]. Nevertheless, the self-provided information in an underground forum may not be trustworthy and cannot be used for the detection [23].

8 CONCLUSION

Analyzing underground forums and marketplaces is of great importance to understand and combat cybercrime and illegal activities. Even though research efforts have been invested in understanding the organizational structure and social activities of underground forums, private messages have been overlooked. In this paper, we analyze an underground forum Nulled.io to understand what users discuss in private messages, why users are contacted privately, etc. In addition, we designed machine learning models that take the characteristics of underground forums into account to detect private interactions between users. The results showed that our models are effective in detecting private interactions and can withstand attacks.

ACKNOWLEDGMENTS

This work was supported in part by grants from the U.S. Army Research Laboratory and the Center for Cybersecurity and Digital Forensics at Arizona State University. The information reported here does not reflect the position or the policy of the funding agency or project sponsor.

REFERENCES

[1] Sadia Afroz, Vaibhav Garg, Damon McCoy, and Rachel Greenstadt. 2013. Honor among thieves: A common's analysis of cybercrime economies. In *eCrime Researchers Summit (eCRS)*.

[2] Sadia Afroz, Aylin Caliskan Islam, Ariel Stolerman, Rachel Greenstadt, and Damon McCoy. 2014. Doppelgänger finder: Taking stylometry to the underground. In *Proceedings of the IEEE Symposium on Security and Privacy*.

[3] Mohammad Al Hasan, Vineet Chaoji, Saeed Salem, and Mohammed Zaki. 2006. Link prediction using supervised learning. In *SDM06: workshop on link analysis, counter-terrorism and security*.

[4] Mohammad Al Hasan and Mohammed J Zaki. 2011. A survey of link prediction in social networks. In *Social network data analytics*.

[5] Mostafa D Awheda and Howard M Schwartz. 2016. A fuzzy reinforcement learning algorithm using a predictor for pursuit-evasion games. In *Proceedings of the IEEE International Systems Conference (SysCon)*.

[6] Fabricio Benevenuto, Gabriel Magno, Tiago Rodrigues, and Virgilio Almeida. 2010. Detecting spammers on twitter. In *Collaboration, electronic messaging, anti-abuse and spam conference (CEAS)*.

[7] Fabrício Benevenuto, Tiago Rodrigues, Meeyoung Cha, and Virgílio Almeida. 2009. Characterizing user behavior in online social networks. In *Proceedings of the ACM SIGCOMM Conference on Internet Measurement (IMC)*.

[8] Moira Burke and Robert E Kraut. 2014. Growing closer on facebook: changes in tie strength through social network site use. In *Proceedings of the ACM SIGCHI Conference on Human Factors in Computing Systems (CHI)*.

[9] Yinzhi Cao and Junfeng Yang. 2015. Towards making systems forget with machine unlearning. In *Proceedings of the IEEE Symposium on Security and Privacy*.

[10] Nitesh V Chawla. 2009. Data mining for imbalanced datasets: An overview. In *Data mining and knowledge discovery handbook*.

[11] Hsinchun Chen, Xin Li, and Zan Huang. 2005. Link prediction approach to collaborative filtering. In *Proceedings of the ACM/IEEE-CS Joint Conference on Digital Libraries (JCDL)*.

[12] Lingwei Chen, Yanfang Ye, and Thirimachos Bourlai. 2017. Adversarial Machine Learning in Malware Detection: Arms Race between Evasion Attack and Defense. In *Proceedings of the IEEE European Intelligence and Security Informatics Conference (EISIC)*.

[13] Nicolas Christin. 2013. Traveling the Silk Road: A measurement analysis of a large anonymous online marketplace. In *Proceedings of the International World Wide Web Conference (WWW)*.

[14] Aaron Clauset, Cristopher Moore, and Mark EJ Newman. 2008. Hierarchical structure and the prediction of missing links in networks. *Nature* (2008).

[15] Jana Diesner and Kathleen M Carley. 2005. Revealing social structure from texts: meta-matrix text analysis as a novel method for network text analysis. In *Causal mapping for research in information technology*.

[16] Yuxiao Dong, Jie Tang, Sen Wu, Jilei Tian, Nitesh V Chawla, Jinghai Rao, and Huanhuan Cao. 2012. Link prediction and recommendation across heterogeneous social networks. In *Proceedings of the IEEE International Conference on Data Mining (ICDM)*.

[17] Greg Durrett, Jonathan K Kummerfeld, Taylor Berg-Kirkpatrick, Rebecca S Portnoff, Sadia Afroz, Damon McCoy, Kirill Levchenko, and Vern Paxson. 2017. Identifying Products in Online Cybercrime Marketplaces: A Dataset for Fine-grained Domain Adaptation. *arXiv preprint arXiv:1708.09609* (2017).

[18] Nicole B Ellison, Charles Steinfield, and Cliff Lampe. 2007. The benefits of Facebook "friends:" Social capital and college students' use of online social network sites. *Journal of computer-mediated communication* (2007).

[19] Jason Franklin, Adrian Perrig, Vern Paxson, and Stefan Savage. 2007. An inquiry into the nature and causes of the wealth of internet miscreants.. In *Proceedings of the ACM Conference on Computer and Communications Security (CCS)*.

[20] Shuang Hao, Kevin Borgolte, Nick Nikiforakis, Gianluca Stringhini, Manuel Egele, Michael Eubanks, Brian Krebs, and Giovanni Vigna. 2015. Drops for stuff: An analysis of reshipping mule scams. In *Proceedings of the ACM Conference on Computer and Communications Security (CCS)*.

[21] Thorsten Holz, Markus Engelberth, and Felix Freiling. 2009. Learning more about the underground economy: A case-study of keyloggers and dropzones. In *Proceedings of the European Symposium on Research in Computer Security (ESORICS)*.

[22] Xia Hu, Lei Tang, Jiliang Tang, and Huan Liu. 2013. Exploiting social relations for sentiment analysis in microblogging. In *Proceedings of the ACM International Conference on Web Search and Data Mining (WSDM)*.

[23] Haruna Isah, Daniel Neagu, and Paul Trundle. 2015. Bipartite network model for inferring hidden ties in crime data. In *Proceedings of the IEEE/ACM International Conference on Advances in Social Networks Analysis and Mining (ASONAM)*.

[24] Aamera ZH Khan, Mohammad Atique, and VM Thakare. 2015. Combining lexicon-based and learning-based methods for Twitter sentiment analysis. *International Journal of Electronics, Communication and Soft Computing Science & Engineering (IJECSCSE)* (2015).

[25] Haewoon Kwak, Changhyun Lee, Hosung Park, and Sue Moon. 2010. What is Twitter, a social network or a news media?. In *Proceedings of the International World Wide Web Conference (WWW)*.

[26] Cliff AC Lampe, Nicole Ellison, and Charles Steinfield. 2007. A familiar face (book): profile elements as signals in an online social network. In *Proceedings of the ACM SIGCHI Conference on Human Factors in Computing Systems (CHI)*.

[27] David Liben-Nowell and Jon Kleinberg. 2007. The link-prediction problem for social networks. *journal of the Association for Information Science and Technology* (2007).

[28] Kar Wai Lim, Changyou Chen, and Wray Buntine. 2016. Twitter-network topic model: A full Bayesian treatment for social network and text modeling. *arXiv preprint arXiv:1609.06791* (2016).

[29] Kuan-Yu Lin and Hsi-Peng Lu. 2011. Why people use social networking sites: An empirical study integrating network externalities and motivation theory. *Computers in human behavior* (2011).

[30] Bing Liu and Lei Zhang. 2012. A survey of opinion mining and sentiment analysis. In *Mining text data*.

[31] Caroline Lo, Dan Frankowski, and Jure Leskovec. 2016. Understanding behaviors that lead to purchasing: A case study of pinterest. In *Proceedings of the ACM SIGKDD International Conference on Knowledge Discovery and Data Mining (KDD)*.

[32] Andrew McCallum, Andres Corrada-Emmanuel, and Xuerui Wang. 2005. Topic and Role Discovery in Social Networks.. In *Proceedings of the International Joint Conference on Artificial Intelligence (IJCAI)*.

[33] Ajay Modi, Zhibo Sun, Anupam Panwar, Tejas Khairnar, Ziming Zhao, Adam Doupé, Gail-Joon Ahn, and Paul Black. 2016. Towards automated threat intelligence fusion. In *Proceedings of the IEEE International Conference on Collaboration and Internet Computing (CIC)*.

[34] Meredith Ringel Morris, Jaime Teevan, and Katrina Panovich. 2010. What do people ask their social networks, and why?: a survey study of status message q&a behavior. In *Proceedings of the ACM SIGCHI Conference on Human Factors in Computing Systems (CHI)*.

[35] Marti Motoyama, Damon McCoy, Kirill Levchenko, Stefan Savage, and Geoffrey M Voelker. 2011. An analysis of underground forums. In *Proceedings of the ACM SIGCOMM Conference on Internet Measurement (IMC)*.

[36] Mor Naaman, Jeffrey Boase, and Chih-Hui Lai. 2010. Is it really about me?: message content in social awareness streams. In *Proceedings of the ACM Conference on Computer Supported Cooperative Work (CSCW)*.

[37] Minh-Thap Nguyen and Ee-Peng Lim. 2014. On predicting religion labels in microblogging networks. In *Proceedings of the ACM SIGIR Conference on Research & Development in Information Retrieval (SIGIR)*.

[38] Brendan O'Connor, Ramnath Balasubramanyan, Bryan R Routledge, Noah A Smith, et al. 2010. From tweets to polls: Linking text sentiment to public opinion time series.. In *Proceedings of the International AAAI Conference on Web and Social Media (ICWSM)*.

[39] Jaziar Radianti. 2010. A study of a social behavior inside the online black markets. In *Proceedings of the International Conference on Emerging Security Information, Systems and Technologies (SECURWARE)*.

[40] Craig Ross, Emily S Orr, Mia Sisic, Jaime M Arseneault, Mary G Simmering, and R Robert Orr. 2009. Personality and motivations associated with Facebook use. *Computers in human behavior* (2009).

[41] Salvatore Scellato, Anastasios Noulas, and Cecilia Mascolo. 2011. Exploiting place features in link prediction on location-based social networks. In *Proceedings of the ACM SIGKDD International Conference on Knowledge Discovery and Data Mining (KDD)*.

[42] Gwendolyn Seidman. 2013. Self-presentation and belonging on Facebook: How personality influences social media use and motivations. *Personality and Individual Differences* (2013).

[43] Brett Stone-Gross, Thorsten Holz, Gianluca Stringhini, and Giovanni Vigna. 2011. The Underground Economy of Spam: A Botmaster's Perspective of Coordinating Large-Scale Spam Campaigns. *LEET* (2011).

[44] Kurt Thomas, Damon McCoy, Chris Grier, Alek Kolcz, and Vern Paxson. 2013. Trafficking Fraudulent Accounts: The Role of the Underground Market in Twitter Spam and Abuse. In *Proceedings of the USENIX Security Symposium (USENIX)*.

[45] Dashun Wang, Dino Pedreschi, Chaoming Song, Fosca Giannotti, and Albert-Laszlo Barabasi. 2011. Human mobility, social ties, and link prediction. In *Proceedings of the ACM SIGKDD International Conference on Knowledge Discovery and Data Mining (KDD)*.

[46] Ziming Zhao, Gail-Joon Ahn, Hongxin Hu, and Deepinder Mahi. 2012. SocialImpact: systematic analysis of underground social dynamics. In *Proceedings of the European Symposium on Research in Computer Security (ESORICS)*.

[47] Ziming Zhao, Mukund Sankaran, Gail-Joon Ahn, Thomas J Holt, Yiming Jing, and Hongxin Hu. 2016. Mules, Seals, and Attacking Tools: Analyzing 12 Online Marketplaces. *IEEE Security & Privacy* (2016).

[48] Juan Zheng, Zhimin He, and Zhe Lin. 2017. Hybrid adversarial sample crafting for black-box evasion attack. In *Proceedings of the IEEE International Conference on Wavelet Analysis and Pattern Recognition (ICWAPR)*.

[49] Yilu Zhou, Edna Reid, Jialun Qin, Hsinchun Chen, and Guanpi Lai. 2005. US domestic extremist groups on the Web: link and content analysis. *IEEE intelligent systems* (2005).

BootKeeper: Validating Software Integrity Properties on Boot Firmware Images

Ronny Chevalier
CentraleSupélec, Inria, Univ Rennes,
CNRS, IRISA
ronny.chevalier@centralesupelec.fr

Stefano Cristalli
Università degli Studi di Milano
stefano.cristalli@studenti.unimi.it

Christophe Hauser
University of Southern California
hauser@isi.edu

Yan Shoshitaishvili
Arizona State University
yans@asu.edu

Ruoyu Wang
Arizona State University
fishw@asu.edu

Christopher Kruegel
University of California, Santa
Barbara
chris@cs.ucsb.edu

Giovanni Vigna
University of California, Santa
Barbara
vigna@cs.ucsb.edu

Danilo Bruschi
Università degli Studi di Milano
bruschi@di.unimi.it

Andrea Lanzi
Università degli Studi di Milano
andrea.lanzi@unimi.it

ABSTRACT

Boot firmware, like UEFI-compliant firmware, has been the target of numerous attacks, giving the attacker control over the entire system while being undetected. The *measured boot* mechanism of a computer platform ensures its integrity by using cryptographic measurements to detect such attacks. This is typically performed by relying on a Trusted Platform Module (TPM). Recent work, however, shows that vendors do not respect the specifications that have been devised to ensure the integrity of the firmware's loading process. As a result, attackers may bypass such measurement mechanisms and successfully load a modified firmware image while remaining unnoticed. In this paper we introduce BootKeeper, a static analysis approach verifying a set of key security properties on boot firmware images before deployment, to ensure the integrity of the measured boot process. We evaluate BootKeeper against several attacks on common boot firmware implementations and demonstrate its applicability.

CCS CONCEPTS

• **Security and privacy** → **Systems security**.

KEYWORDS

firmware, TPM, SCRTM, binary analysis

ACM Reference Format:
Ronny Chevalier, Stefano Cristalli, Christophe Hauser, Yan Shoshitaishvili, Ruoyu Wang, Christopher Kruegel, Giovanni Vigna, Danilo Bruschi, and Andrea Lanzi. 2019. BootKeeper: Validating Software Integrity Properties on Boot Firmware Images. In *Ninth ACM Conference on Data and Application Security and Privacy (CODASPY '19), March 25–27, 2019, Richardson, TX, USA.* ACM, New York, NY, USA, 11 pages. https://doi.org/10.1145/3292006.3300026

1 INTRODUCTION

One of the most critical components of every computer is the boot firmware (e.g., BIOS or UEFI-compliant firmware), which is in charge of initializing and testing the various hardware components, and then transfer execution to the Operating System (OS). As a result of its early execution, the boot firmware is a highly privileged program. Any malicious alteration of its behavior can have critical consequences on the entire system. An attacker that can control the firmware can control any parts of the software and undermine the security of the entire OS. Without any protection of the integrity of the boot firmware, we cannot assure any security properties of the software executing on the system.

To guarantee the software integrity of the machine, the Trusted Computing Group (TCG), an industry coalition formed to implement trusted computing concepts across personal computers, designed a new set of hardware components, the aim of which is to solve various hardware-level trust issues. In their specification, they define the TPM, which is composed of a co-processor that offers cryptographic functions (e.g., SHA-1, RSA, random number generator, or HMAC) and a tamper-resistant non-volatile memory used for storing cryptographic keys [33]. The TPM along with other software components together form a root of trust, which is leveraged as part of several security mechanisms, including the *measured boot* process. With measured boot, platforms with a TPM can be configured to measure every component of the boot process, including the firmware, boot loader, and kernel. Such measurement process is also called the Static Root of Trust for Measurement (SRTM).

The core of trust of the entire process is established based on the integrity of the first piece of code inside the boot firmware which is doing the first measurements, also called the Static Core Root of Trust for Measurement (SCRTM) [41]. In the event where a malicious modification of the SCRTM successfully hides from the self-measurement technique, the whole chain of trust and, consequently, the integrity of the entire system may be broken. In this direction, Butterworth et al. [4] described different examples of attacks against the SCRTM component. In particular, the authors show how a novel "tick" malware, a 51-byte patch to the SCRTM, can replay a forged measurement to the TPM, falsely indicating that the BIOS is genuine. These attacks take advantage of the fact that some vendors do not measure the SCRTM code, thus allowing an attacker to modify it and to forge measurements without being detected.

Recent platforms incorporate an immutable, hardware protected SCRTM [11, 23]. Intel Boot Guard and HP Sure Start are immutable SCRTMs which measure and verify, at boot time, the integrity of the BIOS image before executing it. Such technologies are not directly vulnerable to the aforementioned attacks, since their code cannot be modified by an attacker.[1] Both technologies, however, are only available in recent Intel and HP platforms, *leaving previous hardware implementations, or devices of other vendors, vulnerable against forged measurements*. In such implementations, since the SCRTM is not hardware protected, *it is usually attached to the firmware image itself during the firmware update process*. Even when the firmware image is signed, attacks may compromise this process [14], and consequently allow an attacker to modify both the firmware code and the SCRTM.

In order to solve these challenges in validating the SCRTM code, we design a self-contained approach based on static analysis at the binary level, which is able, starting from a boot firmware image, to validate the correctness of the measurement process. Our system verifies software properties on the SCRTM code embedded in firmware images, including: (1) the completeness of firmware code measurements in terms of fingerprinted memory regions, (2) the correctness of cryptographic functions implemented[2] inside the SCRTM (e.g., SHA-1), and (3) the correctness of the SCRTM's control flow. More in detail, the first property ensures that the code of the entire firmware is measured correctly by the SCRTM, i.e., that none of the instructions to be executed at runtime will be missed by the measurement process. The second property ensures that the implementation of cryptographic functions inside the SCRTM is correct. The third property validates the correctness of the measurement operations performed by the SCRTM in terms of execution order. It also guarantees the atomicity of operations occurring between memory fingerprinting and write operations performed on the TPM component (i.e., ensuring that what is measured is what is written to the TPM). Altogether, this set of properties can prevent attacks aiming to elude the measurement process, and it guarantees that the integrity of a firmware image is properly verified during the *measured boot* process.

We implement a prototype of our system, dubbed BootKeeper, based on the angr program analysis framework [6, 29]. We evaluate our system on different open source boot firmware images, and we implement different attacks against the firmware to show the efficacy of our approach. Our paper makes the following contributions:

- We devise a set of software properties that can be used for validating the measurement process and mitigate firmware attacks aimed to subvert the entire system.
- We design and implement BootKeeper, a binary analysis approach to detect and prevent measurement boot firmware attacks in different attack scenarios.
- We perform experimental evaluation against different attacks and several boot firmware implementations to demonstrate the effectiveness of our approach.

2 BACKGROUND

In this section, we introduce the background technology needed to understand our approach. We first describe the principles of the TPM, then we describe the UEFI specifications and some of the software/hardware components involved in the boot measurement process.

2.1 Trusted Platform Module (TPM)

The TPM specification defines a co-processor offering cryptographic features (e.g., SHA-1, RSA, random number generator, or HMAC), and tamper-resistant storage for cryptographic keys [33].

The TPM provides a minimum of 16 Platform Configuration Register (PCR) which are 160-bit wide registers used to store the measurements done by the SCRTM (usually SHA-1 hashes). The design of these registers allows an unlimited amount of measurements and prevents an attacker from overwriting them with arbitrary values. In order to do this, the only possible operation is *extend*:

$$PCR_i = H(PCR_i \mathbin{\|} m)$$

Where PCR_i is the ith PCR register, H is the hash function and m the new measurement. The TPM *concatenates* each new measurement sent with the previous value of the register, then it hashes the result, which becomes the new value of the register. This mechanism is crucial to establishing a chain of trust, since the only way to obtain a given measurement value from a PCR is to reproduce the same series of measurements in the same order. The measured boot process relies on this mechanism to guarantee that a given software platform is valid and has not been tampered with.

The TPM also relies on these measurements to provide specific features (e.g., secure storage or remote attestation). For instance, with the sealing operation, the TPM offers the ability to encrypt data, with a key only known to the TPM, and it binds the decryption to the PCRs values. During the decryption (i.e., unsealing), the TPM only decrypts the data if the PCRs values match the ones used during the encryption. One common use case for the sealing operation is to store the disk encryption key. It ensures that the disk is decrypted only if the platform has booted with the expected hardware and software, and if no attacker tampered with the boot process (e.g., an evil maid attack).

2.2 Static Core Root of Trust for Measurement

The SCRTM is responsible for the first measurement sent to the TPM in the PCR0 register and it is considered trusted by default on the system. Since the default values of the PCRs are known

---

[1] Nonetheless, Intel Boot Guard has been shown to be vulnerable to some attacks as well [19].
[2] Vendors typically implement the cryptographic functionalities used as part of the measurement process in software.

(either 0x00...0x00 or 0xFF...0xFF), the entire trust in the SRTM relies on the SCRTM. If it is possible for an attacker to modify the SCRTM, then it is also possible for the attacker to forge the first measurement, and the next one, etc.

Therefore, the TCG PC client specific implementation [31] states that the SCRTM must be an immutable portion of the firmware. The specification defines immutability such that only an approved agent and method can modify the SCRTM. Most firmware fulfill this requirement by using signed updates, because the SCRTM can only be modified if the update is coming from the vendor. Recent firmware fulfill the requirement using an immutable hardware protected SCRTM [11, 23]. Unfortunately, legacy platforms do not provide signed updates, or do not require them. Furthermore, Kallenberg et al. [12], and Wojtczuk and Tereshkin [37] have successfully exploited multiple vulnerabilities in the implementation of signed firmware updates by vendors, allowing an attacker to update the firmware with a malicious one. Finally, if the private key of the vendor is compromised, the platform is vulnerable.

2.3 Unified Extensible Firmware Interface

In 2005, 11 industry leading technology companies created the Unified Extensible Firmware Interface (UEFI) forum which defines specifications for interfaces [36] used by the OS to communicate with the firmware [42] and Platform Initialization (PI) specifications [35] which define the required interfaces for the components in the firmware, allowing multiple providers to create different parts. UEFI specifications are about the interfaces, while UEFI PI specifications are about building UEFI-compliant firmware. Manufacturers are now providing, as boot firmware replacing the Basic Input/Output System (BIOS), UEFI-compliant firmware images. UEFI and PI specifications define seven phases, as illustrated in Figure 1, which describe the boot process of a platform:

(1) The Security phase (SEC) is the initial code running, it switches from real mode to protected mode, initializes the memory space to run stack-based C code, and discovers, verifies and executes the next phase.
(2) The Pre-EFI Initialization phase (PEI) initializes permanent memory, handles the different states of the system (e.g., recovery after suspending), executes the next phase.
(3) The Driver Execution Environment phase (DXE) discovers and executes drivers which initialize platform components.
(4) The Boot Device Selection phase (BDS) chooses the boot loader to execute.
(5) The Transient System Load phase (TLS) handles special applications or executes the boot loader from the OS.
(6) The Runtime phase (RT) is when the OS executing, but there are still runtime services of firmware available to communicate with the OS.
(7) The After Life phase (AL) takes control back over the OS when it has shutdown.

The TCG specifies requirements for the measurement of UEFI-compliant firmware in TPM PCRs [34]. The SCRTM in UEFI-compliant firmware is generally formed by the SEC and PEI phases [42], although no strict requirements about its location are specified in the TCG specification as it can also be the entire BIOS [31]. Moreover, in recent platforms, the SCRTM is a hardware-protected component,

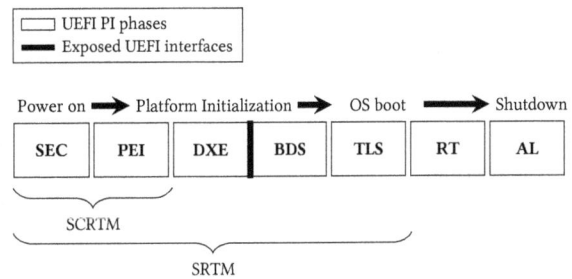

Figure 1: UEFI PI phases with the ones corresponding to the SCRTM and SRTM

outside of the BIOS, that performs measurements on the BIOS before its execution [11, 23]. In our work, however, we only consider a non-hardware protected SCRTM.

3 APPROACH OVERVIEW

BootKeeper is an offline analysis approach leveraging state-of-the-art binary analysis techniques to evaluate the validity and correctness of boot firmware images.

3.1 Threat Model

Our approach targets systems that implement measured boot protection mechanisms by using Trusted Computing technology. From a high-level perspective, an attacker may attempt to tamper with a system's firmware in two ways:

- By exploiting weaknesses of the SCRTM, e.g., a buggy or incorrect SCRTM may only perform partial measurements. In this case, an attacker may be able to inject code within the vendor's firmware image in the non-measured portions of the memory.
- By directly injecting a malicious SCRTM, the attacker may spoof the vendor's golden measurement values to pretend that the legitimate firmware is in place, while executing a malicious version of it.

By successfully circumventing the measurement process, an attacker may not only compromise the integrity of the system while tricking the attestation procedure into reporting a legitimate software platform, but it may also leak secret information from the TPM such as cryptographic keys used for full disk encryption (as used by Microsoft Windows's BitLocker, among other software products relying on this mechanism).

In the remainder of this paper, we assume the following attacker model:

(1) The attacker does not have physical access to the system.
(2) The attacker does not have any form of privileged access to the system (neither local or remote, i.e., no control over the OS).
(3) The system itself has not been infected prior to the attack and is non-malicious (i.e., the SCRTM is invoked from a non-malicious environment).
(4) The SCRTM's code does not implement user input mechanisms (but such mechanisms may be implemented as part of later stages of the EFI boot process).

(5) The attacker has the ability and sufficient knowledge about the target platform to craft malicious firmware images, i.e., access to the vendors' official firmware images, and knowledge about the platform's golden values (i.e., correct measurement values), or the ability to obtain those by reverse engineering.

(6) The attacker may spread malicious images online (e.g., by compromising the vendor's website or through third party websites such as user forums).

(7) Optionally, the attacker may remotely interfere with the automated firmware update process that comes with some systems by compromising the download site, or by mounting a man in the middle attack when applicable (e.g., if this process does not check the validity of SSL certificates), to trick the remote system into applying a firmware update using an attacker-chosen malicious image.

3.1.1 Signature Verification. In order to successfully install a malicious firmware image in the target system, an attacker needs to bypass eventual signature verification mechanisms in place. While this aspect is outside of the scope of this paper, we briefly demonstrate the practicality of this assumption as follows.

A good practice when releasing software updates is to rely on cryptographic signatures in order to guarantee the integrity of the new software image before or during the installation process. Unfortunately, this process is often imperfect, as several vendors do not implement proper signature verification mechanisms, leaving gaps for an attacker to use a forged firmware image. In other situations, attackers may use a stolen certificate [14] to sign malicious firmware images, or may remotely exploit a vulnerability in the firmware update routine, to bypass the signature checks. In the remainder of this paper, we assume that the signature verification mechanism is either absent, or vulnerable.

3.2 Analysis Steps

Our analysis approach relies on the verification of a set of key properties, which we describe in more detail the remainder of this section.

3.2.1 Code Integrity Properties (CIP). The SCRTM code is always implemented with two main fundamental operations: (1) an operation of fingerprinting, which scans the code regions in memory (e.g., using SHA-1) and (2) a TPM write operation, storing the computed fingerprints in the TPM. We define these two operations as the building blocks of any SCRTM measurement process performed on the platform.

In order to elude the measurement process, an attacker may act at two different levels.

- Firstly, as illustrated in Figure 2, the attacker may modify the fingerprint function (e.g., code or parameters) to generate spoofed measurement values which correspond to valid golden values (i.e., values corresponding to correct measurements on the vendor's firmware) even though the original firmware code is modified.

- Secondly, the attacker may modify the results of the fingerprint function just before these are written to the TPM.

The *tick* and the *flea* attacks, described by Butterworth et al. [4], are concrete examples of such attacks.

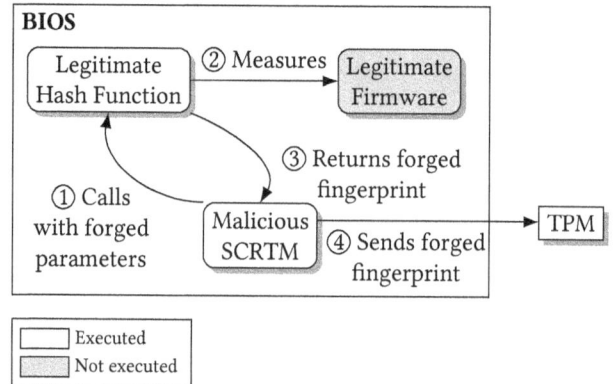

Figure 2: Example of a measurement-spoofing attack where an attacker sends a legitimate fingerprint of non-executed firmware.

In order to prevent these attacks, our system verifies the three following properties:

(1) *The authenticity of cryptographic hash functions.* Regardless of any potential implementation variants, our system must be able to verify the authenticity of the code used as part of the fingerprinting measurement process. BootKeeper leverages binary analysis techniques to verify that the correct hash function is indeed used as part of the firmware's fingerprinting code.

(2) *The atomicity of the measurement process.* A correct SCRTM implementation should also guarantee the atomicity of its measurement process, i.e., that the fingerprinting and TPM write operations are invoked sequentially in the correct order, and that the integrity of the measurement values if preserved between these two operations. In order to verify this property, BootKeeper constructs a Control-Flow Graph (CFG) of the SCRTM, and detects eventual operations modifying the measurement results before those are written to the TPM.[3]

These two properties ensure the correctness of the SCRTM's code measurements process. In addition to these, BootKeeper also ensures that the firmware under analysis does not present risks of certain classes of runtime attacks, as described below.

3.2.2 Code Execution Integrity Property (CEIP). Even if properties (1) and (2) are guaranteed, an attacker may attempt to alter the control-flow of the SCRTM by redirecting the execution to malicious code hidden in the binary firmware image. Fortunately, UEFI firmware runs in an execution environment protected by Data Execution Prevention (DEP). In other words, an attacker cannot trivially execute code injected in arbitrary sections of the binary image.

---

[3]In practice, such operations may either correspond to malicious code attempting to forge measurement values, or to benign buggy code reporting erroneous measurements.

In the execution context of the SCRTM, an attacker does not have the ability to inject code at runtime since the SCRTM's code does not implement user input mechanisms and the SCRTM code is invoked from a non-malicious environment (see rules 3 and 4 of our attacker model in subsection 3.1). However, it remains possible for the attackers to hide code within the binary firmware image, and to attempt to trigger its execution at runtime.

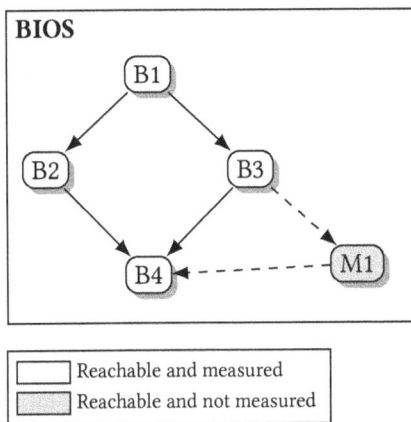

Figure 3: Example of an incomplete measurement of the firmware where reachable (malicious) code is not measured.

BootKeeper addresses this family of attacks as well by relying on an additional property:

(3) *Completeness of the measurements.* The SCRTM must guarantee the completeness of the measurements of the firmware code memory regions. More in detail, every memory region belonging to the CFG of the SCRTM must be measured and reported to the TPM component. By doing so, attempts to hide malicious code within non-measured memory regions is detected, as represented in Figure 3, showing benign (B) and malicious (M) basic blocks forming a CFG.

We emphasize that BootKeeper does not rely on a-priori knowledge of the legitimate CFG of firmware images. Instead, the goal of BootKeeper is to ensure that *all reachable code* will be *correctly* measured and reported to the TPM at runtime. As such, the detection of malicious code is a two-stage process: a static part (BootKeeper) which ensures that the verification code is correctly implemented, and a dynamic part (the measured boot process), which relies on those mechanisms.

Recall the attacker model presented in subsection 3.1: (3) the SCRTM executes in a non-malicious environment (i.e., the initial state of the system is non-malicious, only firmware images are) and (4) it does not implement I/O mechanisms. As a consequence, dynamic code injection attacks are specifically excluded.

4 SYSTEM DESIGN AND IMPLEMENTATION

In this section, we present the algorithmic properties of our analysis components.

4.1 Code Integrity Properties (CIP) Validation

The process of validating the Code Integrity Properties presented in subsubsection 3.2.1 relies on four analysis steps: (1) Detecting TPM write operations inside the firmware code, (2) Detecting hash functions inside the firmware code, (3) Validating the authenticity of hash functions, (4) Validating the atomicity of the measurement process. We now describe how the system achieves each step of the analysis.

4.1.1 TPM Write Operation Detection. The first step of our analysis is to identify the TPM write operations inside the firmware code. Such operations can be identified by searching for standard API prototypes. According to the TPM specification version 1.2 [31, 32], such functions must use a fixed address (0xFED40000 is the default), along with an offset used for distinguishing among different operations (e.g., read and write) on the TPM registers.

Unfortunately, we cannot predict how the compiler organizes the instructions or how the code of the firmware performs the write accesses. Developers tend to create abstraction layers (e.g., to avoid redundancy or to have a modular code), and may use different optimization flags for the compilation of the firmware. As a result of this, TPM read and write operations do not straightforwardly appear as an offset from the specified constant address value in the binary executable version of the firmware. Therefore, in order to tackle this problem and find a state of the program where a write access to the TPM known address happens, we leverage symbolic execution, starting at the entry point of the firmware, and record every instruction writing at the specified address (0xFED40024 in our case). This step of symbolic execution allows BootKeeper to resolve computed addresses for which it would be extremely difficult to reason about in a purely static setup. We leverage the angr [6] platform to perform symbolic execution. During symbolic execution, the system tracks the state of registers and memory throughout program execution along with the constraints on those variables. Whenever a conditional branch is reached, the execution follows both paths while applying constraints to the program state to reflect whether the condition evaluates to True or False. At the end of this analysis step, BootKeeper has obtained a list of addresses in the firmware corresponding to the TPM write operations, if any such operation is present. If the system does not find any TPM write operation, it flags the firmware image as non-valid.

4.1.2 Detecting Hash Functions. The second step of our analysis is to identify hash functions among the functions used by the firmware image to elaborate the measurement values. We apply the following algorithm. The analyzer starts from the TPM write operations and works iteratively on the instructions flow in reverse order. To this end, we leverage a static backward approach [15]. where for each identified TPM write operation, our analyzer computes a backward slice starting from the sensitive data. Sensitive data are the parameters of the TPM write operations, in our case the measurements value of the hash function stored in a particular memory region. The aim of this backward slicing analysis step is to identify modifications on sensitive data, and to find all the data sources from which the modified data is derived.

The backward slice technique allows us to focus our analysis only on the instructions that lead to a single TPM write access, which is important for two reasons. First, for performance reasons, focusing on a subset of the program greatly improves the time needed to perform further analyses. Second, and more importantly, it ensures that the TPM write access is connected to a measurement computed earlier in the execution (i.e., not inserted in an ad-hoc manner). Hence, given a set of instructions related to the TPM write access, BootKeeper detects if an actual measurement is present.

The output of this analysis step is a set of traces corresponding to instructions correlated with the TPM write operations parameters. Such traces could also be leveraged to locate the hash function code as well. However, it is worth noting that the backward slicing algorithm returns an over-approximation of the instructions leading to the program point where the TPM measurements are sent, and therefore, it might include unrelated instructions. For example, functions which simply move computed hash values from one memory structure to another may also be whitelisted by this analysis. For this reason, we cannot simply rely on this technique to accurately locate the hash functions themselves, and we leverage a different approach to precisely locate those, as presented in the following paragraph.

4.1.3 Validating the Authenticity of Hash Functions. After Boot-Keeper has identified the set of instructions related to a particular TPM operation, it extracts the corresponding blocks and attempts to recognize one of the possible valid hash function (e.g., SHA-1). In order to automatically identify cryptographic functions within binary code, we leverage the approach presented by Lestringant et al. [17] which relies on Data Flow Graph (DFG) isomorphism. From a high-level perspective, this approach compares the code structure of known functions with the code structure of unknown functions, to determine if these implement the same algorithm. This approach first employs a normalization step (based on a code rewrite mechanism), which is designed to increase the detection capability by erasing the peculiarities of each instance of an algorithm. Then, by relying on a sub-graph isomorphism algorithm, the normalized DFG is compared to that of known reference functions. We chose this approach to recognize functions of well-known libraries which are used in real-world boot firmware images (including Crypto++ and OpenSSL [21]).

BootKeeper leverages this technique starting from the instruction traces highlighted in the previous analysis step. From there, it creates a DFG for each corresponding function of the firmware image involved in the trace, and attempts to match the signature of a standard hash function, such as the SHA-1 implementation of libOpenSSL. The output of this analysis step is the set of basic blocks belonging to the identified hash function. If no known hash function is found, then *BootKeeper flags the firmware image as non-valid.*

4.1.4 Validating the Atomicity Property. The final step involved in validating code integrity is to ensure that no modification of the computed measurements occurs before those are written to the TPM. From the instruction traces obtained during the backward slicing step (subsubsection 4.1.2), BootKeeper executes the corresponding code paths symbolically, from the hash function's return instruction to the TPM write operation, and rules out the presence of instructions modifying the computed hash value. In order to detect such instructions, BootKeeper performs a last step

of forward reaching definition analysis on each identified code path to ensure that the value stored in the TPM indeed corresponds to the return value of the correct hash function. If any instruction on a given path modifies the measurement value, the atomicity property is violated. In this case, the firmware image is reported as invalid, and BootKeeper reports the faulty instruction and program path.

4.2 Code Execution Integrity Validation

Recall that, in addition to verifying the correctness of the measurement process, BootKeeper also evaluates the risks of runtime attacks through a Code Execution Integrity Property (CEIP) described earlier in Section 3.2.2, which consists in the completeness of measurements.

Conceptually, if the measurement process is incomplete, i.e., leaving out portions of the code section, it becomes possible for an attacker to "hide" malicious code in the non-fingerprinted areas, hence the importance of this property.

4.2.1 Completeness of the Measurements. BootKeeper ensures that every function in the CFG of the SCRTM is measured. The acute reader may wonder what becomes of basic blocks of code which is deemed non-reachable by the control-flow recovery analysis: this point is discussed in section 6. The CFG is computed by a recursive algorithm which disassembles and analyzes each basic block, identifies its possible exits (i.e., successors) and adds them to the graph. It repeats this analysis recursively until no new exits are identified. CFG recovery has one fundamental challenge: indirect jumps. Indirect jumps occur when the code transfers control flow to a target represented by a value in a register or a memory location (e.g., `jmp %eax`). Indirect jumps can be categorized in two main classes: (1) Computed, an example could be an application that uses values in a register or memory to determine an index into a jump table stored in memory; (2) Runtime binding, i.e., function pointers which jump targets are determined at runtime. BootKeeper leverages state-of-the-art analysis techniques for control-flow recovery, as available in the `angr` framework [6]. This process leverages a combination of forced execution, backwards slicing, and symbolic execution to recover, to the extent possible, all jump targets of each indirect jump. While it may not always be possible to recover all jump targets in complex software projects, it is practical in the context of a boot firmware's SCRTM due to the minimal aspect of such a code base. A more detailed discussion of this point and the practical limitations that it may involve is provided in section 6.

Once BootKeeper has obtained a CFG of the SCRTM, it proceeds to verify the coverage of the SCRTM in terms of code fingerprinting. In order to do so, BootKeeper analyses all input values passed to the fingerprinting functions (i.e., hash function identified in subsubsection 4.1.3) to determine the address and size of the memory areas used to compute the measurements. At this point, BootKeeper has statically identified the addresses and sizes of the memory regions that will be fingerprinted by the SCRTM at runtime. Its next step is to ensure that all reachable code in the SCRTM's CFG does indeed fall within the measured memory regions. In order to do so, Boot-Keeper verifies that the address of each basic block belonging to the CFG falls within that range. If it is not the case, it means that a part of the firmware's code will not be measured correctly, and *flags the firmware image as non-valid.*

By ensuring that all the reachable code in the CFG is indeed measured by the SCRTM, BootKeeper prevents firmware modification attacks. where malicious code is inserted within the executable paths of the firmware's code.

5 EXPERIMENTAL EVALUATION

This section presents our experimental results. Our evaluation metrics cover multiple attack vectors representing a large span of the attack surface against the SCRTM. These include the ability of our prototype to identify and recover the location of TPM write instructions, the effectiveness of our approach to detect the presence of forged TPM measurements, and to detect possible hidden code areas which are left unmeasured. In addition to this, we also evaluate the robustness of our analysis against various compiler optimization settings.

5.1 Experimental Setup

We evaluate BootKeeper on two real-world implementations of boot firmware used in the industry, as well as a custom-crafted malicious firmware implementing state-of-the-art attacks.

(1) SeaBIOS [20], a native x86 BIOS implementation with TPM support. It also supports standard BIOS features and calling interfaces that are implemented by a typical proprietary x86 BIOS implementations. This project is meant to provide an improved and more easily extendable implementation in comparison to the proprietary counterparts which come as stock firmware on standard x86 hardware, and can be deployed as replacement firmware on a variety of motherboards.

(2) EDK II [30], a modern, cross-platform firmware platform supported by a number of real Intel and ARM hardware platforms. It is a component of Intel's TianoCore (Intel's reference implementation of UEFI). Major vendors (e.g., Apple, ARM, or HP) contribute to its development, and it serves as a basis for a number of proprietary UEFI-compliant firmware implementations.

(3) A custom-crafted malicious firmware image which we implemented to reproduce multiple variants of the state-of-the-art attacks introduced by Butterworth et al. [4].

For validating cryptographic functions, we are using firmware (EDK II) that implements the SHA-1 function of the OpenSSL [21] libraries and gcc as a compiler.

5.2 TPM Write Access Detection

We evaluated BootKeeper against SeaBIOS, EDK II, and our custom firmware. Our hypothesis is that complex firmware implementations, like SeaBIOS and EDK II, use abstraction layers which tend to obfuscate TPM write instructions, i.e., these do not exhibit such instructions in the form of a fixed address corresponding to the specification (e.g., mov 0xfed40024, al). Additionally, these abstraction layers may invoke several functions to initialize data structures, perform hardware tests, use loop structures or handle different types of errors, thus creating many paths, potentially leading our analysis to path explosion during its symbolic execution phase. In order to test the resiliency of our approach against the aforementioned intricacies, but also against compiler optimizations, we evaluated

Table 1: Detection of the function writing the measurements

Optimization flags	Custom firmware	EDK II	SeaBIOS
-O0	●	○	✗
-O1	●	○	●
-O2	●	●	●
-O3	●	●	●
-Os	●	●	●

● : detected ○ : not detected ✗ : error

BootKeeper in the context of multiple compiler optimization settings. For each firmware implementation, we produced 5 variants using different optimization flags: -O1 to -O3 which optimize for speed, -Os which optimizes for size, and -O0 for no optimization. This process generates 15 firmware variants. We present the results in Table 1.

BootKeeper can successfully detect the TPM write access in 80% of all cases (12 out of 15). During this evaluation phase, we set an analysis timeout threshold of 10 minutes.

It is worth noting that BootKeeper found all the write access instructions within all the tested variants, with the notable exception of *unoptimized* EDK II images. We explain this observation by the fact that a lesser optimization level means more instructions to execute, more loops and therefore more likelihood of path explosion during symbolic analysis. While extending the analysis timeout threshold would be a viable option, we argue that vendors typically compile their code with size optimizations (using -Os) when releasing firmware for production use, to reduce memory footprint, in which case our approach succeeds under the 10 minutes threshold.

In the case of SeaBIOS, the analysis results are missing in the situation where no optimization is used (-O0). Unfortunately, a bug in SeaBIOS prevented the code from compiling with this optimization level at the time of our evaluation, hence we could not test it. Nonetheless, BootKeeper can successfully detect TPM write operations in SeaBIOS in all other optimization settings.

In summary, these experiments demonstrate that our approach can correctly detect the TPM write operations even in intricate cases, in real-world firmware implementations, from legacy BIOS to recent UEFI-compliant firmware.

5.3 Forged TPM Measurements Detection

In order to evaluate the effectiveness of our approach against state-of-the-art attacks, we reproduced multiple variants of the *tick* attack, described by Butterworth et al. [4]. Each developed attack variant attempts to forge the measurements sent to the TPM by relying on several techniques: (1) attacking the SHA-1 function, (2) leaving out non-measured code, (3) modifying the TPM parameters. We now describe how BootKeeper performs against these attacks.

Hash Function Validation. A first attack attempts to subvert the hash function results. In order to test this attack, we create two firmware versions: one without a SHA-1 function, and another with a modified version of SHA-1 which returns a tampered hash value. In either case, BootKeeper reports no match when generating signatures for the function defined inside the instruction traces (compared against a generated database of common cryptographic implementations from Crypto++ and libOpenSSL) and reports a violation of the property "valid hash function".

Completeness of the Measurement. We evaluate this property by implementing an attack that can modify the firmware's code by including new code to the CFG of the program. More specifically, we add new malicious functions to a non-measured code area that is invoked before returning from the SCRTM code. Since this code is not included in any measurement performed by the hash function, BootKeeper can detect it by ensuring that every part of the CFG is correctly measured (as described previously in subsubsection 4.2.1).

Atomicity Property. In order to validate the atomicity property, we define a scenario where an attacker properly measures the firmware with the correct SHA-1 function, but then tampers with the results by overwriting the measurements with other values before sending those to the TPM, thus violating the atomicity property of the measurement operations. During the analysis, BootKeeper can fetch the parameters of the hash function, and more importantly the address of the pointer where the hash is stored. Then, by performing the symbolic execution step described in subsubsection 4.1.4, it can detect the malicious instruction responsible for overwriting the measurements.

In order to fully reflect practical analysis challenges, we also consider the case where an attacker attempts to trick the analysis by incorporating a real measurement using the correct hash function, and later writing the measured value somewhere else before sending a forged value to the TPM. We reproduce this attack scenario to evaluate the resilience of our analysis step presented in Section 4.1.4 against the presence of false positives involved by the backward slicing algorithm. In our evaluation, false positives indeed occur, but these are effectively filtered by the following step of forward reaching definition analysis (as expected). In this situation again, BootKeeper can detect the attack, and report the malicious instruction responsible for overwriting the measurements.

5.4 Performance

While performance is not critical in the context of an offline analysis setting, we demonstrate the practicality of BootKeeper in terms of analysis time and memory usage. In the following, we use a valid firmware for evaluation, and measure the required amount of time BootKeeper takes to proceed, while monitoring the peak of RAM usage. In this experiment, we use a single-thread on an Intel Xeon E312 with 64GB of RAM. The results presented in Table 2 were obtained by running this experiment 100 times, and represent the mean, minimum, maximum values and the standard deviation of both the runtime (in milliseconds) and the RAM usage (in megabytes). Executing the entire analysis (i.e., validating the firmware) takes on average 1 minute and 48 seconds. The memory usage peaks at 522 megabytes.

6 DISCUSSION

BootKeeper is a purely static approach relying on advanced binary program techniques to analyze firmware images. As any static approach, it comes with some challenges. In this section, we describe

Table 2: Time and RAM usage for firmware analysis

Type		Minimum	Maximum	Mean	Standard deviation
Time	(ms)	103 950	108 760	105 704	849
RAM	(MB)	522.3	522.8	522.7	0.1

in more detail the nature of these challenges, and how BootKeeper addresses those. Finally, we point to some practical limits of our approach and propose alternative research directions of interest.

6.1 Theoretical Limitations

In order to detect violations of the properties introduced in Section 3, BootKeeper relies on a combination of state-of-the-art static analysis techniques, which together provide the basis for implementing the verification algorithms presented in Section 4. These techniques, however, are subject to theoretical limits, which prevents our approach from reasoning about certain classes of properties in all possible situations.

BootKeeper relies in particular on:

- Static CFG recovery to determine the set of possible execution paths of a firmware image. The CFG obtained from binary analysis is neither sound nor complete (the general problem of deciding if an arbitrary path in a program is executable is undecidable [22]).
- Symbolic execution and constraint solving, to reason about the possible concrete values of memory and registers at arbitrary points of the execution. Symbolic execution is subject to the well-known state explosion problem due to its exponential growing nature, and the general problem of constraint (SMT) solving is NP complete.
- Data-flow analysis, to isolate program paths involving measurement values, to generate program slices in order to isolate the instructions affecting these values, and more generally, to detect faulty operations. Reasoning about data-flow at the binary level requires accurate models of data structure recovery, and is subject to the pointer aliasing problem [22].

Our approach inherits from these general limitations. We discuss the practical impact of these theoretical limitations in subsection 6.2 below.

6.2 Practical Impact

The following is a discussion of the practical impact of the aforementioned limitations in our approach.

6.2.1 False Positives. In the case where the CFG is too conservative and includes an overestimate of possible code paths in the graph, BootKeeper will accordingly operate conservatively during the verification of property 3, i.e., the completeness of measurements. While this may lead to false positives in certain circumstances, we stress that the CFG we obtain from a binary has a basic-block level granularity. In comparison, vendors typically scan entire memory regions corresponding to sections from the firmware binary. *Why not just measure entire sections then?* Our approach is more fine-grained, and aims to ensure that the vendor conforms to at least a defined minimal code coverage corresponding to (an estimation) of the possible execution paths.

In the case of an incomplete CFG between the return value of the hash function used in the measurements and the subsequent TPM write operation, BootKeeper will not be able to compute a backward slice and therefore will not be able to validate property 2, i.e., the atomicity of the measurement process. In this case, *it will flag the image as malicious*, thus generating a false positive.

6.2.2 False Negatives. Similarly, the CFG may miss edges in the graph corresponding, such as indirect jumps caused by complex instances of runtime binding which cannot be resolved even with symbolic execution. This may happen, among other possible cases, when external information (i.e., external to the program) is required to compute the jump target. The presence of such obfuscated or evasive code in early stages of firmware execution is, by itself, an excellent indicator of maliciousness which our approach could be extended with.

When such constructs are benign and part of the official vendor's firmware, an attacker may succeed in hiding a payload P if: 1) the SCRTM omits one portion of executable memory M_1 during the measurements, 2) BootKeeper is missing a part of the CFG corresponding to a set of basic blocks mapped in memory during runtime as M_2 (in practice, M_2 may not be contiguous), and the following holds true:

$$M1 \cap M2 \neq \emptyset \wedge |M_1 \cap M_2| \geq sizeof(P)$$

Without ruling out the possibility of strong attacker specifically challenging state-of-the-art static analysis techniques, we estimate that BootKeeper significantly raises the bar for an attacker to circumvent the measurement process, and we consider our approach practical in the context of a large span of possible attacks.

The presented limitations are intrinsic to any static approach, and cannot trivially be addressed without additional knowledge of the runtime environment. In the next section, we discuss possible alternatives to overcome these limitations.

6.3 Alternative Solutions

In order to analyze the program paths involved in firmware during execution in a dynamic setting, an emulation of all the hardware components involved during the platform initialization process would be necessary. Implementing such a system is a cumbersome engineering task, especially if numerous targets need to be supported. An alternative approach is to directly instrument the hardware to dump the state of registers and memory as the firmware executes, the knowledge of which would ease offline analysis. Similar to this is the Avatar approach [39] which selectively switches between different execution models, in a setup which is backed by the physical hardware.

While relevant to this discussion, neither of these approaches fits within the scope of this paper. In comparison, BootKeeper requires no hardware nor custom hardware models.

6.4 Obfuscation

Static binary program analysis techniques are vulnerable to the presence of obfuscation, and it is possible that a malicious firmware author could attempt to attack BootKeeper in this manner. For instance, Sharif et al. [27] obfuscate conditional code by using the result of a hash function as a condition replacement. Since cryptographic hash functions have the pre-image resistance property, it is impossible for constraints solvers to solve all the constraints generated by the operations of the hash function.

These weaknesses are inherent to any tool relying on static program analysis [5, 28, 38].

In the context of boot firmware, the problem related to obfuscation is two-fold. First, genuine vendors could use obfuscation techniques to protect their code against reverse engineering. Secondly, by relying on obfuscation techniques, an attacker could attempt to defend against automated program analysis. While the former would affect BootKeeper, the latter may be used as an indicator malice.

7 RELATED WORK

To the best of our knowledge, John Heasman developed the first public BIOS rootkit by modifying Advanced Configuration and Power Interface (ACPI) tables stored in the BIOS [9], and he also showed how to make a persistent rootkit by re-flashing the expansion Read-Only Memory (ROM) of a Peripheral Component Interconnect (PCI) device [10]. Other attacks have been performed since then, Anibal Sacco and Alfredo Ortega discussed how to inject malicious code in Phoenix Award BIOS [24] and Jonathan Brossard showed the practicability of infecting different kinds of firmware [2]. In addition to papers and proof of concepts of attacks, some malware is also taking advantage of the lack of security of the boot firmware. For example, the Chernobyl virus [8], which appeared in 1999, tried to overwrite the BIOS to make it unbootable. In 2011, the malware called Mebromi [18] re-flashed the BIOS of its victims to later write a malicious Master Boot Record (MBR) which infected the OS even when it was re-installed from scratch.

All these attacks can be detected if the vendor is trustworthy, a TPM device is present and used correctly. Several misconfiguration and design issues, however, show that the TPM can be attacked as well. In this direction, Butterworth et al. [4] demonstrated a replay-attack that forges the measurement sent to the TPM to fake an uncorrupted BIOS in case of non-respect of the specifications and recommendations. Bruschi et al. [3] also showed a replay-attack in an authorization protocol of the TPM. Sadeghi et al. [25] and Butterworth et al. [4] revealed that some TPM implementations do not meet the TCG specifications which may have critical security implications. Kauer [13] also demonstrated a TPM reset attack which allows an attacker to forge the PCR values.

Several approaches have been proposed to improve the TPM technology and the boot firmware integrity techniques. For example, Bernhard Kauer proposed a counter measure [13] to the reset attack on the TPM by using a Dynamic Root of Trust for Measurement (DRTM). In the direction of firmware security, dynamic analysis using symbolic execution has been extensively used to find vulnerabilities in firmware [1, 7, 16, 28, 40]. More related to our work, Bazhaniuk et al. [1] used an approach to detect vulnerabilities in boot firmware. Our work is orthogonal to such approach and focuses on boot firmware phases where vulnerabilities are not detected or fixed by the vendor and they can be used by an attacker to tamper with the boot process (e.g., to forge PCRs values).

Butterworth et al. [4] designed a timing-based attestation at the BIOS level as an alternative to the hashing of the firmware. Such a technique provides a reliable way to attest the integrity of a platform even if the attacker has the same privilege level as the SCRTM. The idea, adapted from previous work on timing-based attestation [26], is that in the absence of an attacker the time required to perform a checksum of the firmware will be constant. When an attacker tries to fake the checksum, she requires additional instructions that increase the execution time, hence it can be detected by the system. While this work greatly improves the trust in the remote attestation, and fixes the vulnerabilities discovered in their paper, it requires a complicated architecture for being deployed. In fact, it needs to set up a remote server for the attestation phase and to modify the interrupt signal handling in the OS to obtain a precise measurement of the code execution. On the contrary, our approach works without having an attestation architecture and it only performs static checks on the firmware boot image.

Recent platforms incorporate immutable, hardware protected SCRTMs, called Intel Boot Guard [23] and HP Sure Start [11]. They are immutable SCRTMs that measure and verify at boot time the BIOS before its execution, thus providing firmware integrity and a trusted boot chain with a Root-of-Trust locked into hardware. Such technologies ensure that the first measurement cannot be forged, since the attacker cannot modify their code. Both technologies, however, are only available in recent Intel and HP platforms. In addition, Intel Boot Guard has been showed to be vulnerable to a certain class of attacks [19]. The advantage of our approach with respect to those new technologies is twofold. First, it can be used to protect architectures that are not equipped with such hardware features. Second, our approach is orthogonal to such hardware protections, since BootKeeper can be used as a standalone analyzer from the vendor side for validating the SCRTM code as the last step of the deployment process. The main contribution of BootKeeper is related to the software properties that we devise for validating the measurement process. When BootKeeper is used by the vendor, our analyzer can perform the same analysis (e.g., enforcing software properties) at the source code level, and verify that no one tampers with the measurement task during the developing process.

8 CONCLUSION

In this paper, we introduce BootKeeper, a binary analysis approach to validate the measurement process of a boot firmware. Our system uses static analysis and symbolic execution to validate a set of software properties on the measurement process implemented as part of the UEFI *measured boot* specification. BootKeeper detects incorrect implementations of UEFI firmware which do not exhaustively or correctly implement the measured boot process, as well as malicious images crafted with the intention of bypassing the measured boot process. More specifically, BootKeeper focuses on the SCRTM, which is the most critical component in the verification chain. An incomplete SCRTM implementation leaves room for an attacker to hide code in subsequent parts of the firmware, whereas a malicious SCRTM voluntarily ignores specific regions where malicious payloads are hidden, or attempts to forge measurements in

order to match the measured values of a legitimate vendor firmware (i.e., golden values), among other possible attacks.

This approach can greatly improve trust in boot firmware update procedures. We evaluate BootKeeper against real-world firmware used in the industry as well as custom malicious firmware images, and show that our system is able to detect multiple variants of a variety of attacks from the state-of-the-art in the literature.

REFERENCES

[1] Oleksandr Bazhaniuk, John Loucaides, Lee Rosenbaum, Mark R Tuttle, and Vincent Zimmer. 2015. Symbolic execution for BIOS security. In *9th USENIX Workshop on Offensive Technologies (WOOT '15)*.
[2] Jonathan Brossard. 2012. Hardware backdooring is practical. *BlackHat, Las Vegas, USA* (2012).
[3] Danilo Bruschi, Lorenzo Cavallaro, Andrea Lanzi, and Mattia Monga. 2005. Replay attack in TCG specification and solution. In *Proceeding of the 21st Annual Computer Security Applications Conference (ACSAC '05)*. IEEE, 127–137.
[4] John Butterworth, Corey Kallenberg, Xeno Kovah, and Amy Herzog. 2013. BIOS Chronomancy: Fixing the core root of trust for measurement. In *Proceedings of the 2013 ACM SIGSAC conference on Computer & Communications Security (CCS '13)*. ACM, 25–36.
[5] Vitaly Chipounov, Volodymyr Kuznetsov, and George Candea. 2011. S2E: A Platform for In-vivo Multi-path Analysis of Software Systems. In *Proceedings of the Sixteenth International Conference on Architectural Support for Programming Languages and Operating Systems (ASPLOS XVI)*. ACM, New York, NY, USA, 265–278. https://doi.org/10.1145/1950365.1950396
[6] University California Santa Barbara Computer Security Lab. [n. d.]. angr, a binary analysis framework. https://angr.io/ Accessed: 2018-11-30.
[7] Drew Davidson and Benjamin Moench. 2013. FIE on Firmware: Finding Vulnerabilities in Embedded Systems Using Symbolic Execution. In *Proceedings of the USENIX Security Symposium*.
[8] F-Secure. [n. d.]. Virus:DOS/CIH Description | F-Secure Labs. https://www.f-secure.com/v-descs/cih.shtml Accessed: 2018-11-30.
[9] John Heasman. 2006. Implementing and detecting an ACPI BIOS rootkit. In *Black Hat Europe*.
[10] John Heasman. 2007. Implementing and detecting a PCI rootkit. In *Black Hat DC*.
[11] HP Inc. 2018. HP Sure Start. https://www8.hp.com/h20195/v2/GetPDF.aspx/4AA7-2197ENW.pdf Accessed: 2018-11-30.
[12] Corey Kallenberg, John Butterworth, Xeno Kovah, and C Cornwell. 2013. Defeating Signed BIOS Enforcement. (2013). EkoParty, Buenos Aires.
[13] Bernhard Kauer. 2007. OSLO: Improving the Security of Trusted Computing. In *Proceedings of the USENIX Security Symposium*.
[14] Doowon Kim, Bum Jun Kwon, and Tudor Dumitraş. 2017. Certified Malware: Measuring Breaches of Trust in the Windows Code-Signing PKI. In *Proceedings of the 2017 ACM SIGSAC Conference on Computer and Communications Security (CCS '17)*. ACM, 1435–1448.
[15] Akos Kiss, Judit Jász, Gábor Lehotai, and Tibor Gyimóthy. 2003. Interprocedural static slicing of binary executables. In *Proceeding of the 3rd International Workshop on Source Code Analysis and Manipulation (SCAM '03)*. IEEE, 118–127.
[16] Volodymyr Kuznetsov, Vitaly Chipounov, and George Candea. 2010. Testing Closed-Source Binary Device Drivers with DDT. In *USENIX Annual Technical Conference*.
[17] Pierre Lestringant, Frédéric Guihéry, and Pierre-Alain Fouque. 2015. Automated Identification of Cryptographic Primitives in Binary Code with Data Flow Graph Isomorphism. In *Proceedings of the 10th ACM Symposium on Information, Computer and Communications Security*. ACM, 203–214.
[18] Ge Livian. 2011. BIOS Threat is Showing up Again! https://www.symantec.com/connect/blogs/bios-threat-showing-again Accessed: 2018-11-30.
[19] Alex Matrosov. 2017. Who Watch BIOS Watchers? https://medium.com/@matrosov/bypass-intel-boot-guard-cc05edfca3a9 Accessed: 2018-11-30.
[20] Kevin O'Connor. [n. d.]. SeaBIOS. https://www.seabios.org/SeaBIOS Accessed: 2018-11-30.
[21] OpenSSL Foundation, Inc. [n. d.]. OpenSSL. https://www.openssl.org/ Accessed: 2018-11-30.
[22] Ganesan Ramalingam. 1994. The undecidability of aliasing. *ACM Transactions on Programming Languages and Systems (TOPLAS)* 16, 5 (1994), 1467–1471.
[23] Xiaoyu Ruan. 2014. Boot with Integrity, or Don't Boot. In *Platform Embedded Security Technology Revealed: Safeguarding the Future of Computing with Intel Embedded Security and Management Engine*. Apress, Berkeley, CA, USA, Chapter 6, 143–163.
[24] Anibal L Sacco and Alfredo A Ortega. 2009. Persistent BIOS infection. In *CanSecWest Applied Security Conference*.

[25] Ahmad-Reza Sadeghi, Marcel Selhorst, Christian Stüble, Christian Wachsmann, and Marcel Winandy. 2006. TCG inside?: a note on TPM specification compliance. In *Proceedings of the first ACM workshop on Scalable trusted computing*. ACM, 47–56.

[26] Dries Schellekens, Brecht Wyseur, and Bart Preneel. 2008. Remote attestation on legacy operating systems with trusted platform modules. *Science of Computer Programming* 74, 1 (2008), 13–22.

[27] Monirul Sharif, Andrea Lanzi, Jonathon Giffin, and Wenke Lee. 2008. Impeding Malware Analysis Using Conditional Code Obfuscation. In *Proceedings of the Network and Distributed System and Security symposium (NDSS)*.

[28] Yan Shoshitaishvili, Ruoyu Wang, Christophe Hauser, Christopher Kruegel, and Giovanni Vigna. 2015. Firmalice - Automatic Detection of Authentication Bypass Vulnerabilities in Binary Firmware. In *Proceedings of the Network and Distributed System and Security Symposium*.

[29] Yan Shoshitaishvili, Ruoyu Wang, Christopher Salls, Nick Stephens, Mario Polino, Andrew Dutcher, John Grosen, Siji Feng, Christophe Hauser, Christopher Kruegel, and Giovanni Vigna. 2015. SoK: (State of) The Art of War: Offensive Techniques in Binary Analysis. In *IEEE Symposium on Security and Privacy*. 138–157.

[30] The TianoCore Community. [n. d.]. EDK II. https://github.com/tianocore/tianocore.github.io/wiki/EDK-II Accessed: 2018-11-30.

[31] Trusted Computing Group 2005. *PC Client Specific Implementation Specification for Conventional BIOS*. Trusted Computing Group.

[32] Trusted Computing Group 2005. *PC Client Specific-TPM Interface Specification*. Trusted Computing Group.

[33] Trusted Computing Group 2011. *TPM Main, Part 1 Design Principles*. Trusted Computing Group.

[34] Trusted Computing Group 2014. *EFI Platform Specification*. Trusted Computing Group.

[35] UEFI Forum 2017. *UEFI Platform Initialization Specification* (version 1.6 ed.). UEFI Forum.

[36] UEFI Forum. 2017. *Unified Extensible Firmware Interface Specification*. Version 2.7.

[37] Rafal Wojtczuk and Alexander Tereshkin. 2009. Attacking Intel BIOS. (July 2009). Black Hat USA.

[38] Babak Yadegari and Saumya Debray. 2015. Symbolic Execution of Obfuscated Code. In *Proceedings of the 22nd ACM SIGSAC Conference on Computer and Communications Security (CCS '15)*. ACM, 732–744.

[39] Jonas Zaddach, Luca Bruno, Aurelien Francillon, and Davide Balzarotti. 2014. AVATAR: A Framework to Support Dynamic Security Analysis of Embedded Systems' Firmwares.. In *NDSS*.

[40] Jonas Zaddach, Luca Bruno, Aurelien Francillon, and Davide Balzarotti. 2014. AVATAR: A Framework to Support Dynamic Security Analysis of Embedded Systems Firmwares. In *Proceedings of the 21st Symposium on Network and Distributed System and Security (NDSS '14)*.

[41] Shiva Dasari Zimmer, SR Dasari, and SP Brogan. 2009. *Trusted Platforms: UEFI, PI, and TCG-based firmware*. Technical Report. Intel and IBM.

[42] Vincent Zimmer, Michael Rothman, and Suresh Marisetty. 2010. *Beyond BIOS: developing with the unified extensible firmware interface*. Intel Press.

MimosaFTL: Adding Secure and Practical Ransomware Defense Strategy to Flash Translation Layer

Peiying Wang[*][†]
School of Cyber Security, University
of Chinese Academy of Sciences
Beijing, China
wangpeiying@iie.ac.cn

Shijie Jia[†][‡]
Institute of Information Engineering,
CAS
Beijing, China
jiashijie@iie.ac.cn

Bo Chen
Department of Computer Science,
Michigan Technological University
Houghton, USA
bchen@mtu.edu

Luning Xia[*][†]
School of Cyber Security, University
of Chinese Academy of Sciences
Beijing, China
xialuning@iie.ac.cn

Peng Liu
Pennsylvania State University
University Park, PA
pliu@ist.psu.edu

ABSTRACT

Ransomware attacks have become prevalent nowadays due to sudden flourish of cryptocurrencies. Most existing defense strategies for ransomware, however, are vulnerable to privileged ransomware who can compromise the operating system and hence any backup data stored locally. The out-of-place-update and the isolation nature of flash memory storage, for the first time, makes it possible to design a defense strategy which is secure against the privileged ransomware.

In this work, we propose MimosaFTL, a secure and practical ransomware defense strategy for mobile computing devices equipped with flash memory as external storage. MimosaFTL is secure against the privileged malware by taking advantage of unique characteristics of flash storage. In addition, it is more practical (compared to prior work) for real-world deployments by: 1) incorporating a fine-grained detection scheme which can detect presence of ransomware accurately; and 2) allowing the victim to efficiently restore the infected external storage to the exact point when the malware starts to perform corruption. Experimental evaluation shows that, MimosaFTL can mitigate ransomware attacks effectively with a small negative impact on both I/O performance and lifetime of flash storage.

CCS CONCEPTS

• **Security and privacy → Malware and its mitigation;**

---

[*]Also with Institute of Information Engineering, CAS, Beijing, China.
[†]Also with Data Assurance and Communication Security Research Center, CAS, Beijing, China.
[‡]Corresponding author.

KEYWORDS

Ransomware, Mobile devices, Flash translation layer, Access patterns, Ransomware detection, Binary search

ACM Reference Format:
Peiying Wang, Shijie Jia, Bo Chen, Luning Xia, and Peng Liu. 2019. MimosaFTL: Adding Secure and Practical Ransomware Defense Strategy to Flash Translation Layer. In *Ninth ACM Conference on Data and Application Security and Privacy (CODASPY '19), March 25–27, 2019, Richardson, TX, USA.* ACM, New York, NY, USA, 12 pages. https://doi.org/10.1145/3292006.3300041

1 INTRODUCTION

In recent years, a special type of malware named ransomware has become very popular among cybercriminals. According to a report by Symantec [38], the number of ransomware attacks increased over 36% in 2017, and more than 4,000 ransomware attacks occur daily [41]. The latest notable ransomware instance, WannaCry [25, 39], has spread across 150 countries and infected more than 250,000 machines in a short period.

Different from regular malware, ransomware extorts ransom money from victims by either locking the victim systems (i.e., *locker ransomware*) or encrypting the data (i.e., *crypto-ransomware*). Locker ransomware can be easily defended since data are still there and we can simply unplug storage medium from the infected system and plug it to a clean system to copy out the data. On the contrary, crypto-ransomware is more difficult to be defended since the data have been encrypted by strong encryption with secret key only known to the ransomware attacker. Therefore, the paper focuses on defending against crypto-ransomware.

In the literature, many approaches have been proposed to defend crypto-ransomware. They can be roughly categorized into two families: 1) ransomware detection; 2) data recovery from ransomware attacks. The idea of ransomware detection is to detect ransomware and block it as fast as possible before it can cause significant damage to the valuable user data. The detection usually relies on monitoring file system activities [10, 19, 20, 26, 33] or analyzing cryptographic operations [10, 20, 22]. A pure detection-based solution is unfortunately not sufficient due to the following reasons: First, regardless how fast the detection can be, the ransomware still runs before being blocked and encrypt some data. Second, *if the ransomware can compromise the operating system (OS) and obtain root privilege (i.e., privileged ransomware), it can simply disable the detection capability.* The other category of ransomware defense relies on backing up valuable data, and restoring them after ransomware attacks. The data can be backed up in either local storage [10, 37] or third-party cloud [45]. However, those approaches are all problematic. Backing up data in the third-party cloud results in extra storage and communication cost which may not be acceptable by users [37]. Backing up data locally can eliminate the need of third-party cloud. However, *the backups are vulnerable to privileged ransomware which can compromise the OS and obtain root privilege.*

Mobile devices like smart phones and tablets have been used extensively nowadays. According to statista [36], there are approximately 4.92 billion mobile devices in 2018. Unlike desktop computers, mobile computing devices usually use flash memory as external storage media (e.g., eMMC cards, MicroSD cards and SSD drives).

Compared to traditional mechanical drivers broadly used in desktop computers, flash memory has significantly different characteristics: First, flash memory cannot be over-written before an erase operation is performed, which can only be performed on the basis of a large block (usually a few hundred KBs). However, the write operation is usually performed on the basis of a small page (usually a few KBs). Therefore, directly over-writing a page requires first erasing the entire encompassing block which further requires backing up valid data stored in other pages of this block, causing significant write amplification. Second, flash memory is vulnerable to wear. In other words, frequently writing/erasing the same flash block will eventually deteriorate the integrity of the storage. To accommodate the special nature of flash memory, an out-of-place-update strategy is usually used in flash storage, in which the newly updated data will be written to a new empty page, rather than the page being occupied by the old data.

Flash memory's special nature makes it possible to design a defense strategy secure against privileged ransomware. Mobile computing devices, which are equipped with flash media as external storage, suffer significantly from ransomware attacks recently [3]. Due to the out-of-place-update feature of flash media, the user data being over-written by ransomware[1] will be temporarily preserved in flash memory, which can be utilized later for data recovery. Additionally, the flash memory is usually used in the form of an isolated device being attached to a host system, with independent processor, memory, and software component (i.e., flash translation layer). This prevents the ransomware from having direct access to the raw flash using the limited read/write interface being offered, *even if the ransomware can compromise the entire host OS.* In other words, the ransomware will not be able to corrupt those old data being preserved in flash memory. Taking advantage of the aforementioned properties, it is possible to design more secure strategies specifically for mobile devices to enable data recovery from ransomware attacks.

Limitations of existing ransomware defense strategies utilizing flash memory. FlashGuard [14] and SSD-Insider [4] were designed to allow data recovery from ransomware by utilizing

special nature of flash memory. They, however, both suffer from significant limitations.

The basic idea of FlashGuard is: Having observed that any data being encrypted by ransomware need to be read first and then deleted, it modifies garbage collection strategy in flash translation layer (FTL) such that the invalid data having been read will not be reclaimed. In this way, it ensures that, for those data encrypted by ransomware, their plaintexts are always preserved in flash memory and used for data recovery. Their design, however, is not practical: First, FlashGuard does not employ any detection algorithm or IDS, and hence does not have any knowledge on when ransomware comes. Therefore, it needs to preserve all the historical versions of the "possibly" attacked data for a long period (e.g., 20 days [14]) to maximize probability of successful recovery. This unfortunately may be overkill and impractical for mobile devices which usually have limited storage space. Second, FlashGuard does not provide a concrete recovery component which can take care of data recovery transparently to end users. Therefore, the users need to manually recover data encrypted by ransomware. Specifically, the user needs to unplug the flash storage device, plug it into another clean and isolated computing device [14], manually identify the corrupted data and metadata, and recover them using data preserved by Flash-Guard. This is very impractical considering that the users usually do not have necessary computer skills.

SSD-Insider [4] tries to improve FlashGuard by introducing a ransomware detection and a data recovery component. However, it also suffers from a few significant issues. First, their ransomware detection mechanism is not effective. This is because, they detect ransomware by collecting "run-length" of overwritten blocks within a small fixed time window (e.g., 10 seconds). This relies on their observation that ransomware "conducts overwriting immediately after reading and encrypting the victim's files" [4]. This observation, however, is not necessarily true according to our independent study (Sec. 3). Specifically, we observed a special type of ransomware (Sec. 3), which will not overwrite the original LBAs with random data until attacking a large number of files. In other words, the overwriting pattern of this type of ransomware is difficult to be observed during this small fixed time window. In addition, CPU/IO-intensive applications may slow down activities of ransomware, making it difficult to observe the overwrite pattern of ransomware in this small fixed time window as well. Second, their recovery component is coarsely designed and can only recover data before 10 seconds. In other words, they strongly rely on an implied assumption that the ransomware starts to corrupt data and will be caught within 10 seconds. This assumption usually cannot hold in practice, since real-world ransomware does not necessarily perform attacks within 10 seconds (Sec. 3). In addition, the ransomware may actively play against the victim, after they know the design of SSD-Insider. A key challenge they cannot resolve is to allow the victim to locate and restore the exact point when the ransomware starts to corrupt external storage. Our design can successfully tackle this challenge. Third, they implemented their solution into an open-channel SSD platform, which actually runs on the block device layer [5] and is accessible to the ransomware. Such an implementation unfortunately contradicts the overall design rationale, since security of ransomware defense strategies for flash storage [14] strongly

---

[1]Deletion of user data can be viewed as a special over-write operation, being achieved by over-writing the target data with garbage information.

relies on the close nature of flash memory (which prevents the ransomware from corrupting data preserved in flash memory).

In this work, we aim to eliminate the aforementioned limitations and design a secure yet more practical (compared to Flash-Guard and SSD-Insider) ransomware defense strategy specifically for mobile devices equipped with flash storage. The resulting design, MimosaFTL, is secure against privileged ransomware by taking advantage of the special nature of flash storage. In addition, it incorporates a detection component which monitors access behaviors caused by the ransomware in the FTL and, once the ransomware is detected, an efficient data recovery process will be invoked to restore the infected external storage to a good previous state. Our design relies on two key insights:

First, we introduce a fine-grained detection scheme which can detect presence of ransomware accurately with low overhead. Unlike SSD-Insider which simply relies on counting the number of overwrites, we rely on a few different characteristics, including I/O access type, I/O location and length of I/O. This can result in a more accurate detection result. In addition, our detection is less expensive than SSD-Insider, since we introduce a one-time preprocessing step which uses K-means clustering to distill a few access patterns in the beginning, and during detection, the observed behavior can be compared to the known patterns efficiently. Second, we allow efficiently restoring the infected external storage to the exact point when the ransomware starts to perform corruption. Thanks to the out-of-place-update and the isolation nature of flash storage, by simply manipulating garbage collection, old data can be preserved and the only concern remaining is the metadata. To efficiently restore the metadata to the exact point before ransomware corrupts user data (we call this point "corruption point"), MimosaFTL does the following (Sec. 4.4 and 4.5): 1) It backs up the latest metadata when the detection does not detect ransomware (we call this point "latest good point"); 2) Each change of the metadata from the latest good point is kept in the flash memory OOB area; 3) The metadata in the corruption point is efficiently reconstructed by applying a binary search between the latest good point and the detection point (i.e., when the ransomware is detected), together with a small number of user involvements.

Contributions. Our contributions are summarized as follows:

- We have collected more than five hundred real-world ransomware samples, and analyze their access behaviors in the FTL. By applying K-mean clustering, we have successfully identified a few unique access patterns of ransomware on the flash memory.
- We design a fine-grained detection scheme in the FTL, which can effectively detect presence of ransomware by monitoring access behaviors on the flash memory caused by ransomware. In addition, we design a scheme which can efficiently recover external storage to the exact point when ransomware starts to corrupt data.
- We implement a prototype of MimosaFTL using real-world flash firmware, which was ported to an electronic development board. Experimental evaluation shows that MimosaFTL can effectively mitigate ransomware attacks with a small negative impact on both I/O performance and lifetime of flash devices.

2 BACKGROUND

2.1 Ransomware

Ransomware is a special form of malware that restricts access to a victim computer in order to extort the victim for financial gain [23]. Traditional malware typically aims to collect sensitive information stealthily without raising suspicion. On the contrary, ransomware will notify the victim, after having infected his/her valuable files.

Ransomware can be classified into locker ransomware and crypto-ransomware based on whether cryptographic algorithms are used to restrict data from victims. Locker ransomware is designed to restrict interaction with the system by weak techniques, such as simply locking the screen [44] or modifying the master boot record (MBR) and/or partition table [1], which can be easily restored without paying the ransom. Crypto-ransomware uses cryptographic algorithms to encrypt the victim's valuable files (e.g., documents and images) silently. Once the encryption is completed, the victim will be asked for a ransom to obtain the decryption keys needed for recovering plaintext files.

Crypto-ransomware can be divided into three categories based on types of encryption schemes being used [28]: symmetric key crypto-ransomware, asymmetric key crypto-ransomware, and hybrid key crypto-ransomware. Symmetric key crypto-ransomware simply uses symmetric encryption to encrypt files. The symmetric key may be reverse engineered or even brute forced [2]. Asymmetric key crypto-ransomware uses asymmetric encryption for file encryption. A drawback is that, encrypting large files using asymmetric encryption is usually time consuming. Hybrid key crypto-ransomware mitigates the drawback of asymmetric key crypto-ransomware, by using symmetric encryption to encrypt files, and using asymmetric encryption to encrypt the corresponding encryption key. Hybrid key crypto-ransomware is the mainstream of ransomware [22].

2.2 NAND Flash Memory

NAND Flash stores information in an array of memory cells, which are grouped into blocks of a few hundred Kilobytes. Each block is further divided into a certain number (e.g., 32, 64, or 128) of pages. Typical page size is 512 bytes, 2KB, and 4KB [7]. A page usually contains a small spare out-of-band (OOB) area which is used for storing various metadata (e.g., error correction code) [21].

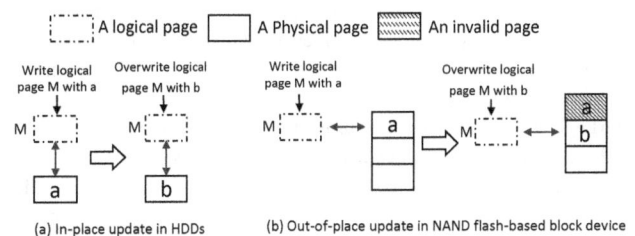

Figure 1: Overwrite operation in HDDs and NAND flash-based block devices.

Different from traditional mechanical hard drives, NAND flash has a few unique characteristics, as described in the following. First, NAND flash has an erase-before-write design, i.e., overwriting a

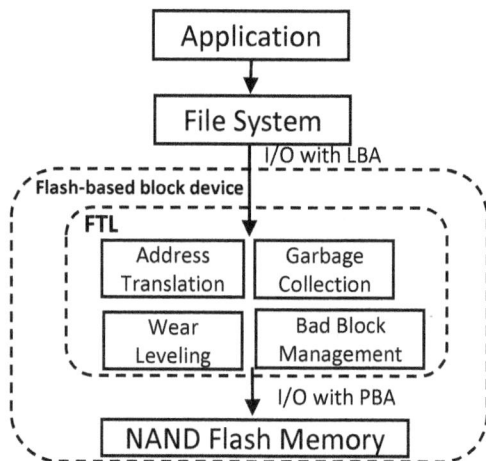

Figure 2: The architecture of a flash-based block device.

flash cell is not feasible before an erasure is performed over it. Second, the unit for reading/programming flash is usually a page, but the unit for erasing flash is usually a block (i.e., block erasure). Therefore, overwriting a page requires first erasing the entire encompassing block. This may cause significant write amplification, since data stored in the other pages of this block needs to be backed up before block erasure and written back after block erasure. Third, each block can be programmed/erased for a limited number of times. Therefore, a block will be worn out if the number of programs/erasures performed over it exceeds a certain threshold. To accommodate this special nature of flash memory, an out-of-place update rather than an in-place update strategy, is used in flash storage (Figure 1), in which when a page is overwritten, the new data will be simply written to a new empty page, while the old data will be temporarily preserved in the old page before garbage collection is invoked.

To be compatible with traditional block-based file systems (e.g., NTFS, EXT4, FAT32), a flash device is usually used as a block device by exposing a block-based access interface (i.e., a *flash-based block device* like SSD drive, USB stick, eMMC card, and SD card). The architecture of a flash-based storage system is shown in Figure 2, in which we can observe that to transparently handle the special nature of flash memory, a piece of special firmware, Flash Translation Layer (FTL), is introduced between the file system and the raw flash. The FTL usually implements four key functions: address translation, garbage collection, wear leveling, and bad block management.

Address translation. Flash-based block devices usually implement out-of-place-update strategy, and therefore location of valid data may change over time. Thus, the FTL needs to keep track of mappings between addresses from upper layer and actual physical addresses in flash memory. Utilizing these mappings, the FTL can translate addresses from the upper layer (we call them Logical Block Addresses, or LBAs) to physical flash memory addresses (we call them Physical Block Addresses, or PBAs), providing a unique block-based access interface.

Garbage collection. Garbage collection is necessary to periodically reclaim those pages which store invalid stale data (we call

these pages invalid pages). The garbage collection runs as follows: 1) It selects those blocks which satisfy a certain reclaim threshold as victim blocks. For example, the victim blocks can be those with the largest number of invalid pages. 2) It copies valid data stored in the victim blocks to free blocks, and meanwhile, updates the corresponding mappings; 3) It finally erases the victim blocks.

Wear leveling. Each flash block has a limited number of program/erase (P/E) cycles. Therefore, to prolong lifetime of flash memory, programmings/erasures need to be distributed evenly across the entire flash memory. This can be achieved by wear leveling.

Bad block management. Due to their limited P/E cycles, flash blocks will eventually turn "bad" and cannot be used to reliably store data any more. Bad block management is thus required to carefully manage those bad blocks.

2.3 K-means Clustering

K-means clustering [18] is a widely used clustering algorithm which is used for unlabeled data. It can be viewed as an optimization problem: given a set of n data points (each is from a d-dimension space), it places k centroids that can minimize the overall squared distance between each data point and its closest centroid.

Silhouette coefficient [32] is usually used to evaluate effectiveness of clustering, which is defined as:

$$s(i) = \frac{b(i)-a(i)}{\max\{a(i),b(i)\}}$$

where, for each data point i in the dataset, $a(i)$ is the average distance between i and all the other data points within the same cluster; $b(i)$ is the smallest average distance of i to all data points in any other clusters, of which i is not a member; the average $s(i)$ over all data points of a cluster measures how tightly grouped all the data points in the cluster. In general, the silhouette coefficient ranges from -1 to $+1$, and a higher value usually indicates a more ideal clustering model.

3 STUDYING ACCESS ACTIVITIES ON FLASH MEMORY CAUSED BY REAL-WORLD RANSOMWARE

Ransomware behaves differently from benign software and other types of malware. For example, the ransomware usually needs to read the victim data, encrypt them, and 1) over-write the victim data with the ciphertext; or 2) write back the ciphertext to a different location and delete the victim data. Our intuition is, the special behaviors of ransomware in the upper layers (e.g, file system) will eventually cause repeated special access behaviors (i.e., access patterns) on the underlying flash memory. Since all the access requests issued by the file system will be handled by the underlying FTL (Sec. 2.2), by hacking into the real-world FTL, we may be able to detect abnormal access behaviors on the flash memory caused by ransomware, which is running in the upper layers.

In the FTL, there is no semantic information from the upper layers. To monitor the access activities of ransomware on flash memory, we can only utilize limited information as follows: access type (i.e., read/write), destination LBA, and size of each I/O request. Note that, the delete operation is usually implemented by writing the target location with NULL data.

Collecting access activities of ransomware on flash memory. To study specific access behaviors on flash memory caused by ransomware, we randomly selected and ran 518 prevalent crypto-ransomware samples collected from VirusTotal [42] and Github [12], including 11 different ransomware families. Column 1 and 2 in Table 1 summarize information about the samples being used. To collect access activities of ransomware on flash memory, we followed a few steps: 1) We ported an open-source FTL framework, OpenNFM [9], to an electronic development board LPC-H3131 [24]. 2) We attached LPC-H3131 as a USB mass storage device of a computer running a virtual machine with Windows 7 and FAT32. 3) We ran each ransomware sample in the virtual machine and used Tera Term Pro [35], a serial debugging tool, to output access activities. After each run, the virtual machine was restored to a clean state.

Extracting access patterns on flash memory caused by ransomware. To distill patterns of access behaviors on flash memory caused by ransomware, we utilize K-means clustering algorithm (Sec. 2.3), a widely used unsupervised learning algorithm. Compared to supervised learning [4], the unsupervised learning algorithm is more suitable for ransomware scenarios, because: the ransomware samples are created by diversified hackers or organizations, resulting in various ransomware categories with different behavior patterns, and such prior knowledge is unknown. We consider a 3-dimensional space. These 3 dimensions include the access type (i.e., read or write), the starting destination LBA, and the size of each I/O request. In other words, each data point for K-means is a 3-dimension vector (access type, starting destination LBA, size of I/O request).

Training. We used half ransomware samples from each ransomware family (Table 1) for training purpose. For each sample, we collected 150 successive access. Note that each access contains the access type (i.e., read or write), the starting destination LBA, and the size of I/O request, and is viewed as a data point (i.e., a 3-dimension vector) for K-means clustering. During training, we changed value of k incrementally from 2 to 8, and calculated the silhouette coefficient for each k value. We found that K-means clustering can obtain the best clustering result[2] when k=4. After the training, we obtain the following results for our K-means clustering model: 1) Centroids of 4 clusters, which can be used to label new data; 2) Labels for the training data (each data point is assigned to a single cluster).

Extracting access patterns. After having fixed the K-means clustering model (i.e., k=4), we extracted access patterns using remaining ransomware samples from each ransomware family. For each ransomware sample, we selected 150 successive access. Each access corresponds to a 3-dimension data point, which was used as an input to the fixed K-means clustering model.

Column 3 to 6 in Table 1 show the classification results corresponding to the four clusters A, B, C, and D. The corresponding four types of access patters are summarized as follows (see Figure 3):

- **Type A**: the ransomware reads from successive LBAs, and writes back ciphertext (after encryption) to these LBAs with the same

Table 1: Real-world ransomware samples and K-means clustering results.

Family	#Samples	A	B	C	D	Time
TeslaCrypt	26(5.02%)	145	5	0	0	12
Locky	131(25.29%)	137	1	9	3	12
Cerber	23(4.44%)	143	4	3	0	2
Ransom32	28(5.40%)	131	8	11	0	8
CTB-locker	71(13.71%)	2	141	5	2	2
CryptoLocker	49(9.46%)	1	146	2	1	2
HydraCrypt	38(7.34%)	0	1	121	28	12
Samas	30(5.79%)	0	0	31	119	19
Bart	6(1.16%)	2	4	10	134	2
CryptoWall	102(19.69%)	1	7	15	127	13
Maktub	14(2.70%)	0	3	15	132	4
Total	518	-	-	-	-	-

starting LBA. The size of the ciphertext being written back is almost[3] the same as the size of the content being read.

- **Type B**: the ransomware reads from successive LBAs, and writes back ciphertext to these LBAs with the same starting LBA. The size of the ciphertext being written back is smaller than the size of the content being read. This is because, the victim file may be compressed before being encrypted or only a portion of a file is encrypted (e.g., CryptoLocker).

- **Type C**: the ransomware reads from successive LBAs, and writes the ciphertext to new free LBAs. The size of the ciphertext being written is almost the same as the size of the content being read.

- **Type D**: the ransomware reads from successive LBAs, and writes the ciphertext to new free LBAs. The size of the content being read/written exhibits certain periodic characteristics, e.g., the length of each successive read is always 32 or 64 (in LBAs), and the length of each successive write is always 8 (in LBAs). Potential reasons for this type of pattern are: To attack victim files quickly, ransomware usually uses symmetric encryption to encrypt files [22]. As plaintext input and ciphertext output of symmetric encryption are commonly divided into groups with fixed size (e.g., 16 bytes in AES), both the successive read/write will exhibit certain periodic characteristics in length. For this type of ransomware, we also observed that it will not overwrite the original LBAs with random data until having attacked a large number of data (i.e., the delay of overwriting the original LBAs with randomness is more than 10 seconds [4]).

For each ransomware family, we also measured their average time of attacking the entire external storage on LPC-H3131 (see column 7 of Table 1, in minutes). The time varies from 2 to 19 minutes, which indicates that different ransomware variants may have a completely different attack throughput. Therefore, detecting ransomware by observing overwrites in a small fixed time window (e.g., 10 seconds [4]) or simply restoring the victim system to a fixed historical check point (e.g., before 10 seconds [4]) may not be proper.

---

[2]During training of K-means clustering, we found the silhouette coefficient is both high when k is either 2 or 4. However, $k = 2$ means there are only 2 clusters, which may easily lead to a situation that mistakenly categorizes normal software behaviors as ransomware behaviors, causing higher false positives. Therefore, we choose k as 4.

[3]Some ransomware samples like Ransom32 append RSA or AES key information at the end of each ciphertext, and hence the size of the data being written back is slightly increased.

R/W	LBA	Length		R/W	LBA	Length		R/W	LBA	Length		R/W	LBA	Length
R	182-1186	1005		R	174-382	209		R	128-5647	5520		R	190-253	64
W	182-1186	1005		W	174-374	201		W	41908-47427	5520		W	12934-12941	8
R	2557-8689	6133		R	594-931	338		R	5648-11055	5408		W	12990-12997	8
W	2557-8690	6134		R	1166-1171	6		W	120-5530	5411		R	254-285	32
R	8861-9123	263		W	594-927	334		R	13460-29839	16380		W	12998-13005	8
R	10023-10844	822		W	1166-1170	5		W	55620-63807	16380		R	286-317	32
W	8861-9123	263		R	3298-5906	2609		W	47428-55619			W	13006-13013	8
W	10023-10845	823		W	3298-5602	2305		R	11056-13456	2401		W	5466-5473	8
								W	5536-7936	2401		R	318-381	64

(1) Type A	(2) Type B	(3) Type C	(4) Type D

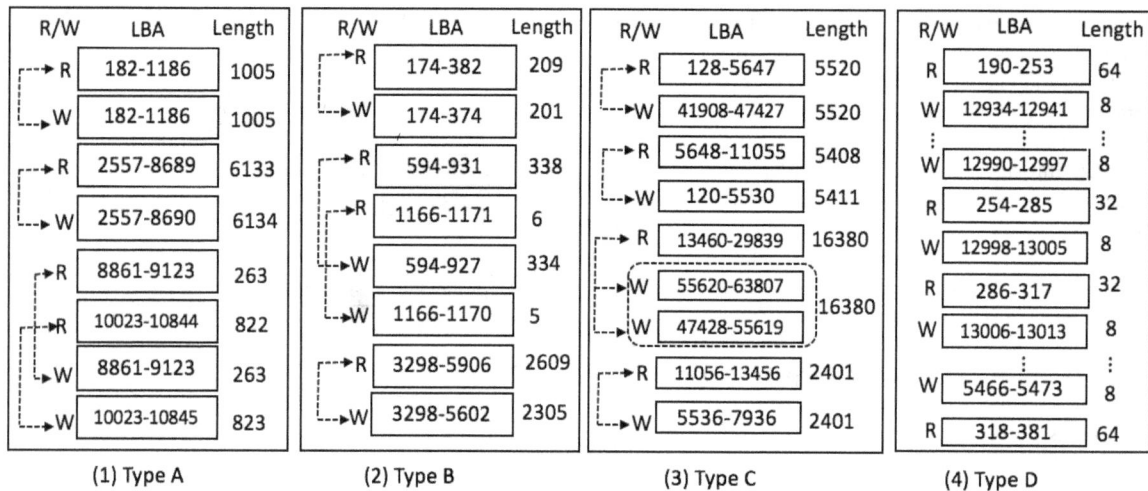

Figure 3: Four types of ransomware access patterns observed in FTL. R:read, W:write, Length: the LBA length of a successive read or write operation.

4 MIMOSAFTL DESIGN

4.1 Model and Assumptions

System model. We consider mobile computing devices which are equipped with flash-based block devices (e.g., eMMC cards, SD cards, MiniSD cards, SSD drives) as external storage. This is the most common form of mobile computing devices nowadays. It can be also applied to desktop/laptop systems which use flash-based block devices (e.g., SSD drives).

Threat model. We consider crypto-ransomware which encrypts the victim's data and asks for ransom money. We do not consider locker-ransomware which simply locks the victim system, since it can be easily defended by copying out the data from the victim system. In addition, the ransomware can compromise the entire host OS. However, the ransomware cannot compromise the FTL. This is because, a flash-based block device usually only exposes a block access interface to the OS, with independent processor, memory, firmware (i.e., FTL), all of which are inside the flash device (Sec. 2.2) and invisible to the OS. Also, once the ransomware has successfully propagated to the victim system, it will run and encrypt the victim data to gain profit.

Assumptions. We assume ransomware will not imitate regular non-malicious software when performing encryption (e.g, slowly encrypt victim data in a long period). Such highly intelligent ransomware is rarely found in practice, since most ransomware tends to encrypt victims' data and ask for ransom in a short period. We also assume the mobile device always has spare storage space in flash memory.

4.2 Design Overview of MimosaFTL

MimosaFTL aims to design a practical ransomware defense strategy, which is secure against privileged ransomware. To achieve this goal, MimosaFTL adds three components to flash translation layer (FTL): ransomware detection, data backup and data recovery. The **ransomware detection** component is running in the FTL and monitoring access behaviours on flash memory, aiming to detect presence of ransomware in a timely manner. Since the privileged ransomware is not able to compromise the FTL (Sec. 4.1), the detection component can always remain secure. The **data backup** component backs up essential data for later recovery of external storage hacked by ransomware. The external storage includes both data and metadata. By utilizing the out-of-place-update feature of the flash-based block device, MimosaFTL simply modifies the garbage collection to preserve the data corrupted by the ransomware. In addition, MimosaFTL periodically keeps the latest version of the "good" metadata after relying on the detection component to identify a good state. The **data recovery** component restores the external storage corrupted by ransomware once ransomware has been detected. Both the data and the metadata will be recovered.

4.3 Ransomware Detection

Based on the access patterns extracted in Sec. 3, our detection scheme can simply monitor access behaviors on the flash memory, and compare them with the known ransomware patterns. We introduce a new data structure, namely, recently requested access (RRA) list, to keep track of the recent I/O requests from the block device. When an access request is received by the FTL, its abstract information will be inserted into the RRA list. Each entry of the list consists of three components: access type (i.e., read/write), starting destination LBA, and length of each access request. Note that the delete (e.g., trim [40]) operation can be treated as an overwrite.

The length of the RRA list is determined by the user. When the list is filled, the detection process will be triggered. After the detection process, MimosaFTL will clear the RRA list and prepare for the next detection process.

We elaborate details of the detection process in Algorithm 1, in which access requests in the RRA list are analyzed to detect presence of ransomware as follows:

1) For ransomware which writes ciphertext to the original LBAs of the victim files (i.e., type A or B): Algorithm 1 first checks the

RRA list, to find out whether there are a read and a write, that start with the same LBA address. It then compares their corresponding read/write lengths. If the length difference is small (e.g., less than 5 LBAs), this is a type-A ransomware pattern. Otherwise, this is type B ransomware pattern. It will accumulate the number of type A patterns, and compute a ratio between the # of type A pattern and the total number of the requests in the RRA. If the ratio is larger than $Threshold\_1$ (will be discussed in Sec. 6), it will conclude with a detection of type A ransomware attack. Similarly, it will accumulate the number of type B patterns, and conclude whether there is a type B ransomware attack.

2) For ransomware which writes ciphertext of the victim files to new free LBAs (i.e., type C or D): Algorithm 1 first compares the length of a read request with the total length of the continuous write requests before the next read request is invoked. If the two lengths are almost the same (e.g., less than 5 LBAs), it will consider it as a type C ransomware pattern. It will accumulate the number of type C patterns, and compute a ratio between the # of type C pattern and the total number of the requests in the RRA. If the ratio is larger than $Threshold\_1$, it will conclude with a detection of type C ransomware attack.

For type D ransomware, Algorithm 1 uses a data structure to help analyze frequency of each length. It then checks whether or not the frequency exceeds $Threshold\_2$ (condition 1). In addition, Algorithm 1 distinguishes type D ransomware from benign applications like file encryption and compression applications, as they may generate similar I/O access patterns. The idea is that benign applications are not designed to deny access to the original files (i.e., the original files will not be deleted/overwritten) during their running time. Therefore, during running time of an application, it further checks whether or not the mappings of the destination LBAs of the continuous read turn invalid gradually (condition 2). If both condition 1 and 2 are true, Algorithm 1 concludes with a type D ransomware attack.

4.4 Data Backup

To allow restoring external storage after ransomware attacks, MimosaFTL needs to back up both data and metadata (e.g., the mapping table, which records mappings between LBA and PBA).

Back up metadata. For creating metadata backup, we take advantage of the fact that MimosaFTL has a detection component. Periodically, if no ransomware is detected, we will create a redundant copy of the current essential metadata and discard old versions of metadata. Note that: 1) The size of metadata is usually much smaller than data, and hence only a few flash blocks are required to store metadata. In addition, the blocks storing metadata backup are usually invisible to the OS, and hence cannot be corrupted by ransomware. 2) The metadata will be correctly backed up when the ransomware is correctly detected, which is of high probability according to our evaluation in Sec. 6.

Back up data. Thanks to the out-of-place-update feature of flash-based block devices, the data will be temporarily preserved and can be used for data recovery from ransomware attack. However, garbage collection will eventually reclaim those data which have been corrupted by ransomware since they have become invalid. Simply disabling garbage collection [13] can prevent those data

---

Algorithm 1 Ransomware detection in MimosaFTL.

Require:
    The *RRA* list, and each access request in the *RRA* list includes the access type (*Type*), the starting destination LBA (*DLBA*) and the length (*Len*).
1: **for** *each access request in RRA list* **do**
2:     **if** *read Type's DLBA == write Type's DLBA && Abs(read Type's Len− write Type's Len) <= 5* **then**
3:         *Dete_A + +;*
4:     **end if**
5:     **if** *read Type's DLBA == write Type's DLBA && write Type's Len < read Type's Len* **then**
6:         *Dete_B + +;*
7:     **end if**
8:     **if** *Abs(the length of a read request − the total length of the continuous write requests before the next read request) <= 5* **then**
9:         *Dete_C + +;*
10:    **end if**
11:    *Set the map < key, value >, where key=Len and value= times of this Len appears. Obtain the first three largest values: value_1, value_2, value_3;*
12:    *Sum = value_1 + value_2 + value_3;*
13: **end for**
14: *ValLen ← the length of RRA list;*
15: **if** *(Dete_A/ValLen > Threshold_1) || (Dete_B/ValLen > Threshold_1) || (Dete_C/ValLen > Threshold_1)* **then**
16:    *Ransomware is detected;*
17: **else if** *(Sum/ValLen > Threshold_2) && Mappings of the destination LBAs of the continuous read requests in RRA list become invalid gradually* **then**
18:    *Ransomware is detected;*
19: **end if**

---

from being removed. This, however, is problematic, since data will fill the entire flash memory shortly without a garbage collection. Taking advantage of the detection component and the out-of-place-update feature of flash storage, we use a phased garbage collection strategy. When detection process is invoked and does not detect presence of ransomware (i.e., the beginning of a phase), the current metadata will be backed up periodically (e.g., one day), and any data being "touched" (e.g., write, delete) in this phase will be frozen (i.e., will not be removed by garbage collection) until the next detection process is invoked (i.e, the end of the phase). Using the out-of-place-update feature, the frozen is possible. In addition, at the beginning of each phase, we will immediately conduct a garbage collection on those blocks storing invalid data coming from last phase.

4.5 Data Recovery

Once ransomware is detected, MimosaFTL will immediately inform the user and make the storage as read-only. Then, the ransomware will be blocked and removed by the user (blocking and removing malware is not our focus in this work). Once the attack is confirmed

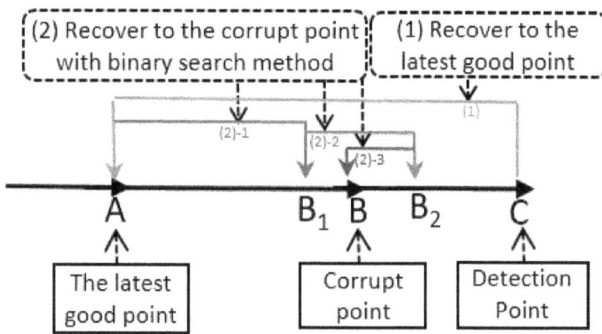

Figure 4: Recovery timeline of MimosaFTL.

by the user, a recovery component will be triggered to interact[4] with the victim user to restore the external storage being corrupted by the ransomware. Since the data are preserved due to the out-of-place-update feature of flash memory, the major problem in the recovery component will be restoring the metadata at the point of time right before the ransomware starts to damage the external storage (we call this point of time "corruption point"). Such a recovery design is advantageous, because: 1) The expensive direct data recovery can be avoided since the "good" data are preserved in flash memory, and by restoring the metadata which point to the "good" data, the external storage can be recovered. 2) The recovery of metadata can be done efficiently, considering their small size.

However, restoring the metadata at the corruption point is challenging, because: The detection component of MimosaFTL relies on observing access behaviors of ransomware for detection, and a few user files will be corrupted unavoidably before the point of time when ransomware is detected (we call this point of time "detection point"). Since MimosaFTL periodically backs up the latest "good" metadata (we call this point of time "latest good point"), we can first restore the external storage to this latest good point, and then approach the corruption point from the latest good point.

To restore the metadata at the corruption point, MimosaFTL needs to rely on information stored in the OOB areas. MimosaFTL will store the following information in the OOB of each page: backup version (which records the version number of the periodic metadata backup), writing sequence number (which records the write sequence number in a specific periodic metadata backup) and destination LBA. Note that we usually only use a small portion of the OOB area, which will not significantly affect its regular use. For example, in our experimental evaluation, we only need to use 8 bytes of the OOB, which is 12.5% of its entire capacity.

When MimosaFTL detects the ransomware and informs the victim user, the user will trigger the recovery component to perform the following steps (see Figure 4): First, it will recover the system to the latest good point (i.e., from point C to A). This step is straightforward, since MimosaFTL has backed up metadata of point A and all the valid data of point A has been preserved (Sec. 4.4). Second, to recover the system to the corruption point (i.e., from point A to B),

MimosaFTL will read the entire OOB areas of the flash physical pages storing the user data to find out the ones with the largest backup version number (i.e., the latest backup version), then build up a list of destination LBA and PBA mappings in the order of their writing sequence number. Next, MimosaFTL will recover the mapping table at point B using an efficient binary search approach as described below:

MimosaFTL first applies half of the entire changes to the metadata at point A, restoring the metadata at point B_1. The user then checks the data (at the OS level) recovered at point B_1. If the user does not find corruption at B_1, the corruption point should be located somewhere between B_1 and C (otherwise, the corruption point should be located somewhere between A and B_1), and the next point being examined should be B_2. The metadata at B_2 can be restored by applying half of entire changes between B_1 and C to the metadata at point B_1. Recursively, the search will reach the corruption point B. Note that interacting with the user for data recovery is necessary since only the user knows the latest good state of the data. However, due to the efficient binary search, the user involvement can be kept small (i.e., log(n), where n is the number of write operations between the latest good point and the detection point).

The recovery process of MimosaFTL requires interacting with the victim user, which can be achieved by taking advantage of the reserved operation codes (i.e., *0x60H* to *0x7FH*) of SCSI commands [15, 46]. Specially, we can adopt an SCSI command with operation code *0x71H* to inform MimosaFTL to modify mapping table forward, and adopt another SCSI command with operation code *0x72H* to modify mapping table backward. If the user confirms that all the victim files have been recovered, we can adopt another SCSI command with operation code *0x73H* to inform MimosaFTL that the recovery process ends. Note that if the detection has false positives, the user will not trigger the recovery component.

5 SECURITY ANALYSIS AND DISCUSSION
5.1 Security Analysis
A pattern-based detection solution usually cannot guarantee 100% accuracy. In the following, we analyze the security of MimosaFTL under two cases: 1) the ransomware is correctly detected; 2) the ransomware is not correctly detected.

Case 1: the detection component correctly detects the ransomware. Clearly in MimosaFTL, both data and metadata will be correctly backed up and the ransomware is not able to bypass the FTL to corrupt those backups even if it can compromise the host operating system (Sec. 4.1). Once the ransomware is correctly detected, the recovery component will be correctly triggered by the user to recover the external storage to the corruption point.

Case 2: the detection component does not correctly detect the ransomware. This usually includes *false positives* and *false negatives*, which will be discussed respectively as follows.

- Rarely, benign applications and regular user operations may exhibit similar access patterns as ransomware, causing false positives. MimosaFTL can handle false positives because, the data recovery component is triggered by the user, and the user can simply not trigger the data recovery component if that is a false positive.

---

[4]User involvement (via customized I/O commands, e.g., SCSI commands) is usually necessary, since only the user knows the latest version of the data.

- Some ransomware variants may escape from being detected (e.g., new ransomware variants), causing false negatives. When the false negative happens, MimosaFTL is at least as good as Flash-Guard [14], which provides the possibility of external storage recovery. Especially, for this case, MimosaFTL is even better than FlashGuard, since a user-friendly recovery component has been built into the FTL, which can allow a more convenient recovery after the actual ransomware finishes hacking the victim mobile device and informs the user.

5.2 Discussion

Working on the FTL layer rather than the upper layers. MimosaFTL is a solution which requires being incorporated into the flash translation layer (FTL). This seems unavoidable since its security strongly relies on the close nature of flash memory. Such an incorporation is not unique, since a lot of existing security defenses [7, 8, 13, 14, 16, 17, 29, 43] for flash memory have a similar requirement of incorporating security strategies into the FTL. The incorporation could be achieved by either collaborating with flash memory vendors or turning the defenses into industry standards.
Handling ransomware-like benign applications. Some special benign applications like encryption, compression, and deletion applications may exhibit ransomware-like access behaviors. MimosaFTL is designed to not mistakenly detect them as ransomware. 1) For benign encryption and compression applications, they commonly treat the original file content carefully, since their ultimate goal is to generate an encrypted/compressed version of the original file, rather than to restrict access to the file [19]. In other words, the original files usually remain intact when they are running, though automatic deletion may be deliberately activated by the user after the encryption or compression is done. MimosaFTL checks the mapping modifications of the destination LBAs of the continuous read requests in the RRA list to differentiate ransomware and this type of benign applications. 2) For secure deletion applications, they commonly open a file and overwrite its contents with new, meaningless data [30], e.g., all zeros, however, they will not read the files during deletion. If the user changes the file content via a benign application (e.g., updating the data of a Microsoft Word file), it may also generate similar access patterns with ransomware. However, there are some key differences. For example, benign applications usually read a single file at a time and modify different parts of the file continuously, but ransomware usually performs reading and rewriting in an interleaved manner.
Protecting SCSI interface. MimosaFTL supports user interaction via SCSI commands. To prevent privileged malware from abusing this new interface to disturb our design, we can introduce a simple authentication using secrets only known by the user. Specifically, every time when the SCSI interface is used, the user needs to provide a secret password which needs to be verified by the FTL (the secret password is stored in the metadata area of the flash which is invisible to the upper layer and hence the ransomware). Since the ransomware does not have this secret password and is not able to pass the authentication in order to use this SCSI interface.
MimosaFTL does not affect data correctness. The out-of-place-update feature of flash storage preserves data being deleted by ransomware, and MimosaFTL only modifies garbage collection to

Table 2: Ransomware samples and portion of the selected benign applications.

Ransomware	#Samples	Benign application	Main capability
Samas	36	7-zip	Compression
Cerber	47	Winzip	Compression
Ransom32	53	WinRAR	Compression
Maktub	14	TrueCrypt	Encryption
Jigsaw	56	DiskCryptor	Encryption
Radamant	36	SDelete	Deletion
CryptoFortress	37	Eraser	Deletion
HydraCrypt	29	Davinci Resolve	Multimedia tools
WannaCry	12	Eclipse	Developers tools
Critroni	20	Anaconda	Developers tools
CryptoDefense	6	SQLite	Developers tools

delay deletion of these preserved data, such that they can be used for potential data recovery later. In addition, the latest metadata are also backed up for potential data recovery. All the aforementioned operations of MimosaFTL do not affect data correctness. In addition, the detection of MimosaFTL mainly reads data which does not affect data correctness either.

6 IMPLEMENTATION AND EVALUATION

6.1 Implementation

We have implemented a prototype of MimosaFTL using Open-NFM [9], an open source NAND flash controller framework. We ported MimosaFTL to LPC-H3131 [24], a development board equipped with 180 MHz ARM processor, 512 MB NAND flash, and 32 MB SDRAM. The block size of the NAND flash is 128 KB and the page size is 2 KB. The entire NAND flash has 4,096 erase blocks, and each block is composed of 64 pages. Moreover, the size of the OOB area in each page is 64 bytes. Each mapping entry can be represented by 3 bytes, and the mapping table occupies approximately 6 blocks.

6.2 Evaluation

6.2.1 Effectiveness of MimosaFTL in Detection. We evaluate effectiveness of the detection component of MimosaFTL by looking into its false positives and false negatives.
Dataset construction. To provide a comprehensive evaluation of the detection component, as shown in Table 2, we collected 346 new prevalent ransomware samples belonging to 11 different families from VirusTotal (73.4%) and Github (26.6%), which are completely disjoint from the training samples used in Sec. 3. Our dataset covers a majority of existing ransomware families that appear from 2001 to 2018. In addition, we built a dataset containing 95 benign application samples (partial of them are shown in Table 2), including: 1) software that has ransomware-like behaviors such as file encryption, compression and data deletion; 2) multimedia tools and applications (e.g., media player, audio/video transcoding applications, and games); 3) developer tools; 4) office tools. Besides these benign application samples, we also collected I/O access requests from installing/upgrading these benign software and web server (e.g., search engine service, web mail server).

Ransomware detection accuracy. In order to evaluate detection accuracy of MimosaFTL, we measured both false negatives and false positives, varying the thresholds to determine the best detection effectiveness.

First, we evaluated whether MimosaFTL can successfully distinguish ransomware from benign applications, following a few steps: 1) We ported MimosaFTL to LPC-H3131, and used the board as an external storage; 2) We ran all the ransomware samples and benign application samples; 3) We varied the thresholds in the detection algorithm (i.e., $Threshold\_1$ and $Threshold\_2$) simultaneously, and kept track of those thresholds by which the detection algorithm successfully detects ransomware samples or mistakenly detects benign application samples as ransomware in Figure 5. The left half of the figure is for ransomware samples (with thresholds vary between 0.8 and 0.97), and the right half of the figure is for benign application samples (with threshold vary between 0.02 and 0.5). A clear difference is observed between the ransomware samples (minimum 0.8) and the benign application samples (maximum 0.5).

Second, to determine thresholds described in the detection Algorithm 1, we measured false positives and false negatives by varying $Threshold\_1$ for type A/B/C ransomware and $Threshold\_2$ for type D ransomware. As shown in Figure 6, MimosaFTL does not have any false positives/false negatives when $Threshold\_1 \in (0.55, 0.78)$ and $Threshold\_2 \in (0.63, 0.87)$.

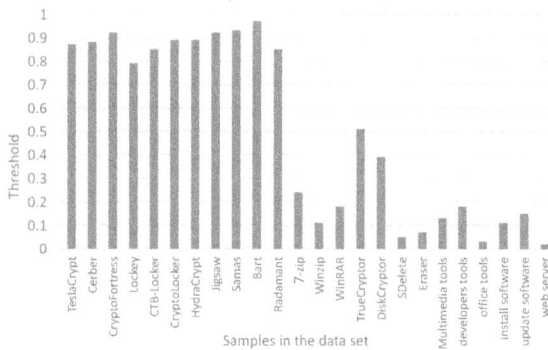

Figure 5: The threshold that the detection component successfully detects the ransomware or mistakenly detects benign applications as ransomware.

6.2.2 Efficiency of MimosaFTL in Recovery. We evaluate how efficiently the MimosaFTL can recover the external storage corrupted by ransomware. Table 3 shows each separate time spent on recovery. We observe that most time is spent on building the LBA and PBA mappings, which requires reading the OOB areas of user data blocks. The time cost of recovering to point A is mainly to read metadata in the system reserved blocks. With binary search process based on limited number of user interaction, the efficiency of data recovery is optimistic.

6.2.3 Impact of MimosaFTL on Flash-based Block Devices. We evaluate impact of MimosaFTL on regular flash-based block devices, in terms of I/O throughput and lifetime of flash memory.

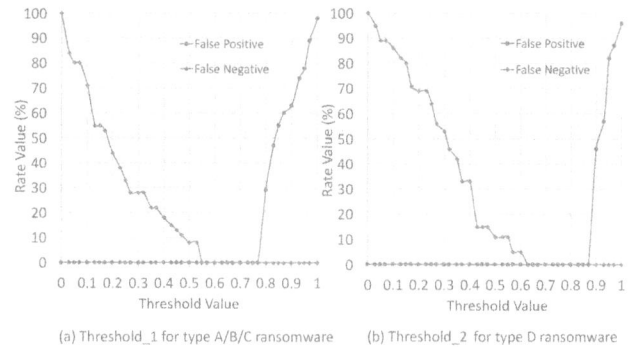

(a) Threshold_1 for type A/B/C ransomware   (b) Threshold_2 for type D ransomware

Figure 6: The false positive rate and false negative rate vary with adjustment of the threshold.

Table 3: Individual time components for recovery (in seconds).

Recover to point A	Build LBA and PBA mappings	Rebuild a mapping table	System restart
0.65	2.83	0.43 to 1.26	1.32

Impact on flash storage I/O throughput. To access impact of MimosaFTL on the storage I/O throughput, we benchmarked the original OpenNFM and MimosaFTL using fio [11] with non-buffered I/O option. We ran fio in a host computer with Intel i5 CPU (3.30GHz, 4GB RAM) and Windows 10 Pro 64-bit. We set the array length of the RRA list as 150 (i.e., the detection component is triggered upon every 150 continuous access requests). We created backup for the essential FTL metadata (e.g., addresses mapping table) once a day if ransomware is not detected.

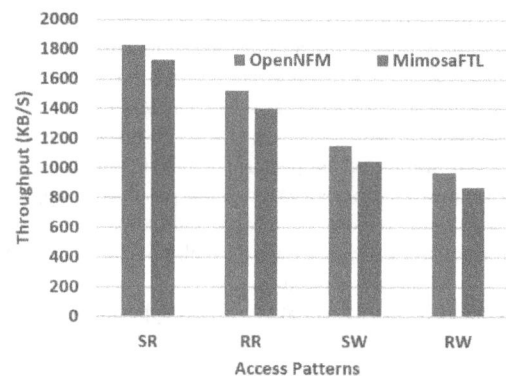

Figure 7: Comparisons of read/write throughput (KB/s) between OpenNFM and MimosaFTL. SR - sequential read, RR - random read, SW - sequential write, RW - random write.

The benchmark results for I/O throughput of the two systems are shown in Figure 7. We observe that MimosaFTL decreases the read (i.e., sequential and random read) throughput by up to 6.8%, and decrease the write (including sequential and random write) throughput by up to 7.2%. We analyze the additional overhead of

MimosaFTL in the following: 1) MimosaFTL running the detection algorithm needs to update the RRA list, and the detection process is triggered when the RRA list is filled. The RRA list is maintained in RAM, which does not incur too much overhead. In addition, the detection process needs to analyze all the entries in the RRA list which may incur overhead. However, it only happens periodically. 2) MimosaFTL needs to back up metadata daily in our implementation, which takes as less as 0.1 seconds for each back up operation. 3) MimosaFTL adopts phased garbage collection, which delays execution of garbage collection on invalid blocks. MimosaFTL schedules the garbage collection during idle time, reducing its impact on the entire performance. 4) To allow restoring mapping tables during recovery, MimosaFTL needs to write relevant information into the OOB area of each page. Compared to OpenNFM, this does not bring extra overhead, as OpenNFM also needs to keep similar information to enable recovery from power lost.

Impact on the flash device's lifetime. To prolong lifetime of flash memory, MimosaFTL utilizes a global wear leveling strategy. In MimosaFTL, when allocating blocks, blocks with smaller P/E cycles will be allocated first. In addition, the blocks having larger P/E cycles will be swapped with blocks having smaller P/E cycles. To evaluate wear leveling effectiveness, we use hoover economic wealth inequality indicator [7, 17, 31], which calculates an appropriately normalized sum of the difference of each measurement to the mean. Assuming erasure counts of all the n erase blocks are e_1, $e_2,..., e_n$, and $E = \sum_{i=1}^{n} e_i$, a wear leveling inequality (WLI) can be computed as: $WLI = \frac{1}{2} \sum_{i=1}^{n} \| \frac{e_i}{E} - \frac{1}{n} \|$. This indicates the fraction of erasures that must be re-assigned to other blocks in order to achieve completely even wear.

We repeatedly wrote data to the board, completely filled the 480 MB flash, and then erased the data. After having written 480 GB data, we calculated the number of erasures performed on each flash block. We then computed the WLI, obtaining 9.2%. This small value indicates a small impact of MimosaFTL on the lifetime of flash memory.

7 RELATED WORK

The existing work of ransomware defense can be categorized into detection and recovery.

Ransomware detection. Existing ransomware detection approaches mainly monitor typical ransomware file system activities [10, 19, 20, 33] or analyze cryptographic primitives [10, 20, 22]. Kharraz et al. [20] were the first to analyze a large number of ransomware samples. They suggest some potential defenses in term of file system interactions, encryption mechanisms and financial incentives. Unveil [19] generates an artificial user environment and monitors desktop lockers, file access patterns and I/O data entropy. CryptoDrop [33] observes file type changes and measures file modifications using similarity-preserving hash functions and shannon entropy to detect ransomware. ShieldFS [10] monitors file system access activities and collects features like folder listing, file read/write/rename, file type and write entropy.

Additionally, some other works utilize honeypot techniques [27], software-defined networking (SDN) [6] or machine learning approaches [34] to recognize ransomware. The detection approaches discussed so far are workable under the assumption that the OS

is trusted and the malware cannot not compromise it. However, advanced ransomware may run with root privileges, and is able to disable or bypass the detection mechanisms. The detection component of MimosaFTL is secure against this type of privileged ransomware.

Data recovery from ransomware attacks. Inspired by copy-on-write file systems, ShieldFS [10] automatically shadows a file whenever the original one is modified. PayBreak [22] leverages the fact that in a hybrid cryptosystem the session key must be used during the symmetric encryption. It observes the use of these keys, holds them in escrow, and is able to decrypt files that would otherwise only be recoverable by paying the ransom. The aforementioned approaches are vulnerable to the privileged ransomware which can compromise the OS and disturb the data (or key) recovery.

FlashGuard [14] can defend against the privileged ransomware by exploiting features present in the lower layer flash memory. However, due to lack of a detection algorithm as well as a user-friendly recovery component, FlashGuard is far from being practical. SSD-Insider [4] incorporates a ransomware detection component based on the overwriting patterns in a small fixed time window (e.g., 10 seconds). However, SSD-Insider is not practical either because: First, it relies on an observation that ransomware "conducts overwriting immediately after reading and encrypting the victim's file", which is not necessarily true according to our study (Sec 3). Second, its recovery component is coarsely designed and can only recover data before 10 seconds.

8 CONCLUSION

In this work, we propose MimosaFTL, the first secure yet more practical ransomware defense strategy for mobile computing devices that are equipped with flash memory as external storage. Security analysis and experimental evaluation show that MimosaFTL can defend against privileged ransomware with a small negative impact on storage performance and device's lifetime.

ACKNOWLEDGMENT

This work was partially supported by the National Natural Science Foundation of China (No. 61802395, No. 61602475, No.61602476 and No.61872357) and National Cryptographic Foundation of China (Grant No. MMJJ20170212). Peng Liu was supported by ARO W911NF-13-1-0421 (MURI), NSF CNS-1422594, NSF CNS-1505664, and NSF CNS-1814679.

REFERENCES

[1] Mohammad Mehdi Ahmadian, Hamid Reza Shahriari, and Seyed Mohammad Ghaffarian. 2015. Connection-monitor & connection-breaker: A novel approach for prevention and detection of high survivable ransomwares. In *Information Security and Cryptology (ISCISC), 2015 12th International Iranian Society of Cryptology Conference on*. IEEE, 79–84.

[2] Mohammad Mehdi Ahmadian, Hamid Reza Shahriari, and Seyed Mohammad Ghaffarian. 2015. Connection-monitor & connection-breaker: A novel approach for prevention and detection of high survivable ransomwares. (2015), 79–84.

[3] Nicolo Andronio, Stefano Zanero, and Federico Maggi. 2015. HelDroid: Dissecting and Detecting Mobile Ransomware. (2015), 382–404.

[4] SungHa Baek, Youngdon Jung, Aziz Mohaisen, Sungjin Lee, and DaeHun Nyang. 2018. SSD-Insider: Internal Defense of Solid-State Drive against Ransomware with Perfect Data Recovery. In *38th IEEE International Conference on Distributed Computing Systems,ICDCS 2018, Vienna, Austria, July 2-6, 2018*. 875–884.

[5] Matias Bjørling, Javier González, and Philippe Bonnet. 2017. LightNVM: The Linux Open-Channel SSD Subsystem.. In *FAST*. 359–374.

[6] Krzysztof Cabaj, Marcin Gregorczyk, and Wojciech Mazurczyk. 2017. Software-defined networking-based crypto ransomware detection using HTTP traffic characteristics. *Computers & Electrical Engineering* (2017).

[7] Bo Chen, Shijie Jia, Luning Xia, and Peng Liu. 2016. Sanitizing data is not enough!: towards sanitizing structural artifacts in flash media. In *Proceedings of the 32nd Annual Conference on Computer Security Applications.* ACM, 496–507.

[8] Bo Chen and Radu Sion. 2015. HiFlash: A history independent flash device. *arXiv preprint arXiv:1511.05180* (2015).

[9] Google Code. 2011. OpenNFM. https://code.google.com/p/opennfm/.

[10] Andrea Continella, Alessandro Guagnelli, Giovanni Zingaro, Giulio De Pasquale, Alessandro Barenghi, Stefano Zanero, and Federico Maggi. 2016. ShieldFS: a self-healing, ransomware-aware filesystem. In *Proceedings of the 32nd Annual Conference on Computer Security Applications.* ACM, 336–347.

[11] Freecode. 2014. fio. http://freecode.com/projects/fio.

[12] Github. 2018. A repository of LIVE malwares for your own joy and pleasure. https://github.com/ytisf/theZoo.

[13] Le Guan, Shijie Jia, Bo Chen, Fengwei Zhang, Bo Luo, Jingqiang Lin, Peng Liu, Xinyu Xing, and Luning Xia. 2017. Supporting Transparent Snapshot for Bare-metal Malware Analysis on Mobile Devices. In *Proceedings of the 33rd Annual Computer Security Applications Conference.* ACM, 339–349.

[14] Jian Huang, Jun Xu, Xinyu Xing, Peng Liu, and Moinuddin K Qureshi. 2017. FlashGuard: Leveraging Intrinsic Flash Properties to Defend Against Encryption Ransomware. In *Proceedings of the 2017 ACM SIGSAC Conference on Computer and Communications Security.* ACM, 2231–2244.

[15] INCITS. 2015. SCSI Command Operation Codes. http://www.t10.org/lists/op-num.htm.

[16] Shijie Jia, Luning Xia, Bo Chen, and Peng Liu. 2016. Nfps: Adding undetectable secure deletion to flash translation layer. In *Proceedings of the 11th ACM on Asia Conference on Computer and Communications Security.* ACM, 305–315.

[17] Shijie Jia, Luning Xia, Bo Chen, and Peng Liu. 2017. DEFTL: Implementing Plausibly Deniable Encryption in Flash Translation Layer. In *Proceedings of the 2017 ACM SIGSAC Conference on Computer and Communications Security.* ACM, 2217–2229.

[18] Tapas Kanungo, David M. Mount, Nathan S. Netanyahu, Christine D. Piatko, Ruth Silverman, and Angela Y. Wu. 2002. An Efficient k-Means Clustering Algorithm: Analysis and Implementation. *IEEE Trans. Pattern Anal. Mach. Intell.* 24, 7 (2002), 881–892.

[19] Amin Kharraz, Sajjad Arshad, Collin Mulliner, William K Robertson, and Engin Kirda. 2016. UNVEIL: A Large-Scale, Automated Approach to Detecting Ransomware.. In *USENIX Security Symposium.* 757–772.

[20] Amin Kharraz, William Robertson, Davide Balzarotti, Leyla Bilge, and Engin Kirda. 2015. Cutting the gordian knot: A look under the hood of ransomware attacks. In *International Conference on Detection of Intrusions and Malware, and Vulnerability Assessment.* Springer, 3–24.

[21] Youngjae Kim, Brendan Tauras, Aayush Gupta, and Bhuvan Urgaonkar. 2009. Flashsim: A simulator for nand flash-based solid-state drives. In *Advances in System Simulation, 2009. SIMUL'09. First International Conference on.* IEEE, 125–131.

[22] Eugene Kolodenker, William Koch, Gianluca Stringhini, and Manuel Egele. 2017. PayBreak: defense against cryptographic ransomware. In *Proceedings of the 2017 ACM on Asia Conference on Computer and Communications Security.* ACM, 599–611.

[23] Xin Luo and Qinyu Liao. 2007. Awareness education as the key to ransomware prevention. *Information Systems Security* 16, 4 (2007), 195–202.

[24] Mantech. 2017. LPC-H3131. http://www.mantech.co.za/.

[25] Mcafee. [n. d.]. WannaCry: Ransomware Spreads Like Wildfire, Attacks Over 150 Countries. https://securingtomorrow.mcafee.com/consumer/

consumer-threat-notices/wannacry-ransomware-attacks/.

[26] Shagufta Mehnaz, Anand Mudgerikar, and Elisa Bertino. 2018. RWGuard: A Real-Time Detection System Against Cryptographic Ransomware. In *International Symposium on Research in Attacks, Intrusions, and Defenses.* Springer, 114–136.

[27] Chris Moore. 2016. Detecting ransomware with honeypot techniques. In *Cybersecurity and Cyberforensics Conference (CCC), 2016.* IEEE, 77–81.

[28] Bharti Nagpal and Vinayak Wadhwa. 2016. Cryptoviral Extortion: Evolution, Scenarios, and Analysis. In *Proceedings of the International Conference on Signal, Networks, Computing, and Systems.* Springer, 309–316.

[29] Joon-Young Paik, Keuntae Shin, and Eun-Sun Cho. 2016. Poster: Self-defensible storage devices based on flash memory against ransomware. In *Proceedings of IEEE Symposium on Security and Privacy.*

[30] Joel Reardon, David A Basin, and Srdjan Capkun. 2013. SoK: Secure Data Deletion. *ieee symposium on security and privacy* 12, 3 (2013), 301–315.

[31] Joel Reardon, Srdjan Capkun, and David Basin. 2012. Data node encrypted file system: Efficient secure deletion for flash memory. (2012), 17–17.

[32] PJ Rousseeuw. 1999. Silhouettes: A graphical aid to the interpretation and validation of cluster analysis. *Journal of Computational & Applied Mathematics.* 20, 20 (1999), 53–65.

[33] Nolen Scaife, Henry Carter, Patrick Traynor, and Kevin RB Butler. 2016. Cryptolock (and drop it): stopping ransomware attacks on user data. In *Distributed Computing Systems (ICDCS), 2016 IEEE 36th International Conference on.* IEEE, 303–312.

[34] Daniele Sgandurra, Luis Muñoz-González, Rabih Mohsen, and Emil C Lupu. 2016. Automated dynamic analysis of ransomware: Benefits, limitations and use for detection. *arXiv preprint arXiv:1609.03020* (2016).

[35] SOFTPEDIA. 2018. Tera Term Pro Web. http://www.softpedia.com/get/Network-Tools/Telnet-SSH-Clients/Tera-Term-Web.shtml.

[36] Statista. 2018. Number of mobile phone users worldwide from 2013 to 2019 (in billions). https://www.statista.com/statistics/274774/forecast-of-mobile-phone-users-worldwide/.

[37] Kul Prasad Subedi, Daya Ram Budhathoki, Bo Chen, and Dipankar Dasgupta. 2017. RDS3: Ransomware defense strategy by using stealthily spare space. In *Computational Intelligence (SSCI), 2017 IEEE Symposium Series on.* IEEE, 1–8.

[38] Symantec. [n. d.]. 2017 Internet Security Threat Report. https://www.symantec.com/security-center/threat-report.

[39] Symantec. [n. d.]. A new breed of threat: WannaCry and Petya. https://www.symantec.com/content/dam/symantec/docs/security-center/white-papers/istr-ransomware-2017-en.pdf.

[40] Cactus Technologies. [n. d.]. Solid State Drive Primer-Controller Functions-TRIM Command. https://www.cactus-tech.com/resources/blog/details/solid-state-drive-primer-12-controller-functions-trim-command.

[41] Thebestvpn. [n. d.]. Cyber Security Statistics. https://thebestvpn.com/cyber-security-statistics-2018/.

[42] virustotal. 2018. Virustotal. https://www.virustotal.com/en/.

[43] Michael Yung Chung Wei, Laura M Grupp, Frederick E Spada, and Steven Swanson. 2011. Reliably erasing data from flash-based solid state drives.. In *Fast*, Vol. 11. 8–8.

[44] Wikipedia. [n. d.]. Trojan.Winlock. https://ru.wikipedia.org/wiki/Trojan.Winlock.

[45] Joobeom Yun, Junbeom Hur, Youngjoo Shin, and Dongyoung Koo. 2017. CLDSafe: An Efficient File Backup System in Cloud Storage against Ransomware. *IEICE TRANSACTIONS on Information and Systems* 100, 9 (2017), 2228–2231.

[46] Qionglu Zhang, Shijie Jia, Bing Chang, and Bo Chen. 2018. Ensuring data confidentiality via plausibly deniable encryption and secure deletion–a survey. *Cybersecurity* 1, 1 (2018).

BlAnC: Blockchain-based Anonymous and Decentralized Credit Networks

Gaurav Panwar, Satyajayant Misra, Roopa Vishwanathan
New Mexico State University
Las Cruces, New Mexico
{gpanwar,misra,roopav}@nmsu.edu

ABSTRACT

Distributed credit networks, such as Ripple [19] and Stellar [23], are becoming popular as an alternative means for financial transactions. However, the current designs do not preserve user privacy or are not truly decentralized. In this paper, we explore the creation of a distributed credit network that preserves user and transaction privacy and unlinkability. We propose BlAnC, a novel, fully decentralized blockchain-based credit network where credit transfer between a sender-receiver pair happens on demand. In BlAnC, multiple concurrent transactions can occur seamlessly, and malicious network actors that do not follow the protocols and/or disrupt operations can be identified efficiently.

We perform security analysis of our proposed protocols in the universal composability framework to demonstrate its strength, and discuss how our network handles operational dynamics. We also present preliminary experiments and scalability analyses.

CCS CONCEPTS

• **Security and privacy** → **Distributed systems security**;

KEYWORDS

Distributed credit network; anonymity; transaction atomicity; blockchain

ACM Reference Format:
Gaurav Panwar, Satyajayant Misra, Roopa Vishwanathan. 2019. BlAnC: Blockchain-based Anonymous, and Decentralized Credit Networks. In *Ninth ACM Conference on Data and Application Security and Privacy (CODASPY '19), March 25–27, 2019, Richardson, TX, USA*. ACM, New York, NY, USA, 12 pages. https://doi.org/10.1145/3292006.3300034

1 INTRODUCTION

Credit networks are distributed systems of trust between users, where a user extends financial credit, or guarantees assets to other users whom it deems credit worthy, with the extended credit proportionate to the amount of trust that exists between the users [2, 26]. Distributed credit networks (DCNs') are essentially peer-to-peer lending networks, where users extend credit, borrow money and commodities from each other directly, while minimizing the role of banks, clearing-houses, or bourses. The rising popularity of DCNs

stem from their capability to enable direct exchanges between users, sidestepping the waiting times and arbitrage fees charged by traditional, regulated financial institutions, in exchange for users accepting counter-party credit risks. In a credit network, two users, Alice and Bob can trade credits directly with each other, if there exists a direct trust relationship between them, or via a path between them through network peers, built on peer-wise credit relationships.

A DCN provides the basic infrastructure for building distributed payment networks, where the payment between users could be remittances of diverse nature (e.g, fiat currency, cryptocurrency, assets' transfer, such as stocks and bonds). The goal of such remittance networks is to create a distributed financial ecosystem, best exemplified by the Ripple payment settlement network [19].

Credit networks have found use in several applications, such as designing and securing social networks [13], Sybil tolerant networks [26], and content rating systems [8]. Popular blockchain-based payment settlement networks (e.g., Ripple [19], Stellar [23]) use credit networks as underlying infrastructure to represent credit between users. Other examples being TrustDavis [3], Bazaar [18], and Ostra [12]. Furthermore, traditional banking systems have begun integrating blockchain-based payment networks such as Ripple into services [21]–an increasingly popular trend.

Conceptually, a credit network can be modeled as a directed graph where users represent vertices, weighted edges represent the credit amount that a user is willing to offer its adjacent neighbor, and the directionality of the edge represents the direction of credit flow. The amount of credit between a given pair of users is usually proportional to the degree of trust that exists between them. A user can route payments to another user over a network pathi with sufficient credit. Once a payment gets routed from a sender to a receiver, all edges along the path get decremented by the transmitted amount.

Both centralized and decentralized credit networks currently exist. In the centralized version [12, 18], a service provider, e.g., a bank, constructs and maintains a database of all link weights, facilitates transactions between users, and performs updates to users' credit links post transactions. In the decentralized version [15, 19, 23], users maintain their own credit links, find credit routes cooperatively, and perform updates locally. Evidently, since there is no central server to manage the network/users, find paths, and route payments, operation and maintenance of such distributed credit networks is more challenging, but the design offers better privacy guarantees and is intuitively more resilient against failures. In this paper we focus on this decentralized version.

Challenges: For broad-based acceptance and use, any credit network has to handle the following three major challenges:

(a) *Concurrency*: In a credit network, several concurrent transactions could occur (e.g., Ripple's XRP processes up to 1500 transactions per second [20]), with many of them potentially using the same credit links. The network design ought to support this, while ensuring the integrity and atomicity of every transaction – either all credit links on the path get decremented, or none at all. This guarantees that the right receiver gets the payment, and prevents double-spending of credits.

(b) *Efficient routing*: Routing of a credit payment, requires finding of a path between a sender and receiver that has sufficient credit, in an efficient way. This needs to be done in a network where the users know only their immediate neighbors, and the network topology is dynamic due to user churn.

(c) *Privacy*: We believe that, at a minimum, a well-designed DCN needs to guarantee sender and receiver privacy (does not reveal their identities), as well as privacy of the amount transacted between them. The DCN also needs to ensure un-linkability of transactions, guarantee the privacy of the intermediate users in the path, as well as hide the network topology from adversaries. We note that today's blockchain-based networks, such as Ripple make their entire transaction history and network topology public.

Contributions: In this paper, we present BlAnC, a fully decentralized blockchain-based credit network that provides:
(1) User and transaction privacy, while providing transaction integrity, and accountability. Users can choose to split their credit requests across multiple paths in the network.
(2) On-demand routing, that can swiftly adapt to changing network topology, with quick on-boarding/off-boarding of users, and very low maintenance overhead.
(3) Capability for *concurrent* transactions.
(4) Distributed blockchain-based approach to publicly document transactions and identify malicious actors in transactions.

In essence, we propose an alternative to proposed landmarks-based routing and DCN maintenance techniques [10, 22, 25], by having a subset of users facilitating transactions, termed *routing helpers* (RHs). The set of helpers can change over time, and our protocols are resilient against possible collusion among the helpers. We also discuss possible optimizations of our work.

Outline: In Section 2, we review relevant work in the area of credit networks. In Section 3, we give our system model and assumptions. In Section 4, we review the adversary model, and required privacy/security properties. In Section 5, we present our protocols. In Section 6, we present our security analysis in the universal composability framework. In Section 7, we analyze the time, space, message, and communication overheads of BlAnC. In Section 8, we present our experiments and performance analysis. In Section 9, we discuss possible optimizations and extensions to BlAnC, and in Section 10, we conclude the paper, and discuss future work.

2 RELATED WORK

Since a credit network is essentially a flow network, intuitively, one can use the Ford-Fulkerson method [6], or push-relabel algorithms [7], for computing available credit on a path, but their computation costs ($O(VE^2)$, $O(V^3)$, respectively, in a graph $G(V, E)$) do not scale to large, dynamic networks (millions of nodes).

Prihodko *et al.* [5] proposed Flare, a routing algorithm for the Lightning Network, in which each node keeps track of its k neighbors, and maintains links to *beacon* nodes. Flare reveals the value of a link between two users to all nodes in the neighborhood, and works only for Bitcoin transactions. Malavolta *et al.* [11] proposed payment-channel networks that make a tradeoff between privacy and concurrency; additionally their network topology is publicly known to every user in the credit network. Designing a distributed credit network, that maintains user and transaction privacy, while supporting concurrency is a challenge.

There is extensive literature on privacy-preserving transactions in Bitcoin which we do not review here, since credit networks have different structure and privacy needs as compared to cryptocurrencies, which do not require credit links or IOU paths, secure path-finding, etc. In Bitcoin and other cryptocurrencies, any user can buy/sell goods and services to other users, whereas in a credit network, users cannot transact with each other, unless they can find a path between them. Although, unlike Bitcoin and fiat currency used by banks, credit networks enable users to transact in *different currencies* expeditiously (e.g., 3-5 seconds for XRP payments, vs. 3-5 days for bank wires), and with much lower transaction fees.

Credit networks are broadly divided into centralized and decentralized architectures. In the centralized version, there has been work into reducing the reliance on the central, trusted server by using trusted hardware and oblivious computations [14, 26]. In the distributed setting, mechanisms using *landmark routing* [25] to perform route computation between users and landmark(s), and stitching the paths together to route between users, have been proposed. The landmarks–analogous to real-world banks–have less control over the network than in the centralized setting. We now discuss the prior work most relevant to this paper [10, 22].

SilentWhispers [10] presented a DCN architecture using landmark routing, in which a subset of paths between a sender and receiver is calculated, via several landmarks. At regular time intervals, each landmark starts two instances of breadth-first-search (BFS) rooted at itself. One between the sender and itself, and the other between the receiver and itself. These two paths are stitched together to form a complete path between sender and receiver. While SilentWhispers provides transaction integrity, accountability, as well as sender/receiver and transaction value privacy, it does not provide mechanisms for concurrent transactions (essential for scalability). It is also vulnerable to deadlocks, and requires users to join the network only at fixed time intervals. Additionally, prior to going offline, a user needs to hand over her signing keys, and other transaction-related data to the landmarks, which will impersonate the user during absence.

Roos *et al.* [22] presented a DCN which uses graph embedding for efficient routing, with support for concurrent transactions. The embedding algorithm constructs a rooted spanning tree of the network graph. Nodes are addressed based on their distance from the root and routing is performed based on prefixes. In [22], (a) senders pick random credit amounts to transmit along a path, without knowing whether there is adequate liquidity on the chosen path, which leads to a high rate of transaction failure, (b) there is a waiting time imposed on a user to join the network, and (c) a path is greedily chosen based on a heuristic estimate of closeness to the receiver. In a network without high dynamicity, this could lead to linkability of transactions, and eventually compromise sender/receiver privacy.

In contrast, in our approach BlAnC, the maximum credit available on a path is computed during the **Find Route** phase (first phase), and users can dynamically choose their transaction amount. Further, the on-boarding process does not require a user to wait. We do not pre-compute routes; all routing is done truly on-demand at the start of a transaction.

While [10, 22] represent progress in this area, their solutions do not provide resilience against transaction failures, capabilities such as rollbacks and timeouts, and cannot easily be adapted to real-world credit networks. We have proactively chosen to design a blockchain-based solution, to create a secure, anonymous, and distributed events ledger for BlAnC, with built-in anonymity. Thus our system can be augmented to fit in with real-world, well-regarded blockchain-based credit networks [19, 23].

3 SYSTEM MODEL

A credit network is a directed graph where the vertices of the graph represent the users or member nodes of the credit network, the weighted edges represent the flow of credit between the nodes. A directed edge with weight γ from node j to node k signifies that k has extended γ credits to j. The in-degree of k signifies the number of nodes that k has extended credit to, while the out-degree of k signifies the number of nodes that have extended credit to k. A node can lose no more than the total credit it has extended to its neighbors. Our DCN consists of nodes with credit relationships, credit senders and receivers, and a group of volunteering nodes called *routing helpers* who facilitate transactions. We assume all credit amounts are non-negative integers. We also assume that credit transfer between a sender-receiver pair happens over multiple paths to increase value privacy. We give our table of notations in Table 1.

Routing Helpers: We assume the existence of a dynamic set of *routing helpers* (RHs) who help route transactions (RHs *do not* know the identities of the sender, receiver, and any intermediate nodes on the path). Any well-connected node can volunteer to be an RH by writing a "volunteer" message to the Blockchain containing its public key. A sender-receiver pair creates a credit transfer path between itself using an on-demand routing protocol with the help of intermediate RHs. Credit may be distributed across multiple paths to improve unlinkability and transaction privacy. In BlAnC, the RHs help set up checkpoints, which minimize the number of rollbacks, shorten the length of a path segment along which a failed transaction (or path set-up) needs to be re-tried, and provide resilience. For simplicity, we do not discuss routing fees or mining incentives in this paper. Incorporating these into an implementation of BlAnC would be trivial, using techniques such as [4].

Blockchain: All nodes, in BlAnC are part of a Blockchain (BC). Unlike in Bitcoin, where transactions are written to the BC, in BlAnC, the miners write signed messages to the BC, converting it into a *distributed events ledger*. Each node is subscribed to the BC, so whenever a new block is written to the BC, it is broadcasted to all subscribed nodes. When a node needs to write a message, msg, to the BC, it calls the function $BC.write(msg)$, which adds the message to the message pool, and at a later point, a miner would

Table 1: Notations

Variable	Definition
λ	Security parameter
RH	Routing helper
$\alpha = \{\alpha_1, \ldots, \alpha_n\}$	α is the total credit amount; each α_i is a fraction of α.
hopMax	Broadcast parameter
txid, txid′ **txid″, txid‴**	Transaction ids
M	Upper-bound on neighbors along a path
seg_{jk}	Path segment between nodes j, k
tS	Current timestamp
tD	Deadline (time) for transaction timeout
currMax$_i$	Max. link weight of user i
currMax$_{seg_{jk}}$	Max. link weight along seg_{jk}
cw_{jk}	Current link weight between nodes j, k
fw_{jk}	Future link weight between nodes j, k
uw_{jk}	Updated link weight between nodes j, k
H_{jk}	Hold contract between Node j, k
P_{jk}	Pay contract between Node j, k
$BC.read()$ $BC.write()$	Blockchain read/write functions
K_{ij}	Shared symmetric key between users i, j
K_{ijk}	Shared symmetric key between users i, j, k
SK_j, VK_j	Temporary signing/verification key-pair of node j
sk_j, vk_j	Long-term signing/verification key-pair of node j
PK_j, DK_j	Encryption/decryption key-pair of node j
C_i	Ciphertext produced by user i
σ	Signature

write the message on to the BC. Message pools are analogous to transaction pools from Bitcoin and other cryptocurrency networks.

The RHs or any nodes in the network can become miners who help in writing transactions from the message pools. The system model calls for a low mining difficulty in the credit network for near instantaneous generation of new blocks on the BC. This will facilitate fast transactions and rollbacks. As the miners themselves are part of the DCN, thus high mining complexity (proof-of-work) is not essential in BlAnC. The blockchain will be used for proof of transactions (and misbehavior); any adjudication and punitive enforcement of misbehavior is out of scope of this work. Consensus protocols used by the underlying blockchain do not affect BlAnC, hence are not discussed here. BlAnC is designed for decentralized anonymity, using a database for storing credit link weights will be more efficient but it may leak private information.

Joining/leaving the network: A node which needs to join any DCN needs to find at least one network node that is willing to extend credit to, and/or receive credit from it. In BlAnC, the joining and the existing node share their pseudonymous identities and their corresponding real identities (verification keys), along with the mutually-agreed upon link weights(credits). They then double sign(each also has the other's signature) the agreed credit values, and store them. The new node also joins the BC network to receive update messages from the BC (including updates about RHs). A node leaving the DCN permanently just needs to set its link weights to zero and inform its neighbors to do the same for its incoming links. Any node going offline temporarily cannot be part of any ongoing transactions in the network. Before going offline, the node needs to inform its neighbors not to send any *Find Route* packets to it until it comes back online. We discuss handling disconnections, etc., in Section 5.5.

4 ADVERSARY MODEL AND SECURITY PROPERTIES

In our system, the adversary can adaptively corrupt a subset of users. Once user i is corrupted, its credit links will be controlled by the adversary, the adversary can misreport i's link credit value, not respond to requests, relay fraudulent messages to neighbors, and try to re-route payments to other adversary(s). An adversary can also corrupt RHs, who could possibly collude with other malicious users, but we assume a honest majority of RHs. We assume that an adversary cannot corrupt *all* users in the DCN, and thus may know partial network topology, but does not have global knowledge.

We assume that all users have a long-term verification/signing key-pair, and user i's long-term key-pair is denoted by (vk_i, sk_i). Further, all users have pseudonymous, temporary key-pairs: let us denote the temporary verification/signing key-pair of user i by (VK_i, SK_i). The temporary verifcation key is signed by the long-term signing key: $\sigma \leftarrow Sign_{sk_i}(VK_i)$. This effectively ties the temporary keys (identities) to the real/longterm identity. Each user i exchanges its temporary key-pair with all of its neighbors, who in turn verify i's pair using i's long-term verification key. A user's pseudonym and temporary key-pair do not change unless there is a dispute or user failure. The long-term verification key of each RH in the system is known to all users, along with the long-term public key of the RH (used for encrypted communication to RH). Sender and receiver in a transaction share each other's temporary key-pairs.

Desired Security/Privacy properties: We now outline the privacy and security properties provided by our system.

Sender/receiver privacy: An adversary will not know the real or pseudonymous identities of the sender/receiver in any successful transaction, unless she is their next-hop neighbor (all neighbors know each others' identities).

Link privacy: An adversary only knows the value of her adjacent credit links.

Value privacy: An adversary not on the sender-receiver path does not know the amount being transacted. A corrupted node on a sender-receiver path will know the fraction of the amount transacted through her (unavoidable), but will not know the sender/receiver identities. Also, an adversary cannot compute the total credit transferred between two node pairs without compromising at least one node on all the credit fraction paths (credit is transferred concurrently along multiple paths for unlinkability).

Accountability: An adversary cannot re-route payments or misreport her credit link value without being detected by her honest neighbors. Malicious users violating the protocol can be identified and barred by their honest neighbors from being in the credit paths.

Integrity/Rollback: If a transaction does not go through successfully (after multiple retries), every credit link on the sender-receiver path will get rolled back to its original value. If a transaction goes through successfully, the credit links on the path will get decremented by the credit amount correctly.

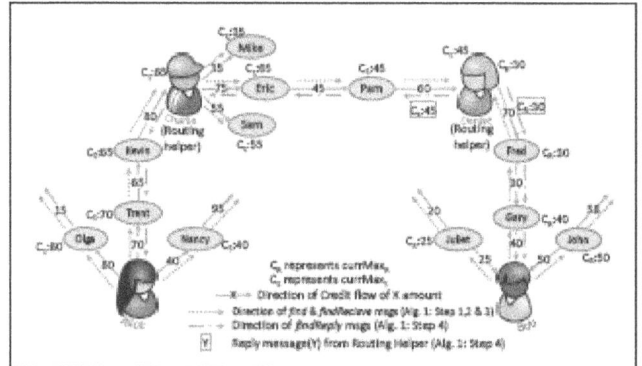

Figure 1: *Find Route* **Phase: Alice and Bob use Charlie and Denise as RHs for one of the transaction-split α_i.**

5 CONSTRUCTION OF BlAnC

The operations of BlAnC can be summed up using three broad phases: *Find Route*, *Hold*, and *Pay*, which we discuss here.

5.1 *Find Route* Phase

In this phase, at a high-level a sender Alice needs to send receiver Bob an amount α, shares of which will be transmitted along different paths. Alice and Bob agree on the number of paths, n, and pick two RHs for each path (to break up the path and improve unlinkability). The maximum transmittable amount along each path, α_i (where $i \in [1..n]$), will be determined dynamically by Alice and Bob after the RHs find a path between Alice and Bob, and report to them the maximum available credit on that path. As shown in the illustration in Figure 1, Alice and Bob use RHs Charlie and Denise. In this phase, the route between Alice and Bob is segmented at the two RHs: seg_{AC}, seg_{CD}, and seg_{DB}, representing segments between Alice and Charlie, Charlie and Dennis, and Dennis and Bob respectively, with corresponding transaction ids **txid'**, **txid''**, and **txid'''**.

Alice broadcasts a *find* message towards Charlie on seg_{AC}; the message is broadcasted forward by each neighbor that receives it until the copies reach Charlie. Bob performs a similar broadcast of the *findReceive* message towards Denise on seg_{DB}. Both RHs only act on the first *find* or *findReceive* messages they receive, respectively, and drop all later duplicate messages. For readability, only a single path (seg_{AC}, seg_{CD}, seg_{DB}) between Alice and Bob is shown. Each node stores the mapping of the incoming, outgoing links, and transaction ID per transaction. This info is stored until transaction completes/aborts.

In case the *find* or *findReceive* did not reach the intended RH, Alice or Bob respectively, can update the **hopMax** value in the tuple before re-broadcasting it. When the *find* message reaches Charlie, he retrieves the maximum credit available on seg_{AC}, $C_s = 65$, and forwards the *find* message to Denise. The max. credit available on seg_{CD} is 45, so Denise sets $C_s = 45$ ($min(max(seg_{AC}), max(seg_{CD}))$ $\Rightarrow min(65, 45)$), and forwards a *findReply* message to Charlie, who

Algorithm 1: *Find Route* Phase

Input : α, n, λ, **hopMax**, hash function H, public ledger BC
Output: Maximum available credit along n paths, $\alpha_1, \ldots, \alpha_n$.
Parties : Sender: Alice, Receiver: Bob

1 **for** $i \in [1..n]$ **do**

    Step 1: Alice and Bob pick RHs Charlie, Denise, broadcast *find* and *findReceive* tuples along seg_{AC} and seg_{DB} respectively, containing **currMax**$_s$ = **currMax**$_A$ and **currMax**$_r$ = **currMax**$_B$. (see Algorithm 6)

    Step 2: Intermediate neighbors (j, k) update **currMax**$_s$ and **currMax**$_r$ along the paths by setting **currMax**$_{seg_{XY}}$ = $min(cw_{jk},$ **currMax**$_{seg_{XY}})$ where $seg_{XY} \in \{seg_{AC}, seg_{DB}\}$, and forward tuples. (see Algorithm 7)

    Step 3: Charlie finds a path to Denise and the max. available credit along seg_{AC}, seg_{CD}. (see Algorithm 8)

    Step 4: Charlie and Denise reply with the maximum credit values, **currMax**$_s$ and **currMax**$_r$, to Alice and Bob respectively. (see Algorithm 9)

    Step 5: Alice and Bob compute out-of-band, $\alpha_i = min($**currMax**$_s,$ **currMax**$_r)$.

2 **end**

3 If $\alpha' = sum(\alpha_1, \ldots, \alpha_n)$, such that $\alpha' < \alpha$, Alice and Bob will repeat Algorithm 1 until α is met, or will choose to transmit α'.

in turn forwards the message back to Alice. The max. available credit on the path from Alice to Denise (seg_{AC}, seg_{CD}) is 45. Denise replies to Bob with maximum credit available on seg_{DB}, $C_r = 30$. Finally, Alice and Bob compute $min(C_s, C_r) = 30$.

Algorithm 1 presents the algorithm (see Table 1 for notations). The steps are self-explanatory. The other algorithms invoked within Algorithm 1 are in the Appendix A.

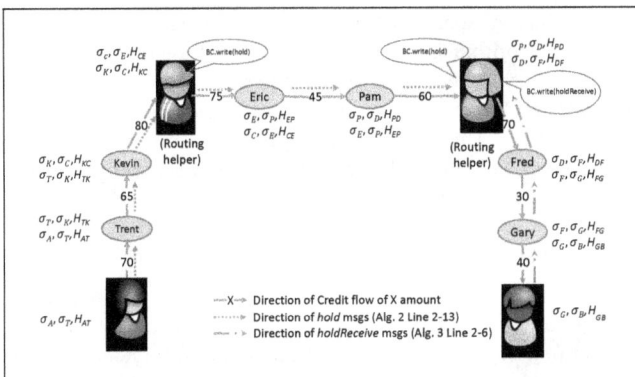

Figure 2: *Hold* **Phase: Between Alice and Denise on segments** seg_{AC}, seg_{CD} **and between Bob and Denise on segment** seg_{DB}.

5.2 *Hold* Phase

After the **Find Route** phase, the path between Alice and Bob is identified. Now, we need to ensure that all the nodes on the path

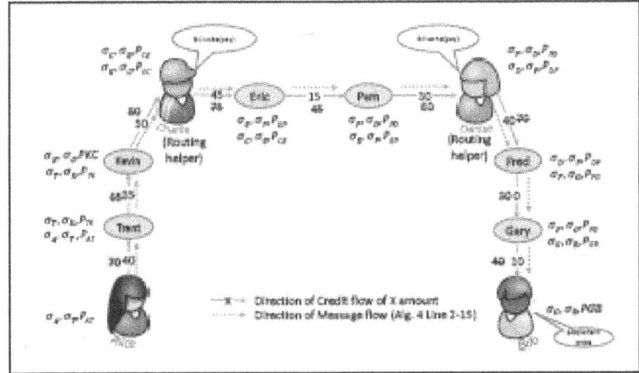

Figure 3: *Pay* **Phase: Alice creates a** *pay* **tuple with** $\alpha_i = 30$, **and forwards it on the Alice-Bob path (in the figure,** α_i **is contained in each** P_{jk} **contract, for nodes** j, k). **Each RH writes a message to the BC whenever they receive the** *pay* **tuple. When Bob receives** α_i **credits, he writes a success message to the BC.**

from Alice to Bob commit to the current transaction by signing contracts with their neighbors on the path. The idea is neighbors j and k (represented by (j, k)) each sign a contract which specifies their current and future link weights (after the transaction), represented as cw_{jk} and fw_{jk} respectively, and store each other's signatures on the contract. This contract will be written to the BC in the event of a dispute or transaction failure, thus providing accountability.

We give a pictorial representation of the **Hold** Phase that happens from both Alice and Bob in Figure 2. Alice constructs a *hold* tuple with $\alpha_i = 30$ and forwards it on the Alice-Denise path (in the figure, α_i is contained in every contract H_{jk}, for neighbors j, k). Each neighboring node-pair on the Alice-Denise path creates *hold* contracts between themselves. In parallel, Bob creates a *holdReceive* tuple with $\alpha_i = 30$, and forwards it on the Bob-Denise path, seg_{DB}. Each node pair(e.g. j, k) on seg_{DB} writes the corresponding contract, and their signatures on the contract (σ_j, σ_k) into their log file for accountability. Each RH writes a message to the BC whenever they receive *hold* and/or *holdReceive* tuples indicating the successful reception of the tuple by them.

Algorithm 2 and Algorithm 3 show the sender and receiver portions of the **Hold** phase.

Alice and Bob pick a pre-image, $x \leftarrow \{0, 1\}^\lambda$ out-of-band, and compute txid $\leftarrow H(x)$ (Line 3 in Algorithm 2). Note that after successful completion of the transaction, Bob will write x to the BC, which will help all nodes on the path verify that the transaction concluded successfully. Alice sends a *hold* message on the seg_{AC} to Charlie, who in turn forwards it to Denise on seg_{CD} (Line 3 in Algorithm 2). The *hold* messages follow the path used by txid$'$ on seg_{AC}, and txid$''$ on seg_{CD} in the **Find Route** Phase. When Charlie or Denise receive the *hold* message, they write a signed message to the BC, which indicates to all nodes on the previous segment that the *hold* message reached the target RH. In the MultiSig algorithm (Line 5, 7, 12 in Algorithm 2), nodes exchange pairwise signatures on contracts; this step is intuitive, and is given in Algorithm 5. The *hold* message will update the transaction id stored by the nodes along the path to the actual transaction id, txid.

Similarly, Bob will send a *holdReceive* message on seg_{DB}, which will follow the path with txid$'''$ and create pairwise contracts for

---

Algorithm 2: *Hold* Phase: Sender and Helpers' Sub-paths

Input : Set of RHs, $\alpha = \alpha_1, \ldots, \alpha_n$, λ, hash function H, a public ledger BC, **txid**′, **txid**″, K_{AD}

Output: *hold* contracts between all nodes on the path on seg_{AC} and seg_{CD}

Parties : Sender: Alice, Receiver: Bob, Helpers: Charlie, Denise

1 **for** $\alpha_i, i \in [1..n]$ **do**

    /* Hold on sub-path from Alice to Charlie   */

2   **begin**

3   Alice picks token, $x \leftarrow \{0,1\}^\lambda$, **txid** $\leftarrow H(x)$, shares token, x, **txid** with Bob; constructs tuple: $hold(\textbf{txid}'||\textbf{txid}||\alpha_i||C_A||\text{tD})$, where, $C_A = E_{K_{AD}}(\text{token}||vk_C||\textbf{txid}||\text{tS})$; sends *hold* to neighbor on path **txid**′.

4   **for** *each pair of consecutive nodes* $j, k \in [1..\textbf{M}]$ *on path* **txid**′ **do**

5   When k receives $hold(\textbf{txid}', \textbf{txid}, \alpha_i, C_A)$ from j, then k runs MultiSig$(j||SK_j||VK_j||k||SK_k||VK_k||\text{tS}||cw_{jk}||$

6          $fw_{jk})$; j, k each locally stores $(\sigma_j, \sigma_k, (H_{jk} = \text{contract}))$ (see Algorithm 5), and k updates current record of **txid**′ to **txid**.

7   **end**

8   Charlie, on receiving *hold*, calls MultiSig(), and updates **txid**, writes a signed message to BC using $BC.write((vk_C||\textbf{txid}||hold)||Sign_{sk_C}(vk_C||\textbf{txid}||hold))$.

9   **end**

    /* Hold on sub-path from Charlie to Denise   */

10   **begin**

11   Charlie updates the tuple to $hold(\textbf{txid}''||\textbf{txid}||\alpha_i||C_A||\text{tD})$, sends it to neighbor on seg_{CD} with **txid**″.

12   The intermediate nodes follow the same procedure as those on seg_{AC}, except with **txid**″ instead of **txid**′ (details omitted due to space constraints).

13   Denise, on receiving *hold* tuple, calls MultiSig(), updates **txid**, writes a signed message to BC by calling $BC.write((vk_D||\textbf{txid}||hold)||Sign_{sk_D}(vk_D||\textbf{txid}||hold))$.

14   **end**

15 **end**

Algorithm 3: *Hold* Phase: Receiver's Sub-path

Input : Set of RHs, total amount $\alpha = \alpha_1, \ldots, \alpha_n$, λ, hash function H, a public ledger, BC, **txid**‴, K_{BD}

Output: *hold* contracts between all nodes on seg_{DB}

Parties : Sender: Alice, Receiver: Bob, Helpers: Charlie, Denise

1 **for** $\alpha_i, i \in [1..n]$ **do**

    /* Hold on sub-path from Bob to Denise   */

2   **begin**

3   Concurrently, Bob constructs tuple: $holdReceive(\textbf{txid}'''||\textbf{txid}||\alpha_i||C_B||\text{tD})$, where $C_B = E_{K_{BD}}(\text{token}||vk_C||\textbf{txid}||\text{tS})$, sends *holdReceive* tuple to next neighbor on path **txid**‴.

4   The intermediate nodes follow the same procedure as those on seg_{AC}, except with **txid**‴ instead of **txid**′.

5   Denise receives the *holdReceive* tuple and then creates *hold* contract with the neighbor on **txid**‴ path. On receiving the *hold* from the neighbor on seg_{CD} Denise establishes a full path marked by **txid** from Alice to Bob. (seg_{AC}, seg_{CD} and seg_{DB}) Finally, Denise writes a signed message to BC by calling $BC.write((vk_D||\textbf{txid}||holdReceive)||$ $Sign_{sk_D}(vk_D||\textbf{txid}||holdReceive))$.

6   **end**

7 **end**

5.3 *Pay* Phase

At the end of the *Hold* phase, all nodes on the path from Alice to Bob would have committed α_i credits to the current transaction, **txid**, by signing contracts with neighbors on the path. In the *Pay* phase, Alice sends a *pay* tuple along the path to Bob: $pay(\textbf{txid}, \alpha_i, \text{tD})$ to complete the transaction. Algorithm 4 shows the steps of the *Pay* phase; we give a pictorial representation of the *Pay* phase in Figure 3.

Each node first signs *pay* contracts, corresponding to its previously signed *hold* contracts, with its neighbors on the path and changes its corresponding link weights: this step is intuitive, and is given in Algorithm 5. Whenever Charlie or Denise receive the *pay* message, they write a signed message to the BC, thus indicating to all nodes on the previous segment that the *pay* message reached the target RH. The *pay* message from Alice, contains a timeout value tD; nodes wait for tD time for the target RH to write the *pay* message to the BC, or abort

5.4 Blockchain Operations

Because of low mining complexity in the BC, we assume that there will not be any shortage of miners. Thus ensuring timely propagation of new blocks containing latest messages from nodes within the network. The relatively higher no. of messages in BC can be dealt by creating an archived snapshot of BC at certain fixed time intervals and starting a new one-block chain. In this model, individual resource constrained user nodes need not store the entire BC, but only the compacted chain from the last snapshot. However, unconstrained devices (users, RHs) can store longer chains of the BC to act as a source of truth for older transaction data.

each link on the path (Line 3 in Algorithm 3). The nodes on seg_{DB} will also get updated with the actual transaction id, **txid**. When Denise receives the *holdReceive* message, she writes a signed message to the BC, thus indicating to all nodes on the seg_{DB} segment that the *holdReceive* message reached the target RH. The *hold* and *holdReceive* messages from Alice and Bob, respectively, contain a tD parameter. This parameter indicates the time at which the *hold* contracts will timeout if the nodes don't see a signed *hold* message or a signed *holdReceive* message on the BC corresponding to **txid** from their target RH. After the *Hold* phase, the three different paths from the *Find Route* phase coalesce into a single path marked by **txid**.

Whenever a new block is mined, and written onto the BC, the underlying consensus algorithm synchronizes it across the network. Our DCN can be deployed on any existing BC as long as it supports individual nodes writing signed messages to the BC as opposed to writing transactions, and has low mining complexity.

5.5 System Dynamics: Handling Timeouts, Node Failures, and Corrupt Nodes

Timeout in *Hold* Phase: All nodes know who the target RH on their respective segment is, e.g., Charlie for seg_{AC}, and so on. If there are no *hold* messages written on BC associated with the current **txid** by either RHs, this means that the *hold* messages timed out in the first segment and never reached Charlie. In this scenario, *hold* contracts are dropped by all nodes on the path and Alice has to retry the transaction. If nodes time out during the ***Hold*** phase and see a *hold* message on BC from their target RH, they wait for the transaction to be retried and completed in the other segment.

However, if the nodes on any segment do not see a *hold* message from their target RH before timing out, they drop the *hold* contracts and reservation on their links, since the transaction timed-out in their segment, and the ***Find Route*** phase will be retried on that segment. All the nodes on the specific timed-out segment also publish the dropped contracts onto the BC. This will expose the offending node's (node which caused the time-out) ephemeral identity and thus its neighbors will not forward the find tuple to this node for the current transaction when the ***Find Route*** phase is retried. The offending node's privacy in the network is still maintained and only its immediate neighbors identify it. The offending node could be an RH, then the sender-receiver can try again or abort the transaction and start with a new set of RHs.

To illustrate, if Charlie had written the *hold* message to BC and Denise did not, then Charlie will retry for seg_{CD} by repeating the ***Find Route*** phase, and ***Hold*** phase to Denise, to find an alternate path. If the timeout occurs after Denise has written a *hold* message on the BC, but the *holdReceive* message is not complete, then Bob will retry the transaction for seg_{DB} on its end.

Timeout in Pay Phase: On timeout, each node j on a path **txid** on the timed-out segment, will call $BC.write(\textbf{txid}||H_{jk}||P_{jk})$ if they had a *pay* contract or just $BC.write(H_{jk})$ if they did not receive a *pay* message from the neighboring node. In the pay phase, seg_{AC} or seg_{CD} time-out if target RH (Charlie or Denise, respectively) did not write a signed *pay* message to the BC indicating successful reception of *pay* message. Segment seg_{DB} times-out if nodes on the segment do not see a **success** message on the BC from Bob, with a correct pre-image for **txid**. When the current transaction cannot be completed because either the timeout occurred on seg_{AC}, or if there are no alternate viable paths on seg_{CD} or seg_{DB}, Alice or Bob can abort the transaction. To abort transaction and initiate a rollback of any changes in the network (from *pay* contracts affecting link weights) tied to **txid**, Bob or Alice write the tuple: (**txid**, x, **failure − rollback**) to the BC. All nodes on path should delete their *hold* contracts and revert back to previous link weights if they had any *pay* contracts associated with transaction **txid**. Rollback won't affect other concurrent transactions; no topology-related info is written to BC.

Algorithm 4: *Pay* Phase

Input : Set of RHs, total amount $\alpha = \alpha_1, \ldots, \alpha_n$, λ, hash function H, a public ledger, BC, **txid**

Output : Updated link weights and corresponding *pay* contracts on each link from Sender to Receiver equivalent to transaction amount

Parties : Sender: Alice, Receiver: Bob, Helpers: Charlie, Denise

1 **for** $\alpha_i, i \in [1..n]$ **do**
    /* Pay on sub-path from Alice to Charlie   */
2   **begin**
3   Alice constructs tuple $pay(\textbf{txid}||\alpha_i||\text{tD})$, sends *pay* tuple to next neighbor on path **txid**
4   **for** *each pair of consecutive nodes* $j, k \in [1..\textbf{M}]$ *in* seg_{AC} *which have* **txid do**
5   When k receives $pay(\textbf{txid}||\alpha_i||\text{tD})$ from j, k runs MultiSig($j \parallel SK_j \parallel VK_j \parallel k \parallel SK_k \parallel VK_k \parallel$ tS$||cw_{jk}||uw_{jk}$) (see Algorithm 5). Nodes j, k each locally store $(\sigma_j, \sigma_k, (P_{jk} = \text{contract}))$.
6   **end**
7   On receiving *pay* tuple, after calling MultiSig(), Charlie writes a signed message to BC by calling $BC.write((vk_C||\textbf{txid}||pay)||\text{Sign}_{SK_C}(vk_C||\textbf{txid}||pay))$.
8   **end**
    /* Pay on sub-path from Charlie to Denise   */
9   **begin**
10   Charlie forwards *pay* tuple to the next neighbor on **txid** path towards Denise.
11   Intermediate nodes follow the same steps as those on seg_{AC}. On receiving the *pay* tuple, and after calling MultiSig(), Denise writes a signed message to BC by calling $BC.write((vk_D||\textbf{txid}||pay)||\text{Sign}_{SK_D}(vk_D||\textbf{txid}||pay))$. Denise forwards *pay* tuple to the next neighbor on **txid** path towards Bob.
12   **end**
    /* Pay on sub-path from Denise to Bob   */
13   **begin**
14   Intermediate nodes on seg_{DB} follow the same steps as those on the other segments. On receiving the *pay* tuple, after calling MultiSig(), Bob writes a success message to BC by calling $BC.write(\textbf{txid}||x||\textbf{success})$.
15   **end**
16 **end**

Alternatively, if the timeout occurred on seg_{CD} or seg_{DB}, then Charlie or Denise, respectively, will retry to find an alternate path. Since all contracts were written to the BC, all honest nodes in the path know which node timed out the transaction (faulty node), either by malicious behavior or by going offline, the honest nodes will route retry packets to neighbors other than the identified faulty node to prevent subsequent failures. If Charlie wrote the *pay* message to the BC, then Charlie will retry the ***Find Route***, and ***Hold*** phases to Denise to find an alternative path, before retrying the ***Pay*** phase again.

In the absence of malicious nodes in the network, i.e., no timeouts in a transaction, only six messages will be written to the BC. Three messages are written by the RHs after the *Hold* and two message in the *Pay* phases. The sixth message is the **success** message written by Bob to the BC. The only information gleaned from BC is that a certain RH pair was involved in a transaction of unknown amount. Since no node involved in the transaction exposed their identity, there is no need to change any node's pseudonymous identities. However, if the transaction was retried, that is, a timeout occurred, all nodes involved in the transaction will need to update their pseudonymous identities and share new pseudonymous identities with their neighbors. This rekeying will help reduce linkability between transactions as now all the nodes' previous pseudonymous identities are in the BC.

Algorithm 5: Multisig Exchange

Input   : $j, SK_j, VK_j, k, SK_k, VK_k, cw_{jk}, \gamma \in \{fw_{jk}, uw_{jk}\}$, **txid**, tS

Output : Tuple $(\sigma_j, \sigma_k, \text{contract})$ stored at node j and k

Parties : Node j and k

1   j sends $\sigma_j \leftarrow \text{Sign}_{SK_j}(\text{contract} = (cw_{jk}, \gamma), \textbf{txid}, \text{tS})$ to k

2   k sends $\sigma_k \leftarrow \text{Sign}_{SK_k}(\text{contract} = (cw_{jk}, \gamma), \textbf{txid}, \text{tS})$ to j

3   **if** $\text{Verify}_{VK_k}(\text{contract}||\sigma_k) \stackrel{?}{=} 1$ **then**

4 | j stores $(\sigma_j||\sigma_k||\text{contract})$

5   **end**

6   **if** $\text{Verify}_{VK_j}(\text{contract}||\sigma_j) \stackrel{?}{=} 1$ **then**

7 | k stores $(\sigma_j||\sigma_k||\text{contract})$

8   **end**

Malicious RHs: In case of misbehaving RHs where the RHs neglects to write *hold/pay* tuple reception messages to the BC, other nodes on the path would timeout. They would then dump all the *hold/pay* contracts for the given transactions on to the BC. This would show that all nodes on the path went through with the transaction and the misbehaving RH did not update the transaction on the BC.

There is a possibility of an RH changing its public identity and coming back as a new one after it is identified as malicious. However, if users choose well-known RHs (e.g., one that has written many transactions to the BC), then the impact of such a malicious RH can be significantly mitigated. Even in the presence of misbehaving RHs the sender/receiver do not end up losing any credits as the transaction will either get re-routed or aborted in case of failure.

6   SECURITY ANALYSIS

We prove the security of our constructions in the Universal Composability (UC) framework [1] which is a well-known framework used to analyze the security of distributed protocols. The UC paradigm elegantly captures the conditions under which a given distributed protocol is secure, by comparing it to an ideal realization of the protocol. To this end, the UC framework defines two "worlds": the real-world, where the protocol, π to be proved secure runs, and the ideal-world, where the entire protocol, ϕ is executed by an ideal, trusted functionality, where all users only talk to the ideal functionality via secure and authenticated channels. The goal then is to

prove that no distinguishing algorithm, commonly called as "environment", $\mathcal{Z}$, can successfully distinguish between the execution (EXEC) of the two worlds. The notion of UC security is captured by the pair of definitions below:

Definition 6.1. (UC-emulation [1]) Let π and ϕ be probabilistic polynomial-time (PPT) protocols. We say that π UC-emulates ϕ if for any PPT adversary $\mathcal{A}$ there exists a PPT adversary $\mathcal{S}$ such that for any balanced PPT environment $\mathcal{Z}$ we have

$$\text{EXEC}_{\phi, \mathcal{S}, \mathcal{Z}} \approx \text{EXEC}_{\pi, \mathcal{A}, \mathcal{Z}}$$

Definition 6.2. (UC-realization [1]) Let $\mathcal{F}$ be an ideal functionality and let π be a protocol. We say that π UC-realizes $\mathcal{F}$ if π UC-emulates the ideal protocol for $\mathcal{F}$.

We define a distributed credit network functionality $\mathcal{F}_{\text{DCN}}$ in the ideal world, which consists of $\mathcal{F}_{\text{FindRoute}}, \mathcal{F}_{\text{Hold}}, \mathcal{F}_{\text{Pay}}$, and $\mathcal{F}_{\text{BC}}$. An adversary can corrupt regular users and routing helpers at any time, upon which the user's responses to queries by $\mathcal{F}_{\text{DCN}}$ will be generated by the adversary. We assume $\mathcal{F}_{\text{DCN}}$ maintains an adjacency matrix of all users in the network, where the entries of the matrix are the link weights, which is regularly updated when $\mathcal{F}_{\text{FindRoute}}$ and $\mathcal{F}_{\text{Pay}}$ are called. Due to space constraints we have given the definitions of $\mathcal{F}_{\text{FindRoute}}, \mathcal{F}_{\text{Hold}}, \mathcal{F}_{\text{Pay}}$, and $\mathcal{F}_{\text{BC}}$, discussion about their design choices and correctness, and the proof of the following theorem in the full version of the paper [17].

THEOREM 6.3. *Let* $\mathcal{F}_{\text{DCN}}$ *be an ideal functionality for* BlAnC. *Let* $\mathcal{A}$ *be a probabilistic polynomial-time (PPT) adversary for* BlAnC, *and let* $\mathcal{S}$ *be the ideal-world PPT simulator for* $\mathcal{F}_{\text{DCN}}$. BlAnC *UC-realizes* $\mathcal{F}_{\text{DCN}}$, *for any PPT distinguishing environment* $\mathcal{Z}$.

Sketch: At a high level, the proof shows that no PPT distinguishing environment $\mathcal{Z}$ can distinguish between the outputs of the ideal-world simulator, $\mathcal{S}$, and a BlAnC adversary $\mathcal{A}$. Ideal-world $\mathcal{S}$ mirrors the actions of a real-world $\mathcal{A}$, and we show that if $\mathcal{A}$ cheats in the real-world, $\mathcal{S}$ would also break the security of the $\mathcal{F}_{\text{DCN}}$, which is not possible.

7   SCALABILITY METRICS

In this section, we analyze the performance of our system with respect to time, space, message, and communication complexities. Time is measured in terms of the average execution time of a cryptographic operation, the space is measured in terms of the total storage required, the message complexity is measured in number of messages, in the worst case, and the communication complexity is the number of bytes of information transmitted. Table 2 shows the asymptotic time, space and message complexities. Table 3 shows the number of encryptions, decryptions, signatures, and hashes at each node during the *Find Route*, *Hold*, and *Pay* phases. Table 4 shows the communication complexity in bytes at different nodes.

Joining the network: When a new node joins the credit network, it shares pseudonymous keys, verification keys, and link weights with nodes that it will be connected to in the network and stores these values. This is a one time setup cost and is linear in the number of neighbors the new node will have in the network. The node also joins the blockchain which incurs a constant time/space overhead and is a one time setup cost.

Key exchange after timeout: When a transaction times out, all nodes involved in the transaction would have published their

Table 2: Asymptotic Complexities: n **denotes the number of fractions of a payment (in Ripple [19], the max. number of paths, and hence** n**, for a single transaction is 7),** d **denotes node degree,** k **is the number of nodes on a single path (**$k \subseteq M$, $|k| << |M|$**),** c **is the max. path length between sender and receiver (from Ripple [19], the max. path length is 10).**

Phases	Time	Space	Messages		
			Regular users	Charlie (RH)	Denise (RH)
Find Route Phase	$O(n)$	$O(n)$	$O(d^c \cdot n)$	$O(d^c \cdot n)$	$O(k \cdot n)$
Hold Phase	$O(k \cdot n)$	$O(k \cdot n)$	$O(k \cdot n)$	$O(n)$	$O(n)$
Pay Phase	$O(k \cdot n)$	$O(k \cdot n)$	$O(k \cdot n)$	$O(n)$	$O(n)$

Table 3: n **is the number of fractions, number of cryptographic operations at a node: E: no. of encryptions, D: no. of decryptions, S: no. of signatures, V: no. of verifications, H: no. of hashes.**

Phases	Sender	Receiver	RH
Find Route Phase	E: $2n$, D: $2n$, H: $3n$	E: $2n$, D: $2n$, H: $3n$	E: $2n$, D: $2n$, S: n, H; n
Hold Phase	E: n, S: $2n$, V: $2n$	E: n, S: $2n$, V: $2n$	D: $2n$, S: $2n$, V: $2n$
Pay Phase	S: $2n$, V: $2n$	S: $2n$, V: $2n$	S: $2n$, V: $2n$

Table 4: Worst case communication complexity (in message size): Using RSA-2048 for PKI, ECDSA signatures (72 bytes), AES-256 for symmetric key encryption and SHA-256 for token/txids' generation.

Type of Message	Size	Phase
find Tuple	166 *bytes*	*Find Route* Phase
findReceive Tuple	134 *bytes*	*Find Route* Phase
findReply Tuple	240 *bytes*	*Find Route* Phase
hold Tuple	272 *bytes*	*Hold* Phase
holdReceive Tuple	272 *bytes*	*Hold* Phase
pay Tuple	80 *bytes*	*Pay* Phase
BC.write hold	172 *bytes*	*Hold* Phase
BC.write holdReceive	179 *bytes*	*Hold* Phase
BC.write pay	171 *bytes*	*Pay* Phase

Table 5: Emulation results for crypto operations in BlAnC

Cryptographic Operation	*Find Route* Phase	*Hold* Phase	*Pay* Phase
RSA-2048 Encrypt Time	202.78 *us*	NA	NA
RSA-2048 Decrypt Time	2.63 *ms*	NA	NA
AES-256 Encrypt Time	4.54 *us*	4.54 *us*	NA
AES-256 Decrypt Time	4.08 *us*	4.08 *us*	NA
ECDSA Sign Time	192.22 *us*	6.38 *ms*	6.17 *ms*
ECDSA Verify Time	1.10 *ms*	31.59 *ms*	31.59 *ms*
SHA-256 Hash Time	24.36 *us*	8.12 *us*	NA

hold and *pay* contracts to the BC, exposing their pseudonyms. All involved nodes need to establish new pseudonyms with their neighbors. The time complexity of this step is $O(k \cdot d)$, where d is maximum node degree in the DCN.

8 EXPERIMENTS AND EVALUATION

The cryptographic operations used in the protocol, which are AES-256, SHA-256, RSA-2048 and ECDSA were implemented using C++ Open-SSL libraries [24]. The simulations were performed on a desktop class machine with Intel(R) Core(TM) i7-7600U CPU @ 2.80GHz and 8GB RAM. We use ns-3 [16], a discrete event network simulator to test BlAnC. The simulations were run on a 100 node network with the nodes connected over WiFi, since a wireless connection is representative of a majority of users. Given that the Internet's diameter is around 18, in our simulation setup, the sender and receiver

are 15 hops apart, on a path passing through the two RH. The network's physical layer delay characteristics are set to the Constant Speed Propagation Delay Model and loss characteristics are set to the Log Distance Propagation Loss Model. The channel coding was set to Orthogonal frequency-division multiplexing at a data rate of 6 Mbps. The simulations were run with multiple concurrent transactions and a total of 200 transactions were simulated.

Table 5 shows the timings for the cryptographic operations performed by nodes on a transaction path for the different phases during a BlAnC transaction. The cryptographic operations in the *Hold* phase and *Pay* phases contribute make the bulk of the cryptographic time delay, that is, ~ 37 *ms* as opposed to 4 *ms* in the *Find Route* phase.

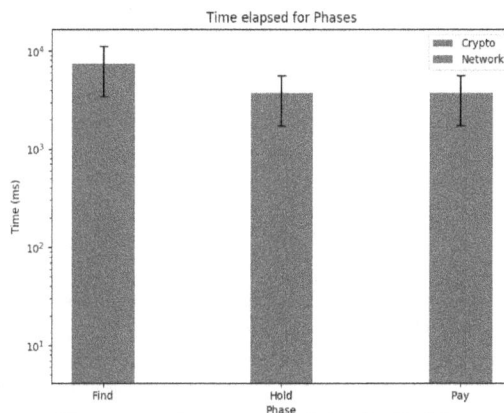

Figure 4: Illustration of average time delay for *Find Route* , *Hold* and *Pay* phases during a BlAnC transaction due to network and cryptographic operations.

Figure 4 shows that majority of the time delay in BlAnC comes from the network when compared to delay incurred due to cryptographic operations. The error bars represent the standard deviations of the delay. From the ns-3 simulations, we observed that the total time taken by the *Find Route* phase to conclude was on average 7.303 *secs*. This is the time taken by Alice and Bob to determine the maximum value of α_i credit that can flow between Alice and Bob in the chosen path for the transaction in question. The delay of 7.303 secs includes network delay, while the delay contributed by cryptographic operations was approximately 4.158 *ms*. In comparison to SilentWhispers [10] which takes 1.349 seconds (the authors only measured cryptographic costs) to determine α_i on a path of length 10 *hops* (BlAnC is three orders of magnitude faster). The significant time delay (in the *Find Route* phase) is attributed to the ad hoc, on demand path finding technique of BlAnC. This delay is a trade-off to ensure that the privacy of sender and receiver is protected as each transaction triggers a new set of path searches and the paths to chosen RHs are not pre-determined.

The *Hold* and *Pay* phases took a total duration of 1.253 secs each. So a complete transaction on average takes 9.809 secs to finish. We did not include the time delays for the BC as those delays would not affect the flow of credit from sender to receiver unless there is an occurrence of a timeout during the transaction.

9 OPTIMIZATIONS

In the *Find Route* phase, the cost of finding a path from sender/receiver to their respective RHs, in the worst case could be $O(d^c)$, where d is the maximum degree of a node on the path, and c is the maximum hop count. In practice, c could be set as the maximum length of a path between two nodes, which, according to empirical data collected from Ripple's datasets is 10 [10, 19]. This is a one-time cost, which, will be amortized over time by having the sender/receiver store information about the paths to their respective RHs, over the course of their transactions. The sender/receiver would then only have to follow a fixed path to their RH, and would incur a cost of $O(d^c)$ infrequently. Another way to optimize this cost would be for every node to choose d' of its neighbors at random ($d' < d$), and send *find* tuples only to them.

Each node in the credit network that is involved in a transaction, could keep track of the identity of the RH, maximum link weight available to RH, and the interface it reached the RH from. By using this information as a forwarding table, the number of broadcasts could be decreased in a stable credit network where the links state do not vary frequently. Broadcasts could be used in-case of a stale forwarding table, in which case the sender would retry the *Find Route* phase with a broadcast instead of a directed *find* message. This would also reduce the cost of the protocol in the *Find Route* phase if the intermediate nodes do not need to use broadcasts and already have a path available to a known RH. Each node could also build a history of all the RHs it has used for prior transactions, and prefer to use the ones with which the transactions completed successfully instead of trying to send payment through new RHs.

Graph embedding, as used in [22] could be used in our *Find Route* phase to construct an optimal path between the sender/receiver and their respective RHs. One could construct a spanning tree of the network rooted at the RHs, and either use tree-base embedded routing (strictly following the edges of the spanning tree), or a more flexible approach, where one greedily chooses the shortest path between two nodes.

Since the BC is being used to publish transaction-related messages, the storage of the BC can become challenging, along with the scaling of the DCN. To tackle this problem, the BC can be compressed at regular time epochs as we discussed before. At the end of a time epoch, all nodes would make sure all the payments and links are settled for past transactions. At this point, the BC can be compacted by replacing all but the last few active blocks (blocks containing active transactions) with a single compacted block that contains the hash of the chain upto that point. At the start of the new epoch, all RHs need to declare themselves as RHs again, as there is no historical information available to new nodes joining the credit network in the new epoch.

10 CONCLUSIONS AND FUTURE WORK

In this paper, we propose BlAnC, a novel, fully decentralized blockchain-based credit network that preserves user and transaction anonymity, enables on-demand and concurrent transactions to happen seamlessly, and can identify malicious network actors that do not follow the protocols and disrupt operations. We performed security analysis to demonstrate BlAnC's strength and presented

scalability metrics. Simulation/emulation-based analysis of the latency of transactions in the DCN demonstrate BlAnC's scalability.

In the future, we intend to implement BlAnC in a real-world testbed like Hyperledger [9] and test impact of real-world network dynamics on the protocols' stability and scalability.

11 ACKNOWLEDGEMENTS

Research supported by NSF awards #1800088; #1719342; #1345232, EPSCoR Cooperative agreement OIA-1757207; and ARO grant #W911NF-07-2-0027. Any opinions, findings, and conclusions or recommendations expressed in this material are those of the authors and do not necessarily reflect the views of the federal government.

REFERENCES

[1] Ran Canetti. 2001. Universally Composable Security: A New Paradigm for Cryptographic Protocols. In *42nd Annual Symposium on Foundations of Computer Science, FOCS*. 136–145.
[2] P. Dandekar, A. Goel, R. Govindan, and I. Post. 2011. Liquidity in credit networks: a little trust goes a long way. , 147–156 pages.
[3] D. B. DeFigueiredo and E. T. Barr. 2005. TrustDavis: A Non-Exploitable Online Reputation System. In *IEEE International Conference on E-Commerce Technology (CEC 2005)*. 274–283.
[4] Felix Engelmann, Henning Kopp, Frank Kargl, Florian Glaser, and Christof Weinhardt. 2017. Towards an Economic Analysis of Routing in Payment Channel Networks. In *Proceedings of the 1st Workshop on Scalable and Resilient Infrastructures for Distributed Ledgers (SERIAL '17)*. Article 2, 6 pages.
[5] Flare [n. d.]. Flare. https://bitfury.com/content/downloads/whitepaper_flare_an_approach_to_routing_in_lightning_network_7_7_2016.pdf.
[6] L.R. Ford and D.R. Fulkerson. 1954. Maximal flow through a network. *Canadian Journal of Mathematics* 8 (1954).
[7] A.V. Goldberg and R. E. Tarjan. 1988. A new approach to the maximum flow problem. *J. of ACM* 35 (1988), 921–940.
[8] A. M. Kakhki, C. Kliman-Silver, and A. Mislove. 2013. Iolaus: securing online content rating systems. In *International World Wide Web Conference, WWW*. 919–930.
[9] Linux Foundation. 2015. Hyperledger Project. https://www.hyperledger.org
[10] G. Malavolta, P. Moreno-Sanchez, A. Kate, and M. Maffei. 2017. SilentWhispers: Enforcing Security and Privacy in Decentralized Credit Networks. In *Annual Network and Distributed System Security Symposium, NDSS*.
[11] G. Malavolta, P. Moreno-Sanchez, A. Kate, M. Maffei, and S. Ravi. 2017. Concurrency and Privacy with Payment-Channel Networks. In *Proceedings ACM SIGSAC Conference on Computer and Communications Security, CCS*. 455–471.
[12] A. Mislove, A. Post, P. Druschel, and P. K. Gummadi. 2008. Ostra: Leveraging Trust to Thwart Unwanted Communication. In *Proceedings of the USENIX Symposium on Networked Systems Design & Implementation, NSDI*. 15–30.
[13] A. Mohaisen, N. Hopper, and Y. Kim. 2011. Keep your friends close: Incorporating trust into social network-based Sybil defenses. In *IEEE International Conference on Computer Communications, INFOCOM*. 1943–1951.
[14] P. Moreno-Sanchez, A. Kate, M. Maffei, and K. Pecina. 2015. Privacy Preserving Payments in Credit Networks: Enabling trust with privacy in online marketplaces. In *Annual Network and Distributed System Security Symposium, NDSS*.
[15] P. Moreno-Sanchez, N. Modi, R. Songhela, A. Kate, and S. Fahmy. 2018. Mind Your Credit: Assessing the Health of the Ripple Credit Network. In *Proceedings of the World Wide Web Conference on World Wide Web, WWW*. 329–338.
[16] NSNAM.org. 2008. Network Simulator 3. https://www.nsnam.org/
[17] G. Panwar, S. Misra, and R. Vishwanathan. 2019. BlAnC. https://eprint.iacr.org/2019/014
[18] A. Post, V. Shah, and A. Mislove. 2011. Bazaar: Strengthening User Reputations in Online Marketplaces. In *Proceedings of the USENIX Symposium on Networked Systems Design and Implementation, NSDI*.
[19] Ripple [n. d.]. Ripple website. https://ripple.com.
[20] Ripple [n. d.]. Ripple XRP charts. https://ripple.com/xrp/.
[21] Ripple [n. d.]. Several global banks join RIpple's growing network. https://ripple.com/insights/several-global-banks-join-ripples-growing-network/.
[22] S. Roos, P. Moreno-Sanchez, A. Kate, and I. Goldberg. 2018. Settling payments fast and private: efficient decentralized routing for path-based transactions. In *Annual Network and Distributed System Security Symposium, NDSS, To appear*.
[23] Stellar [n. d.]. Stellar website. https://stellar.org.
[24] The OpenSSL Project. 1998. OpenSSL: The Open Source toolkit for SSL/TLS. https://{www.openssl.org}
[25] P. F. Tsuchiya. 1988. The Landmark Hierarchy: A New Hierarchy for Routing in Very Large Networks. In *Symposium Proceedings on Communications Architectures*

and Protocols (SIGCOMM '88). 35–42.

[26] B. Viswanath, M. Mondal, P. K. Gummadi, A. Mislove, and A. Post. 2012. Canal: scaling social network-based Sybil tolerance schemes. In *Proceedings of EuroSys*. 309–322.

A FIND ROUTE PHASE ALGORITHMS

We give details of the algorithms called in the steps of the ***Find Route*** Algorithm 1. All the algorithms below have common inputs, CI defined as: CI = {Set of all RHs, no. of paths n, security parameter λ, hash function H, public ledger BC, **hopMax**}.

Algorithm 6: ***Find Route*** Phase: Sender/Receiver Start

Input : CI (defined above)
Output : *find* and *findReceive* tuples of sender and receiver
Parties : Sender: Alice, Receiver: Bob

1 **for** $i \in [1..n]$ **do**
  /* Sender start   */
2 | **begin**
3 | | Alice picks a $x' \leftarrow \{0,1\}^\lambda$, computes **txid**$' \leftarrow H(x')$, finds **currMax**$_A$,
4 | | reserves the amount, sets **currMax**$_s \leftarrow$ **currMax**$_A$.
5 | | Constructs tuple:
     find(**txid**$'||(vk_C||``vk_D)||reserve($**currMax**$_s)$ $||$**hopMax**$||C_A$), where
     $C_A = E_{PK_D}(K_{AD}||y \leftarrow \{0,1\}^\lambda||tS) \parallel K_{AD}$ is a shared symmetric key between Alice and Denise, y is a nonce, PK_D is Public Key of Denise and tS is timestamp for tuple. The *find* tuple is sent to all of Alice's neighbors.
6 | **end**
  /* Receiver start   */
7 | **begin**
8 | | Parallelly, Bob picks a $x''' \leftarrow \{0,1\}^\lambda$, computes **txid**$''' \leftarrow H(x''')$, finds and reserves **currMax**$_B$, sets **currMax**$_r \leftarrow$ **currMax**$_B$.
9 | | Constructs tuple:
     findReceive(**txid**$'''||vk_D||reserve($**currMax**$_r)$ $||$**hopMax**$||C_B$)
10 | | where $C_B = E_{PK_D}(K_{BD}||y' \leftarrow \{0,1\}^\lambda||tS)$; K_{BD} is shared symmetric between Bob and Denise. The *findReceive* tuple is sent to all of Bob's neighbors.
11 | **end**
12 **end**

In Algorithm 6, Alice and Bob generate **txid**$'$ and **txid**$'''$ respectively. They also independently generate symmetric encryption keys and challenge nonces for Denise. Alice creates a *find* tuple, containing the **txid**$'$, **currMax**$_s$, **hopMax**, identity of both Charlie and Denise, and some encrypted information which is broadcast to all her neighbors. Bob also creates a similar tuple called *findReceive*, containing the **txid**$''$, **currMax**$_r$, **hopMax**, identity of Denise, and some encrypted information which is broadcast to all his neighbors. At Alice and Bob **currMax**$_s$ and **currMax**$_r$ are respectively set to their outgoing link weights. If the messages timeout, then sender can retry with a higher **hopMax** value.

Algorithm 7: ***Find Route*** Phase: Path Construction

Input : CI
Output : Sender-helper path, receiver-helper path
Parties : Sender: Alice, Receiver: Bob

1 **for** $i \in [1..n]$ **do**
  /* Sender-helper path construction   */
2 | **for** *neighbors* $j \in [1..M]$ *in credit path between Alice-Charlie* **do**
3 | | **if** (**hopMax** = 0) **then**
4 | | | do nothing
5 | | **end**
6 | | **else**
7 | | | Reserve **currMax**$_j$ by min(**currMax**$_s$, **currMax**$_j$), set **currMax**$_s$ = min(**currMax**$_s$, **currMax**$_j$).
8 | | | Construct tuple:
       find(**txid**$'||(vk_C, vk_D)||reserve($**currMax**$_s)$ $||$(**hopMax** $-$ 1)$||C_A$).
9 | | | Send tuple to all neighbors to whom j has an outgoing credit link.
10 | | **end**
11 | **end**
  /* Receiver-helper and sender-helper path construction done concurrently */
12 | **for** *neighbors* $j \in [1..M]$ *in credit path between Bob-Denise* **do**
13 | | **if** (**hopMax** = 0) **then**
14 | | | do nothing
15 | | **end**
16 | | **else**
17 | | | Reserve **currMax**$_j$ by min(**currMax**$_r$, **currMax**$_j$), set **currMax**$_r$ = min(**currMax**$_r$, **currMax**$_j$). Construct tuple:
       findReceive(**txid**$'''||vk_D||reserve($**currMax**$_r)$ $||$**hopMax** $- 1||C_B$).
18 | | | Send tuple to all neighbors to whom j has an incoming link.
19 | | **end**
20 | **end**
21 **end**

In Algorithm 7, each intermediate node on seg_{AC}, on receiving the *find* tuple will *reserve* the minimum of **currMax**$_s$ and it's outgoing link's credit value. The node updates **currMax**$_s$ (if needed) and also decrements the value of **hopMax** in the *find* tuple before broadcasting it to all its neighbors. Similarly, each intermediate node on seg_{DB}, on receiving the *findReceive* tuple will *reserve* the minimum of **currMax**$_r$ and the available credit on its outgoing link. The procedure is the same as that followed by the intermediate node in seg_{AC}, only now the receiver is Denise. If the **hopMax** value was 0 when the node received the *find* or *findReceive* tuple, then the node drops the message.

In Algorithm 8, when Charlie receives the *find* tuple, it creates a new **txid**$''$, updates the *find* tuple with this new value and broadcasts it towards Denise. Each intermediate node on seg_{CD} from

Algorithm 8: *Find Route* Phase: Helpers' Max. Value Computation

---
Input : CI
Output : Max. transaction value computed by *RHs*
Parties : Sender: Alice, Receiver: Bob

1 **for** $i \in [1..n]$ **do**
  /* Sender-helper max. computation */
2   When Charlie gets the find$(\cdot, \cdot, \cdot, \cdot, \cdot)$ tuple from Alice, he does:
  - Pick $x'' \leftarrow \{0,1\}^\lambda$, compute $\textbf{txid}'' \leftarrow H(x'')$, reserve $\textbf{currMax}_C$ by $\min(\textbf{currMax}_s, \textbf{currMax}_C)$, set $\textbf{currMax}_s = \min(\textbf{currMax}_s, \textbf{currMax}_C)$.
  - Store tuple $(\textbf{txid}'||\textbf{txid}''||vk_D||reserve(\textbf{currMax}_s))$, create new tuple: $find(\textbf{txid}''||(vk_C, vk_D)||reserve(\textbf{currMax}_s)||\textbf{hopMax}||C_A)$. The find tuple is then sent to all of Charlie's neighbors.

  for *neighbors* $j \in [1..M]$ *in path between Charlie-Denise* **do**
    if (hopMax = 0) **then**
    | do nothing.
    end
    else
    | Reserve $\textbf{currMax}_j$ by $\min(\textbf{currMax}_s, \textbf{currMax}_j)$, set $\textbf{currMax}_s = \min(\textbf{currMax}_s, \textbf{currMax}_j)$. Construct tuple: $find(\textbf{txid}''||(vk_C||vk_D)||reserve(\textbf{currMax}_s)||\textbf{hopMax}-1||C_A)$. Send tuple to all neighbors.
    end
  end
  /* Max. in path between *RHs* */
3   When Denise gets the find$(\cdot||\cdot||\cdot||\cdot||\cdot)$ tuple from Charlie, she retrieves $(K_{AD}||y||tS) \leftarrow D_{DK_D}(C_A)$.
4   **if** *decryption fails* **then**
5 | do nothing.
6   **end**
7   **else**
8 | Reserve $\textbf{currMax}_D$ by $\min(\textbf{currMax}_s, \textbf{currMax}_D)$, set $\textbf{currMax}_s = \min(\textbf{currMax}_s, \textbf{currMax}_D)$.
9 | Store tuple $(\textbf{txid}''||K_{ABD}||y||vk_C||reserve(\textbf{currMax}_s))$.
10 | Construct tuple: $findReply(\textbf{txid}''||(vk_C||vk_D)||C_D||(m||\sigma_D))$, where $C_D = E_{K_{AD}}(reserve(\textbf{currMax}_s)||y||tS)$, $m = reserve(\textbf{currMax}_s)$, $\sigma_D = Sign_{sk_D}(vk_C||reserve(\textbf{currMax}_s))$. The *findReply* tuple will be forwarded to the neighbors on the reverse path with Charlie.
11 **end**
12 **end**

Charlie to Denise follows the same steps as nodes on seg_{AC} mentioned earlier. If the *find* tuple does not reach Denise, and Charlie times out, then Charlie can retry with a higher **hopMax** value. When Denise receives the message, she retrieves the encrypted challenge nonce and the symmetric key. She composes a *findReply* tuple with encrypted information for Alice and forwards it to the node on seg_{CD}. This message is forwarded back towards Charlie by each intermediate node.

In Algorithm 9, on receiving the *findReply* tuple from Denise, Charlie updates the tuple with **txid**$'$ and forwards it back towards Alice on seg_{AC}. When Denise receives the *findReceive* tuple from Bob, she retrieves the encrypted challenge nonce and the symmetric key. She composes a *findReply* tuple with encrypted information for Bob and forwards it to the node on seg_{DB}. This message is forwarded back towards Bob by each intermediate node. At the

Algorithm 9: *Find Route* Phase: Helpers Reply

Input : CI
Output : *findReply* tuples of *RHs*
Parties : Sender: Alice, Receiver: Bob

1 **for** $i \in [1..n]$ **do**
  /* Sender's *RH* sending reply */
2   Charlie, on receipt of Denise's *findReply*() does:
3   Retrieve **txid**$'$ stored in same tuple as **txid**$''$, sets his copy of $\textbf{currMax}_s$ to be the $\textbf{currMax}_s$ received from Denise.
4   Compose reply to Alice: $findReply(\textbf{txid}'||vk_C||E_{K_{AD}}(\textbf{currMax}_s||y'||ts)||C_A)$.
5   The *findReply* tuple will be forwarded only to those neighbors on the path from Charlie-Alice, who have used **txid**$'$.
  /* Receiver's *RH* sending reply */
6   In parallel, Denise, on receiving Bob's message will retrieve $(K_{BD}, y', tS) \leftarrow D_{DK_D}(C_B)$
7   **if** *decryption fails* **then**
8 | do nothing.
9   **end**
10 **else**
11 | Reserve $\textbf{currMax}_D$ by $\min(\textbf{currMax}_r, \textbf{currMax}_D)$, set $\textbf{currMax}_r = \min(\textbf{currMax}_r, \textbf{currMax}_D)$.
12 | Compose reply to Bob $findReply(\textbf{txid}'''||vk_D||E_{K_{BD}}(\textbf{currMax}_r||y'||ts)||C_B)$. The *findReply* tuple will be forwarded only to those neighbors on the path from Denise-Bob, who have used **txid**$'''$.
13 **end**
14 **end**

end of the *Find Route* phase, Alice and Bob both have a shared symmetric key with Denise, and can establish how much maximum credit can flow between Alice and Bob over seg_{AC}, seg_{CD} and seg_{DB}.

SKA-CaNPT: Secure Key Agreement using Cancelable and Noninvertible Biometrics based on Periodic Transformation*

Laleh ESKANDARIAN, Dilara AKDOĞAN, Duygu KARAOĞLAN ALTOP, Albert LEVI

Faculty of Engineering and Natural Sciences, Sabancı University, Istanbul Turkey

[leskandarian,dakdogan,duyguk,levi]@sabanciuniv.edu

ABSTRACT

Nowadays, many of the security-providing applications use biometrics-based authentication. However, since each person's biometrics is unique and non-replaceable, once it is compromised, it will be compromised forever. Therefore, it is hard for the users to trust biometrics. To overcome this problem, in this paper, we propose a novel secure key agreement protocol SKA-CaNPT. Here, we use a periodic transformation function to make biometrics cancelable and noninvertible. At the very end of our SKA-CaNPT protocol, the user and the server make an agreement on a symmetric shared key that is based on the feature points of the user's biometrics. Therefore, if the transformed data is compromised, then just by changing one of the inputs of the transformation function, we can renew the cryptographic key. As a proof of concept, we apply our SKA-CaNPT protocol on fingerprints. Besides, we apply different security analyses on our protocol. We use Shannon's entropy and Hamming distance metrics to analyze the randomness and the distinctiveness of the agreed keys. Moreover, according to the low IKGR (Incorrect Key Generation Rate), high CKGR (Correct Key Generation Rate) and high attack complexity possessed by our SKA-CaNPT protocol, we can conclude that our scheme is secure against brute-force, replay and impersonation attacks.

KEYWORDS

Biometrics; bio-cryptography; cancelable biometrics; noninvertible biometrics; periodic transformation; fingerprints; key agreement; security analysis

ACM Reference format:
Laleh ESKANDARIAN, Dilara AKDOĞAN, Duygu KARAOĞLAN ALTOP, Albert LEVI. 2019. SKA-CaNPT: Secure Key Agreement using Cancelable and Noninvertible Biometrics based on Periodic Transformation. In *Proceedings of Ninth ACM Conference on Data and Application Security and Privacy, Richardson, TX, USA, March 25–27, 2019 (CODASPY '19),* 12 pages.
https://doi.org/10.1145/3292006.3300037

*This work was supported in part by the Scientific and Technological Research Council of Turkey (TÜBİTAK) under grant 114E557.
Dilara Akdoğan was supported by TÜBİTAK BİDEB 2228-A.
Duygu Karaoğlan Altop was supported by TÜBİTAK BİDEB 2211-C and Turkcell Academy Technology Leaders Graduate Scholarship Program.

1 INTRODUCTION

In everyday life, people use traditional authentication schemes to verify their identity, in which the secret key is either something they have (e.g. smart card, SIM card in mobile phone), or something they know (e.g. password, PIN code). Despite the wide use of these techniques, there are a lot of limitations. For instance, a personal device like a mobile phone or a smart card could be stolen, lost or borrowed, or a password could be guessed. The problem of the above-mentioned methods is that the difference between the authorized person and the imposter is indistinguishable. One way of solving such a problem is to choose a complex password; however, because of being hard to be kept in mind, people tend to write their passwords down, which causes a security threat. In order to overcome these limitations, authentication using something we are (e.g. biometrics: fingerprint, iris, face, etc) could be useful [23]. There are a lot of advantages of using biometrics-based authentication, such as, users don't need to keep their passwords in a secure place or remember them, or from another point of view, users cannot forget their passwords or loose them. In addition, it is very difficult to forge someone's biometrics in comparison to forging documents.

We have to protect the templates in order to avoid some problematic consequences. First of all, if biometrics is stolen, it is lost forever. In other words, in case that someone's biometrics is stolen or lost, (s)he cannot replace it for his/her whole life. Secondly, because of the fact that the users can apply their biometric traits in many different applications, each one of these applications will be confronted with a risk when the corresponding biometrics is compromised once. This is known as the cross matching problem of biometrics. It means that if the users apply the same biometrics in different applications, they could be potentially tracked. Finally, biometrics are not renewable. Users can renew their passwords or PINs by resetting them, but not their biometric traits.

The technique that can overcome the aforementioned problems is called *cancelable biometrics* [4]. The main idea of cancelable biometrics is to map the original biometric template into a new template prior to the matching process, and to store this new biometric template in the database instead of the original one [23]. Though, if the transformed biometric data is compromised, by only changing the matching characteristics, the biometric template could be renewed. The noninvertibility property can be introduced by applying a one-way transformation function while generating the cancelable biometrics. In that case, the template's protection strength relies on the transformation function.

The combination of biometrics and cryptography, which provides higher security and privacy, is referred to as *bio−cryptography*. In bio-cryptographic applications, common encryption and decryption is applied over the data, but the secret keys are driven from the biometric data itself. These secret keys should be (i) long enough to avoid them being guessed by an attacker, (ii) random enough to contain sufficient entropy, and (iii) distinctive enough to avoid them being forged. Security of the system can be maintained by only this means. However, satisfying these requirements are hard and complex due to the invariant characteristic of biometrics. Moreover, the main obstacle of the above-mentioned combination is that biometrics are noisy. It means that we can only expect an approximate match of the stored template. On the other hand, cryptography requires the exact same key to pass, because otherwise the protocol will fail [12]. Thus, when designing bio-cryptographic systems, this variation should be well analyzed. For instance, error correction codes or fuzzy key binding methods, like *fuzzy commitment* or *fuzzy vault*, can be used to handle the above-mentioned problem.

In this work, we present a novel secure key agreement protocol, SKA-CaNPT: Secure Key Agreement using Cancelable and Noninvertible Biometrics based on Periodic Transformation. Our proposed approach is based on the SKA-PB protocol, introduced by Akdoğan et al. [3], and the idea of using a periodic transformation function to provide the cancelability and the noninvertibility properties, suggested by Dang et al. [7], which are described in detail in Section 2. SKA-CaNPT uses cancelable and noninvertible biometrics while generating the cryptographic keys that will be agreed upon. The reason behind this is to keep the original biometrics safe and secure so that the shared symmetric key can be extracted directly from the stored biometric template. The properties of cancelability and noninvertibility are fulfilled through a periodic transformation function that is applied on the captured biometrics. As a proof of fact, we apply our SKA-CaNPT protocol on fingerprints, which are known to be an unordered set of biometrics. In other words, we apply our protocol on an unordered set of minutiae points. It is important to note here that our approach is not specific to fingerprints, but specific to unordered biometrics. Thus, any biometrics with unordered feature, such as handwritten signature, facial and palm print, can be used with proper adjustments in the algorithm. In order to hide the genuine minutiae points, and thus to decrease the risk of information leakage to the attacker, a number of fake minutiae points are generated randomly. It is important to note here that, in order for the fake minutiae points to be indistinguishable from the genuine minutiae points, the same periodic transformation function is also applied on the fake minutiae points as well.

Our SKA-CaNPT protocol works in rounds, and in each round, server and user try to agree on a symmetric shared key. First of all, they try to find a set of common minutiae points, and then, depending on a pre-defined threshold value and the calculated similarity score, user is either accepted or rejected and a new round starts. In addition, keys generated using our SKA-CaNPT protocol can be renewed/revoked if a transformed data is compromised, only by changing the input of the transformation algorithm and applying it on the original biometric data.

Security performance of our SKA-CaNPT protocol is analyzed from different aspects. From biometrics aspect, our method presents high verification performance proved by the achieved low IKGR (Incorrect Key Generation Rate) and high CKGR (Correct Key Generation Rate) values. Additionally, we show that our SKA-CaNPT protocol is resistant against brute-force, replay and impersonation attacks. On the top of it, the quality of the agreed symmetric shared

keys are high, demonstrated through randomness and distinctiveness evaluations. In this regard, we can use the generated keys as cryptographic keys since each key is different from the other keys, and they have enough randomness. In addition, our protocol is resistant against any attack that compromises the original biometrics since we use a one-way periodic transformation function to make the input biometrics cancelable and noninvertible. Furthermore, we analyze the communication, computation and storage requirements of our protocol. Finally, we compare our protocol with SKA-PB protocol [3] and the cancelable fuzzy vault approach [7].

This paper is organized as follows. Section 2 reviews the related works. In Section 3, we introduce our proposed SKA-CaNPT protocol. Section 4 discusses the performance and the security of our SKA-CaNPT protocol, along with analyzing its complexity and memory requirements. Finally, Section 5 concludes our work and discusses possible future works.

2 RELATED WORK

In this section, we first discuss the literature of the related works, and then, we mention about the problem statement of this paper.

2.1 Literature Overview

Template protection is of great importance in biometric systems. Once a biometric template of a user is compromised, it cannot be replaced. To overcome the this problem, Jain et al. [13] propose two approaches: (i) biometric cryptosystems, and (ii) feature transformation. In biometric cryptosystems, the cryptographic key of the security protocol is either generated from the biometrics itself, or it is binded to the biometrics. In both cases, only the helper data is stored in the database, while the key and the biometrics template are discarded. Therefore, the attacker cannot find any information about the key and the biometrics from the stored helper data.

With regard to biometric cryptosystems, Dodis et al. [8] present *fuzzy extractor* and *secure sketch*, which are the two well-known approaches in biometric cryptosystem. *Fuzzy commitment* [16] and *fuzzy vault* [15] are examples of such methods. Fuzzy commitment is mostly used to secure the biometric features of the individuals, which are in the form of binary vectors, such as the iris code. However, it has been shown that both the key and the original biometric data can be reconstructed using error correction codes and statistical attacks. On the other hand, fuzzy vault is one of most popular biometric template protection schemes, that in contrast with fuzzy commitment, is applicable on unordered set of biometric data, such as fingerprints. There are many researches in the literature about the fuzzy vault scheme that are based on different biometrics [6, 10, 17]. Nevertheless, various attacks against the fuzzy vault scheme are also discovered [18, 26].

On the other hand, in feature transformation, data is transformed prior to the matching process, and then, it is stored in the database. The transformation function is a one-way function that makes recovering the original template from the transformed one hard. This transformation is carried out in either the feature or the signal domain. Moreover, in order to update the templates, the transformation's parameters are modified [22, 23], which makes the original template stay safe. For instance, Ratha et al. [23] recommend 3 types of noninvertible cancelable biometric transformation methods for fingerprint templates: (i) *Cartesian* transformation, (ii) *polar* transformation, and (iii) *functional* transformation. In the former two, after the minutia points are normalized according to a singular point and polar coordinates of the minutiae are calculated based on the position of the core point, respectively, fingerprint images are partitioned into segments, which are then rearranged based on a public information. On the other hand, in the latter, authors propose to apply a local value smoothing function on the captured biometric template using a random key. Unfortunately, several research have showed that the proposed noninvertible cancelable methods in [23] are not resistant against correlation and brute-force attacks [21, 28].

Alternatively, Jin et al. [14] propose another cancelable and non-invertible biometrics approach: BioHash. In this method, authors firstly extract the most specific characteristics of the biometric features, and then, based on a user specific random matrix, these characteristics are placed on a set of randomly generated orthogonal directions. Besides, Farooq et al. [9] propose an approach to implement BioHash. In their model, authors convert fingerprint minutiae into a binary string area. After that, these binary representations are transformed to anonymous representations according to a unique personal key. However, Nandakumar et al. [13] discuss that BioHash is invertible, although it is mentioned to be noninvertible. On the other hand, Chikkerur et al. [5] propose another method to generate cancelable fingerprint templates. In this method, small pieces of minutiae are extracted from the fingerprint image, and then, without changing the distance between each of these small pieces of minutiae, authors transform them to projection matrices. Unfortunately, accuracy of this method is shown to be poor [19].

2.2 Baseline Methods and Problem Statement

In the below paragraphs, we describe the two valuable related works that our proposed key agreement protocol is based upon, a biometric cryptosystem and a feature transformation method.

Akdoğan et al. [3] propose SKA-PB, secure key agreement protocol using pure biometrics, in which the keys are generated using fingerprint's minutiae points that are directly extracted from the fingerprint images, without using any other helper data. SKA-PB has two phases: (i) enrollment phase, and (ii) verification phase. In the enrollment phase, users provide 3 fingerprint images of the same finger. Minutiae values, *(x, y, type)*, are extracted from these fingerprint images and a fingerprint template is generated as follows. Firstly, a distance threshold, T_{dist}, is set up and some representative minutiae, which are utmost T_{dist}-away from any other minutiae with the smallest y- coordinate, are found accordingly. Then, the server considers these 3 minutiae templates and if a minutia shows up in at least 2 out of 3 templates, it is added to the final minutiae template. There is also a neighborhood relation defined in the SKA-PB protocol for the coordinates x_i and y_i of a particular minutia: all the points that are in a particular range are considered as neighborhood minutiae. After each points' neighborhoods are found, the minutia values of each particular point and its neighbors are concatenated separately, and hashed. Then, these hashed values are stored as each user's template in the server side.

In the verification phase, 3 different images of the same finger are captured and their minutiae are extracted. As mentioned above, some representative minutiae are selected according to the predefined distance threshold, the other minutiae are mapped to their representatives, and the most reliable minutiae are calculated. Then, to keep the genuine points safe and secure, chaff points (i.e. fake minutiae points) are introduced such that the fake points also preserve the T_{dist}-neighborhood relation. The authors developed this method to decrease the risk of information leakage to the attacker, who would try to find the original biometric template of a user. Thereafter, concatenation of the minutiae values are computed for both genuine and fake points, and both the single and double hash values of these minutiae values are computed. After that, double hashes and the user ID is transmitted to the server. At this point, server and user try to find a common set of minutiae points: A similarity score is calculated and if the number of common minutiae points is above a predefined score, the user is accepted; otherwise, (s)he is rejected. Since SKA-PB runs in rounds, if the user gets rejected in any round, the protocol can re-start from scratch.

Dang et al. [7] present a cancelable noninvertible fuzzy vault model that uses a periodic transformation function on face features. The proposed scheme includes enrollment and authentication phases. In the enrollment phase, the feature vector X is extracted from the face image and the periods P of this vector are calculated and hashed to be kept safe and stored in the database. In addition, for the proper recovery of the periods during authentication, Reed-Solomon error correction code is calculated for those values. Then, a periodic transformation function, the sine transformation, is applied on the extracted feature vectors, the output of which is called Y. Thereafter, a randomly generated key is utilized as the coefficients of the fuzzy vault polynomial, as usual, which is then applied on the transformed feature vector to produce the genuine points for the vault. Also, a set of fake points are introduced to the fuzzy vault, which are stored in the vault database together with the genuine points and the hash of the randomly generated key.

In the authentication phase, face related feature vector X' and the corresponding period vector P' are extracted from the face image. After that, calculated period vector P' is corrected using Read-Solomon error correction and the hash of this vector is compared to the hash of the original period vector: If they match, the sine transformation is applied on the feature vector X' to find the feature vector Y'; otherwise, authentication fails. If the transformed feature vectors Y' and Y have enough overlap when the fuzzy vault's decoding step is performed, then the key is recovered correctly. Here, the hashed value of the recovered key is compared with the randomly generated key: If they match, the user is verified; otherwise, authentication fails.

In most of the key binding/generation based existing methods proposed for key agreement, helper data is utilized along with pure biometrics, which complicates the overall system and makes it prone to single point of failures. In case that the helper data is compromised, original biometric of the user can be retrieved; such systems rely heavily on the *safe-storage* of the helper data, which makes them prone to single point of failure. Although Akdoğan et al. [3] propose a method that generates the key directly from the captured biometrics without using any helper data, it suffers from being lack of cancelability and noninvertibility properties. Cancelability requires an intentionally distorted biometric data to be used while generating the cryptographic key. However, in Akdoğan et

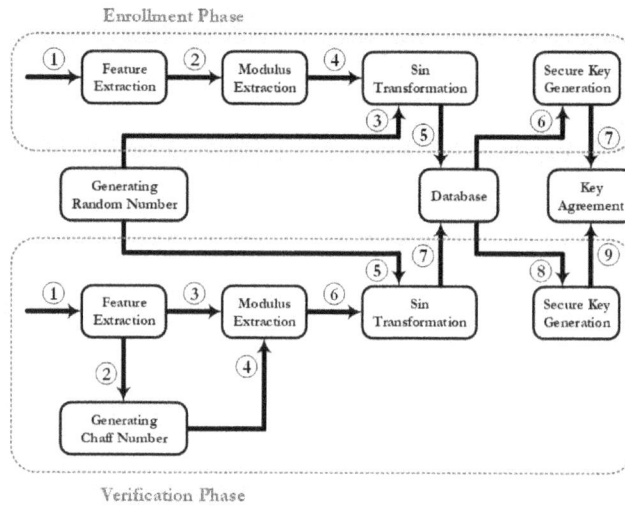

Figure 1: Our proposed cancelable and noninvertible secure key agreement protocol

al. [3], the captured fingerprint itself is utilized to construct the respective key. Besides, noninvertibility can be achieved only if the biometric is cancelable; hence, the proposal of Akdoğan et al. [3] does not either have the noninvertibility property since it does not have the cancelability property. On the other hand, Dang et al. [7] propose a method to overcome this shortage, which makes the fuzzy vault scheme cancelable and noninvertible. Here, the authors apply a one-way transformation function on the captured biometric data to intentionally distort it in a way that it cannot be inverted back to the original biometric, before using it to lock the vault. As discussed in [3], SKA-PB protocol has larger attack complexity and it is stronger against brute-force attacks as compared to the fuzzy vault scheme. In this regard, we combine the idea of cancelable noninvertible transformation with the SKA-PB protocol to overcome the above-mentioned problems and to provide a more secure environment.

3 PROPOSED APPROACH: SKA-CANPT

In this section, we provide a detailed explanation of our proposed protocol SKA-CaNPT: Secure Key Agreement using Cancelable and Noninvertible Biometrics based on Periodic Transformation, which is given in Algorithm 1 and visualized in Figure 2. As a proof of fact, we apply our SKA-CaNPT protocol on fingerprints. Our proposed approach is composed of two phases: (i) enrollment phase, and (ii) verification phase, as shown in Figure 1, each of which is explained in the below subsections. Table 1 gives the definition of symbols that are used in our SKA-CaNPT protocol.

In the enrollment phase, minutiae are extracted from the captured biometric data and they are transformed with our periodic transformation algorithm. After that, the biometric template of the user is calculated through the process of finding the most reliable minutiae and the constructed templates are stored in the server database so that they can be used in the matching process later. Moreover, in the verification phase, the most reliable minutiae are calculated with the user's newly registered fingerprints, after

feature extraction and periodic transformation operations are performed. In this phase, the template is composed of genuine minutiae and the generated chaff points. In the following, the user and the server try to find a common set of minutiae and a similarity score is calculated according to the number of found common minutiae. Depending on this calculated similarity score, our SKA-CaNPT protocol decides whether to reject or to accept the corresponding user. If the user is accepted, then the server and the user make an agreement on a symmetric key. Otherwise, the protocol can start from scratch if required.

As mentioned before, our approach basically combines the SKA-PB protocol [3] and the idea of using a transformation function [7]. The periodic transformation function that we utilize has two important properties. The first one is the similarity preservation property, which means that the similarity of the distances between the original template and the transformed one are preserved. This property ensures that the two transformed fingerprint feature vectors will be close to each other as in the case of the two original fingerprint feature vectors, where closeness is related to the similarity score defined in Equation 5 in Section 3.2. On the other hand, the second important property is noninvertibility, which results in the fact that the original fingerprint templates are protected against compromise forever, by its very nature. This way, the original biometric is neither stored nor transmitted to elsewhere, rather a transformed version is utilized for such purposes. If one cannot get back to the original biometric from the transformed one, then the original biometric can be said to be well-protected.

3.1 Enrolment Phase

In the enrolment phase, user is asked to provide 3 fingerprint images of the same finger using which the minutia are extracted, as in SKA-PB [3]. The stored information per minutiae are composed of 3 attributes: locations of the x and y coordinates, and the *type* of the minutia (*end* or *bifurcation*). In other respects, *cancelability* and *noninvertibility* properties are introduced with the below steps [7].

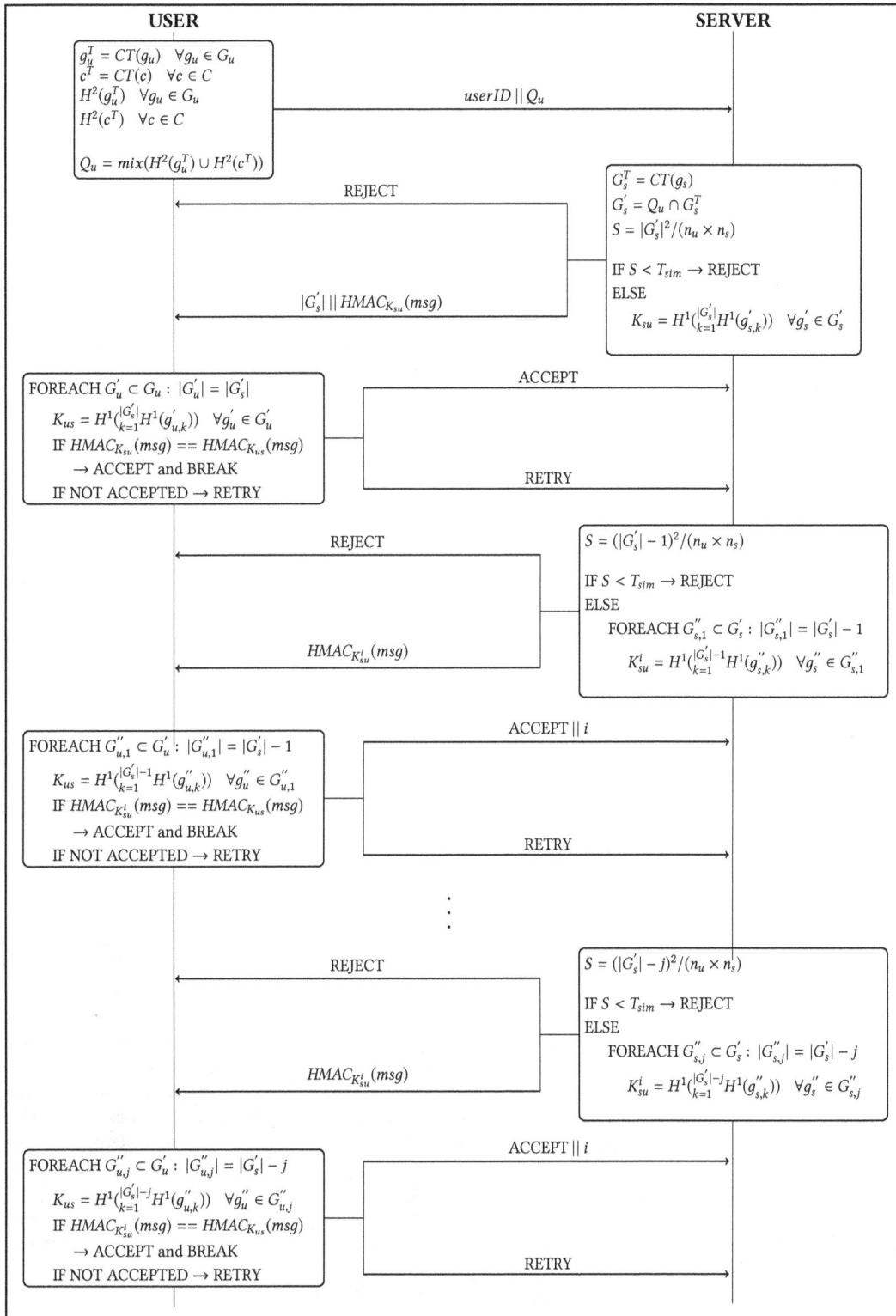

Figure 2: Our proposed cancelable and noninvertible secure key agreement protocol

Table 1: Symbols used in SKA-CaNPT Protocol Definition

Symbol	Description	Symbol	Description
FP	Fingerprint	$type$	Type of a minutia
x	Location of minutia on x-coordinate	y	Location of minutia on y-coordinate
x'	Location on x-coordinate after transformation	y'	Location on y-coordinate after transformation
m_x	Modulus number of x-coordinate	m_y	Modulus number of y-coordinate
r	A random vector with elements (r_i) in $[-1, 1]$	$CT()$	Transformation function
n_u	Genuine minutiae count on user side	n_s	Genuine minutiae count on server side
n_{com}	Number of common minutiae found by the server	n_{com}^{key}	Number of minutiae used in the final key agreement
$H^i(\cdot)$	Hash function applied i times $(i \geq 0)$	att_c	Attack complexity
G_s	Set of genuine minutiae on the server side	G_s^T	Transformed set of genuine minutiae on the server side
G_u	Set of genuine minutiae on the user side	g_u^T	Transformed set of genuine minutiae on the user side
C	Set of fake minutiae on the user side	C^T	Transformed set of fake minutiae on the user side
Q_u	Set of shuffled $\left(H^2(g_u^T) \cup H^2(c^T)\right)$	S	Similarity score
T_{sim}	Acceptance similarity score threshold	T_{dist}	Distance threshold used in neighborhood definition
$HMAC(\cdot)$	Keyed-Hashing for Message Authentication	$HMAC_{K_{us}}(\cdot)$	HMAC generated using K_{us}
$HMAC_{K_{su}}(\cdot)$	HMAC generated using K_{su}	$HMAC_{K_{su}^i}(\cdot)$	HMAC generated using K_{su}^i
K^i	i^{th} key generated $(i \geq 0)$		

(a) Modulus Extraction: We use the sine function as the transformation function. Due to the fact that the sine function is periodic with a period of 2π, we find the modules of each minutia coordinate separately, i.e. we calculate the modulus for the x and y coordinates of each minutiae. Therefore, for each minutiae coordinate, we have a definition as given in Equation 1, where m is the modulus of x and y. Hence, the modules of these coordinates m_{x_i} and m_{y_i} are calculated as in Equation 2.

$$x_i = \alpha_i + m_{xi}2\pi \qquad y_i = \beta_i + m_{yi}2\pi \qquad (1)$$

$$m_{xi} = [x_i \div 2\pi] \qquad m_{yi} = [y_i \div 2\pi] \qquad (2)$$

In the following, you can find a modulus extraction example:

$$x_i = 272 \qquad y_i = 87$$
$$m_{xi} = [272 \div 2\pi] = 43 \qquad m_{yi} = [87 \div 2\pi] = 14$$

(b) Sine Transformation: After modulus extraction, minutiae coordinates are transformed as defined in Equation 4, using the analogy behind Equation 3, where r_i is an individual element from the random vector r, whose range is in $[-1, 1]$. Here, the many-to-one sine periodic transformation function is used as the cancelable noninvertible transformation function. It means that each one of the x_i and y_i coordinate values are transformed to some particular x_i' and y_i' coordinate values, while for each specified x_i' and y_i' coordinate values in the original space, we can find a lot of x_i and y_i coordinate values in the transformed space. Having many different correspondent values for the particular x_i' and y_i' coordinates,

the above-mentioned discourse can be accepted as a proof for the noninvertibility property of the sine transformation function.

$$sin(x_i + x_i') = r_i \qquad sin(y_i + y_i') = r_i \qquad (3)$$

$$x_i' = arcsin(r_i) - \alpha_i \qquad y_i' = arcsin(r_i) - \beta_i \qquad (4)$$

After modulus extraction and sine transformation operations, each fingerprint's template is produced according to its list of minutiae. For template generation, groups of minutiae are categorized with respect to a given distance threshold, T_{dist}, and a representative minutia is selected for each group of minutiae, as described in SKA-PB [3]. Then, the minutiae are quantized according to the selected representative: minutiae having the same minutiae type and being utmost T_{dist}-away to any other minutiae are mapped to the one minutia having the smallest y-coordinate value. Thereafter, the most reliable minutia are found as described in SKA-PB [3] and the final template is constructed. Finally, the concatenation of $(x_i||y_i||type)$ are calculated for each representative minutiae and its T_{dist}-neighborhood, as defined in SKA-PB [3], and their hashed values, $H^1(x_i||y_i||type)$, are stored in the server side, separately for each user. This process is performed only in the server side.

3.2 Verification Phase

In the verification phase, which is depicted in Figure 2, firstly, 3 different fingerprints of the same finger are acquired from the user, as in the enrollment phase, as discussed in SKA-PB [3]. Minutiae are extracted from these fingerprint images and for adding the cancelability and noninvertibility properties to the extracted minutiae, we

Algorithm 1 Template Generation Algorithm

INPUT: FP_1, FP_2, FP_3, r
OUTPUT: G_s^T
1: $G_s^{init} = ExtractMinutiae(FP_1, FP_2, FP_3)$
2: **for** $i = 1 : |G_s^{init}| - 1$ **do**
3:     $m_1 = G_s^{init}(i) = (x_i, y_i)$
4:     $m_x = x_i \div 2\pi; \quad m_y = y_i \div 2\pi$
5:     $\alpha_i = x_i - m_x 2\pi; \quad \beta_i = y_i - m_y 2\pi$
6:     $x'_i = arcsin(r) - \alpha_i; \quad y'_i = arcsin(r) - \beta_i$
7:     $m_1 = (x'_i, y'_i)$
8:     **for** $j = i + 1 : |G_s^{init}|$ **do**
9:        $m_2 = G_s^{init}(j)$
10:        **if** $m_1.x' \geq m_2.x - (2 * T_{dist}) \& m_1.x' \leq m_2.x + (2 * T_{dist}) \&$
11:          $m_1.y \geq m_2.y - (2 * T_{dist}) \& m_1.y' \leq m_2.y + (2 * T_{dist}) \&$
12:          $m_1.type == m_2.type$ **then**
13:           $m_1.visited + +$
14:        **end if**
15:     **end for**
16: **end for**
17: **for** $i = 1 : |G_s^{init}|$ **do**
18:     **if** $G_s^{init}(i).visited < 2$ **then**
19:        Remove i^{th} minutia from G_s^{init}
20:     **end if**
21: **end for**
22: $ind \leftarrow 1$
23: **for** $i = 1 : |G_s^{init}|$ **do**
24:     $m_1 = G_s^{init}(i)$
25:     **for** $j = (-1) * T_{dist} : T_{dist}$ **do**
26:        **for** $k = (-1) * T_{dist} : T_{dist}$ **do**
27:          $G_s(ind) = H^1(m_1.x + j || m_1.y + k || m_1.type)$
28:          $ind \leftarrow ind + 1$
29:        **end for**
30:     **end for**
31: **end for**

---

apply the sine periodic transformation function on these minutiae. After that, the quantization operation is performed to designate the representative minutiae, and the most reliable minutiae are found, as in the enrollment phase.

Differently, in the verification phase, we randomly generate $10 * |G_u|$ fake minutiae in order to mask the genuine minutiae and we transform them with our cancelable noninvertible transformation algorithm, where G_u is the set of genuine minutiae on the user side. The fake minutiae points should also preserve the T_{dist}-neighbourhood relation as well. In other words, since the genuine minutiae points are T_{dist}-away from other genuine minutiae points, the fake minutiae points should be T_{dist}-away from all the other minutiae points, in order to decrease the possibility of information leakage to the attacker and in order not to be distinguishable from the genuine minutiae points. Afterwards, as in SKA-PB [3], features of these minutiae points are concatenated and two different hash values are calculated: $H^1(x_i || y_i || type)$ and $H^2(x_i || y_i || type)$. The single hashes are utilized for generating the key and the double hashes are utilized for verification purposes, as described below.

Following steps are carried out to find the common genuine minutiae, as discussed in SKA-PB [3]. First of all, double hashes of the minutiae points are concatenated with each user's ID in the user side, and then they are transmitted to the server (1st message in Figure 2). Secondly, server compares each of these double

hashed values with the double hashes of its correspondent user's minutiae points. In addition, if the user's genuine minutiae are in the T_{dist}-neighbourhood of the server's minutiae, they are counted as common genuine minutiae as well. Then, a comparison is performed between the minutiae of the user and the minutiae of the server, and a similarity score is computed as given in Equation 5, where n_{com} is the number of common minutiae, n_s is the number of genuine minutiae on the server side, and n_u is the number of genuine minutiae on the user side.

$$S = \frac{n_{com}^2}{n_u + n_s} \times 100 \qquad (5)$$

Key agreement process starts if the calculated similarity score is above a predefined acceptance threshold, T_{sim}, as defined in SKA-PB [3]. When this is the case, server calculates the double hash of all common minutiae, $H^1(G_s)$, to generate the key, K_{su}, using which the communication with the user will be secured. In order to make sure that both the server and the user are using the same key, $HMAC$ of a predefined message, msg, is calculated with K_{su} and it is transmitted to the user together with the number of common minutiae that the server has found, $|G'_s|$ (2nd message in Figure 2). After that, according to the number of common found minutiae, the user tries the possible subsets of the genuine minutiae with the equal number to generate the key. The user sends a positive acknowledgement if (s)he can verify the $HMAC$ (3rd message in Figure 2); otherwise, s(he) tries to generate another key with another subset, until (s)he can verify the $HMAC$ or all the other subsets are tested. The user will send a $RETRY$ message if (s)he cannot verify the $HMAC$ even all the subsets are tried (third message in Figure 2).

As discussed in SKA-PB [3], if the user transmits a $RETRY$ message to the server, a new similarity score is calculated in the server side using $|G'_s| - 1$ as the common minutiae count, and if it is above T_{sim}, server generates all possible keys of all subsets of the common minutiae that it has found, which has the size $|G'_s| - 1$, and then it computes all $HMAC$s of the predefined message with respect to these keys and transmits them to the user (4th message in Figure 2). Thereafter, the user sends a positive acknowledgement if (s)he can verify any of the transmitted $HMAC$ values with any of the keys which are generated based on any subsets of the genuine minutiae with the same size of $|G'_s| - 1$. Along with the positive acknowledgement, user also transmits the index of the verified $HMAC$, i, to the server; otherwise, another $RETRY$ message will be transmitted to the server (5th message in Figure 2). In this case, the aforementioned process will be repeated with $|G'_s| - 2$. The overall process stops at the jth iteration if any of the $HMAC$ values cannot be verified by the user or the similarity score of $|G'_s| - j$ is under the acceptance threshold, T_{sim}. At the very end of the protocol, the server and the user can agree on a symmetric cryptographic key if the user can verify any of the $HMAC$ values (last message in Figure 2). On the other hand, upon a request, the server and the user can start from scratch, if the protocol stops without any key agreement.

In our SKA-CaNPT protocol, we utilize a cancelable noninvertible transformation function, i.e. the sine function, to transform the user's original biometric feature vector to a secure transformed template. By this means, if the key is compromised by an attacker, cancelling the stored biometric template and generating a new one would be easy. To construct a new fingerprint template, a newly generated random vector r' will be replaced with the previous random vector r in the cancelable and noninvertible transformation algorithm, and then the key agreement protocol can be run with this newly transformed biometric template from scratch.

4 PERFORMANCE EVALUATION

For performance evaluation purposes, we have tested our SKA-CaNPT protocol using the Verifinger sample database [2], consisting of 30 different subjects, where there exists 8 images per finger for each user. These fingerprints are captured using Cross Match Verifier 300 at 500 ppi [1].

We use pre-aligned fingerprint images to test our protocol. As explained in SKA-PB [3], fingerprint images are aligned with Matlab R2015a, using their intensity values, and each fingerprint's minutiae are extracted using Neurotechnology Biometric SDK 5.0 Verifinger [2]. In the utilized dataset, we use the first 3 images to produce the fingerprint templates of the server side and the other 5 are used to generate the templates of the user side. Hence, each subject is tested $\binom{5}{3} = 10$ times. Moreover, we also carry out impostor tests, in which we check each subjects' template against all the other subjects' templates. In our SKA-CaNPT protocol, we use SHA-256 hash function [20], hence, all of the generated keys are 256 bits.

4.1 Performance Metrics and Parameters

The most important performance measure of a biometric cryptosystem is the error rate, which in our case is computed through Incorrect Key Generation Rate (IKGR) and Correct Key Generation Rate (CKGR). IKGR is the rate of falsely acceptance of the impostor users, i.e. percentage of the impostors that can agree on a key with the server as if they were genuine, while CKGR is the rate of truly acceptance of the genuine users, i.e. percentage of the genuine users that can agree on a key with the server.

Besides, randomness of the generated cryptographic keys is one of the most important concerns for key agreement/generation protocols. Here, Shannon's entropy [27] is used to measure the randomness, according to which, the entropy value can be within the range of $[0, 1]$, where 1 indicates maximum randomness.

Additionally, distinctiveness of the generated cryptographic keys is another important concern for key agreement/generation protocols: After each round of the protocol, a different key is required to be generated. Here, the distinctiveness of the generated keys are measured by the Hamming distance metric [11], which defines the difference of the element positions in two strings of equal length.

4.2 Verification Results

A similarity score is calculated for each test using Equation 5, which is defined in Section 3.2. Figure 3 illustrates the respective percentages of IKGR and CKGR. As shown in this figure, the optimum error rate of our SKA-CaNPT protocol is achieved when the threshold value is set to 24.762, where IKGR is 0.67% and CKGR is 96.67%, which are absolutely sufficient for a generic bio-cryptographic authentication system.

We find the average number of attempts to make an agreement on the key as 3.068. In addition, 16 out of 30 subjects can correctly generate a key in their first attempts, which corresponds to 67.46%. Moreover, in 1 subject from 30 subjects, the server and the user

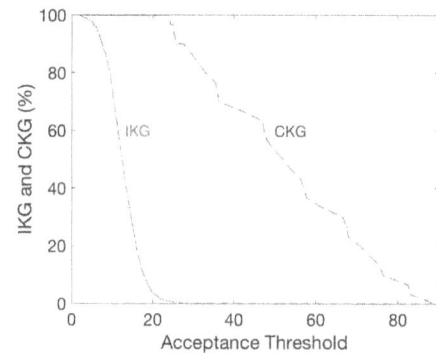

Figure 3: IKGR and CKGR when the threshold sets to 24.762

cannot make an agreement on a symmetric shared key. Therefore, the success rate is 96.67%.

4.3 Security Analysis

In this section, we first specify our threat model and then, we analyze the resistance of our protocol against brute-force, impersonation and replay attacks. Finally, the qualification of the keys generated through our SKA-CaNPT protocol is evaluated according to the Hamming distance and Shannon's entropy metrics.

4.3.1 Threat Model. The attacker's main purpose is as follows: (i) eavesdropping to find the key exchanged between the server and the user, (ii) impersonating a genuine user, and (iii) trying to find the original biometric template of a user. Since we are not assuming any secure channel, the attacker can access all of the protocol messages, including the hash values and the HMACs that are transmitted between the user and the server. Hence, it is possible that the attacker can learn the number of minutiae, using which the key is generated. Therefore, using this value, the attacker can try the passive mode brute-force attack to guess the key. Also, in the active mode, the attacker can apply a replay attack to impersonate a genuine user. However, in the following paragraphs, we discuss how our protocol is resistant against these types of attacks.

4.3.2 Resistance Against Brute-force Attacks. A brute-force attack is always an option for an adversary; (s)he can try all possible combinations of the keys. In fact, this attack is infeasible against our SKA-CaNPT protocol since we are using 256 bit keys in our protocol. Hence, below, we define a more intelligent brute-force attack by using protocol messages.

All possible minutiae locations and their types are generated by this attack. Although in our SKA-CaNPT protocol, we first transform the minutiae points prior to message exchange, due to the similarity distance preservation property of our cancelable noninvertible transformation function, distances among any two minutiae points remain the same. Therefore, since the maximum distance between two minutiae points is 512, and there are 2 types of minutia, *end* or *bifurcation*, the attacker can generate $512 \times 512 \times 2 = 2^{19}$ points for a brute-force attack, and apply the hash function on them once and twice. However, as mentioned before, we do not assume a secure channel, and thus the attacker can also have access to

Q_u, which is the list of the transformed fake and genuine minutiae. For this reason, the search space of the attacker reduces to $|Q_u|$. Nevertheless, as shown below, our SKA-CaNPT protocol is still secure against brute-force attacks.

As mentioned above, Q_u and n_{com}^{key}, the number of minutia for generating the key, are the information that the attacker has. The attacker should try all the subsets of Q_u with the size of n_{com}^{key} for finding all the generated keys, attack complexity of which can be calculated with Equation 6.

$$att_c = \binom{|Q_u|}{n_{com}^{key}} = \frac{|Q_u|!}{n_{com}^{key}!(|Q_u| - n_{com}^{key})!} \qquad (6)$$

If we calculate the attack complexity after each key agreement by using Equation 6 and compute the average, we will have the overall attack complexity of the system. With this calculation, the attack complexity of our SKA-CaNPT protocol is 94 bits, which means that 2^{94} hash and HMAC verifications are required. Juliato et al. [29] discuss that one block of HMAC computation takes 0.8977 microseconds even with a particular hardware implementation. Hence, according to the aforementioned complexity, it will take about 5.6×10^{14} years for an attacker to attack our SKA-CaNPT protocol. Therefore, we can claim that our protocol is sufficiently secure against intelligent brute-force attacks.

4.3.3 Resistance Against Replay and Impersonation Attacks. Impersonating a genuine user to find the correct key is referred to as replay attack. In replay attacks, the attacker replays the previously transmitted messages between the server and the victim user. In order to find the generated key effectively, the attacker needs to know the genuine minutiae; otherwise, (s)he must check all the combinations of Q_u, which is the set of the mixed and hashed genuine and fake minutiae points. Since the transformed version of both genuine and fake minutiae points are listed in Q_u, genuine minutiae points are indistinguishable for the attacker, so (s)he should try all the possible combinations of Q_u using Equation 6. Hence, the complexity of the replay attack is the same as that of brute-force.

In addition, if the attacker tries to generate the key with applying his/her own fingerprint, (s)he will be successful in 0.67% of the cases, since it is the IKGR performance of our protocol. It is important to note here that it is a general problem in all biometrics systems and it is not just specific to our method.

4.3.4 Randomness of the Agreed Keys. Our SKA-CaNPT protocol generates 300 keys from 30 different subjects. These keys are generated using hash functions applied on the common minutiae. Due to the fact that hash functions already introduce randomness to the input string, we calculate the Shannon's entropy of the concatenated common minutiae ($x||y||type$) instead of the entropy of the keys. Respective results are given in Figure 4, where the entropy is above 0.98 for 90.66% of the keys, indicating really good randomness.

4.3.5 Distinctiveness. We cannot expect to generate the same key after each key agreement run, since biometrics are not exactly the same of each other in different acquisitions, which is known as intra-person distinction. Indeed, if we generate the same key and if the key is compromised in one of the sessions, it will increase the risk of compromising messages from the other sessions as well,

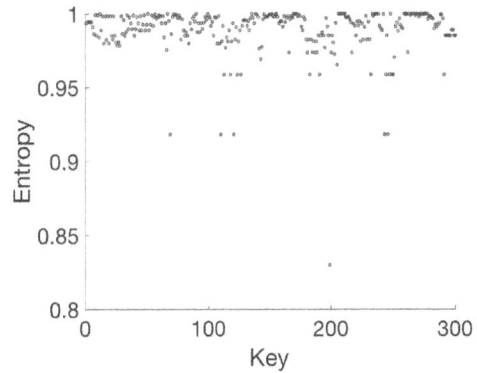

Figure 4: Entropy values of the transformed minutiae

which is a concern for the confidentiality of the system. Thus, generating different keys in different key agreement runs is of great importance. As discussed in SKA-PB [3], according to the quality of the scanner, the finger's pressure, acquisition environment, etc., order of the minutiae and their quality can change. The above-mentioned situation can have either a positive or a negative impact on the key agreement process, depending on the application.

Here, Hamming distance are calculated to find the differences among the keys of the same user, which are generated from the transformed minutiae in different key agreement protocol runs. Results, which are provided in Figure 5, show that 256 bit keys possess an average Hamming distance of approximately $120 - 130$ bits for each different user, where the minimum distance is 103. Additionally, we also computed the average Hamming distance among the keys that are generated from the transformed minutiae of different users in order to show that the keys are distinctive among users as well. Results, which are provided in Figure 6, show that the average Hamming distance varies between $120 - 135$ bits. Hence, we can conclude that the average Hamming distance among different users' keys is close to that of the same user's keys, which means that it is indistinguishable that which of the two keys belong to different users and which ones belong to the same user.

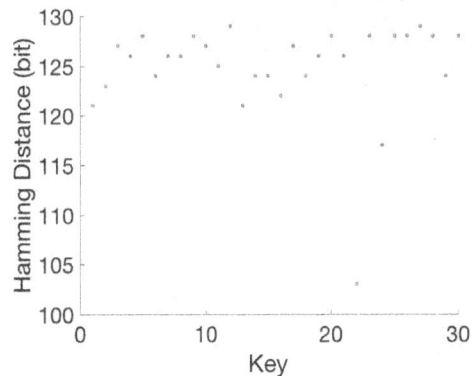

Figure 5: Average Hamming distances - same user's keys

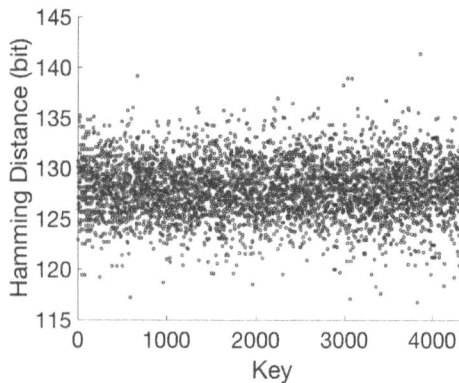

Figure 6: Average Hamming distances - different user's keys

While generating the keys, we hash the concatenation of the minutiae points, as described in Section 3. Due to the hash function's property, a small change in a minutiae concatenation causes a really huge difference on the hash values. Therefore, we need to calculate the Hamming distance of the minutiae concatenations to find out the level of unpredictability of our protocol. By this means, we compute the attack complexity of the *fingerprint similarity attack* over the minutiae concatenations. The length of the minutiae concatenations vary since in each run of the protocol, the number of found common minutiae is different. In this attack, the imposter tries to guess the concatenation of a genuine minutia's length, before the hash function is applied on it, according to his/her fingerprint minutiae, by changing the bits of the minutiae concatenations. If we assume that the Hamming distance of the victim's minutiae concatenation and the imposter minutiae concatenation is clear for the imposter and (s)he knows the length of the minutiae concatenation, we have three different cases: (i) the length of the imposter's minutiae concatenation is the same as that of the victim's minutiae concatenation, (ii) the imposter's minutiae concatenation is longer than the victim's minutiae concatenation, or (iii) the imposter's minutiae concatenation is shorter than the victim's minutiae concatenation. In each of these cases, the bit strings are considered equal-length. The quantity of the combination of the locations which are different shows the attack complexity. In addition, in the third case, the imposter's minutiae concatenation bits and the victim's minutiae concatenation bits are important in the attack complexity, since the imposter should find them as well. This attack complexity is calculated for each protocol run. In addition, we find the median of each person's attack complexities to learn about the average case behavior. As a consequence, the overall complexity of the fingerprint similarity attack becomes 2^{251}. This amount of complexity is completely sufficient for preserving the SKA-CaNPT protocol from fingerprint similarity attack.

4.3.6 Cancelability and Noninvertibility of the Fingerprint Templates. In order to check the cancelability property of our SKA-CaNPT protocol, we checked the Hamming distance among the keys that are generated from the transformed minutiae using different random numbers. As provided in Figure 7, average Hamming distance varies between $120 - 135$ bits. Results show that the Hamming distance among the keys of the same user that are transformed

with different random numbers are similar to the Hamming distance among the keys of the same user that are transformed with the same random number. This shows a really good distinctiveness between these sets of keys, which means that whenever we need to cancel a fingerprint template, we will obtain a new template which is totally different from the previous one and that will preserve the original template to be compromised. In addition, similar to the analysis described in Section 4.3.5, the fingerprint similarity attack complexity can also be calculated for the Hamming distance among minutiae concatenations before applying the hash function on the same user's minutiae points that are transformed with different random numbers, whose result yields to 2^{252}. This amount of complexity shows that, when we cancel the original fingerprint template, the attacker cannot substitute the original minutiae with his/her own minutiae. Therefore, it is easy and safe to cancel a fingerprint template whenever required.

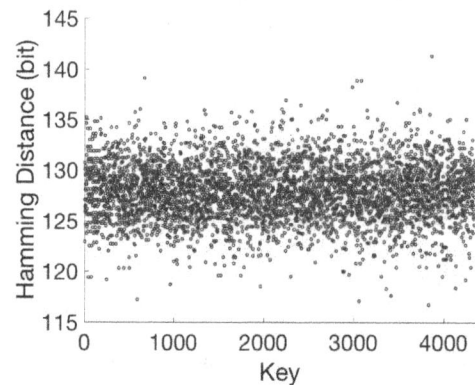

Figure 7: Average Hamming distances - same user's keys with different random numbers

In order to justify the noninvertibility property, if we assume that an attacker finds (X', Y'), where X' is the location of the minutia after transformation on the X-coordinate, and Y' is the location of the minutia after transformation on the Y-coordinate, (s)he will try her/his best to find (X, Y), i.e. original locations prior to transformation using the knowledge of the transformation function and some other public data. First of all, we should mention that the utilized periodic transformation function has the many-to-one mapping property. It means that, based on Equation 3 and Equation 4, X can only be transformed into one and exactly one X', and similarly, Y can only be transformed into one and exactly one Y', while X' and Y' can be transformed into many Xs and many Ys. Besides, if the adversary has X', Y' and r_i, (s)he can find α_i and β_i, but since the modulus m_i is unknown, the adversary cannot infer either X or Y.

4.4 Computational Complexity Analysis

The computational complexity of our SKA-CaNPT protocol is computed for the server and the user separately by calculating the complexity of the transformation function and the number of key generation attempts.

As mentioned in Section 3, the cancelable and noninvertible transformation function that we utilize is the sine periodic function.

As discussed in [24, 25], computational complexity of $sin(x)$ for fixed-point rational inputs are computable in polynomial space. Therefore, both in the server side and the user side, the computational complexity of the transformation function is $O(n)$, where n is the total number of minutiae points. As discussed exclusively in Section 3 and as can be analyzed from Figure 2, computational complexity of the server and the user can be calculated by Equation 7, where n_{com} is the number of common found minutiae, and Equation 8, where n_u is the number of genuine minutiae in the user side, results of which are 2^{17} and 2^{39}, respectively. By this means, the total computational complexity of the server is 2^{17}, while the total computational complexity of the user is 2^{39}, since $O(n) < O(2^n)$.

$$server_{complexity} = \sum_{i=n_{com}}^{n_{com}^{key}} \binom{n_{com}}{i} \qquad (7)$$

$$user_{complexity} = \sum_{i=n_{com}}^{n_{com}^{key}} \binom{n_u}{i} \qquad (8)$$

4.5 Communication Complexity Analysis

The communication complexity of our SKA-CaNPT protocol is computed according to the bits transmitted between the server and the user. The first message that the user sends to the server includes Q_u (set of genuine and fake minutiae) and the user ID, where Q_u has 256 bits and the user *ID* is a 32 bit integer. In the dataset that we utilize, there are 440 minutiae points on average. Therefore, the communication cost of this message is $(440 \times 256) + 32 = 13.75$ KB. The second message transmitted from the server to the user can either be a rejection acknowledgment or n_{com} and *HMAC* values, where the former is 1 bit and the latter is $256 + 32 = 288$ bits.

In the next step of our protocol, the user responds to the server with *RETRY* or *ACCEPT*, both of which requires only 1 bit. If the user sends a *RETRY* message, then the server can transmit a negative acknowledgement or the list of the *HMAC* values, which contains $\binom{n_{com}}{n_{com}-1}$ number of minutiae points. The average of n_{com} is 25 for the utilized dataset; thus, the average communication cost of this kind of a message is $256 \times \binom{22}{21} = 5632$ bits. If the user cannot verify any of the *HMAC* values, (s)he will send another *RETRY* message, but if the SKA-CaNPT protocol continues with an *ACCEPT* message, then the total communication cost will be $32 + 1 = 33$ bits.

In the following steps, the server's communication cost will change according to the following combinatorial value: $\binom{n_{com}}{x}$, where $x = n_{com} - 2, \ldots, n_{com}^{key}$ is the number minutiae that is used in the key generation process. Since the key is generated with an average number of 16 minutiae, the average communication cost in the server side can be approximated as $256 \times \binom{25}{16} = 65.37$ MB.

The total size of the transmitted messages are 65.37 MB for the server and 13.75 KB for the user. Hence, with today's Internet quality, the above-mentioned amounts are reasonable.

4.6 Memory Requirements Analysis

In our SKA-CaNPT protocol, average number of transmitted minutiae is 42.4, which can be approximated as 42, in the server side. Moreover, neighbourhood points of each minutiae are also stored in the server side. As described in Section 3.1, we have a neighborhood relation strategy, by which the neighbor points of the representative minutiae are stored in the server side according to a predefined threshold value, T_{dist}, value of which is assumed as 10. Therefore, each representative minutiae is represented with $21 \times 21 = 441$ points, which means that, for each subject, the average number of minutiae that is stored in the server side is $42 \times 441 = 18522$. In addition, before storing these points on the server, first SHA-256 hash function is applied on them, which means that each point is 256 bits. The utilized dataset consists of 30 subjects, as mentioned before in Section 4.1. Therefore, the total storage size required by the server is $30 \times 18522 \times 30 = 16.9$ MB. In the case that the server needs to store double hashes of the minutiae points and their neighbors as well, the storage amount will become $16.9 \times 2 = 33.8$ MB.

On the other hand, the average number of transmitted minutiae is approximately 40, in the user side. Here, the neighboring points are not stored, but $10 \times |G_u|$ chaff points are added to the original minutiae points, which means that, $10 \times 40 = 400$ chaff points are added to the original minutiae points on average. Therefore, in the user side, total number of minutiae points is 440. Here, we first calculate the single hashes of the minutiae points and then we calculate the double hash values as well. Hence, in total, our protocol requires $440 \times 256 \times 2 = 28.16$ KB of storage for a user.

4.7 Comparative Analysis with Related Work

In this section, we compare our SKA-CaNPT protocol with the SKA-PB protocol that is presented by Akdoğan et al. [3] and the cancelable fuzzy vault approach that is presented by Dang et al. [7], which are described in detail in Section 2.2. These two protocols are compared with that of ours according to IKGR and CKGR, as well as brute-force attack complexity. We also compare our SKA-CaNPT protocol with the proposed SKA-PB protocol [3] with respect to replay and impersonation attack complexities together with the randomness and the distinctiveness of the agreed symmetric keys. The reason behind not being able to compare our SKA-CaNPT protocol with the cancelable fuzzy vault approach [7] against these performance metrics is that the respective authors do not include such analysis in their corresponding proposal.

IKGR and CKGR of our SKA-CaNPT protocol are 0.67% and 96.67%, as discussed in Section 4.2. These values are given as 0.57% and 99.43% in SKA-PB [3]. Nevertheless, our results are still reasonable and acceptable for bio-cryptographic authentication systems. Hence, we can conclude that our SKA-CaNPT protocol successfully improves the SKA-PB protocol by means of adding cancelability and noninvertibility properties, despite degrading the IKGR and CKGR performance a little. Besides, our SKA-CaNPT protocol preserves the attack complexity, randomness and distinctiveness of SKA-PB, which are more or less the same of each other.

In the cancelable fuzzy vault approach [7], Dang et al. apply their proposed scheme on face features with 40 genuine minutiae points and on a polynomial of order 9 for the construction of the fuzzy vault. We applied this proposed method to our utilized dataset as well. The comparison of our SKA-CaNPT protocol with the cancelable fuzzy vault scheme [7] shows that the IKGR and CKGR of our SKA-CaNPT protocol outperforms the IKGR and CKGR of the cancelable fuzzy vault scheme, which are 1.8% and 54.4%. The authors of this approach report their protocol's resistance against brute-force attack as 2^{57}, which is 2^{94} in our proposed SKA-CaNPT protocol. In conclusion, our SKA-CaNPT protocol is stronger against brute-force attack in comparison to the cancelable fuzzy vault scheme. Since the cancelable fuzzy vault scheme is different from our protocol in the manner that the cryptographic keys are generated, comparing these two protocols in terms of randomness and distinctiveness of the agreed keys is not applicable.

5 CONCLUSIONS

In this paper, we present a secure key agreement protocol: Secure Key Agreement using Cancelable and Noninvertible Biometrics based on Periodic Transformation (SKA-CaNPT). As the name of our protocol implies, we use cancelable and noninvertible biometric features while generating the keys to be agreed, and we satisfy these properties through the use of periodic transformation. As a proof of concept, we apply our protocol on fingerprints and we generate the secretly shared keys using minutiae points, without using any other random data while generating the key. Both the cryptographic keys that are agreed upon and the stored biometric templates that are generated using our SKA-CaNPT protocol are cancelable, since if we need to renew the biometric template, we can easily change one of the inputs of the sine transformation function to compute a brand new symmetric shared key. Besides, the stored biometric templates that are generated using our SKA-CaNPT protocol are noninvertible because of the utilized periodic transformation function.

Additionally, in our SKA-CaNPT protocol, we use chaff points in order to hide the genuine minutiae points. We generate these chaff points according to a predefined strategy and then we apply the cancelable noninvertible sine transformation function to make them completely indistinguishable from the genuine minutiae. Since adding chaff points decreases the probability of information leakage to the attacker, it results in higher verification performance. It is important to note here that during the key generation process, our system uses the hash functions and threshold mechanisms.

We analyze the security of our SKA-CaNPT protocol according to a number of different metrics. The *IKGR* value is 0.67%, while the *CKGR* value is 96.67%, which shows the verification performance of our protocol. In addition, we analyze the strength of our protocol against brute-force, replay and impersonation attacks. The attack complexity of our protocol is 2^{94}, which implies that an attacker has negligible probability in succeeding in a brute force attack. We also analyze the randomness of the generated keys, which shows that the entropy of all the keys are greater than 0.97. Hence, it can be concluded that the keys are random enough to be used as cryptographic keys. On the other hand, according to the Hamming distance metric, we evaluate the distinctiveness of the agreed keys, which shows that there is a quite large difference between the same person's keys and different persons' keys, making them completely indistinguishable from each other. Furthermore, we show that the canceled keys do not have any correlation with the renewed keys, again using the Hamming distance metric, but this time, on the keys that are generated using different random numbers in the sine transformation function. From another perspective, we provide the computation and communication complexities of our proposed protocol, as well as its memory requirements, results of which are in reasonable ranges. Finally, we compare SKA-CaNPT with

the baseline protocols [3, 7], and show that our proposed solution successfully improves SKA-PB [3] and outperforms the cancelable fuzzy vault scheme [7].

REFERENCES

[1] [n. d.]. Cross Match Verifier 300 LC. http://www.crossmatch.com/verifier-300-lc/. ([n. d.]). Accessed: 2015-05-01.
[2] [n. d.]. Neurotechnology Verifinger Sample DB. http://www.neurotechnology.com/. ([n. d.]). Accessed: 2015-05-01.
[3] D. Akdogan, D. K.Altop, and A. Levi. 2015. Secure Key Agreement using Pure Biometrics. In *IEEE Conference on Communications and Network Security*.
[4] R. Bolle, J. Connell, S. Pankanti, N. Ratha, and W. Andrew. 2003. Senior, Guide to Biometrics. (2003).
[5] S. Chikkerur, N.K. Ratha, H. Connell, and R.M. Bolle. 2008. Generating Registration-Free Cancellable Fingerprint Templates. *In BTAS08* 2008 (2008).
[6] T. Clancy, D. Lin, and N. Kiyavash. 2003. Secure Smartcard-Based Fingerprint Authentication. *In Proceedings of ACM SIGMM Workshop on Biometric Methods and Applications* 2003 (2003), 45–52.
[7] T.K. Dang, Q.C. Truong, T.T.B. Le1, and H. Truong. 2016. Cancellable fuzzy vault with periodic transformation for biometric template protection. *IET Biometrics* 2016 (2016), 1–7.
[8] Y. Dodis, R. Ostrovsky, L. Reyzin, and A. Smith. February 2006. *Fuzzy Extractors: How to Generate Strong Keys from Biometrics and Other Noisy Data.* Technical Report. Technical Report 235, Cryptology ePrint Archive.
[9] F. Farooq, R.M. Bolle, T.Y. Jea, and N. Ratha. 2007. Anonymous and Revocable Fingerprint Recognition. *In Proceedings of Computer Vision and Pattern Recognition, Minneapolis* 2007 (2007).
[10] J. Fierrez-Aguilar, D. Garcia-Romero, J. Ortega-Garcia, and J. Gonzalez-Rodriguez. 2005. Bayesian Adaptation for User-Dependent Multimodal Biometric Authentication. *Pattern Recognition* 38 (2005), 1317–1319.
[11] R.W. Hamming. 1950. AError detecting and error correcting codes. *Bell System Technical Journal* 29, 2 (1950), 147–160.
[12] F. Hao, R. Anderson, and J. Daugman. 2005. *Combining cryptography with biometrics effectively.* Technical Report. University of Cambridge.
[13] A.K. Jain, K. Nandakumar, and A. Nagar. 2008. Biometric Template Security. *EURASIP Journal on Advances in Signal Processing* 2008, 113 (2008), 1–âĂŞ17.
[14] A.T.B. Jin, D.N.C. Ling, and A. Goh. 2004. Biohashing: two factor authentication featuring fingerprint data and tokenised random number. *Pattern recognition* 37, 11 (2004), 2245–2255.
[15] A. Juels and M. Sudan. 2006. A Fuzzy Vault Scheme. *Designs, Codes and Cryptography* 38, 2 (2006), 237–257.
[16] A. Juels and M. Wattenberg. 1999. A Fuzzy Commitment Scheme. In *ACM Conference on Computer and Communications Security*. 28–36.
[17] Y.J. Lee, K. Bae, S.J. Lee, K.R. Park, and J. Kim. 2007. Biometric Key Binding: Fuzzy Vault based on Iris Images. *In Proceedings of Second International Conference on Biometrics* 38 (2007), 800–808.
[18] P. Mihailescu. 2007. The fuzzy vault for fingerprints is vulnerable to brute force attack. *Computing Research Repository* 2007 (2007).
[19] R. Mukhaiyar. 2015. *Cancellable Biometric using Matrix Approaches.* Ph.D. Dissertation.
[20] National Institute of Standards and Technology. 2002. *FIPS PUB 180-2: Secure Hash Standard.* pub-NIST.
[21] F. Quan, S. Fei, C. Anni, and Z. Feifei. 2008. Cracking cancelable fingerprint template of ratha. *In Proceedings of the International Symposium on Computer Science and Computational Technology. Washington, DC, USA: IEEE Computer Society* 2 (2008), 572–575.
[22] J. Connell R. Bolle and N. Ratha. 2002. Biometrics perils and patches. *Pattern Recognition* 35, 12 (2002), 2727–2738.
[23] N. Ratha, S. Chikkerur, J. Connell, and R. Bolle. 2007. Generating cancelable fingerprint templates. *Pattern Analysis and Machine Intelligence of the IEEE Transactions* 29, 4 (2007), 561–572.
[24] J.H. Reif. 1986. Logarithmic Depth Circuits for Algebraic Functions. *SIAM journal of computing* 15, 1 (1986), 1231–242.
[25] John H. Reif and Stephen R. Tate. 1992. On Threshold Circuits and Polynomial Computation. *SIAM J. Comput.* 21, 5 (1992), 896–908.
[26] W. Scheirer and T. Boult. 2007. Cracking fuzzy vaults and biometric encryption. *Biometrics Symposium* 2007 (2007), 1–6.
[27] C. Shannon. 1948. A mathematical theory of communication. *Bell System Technical Journal* 27, 4 (1948), 623–656.
[28] S.W. Shin, M.-K. Lee, D. Moon, and K. Moon. 2009. Dictionary attack on functional transform-based cancelable fingerprint templates. *ETRI journal* 31, 5 (2009).
[29] M. uliato and C. Gebotys. 2011. *FPGA implementation of an HMAC processor based on the SHA-2 family of hash functions.* Technical Report. University of Waterloo.

Author Index

NOTES